The Biographical Dictionary of British Economists

THOEMMES CONTINUUM

THE BIOGRAPHICAL DICTIONARY OF BRITISH ECONOMISTS

Volume 1
A–J

EDITOR-IN-CHIEF

Donald Rutherford
University of Edinburgh

SUPERVISING EDITORS

Roger Backhouse
Anthony Brewer
Forrest Capie
Leslie Clarkson
Walter Eltis
Geoffrey Gilbert
Peter Groenewegen

G.C. Harcourt
Stephen Littlechild
T.H. Lloyd
Harro Maas
Noel Thompson
A.M.C. Waterman

THOEMMES CONTINUUM

This edition published by Thoemmes Continuum, 2004

Thoemmes Continuum is an imprint of
The Continuum International Publishing Group Ltd

Thoemmes Continuum
11 Great George Street
Bristol BS1 5RR, England

http://www.thoemmes.com

The Biographical Dictionary of British Economists
2 Volumes: ISBN 1 84371 030 7

© Thoemmes Continuum, 2004

British Library Cataloguing-in-Publication Data
A CIP record of this title is available from the British Library

All rights reserved. No part of this publication may be
reproduced, stored in a retrieval system, or
transmitted in any way or by any means, electronic,
mechanical, photocopying, recording or otherwise,
without the written permission of the copyright holder.

Typeset in Sabon.
Printed and bound in the UK by Antony Rowe Ltd.
This book is printed on acid-free paper, sewn, and
cased in a durable buckram cloth.

CONTENTS

Introduction vii

How to use the *Dictionary* xi

General bibliography xiii

List of contributors xv

Biographical entries A–Z 1

Name index 1321

INTRODUCTION

For centuries, Britain has produced writers on economics who have contributed to most branches of the discipline. Many of them have attracted substantial biographies; the lesser figures have often inspired articles in academic journals. Hundreds of writers remain, however, who have been known only through a mention as brief as a library catalogue entry. This *Dictionary* brings together new essays on over six hundred individuals, both major and minor. It has been our intention to give a clear indication of who were these men and women who participated in successive debates on economic theories and issues. We call them 'economists' despite the indisputable fact that until the twentieth century, most of the people celebrated here combined an interest in economics with the pursuit of a different occupation – merchant, cleric, philosopher, journalist, banker or civil servant. But nevertheless, what they wrote is part of an important tradition.

A closer examination of the title of this work indicates its focus. It is a biographical work. Although much of each entry deliberately aims to add to the history of economic ideas, there is enough biographical information to describe the life that gave rise to an interest in economics. This is not, therefore, an account of disembodied minds. Every attempt has been made to discover the family background, education and career of each biographical subject. This has been difficult for some pre-1800 authors, but meagre biographical facts and hints in published works rescue them from total obscurity. A biographical approach to economics has interested many leading economists, who chose a mixture of an analysis of ideas and a chronicle of life events to illuminate an aspect of economics. Hicks, for example, tended to concentrate on an economist's theoretical achievement, as is clear in his essay on Hawtrey in *Economic Perspectives* (1977). Keynes, on the other hand, in *Essays in Biography* (1933), presented vivid portraits of economists before providing a comprehensive survey of their economic thought. This *Biographical Dictionary* will, we hope, be more in the spirit of Keynes the biographer.

This work is identified with Britain so it is necessary to explain what qualifies here to be 'British'. Birth in Great Britain – England, Scotland and Wales – could be a qualification for inclusion. But this has its difficulties, as someone born in Britain could emigrate before taking up any interest in economics at all. A country is chiefly regarded as a group of residents at a particular time, rather than as a land area, so there is a case here for using the criterion of residence as a justification for selection. Through living in a particular place, writers have an opportunity to encounter and join an intellectual community, with common influences and similar concerns. Thus in this work a qualification for inclusion is adult residence, usually for at least ten years, in Britain at the time of writing on economics.

To be ranked as economist means meeting one or more of several criteria. The easiest cases are people who spent their careers teaching or researching the subject, or holding the job title of

Introduction

'economist'. Only economists of the last hundred years are likely to qualify in these ways. Even in the late nineteenth century, few chairs of economics existed in Britain and few people worked exclusively on economics in government or private employment. The term 'economist', originating in the French Physiocratic School of the second half of the eighteenth century, did not indicate full-time specialization in the subject, as the careers of Quesnay and Turgot, for example, demonstrate. To use too narrow a definition of an economist – as a person with a university degree in that subject earning a living from practising economics – would unfortunately exclude thinkers as eminent as David Ricardo, Karl Marx, John Stuart Mill and hundreds of lesser luminaries. As Willie Henderson has perceptively remarked:

> Formal economics for the most of the nineteenth century was not as neatly contained within the boundaries of professional discussion as it has been in the latter part of the twentieth century. It was available to, and written by, specialists and non-specialists alike, and its discourse was seen as significant, in some respects at least, to actions of industry, government and enterprise and even to notions of order, reform and democracy.[1]

Thus it is necessary to be generously broad in the selection of biographical subjects, but this does create another problem. It is possible to be employed as an economist for a bank or a governmental agency and make a significant contribution to economics without any external publications. Including in this *Dictionary* economists whose works have not survived in published form makes an assessment difficult. Without a publication, it is hard to discern the mind of the economist. Sometimes records of parliamentary proceedings provide a 'publication' of thoughts on economics, as with Samuel Bosanquet and Joseph Hume. Fortunately we were able to find pamphlets, books and articles for the majority of these economics writers. An examination of the bibliographies will show how diverse were the interests of these economists. In toto, they are interested in branches of economics as varied as those listed in the subject classification of the *American Economic Review* and the *Economic Journal*. Thus the economics underlying this anthology is a study of particular theories, ideas, models, methods and policies of many related fields of inquiry. Value, money, trade, economic systems, income distribution, population, welfare, markets, planning, taxation, the state, firms, households and industries are recurrent candidates for investigation.

The time period covered by this *Dictionary* is long. We have some medieval writers, including Robert Grosseteste and Duns Scotus. (Admittedly the range of economic thinking of those men who were primarily theologians and philosophers was narrow, but later economists are as prone to limited concerns. In the twentieth century, professional economists have often followed the path of modern science by becoming more and more specialized.) There is room here, after the medieval period, to present the thinking of early Elizabethan writers on trade and money, for mercantilists and then for the neoclassicals, Keynesians, econometricians and abstract theorists. Dissenters who stood outside the prevailing fashions of economics also find a place. Writers whose interest in economics is very peripheral have been included – for example Charles Dickens – as they contributed to a debate, in his case on the dismal and harsh precepts of contemporary political economy. Specialist interests are well represented here. There are many demographers, socialists, philanthropists, bankers and economic historians presented for a new assessment. Living economists have largely been excluded: when a life is concluded an assessment usually begins, providing many rich sources of reminiscence and criticism. There has

---

[1] Willie Henderson (2000), *John Ruskin's Political Economy*. London and New York: Routledge, p. 24.

Introduction

been late inclusion in the *Dictionary* of the recently deceased, for example, Michael Bacharach and John Flemming.

It will be noted that these entries – long, middling or short in length – all attempt to include place and date of birth and death, education, principal life events, a summary and discussion of major economic writings and a bibliography. The leading books, pamphlets and articles of each biographical subject are cited with original dates of publication, and place of publication if other than London. References to useful secondary sources are also included. For economists whose intellectual interests are mainly non-economic, the bibliography concentrates on economics works.

What can the reader gain from this *Dictionary*? First, a summary of what is known of the life and ideas of British men and women who made some contribution to economic thought. Second, an opportunity to acquire a knowledge in context of economic writers by learning of their contemporaries and by being able to trace the precursors and followers of their ideas. Third, these articles with their bibliographies should become an important tool for the historian of ideas. It is hoped that this *Dictionary* will inspire many other writings on British economic thought.

Donald Rutherford, 2004

HOW TO USE THE *DICTIONARY*

The *Dictionary* contains entries on approximately 600 important thinkers and practitioners in the history of economics. The title of each entry gives the subject's name and dates of birth and death, where known. Further biographical details, again where known, are given in the opening paragraph or paragraphs of each entry. The remainder of each entry discusses the subject's work, writings, ideas and contribution to economics.

Bibliographies have been included with each entry. These should not be taken as full and complete bibliographies, which in some cases would take up many pages. Many of the subjects published very widely, often on many subjects apart from economics, and many have also been the subjects of vast bodies of literature. We have tried to restrict bibliographies to the most important and relevant works to the subject at hand. We have in most cases included only published works; only rarely, where there is an unpublished work of major importance, have we given manuscript details.

Within the body of the entries there is a cross-referencing system referring to other entries. Names which appear in small capitals (e.g. JEVONS) are themselves the subjects of entries in the *Dictionary*, and the reader may refer to these entries for more information. In some caes, where there are entries on more than one person with the same name or surname (e.g. Thomas WILSON, ANDERSON, BARING, BLAKE) we have tried to provide identifying information; in other cases, the context should be sufficient to identify the subject.

An index is also provided, which lists each person who is the subject of an entry and lists the page numbers on which cross-references can be found. As many of the entries are quite short, we have opted for this system rather than identifying every occurrence of the individual's name. The use of small capitals for cross-references allows users of the index to spot references easily on the page.

GENERAL BIBLIOGRAPHY

The following are general reference works which may be of use for further information about individuals named in the *Dictionary*.

Dictionary of National Biography (*DNB*), ed. Leslie Stephen and Sidney Lee, first published in May 1885. A new edition of DNB is currently in progress.
Who Was Who.
Arestis, P. and Sawyer, M., *A Biographical Dictionary of Dissenting Economists* (Aldershot, 1992).
Backhouse, R., *Penguin History of Economics* (2002).
Blaug, M., *Economic Thought in Retrospect*, 5th edn (Cambridge, 1997).
Cannan, E., *A History of the Theories of Production and Distribution from 1776–1848*, 3rd edn (1917).
Catalogue of the Goldsmith's Library, University of London Library (1970–83).
Greenaway, D., Bleaney, M. and Stewart, I.M.T., *Companion to Contemporary Economic Thought* (1991).
Heckscher, E., *Mercantilism* (1955).
Himmelfarb, G., *The Idea of Poverty* (1984).
Hollander, S., *Classical Economics* (Oxford, 1987).
Hutchison, T.W., *Before Adam Smith: The Emergence of Political Economy* (Oxford, 1988).
Kadish, A., *Historians, Economists and Economic History* (1989).
Kress Library of Business and Economics Catalogue (1940).
Letwin, W., *The Origins of Scientific Economics: English Economic Thought 1660–1976* (1963).
O'Brien, D.P., *The Classical Economists* (Oxford, 1975).
Schumpeter. J.A., *History of Economic Analysis* (1954).
Thompson, N., *Political Economy and the Labour Party* (1996).

LIST OF CONTRIBUTORS

Timothy Alborn
Associate Professor of History
Lehman College
City University of New York

David Ashbury
London

Marie-Thérèse Maxwell Awadalla
Department of Economics
Brock University
St. Catharine's, Ontario

Roger E. Backhouse
Professor of the History and Philosophy of Economics
University of Birmingham

Michelle C. Baddeley
Fellow and College Lecturer in Economics
Gonville and Caius College, Cambridge

Aldo Barba
Reader, Dipartimento di Scienze Economiche e Sociali
Facoltà di Economia
Università degli Studi di Napoli 'Federico II'

Nicholas Barr
Professor of Public Economics
European Institute
London School of Economics

Logie Barrow
University of Bremen
Bremen, Germany,

Daniele Besomi
Gola di Lago, Switzerland

R.D. Collison Black
The Queen's University of Belfast

Ian Blanchard
Professor of Medieval Economic and Social History
School of History and Classics
University of Edinburgh

Christopher Bliss
Professorial Fellow
Nuffield College, Oxford

Marjorie Bloy
Rotherham, Yorkshire

Katharine Bradley
Barnett Librarian and Archivist
Toynbee Hall
London

Sir Samuel Brittan
Financial Times
London

List of Contributors

Vivienne Brown
Professor of Intellectual History
Faculty of Social Sciences
The Open University

J.M. Bumsted
Fellow of St. John's College and Professor of History
University of Manitoba

Kathleen Burk
Professor of Modern and Contemporary History
Department of History
University College, London
Gresham Professor of Rhetoric
Gresham College, London

Brian Burkitt
Senior Lecturer
Department of Social Sciences and Humanities
University of Bradford

C. George Caffentzis
Professor
Department of Philosophy
University of Southern Maine

Peter Cain
Research Professor in History
Department of History
Sheffield Hallam University

Professor R.H. Campbell
Newton Stewart, Dumfries and Galloway

Forrest Capie
Bank of England

Terrell Carver
Professor of Political Theory
Department of Politics
University of Bristol

John Chapman
Principal Lecturer
Department of Geography
University of Portsmouth

Victoria Chick
Emeritus Professor
University College, London

Leslie Clarkson
Emeritus Professor of Social History
The Queen's University of Belfast

David Collard
Department of Economics,
University of Bath

Selwyn Cornish
Reader, School of Economics,
Australian National University

James E. Crimmins
Professor of Political Theory
Department of Political Science
Huron University College
London, Ontario

Eileen M. Curran
Emerita Professor of English,
Colby College,
Waterville, Maine

Richard R. Danielson
Professor, School of Human Kinetics
Laurentian University
Sudbury, Ontario

Adrian Darnell
Professor, Department of Economics and Finance
University of Durham

Sir Partha Dasgupta
Professor, Faculty of Economics
University of Cambridge

List of Contributors

Phyllis Deane
Cambridge

Lord Desai
Professor, Centre for the Study of Global Governance
London School of Economics and Political Science

H.T. Dickinson
Richard Lodge Professor of British History
School of History and Classics
University of Edinburgh

Robert Dimand
Professor, Department of Economics
Brock University
St. Catharine's, Ontario

N.H. Dimsdale
Emeritus Fellow in Economics
The Queen's College
Oxford

Ian Donnachie
Reader in History
The Open University in Scotland

Alastair Dow
Professor, Division of Economics and Enterprise
Glasgow Caledonian University

Andrew S. Downes
Professor and University Director
Sir Arthur Lewis Institute of Social and Economic Studies
University of the West Indies

Alan Ebenstein
Adjunct Scholar, Cato Institute
Washington, DC

E. Anthon Eff
Associate Professor, Department of Economics and Finance
Middle Tennessee State University

Ben Fine
Professor of Economics
School of Oriental and African Studies
University of London

Gordon Fletcher
Lecturer in Economics
School of Management
University of Liverpool

Geoffrey Foote
Senior Lecturer in History
School of Arts and Media Studies
University of Teesside

J.L. Ford
Emeritus Professor, Department of Economics
University of Birmingham

Andy Forrester
Chiswick
London

Jonathan A. Fowler
Assistant Professor, Liberal Arts Department
Pellissippi State Community College
Knoxville, Tennessee

Elena Gallego
Associate Professor, Department of History of Economic Thought
University Complutense of Madrid

Christian Gehrke
Associate Professor, Department of Economics
University of Graz

Geoffrey Gilbert
Professor of Economics
Hobart and William Smith Colleges
Geneva, New York

List of Contributors

Dr David Gladstone
Senior Lecturer and Director of
Programmes in Social Policy
School for Policy Studies
University of Bristol

Howard Glennerster
Professor of Social Administration
London School of Economics and Political Science

Mark Goldie
Senior Lecturer in the Faculty of History
Fellow of Churchill College
University of Cambridge

Charles Goodhart
Professor and Deputy Director, Financial Markets Group
London School of Economics and Political Science

Nigel Goose
Professor of Social and Economic History
University of Hertfordshire

Kenneth Graham
Professor
Department of English Literature
University of Guelph

Andrew Graham
Master
Balliol College
Oxford

Richard Grassby
Hagerstown, Maryland

A.C. Grayling
Reader, Department of Philosophy
Birkbeck College
University of London

Peter Groenewegen
Professor, Department of Economics
University of Sydney

Martin Haggerty
Scarborough, Yorkshire

Omar Hamouda
Professor, Department of Economics
Glendon College
York University
Toronto

Philip Hanson
Emeritus Professor of the Political Economy of Russia and Eastern Europe
Centre for Russian and East European Studies
University of Birmingham

G.C. Harcourt
Emeritus Reader in the History of Economic Theory
Jesus College, Cambridge

Indra Hardeen
Department of Economics
Brock University
St. Catharine's, Ontario

Keith Hartley
Professor and Director, Centre for Defence Economics
University of York

John T. Harwood
Associate Professor, School of Information Sciences and Technology
Penn State University

John Hatcher
Professor of Economic and Social History
Corpus Christi
Cambridge

Barry Haworth
Assistant Professor, Department of Economics
College of Business and Public Administration
University of Louisville
Louisville, Kentucky

List of Contributors

Rod Hay
Department of Economics,
University of Guelph

James Henderson
Professor, Department of Economics
Valparaiso University
Valparaiso, Indiana

Norriss Hetherington
Director, Institute for the History of
Astronomy
Berkeley, California

Geoffrey M. Hodgson
Research Professor, The Business School
University of Hertfordshire

Michael Howard
Professor, Department of Economics
University of Waterloo
Waterloo, Ontario

Thomas M. Humphrey
Senior Economist and Research Advisor
Research Department
Federal Reserve Bank of Richmond

Anne Humpherys
Professor, Lehman College
City University of New York

Sir Laurence Hunter
Emeritus Professor and Honorary Senior
Research Fellow
School of Business and Management
University of Glasgow

Frances Hutchinson
Honorary Visiting Research Fellow
Department of Social Sciences and
Humanities
University of Bradford

Alan Hutton
Division of Economics and Enterprise
Glasgow Caledonian University

Joanna Innes
Fellow and Tutor
Somerville College, Oxford

Joyce Jacobsen
Professor of Economics
Department of Economics
Wesleyan University

Simon James
Reader in Economics
School of Business and Economics
University of Exeter

Kevin Jefferys
Professor of Contemporary History
School of Humanities
Faculty of Arts
University of Plymouth

Ralph Jessop
Senior Lecturer in Literature and
Philosophy
The University of Glasgow

Sir Richard Jolly
Professor, Institute of Development Studies
University of Sussex

Priti Joshi
Assistant Professor, Department of English
and Comparative Literature
San Diego State University

Professor Anastassios Karayiannis
Associate Professor
Department of Economics
University of Piraeus
Athens

List of Contributors

Prue Kerr
Perth, Western Australia

Ann Kimber
London

J.E. King
Professor of Economics
Department of Economics and Finance
La Trobe University

Matthias Klaes
Director, Stirling Centre for Economic Methodology
Department of Economics
University of Stirling

Robert H. Koehn
Lecturer, Department of Economics
Brock University
St. Catharine's, Ontario

Gerard M. Koot
Professor, Department of History
University of Massachusetts Dartmouth

Heinz D. Kurz
Professor, Department of Economics
University of Graz

Bruce Larson
Professor of Economics
University of North Carolina at Asheville

Colin W. Lawson
Reader, Department of Economics
University of Bath

Frederic S. Lee
Professor of Economics
University of Missouri, Kansas City

Robert Leeson
Associate Professor of Economics
Murdoch University

Enrico Sergio Leverero
Researcher, Dipartimento di Economia
Universita di Roma Tre

David M. Levy
Professor of Economics
George Mason University

Jack Little
Professor and Chair, Department of History
Simon Fraser University
Burnaby, British Columbia

Stephen C. Littlechild
Honorary Professor
University of Birmingham Business School
Principal Research Fellow
Judge Institute of Management Studies
University of Cambridge

Marilyn Livingstone
Northlew, Devon

Brian Loasby
Professor, Department of Economics
University of Stirling

Donna Loftus
Lecturer, Department of History
The Open University

John Loxley
Professor, Department of Economics
University of Manitoba

Sarah Lumley
Senior Lecturer, Faculty of Natural and Agricultural Sciences
The University of Western Australia

Harro Maas
Assistant Professor, Department of Economics
University of Amsterdam

List of Contributors

Fiona C. Maclachlan
Professor of Economics and Finance
Manhattan College

Vincenzo Maffeo
Researcher, Dipartimento di Scienze giuridiche,
Facoltà di Giurisprudenza,
Università degli studi di Roma 'La Sapienza'

Lars Magnusson
Professor and Chair in Economic History
Department of Economic History
University of Uppsala

John Maloney
Reader in Economics
School of Business and Economics
University of Exeter

D.E. Martin
Senior Lecturer in History
Department of History
University of Sheffield

Roger Ashton McCain
Professor, Department of Economics and International Business
Drexel University

Roger Middleton
Reader in the History of Political Economy
Department of Historical Studies
University of Bristol

Dale E. Miller
Assistant Professor, Department of Philosophy
Old Dominion University

Wallace G. Mills
Associate Professor, Department of History
St Mary's University
Halifax, Nova Scotia

A.L. Minkes
Oxford

D.E. Moggridge
Professor of Economics
Department of Economics
University of Toronto

Pat Moloney
Senior Lecturer, School of History, Philosophy, Political Science and International Relations
School of Political Science
Victoria University of Wellington

Catherine Molyneux
Edmonton, Alberta

Seàn D. Moore
Assistant Professor of English,
University of New Hampshire

Dr Gregory C.G. Moore
Senior Economist
College of Business
University of Notre Dame, Australia

Mr James Ashley Morrison
Trinity College, Cambridge

Cary J. Nederman
Professor, Department of Political Science
Texas A&M University

Katharine Norley
London

D.P. O'Brien
Professor Emeritus of Economics
University of Durham

John J. O'Connor
Mathematical Institute
University of St Andrews

List of Contributors

Julie O'Neill
Burton Joyce, Nottinghamshire

Terry J. O'Shaughnessy
Tutor and Fellow in Economics
St Anne's College, Oxford

Shepley Orr
Senior Research Associate, School of
Economics and Social Studies
University of East Anglia

James R. Otteson
Associate Professor of Philosophy
Department of Philosophy
University of Alabama

Morton Paglin
Emeritus Professor, Department of
Economics
Portland State University
Portland, Oregon

Antonella Palumbo
Researcher, Departimento di Economia
Università di Roma Tre

Joseph L. Pappin III
Professor, Division of Continuing
Education
University of South Carolina, Columbia

Sir Alan Peacock
The David Hume Institute
University of Edinburgh

Robin Pearson
Reader, Department of History
University of Hull

Sandra Peart
Professor, Department of Economics
Baldwin-Wallace College
Berea, Ohio

M. Hashem Pesaran, FBA
Professor of Economics
Faculty of Economics and Politics
University of Cambridge

Ray Petridis
Associate Professor in Economics
Murdoch University

Massimo Pivetti
Professor of Political Economy
Istituto di Economia e Finanza,
Università di Roma 'La Sapienza'

Geoffrey Poitras
Professor of Finance
Faculty of Business Administration
Simon Fraser University
Burnaby, British Columbia

Cliff Pratten
Emeritus Fellow
Trinity Hall, Cambridge

Betsey Barker Price
Department of the History of Science
Harvard University
Cambridge, Massachusetts

Iorwerth Prothero
Robinson College, Cambridge

John Pullen
Professor, School of Economics, Business
and Law
University of New England
Armidale, New South Wales

Salim Rashid
Professor of Economics
University of Illinois Urbana-Champaign

David R. Raynor
Associate Professor, Department of
Philosophy
University of Ottawa

List of Contributors

David Renton
Senior Research Fellow in History
Sunderland University

Kenneth Richards
Aberystwyth

Martin Ricketts
Professor of Economic Organisation
Department of Economics and Interational Studies
University of Buckingham

Edmund F. Robertson
Mathematical Institute
University of St Andrews

Hugh Rockoff
Professor, Department of Economics
Rutgers University

Alessandro Roncaglia
Professor of Economics
Department of Economic Sciences
Università di Roma 'La Sapienza'

Jeffery I. Round
Reader, Department of Economics
University of Warwick

Donald Rutherford
Department of Economics
University of Edinburgh

Keith A.P. Sandiford
Emeritus Professor
University of Manitoba

Claudio Sardoni
Professor, Dipartimento di Scienze Economiche
Università di Roma 'La Sapienza'

Mona Scheuermann
Professor, Department of English
Oakton Community College
Des Plaines, Illinois

Stefan W. Schmitz
Research Unit for Institutional Change and European Integration
Austrian Academy of Sciences
Vienna

Maurice Scott
Oxford

Neil T. Skaggs
Professor, Department of Economics
Illinois State University

Andrew Skinner
Professor
Department of Political Economy
University of Glasgow

Anthony Slaven
Professor, Centre for Business History in Scotland
University of Glasgow

Barbara Smith
Edgbaston, Birmingham

William D. Sockwell
Associate Professor of Economics
Department of Economics
Berry College
Mount Berry, Georgia

Mark G. Spencer
Postdoctoral Research Fellow
Department of History
University of Toronto

Michael F. Sproul
Lecturer, Department of Economics
Loyola Marymount University
Los Angeles

David Stack
Lecturer in Modern British History
School of History
University of Reading

List of Contributors

Richard Sturn
Associate Professor, Institute of Public Economics
University of Graz

John Taylor
East Alton, Illinois

Michael W. Taylor
Senior Economist, Monetary and Financial Systems Department
International Monetary Fund

A.P. Thirlwall
Professor of Applied Economics
Department of Economics
University of Kent

J.H. Thomas
Porthcawl, Mid-Glamorgan

Jim Thomas
Emeritus Reader in Economics
Department of Economics
London School of Economics and Political Science

Martyn Thompson
New Orleans

Noel Thompson
Professor, Department of History
University of Wales Swansea

Tom Tomlinson
Faculty of Arts and Humanities
School of Oriental and African Studies
University of London

Attilio Trezzini
Researcher, Dipartimento di Economia 'Federico Caffe'
Università di Roma Tre

Michael J. Turner
Reader in Modern British History
University of Sunderland

Liz Varley
Catterick Garrison, Northumberland

William Veloce
Associate Professor, Department of Economics
Brock University
St. Catharine's, Ontario

Alan Ventress
Associate Director, State Records Authority of New South Wales
Sydney, NSW

Izumi Watanbe
Professor of Economics
Osaka University of Economics

A.M.C. Waterman
Fellow of St John's College, Winnipeg
Professor of Economics
University of Manitoba

Norman West
Professor of History
Social Science Department
Suffolk County Community College
Selden, New York

John K. Whittaker
Emeritus Professor of Economics
Department of Economics
University of Virginia

Morgen Witzel
Honorary Senior Fellow
School of Business and Economics
University of Exeter

Barbara Wood
Richmond, Surrey

Geoffrey E. Wood
Professor of Economics
Cass Business School
London

List of Contributors

John H. Wood
R.J. Reynolds Professor of Economics
Wake Forest University

Thomas Worth
London

Basil Yamey
London

John T. Young
Research Associate
Centre for History of Science,
Technology and Medicine
Imperial College
London

Jesùs M. Zaratiegui
Associate Professor, Department of
Economics
University of Navarra
Dpt de Economia
Universidad de Navarra

A

ACLAND, John (*c*.1729–after 1796)

Acland was born around 1729, the son of John Acland, vicar of Broad Clyst in Devon. He died some time after 1796. He entered Balliol College, Oxford in 1747, aged 18, gained his BA in 1751, and followed his father into the Broad Clyst living. He was a member of the Devon county bench, and cousin to MPs Sir Thomas Acland and John Dyke Acland.

Acland's interest in friendly societies was undoubtedly prompted by his Devon experience, as both minister and magistrate. Clothworkers in Devon, as in other parts of the West Country, may have been precocious in forming friendly societies. Certainly in the 1760s, a decade of rising prices which saw much interest in new approaches to the relief of the poor, it was to such societies that Devon magistrates turned as they sought a route forward appropriate to local conditions. In 1769, a local act was obtained, permitting the establishment of a county-wide network of contributory friendly societies, under parish auspices, and with an element of subsidy from the poor rates (9 Geo 3 c 82). The project apparently ran into difficulty, however, and the act was repealed at local initiative in 1772 (12 Geo 3 c. 18).

In 1786, Acland published *A Plan for rendering the Poor independent on Public Contributions, founded on the basis of the Friendly Societies, commonly called Clubs*. This proposed that a similar scheme might be extended throughout the country. Acland hoped that publicly organized friendly societies (membership of which was to be compulsory) would dispense with undesirable features of existing benefit clubs (too much drinking in pubs; too much money devoted to supporting 'mutinous secessions from labour', or wasted on extravagant funerals), while encouraging the poor to be frugal and reducing or eliminating rate-expenditure on doles. Friendly societies were probably increasing in number at this time, and their potential was widely noted and discussed. Acland's pamphlet, which was much praised and cited (it included within its pages a supporting letter from Richard PRICE) attracted notice not on any count of originality, but rather because it put flesh on widely touted ideas. One immediate effect was to spur John Rolle, MP for Devon, to introduce a general bill incorporating the proposal into the House of Commons. However, this failed to pass. What did pass, in 1793, was a bill drafted by the secretary to the Treasury, George ROSE (33 Geo 3 c 54), which offered legal support to friendly societies which registered their existence with local magistrates.

A second pamphlet, published in 1796, took issue with Edward KING's attempt to prove the public utility of the national debt. The pamphlet was heavily politically biased: the policy of sustaining a debt was identified with the prime minister, William Pitt (though in fact, he tried to shift fiscal policy away from dependence on borrowing). Acland admitted that someone expert in trade and banking might have been better placed to analyse the case. He himself focused especially on the argument that public debt made for national prosperity. In his view, the earth's produce had natural limits. Taxation and fashionable living together acted to raise prices, ensuring that supposed prosperity was certainly not shared by the poor.

BIBLIOGRAPHY
A Plan for rendering the Poor independent on Public Contributions, founded on the basis of the Friendly Societies, commonly called Clubs (1786).
An Answer to a Pamphlet, published by Edward King, Esq.... in which he Attempts to Prove the Public Utility of the National Debt. A Confutation of that Pernicious Doctrine, and a True Statement of the Real Cause of the Present High Price of Provisions (Exeter, 1796).

Further Reading
Gosden, P.H. (1961) *The Friendly Societies in England* (Manchester, 1961).
Keith-Lucas, B. 'A Local Act for Social Insurance', *Cambridge Law Journal* (1952), vol. 2, no. 2, pp. 191–7.
Steer, W.S., 'Devon Pioneers of Social Insurance', *Transactions of the Devon Association for the Promotion of Science, Literature and Art* (1964), vol. 96, pp. 303–17.
Poynter, J.R., *Society and Pauperism. English Ideas on Poor Relief 1795–1834* (1969).

Joanna Innes

ACWORTH, William Mitchell (1850–1925)

Acworth was born 22 November 1850 at Rothley in Leicestershire, and died in London on 2 April 1925. He was the third son of the Rev. William Acworth and his wife, Margaret Dundas, of Glasgow. Acworth was educated at Uppingham School and Christ Church, Oxford where he was awarded a BA (second class) in modern history in 1872. In that year he began work as the private tutor to princes William (later to become Kaiser Wilhelm II) and Henry of Germany. In May 1875 and again in 1885, Acworth was an assistant teacher at Dulwich College. In 1890, the Inner Temple called him to the bar.

In 1878 Acworth married Elizabeth Louisa Oswald, the eldest daughter of James Brown from Ayrshire. She died in 1904. Acworth then married Elizabeth Learmonth from Hundleshope, Peeblesshire in 1923. Both marriages were without issue. Acworth was knighted in 1921, and was created a Knight Commander of the Star of India (KCSI) in 1922.

Acworth became interested in the administration of asylums and in 1886 he was elected to the Metropolitan Asylums Board, later becoming its chairman. Politically, Acworth was a unionist and an advocate of private enterprise. He was a member of the London County Council between 1889 and 1892, and stood unsuccessfully in 1906, 1910 and 1911 for election as MP for Keighley in the West Riding of Yorkshire.

In the 1880s, Acworth became interested in the economics of railway transport, publishing his first book in 1889. This was followed by a number of other railway publications. In *The Railways and the Traders* (1891) he was critical of railway accounts in Britain, comparing them with the more efficient American statistical methods. The changes that Acworth suggested in 1906 were not implemented until 1911; his recommended system of accounting did not become a requirement until 1920.

Soon after the foundation of the London School of Economics in October 1895, Acworth introduced lectures for railway students. From his lectures he published *The Elements of Railway Economics* (1905), going on to publish many other articles on railway economics in Britain and the United States. Acworth was a director of the Underground Electric Railways of London Limited and also of the Midland and South-Western Junction Railway. He was also a member of the council of the Royal Economic Society and of the Institute of Transport. The LSE now possesses Acworth's collection of transport literature.

Acworth was a member of many official bodies concerned with railways. He sat on the Royal Commission on accidents to railway servants (1899), the vice-regal commission on Irish railways (1906) and the Royal Commission of Enquiry into Canadian railways (1916) that recommended that the government should operate all Canadian railways as a single system. He chaired the East India Railway committee (1920); its report, recommending state management of the entire network and the separation of railway and general government finances, was implemented. As a world expert on the relationship between governments and railways, Acworth investigated Austrian railways for the League of Nations and German railways for the Reparations Commission (1924).

Despite his views on economics, Acworth found himself suggesting some element of state control in the years following the First World War, although he strongly favoured the separation of railway budgets from national finances and promoted safeguards against any political interference in the transport system.

BIBLIOGRAPHY
Railways of England (1889).
Railways of Scotland (1890).
Railways and the Traders (1891).
Government Railways in a Democratic State (1892).
Railway Economics (1892).
The Nationalisation of Swiss Railways (1898).
A Historical Sketch of State Railway Ownership (1920).

Marjorie Bloy

ALLEN, George Cyril (1900–82)

Allen was born 28 June 1900 at Kenilworth, and died 31 July 1982 at Oxford. He joined the newly created Royal Air Force as an officer in 1918. Following the war he attended the University of Birmingham where he studied under William ASHLEY, graduating BCom in 1921 and MCom in 1922. Chance brought him a job as a lecturer in economics at Koto Shogyo Gakko in Nagoya, Japan, which he held from 1922–5; he retained a lifelong interest in the Japanese economy and culture. Returning to Birmingham in 1925, Allen was a research fellow and lecturer in industrial economics, and also studied for his PhD, which he received in 1928. His thesis was published as *The Industrial Development of Birmingham and the Black Country* (1929). In 1929 he moved to University College of Hull as professor of economics; in 1933 he moved to Liverpool as Brunner Professor of Economic Science; and in 1947 he was appointed professor of political economy at the University of London. He became emeritus professor in 1967. He was made a fellow of the School of Oriental and African Studies in 1973, and of St Anthony's College, Oxford in 1982.

Allen also had a long record of public service. During the Second World War he served as an assistant secretary to the Board of Trade, and following the war was a member of the Price Regulation Committee until 1953. He was a member of the Monopolies Commission from 1950–62, and served on several commissions and enquiries. He was president of the economics section of the British Association for the Advancement of Science (1950), vice-president of the Royal Economic Society (1933–63) and was elected a fellow of the British Academy in 1965. He married Eleanora Shanks in 1929.

Two issues dominated Allen's writings over the course of some fifty years of activity: the failing response of British industry to competitive pressures, and the much more successful response of Japan to those same pressures. His critique of British industry begins with one of his best and most important works, *British Industries and Their Organization* (1933). Here Allen charts the development of British industry from the Industrial Revolution to the First World War, noting that the initial advantages to Britain of early industrialization had been eroded by the middle of the nineteenth century by increased foreign competition. British industry had by the end of the century effectively restructured itself, with certain areas concentrating on specialist industries and abandoning others; as an example, he cites the rise of shipbuilding on the Clyde and the simultaneous decay of the Glasgow textile industry.

However, fundamental weaknesses remained in the system. In particular, Allen argued that in a *laissez-faire* economy, certain industries would tend to concentrate and reach a size beyond which the economies of scale no longer operated: 'while industrial individualism stimulated the adoption of improved methods of production and might be justified in a period in which communities were lifting themselves from a plane of primitive equipment and scanty wealth, it did not promote the optimum distribution of resources' (1933: 10). Unrestrained competition, Allen believed, led ultimately to wasteful practices. He called for more planning, more co-operation between firms, and more professional management to create greater efficiency. In the 1960s he returned to this theme with more vigour, notably in *The British Disease* (1976) and *British Industry and Economic Policy* (1979) in which he attacked government and industrialists alike for failure of planning and foresight.

Allen was an early prophet of the competitive threat posed by Japanese industrialization, and in *Japan: The Hungry Guest* (1938) and *Japanese Industry: Its Recent Development and Present Condition* (1940) he warned that Japanese economic expansion could have serious consequences for the rest of the world. In the post-war period he was an interested observer of the rapid recovery of the Japanese economy, and in the 1970s wrote several works praising Japanese industrial structure and the relationship between industry and the state, most notably in *How Japan Competes* (1978). Subsequent economic problems in Japan have shown that not all of Allen's conclusions about the Japanese economic system were valid, but his role in alerting the West to the potential – and commercial threat – of a resurgent Japan was very important at the time.

BIBLIOGRAPHY
Modern Japan and its Problems (1928).
The Industrial Development of Birmingham and the Black Country (1929).
British Industries and Their Organization (1933).
Japan: The Hungry Guest (1938).
Japanese Industry: Its Recent Development and Present Condition (1940).
(with A.G. Donnithorne) *Western Enterprise in Far Eastern Development* (1954).
Japan's Economic Recovery (1958).
Japan as a Market and Source of Supply (1966).
The British Disease: A Short Essay on the Nature and Causes of the Nation's Lagging Wealth (1976).
How Japan Competes (1978).
British Industry and Economic Policy (1979).

Further Reading
'Allen, George Cyril', in Contemporary Authors, New Revision Series, vol. 32 (1988).

Morgen Witzel

ALLEN, Roy George Douglas (1906–83)

Allen was born 3 June 1906 at Stoke-on-Trent, Staffordshire, and died 29 September 1983 at Southwold, Suffolk. He was educated at the Royal Grammar School, Worcester and Sidney Sussex College Cambridge, where he read mathematics. He graduated with a first-class degree in 1927. From 1928 he taught statistics at the London School of Economics; he was appointed a reader in 1940, and a professor in 1944. He retired in 1973 but continued to teach. He established and developed the statistics and econometrics department at the LSE until it was ranked among the leading departments of its kind.

During the Second World War Allen held important administrative posts. From 1939 until 1941 he was a statistician at HM Treasury. In 1941, he was sent to Washington, where from 1941 to 1942 he was Director of Records and Statistics for the British Supply Council. From 1942 to 1945, he was British Director of Research and Statistics for the Combined Production and Resources Board in Washington. In a 1946 paper in the *Journal of the Royal Statistics Society*, Allen described the terms of lend-lease and compared the degree of mobilization of the USA and the UK. By mid-1944, the UK had 55 per cent of its labour force employed on war duties, compared to 40 per cent in the USA.

After returning to London at the end of the war, Allen was a statistical adviser for HM Treasury from 1947 to 1948. From 1960 until 1972 he was a member of the Air Transport Licensing Board, and from 1972 until 1973 he served on the Civil Aviation Authority. He was chairman of the Departmental Committee on the Impact of Rates on Households, and a foundation member of the Social Science Research Council; he was first chairman of its Statistics Committee. He was president of the Econometric Society in 1951 and President of the Royal Statistical Society in 1969–70. Allen was knighted in 1966.

Allen was an economic statistician and mathematical economist. In the 1930s he worked with John HICKS and Arthur BOWLEY. With Hicks he published the two-part article 'A Reconsideration of the Theory of Value' in *Economica* in 1935. With Bowley, Allen worked on the statistics of family budgets. His book with Bowley, *Family Expenditure* (1935), reported a study aimed to discover how far the expenditure of individual families or groups of families could be described by rules and formulae. The authors broke new ground in applying statistical methods to the study of consumers' expenditure.

In a paper in *Economica* in 1949 Allen examined the properties of index numbers where preferences change. He identified the characteristics of quantity indices and what became 'Allen' quantity indices. His conclusion was that index numbers should be limited to short-run comparisons. In *Index Numbers in Theory and Practice* (1975), he noted that the concept of index numbers is straightforward but there are important assumptions and potential hazards in constructing and using index numbers. He goes on to give a comprehensive description of their design, construction and use.

Starting with *Mathematical Analysis for Economists* (1938), a book that was based on a course of lectures aimed to provide a course of pure mathematics in directions most useful to students of economics, Allen published a series of widely used textbooks providing an introduction to mathematical economics and to economic statistics. *Mathematical Economics* (1956) was an advanced textbook and a standard text for a generation of students taking courses in mathematical economics.

BIBLIOGRAPHY

(with J.R. Hicks) 'A Reconsideration of the Theory of Value': parts 1 and 2, *Economica* (1934), new series, vol. 1, pp. 52–76 and 196–219.

'A Note on the Determinateness of the Utility Function', *Review of Economic Studies* (1935), vol. 2, pp. 155–8.

(with A.L. Bowley) *Family Expenditure* (1935).
Mathematical Analysis for Economists (1938).
'Mutual Aid between the US and British Empire, 1941–45', *Journal of the Royal Statistical Society* (1946), vol. CIX, pp. 243–77.
'The Economic Theory of Index Numbers', *Economica* (1949), new series, vol. 16, pp. 197–203.
Statistics for Economists (1949).
(with J.E. Ely) *International Trade Statistics* (1953).
Mathematical Economics (1956).
Basic Mathematics (1962).
Macro-Economic Theory (1967).
Index Numbers in Theory and Practice (1975).
An Introduction to National Accounts Statistics (1980).

Further Reading
Cairncross, A., 'Roy Allen 1906–1983', *In Proceedings of the British Academy*, vol. 70 (Oxford, 1985).
Grebenick. E., 'Roy George Douglas Allen, 1906–1983', *Journal of the Royal Statistical Society* (1984), pp. 706–7.

Cliff Pratten

ANDERSON, Adam (*c*.1692–1765)

Anderson was probably born in Aberdeen in 1692, and died in Clerkenwell, London on 10 January 1765. Little is known of his life until he went to London, where he worked as a clerk for the South Sea Company for forty years until his death, rising to the post of chief clerk of the Stock and New Annuities. He was also one of the court of assistants of the Scots Corporation in London in 1762, and a trustee in 1765 for the establishment of the colony of Georgia.

Anderson is chiefly remembered for his *A Historical and Chronological Deduction of the Origin of Commerce* of 1764, which was subsequently revised and expanded by David MACPHERSON from two volumes to a four-volume edition in 1805. Anderson's industry in compiling so much information covering centuries of economic history was massive. His ambitious aim was to establish the causes and instruments of commerce by analysing his collected data. Many causes of commerce were mentioned. Commerce is possible because every habitable country has a superfluity of produce and the erosion of feudalism through the granting of exclusive privileges to maritime towns. Also the discovery of the mariner's compass and then the invention of gunpowder artillery, which allowed ships to become larger, were crucial.

True to his Scottish roots, Anderson asserted that Protestant countries have advantages over 'the Popish' in both commerce and manufactures as there are no useful workers shut up in convents, no obligation to celibacy, no interruption to employment through religious holidays and processions, and useful people are encouraged to take up residence. He estimated that the whole rental of land and houses of England had risen from £5m to £10m in the past 250 years through the increase in commerce and manufactures. He reminded his readers that England's commerce with America exceeded its trade with Europe. Also he was sufficiently far-sighted to argue for the same weights and measures and same decimal coinage to be employed in all Christian countries.

With justification, Adam SMITH praised Anderson and, according to the CANNAN edition of the *Wealth of Nations*, drew more from the *Origin of Commerce* than from any other book. Dorfman mentions the breadth of the book in its use of foreign economic data to consider the fortunes of Britain and America.

BIBLIOGRAPHY
A Historical and Chronological Deduction of the Origin of Commerce, from the earliest accounts to the present time, containing a history of the large commercial interests of the British Empire (1764; repr. New York, 1967).

Further Reading
Dorfman, J., 'An Eighteenth Century Guide Book for Economic Policy', introduction to A. Anderson, *A Historical and Chronological Deduction of the Origin of Commerce* (New York, 1967).

Donald Rutherford

ANDERSON, James (1739–1808)

Anderson was born in a village near Edinburgh some time in 1739, and died in London on 15 October 1808. Orphaned as a young child, he was reared by a relative who encouraged him, while still in his teens, to take over the management of his father's tenant farm (Mullet 1968). His early education included paid instruction in Edinburgh, which gave him some familiarity with foreign languages. Subsequently he attended the lectures of William Cullen at Edinburgh University in order to understand chemistry in its relation to agricultural improvement. Cullen was a leading member of the scientific school in the Scottish Enlightenment and a formative influence on Anderson. From Cullen, and in related classes at the university, Anderson absorbed an inductive, empirical method which infused his many publications, weighing them down with carefully observed detail.

Agricultural improvement, broadly conceived, was the great love of Anderson's intellectual life. By improvement, of course, was meant technical advance in agriculture. He married in July 1768 and, in the next year, took a lease on a 1300–acre farm in Aberdeenshire near his wife's family estate. There he practised and wrote on improvement in a stream of articles which began in 1769. At Monkshill Farm he conceived, among his many practical notions, the abstract, economic construct of differential rent (*An Enquiry into the Nature of the Corn Laws, with a View to the new Corn Bill proposed for Scotland*, 1777). As his fame grew, Aberdeen University conferred on him an honorary LLD. It is ironic that by 1783 the farm's finances were insufficiently sound to educate his many children, and the family moved back to Edinburgh.

Intellectual concerns absorbed Anderson for the rest of his life. The British Treasury asked him to report on the fishery in the West of Scotland (*An Account of the Present State of the Hebrides and Western Coasts of Scotland*, 1785). Regular publications continued on topics ranging from agricultural improvement in Scotland to slavery in the West Indies. He founded and was editor of two periodicals, *The Bee* (1790–94) and *Recreations in Agriculture* (1798–1802). His correspondents included George Washington and Jeremy BENTHAM. Returning to the subject of the Corn Laws, Anderson wrote *A Calm Investigation of the Circumstances that have led to the Present Scarcity of Grain in Britain* (1801). A widower living in London from 1797, he remarried in 1801.

MALTHUS read and criticized the optimistic population theory of *A Calm Investigation*, but there is only limited evidence that Malthus was aware of the statement of rent made by Anderson in 1777 (Prendergast 1987). RICARDO may have known of Anderson, but no evidence exists of his having read the *Enquiry*. It seems likely that no strong intellectual thread linked Anderson's theoretical advance with later developments. Malthus elaborated differential rent theory independently, along with Ricardo, and incorporated the construct into systems much more sophisticated than that of Anderson. Thus, Malthus and Ricardo have received the principal credit for the introduction of economic rent into economic analysis.

Observations on the Means of exciting a Spirit of National Industry was written mostly in 1775 but published in 1777. In this work Anderson offered a prescription for economic development in contemporary Scotland, with emphasis on the backward Highlands. Agriculture and manufacturing were seen as complementary in a framework that development economists would call balanced growth (1777: 305). An internal growth dynamic was sought with only a supplementary contribution by exports. Agriculture was for him the most important sector of the economy, but to flourish, agriculture required the demand of growing manufacturing districts with their wage labour. While generally favouring trade, Anderson saw agricultural protection as promoting technological advance, and so he favoured the Corn Laws. The state had a role along with the market in securing development (Gee 1998).

The fundamental difference between Anderson and Adam SMITH – and Anderson was an early critic – was in their attitude to state involvement in agricultural regulation. In contrast with Smith's pro-market views, Anderson advocated a price stabilization policy which would, he claimed, in the long run lead to increased output in an average year, lower prices and freedom from want in times of crop failures. These benefits would more than compensate for the costs of the programme, the funds taken from general revenues to pay the export bounty in good crop years. In his two 1777 publications he also pointed towards an equilibrium notion of value, attacking Smith's view of the corn price and the cost of living as being indistinguishable. Anderson's writings did cause Smith to modify, in a minor way, his analysis of corn bounties (Dow 1984).

Though now forgotten by most economists not specializing in economic doctrine, Anderson's treatment of economic rent was widely praised in the nineteenth century. For example, J.R. MCCULLOCH was quite laudatory of Anderson's contribution. Both Karl MARX and Henry George acknowledged Anderson as the originator of differential rent. Stanley JEVONS was aware of his contribution, and later Edwin CANNAN and Joseph Schumpeter subjected his rent formulation to critical appraisal. Then near oblivion fell. Neither Eric Roll nor Maurice DOBB mentioned Anderson in their widely read books on economic thought. Alexander Gray was similarly silent. More recently some renewed recognition is evident; for instance, Phyllis Deane acknowledged Anderson's contribution (Deane 1978), and in his commentary in *James Mill*, Donald Winch noted that Mill's first pamphlet was a response to Anderson's later writing on the corn bounty in 1801 (Winch 1966: 25). D.P. O'Brien deals with Anderson's rent concept in J.R. McCulloch: A Study in Classical Economics (O'Brien 1970) and Samuel Hollander, in *The Economics of David Ricardo*, devotes several pages of text and an interpretative appendix to Anderson's theory of differential rent (Hollander 1979). Two full articles on Anderson's contributions appeared in academic economics journals in the 1980s and 1990s (Prendergast 1987; Gee 1998). The article by Gee looks beyond rent to Anderson's wider perspective on economic development.

Anderson was an intellectual innovator ahead of his time. His natural place is in the vanguard of that pragmatic Scottish tradition of political economy which flourished until recent decades, but which is now, unfortunately, extinct (Dow *et al.* 2000). Drawing on the more inductive strand of Enlightenment thinking, which he absorbed in his scientific studies, Anderson favoured careful observation and generalization based on experience. His arguments contained short chains of logic designed to buttress and explain a policy recommendation. That a man such as Anderson should emerge with profound insights is evidence of the breadth of the Scottish Enlightenment in the society of Scotland in the late eighteenth century.

BIBLIOGRAPHY
An Enquiry into the Nature of the Corn Laws, with a View to the new Corn Bill proposed for Scotland (Edinburgh, 1777).
Observations on the Means of exciting a Spirit of National Industry (Edinburgh, 1777).
An Account of the Present State of the Hebrides and Western Coasts of Scotland (Edinburgh, 1785).
Recreations in Agriculture, Natural History, Arts and Miscellaneous Literature (1799–1802).
A Calm Investigation of the Circumstances that have led to the present Scarcity of Grain in Britain (1801).

Further Reading
Dow, A.C., 'The Hauteur of Adam Smith: An Unpublished Letter from James Anderson of Monkshill', *Scottish Journal of Political Economy* (1984) vol. 31, no. 3, pp. 284–5.
Dow, A.C., Dow, S. and Hutton, A., 'Applied Economics in a Political Economy Tradition: The Case of Scotland from the 1890s to the 1950s', *History of Political Economy supplement, Towards a History of Applied Economics*, vol. 32.
Deane, P., *The Evolution of Economic Ideas* (Cambridge, 1978).
Gee, A., 'James Anderson, Development Economist: A Cautionary Tale', *The Manchester School* (1998), vol. 66, no. 5, pp. 581–606.
Hollander, S., *The Economics of David Ricardo* (Toronto, 1979).
Mullet, C.F., 'A Village Aristotle and the Harmony of Interests: James Anderson of Monks Hill', *The Journal of British Studies* (1968), vol. 8, no. 1, pp. 94–118.
O'Brien, D.P., *J.R. McCullouch: A Study in Classical Economics* (1970).
Prendergast, R., 'James Anderson's Political Economy', *Scottish Journal of Political Economy* (1987), vol. 34, no. 4, pp. 388–409.

Winch, D., *James Mill: Selected Economic Writings* (Edinburgh, 1966).

Alistair Dow

ANDREWS, Philip Walter Sawford (1914–71)

Andrews was born in Southampton on 12 March 1914, and died in Lancaster on 5 March 1971. He was one of six children. His mother was Ethel Sawford, the daughter of an agricultural and iron stone labourer and had been a domestic servant before her marriage. His father was Frederick Walter Andrews, son of a ship's steward and stevedore, who worked as an able-bodied seaman and shunter and retired as chief inspector, traffic department, at the Southampton Docks. His sister, Evelyn Mary, married Richard W. Marsh MP.

Andrews was educated in Southampton at St Denys Elementary School and Tauton's School (1925–31), where he was a modern studies prizeman. He entered University College, Southampton as an Open Foundation Scholar in 1931 to read for a University of London external degree. Driven by a desire to improve the world in which he lived, Andrews specialized in economics, attending lectures on economic theory, money, banking, public finance, international trade, and applied economics. In 1934 he graduated with a second-class degree in economics. Awarded a research grant by Southampton, he remained there for the next three years as a research student, temporary assistant lecturer and honorary tutor-organizer for the Workers' Educational Association. In 1934 he attended the Aberdeen meeting of the British Association for the Advancement of Science where he met David H. MACGREGOR, who was giving a paper on joint stock company registrations. MacGregor encouraged Andrews to do a research degree at Oxford, and so in 1937 he entered Oxford to study for a D. Phil in economics.

Once at Oxford, Andrews became involved in the Oxford Economists' Research Group. He became enthralled at seeing economists actually finding out what businessmen did instead of assuming that they already knew. The Group's inquiry into price determination caught his attention and was destined to have a major influence on him. With the outbreak of war in 1939, the Group suspended its work. Andrews, who was a conscientious objector to military service, remained in Oxford and became involved with the Nuffield College Social Reconstruction Survey under the direction of G.D.H. COLE. Cole and the Survey were concerned about the post-war economic and social prospects of the main industrial regions of Great Britain, and formulated proposals about general problems of social and economic reorganization after the war. Andrews was the Survey's chief statistician and, in this role, he supervised Elizabeth Brunner's work on *Holiday Making and the Holiday Trades* (1945). As a result, Brunner became his research associate and colleague for the next twenty-five years.

In 1943 Cole received a letter from Samuel Courtauld, the chairman of the board of textiles firm Courtaulds, expressing doubt about the dictum that the bigger the enterprise or plant the more efficient it would be. Because he did not believe that any thorough investigation into the economics of large-scale production had been carried out, Courtauld asked Cole whether it would be possible to establish such an investigation. With funds provided by Courtauld, Cole established the Courtauld Inquiry with Andrews in charge of the empirical and statistical investigation into the economies of scale. Later the terms of the Inquiry were extended to investigating the relative efficiency of small-scale and large-scale business and allied problems of industrial structure and organization. The Inquiry continued until 1949.

In 1946 Andrews was appointed Official Fellow of Nuffield College, Oxford, and he remained at Nuffield until 1967. He then became the Professor of Economics at the University of Lancaster. The move was, in part, prompted by the relationship between Elizabeth Brunner and Nuffield College. In spite of being diagnosed with cancer, Andrews maintained a heavy workload until the end of his life. In addition to his research and teaching, Andrews engaged in other activities: in 1947 he helped to revive the Oxford Economists' Research Group and participated in it until 1957, and in 1948 he was a founding member of the Oxford Management Club. In 1952 he established the *Journal of Industrial Economics* with the purpose of encouraging both academic and industrial economists to use economic analysis when writing on industrial and commercial topics. Andrews maintained the general editorship of the journal until 1971. From 1958–62 he was on leave from Nuffield College and during this period advised private businesses on their defence before the Monopolies Commission or in the Restrictive Practices Court.

Ever since his involvement with the Oxford Economists' Research Group and involvement in the Courtauld Inquiry, Andrews had become progressively disenchanted with marginalism, dismissing the firm demand curve, declining marginal products and increasing marginal costs, firm equilibrium, and profit maximizing pricing through the equation of marginal costs and marginal revenue. He became increasingly determined to develop an alternative theory of the business enterprise. His first presentation of his alternative theory was in the publication of *Manufacturing Business* (1949), arguably his best-known and most infamous work.

The manufacturing business that concerned Andrews was a going concern and existed in real time, and its goals were survival and growth. It did not face internal cost constraints on sales in the short term or on the expansion of the scale of production in the long term.

Neither was it impelled to sell at a price determined by the interaction of costs with an external demand constraint; rather, it would decide on a pricing policy and administered its own price. But the absence of such internal constraints did not mean the absence of any constraints at all. The business enterprise existed in an industrial environment, a system of inter-related enterprises which exerted competitive pressure on pricing behaviour which could be ignored only at the risk of the enterprise's own demise.

However, Andrews could not claim that, in *Manufacturing Business*, he had produced a theoretical alternative to marginalism. In particular, his theory of the business enterprise lacked a grounding in a theory of markets, a discussion of industry and markets, an analysis of retail trade and consumer behaviour, and a discussion of enterprise investment decision-making. It was also a negative critique of marginalism. Between 1950 and 1964 Andrews repaired these omissions, and by doing so transformed his theory of the manufacturing business into a theory of industrial markets and then finally into a general theory of markets, which included retail trade and consumer markets, called the theory of competitive oligopoly. Incorporated in the theory were his theories of normal cost pricing and prices.

With *Manufacturing Business* and subsequent publications, Andrews created the potential for a theoretical revolution in terms of replacing neoclassical price theory and its marginalist approach to the theory of the firm with a non-neoclassical theory of prices and the firm. Consequently, upon the publication of *Manufacturing Business*, his theory of normal cost pricing was subject to withering criticism from neoclassical economists. Unable to dismiss his work on empirical grounds, critics attacked the book as hard to read and full of wrong-headed theorizing, discrediting Andrews as an economic theorist and attempting to prevent the renewal of his Nuffield Fellowship. Although he was able to retain his fellowship, the experience left him reluctant to defend his theory publicly. It may have also contributed to his turning away after 1953 from systematic development of his theory of competitive oligopoly to work more with businessmen and their practical issues. Consequently, Andrews never wrote a book in which he presented his theory in a systematic manner. Thus the promise of a well-developed alternative to neoclassical price theory and its marginalist analysis of the firm, which had seemed quite imminent in 1952, never materialized although Andrews wrote a very good and pointed critique of marginalism in *On Competition in Economic Theory* (1964).

Although consigned to oblivion by neoclassical economists, Andrews and his work were discovered by post-Keynesian economists in the 1970s and become an essential foundational component of a heterodox microeconomic theory. Today, Andrews is better known than at any time in the last thirty years.

BIBLIOGRAPHY

'A Further Inquiry into the Effects of Rates of Interest', *Oxford Economic Papers* (1940), vol. 3: 32–73.

Manufacturing Business (1949).

(with E. Brunner) *Capital Development in Steel* (Oxford, 1951).

(with T. Wilson) *Oxford Studies in the Price Mechanism* (Oxford, 1951).

On Competition in Economic Theory (1964).

(with E. Brunner) *Studies in Pricing* (1975).

(with F.A. Friday) *Fair Trade: Resale Price Maintenance Re-examined* (1960).

Further Reading

G.D.H. Cole Papers, Nuffield College, Oxford.

King, J.E., *Economic Exiles* (New York, 1998).

Lee, F.S., 'D.H. MacGregor and the Firm: A Neglected Chapter in the History of the Post Keynesian Theory of the Firm',

British Review of Economic Issues (1989), vol. 11, no. 24, pp. 21–47.
———, *Post Keynesian Price Theory* (Cambridge, 1998).
Lee, F.S. and Earl, P.E., *The Economics of Competitive Enterprise: Selected Essays of P.W.S. Andrews* (Aldershot, 1993).
Lee, F.S. and Irving-Lessmann, J., 'The Fate of an Errant Hypothesis: The Doctrine of Normal Cost Prices', *History of Political Economy* (1992), vol. 24, no. 2, pp. 273–309.
Philip Walter Sawford Andrews Papers, British Library of Political and Economic Science, London School of Economics, London.
Young, W. and Lee, F.S., *Oxford Economics and Oxford Economists* (1993).

Frederic S. Lee

ANGELL, Norman (1872–1967)

Angell was born Ralph Norman Angell Lane on 26 December 1872 in Holbeach, Lincolnshire. He died on 7 October 1967 in Croydon, Surrey. He was brought up in a well-to-do but unpretentious middle-class household. His father, Thomas Angell Lane, had established a chain of local shops before retiring to become a gentleman magistrate with a taste for French classics. He quietly encouraged his son in his precocious reading of political texts.

Angell attended elementary schools in England, but had the good fortune to be sent to a French lycée at St.-Omer. Having escaped the confining influences of the conventional English public (that is, private) boarding school, he found himself at the age of seventeen editing a bi-weekly English language newspaper in Geneva, catering mainly for tourists. Simultaneously he was taking courses at Geneva University.

He was, however, essentially self-taught. He happened to read John Stuart MILL's *On Liberty* during an illness at the age of twelve, and this was for a long time his guiding light. But he also devoured the work of other 'public intellectuals', such as Voltaire, Huxley, SPENCER and CARLYLE.

His family would gladly have financed a British university course, probably in Cambridge, but at the age of seventeen Angell was so appalled by the lack of interest of many of his family and friends in his ideasthat he despaired of the rulers of Europe adopting rational policies. He decided to immerse himself in manual labour in California. Despite being only five feet tall and of a frail appearance, he was physically very resilient. For seven years he worked as a vine planter, irrigation ditch digger, cow puncher, and smallholder in the new western state. But eventually he concluded that life in the wilderness posed quite as many problems as life in a city, and he accepted offers to be a reporter first for the *St Louis Globe Democrat* and later the *San Francisco Chronicle*. It was not the physical hardships that made for unhappiness: 'This came from the anxieties and uncertainties, the fear of debt, the presence of creditors whenever I should go to town.'

Angell returned to England for family reasons in 1898 and then earned his living working for small journals, both in French and in English, in Paris. He was in that city during the Dreyfus case, where French anti-semitism made a deep impression on him, as had American aggression in the Spanish-American War and British jingoism in the Boer War. This led to the publication of his first book, *Patriotism under Three Flags: A Plea for Rationalism in Politics* (1903). This fell still-born from the press; but in the course of occasional contacts he impressed Lord Northcliffe, who appointed him as the first editor and manager of the Paris edition of the *Daily Mail*, a post he occupied from 1905 to 1912 . It was during this period that he wrote in his spare time the book for which he achieved lasting fame, and in some quarters notoriety.

The Great Illusion originated in 1909 as a short essay, issued at his own expense, called *Europe's Optical Illusion* by 'Norman Angell' a style he later legalized as his own name. Gradually news of it spread by word of mouth among the English establishment. It influenced people such as Lord Esher, the confidante of Edward VII and chairman of the Imperial Defence Committee. This unexpected attention enabled Angell to expand the work, which was republished in 1910 as *The Great Illusion*, in which form it sold over two million copies and was translated into twenty-five languages. The Garton Foundation was established to promote his ideas. In his autobiography he described the book as 'a publishing success but political failure'.

From 1912 onwards Angell supported himself as a freelance writer, lecturer and journalist. In all he wrote forty-one books: 'too many', he afterwards wrote. It is for *The Great Illusion* that he will be remembered. He obviously had practical managerial and journalistic abilities; otherwise Northcliffe would hardly have tolerated someone with opinions almost diametrically opposed his own aggressive anti-Germanism as a collaborator. Indeed, Northcliffe continued to see Angell after 1912 and offered him the hospitality of the *Daily Mail* for articles which took issue with his own positions.

Angell never seemed to have ambitions for an academic position and wrote mainly for the educated general public. He laboured at telling home truths which academic economists acknowledged but were too ready to take for granted. He was warmly praised for his efforts by KEYNES. His chief sorrow was that the wider public, such as the mass readers of the *Daily Mail*, would not abandon their prejudices and perform a little rational analysis. It is perhaps as well that he did not live into the age of late twentieth-century tabloid journalism, television and spin doctors. He was not a conventional pacifist, but he advocated British neutrality during the period leading up to the First World War. This brought him into the company of Labour leaders such as Ramsay MacDonald, who opposed participation in the war, and also of course intellectuals such as Bertrand Russell. The fact that most of his political supporters came from one wing of Labour Party propelled him into that party, and from 1929 to 1931 he was Labour MP for North Bradford.

Doctrinally, Angell was from the beginning a classical liberal and a strong opponent of Marxist theories that war was the product of capitalism; theories that were influential even among Labour Members who disavowed Marx. Although his primary interest was international affairs, he was equally infuriated when such MPs took the view that nothing could be done about the gathering economic depression unless capitalism was abolished. He did not stand for re-election in 1931 because he felt 'better fitted to present the case for internationalism to the public direct, freed from party ties'. He was knighted in 1931; a dinner in his honour was presided over by the very same man, Lord Cecil, who had refused him a passport in 1916. He was far more pleased with the Nobel Peace Prize, awarded in 1933.

In the inter-war years, Angell was concerned to promote collective security against the dictators, and he devoted some years of his life, before, during and after the Second World War trying to convince the Americans to come to Britain's side in defence of civilization. He found himself having to fight on two fronts, against the right-wing isolationists and against the American left who, with some sympathizers in the Roosevelt household, wanted to back Stalin in his confrontations with Churchill. Not surprisingly, he was later a strong supporter of Western defence efforts in the Cold War period.

The urge to bury himself in physical activity never deserted Angell, even though from his sixties onwards he developed severe migraines which prevented him from getting more than four or five hours sleep a night. He was a keen sailor all his life and bought Northey Island, a small island on the Blackwater Estuary. As far as is known, he showed no interest in partners of either sex and, as he put it, craved his 'daily bath of solitude', but was delighted to entertain his nephew and niece on boating holidays. Despite his health problems, he continued lecturing in the USA until the age of ninety. He was too rational to believe that he could defeat mortality, and he died in a Surrey nursing home at the age of ninety-four.

Angell's lifelong sorrow was the frequent misrepresentation of *The Great Illusion*. He was alleged to have said that war was impossible because of its great expense, a misrepresentation still current in the twenty-first century. As he so often remarked, he would hardly have gone to the trouble to write and promote this book if he believed that war could not happen or would fizzle out very quickly. On the contrary, the illusion which he tackled was that wars could be economically advantageous. He was writing against a background of the German drive to build battleships and acquire colonies. In a curious way these German beliefs were supported by British jingoists, who believed that the Germans were bound to break out in search of *Lebensraum* and that a clash was therefore inevitable.

The Great Illusion did not, of course, contain equations and was quite sparse in statistics. But it gave illustration after illustration to show the fallacy of treating nations as if they were individual people. He cited for instance the 'German' acquisition of Alsace-Lorraine after the Franco-Prussian war. Did it give the German people access to steel and coal? No. They had to buy the products of former French provinces just as they did before. Another example was the British conquest of South Africa. The gold and diamond mines remained with their original owners, and the British had to purchase their products as before. He also cited the case of small countries such as Norway and Switzerland which attained high standards of living without colonies or conquests, simply by trading in the open market. War was a waste of resources, or as later economists would put it, a negative-sum game.

The basic Angell thesis stands the test of time pretty well. An opponent might cite the success of cartels in forcing up the prices of key commodities for periods of years. But such cartels have never been a main feature of the world economy. The period when the oil producers' cartel (OPEC) did most harm – after the Yom Kippur war of 1973 – was also a period when inflationary overheating in all in the main industrial countries was in any case pushing up the market price of fuel and gave OPEC its opportunity. Given the role of Middle Eastern wars in acting as a trigger for such cartel action, it would have been ludicrous to suggest that Western economies would have benefited from a punitive expedition to Saudi Arabia, which was the lynchpin of OPEC.

Victors in war have sometimes implicitly supported the Angell thesis by trying to force the defeated governments to cover their wartime losses of the winning side. An indemnity was imposed on France after the Franco-Prussian war of 1870–1, and a reparations burden was imposed on Germany after the First World War. The French indemnity was never more than a tiny fraction of the imperial German national income; and it was notorious that German reparations were never paid, as Keynes, along with Angell, had warned they could not be.

A more telling criticism might be that Angell assumed too readily the moral standards of nineteenth-century capitalism under which a victorious government continued to buy on world markets and did not just seize the assets of the defeated country. He took for granted, for instance, that the British government would not have wished to destroy its international credit rating by seizing the South African mines after the Boer War. The Soviet Union did not of course always accept the rules of capitalist trade: notoriously so when the Red Army simply seized machinery and industrial plant from the eastern part of Germany which it occupied after the Second World War. But again the benefit, if any, of this captured material to the USSR was far less than the horrendous economic damage inflicted by the German invasion.

The Angell argument is more vulnerable when the enemy is not a conventional state but international groupings of, say, religious fundamentalists who purport to despise the materialism of the West and regard death in terrorist action against the USA and its allies as the most honourable fate that can befall a young man. This was not of course a new phenomenon. There had been the *kamikaze* Japanese pilots in the Second World War; and for centuries in Europe the feudal code treated honour as infinitely superior to worldly riches. Shakespeare's plays contain numerous speeches on these lines, as well as, on the other side, the famous dismissal of honour put into the mouth of Sir John Falstaff. Neither Angell or any other political economist can 'refute' such codes of honour. Indeed, Angell was careful to point out that he did not regard economic rivalries as the only cause of war, but wanted to dispel them as a contributory factor. Nor was he worried by the assertion that 'you can't change human nature'. He did not dispute this, but argued that human behaviour could be changed by the equivalent of a Hobbesian sovereign in international affairs. He gave numerous instances where barbaric practices such as duelling, judicial torture or burning religious nonconformists had been eliminated or forced to the margin inside individual countries. He did live long enough to see how easily this moral progress could be put into reverse even in domestic politics and was thus – to the pain of some of his earlier friends on the left – one of the first to argue for rearmament against Nazi Germany and for an alert western defence against the Soviet threat. Indeed the limited part that reason plays in human affairs makes it all the more important that this should be true reason rather than the false arguments of the geo-politicians against whom Angell fought all his life. The fallacies he fought continued well into the twenty-first century. One example was the frequent belief that the USA desired or needed to dominate the Middle East for the sake of oil without realizing that Middle Eastern countries needed to sell the oil as much as the West needed to buy it.

Angell made one venture into economics, more narrowly understood, when he invented a card game described in *The Money Game* (1928). This was an attempt to explain matters such as deflation and inflation in visual terms which the ordinary person could understand. It could be regarded as the precursor to the National Income Machine which A.W. PHILLIPS invented at the London School of Economics after the Second World War, in which the flow of spending through the economy was shown by means of coloured water with taps that could be turned on and off.

Such devices went out of fashion with the increasing mathematical complexity of economic models which were more difficult to illustrate by visual devices. Opponents also said that such teaching devices ignored the subtle complexities introduced by the vagaries of human nature into the workings of the economy. But the more sophisticated mathematical models were even more mechanistic and the governing principles were more difficult even for their inventors to discern. If there were ever a serious attempt at mass economic education, there would be a case for returning to the Angell–Phillips tradition, so long as it was made clear that these devices can only illustrate guiding principles and cannot encompass the institutional variety of actual economies.

BIBLIOGRAPHY
Patriotism under Three Flags: A Plea for Rationalism in Politics (1903).
The Great Illusion (1910).
The Great Illusion Now (1938).
After All: The Autobiography of Norman Angell (1951).

Further Reading
Bisceglia, L., *Norman Angell and Liberal Internationalism in Britain 1931–1935* (New York, 1982).

Miller, J.D.B., *Norman Angell and the Futility of War* (1986).

Samuel Brittan

ANSTEY, Vera (1889–1976)

Anstey was born Vera Powell in 1889. She died in London on 26 November 1976. She was educated at Cheltenham Ladies College and Bedford College, London and then the London School of Economics. She graduated from the latter with first-class honours in economic history in 1913. She married a fellow student, Percy Anstey, in the same year, and in 1914 the couple moved to Bombay. Vera Anstey returned to England after her husband's death in 1920, and joined the faculty of the LSE as an assistant in 1921. She remained there until her retirement in 1964, becoming successively lecturer in commerce (1929), Sir Ernest Cassel Reader in Commerce (1941), and then a part-time member of the academic staff (1954). She served as dean of the Faculty of Economics from 1950 to 1954, and as a member of the Royal Commission on the Taxation of Profits and Income from 1950 to 1955.

Anstey's encounter with India was the turning point of her long and productive career of teaching and research. A pioneer of development economics before it was a recognized field, she shaped economics in India through the successive editions of her influential book on *The Economic Development of India* (1929), and through her teaching and mentoring of Indians studying economics at LSE. In the words of Tarlok Singh, secretary to the first prime minister of independent India, 'For generations of students at LSE, from India and the sub-continent, she had been a friend and guide who had cared for each of them' (Singh 1977, quoted in Dahrendorf 1995: 408). Her work is appropriately commemorated by the annual Vera Anstey Memorial Lecture to the Indian Economic Association (Chakravarty 1989). She also published a monograph on *The Trade of the Indian Ocean* (1929), an introductory textbook for economics students in India and Pakistan (1964), and journal articles on the Indian economy (Anstey 1923, 1936, 1947, 1952, and Anstey and Taraporevela 1956).

Anstey's approach to Indian development was inspired by the work of her senior LSE colleague, the economic historian R.H. TAWNEY, on Chinese agriculture. Like Tawney, she took an historical approach, and stressed the importance of technical training and education. She emphasized agricultural development, and was critical of protectionist measures to promote industrialization. She paid particular attention to institutions and social customs as barriers or aids to development. Chakravarty (1989) drew attention to Anstey's example of how the productivity of women picking cotton in Dharwar, in the Deccan, quintupled when the system of contract was changed, improving incentives.

When the London School of Economics moved to Cambridge for the duration of the Second World War, Anstey took on the challenging additional role of accommodation officer. She found, as she put it, that, 'The need to pander to the proclivities of hostesses or landladies indeed the great inequality of billeting conditions posed very delicate problems to the harassed, but withal amused, billeting officer' but she achieved her twin goals, 'that no student should have nowhere to sleep; and that no court case should be instituted' (Anstey 1951, quoted in Dahrendorf 1995: 346–7). Amusing as well as amused, her sense of humour managed to ease clashes between landladies and lodgers.

BIBLIOGRAPHY
'Some Recent Literature on Finance and Politics in India', *Economica* (1923), vol. 3, June, pp. 133–8.

The Trade of the Indian Ocean (1929).
The Economic Development of India (1929; 4th edn, 1952).
'India's Economic Position and Policy in Relation to the New Constitution', *Economica* (1936), new series, vol. 3, August, pp. 235–6.
'Social Accounting in India', *Indian Journal of Economics* (1947), vol. 27, January, pp. 271–77.
'LSE Yesterday, Today and Tomorrow, Part One', *LSE Magazine*, January, pp. 2–4.
'LSE Yesterday, Today and Tomorrow, Part One', *LSE Magazine*, July, pp. 2–5.
'The Colombo Plan: With Special Reference to India and Pakistan', *Economia Internazionale* (1952), vol. 5, February, pp. 134–47.
(with R.J. Taraporevala) 'Some Aspects of the Structure of Indian Industry', *Journal of the Royal Statistical Society* (1956), vol. 119, no. 1, pp. 62–82.
An Introduction to Economics: For Students in India and Pakistan (1964).

Further Reading
Chakravarty, S., 'British Perceptions of Indian Economic Problems: Dr. Vera Anstey and Her Book', *Indian Economic Journal* (1989), vol. 37, October–December, pp. 1–7.
Dahrendorf, R., *LSE: A History of the London School of Economics and Political Science 1895–1995* (Oxford, 1995).
Singh, T., 'Vera Anstey's Work for India', *LSE Magazine* (1977), June, p. 6.

Robert W. Dimand
Marie-Thérèse Maxwell Awadalla

ARMSTRONG, Clement (*c.*1477–1536)

Clement Armstrong (sometimes Ormestrong, Ormyston or Ormeston) was born in London around 1477, and died there after a short illness some time between January and early May 1536; his will was proved on 4 May of that year (Bindoff 1944). His father may have been Ralph Ormeston, a mercer and stapler of London who in 1493 become warden of the Mercers' Company and who died in 1496. Armstrong himself was admitted a freeman of the Grocers' Company in 1502. Of his career as a grocer nothing is known, but in 1516 he appears in the official records as a provider of building materials for royal buildings. Bindoff describes his new career as 'high-class interior decorating' (1944: 71); he worked on the buildings for the Field of the Cloth of Gold in 1520, and also undertook a commission for the Duke of Suffolk. It is around this time that Armstrong made the acquaintance of the printer and lawyer John Rastell who helped him secure further commissions. In 1527, when Rastell wrote and staged a masque in the great hall at Greenwich palace to welcome ambassadors from France, Armstrong provided the furnishings and stage scenery.

Rastell and Armstrong were more than just sometime colleagues; they also shared an interest in government and politics. Rastell had converted to Protestantism around 1530, and by 1532 was an active propagandist for the government during the time of the break with Rome. He was also close to Thomas Cromwell, and probably encouraged Armstrong to form a connection with Cromwell as well. However, Rastell fell out with Cromwell over the question of tithes, to which he was opposed; and the execution of his brother-in-law, Sir Thomas MORE, in 1535 cast a further shadow over him. Rastell was imprisoned and died in 1536, not long after Armstrong.

In 1535, Armstrong wrote to Cromwell and sent manuscripts of two treatises, works on which, he says, he had been working for some three years. The two works, *A Treatise concerning the Staple and the Commodities of this Realm* and *How to reform the Realm in setting them to work and to restore Tillage*, concern issues in which Armstrong is likely to have been personally interested, namely trade (thanks to his connection with the Grocers' Company) and agriculture and the consequences of enclosure (his mother is believed to have come from a landed family).

A Treatise concerning the Staple reflects the turmoil of the rapidly changing economy and society of Tudor England. Armstrong laments the rising levels of wool exports from England, and the consequent collapse of the domestic cloth industry. The demand for English wool on the continent was so strong that prices were rising rapidly, making it more profitable to export wool than to make cloth. Indeed, so great were the profits to be made from wool that landlords were enclosing agricultural land and converting it to pasture in order to raise more sheep, which was in turn leading to rising poverty. Armstrong attacks the enclosing landlords in no uncertain terms: 'what wretchis are those, that for theyr own syngler weale werkith ageynst Goddes wille and ordinaunce, to distroy the common weale of the holl realme...' (1535: 98). One wool merchant, or stapler, can destroy the living of several thousand common people (1535: 104). He also attacks the importation of foreign goods, which leads to the export of money from the kingdom, and calls for government measures to protect native industry. He suggests that there might even be too many merchants in the city of London, and that 'reforms' might be introduced in order to reduce competition and ensure that fair prices were paid for goods, arguing that the crown needed to undertake these reforms for the good of the people.

The second treatise, *How to Reform the Realm*, is a more direct attack on enclosure and argues for the restoration of agriculture which will in turn create employment and reduce poverty, begging and vagrancy. There is no evidence that Cromwell responded to Armstrong's treatises, although a letter from the latter to the former in late 1535 requested their return, as the author wished to make certain amendments. Armstrong's relationship with Rastell, who was by now in disgrace, would not have helped his cause. Cromwell did not return the treatises, and they were found among his papers in 1878 by the scholar Reinhold Pauli (the question of their dating remained open, and was finally settled by Bindoff). There was considerable interest in Armstrong for a time; John Maynard KEYNES considered him a forerunner of the mercantilists, and R.H. TAWNEY and Eileen POWER included the treatises in their collection of reprinted Tudor economic documents.

BIBLIOGRAPHY

A Treatise concerning the Staple and the Commodities of this Realm (1535; repr. in R.H. Tawney and E. Power, *Tudor Economic Documents*, 1924, vol. 3, pp. 90–114).

How to reform the Realm in setting them to work and to restore Tillage (1535; repr. in R.H. Tawney and E. Power, *Tudor Economic Documents*, 1924, vol. 3, pp. 115–29).

Further Reading

Bindoff, S.T., 'Clement Armstrong and his Treatises of the Commonweal', *English Historical Review* 1st ser., 14 (1944), pp. 64–73.

Morgen Witzel

ASGILL, John (1659–1738)

Asgill was born 25 March 1659 at Hanley Castle, Worcestershire and died in London on 10 November 1738. He entered the Middle Temple in 1686 and was called to the bar in

1792. Early patronage, notably by one of William III's judges, Robert Eyre, helped him build a successful legal practice. In the early 1690s he became friendly with Nicholas BARBON, the property developer and promoter of the Land Bank, and became Barbon's partner in the Land Bank, and helped merge it with John BRISCOE's National Land Bank in 1696. The Land Bank was never a strong business proposition, and Barbon's death in 1798 weakened it still further; the bank finally collapsed in 1700. Barbon had made Asgill his executor, and the debts and encumbrances of the Land Bank remained with him for almost all the remainder of his life.

Asgill's career after this point is increasingly tortuous. Thanks to a legacy from Barbon he was elected MP to the latter's old seat in Bramber in 1699, but was almost immediately in trouble for publishing a pamphlet claiming that for Christians, death was not inevitable; true believers were in fact immortal. Even his printers thought he had lost his reason. He then proceeded to Ireland, where an advantageous marriage brought him considerable estates, and he was elected MP for Enniscorthy in the Irish House of Commons and attempted very briefly to set up an Irish version of the Land Bank. Two weeks later he was expelled from the Irish house, his pamphlet on death having been burnt in Dublin by the public hangman. Returning to England, he resumed his seat in parliament but played no significant role. Mismanagement of his Irish estates coupled with debts from the Land Bank had ruined him, and upon prorogation in 1707 he was arrested for debts totalling around £10,000. Committed to the Fleet prison, he appealed to parliament and a committee of the House of Commons was set up to study his case; he was ordered released and reinstated in his seat, but was then formally charged with blasphemy for his earlier pamphlet, was ejected from the house, and was once more arrested and returned to the Fleet. A few years before his death, his creditors finally agreed to accept a small annuity in settlement of his debts and he was released.

Asgill's writings on money stem from the period of his involvement with Barbon and the ill-fated Land Bank, and consist of two pamphlets, *Several Assertions Proved, in Order to Create another Species of Money than Gold and Silver* (1696) and *An Essay on a Registry, for Titles of Land* (1698). His remaining writings were of a highly speculative theological nature. *Several Assertions*, published as the Land Bank scheme began to show signs of failing, is a bold call for reform of the currency. Asgill blames current economic problems in England on the shortage of currency, arguing that there is not enough circulating money to fulfil all the contracts currently outstanding. The shortage of money is in turn leading to speculation and stock jobbing. There are only two alternatives: to restrict economic activity, or to invent a new kind of money.

Current proposals for making bills of credit into current money will not work, says Asgill; these merely 'represent' money and will not stop the demand for it. Any new kind of money must have all the qualities of money itself: it must be durable and incorruptible, be easily transferable, and have intrinsic value. This view leads to an argument that land has all these properties, and therefore securities on lands can be exchanged as money. The remainder of the pamphlet is a thinly disguised advertisement for the land bank. However, Asgill's views on the necessary properties of money if it is to have public confidence form an interesting contribution to the wider debate.

An Essay on a Registry also reflects the affairs of the Land Bank, and takes up the earlier call of Andrew YARRANTON for the establishment of a public register of lands. Such an institution would, by making it plain to all who had title to land and what encumbrances might be upon it, make it much easier to use land as security for loans, which would in turn allow more credit and more money to enter the economy. Like Yarranton, Asgill deplores the excessive legal formality of transactions that use land as security, and maintains that the only parties to benefit from the system are lawyers. Ironically, it was just such transactions and legal formalities that would later help entangle him in further debt in Ireland.

BIBLIOGRAPHY
Several Assertions Proved, in Order to Create another Species of Money than Gold and Silver (1696; 2nd edn, 1720).
An Essay on a Registry, for Titles of Land (1698; repr. 1701, 1702).
An Argument Proving that According to the Covenant of Eternal Life Revealed in the Scripture, Man May be Translated Hence into that Eternal Life without Passing Through Death (1700).
Mr. Asgill's Defence upon his Expulsion from the House of Commons (1707).
An Essay Upon Charity (1731).

Morgen Witzel

ASHBY, Arthur Wilfred (1886–1953)

Ashby was born on 19 August 1886 at Tysoe in Warwickshire and died at Oxford on 9 September 1953. His upbringing in a reforming rural family in Tysoe coloured his academic interests. His father was a self-taught surveyor as well as a small farmer, a Methodist lay preacher, poor law guardian and local agent for the Labour party. Ashby's initial schooling ended early, at age twelve, when he went to work with his father. His father's Labour Party connections may have been responsible for his attendance at Ruskin College with a Charles Buskin scholarship in 1909. His diploma (with distinction) led to the publication of his first book, *One Hundred Years of Poor Law Administration in a Warwickshire Village* in 1912, the same year that he was given a scholarship to the Institute for Research in Agricultural Economics at Oxford.

After a short time as an honorary fellow to the University of Wisconsin, Ashby returned to Oxford in 1915, moving on in 1917 to work at the Board of Agriculture until 1919. He returned to the Institute at Oxford again in 1919 and remained there until 1924, when he was asked to head up a new department of agricultural economics at University College, Aberystwyth; he became the first professor of agricultural economics there in 1929. Ashby spent over twenty years at Aberystwyth until, in 1946, he succeeded C.S. ORWIN as director of the Institute for Research in Agricultural Economics at Oxford, a position he filled until his retirement in 1952. He served as a JP in both Cardiganshire and Oxfordshire, and was awarded the CBE in 1946.

The influence of Ashby's background can be seen in his first book, a detailed study of the poor law in his home village of Tysoe, using copious original sources and extending the examination of the poor law beyond the timeframe indicated by the title. He looks closely at the origins of the Elizabethan poor law system and further back at the more *ad hoc* poor relief arrangements that proceeded it. He also examines the economic and social consequences of the poor law system, such as wages and prices, poor rate assessment and illegitimacy. The numerous tables and extracts from original documents make this work a very valuable resource for anyone looking at both the theory and practice of the poor law.

Ashby's published work can be divided into two categories, academic works and those aimed at practitioners. In the first category are his four major monographs, beginning with the poor law volume discussed above. The other three books are *Allotments and Small Holdings in Oxfordshire* (1917), which was the standard work on the subject for many decades; *Rural Education* (co-authored with Phoebe Byles) and *The Agriculture of Wales and Monmouthshire* (co-authored with I.L. Evans). These three works encompass many of Ashby's concerns. The book on allotments stresses the importance of small-scale agricultural production, while the volume on rural education recognizes the value of evening classes and workers institutes, and reflects Ashby's interest in encouraging those who came to higher education through non-traditional routes, as he himself had done.

The survey of Welsh agriculture was published near the end of his time at Aberystwyth and draws on statistics from seventy years to 1939 to illustrate the changes that had taken place in Welsh agriculture, particularly the shift from grain production to animal products. Ashby sees foreign competition as the key driver of this change, and concludes that concentration on fresh milk can alleviate such competition. He also stresses the need for central marketing of produce, which is unsurprising given his involvement in the establishment of the Milk Marketing Board. The need for implementing new technology is also stressed and the book provides statistics for the limited impact which tractors and other mechanical devices had had on Welsh agriculture to date.

In addition to these major monographs, Ashby had a copious output of pamphlets on a variety of practical subjects, such as milk marketing, land tenure, agricultural co-operatives, Young Farmer's Clubs, farmers' credit and agricultural wages. The latter subject was a particular interest; he had been involved in the first Agricultural Wages Board during the First World War and was a member of the Board for nearly thirty years. Ashby also published a large number of papers in a variety of journals, and was a frequent participant at conferences (in whose proceedings his papers were published) as well as a popular teacher.

BIBLIOGRAPHY

One Hundred Years of Poor Law Administration in a Warwickshire Village (1912).
Allotments and Small Holdings in Oxfordshire (1917).
(with P. Byles) *Rural Education* (1923).
(with I.L. Evans) *The Agriculture of Wales and Monmouthshire* (1944).

A full list of Ashby's articles is to be found in *Journal of Agricultural Economics* (1956), vol. XII.

Marilyn Livingstone

ASHLEY, William James (1860–1927)

Ashley was born on 25 February 1860, in Bermondsey, South London, and died in Canterbury on 23 July 1927. He was the eldest of the six children (out of eight born) of a Baptist journeyman silk hat finisher. Educated principally at St. Olave's Grammar School, Southwark, he won the Brackenbury scholarship in 1878 to enter Balliol College, Oxford where he obtained a first-class BA in modern history (later converted to an MA) but was unable to afford to pursue *literae humaniores* (greats). Funding himself through tutoring, lectures and articles, he was introduced to economics and, attending Arnold TOYNBEE's lectures on the industrial revolution in 1881–2, became enthusiastic about the subject. At Toynbee's suggestion, he followed issues such as wages through the writings of economists starting with Adam SMITH. The history of economics became one of the main themes in his studies of mediaeval economic history. Soon he was also commenting on contemporary social and economic events and ideas, notably business education, trusts, tariffs and trade unions.

Starting with *James and Philip van Artevelde* (1883), which won the Lothian prize in 1882, Ashley published dozens of papers on the mediaeval period in England, France and Germany (many collected in *Surveys, Historic and Economic*, 1900). In 1885 he was awarded a fellowship and lectureship at Lincoln College, Oxford and a few months later an additional lectureship at Corpus Christi. This included lecturing in political economy to 80–100 students. He became a founder and secretary of the Oxford Economic Society. At this time too, he met (Annie) Margaret Hill, daughter of George Birkbeck Hill, but the wedding waited until the spring of 1888 when Ashley was appointed to a newly created professorship in the department of political science, shortly changed to political economy and constitutional history, at the University of Toronto. It was his task to set up the department to teach future lawyers and businessmen.

Before leaving Oxford, Ashley published what was then considered to be an important landmark in the development of economic history, *An Introduction to English Economic History and Theory, Part I: The Middle Ages* (1888). The preface indicates that the work was intended as a challenge to classical economic ideas, drawing inspiration instead from German historical methods. *Part II: The End of the Middle Ages* followed in 1893.

Ashley was at Toronto from 1888 to 1892. Largely due to the reputation of his 1888 book, he then received an invitation to take up a newly created professorship in economic history at Harvard, the first in the English-speaking world. He was at Harvard from 1892 to 1901. While there he taught an elementary economics course with sometimes as many as 400 students in attendance, and shared administrative work that he found congenial. He also became editor of the *Quarterly Journal of Economics*, in which many of his articles appeared. To make ends meet, he repeated his lectures to women at Radcliffe College and wrote articles for the New York *Nation*. One outcome was that no further volumes of his *Economic History* ever appeared, but he did produce several contemporary studies of Canadian and US subjects.

Ashley's two inaugural addresses reveal significant views on contemporary political economy. In that at Toronto (1888), he said that, until about 1870–5, political economy 'occupied...no very dignified or useful position', only suitable for 'Passmen' and 'women' (1888: 10), as the assumptions made 'rendered the "pure theory" of little avail'. He said that the term 'stank in the nostrils of intelligent working men' (1888: 11), while Gladstone thought its principles should be relegated to the planet Saturn (1888: 12). But, in Germany, a revolution had occurred in the subject and the 'historical method', applied first to law, had now been applied to political economy 'after an onslaught on economic orthodoxy' (1888: 15). The approach spread to England via T.E. Cliffe Leslie, a professor at Dublin, and Dr D.K. Ingram at the British Association Economic Section and, more recently, through Toynbee. Political economy, once it discarded the 'abstract deductive method' (1888: 16) for the 'historical, statistical, inductive', could 'directly tackle the pressing economic questions of the present', being 'inductive if you wish to be polite, or empirical if you wish to indicate scorn' (1888: 18–9) and dismissing *laissez-faire* 'as a general principle' (1888: 23).

Although his Harvard inaugural address of 4 January 1893, was entitled 'On the Study of Economic History' (1893), Ashley repeated to this new audience his views on political economy, although he estimated that the tolerance of political economists had improved with a change in their attachment to one method, their recognition that 'economic conclusions are relative to given conditions' and 'possess only hypothetical validity', and a start on their 'true field of work' (1893: 117). The outcome of this new attitude was the discipline of economic history, investigating 'the character and sequence of the stages of economic development' (1893: 121), dynamic, collective, institutional and representing 'economic evolution' (1893: 122) and examining 'modern industrial life in the piece' (quoted in A. Ashley 1932: 35). He added: 'We can leave to the Cambridge people hair-splitting analysis of abstract doctrine'. He distinguished what he called 'political economics', comprising general theories that might guide statesmen, from 'business economics' dealing with the 'practical problems which arise in the handling of any industrial or commercial enterprise' (MacDonald 1942: 34). Economic history represented a fresh division of labour within history or economics, often identifying precedents for modern discussions on, for example, the nature of private property or serfdom, not some primitive suffrage, in the mediaeval village (1893: 135). Ashley's address to the American Historical Association on 28 December 1899 added: 'The historian and the economist...may expel Nature with the fork of the Seminary or the Deductive Method; but Nemesis stands very near the shoulder of "Pure Economics" or "Pure History"'and in America it usually calls itself "Sociology"' (1900: 30).

Soon after this, Ashley moved on to another challenge and variant of economics with his appointment to be the 'Organizing Professor for Proposed Faculty of Commerce' at an annual stipend of £750 at the new University of Birmingham (Smith 2003: 12). Ashley's father had sent him the advertisement for the post, aware that he was tiring of Harvard life. Ashley, backed up by references from Alfred MARSHALL and William CUNNINGHAM, got the job and was appointed on 31 July 1901. Important qualifications must have been his administrative experience in Toronto and Harvard, his considerable list of publications and his ideas about educating businessmen and the new economics already apparent at Harvard.

Ashley arrived in Birmingham as a man of forty-three years with a wife, two daughters and a son. He found a house in Edgbaston, Birmingham, fetched his family from their holiday in Canada, and settled down to organize the new faculty, the first students of which were expected in October 1902. The family continued to live, and entertain staff, students and friends regularly at this house until 1920. Ashley's wife died in 1922 and he finally retired to Canterbury in 1925. His sister lived with him in the last few years in Birmingham and Canterbury.

Ashley's immediate task in 1902 and for the rest of his stay at Birmingham was to attract students to his new faculty, but he soon widened this to persuading business men (fathers mainly) and then the wider 'commercial community' (1926: 147) to send their sons to the many new departments and faculties of higher commercial education (LSE, Manchester, and others) in England. This wider effort is reflected in half a dozen papers and talks from 1903–26. Before settling his plans for Birmingham, he visited Germany for ideas, his report on the journey appearing in *The Times* on 2 April 1903. The Germans, he found, were not so much training businessmen as civil servants.

Ashley published his first brochure, *The Faculty of Commerce in the University of Birmingham: Its Purpose and Programme*, in 1902. As justification for vocational rather than cultural training, he argued that university education had always been 'professional' though the professions had expanded from the church through law, medicine, and engineering to now include the business profession (1926: 143). In 1902, he wrote that 'The instruction provided by the Faculty of Commerce furnishes a systematic training' and 'consists of study of two kinds'. There are parts that are of 'concern to the future man of business', but are elements of true education, and others that are recognised as elements of liberal culture but 'are peculiarly valuable for those engaged in commerce and manufacture' with others 'serviceable to all classes of business man' (*University Calendar* 1902: 276). The curriculum was to be utilitarian, aimed at producing successful business men 'not the rank and file, but the officers of the industrial and commercial army' (1906: 1). Businessmen had to be persuaded of the value of the course for their sons. Graduates had to be found jobs. Ashley was sure that business men were repelled by economics, so he played down the word economics as much as possible: 'If we ask too much they will not come at all' (1926: 148).

Ashley's teaching was supplemented in 1902 by that of Lawrence Dicksee, the first professor of accounting in Britain, and in 1903 by Adam KIRKALDY; otherwise, staff from the Arts and Science Faculties were called upon. In 1906, Ashley, extending his concept to a 'science of commerce', described foreign languages (usually two) and commercial law as on the 'circumference of [the] subject' (1906: 7). To 'penetrate' to the centre was to reach 'training of the judgement to deal with the actual problems of commercial life' (1906: 7). Accounting was part of this centre.

An important issue involved the place and type of economics to be included. Ashley went on to state that 'the really constitutive and most characteristic part of a commercial curriculum at the University must, however, be found in Economics', but not as taught in this country (1906: 8):

> Political economy as represented by the usual textbooks, is defective in both its character and in its scope for the purposes of business education. In its character, because of its tendency – with 'marginal utility' and 'consumers' rent', and the like – to become a branch of psychology; in its scope, because it gives a quite inadequate amount of attention to the concrete facts of industrial and commercial life.
> (1906: 8–9)

Two new directions for economics were needed. The first was a 'descriptive survey of the actual forms of economic activity', such as 'the really large facts of all the great industries of England and its rivals'; 'tendencies in their historical development'; being selective and relating one element to another to include the 'noise and turmoil of real life' (1906: 9).

The second direction involved the 'heart of the matter'. 'What is absolutely requisite and quite feasible, though certainly difficult, is the creation of a 'science of commerce', in the sense of a systematic consideration of the problems of business policy. What is wanted is 'private economics' for the business man, as distinguished from 'political' and 'social' economy' (1906: 7–8). By 1906, his aim had widened to turning out 'competent men of business' rather than simply leaders (1906: 8).

The curriculum at Birmingham included commerce, accounting and a foreign language in each year. European history in the first year was followed by public finance and economic analysis in the second and commercial law and transport in the third. Students had a choice of one subject in each year, ranging widely into subjects like technique of trade, brewing, logic or factory hygiene and including the study of institutions in Britain and Europe. Economics appeared only as 'economic analysis' in the second year. The course involved a 'rapid survey of the whole of the wealth-producing and wealth-distributing activity of society' and sought to 'disentangle the larger forces at work, to direct attention to the complex relations of cause and effect, and to indicate the general causes and criteria of national prosperity' (*University Calendar* 1902: 288).

The novel, specialist parts of the programme were the three years of commerce. Given by Ashley himself, these lay at the heart of his concept of education for businessmen. The first two years covered the 'modern development and present structure and position of industry and trade in the leading countries of the world' including their geography, resources, technology, capital, labour and commercial relations. Commerce III, the 'arduous' course Ashley needed time to prepare, introduced higher business policy questions as confronted by a manufacturer or merchant with an eye on business efficiency and success. Examples included such topics as the location and layout of works, production on a large and small scale, and combinations.

The problem was to attract students to the courses, especially from Britain; much less so from abroad. Many came from Japan, for example. The intake of five students in 1902 had only risen to forty across all three years by the time of the First World War (Smith 2003: 27–31). No wonder Ashley's mission became the publicizing of the value of higher commercial education for businessmen.

Ashley often presented his views on economic questions in prefaces such as that to his *English Economic History and Theory* (1888) where he referred to the divergence between those, like RICARDO, MILL and CAIRNES, who practised deduction and those who used the 'way of historical inquiry, and the observation of facts' (1913 edn: xii). The final chapter of the book focused on 'economic theories and legislation'. He apparently edited a series of 'economic classics', but these have not been traced. An exception is the editing and addition of an introduction to John Stuart Mill's *Principles of Political Economy* (1909). Ashley exhaustively traced the movements in Mill's thinking between the 1848 and 1871 editions of his *Principles*, implementing Toynbee's earlier suggestion. He felt Mill had moved a very modest way from abstract theory towards Ashley's position.

Ashley gave the address as president of the Economic Science Section of the British Association for the Advancement of Science held in Leicester in 1907. He reviewed the 'progress' over the last twenty years: 'The orthodox economics of the middle of the nineteenth century has for some time been quite dead' (1907: 2), though some doctrines may earn permanent places in thinking. The first phase of English economics 'as a system of thought' had 'become a closed chapter in intellectual history'; likewise the deductive method, though the 'fashionable modern term analysis' is elastic enough to cover different approaches. Meanwhile, while theory 'has almost monopolized the attention of professional economists – there has been a remarkable awakening of interest in the actual history of our land' (1907: 16). Examples included the work of Toynbee, Cunningham, SEEBOHM, MACROSTY and the WEBBS. Economics could now offer a career to a young man of ability (1907: 18-1-9, 21). However, professors of political economy in Britain were still poorly paid, subject to the 'sport of election' (1907: 21) to their post and, at first, often appointed for a term of years. He noted Marshall's appointment at Cambridge twenty-two years earlier as the first head of a living department. The *Economic Journal* and *Economic Review* both first appeared in 1891. There was also much private work outside universities. The change followed a new interest in social questions and the need for systematic training for municipal and political administrators as well as business men. The deepening 'purely scientific understanding of economic problems' (1907: 23) provided a context for studies like those of Charles Booth and Rowntree, while CHAPMAN and CLAPHAM's books on the cotton and woollen trades, using the historical method, were remedying a gap in the literature (1908: 189).

Writing on the enlargement of economics in 1908, Ashley sought a move away from political or social economy treating society as a whole to a 'sustained and systematic treatment of economic questions as they present themselves to men actually engaged in business' or a 'consecutive treatment of business problems' (1908: 190). While sources such as financial, trade and technical journals, blue books and company records existed, they were all fragmentary and disconnected. What was needed was a 'science of commerce' or business economics (1908: 191) to make these connections. Businessmen could gain from studying fluctuations, price and output records and cost accounting. The urgent task for academics was to observe, mediate and write the needed books on the 'business man's point of view' (1908: 203–4).

After Ashley retired from Birmingham in September 1926, he delivered three lectures on this business economics at the Commercial College at Copenhagen. The lectures were published as a book under the title *Business Economics*, written in Canterbury in 1926 and subsequently translated into Japanese. By business economics, he meant 'the study of the organization and financing of business concerns, of the manufacturing policy of business concerns, of their price policy, their labour policy and so on, as they present themselves in effort to secure profit' (1926: 9). Business economics would serve as a 'new sister in the house of Economics', subdivided into 'Business Policy' in relation to the supply of capital and outside markets and 'Business Administration' in relation to internal working (1926: 9–10). He concluded that 'political economy can afford to disregard the fortunes of particular undertakings; Business Economics is bound to consider them' (1926: 70–1). However, Ikema *et al.* (2002: 163) point out that 'Ashley's pioneering efforts in both organizing and introducing business economics were less successful in England than in Germany, the US and Japan', and were especially developed in Japanese commercial schools and universities of commerce.

Another major book was *The Tariff Problem* (1903), written after Ashley refused to sign a manifesto of economic teachers designed to close down the arguments (*Edgbastonia* 1904: 29). Examining both sides of the arguments, Ashley concluded the decision rested with political economy rather than economics (Clapham 1927: 682). He was concerned that skilled jobs were being pushed out by unskilled jobs, and this influenced his move to support imperial preference not least as a response to the wishes of much of the empire. He still held that view in 1926 in his book, *Imperial Preference*.

Ashley also wrote on inflation and the cost of living, explained in his book on gold prices (1912) as a response to the expansion of gold production in the 1900s. He was a strong supporter of trade unions, conciliation and wages boards, but opposed F.W. Taylor's system of scientific management, which he considered inhumane. A major interest throughout his career was the spread of trusts and combinations, which he considered inevitable. His writing and lectures reached a European and Japanese audience, as is evident from the translations of many of his works. Germany was particularly important to him and he was very proud of the honorary PhD awarded him by Berlin in 1910: until the horror of the First World War.

As the war cut academic work, Ashley took up many public duties which continued until his death in 1927. He was knighted in 1917 for his efforts. His specialisms were in food supplies, prices and the cost of living, agriculture and industrial relations. He spent six months in 1915–16 on the committee on 'trade relationships after the war'. He wrote a paper on the food supply and economic situation in Germany for the Royal Society in 1915, while his training for the 'task of welfare supervisor' proved of wider application. Often his service on these government bodies was quite brief, as another task then took up his time and attention. His first activity was as an intelligence officer to the Birmingham Citizens Executive Committee (1914) to whom he reported on the local situation. He served on the Departmental Committee on Food Prices from January to December 1916; the committee of the Royal Society on food supplies and their impact on physiology, where he opposed bread rationing; the Consumers Council from February to July 1918; and the Sumner Committee on the cost of living in mid-1918. He was on the Departmental Committee on Retail Coal Prices from 1915 to 1926.

At the request of the Ministry of Labour, Ashley helped establish Whitley Councils in Birmingham, presiding over a meeting of workers on 19 January and of employers on 28 January 1918, followed by the formation of Councils for hollow-ware and bedsteads trades later that year. Ashley served on the committee appointed by the Agricultural Wages Board on prices and the rural cost of living for a year from April 1918, going on to membership of the Royal Commission on Agriculture during its brief life (1919–20) and to being one of three members of the Agricultural Tribunal (1922–4). This Tribunal enquired into the methods adopted in other countries to increase the prosperity of agriculture; to secure the fullest use of the land for food production and the employment of labour at a living wage. Tariffs were one issue under consideration. From the latter post he went on to be chair of a Departmental Committee on the Glassware Industry, set up under the Safeguarding of Industries Act (1921) and leading to a recommendation for a duty on some glassware in August 1922. Until the election killed the proposal, Ashley sat on a committee to devise tariff reform. His final and perhaps grandest commitment occurred when he took a vacancy on the Balfour Committee on Industry and Trade in December 1924, but his contribution was aborted by his final illness in November 1926. His memorandum, already prepared before his operation, was circulated to members after his death in July 1927 (abridged in appendix to A. Ashley 1932: 165–71). Alongside these public activities, Ashley was appointed vice-principal of Birmingham University in June 1918 and served until his retirement in 1925. He was bitterly disappointed not to have received the vice-chancellorship at the retirement of Sir Oliver Lodge in 1919.

Politically, Ashley considered the tasks of a politician to be 'to urge a new organisation of existing Government works on the basis of a fair wage and not competition wage'; to seek 'the extension of State ownership to railways, waterworks and gasworks' and to increase 'municipal property in land and houses' (A. Ashley 1932: 35). He still called himself an 'evolutionary socialist' at the age of sixty, remaining an advocate of government intervention in many fields. In practice, the radical element in his politics was 'diverted into Unionist and Imperialistic channels' suggesting 'a Democratic Imperialism with a genuine Social-Amelioration intent and content' (A. Ashley 1932:109). He sought to switch the Unionists away from *laissez-faire* and to support for many of the social measures being proposed by the Liberals in the 1900s, notably proposing a draft unemployment insurance scheme in 1908. Having been co-opted on to a Unionist sub-committee on industrial unrest in 1912, his hand can be seen in its report supporting conciliation but rejecting a minimum wage.

In religion, although brought up a teetotal Baptist and attending a Wesleyan school in his youth, Ashley later moved, via the American Episcopal Church and Church Social Union while at Harvard, into the Church of England as an evangelical Christian. He became a churchwarden at Birmingham Cathedral, delivered sermons as an economist and, after his move there, was a diocesan lay reader in Canterbury, where he enjoyed the church music. One pleasure of these last years was his appointment as an honorary fellow of Lincoln College, Oxford in 1920, thirty-five years after his original fellowship. Apparently in relatively good health at sixty-six years, as evidenced by his travels abroad, he had to have a serious operation in November 1926 and then grew steadily worse. He kept working on his memo to the Balfour Committee and his last book, *The Bread of our Forefathers* (1928).

His daughter and biographer considered Ashley as an economic historian (A. Ashley 1932), but Clapham (1927: 679) wrote that he was 'by training and disposition a Political economist [sic] in the proper sense of that now undeservedly neglected term. (It is true that…he rarely so described himself)'. He added that Ashley was a first-rate historian but a 'somewhat undistinguished economist'.

BIBLIOGRAPHY
James and Philip van Artevelde (1883).
An Introduction to English Economic History and Theory, Part I: The Middle Ages (1888); *Part II: The End of the Middle Ages* (1893; 2nd edn both volumes, 1913).
What is Political Science? An Inaugural Lecture Given in the Convocation Hall of the University of Toronto, 9 November, 1888 (Toronto, 1888).

'On the Study of Economic History', *Quarterly Journal of Economics* (1893), vol. 7, January.
Surveys, Historic and Economic (1900).
The Faculty of Commerce in the University of Birmingham: Its Purpose and Programme (Birmingham, 1902).
The Tariff Problem (1903; subsequent edns 1904, 1911, 1920).
The Universities and Business (Brierly Hill, 1903).
'A Science of Commerce and Some Prolegomena', *Science Progress in the Twentieth Century* (1906), vol. 1, July, pp. 3–11.
'The Present Position of Political Economy in England', *Economic Journal* (1907), vol. 17, December.
'The Enlargement of Economics', *Economic Journal* (1908), vol. 18, June.
Gold and Prices (1912).
The Economic Organisation of England: An Outline History (1912; subsequent edns 1930, 1949).
Scientific Management and the Engineering Situation (1922).
'Considerations of National Defence; Considerations of National Health; Considerations of Economic Stability', appendices to Agricultural Tribunal Investigation, Second Interim Report (1923).
Imperial Preference (1926).
Commercial Education (1926).
Business Economics (1926).
'The Place of Economic History in University Studies', *Economic History Review* (1927), vol. 1, pp. 1–11.

Further Reading
Ashley, A., *William James Ashley: A Life* (1932).
Ashley, J., *My Autobiography by James Ashley, Written in 1907*, typescript in Birmingham University Collection 9/iii/30.
Clapham, J.H., obituary in *Economic Journal* (1927) pp.679–83.

Edgbastonia (1904) February, pp. 23–9.
Ikema, M. et al., *Hitotsubashi University 1875–2000* (Basingstoke, 2002).
Kadish, A., *Oxford Economists of the Late Nineteenth Century* (Oxford, 1982).
——, *Historians, Economists and Economic History* (1989).
MacDonald, J.L., 'Sir William Ashley (1860–1927)' in B.E. Schmitt (ed.), *Some Historians of Modern Europe* (Chicago, 1942), pp. 20–44.
Nishizawa, T., 'Marshall, Ashley on Education of Businessman and "Science of Business", *Marshall's School of Economics in the Making*' (Tokyo, 2002).
Smith, B.M.D., *A Hundred Years of Business Studies at the University of Birmingham 1902–2002* (Birmingham, 2003).
——, *Sir William James Ashley (1860–1927)* (Birmingham, 2003).
University Calendar 1902–3 (Birmingham, 1902).
University Collection, in University of Birmingham Archives.

Barbara M.D. Smith

ASHTON, Thomas Southcliffe (1889–1968)

Ashton was born on 11 January 1889 in Ashton-under-Lyne, a few miles east of Manchester, the son of Thomas Ashton, a bank manager, and Susan Sutcliffe. He died in Oxford on 22 September 1968, a few months before his eightieth birthday. He was educated at Ashton-under-Lyne secondary school, and at Manchester University, where he read history and political economy, obtaining his MA in 1920. His career started in Dublin, teaching history and English in the Masonic Boys' School; but having learned that his vocation lay in teaching, he soon resigned to take up lecturing, at a quarter of the income, on trade and tariffs for the Free Trade Union. In 1912, after two months in Germany to learn the language, he was appointed assistant lecturer in economics at Sheffield University, a post he held during the First World War after his application for military service was rejected on the grounds that one of his fingers had been crushed in an accident. From 1919 to 1921 he was lecturer and tutor at the University of Birmingham, and in 1921 was appointed senior lecturer in economics at Manchester University, where he remained until 1944, becoming dean of the Faculty of Commerce and Administration from 1938–44. His last position was as professor of economic history at the London School of Economics from 1944–54.

In 1949 Ashton took two terms' leave, spending five months at Johns Hopkins University and giving many lectures elsewhere in the United States. He visited Scandinavia in 1954. To the surprise of some people, but consistent with his belief in the self-organizing abilities of the working class and scepticism about large organizations, he was a member of the Mont Pelerin Society. He was elected a fellow of the British Academy in 1951; an honorary vice-president of the Royal Historical Society in 1961; an honorary vice-president of the Royal Economic Society in 1964; president of the Manchester Statistical Society in 1938–40; and president of the Economic History Society in 1960–3. He received honorary doctorates from the Universities of Nottingham (1963), Manchester (1964) and Stockholm (1964), but declined non-academic honours. For the last eleven years of his life he lived at Blockley in the Cotswolds

For significant parts of his career, Ashton's academic situation was far from ideal. His position at Sheffield, with a high workload of adult education and other activities, left him little time or energy for research. In moving to Birmingham, he hoped to further his studies of the iron and steel industry with William ASHLEY. However, Ashley had become more interested in politics and university administration and offered little encouragement. Though he managed to make some progress on his research in Birmingham, when George UNWIN invited him to return to Manchester, he jumped at the opportunity. There he received from Unwin the encouragement he had not received at Birmingham. Even when he had moved to LSE, two decades or more after Unwin's death, Ashton had the latter's portrait on his office wall.

At Manchester, though he was establishing his reputation in economic history, Ashton taught monetary economics and public finance in the economics department. He later edited, with R.S. SAYERS, a volume of papers on monetary history. The change came when R.H. TAWNEY invited him to succeed Eileen POWER as professor of economic history at LSE. Tawney invited him specifically because of his reputation in economic history, and he then had the opportunity to teach the subject he had specialized in for the first time.

Ashton's background was in the Lancashire cotton industry, non-conformist religion and Liberal politics. Perhaps typical of his day, he studied political economy along with history and geography, having come to see economic improvement rather than religion as the route to a better life. His first academic work was a paper, presented to the Royal Statistical Society, on the size distribution of firms, written with Sidney CHAPMAN, a colleague at Manchester University. This was an exercise in Marshallian, realistic economics. Using statistical analysis, Ashton and Chapman concluded that a variety of factors affected the size distribution of firms, including legal constraints as well as random effects. The book that made Ashton's reputation, *Iron and Steel in the Industrial Revolution* (1924), continued this tradition of industrial analysis. In a style that became characteristic of his work, Ashton shunned broad generalizations and focused on individual iron-masters, individual workers, trade organizations and relationships between them. While still at Manchester, this was followed by *The Coal Industry of the Eighteenth Century* (1929), and a book on an individual industrialist, Peter Stubbs, an archive of whose papers he had discovered. Apart from his history of the Manchester Statistical Society, with which he was closely involved around the time of its centenary (1933), and considerable writing for *The Manchester Guardian* (which brought him into contact with J.L. HAMMOND), his work focused on industrial history.

At LSE, his work broadened. *The Industrial Revolution* (1948) rapidly became a classic text on its subject that remained important reading for students of this period for many years. This attached great importance to the role of inventions, but was the first to synthesize interpretations of the period that emphasized both gradual change and radical breaking with the past. Ashton looked not only at industrial change but also at the broader social and political context. The connection between nonconformity and industrial development was explained by nonconformists being better educated than much of the middle classes. As an economist, lecturing for decades on monetary economics, he focused on the rate of interest, discussing factors such as the public debt and the supply of capital to industry. The importance of a low rate of interest, perhaps obvious to an economist, was, he argued, something that historians had never properly emphasized.

This book was followed by two others. *An Economic History of England: The Eighteenth Century* (1955) was intended as one volume in a five-volume work, the remaining volumes being written by his colleagues at LSE. This marked a further broadening of his work and, like his previous book, is still used by students. The other, *Economic Fluctuations in England, 1700–1800* (1959) was perhaps even more remarkable. Though influenced by economists (he cites conversations with John HICKS, Lionel ROBBINS and Jacob Viner in the preface), he did not use economic theory to structure the book, but patiently traced the influence of a variety of factors, starting with the effects of nature and the harvest, proceeding through war to discussions of building and finance. Where possible, statistical methods were employed. He showed that it was possible to describe in considerable detail the fluctuations experienced by the English economy in the eighteenth century, summarizing his work with a table showing cyclical turning points, including the dates of crises, for the entire century. Though of relevance to theories of the cycle, his generalizations were modest, concerning the irregularity of fluctuations, the importance of agriculture and the pervasiveness of international trade in economic life.

In his account of the discipline of economic history in Britain, D.C. Coleman (1987) divides it into two categories: 'reformers', who sought to use economic history to promote social change; and 'neutralists', who tried to avoid making moral judgements about the past. He places Ashton firmly in the latter group, unlike his LSE colleague Tawney who, though also influenced by Unwin, was a reformer. He played a major role in establishing the direction taken by British economic history. Despite his importance to the subject, he acquired a reputation for modesty and a dislike of ceremony. The latter jarred with Ashley's very formal style while he was at Birmingham, and he was uncomfortable during the tail-end of LSE's wartime period in Cambridge. His *Festschrift* was written entirely by former students, many of whom he kept in contact with long after his retirement.

BIBLIOGRAPHY
Iron and Steel in the Industrial Revolution (Manchester, 1924; 2nd edn, 1951).
(with J. Sykes) *The Coal Industry of the Eighteenth Century* (Manchester, 1929).
Economic and Social Investigations in Manchester, 1833–1933: A Centenary History of the Manchester Statistical Society (1934; repr. Brighton, 1977).
An Eighteenth-Century Industrialist: Peter Stubbs of Warrington, 1756–1806 (Manchester, 1939).

The Industrial Revolution, 1760–1830 (1948).
Letters of a West African Trader, Edward Grace, 1767–70 (1950).
(with R.S. Sayers) *Papers in English Monetary History* (Oxford, 1953).
An Economic History of England: The Eighteenth Century (1955).
Economic Fluctuations in England, 1700–1800 (Oxford, 1959).

Further Reading
Coleman, D.C., *History and the Economic Past: An Account of the Rise and Decline of Economic History in Britain* (Oxford, 1987).
John, A.H., 'Obituary: Thomas Southcliffe Ashton, 1889–1968', *Economic History Review* (1968), vol. 21, no. 3, pp. iii–v.
Pressnell, L.S. (ed.), *Studies in the Industrial Revolution, Presented to T.S. Ashton to mark his 70th birthday* (1960). (Includes bibliography of T.S. Ashton's academic writings.)
Sayers, R.S., 'Thomas Southcliffe Ashton', *Proceedings of the British Academy* (1970), vol. 56, pp. 263–81.

Roger Backhouse

ATTWOOD, Thomas (1783–1856)

Attwood was born in Shropshire on 6 October 1783, the third son of Matthias Attwood, a wealthy Birmingham banker and iron manufacturer. He died in Birmingham on 6 March 1856. He attended Wolverhampton Grammar School before joining his father's bank, Attwood & Spooner, in 1799. A keen community servant, he was appointed High Bailiff of Birmingham in 1811 and made a name for himself by presenting petitions to parliament on behalf of that city. He successfully challenged the orders-in-council promulgated in response to the Napoleonic Blockade and helped, in 1812, to persuade the government to rescind the East India Company monopoly.

Attwood was mainly interested in currency reform, and devoted most of his public life to systematic attacks on the Currency Bill of 1819, by which Sir Robert Peel had restored the gold standard. He began from the premise that gold was but one of many indicators of national wealth, and should not be used as the sole criterion for the issue of bank notes. He promoted the radical notion of a managed currency aimed at maintaining higher prices to encourage the production of the maximum number of goods and services by which alone could full employment be guaranteed. In Attwood's view, economic prosperity ought to be measured in terms of production and employment which provided the securest means of achieving social and organic harmony. This was the kernel of his message delivered in such pamphlets as *The Remedy; or Thoughts on the Present Distress* (1816), *Prosperity Restored; or Reflections on the Cause of the Present Distresses, and on the Only Means of Relieving Them* (1817), *An Exposition of the Cause and Remedy of the Agricultural Distress* (1828), and *A Correspondence...on the Subject of Restoring Cash Payments* (1832).

By attributing all of the economic crises of the post-Waterloo age to the mismanagement of the monetary system, Attwood eventually came to the conclusion that only through political reform could an efficient legislature be secured. The contemporary political elite, in his judgement, were interested only in vested landed interests and too prone to neglect the needs of the workers and the industrial middle classes. These considerations persuaded him, in the winter of 1829–30, to form the Birmingham Political Union 'to obtain by every just and legal means such a reform in the Commons House of Parliament as may ensure a real and effectual representation of the lower and middle classes of people in that House' (quoted in Finlayson 1970: 7).

In a period of severe economic slump, the Birmingham Political Union soon became the model for a number of urban centres and so powerful was the extra-parliamentary pressure upon the Government throughout 1831 that the Reform Bill of 1832 could no longer be delayed. Like the majority of contemporary radicals, however, Attwood was most disappointed with its results. Not only did the reformed legislature refuse to follow his advice with respect to the currency question, but it passed the Poor Law Amendment Act of 1834 which seemed to present the poor with additional hardships. Attwood also attributed the economic depression of the late 1830s to governmental ineptitude and consequently sided with the Chartists even though he disagreed with the aggressiveness of the majority of that pressure group.

Attwood, who had been elected as Birmingham's first representative in the reformed House of Commons in 1832, agreed to introduce the Chartist petition to the national assembly in 1839. This called for annual parliaments, universal male suffrage, equal electoral districts, payment for members of parliament, secret ballot and the removal of property qualifications for membership of parliament. However, he was so disillusioned by its reception that he retired from public life shortly afterwards. He was also very disappointed by the refusal of the Chartists to accept his currency proposals.

Attwood was an influential politician in the early 1830s when he could be seen at Westminster as the mouthpiece of Birmingham, then one of the fastest growing cities in the world. But his tendency to connect every subject with the management of the national currency led to his loss of prestige and respect. Other politicians began to regard him as little more than a boring 'currency crank', especially since his economic principles and philosophy differed so sharply from the conventional ideas then preached by Thomas MALTHUS, David RICARDO and Nassau SENIOR. But Attwood recognized, much sooner than did the majority of his contemporaries, that it was necessary to reshape traditional political economy to suit the changing needs of an industrializing society.

Attwood's generosity of spirit and devotion to public duty led to a sad neglect of his personal affairs. He thus left an estate grossly depleted in comparison to the one he had himself inherited. He considered himself a political failure, and this was also the generally accepted view of him by historians and economists throughout the nineteenth century and much of the twentieth century. His ideas were widely ridiculed while he lived, but Attwoodian economics became increasingly acceptable after his death. He was among the first to realize that bank notes, bills of exchange and even transfers made for more flexible business transactions and could stimulate production in a way in which gold and silver could not. He recognized that neither the supply nor the price of gold, dependent as they were on international circumstances, could be properly controlled by any individual government. Moreover, the supply of gold could seldom reflect the economic conditions prevailing in any one country at any given time. It was therefore absurd to use bullion as the sole basis for a monetary system. By following the advice of such classical economists as Malthus and Ricardo, the government, in Attwood's opinion, was merely ensuring that money remained dear and credit scarce.

Attwood's critics considered his own recommendations too dangerously inflationary, even though he was always careful to suggest that the issue of bank notes had to be strictly monitored and controlled. Twentieth-century economists, more conscious of the evils of deflation, came steadily to recognize the value of Attwood's suggestions, some of which appear to have influenced John Maynard KEYNES and others (even though there is little evidence that they read his pamphlets).

While Attwood was ridiculed by the London press throughout his parliamentary career and generally ignored by the British public during his final years, modern historians such as G.D.H. COLE and David Moss have tried to rehabilitate him; and it is significant that, in 1983, the bicentenary of his birth was commemorated in Birmingham. A plaque was placed on the site of his house in the Crescent and the city council also voted to clean up his statue and its surroundings.

BIBLIOGRAPHY
The Remedy; or Thoughts on the Present Distress (1816).
Prosperity Restored; or Reflections on the Cause of the Present Distresses, and on the Only Means of Relieving Them (1817).
An Exposition of the Cause and Remedy of the Agricultural Distress (1828).
A Correspondence...on the Subject of Restoring Cash Payments (1832).

Further Reading
Briggs, A. 'Thomas Attwood and the Economic Background of the Birmingham Political Union', *Cambridge Historical Journal* (1948), vol. 2, pp. 190–216.
Checkland, S., 'The Birmingham Economists, 1815–1850', *Economic History Review* (1948), second series, vol. 1, pp. 1–19.
Cole, G.D.H., *Chartist Portraits* (New York, 1965).
Finlayson, G.B.A.M., *Decade of Reform: England in the Eighteen Thirties* (New York, 1970).
Flick, C., *The Birmingham Political Union and the Movements for Reform in Britain, 1830–32* (1978).
Hollis, P. (ed.), *Pressure From Without in Early Victorian England* (1974).
Hovell, M., *The Chartist Movement* (Manchester, 1918).
Moss, D.J., *Thomas Attwood: The Biography of a Radical* (Montreal, 1990).

Keith A.P. Sandiford

AUCKLAND, Lord *see* Eden, William

AVES, Ernest (1857–1917)

Aves was born in Cambridge in 1857, and died on 19 April 1917 at Haslemere, Buckinghamshire. He attended Trinity College, Cambridge, where he took a first in the moral sciences tripos. Shortly after his graduation, he became a resident at Toynbee Hall, the universities' settlement in East London, where he remained from 1886 until his marriage in 1897 to Eva Maitland.

Aves came to the settlement with a strong interest in social issues. He developed this interest both in theoretical and practical ways during his time as a resident, and later as secretary to the Council and sub-warden of the settlement. From the start, he threw himself into investigative social work, assisting Beatrice Potter (later WEBB) with her research into the sweated trades. This led him into his work with Charles Booth and the *Life and Labour of the People* survey. A number of other Toynbee Hall residents participated in the survey, including Hubert Llewellyn SMITH. Aves was to become one of Booth's most dedicated assistants, contributing to the Building Trades section in the Industry series, as well as to the Religious Influences series. Aves was a member of the Royal Statistical Society, and also of the Junior Economic Club established by Clara COLLET in 1890 at University College, London. He was involved in the Toynbee Economic Club from its foundation in 1890 until shortly before his death in 1917.

Like Hubert Llewellyn Smith, Aves was directly involved in the trade disputes that erupted at the end of the 1880s in East London. He assisted the Dockers' Strike, and in 1889 became the first president of the Dockers' Union Trafalgar Branch, which met at Toynbee Hall. In 1903, he was a member of William BEVERIDGE's committee examining the nature of unemployment in East London. Aves would also work with E.F. WISE and Jimmy MALLON on the anti-sweating campaigns of the Edwardian period, which would culminate in the Trades Board Act of 1909. By 1907, Aves's research and campaigning would make him the ideal candidate for the position of Home Office Commissioner on working conditions in Australia and New Zealand, with a special interest in sweated labour. Aves reported back to the Home Office in 1908, and was appointed as chair of the Trades Boards.

Despite his move into the Civil Service, Aves was still able to maintain his links with social work. Besides his continuing connection with Toynbee Hall, he was involved with the Passmore-Edwards Settlement, and also the Hampstead Garden Suburb housing project. He was a director of the Suburb Trust, and became a member of the executive committee of the Hampstead Council of Social Welfare in 1910.

Aves's career was marked by his concern for workers' welfare. He had a deep and abiding empathy with the workers he had come into contact with through his research and social work, and was a dedicated advocate of a more benevolent industrial system. His book, *Co-operative Industry* (1907), is a masterful exploration of the origins and development of co-operation, firmly rooted in its potential to benefit those whose efforts created goods and wealth. He was eager to eradicate the evils of sweated labour and other exploitative practices. Aves is particularly notable for his practical as well as theoretical work, but perhaps his most enduring contribution to British economics is his seventeen years' service to Booth's *Life and Labour*. This thorough and meticulous survey of late Victorian conditions is indispensable to studies of the development of the industrial system, and its effects on people of all backgrounds.

BIBLIOGRAPHY
Co-operative Industry (1907).
(with C. Booth and H. Higgs) *Family Budgets: Being the Income and Expenses of Twenty-Eight British Households 1891–1894* (1896).
'Labour Notes', *Economic Journal* (1898–1906).
'Furniture Trade', in C. Booth (ed.), *Life and Labour of the People*, vol. 1 (1889).
'The Building Trades', in C. Booth (ed.), *Life and Labour of the People*, vol. 5 (1895).
Aves's research notes for the *Life and Labour of the People* survey are held in the Charles Booth archives at the London School of Economics.

Further Reading
Barnett, H., *Canon Barnett, His Life, Work and Friends by his Wife*, vol. 2 (1918).
——, 'Mr. Ernest Aves', *Toynbee Record* (1917), June, pp. 63–4.
Briggs A. and Macartney, A., *Toynbee Hall: The First Hundred Years* (1984).
Englander, D. and O'Day, R., *Retrieved Riches: Social Investigation in Britain 1840–1914* (Aldershot, 1998).
G.T.R, 'Obituary: Ernest Aves', *Economic Journal* (1917), p. xxvii.
Nunn, T.H., 'Ernest Aves', *Toynbee Record* (1917), June, pp. 56–9.
Simey, T.S. and Simey, M.B., *Charles Booth, Social Scientist* (1960).

Katharine Bradley

B

BABBAGE, Charles (1791–1871)

The circumstances of Babbage's birth are vague; he was born on 26 December of either 1791 or 1792. Teignmouth, Devon is usually given as his place of birth, but Wandsworth, Surrey is also mentioned. He died in London on 18 October 1871. He came from an upper middle-class family; his father, Benjamin Babbage, made a fortune in banking. Educated at various schools in Devon and Middlesex, Babbage entered Trinity College, Cambridge in 1810, moving in 1812 to Peterhouse College. Generally considered as one of the most gifted students, he ruined his chances to win honours in the final examinations by choosing to defend a thesis that God was a material agent, which caused uproar. At Cambridge, Babbage and a number of like-minded individuals such as John Herschel and the mathematician George Peacock, formed the famous and short-lived Analytical Society (1811) that aimed to promote the clarity and rigor of continental mathematics over British geometry. George Biddell Airy, later to be astronomer royal, and William WHEWELL were initially sympathetic to its purposes, and the Analytical Society would prove highly instrumental in reforming the Cambridge mathematical tripos. Its ideas were also formative for Augustus De Morgan, the first and influential professor of mathematics at University College, London.

At age twenty-three Babbage married Georgiana Whitmore, much against the wishes of his father. John Herschel, close friend of Babbage who saw him almost daily, did not learn of Georgiana's existence for over two years. Babbage himself, on leaving Cambridge, chose to devote his life to science. He moved to London in 1815, where he joined a scientific and intellectual circle which included many dissenters and utilitarians. He himself was a political Whig, but he did not hesitate to criticize the scientific establishment from within, even after becoming a fellow of the Royal Society in 1816. He particularly shared the view that scientific education in Britain was largely out of date, and set out to alter this state of affairs. His *Decline of Science in England* (1830) that contained a vehement, and sometimes even personal attack on the Royal Society was influential in the establishment of the British Association for the Advancement of Science (BAAS) in 1833. In the following year Babbage also helped to fund the Statistical Society in London, along with Whewell and Richard JONES. Babbage made some contributions to the *Journal of the London Statistical Society*, but soon lost interest. As Jones and Whewell, he considered the general quality of the papers in the journal too low to merit the predicate 'scientific'. Also, by the end of the 1830s Babbage had become too involved in the design of this 'analytical engine', the first programmable computer, to spare time for other things. He had been appointed Lucasian Professor of Mathematics at Cambridge in 1828, but in 1839 he gave up this post as well in order to concentrate on his own work.

Three elements are of importance in the initial idea and development of Babbage's calculating engines: his commitments to science, to mathematics, and to modern industry. Tables of numbers were notoriously unreliable in the early nineteenth century. The sources for errors were numerous, and stretched from the process of computing a table of logarithms to the setting and printing of such tables. Tables were used everywhere, in astronomy, life-insurance, navigation, and errors became more and more important and costly. Babbage, on one occasion in the early 1820s when checking tables with John Herschel, exclaimed in exasperation he wished 'to God these calculations had been executed by steam'. The idea of performing these computations by means of machines would occupy him for the rest of his life.

There had been earlier examples of counting machines, famously by Blaise Pascal in the sixteenth century, but Babbage's project was of a much more grandiose scale. He envisioned the computation and printing of tables of numbers in one unbroken mechanical chain so as to exclude all human sources of errors. Adam SMITH's concept of the division of labour proved central to the process and this concept found its mathematical counterpart in the so-called 'method of differences'; hence the name of Babbage's first calculating engines. Babbage mechanized the lowest part of the whole process of tabulation using wheels and gears, thus extending the substitution of machines for man from manual to mental labour. The upshot of this is an important modification and extension of the theory of the division of labour to the division of skills. A major part of Babbage's *On the Economy of Machinery and Manufactures* (1832) is devoted to this issue.

When Babbage first presented his calculating engine project to the Astronomical Society in 1822, it was greeted with enthusiasm and the government quickly promised financial support for a larger and more complex version. However, quarrels between Babbage and his partner, the tool-maker Joseph Clement, led to the collapse of the project in 1828. Babbage himself was already at work on a far more ambitious calculating machine, which he called the analytical engine. Unlike the difference engine, which was intended only for making tables, the analytical engine was a programmable automatic calculator capable of a number of different functions. It used a punched-card system, previously developed for Jacquard power looms, to input instructions, and returned data in printed form. Most important of all, the machine was intended to be able to store data in memory, and it is this last feature in particular that led Alan Turing in the 1940s to credit Babbage with the invention of the computer.

However, the analytical engine was destined never to be completed. Babbage approached the government in the 1840s for financial support, ministers sought the advice of George Biddell Airy, who advised against it; he considered Babbage's engines too inflexible in use, too vulnerable to breakdowns and, more importantly, impracticable because the numerous instances for which initial settings had to be computed by hand. The mathematical and mechanical complexities were also immense. Babbage and his partner, the even more talented mathematician Ada, Countess of Lovelace, only legitimate child of Lord Byron, could not easily solve them, especially as by the mid-1840s they were running out of money. A mathematical scheme for winning large sums of money by betting on horse races was an inevitable failure, leading to more financial losses, and the premature death of the Countess of Lovelace was a further blow. Babbage became increasingly solitary and irascible in later years, and died virtually alone; only two people attended his funeral.

On the Economy of Machinery and Manufactures has been praised for its encyclopaedic knowledge of manufacturing techniques, for its many insightful suggestions into the relation between technological innovation and gluts in the market, for his remarks on economies of scale and technology transfers, and in particular for its penetrating insights into the social organisation of labour. These insights were quickly taken up by his most perceptive readers, John Stuart MILL and Karl MARX.

Many of Babbage's insights can be traced back to his striving to rule out error and to reach the highest level of precision attainable by means of machines. Once Babbage realized that the principle of the division of labour did not just relate to manual labour, but extended to the skills of the workman as well, he opened new vistas in calculating the efficiency of production and suggested (analogous to his calculating engines) means of mechanizing mental labour where possible. By dividing skills into separate activities, mental labour could be routinized, could be paid according to its separate contribution to the produce, and could, in fact, be mechanized, as witnessed by his difference engine. Babbage's own description of the working of his calculating engine in *On the Economy of Machinery and Manufactures* reads like a Taylorized scheme of labour organisation (*Works*, vol. 8: 140–42). The reduction of a mental skill into a precise order of wheels and gears fits precisely to the exact timing of different manual activities by means of a clock. In Philip Mirowski's words, 'the very architecture of the Analytical Engine...constituted a projection of a more perfect factory' (Mirowski 2002: 34).

Babbage approached this 'more perfect factory' from the viewpoint of efficiency. In contrast with Marx, it was not the inequality in labour relations that drove his analysis, but the urge to improve precision and hence their efficiency. His topical remarks on profit sharing and trade unions should be seen as improved technologies of control, that is, as efficient means to fit the workmen into the factory. He showed how mental skills could be subdivided into separate parts, and then how these subdivided skills could be built into a machine. Technology, Babbage believed, was on the verge of revolutionizing production.

This would have many benefits, not only for the economy but also in improving conditions for workers in industrial concerns. But he also warned that increasing mechanization would lead to problems in society and the workplace, and called for a change in the organization of labour in manufacturing industries. Babbage was an early advocate of schemes such as profit-sharing and paying bonuses for production that would be part of orthodox thinking in Britain by 1900, and his ideas on motivating workers stand comparison with those of Robert OWEN.

Today, Babbage is seen as a founding father of the computer age, but he made important contributions in a wide variety of other fields, including political economy. To understand the age of machinery, it is essential to take account of Babbage's pioneering work on his calculating engines and *The Economy of Machinery and Manufactures*.

BIBLIOGRAPHY
Reflections on the Decline of Science in England and Some of its Causes (1830).
The Economy of Machinery and Manufactures (1832).
The Works of Charles Babbage, ed. M. Campbell-Kelly and P.M. Roget (1989).

Further Reading
Berg, M., *The Machinery Question and the Making of Political Economy 1815–1848* (Cambridge, 1980).
Dubbey, J.M., *The Mathematical Work of Charles Babbage* (Cambridge, 1978).
Hyman, A., *Science and Reform: Selected Works of Charles Babbage* (Cambridge, 1985).
Mirowski, P., *Machine Dreams : Economics Becomes a Cyborg Science* (Cambridge, 2002).
Morrison, P. and Morrison, E., *Charles Babbage and his Calculating Engines* (New York, 1961).
Moseley, M., *Irascible Genius: The Life of Charles Babbage* (Chicago,1964).

Romano, R.M., 'The Economic Ideas of Charles Babbage', *History of Political Economy* (1982) vol. 14, no. 3, pp. 385–405.

Swade, D., *The Cogwheel Brain: Charles Babbage and the Quest to Build the First Computer* (2000).

Harro Maas

BACHARACH, Michael Owen Leslie (1936–2002)

Bacharach was born in London on 9 November 1936, and died in Italy on 12 August 2002. His parents were Elizabeth Owens, a seamstress, and Alfred Bacharach, a research chemist who also edited a series of books on 'Lives of the Great Composers'. This musical influence nurtured in Bacharach a life-long love of playing classical and jazz piano. He attended St Paul's School, and then Trinity College, Cambridge, studying maths and economics. He refused a teaching post at Trinity, instead studying econometrics at Stanford for a year, and then returned to Cambridge to take a doctorate, which he completed in 1965.

Bacharach subsequently moved to Oxford where, after taking temporary lectureships at Nuffield College (1965–7) and Balliol College (1968–9), in 1969 he was made a student (fellow) of Christ Church and a university lecturer in economics. He was made a professor of the university in 1996, and was also the director of the research unit on bounded rationality in economic behaviour, and the founder of Oxford's laboratory in experimental economics.

Bacharach's early career was in the then mainstream economic topic of input-output analysis which concerned inter-industry relations. His doctoral thesis was published as *Biproportional Matrices and Input-Output Change* (1970), which was influential and is still cited.

In the early 1970s Bacharach turned his analytic rigour to the emerging field of game theory, before it became a pillar of modern economic theory. In 1976 he published a textbook entitled *Economics and the Theory of Games*. Although the fundamental developments in game theory took place in the 1940s and 1950s through two large tomes and a series of articles, Bacharach managed, with characteristic brevity, to convey the fundamentals in a mere 156 pages.

Bacharach devoted the rest of his career to the foundations of decision and game theory. He both challenged and developed the assumptions of rationality used in economics, focussing in particular on three foundational problems in game theory (1987). First, he addressed the 'common knowledge problem' with what he called the depth limits of reasoning. Employing the idea that humans have cognitive limitations on the depths to which they can reason about each others' rationality, he avoided a logical infinite regress, and solved a little understood problem. By then applying epistemic logic to the repeated play of games, Bacharach showed how the common knowledge axiom could be reformed and used to explain observed behaviour (1992a, 1992b, 1997).

Second, Bacharach addressed the problem of how people with common aims co-ordinate in the absence of communication. Here he developed a theory of framing and salience which showed how people reason in a common decision frame which enhances co-ordination (1993, 1997). Third, he was concerned with the problem of explaining the widespread observation of co-operation when the received theory predicted non-co-operation. Following his work on framing and salience, Bacharach developed the idea of 'we-thinking', or reasoning as a part of a larger unit than the individuals involved (1999). It was a theory he hoped would expand both economic and policy thinking about promoting co-operation.

As part of his project Bacharach wrote a series of influential essays, co-edited two books, *The Foundations of Decision Theory* (1991) and *Epistemic Logic and the Theory of Games and Decisions* (1997), and left behind a partially completed monograph summarizing his theory, *Beyond the Individual: A Study of Framing and Co-operation*.

Bacharach was largely unconcerned with self-promotion. Because of his dense, uncompromising writing style, it was often the case that his most important essays were published in more obscure locations, while essays less central to his main project were published in well-known venues such as the *Journal of Philosophy* and prestigious edited collections for social scientists in general.

To his friends, students and colleagues, his enormous academic and intellectual contributions stood side-by-side with his personality. He was considerate in the broadest possible sense of the word, and was happily not content with contemplation alone. This was most apparent in his house, which contained a large collection of music and musical instruments, toys for his children, tools and a small shed for fixing whatever might be broken, a fountain, garden, excellent food, drink, books and art, all of which were important to him and eagerly shared. He approached everything with a commitment that was contagious and admirable.

Michael Bacharach was an innovative and rigorous economist whose work ranged from the empirical to the most abstract theory, and inspired a great many students and colleagues. He was often significantly ahead of mainstream economics in his thinking, and the reception of his work frequently would take some time, and his latest work may still do. Nevertheless, he was concerned that his theories could be applied to concrete issues in the social sciences at large. To this end he collaborated with faculty and supervised graduate students not only from economics, but also from artificial intelligence, philosophy, political science, psychology and sociology.

BIBLIOGRAPHY
Biproportional Matrices and Input-Output Change (1970).
Economics and the Theory of Games (1976).
'A Theory of Rational Decision in Games', *Erkenntnis* (1987), vol. 27, pp. 17–55.
(with S. Hurley) *Foundations of Decision Theory* (Oxford, 1991).
'Commodities, Language and Desire', *Journal of Philosophy* (1990), vol. 87, pp. 346–68.
'Backward Induction and Beliefs about Oneself', *Synthese* (1992a), vol. 91, pp. 247–84.
;The Acquisition of Common Knowledge', in C. Bicchieri and M.L. Dalla Chiara (eds), *Knowledge, Belief and Strategic Interaction* (Cambridge, 1992b, pp. 285–315).
'Variable Universe Games', in K. Binmore, A. Kirman and P. Tani (eds), *Frontiers of Game Theory* (Cambridge, Massachusetts, 1993, pp. 255–75).
(with M. Bernasconi) 'The Variable Frame Theory of Focal Points: An Experimental Study', *Games and Economic Behavior* (1997), vol. 19, pp. 1–45.
'The Epistemic Structure of a Theory of a Game', in P. Mongin, M. Bacharach, L. Gerard-Valet and H. Shin (eds), *Epistemic Logic and the Theory of Games and Decisions* (Boston, 1997, pp. 303–44).
'Interactive Team Reasoning: A Contribution to the Theory of Co-operation', *Research in Economics* (1999), vol. 53, pp. 117–47.

Shepley Orr

BACON, Francis (1561–1626)

Bacon was born 22 January 1561 at York House in the Strand in London. He died near London on 9 April 1626. He was the second child of Anne Cooke and last of at least eleven offspring of Nicholas Bacon who, at Francis's birth, held the title of Lord Keeper of the Seal of Queen Elizabeth I with the authority to exercise the full jurisdiction of Lord Chancellor. Francis was the full brother of Anthony Bacon, secretary to Robert Devereux, 2nd Earl of Essex, from at least 1590 until shortly before his death in 1601.

Francis Bacon was educated at Trinity College, Cambridge (1573–5, leaving without a degree) and at Gray's Inn, where his almost fifty-year presence is commemorated by a famous statue in the courtyard, South Square. Admitted to Gray's Inn in 1576, Bacon engaged seriously in study of the law only the death of his father in 1579. In 1582, he received his first of numerous subsequent judicial appointments. In 1584, he was elected to his first parliamentary seat, for Melcomb in Dorsetshire and the borough of Catton, at the age of twenty-three.

As reflected in his first publication, 'Of Studies', the first in a collection of ten essays, in 1597, Bacon had already gleaned from his university days that, while studies hone aspects of a man's character, 'they teach not their own use'. By the time he was thirty, Bacon had nonetheless devised his unique direction for the application of learning. Although he found the minds of his early educators, such as his Cambridge master Dr John Whitgift, who later became Archbishop of Canterbury, encloistered in the unfruitfulness of Aristotle, he was inspired by two other types of effective endeavours: exploration, or 'observation' in the generic, and 'industry', or creative productivity.

During Bacon's first year at Cambridge, Sir Francis Drake returned from the coast of Panama loaded with silver and gold, and in 1576 Sir Martin Frobisher further heightened interest in geological riches across the Atlantic, stimulated by finds of 'black ore' on Baffin Island. The manuscript by Richard Hakluyt, known as the *Discourse on Western Planting*, was one of the earliest works designed specifically to secure political support for English exploration, and was presented to Queen Elizabeth during Bacon's first year in parliament. In 1592, the treasurer to the Queen and Bacon's uncle, Lord Burghley, received a plea from his penniless nephew for support in a livelihood devoted to bringing 'industrious observations' and 'profitable inventions and discoveries' into the body of schooled knowledge. Almost all of Bacon's writings well-known today, from *Mr Bacon in Praise of Learning* (produced exclusively for Queen Elizabeth in 1592) to the unfinished *The Great Instauration* (Part II *New Organon* (1620); Part I, the enlarged version of *The Proficience and Advancement of Learning*, 1605 (1623)) and *New Atlantis* (1627), set out systematically Bacon's persuasion that knowledge in the form of discoveries, inventions and new techniques was the most powerful force in history.

In 1606, Bacon was knighted by King James I, and had married Alice Barnham, the daughter of an alderman, Benedict Barnham and Lady Dorothea Smith. It was as a lawyer, parliamentarian and advisor to Queen and King that Bacon participated in national affairs and took up many economic issues. From 1584 to 1617 he successfully held numerous parliamentary seats, representing variously Taunton, Liverpool, Middlesex, Southampton, Ipswich, St Albans and Cambridge University. In 1618 he was created Baron Verulam, and in 1620 was made Viscount St Albans. His political career came to an end, however, in 1621. Only four years after having attained his father's post of Lord Keeper of the Great Seal, Bacon was convicted of having accepted bribes and was barred further from holding political office.

In 1595, after expiry of a lease to one of his half-brothers, Edward Bacon, Bacon was granted Twickenham Park, an eighty-seven-acre estate, and leaving his lodgings at Gray's Inn, he resided there after 1601 for almost a decade. In 1608, however, Bacon retreated for the rest of his days to the property his father had acquired in Bacon's youth, Gorhambury at St Albans in Hertfordshire. Burdened by debt inherited from his brother Anthony, Bacon left upon his death in 1626 an estate worth far less than the claims against it, which amounted to £20,000. Bacon's widow, aged thirty-nine and without children, immediately married Sir John Underhill, at the time serving as a member of the Bacon household, but, given that Bacon had earlier struck Alice from his will, Gorhambury did not pass to her. By the mid-1600s the estate was, however, still in the Bacon family, owned by Bacon's principal secretary Sir Thomas Meautys, who had married the daughter of Nathaniel Bacon, another of Bacon's half-brothers.

Although the state of his personal affairs did not show any astute financial expertise on Bacon's part, in his essays, histories and parliamentary declarations, Bacon reflected dissent from many of the more dogmatic economic positions of those blindly loyal to the English throne. Bacon's sympathies lay more with balancing the powers of the Crown and the English nation, and with issues of taxation, monopoly, trade and, of course, legal rights of Royal Court and Parliament until his death. He opposed, for example, many views favourable to the monarch: that expenditures by the Crown, supported by taxation, were inherently economically beneficial, that the Crown could encroach on the right of the House of Commons to set taxation levels, and that taxing merchants was a good source of royal revenue. He observed 'that taxes levied by consent of the estate, do abate men's courage less: as it hath been seen notably, in the excises of the Low Countries; and, in some degree, in the subsidies of England...although the same tribute and tax, laid by consent or by imposing, be all one to the purse, yet it works diversely upon the courage' (1612). For fear of sedition against the Crown, the material well-being of the nation ought not be overly taxed, he argued in 'Of Seditions and Troubles' (1625), noting numerous ways in addition to 'the moderating of taxes and tributes' by which 'want and poverty in the estate' can be kept at bay: 'the opening, and well-balancing of trade; the cherishing of manufactures; the banishing of idleness; the repressing of waste, and excess, by sumptuary laws; the improvement and husbanding of the soil; the regulating of prices of things vendible...' To Bacon, the most expedient avenue to a healthy national economy was the encouragement of cultivative agriculture, free trade, and flourishing manufacturing activity.

Errors in defining wealth repeatedly excited Bacon's disapproval. He challenged the assumption that 'works of ostentation', 'little stones', even 'rarieties' were truly riches and questioned the role of parsimony as a route to sound enrichment. Observing that 'all men are drawn into actions by three things, – pleasure, honour, and profit' (1608–9), Bacon nonetheless refuted the notion that wealth in and of itself is 'useful'. He offered both example and proverbial evidence that riches are those means which are obtained justly and preferably slowly, used soberly, distributed cheerfully and left contentedly.

Linked to Bacon's interest in individual wealth was his examination of a country's well-being and of the extension of its borders to assure it. Colonization could not replace the need for a country's own enterprise, but it was a good strategy to enhance it. In 'Of Seditions and Troubles' (1625), he laid out his mercantilist vision for England: 'the increase of any estate must be upon the foreigner (for whatsoever is somewhere gotten, is somewhere lost)'. The economic increase by 'union' of different political entities was appropriate despite diverse historical patterns, he argued in *A Brief Discourse Touching the Happy Union of the Kingdoms of England and Scotland* (1603), *Certain Articles or Considerations Touching the Union of the Kingdoms of England and*

Scotland (1604), *Certain Considerations Touching the Plantation in Ireland* (1608–9), and in his Lord Chancellor's speech at the election of Serjeant Richardson as parliamentary speaker (1620). Bacon distinguished between an area's enhancing 'superficially' different characteristics, such as language, and those which would affect the Crown's income: independent finances, taxation, and rival employments. When the process of harmonization was overseen by royal officers, such as the councils of plantation in England and in each of her colonies, he asserted, it would be as natural as the blending of lesser and greater illuminations or the settling of fermenting liquors.

In the context of strengthening the English economy, Bacon proposed the harmonization of regulations within the British Isles to include, among other matters, restrictions on the transport of gold and silver and the marking of coins. Like most contemporary mercantilists, he was concerned with national gold and silver reserves. In his essay, 'Of Seditions and Troubles' (1625), Bacon called, however, not for mere conquest, but for a tripartite mercantile economy, 'if these three wheels go, wealth will flow as in a spring tide': 'the commodity as nature yielded it, the manufacture, and the vecture, or carriage'.

At the centre of Bacon's vision of territorial expansion was undoubtedly his support for a wider, or at least a sustained range of agricultural commodities. He had successfully, with the last Act of Parliament against enclosure, continued the battle against the replacing of tillage by pasture, of people by sheep, right through the final Elizabethan parliament in 1601. Leading up to 1624 when the long series of enclosure laws were repealed during the reign of James I, Bacon held out, perhaps in the same spirit, for the 'plantation' of Ireland to be undertaken by men of 'plenty', meaning those with an estate worth £1,000 a year in land, and able to pay enough into the Exchequer to support thirty foot soldiers in local militias. Bacon argued for low tax rates for planters, government financial aid, freedom from custom duties, and free commodity movement, all of which, he felt, would bring profit and strength to the Crown.

Behind virtually every one of Bacon's economic policy proposals was, however, his plea for 'manufacture', 'work' being 'worth more than the material'. By following the model of the Low Countries, England too, he wrote, could have the 'best mines above ground in the world'. Central to this perspective were his theories on invention, innovation and monopoly. He believed that patent or monopoly protected manufacturing endeavour from competition quite well. Nonetheless, widespread economic gain would not spring from allowing patents or monopolies to be permanent or from giving the Crown free rein in obtaining monopolies. While he insisted that 'we ought not meddle with her Majesty's Prerogative', he also supported Parliament in its 1624 Statute of Monopolies, which declared that only Parliament might grant statutory monopolies, limiting them to new inventions, and to a period not to exceed fourteen years. Thus, in the same decade, he unsuccessfully attempted to establish staple towns in Ireland as monopoly locations for trade (1617), and subsequently recommending support of free trade into England of the 'wools, woolfells, morlins, shorlings, lambskins, woolen yarns and flocks' from Ireland. While the Crown would benefit from a monopoly on the manufacture of gold and silver thread in England, the process would, he noted, allow for important precious metals to be kept and controlled within the realm, and employ the poor in gainful labour.

Bacon was an important and even politically daring thinker on economic issues. Schumpeter credits Bacon with one of the earliest uses of the term 'favourable balance of trade' in 1615 (1954: 345n), and found in his writings the proverbial 'beggers should not be choosers' and 'all is not gold that glitters', (as well as the perhaps less frequently quoted 'if money be not thy servant, it will be thy master', 'the tooth of usury be grinded that it not bite too much', and 'money is like muck, best when it is spread out'). But rather than an innovator of economic concepts, Bacon was the adaptor of his philosophical principles of the dignity and worth of the human mind and its expression to the contemporary context in which economic life was being led under an extremely powerful constitutional Anglo-Saxon monarchy. 'Lastly, I would address one general admonition to all; that they consider what are the true ends of knowledge, and that they seek it not either for pleasure of the mind, or for contention, or for superiority to others, or for profit, or fame, or power, or any of these inferior things; but for the benefit and use of Life; and that they perfect and govern it in charity' (1623). While his contribution to the development of post-Aristotelian experimental philosophy is by far the best-known aspect of his work, he also had a high respect for social endeavours and concern for each individual's plight in the material world which reverberated in his economic ideas.

BIBLIOGRAPHY
Mr. Bacon in Praise of Learning (1592).
Essays (1597).
A Brief Discourse Touching the Happy Union of the Kingdoms of England and Scotland (1603).
Certain Articles or Considerations Touching the Union of the Kingdoms of England and Scotland (1604).
Certain Considerations Touching the Plantation in Ireland (1608–9).
'Of the True Greatness of Kingdoms and Estates' (1612).
The Great Instauration (1623).
'Of Seditions and Troubles' (1625).
New Atlantis (1627).
Works of Francis Bacon, ed. J. Spedding, R.L. Ellis and D.D. Heath (1857–74, 1881).
The Letters and Life of Francis Bacon, Including All His Occasional Works, ed. J. Spedding (1861–74).

Further Reading
Cunningham, W., *The Growth of English Industry and Commerce during the Early and Middle Ages* (1910; repr. 1968).
Fischer, K., *Francis Bacon und seine Nachfolger. Entwicklungsgeschichte der Erfahrungsphilosophie* (Francis Bacon and his Followers. History of the Development of Experimental Philosophy) (Leipzig, 1875).
Heckscher, E.F., *Mercantilism*, trans. M. Shapiro (1935).
Levi, A., *Il Pensiero di Francesco Bacone considerato in relatione con le filosofie della natura del Rinascimento e col razionalismo cartesiano* (The Thought of Francis Bacon Considered in Relation to the Philosophy of Nature of the Renaissance and Cartesian rationalism) (Torino, 1925).
Perlman, M. and McCann, C.R., Jr, *The Pillars of Economic Understanding: Ideas and Traditions* (Ann Arbor, Michigan, 1998).
Rossi, P., *Francis Bacon: From Magic to Science*, trans. S. Rabinovich (1968).
Schumpeter, J., *History of Economic Analysis* (1954).
Unwin, G. *Industrial Organisation in the Sixteenth and Seventeenth Centuries* (1904; repr. 1963).

Betsey Barker Price

BAGEHOT, Walter (1826–1877)

Bagehot was born at Langport Somerset in 1826, and died there on 24 March 1877. His father, Thomas Bagehot, managed the local branch of Stuckey's, a prosperous country bank; his mother, Edith Stuckey, was a niece of the founder. The Bagehots lived in rooms above the bank and it was there that Walter Bagehot was born, the ideal birthplace for a man whose ideas about central banking would influence monetary policy from the late 1800s to the present.

Bagehot was educated at the local grammar school, at Bristol College and at University College, London. It is said that his father, a keen Unitarian, would not think of sending his son to Oxford or Cambridge. He was a capable student, and took BA and MA degrees with honours. He began reading law, but the law with its emphasis on detail did not appeal, and in 1852 he joined his father in the bank at Langport. In the following years, he continued at Stuckey's while contributing essays to various periodicals. In 1854, he began co-editing the *National Review* with Richard Hutton, a college friend. In 1856 Hutton was asked by James WILSON, the founder, owner and first editor of *The Economist*, to become the second editor. Shortly thereafter Bagehot, on a visit to Wilson's home to discuss the possibility of a series of articles on banking, met Wilson's eldest daughter Eliza. They were soon engaged, and were married in 1858. The following year Bagehot was made director of *The Economist* when his father-in-law was given an important government post in India. Following Wilson's death, Bagehot became the third editor of *The Economist* in 1861, and Hutton moved on to *The Spectator*.

The Economist was to be Bagehot's main creative outlet for the remainder of his life. He made four attempts to enter Parliament, but without success. His influence on politics, however, was significant. *The Economist* of course was by then an influential journal and politicians from both parties sought his advice, so much so that Alistair Buchan entitled his biography of Bagehot *The Spare Chancellor* (1959). As well as his involvement in Stuckey's and in editing *The Economist*, Bagehot wrote three of his landmark works over the next six years: *The English Constitution* (1867) and *Physics and Politics* (1872), his major contributions to political science, *and Lombard Street* (1873). He had suffered from ill health since his youth, and died at the age of fifty-one, still at the helm of *The Economist*.

Although Bagehot followed Wilson and *The Economist* in advocating free trade, he was not always opposed to what would be considered leftist positions in our day. He supported, for example, the right of labour unions to organize and fight for a larger share of business income. Perhaps even more notable was his eventual support for the Factory Acts, which regulated working conditions in British industry. James Wilson and other prominent liberals had opposed the Factory Acts because they interfered with the rights of capitalists to use their property as they saw fit, and with the rights of employers and employees to enter into whatever bargains they wished. Bagehot, however, was able to write in 1864 that 'no one had any doubt now' of their wisdom (quoted in Buchan 1959: 132). He also supported the income tax – partly, to be sure, because the policy of free trade meant that tariff revenues would be low – and he thought that nationalization of the railroads might be in order. In 1865 he wrote in *The Economist*:

> A transfer of the ownership of the railways to the Government might be made so as to diminish their danger, economise their cost, and augment their utility. It would be very difficult so to transfer, we know. But when great results are *possible*, we should carefully examine whether they are not also *attainable*.
>
> (quoted in Buchan 1959: 211)

Initially, Bagehot held a low opinion of Abraham Lincoln and, despite his intense opposition to slavery, denounced the Emancipation Proclamation as a fraud. Eventually, however, he came to recognize Lincoln's greatness. Bagehot claimed to lay great stress on the principle that opinions should be based on a close and fair reading of the data, and as these examples show, he adhered to this principle far better in practice than most who make this claim.

Undoubtedly Bagehot's major claim to fame as an economist rests on *Lombard Street, a Description of the Money Market*. Lombard Street was the site of the bill brokers, who supplied short-term capital to financial markets. Bagehot tells us that he chose this title rather than 'the money market' to stress his emphasis on the concrete realities of the market. This emphasis sets *Lombard Street* apart from academic writings about banking. Bagehot knew the money market and the people who participated in it intimately and he had the skill to make them come alive. *Lombard Street* is one of the few classics in economics that is a pleasure to read. But the central question addressed in *Lombard Street* was a serious one: what should be the relationship between the Bank of England and the money market?

Lombard Street grew out of a response to a particular problem at a particular time and place. Late in 1866, Lancelot Holland, Governor of the Bank of England, recalled with pride the Bank's response to a financial panic in May of that year: 'We did not flinch from our post...we made advances which would hardly have been credited...before the Chancellor of the Exchequer was perhaps out of his bed we had advanced one-half of our reserves' (Clapham 1970: 283). Bagehot heartily endorsed this statement in *The Economist*, emphasizing that the words 'our post' reflected recognition of responsibility for the market. A faction at the Bank, however, led by one of the directors, former governor Thomson Hankey, denied that the Bank had a special responsibility to support the market as a whole. The Bank should do its part, a large part to be sure given its size, alongside others in the event of a crisis, but the Bank was under no obligation to sacrifice itself in the national interest. *Lombard Street* was written in response to this position.

There was another reason, when Bagehot wrote, for emphasizing the Bank's responsibility to the market and its need, derived from that responsibility, to hold a large gold reserve. The Bank of France had suspended cash payments in the wake of the Franco-Prussian War of 1870–1. The Bank of England therefore held the only large gold reserve in Europe. Indeed, since the USA was on a paper standard (the USA returned to gold in 1879, and created a central bank in 1913) one could say that the Bank's reserve was the only large gold reserve in the world. Germany, moreover, was owed large reparation from France to be paid in gold; gold that would be drawn from London. There was, Bagehot thought, a danger that the Bank of England's gold reserve would be depleted to the point that the market would become alarmed.

The argument of *Lombard Street* can be summarized in five key propositions. The first of these was that the Bank of England had become the main holder of England's gold reserve. This was a fact from which all discussions of the role of the Bank had to begin. It was not necessarily, Bagehot thought, the best of all possible worlds. He believed that if a system of competitive banking had been established in Britain, a system might have evolved in which each bank held its own reserve. Each bank would then be responsible for itself in good times and bad, and would hold a reserve adequate to the purpose. Bagehot thought that such a system, which many at the time and since have referred to as a free banking system, might well work better than the system that had evolved. However, there was no way in 1873, Bagehot believed, to introduce a free banking system. The Bank had been given various government privileges during its long history, in particular the sole right in London to issue bank notes, and as a result a system had evolved in which most banks held relatively low gold reserves and relied on the gold reserve of the Bank of England to carry them through emergencies. Reform, Bagehot believed, must be based on what the system is, and not on what it might have been. Many modern-day advocates of free banking have pointed to Bagehot's kind words about free banking to support their position. Few, however, have taken to heart Bagehot's understanding that reform must take account of long-established institutions.

Bagehot's second proposition was that the Bank must hold at all times an adequate reserve of gold. It followed that the Bank must then hold enough gold to meet any plausible demand. How much was enough? It was difficult to give a simple rule. The money market, however, had an idea about what the minimum should be, and the Bank must be sure that it always holds a bit more. If the reserve should approach the amount that the market considered the bare minimum, the market would become apprehensive. If the reserves fell below this amount, what Bagehot referred to as the 'apprehension minimum', apprehension might turn to alarm and finally to panic. Whenever the Bank's reserve approached the apprehension minimum the Bank must take every precaution to conserve and if possible increase its reserve, perhaps by raising the discount rate and limiting its lending. Bagehot argued that at the time he wrote, the Bank needed to hold at least £10,000,000 to remain well above the apprehension minimum.

Third, the Bank of England should act as lender of last resort during panics by lending freely. It should provide money for bill brokers and other borrowers when they were in a panic, because panics, if allowed to go unchecked, had a devastating effect not only on the money market but also on the economy as a whole. In an oft-quoted passage – Bagehot himself quoted it twice – he praised the Bank's account of how it met the crisis of 1825:

> The way in which the panic of 1825 was stopped by advancing money has been described in so broad and graphic a way the passage has become classical. 'We lent it,' said Mr. Harman on behalf of the Bank of England, 'by every possible means, and in modes we have never adopted before; we took in stock on security, we purchased Exchequer bills, we made advances on Exchequer bills, we not only discounted outright, but we made advances on the deposit of bills of exchange to and immense amount, in short, by every possible means consistent with the safety of the Bank, and we were not on some occasions over-nice.
> (1873: 51–2)

While the Bank did need to lend freely, and had to avoid being 'over-nice', there was no need, Bagehot thought, to take collateral on which the Bank would ultimately lose. This qualification has been taken to mean that a central bank should not lend to insolvent institutions even in a crisis. This is a reasonable extension, but it should be noted that Bagehot had in mind a crisis in which the Bank would be lending on the basis of collateral, collateral that Bagehot believed almost always would prove good in ordinary times. Bagehot might well have given more weight to not being 'over-nice' in some modern circumstances in which central banks are asked to make unsecured loans to institutions whose solvency is difficult to evaluate in the short-run.

Fourth, the Bank should be ready to lend freely during a panic, but it should do so only at a high rate of interest. The combination of (3) and (4) – lend freely at a high rate during panics – is the 'Bagehot's rule' or the 'Bagehot Principle'. There were several reasons for lending at high rates. The most important, which would apply in all circumstances, was that a high rate would discourage unnecessary borrowing – that is borrowing to build up reserves against remote dangers – and thus help preserve the Bank's gold. Also, a combination of a panic and an external drain was a special case that gives extra weight to the necessity for a high rate. The high rate (compared with foreign rates) would slow or reverse the drain: '10 per cent bank rate will bring gold from the moon,' as the old saying went, while lending freely would calm the panic. Finally, a third reason for a high rate was to punish 'unreasonable timidity'. Those brokers who lacked the courage to borrow to save their own businesses should pay a heavy price.

Fifth, the Bank must accept its responsibility and announce in advance its willingness to act in a panic. A frank acknowledgement by the Bank of its responsibilities would make the market rest easier, especially at those times when the market had become apprehensive about weakening economic conditions and a falling Bank reserve. If brokers knew that the Bank would always be there for them, there would be no need for brokers to try to turn their assets into cash when money was tight, or the Bank's reserve seemed low. This point, as much as any, was the central theme of *Lombard Street*. The Bank had acted appropriately on several past occasions, and probably would do so again. A commitment to act might prevent the need to act.

Much of the modern interest in *Lombard Street* among economists, especially among American economists, stems from Milton Friedman and Anna J. Schwartz's *A Monetary History of the United States* (1963). The authors claimed that if only the Federal Reserve had followed Bagehot's advice, the Great Depression would have been avoided, or at least greatly ameliorated:

> The actions required to prevent monetary collapse did not call for a level of knowledge of the operation of the banking system or of the workings of monetary forces or of economic fluctuations which was developed only later and was not available to the Reserve System. On the contrary, as we have pointed out earlier, pursuit of the policies outlined by the System itself in the 1920s, or for that matter by Bagehot in 1873, would have prevented the catastrophe.
>
> (Friedman and Schwartz 1963: 730)

Why was Bagehot's advice ignored? There are two possibilities. First, Bagehot's advice may have been ignored because it was forgotten. Second, Bagehot's advice, even if known, may have been ignored because it did not seem to apply to the United States during the early 1930s. Bagehot, moreover, never explained how one was to recognize a panic. For him, the question might have seemed foolish: panic was something you could see in a man's eyes. The lack of a quantitative indicator was made more problematic because Bagehot defined a state of the money market closely related to panic, apprehension or alarm about the size of the Bank's reserve, that required the exact opposite of lending freely. Apprehension required that the Bank refrain from lending in order to protect and if possible increase the reserve. Bagehot praised the Bank for lending freely to calm the panic of 1825; but he also blamed the Bank for causing the panic by allowing its reserve to fall from £10,721,000 on 24 December 1824 to £1,260,000 on 25 December 1825.

While the distinction between an apprehensive market and a panicked market apparently was obvious to Bagehot, and probably was obvious to most observers in some of the British crises, it was far from obvious in America in the 1930s. The acute need to distinguish between apprehension and panic was a by-product of the gold standard. A central bank, such as the Federal Reserve or the Bank of England operating under a modern fiat standard, and faced with an internal drain, can print money freely and lend it freely to any extent. A Bank in a developing country, faced with failures by banks that have liabilities denominated in foreign currencies, however, is very much in Bagehot's world. When does it protect its reserve, and when does it lend freely? If Bagehot had been asked for a quantitative indicator panic, he would probably have cited the nominal rate of interest. After all, if brokers were desperate for cash one would expect the rate being charge for money to go up. Certainly, Bagehot discusses the determinants of the nominal rate in *Lombard Street* in some detail.

Although *Lombard Street* is Bagehot's greatest work in economics, his other economic writings are still of value, particularly to those with an interest in the history of economic thought or in British economic history, especially his brilliant essays on individuals such as Adam SMITH, John BRIGHT, Richard COBDEN and William Gladstone. A number of his essays on economic subjects were collected by Hutton and published in 1879. Although the discipline of economics has moved on in terms of exactness, mathematical expression and thoroughness, these essays are still worth reading for Bagehot's ability to illustrate basic economic principles with clever examples and to encapsulate them in telling epigrams.

How important have been Bagehot's contributions in the long run? Anna J. Schwartz has argued that there was no real banking panic (in the sense of one in which the payments system was seriously disrupted) in England after 1866. The reason was that policy makers had learned that: 'A financial crisis *per contra* could be averted by timely predictable signals to market participants of institutional readiness to make available an augmented supply of funds' (Schwartz 1987: 28). Schwartz does not describe the exact role of *Lombard Street* in the learning process, but there is certainly no other text with as strong a claim to have influenced policy makers. To be sure, proving that a change in attitudes at the Bank of England, let alone *Lombard Street*, deserves credit for what did not happen is extremely difficult. John H. Wood (2003) has recently argued that the Bank did not adopt Bagehot's policies until well into the twentieth century. Its reserve, one thing that we can readily check, did not keep pace with the growing size of British financial markets despite Bagehot's insistence on a large reserve. Moreover, Wood maintains that other economic developments, such as the declining importance of harvest failures (in part because of the repeal of the Corn Laws) can account for the stability observed after 1866. Nevertheless, to the extent that *Lombard Street* played even a small role in eliminating panics in Britain and other industrial countries, it must be regarded as a major achievement. Financial panics were a major cause of economic distress in the industrial countries until the middle of the twentieth century. Financial panics, moreover, have not disappeared; they are a continuing problem in developing countries. Economists continue to read and cite *Lombard Street* as they grope for policies that will provide stability in an increasingly integrated world financial system.

As J. Shield NICHOLSON (1914) pointed out long ago, Bagehot resembles Adam Smith more than most economists of the same or later eras. Both were interested in literature, including poetry. Both, perhaps as a result, expressed themselves in clear vigorous prose. Both got along well with men of affairs, and partly as a result, were superb economic psychologists. In John Maynard KEYNES's assessment of Bagehot, which appears in a review of *The Works and Life of Walter Bagehot* by Mrs. Russell Barrington (1915), he argued that Bagehot was not a great abstract thinker, but rather a great psychologist, and was at his height in writing about men and events with which he was intimately familiar. Bagehot probably learned more about people from real life, and Smith more, to judge by *The Theory of Moral Sentiments*, from his extensive reading. Both Bagehot and Smith, moreover, relied on their understanding of the irrational side of human nature to suggest limits to *laissez-faire*. Both recognized that even the most hard-bitten men of money could succumb to panic. They believed strongly in the civilizing force of free markets, but neither was a fundamentalist.

An account of Bagehot the economist, one must emphasize, describes only a small part of Bagehot the man. He was, as Ruth Dudley Edwards, the historian of *The Economist*, put it, 'a banker, editor, essayist, journalist and failed politician who wrote on economics, education, history, law, literature, politics, religion, and social psychology' (Edwards 1995: 226). Bagehot was one of the great economists of the nineteenth century, and his classic, *Lombard*

Street, should still be read by every aspiring economist.

BIBLIOGRAPHY
Lombard Street: A Description of the Money Market (1873).

Further Reading
Barrington, R., *The Works and Life of Walter Bagehot* (1915).
Buchan, A., *The Spare Chancellor: The Life of Bagehot* (Ann Arbor, Michigan, 1959).
Clapham, J.H., *The Bank of England, a History* (Cambridge, 1970).
Edwards, R.D., *The Pursuit of Reason: The Economist 1843–1993* (Boston, 1995).
Friedman, M., and Schwartz, A.J., *A Monetary History of the United States, 1867–1960* (Princeton, 1963).
Keynes, J.M., 'The Works of Bagehot and The Works and Life of Walter Bagehot, by Russell Barrington', *The Economic Journal* (1915), vol. 25, September, pp. 369–75.
Nicholson, J.S., 'Walter Bagehot', *The Economic Journal* (1914), vol. 24, December, pp. 543–50.
Rockoff, H. 'Walter Bagehot and the Theory of Central Banking', in F. Capie and G. Wood, *Financial Crises and the World Banking System* (New York, 1986, pp. 160–80).
Schwartz, A.J., 'Real and Pseudo-Financial Crises', in F. Capie and G. Wood, *Financial Crises and the World Banking System* (New York, 1986, pp. 11–40; repr. in A.J. Schwartz, *Money in Historical Perspective*, Chicago, 1987, pp. 271–88).
St John-Stevas, N. (ed.), *The Collected Works of Walter Bagehot* (Cambridge, Massachusetts, 1965–86).
Wood, J.H., 'Bagehot's Lender of Last Resort, a Hollow Hallowed Tradition', *The Independent Review* (2003), vol. 7, pp. 343–51.

Hugh Rockoff

BAILEY, Samuel (1791–1870)

Bailey was born in Sheffield in 1791, and died there of a heart attack on 18 January 1870. He was the fourth son and ninth child of Mary and Joseph Bailey, a scissor-maker who had risen to become a wealthy merchant and factory owner. From c.1796–1805 he attended the Sheffield Free Writing School and the Moravian School in Fulneck. Around 1806 he joined the family business, probably as a clerk and book-keeper. After a brief but profitable sojourn to America around 1812–14, establishing a new branch of the family business, he returned to Sheffield and in 1824 took over his father's firm. He retired from active business a few years later around 1831 to devote himself entirely to the pursuit of his intellectual interests. He spent the rest of his life in Sheffield, unmarried.

Bailey was a founding member, frequent lecturer and four-times president of the Sheffield Literary and Philosophical Society, and served on various local committees such as the Sheffield Town Trust, Gas Company, Water-works, Library, Mechanics Institute, Fire Office (an insurance company) and Banking Company. After 1831 he was also active in the Sheffield Reform movement, stood twice as candidate for parliament, and was narrowly defeated in the second Reform election of 1835. In 1818 Bailey published a series of newspaper articles, followed in 1821 by his first book, *Essays on the Formation and Publication of Opinions and on Other Subjects*, which drew praise from some of the philosophical radicals, including James MILL. Subsequently, Bailey made a number of further contributions to philosophy, including *Essays on the Pursuit of Truth* (1829), a tract on representative government (1835), a criticism of BERKELEY's theory of vision (1842), *The Theory of Reasoning* (1851), and a tripartite series of *Letters on the Philosophy of the Human Mind* (1855–62). With these writings Bailey acquired some fame as a philosopher, and in 1837 he seems to have been one of the most promising candidates for the professorship of moral philosophy at Glasgow (see De Vivo 1984: 139). Apart from his philosophical and economic writings, Bailey also published various tracts on religious matters as well as a poem (*Maro; or, Poetic Irritability*, 1845) and a literary criticism of Shakespeare's plays (*On the Received Text of Shakespeare's Dramatic writings and its Improvement*, 2 volumes, 1862 and 1866).

Bailey's first deliberations on economic issues in *Questions on Political Economy, Politics, Morals, Metaphysics, Polite Literature, and other Branches of Knowledge...* (1823), are noteworthy only for their amateurish and rather deferential character. His main contribution to economics was his *Critical Dissertation on the Nature, Measure and Causes of Value* (1825), in which he criticized RICARDO's concept of absolute value on the ground that value was something essentially relative that denotes nothing positive or real, but merely the relation in which two objects stand to each other as exchangeable commodities. Accordingly, he declared the SMITH-Ricardo-MALTHUS idea of having to find an invariable measure of value for intertemporal and interspatial value comparisons a pointless exercise. Bailey made some valid criticisms of the Ricardian theory of value, which prompted James Mill and MCCULLOCH to reformulations and amendments. But his criticisms of Ricardo's concept of the inverse wage-profit relationship were clearly based on grave misunderstandings. The *Critical Dissertation* provoked extensive responses from Malthus (1827) and from DE QUINCEY (1844), to which Bailey made no reply, but a critical review in the *Westminster Review*, probably written by James Mill, drew a long rejoinder from Bailey (1826), in which he repeated his earlier argument.

It has been variously suggested that Bailey may also be the author of two anonymous pamphlets, *Observations on Certain Verbal Disputes* (1821) and *An Inquiry into those Principles advocated by Mr. Malthus* (1821).

However, in his unpublished notebooks Bailey explicitly repudiated his authorship (see Dennis 1973), and inscribed copies in Piero SRAFFA's library seem to confirm that these pamphlets were indeed authored by somebody else.

Bailey's third economic treatise, *Money and its Vicissitudes in Value* (1837), was not a particularly noteworthy performance. While endorsing HUME's argument that a rise in money supply may temporarily stimulate production, Bailey argued that attempting to regulate the value of money was not a legitimate object of monetary policy. In the appendix on joint stock banks, he argued in favour of a competitive banking system and protested against the then-pending proposal to legislate the conduct of joint stock banks (*A Defence of Joint-Stock Banks and Country Issues* (1840) was a slightly revised version of the 1837 appendix).

The importance that is sometimes attributed to Bailey's *Critical Dissertation* as a landmark contribution to value theory owes much to fact that TORRENS had declared, in 1831, that this treatise had been decisive for the abandonment of Ricardo's doctrines. However, this was as much an overstatement as the claims that have later been made by Seligman and others, who depicted Bailey as a precursor of 'modern', that is marginal utility value theory and an early exponent of the abstinence theory. Bailey's remarks on the 'causes of value' fell far short of anything that could be called an alternative theory, and indeed did not get beyond the vague suggestion that a theory of value must take into account 'mental states' and 'estimations'. If Bailey contributed to the abandonment of the surplus approach and its gradual replacement by the supply and demand approach, then this did not so much concern the demand side, but rather the supply side. More specifically, with his division of reproducible commodities into those which can be supplied at constant costs and those which are only producible at increasing costs Bailey introduced the idea of a relationship between cost and quantity produced. It was this idea, later taken up by John Stuart MILL (who silently adopted several of Bailey's ideas in Book III of his *Principles*), which eventually paved the way to MARSHALL's attempted reconciliation of 'cost of production' and 'marginal utility' in the determination of price (see De Vivo 1984: 133ff).

BIBLIOGRAPHY
Essays on the Formation and Publication of Opinions and on Other Subjects (1821).
Questions on Political Economy, Politics, Morals, Metaphysics, Polite Literature, and other Branches of Knowledge; for discussion in literary societies, or for private study, with remarks under each question, original and selected (1823).
A Critical Dissertation on the Nature, Measures, and Causes of Value; chiefly in reference to the writings of Mr. Ricardo and his followers (1825).
A Letter to a Political Economist; occasioned by an article in the Westminster Review on the subject of value (1826).
Essays on the Pursuit of Truth, On the Progress of Knowledge, and on the Fundamental Principle of all Evidence and Expectation (1829).
A Discussion of Parliamentary Reform (1830).
Essays on the Pursuit of Truth (1829).
The Rationale of Political Representation (1835).
Money and its Vicissitudes in Value; as they affect National Industry and Pecuniary Contracts: with a Postscript on Joint-Stock Banks (1837).
A Defence of Joint-Stock Banks and Country Issues (1840).
The Theory of Reasoning (1851).
Letters on the Philosophy of the Human Mind (1855–62).

Further Reading
Dennis, K., 'The Bailey Notebooks and Authorship of "Verbal Disputes"', *History of Economic Thought Newsletter* (1973), vol. 11, pp. 17–18.

De Quincey, T., *The Logic of Political Economy* (1844; repr. in T. De Quincey, *Political Economy and Politics*, New York, 1970).
De Vivo, G., *Ricardo and his Critics. A Study of Classical Theories of Value and Distribution* (Modena, 1984).
Malthus, T.R., *Definitions in Political Economy* (1827; repr. Fairfield, New Jersey, 1986).
Rauner, R.M., *Samuel Bailey and the Classical Theory of Value* (Cambridge, Massachusetts, 1961).

Christian Gehrke

BAILEY, William (d. 1773)

Bailey died in London in January 1773. His origins are obscure; the first knowledge of him comes with the publication of *A Treaties on the Better Employment and More Comfortable Support of the Poor in Workhouses* in 1758, from which it is clear that Bailey is connected in some way with the Society for the Encouragement of Arts, Manufactures and Commerce (later the Royal Society). He may be the William Bailey who in 1770 won a prize of twenty guineas, awarded by the Society, for the design of an improved straw-cutting machine. He was definitely appointed registrar of the Society in 1766, and served until his death in 1773.

Shortly after his appointment he conceived the idea of producing a volume describing many of the inventions and devices that had been registered with the Society, and in 1769 he was advanced the sum of 50 guineas for production of drawings. Some of these were done by himself, others by his sons Alexander and William. The resulting work, *The Advancement of Art, Manufactures, and Commerce, or Descriptions of the Useful*

Machines and Models contained in the Repository of the Society (1772), was published shortly before Bailey's death. It contains good descriptions of many and varied machines, and shows clearly the state of the art in agricultural and manufacturing technology at the time. The work was updated by Alexander Bailey, who succeeded his father as registrar in 1773 and held the post in 1779, at which point he fell out with the Society and resigned.

The *Treaties* of 1758 takes the view that the poor are best off when they are usefully employed, and that to provide a comfortable subsistence for the poor is a duty consistent with moral virtue and Christian charity. Giving work to the unemployed also benefits the economy, as people become productive rather than being an economic burden. Bailey proposes that the Society for the Encouragement of Arts, Manufactures and Commerce should become directly involved by encouraging workhouses to develop manufacturing industries, making payments or awarding prizes to those that are particularly productive or invent new ways of working and making goods. This commercial encouragement would benefit the poor in those workhouses and would stimulate others to emulate them.

Bailey goes on to set out rules for governance of workhouses, including the duties of governors and officers, meals to be served, industries to be pursued and so on. Among the useful occupations residents of workhouses can perform are spinning flax, twisting linen and woollen yarn, weaving linen and woollen cloth, bleaching linen, knitting stockings and caps, making pegs for tilers, making gloves, making wicker ware and matches, cutting corks, weaving carpets and making papier maché. The work also contains some remarks on flax and the linen industry, and engravings of some new inventions for the manufacture of linen.

BIBLIOGRAPHY
A Treaties on the Better Employment and More Comfortable Support of the Poor in Workhouses (1758).
The Advancement of Art, Manufactures, and Commerce, or Descriptions of the Useful Machines and Models contained in the Repository of the Society (1772).

Further Reading
Wood, H.T., *A History of the Royal Society of Arts* (1913).

Morgen Witzel

BAINES, Edward (1774–1848)

Edward Baines was born on 5 February 1774 at Walton-le-Dale in Lancashire, the son of Richard Baines and his wife Jane. He died in Leeds on 3 August 1848. He was educated at Hawkshead school and Preston grammar school, and then in 1790 he was apprenticed to a printer in Preston, where he worked until 1794. He moved to Leeds and found work with the *Leeds Mercury*, which he bought in March 1801, then aged twenty-seven. Contrary to normal practice, Baines wrote political editorials for the *Mercury*, making the paper the mouthpiece of Whig opinion in the West Riding. In Baines's hands, the newspaper soon became recognized as the leading Whig paper in Yorkshire and its circulation increased rapidly to become one of the most important provincial publications.

In 1798, Baines married Charlotte Talbot of Leeds and the couple had eleven children. Baines was a founder member of the Leeds Philosophical and Literary Society (1819) and became a magistrate in the town. In 1834 Baines became an MP for Leeds, a seat he held until he was forced to retire in 1841.

A staunch Methodist, Baines supported the campaigns for political and religious freedoms that were being demanded by Dissenters, including the abolition of church rates and removal of civil disabilities. He also campaigned for parliamentary reform although he opposed universal suffrage. In 1817 he was instrumental in exposing the activities of the government's *agent provocateur*, 'Oliver the Spy', who had masterminded the Pentrich rising. The *Mercury* was also used to support the anti-slavery campaign of Clarkson and Sharp. Baines was not averse to attacking the government, and the *Mercury's* reports of the Peterloo Massacre (1819) were very critical of both the organizers of the meeting and of the officers of the yeomanry.

Baines became prominent in the affairs of Leeds. He was instrumental in the establishment of the Leeds Mechanics Institute, and advocated local improvements. He used the *Leeds Mercury* to promote the causes of Catholic Emancipation and the Anti-Corn-Law League and to oppose government control over education. He encouraged the reclamation of a large part of Chat Moss, living long enough to see it become productive farmland.

During the 1830s the factory movement campaigned for legislation to control working conditions. Baines published his *History of the Cotton Manufacture* (1835). This is largely a favourable work, describing the historical evolution of the cotton industry but with the main concentration on the events of the last fifty years. He discusses the contributions of inventors and entrepreneurs such as Kay, Wyatt, Arkwright and Crompton, then subsequent developments such as the harnessing of steam to create the power loom. There are chapters on bleaching, calico printing, cotton wool, extent and value of the manufacture. The book contains much statistical data on cotton manufacturing, illustrations of factories and descriptions of cotton machinery. Baines describes these developments as 'a spectacle unparalleled in the annals of industry' (1835: 6), describing how science and art allied to nature have created wealth.

Chapter 16 looks at the darker side of these advances, however, describing the poverty of the mill workers and conditions in the workplace. Although he regretted the health problems and problems of morals in the factories, he attacked those who opposed child labour. He claimed that 'factory labour is far less injurious than many other forms of employment' and said that factory children invariably suffered ill-health from birth. He believed that the inventions of textile machinery enabled working people to better themselves. In the preface to the book, Baines maintained that the manufacture of cotton 'is the very creature of mechanical invention and chemical discovery...which has ...rendered the most important service to science, as well as increased the wealth and power of the country'.

BIBLIOGRAPHY
History of the Reign of George III (1823).
History, Directory and Gazetteer of the County of York (1823).
On the Moral Influence of Free Trade, and its Effects in the Prosperity of Nations (1830).
History of Cotton Manufacture (1835).
History of the County Palatine and Duchy of Lancaster (1836).

Marjorie Bloy

BALOGH, Thomas (1905–85)

Balogh was born in Budapest on 2 November 1905, the elder of two sons, and died at his home in Hampstead in London on 20 January 1985. His brother, Dennis, was an agricultural economist. His father, Emil, was a railway engineer and the Director of the

Transport Board in Budapest, and his mother Eva was the daughter of Professor Bernard Levy of Berlin and Budapest.

Balogh was educated in the Modelgymnasium in Budapest and then studied law and economics at Budapest University. His thesis on German inflation earned him his doctorate and a fellowship of the Royal Hungarian College that allowed him in 1927–28 to move to the University of Berlin. In Germany he worked for the Reichsbank, and from Berlin he won a Rockefeller Fellowship to Harvard (1928–30). While based in Harvard, he managed spells in the statistical department of the Federal Reserve and, in 1930, in the research department of the Banque de France. In June 1930, armed with a letter of introduction from Joseph Schumpeter, he met KEYNES. Keynes not only published Balogh's first article in English, 'The Import of Gold into France', but also helped him to his first job in England with the banking firm of O.T. Falk & Co. (Falk had been Keynes's deputy at the Treasury during the First World War and his successor as Treasury representative at Versailles.) From 1934–40 Balogh was a lecturer at University College, London, from 1938–42 he was attached to the National Institute of Economic Research, and from 1940–5 he combined a post at the new Institute of Statistics in Oxford, a connection he maintained until 1955, with a lectureship at Balliol College. In 1945 he was elected to a fellowship at Balliol, a position that he held until his retirement in 1973. In 1960 he was promoted to a university readership.

Balogh married twice. The first, in 1945, was to Penelope Gatty (née Tower), a psychotherapist and the widow of Oliver Gatty, a fellow of Balliol. This marriage was dissolved in 1970 and the same year he married Catherine Storr (née Cole), a psychologist and author of children's books.

The bare facts of Balogh's life convey little of the man. The titles of his main books, listed in the bibliography, indicate something of his range of interests, but even these do not display the power of his intelligence or the trenchancy of his personality. He had extraordinary intellect with an uncanny ability to absorb ideas, information and gossip about everything. Wilfred Beckerman recalls Balogh arriving in Athens when Beckerman was economic adviser to the Greek government, and within an hour Balogh knew more than Beckerman about everything going on in Greece. Balogh was also constantly on the attack, especially against the establishment and against what he regarded as stupidity and injustice. For him, everything and everybody was black or white, and he was loved and hated in equal measure; and everyone, whatever their feelings about him, had stories about him.

Above all, Balogh was a political economist with a passionate concern with policy and with such a command of events and ideas that his advice was constantly sought at the highest levels. He advised the governments of more than a dozen countries; he worked for the League of Nations, the Food and Agriculture Organization, the United Nations and the Organization for Economic Cooperation and Development; and he was a friend of as well as adviser to Michael Manley (Prime Minister of Jamaica), Jawaharlal Nehru (Prime Minister of India) and Dom Mintoff (Prime Minister of Malta). On one occasion when a ferry to Malta had broken down, Mintoff sent a destroyer to collect Balogh from Sicily.

Balogh's longest link was, however, with the British Labour Party. In the 1930s and 1940s he advised 'Manny' Shinwell and Aneuran Bevan and, from the late 1940s to the 1970s, Harold Wilson, as President of the Board of Trade, Shadow Chancellor, Leader of the Opposition and as Prime Minister. As a result, in October 1964, Balogh was appointed economic adviser to the Cabinet. At least this was the formal name: the reality was that he was the economic adviser to the Prime Minister, and he set up the first policy unit in Downing Street. In this role he was especially influential in the establishment of the Industrial Reorganisation Corporation, in the policy to develop North Sea Gas and in the continuing attempts of the Labour Party to find a workable incomes policy. However, his star gradually waned and in 1968 he was made a life peer and returned to Oxford. Nevertheless, he returned to government in 1974 as Minister of State at the Department of Energy and, having played a key role in the creation of the British National Oil Corporation, became its deputy chairman from 1976–8.

Throughout his career as an economist, Balogh's ideas spewed forth in a constant stream of pamphlets and newspaper contributions and, later, in speeches in the House of Lords. They cover a huge range, but one thing is typical: a contempt for mainstream economics. Indeed, his last book carries the title *The Irrelevance of Conventional Economics*. His greatest hates were neoclassical economics and monetarism, but even Keynesianism, as encapsulated in either the Hicks IS/LM model or, in conjunction with the Phillips Curve, as any form or menu for policy choice, was subject to attack. What was wrong with neoclassical economics was, as he would say, the 'absurd' assumptions of perfect competition and perfect knowledge. What was wrong with *all* formal models were that they were deterministic and a historical. Balogh believed passionately in the use of economic analysis, but it had to be economics in context, and the context was, of course, inevitably different.

A second feature of Balogh's writings, and herein lies his main claim to importance in economics, was his ability to see, very early, to the heart of the matter. Extraordinarily, as early as 1941 he was commenting on how the Keynesian commitment to full employment would alter the whole context of wage bargaining and how, as a result, an incomes policy would be essential if full employment were to be combined with price stability. He never believed in the Phillips Curve.

A second example was his opposition to the monetary arrangements agreed at Bretton Woods in 1944 and, in particular, as he saw it, to the conditions imposed on the UK by the USA in the subsequent loans. His argument was that the arrangements ignored the unequal power of the USA in the immediate post-war period and that, as a result, any attempt to move to full convertibility of currencies would only result in runs on the currency. This is, of course, exactly what happened in the UK in 1947, and convertibility had to be reversed almost immediately. Balogh maintained that in the debates in Parliament about the terms of the loans only four people seriously criticized the terms, and that he had advised all four!

A third example was his analysis of the North Sea and the discovery of gas and then of oil. Faster than anyone, he saw not only that there were potentially huge monopoly profits (prevailing gas and oil prices were well above extraction costs), but also how these could be captured by the UK rather than by the multinational companies. The mechanism in the case of gas was to use the power of British Gas as the single purchaser to impose a monopsony price. With this route unavailable for oil, the solution was a special Petroleum Revenue Tax. In both cases he had to fight a sustained campaign, against great opposition, and in both cases he was, at least partially, successful.

Balogh left his mark, not just in changing policy, but also on the civil service. His 1959 essay 'The Apotheosis of the Dilettante' – an attack on the amateur nature of much advice – undoubtedly contributed to subsequent reforms in the structure of advice in the civil service. Three ex-prime ministers attended his memorial service. However, it was Lord Lever who described him as a talented political economist and a devoted public servant. Balogh, the scourge of the establishment, would have regarded the latter as highly ironic. Yet, if we add to this the power of his insights and the flamboyancy (his enemies would say the impossibility) of his character, the verdict is not unfair.

BIBLIOGRAPHY
'The Import of Gold into France', *Economic Journal* (1930), September.

Studies in Financial Organisation (Cambridge, 1947).
The Dollar Crisis: Causes and Cure; a Report to the Fabian Society (Oxford, 1949).
'The Apotheosis of the Dilettante' in H. Thomas (ed.), *The Establishment* (1959).
Unequal Partners (Oxford, 1963).
The Economics of Poverty (1966).
Labour and Inflation, Fabian Tract 403 (1970).
(with P. Balacs) *Fact and Fancy in International Economic Relations: An Essay on International Monetary Reform* (Oxford, 1973).
The Irrelevance of Conventional Economics (1982).

Andrew Graham

BANFIELD, Thomas Collins (1802–55)

Banfield was born on 3 April, probably in 1802 (the date he preferred), in Castle Lyons, co. Tipperary. He died at Bucharest on 23 November 1855, following a stroke. He was the eldest son of the eldest son in a large Quaker family in Clonmel, who owned farms, flour mills and tanneries, and were involved in the bacon trade and in banking. Nothing is known about Banfield's first twenty-five years. Family tradition has him leaving Clonmel as a young man because he was bored. He appears first in 1828, in Brunswick, Germany, where after giving private English lessons he began a brief, uneasy academic career: professor of English at the Collegium Carolinum in Brunswick until dismissed a few months later for insubordination, and then lektor of English at the University of Göttingen 1829–33, though on leave in 1831–3 to work in Vienna on a 'practical English grammar (1832) and to study Slavic languages. At Göttingen he gave English lessons to Prince Maximilian of Bavaria, later King Maximilian II, whose letter of introduction opened the Vienna homes of scholars, important government officials and other eminent citizens. In 1832 Banfield accompanied Count Alfred Potocki on a four-month trip through Galicia; in 1835 he married Josephine Frech, from a cultivated, well-to-do Viennese family. He became librarian to Maximilian in 1837 with the duties of a private secretary.

In December 1838–January 1839, with other 'gentlemen lately arrived from Munich', Banfield warned English Chartists, Corn Law opponents and Turkish sympathizers of the dangers posed by Russia. On the same trip he sent Maximilian impressions of 'Princess A.' (Princess Augusta of Cambridge) as a royal marital prospect. He also found in the *British and Foreign Review* an outlet for his own frequent articles on economic questions. Returning to Bavaria, he accompanied Maximilian on an Italian tour, during which Maximilian confided to him some of his plans for Germany.

When he declined to accompany Maximilian on a proposed Greek tour, Banfield effectively ended his employment. For much of the 1840s he had lodgings in London, his family was in Wiesbaden, and he was travelling widely. In London he met Nassau SENIOR, thereafter his strongest supporter. He became a functionary of the British government, reporting on Continental political and economic conditions. Late in 1843 he applied for the long vacant chair of political economy at University College London; no appointment was made. In April and May 1844 he received permission to lecture at Cambridge University, introducing the work of Continental, particularly German, economists. Revising the lectures for publication as *Four Lectures on the Organization of Industry* (1845), he again was short of funds and humbly, and unsuccessfully, asked Maximilian for his old position. The book was well received but did not lead to academic employment. The *British and Foreign Review* ceased publication.

Despite these setbacks, Banfield began to make headway. The first volume of his *Industry of the Rhine*, subtitled *Agriculture*, was published in 1846, a busy year. He contributed to the *Mining Journal*. Probably about this time he was director of works for a mining company in which he owned shares; in 1846 he applied for permission to introduce new methods of preparing ore, and he travelled through the iron and steel areas that he then discusses at length in the second volume of *Industry of the Rhine*, on manufactures (1848). His work for the British government became visible when he was named secretary to the Privy Council. In 1849 he was appointed to the Commission of Metropolitan Sewers. He managed also to publish regularly on economic history and co-edited, then edited the biennial *Statistical Companion*.

Banfield belonged to the Reform Club and the Statistical Society, and was a corresponding member of the Central Statistical Commission at Brussels. He was reportedly decorated with several European orders. Then in 1855, to his dismay, he was sent to the Crimea, with the 'comparative rank' of colonel, to straighten out the Land Transport Corps's accounts. Much of the work was physically and emotionally draining, under appalling conditions, all the more difficult for a man in his fifties. Banfield suddenly took ill, and then suffered a stroke and died after being brought to Bucharest. He was buried with military honours in the Protestant Cemetery at Bucharest. R.G. Colquhoun, the British consul general in Bucharest, reported to Lord Clarendon: 'I had simply informed the acting Commander in Chief of the Austrian Forces of the death, as is usual here in such cases and I was greatly surprised by the presence at the Ceremony of the four generals now in garrison here...The Pasha Suleyman sent an escort of 80 men and his music, and the Wallachian staff also attended' (transcript in family possession). Maximilian, now King of Bavaria, again aided the family, ordering a pension for Banfield's widow, who moved to Munich. She had been left destitute, with ten children aged between one year and nineteen. Lord Panmure, at the War Office, declared that he could not grant a pension.

Nassau Senior judged Banfield to be 'a good, indeed in some respects an original, political economist & a sound liberal politician (to M. Napier, 8 Sept 1843; BL Ad.Ms. 34,624/80-1), with 'an acquaintance with continental manufactures & trade very unusual in this country (to Ld. Brougham, 2 Feb. 1844; Brougham Papers, University College London). Add a thorough acquaintance with the economic literature of France, Italy, the Low Countries and the German-speaking states, all in their original languages, and one sees his historical importance.

The *Industry of the Rhine* volumes addressed a more general audience than *Organization of Industry*, in part imitating the popular travel books of the time; we follow the narrator, who feels like a real person, from town to town, into farm yards and farm houses, while absorbing charts, statistics, economic theory and Banfieldian principles, all brief and accessible. Those principles are good Quaker ones: the value of education, simplicity, 'intelligence, sobriety, morality. To put it more in the economist's terms, he discusses free trade, laws and taxes that treat all equally and equitably, cultivation of human and natural advantages rather than misplaced protection of weaknesses, an acceptance of fair competition, and even a prescient acceptance of globalization. Enterprises, agricultural or industrial, will go where costs are lowest; this is acceptable even when it takes them out of the country to less developed countries, for the country they have left then develops advanced products, advanced populace, higher wages and profits.

Note: this entry is based on documents in the family's possession and in German and English archives. I am deeply indebted to Banfield's great-granddaughter, Karin Banfield Dilling of Ratzeburg, Germany, for much information and for her great generosity and patience.

BIBLIOGRAPHY

The Austrian Empire Her Population and Resources (1842).
Six Letters to the Right Honourable Sir Robert Peel, Bart., being an attempt to expose the dangerous tendency of the theory of rent advocated by Mr. Ricardo and the writers of his school. By a political economist (1843).
Four Lectures on the Organization of Industry (1845; repr. New York, 1873).
Industry of the Rhine, 2 vols (1846–8; repr. New York, 1869).
The Progress of the Prussian Nation (1847).
The Economy of the British Empire (1849; repr. 1850).
A Letter to William Brown, Esq., MP., on the Advantages of his Proposed System of Decimal Coinage (1855).

Further Reading
Burke, W.P., *History of Clonmel* (Waterford, 1907).
Curran, E.M., 'Banfield, Thomas C.', http://victorianresearch.org/Obscure_contributors.htm (2003).
de Groot, H.B., '*British and Foreign Review*: Introduction', *Wellesley Index to Victorian Periodicals* (1979), vol. 3, pp. 62–76.

Eileen Curran

BANKS, Joseph (1743–1820)

Banks was born in London on 13 February 1743, and died on 20 June 1820 at Isleworth, Middlesex. The only son of William Banks and Sarah, née Bate, he was educated by a private tutor before being sent to Harrow and then Eton. In 1760 he began his studies at Christ Church College, Oxford, but was unable to absorb himself in botany, the subject that most interested him, because it was not offered there. He then employed Isaac Lyons from the University of Cambridge as a private botany tutor. Banks did not complete his degree, and left Oxford in 1763.

Banks travelled to Newfoundland and Labrador in 1766–7 to collect botanical and geological specimens, and was elected a fellow of the Royal Society that same year. He successfully lobbied the Royal Society and the Royal Navy to be included on James Cook's first voyage to Tahiti on board the Endeavour (1768–71), a privilege for which he paid £10,000. This voyage commenced Banks's great career in science, particularly botany. Returning home, he continued to travel in Euope and also to Iceland, gathering more samples and information. He was elected president of the Royal Society in 1778 and held the position until 1820, making him the Society's longest serving president. As president, he participated in the work of the British Museum, Greenwich Royal Observatory and the Boards of Longitude and Agriculture. He was knighted in 1781, and appointed to the Privy Council in 1797. On 23 March 1779, he married Dorothea Hugessen (1758–1828); they had no children.

Throughout his career Banks was alert to the economic opportunities that flowed from his work, whether it was the encouragement of the geological mapping of Britain, the economic benefits of Spanish Merino sheep, the establishment of sheep farming in Australia or through his advocacy of Captain William Bligh's breadfruit voyages, testing the theory that breadfruit would be a suitable staple for African slaves. Banks was one of the first advocates of economic botany and employed botanists to collect plants for him from all parts of the world. He was also special director of the Royal Botanic Gardens, and corresponded with George CHALMERS with a view to setting up a network of botanical gardens to collect and study specimens.

Banks maintained an impressive circle of correspondents on a wide variety of subjects that interested him. He was a magnificent facilitator, who established scholarly networks throughout the world. One of his more influential activities was his involvement in the decision to select Botany Bay as the site for a convict settlement. Between 1788 and 1820 Banks was the unofficial expert on all matters Australian, and succeeding generations in that country called him the 'Father of Australia'. Regrettably, though a polymath, Banks did little to publish the results of much of his work. His great plan to publish a botanical account of the Endeavour voyage only coming to fruition two hundred years later, in 1990, with the publication of *Banks's Florilegium*.

An interest in metallurgy led Banks to consider questions of currency, and while a privy councillor he served on the Coin Committee. His achievements here included the re-establishment of the Royal Mint on Tower Hill in 1810. Banks was friendly with Matthew Boulton, one of the pioneers of the modern steam engine who was in the process of introducing steam power into manufacturing and had already shown the efficacy of steam-driven machinery in minting, and together they introduced steam technology into the Royal Mint. This in turn led Banks to consider issues such as standardization of the currency. He was in favour of reminting, which he felt would strengthen the value of the currency, and he also was an early proponent of decimalization. Banks's ideas on the currency are contained in his correspondence with Boulton and others.

BIBLIOGRAPHY
Banks's Florilegium (1990).
The Endeavour Journal of Joseph Banks 1768–1771 (Sydney, 1962).
Papers of Sir Joseph Banks (16 January 2004).
The Propriety of Allowing a Qualified Exportation of Wool (1782).
A Short Account of the Causes of the Disease in Corn called by Farmers the Blight, the Mildew and the Rust (1805).

Further Reading
Carter, H.B., *His Majesty's Spanish Flock: Sir Joseph Banks and the Merinos of George III of England* (1964).
——, *The Sheep and Wool Correspondence of Sir Joseph Banks* (1979).
——, *Sir Joseph Banks, 1743–1820* (1988).
Maiden, J.H., *Sir Joseph Banks: The 'Father of Australia'* (1907).
O'Brien, P. *Joseph Banks* (1987).

Alan Ventress

BARBON, Nicholas (*c*.1640–1698)

Barbon was born in London around 1640, and was probably the son of the famous Praisegod Barbon, or Barebone, after whom the Barebone parliament was named. He died in London in 1698. He graduated MD at Utrecht in 1661, and became a honorary fellow of the college of physicians there in 1664. Taking use of the opportunity which the Great Fire of London 1666 offered, he became a considerable and speculative builder, and was also the first to introduce a system of fire insurance in England. He was MP for Bramber in 1690 and 1695, and the founder of a speculative land bank in partnership with John ASGILL.

Barbon was not a very prolific writer. Rather, his pamphlets are short and condensed, but reveal great analytical abilities. In his earliest known text, *Letters to a Gentleman in the Country giving an Account of the Two Insurances-Offices; the Fire Office and Friendly Society* (1684), he sought to demonstrate the advantages of his own fire insurance company and the disadvantages of its rival. The pamphlet *Apology for the Builder; or a Discourse showing the Cause and Effects of the Increase of Building* (1695) was likewise an exercise in self-interest. Here he argued for the massive re-building of London, and against those who argued that the rest of England was drained of population and capital because of massive and speculative building in the capital.

However, Barbon is mainly remembered for two small but remarkable tracts, *A Discourse of Trade* (1690) and *A Discourse Concerning Coining the New Money Lighter* (1696). The general tone of the first of the treatises can also partly, at least, be explained by Barbon's experience as a builder and banker. His aim was most probably stimulated by his wish to combat regulations which, according to him, had hampered a healthy increase of trade and production. The second treatise was in effect quite different; it was mainly a critical response to John LOCKE during the re-coinage discussion in the middle of the 1690s.

In *A Discourse of Trade*, Barbon sets out to discuss the advantages of nature of trade in general. Here, at some length, he discusses the concepts of value and riches. 'Things of no use have no value', he pointed out (1690: 13). The value of a country lies in its native production, he stresses, and thinks that this shows the error of Thomas MUN's definition which leads to the conclusion that nations can get rich by parsimony like individuals. Moreover, as he continues, 'the market is the best judge of value: for by the Concourse of Buyers and sellers, the quality of wares, and the occasion for them are Best known' (1690: 20). He took the same position with regard to money, and pointed out that it would be a grave mistake to believe that money had an 'intrinsick value by itself' (1690: 24). Instead, like any commodity it varied in its value. Barbon, was in fact – as Douglas Vickers (1959) has pointed out – the first money 'cartelist' on principal terms. Hence he argued that public acceptability was the essential quality of money. It was considered legal tender not because of its 'intrinsic' or metal value but because of the stamp put on it by a central governmental body.

Barbon also discussed the general benefits of trade. An abundant foreign trade would raise the value of land, improve the natural stock of the country and increase wages as well as the revenues of the state. Moreover, by its civilizing effects trade would bring not only increased wealth but also peace. Contrary to, for example, his contemporary Josiah CHILD, Barbon did not emphasize the visible hand of governments in order to make trade prosperous. Instead, trade was mainly promoted by the 'industry of the poor' and the 'liberality in the Rich'. Thus the consumption of luxury wares among the richer classes should not be opposed but rather encouraged. Barbon even went so far as to defend 'prodigality' with the argument that although it was vicious from the individual point of view, it brought social benefits by raising demand: 'Prodigality is a vice that is prejudicial to the Man, but not to the Trade; It is living a pace, and spending that in a Year, that should last all his life; Covetousness is a Vice, prejudicial both to Man & Trade; It starves the Man, and breaks the Trade: and by the same way the Covetous Man thinks he grows rich, he grows poor' (1690: 63).

As to the causes behind the prevailing and much debated decay of trade in England, he especially pointed out the 'many prohibitions and high rents' (1690: 71). On the whole, in this pamphlet his tone was quite 'liberal'. Barbon of course admitted that the best for England would be 'if our Serges, Stuffs, or Cloth are Exchanged for Unmanufactured Goods...because of the difference in Number of Hands in the making of the First, and the Later' (1690: 76f). However, to draw the conclusion from this that more prohibition should be introduced was wrong. Rather, a better solution was that English wares should be made more competitive by low interest rates, low prices on provisions and low wages. For this purpose, not the least, an 'increased industry' among the poor was most necessary.

In the second treatise, *A Discourse Concerning Coining the New Money Lighter*

(1695) Barbon's direct aim was to attack Locke and especially his view on money and interest which the latter had developed in the 1691 pamphlet *Some Considerations of the Consequences of the Lowering of Interest and Raising the Value of Money*. Here Locke had criticized – as in his forthcoming tract *Further Considerations Concerning Raising the Value of Money* (1696) – the re-coinage project of William LOWNDES, the aim of which was to coin money with less gold and silver in it (hence to 'increase the value of money', according to the contemporary vocabulary; while we would rather speak of an increase of price in monetary terms). Locke argued that the old ratio between nominal money and silver and gold must be retained, perceiving Lowndes's project as a form of debasement hurtful to the country. Barbon argued instead that although 'Nothing can be of greater Advantage to Banks than scarcity of Money', the same is not always the case with the rest of the community. For one thing, 'it has been a Custom in all Ages, and amongst all Nations, to Raise the Value of their Money' (1696: 187). Princes and states have always raised the value of their money because of two causes, 'ordinary' causes and second 'extraordinary' causes. 'The Ordinary and Common use of Raising the Value of the Coin is the rise of Bullion' (1696: 198), and this is most valuable for trade and commerce. To lower the value of money, on the other hand, may be profitable for banks but will depress the trades. Hence Barbon emphasizes: 'The cause of raising the Money here in Europe will always continue, as long as the Europeans continue in Traffick and Commerce: for Trade makes a People rich, and Gold and Silver are Badges of Riches; and therefore as the People grow rich, the price of Gold and Silver will rise, because the occasion for Gold and Silver will still increase' (Barbon 1696:197). Hence Barbon also drew some interesting conclusions regarding the fears of the inflow of silver and gold from the Americas, which were widespread during the seventeenth century: 'This continual Rise of Gold and Silver will be no prejudice to the Princes and States'. The only difference will be that there will be more money 'in every man's House' (1696: 198).

However, there might also be extraordinary causes for the raising of the value of money and this can cause problems: 'When Princes and States have been engag'd in great Wars, and wanting money they have sometimes...not observ'd the usual Bonds and Limits of raising the Value of money Ten or Fifteenth per cent above the Market Price of Bullion: but have greatly exceeded to it to Thirty, Forty, Fifty per cent, and more' (1696: 198). Hence in cases where the price of money is lowered by the price of gold and silver metal, coins would of course be drawn from exchange and melted down and instead be used in their bullion form.

In his argument against Locke, Barbon began by firmly stating that Locke's main mistake was his belief that there existed an 'intrinsick' value in silver. As mistaken was the view that this intrinsic value should be 'the instrument and measure of commerce'. Instead, according to Barbon, silver as well as money in general were commodities which price varied depending on use and quantity. Thus, there was neither an 'intrinsick' value in silver nor a necessary relationship between nominal money and silver. Here he returned to his demand and supply model. Thus 'value' is defined as 'the price of things' determined mainly by use: 'There are two general uses by which all Things have a Value: They are either useful to supply the Wants of the Body, or the Want of the Mind'. Riches, in turn, he defines as 'all such Things as are of great value' (1696: 159).

On the basis of this definition of value, Barbon went on to criticize the theory of the favourable balance of trade. The opinion, he argued, that silver and gold have an 'intrinsick' value stemmed from the same confusion which had haunted King Midas. This mistake was granted upon the false supposition 'that Gold and Silver are the only Riches' (1696: 160). Hence, the notion of a favourable balance of trade was a simple mistake. He based his critique upon two different arguments. First, he repeated Child's conviction that it would be almost impracticable to account for such a balance. Not even the fact that foreign exchange 'run high upon a Nation' is a true sign of an unfavourable balance of trade; especially as bills of exchange 'rise and fall every week and of some particular times in the year run high against a Nation'. From this he carried on to stress a second and more principal point:

> But if there could be an account taken of the Balance of Trade, I can't see where the advantage of it could be. For the reason that's given for it, That the Overplus is paid in Bullion, and the Nation grows so much the richer, because the balance is made in Bullion, is altogether a mistake: For Gold and Silver are but commodities; and one sort of commodity is as good as another, so it be of the same value. A hundred pounds of worth of Copper is as good to a merchant, as if he imported an hundred pounds worth of Silver, and he may get as much by it...For a Nation grows rich, by the Inhabitants growing rich...
> (1696: 177)

Instead of an account of the balance of trade, Barbon suggested another method to judge whether a nation grow rich or poor by its trade. First, it might be judged by observing whether the inhabitants were 'growing rich' or not. Secondly, to know whether a nation gained or lost in its trade, the method would be to consider 'what sort of Goods employ most hands by importing and manufacturing'. Thus, a well-regulated trade should be ordered so that a maximum of people are employed, as 'the more there are employ'd in a nation the richer the Nation grows' (1698: 178).

Moreover, besides presenting an alternative to the balance of trade 'doctrine' in such terms, Barbon developed a critique of the generally accepted view that an 'overballance' of trade must lead to that 'money is carried out' of the realm. In fact anticipating the specie flow mechanism later developed by GERVAISE, HUME and others, he stated that a negative trade balance would merely mean that the price of English bills of exchange would fall, and with them export prices measured in value: 'That all sorts of Goods of the value of the Bill of Exchange, or the Balance of the accompt, will answer the Bill, and Balance the Accompt as well as Money' (1696: 187). Thus, a net outflow of money would not be feasible, at least not in the long run. However, he did not explicitly mention that such a neat balancing-out in the long run necessitated, for example, that demand on foreign markets was elastic and that a lower export price would mean higher foreign demand. But at the same time, he was clearly aware of the principle of elasticity. Therefore, it is highly plausible that he pre-supposed this condition without spelling it out clearly.

Against this background, it is not strange that Barbon today is acknowledged for having a rather modern view, especially with regard to the formation of value and price. In the first chapter of *A Discourse of Trade* he puts forward – for his time – a quite sophisticated demand and supply model. 'The Price of Wares', he says, 'is the present Value; and ariseth by Computing the occasions or use for them with the Quantity to serve that Occasion; for the Value of things depending on the use of them, the Over-plus of Those Wares which are more than can be used, becomes worth nothing; So that Plenty in respect of the occasion, makes things cheap and Scarcity dear' (1690: 15). The second chapter, on money, credit and interest, also contains interesting new ideas. In contrast to John Locke, Barbon argues that the value of money is a convention; it is not intrinsic, but something which is established by law. This view he later developed more thoroughly in his 1696 pamphlet. In this chapter, too, Barbon is keen to point out that interest is paid not for money but for stock: 'Interest is commonly reckoned for Mony...but this is a mistake: for the Interest is paid for Stock...No Man takes up Mony at Interest to lay it by him, and lose the Interest by it' (1690: 31f). To regard interest as something different than a mere price of borrowing and lending money was quite a novelty at the time.

Thus with Barbon we seem far from the stylized version of a mercantilist writer of the seventeenth century. Instead of the advantages of a trade surplus, he stressed rather the role of production and demand as dynamic economic forces propelling growth and increased wealth. He noted the relationship between interest as a price paid for the loan of money – the definition employed by most economic pamphleteers of the age – and the real rate of interest. This line of reasoning would in the eighteenth century be further developed by, for example, Joseph MASSIE, Josiah TUCKER and David Hume.

However, if we take an even broader view of Barbon's accomplishment it is impossible not to notice the influence from the contemporary moral philosophical and political discussions. As Barbon did not explicitly cite any works of this kind, we can not be exactly sure of the exact influence he gained from this literature. But most of the discussion on political, moral and judicial matters during this period was carried out within the context of natural rights discourse. Barbon's *A Discourse of Trade* contained several such references to the civilizing function of trade, which was a typical feature of this tradition. Moreover, he presented a historical sequence – almost a stage theory – of a rise from barbarism to modern civilization in much the same mode as would become popular during the eighteenth century. Against this background, it is right to acknowledge Barbon as an important predecessor to the classical English school of economics, including Adam SMITH, rather than simply to regard him as some form of 'mercantilist'.

BIBLIOGRAPHY
A Discourse of Trade (1690).
A Discourse Concerning Coining the New Money Lighter (1696; repr. in L.

Magnusson (ed.), *Mercantilism: Critical Concepts in the History of Economics*, vol. III, 1995).

Further Reading
Bowley, M., *Studies in the History of Economic Ideas before 1870* (1973).
Hutchison, T., *Before Adam Smith* (Cambridge, 1988).
Johnson, E.A., *Predecessors of Adam Smith* (New York, 1939).
Magnusson, L., *Mercantilism: the Shaping of Economic Language* (1994).
Vickers, D., *Studies in the Theory of Money 1660–1776* (Philadelphia, 1959).

Lars Magnusson

BARING, Alexander (1774–1848)

Baring was born in England on 27 October 1774, and died at Longleat, the seat of the Marquis of Bath, on 13 May 1848. His father, Sir Francis Baring (1740–1810), was a director of the East India Company, financial advisor to William Pitt the Younger and founder of the merchant banking firm John & Francis Baring & Company (1763). Under Sir Francis's management the firm became, by the end of eighteenth century, one of the most stable financial houses in Europe, playing a prominent role in financing the British war effort against France. In the early part of his life Alexander Baring went to America where, in 1798, he married the daughter of Senator William Bingham of Philadelphia, from one of the wealthiest families of Pennsylvania. Through this union he came into contact with the main mercantile firms of America, and the bank attained a leading position in the financing of US foreign trade.

In 1803 Baring signed in Paris an agreement on behalf of his bank and Hope bank from

Amsterdam, promising a loan to the Treasury of the United States to finance the Louisiana Purchase. Since the French were frightened of marketing American bonds, the American diplomats Livingston and Monroe and the French Treasury Minister Barbé-Marbois made an arrangement with the two banking houses to convert bonds into cash. During the war between America and England (1812–14), Baring's bank continued to pay interest in the absence of remittances and clear instructions from the USA. At the death of Sir Francis in 1810, Alexander Baring became the head of the firm (renamed in 1806 Baring brothers and Company).

From 1806 to 1835 Baring sat in the House of Commons, representing in turn Taunton (1806–26), Callington (1806–31), Thetford (1831–2) and North Essex (1832–5). He took an assiduous part in the parliamentary debates on commercial and financial affairs. A supporter of free trade, he strongly opposed the protectionist legislation that Britain was introducing to counteract the Continental System. In 1820, he presented the free trade petition of the London merchants in the House of Commons. A critic of the inflationary policy of the war years, Baring supported RICARDO's Ingot Plan and the resumption legislation of 1819. In 1821, however, he pioneered the opposition to the 1819 Resumption Act, maintaining that its content had to be reconsidered on the ground that it was producing economic distress, and proposing a bimetallic standard of value. The preference for a mixed standard he retained throughout his life, a position that allowed him to distance himself from both the supporters of gold and from the Birmingham economists. He also took part in the debate on the Reform Bill of 1832, firmly opposing any proposals for strengthening the Commons. According to Baring, the Bill would create a division in the legislature between rural and industrial interests, favouring the more organised population of manufacturing districts. He was President of the Board of Trade in Sir Robert Peel's first administration (1834). In May 1835 he was raised to the peerage as Baron Ashburton, taking the title formerly held by John DUNNING, who had been married to Baring's aunt.

In 1841, with the formation of Peel's second ministry, the anti-American Foreign Secretary Lord Palmerston was replaced with the pro-trade Lord Aberdeen. In the following year, Baring was appointed as special commissioner to settle the Northeast Boundary Dispute, a controversy about the position of the US-Canada border in the region between Maine and New Brunswick, which in 1839 had triggered a conflict (the Aroostook War). Baring and Daniel Webster (US Secretary of State and legal advisor to the Baring's bank since 1831) reached an agreement favourable to the USA, the Webster-Ashburton Treaty, which started a co-operative intercourse that restored free trade between the two countries. A milestone in the history of Anglo-American relations, the treaty represents Britain's definitive renunciation to challenging the supremacy of the USA in North America.

Baring opposed Peel's repeal of the Corn Laws in 1846. This position, ascribed by his critics to his interests as a landlord, was not an abjuration of his free trade credo, but rather the restatement of an ambiguous attitude regarding free trade that he maintained in the later part of his life. Indeed, he had been an agricultural protectionist since the years of the Reform Bill debate, justifying this exception to free trade principles on the ground that the tariff was to be used to balance economic interests between landowners and manufacturers, a position coherent with his constitutional conservatism. As he wrote to Peel in 1841, 'I am aware to what extent our Conservative party is a party pledged to the support of the land and that, that principle abandoned, the party is dissolved' (Gash 1965: 137–8). He also strongly opposed Peel's financial policy, resisting the Bank Charter Act of 1844.

Baring published several speeches and two tracts. In his first work, *An Inquiry into the*

Causes and Consequences of the Orders in Council, and an Examination of the Conduct of Great Britain toward the Neutral Commerce of America (1808), he firmly contested the protectionist legislation that Britain was introducing as a reaction against the Berlin and Milan Decrees. One of several written at that time to resist the widespread anti-trade climate, the tract focuses on the effects which the British counter-blockade measures would have on the political and economic relations between Britain and the USA. Worried by the strategy of adding the USA to Britain's European enemies, Baring took to task the supporters of a war against the Americans, and opposed the imposition on USA vessels of touching at British ports before proceeding to ports from which the British flag was excluded (1808: 103–17).

Baring's second book, *The Financial and Commercial Crisis Considered* (1847), is linked to his interest and competence in financial affairs. It discusses Peel's Act of 1844 and the principles of the currency school. He dissented from a mechanical rule for the regulation of note issue, centring upon the distinction between withdrawal of metals from the Bank of England's coffers caused by panic or distrust within the country, and a drain on the Bank's gold caused by a demand to send it abroad due to an unfavourable state of the foreign exchanges. In considering the first possibility, he offered a detailed analysis of the financial distress of 1825, when a rush upon the banks by depositors and holders of notes completely drained the gold of the Bank. A large addition of notes not covered by specie was made, the panic ceased and gold and notes flowed back to the Bank. Warning the reader that from this it cannot be supposed that 'an increased issue of paper is an invariable remedy against a drain of specie', since 'a contrary treatment might have suited a drain caused by adverse exchange', he regarded the experience of 1825–6 as 'a clear proof that the act of 1844 not only would not have suited that case, but would have aggravated all the difficulties' (1847: 14).

As far as the second possibility is concerned (a drain of external origin), Baring elaborated a more articulate opposition to the restrictions of Peel's Act basically revolving around the distinction between a drain due to temporary causes from one determined by a fundamental disequilibrium of the price level. In his opinion, the strategy of correcting an adverse state of the foreign exchanges by making money scarce could not have avoided a rising rate of interest, a paralysis of credit, and an abrupt devaluation of the capital. He asked the supporters of the Bank Charter Act whether they 'comprehend the losses occasioned by this depreciation of all property when this screw is applied to correct every occasional fluctuation of the exchange?' (1847: 27). According to Baring, that was the situation in that very moment, with an abundant treasure in the Bank and an external demand for gold that, due to the failing harvest, was due to a sudden demand for food:

> if those wants continue, we must have the supply or starve, whatever may be the state of our paper circulation; and how can it be supposed that you can suddenly create by cheapness new markets for goods rather of luxury than of necessity, a creation that all practical men know to be a work of time, and therefore wholly unfit as a remedy for an immediate emergency?
>
> (1847: 28)

This double distinction between internal and external drains, and, among the latter, between occasional and permanent drains, was a well-established argument among the members of the banking school. Palmer, in 1840, had argued against a mechanical rule for note issues drawing similar distinctions, although he considered 1825 as an example of an external drain due to a disequilibrium in the price levels (Viner 1965: 261–2). FULLARTON devoted an entire chapter of his book *On the Regulations of Currencies* to a detailed analysis of these distinctions, denying the prolonged nature of all drains and maintaining that even a substantial external drain does not justify a contraction in circulation since the Bank of England cannot act before its natural termination (Fullarton 1845: 145–73). J.S. MILL in his 1848 *Principles of Political Economy* reached conclusions close to Baring's point of view, considering the contraction of circulation an improper response but in the case of a non occasional external drain (Viner 1965: 262–3).

Having singled out the main cause of the high market rate of interest in the artificial restraints of the Bank Charter Act and in the absorption of capital for a plethora of railroads projects of those days, Baring suggested the overcoming of the financial and commercial distress by the removal of the restraints of the Act, and the enforcement of regulatory bodies that would allow the public to have correct information about the condition and proceedings of the railroad companies. In this way it was possible, according to him, to check the excess of speculation at home and to make available about one-third of the Bank's treasure to satisfy the need for food with no restraints on circulation, and without putting pressure on the rate of interest. He emphasized the importance of deposits as a means of payment and, even recognizing that their offices 'are different from those performed by paper' (1847: 21), he denied that the provisions of the Bank Charter Act could avoid a depletion of the Bank's reserves since the Act regulated notes while it disregarded deposits, although the 'power of these two descriptions of claims is exactly the same over the treasure of the Bank' (1847: 21).

While strenuously maintaining that the Bank could not be managed by mechanical rules, ignoring all the specific surrounding circumstances, Baring stressed the importance of a clear definition of the aims that the directors should attain by discretion. In his opinion, 'the support of our own industry in all its branches is a sacred duty of an institution established mainly for that purpose by public authority' (1847: 24). Assistance to the wants of the Exchequer he also considered a proper function of the Bank, provided it be occasional and not systematically forced by 'the modern practice of yearly throwing over our source of revenues' (1847: 26). According to Baring, it is this very function that justifies the great privileges that the Bank enjoys.

Baring criticized abstract thinking and stressed the importance of the point of view of the practical man. Nevertheless, he was well aware of the theoretical dimension of the economic debate, and in his works he refers to economic theory and to its policy implications even when his reasoning revolves mainly around positive facts. This circumstance, coupled with his authority as a banker and statesman, made his opinions extremely influential among the theorists of the time. MCCULLOCH referred to Baring's *Inquiry* as a 'very able tract; rather too favourable to the pretensions of neutrals; but the best by far, in a commercial point of view, of those published on the interesting subject of which it treats' (McCulloch 1845: 121). Baring's other book, *The Financial and Commercial Crisis Considered,* was very often referred to by members of the banking school: it was judged by NEWMARCH as 'a just and vivid picture of the practical evils which may either be traced altogether to the direct operation of the Bill of 1844, or which it has greatly contributed to aggravate' (Newmarch 1847: 273).

BIBLIOGRAPHY

An Inquiry into the Causes and Consequences of the Orders in Council, and an Examination of the Conduct of Great Britain toward the Neutral Commerce of America (1808).

Mr. Alexander Baring's speech in the House of Commons, on the 15th day of May, 1823, on Mr. Buxton's motion for a resolution declaratory of slavery in the British colonies being contrary to the English constitution and to Christianity (1823).

Speech of Alexander Baring, Esq., M.P. in the House of Commons, on Thursday, the 3d of March, 1831, on Lord John

Russell's Motion for Reform of Parliament. Extracted from the Mirror of Parliament (1831).
Speech of the Right Honourable Lord Ashburton, (in the House of Lords) on the second reading of the Canada government bill. Friday, February 2, 1838 (1838).
The Financial and Commercial Crisis considered (1847).

Further Reading
Fetter, F., *Development of British Monetary Orthodoxy* (Cambridge, Massachusetts, 1965).
Fullarton, J., *On the Regulation of Currencies* (1845; repr. New York, 1969).
Gash, N., *Reaction and Reconstruction in English Politics 1832–1852* (Oxford, 1965).
Jones, H., *To the Webster-Ashburton Treaty: a Study in Anglo-American Relations, 1783–1843* (Chapel Hill, North Carolina, 1977).
McCulloch, J.R., *The Literature of Political Economy* (1845).
Newmarch, W., 'The Financial Pressure', *The Quarterly Review* (1847), vol. CLXI, pp. 230–73.
Viner, J., *Studies in the Theory of International Trade* (New York, 1937; repr. New York, 1965).

Aldo Barba

BARING, Francis (1740–1810)

Baring was born at Larkbear, near Exeter in Devon, on 18 April 1740, and died at Lee, Kent on 11 September 1810. His father John Baring, himself the son of a Lutheran pastor, had emigrated from Hamburg to Britain and settled at Larkbear, where he had founded a cloth manufacturing business. Despite having been rendered deaf by a childhood illness, Francis Baring exhibited a remarkable aptitude for business, first with the Anglo-German merchant house of Boehm, where he served an apprenticeship, and then in business on his own account. In partnership with his brother John, Baring founded the import-export business John and Francis Baring in 1763 while he was still in his early twenties (the name was changed to Baring Brothers in 1806). This firm prospered and soon became involved in banking activities as well. In 1784 Baring entered parliament as MP for High Wycombe, taking the seat left vacant by the resignation of Admiral Sir John Jervis, and represented that constituency until 1790. From 1794–6 and 1802–6 he represented Chipping Wycombe, and from 1796–1802 held the seat for Calne. Shrewdly gauging the direction of the political wind, Baring became close to William Pitt the Younger, and used his political connections to great effect in furthering his business.

In 1779 Baring had become a director of the East India Company, and from 1792–3 was chairman of the Company, for which service he was made a baronet in May 1793. He continued to be closely involved with the Company and often advised the government on matters concerning Indian trade and finance. During the Napoleonic wars Baring, along with other bankers with continental connections such as Rothschild, played a major role in raising funds to finance British military and naval operations against France and the payment of subsidies to foreign allies. His wealth was such that a contemporary described him as 'the first merchant of Europe', and he used his money to acquire a considerable collection of paintings (purchased from his estate by the Prince Regent after his death) and the manors of Lee in Kent and Micheldever in Hampshire.

Baring was a frequent speaker in and out of Parliament on financial affairs, and in the opinion of contemporaries was a notable authority on finance. He left few writings, the most important of which is *Observations on the Establishment of the Bank of England, and on the Paper Circulation of the Country* (1797). This short work contains a shrewd appreciation of just how important the Bank of England had become to the national economy, both as the lender of last resort (a term which Baring is credited with having invented) and the guarantor of the paper currency. Writing in the immediate aftermath of the Restriction Act of 1797 which suspended payments of gold and silver and, to all practical purposes, made bank notes the circulating currency of the kingdom, Baring observed that this system would only work if confidence in the Bank of England remained strong. He was against increasing the supply of paper money in circulation because, he said, if too much money circulated, confidence would decrease and this would cause the value of paper money to fall.

Baring was quick to point out that paper money is no different from gold in this respect: 'any thing may become a circulating medium; paper is as good a representative sign as gold, and in many instances it is better' (1797: 3). If an excessive quantity of gold were to be in circulation, he says, then confidence in gold would decline in just the same way. The amount of money in circulation must match the demand for money: 'in the case of too great an excess [of money in circulation], depreciation, distress and convulsion must follow; but if too much curtailed, the exertion and industry of the country is chilled, or palsied, and its growing prosperity thereby prevented' (1797: 42). The agency best placed to determine the amount of money that should be in circulation, Baring says, is the Bank of England itself, which has the experience and knowledge to manage money supply effectively.

In 1801 Baring responded to a publication by his fellow MP Walter BOYD in which the latter argued that price inflation, particularly affecting foodstuffs, was directly attributable to the widespread use of paper money. Boyd believed also that there was too much money in circulation, which was in turn leading to a depreciation in value on the foreign exchanges, notably Hamburg. Baring defended the use of paper money in *Observations on the Publication of Walter Boyd, Esq, M.P.* (1801), arguing that there was no connection between the supply of paper money and domestic price inflation, although he was rather more hazy about the impact on foreign exchanges. A promising debate between the two men was cut short when Boyd was detained in France following the renewed outbreak of war in 1802.

BIBLIOGRAPHY
Observations on the Establishment of the Bank of England, and on the Paper Circulation of the Country (1797).
Further Observations on the Establishment of the Bank of England, and on the Paper Circulation of the Country (1797).
Observations on the Publication of Walter Boyd, Esq, M.P. (1801).

Further Reading
Ziegler, P. *The Sixth Great Power: A History of One of the Greatest of All Banking Families, the House of Baring* (New York, 1988).

Ann Kimber

BARNARD, John (1685–1764)

Barnard was born in Reading, Berkshire in 1685 (exact date unknown), and died in Clapham, Surrey on 20 August 1764. His family were Quakers, but Barnard converted to the Anglican church in 1703. At age fifteen he followed his father into the family wine business, starting as an apprentice and learning the skills of book-keeping and accounting before going on to become a partner in the firm some time before 1710.

As well as his career in business, Barnard had a highly distinguished record of public service. He was an alderman of the City of London from 1728 to 1756, representing first the Dowgate ward and later that of Bridge Without. He served as member of parliament for the City of London from 1722–61. Knighted by George II in 1732, he went on to become sheriff of London in 1735 and lord mayor in 1737. In 1745 he rallied his fellow London merchants to support the Bank of England when public confidence in that institution was threatened following the outbreak of the Jacobite rebellion. He retired from public life in the late 1750s, spending most of his time in seclusion at his house in Clapham.

In parliament, Barnard was known as a strong and persuasive speaker, and was regarded as an authority on matters of state finance. Along with fellow MPs such as William Pulteney (later Earl of Bath), Barnard frequently opposed Sir Robert Walpole's financial policies; they also clashed over a bill introduced by Barnard to limit the number of theatres and playhouses in London, which Walpole opposed. In 1737 Barnard proposed a scheme for reducing the interest paid on the national debt from 4 per cent to 3 per cent. This was not at first carried through, as Walpole was opposed and Pulteney failed to give his support; according to rumours, a considerable part of Pulteney's wife's fortune was tied up in government stocks. A number of pamphlets supporting the measure appeared and public pressure begin to grow, until the scheme was finally adopted during the Pelham ministry. Barnard's opposition to Walpole was not personal (unlike that of Pulteney), and he continued to be critical of succeeding governments. In 1746 he turned down the chance to serve as chancellor of the exchequer.

Barnard was strongly aware of his responsibilities as a member of parliament, and insisted on bringing a moral dimension into finance and politics. He insisted that 'every Member of Parliament is a Trustee of the People, and bound in Duty to manage the Publick Affairs for their greatest Advantage' (1737: 1). He opposed indirection taxation, especially on necessities such as salt, coal, beer and ale – the latter two then considered as necessities – on the grounds that the poor paid a disproportionately high amount of these taxes. He was prepared to accept higher taxation in time of war, but argued that taxes should be immediately reduced once peace was returned, and that 'no more money ought in any Year to be raised, or continue at any time to be raised, than is absolutely necessary for the Well-being of the Nation' (1737: 1). The national debt should be reduced as far as possible in order to reduce the tax burden still further. Barnard believed that low taxes were essential to both the security of the state and the well-being of the people.

BIBLIOGRAPHY

Reasons for the Representatives of the People of Great Britain to take advantage of the present Rate of Interest for the more speedy lessening of the National Debt (1737).

Some Thoughts on the Scarcity of Silver Coin; with proposals for remedy thereof (1759).

Further Reading

Anon., *Considerations occasioned by a Proposal for Reducing Interest to Three per Cent, with some general thoughts upon reductions* (1737).

Venn, H., *Memoirs of the Late John Barnard* (1776).

Morgen Witzel

BARRINGTON, Shute (1734–1826)

Barrington was born 26 May 1734 at Becket in Berkshire, and died 25 March 1826 at his residence in Cavendish Square, London. His father, born John Shute (1678–1734), took the surname of Barrington after a relative who left him a substantial legacy and was subsequently created first Viscount Barrington in the Irish peerage; his wife Anne (died 1763) was the daughter and co-heiress of Sir William Daines, MP, mayor of Bristol. Barrington, their sixth and youngest son, was only six months old when his father died in a carriage accident. He was educated at Eton and Merton College, Oxford (BA 1755, ordained 1756, MA 1757, DCL 1762). He married in 1761 Lady Diana Beauclerk, daughter of the Duke of St. Alban's, who died in 1766 bearing a stillborn child. In 1770 he married Jane, only daughter of Sir Berkeley William Guise, baronet, of Rendcombe, Gloucestershire; her dowry included extensive property. The marriage was childless except for an adopted daughter.

Able, well-connected and devout, Barrington was a particular favourite of George III, who made him a royal chaplain in 1760. Barrington's eldest brother William, second Lord Barrington, became Secretary for War in 1760 and after much lobbying secured his brother a Hereford prebend in September 1761, adding a Christ Church canonry in October 1761 and a St. Paul's prebend in 1768. In 1769, aged only thirty-five, Barrington became Bishop of Llandaff. He gained notoriety in 1771 by an energetic defence of subscription to the Articles of Religion, although his own father had been a leading opponent of the subscription principle. He was one of the first bishops to oppose the slave trade, denouncing it in a 1775 sermon as 'a traffic as inhuman in the mode of carrying it on, as it is unjustifiable in it's principle'.

In 1782 George III secured him the plum diocese of Salisbury where he won an immediate reputation for generosity, providing endowment for the Cathedral almshouses and setting up a relief fund for necessitous clergy. Barrington was a convinced believer in harnessing private charity: besides financing extensive repairs to the episcopal palace from his own revenues, he launched boldly into major cathedral restoration, trusting public subscription would come in. The public lived up to his hopes: among many subscribers, George III on an incognito visit to the works personally handed over a £1,000 bank bill.

As a bishop, Barrington was ex-officio a governor of Queen Anne's Bounty and took his duties seriously, playing a full part in the reform of the Bounty's procedures which began about 1780. Through his Bounty work he developed a keen interest in church finance. In a letter to his Salisbury clergy, he not only explained to them in detail how and why the Bounty administered its funds to improve the income of poor parishes, but also advised them on the vexed subject of tithe. He warned that commutation, the practice of exchanging entitlement to tithe payment for permanent ownership of a piece of land, transferred all the headaches of landowning from tithe-payer to clergyman: repairs to buildings and fences, losses from bad or insolvent tenants, soil exhaustion and mismanagement. Farming the land direct required capital to stock it, agricultural skills, and more time than a conscientious clergyman could spare from his professional duties. Barrington also set out principles for deciding a fair stipend for curates, and gave clear instructions for ensuring that parochial charities were properly applied to their intended objects.

In the same letter Barrington turned his mind to financial support for the infant Sunday Schools movement, of which he was a committed supporter. His suggestion of a county-based structure of general funding and a unified approach co-ordinating the new parish educational ventures with the existing charity schools looked far beyond the early nineteenth-century answer of voluntary schools societies to the need for a state education system.

A pragmatist all his life, Barrington was strongly attracted by the practical philanthropy of William Wilberforce. By 1786 he was working closely with Wilberforce's friend and ally Beilby Porteus, Bishop of London, and after Porteus's death in 1809 Barrington was Wilberforce's main episcopal patron. His 1791 translation to the wealthy palatine bishopric of Durham greatly increased his scope for financial and political usefulness. Barrington's liberality, high standing and influence were invaluable to Wilberforce, who described him to Hannah More as 'a very sun, the centre of an entire system'. By the end of his life he belonged to at least forty-seven of Wilberforce's charitable societies, serving as president of five, vice-president of twelve, governor of six and patron of two.

In 1796, Barrington and his kinsman Sir Thomas BERNARD joined with Wilberforce to found the Society for Bettering the Condition of the Poor. The Society worked by means of a committee, subscriptions, correspondence, published reports and the circulation of hortatory tracts to collect and disseminate good practice in relieving poverty. When Barrington had his 1797 episcopal visitation charge printed for circulation, he appended to it a tract by John Stonehouse entitled *Various Means of Doing Good Bodily and Spiritually*, which made it clear that Barrington expected his clergy to care for their needy parishioners not only by comforting the sick and encouraging family Bible reading, but also by such practical measures as helping with house rent, supplying appropriate nourishment to invalids and convalescents, paying part or all of their apothecary's bill, providing work tools such as rakes and spades, or contriving work for the unemployed. Barrington's charge urged his clergy to see the importance of helping their wealthy and benevolent parishioners to translate goodwill into effective practice, and Stonehouse's tract proposed using the superior buying power of the rich to provide necessities such as food, fuel and clothing 'which may be bought much cheaper than *they* can buy them', and to endow infirmaries where the medical needs of many unable to afford the existing provision could be met. Giving money was advised only if the needy person lived at a distance and their needs could be met in no other way.

Following the bad harvest of 1799, Barrington used his position as Prince Bishop and Custos Rotulorum of the County Durham magistrates to send a circular letter calling their attention to the need for speedy and effectual steps to avoid a general famine. He wanted to establish a committee structure and public subscription fund before the hardship became acute. He warned that raising money to buy food locally for those in need would only inflate the price without increasing the overall supply. Instead, he proposed a campaign to reduce wastefulness in prosperous households coupled with emergency aid in the form of subsidized supplies of wholesome meat soups and a longer term strategy of educating the poor to use imported rice and maize in place of their usual wheat and potatoes. The Society for Bettering the Condition of the Poor, two of whose publications he recommended for further reading, had assembled experimental data on the food value of rice as a dietary staple and accounts of how an enlightened Warwick nobleman used rice dishes from his own table to overcome his tenants' initial resistance.

As the bad harvests continued and the crisis deepened, Barrington in 1801 issued a charge to the churchwardens of his diocese concerning their duties under the poor law. Having set out the economic argument that raising agricultural wages to cope with the high price of corn would simply destroy jobs, he urged that every possible step be taken to assist the labouring poor to survive by their own efforts, offering detailed practical suggestions on how families might be helped through crisis to avoid the shattering loss of self-esteem caused by becoming dependent on the parish, and suggesting that this be financed by keeping parish alms separate from the general parochial relief funds. In an interesting precursor to the allotments movement, one of his suggestions was to provide struggling families with 'potatoe grounds, cow pastures, and other objects of occupation and attention for their vacant hours' (1811: 271–2).

Barrington's hands-on charitable work, ably assisted by his wife Jane, was extensive and imaginative. On one occasion Jane personally presented every cottager in a Durham village with a hive of bees. During the years of the French Revolution, Barrington's staunch Protestant principles led him to blame the outbreak of revolution on the debilitating effects of 'Popery', and he was accused of preaching a crusade against Catholics. At the same time he not only gave generous help to exiled French Catholic bishops and clergy, but also had the tact to do this through his confidential lawyer, the prominent Catholic Charles Butler.

His shrewd uprating of the episcopal mining leases financed the building of schools in the mining communities: the Barrington School, established at Bishop Auckland in 1810, became the National Society's first 'model school' training future teachers. In his last years of life a major court action for restitution of lapsed lead-mining royalties brought in £70,000 with which he established the Barrington Fund for needy clergy and their widows and orphans, and the Barrington Schools Fund for educational work.

Despite the paternalism which characterizes much of Barrington's social thought, he and Porteus were the first two bishops to defend the interdenominational British and Foreign Bible Society, founded in March 1804 to ensure an open supply of Bibles for anyone wanting to buy one. The cherished principle of the rival Society for Promoting Christian Knowledge was that the Bible must be supplied with the Prayer Book to ensure correct interpretation, and the Bible Society came under heavy pamphlet fire from outraged senior churchmen. For Barrington and Porteus, the key consideration was satisfying the public demand for Bibles. Their support 'was the most important thing that happened to the Bible Society for some years, perhaps decisive for its success' (Brown 1961: 246).

Barrington did not regard himself as an economist: apart from a biography of his brother William and an edition of his father's theological writings, his main publications were polemics against Roman Catholic 'corruptions'. His surviving writings on economic themes are in the collected edition of his sermons and episcopal charges published in 1811. His chief influence was through his practical impact on the development of philanthropy and church-sponsored education. He defined 'genuine Christianity' as 'the union of pure devotion with universal benevolence', and did his conscientious best to live by what he preached. He sustained an extraordinary level of public charity and unobtrusive private giving by a domestic regime of strict economy. As his obituary in the *Durham County Advertiser* put it: 'No one…ever better understood the true value of money, or employed it more judiciously as the instrument of virtue.'

BIBLIOGRAPHY
Sermons, charges, and tracts, now first collected into a volume (1811).

Further Reading
Best, G.F.A, *Temporal Pillars: Queen Anne's Bounty, the Ecclesiastical Commissioners, and the Church of England* (Cambridge, 1964).
Brown, F.K., *Fathers of the Victorians: The Age of Wilberforce* (Cambridge, 1961).
Durham County Advertiser, 1, 8, 22, 29 April 1826.
Hughes, E., *North Country Life in the Eighteenth Century* (Oxford, 1952).
Maynard, W.B., 'The Ecclesiastical Administration of the Archdeaconry of Durham, 1774–1856', PhD dissertation, University of Durham (1973).

E.A. Varley

BARROW, Isaac (1630–77)

Barrow was born in London in October 1630, and died of fever in London on 4 May 1677. He was the son of Thomas Barrow, a linen draper, and his wife Ann, daughter of William Buggin of North Cray, Kent. Barrow was educated at Charterhouse, where his education suffered and he acquired a reputation as a bully; he was then sent to Felstead in Essex, where the headmaster had a reputation for strict discipline. Here Barrow made rapid progress, learning Greek, Latin, Hebrew and logic in preparation for university. After he had been at Felstead for two years, Barrow's father incurred debts in the Irish rebellion and was unable to pay his son's fees. However the headmaster, realizing Isaac's potential, took him in and later appointed him as a tutor to Thomas Fairfax.

In 1643 Barrow was admitted as a foundation scholar at Peterhouse College, Cambridge, where his uncle was a fellow. The latter lost his post due to his Royalist views, and Barrow then went to Oxford where his brother had become the King's Linen Draper. In 1644 he went to London; in 1646, destitute, he returned to Cambridge and enrolled at Trinity College, Cambridge. Barrow enrolled in 1646 and performed menial duties in return for instruction, board and lodging. Duport, the Regius Professor of Greek at Cambridge, tutored Barrow without taking any fees, partly because of Barrow's talent and partly because both were royalists. Under Duport, Barrow studied languages, literature, chronology, geography and theology and also arithmetic, geometry and optics; but, like all students at the time, he was encouraged not to specialize in a subject such as mathematics before graduating.

Barrow graduated in 1649 and successfully competed for a college fellowship in the same year. He gave a speech in which he praised the teaching of the classics but criticized the lack of mathematics and science. He started to study mathematics in depth immediately after his graduation. His enthusiasm and willingness to teach enabled him to attract enough people to the subject to help begin to lay the foundations for the study of mathematics at Cambridge. In 1648 he was considered to be the ringleader of a group of royalists at Cambridge and was threatened with expulsion. Another threat came in 1650 as a result of a speech Barrow made on the anniversary of the Gunpowder Plot. He survived, however, and received his MA in 1652. In 1654 he defended the university in a speech in which he spoke of the importance of learning Greek, Latin and literature for the purpose of acquiring a firm basis for learning. He also praised the advances the university had made in subjects such as Arabic, modern languages such as French, Spanish and Italian, mathematics and science.

Barrow now went on to study divinity, but his study of church history led him to astronomy, which in turn led him to study geometry. He taught himself geometry, compiling a simplified edition of Euclid's *Elements* which was printed in 1655 and remained the standard textbook for half a century. He received a college lectureship, and was widely expected to replace Duport as Professor of Greek when the latter was finally forced out of the university, but was told he did not have enough experience; in fact, his political views were almost certainly the cause of his rejection.

In 1655 Barrow went to France to study mathematics at Paris, but found this experience disappointing; apart from Roberval, there were few mathematicians from whom he could learn. In February 1656 he went to Florence, where he remained for eight months; a planned visit to Rome had to be cancelled because of an outbreak of the plague. While in Florence Barrow spent much of his time in the Medici Library, where there was a fine collection of coins. Barrow later used the expertise he had acquired here to act as a collector of coins and medals for a London merchant, and this in turn helped Barrow with much needed finance. While in Florence also, Barrow met Carolo Renaldini, who was writing a paper on algebra, and Vincenzo Viviani, Galileo's last pupil. Barrow then travelled on to Turkey, avoiding an attack by pirates, and spent seven months in Smyrna and a year and a half in Constantinople. His homeward journey in 1659 was also fraught; his ship was destroyed by fire while docked at Venice, and all his possessions were lost. He returned to Cambridge in September 1659.

The Restoration brought about many changes at Cambridge, not least of which was the resignation of the Professor of Greek who had replaced Duport. The latter was then offered the post but declined. This left the way open for Barrow, who was elected without opposition. However, the salary was only £40 a year, and in 1662 Barrow accepted the post of Professor of Geometry at Gresham College. He was a founder member of the Royal Society in 1663, but his contribution was minimal, and at one point he was nearly expelled for failing to pay his dues.

In the summer of 1663 the position as Lucasian Professor of Mathematics was created at Cambridge thanks to an endowment left by Henry Lucas. Barrow was an obvious choice for this position and he relinquished the Greek chair for that in mathematics. In the spring of 1664 he delivered the first six of his mathematics lectures, which consisted of basic material. In the autumn he delivered nine more lectures and, in the spring of 1665 the first five of his geometrical lectures. Further lectures followed on other topics, including a series of lectures on optics in the 1668–9 session. Isaac NEWTON attended these lectures, and had many private discussions with Barrow about the work. In the later lectures he covered such topics as divisibility, congruence, equality, time and space. The final lectures cover measurement, proportion and ratio.

In 1669 Barrow resigned from the Lucasian Chair in favour of Newton and did no further mathematical work. He was appointed as royal chaplain to Charles II at Salisbury in 1670, then, in February 1673, as master of Trinity College. At Trinity, Barrow was occupied with two major issues: limiting the number of Royal interventions, and the building of the Wren library. On the first of these issues he had some success while on the second he spent much time and effort on generating interest in the project and the necessary funds. He did not live to see the result of this work. In April 1677 Barrow travelled to London where he contracted malignant fever. He tried to cure it by fasting and taking opium, a formula which had previously worked for him while ill in Constantinople. He died, and was buried a few days later at Westminster Abbey.

John COLLINS later published most of Barrow's lectures: *Lectiones Opticae* was published in 1669, *Lectiones Geometricae* in 1670 and *Lectiones Mathematicae* in 1683 (a complete collection of all Barrow's lectures in English was published in 1734). These three books show the extent of his work. *Lectiones Mathematicae* were lectures designed to revive interest in mathematics at Cambridge while trying to point it in a new direction by introducing modern techniques. Barrow tried to classify the different branches of mathematics arguing that algebra is not part of true mathematics and should be considered to be logic, while geometry is a basic mathematical science. The *Lectiones Geometricae* probably represent work which Barrow studied while at Gresham. They contain the important work on tangents which was to form the starting point of Newton's work on the calculus. The *Lectiones Opticae* were more theoretical than practical, which was unusual for his time. The content is mainly geometrical optics.

Though Barrow did not lecture on economics, he exercised considerable influence at a time when economics thinking was at a formative stage. This influences was exerted in part through Newton and others who went on to develop mathematical principles which ultimately were adopted by economists for theory and measurement. Barrow himself, who believed that the principles that guided mathematics could guide other spheres of life as well, would have approved of this. More directly, however, his reputation for scholarship influenced the thinking of contemporaries in other spheres. This can be seen clearly, for example, in his lecture on measurement, when he discusses the importance of measurement in determining the value and utility of all kinds of things. Here Barrow distinguished between natural and arbitrary measure. An arbitrary measure is a unit of measure decreed by an authority, while a natural measure is:

> the measure of every natural thing is that which is the first and most perfect in the genus; as the divine nature is the measure of goodness and wisdom, because God alone is originally of himself good and wise...Every thing, according to Plato, has such a measure, the eternal and indefectable idea of itself, viz. some most exact pattern, from its similitude or correspondence with which it is accounted true, comely and perfect...
> (1734: 252)

This distinction between natural and arbitrary measure became very important in the instrinsic v. extrinsic value argument related to the currency, and later in the whole question of sources of value and utility.

BIBLIOGRAPHY

The Usefulness of Mathematical Learning Explained and Demonstrated: Being Mathematical Lectures read in the Public Schools at the University of Cambridge (1734).

Further Reading

Feingold, M. (ed.), *Before Newton: The Life and Times of Isaac Barrow* (Cambridge, 1990).

Osmond, P.H., *Isaac Barrow, His Life and Times* (1944).

John J. O'Connor
Edmund F. Robertson

BARTLEY, George Christopher Trout (1842–1910)

Bartley was born in Hackney, East London on 22 November 1842, and died in London on 13 September 1910. In 1864 he married Mary Charlotte Cole, by whom he had four sons and one daughter. Bartley was educated in Blackheath, Clapton and University College school before becoming a science examiner for the Committee of the Council on Education. Here he was promoted firstly to official examiner, and then assistant director of the science division of the Committee, where he served until his resignation in 1880. In that year Bartley decided to pursue a political career, and sat as the Conservative MP for North Islington between 1885 and 1906. He was also a JP for London and Middlesex. He was awarded a knighthood in 1902.

Bartley's interest in the economic side of social issues came from his concerns about the education of deprived children. In *The Educational Condition and Requirements of One Square Mile at the East End of London* (1870) and *The Schools for the People* (1871), Bartley argued that the voluntary organization of education had failed children from poorer backgrounds. Bartley recognized that not only did education need funding from the government, but that it needed an overarching mechanism to maintain standards. To his mind, the Education Act of 1870 had the potential to achieve this.

Around the same time, Bartley began to apply his ideas to other social problems, notably the new poor law and his notion of thrift. His thoughts and proposals were published in by the National Provident Society as the *Provident Knowledge Papers*. Bartley was concerned that the new poor law was a deterrent to thrift, in that relief was only available to the destitute. In addition, he was particularly critical of well-meaning but ultimately destructive charity work in poorer areas which, he noted in his educational studies, exacerbated the problems caused by the poor law. Those on low or seasonal wages were discouraged from saving, as this would count against them if they had to approach the parish relieving officer for relief in times of crisis. He wrote in *The Seven Ages of a Village Pauper* (1874) that the 'Parish gives her comforts, but on one condition, and that condition is destitution and thriftlessness' (1874: 41).

One of Bartley's solutions was to create a financial establishment that would benefit workers: the Penny Bank. In 1872, he established the first Instalment Club on the Edgware Road, which allowed workmen to buy clothes and tools by making regular payments. He established the Middlesex Penny Bank in the same year; and in 1875 he set up the National Penny Bank with Sir Henry Cole, his father-in-law. The Penny Bank operated on the principle that a small amount could be invested by anyone without it causing them hardship, and that if the regular investments were continued over a period of time, the saver could have a significant sum for emergencies or a change in circumstances. By 1911, over 2,900,000 accounts had been opened and the Penny Bank had 22,000,000 depositors.

Bartley also argued that the thrifty should be rewarded for their efforts with certificates and other gifts, but more importantly that they should receive relief over the unthrifty, as they had taken steps to add to that relief. Bartley's views on relief and thrift are consistent with the often derided Charity Organisation Society, but his ideas on more accessible banking and his recognition that relief can demoralise the claimant are just as relevant to today as they were to the late nineteenth century.

BIBLIOGRAPHY

The Educational Condition and Requirements of One Square Mile at the East End of London (1870).
The Schools for the People (1871).
Provident Knowledge Papers, nos 1–18 (1872–8).
The Poor Law in its Effects on Thrift (1873).
Seven Ages of a Village Pauper (1874).
The Parish Net: How It Is Dragged and What It Catches (1875).
A Handy Book for Guardians of the Poor (1876).
The Penny Bank News (1877).
Domestic Economy: Thrift in Everyday Life (1878).
London and the Unemployed Problem (1905).

Katharine Bradley

BARTON, John (1789–1852)

John Barton was born on 11 June 1789 into a Quaker family in Southwark, London. He died at Chichester, Sussex, on 10 March 1852. He was brought up in Tottenham and London in the household of his maternal grandfather, Thomas Horne, because his father had died shortly before his birth. Details of his education are not known, but it was certainly a good one: he knew German, French and Latin, and was well read in both modern and ancient literature. From his grandfather, Barton seems to have inherited a handsome fortune, enabling him to settle down with his family on a landed estate at Stoughton, Sussex, after his marriage. In 1833 the household was moved to Eastleigh, Hampshire. He became paralyzed in 1851.

A well-to-do Sussex landowner, Barton had means and leisure for extensive travels and for pursuing his wide-ranging intellectual interests in botanical, mechanical, philosophical, socio-economic and other subjects. He was one of the original promoters of the Chichester Savings Bank, the Lancasterian School and the Mechanics Institution, where he also lectured for many years. In 1847 he was elected a fellow of the London Statistical Society, to which he read a paper in 1849 on 'The Influence of the Subdivision of the Soil on the Moral and

Physical Well-being of the People of England and Wales'.

Barton is best known for his *Observations on the Circumstances which Influence the Condition of the Labouring Classes of Society* (1817), which contains an early critical discussion of the impact of machinery on employment and which was noticed favourably by RICARDO, MALTHUS, MCCULLOCH, Sismondi and MARX. The writing of the *Observations* was apparently prompted by Barton's dissatisfaction with Ricardo's reply to some objections he had put forward (in a letter which has not been preserved) to some propositions in the latter's *Principles*. In his *Observations*, Barton challenged the SMITH-Ricardo claim that the demand for labour will increase in proportion with the increase of the capital and wealth of a nation, arguing that, 'the demand for labour depends...on the increase of circulating, and not of fixed capital... As arts are cultivated, and civilisation is extended, fixed capital bears a larger and larger proportion to circulating capital' (1817: 16). By means of numerical examples, Barton sought to demonstrate that a continuous process of capital accumulation and output growth can be attended with a decrease in total employment as a consequence of the conversion of circulating capital into fixed capital. In the famous chapter 'On Machinery', newly inserted in the third edition of the *Principles* (1821), Ricardo acknowledged the force of part of Barton's argument.

In his second book, the *Inquiry into the Causes of the Progressive Depreciation of Agricultural Labour in Modern Times* (1820), Barton attacked Malthusian population theory and disputed the prevailing opinion that excess population and low wages were caused by the old poor laws. Assembling population figures from the sixteenth to the eighteenth centuries, Barton sought to show that the main determinant of marriage age was custom and work prospects rather than the level of wages, and that population growth was not causally linked to capital accumulation. He presented his argument in terms of a skilful combination of abstract reasoning and statistical data, in particular demographic time series.

In the 1830s and 1840s Barton wrote several tracts on the Corn Laws, population growth and colonization, in which he extended his earlier analysis into a general critique of industrialism and of the free-trade doctrine (see 1830, 1833, 1844). He defended the Corn Laws on the ground that the workers displaced in agriculture could not easily be transferred to manufacturing and that the industrialization process must lead to a concentration of income and wealth. As a means of relieving the problem of excess population he recommended supportive measures for emigration and colonization. In a newspaper article of 1846 (re-published in Barton 1847) he correctly predicted the monetary crisis of 1847.

BIBLIOGRAPHY
Observations on the Circumstances which Influence the Condition of the Labouring Classes of Society (1817).
An Inquiry into the Causes of the Progressive Depreciation of Agricultural Labour in Modern Times (1820).
A Statement of the Consequences Likely to Ensue from our Growing Excess of Population, if not remedied by Colonization (1830).
An Inquiry into the Expediency of the Existing Restrictions on the Importation of Foreign Corn, with Observations on the Present Social and Political Prospects of Great Britain (1833).
The Influence of the Price of Corn on the Rate of Mortality (1844).
The Monetary Crisis of 1847, Prediction and Counter-Prediction (1847).

Further Reading
Sotiroff, G., 'John Barton (1789–1852)', *Economic Journal* (1952), vol. 62, pp. 87–102.
—— (ed.), *Economic Writings of John Barton* (1962).

Christian Gehrke

BASTABLE, Charles Francis (1855–1945)

Bastable was born in County Cork in 1855, and died in Dublin in 1945. He was educated at Trinity College, Dublin where he studied history and political science (BA 1878) and then went on to study law. He was called to the bar in 1881. In 1882 he was offered and accepted the post of Whately Professor of Political Economy at Trinity College, Dublin. He held this post until his retirement in 1932. In Britain, Bastable was also a prominent figure; he was a member of the first Council of the Royal Economic Society, and in 1894 was elected president of Section F of the British Association for the Advancement of Science. He was elected a fellow of the British Academy in 1921.

As a writer Bastable was most active during the 1880s and 1890s, when he produced his three major works: *The Theory of International Trade* (1887), *The Commerce of Nations* (1891) and *Public Finance* (1892). *The Theory of International Trade* is, as Bastable himself plainly says in his preface, a restating and updating of classical economic theory on trade. Adam SMITH, David RICARDO and J.S. MILL are cited throughout. In the opening pages of the work Bastable shows a gentle impatience with succeeding authorities whose work, he says, has tended to cloud the picture and obfuscate the details. His aim is to peel back some of these layers of later theory and look at the fundamentals – as presented in classical theory – of such issues as the role of money in foreign trade, foreign exchange, the balance of trade, and taxation and tariffs. Bastable emerges as a strong supporter of free trade very much in the tradition of Adam Smith.

The Commerce of Nations, possibly written for a more popular audience, makes many of the same points but is more focused on free trade and contains a strong attack on protectionism. Free trade is justified, says Bastable, by historical study. The past shows that protectionist measures have always failed; it can be deduced, then, that all present and future protectionism is likewise doomed to failure. The reason for this, he says, is that protectionism is founded on 'ideas and sentiments unsuited for industrial civilization' (1891: vii), but this is not always immediately apparent, and politicians have often been seduced by the apparent benefits that protection seems to offer. Studying its history shows 'how so many able and enlightened men have adopted a system that is notwithstanding both to social and economic progress' (1891: vii).

Public Finance, written as a textbook but again with a popular message, is a discussion of the basic principles of public revenue and administration. It again contains a strong *laissez-faire* element. The key theme is a warning that public expenditure is on the rise, and this in turn means that government revenues will need to rise as well; there is a strong threat of higher taxation. Both taxation and expenditure need to be held in check. The best method of achieving this is for the public to become better informed about state finances, and thus better able to hold political leaders to account.

An able and entertaining lecturer, Bastable was very much in the tradition of classical economic thinking, with roots in the late seventeenth and early eighteenth century liberal tradition. His approach was historical and reflective, and he never entered into the realms of grand theory. Nor, although he occasionally cited Alfred MARSHALL, does he appear to have much time for contemporary neoclassical economics. His modern influences, if any, were from the German historical school and contemporary sociology, as evidenced by his occasional insistences on understanding the human element when discussing ideas in economics.

BIBLIOGRAPHY
The Theory of International Trade (1887).
The Commerce of Nations (1891).
Public Finance (1892).

Further Reading
Bristow, J.A., 'Bastable, Charles Francis', in J. Eatwell *et al.* (eds), *The New Palgrave: A Dictionary of Economics* (1987, p. 203).

David Ashbury

BAUER, Peter Thomas (1915–2002)

Bauer was born Peter Thomas (Tamas) Bauer in Budapest on 6 November 1915 of Jewish parents (his father was a bookmaker), and died in London on 2 May 2002. He was educated at the Scholae Piae in Budapest, and at Gonville and Caius College, Cambridge. Apart from a few years as an employee of Guthrie and Company, a leading firm of Far Eastern merchants and rubber growers, and as a monitor of foreign broadcasters in the BBC, Bauer spent his working life in academia. He was a fellow of Caius College, Cambridge (1946–60 and 1968–2002), reader in agricultural economics at the University of London (1947–8), university lecturer in economics at Cambridge (1948–56), Smuts Reader in Commonwealth Studies (1956–60) and emeritus professor of economics, 1960–84; he was also professor of economics at the London School of Economics from 1960–84. He was a fellow of the British Academy, and was elevated to the peerage as Baron Bauer of Market Ward in the City of Cambridge in 1983. Shortly before his death he was the first recipient of the Milton Friedman Prize for Advancing Liberty, established by the Cato Institute in Washington DC.

Bauer was a pioneer of modern development economics. He was the major theorist of the process of change that transforms a subsistence or near-subsistence economy into an exchange economy. His publications, from the earliest to the most recent, have emphasized and analysed the crucial role of domestic trade as well as foreign trade in the early stages of economic development. He was also among the first economists to question the need for and role of foreign aid in less-developed countries, and concluded that, contrary to the conventional wisdom when his studies began, foreign aid was likely to retard the development of the recipient countries rather than to promote it. At best its contribution to economic growth could be significant. On the other hand, it had adverse effects in many recipient countries, including the politicization of life.

Bauer took the use of economic reasoning in development studies well beyond what was achieved by other pioneers, combining a robust command of economic analysis with extensive empirical research, exceptional in scope and depth. For example, his *West African Trade* (1964) analysed in great detail the commerce of several West African companies, and in particular identified the structural elements of their economies that differed from those of Western countries and thus limited compatibility and transferability of Western economic concepts.

Bauer successfully challenged a number of central propositions of what, until quite recently, have been orthodox mainstream development economics. These propositions include the following: that the poverty of poor countries imposes constraints that perpetuate that poverty (the vicious circle); that the interests of the Third World countries are damaged by commercial contacts with the West; that the terms of trade persistently worsen for Third World countries; that economic advance in the Third World cannot proceed without extensive government planning and control; that population growth is a major obstacle to progress and prosperity in the Third World; that peasant producers do not take long views and contribute little to capital formation; and that internal trade is inefficient and unproductive.

Bauer insisted on the crucial importance of cultural and political factors in economic development. He emphasized the significance for economic advance of the attributes, attitudes and mores of people and groups. He had observed their importance in his own firsthand in-depth studies of the multi-ethnic societies of Malaya (1948) and West Africa (1964). He showed that such factors are much more important than those singled out by mainstream development economics, such as the volume of (monetary) investment, the supply of education or the presence of natural resources.

Bauer also insisted that a proper understanding of a given situation required a thorough study of that situation's antecedents. He deplored the ignorance of the past and the neglect of the time dimension in cultural and social (including economic) phenomena that were so notable a feature of contemporary discourse. He has been criticized for not presenting a theory of development, in the sense of an over-arching theory or explanation of material progress. But it was Bauer's view that a theory of economic development is tantamount to a theory of history; and for Bauer a theory of history was a will-o'-the-wisp, albeit a seductive one. He expounded his thinking in a review article on John HICKS's *A Theory of Economic History*. Hicks found that rather critical review of sufficient interest to have it included as an appendix in the Spanish edition of his book.

In the course of his career, Bauer wrote (or co-authored) a series of articles that reviewed major publications in development economics. These included review articles on three international reports (including those associated with the names of Lester Pearson and Willi Brandt) and on major works by Arthur LEWIS, Benjamin Higgins, W.W. Rostow, Gunnar Myrdal and Ragnar Nurkse. Bauer generally found little reason to be impressed by new analytical approaches put forward in these publications: whether these novelties related, for instance, to the supposedly unlimited supply of unskilled labour in poor countries or to the stages of growth through which a developing country had to proceed. His criticisms stemmed largely from his confrontation of what he read with what he had observed and studied in various Third World countries.

Bauer lived long enough to see the growing influence of his work and his ideas. His views on development are no longer dismissed or derided, as they were originally, as eccentric, misguided, economically illiterate or simply ideological. While resisted at the time, his ideas have become a part of the new 'establishment of ideas' (Sen 2000). Bauer was apt to say that he was doing little more than stating the obvious, by contrasting the then reigning orthodoxy with the facts he observed. He was being far too modest.

BIBLIOGRAPHY
The Rubber Industry (1948).
(with B.S. Yamey) *The Economics of Underdeveloped Countries* (1957).
West African Trade (Cambridge, 1964).
(with B.S. Yamey) *Markets, Market Control and Marketing Reform* (1968).
Dissent on Development (1972).
Equality, the Third World and Economic Delusion (1981).
Reality and Rhetoric: Studies in the Economics of Development (1984).
The Development Frontier: Essays in Applied Economics (Cambridge, Massachusetts, 1994).
From Subsistence to Exchange and Other Essays (Princeton, 2000).

Further Reading
'Development Economics After 40 years: Essays in Honour of Peter Bauer', *The Cato Journal* (1987), vol. 7.
A Tribute to Peter Bauer (2002).
Sen, A., 'Introduction to Peter Bauer', in P.T. Bauer, *From Subsistence to Exchange and Other Essays* (Princeton, 2000).

Basil S. Yamey

BAYES, Thomas (1702–61)

Thomas Bayes was born in London in 1702, the eldest son of the Rev. Joshua Bayes, a non-conformist minister, and Ann Carpenter. Following in his father's footsteps, Bayes was appointed non-conformist minister in 1728. He assisted his father at the Leather Lane chapel until 1729, and in 1731 he became the Presbyterian Minister at Mount Sion in Tunbridge Wells, where he remained until his death. There is evidence that he studied at Edinburgh University. In 1742, he was elected as a fellow of the Royal Society. He retired from the ministry in 1752 and died in April 1761.

Bayes wrote two theological tracts. In the first, published in 1731, Bayes argued that the principal desire of God is for the happiness of his creatures. In 1736, in his second tract, he defended the new mathematical methods of Newton against attacks from theologians of his time. More significantly, in 1764 two of Bayes's mathematical papers were found by his renowned friend Richard PRICE and were published posthumously in the *Philosophical Transactions* of the Royal Society. In the first of these, Bayes was among the first to recognize the asymptotic behaviour of a series expansion deriving the expansion of the series for log x!. Bayes's fame, however, rests entirely on a single mathematical paper communicated to the Royal Society in December of 1763, two and one-half years after his death. Barnard (1958: 295) states that 'his [Bayes's] mathematical work, although small in quantity, is of the very highest quality'.

The title of the paper for which Bayes has become famous is 'An Essay Towards Solving a Problem in the Doctrine of Chances'. Price contributed an introduction and an appendix to the paper. The novel problem addressed by Bayes (1764 : 376) was clearly stated as: 'Given the number of times in which an unknown event has happened and failed: Required the chance that the probability of its happening in a single trial lies somewhere between any two degrees of probability that can be named'.

Bayes's solution depended on two original ideas. The first, labelled as Bayes's Theorem by P.S. Laplace in 1774, refers to reversing the order of the events A and B in a conditional probability, $P(A/B)$, written in its simplest form as

$$P(B/A) = P(A/B) \, P(B)/P(A)$$

Bayes's Theorem gave a solution to the inverse probability question working backwards from effect to cause by estimating the conditional probability of the cause B given that certain effects A have occurred. Bayes's Theorem appears in all modern texts of probability and statistics. There is no controversy in the use of this theorem to obtain the inverted conditional probabilities.

The second and more controversial idea arises from recognizing that this law of inverse probability can be viewed as a basis for the subjective personal degree of belief view of probability. By generalizing Bayes's Theorem to any hypothesis H and any evidence S, one can rewrite the theorem as

$$P(H/D) = P(H) \times P(D/H) \,/\, P(D),$$

or in words as posterior distribution prior distribution ∞ likelihood function where $P(H/D)$ represents the probability statement or posterior belief about H after obtaining data D, $P(H)$ represents the probability statement or prior belief about the hypothesis H before obtaining data, and $P(D/H)$ is the likelihood function. This view gives a method for showing how beliefs are updated or modified in the light of experience. This interpretation forms the basis of an alternative approach to statistical inference known as Bayesian statistical inference. Zellner (1971) was one of the major proponents of this new approach for the study of econometrics.

The main controversy surrounding Bayesian inference is the use and formulation of the prior belief $P(H)$. Bayes also struggled with this issue in his essay, which may account for his withholding the paper. Bayes adopted the uniform distribution when nothing is known about the prior probabilities for the probability of success in the binomial distribution. This approach to the prior beliefs is now known as Bayes's Postulate.

The significance of Bayes's paper was not fully appreciated until the 1960s, some two hundred years after his death, when Bayes's Theorem took on a new importance and provided the basis for the flourishing but controversial theory of statistical inference known as Bayesian statistical inference. Gillies (1987: 328) addresses the interesting question, 'Was Bayes a Bayesian?' and concludes that 'yes, he was a Bayesian, but a cautious and doubtful Bayesian'.

BIBLIOGRAPHY

Divine Benevolence, or an Attempt to Prove that the Principal End of the Divine Providence and Government is the Happiness of his Creatures (1731).

An Introduction to the Doctrine of Fluxions, and Defence of the Mathematicians against the Objections of the Author of the Analyst, so far as they are Designed to affect their General Method of Reasoning (1736).

'A Letter from the Late Reverend Mr. Thomas Bayes, F.R.S. to John Canton, M.A. and F.R.S.', *Philosophical Transactions of the Royal Society of London* (1764), vol. 53, pp. 269–71.

'An Essay towards solving a Problem in the Doctrine of Chances, By the late Rev. Mr. Bayes, F.R.S. communicated by Mr. Price, in a letter to John Canton, A.M. F.R.S.', *Philosophical Transactions of the Royal Society of London* (1764), vol. 53, pp. 370–418 and vol. 54, pp. 296–325; reprinted in *Biometrika* (1958), vol. 45, pp. 293–315, with a biographical note by G.A. Barnard.

Further Reading

Bernardo, J.M. and Smith, A.F.M., *Bayesian Theory* (New York, 1994).

Dale, A.I., *A History of Inverse Probability from Thomas Bayes to Karl Pearson* (New York, 1991).

Gillies, D.A., 'Was Bayes a Bayesian?', *Historia Mathematica* (1987), vol. 14, pp. 325–46.

Laplace, P.S., 'Mémoire sur la probabilité des causes par les évènemens', *Mémoires de l'Académie royale des sciences presentés par divers savans* (1774), vol. 6, pp. 621–56; trans. in Stigler (1986).

Pearson, K., *The History of Statistics in the 17th and 18th Centuries: Lectures by K. Pearson 1921–1933*, ed. E.S. Pearson (1978).

Stigler, S.M., *The History of Statistics : The Measurement of Uncertainty before 1900* (Cambridge, Massachusetts, 1986).

Zellner, A., *An Introduction to Bayesian Inference in Econometrics* (New York, 1971).

William Veloce

BAZLEY, Thomas (1797–1885)

Bazley was born on 27 May 1797 at Gilnow near Bolton in Lancashire. He died at Lytham, Lancashire, on 18 March 1885 and was buried at St John's Church, Manchester. He was the son of Thomas Bazley, a textile manufacturer who later became a journalist, and his wife, Anne Hilton of Horwich. Bazley was educated at Bolton grammar school. In 1818, at the age of twenty-one, he set up a business in Bolton as a yarn agent for the cotton industry. In 1826 he moved to Manchester, going into partnership with Robert Gardner, a cotton spinner and cotton merchant. On 2 June 1828 he married Mary Maria Sarah Nash of Clayton, near Manchester; they had one son, Thomas Sebastian. From 1858 to 1880, Bazley sat as one of Manchester's MPs; he was re-elected on four separate occasions. He was given a baronetcy by Gladstone's government in 1869.

In the 1820s, Bazley and Gardner established a model industrial village at Barrow Bridge. By 1835, the complex included a cotton spinning and doubling mill, and the following year a cooperative shop was opened, managed by a committee of workmen from the mills. Bazley was one of the first employers to introduce the payment of wages on Fridays instead of Saturdays. He then implemented a Saturday half-day closing of the works so that his female workers could go shopping. The village became a self-contained unit, having its own economic, social and educational facilities. Eventually, Bazley's factories became the biggest manufacturing concerns in Britain.

Disraeli visited the village in 1840 and used it as 'Millbank' in his novel *Coningsby* (1844). According to Disraeli, it was 'a village of not inconsiderable size, and remarkable from the neatness and even picturesque character of its architecture, and the gay gardens that surrounded it...In the background rose a church...and near it was a clerical residence and a school-house of similar design. The village, too, could boast of...an Institute where there were a library and a lecture-room; and a reading-hall'. Prince Albert visited Barrow Bridge on 11 October 1851. The mills closed in 1877 and were demolished, although many of the cottages still remain.

Bazley was one of the earliest supporters of the Lancashire Public Schools Association, set up in 1837. The Association was instrumental in changing the funding of popular education, suggesting that levying a local tax could finance free non-sectarian schools. Also in 1837, Bazley made his first public speech, at the launch of the free trade campaign in Liverpool. He went on to become one of the founder members of the Anti-Corn-Law Association (1838) and a member of the Anti-Corn-Law Leagues' council. In 1845 the Manchester Chamber of Commerce was formed, and Bazley became its first chairman.

He held the position from 1846 until 1859, although he remained as one of the directors until 1880. In 1851, Bazley was a royal commissioner of the Great Exhibition and a member of the royal commission that investigated amalgamating British commercial laws. He became a commissioner of the Paris Exhibition (1855), and in recognition of his work received the Legion of Honour from Napoleon III. In 1862 Bazley retired from his business ventures in order to devote his time to his parliamentary and public work.

Bazley's writings reflected his public interests. He supported the cotton industry and believed that manufacturing represented progress, but only so long as workers as well as owners were able to prosper. In *Trade and Commerce the Auxiliaries of Civilisation and Comfort* (1858) he described the huge advances in material prosperity of the past century, but in other works he called for more education and chances for the working classes to better themselves, and for factory owners to give their employees a decent standard of living.

BIBLIOGRAPHY
Cotton as an Element of Industry (1852).
Lecture upon the Labour of Life (1856).
National Education: What Should It Be? (1858).
Trade and Commerce the Auxiliaries of Civilisation and Comfort (1858).
The Barton Aqueduct (1859).

Marjorie Bloy

BEALES, Hugh Lancelot (1889–1988)

Lance Beales was born on 18 February 1889, the third son of the Reverend W. Beales, and died on 19 April 1988. He was educated at Kingswood School, Bath, and at the University of Manchester. After his initial post as a lecturer in economic history at the University of Sheffield (1919–26) he moved to London, where he taught economic history at the London School of Economics, and was promoted to a readership in 1931. Beales edited *Agenda*, the LSE's war-time journal of reconstruction. He remained at the LSE until his retirement in 1956. In the 1950s he held several visiting professorships at American universities, including Columbia (1954–5), Harvard (1956) and Washington (1959). He was made an honorary doctor of letters by Exeter University in 1969 and by Sheffield in 1971, and was elected to an honorary fellowship at the LSE in the latter year.

After completing his undergraduate studies, Beales spent several years teaching extra mural classes for the Workers' Educational Association (WEA), an employment that he was able to continue while working for Sheffield and then at the London School of Economics. He contributed to the early years of the Economic History Society, and wrote broadcasts for radio and an early educational film for schools. Beales was happiest at LSE under the influence of Eileen POWER, during which time he found the department 'informal, associative and free', than the post-war auspices of T. S. ASHTON. Through his time at the School, Beales was uncommonly active. He taught a large number of research students, rarely less than a dozen a year. Throughout his research career, Beales saw his own role as being 'to bring the social background to any kind of economic behavioural system into association with both the theorising and the history telling of this kind of period'.

Many of Beales's books were textbooks, reading lists or other teaching aids. Through the WEA, he published various bibliographies and an early history of industrialization. Together with R.S. Lambert, Beales edited *Memoirs of the Unemployed*, a series of autobiographical accounts written by the victims of inactivity, and published in 1934. The editors' introduction complained that unemployment reduced industrious workers to the condition of 'fruitless aliens'. McKibbin (1991) describes this text as 'one of the most important studies of inter-war unemployment'.

Beales's main contributions were made in the teaching of his subject, and in the promotion of collaborative research. In both areas, Beales advocated an economic form of what would later become known as 'history from below'. Such views are most clear in his study of The Industrial Revolution. Beales's concern was with the losers in this grand historical change. Describing the village labourers, Beales wrote, 'No class in the nineteenth century has so sombre a history.' The factory system he described as a means to oblige male workers to share their employment with women and children: 'It systematized child labour, pauper and free, and exploited it with persistent brutality, creating a proletariat of stunted weaklings.' Of Robert OWEN, Beales wrote, 'The modern labour movement has no need to be ashamed or forgetful of its parentage.' Such sympathy was not extended to those historical figures who Beales associated with the historical right. His essay on MALTHUS described the economist as an opponent, 'a godsend to the conservatives and frightened people who feared the spread in England of French revolutionary ideas and behaviour'. Fortunately, the ideas of the 'black parson' had been defeated, 'the social policies of industrialized societies are all alike, and Malthus could approve of none of them'. Asked to give the Hobhouse Memorial Trust lecture in 1946, Beales praised the ascendancy of social collectivism, which he described as the best and future condition of things: 'I find it difficult to understand how we can get back to the primitive simplicities of economic liberalism.'

A historian of working-class organization, with generous, diverse tastes, Beales's other books included a history of industrialization, and a study of *The Early English Socialists* (1933). This revealed a strong regard for such figures as HODGSKIN and the Tolpuddle Martyrs, as well as the English followers of

MARX. Beales edited Penguin's Pelican series for its first ten years, and vigorously promoted the work of his fellow historians. He also republished Prince Kropotkin's *Mutual Aid*, terming it 'a co-operator's classic, one of the sacred texts of Marxism and socialism, a book that may yet help to make an epoch'. He collected an extensive library of over ten thousand books and pamphlets dealing with social and economic reform in Great Britain. This collection was purchased by Wesleyan University in 1958, and remains on display there.

BIBLIOGRAPHY
The Industrial Revolution 1750–1850 (1928).
The Early English Socialists (1933).
(with R.S. Lambert) *Memoirs of the Unemployed* (1934).
'The Great Depression in Industry and Trade', *Economic History Review* (1934–5), vol. 5, no. 1.
'The "Basic" Industries of England 1850–1914', *Economic History Review* (1934–5), vol. 5, no. 2.
The Making of Social Policy (1946).
'Malthus and the Limits of Population Growth', in D.V. Glass (ed.), *Introduction to Malthus* (1953).

Further Reading
McKibbin, R., *The Ideologies of Class: Social Relations in Britain 1880–1950* (Oxford, 1991).

David Renton

BECHER, John Thomas (1769/70–1848)

John Thomas Becher was born in Ireland in 1769/70, the son of the Rev. Michael Becher. He lived in Nottinghamshire from the 1790s until his death on 3 January 1848 at Southwell. He was educated at Westminster and Christ Church, Oxford (BA 1792, MA 1795). He married in 1802 a distant cousin, Mary Becher, and they had two children. After graduation, Becher was ordained in the Church of England, where his main posts were perpetual curate of Thurgarton and Hoveringham (Nottinghamshire) 1799–1848, prebendary of South Muskham (1818–48) and vicar-general of the collegiate church, Southwell (1830–48). He held several other church livings and was one of the pluralists named in Wade's critical *The Extraordinary Black Book* (1832). As prebendary and vicar-general of the collegiate church, he put the chapter's chaotic business affairs on a proper footing.

As land-owner and magistrate, Becher was involved in a wide range of affairs in Nottinghamshire. He played an important part in preserving law and order during Luddite troubles in the early nineteenth century. He was responsible for replacing Southwell's outdated House of Correction. He helped establish the first County Lunatic Asylum in Nottingham. He organized an emigration scheme to Africa for unemployed people and established two workhouses, a friendly society, a savings bank and an endowment society. The value of Becher's work was nationally recognized and he was invited to give evidence to parliamentary committees and commissions concerned with prisons, lunacy, friendly societies, emigration, agriculture and the poor law. He was also one of three supervisors appointed to build Millbank Penitentiary, London in 1812.

Becher's abiding interest was in the poor law, about which he expounded his views in *The Anti-pauper System* (1828). He sought to achieve a balance between the needs of the poor and the burden on poor rate payers. He distinguished between those who could not be held responsible for their poverty – the old, the infirm, children, lunatics – for whom the parish should assume responsibility, and the idle able-bodied, who should be deterred from seeking help. He was also committed to the idea of preventing pauperism by encouraging self-help amongst working people by providing, for example, allotments, savings banks, friendly societies, endowment societies, penny clubs and funds to enable emigration. The Select Committee of the House of Lords (1831) and the Royal Commission on the Poor Laws (1832–4) paid much attention to Becher's work but, to his disappointment, the new Poor Law Act of 1834 incorporated the deterrent workhouse test while ignoring the preventive self-help measures he had advocated.

Becher understood the multi-causality of contemporary problems. Like Jeremy BENTHAM, he was concerned with the efficient organization of society and, like Edwin CHADWICK, he collected detailed evidence and studied current good practice as a prelude to policy or decision making. Whether dealing with inmates in prisons, lunatic asylums or workhouses, he identified and categorized different needs and advocated ways of providing for them. He also devised and promoted systems of book-keeping for savings banks and actuarially sound tables of contributions for friendly societies. Although Becher advocated self-help, he believed that working people lacked the expertise to manage their own affairs and that organizations such as friendly societies should be managed for them. In this respect, Becher failed to keep in touch with the evolving social and political climate.

BIBLIOGRAPHY
Observations on Friendly Societies and on Banks for Savings (1823).
The Constitution of Friendly Societies upon Legal and Scientific Principles (1824).
Tables of Contributions (1825).
Observations on the Report of the Laws Respecting Friendly Societies (1826).
The Anti-Pauper System (1828; 2nd edn 1834).
A Compendium and Practical System of Book-Keeping for Savings Banks (1829).
Evidence to the Select Committee of the House of Lords on the Poor Law (1831).

Further Reading
O'Neill, J., *The Life and Times of J T Becher of Southwell* (Nottingham, 2002).

Julie O'Neill

BEEKE, Henry (1751–1837)

Beeke was born in Kingsteighnton, Devon on 6 January 1751, the son of a vicar, and died at Torquay on 9 March 1837. He entered Corpus Christi College, Cambridge in 1769 (BA 1773, MA 1776) and went on to study divinity (BD 1785, DD 1800). Ordained in 1782, he was vicar of St Mary the Virgin, Bristol (1782–9), rector of Ufton Norcot, Berkshire (1789–1813) and Dean of Bristol from 1813 until his death. At the same time he was a fellow of Oriel College from 1775, and in 1801 took up the post of professor of modern history at Oxford.

A learned and scholarly figure, Beeke published his *Observations on the Produce of the Income Tax* in 1799, and was thenceforth regarded as an expert on financial matters. He was a good friend of such prominent Tories as Nicholas VANSITTART, later Lord Addington, and J.C. Herries. It is probable that the publication of the *Observations* led to a meeting with William Pitt at Addington's house in 1800. Thereafter Beeke regularly provided advice on a variety of economic topics to the Tory administration and became something of an unofficial economic advisor to the government. However, the rivalry between Pitt and Addington spilled over to their advisers, and George ROSE seems to have been suspicious of Beeke. His appointment of Beeke as professor of modern history at Oxford may well have been a reward for the services he provided the Tory administration.

The contribution of Beeke to the study of the distribution of income and wealth has hitherto been largely unnoticed, despite its influence upon contemporary French economists. In *Observations upon the Produce of the Income Tax*, Beeke is led to conjecture upon the 'expected' inequality of both income and wealth. He applies his ideas explicitly to income, but since he also refers to the inequality of property, he presumably means to apply it also to wealth. He believes the natural scale of inequality will be an arithmetical progression. This pattern is based on a set of moral causes which are presumably permanent in character. These causes he finds to be (1) unequal ability and diligence in acquiring property; (2) unequal success and prudence in preserving it; and (3) unequal numbers inheriting any given property. This is one area where income and wealth ('property') are conflated.

Beeke makes many acute and perceptive observations upon the factors modifying his predicted pattern. Thus the tendency of England's popular institutions is to lessen inequality, and this has operated historically in many ways, such as intermarriage between wealthy lords and merchant families. But he is careful to point out that inequality is being considerably accentuated in favour of the rich in his time: 'for to them almost exclusively belong the vast remittances of the gains by foreign enterprise, and income from foreign possessions'. One wishes Beeke had taken the trouble to compare in some detail the results of his hypothesis with the well-known table of Gregory KING of the 1680s or the later account of the social structure drawn up by Joseph MASSIE in the 1750s.

Beeke favoured a free trade in corn, despite being a Tory, and wished England could follow the lead of Holland in this respect. During Nicholas Vansittart's tenure as Chancellor of the Exchequer, Beeke served as his financial advisor and provided reports on the economic conditions prevailing in the country. The topics on which Beeke provided the most regular advice were funding and paper money. During the scarcity of 1800, he sent a careful and somewhat detailed memorandum on the dearness of corn, and it is this period of observation that led him to hypothesize upon what has come to be known today as the Giffen good:

In all times of Dearness, there is an *Increase* in the consumption of whatever forms the *Basis* of the Food of the People, so long as by retrenching all other expense in Provisions they can possibly find Money to purchase it. They do not understand the Arts of Economical Cookery, they have not Utensils for it, their Stomachs are not used to novelties. With us the Consumption of Bread always increases when their Money, if divided, will not purchase an addition to Meat to the Diet which they cannot abandon. And this is true even when Bread is become in comparison far more costly.

It is not known whether this report, an unpublished memorandum prepared for the Chancellor, was widely circulated, but if it was, then other early statements, such as that of the bureaucrat Simon Gray, may be indebted to Beeke.

As well as the *Observations*, he was the author of *Letter to a County Member on the Means of Securing a Safe and Honorable Peace* (1798) and *Observations on the Roman Roads in Great Britain* (n.d.), and also published a few sermons.

BIBLIOGRAPHY

Letter to a County Member on the Means of Securing a Safe and Honorable Peace (1798).

Observations on the Produce of the Income Tax, and on its Proportion to the Whole Income of Great Britain (1799; revised edn, 1800).

Observations on the Roman Roads in Great Britain (n.d.)

Salim Rashid

BEESLEY, Michael Edwin (1924–99)

Beesley was born in the Birmingham suburb of Edgbaston on 3 July 1924, the son of Edwin and Kathleen Beesley. He died on 24 September 1999, in University College Hospital, London, after a short illness. His father was a manager at the engineering firm of Stewart and Lloyd. His schooling at King Edwards Grammar School, Five Ways, Birmingham, was interrupted when he was knocked down by a bus at the age of thirteen. The main damage was to his leg, and he remained disabled and often in pain throughout his life. He exhibited great fortitude in the face of this disability and determined to live a normal life, playing cricket, golf and table tennis with flair and enthusiasm. He was later to say that the accident changed his career from sportsman to scholar. He took a Bachelor of Commerce degree at Birmingham University, graduating with first-class honours in 1945. Rejecting the offer to stay on for a PhD, he worked in a jewellery business for a year, acquiring practical experience in costing and pricing, as well as other valuable knowledge.

Intellectual starvation led him back to do a PhD at the University of Birmingham, which he completed in 1951. His undergraduate studies there had been inspired by Arthur Shenfield's 'unfailingly brilliant defence of the competitive paradigm', and by the emphasis of Philip Sargant FLORENCE on the development and interpretation of empirical data. On the basis that anti-trust law was preferable to other forms of government intervention, he studied cartels (trade associations) with the aim of working out effective counter-measures.

After standing unsuccessfully as a Liberal candidate in the 1950 general election, Beesley was appointed to a lectureship in commerce at Birmingham in 1951. Stimulated and assisted by their mentor Gilbert WALKER, he and his colleague Alan Walters published their first article, on transport policy and investment in roads, with a follow-up article on investment in railways. Thus began a lifelong interest in the inter-relationships between investment criteria, pricing and regulation. Beesley also published various empirical papers on firms, and on the British motor car industry. Walker organized a visiting post for Beesley as associate professor at the Wharton School in Philadelphia in 1959. This gave a further insight into, and appreciation of, a consumer-orientated society; not least including the student body, where the burden of proof for failure in tests rested on the lecturer. Walker also asked him to tour eight US business schools and advise on future development in Birmingham.

In 1961 Beesley took up the Rees Jeffreys Research Fellowship in transport economics at the London School of Economics, becoming reader in economics there in 1964, and part-time chief economic adviser at the Ministry of Transport from 1964 to 1970. This provided the opportunity to develop, with Christopher Foster and others, the first major UK applications of cost-benefit analysis, not least to the M1 motorway and the Victoria underground line. Later they explored how this return depended on the pricing policy adopted and on values of less quantifiable factors such as comfort (see Foster 2001). Assumptions on consumer valuations were crucial to these analyses. Beesley made pioneering empirical estimates of the value of time spent travelling, based on choices made by over a thousand civil servants in their journey to work. This much-cited research showed that the value of travel time was of the order of one-third the value of the hourly wage.

Beesley concluded from his experience at the Ministry of Transport that, for an economist to have influence, his or her advice must anticipate policy needs, be produced quickly when needed, and be couched in easily understood terms. If his advice was not always easily understood – in part because he was ahead of his time and some of his concepts were unfamiliar – it certainly anticipated policy needs and was produced quickly. It was also presented with irrepressible enthusiasm.

In 1965, Beesley moved from the LSE to the London Business School. The multi-disciplinary context there influenced the nature of his research. For example, he published several papers with Geoff White on mergers policy, industrial restructuring and competition policy. He brought to these his cost-benefit approach, and an emphasis on the information necessary to effective operation of such policies. Importantly, they extended the appraisal beyond the cost-benefit phase to the whole process of intervention. This provided a richer and more complete organizational framework for analysing the effectiveness of alternative agencies and processes, though it does not seem to have been taken up by others.

During the 1970s and 1980s Beesley continued his research on transport with many colleagues, including several papers on the taxi market and its regulation, and others on maximizing the benefits from subsidies to bus and rail operators. A consistent theme in his work was how to improve the performance of public undertakings in terms of the service provided and the costs of provision. In addition to his teaching and research, he was active in administration at the School. In 1976 he established the Small Business Unit, and in 1977, with Tom Evans and David Chambers, established the Institute of Public Sector Management, of which he was director and then chairman for nine years. After retiring in 1984 at the age of sixty, he immediately returned as visiting professor and director of the PhD programme from 1985–89. In 1990 he was made the School's first emeritus professor. He was awarded a CBE in 1985 in recognition of his work on public sector management.

In 1980 the Secretary of State for Industry, Sir Keith Joseph, had asked Beesley to conduct an enquiry into the scope for liberalization of the use of British Telecom's network. Beesley urged more competition, at that time an unfamiliar policy and difficult for the government, company and unions. Yet his report was influential in persuading the government to press ahead with liberalization, and BT to accept more competition. At the time of BT's privatization, the government invited Stephen Littlechild to advise on the regulation of BT's profitability. Littlechild and Beesley together discussed and developed the RPI-X form of price cap regulation proposed in Littlechild's 1983 report. Sensing the opportunity and need to give some shape to emerging government policy, they set out the principles, problems and priorities of privatization later in 1983. Their follow-up paper on the regulation of privatized monopolies contrasted the UK and US approaches, and urged the need to use both neo-classical and Austrian analyses of competition. Both papers were much reprinted and studied around the world, since policy was moving in a similar direction internationally.

In parallel with his work on telecommunications, Beesley was advising the Department of Transport. In late 1982 he recommended bus deregulation. He was subsequently asked to join a cross-departmental committee on bus privatization, and argued the case for competition against other transport economists who advocated competitive franchising. In 1988 he advised the Government on water privatization and regulation. As competition in the product market was potentially non-existent, he emphasized the need for competition in the capital market, by maximizing the threat of take-over of the incumbent management. Preferring take-overs from outside the sector, he also argued for automatic reference to the Monopolies and Mergers Commission (MMC) of large mergers within the water industry, with the MMC decision explicitly to be taken in the light of the regulator's need to maintain effective comparisons across the industry. Paradoxically, that policy has effectively limited larger mergers and take-overs within the water industry, and has been challenged on that account. Whether he would have maintained it in the light of experience is an interesting speculation.

Beesley was a member of the MMC itself from 1988–94. Reports to which he contributed, typically diligently and innovatively, included those on petrol, photocopiers and recorded music. He was an influential member of the group investigating British Gas in 1993. This report contained far-reaching recommendations on market deregulation and the future structure of the gas industry, not least the divestment of all British Gas trading activities. He was also an economic adviser to the Office of Electricity Regulation from its inception in 1989, to the Office of Gas Regulation from 1994, and to Ofgem from its inception in 1999. His work thus increasingly covered all aspects of privatization, competition, regulation and deregulation in all the major UK utilities. To him more than to any other individual is attributable the intellectual framework of government and regulatory policy in all these areas. His collected papers embody his innovative and influential yet disciplined thinking on privatization.

Beesley travelled widely, with academic positions as visiting professor at the University of British Columbia (1968), Harvard Business School and Economics Department (1974), and MacQuarie University, Sydney (1979–80). In addition, his work on transport economics and telecommunications policy took him to India, Pakistan, Hong Kong, South Korea, Cyprus and many European countries. His teaching and advice were enriched by his own practical experience, not least as chairman of London Express Aviation Ltd, a company formed in the 1980s to enter the air traffic market. The experience proved costly, not least in time, but gave valuable insights into the risks of business. He also experienced the problems faced by 'customers' dealing with regulators.

His teaching, administration, research and consultancy workloads (including over 150 publications) would have kept several men busy, but despite all the pressures on his time, he was always instantly willing to give generously both time and original ideas to his students and junior colleagues. In addition, he was instrumental in setting up the *Journal of Transport Economics and Policy*, served on its editorial board from its inception in 1967 until his death, and was managing editor for thirteen years. He was an unpaid but active member of Harrow Health Authority for fifteen years. He was a trustee of the Institute of Economic Affairs. From 1991, he and Colin Robinson instigated, organised and contributed to the joint Institute and London Business School annual regulation lecture series; after his death they were renamed The Beesley Lectures.

Beesley met his wife, Eleanor Yard, in November 1943 in Birmingham University's Barber Institute for Fine Arts. They married on 1 April 1947. He was an accomplished pianist, frequently accompanying his wife's cello playing at concerts. He could also be persuaded to produce an impromptu rendition of Scott Joplin. P.G. Wodehouse and Conan Doyle (whom he was fond of quoting) were his literary heroes; *The Times* crossword was his bedtime reading. He was a devoted family man (he and Eleanor had two daughters and three sons), and in latter years the family took an annual winter break in Australia. But research was his all-pervasive interest, and he could not resist working in Australia as well, importing and exporting ideas and experience.

BIBLIOGRAPHY

'The Birth and Death of Industrial Establishments', *Economica* (1955), vol. IV, no. 1, October.

'Financial Criteria for Investment in Railways', *Bulletin of the Oxford University Institute of Statistics* (1962), vol. 24, no.1, February.

'Some Aspects of the Economics of the M1', *Journal of Industrial Economics* (1962), vol. X, no. 3, July.

(with C.D. Foster) 'Estimating the Social Benefit of Constructing an Underground Railway in London', *Journal of the Royal Statistical Society,* (1963), Series A (General), vol. 126, part I; reprinted in K.J. Arrow and T. Scitovsky (eds), *AEA Readings in Welfare Economics* (1969), vol. XII, pp. 462–520.

(with J.F. Kain), 'Urban Form, Car Ownership and Public Policy: an Appraisal of Traffic in Towns', *Urban Studies* (1964), vol.1, no. 2, November.

'The Value of Time Spent in Travelling: Some New Evidence', *Economica* (1965), May.

(with G.M. White) 'The Control of Mergers in the UK: An Analysis of Government Institutions and Attitudes', in J.M. Samuels (ed.), *Readings on Mergers and Takeovers* (1972).

'Competition and Supply in London Taxis', *Journal of Transport Economics and Policy* (1979), vol. XIII, no. 1, January.

Liberalisation and the Use of British Telecommunications Network (1981).

(with S.C. Littlechild) 'Privatisation: Problems, Principles and Priorities', *Lloyds Bank Review* (1983), July.

(with S. Glaister), 'Information for Regulating: The Case of Taxis', *The Economic Journal* (1983), vol. 93, September.

(with P Gist and S Glaister) 'Cost-Benefit Analysis and London's Transport Policies', *Progress in Planning Series* (1983), vol. 19, part 3.

(with S.C. Littlechild) 'The Regulation of Privatised Monopolies in the United Kingdom', *Rand Journal Of Economics* (1986).

'Commitment, Sunk Costs and Entry into the Airline Industry: Reflections on Experience', *Journal Transport and Economics Policy* (1986), pp. 173–90.

(with B. Laidlaw and P. Gist) 'Prices and Competition in Voice Telephony in the UK', *Telecommunications Policy* (1987), vol. 11, no. 3, September.

(with B Laidlaw) *The Future of Telecommunications* (1989).

'Collusion, Predation and Mergers in the UK Bus Industry', *Journal of Transport Economics and Policy* (1990), September.

Privatisation, Regulation and Deregulation: Collected Essays and Papers (1992; 2nd edn, 1997).

Further Reading

Foster, C.D., 'Michael Beesley and Cost Benefit Analysis', *Journal of Transport Economics and Policy* (2001), vol. 35, part 1, pp. 3–30.

Littlechild, S.C., 'Michael Beesley's Contribution to Privatisation, Competition and Regulation', in C. Robinson (ed.), *Utility Regulation and Competition Policy* (Cheltenham, 2002, pp. xxvii–xxix).

Robinson, C., 'Professor Michael Beesley: An Appreciation", *Economic Affairs* (1999), December, p. 30.

Stephen Littlechild

BELLERS, John (1654–1725)

Bellers was born around 1654, probably in Gloucestershire, and died in London on 8 February 1725. He came from a background of minor gentry, from a Quaker family, and likewise married a Quaker, Frances Fettiplace, through whom he inherited the manor of Coln St Aldwyn's, Gloucestershire. Well to do, he spent much of his life engaged in various forms of philanthropy in both London and the countryside. He visited prisons and urged the reform of the prison system and the improvement of conditions for inmates, and continually urged his fellow Quakers to devote more of their efforts and money to useful causes. Sir Hans Sloane and William Penn were among his friends.

Bellers wrote very widely on social issues, but his best-known work was *Proposals for Raising a Colledge of Industry of all useful Trades and Husbandry*, originally published in 1696. Renewed attention was drawn to his work on 25 July 1817 when Robert OWEN wrote to the daily newspaper explaining several ideas about a new view of society. In this correspondence, he credited Bellers with the original discovery of a plan that could have substantial and permanent benefits for mankind. Owen described Bellers's work as curious and valuable, noting that it had been produced without any aid from practical experience and that the author had anticipated the needs of society by 120 years.

Bellers's motto was 'Industry brings Plenty'. In his proposal, the improvement of society and the alleviation of poverty were to be accomplished by creating self-sufficient colleges or communities. Bellers proposed that the rich could benefit from taking care of the poor. The poor also could have plenty if villages for agriculture and manufacturing were established based on unity and mutual co-operation. The rich could monitor their investment, enjoy the benefits of participation, and get better results than they would from giving to charities. The poor would have security, protection from competitive intrigues and the flexibility to exchange goods without using money. He calculated that two hundred working people could provide the necessities of life for three hundred people.

Robert Owen republished Bellers's proposal in 1818. The material was a component of the documentation that Owen circulated and was received in essentially the same manner. Thus Bellers's concern for the poor and his emphasis on interdependence eventually became important social issues. His proposal was neglected however, because it was paternalistic. This approach was seen to be incompatible with the development of increasingly efficient free markets within the mainstream economy.

Interest in Bellers's proposal has been sustained by the need for an organic approach that integrates daily life, efficient production and social welfare. He understood that easy living could have negative effects, and he recommended a practical approach to daily life for everyone. Labour, he wrote, 'is as proper for the bodies health, as eating is for its living; for what pains a man saves by ease, he will find in disease'. Several pamphlets on the relief of the poor echoed these themes. As well as Robert Owen, several later writers, including Frederick Morton EDEN, H.M. HYNDMAN and Karl MARX, were familiar with his ideas and quoted Bellers with approval.

BIBLIOGRAPHY
Proposals for Raising a Colledge of Industry of all Useful Trades and Husbandry, with profit for the rich, a plentiful living for the poor, and a good education for youth. Which will be advantage to the Government by the Increase of the people and their riches (1696).
A Supplement to the College of Industry (1696).
An Essay for Imploying the Poor to Profit (1723).
An Epistle to the Friends...Concerning the Prisoners and Sick, and the Prisons and Hospitals of Great Britain (1724).

Further Reading
Owen, R., *A New View of Society: Tracts relative to this subject.*(1818: repr. New York, 1972).

Richard Danielson

BELLMAN, Charles Harold (1886–1963)

Harold Bellman was born in London on 19 February 1886, and died there on 1 June 1963. Although he was born in Paddington in London, Bellman considered himself a Cornishman (both his parents were from Penzance). He was a lifelong Methodist and popular lay preacher. Within a year of leaving school at age fourteen, Bellman had passed the clerks' examinations for the Railway Clearing House and gained promotion (despite finding the job extremely boring). Barred from active service in the First World War on medical grounds, Bellman joined the Ministry for Munitions, where his wartime services won him an MBE. In 1918 he became a part-time board member of the Abbey Road & St John's Wood Building Society, and by June 1920 was a full-time member of management. He became managing director in 1930, and chairman in 1937. Knighted in 1932, Bellman was also granted the Légion d'Honneur and Australian Order of Merit. He was for many years a member of the court of governors of the London School of Economics.

As chairman of the Abbey Road Building Society, Bellman oversaw a unique period of growth in the building society movement. He believed in growing the market rather than winning market share from competitors, and sought wherever possible to publicize the building society movement as a whole. From 1933 he sought to establish a code of practice to protect building societies against rash loans, and in January 1944 he presided over the merger of Abbey Road with the National Building Society, becoming joint managing director and chairman of the new Abbey National. Before the First World War, Abbey Road had been the fifteenth largest building society in Britain with assets of around £1 million and it was still operating from a single office until the early 1930s; but by the Second World War it had become the second largest building society. After the 1944 merger, the Abbey National's combined assets were £82 million, 10.3 per cent of the total assets of all British building societies.

A highly successful businessman, Bellman was also an evangelist for the building society movement as a whole. He produced a number of pamphlets and articles spelling out his position, but the best summary of his views is probably to be found in *The Thrifty Three Millions* (1935) a history of the movement and of the Abbey Road society, updated under the title *Bricks and Mortals* (1949) following the merger with the National. Bellman believed that the aim of building societies was to bring investors and borrowers together almost in the manner of a co-operative – there is a strong echo of the co-operative movement in Bellman's writing – to promote the twin virtues of thrift and home ownership. The first was particularly important in the years after the First World War, when the level of national savings had drastically declined, and Bellman saw building societies as a means of stimulating savings. At the same time, the societies could serve a social purpose in helping to alleviate the shortage of housing. By making home ownership possible for people, he believed, the building societies had stimulated house building and increased the national housing stock. Both these ultimately led to an increase in the nation's capital and would further stimulate economic growth.

Writing during the economic depression of the 1930s, Bellman clearly believed that savings and home ownership were a recipe for economic recovery. He preached this message not only in Britain but also in America, which he visited several times and where he gave a number of speeches, later collected in the volume *Capital, Confidence and Community* (1938). An optimist, Bellman believed that democracy and co-operation would solve most economic, and indeed political, problems. He believed governments should intervene in the economy where necessary, and among other measures, proposed the use of high sales taxes on alcohol to limit consumption and deal with the drink problem.

BIBLIOGRAPHY
The Building Society Movement (1927).
The Silent Revolution: The Influence of Building Societies on the Modern Housing Problem (1928).
Architects of the New Age (1929).
Building Societies: Retrospect and Prospect (1930).
The Thrifty Three Millions: A Study of the Building Society Movement and the Story of the Abbey Road Building Society (1935).
Capital, Confidence and Community (1938).
Christianity and Commerce (1939).

A Cornish Cockney: Reminiscences and Reflections (1947).
Bricks and Mortals: A Study of the Building Society Movement and the Story of the Abbey National Building Society (1949).

Further Reading
Cleary, E.J., *The Building Society Movement* (1965).
Jeremy, D.J., *A Business History of Britain, 1900–1990s* (Oxford, 1988).

Simon Coppock
Morgen Witzel

BENHAM, Frederic Charles Courtenay
(1900–62)

Benham was born 6 March 1900 at Bristol, Gloucestershire, and died 7 January 1962 at St Mary's Hospital, London, of rheumatic heart disease. The son of Charles Courtenay Benham, leather merchant, and his wife Kathleen Grace, née Taylor, he married Suzanne Henriette, née Paitre, of Paris in 1932; they had one daughter. He was educated at Katharine Lady Berkeley's Grammar School and at the London School of Economics (BSc (Econ.) 1922; PhD 1928), where he took first class honours and was a student of Edwin CANNAN.

Upon graduation, Benham worked briefly at the LSE as a research fellow. In 1923 he was appointed lecturer at the University of Sydney. There he confirmed the belief of the dean of the Faculty of Economics, Professor R.C. Mills, that the 'best way for Australian universities to build up small departments was to gamble on young men of promise rather than seek the security of limited achievement' (S.J. Butlin 1962: 386). He left Sydney in 1929 when he accepted a Rockefeller research fellowship. He taught at LSE from 1931–42 and was a *rapporteur* to Chatham House on international economic issues. In 1938 he advised the government of Turkey. Between 1942 and 1945 he was economic adviser to the comptroller for development and welfare in the West Indies, and from 1947–55 advised the commissioner-general for the United Kingdom in south-east Asia, stationed at Singapore. Between these two appointments he was professor of commerce (with special reference to International Trade) at the University of London. From 1955 until his death he occupied the Sir Henry Price chair of International Economics at the Royal Institute of International Affairs. He was awarded the CMG (1950) and the CBE (1945).

In Australia, Benham contributed to the emergence of economics as an academic discipline and to policy discussion. He took a heavy teaching load and published several articles and essays. His book *The Prosperity of Australia* (1928), which he submitted as his doctoral thesis, is arguably the first serious analytical examination of the Australian economy. His publications were heavily influenced by the simple welfare economics that he had been taught by Cannan, taking a decidedly free market stance that was often at variance with the mildly interventionist position adopted by many Australian economists.

Benham consistently applied the test of per capita income when judging the efficacy of policy proposals. On this basis he was highly critical of many fundamental policies that had been applied in Australia in recent decades, especially tariff policy, which had led to an inefficient allocation of resources and reduced the growth of per capita income. He refuted emphatically the conclusion of the famous 'Brigden Report' (*The Australian Tariff: An Economic Enquiry*, 1929) that moderate protection for manufacturing industries could be justified; arguing to the contrary, Benham claimed that the tariff had reduced per capita income in Australia and had lowered the optimum size of its population.

Benham contributed also to the measurement and conceptual development of national income estimation in Australia. Of his work, N. G. Butlin adjudged that:

> Here was the first attempt, in Australia, to explore with some attention to conceptual meaning the various measures and the content of the concepts. In this sense, Benham's estimate was the first estimate for Australia which consciously attempted to measure a carefully devised concept approximating the modern idea of national income.
> (N.G. Butlin 1962: 39)

Later Benham was a pioneer of national income estimation in developing countries, including the West Indies, Singapore and Malaya.

After leaving Australia, Benham published on a variety of subjects, including monetary policy, protection, economic welfare, national income, public finance, economic assistance, and the problems of developing countries. As a teacher and communicator he won an enviable reputation for lucid expression, a facility he used to good effect in his textbook *Economics: A General Textbook for Students*. First published in 1938, this work was widely adopted in universities in Britain and the Commonwealth. In his approach to the economics of less developed countries, Benham's policy advice was based on the application of free market processes, rather than government direction and planning, and exploiting comparative advantage in international trade rather than fostering import replacement. He stressed the importance of a competent and honest public administration.

BIBLIOGRAPHY
(with R.C. Mills) *Lectures on the Principles of Money, Banking and Foreign Exchange and their Application to Australia* (Sydney, 1925).
The Prosperity of Australia: An Economic Analysis (1928).
British Monetary Policy (1932).
Economics (1938).
Great Britain Under Protection (New York, 1941).
The Colombo Plan and other Essays (1956).
The National Income of Singapore (1959).
(with H.A. Holley) *A Short Introduction to the Economy of Latin America* (1960).
Economic Aid to Underdeveloped Countries (1961).

Further Reading
Government of Australia, *The Australian Tariff: An Economic Enquiry* (Melbourne, 1929).
Butlin, N. G., *Australian Domestic Product, Investment and Foreign Borrowing* (Cambridge, 1962).
Butlin, S.J., 'Frederic Benham: 1900–62', *Economic Record* (1962), vol. 38, no. 83, pp. 386–88.
Cain, N.G., 'Benham, Frederic Charles Courtenay (1900–1962)', *Australian Dictionary of Biography*, vol. 7 (Melbourne, 1979).
Goodwin, C.D., *Economic Enquiry in Australia* (Durham, North Carolina, 1966).

Selwyn Cornish

BENTHAM, Jeremy (1748–1832)

Bentham was born in London 15 February 1748 and died there on 6 June 1832. He was the elder son of a London attorney, Jeremiah Bentham, and his first wife, Alicia Whitehorn, née Grove. He was educated at Westminster School and The Queen's College, Oxford, from which he obtained his BA in 1763 (MA 1766). Called to the bar in 1769, he chose to devote his life to applying scientific principles to the reform of English law rather than to the practice of the law itself.

A Fragment on Government (1776) was the first product of Bentham's project to critically analyse law and to set it on the new foundation of the principle of utility. Here he stated the 'fundamental axiom' that 'it is the greatest happiness of the greatest number that is the measure of right and wrong', and that 'the obligation to minister to general happiness, was an obligation paramount to and inclusive of every other' (1776: 393, 441n). In 1780 Bentham printed but did not publish (until 1789) *An Introduction to the Principles of Morals and Legislation*, intended as an introduction to his planned 'Pannomiom' or complete legal code based upon the utility principle. In 1781 Bentham coined the term 'utilitarian', as a practical approach to moral and legal philosophy using pain and pleasure as the basis for choosing both individual actions and public policy.

In 1776–8 Bentham visited his brother Samuel, a diplomat, in Russia, where he hoped to present a code of law to Tsarina Catherine II. Here he busied himself with *Defence of Usury* (1787) and the Panopticon project. *Defence of Usury* was his first essay in political economy and shows him as a disciple of Adam SMITH, albeit one critical of the restrictive lending laws supported by Smith. *Panopticon; or the Inspection-House* (1791), based on an architectural idea by Samuel Bentham, described detailed plans for the construction of a prison (and other controlled institutions, such as factories, schools, hospitals and workhouses) based on a circular design and centrally located watchtower. He went on to consider issues related to poor law reform, the rules of evidence and other judicial practices, as well as economic and finance policy.

In 1815 Bentham published *Chrestomathia* (1815–17), expounding a new system of education for the children of 'the middling and higher ranks'. The curriculum was utilitarian in intent ('chrestomathia' meant useful learning) and stressed science and technology rather than the classics and religion. His major tract on politics of this time was *Plan of Parliamentary Reform, in the Form of a Catechism* (1817), much of which he wrote in 1809–10 after his meeting with James MILL. He was convinced that without democratic reform England risked a revolution, and this lent all the more urgency to the need for political change. Thereafter, Bentham was widely recognized as the foremost philosophical voice of political radicalism in Britain. He dedicated the last ten years of his life to the *Constitutional Code*, a complete code of fundamental laws, including the administrative arrangements for a liberal state based on efficiency and accountability.

Economics was one of the many fields of action to be mastered by anyone concerned with the general field of politics and legislation. Most of Bentham's views on political economy appeared between 1793 and 1801 in the context of the Napoleonic Wars, and are responses to questions of war finance and inflation. In various of his works, he addressed many of the core issues in economic theory, including value, investment, savings, taxation, production, growth, distribution, employment and money. The influence of Smith on Bentham's political economy was substantial and apparent from the first. Bentham explicitly followed Smith in basing his analysis on the proposition that in commerce, each individual is a better judge of his own interests than government. The central issue 'is to know what ought and what ought not to be done by government. It is in this view, and in this view only that the knowledge of what is done and takes place without the interference of government can be of any practical use' (1952–4, vol. 1: 224). In general, experience tells us that the economy prospers when individuals are left alone to pursue their own interests. Where departures from the general rule of non-interference are required by utility, they are 'agenda' items for government, otherwise they remain 'non-agenda'. This seems to point to a political economy that is 'liberal' in a distinctly modern sense, one in which *laissez-faire* holds general sway, the basic rules of which are maintained by government, with exceptions justified on the grounds of utility.

Bentham's commitment to *laissez-faire* is evident in *Defence of Usury*, where he claimed it as axiomatic that 'no man of ripe years and of sound mind, acting freely, and with his eyes open, ought to be hindered with a view to his advantage, from making such bargain, in the way of obtaining money, as he thinks fit: nor...any body hindered from supplying him, upon any terms he thinks proper to accede to' (1952–4, vol. 1: 129). The *Manual of Political Economy* (1793–5) sets out the argument that a free economy is the most productive, and listed the 'non-agenda' of government, including providing financial subsidies and loans, imposing taxes and duties on exports and competing imports, non-importation agreements, and restrictions on industrial competition. In the *Institute of Political Economy* (1801–4) Bentham advanced the view that 'security' is the legislator's primary objective in the field of economic activity. Government should be restricted to offering rewards and prizes for inventions and advertising them, and to removing archaic legal obstacles in the way of enterprise. He opposed subsidies to encourage industry because they presuppose taxes, which are in themselves a 'vice' to be avoided wherever possible. In *Observations on the Restrictive and Prohibitory Commercial System* (1821), he criticized the Spanish Cortes for introducing import duties to protect newly emerging industries.

For Bentham, the 'agenda' of government was largely constituted of monetary strategies designed to enhance wealth, limit runaway prices, and control inflation. He described in detail the benefits of circulating an interest-bearing government-backed paper currency, intended to serve both as a means of exchange and as small savings certificates, and argued for government regulation of the issue of coins and notes as a way to stem inflationary tendencies. He argued that all value is founded on utility and not on exchange, and also gave voice to the doctrine that an expansive monetary policy can raise the level of economic activity. He advocated price controls on basic foodstuffs during times of scarcity. Finally, on the grounds that the government's longevity offered enhanced security and national economic advantages, Bentham advanced the case for state management of the life insurance business.

Other instances of Bentham's willingness to entertain state intervention can be found in writings of the 1790s on the poor law and in the later *Constitutional Code*. In the first, Bentham revealed how little he was prepared to leave to the poor and unemployed to decide for themselves where their best interests lay (Long 1978). In advance of MALTHUS, he argued that 'over-population' was a source of misery among the poor, and the promotion of contraception was the means to lessen the pressures of subsistence on large families unable to provide for themselves. Further, he recommended the establishment of a system of independent, self-sufficient and profitable poor houses to replace the arbitrariness and chaos of parish home relief. In the *Constitutional Code* Bentham set forth arguments for nationalization of the Bank of England, government involvement in education, agricultural and scientific research, elements of government responsibility for health services, transport and other means of communication, and government regulation of the insurance business, lotteries and friendly societies.

Few of Bentham's economic writings were available to nineteenth-century economists, who became acquainted with his general position through his moral and legal philosophy. In his work on civil law can be found the basic principles of Bentham's approach to economic matters. He argued that 'the care of his enjoyments ought to be left almost entirely to the individual', and that 'the principal function of government is to guard against pains'. The best way for government to protect individuals is to create and confer rights, such as the 'rights of personal security, rights of protection for honour, rights of property, and rights of receiving aid in case of need'. Infringements of these rights should be regarded as offences punishable by law (1840: 95).

The operational principles of the civil law were rendered by Bentham in the form of four 'subordinate ends' of the utility principle – security, subsistence, abundance, and equality, in that order – which were meant to guide the legislator in the application of policy and law. At the root of Bentham's understanding of security as the principal object of law is the security of 'expectation': the guarantee against future loss, which enables individuals to confidently plan for the future in their labour and contractual arrangements, knowing that they will not be disappointed in their legitimate expectations. The maximization of well-being is achieved by extending to each agent as wide a sphere of personal inviolability as possible, in ways that are compatible with the same security for others. As Bentham put it, 'The goodness of the laws depends upon their conformity to general *expectation*. The legislator ought to be well acquainted with the progress of this expectation, in order to act in concert with it' (1840: 148). Beyond this, in so far as social well-being depends on the provision of subsistence, this too is best secured through the provision of security of expectations, enabling each individual to secure his subsistence through productive labour. For those who are unable to provide for themselves, the legislator must guarantee the provision of the means of subsistence, since only on the basis of continued existence can interest formation and realization take place.

In his civil law writings we find the first development of what Bentham later (in the 1820s) termed the 'disappointment-preventing principle', intended as a practical strategy to be followed by the legislator when the effect of new legislation would be to thwart an individual's legitimate expectations. Where possible, disappointment must be avoided, but where it cannot be avoided, it must be adequately compensated. This was intended as a safeguard against wide-ranging and ill-conceived plans to redistribute property, such as occurred in France after the Revolution. It was also here that Bentham first posited the diminishing marginal utility of pleasure (1840: 102–7). One of the practical consequences of this idea is that where choices present themselves between giving an additional increment to a rich man or to a poor man, more happiness will generally result from giving it to the poorer of the two. From this, it could be concluded that an equal distribution of money would produce the maximum possible amount of aggregate happiness in terms of the total money available at any given time. However, Bentham resisted this re-distributive outcome, because of the premium he placed on the pleasures associated with security of expectations. Once a system of property is established, the pain associated with changing it (the frustration of the desires of the propertied) determines that security is given priority over the potential benefits to be gained from a forced re-distribution. Nevertheless, according to Bentham's own analysis this cannot hold absolutely. There must come a point when the loss to an extremely wealthy person will be outweighed by the gains to others if a portion of his wealth were dispossessed for redistribution. Bentham would respond that even the smallest coerced dispossession of property would be viewed as an attack on the general security of all, and thus undermine the general confidence that property would be protected.

Bentham's ideas had a substantial influence in the British tradition of political economy. John Stuart MILL closely followed his pragmatic utilitarian attitude in *Principles of Political Economy* (1848), balancing a commitment to *laissez-faire* with the dictates of utility. The utilitarian theory of value and the theory of marginal utility have had an abiding influence. W. Stanley JEVONS explicitly acknowledged his debt to Bentham in this regard in *The Theory of Political Economy*

(1871), and F.Y. EDGEWORTH was convinced that the first principle of economics is that every agent is motivated by self-interest. In *Mathematical Psychics* (1881) Edgeworth adopted Bentham's position on the commensureability of pleasures, and followed him in applying mathematics to the moral sciences. In *The Principles of Political Economy* (1883), Henry SIDGWICK explicitly borrowed from Bentham the idea of diminishing marginal utility, positing that the closer a society came to equality in the distribution of wealth, the greater would be the satisfaction derived from it. Alfred MARSHALL gave courses on Bentham at Cambridge in the early 1870s, but mistakenly supposed he 'wrote little on economics'. In *The End of Laissez-faire* (1927), KEYNES believed the essence of Bentham's political economy to be an unequivocal faith in *laissez-faire*, and pronounced that 'Bentham was not an economist at all'. Later, informed of the range of Bentham's investigations, he suggested that the Royal Economic Society prepare a comprehensive edition of Bentham's economic writings. Since then economists have generally accepted that Bentham should be 'ranked as one of the founding fathers of [the] discipline' (Taylor 1955: 170).

BIBLIOGRAPHY

Theory of Legislation by Jeremy Bentham, English translation of vols 1–2 of E. Dumont, *Traités de législation civile et pénale*, trans. R. Hildreth (Boston, 1840; 2nd edn, 1864).
An Introduction to the Principles of Morals and Legislation, ed. J.H. Burns and H.L.A. Hart (1970).
Of Laws in General, ed. H.L.A. Hart (1970).
A Comment on the Commentaries and A Fragment on Government, ed. J.H. Burns and H.L.A. Hart (1977).
Chrestomathia, ed. M.J. Smith and W.H. Burston (1983).
Constitutional Code, vol. 1, ed. F. Rosen and J.H. Burns (1983).
First Principles Preparatory to Constitutional Code, ed. T.P. Schofield (1989).
Securities Against Misrule and other Constitutional Writings for Tripoli and Greece, ed. T.P. Schofield (1990).
Official Aptitude Maximized; Expense Minimized, ed. T.P. Schofield (1993).
'Legislator of the World': Writings on Codification, Law, and Education, ed. T.P. Scholfield and J. Harris (1998).
Political Tactics, ed. M. James, C. Blamires and C. Pease-Watkin (1999).
Writings on the Poor Laws, vol. 1, ed. M. Quinn (2001).
The Works of Jeremy Bentham, 11 vols, ed. J. Bowring (Edinburgh, 1838–43).
Jeremy Bentham's Economic Writings, 3 vols, ed. W. Stark (London, 1952–4).

Further Reading

Black, R.D.C., 'Bentham and the Political Economists of the Nineteenth Century', *The Bentham Newsletter* (1988), vol. 12, pp. 24–36.
Crimmins, J.E., 'Contending Interpretations of Bentham's Utilitarianism', *Canadian Journal of Political Science* (1996), vol. 29, no. 4, pp. 751–77.
Harrison, R., *Bentham* (1983).
Parekh, B. (ed.), *Jeremy Bentham: Critical Assessments*, 4 vols (1993).
Stark, W., 'Liberty and Equality or: Jeremy Bentham as an Economist', *Economic Journal* (1941), vol. 51, pp. 56–79.
———, 'Jeremy Bentham as an Economist', *Economic Journal* (1946), vol. 56, pp. 583–608.
Taylor, W.L., 'Bentham as an Economist; A Review Article', *South African Journal of Economics* (1955), vol. 23, pp. 66–74.

James E. Crimmins

BERKELEY, George (1685–1753)

Berkeley was born 12 March 1685 near Dysert Castle, Thomastown, Ireland of Anglo-Irish parents. He died at Oxford on 14 January 1753 and was buried in Christ Church, Oxford. His father, William Berkeley, was a collector of tariff and customs fees, a 'gentleman farmer', and a military officer. Berkeley was educated in the Kilkenny School and at Trinity College, Dublin. He then went to London with a view to securing patronage and a position in the Church of England. Dean Jonathan Swift, a court insider and a fellow Anglo-Irish clergyman, introduced Berkeley to leading Tory ministers and intellectuals, but Berkeley's fortunes changed with the death of Queen Anne and the succession of George I in 1714. Upon the defeat of the Jacobite rebellion in 1715, many of Berkeley's friends and acquaintances fled the country. He himself was suspected of Jacobite leanings, due to his political associations and a set of sermons he published in 1712 on a favourite Jacobite theme, *Passive Obedience*. That suspicion put a cloud over his ambitions and he too spent most of the next five years on the continent.

Returning in 1721, Berkeley again applied for a position in the church. After serving in a number of modest positions, in 1724 he received the very lucrative post as the Dean of Derry in northern Ireland. Before taking that position, he launched an extraordinary effort to found a college in Bermuda that would educate native American and English colonists' children together. He wrote a prospectus for the college and spent nearly a decade in recruiting personnel and finding funding for this multicultural institution. He apparently succeeded in his project when Parliament granted land for the college and voted £20,000 for the effort in 1726, but the money was not disbursed. After waiting in vain for more than a year for the grant, Berkeley, with his new bride, Anne Foster, the daughter of Ireland's Chief Justice, set sail in 1728 for Newport, Rhode Island, which he hoped to use as his base. He apparently hoped that his precipitate action would force parliament's hand, but back in London Robert Walpole, manoeuvred to have parliament rescind the grant. Berkeley returned to London in 1731.

However, his book of philosophical dialogues during his 'American sojourn', *Alciphron or the Minute Philosopher*, was very successful and caught the eye of Queen Caroline, the 'philosopher' queen, who frequently invited him to the court. This royal connection most likely led to Berkeley's being promoted to the bishopric of Cloyne in 1734. He spent nearly all the rest of his life in Cloyne, leaving only in the last year of his life to join his son, who was studying in Oxford.

A gifted scholar and intellectual, Berkeley wrote and published some of the most remarkable works in the history of philosophy in his twenties: *An Essay Towards a New Theory of Vision* (1709), *Treatise on the Principles of Human Knowledge* (1710) and *Three Dialogues between Hylas and Philonous* (1713). In these works Berkeley presented a bold philosophical vision that supported orthodox theological beliefs in totally unorthodox ways. He published his major work on money and banking, *The Querist*, while in his fifties.

Berkeley directly experienced a number of decisive moments in economic history that shaped his views on money and banking. He was in France during the collapse of the Mississippi Bubble, and on returning to England he observed the Parliamentary hearings on the corruption occasioned by the similar collapse of the South Sea Bubble. These led Berkeley to write *An Essay toward Preventing the Ruin of Great Britain*, an attack on the moral depravity of the 'get rich quick' economy of the period. The second experience that undoubtedly influenced his thought on money and banking was his observation of the effects of the Rhode Island government-issued paper money. Rhode Island was, even among the American colonies, in the forefront of monetary experimentation (others at the time called it monetary degeneration). Almost all transactions internal to the colony were carried on with paper currency. In his nearly three years in the colony, Berkeley purchased land, built a house for his family, bought slaves and entered into the vibrant intellectual life of the 'specie-less' colony. He was clearly impressed with the positive effects of such a monetary system. His final monetary decisive experience was the chronic economic depression of Ireland in the first third of the eighteenth century, which he thought to be the result of the hedonism of the rich and the almost cataleptic depression of the poor. Berkeley's own fortunes were directly affected by this recession when he returned to Ireland as a bishop in 1734.

The Querist is composed entirely of questions, more than a thousand of them. Berkeley was a careful student of literary composition, and so his unusual choice of expression for economic topics that had largely been dealt with in the declarative (even exclamatory) mode was rooted in his conception of money itself. For Berkeley, money was not a symbol representing a given quantity of any already existing thing or value, but it should be a stimulus to future action, production and empowerment. Whatever its phenomenal form (be it coin or paper currency), money only plays its proper role when it guides action, not when it simply stores it. Thus, like the question, money only becomes itself when it provokes a response from an interlocutor. In itself, it is always incomplete.

Berkeley questioned the conceptions of money proposed by his predecessors in the philosophy of money and queried a new approach: 'Whether money is to be considered as having an intrinsic Value, or as being a Commodity, a Standard, a Measure, or a Pledge, as is variously suggested by Writers? And whether the true Idea of Money, as such, be not altogether that of a Ticket or Counter?' (Part I Query 23). For tickets and counters, like algebraic variables, take on meaning when they allow certain 'moves' and transformations to take place. In themselves, they do not refer to any particular thing (abstract or concrete). In this view, money has a peculiar 'spiritual' or 'notional' character, in that its significance is only apparent when it affects human wills. Thus, the idealistic philosopher who refuted the reality of matter in his epistemological works became the protagonist of a monetary theory questioning 'materialist' concepts of money.

Such an innovative conception of money was crucial for Berkeley's proposal of a National Bank that would issue paper money bills, a project that challenged the almost universal disgust with the crash of the Law 'system' a decade and a half before. Much of Part II of *The Querist* is a review of Law's system, especially his General Bank (later Royal Bank) of France, with an eye to showing how his own projected bank would escape precipitating a bubble. For example, his projected bank would not issue stock certificates or be involved in commercial enterprises; it would be owned by the public and not by a set of wealthy investors; it would be controlled by a legislature and not by an absolute monarch; as a consequence, it would not make 'making money' as an end, but its monetary production would be a means to 'exciting the industry of Mankind'. Thus Berkeley's bank would not enter into the temptation of issuing new notes beyond their use 'for supplying Manufactures and Trade with stock, for regulating Exchange, for quickening Commerce, for putting Spirit into the People' (Part II, Query 142). Most importantly, the managers of the bank were to be intensely and continuously interrogated by the Legislature to prevent any 'privatization' of interest in the Bank's activities.

Berkeley suggested that a paper note currency issued by a bank of the sort he had outlined in his questions (as well as a national mint that would issue small change tokens) would help solve the major class impediments to economic growth. On the one side, the 'native Irish' poor had been so disenfranchised after the defeat of the rebellion against William

III that they had almost no contact with the monetary economy and lived in 'that cynical content in dirt and beggary' (Part I, Query 19); on the other side, the Anglo-Irish gentry spent their rents and interest in frivolous consumption of foreign luxuries or simply lived abroad and spent their income there.

Berkeley suggested that a paper note and small change token currency (if properly managed) could transform both classes. Instead of being obstacles to economic growth, they would become its engines. With the increase in the money supply and its penetration into the 'pores' of the economy, the native Irish poor would begin to experience the power of having and using money. They would begin to work above and beyond the satisfaction of 'cynical contentment' because they would be able to earn money (instead of simply sharecropping or working for a subsistence wage paid in kind) and buy commodities they never dreamed of. This increased consumption is not, in Berkeley's eyes, a good in itself, but simply a sign of and vehicle for the arousal of 'the spirit of the people' and their increased activation which are goods in themselves.

The Anglo-Irish gentry would be paid their rents and interest in paper currency and small change tokens which they could not use in their buying sprees in London and Paris, since the haberdashers and tailors there would not accept Irish currency, but would expect specie. The new monetary regime would force the gentry to spend their incomes in Ireland. As a result, they would both moderate their near-hysterical desire to emulate their English cousins and stimulate local Irish production of art, architecture and manufacture. Thus this currency would create an economy where the different class elements would reinforce each other's activity, instead of increasing pulling away from and subverting each other.

Although Berkeley's writings on money, banking, and development are not as well known in the history of economics as those of two other British empiricist philosophers, John LOCKE and David HUME, Berkeley's sophisticated defence of paper money and national banks in the wake of the catastrophe of John Law's system was an important moment in the revival of the intellectual fortunes of what is now the dominant form of monetary and banking institutions. *The Querist* was a very popular work, often reprinted and quoted in the eighteenth century. It was well known among the Scottish enlightenment economists such as David Hume and Adam SMITH, and it helped stimulate their increasing functionalization of money. Ironically, although *The Querist* was one of the most sophisticated early defences of a paper money economy regulated by the state, a concept that was to become the standard for monetary organization in the twentieth century, it began to lose its own currency in the nineteenth. Interest in *The Querist* was revived with the rise of Keynesian and development economics which studied the impact of money on economic growth. More recently, the anti-representational conception of money that Berkeley pioneered has become an important theme in the postmodern philosophy of money associated with Derrida, Goux and Baudrillard.

BIBLIOGRAPHY
Passive Obedience (1712).
Alciphron or the Minute Philosopher (1732).
An Essay Towards a New Theory of Vision (1709).
Treatise on the Principles of Human Knowledge (1710).
Three Dialogues between Hylas and Philonous (1713).
An Essay toward Preventing the Ruin of Great Britain (1721).
The Querist (1735-7).
The Works of George Berkeley, Bishop of Cloyne, ed. A.A. Luce and T.E. Jessop (1948-57).

Further Reading
Berman, D., *George Berkeley: Idealism and the Man* (Oxford, 1994).

Caffentzis, C.G., *Exciting the Industry of Mankind: George Berkeley's Philosophy of Money* (Dordrecht, 2000).
Kelly, P., 'Ireland and the Critique of Mercantism in Berkeley's *Querist*', in D. Berman (ed.), *George Berkeley: Essays and Replies* (Dublin, 1985).
Leyburn, E.D., 'Bishop Berkeley: *The Querist*' *Proceedings of the Royal Irish Academy* (1937), vol. 44, sect. C, December, pp. 75–98.
Johnston, J., *Bishop Berkeley: The Querist in Historical Perspective* (Dundalk. 1970).
Rashid, S., 'Berkeley's *Querist* and its Influence', *Journal of the History of Economic Thought* (1990), vol. 12, pp. 38–60.
Vickers, D., *Studies in the Theory of Money: 1690–1776* (Philadelphia, 1950).
Ward, I., 'George Berkeley: Precursor of Keynes or Moral Economist on Underdevelopment?', *Journal of Political Economy* (1959), vol. 67, pp. 31–40.

C. George Caffentzis

BERNARD, Thomas (1750–1818)

Bernard was born on 27 April 1750 in Lincoln, and died at Leamington Spa on 1 July 1818. He was the third son of Sir Francis Bernard, the penultimate royal governor of Massachusetts. Educated at Harvard College in Massachusetts (AB 1767, AM 1770), he studied under Professor John Winthrop, astronomer and member of the Royal Society, gaining from his mentor a keen interest in the practical applications of science. In 1770, shortly after colonial unrest led to the recall of Governor Bernard, he followed in his father's footsteps by reading law at the Middle Temple. Ten years later he was called to the bar, after which he practised conveyancing for over twenty years, holding simultaneously two War Office posts, Commissary-General of Musters and Agent and Solicitor of Invalids. Although essentially retired from the law after 1795, he continued to hold the Invalid Office post until 1806 when it passed to his nephew, Francis Bernard-Morland. Although the Bishop of Durham, SHUTE BARRINGTON made him diocesan chancellor in 1801, he was effectively a full-time philanthropist from 1795 until his death in 1818. He inherited the baronetcy from his elder brother, Sir John Bernard, in 1810.

In 1782 Bernard married Margaret Adair, a prominent London merchant's daughter. The couple alternated their residence between a London townhouse in Great Russell Street and a country estate at Iver in Buckinghamshire. Inspired by the charitable example of his parents, siblings and wife, Bernard increasingly devoted less time to the law and more to philanthropic pursuits, most notably the London Foundling Hospital where he became a governor in 1785. From 1795 to 1806 he served as treasurer and director of daily operations for the financially strapped orphanage. By developing about nine acres of the charity's estate, he raised rental revenues that sustained the hospital for the remainder of its existence. He also cut costs, introducing the latest heating and cooking technology of Count Rumford. The treasurer greatly publicized Rumford's plans and was instrumental to their use by workhouses throughout Britain, including Iver, where Bernard served as magistrate. During the dearth of 1795–6, he and his wife also set up a Rumford-style soup kitchen that distributed soup as emergency relief for the rural poor. These initial experiences reinforced Bernard's confidence in the practical applications of science and inspired his collaboration with Rumford on the formation of the Royal Institution of Great Britain (1799). The Institution housed a museum of working models of useful mechanical inventions such as Rumford's pressure cooker, but it also maintained lecture halls and labs where, Sir Humphry Davy, Michael Faraday and other scientists conducted experiments and presented lectures to the public.

In 1796 Bernard founded the Society for Bettering the Condition and Increasing the Comforts of the Poor (SBCP) with William Wilberforce, E.J. Eliot and the Bishop of Durham, Shute BARRINGTON. The SBCP acted as a clearing house for charitable schemes by publishing brief accounts in a periodical titled *The Reports* (1796–1817). As chief author and editor, Bernard outlined the Society's philosophy in introductory essays for each volume. He proposed that empirical methods be used to gain a better understanding, even a 'science' of poverty and poor relief. *The Reports* contained practical information regarding friendly societies, soup kitchens, education, workhouses, savings banks, and cottage gardens and land allotments. Typically, schemes offered advice or relief from environmental conditions, or presented positive incentives such as education, but almost always adhered to Frederick EDEN's dictum that 'the best relief that the poor can receive *must come from themselves*'.

Convinced also that a distinct sense of home was essential to promoting self help, Bernard eschewed workhouses, even the new and improved national institutions proposed by BENTHAM. In *Information for Overseers* (1799), he argued that workhouses were impersonal and failed to discriminate between dependent pauper and independent labouring poor. Treating the needy indiscriminately, as the parochial relief of the poor laws generally did, would, he feared, injure the pride and dampen the will to work of those able to do so, resulting ultimately in increased 'pauperization' and dependence. Instead of workhouses, he promoted outdoor relief administered by local officials who, through in-home visitation and other investigative means, were capable of tailoring relief so that the independence of the labouring poor was preserved.

Through the SBCP Bernard pursued many additional projects, especially in the realm of public health. He re-published Dr Haygarth's advice for preventing contagious fevers and wrote extensively about the success of a fever hospital in Manchester. He used the Manchester hospital as a model for the London Fever Institution that he helped establish in 1801. That same year he and Dr Thomas Denman founded the Cancer Institution. In 1803 he collaborated with Dr Edward Jenner in promoting small pox vaccination among the poor. Although generally an advocate of private voluntary organizations, he frequently turned to the paternal hand of the state in matters of public health. In 1804 he won a grant of £3000 from parliament for the London Fever Hospital and was instrumental in getting additional parliamentary backing for Jenner's work. He also turned to the state to provide protection for child labourers in factories and in hazardous occupations such as chimney sweeps. He and the SBCP firmly endorsed, and helped frame, the limitations on work hours and the improved treatment of children in cotton mills afforded by Sir Robert Peel's Factory Act of 1802.

In 1805 Bernard turned his attention to the creation of the British Institution for Promoting the Fine Arts in the United Kingdom. The British Institution served as a school where domestic artists could study the history paintings of Old Masters in its British Gallery, a privately supported predecessor to the publicly funded British National Gallery that opened in 1824. In *An Account of the British Institution* (1805), Bernard argued patriotically that this institution would develop more skilled artists who could produce impassioned works capturing British glories, but he also maintained that Britain's commercial superiority depended upon 'that degree of taste and elegance of design, which are to be exclusively derived from the cultivation of the Fine Arts' (1805: 3).

Throughout *The Reports* Bernard confidently endorsed the general education of the poor. and in 1808 joined his SBCP co-founder, the Bishop of Durham, in founding a collegiate school at Bishop Auckland for training new teachers. In *The New School* (1809) and *The Barrington School* (1812), he outlined advantages of the teacher training system of an Anglican cleric, Dr Andrew Bell. At the same time a Quaker educator, Joseph Lancaster, was touting his own similar teaching system. Competition between these educational reformers digressed into a religious rift among many supporters of general education. Although Anglican and supporter of Bell, Bernard argued in *Of the Education of the Poor* (1809) that 'to deal out education to the poor only on the terms of religious conformity, is a species of persecution' (1809: 53n). Though sanguine that moral instruction was essential to vocational and other forms of training, he remained aloof from the sectarian fray.

During the trade depression of 1812–13 Bernard backed two new emergency food charities, the Association for the relief of the Manufacturing Poor (AMLP), and the Fish Association for the Benefit of the Community. Both revived a practice, the distribution of salted fish to the poor, that the SBCP used in previous period of dearth, especially 1800–01. In 1814 an excise officer informed the AMLP that they would have to adhere to the statute (41 Geo.III c.89) that limited how much duty-free salt could be used to transport fish for domestic consumption. Seeing this as state interference of the worst sort, Bernard embarked on a campaign to repeal all of the salt duties. In a series of pamphlets, a public letter and two postscripts to Nicholas VANSITTART, Chancellor of Exchequer, Bernard argued that the taxes bore unequally on the poor and inhibited the AMLP's attempts to relieve the poor. In *Case of the Salt Duties* (1818), he cited Adam SMITH's taxation theories from the *Wealth of Nations* and Montesquieu's *Spirit of the Laws* to argue that the salt taxes were too complex to be generally understood, were wrongly levied on a basic necessity and as such weighed disproportionately on the poor. He also made an economic argument for repeal, stating that because salt had so many uses in manufacturing, fisheries and in agriculture its taxation hindered Britain's economic recovery from trade depression. If the duties were repealed, then fisheries would expand, more land would be brought under cultivation, and manufacture would also grow, bringing new employment opportunities. Repeal, he stated in *On the Supply and Employment of Subsistence for the Labouring Classes* (1817), 'would instantaneously supply new and beneficial objects of industry and speculation to all the members of the community.' (1817: 23–4). Later that year Bernard's work bore fruit with a partial repeal for the use of rock salt in agriculture (57 Geo. III c 49). Although Bernard died in July 1818, the repeal campaign continued. Indeed, John Calcraft and other MPs used some of Bernard's arguments and the evidence he collected to achieve final repeal of all salt duties in 1825 (5 Geo. IV c.65).

Although not an original economic theorist, Bernard was unmatched as a publicist. His numerous publications popularized pioneering plans for a system of general education, public health measures and government regulation of child labour. At the same time his campaign against the salt duties marked him as a disciple of Adam Smith and an early proponent of free trade. His main importance, however, rested with his philanthropic work, where he helped establish the empirical study of social problems, an emphasis on self-help charity and the preservation of the basic family as 'part of the stock-in-trade of philanthropy' (Prochaska 1988: 32). Untold philanthropists and social reformers mined the many account of the SBCP's *The Reports*, including Robert OWEN and George Jacob HOLYOAKE, leader of the co-operative movement of the late nineteenth century. Holyoake cited Bernard as the first 'to use the term 'science' in connection with social arrangements.' Lord Shaftesbury took up many of Bernard's causes, especially that of climbing boys and factory workers. Bernard's influence may also be seen in the Charity Organization Society's (1869) promotion of 'scientific charity' seventy years after the SBCP pioneered the concept. He was 'an indefatigable philanthropist' and his SBCP was 'one of the most innovative institutions of its day, or any other' (Poynter 1969: 91; Prochaska 1988: 31).

BIBLIOGRAPHY

The Reports of the Society for Bettering the Condition and Increasing the Comforts of the Poor, 7 vols (1797–1817).

An Account of the Foundling Hospital (1799).

Information for Overseers collected from the first volume of the Reports of the Society for Bettering the Condition and Increasing the Comforts of the Poor (1799).

An Account of the British Institution for Promoting the Fine Arts in the United Kingdom (1805).

A Letter to the Honourable and Right Reverend the Lord Bishop of Durham, on the Principle and Detail of the Measures now under the consideration of Parliament, for Promoting and Encouraging Industry, and for the Relief and Regulation of the Poor (1807).

Of the Education of the Poor; being the first part of a digest of the Reports of the Society for Bettering the Condition of the Poor (1809).

The New School: being and attempt to illustrate its principles, detail, and advantages. (1809).

An Account of the Supply of Fish for the Manufacturing Poor, with Observations (1813).

The Barrington School; being an illustration of the principle, practices, and effects of the new system of instruction, in facilitating the religious and moral instruction of the poor (1815).

A Postscript to a letter to the Right Honourable Nicholas Vansittart, in which some particular objections to the repeal of the salt duties are considered (1817).

Case of the Salt Duties with Proofs and Illustrations (1817).

On the Supply of Employment and Subsistence for the Labouring Classes, in fisheries, manufactures, and the cultivation of waste lands, with remarks on the operation of the salt duties, and a proposal for their repeal (1817).

On the Repeal of the Salt Duties, and its effect on relieving the present distress of the poor, being a second postscript to a letter addressed to the Right Honourable Nicholas Vansittart (1817).

Further Reading

Andrew, D.T., *Philanthropy and Police: London Charity in the Eighteenth Century* (Princeton, 1989).

Baker, J., *Life of Sir Thomas Bernard, Baronet* (1819).

Dibdin, T.F., *Reminiscences of a Literary Life* (1838, pp. 230–4).

Fowler, J.A., '"The Philanthropy of Fish": Sir Thomas Bernard and the Salt Duties', *Consortium on Revolutionary Europe: Selected Papers* (2000, pp. 386–95).

———, 'Adventures of an 'Itinerant Institutor;' The Life and Philanthropy of Thomas Bernard', PhD dissertation, the University of Tennessee (2003).

Gray, B.K., *A History of English Philanthropy from the Dissolution of the Monasteries to the taking of the First Census* (1905).

Owen, D., *English Philanthropy 1660–1960* (Cambridge, Massachusetts, 1964).

Poynter, J.R., *Society and Pauperism English Ideas on Poor Relief, 1795–1834* (1969).

Prochaska, F., *The Voluntary Impulse: Philanthropy in Modern Britain* (1988).

Jonathan Fowler

BEVERIDGE, William Henry (1879–1963)

Beveridge was born in Rangpur, Bengal on 5 March 1879, and died at home in Oxford on 16 March 1963. His parents, Henry Beveridge, a judge in the Indian civil service, and Annette née Ackroyd, were both devoted to India and supported many social and educational causes, and were in favour of home rule for India. Beveridge was sent back to Britain for his education, and after boarding school in Worcestershire and then Charterhouse, went in 1897 to Balliol College, Oxford. Here he excelled at mathematics and classics, taking first-class honours in both. He moved to University College in 1902, graduating with bachelor's degree in civil law in 1903.

Beveridge's father had intended that his son follow him into the legal profession, but Beveridge himself now rebelled, and turned instead to the study of social problems and education for the poor. His interest and science and mathematics had persuaded him, as he later said, that the application of scientific methods to social problems could produce practical solutions. A connection with Samuel Barnett helped secure him the post of sub-warden of Toynbee Hall, and here he met and was influenced by a wide variety of reformers and thinkers on social affairs, most notably Beatrice and Sidney WEBB. Although Beveridge did not agree with the Webbs' views on economics, he found much in them to admire. He worked as an assistant to Beatrice Webb on the Royal Commission on the Poor Laws, to which she submitted a minority report calling for a detailed programme of social security. It was during this period too that he collected much of the material for his later book *Unemployment: A Problem of Industry* (1909).

In 1905 Beveridge embarked on a brief career in journalism, as a leader writer for the *Morning Post*, in whose pages he argued passionately the case for education, welfare provision and social reform. In 1907 he met Winston Churchill, then President of the Board of Trade, and in 1908 accepted the latter's offer to become his personal assistant. Here he worked closely with, among others, Hubert Llewellyn SMITH, and had an important role in drafting legislation such as the Labour Exchanges Act (1909) and the National Insurance Act (1911). He joined the civil service on a permanent basis in 1909, and had reached the rank of assistant secretary by 1913. During the First World War Beveridge, along with Llewellyn Smith, went to Lloyd George's Ministry of Munitions, where he worked until 1916. His authoritarian views, particularly on labour, caused some friction with the trades unions, and Beveridge was not invited to join the new Ministry of Labour, established in 1916, being sent instead to the Ministry of Food. At the close of the war he helped co-ordinate famine relief efforts in central and eastern Europe. He was knighted in 1919 for his services.

Harris (1997) has commented that his war experiences changed Beveridge's views to some extent. Before the war he was a supporter of a strong central administration and of state controls, but by the end of the war he was becoming more sympathetic to *laissez-faire* ideas. If so, this attitude did not extend to his next appointment, as director the London School of Economics. Recommended to this post by Sidney Webb, Beveridge took over at the LSE late in 1919. His years at the school coincided with its period of greatest expansion to date. As he recounted in his autobiography (1953), while he was director, the number of full-time academic staff increased from eight to seventy-six, with another forty-five part-time faculty. The numbers of students increased greatly as well, coming now from all over the world, particularly the Commonwealth. The list of scholars whom Beveridge was able to attract to the LSE is almost endless, but includes such luminaries as Richard TAWNEY, Hugh DALTON, Lionel ROBBINS, Friedrich HAYEK, John HICKS, Nicholas KALDOR, Arthur LEWIS and Ronald

Coase. Four on this list – Hicks, Hayek, Lewis and Coase – later received the Nobel Prize in Economic Sciences. However, the Beveridge years at the LSE were not entirely harmonious. He clashed frequently with the staff, and his autocratic manner eventually created an unusual left-right opposition group led by, among others, Robbins and Harold Laski. Harris (1997) comments that there was general relief among the faculty with Beveridge left to become master of University College, Oxford in 1937.

In 1940, Beveridge was asked by Ernest Bevin to join the Ministry of Labour. Again there were clashes, as Bevin rejected Beveridge's autocratic approach to the control of wartime labour (doubtless recalling, as Harris suggests, the problems that had arisen at the Ministry of Munitions in the previous war). In 1941 Beveridge was effectively pushed out of the mainstream at the ministry and given the task of chairing an inquiry into the provision of social services. He himself saw this as an effective demotion and at first resented his new role. However, he soon found himself warming to his task. The earlier ideals that had led him to Toynbee Hall were rediscovered, and his commitment to the idea of social justice became intense. He even found himself working in harmony with the trades unions, having discovered a common cause. The end result was the 'Beveridge Report', more properly the *Report on Social Insusrance and Allied Services*, which appeared in 1942 and provided a blueprint for expanding the welfare state in Great Britain following the war.

The initial government response to the report was largely negative, but the public overwhelmingly supported the proposals; by early 1943 public pressure had forced the government to backtrack, and Beveridge's proposals were formally accepted for implementation at war's end. He himself spent the next year travelling the country presenting his proposals to largely appreciative audiences. In 1944 he resigned his mastership of University College and was elected as Liberal MP for Berwick-upon-Tweed, fully expecting to have a major role in pushing his reforms through. However, he lost his seat in the postwar election that brought the Labour Party to power, and was instead created Baron Beveridge and elevated to the House of Lords. He served for a time as Liberal leader in the Lords, but never held a major office again, and watched from the sidelines as new welfare state took shape; a shape that was not always to his liking. He published his autobiography in 1953, and then largely retired from public view.

His most famous work, the Beveridge Report, called for a comprehensive approach to and substantial increase of social services in Great Britain. As in most Western nations, these had expanded in haphazard and piecemeal fashion since the last decades of the nineteenth century, and something more systematic was now required. Beveridge used graphic language to describe his goal. He sought a social system that would slay the five 'giants' of Want, Sickness, Squalor, Idleness (through unemployment) and Ignorance. Henceforward, it would be the purpose of government to ensure that every person in Britain had a minimum and decent standard of living. Every person had a right to a standard of living encompassing housing, food, medical care, unemployment insurance and education. Moreover, government would undertake many positive functions to ensure that the economy grew and that income and wealth are fairly distributed. This included heavily progressive income and estate taxation, policies favorable to labour unions, and great expansion of government services, activities and programmes apart from income transfers.

Beveridge's core idea was that all working individuals should pay into a National Insurance Fund that would provide the same benefits to all as a result of unemployment, disability, retirement or death. Additionally, there would be a government safety net for those unable to pay national insurance. Significantly, medical care would be nationalized and free medical treatment would be provided to all. This marked a change in the role of government from the nineteenth century, when government had been inexpensive and small in domestic scope and responsibilities. Now, government was to take the leading role in domestic affairs in creating a better, more prosperous, happier and just society. Following the economic experience of the 1930s, it was believed by most economists that, practically, it was inevitable and necessary for government to take the role it did following the Second World War. This was so not merely, or even mostly, for reasons of social justice. It was necessary because, without significant government intervention and participation in an economy, an economy could not maintain itself and grow at an adequate level. Furthermore, arguments of justice were now paramount. This was the beginning of the 'cradle-to-grave' welfare state, a concept with which Beveridge's name has become widely associated.

Beveridge's major economic work following the Beveridge Report was his 1944 report on unemployment, *Full Employment in a Free Society*. He here broadened his analysis from social insurance to the larger macroeconomic conditions required for full employment, which he interpreted in a largely Keynesian manner. Beveridge was assisted in this work by a number of leading young economists, including Kaldor, Joan ROBINSON and E.F. SCHUMACHER. Earlier, in 1931, he had edited *Tariffs: The Case Examined*, a work by eight of his LSE colleagues including Robbins, Frederic BENHAM and William Hutt, a more traditional work of liberal economics which supported free trade as a means of recovering from the global depression. His other significant works in economics included the massive *Prices and Wages in England from the Twelfth to the Nineteenth Century* (1939) and *Voluntary Action* (1948), written partly in protest at the de-emphasis of the voluntary sector in the post-war welfare reforms.

BIBLIOGRAPHY
Unemployment: A Problem of Industry (1909).
Tariffs: The Case Examined (1931).
Prices and Wages in England from the Twelfth to the Nineteenth Century (1939).
Report on Social Insurance and Allied Services (1942).
Full Employment in a Free Society (1944).
Voluntary Action (1948).
Power and Influence (1953).

Further Reading
Harris, J., *William Beveridge: A Biography*, 2nd edn (Oxford, 1997).
Williams, K. and Williams, J. (eds), *A Beveridge Reader* (1987).

Alan Ebenstein

BICHENO, James Ebenezer (1785–1851)

Ebenezer Bicheno was born in Newbury, Berkshire on 25 January 1785, the eldest of five children, and died in Hobart, Tasmania on 25 February 1851. His father, James Bicheno, was a Baptist minister and schoolmaster and also the author of books on Biblical prophecy. Bicheno married Elizabeth Lloyd from Newbury in 1821, but she died in childbirth a year later. He was called to the bar in 1822, and was elected a Fellow of the Royal Society in 1827.

In 1819 Bicheno wrote a book entitled *Observations on the Philosophy of Criminal Jurisprudence*, in which he argued against transportation. In the 1820s he also questioned the administration of the Poor Laws. He also wrote on botany, and several of his botanical articles appeared in the *Transactions of the Linnaean Society*. He was elected secretary of the Linnaean Society in 1825, remaining so until 1832 when he moved to South Wales to live in Tymaen, Pyle, near Bridgend.

In the late 1820s Bicheno toured Ireland with a friend, and a year after his return his book *Ireland and Its Economy* (1830) was published. In this work, Bicheno emphasized the importance of the potato in the Irish diet 'because when it does not thrive fever spreads'. He thought the poor law would 'prevent the poor from being kind to one another', because 'the rich, neither Catholic nor Protestant, do much to help, the poor help themselves'. Absentee landlordism meant that 'an estate has been regarded in Ireland as a money interest alone'.

While living in London Bicheno had invested heavily in the two ventures in South Wales, the ironworks in Maesteg and the tramway to Porthcawl. After arrival in Bridgend he also participated in the management of both. He became a justice of the peace, and in 1836 the Marquis of Lansdowne invited him to join Archbishop WHATELY's commission to investigate the effect of introducing the Poor Laws into Ireland. Bicheno accepted, and later wrote a detailed minority report questioning the value of the commission's conclusions. In his view, real improvement had to spring from within Ireland itself, from its own inhabitants and its own institutions.

When Bridgend's workhouse was built in 1837, Bicheno was chairman of the Board of Guardians, and he remained active in this capacity until he left for Van Diemen's Land in 1842, to become its colonial secretary at a salary of £1,200 a year. Before leaving, he was a member of the committee that established the Glamorganshire Constabulary and was chairman of another committee that assessed the county's rateable values.

Bicheno arrived in Hobart, with five servants, on the ship *John Renwick* in April 1843. As well as his official duties, he became vice-president of the Mechanics' Institute and, with Dr Story, a doctor from Edinburgh, established the Royal Society there. In 1851 his lecture on 'The Potato Disease in Connection with Distress in Ireland' appeared in its journal. Bicheno was fond of art and music, and arranged the colony's first exhibition of paintings. He continued to be interested in botany, and in his will donated his herbarium to Swansea museum in Wales, while his 2,500 books were left to the Legislative Council in Hobart to start Tasmania's first public library in his house. His estate was valued at £1,600. The seaside town of Bicheno is named after him, and there is a memorial in St David's Park, Hobart.

BIBLIOGRAPHY
Observations on the Philosophy of Criminal Jurisprudence (1819).
Ireland and its Economy (1830).

Further Reading
Thomas, J.H., 'James Ebenezer Bicheno', *The Green Dragon: A Magazine of the Irish in Wales* (1999), vol. 9, pp. 13–18.

J.H. Thomas

BICKERDIKE, Charles Frederick
(1876–1961)

Bickerdike was born on 15 May 1876 in India, and died on 3 February 1961 in Wallington, Surrey. One of seven children, he was the second son of Robert E. Bickerdike, an East India merchant, and Mary C. Bickerdike, of Scottish birth. Bickerdike's early education was at the Whitgift School in Croydon, where he was head of school. In 1895 he entered Merton College at Oxford, where he was a postmaster, studying mathematics and modern history (BA 1899). Bickerdike won the Cobden Prize in 1902 for an essay on land value taxation, an interest of F.Y. EDGEWORTH; he published numerous book reviews and articles during Edgeworth's editorship of the *Economic Journal*. In 1906 Bickerdike submitted a DSc thesis on 'The Theory of Tariffs' to the London

School of Economics, with Edwin CANNAN and Edgeworth as examiners, but the degree was not awarded. In 1910 he was appointed lecturer of economics and commerce at the University of Manchester, under Sydney CHAPMAN, but left about 1912 to take the position of registrar of the Office of Empire, a sub-department of the Board of Trade. Thereafter he remained in the civil service, receiving the OBE in 1937.

Bickerdike's writings employ economic, often mathematical, reasoning to assess contemporary concerns. He is best known for his elasticity approach to optimal tariffs and exchange rates, which was published in 'The Theory of Incipient Taxes' (1906) and restated in 'The Instability of Foreign Exchange' (1920) and 'Internal and External Purchasing Power of Paper Currencies' (1922). He also developed and applied an early monetary growth model to aggregate saving in 'Individual and Social Interests in Relation to Saving' (1924) and 'Saving and the Monetary System' (1925), stressing the importance of savings in creating economic strength and stability. The remainder of his work tends to be occasional, relating to economic events, journal literature or employment.

Bickerdike was effectively a policy analyst at a time when the requisite tools were just being formed. The policies he analysed were those of contemporary life and the tools he used drew from Alfred MARSHALL, embraced the broadened social perspective characteristic of A.C. PIGOU, embodied the mathematical methods of Edgeworth and pointed toward the aggregative analysis of J.M. KEYNES. As such, his work provides a useful glimpse of the workings of internal and external influences in the development of economic thought.

BIBLIOGRAPHY
'Taxation of Site Values', *Economic Journal* (1902), vol. 12, pp. 472–84.
'The Theory of Incipient Taxes', *Economic Journal* (1906), vol. 16, pp. 529–35.
Review of *Protective and Preferential Import Duties* by A. C. Pigou, *Economic Journal* (1907), vol.17, pp. 98–102.
'Relation of the General Supply Curve to a "Particular Expenses" Curve', *Economic Journal* (1907), vol. 17, pp. 583–85.
'Monopoly and Differential Prices', *Economic Journal* (1911), vol. 21, pp. 139–43.
'International Comparisons of Labour Conditions', *Transactions of the Manchester Statistical Society* (1911–12), pp. 61–83.
'The Principle of Land Value Taxation', *Economic Journal* (1912), vol. 22, pp. 1–15.
'A Non-Monetary Cause of Fluctuations in Employment', *Economic Journal* (1914), vol. 24, pp. 357–70.
'On Paying for War by Loans', *Economic Journal* (1915), vol. 25, pp. 433–42.
'Economics and the New Agricultural Policy', *Economic Journal* (1917), vol. 27, pp. 471–85.
'The Instability of Foreign Exchange', *Economic Journal* (1920), vol. 30, pp. 118–22.
'Internal and External Purchasing Power of Paper Currencies', *Economic Journal* (1922), vol. 32, pp. 28–38.
'Individual and Social Interests in Relation to Saving', *Economic Journal* (1924), vol. 34, pp. 408–22.
'Saving and the Monetary System', *Economic Journal* (1925), vol. 35, pp. 366–78.
'Essay by C.F. Bickerdike', *Pollak Prize Essays*, Newton, Massachusetts, 1927, pp. 72–88.

Further Reading
Chipman, J.S., 'Bickerdike's Theory of Incipient and Optimal Tariffs', *History of Political Economy* (1993), vol. 25, no. 3, pp. 461–92.
Larson, B., 'Bickerdike's Life and Work', *History of Political Economy* (1987), vol. 19, no. 1, pp. 1–21.

Tarascio, V.J., 'Bickerdike's Monetary Growth Theory', *History of Political Economy* (1980), vol. 12, no. 2, pp. 161–73.

Tower, E., 'Separability: The One Principal and Serious Defect of Bickerdike's and Edgeworth's Elasticity Approach to Balance-of-Payment Problems?', *History of Political Economy* (1993), vol. 25, no. 3, pp. 493–7.

Bruce Larson

BLACK, Duncan (1908–91)

Duncan Black was born on 23 May 1908 in Motherwell, near Glasgow, and died 14 January 1991 at Paignton, Devon. His father was a boilermaker and his mother, Margaret Brown Muir, was a milliner. Black was educated at Dalziel High School and the University of Glasgow. He studied mathematics and physics for his first degree, graduating with second-class honours in 1929. His first intention was to enter the civil service, but a scholarship enabled him to take a postgraduate course at Glasgow in political economy and political philosophy. In this, Black was much influenced by the professor of political economy, W.R. Scott, whose interests lay in the relationships between philosophy and economics, and by A.K. White, a lecturer in politics who was concerned with the possibility of constructing a pure science of that subject.

These influences evidently fired Black's enthusiasm in a way which the mathematics and physics of his first degree had failed to do. In 1932 he was awarded the MA in economics and politics with first-class honours and later in that year was appointed, not to a civil service post but to an assistant lectureship at the School of Economics and Commerce in Dundee. In 1934 he became a lecturer in economics at the University College of North Wales, Bangor. Like many British academic economists, Black went to a temporary civil service post during the Second World War. In 1945 he moved to a senior lectureship in economics at Queen's University, Belfast; but in 1946 an invitation to take a similar post in social economics attracted him back to the University of Glasgow where he remained until 1952. Black was then appointed professor of economics at the University College of North Wales, a post he held until his retirement in 1968.

Already in 1934, when he left Dundee for his first appointment at Bangor, Black had started work on the idea of using the concepts of economics, notably certain aspects of the theory of choice, in the development of a theory of politics. But at that time he thought that he had not progressed sufficiently to publish any of his results. He then decided to return to work which he had done at Glasgow under Scott on the incidence of income taxes and develop it further. For this he was awarded a PhD by Glasgow University in 1937, and the work appeared in book form in September 1939. War had already broken out, and as it went on Black's duties in the war-time civil service left him no opportunity for writing up his ideas about a theory of politics. Yet already in Belfast in 1945–6 he was developing his 'theory of committee decisions', drafting a paper which he gave to the Economics Section of the British Association for the Advancement of Science at its first post-war meeting in Dundee.

The idea of a quasi-mathematical theory of committee decisions was to most economists at that time an interesting curiosity at best. In a brief article in the *Economic Journal* (1950), Black sought to explain how 'in getting a theory of the committee...we at the same time get a sufficient means to construct a Theory of Politics'. Then 'a theory of the committee that is sufficiently comprehensive' could be used to explain elections to Parliament, the workings of Parliament itself and cabinet government. At the highest level, 'international agreements are reached by committees, which require unanimity in their decisions'.

These ideas were further developed by Black in his book *The Theory of Committees and Elections* (1958) but still failed to find widespread acceptance or interest in Britain. In the United States the reception of Black's ideas was different. From the early 1960s, a school of 'public choice theory' developed and grew in importance. As one of its leading members has written, 'Black can be called the father of modern Public Choice, which is in essence the use of economic tools to deal with the traditional problems of political science' (Tullock 1987).

After his retirement, Black held a series of visiting fellowships and professorships at the University of Chicago, Virginia Polytechnic and Michigan State University. In all these he found great interest in and appreciation for his ideas among faculty and graduate students alike. After 1977, when his wife, Almut, died, he made no further visits abroad, but moved his residence from Cambridge, where he had settled after retiring from Bangor, to Paignton in Devon, where he died at the age of eighty-two.

BIBLIOGRAPHY
The Incidence of Income Taxes (1939).
'The Unity of Political and Economic Science', *Economic Journal* (1950), vol. 60, pp. 506–14.
(with R.A. Newing), *Committee Decisions with Complementary Valuation* (1952).
The Theory of Committees and Elections (1958).

Further Reading
Coase, R.H., 'Duncan Black, 1908–1991', *Proceedings of the British Academy* (1992), vol. 82, pp. 353–65.
Grofman, B., 'Black, Duncan', *The New Palgrave: A Dictionary of Economics* (Basingstoke, 1987).

Tullock, G., *Towards a Science of Politics: Essays in Honor of Duncan Black* (Blacksburg, Virginia, 1981).
——, 'Public Choice', *The New Palgrave: A Dictionary of Economics* (Basingstoke, 1987).

R.D. Collison Black

BLACK, William (d. 1749)

Black's identity is uncertain, but he may be the William Black who signed a petition in support of union with England in 1706 and was clerk to the regality of Dunfermline from c.1712 until at least 1745. Around the time of the union Black published two pamphlets, *Some Considerations in Relation to Trade* (1706) and *Some Overtures and Cautions in Relation to Trade and Taxes* (1707). Both are broadly in favour of union, but both urge that the commissioners negotiating the union protect Scottish trade from dominance by its larger neighbour.

In the first pamphlet, the content of which is largely repeated in the second, Black begins by enumerating the advantages Scotland has in trade, and urges greater government support for Scottish trade. While supporting union with England in political terms, he is concerned that the terms of union as presently proposed will lead to the loss of Scottish control over trade policy. He believes that trade policy should be merged where the two nations have interests in common, but in cases that concern Scotland in particular, such as the Scottish fishing industry and livestock, the country should have a policy independent from that of London. He also calls for some local control over taxation of commodities like salt, worrying that England will impose a salt tax in Scotland which will put Scottish exporters of salt fish and beef at a disadvantage. He also believes that proposed

English restrictions on the shipping industry will hinder Scottish shipbuilders and ship owners.

Another concern is that England already dominates overseas trade, and following union that dominance will only increase. In particular he would like to see some sort of protection for the Indian and African Company, which had suffered heavy losses in the Darien adventure while the English overseas trading companies had continued to thrive. In the short term at least, the former could not hope to compete with its English rivals, and without protection must surely sink, to the detriment of Scottish interests.

Although he supported union, Black was not always in agreement with DEFOE and challenged some of the presumed benefits that the latter urged would flow from union. In the preface to his *Fifth Essay*, Defoe retaliated and attacked Black's calculations and conclusions.

BIBLIOGRAPHY
Some Considerations in Relation to Trade (Edinburgh, 1706).
The Privileges of the Royal Burrows (Edinburgh, 1707).
Some Overtures and Cautions in Relation to Trade and Taxes, Humbly Offered to Parliament (Edinburgh, 1707).

Further Reading
Defoe, D., *The Preface to the Fifth Essay, at Removing National Prejudices, &c. considered, in a Letter to the Author of the Consideration upon Trade* (1706).

Thomas Worth

BLAKE, Francis (1738–1818)

Blake was born sometime in the first six months of 1738, most probably at Twizel in Northumberland, the son of Sir Francis Blake. He died at Twizel on 2 June 1818. Blake graduated with the degree of LL.B. from Trinity Hall, Cambridge in 1763, and succeeded to his father's baronetcy in 1780. He wrote a number of tracts and pamphlets on political and financial issues, which were published together in the volume *Political Tracts* in 1788. Much of Blake's life after this time, however, revolved around Twizel, where his father had begun converting a medieval peel tower into a large mansion. Blake continued this work, which was vast and grandiose even by the standards of the time and which consumed all of his resources and energy. The costs of the project meant that Blake was continually in debt, at one point reportedly being forced to seek sanctuary in Holyrood Abbey to escape arrest for debt. In 1812 the architect George Wyatt was brought in to manage the project and succeeded in getting costs under control, but the house was still unfinished at the time of Blake's death. His son, also Francis, was MP for Berwick for a number of years and took an active part in the debate over the repeal of the Corn Laws.

Blake had an interest in taxation and the national debt, and produced several proposals for reducing or paying off the debt. The most important and innovative of these ideas are to be found in *A Proposal for the Liquidation of the National Debt* (1783). Here he argues for paying off the national debt by transferring the debt from the state to individuals. His proposal is that all property owners would assume a portion of the debt in proportion to their income. Using admittedly notional figures, Blake estimates the national debt at £240 million, and the income of the inhabitants of the country at £60 million; the ratio of debt to income is thus four to one. In Blake's scheme, any person owning lands with an income of £100 per annum would assume £400 of debt, and so on. The debtholders would not be required to raise the money in full, merely to pay interest on it at a rate of four per cent, equivalent to a tax of about three shillings in the pound.

Blake had originally believed that this measure would eradicate the need for all taxes, with the interest paid by debtholders sufficing to cover all national expenditure. He indicates, however, that he revised his thinking upon seeing new calculations of government expenditure, and agrees that some smaller taxes such as the salt tax and tax on stamps could be retained. His goal remains, however, to reduce taxation to its lowest possible level. He blames high taxation on a wide variety of evils, ranging from emigration (where he argues that thousands of people have fled Britain for states with lower levels of taxation) to unemployment. In the case of the latter, he believes that lower taxation would result in more money being invested in enterprise, thus creating employment and trade.

Blake's most thoughtful work, *On the Principles Which Regulate the Course of Exchange* (1811), is now lost, but the contents can be partly reconstructed from Sir Edward Thornton's reply, also published in 1811. According to Thornton, Blake divided exchange into three types: real, nominal and computed. (Thornton takes this to be too restrictive, believing that exchange can take many forms, and argues for a single definition, the conversion of the currency of one country into that of another country.) Blake was not entirely opposed to paper money, but believed it to be risky and subject to fluctuations in value and runs on banks, whereas he saw gold as more reliable. He argued that there was too much paper money in circulation, and this represented a risk to the economy. Again according to Thornton, Blake appeared to support the idea of an intrinsic value for gold and silver coin, suggesting that the only way the value of a currency could be altered was to alter the physical state of the coins, or to restrict or increase the quantity of coinage in circulation.

BIBLIOGRAPHY
A Proposal for the Liquidation of the National Debt (Berwick, 1783; repr. with *An Explanation of the Proposal* in *Political Tracts*, Berwick, 1788; 2nd edn, London, 1795).
The Efficiency of a Sinking Fund of One Million per annum Considered (1786).
The Propriety of an Actual Payment of the National Debt Considered (1786).
On the Principles Which Regulate the Course of Exchange, and on the Present Depreciated State of the Currency (1811?).

Further Reading
Edward Thornton, *Observations on the Report of Committee of the House of Commons, Appointed to Inquire into the High Price of Gold Bullion...together with some remarks on the work of Francis Blake, Esq.* (1811).

Ann Kimber

BLAKE, William (c.1774–1852)

Blake was born probably in 1774 and died in London some time in 1852. Little is known about his life, save that he was a fellow of the Royal Society and in 1815–16 served as president of the Geological Society. In 1831 he was elected to the Political Economy Club. He remains known largely thanks to his two books on the currency.

Blake's first book, *Observations on the Principles Which Regulate the Course of Exchange; and on the Present Depreciated State of the Currency* (1810), was highly influential among the theorists of the time, and caused its author to be regarded as one of the leading authorities in matters of foreign exchange. The tract revolves around the point that deviations of the rate of exchange from par are determined by two sets of factors, independent of each other. The first, which Blake called the real exchange, depends upon the payments a country has to make and receive in connection with its annual imports and exports, and its foreign expenditure (expenses for foreign establishments and expeditions, subsidies to foreign powers and remittances to absentee proprietors). The second, labelled nominal exchange, is unconnected with the state of the country's debts and credits, and arises from an alteration of the currency (changes in the metal's standard of purity, degradation of the weight below the mint standard, and depreciation of the currency from relative over-issue). According to Blake, nominal deviation from par exerts no influence on imports or exports of ordinary produce, given that price and exchange rate variations compensate each other, leaving the terms of trade unaffected. For analogous reasons, no transit of bullion will occur. In the words of FULLARTON, who gave great emphasis to this distinction in his book *On the Regulation of Currencies*, 'the only result would be, that the term "sovereign" would signify a different coin from that which it had expressed heretofore. *Things* would remain the same: the only variance would be in the application of a *name*' (Fullarton 1845: 115). The distinction between real and nominal variations is based on the indispensable premise that the price of a bill of exchange also moves for reasons other than the law of supply and demand, otherwise the depreciation may only affect exchange rate through its action on net exports, thus rendering the distinction meaningless (De Vivo 1987: 251). In this respect, Blake's argument seems to revolve around the practical consideration that an oscillation of the currency in relation to goods and gold suddenly spurs a correspondent alteration of the amount of it needed to purchase the same sum of foreign money as before (1810: 45–8).

Although Blake denied the influence of depreciation on the export of bullion, he maintained the view that a convertible paper currency can never be permanently overissued. When the market price of bullion exceeds the mint price, 'the paper of the Bank would be returned to be exchanged for coin, which would be immediately melted, and sold in the form of bullion, for notes, at the advanced nominal price. These, in their turn, would be sent to the Bank to be in the same manner exchanged for coin, which would be melted and sold as soon as procured' (1810: 66). The drain upon the Bank of England would compel its directors to diminish the issue of notes, bringing the currency back to its natural level. This process, on which also Fullarton put great emphasis (1845: 116–17), has a truly domestic nature and does not necessarily imply an excess of imports over exports and a consequent efflux of bullion abroad, postulated by the specie flow mechanism.

Allowing that the prices of gold and of all commodities were raised by an over-issue of paper currency, and offering an explanation of the self-corrective power of a convertible paper that, though based on the denial of the specie-flow argument, respected the substance of the bullionist doctrine, Blake's *Observations* of 1810 were well received by RICARDO, who referred to it as 'one of the few good pamphlets which were published on the bullion question in that year' (Ricardo 1951–73, vol. IV: 353). Ricardo's favour was probably also due to Blake's contention that, in practice, the variations in the real exchange rate correct themselves without requiring a transit of bullion: 'the natural limit to the amount of the real Exchange is the expense of the transit of Bullion; and long before it has arrived at that point, the export of ordinary produce will be forced, and its import restrained; so that the real exchange can scarcely begin to deviate from par without calling into action a principle that will correct its deviation' (Blake: 1810: 23). Indeed, Blake's position well fitted Ricardo's firm belief that the adjustment of temporary disturbances (for example, those resulting from crop failures) would not activate the specie flow mechanism. However, while extending the analysis of the ability of exchange rate variations within the gold points of restoring the par to the case of foreign expenditures abroad, Blake introduced a significant departure from bullionist orthodoxy:

a possible case may, nevertheless, be supposed, where the government may, from political causes be induced to continue a scale of warfare, demanding a large foreign expenditure that can be supplied by a proportional excess of exports over imports; and, consequently, if the quantity of Bullion in the country were extremely limited, the *real* Exchange might, notwithstanding the usual causes that check and prevent its fluctuations, deviate so much from par, and create so a great drain of Bullion, as to raise its market price above its mint price.

(1810: 26)

Here we find a restatement of the specie flow adjustment to unilateral transfers formulated by THORNTON, and thus the anti-bullionist idea that the specie flow adjustment could be activated in circumstances other from the domestic over-issue of paper (Mason 1956: 498).

The analysis of unilateral payments assumed a prominent role in Blake's *Observations on the Effects Produced by the Expenditure of Government During the Restriction of Cash Payments* (1823). In the first part of this work, the author investigates the process through which foreign loans generate an equivalent flow of exports under inconvertible paper currency. The paper being inconvertible into specie:

some of the essential correctives which tend to restore the exchange are removed: for, first, the price of bullion will then rise exactly to the point where it ceases to be profitable to export it; and consequently the remedy from the export of bullion can no longer be applied. And, secondly, the prices of all other commodities will *not fall*. Now it is the fall of price, arising from the forced contraction, that enables the exporting merchant to gain augmented profits upon all his exports...For the same reason he could not *import* so advantageously as before...The exchanges, therefore, could not, after the restriction [of cash payments], right themselves so rapidly. There would then be left but one correcting remedy; viz. the extra profit arising from the premium of the exchange on all exports, and the corresponding diminution of profit upon all import.

(1823: 31)

In other words, since during the restriction there is no mint price of gold and thus no gold points, it is the unlimited movement of the exchange rate that modifies the terms of trade allowing a trade surplus that compensates the transfer.

The argument that the premium on gold was not explained exclusively by the domestic money supply was hardly reconcilable with the bullionist position; it was in fact by denying that foreign disbursements and loans caused the premium that was based the estimation of the depreciation of an over-issued inconvertible currency by the discrepancy between the market price of gold and its former mint price. Indeed, Ricardo did not fail to recognize that Blake had expounded the anti-bullionist contents of his former work, expressing his disagreement in an unfinished review of *Observations*: 'we must confess we finished the perusal of his tract with regret and disappointment. Mr Blake appears to us to agree with those whose theory he attacks without being himself aware of it, and to confirm by his authority every principle which he has with so much pains attempted to overturn' (Ricardo 1951–73, vol. IV: 353).

Ricardo's disappointment was motivated not only by Blake's adherence to the view that the difference between gold and paper was due to a rise in gold rather than a fall in paper, but also by Blake's unconventional conception of the relationship between savings and investments. While dealing with the general increase of prices of that day, Blake argues that the increase of prices 'depended upon causes connected with the war, and the increased internal expenditure of government, and would have occurred although the currency had remained at its natural level' (1823: 39). Further, he denied, in a language familiar to a Keynesian reader, the view that government cannot be the source of additional demand since it displaces the capitalist's demand for productive power. According to Blake, such a conclusion derives from the erroneous suppositions 'that the whole capital of the country is fully occupied; and, secondly, that there is an immediate employment for successive accumulation of capital as it accrues from saving'. Moving from the premise that 'there are at all times some portions of capital devoted to undertakings that yield very slow returns and slender profits...some portions lying wholly dormant in the form of goods, for which there is no sufficient demand' and 'that when capital accumulates rapidly from savings, it is not always practicable to find new modes of employing it', Blake reached the unorthodox conclusion that 'if these dormant portions and savings could be transferred into the hands of government in exchange for its annuities, they would become source of new demand, without encroaching upon existing capital' (1823: 54–5).

In several remarks written on his copy of *Observations* that refer to this issue, Ricardo criticized Blake's argument on the grounds that a glut could only arise from miscalculation and never be general. For example, commenting on Blake's assertion that 'if every one consumes what he has a right to consume, there must be of necessity a market. Whoever saves from his revenue, foregoes this right, and his share remains undisposed of' (1823: 57), Ricardo wrote: 'I deny this, it is disposed of when it becomes a fund for future production' (Ricardo 1951–73, vol. IV: 343). A review by J.S. MILL of the *Observations* moves along similar lines, inferring from the unquestioned proposition that savings and investments necessarily coincide, that a general glut of commodities is an impossible occurrence.

Blake's works deserve attention for quite a few reasons. His description of the adjustment to unilateral payments during inconvertibility antedated Taussig's treatment of the subject by a century (Mason 1956: 502), while his antibullionist arguments, although plagued by some ambiguities and contradictions, anticipated many themes of the banking school supporters. Blake's analysis of the stimulus that government expenditure exerts on production is among the clearest expositions that questioned the saving-investment identity prior to the Keynesian revolution (Corry 1962: 162–8).

BIBLIOGRAPHY

Observations on the Principles Which Regulate the Course of Exchange; and on the Present Depreciated State of the Currency (1810).

Observations on the Effects Produced by the Expenditure of Government During the Restriction of Cash Payments (1823).

Observations in reply to a Pamphlet by the Rev. Richard Jones, on the Assessment of Tithes to the Poors' Rate (1839).

Further Reading

Corry, B.A., *Money, Saving and Investment in English Economics* (1962).

De Vivo, G., 'William Blake', in J. Eatwell *et al.* (eds), *The New Palgrave: A Dictionary of Economics* (1987).

Fullarton, J., *On the Regulation of Currencies* (1845; repr. New York, 1969).

Mason, W.E., 'The Stereotypes of Classical Transfer Theory', *Journal of Political Economy* (1956), vol. 64, pp. 492–506.

Ricardo, D., *The Works and Correspondence of David Ricardo*, ed. P. Sraffa with the collaboration of M.H. Dobb (Cambridge, 1951–73).

Thornton, H., *An Enquiry into the Nature and Effects of The Credit of Great Britain* (1802).

Viner, Jacob (1937) *Studies in the Theory of International Trade* (New York, 1937; repr. New York, 1965).

Alda Barba

BLANCH, John (c.1670–1756)

Blanch is described variously as a merchant or clothier, and as a gentleman of Gloucestershire. He is probably the John Blanch of Wotton-under-Edge, Gloucestershire, who died in 1756 leaving £300 to the hospital of St Margaret's in Gloucester, on condition that his fellow residents of Wotton raised another £100. His first writings were published in 1694, putting his probable date of birth some time before 1670; his last work, a pamphlet on the cloth industry, appeared in 1731. Blanch wrote two plays, *Swords into Anchors* (1707) and *The Beaux-Merchant* (1714), and several works on the woollen cloth industry and the economy of England.

In his writings, Blanch consciously represented the interests of the country against those of the city. He argued that the trade in luxury goods, which was primarily confined to the city, was harmful to the best interests of the English economy, and he criticized those who encouraged extravagant expenditure. In an addendum to his *The Interests of England Considered* (1694), Blanch attacks Sir Joshua CHILD's *New Discourse on Trade* for putting too much emphasis on London as the main source of national wealth. Wealth is created throughout the country, says Blanch, not just in London. He also attacks Child's views on the East India Company, stating that Child's defence of the Company was motivated primarily by self-interest (Child was a director of the Company).

Blanch also disagreed with Child's assessment of the state of English trade. He believed that England's trade was declining, and in *The Interests of England Considered* and *Abstract on the Grievances of Trade* (1694) he assigned the cause of this decline to the exportation of English wool to manufacturers overseas and the consequent decline of domestic cloth manufacturing. In *Abstract*, he argues that this trend has two unfortunate consequences: first, the decline of manufacturing is leading to unemployment and poverty, and second, imports of cloth manufactured in France and Holland – made from English wool – are leading to an unfavourable balance of trade. In *The Interests of England Considered*, he states the case more forcibly, arguing that since the fourteenth century and the establishment of the Staple, the trade in wool and woollen cloth has been the chief source of national wealth. The neglect of this trade is in turn creating more general economic decline. His solution to the problem is that the export of wool and fleeces should be banned, and that domestic manufacture of cloth should be encouraged. England has, says Blanch, the ability to make the best cloth in Europe; establishing a thriving export business in cloth could create a favourable balance of trade.

In *The Naked Truth* (1696) Blanch again calls for the export of wool to be prohibited, and also attacks the East India Company, whose imports of Indian cloth and luxury goods are also seen as contributing to the national economic decline. These imports, Blanch says, are not balanced by exports to India and can only be paid for with silver. This is impoverishing the country and leading to a shortage of coin, while only the directors of the East India Company are seen to profit. His final work was a pamphlet in support of protectionist legislation, a few years before the passage of the Act of Parliament for the protection of the woollen and silk cloth industries in 1735.

BIBLIOGRAPHY
An Abstract of the Grievances of Trade, which oppress our Poor (1694).
The Interest of England Considered, in an Essay upon Wooll, Our Woollen-Manufactures, and the Improvement of Trade, with some Remarks upon the Conceptions of Sir Joshua Child (1694; 2nd edn, 1707, under the title *The Interests of Great Britain Consider'd...*)
The Naked Truth, in an Essay upon Trade (1696).

Observations on the Bill now depending in the House of Lords, with relation to the Woollen Manufacture (1731).

Morgen Witzel

BLATCHFORD, Robert Peel Glanville
(1851–1943)

Blatchford was born 17 March 1851 at Maidstone, Kent, and died 17 December 1943 at Horsham, Surrey. His parents were peripatetic provincial actors, but his father died when Blatchford was two. His mother insisted on apprenticing both he and his elder brother Montague to 'proper' trades. Blatchford endured six years of a seven-year apprenticeship to a Halifax brushmaker before, at age twenty, tramping to London where he starved some weeks before enlisting in the army. Within eighteen months, he had reached the rank of sergeant, leaving in 1878 to become a timekeeper for a canal construction company at Northwich in Cheshire.

In 1884, Blatchford met the journalist A.M. Thompson, who in the following year persuaded his employer to take Blatchford on for a salary of £4 a week. Within a year, Blatchford was writing leaders for the *Sunday Chronicle* for £1,000 a year. Research for articles on the Irish 'Land War' and on the Manchester slums turned him into a convinced socialist, and in 1891 he left to found a socialist weekly, the *Clarion*. Financially the first years were hard, but in 1894 the editors risked a penny edition of Blatchford's socialist manifesto, *Merry England*. Its massive sales won the paper a following which withstood its author's support for the South African War (1899–1902) and his attack on orthodox religion (from 1903). That support wobbled at his pre-1914 warnings against what he saw as the German threat, and finally collapsed after he expressed his total support for the Great War. With the *Clarion* no longer prospering, Blatchford was reduced to earning well from non-socialist and anti-socialist newspapers.

Blatchford produced for several decades the most readable socialist propaganda in the English language. He attractively sketched his idea of utopia or 'ideal socialism' in *The Sorcery Shop* (1907). This owed much to William MORRIS's eco-socialist *News from Nowhere*. Unlike *Nowhere*, though, there would be no moment of violence during implementation. For Blatchford, such worries were unnecessary: 'Give us a Socialist people, and Socialism will accomplish itself'. Thus his breathtakingly calm but moralistic style accompanied a strategy entirely oriented towards political education and an aim defined as rule by the people, never by loud-mouthed politicians or know-all Fabian experts. This went with what would now be called a 'Whig' version of Britain as uniquely free, and thus open to democratization. Conversely, any 'socialism without democracy' would be 'abominable tyranny'.

Thus both politics and economics were unproblematic. How far this was so can be gleaned from an appealingly tongue-in-cheek warning to British workers, published among the *Clarion Ballads* (1896). Here, 'The Noble Lord De Benture' persuades all peers and their obsequious 'business men' allies to counter a surfeit of 'Socialistic blether' by carting abroad all their 'estates...mines...mills...railways and canals', literally and physically. At this, 'The workers gazed in wonder.../Then sucked their thumbs,/And to their slums/ Disconsolately crept', merely to lament and die. The transparent message was that landlords and capitalists had merely to remove themselves to reduce any economic problem to one of physical organization alone.

Consistent with this confidence was Blatchford's conviction that agriculture was the basis of national wealth. Here, he consciously owed something to the American land reformer Henry George, and thus, unconsciously perhaps, even to the French physiocrats. But this deepened his anxiety that Britain's dependence on imported foodstuffs was aggravating her vulnerability to foreign blockade. At first, most socialists probably viewed this as part of his patriotic heresy. But by 1914, much of the Marxist Social Democratic Federation shared this anxiety along with a broad spectrum of others ranging from tariff reformers to military heroes such as Lord Roberts of Kandahar. On literally physicalist assumptions, autarky remained conceivable, even or particularly in a country with unprecedented investments overseas.

BIBLIOGRAPHY
The Living Wage and the Law of Supply and Demand (1893).
Merry England (1894).
Clarion Ballads (1896).
Dismal England (1899)
The Sorcery Shop: An Impossible Romance (1907).
What is this Socialism? (1908).
Germany and England (1911).
My Eighty Years (1931).

Logie Barrow

BLAXTON, John (*fl. c.*1630–5)

Nothing is known for certain of Blaxton's life, but internal evidence in his works indicates that he was a Church of England clergyman, probably from London. He is best known for *The English Usurer*, a condemnation of usury published in 1634.

The English Usurer is a collection of views on usury by British theologians, all apparently contemporaries of Blaxton. He does not tell us whether these views were deliberately sought for this publication, or were collected from other sources. Blaxton himself takes on the role of editor, arranging the materials by subject matter and contributing a two-page introduction. After providing several definitions of usury and quoting scriptural and canon law authorities on the subject, Blaxton then arranges the material under several headings, including the differences between usury and other forms of commercial activity, the harm done by usury, and a refutation of the primary arguments advanced by those in favour of usury.

Although the great majority of the views expressed are based on either purely religious beliefs that usury is displeasing to God, or on conceptions of natural justice which hold that it is wrong for one person to profit at the expense of another, the work does also contain some ideas relating to economics. Careful distinction is made between lawful forms of lending and usury *per se*, the latter defined as 'lending for gaine without covenant, that is, when the creditor onely intendeth and looketh for gaine by lending and forebearing his money, but doth not indent or covenant with the borrower for gaine' (1634: 4). Lending where the lender shares in the risk, such as sea loans, or where the borrower can share in the gain, such as investments, are acceptable, other forms of lending are not.

The chief objection to usury seems to be related to a conception of money-lending as destructive of value. Usurers are described as perverting 'the end for which money was appointed, which was for commutation, and to be a means to the end; but they make [money] itself the end' (1634: 31). Money, in this view, plays a social function and spreads its benefits around society; but money which is lent for interest becomes static. If money, once lent, is returned directly to the usurer with interest, society as a whole is held to gain less than if the same sum of money had been invested in agriculture or production. The argument, far from internally consistent, does give an idea of the conflicts between moral and social values on the one hand and economics on the other.

Blaxton's only other works were a moderately unpleasant tract against foreigners, arguing that they should not be allowed to live in England and purporting to offer scriptural justification for this view, and a few sermons.

BIBLIOGRAPHY

The English Usurer; or Usury Condemned, by the most learned and famous Divines of the Church of England (1634; repr. Amsterdam, 1974).

Morgen Witzel

BOLTON, Robert (1572–1631)

Bolton was born at Brookhouse near Blackburn, Lancashire in May 1572. He died at Broughton, Northamptonshire, on 17 December 1631. After education at Queen Elizabeth's Grammar School in Blackburn, he went to Oxford in 1592, attending first Lincoln College and then Brasenose. He received his BA in 1596 and MA in 1602, becoming a fellow of Brasenose in the latter year. He lectured at the university on logic and moral philosophy for several years.

Until this point Bolton had shown no signs of strong religious conviction, but around 1607 he was nearly persuaded to become a Roman Catholic. According to his friend and biographer Edmund Blagshawe (1635), Bolton then suffered an attack of conscience and resolved instead to embrace the Church of England more closely. He studied for a degree in divinity, which he received in 1609, and in 1610 became rector at Broughton, where he remained until his death.

An outstanding preacher and writer, Bolton became famous for his piety and wisdom. He focused on the innate goodness of God; unlike some other Puritan evangelists, he argued that God's nature tended towards kindness and the forgiving of sins. True happiness and spiritual comfort could be found in belief in God and obedience to the divine will. Many of his works have a strong element of mysticism.

Yet Bolton could also be practical, as is shown in his single work on usury, published after his death as *A Short and Private Discourse between Mr Bolton and one M.S. concerning Usury* (1637). Blagshawe, who published the work, tells us that it grew out of a conversation between Bolton and one of his congregation who had attempted to defend usury, and that at the time of his death Bolton had been planning to develop this into a larger work on the same subject. The bulk of the work consists of an attack on those who would justify usury. Lending money for gain, says Bolton, is never justified in any circumstance. He demolishes the view that it is acceptable to lend money to the rich but not the poor, arguing that the idea of lending to the rich is inherently contradictory: 'to those who have no need to borrow, we need not lend' (1637: 40).

Bolton rejects the idea that some forms of usury are less harmful than others, and that the Bible and the Church Fathers only intended to prohibit 'biting' usury (that is, usury at rates that are harmful to the borrower's interests). He makes the point that even if the borrower does not suffer from usury, 'yet the Commonwealth, and especially the Communalty pay for it' (1637: 14). His economic argument against usury is as follows. Suppose that a merchant borrows money from a usurer at a moderate rate of interest, say 10 per cent, and the merchant invests this in a business venture that stands to make him a 'reasonable gaine'. But in order both to realize his own gain and pay off the interest on the loan, he will have to earn a larger profit than if he had funded the venture himself. This, says Bolton, leads to a choice between two evils:

If He doe not exceed [this reasonable gain], and that in some proportion, Hee hath lost His labours, and shall feele Himselfe sore bitten. And if the Borrower doe exceed the Usurer's gaine, to maintaine Himself, I demand then who paieth this excessive gaine over and above that reasonable gaine of ten in the Hundred? Who but the Common-Weale? (1637: 15).

In other words, the costs of usury are met by charging higher prices to the people who buy the merchant's goods. This burden is mostly likely to be felt by the poor, who are always most affected by high prices. Similarly, landholders who fall into debt must extract more value to the land in order to pay the interest on the money they borrow.

BIBLIOGRAPHY
A Short and Private Discourse between Mr Bolton and one M.S. concerning Usury (1637).

Further Reading
Blagshawe, E., *The Life and Death of Mr Bolton* (1635).

Morgen Witzel

BONAR, James (1852–1941)

Bonar was born 27 September 1852 in the Free Church manse in Collace, near Perth, and died in Hampstead, London on 18 January 1941. He was brought up in Glasgow from the age of four, where his father, Andrew Bonar, moved to be minister of Finneston in 1856. Bonar's uncles, Horatius and John were also ordained ministers of the Church of Scotland and 'came out' in the Disruption of 1843. Andrew and Horatius Bonar both served as Moderators of the Free Church General Assembly.

James Bonar left Glasgow Academy at the age of sixteen, and his lengthy and distinguished undergraduate career followed the path of Adam SMITH from Glasgow University, where he graduated after five years with first-class honours in mental philosophy, by obtaining a Snell Exhibition to Balliol College, Oxford. There he gained a first in *literae humaniores* in 1877. Just as Smith lauded Frances HUTCHESON, so the major influence on the Bonar was Edward Caird, like Hutcheson a professor of moral philosophy at Glasgow, and later Master of Balliol.

The influences of his family and educational background can perhaps be seen in Bonar's decision to spend the next three years in East London teaching economics in the newly established University Extension Movement. The development of Toynbee Hall in Whitechapel made this work less necessary, and in 1881 Bonar began a career in the civil service as a junior examiner in the Civil Service Commission. He became a senior examiner in 1895 and in 1907 was appointed deputy master of the Ottawa branch of the Royal Mint, from which post he retired to Hampstead in 1919 at the age of sixty-seven.

Before leaving his teaching work in East London Bonar founded an Adam Smith Club with the object of meeting about six times a year to discuss economic questions and, as president, remained its animating force for many years. In 1903 he made a further contribution to general economic education with the publication of *Elements of Political Economy*.

Bonar's gift for friendship was reflected in a network of close relationships throughout the relatively small community of economists of his day in Britain, the USA and continental Europe. As well as interpreting the works of the founding fathers to his own generation, he is credited (along with Professor William Smart of Glasgow) with a major role in bringing the Austrian School to the attention of an English-speaking audience. This he did most notably through an article in the *Quarterly Journal of Economics* (1888) and some of over seventy entries which he contributed to PALGRAVE's *Dictionary of Political Economy* (1894).

In his day Bonar was most widely recognized for his work on MALTHUS, Smith, RICARDO and J.S. MILL, but his scholarly output, though important for his own generation has to a greater or lesser extent, even in the history of economic thought, been superseded. The intended definitive biography of Malthus, the culmination of a lifetime of scholarship, in which he could have drawn on the new materials discovered by others in the 1930s, remained unfinished at his death in 1941 and now lies incomplete and unpublished in the library of the University of Illinois, Urbana. His work on the inter-relationships between economics and philosophy (*Philosophy and Political Economy*, 1893) for which he was perhaps uniquely qualified but which gained much greater recognition on the continent than in Britain when first published, may have the most lasting value.

In a 'career of eminent usefulness' (Shirras 1941) the importance of Bonar's contribution to the institutionalization of the profession of economics in Britain is, however, unquestionable. It is reflected in the offices that he held in the major professional organizations through which the organization of the discipline of economics in Britain evolved. He served as vice-president of the Royal Statistical Society (1920–39) and as president of Section F of the British Association for the Advancement of Science (1929), but it was to the developing work of what became the Royal Economic Society that he made his greatest contribution. A founder member, he served continuously on its council, becoming vice-president in 1925, and from his retirement in 1919 until the mid-1930s he was the most frequent attender at council meetings. Five of his contributions to debates on economic issues along with a number of book reviews and obituaries were published in the *Economic Journal*. His scholarly standing is demonstrated by the award of honorary degrees from the Universities of Glasgow and Cambridge, by the invitation to give the 1929 Newmarch Lectures at University College London and, in 1930, by his election as a fellow of the British Academy.

BIBLIOGRAPHY

Parson Malthus (Glasgow, 1881).
Malthus and his Work (1885; 2nd edn, 1924).
Letters of David Ricardo to Thomas Malthus 1810–1823 (Oxford, 1887).
'Austrian Economists and Their View of Value', *Quarterly Journal of Economics* (1888), vol. 3, October, pp. 1–31.
Philosophy and Political Economy in Some of Their Historical Relations (1893; 4th edn, 1927).
Catalogue of the Library of Adam Smith (1894; 2nd edn, 1932).
Elements of Political Economy (1903).
The Tables Turned: A Lecture and Dialogue on Adam Smith and the Classical Economists (1926).
'Ricardo on Malthus', *Economic Journal* (1929), vol. 39, June, pp. 210–18.
Moral Sense (1930).
Theories of Population from Raleigh to Arthur Young (1931).

Further Reading
Shirras, G.F., 'Obituary: James Bonar', *Economic Journal* (1941), vol. 51, April, pp. 145–56.

Alan Hutton

BOOTH, David (1766–1846)

Booth was born on 9 February 1766 in Kennetles, Forfarshire, in Scotland. He died on 5 December 1846 in Fifeshire. His formal education consisted of less than one year at a parish school. For a time he ran a brewery in

Fifeshire, but his intellectual interests pulled him towards another career, that of schoolmaster and author. He published his *Introduction to an Analytical Dictionary of the English Language* in 1806 and his *Tables of Simple Interest on a new Plan of Arrangement* in 1818. Around 1820 Booth, like many talented Scotsmen of his day, moved to London. There he became acquainted with men of letters like William GODWIN, continued his own writing, and helped supervise publications of the Society for the Diffusion of Useful Knowledge. He wrote, for the SDUK, *The Art of Brewing* (1829), and was the inventor of the brewer's saccharometer.

Booth was an important participant in the 'Malthusian controversy' of the 1820s. Decades earlier, MALTHUS, in the first edition of his *Essay on the Principle of Population* (1798), had argued that an equal-sharing society of the kind envisioned by William Godwin would collapse under the weight of excessive numbers. He put much stress on a supposed tendency of population to increase at a 'geometric' rate, with food supplies only augmentable at a slower, 'arithmetic' rate. These unequal tendencies made 'misery' and 'vice' an inevitable part of the human condition. Radicals and progressives fiercely resisted such a pessimistic doctrine, but it also gained influential adherents. Godwin himself re-entered the fray in 1820 with his lengthy *Of Population*. In the preface, he credited Booth with encouraging him to undertake the project. He also incorporated a forty-five page 'dissertation' by Booth into the work. *Of Population* did not fare as well as Godwin and his allies had hoped, but many readers, including Malthus, recognized a serious challenge to the population principle in the arguments Booth made.

Booth directed a frontal attack on Malthus's assertion that population could double every twenty-five years, as proved by the growth of the American population. This was a point on which Malthus insisted so stubbornly throughout his career that it came to appear a pillar of his entire doctrine, yet Booth showed it to be a demographic impossibility. Through an ingenious technique of 'back projection' from census data, he was able to show that much of the vaunted US population growth was due to immigration, not natural increase. American population was growing at nothing like a geometric rate. In an anonymous 1821 review of Godwin's (and Booth's) work published in the *Edinburgh Review*, Malthus was harshly dismissive of his old opponent but grudgingly complimentary toward Booth for the ingenuity of his immigration calculations. He disputed Booth's mortality estimates for the USA and, more generally, stuck to his guns regarding the 'geometric' thesis. Booth responded with an 1823 pamphlet that demonstrated anew his demographic sophistication. He must be counted among the critics who put Malthusian orthodoxy on the defensive by the end of the 1820s.

BIBLIOGRAPHY
Introduction to an Analytical Dictionary of the English Language (1806).
Tables of Simple Interest on a new Plan of Arrangement (1818).
'Dissertation on the Ratios of Increase in Population, and in the Means of Subsistence', in W. Godwin, *Of Population: An Enquiry Concerning the Power of Increase in the Numbers of Mankind, Being an Answer to Mr. Malthus's Essay on that Subject* (1820).
A Letter to the Rev. T. R. Malthus, M.A., F.R.S., being an answer to the criticism on Mr. Godwin's work on population which was inserted in the LXXth number of the Edinburgh Review (1823).
The Art of Brewing (1829).

Further Reading
Malthus, T.R., 'Review of Godwin's *Of Population*', *Edinburgh Review* (1821), vol. 35, pp. 362–77.
Smith, K., *The Malthusian Controversy* (1951).

Geoffrey Gilbert

BOSANQUET, Charles (1769–1850)

Charles Bosanquet was born on 23 July, 1769 at Forest House, Monmouthshire, the second son of Samuel Bosanquet and Eleanor Hunter. He died at Rock Hall, Northumberland on 20 June, 1850, and is buried in the church there. He married Charlotte Anne Holford on 1 June, 1796 and fathered seven children, three of whom survived him. He served as sub-governor of the South Sea Company from 1808–38, and governor from 1838–50. From 1823–36 he was chairman of the exchequer bill office. He served as Justice of the Peace and Deputy Lieutenant for the county of Northumberland, and was high sheriff of Northumberland in 1828. In 1819 he was lieutenant-colonel of light horse volunteers, later rising to colonel. He maintained a London residence at the Firs, Hampstead, and spent his later years at his estate of Rock Hall, near Alnwick in Northumberland.

Between 1807 and 1808 Bosanquet produced three short works on commercial themes: *Letter on the Proposition submitted to the Government for taking the Duty on Muscavado Sugar ad valorem*, *A Letter to W. Manning, Esq., M.P., on the Depreciation of the West India Property*, and *Thoughts on the Value to Great Britain of Commerce in general, and of the Colonial Trade in particular*. In the second work, Bosanquet blamed the depreciation on ill-considered taxes and other restrictions placed on the colony. He proposed that British breweries should use colonial sugar and that the British navy should use colonial rum. In the third work he pointed out the benefits yielded by the West India trade.

In 1810 Bosanquet published his most important work, *Practical Observations on the Report of the Bullion-Committee*. In this work he criticized the *Report* as being 'altogether at variance with (the opinions) of the persons selected for examination', of relying on propositions that 'are not generally true, and do not therefore form a solid foundation for the abstract reasoning of the Report', and of relying upon facts that 'are erroneously stated; and, when corrected, lead to opposite conclusions'.

Inflationary pressure in early 1809 had prompted David RICARDO to write three letters to the *Morning Chronicle*, the first of which appeared on 29 August (Ricardo's first published work on economics). The public attention aroused by these letters and subsequent pamphlets led Parliament to appoint a select Committee to 'Inquire into the cause of the high price of bullion, and to take into consideration the state of the circulating medium, and of the exchanges between Great Britain and foreign parts.' The Committee, along with Ricardo, took the 'bullionist' position. It stated that inflation had resulted from over-issue of currency, primarily by the Bank of England but also by country banks; and that as a means of preventing over-issue, the Bank of England should resume convertibility of the pound into gold.

Bosanquet held to the 'anti-bullionist' (or 'real bills') position, which was that over-issue would be avoided if banks issued paper money only in exchange for 'solid paper, given, as far as we can judge, for real transactions'. Any over-issue of paper money, in the words of the Bank directors, 'would revert to us by a diminished application for discounts and advances on government securities'. This latter principle became known as the 'Law of the Reflux'.

Ricardo had likened the issues of the Bank of England to a gold mine, insofar as an increased issue of paper money would have the same effect on prices as increased production of gold. Bosanquet countered that the Bank of England issued paper money only on loan, and that since loans must ultimately be repaid, the newly-issued paper money would not cause inflation. Newly-mined gold, in contrast, did not have to be repaid, and therefore would cause inflation. On these grounds, Bosanquet denied the analogy between gold and paper money.

Ricardo's *Reply to Mr. Bosanquet* (1811) has been described by MCCULLOCH (1845) as 'perhaps the best controversial essay that has ever appeared on any disputed question of Political Economy'. In response to Bosanquet's statement that the supply of currency was adequately limited by the Bank's policy of making loans only for 'solid paper', Ricardo answered that as long as the Bank is willing to lend, borrowers will always exist, so that there is no practical limit to the over-issue of money unless the Bank either maintains convertibility, or otherwise acts to maintain the quantity of money within reasonable bounds. Ricardo argued that the simple fact of the pound's depreciation was proof of its over-issue, a circular argument that nevertheless carried the day.

Bosanquet never published a reply to Ricardo, and he has consequently been much abused by historians of economic thought. J.K. Horsefield (1941) wrote of 'the lamentable decline from the counsels of Samuel Bosanquet in 1783 to the apologia of Charles Bosanquet in 1810', while R.S. SAYERS (1952) observed that 'poor Bosanquet is left cutting a very sorry figure'. But Ricardo's victory over Bosanquet was in fact far from complete. The arguments concerning money issued on loan were resurrected intact during the currency school/banking school debates of the 1840s. The issue has remained unsettled ever since, and featured prominently in the monetarist/Keynesian debates of the 1960s and 1970s. Beginning in the 1980s, the real bills viewpoint has seen a small revival of interest. It appears that Bosanquet's writings, like the man himself, are entitled to more respect than they have received.

BIBLIOGRAPHY

A Letter to W. Manning, Esq. M.P. on the Causes of the Rapid and Progressive Depreciation of the West India Property (1807?).

A Letter to W. Manning, Esq. M.P. on the Proposition Submitted to the Consideration of Government, for Taking the Duties on Muscavado Sugar ad valorem (1807?).

Thoughts on the Value, to Great Britain, of Commerce in General and on the Importance of the Colonial Trade in Particular (1808?).

Practical Observations on the Report of the Bullion-Committee (1810).

Further Reading

Horsefield, J.K., *The Duties of a Banker* (141; repr. in T.S. Ashton and R.S. Sayers, *Papers in English Monetary History*, 1953).

McCulloch, J.R., *The Literature of Political Economy* (1845).

Sargent, T.J., 'The Real Bills Doctrine versus the Quantity Theory: A Reconsideration', *The Journal of Political Economy* (1982), vol. 90, no. 6, pp. 1212–36.

Sayers, R.S., *Ricardo's Views on Monetary Questions* (1953).

Samuelson, P.A., 'Reflections on the Merits and Demerits of Monetarism', in J.J. Diamond (ed.), *Issues in Fiscal and Monetary Policy: The Eclectic Economist Views the Controversy* (Minneapolis, 1971).

Sproul, M.F., 'Backed Money, Fiat Money, and the Real Bills Doctrine', *UCLA Working Paper #774B*, http://econpapers.hhs.se/paper/clauclawp/774b.htm (1978).

Tobin, J., 'Commercial Banks as Creators of Money', in D. Carson (ed.), *Banking and Monetary Studies* (Homewood, Illinois, 1963).

Michael F. Sproul

BOSANQUET, Samuel (1744–1806)

Bosanquet was born on 8 June 1744 at Leyton, Essex, and died there aged aixty-three on 4 July 1806. He was the son of Samuel Bosanquet the elder (1700–1765) and Mary Dunster only daughter of William Dunster of Leytonstone. His grandfather, Daniel, was a Huguenot émigré, who fled to London in 1686 following the revocation of the Edict of Nantes and who became a successful City merchant, and Samuel the elder followed his father into the family business. The Bosanquets were one of the most successful émigré families, establishing themselves as prosperous members of the City community.

Bosanquet married his cousin Eleanor, daughter of Henry Hunter and they had three sons (Samuel, Charles and John Bernard) and a daughter, Eleanor, who died young. He studied law but was not called to the bar. He succeeded to the Forest House estate at Leyton, Essex, which had been purchased by his father, and lived the life of a country gentleman, becoming high sheriff at the age of twenty-six. In 1789 he acquired Dingestow Court in Monmouthshire, using a large legacy from his uncle Claude, but continued to live at Leyton. He was active in the family business until his duties at the Bank of England obliged him to reduce his commitments, and he became a deputy director of the Levant Company. He was elected as a director of the Bank of England for the first time in April 1771. His periods of office as a director of the Bank were 1771–3, 1774–7, 1778–81, 1782–5, 1786–89 and 1793–1806. He was deputy governor from 1789–91 and governor from 1791–3. He is chiefly known for his clear exposition of the Bank's views and policies when giving evidence as a witness before the two Secret Parliamentary Committees in 1797. These were appointed to investigate the reasons for the suspension of specie payments by the Bank as a result of financial pressures arising from the Napoleonic Wars. The evidence which Bosanquet gave to the Committees did much to establish his reputation as a practical central banker. He drew upon his extensive experience of decision making at the Bank rather than from abstract monetary theory.

He impressed both contemporaries and later commentators by the sound common sense of his views.

Bosanquet was asked by both Committees to explain why it was necessary to suspend cash payments in 1797 even though the Bank had even lower reserves in 1783, when suspension of payments was avoided. He gave an account of the Bank's actions in 1783, when its reserves had been severely depleted as a result of the American War of Independence. This has been held to be the first occasion that the Bank made a deliberate attempt to manage the money market (Feavearyear 1963).He explained that the Bank had restricted credit through refusing to make its customary advances on the security of new loan stock. This put pressure on the money market, which was denied a normal source of liquidity. No further restriction took place despite a further decline in the Bank's reserves, because the Directors anticipated that a post-war export boom would generate a positive trade balance and an inflow of gold. Their expectations proved to be correct. The success of the Bank's policy in 1783 has been attributed to Bosanquet's foresight (Horsefield 1941). He concluded that: 'Whenever there is an influx of bullion into the country, the Bank have nothing to fear, when a drain takes place from the country, is in general the time for them to be alarmed' (House of Commons 1797).

A major financial crisis occurred in 1793 near the end of Bosanquet's governorship. There was a vigorous boom in the early 1790s associated with an upsurge in canal building. A crisis of confidence was then precipitated by the outbreak of war with France, leading to a severe crisis in the banking system. There was extreme distress among the country banks, many of which failed, leading to an acute shortage of liquidity outside London. The Bank increased its discounts but largely confined its assistance to short-term loans to 'respectable gentleman in London' (Clapham 1944, vol. 1: 197). These included the Lord Mayor of London, to whom advances of more than £60,000 were made. It refused assistance to the Corporation of Liverpool and to banks outside London. The Directors introduced £5 notes, of smaller denomination than the notes previously issued. This measure was intended to increase the circulating medium which had been depleted by the contraction of note issues by the country banks. Despite an increase in the Bank's discounts, the panic was not brought to an end until the government took steps to issue Exchequer bills to merchants offering good security. Although not cash, the Bills were widely acceptable and provided traders with the liquidity they sought so urgently.

The Bank has been severely criticized by HAYEK (1962) for its lack of support to the financial system in the crisis. The responsibility of the central bank to provide liquidity at a time of an internal drain on its bullion was not fully appreciated by the directors (Fetter 1965). The Bank, however, was not in a position to give assistance freely in the face of an internal drain as later advocated by Bagehot in *Lombard Street* (1873). It was not able to lend at a penal rate appropriate for crisis conditions on account of the Usury Laws, which set the maximum rate of interest rate on loans at 5 per cent. Hence it had no alternative but to ration its assistance, which was done on a geographical basis, and this led to complaints of inequitable treatment of applicants for loans.

Before the financial crisis had fully subsided, Bosanquet became concerned about the Bank's practices in lending to the government on Exchequer bills. He considered that advances were being made on inadequate security, which could mean that the directors were in breach of the Bank's charter. He expressed his concerns to William Pitt, the Chancellor of the Exchequer. Pitt readily granted the directors the immunity they sought, and also laid the Bank open to meeting the rapidly expanding needs of the government for war finance. The directors had envisaged that a maximum limit of £500,000 would be set on the Bank's advances to the government, but, as Bosanquet pointed out in his evidence to the House of Commons Committee in 1797, the limit was omitted from the legislation. This set the scene for a series of urgent exchanges between the Chancellor and the Bank over the scale of borrowing in excess of the limit which the directors had proposed. Both excessive government borrowing on Exchequer bills and loans to assist allies were seen by the Bank as weakening the exchange rate and reducing its reserves due to a drain of specie overseas, as Bosanquet explained to the Committee of 1797. For his part, Pitt was unwilling to sacrifice his war aims in response to repeated protests from the Bank, which became increasingly vigorous by 1795, when the exchange rate was weakening.

Bosanquet was heavily involved in representing the Bank's views in discussions with Pitt and gave a detailed account of the Bank's relations with the Chancellor in his evidence in 1797. Because of the pressure of financing government borrowing, the Bank sought to reduce its lending to the private sector by restricting the discounting of commercial bills in December 1795. This led to strong objections from traders, but it reduced the external drain on the Bank's reserves. In focussing on public borrowing, it appears that Bosanquet and his fellow directors overlooked another factor which was weakening the exchange rate and the reserves (Clapham 1944). The expected demonetization of the assignant, the paper currency issued by the revolutionary government in France, increased the French demand for specie in anticipation of the stabilization of the currency. The strong demand for gold forced its price to a premium, making the illegal export of gold from Britain highly profitable, as argued by Hawtrey (1927).

By the end of 1796 the external drain of bullion had abated and the exchange rate strengthened, but the holdings of bullion in the Bank continued to decline. In his evidence, Bosanquet distinguished clearly between the internal drain now reducing the Bank's gold and the previous external drain. He attributed the growth of internal demand for currency to a loan to Ireland and an increased demand for liquidity due to fears of a French invasion. There was a panic demand for gold, putting pressure on the country banks and reducing the Bank's reserves. He argued that a suspension of specie payments by the Bank was the appropriate step in 1797, which was quite different from the situation in 1783, The Bank now faced the threat of invasion rather than an economic fluctuation His argument implied that the Bank should lend freely to accommodate the growth of demand for currency. It did this by asking the government to be relieved of the need to maintain specie payments, to which Pitt agreed, and then issuing inconvertible notes of small denomination.

Bosanquet showed considerable skill in dealing with the practical problems faced by the Bank of England, and provided a lucid exposition of the Bank's views. However, he did not have the insight into monetary issues of a leading theorist, such as Henry THORNTON. In the late eighteenth century the Bank was acquiring the knowledge and experience required for managing a convertible currency. Bosanquet made a major contribution to this learning process. Once specie payments were suspended and the Bank was free to issue inconvertible paper currency, the sophistication of its monetary thought appears to have declined. The directors argued before the Bullion Committee of 1810 that the note issue had no effect on the exchange rate, and asserted that they took no account of the exchange rate in deciding their discount policy (Feavearyear 1963). This was in sharp contrast to the view of Bosanquet, that the Bank should be guided by the behaviour of the exchange rate in assessing monetary conditions. While he distinguished clearly between external and internal drains, he did not fully appreciate the Bank's responsibility for providing assistance to the banking system in the event of an internal drain.

Bosanquet was a capable administrator, who took a keen interest in the internal organization of the Bank. He took steps to check insider trading by members of the Bank's staff, and recommended that clerks should not be permitted to have financial connections with stockbrokers. Clerks should be warned that if found to be associating with stockbrokers, they would face immediate dismissal (Acres 1931). His concerns with the problems of financing government borrowing, maintaining the exchange rate, relieving internal financial crises and curbing insider trading distinguish him as a forerunner of a modern central banker.

When Bosanquet died in 1806, he was buried in the churchyard at Leyton. He is commemorated in the church by a monument designed by Sir John Soane, who was also the architect of the Bank.

Further Reading
Acres, W.M., *The Bank of England from Within, 1694–1900*, 2 vols (Oxford, 1931).
Bagehot, W., *Lombard Street* (1873; repr. Homewood, Illinois, 1962).
Clapham, J. *The Bank of England: A History*, 2 vols. (Cambridge, 1945).
Feavearyear, A.E ., *The Pound Sterling: A History of English Money*, 2nd edn (Oxford, 1963).
Fetter, F.W., *Development of British Monetary Orthodoxy 1797–1875* (Cambridge, Massachusetts, 1965).
Hawtrey, R.G., *Currency and Credit*, 3rd edn (1928).
Hayek, F.A. (1962) 'Introduction' to H. Thornton, *An Enquiry into the Nature of the Paper Credit of Great Britain*, ed. F.A. Hayek (1962).
Horsefield, J.K., 'The Duties of a Banker: The Eighteenth Century View' (1941; repr. in T.S. Ashton and R.S. Sayers (eds), *Papers in English Monetary History* (Oxford, 1953).
Lee, G.L., *The Story of the Bosanquets* (Canterbury, 1966).
House of Commons, *Committee of Secrecy on the Outstanding Demands on the Bank*

of England (1797), Reports and Minutes of Evidence; repr. in *Parliamentary Papers* III (1826).

House of Lords *Committee of Secrecy relating to the Bank of England* (1797), Report and Minutes of Evidence; repr. in *Parliamentary Papers* III (1810).

N.H. Dimsdale

BOWLEY, Arthur Lyon (1869–1957)

Bowley was born 6 November 1869 in Bristol, and died at Haslemere on 21 January 1957. He was the son the Reverend James William Lyon Bowley, vicar of St Philip and St Jacob, and Maria Johnson, his second wife. Bowley's father died of colitis in 1870, leaving his widow to bring up three children from his first marriage and four from their marriage. Bowley was educated at Christ's Hospital (1879–88), and entered Trinity College, Cambridge in 1888 on a mathematics scholarship. He sat his finals in 1891 and was placed tenth in the first class; however, because of earlier illness, in order to take his degree he was required to stay at Cambridge for a further period and from October 1891 to March 1892 he studied physics, chemistry and economics. Significantly for his future career, it was through these studies that he was introduced to Alfred MARSHALL.

On Marshall's suggestion Bowley entered and won the Cobden Essay Prize in 1892 with an essay on 'Changes in the Volume, Character and Geographical Distribution of England's Foreign Trade in the 19th Century and their Causes'. The work subsequently became a successful publication (1893), and is notable for its detailed analysis of the balance of trade. Bowley's skills as an economist and statistician were confirmed in 1894 when he won the Adam Smith Prize with a paper on changes in average wages. On leaving Cambridge, Bowley took employment as a mathematics school teacher, first at Brighton College, then St John's School, Leatherhead. In 1895, Bowley was appointed to the newly founded London School of Economics as part-time lecturer in statistics. This appointment was brought about largely though Marshall's recommendation; Sidney WEBB wanted a practical statistics course on the curriculum which would be sufficient to prepare civil servants. The director of the LSE, W.A.S. HEWINS, approached and appointed Bowley on Marshall's advice, and Bowley taught a statistics course at the LSE almost continuously from 1895 to his retirement in 1936. With Marshall's encouragement, Bowley had been transformed from a mathematician to an economic statistician. Almost all the lecturers at the LSE at that time were part-time and in 1900 Bowley also took employment as lecturer in mathematics at University College, Reading, where he subsequently became professor of mathematics and economics in 1907. There he met Julia Hilliam, an instructor in wood carving and one of the most accomplished women carvers in the country, whom he married in 1904; they had three daughters.

While at Reading, Bowley maintained his part-time appointment at the LSE and was promoted to reader there in 1908, having added mathematics to the curriculum. In 1915 he was awarded the title of professor at the LSE and four years later, in 1919, he was appointed full-time to the newly created and first ever chair in statistics in the social sciences, at which point he resigned his Reading post. He retired in 1936, was made professor emeritus and in 1937 he was awarded the CBE; in 1950 he was made knight bachelor. Bowley was awarded countless academic honours, including a DSc from Cambridge in 1913, but perhaps his most notable honours were the award of both the Silver and Gold Guy Medals by the Royal Statistical Society (1895 and 1935 respectively). He was invited out of retirement in 1940 to become acting director of the Oxford Institute of Statistics. Although then over seventy, he was far from a figurehead, devoting great energy to the post. He retired (for a second time) in December 1944.

Bowley was a most conscientious inquirer in all that he studied. He spread his talents widely, as a teacher and as a researcher in economics, statistics and economic statistics. His reputation and abilities led to numerous positions of importance and influence on national and international bodies, including fellow of the Royal Economic Society from 1893 (and election to its council in 1901); member of the Council of the Royal Statistical Society from 1898 (president during 1938–40); member of the International Statistical Institute from 1903 (treasurer 1929–36 and also 1947–9); member of the editorial board of the newly founded journal *Economica* from 1921 (with Edwin CANNAN and Graham WALLAS); fellow of the British Academy (1922); and editor and member of the executive committee of the London and Cambridge Economic Service from its foundation in 1923 to 1945 (his final contribution was in 1953). He was elected a member of the Senate of the University of London (1930), and was a founder member of the Econometric Society in 1933 (president 1938–9). Also, as he was an acknowledged authority on the measurement of subsistence levels and the cost of living, Sir William BEVERIDGE invited him to membership of a small committee to advise him on the Report on Social Insurance and Allied Services in 1941.

Bowley's major contributions to economics were made as a collector and compiler of economic statistics (particularly wages and national income), as a pioneer of statistical techniques in the social sciences, in the development of mathematical economics and econometrics and, most notably, as a pioneer of sampling techniques. His work on wages and national income accounting began in 1894 when he won the Adam Smith prize essay examining changes in UK average wages from 1860–91. His method was to construct index numbers using ratios rather than levels, and this foray into index numbers led him, in 1899, to propose in *Palgrave's Dictionary* the formula for what has become known as Fisher's ideal index number. Bowley developed his work on wages and, over eight years to 1906, published 'The Statistics of Wages in the United Kingdom during the Last Hundred Years' in fourteen parts. The statistical techniques used, and the economic concepts employed, became more refined in the later parts. There is, for example, a detailed explanation of why changes in earnings would diverge from those of wage rates and although he does not use the term 'wage-drift', Bowley was the first to draw attention to this important phenomenon. His work on wages was primarily statistical in character, but the economic content may be seen to grow over the years. Bowley's causal economic analysis of changes in wages concentrated on the changes in the demand for labour, the increasing market power of combined workers and labour's increasing efficiency. Bowley also produced comparative results for the UK, the USA and France.

His concern with wages became a motivating force in his inter-war work on national income estimation. 'The Definition of National Income' (1922) is a landmark, containing the distinction between market price and factor cost evaluations, and the term 'transfer payments' was explicitly introduced. The treatment of taxation was clarified, and the work culminated in the seminal 1927 joint publication with his one-time postgraduate student, Sir Josiah STAMP, *The National Income, 1924*. The first official estimates of national income, made during the Second World War, relied heavily upon Bowley and Stamp's truly pioneering studies.

Bowley's concern with wages and national income led to a broader concern with the analysis and measurement of social change, exemplified in *The Measurement of Social Phenomena* (1915), which set out a structure for a systematic research programme for a comprehensive socio-economic analysis of society. The emphasis on dynamics is surprising for such an early work, and the analysis of inter-generational mobility is of particular interest.

Bowley's studies of wages, national income, unemployment and poverty were frustrated by both an underdeveloped relevant statistical method and the lack of data. Elementary statistics was not commonly taught as a prescribed component of an economics degree in the nineteenth century; however, from its foundation in 1895 the LSE was unique, and Bowley's lecture courses in statistics became the subject matter of his very successful *Elements of Statistics* (1901), which was very well received and went through six editions (the last in 1937). It was followed by his second text on statistics, the *Elementary Manual of Statistics*, first published in 1910 and going through seven editions by 1951. In the *Manual* he articulated his desire to see established a national office of statistics: 'There is urgent need for more systematic and more complete national statistics', and also warned against the potential dangers of statistical analysis which 'is dangerous in the hands of those who do not know its use and deficiencies. A knowledge of methods and limitations is necessary, if only to avoid being misled by unscrupulous or unscientific arguments' (1910: 5).

Bowley devoted considerable effort to the determination and accumulation of high-quality data. In *Statistical Studies relating to National Progress* (1904) he identified five stringent criteria for the acceptability of statistics. Having put much of the publicly available data to these tests and having found, not surprisingly, that most failed, he said of official publications in his presidential address of 1906 to Section F of The British Association for the Advancement of Science: 'It is a sad reflection that, while so much care and labour are spent in accumulating and printing statistical tables, so few of them are of any real importance, and so few are intelligible, even to one who studies them carefully' (1906: 542). In that same address Bowley complained bitterly of the lack of co-ordination between the various government departments, and declared 'We need a central thinking department in statistics' (1906: 543). The efforts to establish such a department did not come to an early fruition but the arguments of Bowley and others, plus the impetus of the Second World War, eventually saw the establishment of the Central Statistical Office in 1941.

Bowley was, not surprisingly given his undergraduate degree, a most accomplished mathematical economist and in 1924 published his landmark text *The Mathematical Groundwork of Economics*. This was the first text, in English, of economic theory in mathematical language, and it represents the vehicle by which a number of techniques came to be generally accepted. Bowley's intention was 'to reduce to a uniform notation, and to present as a properly related whole, the main part of the mathematical methods used by Cournot, Jevons, Pareto, Edgeworth, Marshall, Pigou and Johnson...' (1924: v). At the time of writing, mathematical economics was in its infancy. The main achievement of the *Groundwork* was to promote the value of mathematical economics, and to elucidate and make known certain concepts best approached through the use of mathematics. For example, the indifference curve, the contract curve, and the derivation of properties of the demand curve, all appear in the first chapter alone. In his treatment of duopoly he introduced both the reaction curve and the concept of conjectural variations. Bowley, quite typically, is concerned with the conditions of solutions to practical problems; this is illustrated most admirably by his analysis of production and exchange under various market structures. It is a remarkable book and was well received by the profession and in reviews.

Although Bowley recognized that the statistical method might be used to test theories, his own empirical work is more descriptive and exploratory. Bowley's major written contribution to econometrics was the pathbreaking text *Family Expenditure* (1935), with R.D.G. ALLEN. The work is an exemplar of its time, whose purpose was 'to discover how far the expenditure of individual families...can be described by rules and formulae, to relate any rules that are found to the postulates of economic theory and to describe the variations from the averages that result from the different choices of individual families'. The methodology was strictly 'measurement before theory'. Bowley and Allen demonstrated, for example, that each family's expenditures on items such as rent, fuel and lighting were less sensitive to family size than expenditures on food and clothing. To incorporate family size and composition into their empirical work they generated the concept of equivalent adult scales whereby family expenditures were weighted by the number in the household but, importantly: 'this number should be, not the actual number of individuals, but a number based on a scale of needs in which allowance is made for age and sex' (1935: 19).

Bowley was one of the early pioneers of the sampling technique, and first drew attention to the method in his 1906 presidential address to the BAAS when he observed: 'The simple method of samples...for which all the materials have existed for at least twenty years...has been completely ignored...progress in the development of theory has...been rapid...but there has been remarkably little application to practical statistical problems. The attention of mathematical statisticians has been mainly directed to theory...it is time that it was brought to bear on the...analysis of existing industrial statistics' (1906: 548–9). Bowley's great success in this field extended from questionnaire design to the analysis of the results, and he set an exemplary standard. His first sample survey of Reading, published in 1913, provides a model of socio-economic investigation and it was quickly followed by similar surveys of Northampton, Warrington, Stanley and Bolton, which were brought together in the famous Five Towns Survey, *Livelihood and Poverty* (1915).

Bowley's understanding and appreciation of the technical aspects of the subject are well illustrated on the one hand by his *Measurement of the Precision Attained in Sampling* (1926), and on the other by his extensive appreciation of EDGEWORTH's contributions to statistical theory (1928). The significance of the former report cannot be over-stated. Bowley's concern was not only with simple summary statistics, but also with the functional form of distributions, a concern born of his Bayesian standpoint. Bowley's Bayesian perspective was never more evident that in 1934 when, of Neyman's newly introduced concept of the 'Confidence Interval'; he remarked: 'I am not at all sure that the "confidence" is not a 'confidence trick' (1934: 609), and he was equally sarcastic and acerbic in the same year towards FISHER. Bowley did not appear to welcome non-Bayesian advances. and Fisher observed that while Bowley may have failed to fully appreciate Neyman and Fisher's work, 'at least Dr. Newman and myself have not been left in his company' (Fisher 1935: 76).

Bowley was an economic statistician of the highest rank. He made numerous pioneering contributions to theory and practice, and made very substantial contributions to the profession via his active involvement in the major national and international professional organizations. There was nothing he did that was without practical, or at least potentially practical, application and he was quick to protect, preserve and promote the areas, techniques and methodologies of economics and statistics which had the benefit of his patronage.

BIBLIOGRAPHY
A Short Account of England's Foreign Trade in the Nineteenth Century (1893; 3rd edn, 1922).
'Wages, Nominal and Real', *Palgrave's Dictionary of Political Economy* (1899), vol. III, pp. 639–41.

(with G.H. Wood) 'The Statistics of Wages in the United Kingdom during the last Hundred Years', 14 parts, *Journal of the Royal Statistical Society* (1898–1906), vols 61–9.
Elements of Statistics (1901; 6th edn, 1937).
Statistical Studies Relating to National Progress in Wealth and Trade since 1882 (1904).
'Presidential Address, British Association, Section F', *Journal of the Royal Statistical Society* (1906), vol. 69, pp. 540–58.
An Elementary Manual of Statistics (1910; 7th edn, 1951).
'Working-Class Households in Reading', *Journal of the Royal Statistical Society* (1913), vol. 76, pp. 672–701.
The Nature and Purpose of the Measurement of Social Phenomena (1915; 2nd edn, 1923).
(with A.R. Burnett-Hurst) *Livelihood and Poverty* (1915).
'The Definition of National Income', *Economic Journal* (1922), vol. 32, pp. 1–11.
The Mathematical Groundwork of Economics (Oxford, 1924).
'Measurement of the Precision Attained in Sampling', *Bulletin de l'Institut International de Statistique* (1926), vol. 22, pp. 1–62.
(with Sir Josiah Stamp) *The National Income, 1924* (Oxford, 1927).
F.Y. Edgeworth's Contributions to Mathematical Statistics (1928).
(with R.G.D. Allen) *Family Expenditure* (1935).

Further Reading
Allen, R.D.G. and George, R.F., 'Professor Sir Arthur Lyon Bowley (with bibliography)', *Journal of the Royal Statistical Society* (1957), vol. 120, pp. 236–41.
Bowley, A.H. (1972) *A Memoir of Professor Sir Arthur Lyon Bowley (1869–1957) and His Family*, privately printed (1972).

Darnell, A.C., 'A.L. Bowley 1869–1957', in D.P. O'Brien and J.R. Presley (eds), *Pioneers of Modern Economics in Britain* (1981, pp. 140–74).
——, 'Bowley, Wicksell and the Development of Mathematical Economics', *Scottish Journal of Political Economy* (1982), vol. 29, pp. 156–80.
Fisher, R.A., 'The Logic of Inductive Inference', *Journal of the Royal Statistical Society* (1935), vol. 98, pp. 39–82.
Neyman, J., 'On Two Different Aspects of the Representative Method' and 'Discussion', *Journal of the Royal Statistical Society* (1934), vol. 97, pp. 558–625.

Adrian Darnell

BOYD, Walter (1753?–1837)

Walter Boyd was probably born 18 November 1753 in the north of Scotland, though the names of his parents are unknown. He died at Plaistow Lodge, near Bromley, Kent, on 16 September 1837. Other than a brother, Archibald, it is not known if he had other siblings. Little is known of his early life. It is possible that he was educated abroad, in Amsterdam and Switzerland, and served as a merchant apprentice in France. Reliable records about his life start only in 1774, when he undertook the position of agent to manage farms in Lincolnshire. Having left this position in 1781 seeking better prospects, in 1782 he began a career as an assistant manager for a newly formed merchant bank in the Austrian Netherlands. This was the beginning of a merchant banking career that was to continue, in fits and starts, until his death. Boyd also served in Parliament, being elected MP for Shaftesbury (1796–1802) and Lymington (1823–30).

In addition to being recognized for writing three significant pamphlets on financial matters, Boyd is also remembered for his activities as a merchant banker with close connections to Prime Minister William Pitt (1759–1806). Boyd rose to this position of influence by a circuitous route. Following three successful years managing the merchant bank in the Austrian Netherlands, Boyd entered a partnership with John William Ker, another manager at the bank, to form the banking firm of Boyd, Ker et Cie in Paris around the middle of 1785. The primary activities of Boyd, Ker et Cie involved performing banking services for well-to-do foreigners, dealing in securities and foreign exchange and making loans to French aristocrats. Included in the client list of Boyd, Ker et Cie were Thomas Jefferson, Lord Bolingbroke and the Duc d'Orléans. By 1791, Boyd, Ker et Cie had risen to be one of the leading banking house in Paris with an extensive network of correspondents throughout France and elsewhere in Europe. These connections were to be valuable to Boyd following the rapid deterioration of the political situation in Paris associated with events surrounding the French Revolution.

Even though the storming of the Bastille occurred in July of 1789, it was still possible for foreign bankers to conduct a profitable banking business in Paris for some time thereafter. There was a gradual deterioration of both the political and economic situation, culminating in the 'Reign of Terror' that began in September of 1793. In October 1793, the National Convention decreed that all British subjects be arrested and their property confiscated. This had a direct impact on the firm of Boyd, Ker and Cie, where all property was seized, and on Boyd himself, who had considerable personal wealth tied up in the firm. In anticipation of such events, in September 1792 Boyd left Paris for London and set about establishing another merchant banking venture 'Boyd, Benefield & Co.' with Paul Benefield, a notorious British nabob. Expelled from India in November 1788 with a substantial amount of wealth intact, Benefield still faced considerable debts in England as a result of failed dealings in India. Benefield likely met Boyd while being sequestered on the Continent waiting to clear up his financial difficulties in England. Benefield was able to return to England in 1790, gaining protection from creditors by purchasing a safe seat in Parliament.

Though the roots of the partnership start in June 1792, the new firm was officially launched in March 1793, with Boyd as the senior partner responsible for banking activities. Boyd was almost certainly aware of Benefield's reputation and prior conduct. However, Boyd was badly in need of capital and Benefield was willing to provide that capital through the purchase of life annuities held by Boyd, Ker et Cie. The firm was successful almost immediately. In addition to a rapid expansion in banking services, such as discounting bills of exchange, Boyd, Benefield & Co. were successful in securing the contract for the £4.6 million Austrian Imperial Loan of 1794. Loans to foreign governments in London were unusual and Boyd demonstrated considerable abilities in bringing the loan to market. In this transaction, Boyd had considerable contact with Prime Minister Pitt, who was anxious to provide support to a key ally in the war against France that had been declared in February 1793. The success of the Austrian loan led to Boyd being able to secure a substantial amount of additional contracting business for loans to the British government.

The period leading up to the suspension of cash payments (convertibility) by the Bank of England in February 1797 was characterized by severe financial difficulties for the British government. These difficulties were brought on largely by problems arising from the war with France. Pitt sought to pay for the war largely through increased borrowing. Having served the government successfully in arranging the Austrian Loan of 1794, Boyd, Benefield and Co. was asked by Pitt to play a lead role in the £18 million government loan of 1795–6 and a number of subsequent borrowings. Such loans were paid by instalments and, while money was plentiful in the summer of 1795, at the end the year the Bank of England implemented a policy of restricting discounts. This action was precipitated by a number of factors including: the increasing demands on the Bank of England by the government for short-term accommodation bills; the large supply of short-term government paper in the market; and a significant drain on the Bank's specie reserves. This action by the Bank had a severe impact on Boyd, Benefield and Co. and, in combination with a number of other negative developments such as the failure of a major foreign correspondent, by the summer of 1796 the firm was in severe difficulties.

By March of 1797, the situation at Boyd, Benefield and Co. had deteriorated to the point where Boyd appealed to Pitt for assistance and was able to obtain a £100,000 advance for the firm. Such assistance was sufficient to permit the firm to continue temporarily. By April 1798, the position of the firm was still solid enough that Boyd was able to be the lead contractor on the £17 million government loan proposed at that time. However, the financial difficulties of the firm weighed heavily on the relationship between Boyd and Benefield. While still able to maintain a position as an important loan contractor, the deterioration of the overall business was such that the Boyd and Benefield were forced into bankruptcy in March 1800. Boyd was forced to dispose of his assets and was obliged to rely on the kindness of friends to sustain his much reduced lifestyle. This dire situation changed abruptly in March 1801 with the resignation of Pitt and the commencement of negotiations to end the war with France. This meant that the assets of Boyd, Ker and Cie, estimated by Boyd to be worth £600,000, were potentially eligible for recovery. However, negotiations between England and France dragged on throughout the year. Anxious to deal with the matter of recovering the assets of Boyd, Ker and Cie, Boyd left for Paris in the latter part of 1801.

Boyd's decision to travel to Paris was to be ill-fated as war between the two countries broke out again in May 1802. Boyd was detained and did not obtain a release until the fall of Napoleon in 1814. Though the resulting peace provided for British citizens to recover seized assets, the process was slow. By the middle of 1816 payments on *rentes* still owned by Boyd, Ker and Cie were being received, though it was not until 1821 that sufficient funds had been obtained to settle the outstanding debts of Boyd, Benefield and Co., permitting Boyd to return to a relatively prosperous life in England. Using the funds secured from the liquidation of Boyd, Ker and Cie, Boyd purchased Plaistow Lodge near Bromley, Kent in 1823 and sat as MP for Lymington from 1823–30. It is estimated that the value of his estate at the time of his death exceeded £200,000, a significant recovery for someone who had faced bankruptcy and been forced to rely on the charity of friends for many years.

As an economist, Boyd is most remembered for the *Letter to the Right Honourable William Pitt on the Influence of the Stoppage of Issues in Specie at the Bank of England on the Prices of Provisions and other Commodities* (1801). Though the importance of the *Letter* in the history of economic thought has been superseded by other contributions to the bullionist controversy, such as Henry THORNTON's *Paper Credit* (1802) and the *Report* of the Bullion Committee (1810), the *Letter* does represent the first reasoned attempt to make a connection between commodity price inflation and the restriction of convertibility by the Bank of England. However, the argument is clouded by a hostility to the Bank that causes Boyd to make claims that could not be supported with the theoretical arguments that are proposed. The essence of the argument in the *Letter* is that suspension of convertibility enabled the Bank to issue notes in excess of what would have been possible under a convertible note issue. This excess issue of notes was the primary cause of the rise in the price of commodities and the fall of the exchanges.

In the *Letter*, Boyd makes reference to 'the great rise in the price of commodities and every species of exchangeable value' and attributes the principal cause to an increase of banknotes. This position was challenged by Sir Francis BARING in *Observations on the Publication of Walter Boyd, Esq., M.P.* (1801). A number of key issues that were central to the later bullionist debates were raised in this exchange. In particular, Boyd argued for using specie convertibility as the appropriate basis for monetary circulation. Observing that the rise in commodity prices was considerably greater than the fall of the exchange in Hamburg and that there was no premium on guineas, Baring observed that there was an inconsistency in Boyd's position. The exchange between Baring and Boyd also raised the issue of the connection between depreciation of the exchanges and the level of domestic commodity prices, though this issue was not fully explored. Finally, there is the issue of determining the sources of exchange rate fluctuations. Boyd argued strongly that by causing the circulation of banknotes to be larger than would be the case under convertibility, the Bank was responsible for the depreciation of the exchanges.

Boyd's other two contributions both dealt with the sinking fund for retiring the outstanding debt of the British government. Boyd was a strong supporter of the principle of a sinking fund but found some shortcomings in implementation. *Reflections on the Financial System of Great Britain, and particularly on the Sinking Fund: written in France in the summer of 1812* (1815) was composed while Boyd was in his tenth year of captivity in France and was not published until his return to England in 1815. In *Reflections*, Boyd argues that the sinking could impose too heavy a burden on the government budget and proposed a reduction in sinking fund payments. Written at the age of seventy-five, *Observations on Lord Grenville's Essay on the Sinking Fund* (1828) is a sixteen-page rejoinder to a pamphlet by Lord GRENVILLE where the advantages a sinking fund not covered by a revenue surplus were questioned. Boyd questioned this position. He argued that even if expenditures exceeded revenues due, say, to war requirements and more debt was issued in a given year than was retired, sinking fund clauses in government loan contracts served to increase the confidence of investors.

BIBLIOGRAPHY
Letter to the Right Honourable William Pitt on the Influence of the Stoppage of Issues in Specie at the Bank of England on the Prices of Provisions and other Commodities (1801; 2nd edn, 1801; 2nd edn corrected, 1811).
Reflections on the Financial System of Great Britain, and particularly on the Sinking Fund: written in France in the summer of 1812 (1815; 2nd edn, 1828).
Observations on Lord Grenville's Essay on the Sinking Fund (1828).

Further Reading
Baring, F., *Observations on the Publication of Walter Boyd, Esq., M.P.* (1801).
Cope, S.R., *Walter Boyd, A Merchant Banker in the Age of Napoleon* (1983).
Fetter, F., *Development of British Monetary Orthodoxy, 1797–1875* (Cambridge, Massachusetts, 1965).
Grenville, W.W., *On the Supposed Advantages of a Sinking Fund* (1828).
Horsefield, J., *Duties of a Banker, II: The Effects of Inconvertibility*, in T. Ashton and R. Sayers, *Papers in English Monetary History* (Oxford, 1953).

Geoffrey Poitras

BRADLAUGH, Charles (1833–91)

Bradlaugh was born on 26 September 1833 in Hoxton, East London, and died in London on 30 January 1891. His parents were highly religious, as was he in his youth. However, during his teens Bradlaugh became interested in Chartism, and began to question his faith. This led him into serious conflict with his father, and Bradlaugh had to leave home. He lodged with freethinking friends before joining the Seventh Dragoon Guards in 1850. Bradlaugh disliked army life and was bought out of the army in 1853. He began work for a solicitor, and married Susannah Hooper in 1855. Despite having a growing family, he dedicated his spare time to lecturing on political issues.

Bradlaugh's political and religious radicalism deepened during the course of the 1860s. In 1860 Bradlaugh and Joseph Barker established *The National Reformer*, a freethinking journal. By 1866, Bradlaugh had started the National Secular Society. Around this time he came into contact with Annie Besant, who went on to write for the *National Reformer* and to work with Bradlaugh on his Freethought Press. This would prove to be an eventful friendship, for in 1877 the pair were prosecuted for publishing Charles Knowles's *The Fruits of Philosophy*. Knowles's book was deemed obscene for its promotion of birth control. Bradlaugh and Besant were found guilty and sentenced to six months' imprisonment, which was later overturned on appeal.

Bradlaugh had great difficulty in achieving his aim of election to parliament. His atheist views won him many enemies in parliament when he was successfully returned as MP for Northampton in 1880. He refused to take the oath of office, preferring to affirm on account of his atheism. When he attempted to take his seat in the Commons, he was expelled and imprisoned in the Tower of London. Although both Benjamin Disraeli and William Gladstone were supportive of him (the latter proposing an Affirmation Bill to allow atheists to affirm the oath), Bradlaugh was forcibly removed from parliament on both occasions when he attempted to take his seat. Despite continued opposition, Bradlaugh finally took his seat in January 1886.

Although many of Bradlaugh's policies were centred upon the radical reform of parliament, he did not neglect economic issues. He argued for land reform in his Freethought Press publications. He was concerned with the abolition of life estates and the aristocracy's domination of agriculture, wishing instead to put land ownership and farming in the hands of agricultural labourers. He also believed that too much was being spent on an ever-expanding bureaucracy. This money was being taken from the lower middle and working classes and being spent on maladministration. He also believed that wages should not be regulated by the government or other agencies, but by the workers and their employers agreeing the terms and conditions of wages and hours to suit them. Bradlaugh was a friend of the worker and small trader, as his work on the Royal Commission on Market Rights and Tolls demonstrated. He argued in *Capital and Labour*: 'I affirm that every laborer willing to work has the right to life; and by life I do not mean merely existence from day to day' (1888: 6). Throughout his career, Bradlaugh was committed to a form of economics that would have the broadest benefit.

BIBLIOGRAPHY
England's Balance-Sheet (1884).
Capital and Labour (1888).
The Eight Hours Movement, Reprinted from the New Review (1889).
Parliament and the Poor: What the Legislature can do: What it Ought to Do (1889).
The Radical Programme (1889).
Labor and Law, with a Memoir (1891).

Further Reading
Bonner, H.B., *Charles Bradlaugh* (1908).
Manwell, R., *The Trial of Annie Besant and Charles Bradlaugh* (1976).
Tribe, D., *President Charles Bradlaugh MP* (1971).

Katharine Bradley

BRAND, John (1743–1808)

Brand was born in Norwich some time in 1743, the son of a tanner, and died in London on 23 December 1808. He studied mathematics at Caius College, Cambridge, taking his BA in 1766 and MA in 1772. He then took holy orders and, after a short spell as reader at the church of St Peter's Mancroft in Norwich, became vicar of Wickham Skeith, Suffolk. He supplemented his income through writing, primarily on mathematics and politics; in 1797 one of his papers appeared in the *British Critic*, where it was read by the Lord Chancellor, Lord Loughborough. The latter was favourably impressed and asked to meet Brand, afterwards appointing him rector of St George's Southwark. Brand held this post for the next eleven years until his death, enjoying some financial security for the first time in his life.

Brand's writings on economics were based on attempts to use mathematics to solve political problems. His *Observations on Some of the Probable Effects of Mr Gilbert's Bill; to which are added Remarks deduced from Dr Price's Account of the National Debt* (1776) is effectively two works combined: a commentary on Thomas GILBERT's proposals for reform of the poor law, and a rebuttal of Richard PRICE's views on the national debt. On the former, Brand notes that the amount of money required to support the poor of England is increasing, and the poor rate is becoming an ever heavier tax burden. He sets out some means of restructuring both the tax and the administration of poor relief, and advocates the incorporation of poorhouses and the appointment of directors to improve finances and general management. There is then a long discourse on the need for more and better public education, concluding that educating the poor would stimulate them to become both more industrious and more patriotic.

Turning to Price's work, Brand argues that taxation is not as much of a threat to national prosperity as the former suggests. Price, he says, looks only at the increase in the amount of money collected in taxation. While this has indeed risen dramatically, what is important is not the value of taxes collected, but the burden of taxation: 'Money represents some real value in goods and commodities, and if a tax at two different periods take away the representative 1/10 of our subsistence, the burthen of that tax upon a people at those different times is equal' (1776: 49). By linking the total paid in tax to the value of money, which he calculates based on the price of corn over a nineteen-year period, Brand purports to show that the actual tax burden has increased only very little. If the total tax paid in 1774 is compared to that paid in 1755, there appears to be an increase of 67 per cent. But the reduced value of money means that the real tax burden has only increased by 11 per cent. There is, he says, no cause for concern about the economy, which is well able to withstand a rise of this nature, and fears of bankruptcy occasioned by the high national debt are groundless.

BIBLIOGRAPHY

Observations on Some of the Probable Effects of Mr Gilbert's Bill; to which are added Remarks deduced from Dr Price's Account of the National Debt (1776).
Political Arithmetic (1797).

Ann Kimber

BRASSEY, Thomas (1805–70)

Brassey was born 7 November 1805 at Buerton in Cheshire, and died at Hastings on 8 December 1870. He was the son of John and Elizabeth Brassey, a farming family whose ancestors had arrived in England with William the Conquerer. Brassey's formal education in a Chester school ended at the age of sixteen, when he was articled to a land surveying and agency firm. By the age of twenty-one he had been made a partner and sent to establish a new branch at Birkenhead. At the same time he was acquiring experience in road building and amassing substantial assets, including a quarry. While arranging the supply of quarry materials, he met the engineer and inventor George Stephenson. This stimulated Brassey's interest in railway building. After several unsuccessful tenders, he was awarded the tender for the Penkridge viaduct near Stafford. His reputation was already high, and he received financial backing from a major financial institution. Still in his twenties, he concentrated at first on railway projects in Britain. In 1841 he successfully tendered for the Paris-Rouen railway and his career as 'railway builder to the world' was launched.

Between 1834 and 1870 Brassey was awarded in excess of one hundred contracts, either in partnership or alone, to build railways and related works in Britain. In that period he also was awarded in excess of twenty contracts to develop projects in France, Spain, Italy, Norway, Holland, Germany, Poland and Denmark. Outside Europe he had a further twenty contracts in Argentina, Canada, Mauritius, India and Australia. At various periods during his career up to 80,000 persons were employed at one time on his own or on joint projects, although some doubt has been cast on the accuracy of these figures (Helps 1872: ix). From the outset of his career Brassey was an unusually benevolent, conciliatory and popular employer. He always attempted to pay what he regarded as fair wages, and the welfare of his workers was a major objective. Although some of his projects were not a financial success, it was this vast reservoir of experience and his observations of the labour market that informed his views on work and wages.

As he fulfilled his contracts, Brassey observed a positive relationship between his workers' wages and their productivity. He decided to compile more systematic information on work and wages. Through interviews with employees, managers and secretaries, supplemented by data from other employers, he compiled twenty-four volumes on work and wages. In addition to railway construction, the data and information related to manufacturing, textiles and building mainly in Britain, Ireland, Germany, France and India. The results of this research were published by his son, Thomas Brassey, as *Work and Wages* in 1872.

The central proposition was the claimed tendency for output per wage unit to be everywhere the same. Brassey wished this 'impressive' proposition to be used to persuade other employers to emulate his approach to wages policy (and his related management policies as well). Employers should recognize that the payment of higher wages did not rule out large profits because the higher wages would be accompanied not only by increased work effort but also by increased investment and improved management methods. The efficiency of workers (especially unskilled labour such as Brassey mainly employed) would increase as their nutrition improved and as they responded more effectively to on-the-job training. Similar beneficial effects for productivity flowed from reducing hours of work while maintaining wages.

Brassey's most notable example was the construction of the Trent railway. The adoption of an eight-hour day instead of the usual ten-hour day led to an increase in output per worker which comfortably offset the increased cost of the reduced hours. This led to the conclusion that: 'daily wages affords no real measure of the actual cost of work; and it is quite possible that work can be more cheaply executed by the same workmen, notwithstanding that their wages have largely increased' (Brassey 1872: 67). The extension of this proposition to cross-country comparisons was based on Brassey's experience of employing labour in many 'civilized' countries: 'the daily wage of labour was fixed at widely different rates; but it was found to be the almost invariable rule that the cost of labour was the same in that for the same sum of money, the same amount of work was everywhere performed' (Brassey 1872 : 75).

Brassey's arguments found favour in the periodical literature of the time (for example, see *Fortnightly Review* (1872); *Edinburgh Review* (1873) and *Quarterly Review* (1873). However, the understanding and interpretation of the ideas by these writers is questionable. Unsurprisingly, some writers used the analysis to further trade union wage claims and to attack the views of mainstream economists. Some benevolent employers followed Brassey's dictum on wages and over the next thirty years frequent references to his arguments may be found in the literature of those who, like Brassey, may be described as the 'amateur economists'.

Among the professional economists, Alfred MARSHALL and J.E. CAIRNES were two early and notable commentators on Brassey's work. Cairnes wielded considerable authority over English economics until the mid-1870s, and because of his pre-neoclassical, historical approach to economics, including attachment to a dilute version of the wages fund doctrine, he was anxious to refute Brassey's wage arguments. In sarcastic terms he described as 'simple' the argument that 'it often pays better to employ a good workman at higher wages, than an inferior one at lower wages' (Cairnes 1874: 281). The main thrust of his argument was that such a wage policy would ultimately be constrained in competitive markets. However, Brassey never suggested that his analysis was ruled out in competitive markets.

Less than a year after its publication, Alfred Marshall had placed *Work and Wages* on the reading list for students in his *Lectures to Women*. He provided summaries of each chapter of the book. The main lesson he wished his students to take from the book was that high wages improved the physical condition of labour and, therefore, workers' efficiency. Elsewhere in his writing, in 1874 as he commenced work on his famous monograph on international trade, then in 1879 in his book (with Mary Paley Marshall) *Economics of Industry*, and again in 1890 in his *Principles of Economics*, he displayed a strong awareness of the links between wages and efficiency. Thus Marshall's own observations of the workings of industrial labour markets were reinforced by Brassey's observations. In the mid-1890s and again in the 1920s, F.Y. EDGEWORTH read and favourably reviewed Brassey. However, Edgeworth dissented from some aspects of Brassey's interpretation of the facts and his reliance only on 'the inductive parts of political economy' (Edgeworth 1894: 688).

In the USA another amateur economist, Jacob Schoenhof, was also influenced by Brassey's arguments. He referred to them approvingly in his 1892 book with the felicitous title *The Economy of High Wages*. Among academic economists in the United States, only Francis A. Walker referred to the detail of Brassey's evidence on the wages–efficiency link. From this starting point Walker developed a more sophisticated analysis of the economy of high wages and related aspects of the operation of internal labour markets.

Paradoxically, it was the non-conformist economist John A. HOBSON who mounted the most effective critique of Brassey's views while also promoting the benefits of the economy of high wages. Hobson pointed to the major weaknesses in Brassey's argument due to his failure to recognize or take into account variations in purchasing power in different countries and the absence of perfect mobility of labour and capital. Despite this critique, Hobson in his work between 1894 and 1927 consistently held to the view, traceable to Brassey, that the payment of higher wages would lead to increased efficiency. He noted some exceptions and some upper limits. In his later writings Hobson illustrated the benefits and the limits to the economy of high wages with reference to the case of the Ford Motor Company in the United States.

BIBLIOGRAPHY
Work and Wages (1872; updated and reissued by Earl Brassey and Sydney Chapman, 1916).
Lectures on the Labour Question (1872).

Further Reading
Cairnes, J.E., *Some Leading Principles of Political Economy* (1874).
Edgeworth, F.Y., 'Review of Papers and Addresses by Lord Brassey', *Economic Journal* (1894), vol. 4, pp. 288–9.
Harrison, F., 'Mr. Brassey on Work and Wages', *Fortnightly Review*, n.s. (1872), vol. 12, pp. 268–86.
Helps, A., *Life and Labours of Mr. Brassey* (1872).
Hobson, J.A., *The Evolution of Modern Capitalism* (1894).
Jeans, J.S., 'On The Comparative Efficiency of Labour at Home and Abroad', *Journal of the Royal Statistical Society* (1884), vol. 47, pp. 614–55.

Ray Petridis

BREWSTER, Francis (before 1642–1705)

Brewster was born in Dublin some time before 1642, and died there early in 1705. His family came originally from County Kerry. He became a prominent merchant of Dublin, serving as master of the Dublin Guild of merchants from 1670–72, alderman in 1670 and 1695, and mayor in 1674. He was knighted by Charles II in 1670. He owned land and ironworks in Kerry, which he claimed were badly damaged in the fighting between the forces of James II and William of Orange in 1690–91; he estimated his losses during this period at £30,000, and petitioned for restitution from forfeited estates. In the *Essays on Trade and Navigation* (1695), Brewster mentions that he was also involved in overseas trade, although not in the very long-distance trades such as those with East India, Turkey or Muscovy.

Brewster was elected to the Irish parliament as MP for Tuam in 1692, and was a loyal supporter of William of Orange. He represented Tuam until 1693 and then again from 1695–9, and then was MP for Doneraile from 1703 until his death. In 1692–3 he gave evidence before parliament in London on the state of Ireland and the abuses committed by certain officials of the government, and in 1698 he served, not without a measure of self-interest, on the commission of inquiry into forfeited estates in Ireland. He was critical of the Irish government for not taking strong enough measures to root out Jacobites, and was concerned at the strength of Tory support in parts of the country. His son Francis was also an Irish MP and shared his father's anti-Tory political views to a large extent; he appears to have suffered from ill health and died shortly after 1713.

Essays on Trade and Navigation (1695) was intended as the first part of a five-part work, but the remaining parts were never published. *New Essays on Trade* (1702) may have been intended as a continuation, but no further works appeared before Brewster's death. He says that he was motivated to write by a concern for the general state of ignorance about trade. There is, he says, no subject on which more has been written and yet worse understood: 'I think it is a mortal distemper in trade…that we have so few men of university-learning conversant in true mercantile employments: if there were as much care to have men of the best heads and education in it, as there is in the laws, the nation would fetch more from abroad, and spend less in law-suits at home' (1695: iii). He calls for the establishment of colleges in each maritime city and major port in England to teach the theory and practice of commerce to young men and educate them properly in trade.

Like many mercantilists, Brewster sees the existence of a strong navy as being of paramount importance, and he draws a direct relationship between the navy and commerce; one cannot be strong without the other. Indeed, *Essays* opens by saying that Britain derives its strength from trade, but France represents a constant threat to that trade, and therefore a strong navy is required for protection. He opposes free ports, which he says will encourage foreign shipping to the detriment of English shipowners, and this in turn will weaken the navy.

Brewster also believes strongly that the domestic woollen manufacture ought to be encouraged and that woollen cloth is one of the most important commodities that the country produces. He welcomes the arrival of Protestant émigrés from Europe, such as the French Huguenots; these were often skilled craftsmen, and could be usefully employed to revitalize the woollen cloth and other industries. He opposes the export of wool and calls for tighter enforcement of the laws prohibiting it. However, he cautions against banning imports, as this could lead to other countries banning British exports in retaliation. The outright prohibition of imports should only be resorted to in extreme cases. Instead, Brewster suggests a system of sumptuary laws that would work to restrict demand for luxury goods and thus reduce imports.

Other measures Brewster proposes include better regulation and laws to govern trade, the establishment of industries by poorhouses and hospitals to provide employment for the poor, and the establishment of a national bank to fund trade. He also calls for the establishment of a government council to regulate trade. This council should be small in number, and made up of experienced men with wide knowledge of trade, not confined to one speciality.

New Essays on Trade repeats many of these themes, with a few additional ones. Here Brewster expands on the idea of providing employment for the poor, and gives his view that full employment is the best way to increase wealth. If those who are in receipt of charity can be gainfully employed, then the wealth of all will increase. He also expresses bullionist views and is particularly critical of bank notes, which he says do not encourage the import of bullion but rather hasten its export. The apparent increase of money at home leads merchants to buy more goods from overseas, but they cannot purchase goods overseas with banknotes, which the inhabitants refuse to recognize. Therefore the increased imports must be paid for with gold and silver, increasing the outflow.

BIBLIOGRAPHY
Essays on Trade and Navigation (1695).
New Essays on Trade (1702).

Further Reading
Johnston-Liik, E.M., *History of the Irish Parliament 1692–1800*, vol. III (Belfast, 2002).

Morgen Witzel

BRIGHT, John (1811–89)

Bright was born at Greenbank, Rochdale on 16 November 1811. He died of diabetes and Bright's disease at One Ash, the family home in Rochdale, on 27 March 1889. He was buried at the Friends' Meeting House in Rochdale. He was the second son of Jacob Bright, a Quaker cotton spinner, and his second wife, Martha Wood. The couple had seven sons and four daughters. Their eldest son died in 1814, leaving John Bright as the eldest child. He was educated at several Quaker schools in the north of England, firstly in Rochdale, then Ackworth. From there, he moved to York and then Newton, near Clitheroe.

At school, Bright developed a lifelong love of the Bible and of seventeenth-century English Puritan poets, especially Milton. Quaker beliefs shaped his politics, which consisted mainly of demands to end social, political or religious inequalities. On completing his education, Bright participated in the management of his father's cotton mills. His introduction to politics came in 1830 when Henry Hunt was elected as MP for Preston. Concurrently, Bright made his first public speech in Rochdale in support of the temperance movement. In 1833 he became a founder member of the Rochdale Literary and Philosophical Society. His main interests outside politics were fishing and cricket. In 1833 and 1836, Bright travelled on the continent. On his return, he became directly involved in politics.

Between 1834 and 1841, Bright led a successful campaign in Rochdale against the payment of compulsory taxes for the Church of England. He became MP for Durham in 1843 and went on to represent Manchester (1847–57) and Birmingham (1857–89). In 1868 he became President of the Board of Trade and a privy counsellor in Gladstone's first ministry. Bright was the first nonconformist cabinet member. He resigned because of ill health in 1870. In 1839 Bright married Elizabeth Priestman from Newcastle on Tyne; she died of consumption in September 1841, leaving Bright with a daughter, Helen. In 1847 Bright married Margaret Elizabeth Leatham; she died in 1878. The couple had four sons and three daughters.

Throughout his long political career, Bright advocated free trade and was one of the leaders of the Anti-Corn Law campaign. He supported land reform and the disestablishment of the Irish Church; he opposed Britain's belligerent foreign policy, advocated government decentralization in India and opposed legislation for reducing factory hours. Bright favoured parliamentary reform, defended religious toleration and opposed capital punishment.

Bright joined the committee of the Anti-Corn Law Association in October 1838, making his first anti-Corn Law speech in Rochdale that year. He and his father, now business partners, gave £300 to the association's funds. In 1839, the association became the Anti-Corn Law League. Richard COBDEN, whom Bright had met in 1835, persuaded Bright to become more active in the League. By 1841 he had emerged as the chief supporting speaker to Cobden. Bright's workers joined Plug Plot strikes (1842), but he persuaded them not to commit violent acts similar to those of other towns. His argument was that while trade was poor, wages could not rise. He was convinced that political reform, as demanded by the Chartists, was not the answer to his workers' distress, but that repeal of the Corn Laws was. One of Bright's perpetual arguments was that without free trade, the domestic economy would not improve.

For five years, Cobden and Bright frequently spoke on the same platform throughout the country. Cobden's speeches provided persuasive arguments; Bright denounced the privileged political position of the agricultural landlords. Although Bright knew the high moral and economic case for free trade, he usually spoke on behalf of the manufacturers and mill hands who, he said, shared a common interest in overturning the corn laws. He opposed the corn laws in parliament during Peel's second ministry until the legislation was repealed in June 1846.

Bright was prominent in encouraging the emergence of manufacturers as a political force after the 1832 Reform Act. He thought that for economic reasons, the middle classes were more valuable to society than the aristocracy was: the middle classes increasingly were the earners and owners of wealth. After the corn laws were repealed, Bright received many tokens of appreciation from his supporters. These included the gift of a library of books and the offer to become Manchester's MP, which he accepted.

Bright always maintained that free trade would promote world peace and was inseparable from a pacific foreign policy. He maintained that all trade was based on mutual cooperation and encouraged goodwill among nations. Bright firmly adhered to the liberal formula of 'peace, retrenchment and reform'. His maiden speech in the Commons on 7 August 1843 supported a motion for the reduction of import duties on raw materials and manufactures and demanded the implementation of total free trade. He denounced the duties on West Indian sugar until they were repealed in 1848 and he worked for the repeal of the Navigation Acts.

On 1 December 1859, Bright addressed the Financial Reform Association in Liverpool. In his speech, he advocated the repeal of income tax, assessed taxes, taxes on marine and fire insurance and the excise on paper. He also wanted to see the abolition of all other duties except those on wine, spirits and tobacco. Bright suggested that duties should be replaced by a tax of eight shillings per £100 of fixed income instead. His ideas terrified the Tories and also alarmed the middle classes.

In the 1859 parliament, Bright argued for a reduction in military expenditure and suggested a reciprocity treaty with France. This became the Cobden Treaty of 1860. During the negotiations, which were made difficult by Palmerston's anti-French speeches and his building of fortifications, Bright acted as Cobden's spokesman in the commons. The House of Lords opposed Gladstone's budget in 1860 because of concessions made by the Cobden Treaty so Bright began to demand changes to the Lords' ability to interfere with finance bills.

During the American Civil War (1861–5), Bright supported the Unionists, believing that the abolition of slavery was of more importance than the need for cheap cotton, although he argued that emancipated labour would produce more cotton. On this issue, his beliefs were secondary to his business affairs: the ensuing cotton famine hit Lancashire hard and Bright and Brothers' six mills were idle for a long period. After 1879 and influenced by Joseph Chamberlain, the Conservatives encouraged protectionism through the 'fair trade' movement that demanded reciprocity rather than merely a British policy of free trade. Bright opposed the movement, pointing out the improved economic condition of Britain under free trade and the injurious consequences of protectionism to America.

The Brights were benevolent employers, but their faith in self-help and independence placed John Bright at the head of the manufacturers who opposed factory legislation, trade unions and social reform. Bright argued that the real problem with the length of factory hours was the maintenance of the Corn Laws. Consequently, he opposed legislation to limit working hours in factories and denounced John Fielden's *The Curse of the Factory System* (1836). Bright opposed Graham's Factory Bill (1844) and Ashley's Factory Bill (1846). He attacked Ashley's description of the horrors of factory conditions, contrasting them with the condition of agricultural labourers for whom landowners had little concern. In 1847 Bright opposed a government scheme of education for factory children, saying that education should be a private matter, not the affair of the state. His father already had built a school for his workers' children and also had provided a reading room and newsroom for his employees. In 1884 Bright wrote: 'I was opposed to all legislation restricting the working of adults, men or women. I was in favour of legislation restricting the labour and guarding the health of children. I still hold the opinion that to limit by law the time during which adults may work is unwise and in many cases oppressive'. It was Bright's belief that limiting working hours by law would lead to more poverty for factory workers since their earning power would be restricted.

Bright was a member of the Peace Society and denounced the Crimean War (1854–6) as un-Christian, contrary to the principles of international free trade and harmful to British interests. He said that foreign alliances would drag Britain into future conflicts and that the only people to benefit from war were the 'tax-eating' classes, whereas ordinary people suffered by paying the increased taxes that were needed to fund foreign adventures. In a powerful speech opposing the war, Bright said that, 'the Angel of Death has been abroad throughout the land; you may almost hear the beating of his wings. There is no one...to sprinkle with blood the lintel and the two sideposts of our doors, that he may spare and pass on; he takes his victims from the castle of the noble, the mansion of the wealthy, and the cottage of the poor and lowly.'

Bright's opinion was that British foreign policy and the expensive network of diplomatic appointments constituted 'a gigantic system of outdoor relief for the aristocracy'. His anti-war views made him very unpopular in the country and also helped to lose him his Manchester seat in 1857. Within a few months he became MP for Birmingham, which he was to represent for the rest of his life. Frustrated at his failure to stop the Crimean War, Bright suffered a nervous breakdown (1856–8). He went fishing in Yorkshire, then went to Europe for several months.

Despite his unpopularity for opposing the Crimean War, Bright went on to attack Disraeli's interventionist policy in Egypt, to denounce the Afghan war and to demand friendly relations with Russia. In September 1873 Bright had accepted the office of Chancellor of the Duchy of Lancaster, which he resigned on 15 July 1882 over the British bombardment of Alexandria following the massacre of Christians there in June. He said the government had conducted a 'manifest violation both of international law and of the moral law' that he could not support.

In 1845, in partnership with his brothers, Bright managed two of the three mills belonging to his father. This turned his attention to the supply of raw cotton, a shortage of which had led to distress in Lancashire. Bright chaired the committee that looked into the feasibility of cotton imports from India. In 1850 he asked for a commission to visit India to investigate the possibilities of extending the cotton trade. The East India Company and the government opposed his suggestion so he established and funded a private enquiry; the report described India's maladministration by the East India Company. This led to Bright opposing the renewal of the company's charter in 1853. He said that instead of being controlled by a trading company, India should be the responsibility of a government department with a minister of state.

Bright pressed for less authoritarian British rule in India both before and after the Indian Mutiny (1857), for which he blamed British misrule. He argued that the Indian people should be allowed to elect their own government, and demanded the decentralization of the government in India. In February 1879 he again advocated decentralization, without success. In 1868 Gladstone offered Bright the post of Secretary of State for India, which he refused on the grounds that it would link him with the military government there.

Bright favoured parliamentary reform, and campaigned for it from 1848. In 1850 he opposed the Ecclesiastical Titles Bill, and in 1853 he supported the lifting of disabilities on Jews. He launched a speech-making campaign for parliamentary reform in Birmingham at the end of 1858 which faded out within a few months, although Disraeli introduced the proposals to parliament in 1859. Bright thought that there would be no parliamentary reform while Palmerston was prime minister, but as soon as Palmerston died Bright renewed his demands for reform. The campaign marked the beginning of the movement toward the reform agitation of the mid-1860s.

In 1866 Bright attacked the anti-reform Whigs, accusing them of retreating to the 'cave of Adullam': the name 'Adullamites' thereafter entered the political vocabulary. Later in 1866 Bright found himself the hero and chief mouthpiece of the reformers, accepted by those who demanded universal suffrage and those who wanted more limited reform: Bright himself supported universal suffrage and the secret ballot. In October 1866 Bright was in Ireland, speaking in favour of parliamentary reform, land reform and disestablishment of the Irish church. In terms of immediate influence, this was the high point of his career.

Bright opposed Disraeli's reform bill (1867), and voted in favour of the enfranchisement of women. Over this issue he changed his mind, speaking against it in 1876. Bright was satisfied with the 1867 Reform Act, which extended the vote to skilled urban artisans but excluded the town and country labourers. The artisans' intelligence and independence impressed him, and he recommended that every man who wanted the vote should acquire these qualities.

Bright proved to be a consistent supporter of reform for Ireland. In 1847, at the height of the famine, he said that the causes of unrest in Ireland should be dealt with, not just the effects. Bright wanted the Irish poor law unions to be given £50,000 for the relief of poverty. In 1849 he visited Ireland to study conditions there at first hand. He advocated the sale of encumbered estates and the break-up of landed property so that the peasants could become a land-owning group. He spoke against Irish coercion bill of 1848 and said that Irish church should be disestablished. This was an argument to which he returned regularly. For example in 1860, Bright asserted that Fenian activity was the result of maintaining the established church in Ireland; he went on to condemn the British administration of Ireland since 1801. Disestablishment finally occurred in 1869.

In 1870 Bright became ill, and he resigned from the Board of Trade in December. He returned to the Commons in 1872 and promptly opposed Irish home rule on grounds that two legislative bodies in Britain would be 'an intolerable mischief'. He also opposed the idea of 'home rule all round' that was proposed in 1875. Gladstone's 1881 Land Act implemented a measure that Bright had proposed for many years. However, Bright opposed Gladstone's Home Rule policy for Ireland in 1882, announcing that he was not prepared to see power given to Irish nationalists who had made a mockery of parliamentary government.

Bright was important in Victorian liberal politics. His views were firmly based on his religious convictions, and he proved to be influential in the achievement of free trade and later ideas of non-intervention. He was enlightened in his views on Ireland and parliamentary reform and was a consistent defender of individual liberties.

BIBLIOGRAPHY
Women's Disabilities Removal Bill: A Speech of John Bright in the House of Commons, 26th April, 1876 (1876).
Speeches on Questions of Public Policy by John Bright, M.P., ed. J.E. Thorold Rogers (1883).
Selected Speeches of the Rt. Hon. John Bright, M.P. on Public Questions (n.d.).

Further Reading
Ausubel, H., *John Bright: Victorian Reformer* (New York, 1966).
Barnett Smith, G., *The Life and Speeches of John Bright* (1881).
Roberts, K., *John Bright* (1979).

Marjorie Bloy

BRISCOE, John (*fl.* 1695–8)

Very little is known of John Briscoe, founder of the National Land Bank in 1695. He was probably, like his contemporary and sometime colleague Thomas NEALE, a London merchant and property owner. He may have been a brother of Samuel Briscoe, the Covent Garden bookseller and publisher. He first appears on the scene in the early 1690s when, along with Neale and Hugh CHAMBERLEN the elder, he began advancing the idea of a land bank. He was briefly a prominent figure in the National Land Bank until its merger with the Land Bank of Nicholas BARBON and John ASGILL, the merged entity being renamed the National Land Bank of England. Thereafter he produced a number of pamphlets urging support for the land bank concept, but it is not known how actively he was involved in the running of this institution. He disappears from view after the collapse of the Land Bank.

Apart from pamphlets on the Land Bank, Briscoe was also the author of *A Discourse of Money* (1696). Although this falls partly into the category of propaganda for the Land Bank, it is also a detailed and thoughtful theory of money. Briscoe begins with a history of money and says it is as old as human society, being more convenient for commerce than barter or exchange. Money began with base metals like iron or brass that had little intrinsic value, 'but was made currant and received an extrinsic or political value from the stamp and authority of the prince or state' (1696: 10), the latter usually taking the form of an image stamped on the coin. Extrinsic value, then, is the power and authority of the state that authorizes the use of the coins in question. However, as time passed, most states converted to gold and silver which were perceived to have intrinsic value; that is, they constitute wealth in their own right and are imperishable. In their bullion form, gold and silver are intrinsic wealth that not even princes can change; but princes can alter extrinsic value by withdrawing their stamp from the coinage. Gold and silver thus became a 'universal coin' (1696: 14).

A running theme throughout the book is Briscoe's belief that intrinsic value is more important than extrinsic value, being less liable to fluctuation and the whim of rulers. Gold and silver to a nation are like blood to a living being, he says, necessary to sustain life. Labour is more productive and business flourishes when there is plenty of gold and silver with 'a real universal value...a solid unchangeable unarbitrary recompense: wherefore the finer and purer your money is, the more it will charm and incite to the use of those means that conduct men to the possession of it' (1696: 20). The intrinsic value of gold and silver not only stimulates manufacturing and trade, but it also raises the value of land, and this encourages the improvement of husbandry and tillage. But, warns Briscoe, this increased wealth also brings the envy and enmity of others and increases the likelihood of war, so a strong navy and merchant fleet become essential.

Briscoe believes that to be beneficial to the economy, money must be in active circulation and all people must have easy access to it. He condemns hoarding and usury, both of which practices tend to concentrate money in the hands of a few and reduce the circulation of money.

Briscoe turns next to the value of money, looking at the relationship between money and price. He makes a direct link between circulating money and the national income, and argues that the ideal situation is when the quantity of money in circulation exactly equals society's needs; that is, when the amount of money each person earns in a year will equal what they need to spend on consumption in that same year. National income and money supply should correlate exactly. He postulates a 'perfect' situation in which a state, isolated from the outside world, has a population of 10,000 people. To determine what the money supply should be, it is necessary to calculate the cost of all those 'particulars' each citizen will need or be expected to consume within the course of a year. If each person can be expected to spend £20 per annum, then the amount of money the state needs is £20 x 10,000, or £200,000. There would thus be an exact correlation between money supply and national income.

But what if the population of this perfect state begins to increase, while the supply of money does not? Income per head will then fall. Briscoe's answer is not to increase money supply, but rather to force prices down to match income. If the population of a state should double, then prices should decline by 50 per cent. Briscoe recognizes that prices will not fall naturally in this way, and accepts that price regulations should be used to compel this decline. A strong believer in intervention, Briscoe argues that cases of dearth or scarcity of money – and indeed of oversupply – are the result of governments being lax in their regulation of the economy. Preventing money shortages prevents dearth and famine, while preventing oversupply stops wasteful speculation.

Briscoe also accepts that his perfect world where money supply matches national income does not exist. One of the primary problems that upsets the balance is the need for defence and war. Here Briscoe argues that society needs to open up and engage in trade in order to bring in additional money to pay for defence, making explicit the interdependence between defence and trade. Another problem is avarice, which leads people to covet more than their due share of the national wealth, and here Briscoe repeats his attack on usury. While very detailed and considered, *A Discourse of Money* suffers from over-reliance on the theoretical model at its heart.

Briscoe's other writings, as noted, are mainly aimed at making the case for the Land Bank. In *A Discourse on the Late Funds* (1696), he attacks other fundraising expedients such as the lottery and the Bank of England. He claims the government is treating the nation as if it were already bankrupt, and this must be a cause of shame to all English people. If a war must be fought, then rather than borrowing, let the country pay for it directly through taxes and by drawing on its own assets and wealth, especially land. People should pay for their own defence and benefit accordingly, rather than seeing the promoters of schemes like the lottery and the Bank of England profit and grow rich. Ironically, only a few years later the Bank of England was called upon by parliament to clean up the mess left by the collapse of the Land Bank.

BIBLIOGRAPHY

The Freehold Estates of England, or England Itself the Best Fund or Security (1695).
An Account of the Value of the Estates in the Several Counties Subscribed Toward the Fund for a National Land-Bank (1695).
Mr Briscoe's Reply to a Pamphlet, intituled, The Freeholders Answer to Mr John Briscoe's Proposals for a National Bank (1695).
A Discourse of Money (1696).
A Discourse on the Late Funds of the Million-Act, Lottery-Act and Bank of England, Shewing, That they are Injurious to the Nobility and Gentry, and Ruinous to the Trade of the Nation (1696).
Proposals for Raising Money for the National Land-Bank (1698).

Morgen Witzel

BROUGHAM, Henry Peter (1778–1868)

Brougham, the first child of Westmoreland landowners Henry and Eleanora Brougham, was born in Edinburgh on 19 September 1778 and died in Cannes on 7 May 1868. His mother was the only daughter of Rev. James Syme, and the niece of the noted historian and principal of Edinburgh University, William Robertson. Brougham credited his maternal grandmother, Robertson's sister, for instilling in him a thirst for knowledge and a perseverance that allowed him to achieve success in his life. After graduating head of his class at Edinburgh High School, he entered Edinburgh University in 1792 where he initially studied science, mathematics and philosophy. Before the age of twenty he published papers on mathematics and physics in the *Transactions* of the Royal Society and in 1803 was elected a Fellow of the Royal Society. Despite these successes, his interest soon turned to law. He was called to the bar at Lincoln's Inn in June 1800 and after a few years as a briefless barrister moved to London to pursue his legal career and politics. He married Marianne Spalding, formerly Marianne Eden, in 1819. Their first child, Sarah Eleanor, died as an infant in 1820 and their only other child, Eleanor Louise, lived from 1822–39.

Brougham is known principally for his political career, becoming one of the most prominent and popular politicians of his day. He became a member of parliament for Camelford under the patronage of the Duke of Bedford in 1810, but lost his position in 1812 when Bedford sold his seat. He was returned for Winchelsea in 1816 and served until 1830. In the House of Commons he was a powerful Whig, generally recognized as a moderate reformer with forceful oratory. He gained immense popularity in 1819 and 1820 when he defended Queen Caroline's right to the throne against charges of adultery by King George IV. He was at the peak of his popularity in 1830, having been elected as an outside candidate from Yorkshire, when he consented to become Lord Chancellor. But his party was briefly turned out in 1835 and he lost the position of Chancellor. He continued to attend the House of Lords for more than two additional decades, making his last speech in 1856, but he was never able to regain the popularity he had in the Commons.

While he was engaged in numerous activities as a member of parliament, Brougham's efforts on behalf of anti-slavery, law reform and education were the most successful. He was generally not an influential politician after 1835, but he remained active as a scholar and statesmen. Among his voluminous writings were a three-volume book of sketches of statesmen, and works on natural theology and political philosophy. In 1857 he helped form the National Association for the Promotion of Social Sciences and served as its president until he was eighty-seven. He also was elected chancellor of Edinburgh University in 1860.

Early in his career Brougham focused on theoretical issues, especially colonial policy, evidently intending to make an impact as a political economist. In 1803 he wrote the two-volume *Inquiry into the Colonial Policy of the European Powers*. Despite some favourable reviews, his work generally is ignored as a work on political economy because of its poor arrangement, long historical digressions and overall length. Nevertheless, it contained a number of important economic arguments. Among other things, he refuted both Adam SMITH and the Physiocrats, who had maintained that the colonies should be given their independence. In noting several reasons for retaining the colonies yet maintaining free trade, Semmel (1970) argues that Brougham was one of the first of the 'free trade imperialists' and an important forerunner of later imperialists. Brougham also criticized Smith for not distancing himself enough from the Physiocrats who had solely emphasized the importance of agriculture. Smith was particularly concerned that investments in colonies were diverting capital from agriculture, but Brougham maintained that if capital did not have an outlet in the colonies overall demand would contract due to fewer markets, potentially causing the produce of the land to decline. Brougham belonged to the new breed of economist who afforded manufacturing as much importance as agriculture; manufacturing, he argued, gave landowners and farmers an incentive to produce more to obtain goods other than food. Brougham also maintained that the accumulation of wealth in Britain led to smaller profit margins and could lead to an excess supply of goods if demand became stagnant, but concluded that stagnation could be avoided if excess supplies of goods and capital could be sent to the colonies.

During the first decade of the nineteenth century Brougham was one of the leading writers on economic subjects. Most of his written contributions to economics during this time were contained in the *Edinburgh Review*, which was the only journal at that time regularly addressing economic topics. Brougham was one of the founders of the *Review* and quickly became its most prolific contributor, specializing in economic matters. Between 1802 and 1806 Brougham wrote thirteen of the twenty-four economics articles; by 1810 he had written twenty of the forty-five economics articles (Fetter 1953). Many of Brougham's *Edinburgh Review* articles reiterated themes presented in his *Colonial Policy*, consistently advocating free trade and a *laissez-faire* approach to policy.

Brougham's most important economics article (in July 1804) was a scathing critique of Lord LAUDERDALE's *Inquiry into the Nature and Origin of Public Wealth*. This article was important not only for its content, but because it was one of the first major economic debates in a public forum. Lauderdale's spirited rebuttal, *Observations by the Earl of Lauderdale on the Review of His Inquiry into the Nature and Origin of Public Wealth*, appeared in pamphlet form in November 1804, and Brougham's rejoinder pamphlet, *Thoughts Suggested by Lord Lauderdale's Observations upon the Edinburgh Review*, was published in 1805. Among the theoretical contributions of these works was one of the earliest and certainly the clearest criticism of Adam Smith's distinction between productive and unproductive labour. While Brougham acknowledged that Lauderdale had also made this distinction, he suggested that Lauderdale's deductions 'appeared deficient...and narrow' and maintained that a more careful elaboration of Smith's errors was necessary (1804: 278–9). Brougham particularly criticized Lauderdale's attempt to prove that agriculture was inherently more productive than manufacturing. He argued that all 'those occupations which tend to supply the necessary wants, or multiply the comforts and pleasures of human life, are equally productive' (1804: 354–63). Both Brougham and Lauderdale had variations of underconsumptionist theory. Lauderdale's more radical theory indicated that oversaving was probable if insufficient emphasis was placed on all types of spending. Brougham agreed that oversaving of capital as well as overpopulation might be possible in the more refined stages of society, but he did not believe, as did Lauderdale, that Britain had become so refined. Consequently, Brougham argued that Britain should seek every outlet possible, such as new colonies, to delay or avoid oversaving.

After 1810 Brougham's theoretical writing on economics ceased, but his influence continued through parliamentary speeches and debates and through his continuing efforts to popularize economic ideas. In parliament he consistently advocated free trade and *laissez-faire* policies, and was generally a strong advocate of the positions of the classical economists. An example of Brougham's devotion to classical ideas was his strong advocacy of the Poor Law Amendment of 1834. Brougham's speech on behalf of the Poor Law Amendment was strongly Malthusian, arguing that the poor laws as they existed provided adverse incentives to the poor. But Brougham was also a pragmatist who was willing to modify a theoretical position if he felt the times warranted a change. The best example of his willingness to alter his theoretical position is his stance on the Corn Laws, which had imposed tariffs on grain imported during the Napoleonic Wars. In 1816 he argued in favour of the Corn Laws as a necessary transition for farmers who had brought poor land into cultivation to produce needed food during the Wars. By 1822, however, he felt the stress from the war had subsided and he voted for RICARDO's amendment to repeal the Corn Laws; from that point forward he was a consistent advocate for repeal.

After he entered parliament Brougham became one of the leading popularizers of classical economic ideas. His position as a well-known public figure, his early theoretical writing on economics, his legendary level of energy and his support of better education for all classes and age groups, made him ideally suited to promote the ideas of the classical economists. Among numerous activities involving education, Brougham supported bills in parliament to promote universal and cheap education for children, was an energizing force in founding the Mechanics' Institutes, organized and served as chair of the Society for the Diffusion of Useful Knowledge and helped found London University. These activities disseminated economic ideas among the middle and working classes and facilitated the introduction of economic theory into the classrooms of Britain.

As a theoretical economist, Brougham should be remembered for his consistent advocacy of free trade and imperialism and the proposition that colonies provided a needed vent for surplus capital and population, thus preventing oversaving (or underconsumption) and stagnation. He was one of the first to note clearly the weakness in Smith's distinction between productive and unproductive labour, and was one of the earliest economists to argue that all sectors of the economy, including manufacturing, were equally important. Perhaps more importantly, he should be remembered for pragmatically and effectively promoting classical economic ideas in parliament and through various educational schemes.

BIBLIOGRAPHY

'Crisis of the Sugar Colonies', *Edinburgh Review* (1802), vol. 1, pp. 216–37.

An Inquiry into the Colonial Policy of the European Powers, 2 vols (Edinburgh, 1803).

'Canard's Principes d'economie politique', *Edinburgh Review* (1803), vol. 2, pp. 43–50.

'Guineas an Unnecessary and Expensive Incumbrance on commerce', *Edinburgh Review* (1803), vol. 3, pp. 101–16.

'Wheatley's Remarks on Currency and Commerce', *Edinburgh Review* (1803), vol. 5), pp. 231–52.

'Hatchett on the Gold Coin', *Edinburgh Review* (1804), vol. 6, pp. 452–7.

'Bishop Watson on the National Debt', *Edinburgh Review* (1804), vol. 6, pp. 468–86.

'Morgan's Comparative View of the Public Finances', *Edinburgh Review* (1804), vol. 7, pp. 75–83.

'Lord Lauderdale's Inquiry into the Nature and Origin of Public Wealth', *Edinburgh Review* (1804), vol. 8, pp. 343–77.

'Plans of National Improvement', *Edinburgh Review* (1804), vol. 9, pp. 1–22.

'O'Conner's Present State of Great Britain', *Edinburgh Review* (1804), vol. 9, pp. 104–24.

'Talleyrand sur les colonies', *Edinburgh Review* (1805), vol. 11, pp. 63–79.

'Sur l'usage de numeraire', *Edinburgh Review* (1805), vol. 11, pp. 112–21.

'Lord Lauderdale's Hints to the Manufacturers', *Edinburgh Review* (1805), vol. 12, pp. 283–90.

Thoughts Suggested by Lord Lauderdale's Observations upon the Edinburgh Review (1805).

'Lord Liverpool on the Coin', *Edinburgh Review* (1806), vol. 14, pp. 265–95.

'Examination of the Late Orders in Council', *Edinburgh Review* (1808), vol. 22, pp. 484–98.

'Baring and Others on the Orders in Council', *Edinburgh Review* (1808), vol. 23, pp. 225–46.

'Education of the Poor', *Edinburgh Review* (1810), vol. 33, pp. 58–88.

'Education of the Poor', *Edinburgh Review* (1811), vol. 37, pp. 1–41.

'Education of the Poor', *Edinburgh Review* (1813), vol. 42, pp. 207–19.

'Bentham's *Defence of Usury*', *Edinburgh Review* (1816), vol. 54, pp. 339–60.

'Cobbett's *Cottage Economy*', *Edinburgh Review* (1823), vol. 75, pp. 105–25.

'Newspaper Tax', *Edinburgh Review* (1835), vol. 123, pp. 181–5.

'Taxes on Knowledge', *Edinburgh Review* (1835), vol. 125, pp. 126–32.

Works of Henry, Lord Brougham, 11 vols (Glasgow, 1855–61).

The Life and Times of Henry Brougham, Written by Himself (1871).

Further Reading
Aspinall, A., *Lord Brougham and the Whig Party* (Manchester, 1927).
Bagehot, W., 'Lord Brougham', in N. St. John Stevas (ed.), *Bagehot's Historical Essays* (New York, 1966).
Fetter, F.W., 'The Authorship of Economic Articles in the Edinburgh Review, 1802–1847', *Journal of Political Economy* (1953), vol. 61, pp. 232–60.
——, *The Economist in Parliament 1780–1868* (Durham, North Carolina, 1980).
Fontana, B., *Rethinking the Politics of Commercial Society: The Edinburgh Review 1802–1832* (Cambridge, 1985).
Garratt, G.T., *Lord Brougham* (1935).
Gilbert, A., *The Work of Lord Brougham for Education in England* (Chambersberg, Pennsylvania, 1922).
Hawes, F., *Henry Brougham* (New York, 1958).
Lauderdale, Lord, *An Inquiry into the Nature and Origin of Public Wealth* (Edinburgh, 1804).
——, *Observations by the Earl of Lauderdale on the Review of His Inquiry into the Nature and Origin of Public Wealth Published in the VIII Number of the Edinburgh Review* (Edinburgh, 1804).
Mill, J., 'Brougham's Inquiry into Colonial Policy of European Powers', *Literary Journal* (1803) vol. 2, pp. 513–28.
——, 'Lord Lauderdale's Inquiry', *Literary Journal* (1804), vol. 3, pp. 1–15.
Semmel, B., *The Rise of Free Trade Imperialism* (Cambridge, 1970).
Sockwell, W.D., 'Contributions of Henry Brougham to Classical Political Economy', *History of Political Economy* (1991), vol. 23, no. 4, pp. 645–73.
——, *Popularizing Classical Economics: Henry Brougham and William Ellis* (1994).
Stewart, R., *Henry Brougham* (1986).

William D. Sockwell

BROUGHTON, John (*c*.1674–1720)

Broughton was born probably in 1674, and may have come from Barkston in Lincolnshire. He attended Christ's College, Cambridge, receiving a BA in 1694. In 1703 he was appointed chaplain to John Churchill, Duke of Marlborough, and in 1712 became vicar of Kingston-upon-Thames. In 1716 he received a doctorate in divinity, also from Christ's College. He died in London. Broughton is most famous for his *Psychologia; or an Account of the Nature of the Rational Soul* (1703), which set out to demonstrate both the immateriality and the immortality of the human soul. The book is a refutation of parts of John LOCKE's *Essay on Human Understanding* and of William Coward's *Second Thoughts concerning Human Soul*.

Broughton was also interested in economic problems, particularly those concerning finance and credit. His *Remarks upon the Bank of England* (1705) was published anonymously, with the author named only (and quite misleadingly) as 'a Merchant of London'. The occasion for this pamphlet was the Bank's request for an extension or 'prolongation' of its original charter, which was due to expire in 1705; the Bank's directors were asking for an extension of a further twenty-one years. Broughton argued that the request should be denied and the Bank dissolved. He accused the Bank of attempting to secure a monopoly of credit in the country, and warned that such a step could result in the cutting off of credit to small merchants as the Bank would serve to channel all available credit to the government: 'And it will follow from hence, that the Bank will be, in short time, not only the *great*, but the *only* lender to the government' (1705: 28, italics in original).

Broughton went on to argue that the concentration of credit in the hands of the Bank would give it far too much power over government, and this could be dangerous to the country as a whole. His attack provoked a defence of the Bank in the anonymous pamphlet *A Vindication of the Bank of England* (1707). The author of this work ridiculed Broughton and his concerns, arguing that a monopoly of credit such as Broughton envisaged was impossible and that the Bank would never be able to dominate the government.

Broughton went on to argue that the supply of credit should in fact be in the hands of government, in order to ensure a sufficient supply of credit and promote trade. A strong system of credit, he says, is essential for strong trade, especially when trading rivals like the Netherlands already have a well-organized system of public credit. The most important aspects of any system of credit are security and convenience:

> That is certainly the most secure Credit, which is least liable of any other to a Failure, and which is founded upon a good Bottom, large enough to support it. And that is most convenient Credit, which is most easie and dispatchful to receive and pay, and will serve the most sorts of People, and upon most Occasions, to make their payments by, as well as they can do by Money
>
> (1706: 6).

Government, he argues, is best placed to ensure that the needs for security and convenience are met. The power government can command means it can provide ample security, and the apparatus of the state can also be used to ensure convenience. Broughton envisages a scheme whereby the tax system could also double up as a public bank, effectively taking over the functions of the Bank of England; receivers of taxes throughout the country would then lend money to merchants as well as collecting taxes.

BIBLIOGRAPHY
Remarks upon the Bank of England, with Regard more Especially to our Trade and Government (1705).

An Essay upon the National Credit of England; Introductory to a Proposal Prepar'd for Establishing the Public Credit, (n.d.; probably 1706).

Further Reading
Anon., *A Vindication of the Bank of England from the Misrepresentations, and Groundless Suggestions of a late Pamphlet entitled, Remarks upon the Bank of England...by a Merchant* (1707).

Morgen Witzel

BROWN, Ernest Henry Phelps (1906–94)

Brown was born on 10 February 1906 in Calne, Wiltshire, the son of a rather austere Baptist ironmonger. He died in Oxford on 15 December 1994. He was educated at Taunton School and at Wadham College, Oxford, where he was secretary of the Union; he graduated in history in 1927 and in politics, philosophy and economics two years later. After a year in the USA as a Rockefeller Travelling Fellow, he became fellow in economics at New College, Oxford in 1930, where for a time George SHACKLE was one of his research assistants. In the Second World War Phelps Brown served in the Royal Artillery, rising to the rank of lieutenant-colonel; his wartime experiences provided the background for his novel, *The Balloon* (1953).

From 1947 until his early retirement in 1968, Phelps Brown was Professor of the Economics of Labour at the London School of Economics where, as he recalled, he benefited more from contact with a succession of gifted junior researchers (including Peter Hart and Sheila Hopkins) than from the expertise of his more senior colleagues. He remained active well into his eighties, publishing four of his eight books and forty of his 100 articles after he retired to Oxford, the last in 1990. In addition to his academic work, Phelps Brown served on a number of official committees. In 1959–61 he was one of the 'three wise men' who advised the Conservative government on incomes policy; he was an independent member of the National Economic Development Council ('Neddy') in 1962–4; and from 1974–8 he was a member of the Royal Commission on the Distribution of Income and Wealth, for which he was knighted in 1976. He was elected Fellow of the British Academy in 1960.

Phelps Brown was a true political economist. His research ranged over the disciplines of economic theory, econometrics, economic history, labour economics, labour history and industrial relations, almost always from a historical perspective and with a concern for the policy implications of his work. He wrote lucidly and without pretension, and was the author of three well-received textbooks, *The Framework of the Price System* (1936), *A Course in Applied Economics* (1951) and *The Economics of Labour* (1962). His masterly *Growth of British Industrial Relations* (1959) remains the best historical introduction to British trade unions and their interactions with organized employers and the state, written from the viewpoint of an economist but with a profound understanding of the way in which institutions originate and evolve. In *A Century of Pay* (1968, with Margaret Browne) he analysed the macroeconomics of labour markets in Germany, Sweden, the United States and the United Kingdom with the same breadth of historical knowledge, combined this time with some adept, but critical, use of economic theory.

Another side of Phelps Brown was revealed in 1957, when the *Quarterly Journal of Economics* published his critique of the fitted Cobb-Douglas production function. The estimated coefficients for labour and capital closely resembled the actual income shares of wages and profits, and it was often claimed that this provided econometric confirmation of neoclassical distribution theory. Phelps Brown denied that these findings had any theoretical significance; they merely reflected the statistical fact that the historical shares of capital and labour had been roughly constant during the relevant periods. Anyone expecting him to intervene on the side of Cambridge (England) in the capital controversies of the 1960s was, however, disappointed. In his Manchester lectures, *Pay and Profits* (1968), he took a surprisingly sympathetic view of the marginal productivity theory of distribution. But he was no friend of abstract theory or of advanced econometric techniques. His presidential address to the Royal Economic Society was a scathing attack on 'the underdevelopment of economics' (1972), in which, he argued, history, institutions, evidence and policy were increasingly neglected in favour of useless displays of technical virtuosity.

Phelps Brown's later books were taken less seriously than they deserved. *The Inequality of Pay* (1977) offered an incomparable comparative account of the development of wage differentials by occupation and industry, labour market discrimination, and the relationship between status, pay and power. As he wryly reflected in his 'Autobiographical Notes', *The Origins of Trade Union Power* (1983) had the misfortune to appear at a time when its subject was in deep and apparently irreversible decline, and *Egalitarianism and the Generation of Inequality* (1988) was no better timed. 'Once more it seems that I shall have been left stranded by a turn in the tide of public opinion, so rapid has been the recession of egalitarian sentiment in this country since 1979' (1996: 138–9).

In almost his last published paper, the text of an after-dinner speech at the 1989 Malvern political economy conference, he asked: 'Would Keynes have endorsed incomes policies?' Of course he would, Phelps Brown replied. He himself was a political moderate, a Keynesian in macroeconomics, and a lifelong advocate of incomes policy as the only way in which full employment could be reconciled with low inflation. Social justice, he believed, required nothing less.

BIBLIOGRAPHY
The Framework of the Pricing System (1936).
(with G.L.S. Shackle) 'British Economic Fluctuations 1924–38', *Oxford Economic Papers* (1939), vol. 2, pp. 98–134.
(with S.V. Hopkins) 'The Course of Wage Rates in Five Countries, 1860–1939', *Oxford Economic papers* n.s. (1950), vol. 2, no. 2, pp. 226–96.
A Course in Applied Economics (1951).
(with P.E. Hart) 'The Share of Wages in National Income', *Economic Journal* (1952), vol. 62, no. 246, pp. 23–77.
(with B. Weber) 'Accumulation, Productivity and Distribution in the British Economy, 1870–1938', *Economic Journal* (1953), vol. 63, no. 250, pp. 63–88
'The Meaning of the Fitted Cobb-Douglas Production Function', *Quarterly Journal of Economics* (1957), vol. 71, no. 4, pp. 546–60.
The Growth of British Industrial Relations: A Study From the Standpoint of 1906–14 (1959).
The Economics of Labor (1962).
Pay and Profits (1968).
(with M.H. Browne) *A Century of Pay* (1968).
'The Underdevelopment of Economics', *Economic Journal* (1972), vol. 82, no. 325, pp. 1–10.
The Inequality of Pay (1977).
(with S.V. Hopkins) *A Perspective of Wages and Prices* (1981).
The Origins of Trade Union Power (1983).
Egalitarianism and the Generation of Inequality (1988).
'Would Keynes Have Endorsed Incomes Policies?', *Review of Political Economy* (1990), vol. 2, no. 2, pp. 127–37.
'Autobiographical Notes', *Review of Political Economy* (1996), vol. 8, no. 2, pp. 129–39.

Further Reading
Hancock, W. and Isaac, J.E., 'Sir Henry Phelps Brown, 1906–1994', *Economic Journal* (1998), vol. 108, no. 448, pp. 757–78.
Review of Political Economy (1996), vol. 8, no. 2, special issue on Henry Phelps Brown.
Worswick, D., 'Ernest Henry Phelps Brown, 1906–1994', *Proceedings of the British Academy* (1995), vol. 90, pp. 319–44.

J.E. King

BRYDGES, Samuel Egerton (1762–1837)

Brydges was born at Wootton, Kent on 30 November 1762, and died at his house near Geneva on 8 September 1837. He was educated at Maidstone School and the King's School at Canterbury, and entered Queens' College, Cambridge in 1780. He left Cambridge after two years and went to study law at the Middle Temple, and was called to the bar in 1787. He never practised law, however, but retired instead to his country home at Denton, Kent and devoted himself to writing. Between 1787 and 1810 he produced several volumes of poetry, two novels and a number of biographical and literary reference works. He also served as an officer in the local yeomanry, and was captain first in the New Romney Dragoons and then the Denton Yeomanry from 1795.

Although productive, these years were not entirely happy ones for Brydges. His books were moderately successful, but did not earn enough money to support him in the lifestyle he desired, and he was also at odds with his neighbours, whom he later described in his autobiography as 'book-hating squires'. Some of this bad feeling may have been compounded when faulty genealogical research persuaded Brydges that his family had a claim to the barony of Chandos. This claim, taken to the House of Lords, was at once contested bitterly, and many of the gentry of east Kent sided with his opponents. The issue dragged on until 1803 when an investigation by Lancaster Herald found against Brydges. He seems to have been deeply hurt by this failure, but his self-esteem was partly restored in 1808 when he was given a knighthood in the Swedish Order of St Joachim.

By 1812, pressing money troubles forced Brydges to give up on his full-time literary career. He had been trying for some years without success to get a seat in parliament, and in 1812 was finally elected MP for Maidstone. He held the seat until 1818. Nominally a Tory, he in fact had no strong allegiances, and allied with a number of Whig Mps in an attempt to reform the poor laws in 1814. He again attempted to introduce a bill for poor law reform in 1817, but again failed, as he did in his attempt to amend the Copyright Act in 1814. These repeated failures seem to have dampened Brydges's enthusiasm for politics, even though he was created a baronet in 1814.

In 1813 Brydges and his eldest son, Thomas Barrett Brydges, established a printing and publishing business at Lee Priory in Kent. Brydges served as chief editor, and under his direction the business reprinted a number of seventeenth and eighteenth-century literary works; Brydges himself often wrote prefaces for these. He also continued to write and publish poetry. The business, however, was not a commercial success, and in 1818 lack of money forced Brydges to resign his seat in the house and move abroad, first to Paris and then to Geneva, where he settled for the remainder of his life. The Lee Priory publishing business was closed in 1822. While in Geneva Brydges continued to write poetry and literary works, and published his autobiography in 1834. He remained an active writer until shortly before his death.

Brydges regarded himself as being both broad-minded and fair-minded, and believed that as a writer he had a duty to keep an open mind and be receptive to new influences. He tells us that when he travelled abroad he felt it important to immerse himself in whatever culture he happened to be in and learn as much about it as possible; he complained on several occasions of the English practice of 'herding together' when travelling on the continent. He liked to think of himself as an iconoclast, and clearly delighted in taking heterodox opinions. Despite this, his views on literature and politics alike were largely conservative. He was much more interested in reviving older works that were falling into obscurity than he was in the literature of his own day, and in his letters and writings he shows more interest in FIELDING, Johnson and Fanny Burney than in his contemporaries, although he liked SOUTHEY's work and respected Byron's 'boldness and recklessness'.

Brydges's interest in poor law reform is reflected in his pamphlet *Arguments in Favour of the Practicability of Relieving the Poor by Finding Employment for them* (1817). He had initially opposed the Corn Laws, but by 1831 he was coming around to a position of grudging support, as spelled out in *Expositions* (1831). His major work on economic issues, however, is *The Population and Riches of Nations, Considered Together* (1819), written not long after his move to Geneva and motivated in part by his opposition to Peel's Currency Act of 1819. A further motivation, he says, was a reading of RICARDO and also of Say's *Traité d'Économie Politique* while in Paris, during which he became convinced that both men had made serious errors.

With respect to Say, Brydges rejects Say's idea that there are 'immaterial riches' and says that riches are necessarily material things. He also rejects any distinction in economics between producers and consumers. All of us, he says, whether producers or no, are consumers; the distinction is nonsensical. Instead, he suggests a division between producers and non-producers. Producers can in turn be divided into two groups, agricultural producers and manufacturing producers, while non-producers fall into six classes: those who live on the profit of capital, such as bankers; those who live by labour applied to non-productive services, including soldiers, sailors and domestic servants; the poor; those who 'live by intellectual labours, as members of the liberal professions, placemen, literati, artists' (1819: 3); those who have independent incomes from rents or other forms of income; and those who live on salaries or revenues granted by the state.

Wealth created by producers is also divided into various categories: wages to the labourers, profits to those who supply the skill and capital, rent to the landholder, interest to the owner of the capital, and taxes and poor rates to the state. Brydges believes there ought to be a fair division into all these categories – except the poor rates, which he detests – and that excessively high wages damage the economy as they give too much money to the labourers and not enough to the other groups. He is also careful not to stigmatize non-productive labour or regard it is unimportant. Very often, non-productive labour is required for productive labour to be productive. The merchant, the capitalist, the intellectual all have their role to play if the labourer is to be made productive.

Brydges also criticizes utilitarians, and says that utility should never have primacy in economic thinking. The main aim of economic activity and regulation should be the promotion of the happiness and strength of the people, and utility arguments must give way before this paramount consideration.

In his attacks on the poor laws, Brydges was especially critical of the Law of Settlement which, he said, restricted the ability and right of the poor to work, even though many would willingly do so. He was also indignant about the practice of employing the poor as unpaid labour, with the latter receiving their subsistence through the poor rates rather than through wages; this was unjust, as it denied work to other labourers who would work for wages. He felt too that the poor laws stigmatized the poor, and that the 'charity' they received was a source of shame to many of them. His subsequent argument that the able-bodied poor, who are able to work, should be compelled to find work, rather diminishes the liberal tone of the previous pages. In other works, Brydges shows himself to be a bullionist and in favour of free trade (though as noted, he changed his position on the Corn Laws), and in favour of low taxation and reducing the national debt.

BIBLIOGRAPHY
Arguments in Favour of the Practicability of Relieving the Poor by Finding Employment for them (1817).
The Population and Riches of Nations, Considered Together (Geneva and London, 1819).
Expositions (Geneva, 1831).
The Autobiography, Times, Opinions and Contemporaries of Sir Egerton Brydges (1834).

Further Reading
Woodworth, M.K., *The Literary Career of Sir Samuel Egerton Brydges* (Oxford, 1935).

Morgen Witzel

BUCHANAN, David (1779–1848)

Buchanan was born in Montrose in 1779, the son of a distinguished printer and publisher. He died in Glasgow on 13 August 1848. He worked for his father, acquiring a knowledge of the book trade; through helping in the preparation of editions of Guthrie's works, he began a life-long interest in geography. A group of gentlemen in the Liberal Party persuaded him to move to Edinburgh in 1808 to start the

Edinburgh Weekly Register, which lasted for about twelve months. Subsequently he was editor of the *Caledonian Mercury* (1810–27) and of the *Edinburgh Courant* (1827–48).

Buchanan first came to public attention through a pamphlet of 1807 on Pitt's volunteer system. He was also an early contributor to the *Edinburgh Review*. In 'Malthus and the Corn Laws' (1815), Buchanan robustly defended free trade in corn against Malthusian support for protection, and argued that agriculture should not gain at the expense of other sectors of the economy. Buchanan's principal contributions to economics were his edition of Adam SMITH's *Wealth of Nations* and his late work on taxation, trade and the currency.

Buchanan praised *The Wealth of Nations* for being 'a great display of reason on the business of the world; touching society in all its essential relations...' (Smith 1814, vol. IV: viii), with the qualification that it was too narrow because of its focus on wealth, so that a broader study of government was needed to emphasize less interference with the natural course of things. In his edition, one of the most detailed in the nineteenth century, Buchanan found much in *The Wealth of Nations* to criticize or qualify. He found factual mistakes, such as modern states preferring trade to agriculture, and objectionable metaphysical interests including the concept of an invariable value of labour. Smith was accused of exaggeration, as when he discussed corporation laws and apprenticeships, and suggested that the learning of a trade is easy. Buchanan disliked Smith's support for the Navigation Acts and his prediction that free trade in corn would not decrease corn prices. Buchanan's line on taxation was tougher than Smith's, as he would not countenance the idea that agriculture could be improved by taxing its produce. He believed that the tax burden had reached its limit in Britain, Ireland and America. Smith gets praise, on the other hand, for his conceptual distinction between productive and unproductive labour and for noting that manufacturing provides an equivalent for surplus agriculture.

The commentary on *The Wealth of Nations* does more than react to a text: it also allows Buchanan to present his views on many economic topics. He is cautious about paper currency, stating that it, and not the unfavourable trade balance, was the major cause of inflation. MALTHUS also received comment and correction from Buchanan, who believed that subsistence limited marriage, rather than the number of children. The physiocrats were also subject to Buchanan's gaze. He looked hard at their notion of the unique ability of agriculture to create a net product, and asserted that it was in fact selling produce at a high price which generated a surplus.

In his own economic treatise, published in 1844, Buchanan chiefly scrutinized tax and trade policies. Painstakingly, he examined tax after tax to see their incidence, usually finding them bad, as with taxes on manufacturing which interfere with invention and new working methods. He thought that Britain was the most heavily taxed of countries. Increasing indirect taxes, he argued, was failing to increase total tax revenue. His keen support for free trade was to him the logical consequence of accepting the division of labour principle. His arguments against protection were strenuous: 'The only encouragement which trade requires is a free market for its produce...' (1844: 113); 'Such manufactures as cannot stand their ground without protection should be left to their fate' (1844: 115). He argued that the foreigners supply only a small amount of the British domestic corn market, so that repeal of the Corn Laws would not be catastrophic. Navigation laws diverted trade from its natural course and interfered with the assortment of cargo. He asserted that colonies governed by monopoly trading companies injured both parties: Britain had gained from America becoming independent.

Writing about trade led Buchanan to consider price theory. He regarded demand and supply as equal weights, never at rest until in even balance. When equality is achieved, there is a natural price with the cessation of price variations. The determinant of all prices is scarcity. Prices have to be sufficient to cover production expenses and yield a rent to landlords. Buchanan had many objections to RICARDO's value and distribution theories. He disliked the prediction that prices would always go on rising despite supply of corn increasing. Also, extra output in agriculture does not arise solely through using more acres of barren land but can be the consequence of more skilful husbandry and increased employment of capital. The idea that labour is the only true measure of exchangeable value is dismissed as neither original nor sound. The inverse relationship between profits and wages was refuted by Buchanan because profit and wage rates can rise together if more capital is employed.

BIBLIOGRAPHY
'Malthus on the Corn Laws', *Edinburgh Review* (1815), no. XLVIII, pp. 491–505.
Inquiry into the Taxation and Commercial Policy of Great Britain; with observations on the principles of currency, and of exchangeable value (Edinburgh, 1844).

Further Reading
Edinburgh Evening Courant (1848), Thursday, 17 August, p. 3.
Smith, A., *An Inquiry into the nature and causes of the Wealth of Nations with notes and and an additional volume by David Buchanan*, 4 vols (Edinburgh, 1814).

Donald Rutherford

BUCKLE, Henry Thomas (1821–1862)

Buckle was born on 24 November 1821 at Lee in Kent, although the family lived in London. He died in Damascus on 29 May 1862, probably of typhoid fever, having been treated for a throat ulcer and having been leeched and bled by a succession of doctors. He was buried in the Protestant cemetery in Damascus. He was the only son of Thomas Buckle and his Calvinist wife Jane Middleton; the couple also had two daughters. Thomas Buckle was a partner in a ship-owning company. Henry Buckle was a sickly child and had no formal education. At the age of eight, he was barely literate. He went to Holloway's school in London on condition that he should learn only what he chose: while there, he won the mathematics prize. Soon after, he left the school. Buckle maintained that he had read only Shakespeare, *Pilgrim's Progress* and the *Arabian Nights* by the age of eighteen.

Buckle's health improved, and when he was seventeen his father insisted that he should join the family business. Shortly afterwards, Thomas Buckle died: this affected his son's health and he went to recuperate in Brighton. However, Buckle inherited his father's share of the family business. He lived off its proceeds, which allowed him to pursue his interests of historical research and also chess. Buckle resolved not to marry until his income had reached £3,000 a year, believing that he would be unable to educate his sons on less money than that (he never married).

Starting in July 1840 the Buckle family travelled in Europe for a year. Buckle studied the languages of each country, and by 1850 he could read nineteen languages with ease and was fluent in seven. He also proved to be an outstanding chess player, and appears to have had a photographic memory. In 1842 he began a course in mediaeval history in London. The next year he began to write a history of Charles I, then left to tour Europe again. He then decided to devote his time to writing a history of English civilization, but did not live long enough to complete the project. On his return, he and his mother set up house in London, although her health suffered in the city. She died in 1859 and Buckle decided to travel once more, to alleviate his grief. He went to Egypt and the Holy Land, and it was in the course of this journey that he fell ill and died.

Buckle was an exponent of positivism, the belief that there are fixed laws governing historical development and that the duty of historians is to discover them. Consequently, his *History of Civilisation in England*, which traced the intellectual history of England, Spain, France and Scotland, is an attempt to investigate the development of individual liberty in each country and to isolate the reasons why 'freedom' was more prevalent in some countries than in others. The work is invariably critical of religion and government: 'Governments do no intrinsic good, at best they only correct evils previously imposed by governments.' He maintained that interest rates were an inverse indicator of the amount of 'democracy' allowed in a country. He also found that the laws of 'wages, profits and rent' given an indication of the economic health of a nation. Another of the 'laws' that Buckle found was that of climate, by which he demonstrated that only in Europe could humans reach high levels of civilization.

BIBLIOGRAPHY
History of Civilisation in England (1857–1861).
Influence of Women on the Progress of Knowledge (1858).
Review of Mill 'On Liberty' (1859).

Marjorie Bloy

BURKE, Edmund (1730–97)

Burke was born on 12 January 1730 in Dublin, and died in Beaconsfield, Buckinghamshire on 9 July 1797. He was the son of an Irish barrister, Richard Burke, who may have been a convert to Anglicanism from Roman Catholicism in order to enter his profession, though the evidence is not certain (O'Brien 1992: 6; Lock 1998: 6). Burke's mother, Jane, was Catholic, as was her family, the Nagles. His brothers were raised Anglican and his sister was raised Catholic. After completing his early education at a Quaker school at Ballitore in County Kildare (1741–4), then graduating from Trinity College, Dublin (BA, 1748), Burke set off for the Temple Inn, in London, with his father's financial support. He studied for the bar from 1750–5, but did not complete his degree, to his father's chagrin. While in London he came to associate with literary and theatrical people and made acquaintances with certain politicians, for whom he wrote pamphlets and speeches. Among his early writings was an ironic work titled *A Vindication of Natural Society* (1756), a satire on the anti-religious ideas of Lord Bolingbroke. In 1757 he published what remains a recognized work in aesthetics, *A Philosophical Inquiry into the Sublime and the Beautiful*. He also collaborated with his close friend, Will Burke, in the publication of *An Account of European Settlements in America* (1757). This work bears on Burke's political economy, for while he criticizes certain monopolistic practices, he approves of nations' regulating commerce to some extent, with its own colonies and for the public good, primarily through economic incentives.

Burke entered the political world by becoming the Private Secretary of William Hamilton, member of parliament and Chief Secretary for Ireland. He fell out with Hamilton after four years and then became private secretary to Charles Watson-Wentworth, the Marquis of Rockingham, one of the wealthiest and most influential English aristocrats and political leader of the Whigs. This put Burke squarely in the middle of British politics. He was elected MP for Wendover in 1765 and remained in parliament until his retirement in 1794, becoming MP for Bristol in 1774. He led the opposition in parliament against the policy of Lord North and King George III in America, and called for the repeal of the Stamp Act. Throughout his career he championed the removal of legislation against the Catholics in Ireland, and helped push forward the Catholic Relief Acts in 1778. In 1782 Rockingham became prime minister and Burke was chosen as paymaster general. He introduced numerous reforms in his position, and was perhaps the first paymaster who did not leave office a wealthy person.

In the 1780s, after the death of the Rockingham in 1782, the Whig leadership passed into the hands of Charles James Fox. Convinced of widespread corruption on the part of the East India Company and its governor general, Warren Hastings, Burke convinced Fox to impeach Hastings. The latter was ultimately acquitted, but Burke's prosecution in the House of Lords was relentless, and he considered this to be the most important endeavour of his career. He expressed his fear in *Remarks on the Policy of the Allies* (1793) that Britain's virtually unchecked power in much of the world could lead to a combination of nations against Britain, to her ultimate ruin. But it was the French Revolution led to Burke's most significant work, *Reflections on the Revolution in France* (1790) for which he is most famous. This work is now a fixture in the canon of political philosophy, considered to be the leading masterpiece in the history of modern conservatism. In the French Revolution Burke saw a threat to all of Europe and foretold of the Revolution's collapse into tyranny and the emergence of a military general.

Burke's political economy is subject to differing interpretations, as is his political philosophy in general. On the surface there appears to be a contradiction between his political philosophy, with its emphasis upon the natural moral law, order, hierarchy and tradition, preferring prudential reform to radical change, and his political economy, stressing economic individualism in a free market setting, and opposing state intervention or regulation. The interpretation of his political philosophy largely divides itself between two basic views, one construing Burke as a utilitarian and pragmatist, emphasizing expediency in the service generally of the status quo, albeit tinged with certain religious overtones. The other view places Burke's politics squarely within the natural law tradition, not of HOBBES or LOCKE, but of Aristotle and Aquinas. Certainly, Burke emphasizes the importance of prejudice, habit, presumption and expediency in his politics, and that individuals typically act in terms of their self-interest. He also claims that the 'grand prejudice' of civil society is religion. Reconciling the moral ends of man with economic freedom within the context of Burke's political thought is crucial to the problem of coherence in Burke.

Burke's most noted work treating political economy is his *Thoughts and Details on Scarcity* (1795). This work, written near the end of Burke's life, is seen to be a straightforward justification of free-market economics, presenting a minimalist view of government, disavowing any form of public welfare beyond the charity of individuals, and denouncing all forms of regulation of commerce. It was occasioned by a specific problem in Speenhamland, a place in Berkshire not far from Burke's own estate. Two poor harvests in 1794 and 1795 pushed the wages of farm labourers below subsistence. Their wages were in turn subsidized by decree of the justices of the peace out of the rates paid by local ratepayers. This in effect transferred the problem of low wages to other labourers, resulting in a catastrophe for all involved. It was this very specific economic catastrophe that led Burke to urge the prime minister, William Pitt, to avoid governmental interference in the market on pain of greater economic hardship. *Thoughts on Scarcity* is in effect a memorandum to the prime minister, and as such it is not a carefully crafted, formal treatise on economics, but it is the closest work we have from Burke on political economy.

Burke's consideration of the problem of wages in *Thoughts on Scarcity* illustrates his basic support for a free-market, capitalist economy. 'Labour is a commodity like every other', Burke proclaims, 'and rises or falls according to the demand. This is the nature of things.' On the whole the labour market provides adequately for men in their necessities. Human labour for Burke is in effect a commodity, similar to other commodities, an object of trade, subject to the laws that govern trade and commerce. If government forces up farm wages, then one of two things will result: either the need for labour will fall or food prices will rise to the disadvantage of labourers. Thus, it is the market that must determine the 'just price' of goods.

From labour as a commodity, to an 'article of trade', to 'the laws and principles of trade', we are led to one of Burke's more problematic statements. He concludes that 'in breaking the laws of commerce, which are the laws of nature', we are, in effect, breaking 'the laws of God'. The problem here is that Burke appears to equate the laws of economics and commerce with the natural moral law originating from the eternal law of God. Granted, both physical laws of nature and natural moral laws can be construed as laws of God in that God is the divine Creator of the natural order of things both physical and moral. As such the physical laws are descriptive and the moral laws are prescriptive. Thus, while the laws of trade and commerce are the laws of God, they are not the same as the moral law, but reflective of the way in which the natural order functions.

Further, there is a natural inequality 'which grows out of the *nature of things*' over a great length of time, embodied in custom, acquisition, and entailing the 'improvement of property'. Such inequality is for Burke closer to the 'true equality, which is the foundation of equity and just policy', much more than any 'human contrivances' (*Correspondence*, vol. 3, p. 403). Yet this natural inequality, serving as a bulwark against the tyranny of imposed equality, allows the pursuit of our 'own selfish interests'. Thus Burke argues in *Thoughts on Scarcity*, thereby connecting 'the general good within their own individual success'. This has overtones of Adam SMITH's 'invisible hand', which perhaps is no coincidence as Burke knew Smith and was familiar with his work. Burke favourably reviewed in the *Annual Register* Smith's *Theory of Moral Sentiments*, and some have speculated that Smith consulted Burke in writing *A Wealth of Nations*, although this claim is unverified. It has also been generally circulated that Smith claimed that Burke alone had understood his political economy, but there is no known documentation to support this. Regardless, both Burke and Smith opposed most forms of governmental interference in the market through regulation. For Burke, such interference is a method of redistribution, tending towards a forced equality. Thus he criticizes the government in his *Speech on American Taxation* (1774) for confusing regulation with commerce, and revenue with taxes. Burke is more willing than Smith to allow for some government regulation and monopolistic practices within the Empire. And Smith decried the growth of the national debt as being ruinous to a country, while Burke declared in his *First Letter on a Regicide Peace* (1796) that some debt was not only tolerable but a sign of her 'prosperity and greatness'.

Burke considered it 'the common doom of man that he must eat his bread by the sweat of his brow', a plight which the state cannot remove. Writing in his *Reflections on the Revolution in France* (1790) Burke offers his only statement on economic rights, declaring that men 'have a right to the fruits of their industry; and to the means of making their industry fruitful. They have a right to the acquisition of their parents'. Further, each 'has a right to a fair portion of all which society, with all its combinations of skill and force, can do in his favour'. Certainly, the 'fair portion' passage does not imply a form of socialism, but it does refer to a 'partnership' in which 'all men have equal rights but not equal things'. We have a right to that which we have gained through our toil and free labour, our ingenuity and craft, and to what we have accumulated for our family and ourselves. We have a right to the fruits of our labour and to the security of our property. On the other hand, men do not have a right 'to what is not reasonable and to what is not for their benefit'.

In the face of labour's failing, or nature's withholding her natural abundance due to blight or pestilence, Burke turns first to personal charity, especially from the landed aristocracy, for those unable to maintain themselves. In 1796 Burke urged Pitt to oppose providing relief for the poor from the tea tax. Instead, the government should encourage frugality and industriousness for the poor. As harsh as this may sound, it should be placed against Burke's own personal charity and his prudential judgement that there are circumstances calling for exceptions to the otherwise general exclusion of governmental influence in the market. Concerning his personal charity, in 1795 and 1796, during the period in which his 'free market' tract *Thoughts and Details on Scarcity* was written, the price of corn exceeded the ability of purchase for many of the poor. Burke arranged for corn to be ground for the poor of Beaconsfield, and had bread made at his own estate and sold to the poor at a reduced price. He helped organize various local institutions to assist the poor and the elderly, and actively participated in their meetings and personally visited the needy. He assisted others financially, opened his home to needy relatives, and to various political refugees and French émigrés.

It is property that is pivotal in Burke's political economy. Property is not limited to the landed gentry or wealthy merchant class, for property is the right of all, even though this right is capable of qualification by Parliament. It is a natural right because it reflects the natural aspirations of our human nature. Moreover, the possession of property secures individuals against state tyranny. The struggle to preserve what is in one's possession, Burke remarks in the *Reflections*, 'is one of the securities against injustice and despotism implanted in our nature. It operates as an instinct to secure property, and to preserve communities in a settled state.'

The importance of property is more than mere possession, because 'the property of the nation is the nation'. But property and geography do not alone define a nation for, as Burke declares in *First Letter on a Regicide Peace* (1796), the nation is a 'moral essence'. That upon which the public benefit depends is 'good order, religion, morality, security, and property'. In turn, the 'original ground of all property...is the solid rock of prescription', Burke writes in his *Letter on the Affairs of Ireland* (1797). Prescription is the most secure of all titles between men, hallowed by time, rooted in the natural law and grounded in the 'eternal order of things'. Prescriptive right helps secure good order, which is the true 'foundation of all good things', Burke writes in the *Reflections*.

As property is fundamental to a society, Burke considers society to be a contract, but not one forged for the purposes of self-preservation or advantage. Rather, society 'is a partnership in all science; a partnership in all art; a partnership in every virtue, and in all perfection'. But the free-market economy seems more concerned with the benefits necessary to sustain our 'animal existence', being part of our essential nature, but not the highest and most noble part. The 'laws of commerce' which are the 'laws of nature' pertain to that element of our 'animal existence' about which the principles of a free market operates. This is according to the 'nature of things'. Yet for Burke virtue and justice ultimately transcend economic or political categories, for nothing, he concludes in his *Speech at Bristol Previous to the Election* (1780), 'should be necessary for commerce which is incompatible with justice'. Still, commerce functions best for the most part when it is left to itself, granting all possible liberty for both the labourer, broker and property owner alike.

Liberty is crucial in Burke's economics, but not the liberty of mere isolated individuals, for men are 'never in a state of *total* independence of each other'. Our liberties are not according to an abstract theory of 'the rights of man', which supposes 'the absence of a state of civil society'; nor do our liberties flow from a pre-social state of nature. For Burke, the true state of nature is 'the state of civil society...For man is by nature reasonable.' As such, the natural state of human beings is one in which their reason can be developed and cultivated, which is in civil society. Neither is government 'made in virtue of natural rights', for 'by having a right to everything [men] want everything', which turns into a demand that the state meet ever expanding wants. Rather our liberties, as Burke affirms in the *Reflections*, are our 'hereditary right'. Liberty cannot exist without being joined together with order and virtue. This belief in liberty as an entailed inheritance should extend throughout the British Empire. Liberty is manifested in free trade within the empire, yet not without qualification. Free trade is to be 'founded in justice, and beneficial to the whole', with priority given to 'the seat of the supreme power', England. Thus, Burke's devotion to free trade is prominent but limited, for it is placed within the framework of the British Empire, an Empire meant to be an enlightened imperialism. Ultimately, for Burke, free trade, as reflected in this passage, is subordinated to the public benefit, i.e. the common good 'founded in justice'. Burke 'wanted to maintain a traditional order', Francis Canavan concludes, 'that was already a market economy' (Canavan 1995: 130). It was a market economy giving precedence to landed property, 'the soul that animated', with limited government, and a state whose aim was the virtuous perfection of the people subordinated to the common good that informs Burke's political economy.

BIBLIOGRAPHY
A Philosophical Enquiry into the Origin of our Ideas of the Sublime and Beautiful (1757; 2nd edn ed. J.T. Boulton, 1987).
An Account of the European Settlements in America (1757).
Tract on the Popery Laws (1765).
Thoughts on the Cause of the Present Discontents (1770).
Speech on American Taxation (1774).
Speech on Conciliation with America (1775).
Speech on Economical Reform (1780).
Speech on the Nabob of Arcot's Debt (1785).
Speeches on the Impeachment of Warren Hastings (1788).
Reflections on the Revolution in France (1790; ed. J.C.D. Clark, Stanford, California, 2001).
An Appeal from the New to the Old Whigs (1791).
Thoughts and Details on Scarcity (1795).
First Letter on a Regicide Peace (1796).
Letter on the Affairs of Ireland (1797).
Writings and Speeches of Edmund Burke, ed. P. Langford *et al.*, 8 vols published to date (I–III, V–IX) (Oxford, 1981–).
The Works of the Right Honourable Edmund Burke, 8 vols (1854–89).
The Correspondence of Edmund Burke, ed. T.W. Copeland, 10 vols (Cambridge, 1958–78).

Further Reading
Barry, N., 'The Political Economy of Edmund Burke', in I. Crowe, *Edmund Burke: His Life and Legacy* (Dublin, 1997, pp. 104–14).
Bromwich, D., *On Empire, Liberty, and Reform: Speeches and Letters: Edmund Burke* (Yale, 2000).
Canavan, F., *The Political Economy of Edmund Burke* (New York, 1995).
Conniff, J., *The Useful Cobbler: Edmund Burke and the Politics of Progress* (Albany, New York, 1994).
Lock, F.P., *Edmund Burke: 1730–1784* (Oxford, 1998).
Macpherson, C.B., *Burke* (Oxford, 1980).
Mansfield, Jr, H.C., *Statesmanship and Party Government: A Study of Burke and Bolingbroke* (Chicago, 1965).
O'Brien, C.C., *The Great Melody: A Thematic Biography of Edmund Burke* (1992).

Pappin, J.L. III, *The Metaphysics of Edmund Burke* (New York, 1993).
Stanlis, P.J., *Edmund Burke and the Natural Law* (Ann Arbor, Michigan, 1958).
Whelan, F.G., *Edmund Burke and India* (Pittsburgh, 1996).
Wilkins, B.T., *The Problem of Burke's Political Philosophy* (Oxford, 1967).

Joseph L. Pappin III

BURT, William (1778–1826)

Burt was born in Plymouth on 23 August 1778, and died there on 1 September 1826. He was educated at Exeter grammar school, and articled as a solicitor in Bridgwater. Some time after 1800 he established a legal practice in Plymouth, and lived comfortably at Colyton, near Honiton for several years, until he lost most of his money in the collapse of a country bank. The incident left him with an abiding distrust of banks, which colours his later works and career. He then took up residence in Plymouth, and supported himself through writing and through an appointment as secretary to the Plymouth chamber of commerce. He also edited a newspaper, the *Plymouth and Dock Telegraph*, and briefly held a commission as an army officer, though he does not appear to have ever seen service. His son, T. Seymour Burt, records that he had wide-ranging interests in science, history and antiquities, and was a frequent lecturer at the Plymouth Institution.

Burt remains best known for the long poem, *Christianity*, discovered and published by his son some years after Burt's death. During his lifetime he published two works which touch on economic issues. *Desultory Reflections on Banks in General* (1810), probably written not longer after the collapse of his own financial affairs, is a critique of the system of credit, which Burt argues leads to speculation and lack of restraint. People should, he says, be sufficient, funding purchases and investment out of money in hand and not through borrowing. He attacks banks and financiers for encouraging people to borrow excessively.

In 1816 Burt published *Review of the Mercantile, Trading and Manufacturing State, Interests and Capabilities of the Port of Plymouth*, a collection of letters and documents dating from July 1814 and showing the efforts that the authorities in Plymouth, especially the chamber of commerce, were making to revive and stimulate overseas trade through the port. Burt, who compiled the collection, included both items on institutions that facilitate trade, such as the Plymouth Exchange, and those that hamper it, such as inefficient customs houses delaying goods in transit. There is notice of the first ships arriving with merchandise from France in the summer of 1814 following the peace, and summaries of major industries such as fishing and the coal trade. In March 1815, with war threatening again, Burt writes to urge that manufacturing should be made a principal objective of economic focus, and argues Britain should attempt to become self-sufficient and not rely on imports that can easily be disrupted in time of war. Surpluses can be exported, which brings in more money. As far as Plymouth itself is concerned, Burt urges the restoration of the woollen cloth industry, and also suggests reinvigorating or re-founding industries such as sugar refining, button making, mills for linseed and rapeseed oil and china manufacturing.

BIBLIOGRAPHY
Desultory Reflections on Banks in General, and the System of Keeping up a False Capital by Accommodation Paper (1810).
Review of the Mercantile, Trading and Manufacturing State, Interests and Capabilities of the Port of Plymouth (Plymouth, 1816).
Christianity: A Poem (1835).

Further Reading
Burt, T.S. 'A Short Memoir of the Author of "Christianity"', in *Christianity: A Poem* (1835: ix–xxvi).

Ann Kimber

BURTON, John Hill (1809–1881)

Burton was born 22 August 1809 in Aberdeen, the son of an army officer, and died 10 August 1881 in Edinburgh. He was educated at Aberdeen grammar school and at Marischal College, Aberdeen. His training as an advocate at the Scottish bar was only possible because his widowed mother sold her home and moved with him into Edinburgh lodgings. With few briefs to sustain him he turned to journalism, writing on history, philosophy and law. His first book, a manual on law, brought his name to a wide audience. His work on David HUME in 1846 established his reputation for careful research based on original sources. He commented that Hume knew in his writing on political economy when he was getting out of his depth. Burton was appointed secretary to the Prison Board at £700 per annum, with the result that there was less need for him to write for a living. In 1867 he was appointed Historiographer Royal with an annual salary of £190. He married first Isabel Lauder (1844), who died in 1849 leaving three daughters; he subsequently married Katherine Innes (1855), who complained that her husband lacked imagination.

Although primarily remembered as an historian, Burton also contributed to the economic debates of his day. In *Poor Laws and Pauperism in Scotland* (1841) reprinted from the *Westminster Review*, he surveyed post-sixteenth-century schemes to alleviate poverty in Scotland with vivid references to the contemporary state of the poor in Edinburgh and Glasgow. He attributed most of Scottish poverty to the expanding and indolent population of the Scottish Highlands, and recommended emigration. Burton thought CHALMERS's scheme in Glasgow was of limited application, and that a new system of benevolence and kindness that would not affect the industry of the poor had to be devised.

His *Political and Social Economy* (1847) was more ambitious. He wrote: 'One of the main objects of this essay is to convince its readers of the fruitfulness of human industry and energy' (1847: 271). He objected to the distinction between productive and unproductive labour, accepting that anything one is willing to pay for is productive. He asserted that a worker should appreciate his control over his labour and rewards. Burton favoured free labour markets and the payment of wages daily instead of weekly to encourage the indolent to work. Intelligence and education increase productivity, so the Scots, he asserted, have an advantage over the English through more widespread education. Poverty he attributed to low productivity and low skill. Although stern towards the poor, he had an ambivalent attitude towards the rich. Happiness does not increase with riches, although the rich are less liable to disease and provide 'surplus floating capital' of benefit to society. Employing many servants is vanity but wealth can be used productively, as when the canals were built with aristocratic capital.

In his discussion of demographic issues, in contrast to MALTHUS who wanted population control to make labour scarce and better paid, Burton was optimistic that human energy would feed an expanding population and argued that the restraints to population growth are fear of want and of losing caste in society. The population cannot grow too fast if the capital stock is growing faster. He favoured emigration for the 'damaged portions of the people' (1847: 340), for example, the handloom weavers who put too little energy into their work. However, he acknowledged the duty of government to reduce the causes of mortality, including famine.

Burton regarded socialism as an attack on property and incentives. He criticized communists for failing to show how members of society would do their social duty. St.-Simon and other socialists were dismissed by him as hollow and fallacious. His other objections to socialist schemes were that they are a violation of the natural order designed by the Deity, for if wages were uniform, there would be a race to be idle. Also, he asserted that it is wrong to believe the produce of labour is limited and competition wrong.

BIBLIOGRAPHY
A Manual of the Law of Scotland (1839).
Poor Laws and Pauperism in Scotland (1841).
Benthamania (1843).
Law of Bankruptcy, Insolvency, and Mercantile Sequestration in Scotland (1845).
Life and Correspondence of David Hume (1846).
Political and Social Economy: Its Practical Implications (1847).
History of Scotland from the Revolution to the Extinction of the last Jacobite Rebellion (1853).
History of Scotland from Agricola's Invasion to the Revolution of 1688 (1867).
The Book Hunter (1867; repr. 1882 with a memoir by Katherine Burton).
History of the Reign of Queen Anne (1880).

Donald Rutherford

C

CAINE, Sydney (1902–91)

Caine was born on 27 June 1902, the son of Harry Edward Caine, a railway worker. He died on 2 January 1991 and was survived by his third wife and his son from his first marriage, Sir Michael Caine. He was educated at Harrow County School and then studied at the London School of Economics and Political Science from 1919–22. He graduated with first-class honours in the BSc (Econ.), having specialized in economic history. In 1925 he married a fellow student, Muriel Harris, whom he met at one of the LSE's popular and well attended lunch-hour dances. She died in 1962 and in 1965 he married Doris Folkand and, following her death in 1973, Lady Elizabeth Bowyer.

In 1923 Caine entered the civil service as an assistant tax inspector. In 1926 he entered the Colonial Office and worked in government service until 1952. In 1929 he was the secretary of the West Indian Sugar Commission, and of the UK Sugar Industry Inquiry Committee in 1934. He was financial secretary in Hong Kong from 1937–9, and financial advisor to the Secretary of State at the Colonial Office in 1942. In that year he was also a member of the Anglo-American Caribbean Commission. Between 1944 and 1948 he was Assistant Under-Secretary and Deputy Under-Secretary at the Colonial Office. He then moved to the Treasury and was the head of the Treasury and Supply Delegation in Washington from 1949–51. In 1951 he was chief of a World Bank Mission to Ceylon. He received a CMG in 1945 and was knighted KCMG in 1947.

In 1952 Caine's career changed direction and he became a university administrator. From 1952–6 he was vice-chancellor of the University of Malaya, and then in 1957 he succeeded Sir Alexander CARR-SAUNDERS as the director of the London School of Economics and Political Science, a post he held until his retirement in September 1967. His period as director saw a considerable expansion in both the size of the School and the number of students. The final year of his directorship was somewhat overshadowed by the first of the LSE student 'troubles', which led to disciplinary action being taken against a number of students and a mass meeting of over 800 students that decided on a sit-in, 'the first major student strike this country has known' (Dahrendorf 1995: 455).

From 1960–7 he was a member of the Independent Television Authority, and was its deputy chairman from 1964. This experience led him to write a Hobart Paper proposing the abolition of the licensing fee for television (Caine 1968). After retiring from the directorship of the London School of Economics, Caine became closely involved in the founding and development of the independent University College at Buckingham. In January 1969, he was invited to become the chairman of the planning board. In April 1973 he was appointed as the chairman of the College's Council of Management and continued in that capacity until 1976 (see Pemberton and

Pemberton 1979). He received an honorary DSc (Buckingham) in 1974. He was a trustee of the Institute of Economic Affairs from 1968–72.

Caine's economic writings were few in number, but they reflected his experience of observing fluctuations in the prices of primary products and attempts at stabilization. In Hobart Paper 24 (1966), he provides a critical review of various stabilization schemes from the 1930s on and argues the case for letting the market operate as much as possible, with minimal direct government interference: 'Public action, that is action by governments and international authorities, can best be directed to the creation of the right climate or background rather than to detailed control' (1966: 54).

In 1971 Caines was the co-ordinator of an Indonesian Sugar Study and this experience encouraged him to return to the problem of stabilization in Hobart Paper 97 (1983), in which his critique of early stabilization programmes was extended to cover the work of UNCTAD and some particular schemes, such as the Coffee Council. He argued that even though futures markets could be helpful in reducing the effects of price fluctuations, they rarely covered periods of more than eighteen months ahead and therefore they did not provide the long-term stability needed for proper planning over the long production cycle that characterized many primary products. As a possible solution, he proposed the establishment of an international agency, a 'long-term contract agency' along the lines of the UK Export Credits Guarantee Department, with the guarantee providing the extra incentive for suppliers and consumers to take a longer term commitment. However, his proposals did not find favour with policy makers and were never tried out.

While Sir Sydney Caine made interesting contributions to the discussion of the stabilization of the prices of primary products, he will probably be best remembered for his work as a university administrator. He became concerned with the effects of government funding on academic freedom during his period as director of the London School of Economics, and this led to his important role in the creation of the University College at Buckingham, the first financially independent university institution to be founded in England since the Second World War.

BIBLIOGRAPHY

'Reminiscence', *LSE Students' Handbook* (1956).
'On Being a University Vice-Chancellor', *LSE Magazine* (1957), vol. 14, July, pp. 6–7, 24.
The History of the Foundation of the London School of Economics and Political Science, (1963).
'Universities and the State', *Political Quarterly* (1966), vol. 37, July–September, pp. 237–57.
Prices for Primary Producers, Hobart Paper 24 (1966).
Paying for TV?, Hobart Paper 35 (1968).
British Universities: Purpose and Prospects (1969).
'British Universities 1900–70', in J.H.M. Scott (ed.), *University Independence: The Main Questions* (1971).
(1983) *The Price of Stability…? A Study of Price Fluctuations in Primary Products with Alternative Prospects for Stabilisation*, Hobart Paper 97 (1983).

Further Reading

Dahrendorf, R., *LSE: A History of the London School of Economics and Political Science, 1895–1995* (Oxford, 1995).
Pemberton, J. and Pemberton, J., *The University College at Buckingham: A First Account of its Inception, Foundation and Early Years* (1979).

Jim Thomas

CAIRNCROSS, Alexander Kirkland
(1911–98)

Alec Cairncross was born 11 February 1911 in Lesmahagow, Lanarkshire, Scotland, and died 21 October 1998 in Oxford. He was the third of four sons and the seventh of eight children of an ironmonger and a schoolteacher. He was educated at Turfholm village school, Hamilton Academy, Glasgow University (BA with first-class honours, 1931) and Trinity College, Cambridge in 1932, for which he won a research studentship, and by which he was awarded only the second PhD in economics at Cambridge. His thesis, 'British Home and Foreign Investment 1870–1913', was not published until 1953, but it rapidly became a classic of the field. During his three years at Cambridge he was a member of the KEYNES 'circus', enjoying conversations and debates with A.C. PIGOU, Joan ROBINSON, Austin ROBINSON, Dennis ROBERTSON, James MEADE, Richard KAHN and Keynes himself.

In 1935 Cairncross returned to Glasgow University as a lecturer in economics which, with an additional lectureship at the West of Scotland Agricultural College, gave him a total income of £600. The coming of the Second World War, however, propelled him into government service, where he spent the subsequent decade. In January 1940 he joined a small group of professional economists in the War Cabinet Office under Lord STAMP, himself an eminent economist. A primary task was to assemble and circulate series of digests of the secret statistics collected by government departments and official agencies; based on these, the group tackled problems and proposed solutions. In June 1941 Cairncross moved to the Board of Trade, and in November of the same year to the Ministry of Aircraft Production (MAP), where he remained until the end of the war, gathering information and planning production. His final position was director of programmes in the MAP.

In 1945 Cairncross went to Berlin for five months as Treasury representative in the negotiations with economists from the USA, France, the UK and the USSR over the level of German reparations. Believing that Germany should be left with sufficient resources to sustain a reasonable standard of living, he found himself at odds with the other national representatives, leading to some lively arguments. The Reparations Plan was published in March 1946. He was briefly a member of the staff of *The Economist*, but he then returned to government service. He joined the Board of Trade as economic adviser in 1946 for three years, the period which saw the 'bonfire of controls' over trade and industry. He finished this period of his career by spending 1950 in Paris as director of the Economics Division of the Organization of European Economic Co-operation, the mediator between the USA and the European recipients of Marshall Aid. He found most exciting the work he did with Per Jacobsson, of the Bank for International Settlements, on a plan to deal with Germany's only post-war balance of payments crisis.

In 1951 Cairncross returned to academic life, joining Glasgow University as professor of applied economics and establishing one of the UK's first research departments in the field. Much of their work focused on regional policies, particularly with regard to the Scottish economy. Yet during his ten years at Glasgow he continued to spend a portion of his time on national and international commitments. In 1954 the World Bank asked him to organize training for senior administrators from less developed countries; consequently, he spent July 1955–December 1956 in Washington setting up the Economic Development Institute, which over the years developed a cadre of economists trained in development economics to serve in third world countries. Upon his return he was asked to serve on the Radcliffe Committee on the Working of the Monetary System (1957–9), in his words, 'the most important [committee] on which an economist could hope to serve' (1998: 204).

In June 1961 Cairncross joined the UK Treasury as economic adviser and head of its economic section, which had a staff of about twelve professional economists. Until the Conservative Party lost the general election in 1964, he observed (without approval) the government's 'dash for growth', which culminated in the serious balance of payments crisis which greeted the newly elected Labour government. The subsequent three years were difficult ones for Cairncross, who now had the titles of director of the economic section and (first) head of the Government Economic Service. The problem was the weakness of sterling, and the question was whether or not to devalue. The prime minister, Harold Wilson, and the Chancellor of the Exchequer, James Callaghan, were determined not to devalue, and at first Cairncross agreed with them. But gradually he changed his mind: he believed that measures had to be taken to deflate demand and/or to control imports, and when neither policy was adopted, he came to believe that devaluation was inevitable. On 2 November 1967 he confronted Callaghan with the unwelcome news; Callaghan announced the devaluation of the pound to the House of Commons a fortnight later, and then resigned.

In December 1967 Cairncross was elected Master of St Peter's College, Oxford, a post he took up in January 1969 and held until 1978. During this period he continued to serve on a number of public committees as well as holding professional posts, such as presidencies of the Royal Economic Society, the British Association and the Girls' Public School Day Trust. In 1971 he became chancellor of Glasgow University, resigning in 1996 when he reached the age of eighty-five.

Cairncross never actually retired. His pleasure was writing, and during his final decade and a half a stream of books and articles poured out, some of the most interesting of which combined personal involvement and immersion in the archives: *Sterling in Decline: the Devaluations of 1931, 1949 and 1967* (1983); *Years of Recovery: British Economic Policy 1945–51* (1985); *The Price of War* (1986), covering the negotiations over German reparations; *The Economic Section 1939–61* (1989), co-authored with Nita Watts, a colleague in the section; and *Managing the British Economy in the 1960s: A Treasury Perspective* (1996). Although not a participant, he was an observer with strong opinions on the 1976 IMF crisis, which resulted in *"Goodbye, Great Britain": the 1976 IMF Crisis* (1992). For some years he ran a seminar – significantly, in economic history rather than economics – at All Souls College, Oxford, and gave papers at home and abroad. He became a fellow of the British Academy in 1961 and was knighted in 1967.

Cairncross was fundamentally a Keynesian, once informing Conservative Chancellor Nigel Lawson that 'All studies show that higher public spending is a far more efficient way of increasing employment than cutting taxes' (*Daily Telegraph*, 28 October 1998). It is probably true that he never really challenged the beliefs absorbed during his Cambridge years, but he was not a theoretical economist: his forte was applying economic analysis to problems of policy. He was very good at the detail. Certainly, he was sceptical of the more inventive economic theories which could only be expressed in complex mathematical formulae. He himself commented that he had written very few journal articles, largely because he never drew together the ideas which surfaced as he worked. What he was good at was relating economics to everyday life, an example of which was telling those interested in theories of growth to go and study the tin tack trade.

Cairncross married Mary Glynn, member of a military and professional family, in 1943, and they had three sons and two daughters (his eldest daughter, Frances, a journalist with *The Economist* and a broadcaster, was in 2003 elected Rector of Exeter College, Oxford, the first father–daughter heads of house in Oxford's history).

Cairncross was a man of public policy and government. He helped embed economists within government, and he brought the economist's cast of mind to problems of devising and implementing policy. This was important: but what will ensure his afterlife, besides the stream of books of history, is his two million word diary, which resides in the archives of Glasgow University. He was not Pepys, but he has provided a resource of inestimable value for those who wish to know the inward workings of public life.

BIBLIOGRAPHY
British Home and Foreign Investment 1870–1913 (1953).
(with B. Eichengreen) *Sterling in Decline: the Devaluations of 1931, 1949 and 1967* (1983).
Years of Recovery: British Economic Policy 1945–51 (1985).
The Price of War (1986).
(with N. Watts) *The Economic Section 1939–61* (1989).
(with K. Burk) *"Goodbye, Great Britain": the 1976 IMF Crisis* (1992).
Managing the British Economy in the 1960s: A Treasury Perspective (1996).
Living With the Century (1998).

Kathleen Burk

CAIRNES, John Elliot (1823–75)

Cairnes was born on 26 December 1823 at Castle Bellingham, County Louth in Ireland. He died at Blackheath, Kent on 8 July 1875. His father, William Cairnes, was a partner in a brewing firm. In 1825 the family moved to Stameen, close to the east coast port of Drogheda. He was educated first at school at Kingstown, where the headmaster thought him a dull child, and thereafter at home. His family had intended that he should follow his father into the brewing business, but Cairnes himself desired to study, and was finally allowed to enter Trinity College, Dublin, in 1842. Initially he studied logic and metaphysics, obtaining first-class honours in 1845. Two years later he won a gold medal in ethics and logic. After graduation in 1848 he worked briefly as an engineer, but then turned his attention to political economy and law. In 1854 he published his first tract in political economy, *An Examination into the Principle of Currency involved in the Bank Charter Act of 1844*, which drew the attention of Thomas TOOKE. In 1856 Cairnes was appointed Whately Professor of Political Economy at the University of Dublin, and in 1859 was appointed professor of political economy and jurisprudence at Queen's College, Galway. In 1860 he married Charlotte Alexander, daughter of a judge; they had three children.

The publication of the *The Slave Power* (1862) made Cairnes's reputation. In 1865 he moved to England, and in 1866 was appointed professor of political economy at University College, London. By now, however, Cairnes was suffering from severe rheumatoid arthritis and was increasingly unwell. Settling at Blackheath, he continued to teach and write and moved in a circle of friends that included John Stuart MILL, Henry FAWCETT and Leonard COURTNEY, who succeeded Cairnes to the chair of political economy at University College after his resignation in 1872. Cairnes's last years were divided between writing and seeking cures for his painful illness.

Cairnes's years of study in political economy were marked by the publication of John Stuart Mill's *Principles of Political Economy* in 1848. This book was of fundamental influence on Cairnes's views of the subject. He became an ardent defender of classical political economy, for example, attempting to defend Mill from the attacks of THORNTON in his *Some Leading Principles of Political Economy* (1874). Mark Donoghue (1998) has recently forcefully argued that Cairnes's defence of a theory that was by then widely condemned should be sought in the persistent economic stagnation in Ireland, and in the dilemmas created by the spread of trade unionism in Britain.

Some Leading Principles of Political Economy was Cairnes's last and perhaps most important book. His most important innovation here was his theory of non-competing groups. According to Cairnes, both costs of production and 'reciprocal demand' from non-competing groups should be taken into account in the explanation of price formation. While reciprocal demand acted on relative prices of aggregates of commodities, cost of production determined the relative price of particular commodities. Cairnes argued that the 'actual price' would be 'the composite result' of the action of both reciprocal demand and cost of production. He extended his views to the labour market, for which he argued that shifts in non-competing groups (for example through education), influenced both relative wages and prices.

Mill's influence on Cairnes is clearly seen in his most widely read work, *The Character and Logical Method of Political Economy* (1857). The book not only summarized much of contemporary methodological debates on political economy, but also provided the format for Cairnes's own approach to questions of political economy. The book grew from the first series of lectures he gave as Whately Professor. In a highly lucid and transparent style, the lectures stated Mill's views on the definition and method of political economy. Where we find Mill, in the famous 1836 *Essay* as well as in Book VI of *Logic* (1843), groping towards a clear delineation of political economy from the natural and the moral sciences (especially history), Cairnes's exposition was more straightforward in its theoretical assumptions and in its practical illustrations. Indirectly, we see the influence of Dugald STEWART's version of common sense philosophy that, through WHATELY and SENIOR on the one hand, and James MILL and J.S. Mill on the other, passed down in the important distinction between phenomena of mind and matter that was of so much importance in John Mill's *Essay* as well.

Like Mill, Cairnes paralleled the scientificity of political economy with that of the natural sciences. The natural sciences, especially physics and astronomy, were only able to make inductions 'indirectly', that is from individual observations to general laws, and where possible used experiments to do so. Political economy followed a somewhat different route of induction, however. Political economists did not need to 'resort to this circuitous process – for this reason, that we have...direct knowledge of these causes in our consciousness...Everyone who embarks in any industrial pursuit...knows that he does so from a view to his own interest – from a desire, for whatever purpose, to possess himself of wealth' (1857: 54). It was therefore not at all a problem, but rather an advantage that political economists were unable to make those experiments from which natural scientists induced general laws. Having their general principles ready at hand (in man's consciousness), political economists 'are entirely independent of those refined inductive processes by which the ultimate truths of physical science are established' (1857: 55).

Despite the manifest importance of introspection in ascertaining the fundamental principles of political economy, Cairnes asserted that political economy paid equal weight to the mental and physical principles that formed its foundation. Cairnes of course referred here to the law of diminishing returns on land and to MALTHUS's population principle, and concluded that 'the problem' for an economist was solved once the 'fact to be accounted for' was connected to 'the known propensities of human nature and ascertained facts of the external world' (1857: 104).

Setting apart their different modes of establishing first principles, political economy and the natural sciences followed the same deductive reasoning process from them. Cairnes equated this reasoning process with reasoning from 'hypotheses'. The modern reader should be warned that it is quite wrong to think of these hypotheses as Popperian (or other) conjectures of any sort: for Cairnes (as for Mill), the truth of these hypotheses was never in doubt. Having thus granted political economy the same scientific status as the natural sciences, Cairnes discussed the differences between both when it came to the issue of exactness. In this regard, the advantage of political economy in that it was able to grasp its fundamental principles directly was offset by its limited possibilities to give these principles numerical exactness. Cairnes equated a mathematical statement of scientific laws with their numerical statement: mathematics was for him arithmetic, rather than any other and more advanced branch of the science, a matter of some importance during his difference of opinion with Stanley JEVONS on the usefulness of mathematics in political economy. A consequence of Cairnes's limited perception of mathematics was his belief that statistics were only of limited use in the study of economics.

The problem political economists faced, Cairnes felt, was twofold. Insofar as the principles of political economy were related to human motives, their nature excluded their rendering in numerical form. Similar sentiments are to be found in Mill's methodological writings, but Cairnes was more explicit on the issue. Cairnes argued that 'such principles do not, from their nature, admit of being weighed and measured like the elements and forces of the material world'. And 'on this account', political economy 'seems necessarily excluded from the domain of exact science' (1857: 80). The other problem was complexity, on which Cairnes by and large followed Mill's views. Complexity, that is, a concurrence of causes, obscured the working of and therefore the possibility of actually observing the 'tendency laws' of political economy.

Though both issues – the unfitness of motives for measurement and complexity, the concurrence of causes – were different, they merged in that they limited the use and usefulness of statistics for political economy, and thus excluded an exact statement of its principles. According to Cairnes, the proper use of statistics was not in discovering the fundamental principles of political economy, but in helping to trace disturbing causes obfuscating their working. Cairnes argued that in thus using statistics there was no difference with the natural sciences. In line with received views rather than facts, Cairnes argued that in astronomy or chemistry statistics only came into play *after* the general principles of the science were clearly exposed. In the deductive stage of the science, statistics served the explanation of 'residual phenomena', not the discovery of fundamental laws, and this was where Cairnes considered the use of statistics in political economy legitimate and useful (1857: 57–8).

Cairnes illustrated his account with a broad array of examples. Some of these he had written on earlier, or would write on extensively in later life, such as the influence of a gold influx on the economy. Others, like the so-called King–Davenant table that had been discussed by precursors like Thomas Tooke and William WHEWELL in relation to the exactness of political economy, naturally presented themselves to Cairnes as something to ponder upon. Cairnes extensively quoted Tooke, who argued in his *History of Prices* that not only all the different influences on the price of corn, but also the 'speculative views operating in the minds of both buyers and sellers' should be taken into account to be able to make exact statements in political economy, and that, even if this was all granted, it still would remain 'an insoluble problem' to predict 'what the price ought in consequence to be' (1857: 81–2).

As a consequence, political economists were only able to make qualitative statements, as for example that 'human beings will more readily dispense with luxuries and vanities than with the necessaries of life', but it was simply impossible to bring such statements 'within the limits of a formulated statement', as it was possible in physics (1857: 88). In the same context Cairnes ardently opposed and criticized contemporaries like Henry Dunning MACLEOD and Richard JENNINGS, who in his view put completely illegitimate and overstrained expectations on analogies of political economy with the science of mechanics, or in reductionist views of mental phenomena to their physiological substratum. For Cairnes, 'nothing but confusion and error could arise' from such reductionist efforts, turning the subject into 'a wholly different study from that which the world has hitherto known it' (1857: 181–2). It is well known that Jevons explicitly endorsed the views of Richard Jennings, and opposed those who, like Cairnes, despaired at the measurement of the phenomena that on a priori grounds might seem unfit for such purposes.

Although Cairnes subscribed essentially to Mill's a priori method in political economy, he showed a somewhat greater willingness than Mill to accept the usefulness of statistics in shedding light on the many contributing causes to concrete historical events. The approach to concrete issues was to start reasoning from a priori principles, and then to use statistics to illustrate and further explain the concrete complexity of historical events. This approach came close to Mill's concrete deductive method, as explained in the the latter's *Logic*. Cairnes (as Mill) distinguished this approach from the one favoured by Comte, who argued that social explanations should start by taking into account the full complexity of society. If this was to mean that the social scientist was forbidden to abstract to a limited set of first principles, then Comte's approach was clearly at odds with that of Mill and Cairnes. If it was to mean that a more limited picture of society should be completed by subsequently integrating additional explanatory elements, then this was just the method Cairnes favoured. His extensive use of this method of detailing a priori principles moved him into the direction of its apparent opposite, the historical school.

Cairnes practised the method outlined above in his empirical studies. He considered these studies, in the introduction to his *Essays in Political Economy* (1873), as 'applied economics', that is, as attempts to apply the theoretical principles of political economy to concrete economic phenomena. His studies on the effects of the gold discoveries are a case in point. Rather than starting from an empirical base, Cairnes approached the topic from a priori principles. He considered what the effect would be from an increase in the gold influx on trade and prices. In the original essays, statistical data did not play any formative role in the argument. If they were there at all, they served illustrative purposes and it is typical for Cairnes's apriorism that statistical materials were added later on, sometimes only to illustrate and underline later developments. Cairnes's primary interest in these essays was theoretical, rather than practical. He aimed to delineate the 'modus operandi', that is, the transmission mechanism, of monetary shocks on the economy, not to estimate their numerical effects. In some instances, statistical materials helped him to add further nuances to his explanations, thus gradually coming to a more complete grasp of the complexity of the economy. Cairnes's awareness of his own apriorism transpires most clearly from his correspondence with Stanley Jevons, for whom statistical data were essential materials to make grounded inferences about the influence of the new gold influx on prices. Cairnes considered the 'entirely distinct methods of inquiry' they used to arrive at the same conclusions as a most welcome enforcement of his own case (Black 1960: 17–18). For Cairnes, Jevons's results confirmed 'what theory applied to facts had led me to anticipate' (1873: 14).

Cairnes's most impressive use of his a priori method was his study into the American slave economy, *The Slave Power*. First published in 1862, the book soon became an important instrument in questioning the widespread English support for the secession movement of the southern states of the USA. The southern states strongly argued for free trade, in contrast with the protectionism favoured in the north, and there was nothing much to be said against their expressed will to become independent. Moreover, the southern states were convinced that the wealth of nations was fundamentally dependent on the flourishing of their cotton industry. These reasons and circumstances provided wide support for the secession movement in England.

Encouraged by Mill, Cairnes looked under the surface of the debate to show that the slavery issue was really the heart of the matter. Using some basic notions of classical economics, Cairnes argued that the economy of the southern states crucially depended on slavery, and then showed how this economic system of its own affected the whole of society, turning it into an aggressive and fundamentally degenerative force, that in the end threatened the progress of civilization in other countries as well. Cairnes pictured the 'slave power' as a system of production striving at complete control over the labour force. But this control came at a cost. Agriculture based on slavery favoured large-scale monoculture production, and as a consequence only made use of unskilled (slave) labour. This was in contrast with the emphasis in manufacturing on skilled labour, and it was no coincidence that manufacturing was largely neglected in the southern states. To increase (or maintain) their profits, planters occupied the most fertile lands, and when the land was exhausted moved to new lands of high fertility. Hence the inherently expansionist and aggressive character of the southern states: the planters squeezed out petty farmers, who could not benefit from the short-term advantages of large-scale production on fertile grounds, and thus produced the famous class of 'poor whites'. The unwillingness of the planters to invest in the quality of the slaves or to improve the quality of the land combined with their excessive expenditures on luxuries.

Thus, partly due to motivational characteristics of the planters and partly due to the inherent long-term drawbacks of a slave based system of production, the 'slave power' corrupted not only the southern states themselves, but extended this corruption beyond its boundaries. What was sold under the labels of democracy and free trade was in fact nothing else than the most perverse social and economic system. Cairnes made it no secret that once the perversity of the slave power was clearly diagnosed, all and every support to the secession states should be withdrawn. Given this overt aim of the book, Cairnes's argument for an English politics of strict neutrality, rather than one of open support to the case of the Union came somewhat as a surprise. Cairnes was however afraid that a complete victory of the Union over the southern states might allow the slave economy survive rather than being extinguished completely. To this last end, he considered a politics of containment more effective.

The Slave Power provides a fine example of how Cairnes made practical inferences from a priori principles. Despite Cairnes's assertions in his *Lectures* that one should distinguish between the science and the art of political economy, *The Slave Power* showed that once a complete picture of an historical state of affairs or development was reached, there was only a very thin line separating science from politics. From Cairnes's complete picture of the 'slave power', the political conclusions followed with almost inescapable logic. In this sense, Cairnes paid full tribute to the political side of political economy. This also was how the public received the book, and as noted, it significantly influenced perceptions in England of what was at stake in the American Civil War. Cairnes's aprioristic view did not lack criticism, of course, some of it politically motivated, some questioning the empirical evidence. Jevons, for example, considered Cairnes's work 'a nearly or quite irrefragable piece of reasoning', (Black 1960: 223), but he questioned Cairnes's claims about slave agriculture necessarily exhausting the soil, and asked for comparative evidence. Others questioned Cairnes's claims about the class of marginalized whites. These criticisms did not affect the fundamentals of his a priori theory, and Cairnes ardently collected additional materials to further substantiate and detail his case.

Looking back at his *Character and Logical Method of Political Economy*, in the preface to the 1875 re-edition, it is quite understandable that Cairnes did not see any reason to alter his views. The appearance of Jevons's *Theory of Political Economy* (1871) notwithstanding, Cairnes still did not believe that mathematics or statistics might contribute much to the advancement of political economy as a science. His empirical studies in economics and especially *The Slave Power* showed a rather different approach pointing in the opposite direction: towards the British historical school, rather than towards the newly emerging mathematical economics. Standing at the crossroads of British political economy in the second half of the nineteenth century, John Elliot Cairnes is rightly considered the 'last of the classical economists'.

BIBLIOGRAPHY
The Character and Logical Method of Political Economy: Being a Course of Lectures Delivered in Hilary Term, 1857 (1857; 2nd edn, 1875).
The Slave Power: Its Character, Career, and Probable Designs (1862; repr. New York, 1969).
Essays in Political Economy (1873; repr. New York, 1965).
Political Essays (1873; repr. New York, 1967).
Some Leading Principles of Political Economy Newly Expounded (1874).
Collected Works, ed. T. Boylan and T. Foley, 6 vols (2003).

Further Reading
Black, R.D.C., 'Jevons and Cairnes', *Economica* (1960), vol. 27, pp. 214–32.
Boylan, T.A. and Foley, T.P., 'John Elliot Cairnes, John Stuart Mill and Ireland: Some Problems for Political Economy', *Hermathena* (1983), vol. 135, p. 96.
De Marchi, N., 'Mill and Cairnes and the Emergence of Marginalism in England', *HOPE* (1972), vol. 4, no. 3, pp. 344–63.
Donoghue, M., 'John Elliot Cairnes and the 'Rehabilitation' of the Classical Wage Fund Doctrine', *The Manchester School of Economic and Social Studies* (1998), vol. 66, pp. 396–417.
Kim, J., Jevons versus Cairnes on Exact Economic Laws', in I.H. Rima (ed.), *Measurement, Quantification, and Economic Analysis: Numeracy in Economics* (1995, pp. 140–56).
Levy, D. and Peart, S.J. *The Secret History of the Dismal Science* (2001–2), www.econlit.org.
O'Brien, G., 'J.S. Mill and J.E. Cairnes', *Economica* (1943), vol. 10, pp. 273–85.
Vint, J., *Capital and Wages: A Lakatosian History of the Wages Fund Doctrine* (Aldershot, 1994).
Weinberg, A., *John Elliot Cairnes and the American Civil War: A Study in Anglo-American Relations* (1970).

Harro Maas

CAMPBELL, Alexander (1796–1870)

Campbell was born in 1796 near the point of Skipness, in Kintyre, Argyllshire. He died at his home in North Coburg Street, Glasgow, on 10 February 1870. He was apprenticed as a joiner in Glasgow, and set up a business that met with some success. In the period immediately following the Napoleonic wars he was influenced by the ideas of Robert OWEN and began to articulate what he termed a 'practical socialism'. This led to his involvement with the Bridgeton Co-operative Society, as its treasurer, and, more importantly, with the ill-fated community established at Orbiston, near Motherwell, in 1825, where he was made superintendent of the foundry department. When this community disintegrated in 1828, Campbell, having made himself liable for some of its debts, was imprisoned for a time in Hamilton jail.

After release his continued enthusiasm for Owenite socialism led to involvement in the creation of a co-operative society in Glasgow (1829), with an associated bazaar (1830) where exchanges were conducted on the basis of labour time. He also published *An Address on the Progress of the Co-operative System* (1831), which, he was to claim, envisioned the 'Rochdale' idea of a dividend to customers on purchases from co-operative stores.

In the early 1830s Campbell engaged with an increasingly militant trade unionism. He was instrumental in the creation of a general union, the Glasgow and West of Scotland Association for the Protection of Labour, and there is evidence too that he was the secretary of the Glasgow United Committee of Trades, an embryonic Trades Council. It is also possible that he edited its newspaper, the *Herald to the Trades Advocate* (1830–1), one of the liveliest of the many lively unstamped, working-class papers of the time. In this period he came to see trade unions as a crucial means of promoting co-operative enterprises. Through the direct employment of their members, in periods of trade dispute or unemployment, they could furnish a flow of products to be purchased in labour exchange bazaars. Such activity would strengthen the position of their members in the labour market, provide goods that would exchange fairly on the basis of their labour cost and raise funds that might ultimately be utilised for the formation of co-operative communities. In this regard, Campbell articulated a socialist political economy that dovetailed short-term palliative measures with co-operative activity that had, as its long-term goal, the creation of a new moral world.

This emphasis on working-class organizations as the agent of change also set him apart from those Owenites, including Owen himself, who looked to philanthropic patrons to furnish the means by which that world could be created. In this regard, and throughout his life, Campbell believed that the interests of the capitalist and the labourer were fundamentally opposed and that therefore the working classes should therefore be responsible themselves for organizing and funding their communitarian emancipation.

In the mid-1830s Campbell was associated with the political agitation resulting from the working-class disappointment that followed the passage of the 1832 Reform Act. However, he always saw political reform as a means to social transformation rather than simply improving existing economic and social arrangements. He was also appointed as a 'social missionary' for the Association of All Classes of All Nations to preach the Owenite gospel (1838). This he did for the next two years, taking part in many public debates and earning the encomium of 'Owen's principal Scottish disciple' (Marwick 1964: 11). It was during this period of proselytization that Campbell fell under the influence of the ascetic transcendentalism and Pestalozzian educational principles of James Pierrepont Greaves. This led to his involvement with the Ham Common Concordium, established in 1843 and wedded to the notion of simple food, sexual abstinence, pure water and cold plunges as the basis of a heightened social and spiritual awareness.

In 1848 Campbell became editor of a paper, *The Spirit of the Age* and, in addition, managed the Canadian Land and Railway Investment Association which aimed to promote working-class investment in railway developments and industrial self-supporting colonies in New Brunswick. These were to be organized 'on the associative principle' and embody 'dwellings, schools, workshops, machinery and manufactures' (Fraser 1966: 138). By this date too, Campbell had come to see the state as an important agent of social progress and advocated a socio-economic programme that included the nationalization of the land, a graduated property tax, home colonies and government provision of employment along the lines of the national workshops established by the French Provisional Government in 1848.

In 1856 Campbell became editor of the *Weekly Chronicle* in Glasgow, a paper concerned with trade union affairs. When this was merged with the *Glasgow Sentinel*, Campbell became its industrial reporter and then, in 1863, its editor. Journalistic activity was also combined with support for producer co-operatives, such as the West of Scotland Painting Company, and for consumer co-operation, that was ultimately to bear fruit in the formation of the Scottish Co-operative Wholesale Society in September 1868.

Campbell also assisted in the re-formation of the Glasgow Trades Council in 1858 and through it campaigned for the repeal of the Master and Servants Act. In connection with this agitation, a national conference of trade union delegates took place in May 1864 (Campbell attending as one of the Glasgow delegates) which some subsequent commentators have seen as presaging the first Trade Union Conference of 1868 (Webb and Webb 1920: 235).

BIBLIOGRAPHY
An Address on the Progress of the Co-operative System (Glasgow, 1831).

Further Reading
Claeys, G., *Saints and Citizens, Politics and Anti-Politics in Early British Socialism* (Cambridge, 1989).
Cullen, A., *Adventures in Socialism* (Glasgow, 1910).
Fraser, W.H., *Alexander Campbell and the Search for Socialism* (Manchester, 1996).
Harrison, J.F.C., *Robert Owen and the Owenites in Britain and America, the Quest for the New Moral World* (1969).
Marwick, W., *The Life of Alexander Campbell* (Glasgow, 1964).
Maxwell, W., *The History of Co-operation in Scotland* (Glasgow, 1910).
Webb, S. and Webb, B., *The History of Trade Unionism* (1920).

Noel Thompson

CANNAN, Edwin (1861–1935)

Cannan was born in Funchal, Madeira in February of 1861, and died in Bournemouth on 8 April 1935. He was the son of David Cannan, a Scot who had worked in Australia during the Victoria gold rush, and his wife Jane, who died a few days after Cannan's birth. The scholar and publisher Charles Cannan was his elder brother. Cannan himself suffered from severe ill-health as a child, but in later life he was physically robust. He was an avid cyclist: once, being told that a book was not available in Oxford, where he lived, he responded that he would then cycle to London, fifty miles away, to fetch it.

Cannan was educated at Clifton and Balliol College, Oxford, where he underwent 'in regard to my social philosophy the kind of change which in regard to religion is described as 'conversion''. As he 'listened to [Oxford tutor and later master] Mr. A.L. Smith, the Historical Spirit entered into me, and I became a new man. I took to hear the truth that all important change is gradual, and that social institutions are not created by the sudden efforts of inspired geniuses but grow "of themselves" usually slower than oak-trees.' His health continued to be problematic, and he did not take an honours degree. He did, however, apply himself to the study of political economy, and an essay of 1886 was later developed as *Elementary Political Economy* (1887), which brought him into contact with the Fabian Society. A study of the works of earlier political economists led to the noted *A History of the Theories of Production and Distribution in English Political Economy 1776–1848* (1893). In 1895 he was among the founder members of staff of the new London School of Economics and Political Science, and lectured on economics from then until his retirement in 1926. Of independent means, Cannan was never formally a full-time member of faculty and he continued to live in Oxford, but nevertheless the LSE became the centre of his work and career from then on. He was finally appointed professor of political economy in 1907, by which time he had become the central focus of the LSE's teaching and research on economics.

Following retirement, Cannan produced one more major work, *A Review of Economic Theory* (1929) and several other books including *An Economist's Protest* (1927). He served as president of the Royal Economic Society in 1932. He married Mary Cullen in 1907; they had one son, who died young.

Cannan possessed a material view of the subject matter of economics. He defined economics in *Elementary Political Economy* as the 'explanation of the general causes on which the wealth or material welfare of human beings depends'. While he was 'not prepared to lay down any rules for determining exactly where 'material' ends and non-material begins', he had a more physical view of the subject matter of economics than many succeeding economists. 'The ultimate object of the science of economics seems to be the more material side of human welfare,' he wrote. He put forward both the necessity of private property to capitalism and the possibility of a communist future; another of his works of the 1880s was the unpublished 'Communism in Relation to Production'. In *A History of the Theories of Production and Distribution*, he concluded:

> A great quantity of that part of the produce of industry which is created by men and women working, not for money rewards, but from other motives, such as family affection or duty to the community, is for all practical purposes incapable of being valued and set down in the sum-total of commodities and services with exchange value.
> (1893)

A History of the Theories of Production and Distribution is among Cannan's most celebrated works. It contains a rigorous analysis of the logic of early economic doctrines, and is unhesitating in pointing out the errors made by earlier economists, no matter how celebrated their stature. Cannan's interest in and facility with the history of ideas, acquired at Oxford, turns this from being a mere work of criticism into an understanding of causality in economic thinking. In particular, he regards Adam SMITH's view of the theory of distribution as mistaken. It is not the rates of wages, profits and rents that should be considered and measured, he says, but the share of these in terms of total production. He repeated this theory in later works, and it became one of the key themes in his consideration of classical economics. Joseph Schumpeter, in his *History of Economic Analysis* (1954), called *A History of the Theories*, along with Cannan's editions of Adam Smith (1896, 1904) and his *The History of Local Rates in England*, 'his main scholarly achievements,' though Schumpeter also said that no one can read Cannan's 'lively short tracts on money and monetary policy without pleasure and profit.' Lionel ROBBINS, another Cannan student, wrote that *A History of the Theories* 'established [Cannan's] standing in the profession', and Friedrich von HAYEK called it Cannan's 'first great work'.

In Britain, Cannan's influence as an economics textbook writer was perhaps second only to that of MARSHALL during the period from 1885 to 1935. In addition to *A History of the Theories of Production and Distribution* and *Elementary Political Economy*, other largely textbooks he wrote included *The History of the Local Rates in England* (1896), *Wealth: A Brief Explanation of the Causes of Economic Welfare* (1914), *Money: Its Connexion with Rising and Falling Prices* (1918), and *A Review of Economic Theory* (1929). Most of these went through multiple editions. All show his commitment to classical economic thinking, which he privileges over modern theory. He rejected Alfred Marshall's claim that the latter's neoclassical theory was an extension of earlier ideas, seeing instead a break in the tradition of thought after J.S. MILL. *A Review of Economic Theory* contains little of contemporary economic thought, and focuses almost entirely on the classical economists.

Cannan also played a pre-eminent role in renewing and expanding interest in Adam Smith. In 1896, he published a set of student's notes of Smith's lectures on jurisprudence, with an introduction. Two years later he published two letters of Smith, with notes. In 1901, largely as a result of his work on Smith, he received an honorary doctorate from the University of Glasgow. His great contribution to Smith scholarship was his 1904 edition of *The Wealth of Nations*, of which Henry HIGGS wrote that it is 'incomparably the best edition. In industry, scholarship, and utility to the serious student, it eclipses all its predecessors.' The Cannan edition of Smith remains widely in use.

Cannan's early interest in socialism was very much of the British version. He opposed the idea of state socialism that emerged during the twentieth century, in which the government replaced private ownership of the means of economic production. In economics, he came to be considered a classical liberal because, like John Stuart Mill, he favoured an evolutionary approach to societal change and did not know in advance what the future of society might have in store. At the LSE, he was the founder of a classical liberal tradition that would later include such luminaries as Lionel ROBBINS, Friedrich von Hayek, Arnold PLANT, Ronald Coase, Arthur Seldon, Peter BAUER and Alan Walters.

Cannan was known for his 'common sense' approach to economics. In his final presidential address to the Royal Economic Society, he inveighed against the tendency of academic economics at that time (and subsequently) to retreat into sterile worlds of mathematical theory distinct from the real world of sensory experience. For Cannan, economic theory is justified by one thing and one thing alone: the ability to influence the actual world of economic practice. Economic theory, he believed, does not exist for its own sake, for the amusement or even edification of academic economists. The economic theory of academic economists that does not lead, either proximately or mediately, to salutary changes or reinforcement particularly of government policy is all but useless. Cannan would have considered most of post-Second World War economic theory to be useless in its mathematical garb. To what extent, he would have asked, do these mathematical formulae add to the understanding of economic activity or influence government policies? 'Do not let them', he inveighed against the purveyors of the new mathematical economic theorizing in 1933, 'avert their eyes from the disgusting mess and run back to find contentment in neat equations and elegant equilibria...The mind of the public is an Augean stable.' The public, he believed, is 'at the mercy of quacks', and he thought the role of the academic economist is 'to assist common sense to grasp the basic elements of economic science.'

Again in the tradition of Mill, Cannan saw maximization of the common material good to be one of the constituents of the best society. He recognized goods other than simple manufactured material ones – that is, goods of the spirit, of nature, of beauty, of kindness – and that distribution as well as production is of importance in considering the maximization of economic life. The highest standard of living for all is the optimal goal for government to seek or to seek to encourage. He preferred the term 'political economy' to 'economics' to describe his craft, better conveying the idea of the purpose of political economy being to explain economic activity and to influence public policy.

Cannan's influence extended beyond conservative economists, however. While Milton Friedman respected him and borrowed the title *An Economist's Protest* for one of his own books, the socialist Hugh DALTON was also an admirer. In his own time he was an influential public economist as well as academic figure. In 1904, he joined with Alfred Marshall and others to sign what became known as the 'professor's manifesto', a letter to the *Times* by fourteen professional economists opposing protectionist trade policies. Later in his career, he took an active role in taxation, government spending, and currency questions, both directly through testimony before government commissions and indirectly through published work.

Cannan's greatest influence was as a teacher. Lionel Robbins, a student of Cannan's during the 1920s, remembered that Cannan 'dominated our horizon. Why he did so and how he did so are extraordinarily difficult to say. Yet no one who ever sat under him would deny it for a moment...if there is a difference between a Cannan man and others, it is, I think, that he will perhaps feel a greater instinctive disgust than most at discussions in terms of the desirability of this or that limited advantage for this or that national area – a greater sense of betrayal at the spectacle of economic analysis in the service of economic nationalism' (Robbins 1971).

BIBLIOGRAPHY
Elementary Political Economy (1887).
A History of the Theories of Production and Distribution in English Political Economy 1776–1848 (1893).
History of Local Rates in England (1896; 2nd edn, 1912).
Lectures on Justice, Police, Revenue and Arms delivered in the University of Glasgow by Adam Smith (1896).
The Economic Outlook (1912).
Wealth: A Brief Explanation of the Causes of Economic Welfare (1914).
Money: Its Connexion with Rising and Falling Prices (1918).
The Paper Pound of 1797–1821 (1919).
An Economist's Protest (1927).
A Review of Economic Theory (1929).
Economic Scares (1933).

Further Reading
Ebenstein, A., *Edwin Cannan: Liberal Doyen* (1997).

Hayek, F. von, 'The Transmission of the Ideals of Economic Freedom', in *Studies in Philosophy, Politics and Economics* (New York, 1967).
Kadish, A., *The Oxford Economists in the Late Nineteenth Century* (Oxford, 1982).
Robbins, L., *Autobiography of an Economist* (1971).
Schumpeter, J., *History of Economic Analysis* (Oxford, 1954).
Smith, A., *Wealth of Nations*, ed. E. Cannan, 2 vols (1904).

Alan Ebenstein

CARLYLE, Thomas (1795–1881)

Carlyle was born at Ecclefechan, Dumfriesshire on 4 December 1795, and died at Chelsea in London on 4 February 1881. Educated at the University of Edinburgh between 1809 and 1814, where he principally studied mathematics and demonstrated some prowess in the discipline, he published numerous works during the 1820s on a variety of topics. He knew many of the leading figures of the Edinburgh intelligentsia during the 1820s and early 1830s, including the editor of the *Edinburgh Review*, Francis Jeffrey, and the philosopher, Sir William Hamilton.

During the course of some twenty years (from 1829), Carlyle produced a number of influential discourses on economic matters and the so-called condition of England question. At Craigenputtoch, a remote Dumfriesshire farm, between 1830 and 1831 Carlyle wrote his most famous and most complex text, the literary-philosophical and highly humorous rhapsodic satire of the times and first major counterblast against the Scottish Enlightenment, *Sartor Resartus*. Eventually moving from Scotland to London in 1834, Carlyle settled at 5 Cheyne Row in

Chelsea. Following the publication of *The French Revolution* (1837), he became a well-known public figure and one of the most exciting writers of his times. He was frequently visited by eminent figures of the day, including the philosopher John Stuart MILL. The manuscript first volume of *The French Revolution*, according to several accounts, was accidentally destroyed by Mill's maidservant and consequently had to be re-written by Carlyle from scratch.

Often referred to as the Sage of Chelsea, Carlyle maintained a significant presence as a social and political moralist throughout much of the century. Though he cannot be described as an economist, several of his ideas on economic principles and work, and his sustained opposition to utilitarianism and the 'classical' economists, Adam SMITH and Thomas MALTHUS, played a not insignificant role in influencing the economic theories, standpoints and practice of a number of eminent Victorian thinkers, most of whom were critics and opponents of Victorian capitalism. A complex and arguably inconsistent writer, Carlyle has often been castigated as a political reactionary. This notion is perhaps best supported by his famous *Past and Present*, an imaginative recreation of a medieval past starkly contrasted to the present condition of England, with especial regard to the nature of work. Seemingly regarding work as an absolute good to the point where he virtually sanctifies all manifestations of work, denying the moral importance of pain and pleasure and of self-interest (in sharp contrast to Benthamite utilitarianism and Malthusian economics), extolling the virtues of humility and *Entsagen* (renunciation of worldly pleasures), advocating emigration as an answer to the problems of a rapidly increasing population – in all these things Carlyle may be said to espouse politically reactionary or extreme or authoritarian views. But against or mitigating the apparently reactionary character of such points, it is important to note that some of the notable figures Carlyle influenced included the political radical and Chartist leader and poet, Thomas Cooper (1805–92), Friedrich ENGELS, Karl MARX, the painter, designer, writer, and leading figure in the arts and crafts movement, William MORRIS, and the famous art critic John RUSKIN.

Carlyle's influence is perhaps much more pervasively evident in the realms of literature and philosophy than it is in the realm of economics, a discipline towards which he was clearly antagonistic. Somewhat famously, in his highly controversial *Latter-Day Pamphlets* (1850), he described economics as 'the *dismal science*'. However, as one of the leading men of letters in nineteenth-century Britain who met and influenced many of the most notable Victorian novelists, poets, writers of non-fiction and political figures, the bias of Carlyle's ideas on economic matters can be detected in many writings of vastly more popular appeal than the works of economists. Of those he most conspicuously influenced, perhaps the most famous writer was the novelist Charles DICKENS. Dickens's 'A Christmas Carol' and *Hard Times*, among other of his works, resonate with well-known Carlylean standpoints on several economic matters such as Carlyle's sympathies for the plight of the worker and the unemployed, and his disaffection towards the more harmful effects of Victorian industrial capitalism.

Carlyle regarded the underpinning economic principles of industrial capitalism, its philosophical assumptions and its attendant progressive liberal philosophy of utilitarianism as deeply dehumanizing and misleading in their materialism/mechanism, their generation of and reliance upon greed and narrow self-interest, their reduction of the employer–employee relationship to one that solely consisted of a mere 'cash nexus', and their implications for society, particularly with regard to the notion of social atomization which seems implicit in that major principle of Smithian economics, the division of labour. Vehemently opposed to an idle aristocracy – he humorously dubbed them 'double-barrelled game-preservers' – Carlyle coined the term 'captains of industry' in advocating a new aristocracy of talent which would concentrate on and direct the world of work, as the most ennobling activity for mankind. Similarly opposed to what he called 'cheap and nasty', he regarded the production of poorly made, mass-produced cheap goods as something verging on an atrocity – in this, and in his sanctification of true or genuine work, his influence upon the arts and crafts movement is obvious. Lines of influence may also be traced to the so-called aesthetic movement in art, which attempted to eschew utterly utilitarian notions of art as having a use-value and the general tendency of this towards the commodification of art. Carlyle was also opposed to advertising or 'puffing', seeing this as part of what was making the nineteenth century an age of mere semblance or sham.

Though his sympathies towards the poor can be clearly detected, Carlyle detested laziness, the indolent condition of the poor and *laissez-faire* governance, which he saw as tantamount to an abnegation of responsibility towards those who needed both assistance and firm control to prevent them from starving or descending into the squalor so pressingly evident in many Victorian cities. Though his views could be extreme in some particulars, and though his distinctive manner of expression and literary allusiveness has always tended to confuse the majority of readers, a careful reading of his work tends to suggest a political standpoint with regard to economics which is much less easily aligned with right-wing or High Tory politics than it may at first seem. Furthermore, Carlyle's criticisms of capitalism are more substantial than may be inferred by a less careful reading of his texts. According to one of the best accounts of Carlyle's views on political economy, Carlyle's critique, 'though neither so thorough nor so subtle as Marx's, is as surprisingly comprehensive as it is unsystematic' (Rosenberg 1974: 153, and also 149–75). However, the unsystematic anti-rationalism (or anti-Enlightenment) manner of Carlyle's writing is one of the ways in which his work, perhaps all too subtly, stands in opposition to the prevalent economic theories and practices of Victorian capitalism which in largely caricatural form he dismisses as typifying all that was most vile within the Victorian economic system. The literary style of Carlyle's writing presents an enormous challenge to the reader's abilities to interpret the complexity of his ideas on economics. But since Carlyle exerted such a prodigious influence on so many contemporary critics of capitalism, his critique and general position on the economic tendencies and underlying principles of Victorian capitalism, as inherited from the classical economists of the Enlightenment, deserve the attention of any student of the period interested in enriching his or her understanding of how the prevalent economic system of capitalism was both perceived and most staunchly criticised by many of Carlyle's contemporaries, some of whom remain without question among the most significant economic theorists of the century. Carlyle's extensive letters are currently being published.

BIBLIOGRAPHY
'Signs of the Times' (1829).
Sartor Resartus (1833–4).
The French Revolution (1837).
Chartism (1840).
On Heroes, Hero-Worship, & The Heroic in History (1841).
Past and Present (1843).
Oliver Cromwell's Letters and Speeches (1845).
Latter-Day Pamphlets (1850).
Frederick the Great (1858–65).
Reminiscences (1881).
The Works of Thomas Carlyle, ed. H.D. Traill, 30 vols (1896–9).
The Collected Letters of Thomas and Jane Welsh Carlyle (Durham, North Carolina, 1970–).

Further Reading
Burrow, J.W., *Whigs and Liberals: Continuity and Change in English Political Thought*, (Oxford, 1988).
Goldberg, M., *Carlyle and Dickens* (Athens, Georgia, 1972).
Gribble, B.Y., 'To Grow to be a Hero: The Influence of Thomas Carlyle upon the Late Prose Romances of William Morris', unpublished doctoral thesis, University of Tennessee (1981).
Heffer, S., *Thomas Carlyle: Moral Desperado* (1996).
Kaplan, F., *Thomas Carlyle: A Biography* (Cambridge, 1983).
Rosenberg, P., *The Seventh Hero: Thomas Carlyle and the Theory of Radical Activism* (Cambridge, Massachusetts, 1974).
Rutherford, D., 'Dismal Carlyle and the "Dismal Science"', *The Carlyle Society Papers* (1996–7), no. 8, pp. 24–36.

Ralph Jessop

CARR-SAUNDERS, Alexander Morris (1886–1966)

Carr-Saunders was born on 14 January 1886 in Reigate, Surrey. He died on the night of 6 October 1966 after trying, at the age of eighty, to push his car uphill following a breakdown at Thirlmere in his beloved Lake District. He was one of five children, and the youngest by some fifteen years, of a wealthy underwriter, James Carr-Saunders, and his wife Flora. A sister married Admiral Sir John Slade, and their youngest daughter became Gandhi's disciple Mira Behn. Carr-Saunders was quietly proud of his descent from Roger Morris, the eighteenth-century architect and after whom he was named. He also felt an affinity with his great-uncle William Wilson Saunders, who was elected to the Royal Society for his studies in entomology, and Edward Saunders, who was also an entomologist and an FRS. In 1929 Carr-Saunders married Teresa Molyneux-Seel and they had three children, Edmund, Flora and Nicholas. Apart from the considerable achievements described below, he also had a lifelong interest in both mountaineering and farming.

Carr-Saunders was educated at Eton and Magdalen College, Oxford. Henry Phelps BROWN (1981: 175) reports that he was lonely in childhood and intensely unhappy at Eton, leaving at sixteen to spend two years in Paris and the French Alps. However, during that time he concluded that biology held the most promise for scientific advance in the coming years and therefore chose to read that subject at Oxford. He was awarded first-class honours in zoology in 1908. He then held the Biological Scholarship at Naples for a year, after which he returned to Oxford to work as a demonstrator. In 1910 he moved to London and studied biometrics under Karl Pearson.

However, Carr-Saunders's interests were widening and he decided not to pursue a career as a natural scientist. He read for the bar, was secretary of the research committee of the Eugenics Education Society, and resided for a time at Toynbee Hall where he was made sub-warden and was also elected to the Stepney Borough Council. During the First World War he held a commission in the Royal Army Service Corps and was posted to a depot at Suez. He was kept there for the remainder of the war, though he used this time, among other things, to plan his future study of population.

After the war Carr-Saunders returned to Oxford as a demonstrator in zoology, taking a particular interest in the issue of population. This soon bore fruit. His book *The Population Problem* was published in 1922. This made his reputation as a serious scholar, being well-received among his contemporaries, though it was some time before its contribution was more fully appreciated. His work effectively straddled the relevant disciplines in applying biological knowledge to human society and examining behaviour that promotes group survival. With Dr C.P. Blacker, Carr-Saunders went on to establish the Population Investigation Committee, which he chaired from 1936 to 1958 and continued as a member until his death. The Committee had the aim of sponsoring and undertaking systematic demographic research, and under Carr-Saunders's active chairmanship did much to improve statistics in this area before the Second World War. Furthermore, many members of that committee were involved with Carr-Saunders's pioneer work carried out by the Royal Commission on Population, on which he served from 1944–9. He was also chairman of its Statistics Committee. In addition, as David GLASS (1966) pointed out, it was through the work of Carr-Saunders and the Population Investigation Committee, continuing under the auspices of the Royal Commission, that demography became established as a university discipline in the UK.

Carr-Saunders also made a more general contribution to university development and in particular the London School of Economics and Political Science (LSE) through very challenging times. Initially, the success of *The Population Problem* led, apparently much to his surprise, to an invitation in 1923 to be the first holder of the Charles Booth Chair of Social Science at the University of Liverpool, a post he held for fourteen years. It was a very appropriate appointment, enabling him to develop his social research and analysis of social structure. In 1927 he published, with D. Caradog Jones, the *Social Structure of England and Wales*, which used social surveys and census data to produce an enlightening account of society and economy. For some years he made a particular study of the professions. This was the subject of his Herbert Spencer Lecture delivered at Oxford in May 1928, and of the pioneering work *The Professions* (with P.A. Wilson) which appeared in 1933. At Liverpool he also contributed to the development of the position of social science in universities and demonstrated his effectiveness in university administration.

In 1937, Carr-Saunders was invited to succeed Sir William BEVERIDGE as Director of LSE, a post that he held until his retirement in 1956. He had some pertinent views on university education in economics as made clear, for example, in his presidential address to the Royal Economic Society, reprinted in the *Economic Journal* in 1958. One was that a particular effort should be made to cater for students who were not going to pursue economics at university after graduation. He suggested that university teachers were so habituated 'to thinking of degree courses in relation to the needs of the scholar that a true wrench of the mind is required in order to construct a course suitable for the student whose future will be in affairs'. Another issue was that economics should be firmly related to social studies more generally. He was clear that to achieve a balanced view of society it is not enough that a student should simply study related disciplines, he or she must be able to relate them to the main subject. He even suggested that perhaps economists and those in close disciplines should sometimes take time to examine the problems of social studies as a whole. It is a view as true now as it was then, and a general approach that he himself had followed in his own studies to excellent effect.

Carr-Saunders's contribution to the development of LSE is ably described by Dahrendorf (1995) in his history of LSE. One of his first achievements was to hold LSE together during the Second World War. The government had planned for half of LSE to go to Glasgow and the other to Aberdeen. However, Carr-Saunders had the foresight in July 1939 to arrange for the whole school to move to Peterhouse College, Cambridge, which became its home for the next six years. Other colleges were less fortunate: for example University College, London ended up split in many ways with parts going to Aberystwyth,

Bangor, Cambridge, Cardiff, Swansea, Sheffield and Southampton. Perhaps surprisingly in the difficult circumstances of the war, under Carr-Saunders's effective directorship the LSE did well at Cambridge and even experienced some expansion. On returning to London, it was thus in a healthy state and ready for post-war growth and development and a continuation of what has been described as its 'golden years' (Darhendorf: 1995: 389–93).

A further substantial contribution to university development began when Carr-Saunders was appointed in 1943 to the Commission on Higher Education in the Colonies, chaired by Sir Cyril Asquith. In 1945 the Commission produced its report with proposals for university development in the then colonies. Carr-Saunders also set up and became chairman of both the University of London Senate Committee and the Inter-University Council, which provided assistance including accreditation to developing colleges and universities overseas. From 1945 to 1951 he chaired the Colonial Social Science Research Council. In 1947 he was appointed chairman of the Commission on University Education in Malaya; in 1953 he was chairman of the Commission on Higher Education for Africans in Central Africa and in 1961 of the Mission on University Education in Northern Nigeria. In 1962 he became a member of the Committee on the University of East Africa.

Carr-Saunders was knighted in 1946, became a fellow of the British Academy in the same year, and was appointed KBE in 1957. He was awarded honorary doctorates from nine universities and was also an honorary fellow of Peterhouse, Cambridge, of the University College of East Africa and of the London School of Economics.

BIBLIOGRAPHY
The Population Problem, A Study in Human Evolution (Oxford, 1922).
Eugenics (1926).

(with D. Caradog Jones) *A Survey of the Social Structure of England and Wales: as Illustrated by Statistics* (1927; 2nd edn, 1937; 3rd edn, 1958 with D. Caradog Jones and C.A. Moser).
Professions, Their Organization and Place in Society (Oxford, 1928).
(with P.A. Wilson) *The Professions* (Oxford, 1933).
'Europe Overseas', in J.S. Huxley and A. Haddon (eds), *We Europeans* (1935, pp. 241–61).
World Population: Past Growth and Present Trends (Oxford, 1936).
(with P.S. Florence and R. Peers) *Consumers' Co-operation in Great Britain; An Examination of the British Co-operative Movement* (1938; revised edn, 1942).
The Biological Basis of Human Nature (1942).
(with H. Mannheim and E.C. Rhodes) *Young Offenders: An Enquiry into Juvenile Delinquency* (Cambridge, 1942).
'The Place of Economics and Allied Subjects in the Curriculum', *Economic Journal* (1958), vol. 68, pp. 433–48.
New Universities Overseas (1961).

Further Reading
Brown, H.P., 'Sir Alexander Morris Carr-Saunders, 1886–1966', Proceedings of the British Academy (1967), vol. 53, pp. 379–89.
Dahrendorf, R., *A History of the London School of Economics and Political Science 1895–1995* (Oxford, 1995).
Glass, D., 'Sir Alexander Carr-Saunders' *The Times* (1966), 15 October, p. 10.
Morris, C, and Fulton, Lord, 'Sir A. Carr-Saunders' *The Times* (1966), 14 October, p. 14.

Simon James

CARTER, William (*c*.1640/45–1703)

Carter was born in the early 1640s, probably in London. No certain information is known about his background, but his first book was published in 1669 while he was still a relatively young man, while in 1698 he notes that he has spent thirty years in the clothing trade and is now growing old. A birth date much past 1645 seems unlikely, and he certainly reached his maturity in the years following the restoration of the monarchy. Carter died in London in 1703.

A clothier by trade, Carter spent most of his career trying to suppress the smuggling of wool from England to the continent. He frequently lobbied the king and parliament to this end, and wrote a series of pamphlets urging stronger measures. Although the export of wool had been outlawed in 1660s, smuggling continued unabated for many years, and Carter urged that more men and ships should be sent to police the coasts and cut off the trade.

Unlike other pamphleteers of his day, however, Carter also took direct action. In 1669, following his first pamphlet, Carter secured a warrant from the crown and rode to Dover, where he arrested the master of a smuggling ship then lying in the port. He then attempted to take his prisoner to Folkestone for trial, but was balked when the master's wife hurried to Folkestone ahead of him and roused a mob, who attacked Carter and his followers with stones. Carter was forced to abandon his prisoner and retreat. He continued his attempts to arrest the smugglers or 'owlers' of Romney Marsh, however, and in 1688 he and a group of fellow clothiers arrested ten smugglers and took them to Romney for trial. The local authorities were fearful of the consequences, for the smugglers enjoyed much local support, and released the suspects on bail. The freed men then roused their own supporters and some fifty armed men then chased Carter and his men as far as Lydd and then Camber. Here they were able to commandeer a boat and escape to the safety of Rye, saving themselves from almost certain death at the hands of the smugglers.

During his eventful life, Carter never ceased to rail against the smuggling of wool. As a clothier he was of course motivated by self-interest, but he was also an advocate of developing a cloth manufacturing base in England in order to improve the balance of trade. In *Englands Interest by Trade Asserted* (1671), Carter argued that the export of wool to France was harmful in two ways: first, England lost the potential revenue to be gained from manufacturing and selling cloth abroad, and second, it gave French manufacturers access to supplies of high-quality wool which would otherwise be denied to them. Cutting off the export of wool, Carter believed, would both help domestic industry and harm the overseas competition.

Carter argues further that all the trades to some extent influenced each other, and increasing the volume and revenue of any one trade would produce general economic benefits, 'there being such a connexion of trades one to another, and the whole of trade being enlarged by the abounding of laborious people' (1671: 12). He describes how the wealth created by trade circulates throughout the kingdom, providing employment and reducing poverty: This [trade] rationally is the strength of any people, poverty and idleness bring their shame and ruine, which would unavoidably follow want of trade. And so much the more where the greatest trade hath been; if it fails, the greater poverty is and will be' (1671: 13).

Englands Interest by Trade Asserted is Carter's most important work, and he refers back to it and quotes from it in nearly all his succeeding works. In later years he became a strong Francophobe. In *The Usurpations of the France* (1698) he argued that France's rapid growth in political and military strength could be traced back to the more than four millions sterling per annum that France gained by exporting cloth made from English wool, and he called on the English people to boycott French imports. In *An Alarum to England*

(1700) he went so far as to accuse the French of deliberately undermining the English economy and impoverishing the country by flooding the market with cheap cloth. He also attacked the East India Company, whose cloth imports from India were, he said, similarly damaging to the domestic cloth industry.

BIBLIOGRAPHY
England's Interest Asserted in the Improvement of its Native Commodities and more especially its Manufacture of Wool (1669).
Englands Interest by Trade Asserted, showing the Necessity & Excellency Thereof (1671).
A Brief Advertisement to the Merchant and Clothier about the present state of the Woollen manufactures of this Nation (1672).
An Abstract of the Proceedings to Prevent Exportation of Wooll Un-manufactured, from 1667 to this present year, 1688 (1688; 2nd edn, 1689).
England's Interest in Securing the Woollen Manufacture of this Realm (1689).
The Usurpations of the France upon the Trade of the Woollen Manufacture of England (1698).
An Alarum to England, to prevent its destruction by the loss of trade and navigation (1700).

Further Reading
Platt, R., *Smuggler's Britain* (1991).

Morgen Witzel

CARUS-WILSON, Eleanora Mary (1897–1977)

Eleanora Mary Carus-Wilson was born in Montreal, Quebec on 27 December 1897, the youngest of three children of Charles Ashley Carus-Wilson and Mary Petrie. She was educated at St Paul's Girls' School and Westfield College, University of London. At the time of her birth her father was professor of Electrical Engineering at McGill University, but her family soon returned to England to live in Hanover Lodge, near Holland Park, which remained her home until her death in London on 1 February 1977.

After graduating in 1921 Carus-Wilson moved, somewhat reluctantly, into school teaching. Her first love remained medieval economic history, and she soon embarked on an MA which she completed with distinction in 1926. She also became a regular member of the famous research seminar run by Eileen POWER and M.M. POSTAN at the London School of Economics. Although able to research and write only on a part-time basis, with the guidance and inspiration of Eileen Power and Caroline Skeel, she published a series of substantial papers. Eventually, in 1936, she was awarded a Leverhulme Fellowship which enabled her to settle down to two years' uninterrupted research. A shortage of university positions, a reluctance to leave her splendid London home and the onset of the Second World War contrived to delay the start of her academic career, and it was not until 1945 that she finally secured a full-time lectureship at the London School of Economics. Thereafter, however, promotion and scholarly recognition advanced rapidly. Carus-Wilson became a reader in 1948, and in 1953 a personal chair was created for her. In 1965 she gave the Ford Lectures at Oxford, and election to a fellowship of the British Academy followed in 1963.

Carus-Wilson played a major role in the development of the relatively new subject of medieval economic history. From the 1930s to her death, her careful and often closely-focussed scholarship, devoted largely to industry, towns and trade, provided a fertile counterpoint to Postan's grand, imaginative and theoretical generalizations on the medieval economy, with their special emphasis on population, settlement and agriculture. This was a most distinguished era for medieval English history, and the importance of Carus-Wilson's contribution was recognized when in 1969 she succeeded Postan as president of the Economic History Society, the first woman to occupy that post.

Carus-Wilson is best known for her pioneering studies of England's textile industry in the Middle Ages, but the significance of her early work on overseas trade should not be underestimated. Her interest in overseas trade had been stimulated by the supervisor of her MA thesis, Eileen Power, and she contributed two lengthy essays on the the Iceland venture to Power and Postan's notable *Studies in English Trade in the Fifteenth Century* (1933). As she was to note later, these essays were written at a time when the study of English medieval customs accounts was in its infancy, and when she looked at them it was revealed at once that the basis of Bristol's trade was the export of manufactured woollens, and that the export of raw wool, which played a major part in the trade of most ports, was never of any significance there. This concern with the quality of sources, and with the necessity of basing description and argument on the evidence, was always firmly at the heart of Carus-Wilson's view of the historian's craft, and it led her to produce, with the assistance of Olive Coleman, a comprehensive and definitive edition of the statistics of England's export trade from 1275 to 1546. This is an invaluable work of reference which pays full tribute to the quality of England's surviving customs accounts, and the overwhelming importance of wool and cloth in her export trade.

The history of towns was a further field in which Carus-Wilson produced major works of scholarship. Bristol featured prominently in her urban writings, and was the subject of her first and last publications; the latter being a masterly account of the development of the medieval city. In the 1960s she produced a stimulating account of the expansion of Exeter at the close of the Middle Ages, and her paper on the rise of Stratford-upon-Avon broke new ground by focusing on a small market town and utilising surname evidence to demonstrate that most of the burgesses who swelled its population were recruited from the surrounding countryside. At the time of her death she was engaged on a history of King's Lynn which was planned as a 'thorough coordination of archaeological with architectural and documentary evidence, so as to build up a complete picture as possible of a medieval English town'. This was a prescient project that foreshadowed much of the interdisciplinary strategy which was to underpin later studies of Winchester and Cheapside, London.

In her pioneering studies of England's most important industry, the manufacture of cloth and clothing, Carus-Wilson adopted the same multi-disciplinary approach. In advance of her time, she incorporated archaeology, art history and technology into a series of seminal historical studies of the rise of the English industry from being a small-scale exporter of high-quality products to becoming the leading supplier of woollen textiles to the international market. In addition to displaying an exemplary command of documentary sources, Carus-Wilson's work derived great strength from a close attention to surviving pieces of medieval cloth, from illustrations of clothworking in a variety of media, including manuscript illuminations and stained glass windows, and from a practical grasp of the equipment used in the various processes of manufacture. These skills were much in evidence in a series of publications which ranged from the inadequacy of certain fourteenth-century aulnage accounts, to the trade in French woad, the nature of 'haberget' cloth, broad surveys of the woollen industry of Europe, the English cloth industry in the twelfth and thirteenth centuries, and industrial growth in the fifteenth-century countryside.

The rise in the scale of England's commercial cloth industry and the shift in its prime location from large towns to countryside, and from highly-regulated gild workshops to free and flexible production based largely on the labour of people working part-time in rural cottages, were leading themes defined and clarified in Carus-Wilson's work. Though burdened by pressing administrative duties during the war, during which she served as head of the Intelligence Branch of the General Department of the Ministry of Food, Carus-Wilson found time to produce two of her most important articles, those on the fortunes of the English cloth industry before 1350 and on the mechanization of fulling. In her classic study of the zenith of the urban cloth industry in the late twelfth and thirteenth centuries, a persuasive case was made for the restraints of trade which came to exist in many leading centres of production.

In the best-documented town, Leicester, she identified the presence of a class of entrepreneurs, dominated by the dyers, who attempted to control all processes of production, except carding and spinning, and to reduce the weavers and fullers to virtual employees. In what was arguably her most controversial paper, 'An Industrial Revolution of the Thirteenth Century', she claimed that historians had been mistaken in assuming that England's cloth industry was in decline in this period, and that any contraction in the older urban centres was more than compensated by growth in rural areas, stimulated by the rapid rise of mechanized fulling undertaken in mills located on the banks of fast-running streams.

Carus-Wilson's special skills lay in the scrupulous use of evidence, and in the ability to establish firm and seemingly indisputable lines beyond which the sources should not carry the eager researcher. Yet her interest in surveying and explaining the fortunes of the English textile industry in the Middle Ages led her into broader and unavoidably more speculative terrain. For some time Carus-Wilson had planned a full-length study of the medieval English textile industry, and her Ford Lectures of 1965 were expected to culminate in just such a book. But her pioneering work had inspired others to study England's leading industry, and inevitably differences of emphasis and view began to emerge. She was criticized for the heavy weight which she had placed on fulling mills in determining the location of the industry, and for exaggeration in the use of the term 'industrial revolution'. Edward Miller, in an article published in the *Economic History Review* in 1965, reasserted the old view that the English industry was in decline in the later thirteenth century, and cited as a major cause the rise of international competition, especially from Flanders; he also expressed the view that it was only in the late Middle Ages that England's rural industry truly flourished. As a consequence of the emergence of these alternative views, the subject matter of her Ford Lectures remained under review and sadly the eagerly awaited volume never appeared.

Much of Carus-Wilson's published work, on the cloth industry as well as on a range of other topics, was of outstanding and enduring quality. The publication of her collected essays in *Medieval Merchant Venturers* in 1954 was a major event for the subject, and remains essential reading for all medieval economic historians. A glowing testimony both to the importance of her contributions and the high regard in which she was held across continental Europe and North America, as well as in Britain, is the remarkable *festschrift* published after her death, which contained seventeen articles on cloth and clothing in medieval Europe written by scholars from eleven different countries.

BIBLIOGRAPHY

'The Overseas Trade of Bristol in the Fifteenth Century', in E. Power and M.M. Postan, *Studies in English Trade in the Fifteenth Century* (1933).

'The Iceland Venture', in E. Power and M.M. Postan, *Studies in English Trade in the Fifteenth Century* (1933).

'The Woollen Industry', in M.M. Postan and E.E. Rich (eds), *The Cambridge Economic History of Europe* (Cambridge, 1952).

Medieval Merchant Venturers (1954).
'Evidences of Industrial Growth on Some Fifteenth-Century Manors', *Economic History Review* (1959), 2nd series, vol. XII, no. 2.
'The Woollen Industry Before 1550', in *The Victoria History of the Counties of England: Wiltshire* (1959).
The Expansion of Exeter at the Close of the Middle Ages (Exeter, 1963).
(with O. Coleman) *England's Export Trade 1275–1547* (Oxford, 1963).
'The First Half-Century of the Borough of Stratford-upon-Avon', *Economic History Review* (1965), 2nd series, vol. XVIII, no. 1.
'Haberget: A Medieval Conundrum', *Medieval Archaeology* (1969), vol. XIII.
(with M.D. Lobel) 'Bristol', in M.D. Lobel (ed.), *Historic Towns* (1975).

Further Reading
Coleman, D.C., 'Industrial Growth and Industrial Revolutions', in E.M. Carus-Wilson (ed.), *Essays in Economic History*, vol. III (1963).
Harte, N.B. and Ponting, K.G. (eds), *Cloth and Clothing in Medieval Europe. Essays in Memory of Professor E M Carus-Wilson* (1983).
Miller, E., 'The Fortunes of the English Textile Industry in the Thirteenth Century', *Economic History Review* (1965), vol. XVIII, no. 1.

John Hatcher

CARY, John (1649?–1717/22)

John Cary was probably born in March 1649 in Bristol, the son of Shershaw and Mary Cary. He died sometime between 1717 and 1722. After apprenticing as linen draper, he became a free merchant in 1672 and began trading goods that ranged from Caribbean sugar to Madeira wines. In 1677 he followed his father into the Bristol Society of Merchant Venturers, and became its warden in 1683. In 1690, his support for Whig MPs Sir Robert Yate and Major Thomas Day prompted rival Tories to have him charged with treasonably encouraging trade with France. Cary, however, defended himself successfully. By 1691 he was the Society's proxy in London, and presented petitions ranging from requests for naval protection of shipping convoys to calls for an expansion of the slave trade through a revocation of the Royal Africa Company's monopoly charter.

Cary drew upon these experiences to develop his first published treatise, *An Essay on the State of England* (1695). His attempts to use the book's fame to secure an appointment to the Board of Trade failed, but they brought him into contact with John LOCKE, who praised the tract. In 1696, Cary founded the Bristol Corporation of the Poor, which he later presented to parliament as a model for a national scheme then being drafted. In 1698, however, his bid for a seat in Parliament failed and his calls for a conquest of Newfoundland went unheeded. The same year, he published *A Vindication of the Parliament of England* (1698), a refutation of William Molyneux's claim that the English parliament had not historically enjoyed sovereignty over Ireland. Two years later he was appointed a trustee for the sale of forfeited estates in Ireland. In 1704, he proposed a plan to develop an Irish linen industry. Late in life, he was held briefly in a debtors' prison after he refused to pay several disputed bills.

Cary expounded mercantilist political economy. Recognizing the world-wide use of gold and silver as money, he asserted that the value of coins was determined by the international market as a function of the weight and fineness of their bullion content. He attacked William LOWNDES's plan to devalue English currency, arguing that reducing the bullion content of coins would only spread the money supply over less valuable coins and might encourage older, heavier coins to be melted down, thus necessitating further recoinage. Instead, he proposed founding a new national bank and credit. Whereas the Bank of England discounted its notes when exchanging them for specie, Cary's bank would issue bills that were on a par with specie or earned interest. With their value maintained, these notes would circulate as currency, and the bank could design its issuance and retirement of them for the purpose of influencing interest rates and multiplying the money supply to match the growing economy.

The universal use of specie centred purchasing power in those nations with positive balances of trade. Cary proposed the establishment of a committee comprised of seasoned merchants to ensure that England sold more to its competitors than it bought from them. This could be accomplished through an integration of the empire's economies. The colonies would specialize in husbandry and provide raw materials while England produced manufactured goods. Such diversification would decrease the empire's dependency on its neighbours. To increase its competitiveness in foreign markets, tariffs could be co-ordinated to encourage the production of complementary rather than substitute goods, as in the case of English wool and Irish linen. Like many mercantilists, Cary was more concerned with propelling England beyond its rivals than with considering the potential inhumanities of slavery and inefficiencies of protectionism.

BIBLIOGRAPHY

An Essay on the State of England in Relation to its Trade, its Poor, and its Taxes, For Carrying on the Present War Against France (Bristol, 1695).

An Essay on the Coyn and Credit of England As they stand with Respect to its Trade (Bristol, 1696).

An Essay Towards the Setlement of a National Credit, In the Kingdom of England, Humbly presented to the two Honourable Houses of Parliament (1696).

A Vindication of the Parliament of England, In Answer to a Book written by William Molyneux of Dublin, esq. Intituled The Case of Irelands being bound by Acts of Parliament in England, stated (1698).

An Account of the Proceedings of the Corporation of Bristol, in Execution of the Act of Parliament for The better Employing and Maintaining the Poor of that City (1700).

A Proposal Offered to the Committee of the Honourable House of Commons, Appointed to Consider of Ways for the Better Providing for the Poor, and Setting them on Work. And now under their Consideration (1700).

Reasons For Passing The Bill For Relieving And Employing The Poor Of This Kingdom Humbly Offered (1700).

Some Considerations relating to the Carrying on the Linnen Manufacture in the Kingdom of Ireland, By a Joint-Stock (1704).

A Proposal for the Paying off the Publick Debts by erecting a National Credit (1719).

The Letters and Papers of John Cary, British Library Add. Ms. 5540 (1819).

Further Reading

Lane, H.J., 'The Life and Writings of John Cary', MA thesis, Bristol University (1932).

Public Records Office, Colonial Office 391/10 Board of Trade Papers: Minutes, Journal B. 1697–1698.

Public Records Office, Colonial Office 388/5 Board of Trade Papers: Original Correspondence, Domestic Trade A.B. 1696–1698.

James Ashley Morrison

CAWOOD, Francis (fl. 1710–21)

Little is known about Cawood save that he was a merchant of London. He was probably born there, and there may be a connection with the family of John Cawood, printer and stationer to the court of Elizabeth I, who died around 1565, but this is not certain. He is almost certainly the Francis Cawood who wrote *Navigation Compleated* in 1710, an attempt to solve the problem of the calculation of longitude, and at this point he is described as a 'student of mathematics'. He is first mentioned as a merchant of London in 1713, and still held that status in 1721, but thereafter nothing is known of him.

Cawood wrote two books on economic subjects, *Britain's Honour, and True Way to obtain Wealth* (1717) and *An Essay, or Scheme: Towards Establishing the Fishery, and other Manufactures, of Great-Britain* (1721). The first work is largely a description of how the Netherlands rose to be a commercial power in the seventeenth century and includes a detailed examination of Dutch commerce, especially in the Baltic but also in the Mediterranean. In the case of the former, Cawood points out that it was the English who pioneered the first trade routes between Russia and western Europe, but English traders had since abandoned these routes to their Dutch rivals. He describes the value and volume of the Russia trade, and urges British merchants to open up these routes once again; an interesting precursor of the more detailed later work on this subject by ODDY.

In a postscript to the work, Cawood comments that it was trade that had made England powerful, and it was the loss of trade that was now dragging the country down: 'If trade has raised our nation (as certainly it has), the loss of trade must necessarily sink our nation. By the decay of commerce our rich lands will be uncultivated; the rents will fall, the tenants starve, the poor multiply, the parishes be burthened...every family [will] bear a share in the declining fate' (1717: 144). Loss of trade will mean that the country will lose the ability to defend itself, as it cannot then raise armies or fleets save through taxation or increasing the public debt, and these will be insufficient for national defence.

In the second work, Cawood urges that measures be taken in hand to stimulate the herring trade, once a major industry in Britain but now largely removed to the Low Countries. He suggests there is a close relationship between shipping and navigation on the one hand, and trade on the other; the two are essential to each other. Therefore, enlarging the herring trade would also provide more shipping and this would be to the good of trade as a whole.

Rather than legislating against foreign traders, however, Cawood believes that the best way to stimulate trade is to create conditions favourable to its existence. If constraints are placed on trade, then trade will go elsewhere: 'It must be acknowledged for incontestable truth, that whenever trade is constrained in any government, it will retire to others, where it may have greater encouragement, and be more favourably used' (1721: 2). He enlarges on the need for trade if the country is to flourish: 'It is certain the interest of princes, that commerce should flourish in their dominions; for never were greater things perform'd by sovereigns, than when the trade of their subjects has offered them the means to put them in execution; which may be proved by infinite examples, both ancient and modern' (1721: 2). He contrasts Spain, rich in gold and silver mines at home and in its colonies and yet impoverished, and the Netherlands, which produces almost nothing but thanks to trade is the wealthiest nation in Europe. Without trade, says Cawood, there can be no wealth.

BIBLIOGRAPHY
Navigation Compleated: Being a New Method never before attain'd to by any: whereby the True Longitude of any one Place in the World may be found... (1710).

Britain's Honour, and True Way to obtain Wealth (1717).
An Essay, or Scheme: Towards Establishing the Fishery, and other Manufactures, of Great-Britain (1721).

Morgen Witzel

CAZENOVE, John (1788–1879)

Cazenove was born in London on 12 May 1788, a son of James Cazenove, merchant, who had emigrated from Geneva. He died 15 August 1879 at New Wandsworth, Surrey. He was educated at Charterhouse School in London and then worked for a time in his father's firm, James Cazenove & Co., until its collapse in 1831. No evidence has so far been found to link him to the modern stockbroking firm, Cazenove and Co., founded by a younger brother. He is known to have published eleven books and pamphlets, the latest at about the age of eighty-seven. Seven of the eleven publications were anonymous. His habit of publishing anonymously raises the possibility that some further publications remain to be discovered.

In addition to his books and pamphlets, Cazenove is thought to have contributed one or more reviews to the *British Critic*, and to have been the anonymous editor of the second (posthumous) edition of MALTHUS's *Principles of Political Economy* (1836). The extent of his editorial interventions in Malthus's *Principles* is unclear, but was possibly considerable. He was also mainly responsible for editing the *Literary Remains* (1859) of Richard JONES, as acknowledged by the editor, William WHEWELL. Amongst the Malthus manuscripts held at Kanto Gakuen University in Japan, there are anonymous papers in Cazenove's hand entitled 'Letters to David Ricardo' that are critical of RICARDO and appear to have been intended at one stage for publication. His extant correspondence includes letters to John Murray, Thomas CHALMERS, William Stanley JEVONS and William Whewell.

Cazenove's ideas on political economy are particularly notable for their anti-Ricardian nature, and for their similarity in certain respects to those of Malthus, although it is not known whether he gained them from Malthus or reached them independently. He was a member of the Political Economy Club from 1821 to 1830, having been proposed by Malthus, and in discussions at the club sided with Malthus against David Ricardo and James MILL. His writings frequently show his affinity with Malthus's ideas. He rejected Say's law of markets, arguing that there is no necessary equality between supply and demand, and no guarantee that general stagnation and gluts will not occur. Like Malthus, he emphasized the importance of demand as a stimulus to growth. He also agreed with Malthus in insisting on a distinction between productive and unproductive labour; and on the need for a body of unproductive consumers, because the productive labourers can not generate an adequate demand for their own products. Against Ricardo, he reiterated Malthus's view that the only measure of value is labour commanded, not labour employed, and in line with Malthus's 'doctrine of proportions', but without using the phrase, he emphasized the danger of over-saving and the need to establish a balance between saving and consumption in order to ensure economic growth. Both Cazenove and Malthus insisted that although capital accumulation is essential, it alone will not guarantee growth, but they both agreed on the difficulty of specifying the precise point of balance.

But Cazenove's writings were not limited to a repetition of Malthus's ideas. They included matters not explicitly addressed in print by Malthus – for example, the notion that bank credit is equivalent to a fresh issue of money (1832, ch. 21) – and on some other matters he criticized Malthus and adopted an independent stance. In editing a second edition (1853) of Malthus's *Definitions in Political Economy* he omitted an entire chapter in which Malthus had criticized J.R. McCULLOCH.

Although it cannot be claimed that Cazenove was a major figure in the history of economics, his writings represent a significant contribution to the anti-Ricardian tradition. The fact that they have been relatively neglected could perhaps be explained in part by his preference for anonymity.

BIBLIOGRAPHY

(Anon.) *A Reply to Mr Say's Letters to Mr Malthus on the Subject of the Stagnation of Trade* (1820).
(Anon.) *Considerations on the Accumulation of Capital* (1822).
(Anon.) *Outlines of Political Economy* (1832).
An Elementary Treatise on Political Economy (1840).
Thoughts on a Few Subjects of Political Economy (1859).

Further Reading

Cazenove, Q.M.A. de, *Quatre siècles* (Four Centuries) (Nimes, 1908).
Gordon, B., 'John Cazenove (1788–1879): Critic of Ricardo, Friend and Editor of Malthus', unpublished paper (1993).
Kynaston, D., *Cazenove & Co.: A History* (1991).
Pullen, J.M., 'The Editor of the Second Edition of T.R. Malthus' Principles of Political Economy', *History of Political Economy* (1978), vol. 10, no. 2, pp. 286–97.
———, 'Two Anonymous Pamphlets by John Cazenove', *Journal of the History of Economic Thought* (1997), vol. 19, no. 2, pp. 301–10.

John Pullen

CHADWICK, Edwin (1800–90)

Chadwick was born in Longsight, near Manchester on 24 January 1800, and died in London on 6 July 1890. The grandson of a prominent Lancashire Methodist and son of an active radical, Chadwick was schooled primarily by his father and private tutors. In 1839 he married Rachael Kennedy; they had two children, Osbert and Marion.

In London in the 1820s, while reading for the bar, Chadwick was introduced to a circle of young radicals and utilitarians who congregated around the James MILL household. In 1828 Chadwick wrote 'The Means of Insurance Against Accidents', followed by 'On a Preventive Police'. Both essays offered administrative interventions to ameliorate poverty, crime and disease, and they brought him to the attention of Jeremy BENTHAM. By the time Chadwick was called to the bar in 1830, he was no longer interested in practising law. He worked instead, first as Bentham's private secretary, and then during the remainder of his life on various legislative reforms, primarily in poor law and public health. In 1889, he was knighted in recognition of his services to the nation as 'father of the sanitary idea'.

Bentham, who was completing the *Constitutional Code* at the time Chadwick was working for him, was a powerful influence on the young barrister. The older philosopher's belief that the role of legislation was to mitigate between individuals' 'self-regard' and the good of the greatest number shaped Chadwick's own approach to legislation and state intervention. In 1832, shortly after Bentham died, Chadwick was approached by Nassau SENIOR to serve on a Royal Commission inquiry into the poor laws. The resulting report, upon which the 1834 New Poor Law was based, was largely Chadwick's work and his earliest and most notorious foray into revising the creaky administrative apparatus of a rapidly industrialising state. The New Poor Law's prohibition of out-relief, introduction of the less-eligibility test and reorganization of parishes into centralized unions drew the ire equally of radicals, humanitarians and local elites, who stood to lose considerable authority in managing local affairs. Chadwick was the primary spokesperson for the law, dogmatic about rigidly implementing its principles, and the one credited with creating the dreaded 'poor bastilles' or workhouses that DICKENS, amongst others, angrily attacked. Without denying the harshness of the New Poor Law, its repressive measures and effort to create a docile, frugal, self-sufficient, independent and procreatively prudent working man (Dean 1991: 154–5), it is worth pointing out that the version of the law that was passed excised many of the preventive measures that Chadwick had written into earlier drafts, such as elementary education for working-class children and sanitary regulations. Without these measures, the law 'took on harsher, more unsympathetic lineaments than he had intended' (Lewis 1952: 18–19).

Despite his expertise and defining hand, Chadwick was not named a commissioner to the Poor Law Commission. With characteristic Victorian energy, he converted his disappointment into his greatest achievement, an inquiry into the sanitary conditions of the working classes. Chadwick turned to sanitation in order to reintroduce preventive measures and to address the poor laws' ongoing expenditure on sickness. Noting that working-class neighborhoods were appallingly and dangerously filthy and that the poor were getting sicker more frequently and dying at a younger age than the better-off, Chadwick concluded that disease arose from dirt. In 1839, keen to demonstrate that much of the disease amongst the lower classes was preventible, he contacted over two thousand poor law guardians, medical officers, factory inspectors, clerks and clergymen from all over the British isles and asked them to respond to detailed questionnaires on the conditions of poor homes, streets, drains, morals and manners. Chadwick sorted, labeled, selected, excerpted and framed their responses into a lengthy report which was published under his name in 1842 as *The Report on the Sanitary Condition of the Labouring Population of Great Britain* (*Sanitary Report*).

The *Sanitary Report* drew a harrowing picture of the deteriorated state of Victorian cities and towns, but offered a clear diagnosis: 'The amount of pauper sickness is considerable, the deaths not few... There is, however, no mystery in the causation. Ill-constructed houses...with decomposing refuse...open drains bringing the oozings of pigsties and other filth to stagnate at the foot of a wall...such are a few of the sources of disease' (Chadwick 1848: 81). Sewage, water, buildings: this trinity was the target of Chadwick's sanitary zeal. Furthermore, he argued that the costs of the lack of sanitation were not merely economic, but also social in the growing immorality of the poor. Chadwick's solutions were clear: he recommended (1) the construction of a vast arterial system of pipes and sewers that would bring water into houses and remove wastes from them; and (2) a central administrative authority to replace local municipalities and oversee the entire system.

The report reverberated widely. Reviewed by all the daily journals, read by legislators as well as novelists, politicians and philosophers, this government document gave Victorians a sense of sight and smell that they seemed to have lacked until now. Required reading at all the engineering colleges, Chadwick's report put the 'sanitary idea' on the legislative and social agenda. The momentum the *Sanitary Report* created and the friends it attracted (notably Lord Shaftesbury and Prince Albert) were so immense that, despite opposition from vested interests – water companies, building contractors, municipal authorities – it led to the Public Health Act of 1848. The date is significant: both cholera and working-class discontent were hovering on the continent. The bill's provisions for cleanliness held out the promise of containing both the 'Indian' disease as well as the 'domestic' disease of social instability and unrest.

In 1848 Chadwick's contribution and expertise could not be neglected, and he was appointed one of the commissioners to the Board of Health. For six years he was in charge of the nation's health, and in those years he racked up victories and also many enemies, most notably in the localities opposed to the Public Health Act's perceived 'Prussian' centralization. The opponents eventually prevailed and in 1854 Chadwick was dismissed from his post (he received a lifelong pension of £1,000 a year for his services) and the Board dismantled. Nevertheless, the sanitary idea had captured the Victorian imagination and prevailed: although the years immediately after 1854 were dismal where public health was concerned, the commitment to sanitation never faded and was renewed in the Public Health Act of 1875. Moreover, the sanitary movement had opened the door to the state's obligation in prevention (Brundage 1988: 104; Flinn 1965: 73). As for Chadwick, although he never again held an official position, during the next thirty-six years he continued his inquiries and pamphlet-writing, covering an astonishing range of topics from the railways to working-class education to the Indian army to competitive exams for civil service, but always faithfully returning to sewage and sanitation (in his will he left £47,000 in trust for the 'advancement of sanitary science'; Finer 1952: 512).

Chadwick played a formidable role in shaping the contours of two particularly Victorian phenomena: state bureaucracy and public health. While by no means the pioneer in developing the bureaucratic machinery of a growing state apparatus, he was at the forefront of this development and, largely because of his brash personality and lack of tact, all too often the public face of what was frequently a bitterly fought battle against 'centralisation'. Thanks to CARLYLE and Dickens, the early Victorian years are often popularly conceived of as a period of rampant *laissez-faire*. Nothing could be further from the truth. Between 1833 and 1850, the state intervened in a number of crucial areas to regulate the lives of its citizens.

The 1833 Factory Act, 1834 New Poor Law, 1835 Municipal Corporations Act, 1836 Registration Act, 1839 Constabulary Act, 1845 Lunacy Act and, of course, 1848 Public Health Act are only the most notable examples. All are marked by the establishment of a bureaucratic infrastructure to systematize and regulate governmental intervention in social affairs. And in almost all of them Chadwick had a hand. His contribution to each was the introduction of a regulatory mechanism. Thus, he inserted an inspectorate in the 1833 Factory Act, while the 1834 New Poor Law not only reorganized parishes into unions, thereby considerably attenuating the authority of local elites, but also appointed salaried poor law guardians. Admittedly, the guardians' powers were limited, but the principle of central oversight was established. Similarly, the Public Health Act allowed the central board to intervene in localities when the death rate rose above 23 per 1,000. Such regulation required a body of trained professional bureaucrats, and these years saw a steady rise in the number of civil servants: in 1833 the Home Office staff numbered only twenty-nine employees (as compared to France's 200,000), but by 1854 the number of inspectors alone had risen to 140 (Roberts 1960: 13, 152). Chadwick was an unabashed centralizer. As he loftily remarked to an associate: 'The Devil was expelled from heaven because he objected to centralisation, and all those who object to centralisation oppose it on devilish grounds!' (Lewis 1952: 11).

Chadwick's method of investigating social questions also played a considerable, if not always salutary, part in the development of government growth in this period. His approach to data collection – contacting an exhaustive number of informants, sending out questionnaires, going on location, taking first-hand testimony – was not new but was used strategically to establish the 'scientific' basis of his inquiries and was much emulated. Chadwick was well aware of the authority his methods garnered; he once boasted 'John

Stuart Mill always deferred to me on any question I had examined because as he said, I always got my information first hand, whilst he could only get it second hand or from books' (Lewis 1965: 15). In addition, Chadwick's mode of organizing data – using tables, graphs, charts, line drawings and maps – was novel and established the norm for future reports and social investigations. The historian M.W. FLINN contended that modern sociology was born not with Charles Booth, but with Chadwick (Flinn 1965: 37).

In the arena of public health, Chadwick's mark was both powerful and constricting. Although he had no medical training, he made the most crucial intervention in defining the parameters of public health for over a century. Chadwick's insistence that dirt caused disease was a perfectly reasonable conclusion and a necessary one in the wretchedly overcrowded cities of nineteenth century Britain. But his equation suffered from a dogged refusal to allow any other cause for the rapid spread of disease. As the historian Christopher Hamlin (1988) has demonstrated, an alternative to Chadwick's version of public health existed in the years before the publication of the *Sanitary Report*. This approach, which Hamlin calls 'political medicine', while not denying the importance of sanitation, insisted that the health of the poor be linked to wages, work conditions and food. Its most powerful advocate was William Pulteney Alison, the leading Scottish Poor Law reformer. Chadwick knew Alison's work well, but denied his broader approach. Largely as a result of Chadwick's formulation, political medicine was unable to find institutional voice and following 1848 was almost entirely silenced. Chadwick's framing of the sanitary idea, while undoubtably commonsensical, was also markedly ideological.

Finally, while Chadwick's reforming energies targeted structural questions of sewers, water and building codes, his greatest anxiety and rhetorical emphasis in the *Sanitary Report* were reserved for the shocking morality of the lower classes. Reading his text, one comes away persuaded that the poor and working classes were uniformly beggars and thieves, prostitutes and vagrants, that incest and bastardy were rampant amongst them. Furthermore, the report repeatedly targeted the poor themselves for the conditions in which they lived. Thus, in the opening pages we read: 'Charles, Calenick, and Kenwyn-streets present some of the worst specimens of defective arrangement, rendered worse still by the recklessness of the very poor' (1842: 81). This unself-conscious marriage of environmental and moral condemnation is the greatest paradox of the *Sanitary Report* and one that dogged Victorian social science. As the historian Michael Cullen (1975) has characterized it, early Victorian social science was marked by a 'semi-voyeuristic fact-gathering' with the result that we know a great deal about how many of the poor cultivated flowers or the books they read, but precious little about their income or expenditures (1975: 137). In Chadwick's case, the 'voyeurism' and its attendant moral censure are particularly acute when it comes to the women of the working classes: 'The improvidence of which we are speaking is to be traced in very many instances to extreme ignorance on the part of the wives of these people.... The minds and morals of the girls become debased, and they marry totally ignorant of all those habits of domestic economy which tend to render a husband's home comfortable and happy' (1842: 205). As is frequently the case, women are the fulcrum on whom social change is justified and initiated. Chadwick was no exception: his plan simultaneously blamed lower-class women for the filth of poor homes – Chadwick inexplicable shifts from the urban to the domestic – and elevated them to the role of junior partners in his sanitary projects.

In Chadwick's reform efforts, we see the desperate attempt to order a rapidly changing and chaotic world in which the chasm between classes was widening. We also glimpse the constricting force of preventive measures that increasingly moved towards social engineering. No doubt the reforms Chadwick introduced ameliorated some of the worst ills of a rapidly industrializing nation and saved many lives. But any narrative of his legacy must also include an account of the hostility he generated: from local elites opposing the administrative bureaucracy he helped create, from the working classes who chafed against the heavy boot of the interventionist but unyielding state apparatus he produced, and from many contemporary scholars who highlight the repressive force of his reforms.

BIBLIOGRAPHY
Report on the Sanitary Condition of the Labouring Population of Great Britain (1842; repr. Edinburgh, 1965).
'The Means of Insurance Against Accidents', *Westminster Review* (1828), vol. 9, pp. 384–21.
'On a Preventive Police', *London Review* (1829), vol. 1, pp. 252–308.

Further Reading
Brundage, A., *England's 'Prussian Minister': Edwin Chadwick and the Politics of Government Growth, 1832–1854* (University Park, Pennsylvania, 1988).
Cullen, M.J., *The Statistical Movement in Early Victorian Britain: The Foundation of Empirical Social Research* (New York, 1975).
Dean, M., *The Constitution of Poverty: Toward a Genealogy of Liberal Governance* (1991).
Finer, S.E., *The Life and Times of Sir Edwin Chadwick* (New York, 1952).
Flinn, M.W., 'Introduction', *Report on the Sanitary Condition of the Labouring Population of Great Britain* (Edinburgh, 1965).
Hamlin, C., *Public Health and Social Justice in the Age of Chadwick: Britain, 1800–1854* (Cambridge, 1998).
Joshi, P. (2004) 'Edwin Chadwick's Self-Fashioning: Professionalism, Masculinity, and the Victorian Poor', *Victorian Literature and Culture* (2004, forthcoming).

Lewis, R.A., *Edwin Chadwick and the Public Health Movement, 1832–1854* (1952).
Roberts, D., *Victorian Origins of the British Welfare State*, New Haven, Connecticut, 1960).

Priti Joshi

CHALMERS, George (1742–1825)

Chalmers was born at Fochabers, Morayshire, at some time in 1742, and died in London on 31 May 1825. He was educated at the local parish school and then at King's College, Aberdeen, and went on to study law at Edinburgh. In 1763 he emigrated to Maryland, where he established a successful legal practice in Baltimore and invested in property, becoming quite wealthy. A staunch Tory, he supported Governor Eden and repeatedly urged the latter to take stronger measures to ward off rebellion, including raising and arming a loyalist militia, but Eden preferred a more conciliatory approach. Chalmers believed the dispute over duties on tea imports was merely an excuse for the radicals, who had sought independence from Britain from the outset, and he campaigned against the radical cause, but to little effect.

Chalmers and many of his fellows were caught up in the rising tide of violence in Maryland beginning in 1774. A merchant friend who had tried to import tea into the colony was forced by a mob to burn not only the cargo but the ship as well; others were physically assaulted or threatened, and Chalmers himself slept with a brace of loaded pistols beside his bed. In September 1775, having incurred the enmity of the leading radicals, he was forced to flee the colony for his own safety, taking passage to Dublin and thence to London, where he arrived in

December. Virtually all his money and property had been left in America and, almost penniless, Chalmers was forced to accept a refugee's stipend from the British government.

To help support himself, he turned to writing. His first works were a series of pamphlets attacking the American rebels, and especially their sympathizers in Britain, but he went on to become a prolific historian and biographer, producing notable biographies of figures as diverse as Daniel DEFOE, Gregory KING, Mary Queen of Scots and Thomas Ruddiman. In 1786 a measure of financial stability returned when he was appointed chief clerk to the Committee for Trade (later Office for Trade), thanks to the patronage of its chairman, Charles Jenkinson (later Earl of Liverpool), and he held this post until his death. From 1792–1804 he served as colonial agent for the Bahamas. In 1789 he was involved in the Committee's collection of evidence on the slave trade. Like Jenkinson, he defended the trade and slavery in general, and believed Parliament had no right to interfere with the property of individuals. Chalmers continued be an ardent anti-abolitionist all his life. His Tory politics also extended to a vehement repudiation of the French Revolution and all who supported it; he wrote, under a pseudonym, a bitter attack on Thomas Paine. When James CURRIE wrote a pamphlet opposing war with France, Chalmers attacked him in language so strong that even his own friends wondered if he was not going to extremes. Showing another side to his character, Chalmers became a noted antiquarian, collector and writer, and was elected to both the Society of Antiquaries and the Royal Society in 1791.

An Estimate of the Comparative Strength of Great Britain (1794) is Chalmers's first work to focus specifically on economics, though an interest in political economy can be detected in many of his works. This is a work of no great subtlety, which argues that Britain has recovered well from the losses suffered during the American war, and should be capable of meeting the threat posed by France. Its growing population, manufacturing, trade, fisheries and agriculture give the country a strong economy and resources with which to fight a war if necessary. The book contains an ironic dedication to James Currie, effectively accusing him of collaboration with the Jacobins.

More substantial is *Considerations on Commerce, Bullion and Coin, Circulation and Exchanges* (1811). This again was written with a view to arguing that the economy is strong and the country can and should continue to prosecute the war with France. Chalmers criticizes the report of the Bullion Committee, and attacks William HUSKISSON, who had argued that the economy was deteriorating. He argues that the main problems affecting the economy are foreign, the exigencies of war and the need for remitting large sums overseas to pay armies and fleets and also to pay subsidies to foreign rulers in the fight against Napoleon. The domestic economy, he says, remains sound and healthy and the bank note system works; he rejects Huskisson's view that Bank of England notes are depreciating in value. He rejects also the Bullion Committee's view that bullion regulates the price of exchanges, but exchange does not regulate the price of bullion; like Francis ELIOT, with whom he was on friendly terms, Chalmers sees bullion as a commodity affected by market prices like any other. Gold and silver, he says, are not measures of value: 'the money of account, and pound sterling, or in other words, the lawful money is the proper measure. And a paper currency might almost as well be established on the security of lead, tin, iron or any other metal, or thing' (1811: 125). The stability of the government and the security of the Bank of England, he says, are the foundations on which money is based, not on the value of gold or silver. He was familiar with the ideas of Sir James STEUART, and quotes him with approval on several occasions.

BIBLIOGRAPHY
An Introduction to the History of the Revolt of the Colonies (1782).

Life of Daniel De Foe (1786).
Life of Thomas Paine, by Francis Oldys, A.M. of the University of Pennsylvania (1794).
An Estimate of the Comparative Strength of Great Britain (1794; repr. New York, 1969).
Vindication of the Privilege of the People in Respect of the Constitutional Right of Free Discussion (1796).
Observations on the State of England in 1696, by Gregory King, with a Life of the Author (1804).
Caledonia, or an Account, Historical and Topographical, of North Britain (vol. 1, 1807; vol. 2, 1810; vol. 3, 1824).
Considerations on Commerce, Bullion and Coin, Circulation and Exchanges; With a View to Our Present Circumstances (1811; 2nd edn, 1811; 3rd edn, 1819; repr. New York, 1969).
An Historical View of the Domestic Economy of Great Britain and Ireland (1812).

Further Reading
Cockroft, G.A., *The Public Life of George Chalmers* (New York, 1939).

Ann Kimber

CHALMERS, Thomas (1780–1847)

Chalmers was born on 17 March 1780 at Anstruther, Fife, the son of a textile merchant, and died 30 May 1847 in Edinburgh. He was educated at the parish school and St Andrews University, matriculating in 1791 and completing the arts course in 1795, and then proceeding to divinity. He was licensed to preach at the age of nineteen in 1799. For two years he attended Edinburgh University where he found Dugald STEWART's lectures shallow.

He was assistant minister at Cavers and then minister at Kilmany (1803–15), where he neglected many parochial duties to lecture on mathematics at his university. After a religious conversion in 1811 he became an immensely popular preacher, both propounding evangelical doctrine and supporting the working classes. He was minister of the Tron Church, Glasgow (1815) and founder of the first Sabbath school of the city. He moved in 1819 to the new Glasgow parish of St John's to practise his approach to poor relief.

Chalmers was professor of moral philosophy at St Andrews from 1823–8. His lectures were a combination of theology and practical Christian ethics; from his second session he included lectures on political economy which largely expounded Adam SMITH's *Wealth of Nations*. As professor of divinity at Edinburgh University (1828–43), he became increasingly involved in the affairs of Church of Scotland. He was prominent in the debate over patrons appointing ministers, in effecting the building of churches in working districts through a church extension programme and in attacking the threats to withdraw state funding for the established church. Chalmers had a large following by 1843, the year of the 'Disruption' when the Free Church of Scotland separated from the Church of Scotland. He was the Moderator of the new church, and principal and professor of divinity at its New College. To finance the ministers of the Free Church he devised a Sustentation Fund, using subscriptions of one penny per week per church member to pay 500 ministers annual stipends of £150. He married a Fife neighbour, Grace Pratt, in 1812; there were six daughters to the marriage.

Early in his career Chalmers wrote on political economy in his *An Inquiry into the Extent and Stability of National Resources* (1808). Within an implicit accounting framework he described the national labour force as having three sectors: producers of food, producers of 'second necessaries', such as clothing and housing, and the disposable population. The last consists of indolent proprietors, the professions and luxury manufacturing. In a way which echoed Richard Cantillon, Chalmers asserted that because there was surplus food above agricultural workers' own consumption, there was food to sustain those in the other two sectors. In this economy, 'The great end and advantage of wealth, is to give accommodation to the desires and necessities of the species' (1808: 41). He pointed out that if the wages fund is intact then the cessation of foreign trade merely has the effect of diverting production from one set of activities to another, although he did admit that some capital could be redundant through possessing no alternative use. Trade also has the disadvantage of wasting labour in transporting goods.

At a time of war and exclusion of British trade from the rest of Europe, Chalmers vigorously argued that a closed economy was viable. The war was financed by taxation of luxuries with the effect of reducing employment by luxury manufacturers to release labour for the armed forces. This taxation is justified as the means of financing cheap national security by the government. Chalmers believed that taxation was low and only required the sacrifice of some luxuries. The treatise had a poor critical reception and London publishers refused to produce a second edition. More popular were his *Discourses on the Christian Revelation, Viewed in Connection with Modern Astronomy* (1817), an expression of his view that science describes but does not explain the natural order. In a year, 20,000 copies in nine editions were sold.

Chalmers returned to economics in his *Political Economy*. With modesty, he stated that he intended no new system of political economy but an application of existing principles to the increase of morality and comfort. Chiefly relying on Smith and MALTHUS, he preached the stern message that there is a limit to improvement because of a limit to the means of subsistence, and that the economical and the moral are closely connected. He derided the notion of being optimistic because of free trade, lower taxes, emigration or more payments to the poor: only moral restraint, saving and personal industry can bring hope for the masses. MCCULLOCH, reviewing the book in the *Edinburgh Review*, rejected Chalmers's pessimism. Chalmers swiftly replied with a pamphlet conceding that industrialization had occasioned improved living standards but at the expense of degrading working conditions. Thus as Harper (1910) has explained, to engage in foreign trade would be to multiply workshops and make men mere machines. The economy would be more secure if it concentrated on home agriculture (Wilson 1910: 338–9). There was a strong physiocratic streak in Chalmers's works, emphasizing the fundamental role of agriculture and arguing for taxation to be solely on land. However, in one of the better stretches of analysis, fuller than the discussion in his 1808 book, he attacked the distinction between productive and unproductive labour, partly to defend the usefulness of the clergy.

In his Bridgewater Treatises *On the Power, Wisdom and Goodness of God*, Chalmers asserted that a sense of property is implanted in us by nature. He strongly stated the classical assumption of self-interest: 'when each man is left to seek, with concentrated and exclusive aim, his own individual benefit...that commodities are furnished for general use, of best quality, and in greatest cheapness and abundance; that the comforts of life are most multiplied; and the most free and rapid augmentation takes place in the riches and resources of the commonwealth' (1833, vol. II: 34). A strong supporter of *laissez-faire* principles, he was keen to emphasize 'the spontaneous workings of human nature' (1833, vol. II: 45); with self-regulation, there was no need to worry about population or capital. A trade depression would cause few problems if wealth were accumulated at times when wages were high.

In publications spanning thirty years, Chalmers reiterated his central message on pauperism. As early as 1817 in the *Edinburgh*

Review, he explained his solution to poverty, a voluntary approach. In *The Christian and the Civic Economy of Large Towns* (1821), he argued that legislation had frozen the fountains of charity. Four fountains would supply enough help for the poor: the habits and economies of the people themselves, the kindness of relatives, the sympathy of the wealthy for the poor, and the sympathy of the poor for each other. Because he regarded the last as so important a source of charity, it is not surprising that church colleagues in their criticisms argued that a wider scheme was needed to redistribute income from rich to poor parishes.

It was Chalmers's earnest belief that the current compulsory system of assessing the rich to give benefits to the poor was exacerbating the problem and was responsible for the increased number of paupers. By contrast his scheme was simple, in a sense attempting to re-create in an overpopulated city the mutual benevolence within the small rural communities in which he had lived for the first thirty five years of his life. A parish would be divided into small districts, twenty-five in the case of St John's, Glasgow, each with a deacon (a type of church officer revived by Chalmers) to investigate social conditions and the validity of paupers' claim for help. The scheme had most chance of success through instituting a tight reign of social control in the Presbyterian tradition. Collections at parish church services would finance the scheme. It was to be through the parish churches, not through charity societies despised by Chalmers, that this voluntary scheme would function. After a transitional period in which the old system of assessment would help the registered paupers, new claimants would be subject to the new approach.

The success of this approach to the relief of poverty was disputed. Statistics produced by Chalmers were suspect, as no information was provided on the occasional poor and on those who were turned down for help (Furgol 1987: 143–56). The St John's experiment ran for eighteen years to 1837, but in some years contributions were too low to finance the scheme. Although not popular in the rest of Glasgow, it was followed elsewhere, including in Edinburgh's Canongate and in Norwich. In his last years Chalmers repeated his St John's method in West Port, a slum district of Edinburgh, building a church and establishing schools. Malthus, in his correspondence with Chalmers, showed a reluctance to be as radical. In a letter of 23 August 1821, Malthus mused that it would be difficult to give up a 'compulsory provision without the sacrifice of too many individuals to the good of the whole'. In a subsequent letter of 22 July 1822 Malthus called Chalmers 'my ablest and best ally'.

BIBLIOGRAPHY

An Inquiry into the Extent and Stability of National Resources (1808).
'Causes and Cure of Pauperism', *Edinburgh Review* (1817), no. LV, pp. 1–31.
On Political Economy (1832).
On the Power, Wisdom and Goodness of God as Manifested in the Adaptation of External Nature to the Moral and Intellectual Constitution of Man (1833).
The Christian and Civic Economy of Large Towns (1821).
The Supreme Importance of a Right Moral to a Right Economical State of the Community: With Observations on a Recent Criticism in the Edinburgh Review (1832).
Tracts on Pauperism (1833).

Further Reading

Brown, S.J., *Thomas Chalmers and the Godly Commonwealth in Scotland* (Oxford, 1982).
Cheyne, A.C. (ed.), (1985), *The Practical and the Pious: Essays on Thomas Chalmers* (Edinburgh, 1985).
Furgol, M.T., 'Thomas Chalmers's Poor Relief Theories and Their Implementation', PhD thesis, Edinburgh University (1987).

Hanna, W., *Memoirs of the Life and Writings of Thomas Chalmers*. (Edinburgh, 1850–2).
Harper, J.W., *The Social Ideal and Dr Chalmers' Contribution to Christian Economics* (Edinburgh, 1910).
Roberts, R.O., 'Thomas Chalmers on the Public Debt', *Economica* (1945), new series, vol. 12, pp. 111–16.

Donald Rutherford

CHAMBERLAYNE, Edward (1616–1703)

Chamberlayne was born at Oddington, Gloucestershire on 13 December 1616, into a family of country gentry. He died in London in May 1703, exact date unknown. He was educated at St Edmund Hall, Oxford, receiving a BA in 1638 and an MA in 1641. He then left England upon the outbreak of the Civil War and went into voluntary exile on the Continent, where he travelled widely. Only after the restoration of the monarchy in 1660 did he return to England. He then devoted himself to writing and translating. In 1669 Chamberlayne took up a post as secretary to the Earl of Carlisle; in 1779 he was appointed tutor to Henry Fitzroy, illegitimate son of Charles II, and he also served for a time in the household of Prince George of Denmark.

Chamberlayne was a versatile and respected scholar, who is listed as one of the founding members of the Royal Society. His primary interest was in literature: he is said to have had several of his own books embalmed and buried with him. His early years back in England after the Restoration were spent compiling the first edition of the work for which he is best known, *Angliae Notiae, or the present state of England*. This work, which first appeared in 1669, was a collection of statistics and factual information concerning English politics, society and trade, and was very well-received; two further editions came out in the same year, and Chamberlayne was to publish twenty editions in all by the time of his death. His son John Chamberlayne then took over the project and published two more editions before his own death; other editors brought out a further fourteen editions, the last appearing in 1755. Probably based on a similar French work, *L'Estate Nouveau de France* (which first appeared in 1661 while Chamberlayne was living in Paris), the *Angliae Notiae* became a standard reference work in its day.

Chamberlayne was concerned to see England recover its former prosperity and greatness after the Civil War and Commonwealth, and he argued that government investment was required in order to strengthen the country politically, socially and economically. *England's Wants: or, several proposals probably beneficial for England*, which appeared in 1685, argued that the government should devote itself to raising more revenue through issues of public stocks and through higher taxation, primarily of luxuries but also of some staples such as salt. He also proposed that taxes should be levied on the legal fees paid for marriages and other contracts, and on inheritances and legacies. Some of his priorities for spending, such as repair of churches and ransoming captives held in Turkey, were somewhat anachronistic, but others included spending on social welfare provision, improvement of roads and improvement of river and maritime navigation to facilitate trade. Among his more enlightened ideas was a proposal for the naturalization for Huguenot refugees, whose industry and craft skills would greatly help the economy. Another proposal was for standard weights and measures and standard coinage to reduce price disparities across the country.

BIBLIOGRAPHY
Angliae Notiae, or the present state of England (1669; subsequent editions by the author to 1702, continued after his death to 1755; 36 editions in all).

England's Wants: or, several proposals probably beneficial for England (1685).

Morgen Witzel

CHAMBERLEN, Hugh (1630/4–after 1720)

Chamberlen was born in London some time between 1630 and 1634, and died in Amsterdam shortly after 1720. He was the eldest son of the physician Peter CHAMBERLEN, and followed his father into the medical profession, although there is no record of his ever having received a degree in medicine. Nonetheless he practised medicine with some success and wrote several important works; his translation of François Mauriceau's treatise on midwifery from the French became a standard text on the subject for a number of years. In 1673 he was appointed physician ordinary to Charles II. However, by the 1680s he was becoming increasingly involved in conflicts with authority. Although he continued as physician ordinary to James II, his anti-Catholic views led to his falling out of favour at court, and around the same time his medical treatise *Manuale Medicum* (1685) brought him the censure of the Royal College of Physicians, which fined him £10 for professional misconduct. By the early 1690s he seems to have ceased the practice of medicine altogether.

The early 1690s saw Chamberlen heavily involved in the promotion of a land bank, claiming credit for the invention of the idea and publishing a series of letters to parliament and other pamphlets aiming to rouse support for the idea. He corresponded with John BRISCOE and was involved in the National Land Bank from its inception, and continued to be a tireless promoter of the scheme right up until its crash in late 1698 and early 1699. His high profile in connection with the land bank seems to have convinced Chamberlen that he should leave the country (he later claimed he was forced into exile, but there is no evidence of this). He spent the following two years in Edinburgh, where he tried briefly to raise support for a land bank in Scotland, and then moved to Amsterdam where he resumed the practice of medicine. He was now at least seventy years of age and his health was failing, and his practice did not fare well. He slips into obscurity around 1708; there is a legal document bearing his signature dated November 1720, and it can be assumed that he died not long after.

Chamberlen's interest in the land bank was twofold. He saw it first as means to manage the national debt, an area where he thought the government ought to be taking a larger role, but he also believed the bank could help to stimulate trade. He first raised the idea in *Dr Chamberlen's Petition, and Proposals for a Land Bank to Increase Trade* (1693); this brought an immediate critical response, which he rebutted in *A Rod for the Fool's-Back, or Dr Chamberlen and his Proposals Vindicated* (1694) and again in *A Brief Narrative of the Nature, & Advantages of the Land-Bank* (1695).

Chamberlen's involvement with the land bank has overshadowed his other interest, namely in the nature and value of money. *A Collection of some Papers writ upon Several Occasions* (1696), which includes letters and pamphlets produced over the previous three years, argues that money is a commodity and that its value is accordingly determined by the market, not by government. The value of all commodities 'is the expense of labour, charge, and hazard, in raising and bringing the same to a market, and this varies it accordingly' (1696: 1); thus gold is cheaper in Guinea or Peru than it is in Amsterdam or London. Scarcity also has an impact on value; gold is cheap in Africa but iron, being scarce, is more valuable. In the home market this has ramifications for the comparative values of gold and silver. When gold is scarce its value relative to silver will rise, but when gold is more plentiful its value will fall: 'that which makes the variety of value here at home betwixt gold, silver and bullion, is the disproportion amongst themselves' (1696: 3).

Because gold and silver are not native to England, they must be brought into the country through economic activity. He argues for a positive balance of trade, but unlike other writers of the period who focus almost exclusively on exporting goods in exchange for money, Chamberlen adds two other types of earnings, 'what our natives can return from foreign service for their labour; or what foreign travellers spend here to see the country' (1696: 2). This represents a very early recognition of the potential value of tourism and of overseas remittances to an economy.

BIBLIOGRAPHY

Manuale Medicum: or, a Small Treatise of the Art of Physick in General (1685).
Some Few Considerations...Concerning the vote of the House of Commons...upon the Bill, for Hindering the Exportation of Gold and Silver... (1693).
Dr Chamberlen's Petition, and Proposals for a Land Bank to Increase Trade (1693).
A Rod for the Fool's-Back, or Dr Chamberlen and his Proposals Vindicated (1694).
A Brief Narrative of the Nature, & Advantages of the Land-Bank (1695).
A Collection of some Papers writ upon Several Occasions, concerning Clipt and Counterfeit Money, and Trade, so far is it relates to the Exportation of Bullion (1696).
A Few Proposals Humbly Recommending...the Establishment of a Land-Credit in the Kingdom (Edinburgh, 1700).

Further Reading

Aveling, J.H., *The Chamberlens and the Midwifery Forceps: Memorials of the Family, and an Essay on the Invention of the Instrument* (1882).

Morgen Witzel

CHAMBERLEN, Peter (1601–83)

Chamberlen was born in London on 8 May 1601, and died at Woodham Mortimer, Essex on 22 December 1683. Chamberlen's father and grandfather were both surgeons, and his grandfather invented, or at least commercially exploited, a new design of surgical forceps which proved especially useful in midwifery, as the instrument could be used to grip tightly but without harming the patient. According to Aveling (1882), the making and selling of these forceps earned a minor fortune for the family. Peter Chamberlen was educated at the Merchant Taylors School and Emmanuel College, Cambridge before going on to study medicine at Padua. He chose to become a physician rather than a surgeon, and graduated MD in 1619.

Returning to England, Chamberlen was at first highly respected for his erudition. He gave lectures on anatomy, and secured a post as physician extraordinary to King Charles I. He was admitted to the College of Physicians in 1628. However, he seems to have quickly damaged his popularity through a series of increasingly cranky schemes which he promoted through public pamphlets. These included the use of public baths for medical treatments and a design for wind-propelled carriages, as well as some rather incoherent dabblings in theology. At one point he seems to have espoused Anabaptism; he was also accused of having converted to Judaism, and wrote at least one pamphlet refuting this charge. By 1660 some of his contemporaries were convinced he had gone mad, for there are references to this in some of his later writings. Certainly his writing became increasingly incoherent as he entered old age.

Chamberlen's only foray into economics was the pamphlet *The Poore Mans Advocate* which appeared in 1649, following the end of the civil war. Here he argued that government has a duty to the poor, not only for moral and spiritual reasons but for economic ones as well: 'The wealth and strength of all countries are in the poore; for they do all the great and necessary workes, and they make up the maine body and strength of armies' (1649: 1). Without the labour provided by the poorer classes, the country would be impoverished.

To ensure the welfare of the poor, Chamberlen proposed that parliament should, first, pay off the national debt, and second, institute programmes of public works such as developing mines, or diking and draining lands near seacoasts to create new agricultural lands. He also believed that government should encourage husbandry, invention and manufacturing in order to boost trade, and favoured setting up colonies and plantations in foreign lands. He defended the rights of the poor to common lands and argued against enclosure, believing that it would lead to an increase in rural poverty; instead, he suggested that the state should take over all common lands in order to preserve them. He proposed that the common lands along with the estates of the former royal family should form the basis of a public stock, the income from which would generate wealth to pay for the army and provide relief for the poor. He also called for the establishment of a public bank to manage this wealth, a proposal that would be taken further by his son, Hugh CHAMBERLEN.

Like others of Chamberlen's writings, *The Poore Mans Advocate* is not always very coherent, and consists for the most part of a series of short statements that are presented as fact, with little argument or evidence. Its views on trade are vague. The chief interest of the work lies in its call for state intervention on behalf of the poor.

BIBLIOGRAPHY
The Poore Mans Advocate, or, Englands Samaritan Powring Oyle and Wyne into the wounds of the Nation (1649).

Further Reading
Aveling, J.H., *The Chamberlens and the Midwifery Forceps: Memorials of the Family, and an Essay on the Invention of the Instrument* (1882).

Morgen Witzel

CHAMPERNOWNE, David Gawen (1912–2000)

Champernowne was born on 9 July 1912 in Oxford where his father, Francis Gawayne, was the bursar of Keble College. He died in Cambridge on 19 August 2000. He belonged to the Dartington line of the Champernowne Family who had lived in South Devon for over 500 years, for the most part in the splendour of Dartington Hall and its picturesque surrounding countryside.

Champernowne, known as 'Champ' to his friends, attended Winchester College as a scholar where he excelled in mathematics. He crowned his school career by winning a mathematical scholarship in 1931 to King's College, Cambridge alongside Alan Turing, the pioneer in modern computing and the chief codebreaker at Bletchley Park. Champernowne and Turing became close friends, sharing a love of mathematics, intellectual games and a similar sense of humour. They continued their friendship well after their undergraduate years and embarked on a number of joint projects. Their friendship however, was rather detached, being more intellectual than personal in nature. They discussed Turing's idea of the 'universal machine', speculated on silver bullion (on Champernowne's advice), and designed one of the first chess computer machines, code named 'Turochamp'. The silver speculation was based on an observation by Champernowne that silver had gained real value during the First World War, an event that he thought was very likely to be repeated. The speculation proved right and earned a handsome profit for Champernowne after the Second World War. The chess machine was built but did not come up to expectations and apparently managed only to beat Champernowne's wife, a novice chess player at the time.

During his first two years at King's, Champernowne completed the maths tripos *par excellence*, obtaining a double first one year early. He also acquired the rare distinction of publishing a scientific paper as an undergraduate. In this paper, published in the *Journal of the London Mathematical Society* in 1933, he was the first to produce an actual example of a 'normal number' in base 10, which has come to be known as Champernowne's Constant (or Number), 0.123456789101112.... It is obtained by concatenating positive integers from one upwards and interpreting them as decimal digits to the right of a decimal point. It has the important property that each digit 0–9 is expected to occur with frequency 1/10, each pair of digits 00–99 is expected to occur with frequency 1/100, and etc. This short paper (seven pages) is one of Champernowne's most cited publications and provides an early signal of his considerable intellect and the type of problems and puzzles that interested him most.

Despite this promising start in mathematics, influenced by the Great Depression and the huge army of unemployed that it left behind, and enticed by John Maynard KEYNES and his ideas aimed at solving the unemployment problem, Champernowne decided to switch to economics. This decision was also most likely helped by his encounters with other leading Cambridge economists, notably Dennis ROBERTSON at Trinity and PIGOU at King's. Starting in October 1934 he came under Keynes's supervision, attended his lectures on the general theory of unemployment and took part in Keynes's Political Economy Club that met regularly on Monday evenings in term. Champernowne's notes of these lectures clearly capture the mood of the moment and the tension that existed between Keynes's ideas and those of the classical economists

Champernowne was an active member of the Political Economy Club and contributed papers on MARX, the conditions of short-period and long-period equilibrium (with Cuthbertson and REDDAWAY) and on the theory of the rate of interest (with Reddaway). Having obtained another first, this time in part two of the economics tripos, Champernowne went on to play an important role in the ensuing debate on the fundamental differences between the general theory of employment as advanced by Keynes and the classical theory, as typified by Pigou in his 'Theory of Unemployment'. One of the main issues separating the two camps was on whether it is the money wage or the real wage that is determined by the wage bargaining process between workers and firms. Keynes argued for the former, while the classical economists argued for the latter. In 1935, Champernowne published an influential review of Keynes's *General Theory* acknowledging the plausibility of Keynes's position only as far as immediate effects were concerned but not from a longer-term perspective. He argued that in the long run where price expectations are updated, workers' pre-occupation with money wage would be a temporary phenomenon and the maintenance of real wage will be their primary concern. This was a courageous intellectual act that struck at the heart of Keynes's arguments, and it could not have helped Champernowne's academic position in Cambridge economics.

After completing his undergraduate training, Champernowne started researching the size distribution of incomes across persons, with the aim of providing a conceptual framework for the explanation of the shape of the upper tail of income-distribution identified by Pareto. Champernowne was the first to provide a stochastic model of this type, which earned him a prize fellowship at King's in 1937. An account of this work was first published in the *Economic Journal* in 1953, but it was not until 1973 that the full text of the prize fellowship was offered for publication to Cambridge University Press (*The Distribution of Income between Persons*, 1973). In the introduction to the published version, Champernowne with characteristic modesty explains the reason for its belated publication as being a response to frequent requests by researchers to consult the fellowship dissertation in the library of King's College.

This was a path-breaking and remarkable contribution. Hitherto most research into income distribution had been purely data-driven and largely descriptive in nature. Champernowne was able to demonstrate the potential of stochastic models in generating empirically plausible features in economics. As his basic framework, he used a Markovian process to characterize the transition probabilities of an individual in one income class to the adjacent income classes, from one period to the next. Assuming that probability of shifts downwards and upwards along the income ladder are reasonably constant both across time and across different income groups, he was able to derive the exact Pareto distribution as the limiting property of his stochastic model. Thus providing a neat theoretical explanation for Pareto's empirical finding that the frequency distribution of wealth, W, is proportional to a power of wealth, $W-1$, at least for relatively large values of W. In his King's fellowship dissertation, Champernowne laid the foundation of many stochastic models of income and wealth distributions that have been advanced in the literature since his pioneering contribution back in 1937.

Champernowne continued his research on income distribution during most of his academic career, producing many scientific papers on the subject, including various refinements of his stochastic model, alternative measures of income inequality, and the analysis of likely factors responsible for the observed worsening of income distribution in many economies. In particular, he argued that there was no 'best coefficient of inequality' rather that different indices were suited to measuring different aspects of inequality. This long-term endeavour culminated in the publication of his last book in 1998, entitled *Economic Inequality and Income Distribution*, written jointly with Frank Cowell, one of his PhD students and later a professor at the London School of Economics.

Champernowne's work on economic theory covered many other areas. But apart from the study of income distribution, his research efforts for the rest of his life focussed on statistics and the application of statistical techniques to economic problems. On completion of his prize fellowship at King's in 1936, he was made an assistant lecturer at the London School of Economics, and returned to Cambridge in 1938 as a university lecturer in statistics and Fellow of King's. But his academic career in Cambridge was cut short by the outbreak of the Second World War. He was recruited first to the statistical section of the prime minister's office and then to the Ministry of Aircraft Production, where he worked as an assistant director in statistics and programming.

After the war Champernowne went to Oxford as director of the Oxford Institute of Statistics, and was subsequently made professor of statistics in 1948. In the same year he married Wilhelmina Dullaert (Mieke) from the Netherlands, who worked at the Institute, and he read a major paper on the time series analysis of autoregressive processes to the Royal Statistical Society. This paper was important for two reasons. First, it provided new theoretical insights into a difficult problem, which was being investigated at the time by Cochrane and Orcutt at the Department of Applied Economics in Cambridge using brute force Monte Carlo techniques. Second, this paper presented a first serious attempt at the application of Bayesian techniques to time series analysis. In a related paper (*Journal of the Royal Statistical Society*, Series A, 1960) Champernowne using computer simulations largely anticipated the highly influential work of Granger and Newbold on the spurious correlation problem that has come to haunt many applied time series economists ever since.

Despite having been made a professor at Oxford, Champernowne preferred the intellectual and work environment in Cambridge and resigned from his Oxford chair in 1959, accepting a readership at Cambridge with a teaching fellowship at Trinity. Over the subsequent decade, he embarked on a major project into the role of uncertainty in economic analysis and decision-making. The result was a three-volume book on *Uncertainty and Estimation in Economics* (1969). One can clearly see

Champernowne's brilliant mind at work on a wide range of problems, from probability theory and statistical methodology to decision-making under uncertainty. These volumes were concerned with the problem of how imperfect information might be used for estimation, statistical inference and decision-making in economics. Volume 1 covers basic concepts in probability and statistics, discusses decision making under uncertainty (inspired by the work of von Neumann), and provides a most interesting account of Bayesian estimation techniques. Volume 2 considers further statistical developments (point and interval estimation, significance testing), social surveys, sequential sampling and time series techniques. Volume 3 discusses problems of insurance, how to prepare for disasters, portfolio selection, and the general problem of planning and decision making under uncertainty. In a tongue-in-cheek example of a successful effort at forestalling the worse effects of disasters, he cites Noah's Ark:

> By means of an accurate and detailed weather forecast Noah was able to ensure the survival of his household and a considerable quantity of livestock throughout a prolonged period of very severe flooding. His precautions involved a mass investment of skilled manpower in the construction of a suitable floating home for his community, and the development of an ingenious means of ascertaining the flood-level during the phase of recovery. He must also have had considerable powers of persuasion to put his scheme across at a time when the subsequent events would have appeared most unlikely.
>
> (1969, vol. 3: 2)

One year after the publication of this study, in 1970, Champernowne was promoted by Cambridge to a personal chair in economics and statistics and elected as a fellow of the British Academy.

Champernowne also made important contributions to the teaching of statistics in the Faculty of Economics and Politics and played, in his own modest and quiet way, an important role in laying the necessary foundations for establishing Cambridge as an important international centre in the area of econometrics and quantitative analysis. He also acted as one of three co-editors of *The Economic Journal* over the period 1971–5, putting considerable effort in the process.

Champernowne loved music, having been a member of choirs at both Winchester and King's. He very much enjoyed singing hymns (often quite loudly). He combined his joy of music with his interest in computing by developing mechanical techniques for composing and harmonizing music. During the academic year 1960–1, he conducted experiments on EDSAC, an electronic computer at the Mathematical Laboratory of Cambridge University. The objective was to 'compose simple music reminiscent of that employed in hymns for children.' The experiment seems to have been a success. Champernowne enjoyed hiking, regularly walking to Wimpole Hall some thirteen miles to the west of Cambridge. At the age of seventy-four he fulfilled one of his life-long ambitions, scaling Scar Fell.

Champernowne did not much care for publicity and found it difficult to handle. In 1945, the British Council sponsored his visit to Stockholm to contact Swedish economists and see what they had accomplished during the war. When questioned by a large gathering of press about the purpose of his visit, he was reported to have been 'a trifle shy and slightly frightened'. Clearly he had not expected so much attention. He was a kind and generous man who loved playing with children; as my own family and I experienced at first-hand when we arrived unexpectedly in Cambridge just before the Iranian Revolution in late 1978.

Note: This entry is partly based on a text read at the memorial service held for David Champernowne in Trinity College Chapel, Cambridge, February 2001.

BIBLIOGRAPHY
Uncertainty and Estimation in Economics (1969).
The Distribution of Income between Persons (1973).
(with Frank Cowell) *Economic Inequality and Income Distribution* (1998).

Further Reading
Harcourt, G.C., 'David Gawen Champernowne, 1912–2000: In Appreciation', *Cambridge Journal of Economics* (2001), vol. 25, pp. 439–42.
Pesaran, M.H., 'Address Given at the Memorial Service for Professor David Gawen Champernowne, 1912–2000', *Annual Recorder*, Trinity College, Cambridge (2002).

M. Hashem Pesaran

CHAPMAN, Sydney John (1871–1951)

Chapman was born at Wells, Norfolk on 20 April 1871, the son of a businessman, and died at Ware, Hertfordshire on 29 August 1951. His family moved to Manchester when Chapman was young, and he was educated Manchester Grammar School and Owens College. He then attended University of London, taking a degree in history in 1891 and subsequently taught at a school in London; he also contemplating entering the Church of England and training as a priest. He entered Trinity College, Cambridge in 1894, initially to study philosophy, but by chance enrolled in a class on economics taught by Alfred MARSHALL. This convinced him to take up the study of economics, and Marshall became a lifelong mentor and friend. A brilliant student, Chapman won both the Cobden and Smith prizes and took first-class honours, graduating with a BA in economics in 1898.

Leaving Cambridge, Chapman first returned to Manchester where he held a research studentship at Owens College. His subsequent rise was very rapid. In 1899 he was appointed lecturer at University College, Cardiff, where he instituted the first courses in economics, and then in 1901 was appointed Stanley Jevons Professor of Political Economy at Manchester; by 1904 he had also been appointed Dean of the Faculty of Commerce. He was a noted teacher, whose students included T.S. ASHTON, and a prolific writer who in the space of ten years produced major works on economic history including *The Lancashire Cotton Industry* (1904) and *The Cotton Industry and Trade* (1905), and the economics textbooks *Outline of Political Economy* (1911) and *Elementary Economics* (1913). He also formed a partnership with Lord Brassey, son of Thomas BRASSEY, to update the latter's *Work and Wages* (1872) and *Foreign Work and English Wages* (1879). Initially they intended to collaborate, but Brassey later made over the whole of the project to Chapman. The result was the three volumes of *Work and Wages* published between 1904 and 1914. Also while at Manchester Chapman married Mabel Morley, the daughter of a Welsh shipowner, in 1903; they had three children.

Chapman was also involved in university politics and played a role in Manchester's transformation into an independent university. He accepted his first public appointment in 1909, advising the government of South Africa on labour issues. By the outbreak of the First World War he was a rising star in the field of economics, and was one of many talented economists whose services were requested by the government; from 1914–18 Chapman worked as an advisor to the Board of Trade. His work was recognized with the award of the CBE in 1917 and the CB in 1919. In 1918 he was invited to join the civil service on a permanent basis, and after some consideration agreed to do so. By 1919 he had succeeded Sir Hubert Llewellyn SMITH as permanent secretary to the Board of Trade, and held this post until 1927, working with presidents of the Board of Trade such as Stanley Baldwin and Sydney WEBB. During this time he was heavily involved in post-war reconstruction initiatives, both in Britain and further afield. He was knighted (KCB) in 1920.

In 1927 Chapman was appointed chief economic advisor to the government, again in succession to Smith. From 1927–32 he was involved in negotiations at the League of Nations, attempting to formulate international agreements to promote trade. The Great Depression and lack of co-operation among League members brought an end to this, and in 1932 Chapman was called upon to help draft protective legislation in Britain and appointed chairman of the Import Duties Advisory Committee. He retired early in 1939, but the outbreak of war brought him back into public service; among other posts, he was vice-chairman of the Central Price Regulation Committee. He retired again in 1945 and lived quietly in Hertfordshire until his death.

During a long and distinguished career Chapman made many contributions to policy. In terms of his writing, however, he is best remembered for *The Lancashire Cotton Industry* and for his work on *Work and Wages*. The former is effectively a case study in industrial economics. Chapman, as he says in the preface to the work, is concerned to see what internal forces cause an industry to develop as it does. He deliberately excludes external considerations such as environmental forces, and focuses almost entirely on the interdependence of forms of distribution with forms of production. He first focuses on how the cotton industry was organized and how that organization evolved, and then goes on to show how changing forms of organization had impacts for marketing and distribution, and for labour. As production became more concentrated, so too did labour; and labour likewise developed forms of organization to match those of the producers. Marketing, too, had to transform itself and become more sophisticated to match the increased capacity of the producers (it is worth noting that Chapman is one of the first British economists to use the term 'marketing' in its present meaning). In summary, he presents this corner of the Industrial Revolution as being primarily driven by new technologies and concentrations of capital among producers, with distributors and workers both trying, and sometimes failing, to evolve appropriate forms in response.

Chapman is cautious, however, about generalizing from this particular study. Studies of the problems of organization and distribution in general terms have their limits; it is also necessary to study individual industries in more detail, for each has different forms of production in different places and different times. The 'labour problem' is equally complex and exhibits many variations. But, says Chapman, this is right and proper. There is no 'one best way' to organize production, distribution or labour: the choice depends always on the needs of the industry. As he says in the preface to *The Lancashire Cotton Industry*, 'The right form is multiform. Private management, joint-stock companies, large and small, labour co-partnership, co-operation, regulated monopolies, to mention only some general forms, have each their respective spheres of operation' (1904: iii).

Brilliant though it is, Chapman's analysis is open to criticism. His deliberate exclusion of external forces weakens his ultimate argument. More recently, examinations of the cotton industry based on transaction cost analysis such as Langlois (1999) have argued that the need to create more efficient production was driven in part by environmental concerns and in part by end-user market demands. The ultimate benefit of the factory system was to reduce transaction costs, rather than to simply concentrate capital for its own sake. Chapman's argument that distribution follows organization also runs counter to the 'structure follows strategy' argument that emerged from American business history a generation or so later. However, his remarks on the interdependence of organization and business activity remain highly relevant today.

Work and Wages, published in three volumes over a ten-year period, builds on the earlier work of Thomas Brassey and his son, Earl Brassey, in the 1870s. Initially intended merely to update the earlier work, Chapman eventually expanded it to cover a wide range of topics. Volume 1 concerns trade, with chapters on various industries including international comparisons of output and wages, and also on commercial methods and on railways. The book opens with a critical examination of international trade, pointing out that the volume of trade is not necessarily an indication of prosperity. Trade must be thought of as bipolar, with both imports and exports considered; it is not sufficient to think of exports only, for this is to fall into the mercantilist trap.

Volume 2 focuses on wages and employment. Here Chapman returns to his idea that the demand for labour depends on the organization of production. He summarizes the law of wages as defined by Marshall and EDGEWORTH, and looks at the organization of labour, trades unions, industrial peace and unemployment. Some of these topics were expanded upon in his edited volume *Labour and Capital After the War* (1918). Volume 3 concludes with a look at social progress and improvements in housing, health and education for workers and their families. In the interesting opening chapter of this volume, Chapman rejects Darwinism and eugenics, at least partially, in favour of a theory of environmental determinism; the human stock can be bettered most effectively by improving people's environment, better food, health, housing, rather than by selective breeding.

BIBLIOGRAPHY

The History of the Trade Between the United Kingdom and the United States, with Special Reference to the Effect of Tariffs (1899).
Local Government and State Aid (1899).
The Lancashire Cotton Industry: A Study in Economic Development (Manchester, 1904).
Work and Wages, 3 vols (1904–14).
The Cotton Industry and Trade (1905).
Outline of Political Economy (1911; repr. 1913, 1917, 1935).
Elementary Economics (1913).
The War and the Cotton Trade (1915).
Labour and Capital After the War (1918).

Further Reading
R.N. Langlois, 'The Coevolution of Technology and Organisation in the Transition to the Factory System', in P.L. Robertson (ed.), *Authority and Control in Modern Industry* (London: Routledge, 1999), pp. 36–55.
S. Pollard, *The Genesis of Modern Management* (London: Penguin, 1965).

Morgen Witzel

CHECKLAND, Sydney George (1916–86)

Checkland was born 9 October 1916 in Ottawa, Ontario, and died in Cambridge on 22 March 1986. He was the second of three sons of Sydney Tom Checkland, itinerant preacher and journalist, and Fanny Selina Savory Mason. The household was strongly supportive but very strictly Baptist, weekly attendance at the First Baptist Church of Ottawa being an important feature of family life. Checkland's education began in two elementary schools, Slater Street Public School (1921–2), and Elgin Street Public School (1922–9). This was followed by High School at Lisgar Collegiate Institute, (1929–34). From school he took a position as a trainee clerk in the Bank of Nova Scotia, becoming an associate of the Canadian Bankers Association in 1937. By then he was employed as an accountant with the Ottawa

Sanitary Laundry Company. His savings from this post, £250, allowed him to go to England in 1938 to study for the BComm degree at Birmingham University under Philip Sargent FLORENCE. There he became president of the Guild of Undergraduates (1940–1), president of the National Union of Students (1941) and President of the International Union of Students (1942). He graduated with first-class honours in 1941 and married Edith Olive Anthony, a geography student at Birmingham, in 1942. They had two sons and three daughters.

In 1942 he enlisted and attended a six-month officer training course at Sandhurst, passing out as best cadet with the Belt of Honour. As a young lieutenant and tank commander in the Governor General's Footguards with the Canadian army, he was severely wounded during the Battle of Falaise following the Normandy landings. In 1945 he was an unsuccessful parliamentary candidate for the Commonwealth Party for Eccleshall, Sheffield in the general election.

In 1946, Checkland returned to Birmingham to take his MComm, and was then appointed at Liverpool University, successively as assistant lecturer in economic science (1946–8), lecturer (1948) and senior lecturer (1949–59), completing his PhD there in 1953. He was then attracted to Cambridge by Michael POSTAN as lecturer in economic history (1953–6). In January 1957 he moved to the University of Glasgow to take up a chair and to establish the new department of economic history. He held this post until his retirement in 1982, returning then to live in Cambridge.

During his years in Glasgow, Checkland was a prolific scholar. Of particular interest is his fine business history, *The Mines of Tharsis* (1967) and his biography, *The Gladstones: a Family Biography, 1764–1851* (1971), which received the Scottish Arts Council Book Award. In 1975 his distinguished study *Scottish Banking: A History 1695–1973* (1975) won the Saltire Society Prize. His scholarly contribution was recognized in his election as a fellow of the British Academy (1977) and to a fellowship of the Royal Society of Edinburgh (1979).

Checkland's early publications on the classical economists, the Birmingham economists and on economic thought were influential. His writing then broadened to embrace biography, and especially influential studies in business, banking and urban history. His papers on urban methodology strongly influenced the development of urban history in Britain, and retain their importance today. His long concern with the trajectory of economic change was particularly relevant for new town planning and regional development in Scotland in the 1960s and 1970s, when he served as a board member of the East Kilbride Development Corporation. His emphasis on models and concepts in entrepreneurship, banking systems and urban development are essential springboards for current research and thinking in these areas.

BIBLIOGRAPHY
The Rise of Industrial Society in England, 1815–1885 (1965).
The Mines of Tharsis: Roman, French and British Enterprise in Spain (1967).
The Gladstones: a Family Biography, 1764–1851 (Cambridge, 1971).
(with E.O.A. Checkland) *The Poor Law Report of 1834* (1973).
Scottish Banking, a History: 1695–1973 (Glasgow, 1975).
The Upas Tree: Glasgow, 1875–1975, a Study in Growth and Contractions (Glasgow, 1976).
The Upas Tree and After: Glasgow 1875–1980 (Glasgow, 1981).
British Public Policy 1776–1939: An Economic and Social Perspective (Cambridge, 1983).
(with E.O.A. Checkland) *Industry and Ethos: Scotland 1832–1914* (1984).

Anthony Slaven

CHILD, Josiah (1630–99)

Child was born in London in 1630, and died 22 June 1699, probably also in London. He was the second son of the London merchant, Richard Child. He was apprenticed to another London merchant, but by 1655 he was engaged in Portsmouth as a provider of stores for the navy. Here he remained for many years, made a fortune and was even elected mayor of the town. Returning to London during the 1670s, he became involved with the East India Company, of which he became a director and later on chairman. From 1671 to 1673 he bought up stocks of £12,000 which made him into the largest single shareholder of the company. Over the East India Company he was said to rule as absolutely as if it had been his private business. In 1673 he was also elected to parliament, serving as MP for Dartmouth from 1673–8 and then Ludlow from 1685–7.

Child was regarded as a most effective lobbyist for the interest of the East India Company. His strategy was to increase his political influence in order to keep up the Company's position and to retain its *de facto* monopoly. To great extent, he seems to have succeeded. By the time of his death Child was a man of great wealth, leaving a fortune of approximately £200,000. In political terms he had started out as a Whig, but with wealth and fortune his sympathies changed towards the Tories. Especially during the short reign of Charles II, he and the East India Company were highly successful. After 1688, however, things changed for the worse. The zenith of the company's monopoly position had been passed, partly because of increased trade and partly due to the impossibility in the long run of maintaining a monopoly position. However, even more important was the political situation after 1688, with a new and reforming parliament. Child's personal political influence also diminished. He made many enemies during his career, and was said to rule the East India Company in a despotic fashion, using his position to forward the interests of himself and his relatives. He himself seems not to have been financially affected by the Company's increasing problems.

As a writer on economics, Child was able to reach a large audience. During the early eighteenth century, he was probably the most widely read economic author in Britain. His first published tract, *Brief Observations Concerning Trade and Interest of Money* (1668) was mainly written in order to advocate an 'abatement' of interest by law to 4 per cent. According to Child, a low rate of interest was the main 'cause of the prosperity and riches of the nation' (1668: 10). He had written the tract mainly for practical political reasons during his work for the Council of Trade (see below). In 1690, when the issue of a fixed interest rate once again was brought forward, the tract was republished with some additional chapters under the title *A Discourse of Trade* (1690). This book again appeared in print – without any major changes – three years later as *A New Discourse of Trade*. In the additional chapters, Child dealt with topics such as the role of merchant companies, the Navigation Act, the employment of the poor, the overseas plantations and 'the Ballance of trade'.

The ongoing commercial rivalry with the Dutch was a strong theme in most of Child's texts. Hence in *Brief Observations Concerning Trade and Interest of Money*, Child made it explicitly clear that his main object was practical: to explain why the Netherlanders had been able to achieve such a 'prodigious increase' in their 'Domestick and Foreign trade, Riches and multitude of Shipping'. For this purpose he presented a list of fifteen reasons: the Dutch had lower interest rates, they were more experienced merchants, they had established a great fishing industry in the North Sea, they encouraged (and renumerated) new inventors, they had established an outstanding shipbuilding industry, and so on. However, he put the main emphasis on the role of interest rates:

This in my poor opinion, is the *Causa causans* of all the other causes of the Riches of that people [the Dutchmen]; and that if Interest of Money were with us reduced to the same rate it is with them, it would in a short time render us as Rich and Considerable in Trade as they are now, and consequently be of greater damage to them, and advantage to us, then can happen by the Issue of the present War...
(1668: 13)

Hence a lower interest rate would profit most classes of people, including the nobility and gentry, the merchants and tradesmen, 'our Marriners, Shipwrights and Porters' as well as farmers and even the poor. Further, he states:

For the Suffers by such a law, I know none but idle persons that lives at as little expence as labour, neither scattering by their expences, so as the Poor may Glean any thing after them, nor working with their hands or heads to bring either Wax, or Honey to the common Hive of the Kingdom; but swelling their own Purses by the sweat of other men brows, and the contrivances of other men's brains.
(Child 1668: 20)

Child's *Observations* was written against the background of political and other events. In 1665 the plague had hit London, and in 1666 fire destroyed most of the capital. In 1667 there were complaints about a trade depression everywhere. In that year the House of Common appointed a select committee to look in to the state of trade and the year thereafter the King established a new Council of Trade, a large body of statesmen and merchants with the responsibility for advising him on economic issues. Lastly, in 1669 the Lords appointed a committee to consider the causes behind what they saw as the fall of rents and decay of trade within the kingdom. In the Council of Trade and most probably also in both committees, Child played a leading role. The views that he presented in this context appeared in his 1668 tract. His arguments and the causes he presented as to why England seems to loose out in relation to the Dutch were hardly very original, and indeed Child relied heavily on an already published work, Henry ROBINSON's *Englands Safety, in Trades Encrease* (1642). In fact of the fifteen suggestions that Child presented, ten seem to have been taken almost directly from Robinson.

However, in his later *Discourse of Trade* Child was also searching for some more general principles which could make the commonwealth rich and powerful. This book too was published at a specific political moment. As noted, in 1690 parliament was once again considering reducing interest rates by statute from 6 to 4 per cent, and Child was as always eager to support such a scheme. However, at the same time the East India Company was under fierce attack. Child's ambition seems to have been to put before parliament a full programme including more liberal trade legislation and revisions of the laws on religion, inheritance, property and apprenticeship. This would perhaps undermine the most radical onslaughts on the East India Company. To some extent, at least, this was the reasoning behind the new chapters in the *Discourse* when it was published in 1690.

As well as showing a rather liberal policy attitude towards trade – Child even advocated tolerance and naturalization with regard to Jews – the *Discourse* and *New Discourse* also include some more general proposals. Thus according to Child national wealth – the material well-being of its population – is mainly a result of production. Of special significance were modern worked-up goods in manufactures. Thus he pointed out that: 'It is multitudes of People and good Laws, such as Cause an encrease of People, which principally Enrich our Country; and if we retrench by Law the Labour of our people, we drive them from us to other countries that gives better Rates' (1693: preface). To this extent he certainly differed from, for example MUN, FORTREY and PETYT, who had emphasized that England's 'great happiness' lay in increasing foreign trade so as to bring in money. It is noteworthy that the issue of foreign trade surpluses was almost totally ignored by Child. Foreign trade itself was certainly important: if well-organized, it would support production and employment would grow at a faster rate. Basically, however, it was people employed in manufactures and trade that provided the material wealth of the nation.

As well as employment, Child also emphasized the need for good laws. With regard to labour, he shared the view of most of his contemporaries that workers were lazy and behaved in accordance with a backward-bending supply curve: when times were good they simply retreated from work. Hence, such laws which encouraged productive work, stimulated foreign craft workers to immigrate and stay and so on, were necessary. Foreign trade must also be organized in a fashion that encouraged growth and employment. As an example of beneficial regulation – ironically, exactly the same example chosen by Adam SMITH – he pointed to the Navigation Act:

> I am of Opinion that in relation to Trade, Shipping, Profit and Power, it is one of the choicest and most prudent Acts that ever was made in England, and without which we had not now been owners of one half of the Shipping, nor trade, nor Employed one half of the Sea-men which we do at present.
> (1693: 91)

It is clear that Child here spoke in favour of protection particularly for the sake of keeping up employment within the shipping industry. But his arguments extended far outside this narrow context. In fact, *A Discourse of Trade* must to a large extent be understood as an argument for the establishment of more manufactures and increased domestic production. For this purpose, he sometimes proposed protection from foreign competition for some industries. But, domestically, he argued rather for more freedom of trade and fewer restrictions, a dismantling of trade and craft regulations, and so on. It is this insistence upon freedom of trade in general which made him in the economic historian W.J. ASHLEY's eyes a member of the group that he named 'Tory free traders', which also included Charles DAVENANT and Dudley NORTH (Ashley 1900). However, Child's attitudes are not always very consistent. In *New Discourse* he could assert the principle of competition in the following terms: 'They that can give the best price for a commodity shall never fail to have it, by any means or another, notwithstanding the opposition of any laws, or interpositions of any power by sea or land; of such force, subtlety, and violence is the general course of trade' (1693: 129). Yet he was engaged in one of the largest monopoly companies of his time and it is not easy to reconcile this with some of his statements in favour of freedom of trade. Moreover, in order to encourage growth Child always seemed to return to his old proposal that interest rates should be lowered to become equal or lower than the rate prevailing in the Dutch republic. With lower interest rates, Englishmen could compete with the Dutch more easily, he believed. If loanable money became more accessible, the English then would be able to engage in trades and projects which would not be profitable at a higher rate of interest.

However, it is in the light of his preference for production and employment that we must discern Child's critique of the orthodox favourable balance of trade theory. His main argument is that it would be impossible for practical reasons to establish such a balance. He felt that it would not be possible to compute an accurate balance because of all the technical complications involved. On the other hand, he pointed out, even if such a balance could be found, it would not present any conclusive proof of whether a country won or lost through its foreign trade. Child here pointed at Virginia and Barbados which both had a favourable balance, but still lost by their trade (mainly because they exported raw materials and imported manufactured goods).

Thus instead of being so concerned with the balance of trade and payments, he said, England should regulate its trade so that manufacturing and employment are encouraged. And this was best accomplished by keeping to the following formula: 'To encourage those Trades most, that vent most of our Manufactures, or supply us with Materials to be further Manufactured in England' (1693:156). From this point of view, he was prepared to defend the East India Company from its antagonists. England benefited very much by the trade carried out by the Company. In particular, it helped to encourage employment in England through its re-exportation of finished wares and its import of wares which could be worked up by domestic manufacture.

Hence, both in his earlier writing and in his *A Discourse of the Nature, Use and Advantages of Trade* (1694), Child presented an explicit critique of the orthodox doctrine of a favourable balance of trade. Finding such a calculation of trade balances useless, he instead suggested another important 'balance'. This was the famous principle of 'labour balance' or 'foreign paid incomes', which stated that any country gained from trade if it exported goods of greater labour content (value added) than it imported. This idea would appear in many other economic tracts and books during the eighteenth century, for example in the work of James STEUART late in the century, but perhaps most explicitly formulated by Theodore Janssen in his *Maxims of Trade* (1713).

It is often stated that Child was not a very systematic thinker and writer. However, he emphasized production and employment as the main progenitors of material wealth and national power, and was one of the first writers in a line of thought which goes on through Steuart and then into nineteenth and early twentieth-century thinking on protection. His view that, for the promotion of manufactures and industry, good laws must be inaugurated, makes him a promulgator of state *dirigisme*. Thus to call him a free-trade Tory, as Ashley did, is not really accurate. As we saw, he was certainly ready to defend economic freedom to a certain extent, and as a Tory and director of the East India Company, he was very suspicious of the increasing cries for protection which mounted up during the 1690s. But, on the other hand, the achievement of wealth was to him part and parcel of the effectiveness of the state machinery. It was this which made him such a admirer of, for example, the Navigation Acts.

BIBLIOGRAPHY

Brief Observations concerning Trade and Interest of Money (1668; repr. in L. Magnusson (ed.), *Mercantilism. Critical Concepts in the History of Economics*, vol. II, 1995).

A Discourse of Trade (1690).

A New Discourse of Trade (1693).

A Discourse of the Nature, Use and Advantages of Trade (1694).

Further Reading

Ashley, W.J., 'The Tory Origin of Free Trade Policy', in W.J. Ashley (ed.), *Surveys, Historical and Economic* (1900).

Hutchison, T., *Before Adam Smith* (Cambridge, 1988).

Johnson, E.A., *Predecessors of Adam Smith* (New York, 1939).

Letwin, W., *Sir Josiah Child, Merchant Economist* (Cambridge, Massachusetts, 1959).

Magnusson, L., *Mercantilism: the Shaping of Economic Language* (1994).

Parakunnel, J.T. *Mercantilism and the East India Trade* (1926).

Lars Magnusson

CLAPHAM, John Harold (1873–1946)

Clapham was born 13 September at Broughton, near Salford, Lancashire, the son of a well-off jeweller, and died suddenly on 29 March 1946 on a train between Cambridge and London. He was educated at Leys School in Cambridge and then at King's College, Cambridge, taking a first class in the history tripos in 1895. He went on to study under the great Cambridge historians Lord Acton and Frederic Maitland, and became a fellow of King's in 1898. His dissertation on the causes of the war of 1792 appeared in 1899. By that time, however, he had also come under the influence of Alfred MARSHALL, who pressed him to take up the study of economic history.

In 1902 Clapham became professor of economics at Yorkshire College (later the University of Leeds), but returned to Cambridge in 1908 and his fellowship King's. During the First World War he served under the Board of Trade and later was a member of the cabinet committee on priorities; he was made CBE in 1918.

Clapham was appointed professor of economic history at Cambridge in 1928, and retired in 1938; however, the outbreak of the war and the death of his colleague Eileen POWER meant that he was no less active. Among other tasks, he oversaw the editing of the first volume of the *Cambridge Economic History of Europe*, which appeared in 1941. He served as vice provost of King's College from 1933–43. Having been elected a fellow of the British Academy in 1928, he served as its president from 1943–5. He also chaired the Clapham committee on social and economic research in the 1940s. His last important publication was his two-volume history of the Bank of England, which appeared in 1944. John Clapham was knighted in 1943. He married Mary Green in 1905, and they had four children.

Clapham had a balanced approach to economic history. He dedicated the first volume of his massive, three-volume *Economic History of Modern Britain* (1926) to both Alfred Marshall and William CUNNINGHAM, who had in fact been opponents during the 1890s on the question of the direction in which academic economics should go: to continue in a largely historical direction, as advocated by Cunningham, or in a mathematical and ideal direction, as proposed by Marshall. Clapham himself typically refrained from use of algebraic formulae, geometrical figures and calculus to present economic history, but he emphasized quantification of economic activity. He wrote in the first volume of *Economic History of Modern Britain* that his goal was 'to make the story more nearly quantitative than it has yet been made…to offer dimensions in place of blurred masses of unspecified size'. He treated economic history fundamentally as history, but brought a rigorous scientific approach to its study and writing. With Eileen Power and Michael POSTAN, he is to a large extent responsible for the growth of economic history as a discipline in the second half of the twentieth century.

Like T.S. ASHTON, Clapham stood out against those who wanted to make moral judgements about the past. Although he began from a basis in Marshallian economic theory, he showed himself ready to challenge that theory when he felt it right to do so. His article 'On Empty Economic Boxes' (1924) caused considerable controversy in the 1920s and 1930s over the theory of the firm. Clapham questioned whether MARSHALL's categories of industries with increasing and decreasing returns were of any value unless one could fill in the boxes with names of specific industries. This attitude is consistent with his preference for factual historical work over theory. As Coleman (1987: 80) comments, Clapham insisted 'upon a balanced presentation of findings, obtained by asking broadly economic questions, aided by numbers and without the prior assumption that capitalism was a phenomenon conducive to increased misery for the many and, therefore, of itself demanding reproach or reform.'

Again like Ashton, he was a 'neutralist' rather than a reformer.

Clapham's work provided a fundamental basis for the challenge to the traditional conception of conceiving the Industrial Revolution during the post-war period. During the 1930s, he sided in policy terms with the resurgent classical liberal upstarts at the London School of Economics, not with the Cambridge economists who favoured greater state activity to end the world slump. At the same time, however, Clapham always maintained the most cordial of relations with his Cambridge colleagues, and his professional views never spilled over into his personal relationships. This made him an ideal co-ordinator of other people's work, reflected in his editorships of the *Cambridge Studies in Economic History* and the *Cambridge Economic History of Europe*.

BIBLIOGRAPHY
The Causes of the War of 1792 (Cambridge, 1899).
The Economic Development of France and Germany, 1815–1914 (1921).
'On Empty Economic Boxes', *Economic Journal* (1924).
An Economic History of Modern Britain, 3 vols (Cambridge, 1926–38).
The Bank of England: A History, 2 vols (Cambridge, 1944).
A Concise Economic History of Britain from the Earliest Times to 1750 (Cambridge, 1949).

Further Reading
Clark, G.N., 'Sir John Harold Clapham, 1873–1946', *Proceedings of the British Academy* (1946).
Coleman, D.C., *History and the Economic Past: An Account of the Rise and Decline of Economic History in Britain* (Oxford, 1987).
Court, W.H.B., *Scarcity and Choice in History* (1970).

Alan Ebenstein

CLARK, Colin Grant (1905–89)

Clark was born in Plymouth on 2 November 1905, and died at St Lucia, Queensland on 4 September 1989. He was the son of James Clark, a merchant of Scottish descent who migrated to Queensland in 1878. He was educated at the Dragon Preparatory School at Oxford, then Winchester and Brasenose College, Oxford. At Oxford he studied chemistry and graduated in 1927. He did not pursue a career in science, but his training as a scientist had an important influence on his approach to economics; he focused on using data to test theories and to suggest hypothesis. In 1928 he worked with Allyn Young on a comparison of labour productivity in British and American industries. Next, he worked as a research assistant for William BEVERIDGE, who during the Second World War designed the framework for the introduction of a welfare system, studying poverty in London. In 1929 he moved to Liverpool to work with Alexander CARR-SAUNDERS, a leading applied economist, on another study of poverty. Clark's career as an economist got off to a flying start, but his career as a politician did not take off. He stood as a Labour Party candidate in the general elections of 1929, 1931 and 1935 but was unsuccessful in all cases.

Clark joined the staff of the Economic Advisory Council set up by the prime minister, Ramsey MacDonald, in 1930. KEYNES was also a member of the Council. In 1931 Clark declined to prepare a protectionist manifesto for MacDonald and resigned from his position with the Council. (Clark always maintained his pro-free trade stance.) Keynes used his influence on Clark's behalf, and in 1931 he was appointed lecturer in statistics at Cambridge University. Between 1931 and 1937 Clark made path-breaking contributions to applied economics and national income accounting. In 1937 he left Cambridge to visit universities in New Zealand and Australia. Keynes urged him to return to continue his important work and 'to lay the foundations for a proper department of statistical realistic economics at Cambridge'. Clark decided to stay in Australia to work in public administration, and he wrote to Keynes explaining his decision: 'it was too remarkable an opportunity to be missed for putting economics into practice' (Keynes 1983: 802). He held posts as director of the Bureau of Industry and state statistician and financial advisor to the Treasury of Queensland from 1938 to 1952. Clark then returned to the UK as director of the Oxford Institute of Agricultural Economics and held that post from 1952 until 1969. In 1969 he again left the UK for Australia, and ended his career with the title of research consultant at the University of Queensland.

Colin Clark's passion and skill was to use statistics to resolve economic issues. He also used statistics to support his views that were sometimes provocative or controversial. His main contributions to economics were made in the 1930s as a pioneer estimating and using national income statistics. Besides estimating the national income of the UK, and later Australia and Russia, he made methodological contributions to the subject. One example was the introduction of the concept of gross national product to include the net foreign income of agents domiciled in a country.

In 1932, only five years after switching from studying science to social sciences, Clark published *The National Income 1924–1934*, one of his landmark studies. He focused on estimating the national income of the UK in 1924 and 1928, for which data was available, but he also made estimates for the other years between 1924 and 1931. The main sources were Inland Revenue data and the censuses of production. He made adjustments to Inland Revenue incomes data for people with low incomes and 'income evading tax'. Clark also estimated changes in prices, the national income deflator, so that the growth of real income could be identified. In addition, inspired by Keynes, Clark estimated savings and investment. A contemporary assessment of the book was that 'this is of very great interest, and in many ways remarkably stimulating' (Flux 1933: 279). Many of the definitions developed by Clark are still in use.

Clark published four papers in the *Economic Journal* in 1933, 1934, 1937 and 1938. The 1933 paper up-dated the UK national income statistics to 1932 and reported estimates of the national income based on output, expenditure and income. The estimates were remarkably close, within 1 per cent of each other. Clark also made quarterly estimates of national income. An objective of this innovation was to provide estimates of recent movements of national income for purposes of forecasting and setting economic policy. In the 1937 paper, Clark presented annual estimates of UK national income up to 1936. The 1938 paper presented estimates of the multiplier. When he received the draft of the paper Keynes commented to Austin ROBINSON, his co-editor of the *Economic Journal*: 'I have just received an extremely interesting article from Colin Clark...As so often happens with Clark's stuff, it seems to me full of mistakes, obscurities and misapprehensions' (Keynes 1983: 801). Nevertheless, Keynes published the paper. Clark started with the proposition that 'the most important determinant of short period changes in national income is to be found in fluctuations in investment.' He estimated the 'money-income multiplier', relating money expenditure on investment goods to the money level of gross national income. Clark describes the need to include other elements of 'autonomous' expenditure attributable to trade and government to calculate the multiplier. His estimates of the multiplier were 2.07 for 1929–33 and 3.22 for 1934–7. In the final paragraph of the article Clark forecasts that investment will decline rapidly by the first quarter of 1939.

The Conditions of Economic Progress, which spans national income accounting and growth and development economics, was Clark's most ambitious project. It was written between 1935 and 1939 and first published in 1940. The book describes the investigations which have been made in all the principal countries into national income and the economic factors bearing on national income. Clark included both rich and poor countries, making possible comparisons of levels of income in developing and advanced economies. The objective was 'to find the conditions under which we can hope for the greatest degree of economic progress in the future' (1940: vii). Although Keynes's work on macroeconomics dominated economics in the 1930s, theoretical work on growth took place. Clark's earlier work on national income statistics was designed to provide statistics to apply Keynesian economics; in *The Conditions of Economic Progress*, he attempted to do the same for growth theory. The book is crammed with tables of statistics, but Clark always attempts to draw conclusions from his data. In this original study, Clark reports international comparisons of actual and potential national income and rates of growth of national income. He uses the classification of industries between primary, secondary and tertiary sectors, and quantifies and analyses labour productivity in each sector. He reviews the roles of increasing returns for labour productivity and of capital for economic progress, and describes the distribution of income. In order to make the international comparisons of levels of income per head, Clark had to develop purchasing power parities because exchange rates do not reflect international differences in prices. He made the comparisons in terms of 'international units', the quantity of goods exchangeable in the USA for $1 over the average of the decade 1925-34. In his chapter on the role of capital, Clark is cautious about the importance of capital: 'we must not fall into the old-fashioned error of regarding the accumulation of capital as the limiting factor in economic progress. Possibly it is not even the predominant factor' (1940: 374). In the same chapter, Clark estimates Cobb–Douglas production functions. In the final chapter he reports estimates of the marginal propensity to consume and estimates of the multiplier based on estimates of the marginal propensities to consume and to import.

The third edition of *The Conditions of Economic Progress*, expanded to 720 pages from the 504 pages of the first edition, was published in 1957. By the time the third edition was written, the volume of national income statistics available had greatly expanded. Data for 1950 replaced that for 1925–34 for the main comparisons of income. Besides the new data, Clark reported new studies bearing on the determination of labour productivity and the other subjects he considered. The final chapter in the third edition, which was not in the first edition, is 'Economic Comparisons with the Ancient World'.

Clark wrote *The Economics of 1960*, which was published in 1942, while he was the economic and financial advisor to the State of Queensland's Treasury. The book was a response to the need to make long-term forecasts of the relative prices of commodities for deciding economic policy, whether to back a policy of expanding primary production or a policy of developing manufacturing industries. Clark in effect modelled the world economy. The 'original force' making for change in the model was increasing production per occupied person in the secondary and tertiary industries. In the introduction, Clark clearly acknowledges the perils of forecasting. When he looked back in 1984, he commented in typically forthright style: 'it is worth tracing how little went right and how much went wrong in *The Economics of 1960*' (1984: 72). In 1941 he had expected a very large post-war improvement in the world terms of trade for agricultural products. He lists the reasons why, in the event, this did not happen. He had overestimated the income elasticity of the demand for food in the advanced countries and the growth of non-farm employment in developing countries, particularly India and China, and underestimated the rate of growth in productivity per man-year of agricultural labour.

In 1962 and 1964 Clark published two papers, *Growthmanship* and *Taxmanship*, through the right-of-centre Institute of Economic Affairs in London. In *Growthmanship* he repeated and fleshed out a theme from *The Conditions of Economic Progress* that the role of increased investment in spurring the rate of growth had been exaggerated and that the main factors in economic growth were human, the accumulation of knowledge and enterprise. Again he used international comparisons of capital employed per unit of output to support his case. Clark identified policies for improving UK economic performance, including free trade, removal of restrictive practices, a reduction in trade union powers and a substantial reduction in taxation. Margaret Thatcher's governments adopted these policies. In *Taxmanship*, Clark contends that taxation beyond 25 per cent of the net national income produces inflation. He first put forward this proposition in an article in the *Economic Journal* in 1945, where he supported it with international comparisons of taxes as a proportion of income and inflation for the inter-war period. Although taxes now form a much higher proportion of national income than during the inter-war period and inflation is moderate, during the 1960s and 1970s when in the UK the proportion of taxes to income rose from 31.5 to 39.2 per cent, inflation took off. There were, of course other contributory factors, including the oil price rises.

The first edition of *The Economics of Subsistence Agriculture*, which Clark wrote with Margaret Haswell, was published in 1964. The first sentence is a quotation from a former director general of the Food and Agriculture Organization: 'A lifetime of malnutrition and actual hunger is the lot of at least two-thirds of mankind'. The authors attack this popular view. They summarize many studies of calorie requirements per person, of primitive agriculture, of the marginal product of labour and land in agriculture and of the income elasticity of the demand for food. They report historical examples of population growth: for example, they claim that 'it required a rapid growth of urban employment' in England in the nineteenth century to solve the rural unemployment problem (1964: 161). Where rural overpopulation did not lead to urban development, they suggest political failure as the cause. A theme of the book is to disprove the statement in the initial quotation and to present the advantages of population growth.

In the preface to *Population Growth and Land Use*, published in 1967, Clark states that: 'the student of population growth and its consequences [is]...compelled...to assemble information from...biology, medicine, mathematics, archaeology, history, nutrition, agriculture, geography, sociology, politics, economics, town planning and traffic engineering'. He proceeds to deal with all of these perspectives in the book. Clark's own controversial view was that the world could feed a rapidly growing population because of the potential of technical progress to increase the productivity of agriculture and that rapid growth of population has some positive effects on output per person (the socialist economists of the nineteenth century had argued much the same thing). One line of his argument is that there are economies of scale/increasing returns for large and increasing population. It would now be difficult to sustain this argument without qualification, in theory or empirically. The final chapter of the book is titled 'Land Use in Urban Areas'. Clark starts the chapter by reviewing estimates of population densities in the cities of Babylon and ancient Greece and mediaeval Europe. He goes on to deal with modern cities, transport and land values. Clark's assessment that the world population could grow rapidly without creating widespread hunger and famine has proved correct, but there are environmental costs to population growth in many countries.

Colin Clark was a pioneer in using economic statistics. He courageously used the very limited statistics available in the 1930s to prepare the most comprehensive assessment of the national income of the UK. Similarly, his international comparisons based on national income statistics and purchasing power parities showed what could be achieved, set a new standard and created an agenda for a greatly expanded profession of economics.

BIBLIOGRAPHY
The National Income 1924–31 (1932).
'The National Income in 1932', *Economic Journal* (1933), vol. XLIII, pp. 205–16.
'Further Data on the National Income', *Economic Journal* (1934), vol. XLIV, pp. 380–97.
National Income and Outlay (1937).
'Determination of the Multiplier from National Income Statistics', *Economic Journal* (1938), vol. XLVIII, pp. 435–8.
'The National Income at its Climax', *Economic Journal* (1938), vol. XLVII, pp. 308–20.
A Critique of Russian Statistics (1939).
Conditions of Economic Progress (1940).
The Economics of 1960 (1942).
'Public Finance and Changes in the Value of Money', *Economic Journal* (1945), vol. LV, pp. 371–89.
Growthmanship (1961).
Taxmanship (1964).
(with M.R. Haswell) *Economics of Subsistence Agriculture* (1964).
Population Growth and Land Use (1967).
(with I. Carruthers) *The Economics of Irrigation*, 3rd edn (Liverpool, 1981).
Regional and Urban Location (St. Lucia, Queensland, 1982).
'Development Economics: The Early Years', in G.M. Meier and D. Seers (eds), *Pioneers in Development* (New York, 1984).

Further Reading
Arndt, H.W., 'Clark, Colin Grant', *The New Palgrave* (1987).
'Clark, Colin', in *International Encyclopedia of the Social Sciences Biographical Supplement* (New York, 1979).
Flux, A.W., Review of Clark's 'The National Income', *Economic Journal* (1933), vol. XLIII, pp. 279–81.
Keynes, J.M., *The Collected Works of John Maynard Keynes* (1983).

Peters, G. (2001) *Colin Clark (1905–1989) Economist and Agricultural Economist* (Oxford, 2001).

Cliff Pratten

CLARKE, Hyde (1815–95)

Clarke was born in London some time in 1815 and died there on 1 March 1895. Details of his education are lacking, but it is known that he took up engineering at an early age. He worked as a railway surveyor in south-west Scotland in the 1830s, and seems to have made a considerable amount of money; he was one of the founding subscribers of the London and County Bank in 1836. He then spent some years in India, and delivered a report on the Indian telegraph service in 1849. He also founded the Council of Foreign Bondholders, and was an active member of the London (later Royal) Statistical Society, serving on its Council at various times from 1868 until his death. In November 1885, he proposed that the Statistical Society hold periodic meetings devoted exclusively to economic subjects. His motion was passed, with the support of Alfred MARSHALL, but the proposal raised such controversy among the members that such meetings were never held. Clarke contributed several papers on economic subjects to the meetings of the Statistical Society and Section F of the British Association. In addition to his interest in economics, he published numerous papers on philology and the origin of languages and races for the Royal Historical Society, and several books on language and mythology. He was a member of the Ethnological Society of London and the Anthropological Institute. Contemporaries reported that he could speak over a hundred languages.

Clarke's writings on economic matters concern two macroeconomic issues, both of which lay outside of the mainstream of classical political economy of that era. The first was an examination of the real and financial aspects of investment in railways, and is of little interest. In the second, he traced and explained the cyclical phenomena he observed in economic activity. Most importantly, Clarke recognized the existence of business cycles and, as Schumpeter noted, he 'recognised a multiplicity of cycles that ran their course simultaneously' (Schumpeter1954: 743). His most significant findings are found in his 1847 pamphlet, *Physical Economy, A Preliminary Inquiry into the Physical Laws Governing the Periods of Famines and Panics*, which appeared originally as an article in the *Railway Register* that same year.

Clarke's contribution to business cycle theory and analysis is noteworthy for its originality. He was an original discoverer of the cyclical nature of business activity. His efforts to date the cycles, a combination of a series of ten or eleven-year cycles within a fifty-four year long wave, was a striking anticipation of the major cycles or spans of such later economists as N.D. Kondratieff, Clement Juglar and William Stanley JEVONS. He presented his findings and his explanations of these cycles both in his 1847 pamphlet and in papers presented at the meetings of the British Association for the Advancement of Science during the 1880s, where he anticipated hypotheses later developed by Jevons and Schumpeter.

Clarke made a distinction between political economy, which 'restricts itself principally to the moral laws which influence society', and what he proposed to call 'physical economy'. The latter would 'include the laws of life (vital statistics), those which regulate famines and pestilences, and the operations of physical phenomena as affecting mankind and society' (1847: 1). John Stuart MILL later made the same distinction. Clarke adopted an inductive approach to his subject, in keeping with the traditions employed in both Section F (Economic Science and Statistics) of the British Association and the Royal Statistical Society.

In his work on business cycles, Clarke began by examining the 'yearly prices of wheat' found in two sources: 'From 1595 downwards we have the prices of wheat at Windsor market, kept for Eton College, and from 1771 we have the averages returned by the government Comptroller of Corn Returns' (1847: 3). Employing the notion of periodicity, he combed these wheat price data trying to discover regular patterns in the ebb and flow of economic activity. As a result of his initial studies, he concluded that economic crises occurred in the years 1796, 1806, 1817, 1827, 1837, and 1847 (1847: 1). Further study led him to revise his dating. Beginning with the 'famine so strongly felt during the French revolution' and focusing on 'an interval of about ten years', Clarke finally settled on 'a period of about fifty-four years, with five intervals of about ten or eleven years, which I took thus: 1793, 1804, 1815, 1826, 1837, [and] 1847' (1847: 3). To test the fifty-four year long wave hypothesis, Clarke developed a table comparing his dates (calculated backwards from 1847) with the historical estimates of crises using information in SMITH's *Wealth of Nations* and the Eton College wheat price data.

R.D. Collison Black has compared Clarke's fifty-four year-long cycle with the works of Kondratieff. In his 'The Long Waves of Economic Life', Kondratieff identified changes in price, interest rates, and the wages of agricultural workers. His dates for the 'First Cycle' in England closely match Clarke's dates, and the last two measures equal Clarke's fifty-four year period. More importantly, 'Kondratieff offered an explanation of the "rhythm of the long cycles" which traced its source to major capital projects such as railroads – those very projects which Hyde Clarke had sought to show were only passively involved because the rhythm of the long cycles came from exogenous physical factors…So far as the concept of the long wave and its dating are concerned, Hyde Clarke did indeed anticipate Kondratieff; so far as its causation is concerned, he did not'

(Black 1987: 53). The same cannot be said for his work on the shorter ten-year cycles, where he anticipated Jevons.

In addition to Clarke's 1847 *Physical Economy*, three other British authors preceded William Stanley Jevons's work on business cycles: John Wade in 1833 published his *History of the Middle and Working Classes*; William Langton presented his 'Observations on a Table shewing the Balance of Account between the Mercantile Public and the Bank of England' to the 1857–8 session of the Manchester Statistical Society; and ten years later, John Mills, drawing on Langton's observations, identified specific dates for six commercial panics in his paper, 'On Credit Cycles, and the Origin of Commercial Crises', which also appeared in the *Transactions of the Manchester Statistical Society*. The dates that Jevons identified for the ten-year cycles (within Clarke's fifty-four year long cycle) match Clarke's more closely than the other three authors, disagreeing only slightly on two of the six crises studied. Clarke's dating was not a simple listing of years, for he also included short descriptions of the economic activity which occurred during much of this fifty-four year period, paying particular attention to the six decennial cycle dates.

In a letter to Jevons of 31 August 1878, Clarke revealed what motivated his search for periodicity in business activity: 'My results were obtained altogether by computations' though 'many of us were struck by the ten yearly occurrence of these panics no known astronomical period would fit'. He then mentioned his friend, the 'late James T. Hackett, a very fair mathematician and astronomical computer, who had been Secretary of the London Astrological Society, and whose inner craze was astrology and consequently periodicity' (Black 1977, vol. IV: 274–5). So Clarke's conception that there exists a set of 'general elementary laws which govern periodical or cyclar action' derived, at least in part, from the periodicity found in astrology.

While the study of astrology led some to the notion of periodicity in business activity, Clarke did not seriously think that it was a causal factor. Instead, Clarke developed two hypotheses to explain his fifty-four year period. These can be classified as an astronomical hypothesis, based on the Saros eclipse cycle, and a meteorological hypothesis. He showed little enthusiasm for his astronomical hypothesis as an explanation, pursuing instead his meteorological hypothesis. He turned to his friend Hackett, whose interest in astrology and questions of periodicity, led him to develop a large collection of data on the subject. 'Mr. Hackett told me that such a [fifty-four year] period had been suggested by a Mr. [George] Mackenzie, in reference to the weather' (1847: 4–5). Mackenzie had developed a diagram comparing wheat prices and the weather. Essentially, Mackenzie's 'great law in the weather is founded upon a principle of compensation, and that series or lots of wind which have unfavourable weather at one time, have the contrary at another; thus they continually change their properties. Hence he assumes the supposed inexplicable nature of weather had its origin' (1847: 4). The most important cause of these weather cycles in Clarke's and Mackenzie's theory was the 'continued variation of the magnetic axes' (1847: 4). Clarke's 'own impressions and observations' persuaded him 'that the great causes of the phenomena manifested in the seasons and the harvests at present are referable to fluctuations in the electro-magnetic condition of this globe' (1847: 9).

This clearly foreshadowed Jevons's later work, positing that the business cycle was essentially based on a meteorological cycle. While Jevons traced the cause of the meteorological cycle to sunspot activity, which caused variations in the earth's magnetism and thus the weather, Clarke's 1847 hypothesis, that 'the shifting or oscillation of the magnetic poles' was connected 'with the periods of the weather', foreshadowed similar hypotheses pursued by astronomers when they realized, in 1851, that sunspot activity was cyclical and directly affected the earth's magnetic fields. These astronomers' hypotheses, and Clarke's pamphlet, later led Jevons to put forth his sunspot theory of the business cycle. Jevons recommended Clarke's pamphlet as 'well worth reading', because Clarke argued 'in a highly scientific manner in a highly scientific spirit that events so regularly recurring cannot be attributed to accidental causes; there must be, he thinks, some physical groundwork' (Jevons 1884: 222). Jevons distinguished Clarke's contributions to business cycle analysis from those of other writers in these words: 'The peculiar interest of Dr. Hyde Clarke's speculations consists in the fact that he not only remarked the cycle of ten or eleven years, but sought to explain it as due to physical causes' (Jevons 1884: 224). Clarke's contribution to business cycle theory and analysis is noteworthy for its originality.

BIBLIOGRAPHY

'On the Political Economy and Capital of Joint-stock Banks', *The Railway Magazine and Annals of Science* (1838), vol. IV, no. xxvii, pp. 288–93 and no. xxviii, pp. 360–2.

Contributions to Railway Statistics (1846).

Physical Economy: A Preliminary Inquiry into the Physical Laws Governing the Periods of Famines and Panics (1847).

'Discussion on Professor Poynting's Paper', *Journal of the (Royal) Statistical Society* (1884), vol. XLVII, March, pp. 65–8.

'Prospective Prices in Europe, America and Asia', *Report of the 1884 Meeting of the BAAS* (1884), vol. 54, August–September, pp. 868–9.

'On Depression of Prices and Results of Economy of Production, and on the Prospect of Recovery', *Report of the 1885 Meeting of the BAAS* (1885), vol. 55, September, pp. 1168–9.

'The Causes Affecting the Reduction in the Cost of Producing Silver', *Report of the 1886 Meeting of the BAAS* (1886), vol. 56, September, pp. 767–8.

'Effective Consumption and Effective Prices in Their Economical and Statistical Relations', *Report of the 1887 Meeting of the BAAS* (1887), vol. 57, August–September, p. 832.

Further Reading

Black, R.D.C., 'Dr. Kondratieff and Mr. Hyde Clarke', *Research in the History of Economic Thought and Methodology* (1987), vol. 9, pp. 35–58.

—— (ed.), *Papers and Correspondence of William Stanley Jevons*, 7 vols (1977).

Henderson, J.P., 'Astronomy, Astrology, and Business Cycles: Hyde Clarke's Contribution', *Research in the History of Economic Thought and Methodology* (1992), vol. 9, pp. 1–34.

——, 'Hyde Clarke's Publications: Papers Presented at Meetings of Scientific Societies, and Other Notes and Letters of Interest', *Research in the History of Economic Thought and Methodology* (1992), vol. 9, pp. 59–72.

Jevons, W.S. 'Commercial Crises and Sunspots', *Nature* (1878), vol. XIX, 14 November, pp. 33–7 and 24 April, pp. 588–90.

——, *Investigations in Currency and Finance* (1884).

——, 'The Periodicity of Commercial Crises and Its Physical Explanation', *Journal of the Statistical and Social Inquiry Society of Ireland* (1878), vol. VII, August, pp. 334–42.

——, 'The Solar Period and the Price of Corn', in *Investigations in Currency and Finance* (1884).

Schumpeter, J.A. *History of Economic Analysis* (New York, 1954).

James P. Henderson

CLAY, Henry (1883–1954)

Clay was born in Germany on 9 May 1883, but was a Yorkshireman to his fingertips, his family having temporarily located near Munchen-Gladbach where his father, Henry James Clay, a Bradford woollen manufacturer, had formed the firm of Goetz, Clay, & Co. He died 30 July 1954 as a result of a street accident in Holland where he had gone to join his children for a North Sea trip in the family yacht. He was the fourth of six children of Henry Clay senior and his wife, Elizabeth Bulmer.

The German partnership ended after eight years and the family moved back to Yorkshire. Clay was educated at Bradford Grammar School and thence as a scholar at University College, Oxford. Disappointed of his immediate hopes of an academic career because of his second class in *literae humaniores* in 1906, Clay became, first, secretary to a London charity organization, and then for two years, warden of the Neighbourhood Guild Settlement in Sheffield. He married in 1910 Gladys Priestman, daughter of a Bradford worsted manufacturer, by whom he had four children and a family life which was always his first priority. Between 1909 and 1917 he lectured for the Workers' Educational Association under the university extension scheme, an experience leading to the writing of *Economics* (1916). This was an introduction for the general reader which had great success, not just in Britain but also in the USA where it sold widely and even attracted a ten-page extended review in the *Journal of Political Economy* (Hamilton 1919). Thus, like many of the best of this generation of autodidactic economists, a clarity in writing and an eye for effective real-world examples gave Clay a comparative advantage in both diagnosing contemporary economic problems and promoting the economics education of Everyman.

Clay was a temporary civil servant from 1917–19 in the newly established Ministry of Labour, where he worked closely on industrial relations and other labour problems with H.D. Butler, later director of the International Labour Office and the first warden of Nuffield College, Oxford, to which post Clay succeeded in 1944. From 1919 to 1921 he was a fellow and lecturer in economics, New College, Oxford, campaigning for the proposed new honour school, philosophy, politics and economics (PPE). Concurrently, he was a special correspondent on industrial questions to the *New York Evening Post*, making the first of many visits to America in 1921. PPE admitted its first students in autumn 1921 just as Clay was preparing to take up the Stanley Jevons chair of political economy at Manchester, which he held from 1922–7. In 1927 he asked to exchange this chair for the new professorship of social economics, a post relieving him of administrative duties which did not interest him.

Clay was to spend eight years in all at Manchester, extremely productive years for him and marking something of a golden age for the economics department which developed both its links to the local community and as a centre of excellence in applied economics (for example, Clay and Brady 1929). He perceived that applied economics could be strengthened by closer regular contacts between economists and businessmen, and instituted his Manchester Thursday lunches as a successful pioneering effort. It was the influence of such business networks, together with his close observation of local industries (especially the Lancashire cotton industry), much more than his subscribing to any particular school of theoretical economics, that made Clay pre-eminently a man of affairs and a very practical economist whose perceptive commentaries on the industrial situation were much in demand. For example, in 1925 he went to South Africa as a member of the economic and wage commission and was largely responsible for the subsequent report. This was to be the first of many commissions, at home and abroad, to act as an arbitrator and adviser. He was thus more at home writing balanced treatments of contemporary economic issues for the *Manchester Guardian* – where his swift and polished productions were something of a marvel even to its seasoned staff – than reviews and articles in the learned journals, although – when public duties permitted – he was a frequent contributor to the *Manchester School of Economic and Social Studies* and to the *Economic Journal*, the journal of the Royal Economic Society upon whose council he served from 1924–48.

Clay was not a foremost economic theorist, although he could be a very perceptive political economist (for example, Clay (1927) on the implicit social bargain of the unemployment insurance system). Indeed, he often expressed doubts about the value of much of the theorizing then in fashion, as he told Edwin CANNAN, who shared his structural diagnosis of Britain's industrial problems but with whom he would clash in the *Economic Journal* over what he perceived to be an unjust and misleading review of his position (Cannan 1930; Clay 1930). Clay 'always felt that as a Professor of Economics I was a fraud...[for] My reading of English economics has been scrappy...I don't know enough mathematics to follow our Cambridge friends, however suspicious I may be of their results; and I cannot suppress my interest in current political and social questions sufficiently to stick to any one part of the field of economics and so do some serious work on it' (cited in Casson 1983: 18–19). He was thus a tool-user rather than a tool-maker, and frequently impatient of the tools provided. Representative of this phase are *The Post-War Unemployment Problem* (1929) and *The Problem of Industrial Relations* (1929). In Casson's (1983: 9) judgement, these two works when taken together 'afford[ed] a convincing diagnosis of the structural problems of the British economy in the 1920s', and Clay, with Cannan and A.C. PIGOU, although none conforming to Keynes's *General Theory* (1936) stereotype of classical economists, were nonetheless the leading pre-Keynesians.

In 1930 Clay resigned his chair to join the Bank of England, in the first instance as adviser to the newly established Securities Management Trust, a Bank subsidiary charged with financing and promoting the rationalization of the depressed staple industries, problems upon which Clay was now especially qualified to advise. In 1930–1 he was a member of the Royal Commission on Unemployment Insurance, and in 1933 he advised on the organization of Argentina's banking system. Clay's shrewd advice and his knack of getting on with people, especially with Bank of England Governor Montagu Norman (whose biography he would later write), led to his appointment in the same year as the governor's economic adviser, although in practice he had been discharging this broader advisory role since the financial crisis of the summer of 1931 which had led, much to his consternation, to Britain's forced abandonment of the gold standard and later to free trade.

Temperamentally, Clay and Norman were poles apart: the governor a prima donna, Clay gentle, scholarly, sensitive and undogmatic. Yet in many ways their views ran parallel and Clay's pragmatic capacity for swift and clear craftsmanship must have been a godsend to Norman, whose inadequacy in expression was in sharp contrast to his considerable powers of thought and decision. They shared the opinion that, necessary as was a proper budgetary and monetary framework, financial ingenuity by governments in the form of large-scale loan-financed public works did not offer a long-term solution to the problems of British industry. These lay more on the supply-side, where widespread inefficiencies in the use of capital and labour resulted in high costs and low productivity, problems which were being addressed by the Bank in its promotion of industrial rationalization. Ostensibly, both Clay and Norman were antipathetic towards the solution for unemployment being developed by J.M. KEYNES, but as we now know from the Per Jacobsson diaries and from Sayers's official history of the Bank, through

Clay, Norman came to favour a controlled demand expansion by Keynesian means, while by 1936 Clay had 'made himself a monetary economist of a stature that went unrecognised by the academic world from which he had been so completely withdrawn' (Sayers 1976, vol. 2: 462, 489). Clay's, and Norman's, openness to new economic ideas is confirmed by their later joint support for Keynes's influential plan, *How to Pay for the War* (1940).

With Josiah STAMP, Clay was one of the most active in the establishment (1938) of the National Institute of Economic and Social Research, and he guided its research as chairman of its council (1940–9) and later president (1949–52). Shortly before the outbreak of the Second World War, Stamp was called upon by the government to produce a broad survey of national economic resources, and Clay and Hubert HENDERSON were his chief assistants in an organization which became the forerunner of the Economic Section and the Central Statistical Office in the Cabinet Secretariat. To this organization were recruited many of Clay's former Manchester colleagues and students whose applied economics skills were exactly those required for administering the war economy. After Stamp's death in 1941, Clay went to the Board of Trade, as economic adviser and later to the Ministry of War Transport.

In 1944 Clay left Whitehall to become the second warden of Nuffield College, Oxford, where he took particular pleasure in the appointment of visiting fellows chosen for their practical experience in the professions, industry or commerce, thereby meeting at least some of the reservations that the College's benefactor had about the direction of the social sciences and of 'his' college. Knighted in 1946, Clay took early retirement as warden in 1949 but continued to enjoy a busy life. He became part-time economic adviser to Unilever; was actively engaged in the collection and editing of Henderson's papers, published posthumously as Clay (1955); and he pursued his work on a biography of Lord Norman, again published posthumously (Clay 1957) and described by Sayers (1958: 357) as Clay's best and most important book (although this was not how it was viewed by Norman's widow who commissioned a further biography and was then not entirely satisfied with that product either).

Clay's writings from his first and famous book to the papers unfinished at his death show the main lines of his thinking unbroken. He was in many ways a Gladstonian liberal, believing that private enterprise was the most efficient form of organizing production; that the liberty of the individual would be endangered by the continued growth of government; and that Britain should maintain its historic internationalism in its economic policies (see Clay 1929b, ch. 14). However, he was also more than this, although his friendliness and complete absence of stridency in whatever he said or wrote tended to conceal the strength of his convictions. His pragmatism and inventiveness made him open to policy experimentation in times of national emergency. He was, for example, involved in the early days of the Liberal summer schools, lecturing and writing on the distribution of capital (Clay 1929b, chaps 12–13), and wrote a broadly supportive review of its report, *Britain's Industrial Future* (1928), a report typically taken as the epitome of interwar progressive thought on economic policy and as laying some of the intellectual foundations for Britain's post-1945 managed-mixed economy (Clay 1928). However, his views diverged from the main stream of contemporary liberal economic thought in at least two ways: in his doubts about the practical results of the Keynesian solution to unemployment, or more especially of the views of some of Keynes's disciples; and concerning industrial monopoly. Clay was not prepared to agree that a competitive system would inevitably degenerate into monopoly unless safeguarded by the state: anti-monopoly legislation in his view was unnecessary, inexpedient, and inequitable.

BIBLIOGRAPHY
(with K.R. Brady) *Manchester at Work: A Survey* (Manchester, 1929).
Economics: An Introduction for the General Reader (1916; 2nd edn, 1942).
'The Authoritarian Element in Distribution', *Economic Journal* (1927), vol. 37, no. 1, pp. 1–18.
'The Liberal Industrial Report', *Economic Journal* (1928), vol. 38, no. 2, pp. 193–203.
The Post-War Unemployment Problem (1929a).
The Problem of Industrial Relations and Other Lectures (1929b).
'Dr Cannan's Views on Unemployment', *Economic Journal* (1930), vol. 40, no. 2, pp. 331–5.
The Inter-war Years and Other Papers: A Selection from the Writings of Hubert Douglas Henderson (Oxford, 1955).
Lord Norman (1957).

Further Reading
Cannan, E., 'The Problem of Unemployment', *Economic Journal* (1930), vol. 40, no. 1, pp. 45–55.
Casson, M., *Economics of Unemployment: An Historical Perspective* (Oxford, 1938).
Hamilton, W.H., 'An Appraisal of Clay's Economics', *Journal of Political Economy* (1919), vol. 27, no. 4, pp. 300–9.
Sayers, R.S., Review of Clay (1957), *Economic Journal* (1958), vol. 68, no. 2, pp. 353–7.
——, *The Bank of England, 1891–1944*, 3 vols (Cambridge, 1976).

Roger Middleton

CLEEVE, Bourchier (1715–60)

Cleeve was born in London in 1715, exact date unknown, the tenth son of a pewterer. He died on 1 March 1760, either in London or at his country estate at Foots Cray, Kent. Little is known of Cleeve's life and career except that he took over his father's pewter business after the latter's death in 1738 and seems to have made the business highly profitable. Certainly he was able to buy Foots Cray Place and other properties in Kent. His later years were spent in substantially rebuilding his country house, and in writing and leisure pursuits.

Cleeve was particularly concerned with levels of taxation in the kingdom, which he saw as being excessively high and hindering prosperity. In *A Scheme for preventing a further increase of the National Debt, and for reducing the same* (1756), Cleeve acknowledges the influence of Matthew DECKER and the latter's ideas on tax reform, and he refers to Decker on a number of occasions throughout the work.

Cleeve proposes first, to pay off the national debt by raising money through annuities, and second, to reform the tax system by abolishing taxes and duties on commodities 'except such duties as affect our manufactures by exports or imports, or French commodities' (1756: 10). Taxes on commodities are to be replaced by a single graduated house tax, with tax rates ranging from £80 per annum for peers' seats and the houses of archbishops, admirals and generals, down to £1 a year for small cottages; any house with an annual rental of less than £2 being exempt from tax. Cleeve calculates that this will yield £9,141,000 in annual revenues.

Cleeve then justifies his system through a series of elaborate calculations showing the amounts that households pay in taxes on goods, and how they would benefit from the lower taxes proposed under his system. He argues that lower taxes mean more disposable income, which in turn leads to higher spending and greater prosperity.

Cleeve's arguments were criticized by Joseph MASSIE, who showed that Cleeve's arithmetic was at fault and his figures greatly exaggerated. Cleeve, said Massie, had miscalculated both the levels of household expenditure and the amount of tax paid. But although he disparaged Cleeve's methods, Massie did not argue with his conclusion that the level of tax being paid was excessive, and agreed that some form of tax reform was essential to restore national prosperity.

BIBLIOGRAPHY
A Scheme for preventing a further increase of the National Debt, and for reducing the same (1756).

Further Reading
Massie, J., *A Letter to Bourchier Cleeve, Esq; concerning his calculations of taxes* (1757).

Morgen Witzel

CLEGG, Hugh Armstrong (1920–95)

Clegg was born 22 May 1920, the son of a Methodist clergyman. He died 9 December 1995. He was educated at Kingswood School, Bath and Magdalen College, Oxford where he studied politics, philosophy and economics. He had two sons and two daughters.

Clegg was the leading UK scholar of industrial relations of his generation. He was a prolific writer, and many of his publications were based on and described the results of his wide-ranging research on unions and industrial relations. He also took part in a series of public enquiries involving individual labour disputes, the reform of labour relations and the operation of incomes policies.

Clegg was appointed to a fellowship at Nuffield College, Oxford in 1949. While he was at Oxford, the university was the leading institution in the UK for the study of labour relations. Most of the Oxford group of labour economists were 'pluralists'; in Clegg's words, they believed 'that a free society consists of a large number of overlapping groups, each with its own interests and objectives which its members are entitled to pursue so long as they do so with reasonable regard to the rights and interests of others'. They 'were also egalitarians, wishing to see a shift in the distribution of wealth towards those with lower incomes, and a shift of power over the conduct of their lives and environment towards working men and women; and for both those reasons emphasising the importance of trade unions in industry, in the economy and in society' (1990: 2).

Clegg's own research traced the development of trade unions and labour relations. In 1954 he published a study of the General and Municipal Workers Union. He maintained the link with the GMWU, and in the early 1960s ran summer schools for the union's shop stewards at Cambridge. In 1964, with Allan Flanders, he published *A History of British Trade Unions since 1889*.

In 1967 Clegg moved to Warwick University as professor of industrial relations and set up the Industrial Relations Research Unit. Again, partly as a result of Clegg's leadership, Warwick took the lead in the field of labour economics. At Warwick, Clegg and his colleagues paid less attention to the philosophy of industrial relations and more to the detailed practice of labour relations; problems of trade union organisation and government, company employment policies, payment structures and the operation of particular pieces of labour legislation. Clegg was a gifted organizer and teacher who was able to convey his own interest and enthusiasm for the subject to colleagues and pupils. Many of today's leading labour economists and human relations practitioners were taught by him.

In 1970 Clegg published the *System of Industrial Relations in Great Britain*, which succeeded a book with the same title edited by Clegg and Flanders, published in 1954. Clegg published a further, completely re-written version in 1979 with the title *The Changing System of Industrial Relations in Great Britain*.

The need to revise the books reflected the rapid changes in industrial relations and pay bargaining, and changing perceptions of those relationships. For many years these books were the standard texts on the subject. In 1976, Clegg published *Trade Unionism under Collective Bargaining*, a comparative study of trade union structure and collective bargaining in six countries.

In 1958 Clegg was appointed a member of the Railway Pay Committee of Enquiry. During the Labour governments of 1964–70 and 1974–9, he was a member of a succession of enquiries and commissions. Clegg's approach to resolving disputes and problems was to seek compromise through conciliation. He searched for fair solutions and expected union leaders and employers to be reasonable. Potentially the most influential committee on which Clegg served was the Donovan Royal Commission, set up in 1965 to investigate the state of labour–management relations. Clegg drafted important sections of the main report; he favoured a voluntary approach and eschewed the introduction of legislation. In the event, the government did not follow through the recommendations of the Commission, in part because it was drawing on the goodwill of trade unions to implement its incomes policy.

Inevitably, incomes policies involve a reorganization of labour relations towards more centralized bargaining. In 1950 the dominant form of pay bargaining in the UK was industry-wide, one step from national wage negotiations, but centralized bargaining was difficult to reconcile with Clegg's realisation of, and emphasis on, the importance of local, firm and plant level negotiations and bargaining. He was convinced that reform of collective bargaining was an essential preliminary to an effective incomes policy. Labour relations and wage bargaining were Clegg's areas of expertise, and he was involved with the introduction and implementation of incomes policies. He was a member of the Prices and Incomes Board.

It was while he was chairman of the Standing Commission on Pay Comparability (the Clegg Commission) in 1979–80 that Clegg was in the public eye. In 1978 the Labour government's incomes policy disintegrated in the 'Winter of Discontent'. The government set up the Commission to settle public sector pay claims on the basis of comparability, the principle that governments had resisted as a part of their incomes policies. During the general election in 1979 Margaret Thatcher committed the new government to implementing the awards made by the Commission. Clegg's awards for many groups of public sector workers were generous. The awards contributed to an acceleration of inflation, spurred on by the soaring price of oil and the government's policy of raising the rate of VAT.

In retrospect, the period 1960–80 was one of turmoil in UK labour relations, with rapid inflation and industrial strife. If unions had voluntarily reformed and incomes policies had succeeded, Clegg would have been a hero, but it was not to be. In 1979 Margaret Thatcher won the election and brought a different approach.

BIBLIOGRAPHY
General Union: a Study of the National Union of General and Municipal Workers (Oxford, 1954).
(with A.J. Killick and R. Adams) *Trade Union Officers: A Study of Full-time Officers, Branch Secretaries and Shop Stewards in British Trade Unions* (Oxford, 1961).
(with A. Fox and A.F. Thompson) *A History of British Trade Unions since 1889* (Oxford, 1964).
Trade Unionism under Collective Bargaining (Oxford, 1966).
The System of Industrial Relations in Great Britain (Oxford, 1970).
How to Run an Incomes Policy, and Why We Made Such a Mess of the Last One (1971).
The Changing System of Industrial Relations in Great Britain (Oxford, 1979).

'The Oxford School of Industrial Relations'
Warwick Papers in Industrial Relations
(Warwick, 1990).

Further Reading
Donovan Commission, *Report of the Royal Commission on Trade Unions and Employers' Associations* (1968).

Cliff Pratten

CLEMENT, Simon (1654?–1730?)

What little is known of Clement's life comes from the British Library's collection of letters saved by Robert Harley, Earl of Oxford. From these we learn that in 1712 Clement was almost sixty years old, that he had a son, Daniel, in London who attended Oxford, and that he was married to Mary Hollister. Mary's niece was Hannah Callowhill, who became William Penn's second wife in 1696. Through Penn, Clement achieved some influence with Harley.

Clement spent his early career as a stock jobber and merchant. He served in Vienna as secretary to the Earl of Peterborough on his embassy to the Emperor from 1711–12, later acting as Peterborough's chargé d'affaires in Vienna from April 1711 until late 1714.

Clement's writings concerned exchange and specialization, paper money, inflation, the money multiplier, scarcity of coins and international trade. In *A Discourse of the General Notions of Money, Trade, and Exchanges* (1695), Clement explained the advantages of trade and specialization, and the importance of metallic money in facilitating trade. He advocated restricting imports as a means of preventing the export of bullion, and favoured recoinage of worn British coins while opposing devaluation of the coinage. In *A Dialogue Between a Countrey Gentleman and a Merchant Concerning the Falling of Guinea's* (1696), Clement argued against raising the value of the guineas on the grounds that this would undervalue silver and create arbitrage opportunities for currency traders, to the detriment of the nation. In *Remarks Upon a Late Ingenious Pamphlet* (1718), Clement claimed that an unprecedented scarcity of silver had been caused by excessive British imports from India, a problem that would not be remedied 'whilst people have the Vanity to give more for a tawdry Callicoe, than for a good silk of our own making'. The true remedy, he claimed, was for consumers to restrain their consumption of Indian goods. He also argued against 'the absurd Opinion, that the Raising our Coin would advance its Value, and prevent its being carried out of the Nation'.

Clement's most influential work was *Faults on Both Sides* (1710). This was a wide-ranging pamphlet that briefly discussed paper money and the influence of credit on trade. The pamphlet (widely attributed to Harley) produced several replies, which Clement answered in *A Vindication of the Faults on Both Sides* (1710). In it he dismissed what modern economists call the money multiplier, on the grounds that all bank-issued money is backed, either by the 'valuable and sufficient security' offered as collateral by the borrower, or by the 'proper stock' of the banker himself. Thus a banker need only take care to issue money to borrowers who offer sufficiently valuable collateral, and the value of the bank's money will be preserved regardless of the quantity issued. This idea is the basis for what later became known as the real bills doctrine, and Clement was one of the earliest defenders of that doctrine. As recently as 1945, Clement's exposition of real bills principles was attacked by Lloyd Mints, who incorrectly attributed Clement's writings to 'Richard' Harley.

It is noteworthy that Clement's exposition of the real bills doctrine required only that money be issued in exchange for sufficiently valuable collateral, and not necessarily to finance 'productive' activity. Thus he avoided the errors of later writers, including Adam SMITH, who thought that a policy of only issuing money for 'real bills' would prevent inflation by making the quantity of money move in step with real output.

BIBLIOGRAPHY
A Discourse of the General Notions of Money, Trade, and Exchanges (1695).
A Dialogue Between a Countrey Gentleman and a Merchant, Concerning the Falling of Guinea's (1696).
The Interest of England, as it Stands, with Relation to the Trade of Ireland (1698).
A Vindication of the Bank of England (1707).
Faults on Both Sides (1710).
A Vindication of the Faults on Both Sides (1710).
Remarks Upon a Late Ingenious Pamphlet (1718).

Further Reading
Mints, L., *A History of Banking Theory* (Chicago, 1945).
Snyder, H., 'The Authorship of Faults on Both Sides', *Philological Quarterly* (1977), vol. 56, pp. 266–72.

Michael F. Sproul

COBBETT, William (1763–1835)

Cobbett was born at the 'Jolly Farmer' in the village of Farnham, Surrey on 9 March 1763 and died in Botley in Hampshire on 18 June 1835. Cobbett attended a local dame school for a short time, and he also received instruction in reading, writing and arithmetic from his father; he was otherwise self-taught. In his youth Cobbett was employed at farm and garden work and briefly as a clerk to an attorney in Gray's Inn. Having joined the British Army in 1784, Cobbett served in Nova Scotia and rose to the rank of sergeant-major. Following his discharge in 1791 he embarked upon a career as a political pamphleteer and journalist, first in the cause of justice for his former army comrade, then, in the United States from 1792–1800 as an anti-Jacobin opponent of political radicalism, and finally and most significantly, as a trenchant critic of the system of English government that had emerged under the Whigs in the eighteenth century. Cobbett's most famous publication was the periodical *Political Register* (1802–35); he also published *Advice to Young Men*, *Cottage Economy* and *Rural Rides*, works that have remained in print in popular editions up to the present. His books on grammar were used widely by those who, like Cobbett, lacked a formal education. Following the passage of the Reform Act in 1832 Cobbett was elected MP for Oldham; he held this seat until his death.

Cobbett's anonymous debut as a political pamphleteer came with the publication of *The Soldier's Friend* (1792), directed at what he saw as systemic corruption in the British army. Yet it was as a Tory critic of Jacobin France and its supporters in the United States, and as a resolute defender of an idealized British polity that Cobbett was to establish his initial reputation as a political polemicist. Having fled to France fearing prosecution for having brought charges of corruption against representatives of the 'epaulet gentry', the September Massacres persuaded him of the need to flee again to the United States, where he arrived in October 1792. Here he responded to the attacks on Britain of a vehemently pro-Jacobin, Democrat press under the pseudonym of Peter Porcupine, determined 'wherever I meet with any malicious aspersions on Britain, her King, or her subjects' to use 'the bitterest drop on my pen ... in retaliation'. To this pledge Cobbett proved indefectibly faithful, moved, as he put it, by 'the *amor patriae* implanted in my breast' (*Porcupine's Gazette, Collected Writings*, vol. 1, p. 154).

In thus responding, Cobbett constructed an idealized 'Old England' by reference to which he judged the polities of the United States and France, finding them, in most respects, decidedly wanting. His ideal was a multifaceted one, though with decidedly Burkean inflections. Cobbett attacked those supporters of the French Revolution, such as Paine and Priestley, whose hubris had led them to believe that through the exercise of human reason alone they could establish a political system that enshrined the principles of liberty and justice. For Cobbett, such men were:

> system-mongers ... an unreasonable species of mortals [for whom] time, place, climate, nature itself, must give way. They must have the same government in every quarter of the globe; when perhaps there are not two countries which can possibly admit of the same form of government at the same time. A thousand hidden causes, a thousand circumstances and unforeseen events, conspire to the forming of government. It is always done little by little. When completed, it presents nothing like a system; nothing like a system composed, and written in a book.
> (*Observations on the Emigration of Dr. Priestley*, Collected Writings, vol. 1, p. 25)

For Cobbett, as for Burke, it was in such an organic fashion that the British constitution had ineluctably emerged, and therein lay its great virtue and its great strength. It has 'borne the test and attracted the admiration of ages' (*ibid.*, p. 17). It was a growth not a construct, the unreasoned but historically sanctified outcome of the incremental changes which the passage of time had effected. At the head of Cobbett's idealized polity was the 'sovereign who, though his fleets command the ocean, though he is the arbiter of nations, and the acknowledged saviour of the civilized world, makes his chief glory consist in being the defender, the friend, the father of his people' (*The Rush-light*, Collected Writings, vol. 1, p. 194). Below the king in the benevolently paternal hierarchy was an ancient nobility and gentry imbued with a sense of social duty which manifested itself most clearly in the treatment of the poor. For Cobbett, 'the English system of poor relief [was] the best in the world; the fairest for the giver and the least degrading for the receiver', treating the poor man as part of a 'great family of which he is a member' (*Priestley's Charity Sermon*, Collected Writings, vol. 1, pp. 210–11).

Such a polity, sanctified by age, buttressed by tradition, secured by hierarchy and infused with benevolence, yielded a 'real' or 'civil' liberty which contrasted both markedly and favourably with what Cobbett saw as the 'abstract', 'political' or, as he sometimes had it, 'French liberty' embodied in such humbug as written constitutions and declarations of the rights of man (*Observations*, in *op. cit.*, vol. 1, p. 28). 'Political liberty', Cobbett wrote in 1800:

> is a matter of speculation rather than of interest; it is an imaginary something of meaning undefined, and is, at best, a very distant if not a very questionable good. But civil liberty, which is perhaps best expressed by the single word justice, is clearly defined and understood, and is ardently beloved by us all it throws a rampart round our property and a shield around our persons. This is the liberty of which our forefathers are so proud.
> (*The Rush-light*, Collected Writings, vol. 1, p. 192)

'Real' liberty, for Cobbett, resided therefore not in the articulation of abstract political principles but in the real security of property and persons which the British polity guaranteed.

The abstract liberty of France created *de nouveau* by the exercise of human reason had led its citizens to 'oblige every merchant, under the pain of the guillotine, to make a declaration of all property to foreign countries and to give up [their] right and title of such property to the Convention' (*A Bone to Gnaw*, Collected

Writings, vol. 1, p. 37). In its name they had 'ransacked the coffers of the rich, stripped poverty of its very rags, robbed the infant of its birth right, wrenched the crutch from the hand of tottering old age, and joined sacrilege to burglary' by 'plunder[ing] even the altars of God' (*A New Year's Gift, Collected Writings*, vol. 1, p. 87). French republicans and the 'Democrat' fellow travellers in the United States might use the language of political liberty but, with the security of property and person destroyed, theirs was a debased and empty rhetoric which the beneficiaries of real English liberty must hold in contempt.

It was by reference to this ideal of Old England that Peter Porcupine directed his critical fire against the American supporters of republican France during the years that Cobbett spent in the United States (1792–1800). And it was an ideal that, throughout this period of self-imposed exile, was insulated from the realities of late eighteenth-century England. But that was to change on Cobbett's return; a return to an England driven by price inflation and the food riots of 1795–6 and 1799–1801; an England which had experienced an onslaught on civil liberties through the suspension of habeas corpus and the circumscription of freedom of association, speech and the press by the Anti-Sedition Acts of 1795; an England too which had seen the burgeoning of a *nouveau riche* of questionable social pedigree grown wealthy from the speculative gains that the administration and financing of war had made possible. Porcupine's imagined England was thus radically different from the real England that Cobbett now confronted.

It was also an England that shortly after his return concluded the Peace of Amiens with France, a France whose perfidious and Jacobinical character Cobbett had spent the 1790s deriding. The Peace represented a repugnant capitulation to the forces of political evil. It was an 'improvident ... disgraceful ... heartchilling ... courage killing peace' and he vented his fury against those who had concluded it in his *Letters to the Right Honourable Henry Addington* (1802, *Collected Writings*, vol. 3, p. 254); *Letters* that strongly parallel Burke's *Letters on a Regicide Peace* (1796–7). Burke had suggested that the preparedness to sacrifice political virtue to economic expediency was what had driven some to contemplate a negotiated peace with France, and Cobbett similarly began to consider in his *Letters* what material interests had so corrupted the British polity that it was prepared to embrace peace with a regicide republic.

In Cobbett's Old England political virtue had been integral to a polity where an independent, ancient, natural aristocracy, under the beneficent tutelage of the monarch, disinterestedly managed the affairs of the nation in the interests of the nation as a whole. This was an Old England grounded in the stability, security, traditional culture and material abundance that only an agrarian economy could furnish; an Old England where there existed a social symbiosis between landowners and labourers rooted in clearly understood concepts of duty, trust and obligation. But now, as he saw it, the war had set in motion forces which had resulted in 'the ancient nobility and gentry of the kingdom ... with very few exceptions [having] been thrust out of all public employment ... [and] banished from the councils of the state', with 'a race of merchants, and manufacturers, and bankers and loan-jobbers, and contractors hav[ing] usurped their place'. Political virtue had been subverted and public policy corrupted, with the government 'very fast becoming what it must be expected to become in such hands' (*Letters*, p. 261).

At the root of the nation's departure from his remembered ideal was the Pitt System of war finance. It was this system which had promoted the fortunes and produced the political and social apotheosis of those whose mercenary intent had corrupted policy making. It was the Pitt System that had substituted paper for gold with the Bank Restriction Act of 1797 and ignited an inflation which, while beneficial to Jews, money jugglers and avaricious landowners, had caused the impoverishment of the working population. It was the Pitt System that had woven venality into the fabric of the constitution, tying the interests of government to those of 'loan mongers', tax-gatherers and 'stock jobbers'. It was the Pitt System that had furnished the wherewithal for the executive to undermine the independence of the legislature, and that had bent public policy to the pursuit of what Cobbett termed 'factitious wealth'. To understand its pernicious effects Cobbett consulted the works of Adam Smith and George Chalmers, but it was Paine's *Decline of the English System of Finance* (1796), read in 1803, which led him to see 'the whole matter in its true light'. 'Here was no bubble, no mud to obstruct my view: the stream was clear and strong' (*Cobbett's Manchester Lectures, Collected Writings*, vol. 11, p. 95). It was, therefore, 'infamous Tom Paine', damned by Cobbett in his American writings as a Jacobin, atheist and rabble rouser, who provided Cobbett with that understanding of the Pitt System which was subsequently to inform his journalism and pamphleteering.

In his *Letters to Addington* Cobbett wrote that he 'wish[ed] our Constitution to be what it was' (p. 252). In effect he wished it to be the imagined constitution of his American writings. Such an aspiration ultimately moved him in the direction of political radicalism with a critique of the existing order focused on the state, old corruption and the morally corrosive consequences of commercial modernity. But it also imbued his radicalism with a profound conservatism which preferred the rural to the urban, the traditional to the modern, beer to tea, the seeming certainty of gold to the vagaries of paper money and common sense to the sophistical theorizing of Parson MALTHUS and 'the feelosophecal doctor' (Adam Smith). This fusion of radicalism, nostalgia for a traditional pre-industrial order and desire for the reconstitution of an imagined pre-Pitt polity often made for that incoherence and the contradiction in which his contemporary opponents so delighted, but it also gave his political radicalism both its distinctive quality, its underlying unity and, more often than not, its cutting edge. Cobbett wished England to be what he believed it had been, and he execrated everything and everyone who prevented or threatened such a reconstitution. Pensioners and placemen were attacked because they reflected and fostered the subversion of paternalism by venality; stock jobbers because they severed the connection between wealth and the land, and between social status and social pedigree; paper money because it too acted as a solvent of the traditional social hierarchy, and undermined accepted notions of worth and value; Jews because they oiled the wheels and reaped the benefits of such developments; the Great Wen, urbanization and commerce because they threatened the agrarian foundations and the rural values of Cobbett's ideal polity, boroughmongers because they corrupted a constitution and a political process which had made Old England the envy of other nations; political economists because, epitomized by Parson Malthus, they had sought to rationalize the destruction of 'the English system of poor relief that is the best in the world, the fairest for the giver and the least degrading for the receiver' (*Priestley's Charity Sermon, Collected Writings*, vol. 1, p. 210).

Here in particular, as regards poor relief, Cobbett saw a paternally virtuous Old England threatened by the economic and ideological forces which 'The Thing' had unleashed. The cost of poor relief had increased rapidly in the late eighteenth and early nineteenth centuries. But while writers such as Malthus explained this by reference to the old poor laws and the premium they put on incontinent breeding, Cobbett explained the phenomenon by reference to the impoverishment that the increasing taxation had created, and, post-1815, to the deflationary determination to return to gold without an adjustment of the real tax burden. He had no truck with Malthusian pessimism. Correctly farmed and free from the increasingly heavy cost of servicing the national debt, the land could yield an abundance. Poor rates were the symptom not the cause of the nation's financial difficulties. In any case they represented only a small part of the fiscal burden borne by the nation:

> We hear loud outcries against the poor rates, the enormous poor rates, the all-devouring poor rates; but, what are the facts? Why, that, in Great Britain, six millions are paid in poor rates, seven million (or thereabouts) in tithes, and sixty millions to fund people, the army, placemen and the rest. And yet nothing of all this seems to be thought of but of the six millions. Even the six millions are, for the greater part, wages and not poor rates.
> (*Rural Rides, Collected Writings*, vol. 13, p. 100)

Further they represented the cost of assuming those paternal responsibilities for the poor that had laid the basis for the real liberty and familial harmony of Old England.

If the forces of venality set in motion by the Pitt System had corrupted the polity and bid fair to destroy the economic prosperity of the nation, they were also apparent in the religion of the established church. Just as the state was sustained by the fiscal fleecing of the nation, so the church played a comparable role by means of tithes and church rates. Just as the state was corrupted by pensioners and placemen, so the church was defiled by a parasitic hierarchy. And just as Cobbett juxtaposed an undefiled agrarian society and purified constitution to the 'The Thing', so he looked to a pure, rustic, authentic English Christianity that was to lead him to stress the need for a separation of church and state.

It led him too to a particular reading of the English Reformation and to a support for Catholic Emancipation in the 1820s. Thus he argued that during the Reformation England's parasitic Protestant Establishment had purveyed an anti-Catholicism whose purpose was to expropriate from the Catholic Church what had, at least in part, been used to furnish the charity that had been used to sustain the poor. The English Reformation 'despoiled the working classes of their patrimony; it tore from them that which nature and reason has assigned to them; it robbed them of that relief for the necessitous which was theirs by right imprescriptible and which has been confirmed to them by the law of the land' (*A History of the Protestant Reformation in England and Ireland, Collected Writings*, vol. 15, letter iv, para. 127). And, for Cobbett, what the Reformation had encompassed in the sixteenth century, another parasitic parson, a 'check-breeding Parson, an 'impudent and illiterate parson', in proposing the abolition of poor relief, sought to effect some three centuries later.

Given his focus on and conception of 'The Thing', Cobbett's explanation of working-class impoverishment inevitably prioritized the political. In consequence, Cobbett distanced himself, if sympathetically, from those popular protests that focused on the role of industrialists and capitalist farmers. Indeed in post Napoleonic War articles in the *Political Register*, such as his 'Address to Journeymen and Labourers', (1816), and his 'Letter to the Luddites (1816), Cobbett sought to dissipate the antagonism which was being expressed towards employers in a period of falling wages and rising unemployment. In the 'Address' he opined that 'when labourers find their wages reduced they should take time to reflect on the real cause before they fly upon their employers, who are in many cases, in as great, or greater, distress, than themselves' (*Collected Writings*, vol. 8, p. 4). Similarly, in his 'Letter' to those who had reacted to their impoverishment by machine-breaking, while he accepted that such action must have been provoked by some 'faults and follies' on the employers' side, 'I think that we shall see that those circumstances that appear to you to have arisen from their avarice, have arisen from their want of the means, more than from their want of inclination to afford you a competence in exchange for your labour.'

> It is not machinery; it is not improvements in machinery; it is not extortions on the part of bakers, butchers and millers and farmers and corn dealers, and cheese and butter sellers [to which] you ought to attribute your present great and cruel sufferings; but wholly and solely to the great burden of taxes, co-operating with the bubble of paper money.
> ('Letter to the Luddites', *Collected Writings*, vol. 8, pp. 19, 27)

As Cobbett had predicted in *Paper Against Gold* (1815), that bubble had burst in the post-Napoleonic period as the government struggled to create the conditions necessary for the restoration of cash payments by the Bank of England, with price deflation precipitating general economic depression and mass unemployment. This was the awful legacy and, for Cobbett, the inevitable nemesis, of the English system of finance which Pitt had created. Yet if nemesis manifested itself most obviously in the economic sphere, its origins were nonetheless political.

For Cobbett, then, working-class impoverishment was the consequence of a political system that had been corrupted by the manner in which the revolutionary and Napoleonic wars had been financed. Its causes were politically rooted; rooted in the political decisions to suspend cash payments in 1797, in the determination to service a rapidly expanding national debt by recourse to indirect taxation and further borrowing, and in the deflationary decision to restore gold payments once again in 1819. The agents of corruption were those whose material interests were integrated with the political system that had enriched them, and who used the power that had been given them to bend that system to their purposes. The Cobbettian demonology included pensioners, placemen, boroughmongers and tax-eaters, not employers, capitalists, masters and machine owners. The oppressors of labour were defined by reference to the part they played in the drama of Old Corruption. In the final analysis it was 'The Thing' not industrial capitalism that had made the many poor.

Inevitably, then, the solution to the material distress of the labouring classes lay in the political sphere:

> Here it is Gentlemen, that you see the real cause of all the calamities that have fallen upon our country. You have seen these dangers creep up upon us by slow degrees, but you have seen their pace to be steady. They have never stopped, they keep gathering about us; and he is a feeble man who expects any remedy, 'till the great cause of the evil be removed, that is to say until there shall take place a radical reform of the Commons' House of Parliament.
> ('Address to Journeymen and Labourers', *Collected Writings*, vol. 8, p. 3)

To rid the country of Old Corruption, to purify the constitution, to banish food riots, to restore stability to the currency, to reconstruct the economy and society on solid agrarian foundations, to replace the money juggler with the yeoman farmer, and tea with beer, and to exorcise the Malthusian incubus, it was merely necessary to extend the franchise; an extension which Cobbett came to believe should encompass all rate payers. Other radicals such as Henry Hunt and George Cartwright might press the case in terms of the rights of Englishmen, but, for Cobbett, an extension of the franchise was essential to destroy 'The Thing' and all its appurtenances. In this and other respects Cobbett's position was nearer to that of Bolingbroke and the eighteenth-century English country party tradition than it was to the mainstream of English platform radicalism.

Cobbett's political radicalism left its most marked imprint on popular consciousness in the immediate postwar period, when the circulation of the *Twopenny Trash* was at its height and when his pamphlets sold by the tens of thousands. It was to be disseminated too in many of the 'unstamped' papers of the early 1830s, but by that date its empirical basis had been profoundly weakened. Thus even before the war financial and administrative reforms had begun 'to reduce the accuracy of the critique of Old Corruption' and, after the war, there was a period of substantial retrenchment which saw gross public expenditure fall from £112.9 million in 1815 to £55.5 million a decade later. As early as 1810 a Parliamentary Committee had concluded that sinecures were an unacceptable means of rewarding past and present public service and, thereafter, the numbers were substantially reduced. The early nineteenth century saw a similar diminution in the cost of civil pensions and 'economical administration' became the order of the day, both before and after the ending of the war. What all this served to do was to weaken the potency and persuasiveness of Cobbettian political radicalism, while at the same time the hearts and minds of significant sections of the working class were won over to the ideas of those anti-capitalist and socialist writers who located the causes of labour's impoverishment in the economic sphere and saw the agents of that impoverishment as those who wielded economic power.

It is ironic that when Cobbett finally made it to the House of Commons it was as a representative of Oldham because his political economy was characterized by an incomprehension of those developments which, in the early nineteenth century, were bringing industrial capitalism to birth in Britain. In so far as these developments were recognized, it was as another source, or consequence, of political corruption and as a threat to his pre-industrial ideal. Thus commerce was viewed as a major cause of our national decline, corrupting public policy so that 'upon every occasion, the question has been not what is just but what is expedient, the expediency turning solely upon the interests of commerce'. Further, it had 'assembled men together in large bodies, which never fails to enervate the mind and produce an effeminacy of taste and manners, not to mention numerous vices, which now disgrace this country' ('Perish Commerce', *Collected Writings*, vol. 4, p. 346). Per contra, reversing the process of commercialization and urbanization would permit the re-emergence of rural virtues and 'more hale and stout sort of men' (*ibid.*, p. 374.) of a kind that only a rural economy could produce. Cobbett's critique of nascent industrial capitalism, with its reference to effeminacy, corruption, luxury, vice and idleness, was rendered in the eighteenth-century language of civic virtue and not that of nineteenth-century anti-capitalism. In this regard, it is as poignant as it is significant that just before he died he was carried around his farm to view one final time the beauties of rural England and to observe the state of his crops.

BIBLIOGRAPHY

The Collected Social and Political Writings of William Cobbett, ed. N. Thompson and D. Eastwood, 16 vols (1998).

Observations on the Emigration of Dr. Priestley (1794; *Collected Writings*).

A Bone to Gnaw for the Democrats (1795; *Collected Writings*, vol. 1, pp. 37–52).

A New Year's Gift to the Democrats (1796; *Collected Writings*, vol. 1, pp. 85–113).

Porcupine's Gazette (1797; *Collected Writings*, vol. 1, pp. 142–63).

The Rush-light (1800; *Collected Writings*, vol. 1, pp. 191–208).

Priestley's Charity Sermon for Poor Emigrants (1801; *Collected Writings*, vol. 1, pp. 209–11).

Letters to the Right Honourable Henry Addington (1802; *Collected Writings*, vol. 3, pp. 212–53).

'Perish Commerce!', *Political Register* (November/December 1807; *Collected Writings*, vol. 4. pp. 343–96).

'Address to Journeymen and Labourers', *Political Register* (November 1816; *Collected Writings*, vol. 8, pp. 1–17).

'Letter to the Luddites', *Political Register* (November 1816; *Collected Writings*, vol. 8, pp. 18–32).

A History of the Protestant Reformation in England and Ireland (1824–7; *Collected Writings*, vol. 15).
Rural Rides (1830; *Collected Writings*, vols 13–15).
Cobbett's Manchester Lectures in Support of Fourteen Reform Propositions (1832; *Collected Writings*, vol. 11).

Further Reading
Cole, G.D.H., *The Life of William Cobbett* (1924).
Dyck, Ian, *William Cobbett and Rural Popular Culture* (Cambridge, 1992).
Green, Daniel, *Great Cobbett, the Noblest Agitator* (1983).
Hazlitt, W., *The Spirit of the Age* (1825).
Nattrass, L., *William Cobbett, the Politics of Style* (Cambridge, 1995).
Osborne, John, *William Cobbett. His Thought and Times* (New Brunswick, New Jersey, 1966).
Pearl, M., *William Cobbett. A Bibliographical Account of his Life and Times* (Oxford, 1953).
Schweitzer, Karl and John Osborne, *Cobbett and his Times* (Leicester, 1990).
Smith, Olivia, *The Politics of Language, 1791–1819* (Cambridge, 1984).
Spater, George, *William Cobbett, the Poor Man's Friend*, 2 vols (Cambridge, 1982).
Spence, Peter, *The Birth of Romantic Radicalism, War, Popular Politics and English Radical Reformism, 1800–1815* (Aldershot, 1996).
Williams, Raymond, *William Cobbett* (Oxford, 1983).
Wilson, David, *Paine and Cobbett, the Transatlantic Connection* (Kingston, Ontario, 1988).

Noel Thompson

COBDEN, Richard (1804–65)

Cobden was born near Midhurst, Sussex on 3 June 1804, and died of bronchitis in London on 2 April 1865. His father was a small farmer who managed his affairs badly and was forced to sell his farm in 1814 (Cobden later bought back the farm and presented it to his family). His mother then opened a village shop, which became the family's principal source of income. Neither Cobden's background, nor his formal education (in so far he received any at Bowes Hall, to which his parents in all good hope and faith sent him), helped him much in later life; he was largely a man of self-education, who devoted his few spare hours in a working life that started at the age of fifteen to reading and study. Cobden emphasized the importance of education for the commonwealth throughout his life, and actively turned to its improvement in his later years in parliament.

In 1828 Cobden started a calico-printing business in Manchester with two partners. This was a daring step: calico-printing needed a large advance of capital and long storage of materials. The economy was at the time gravely depressed, and became even worse in 1829. But Cobden managed to survive, paid his debts, and within a few years turned his business into a thriving concern.

Once financial support was guaranteed for him and his family, Cobden lost interest in making money for its own sake and turned to politics. He produced no major books, but instead diffused his ideas through a long series of pamphlets and speeches, in parliament and at public gatherings. His first pamphlets, *England, Ireland and America* (1835) and *Russia* (1836), expressed his great faith in free trade as a means of causing nations to prosper, and of preventing the horrors of war. Cobden argued violently against a British political outlook that saw British interests everywhere on the globe, even where there were none in fact. For a 'practical businessman' like Cobden, the politics of privileging trade with the colonies over trade with other countries, for example, and of maintaining high tariffs to pay for the Royal Navy as a means of protecting British commerce, had the detrimental consequence of excluding potential markets elsewhere. It could not be expected that other countries would enthusiastically buy British goods when their own commerce was restricted by British policies. However, said Cobden, a removal of trade barriers might make foreign markets more sympathetic to British products.

Another of Cobden's arguments for the removal of trade barriers emphasized the detrimental effects of taxes on imports on the competitiveness of British manufactures. Without tariffs, raw materials could be imported more cheaply, and hence the produce of British manufacturers would be more competitive on the international markets. Cobden's main argument against trade barriers was that they disrupted the smooth functioning of markets.

Such arguments added up to a sort of 'common sense' political economy, in which *le doux commerce* would automatically produce the most desirable outcome for all, not only in Britain, but worldwide. Cobden consistently argued against the disruptive effects of indirect taxation, and favoured direct taxation instead. Cobden's ideal government was a 'night-watch state' that abstained from interference in the markets as much as possible, and limited its task to the well-ordering of markets (for example by fighting against monopolies). Cobden's support for the Bank Act of 1844, that tied the issuing of paper money to the amount of gold bullion, shows this same argument, as does his introduction to Michel Chevalier's tract *On the Probable Fall of the Value of Gold* (1859), on the effects of Californian and Australian gold discoveries. Refraining from commenting on intricate academic definitions, he gave his advice to the House of Commons committee on paper money 'as a merchant and manufacturer', and favoured a government politicy that 'would allow the operations of the exchange to work tranquil without ever occasioning any shock to trade and commerce'.

Cobden's secular, cosmopolitan belief in the beneficial role of free trade would find its outlet in the Anti-Corn Law League's campaign for the repeal of the Corn Laws from the end of the 1830s onwards. With his close friend John BRIGHT, Cobden pursued this goal with unabated zeal. Corn prices had been protected and regulated long before 1815, but in the aftermath of the Napoleonic Wars the Corn Laws were explicitly installed to protect producers' interests. Imports of corn were only permitted after the price of corn in Britain had risen above a certain ceiling. The laws immediately provoked heavy protests, which were ignored by landowners who put their own interests first. It is highly doubtful the Corn Laws were ever effective in shielding the domestic market from continental corn, but the laws were generally considered to make corn prices much more volatile and hence to disturb the smooth functioning of markets.

Cobden was one of the seven founders of the Anti-Corn Law League in 1838. He had stood for parliament the previous year, unsuccessfully, but was elected MP for Stockport in 1841 and at once carried his campaign into the House of Commons. The Tory prime minister, Sir Robert Peel, eventually forced through the repeal of the Corn Law in 1896, against the wishes of a major faction of his own party. The League's role in this repeal has been questioned historically. However, the importance of the League in the development of a British politics and ideology emphasizing free trade as the universal means to prosperity is unquestioned. Even though British politics had emphasized the importance of free trade before the 1840s, the argument had been made on the basis of reciprocity in trade relations, rather than in a unilateral defence of free trade as such. In the notion of reciprocity, that had been defended most forcefully by William HUSKISSON, the notion of 'British interests' was always present. In Cobden's unilateral defence of free trade, reciprocity was not the issue. The emphasis was rather on the peaceful congregation of men that would emerge out of trade. Peel essentially shared with Cobden the idea of free trade as the natural order of society, but in contrast with Cobden, Peel gave this idea a theological twist. For the Tory Peel, it was no longer the vested institutes of Old Britain, like the Anglican church and the landed interest, that secured the natural order of things, but the providential order of the market. This Cobden–Peel belief in free trade as an expression of the natural order in society would become the trade mark of Victorian foreign policy.

By the time of his death, Cobden was seen as a patriot and politician of the same stature as Peel, and his name was venerated on the continent as that of a great statesman. After his death, the first chair in political economy at Owen's College (held by Stanley JEVONS from 1866 until his resignation in 1876) was named after him. The Cobden Club, set up in 1866, was devoted to the defence and diffusion of his ideas. The Manchester School of political economy became a brand name for free trade and *laissez-faire*, and the word 'Cobdenism' was equally identified with a defence of free trade, peace and international cooperation. His name is also attached to the British–French commercial treaty of 1860 that he negotiated with his friend Michel Chevalier. The negotiation of this was his only official post; despite his great popularity, he never held high office.

BIBLIOGRAPHY
England, Ireland, and America (1835).
Russia: by a Manchester manufacturer (1836).
'Preface' to M. Chevalier, *On the Probable Fall of the Value of Gold* (1859).
(with W.E. Gladstone, J. Bright et al.) *Alarming results of the non-reciprocity system of Free-Trade, promoted by Messrs. Gladstone, Cobden, Bright, and their supporters, the cause of social evils and the high rates of interest* (1865).
The Political Writings of Richard Cobden, ed. L. Mallet (1878).
The American Diaries of Richard Cobden, ed. E.H. Cawley (Princeton, 1952).
The European diaries of Richard Cobden, 1846–1849, ed. M. Taylor (Aldershot, 1994).
The Political and Economic works of Richard Cobden (1995).

Further Reading
Kadish, A. (ed.), *The Corn Laws. The Formation of Popular Economics in Britain*, 6 vols (1996).
Ashworth, H., *Recollections of Richard Cobden, M.P. and the Anti-Corn-Law League* (1876).
Axon, W.E.A.,*Cobden as a Citizen: A Chapter in Manchester History* (1907).
Fay, C.R., *The Corn Laws and Social England* (Cambridge, 1932).
Grampp, W.D., *The Manchester School of Economics* (Stanford, California, 1960).
Hinde, W., *Richard Cobden: A Victorian Outsider* (New Haven, Connecticut, 1989).
Howe, A., *Free trade and Liberal England, 1846–1946* (Oxford, 1997).
McCord, N., *The Anti-Corn Law League 1838–1846* (1968).
Morley, J. *The Life of Richard Cobden* (1881).
Read, D., *Cobden and Bright: A Victorian Political Partnership* (1967).

Harro Maas

CODDINGTON, Alan (1941–82)

Coddington was born in Doncaster on 27 November 1941, and died in London 8 June

1982. He was educated at Archbishop Holgate's Grammar School in York, and then read physics at Leeds University (BSc, 1963). He taught mathematics for a year at his old school, and then turned his attention to economics. Supported first by a Sir Ellis Hunter Scholarship and then a Sir Ellis Hunter Fellowship at the newly founded University of York, he worked on the theory of bargaining under the supervision of Alan Peacock and John Williamson (DPhil, 1966). His thesis was published as *Economic Theories of the Bargaining Process* (1968), with an introduction by G.L.S. SHACKLE, who had been the external examiner.

In 1966 Coddington became an assistant lecturer in economics at Queen Mary College, University of London, where he spent the whole of his academic life. He initially taught mathematical economics, but progressively focussed his teaching on his developing research interest in macroeconomics, particularly the legacy of KEYNES, and methodology. He was promoted to lecturer in 1967, senior lecturer in 1975, reader in 1977 and professor in 1980. He had a fruitful year (1974–5) free from teaching as Hallsworth Fellow in Political Economy at the University of Manchester. The articles developed there formed the basis of the work for which he is best known: *Keynesian Economics: The Search for First Principles* (1983).

Coddington worked out many of his ideas by talking to his fellow economists. He was a softly spoken, courteous interlocutor, but his uncompromising logic demanded careful and accurate thought. He enjoyed writing on economic topics for a wider audience, in *The Guardian* and *New Society*, and he was a successful broadcaster. Among other interests, he was a gifted jazz pianist and lover of football and of Italy.

Coddington's work had three main strands: the theory of bargaining, various aspects of environmental economics and the development of twentieth-century economic thought. Underlying his work in all these areas, right from the beginning of his career until its untimely end, was a concern for the methodology underlying economics. A common thread was how economics might deal with the uncertainty which the real-world economy presented. We see this first in his exploration of bargaining, a field which had concentrated on strategy within a static framework or games that could be played to the end with a single set of instructions. These theories did not allow for changes in expectations about the other bargainer's decision rule, and thus could embody persistent mistakes about these rules. Coddington's theory, following Cross (1964, 1965), analyses the process of action and reaction through which the bargain unfolds. Among the many possible paths that such a process may take, he chose to analyse the one which imposes consistency between expectations and actions over time, in which only fulfilled expectations leave the bargainer's actions unchanged. Mistaken expectations are thus corrected. A unification of the Cross and Coddington approaches has been proposed (Carling, 1977).

For Coddington, theory had to be useful, but the appropriate translation of economic theory to applied work was itself a subject for his lively mind. He wrote on environmental issues, where limited information and time-consistency again played important roles, and on the role of economics in policy making generally. He produced a fine critique (1973) of the influential work of Wilfred Beckerman on the environmental effects of economic growth. But it is for his work in the development of twentieth-century economic thought and its methodological foundations that Alan Coddington is best known. His coverage of modern economic thought included Friedman (1975a, 1979), Hahn (1975a), HICKS (1979), Leijonhufvud (1974), Malinvaud (1978), Shackle (1975b) and of course Keynes (1974, 1976, 1979, 1982, 1983). These articles began with a review of positive economics (1975a), in which Coddington identified the principles on which this approach stood and argued that if these principles were rigorously applied, the theory would be stultified and useless. He denied the possibility of value-free economics and made the observation that the positivist criterion of theory-acceptance – congruence with (variously) evidence, facts, experience, or observation – is far from satisfactory, as these terms do not refer to the same thing, nor is appeal to any or all of them objective, as positivists hope, for all are inescapably theory-laden.

In the same year, in a review of Shackle's *Epistemics and Economics* (1975b), Coddington confronted the problem of imperfect knowledge at the core of Shackle's thinking. He distinguished between the recognition of deficient knowledge and the use of knowledge-surrogates (conjectures, expectations, etc.) and gives the useful insight that the theory of probability conflates these. But deficient foresight worried him: he later argued (1982) that Keynes's appeal to uncertainty was opportunistic, in that he used it selectively, to free the investment decision from current circumstances; that is, from current income. But used generally, it would destroy the possibility of doing theory.

He had a similar anxiety about Keynes's theory of speculation, calling it the economics of pure chaos (1983: 81). On liquidity preference more generally he accepted Hicks's argument that liquidity preference and loanable funds were equivalent and accordingly treated Keynes's argument as suspect. His article on Hicks (1979) is a scrupulously fair-minded evaluation of Hicks's contribution to Keynesian theory, scaled down from a projected book which unfortunately was not published.

These last two works found their way into Coddington's posthumously published *Keynesian Economics: The Search for First Principles* (1983), which begins with two new essays. In 'The Keynesian Dichotomy', he is sceptical of the proposition that Keynes integrated monetary and value theory, as the latter had claimed. Rather, Coddington argues, Keynes used a dichotomy between the mechanisms by which price and output are determined as a simplifying device, just as the quantity theory had used a dichotomy between real and monetary variables to simplify. The following chapter tries to restore the cyclical context of Keynes's analysis.

But it is the final chapter of the book (first published in 1976) which gives the most original insights. Coddington's aim is to analyse three types of interpretations of Keynes and the different challenges they pose to the mainstream reductionist method. The interpreters – the fundamentalists, hydraulicists and reconstituted reductionists – are distinguished by their own methodologies. The fundamentalists posed the strongest challenge, as they reject static equilibrium theorising altogether – unlike Keynes himself – and see Keynes's work as just the beginning of a wholesale reconstruction of economics. The 'hydraulicists' – Coddington's coinage for those who saw the macroeconomic system as flows of income which could be manipulated by fiscal policy – undermined reductionism in another way, by not giving a special place to prices, which for reductionists constitute the incentive or signal for individual choice. Finally, Coddington shows that the third group, led by Clower (1965) and Leijonhufvud (1968) try to accommodate Keynes's involuntary unemployment and other malfunctions by abandoning equilibrium, allowing individual choice to be preserved. This approach was, at the time, a rare case of ascribing disputes among economists to their methodology. Unfortunately, Coddington left the stage just as development along these lines was beginning to proceed rapidly.

BIBLIOGRAPHY
'A Theory of the Bargaining Process: A Comment [on Cross (1965)]', *American Economic Review* (1966), vol. 56. no. 3, pp. 522–30 (Cross's reply, pp. 530–33).
Theories of the Bargaining Process (1968).
'Positive Economics', *Canadian Journal of Economics and Political Science* (1972), vol. 5, no. 1, pp. 1–16.

'Professor Beckerman in Perspective', *Environment and Planning* Series A (1973), vol. 5, no. 6, pp. 667–72.

'What *Did* Keynes Mean?', *Challenge: The Magazine of Economic Affairs* (1974a), vol. 17, no. 5.

'The Economics of Conservation', in A. Warren and F. B. Goldsmith (eds), *Conservation in Practice* (New York, 1974b, pp. 453–64).

'The Rationale of General Equilibrium Theory', *Economic Inquiry* (1975a), vol. 13, no. 4, pp. 539–58; repr. in D.A. Walker (ed.), *Equilibrium* (Cheltenham, 2000, pp. 408–27).

'The Creaking Semaphore and Beyond: A Consideration of Shackle's *Epistemics and Economics*', *British Journal for the Philosophy of Science* (1975b), vol. 26, pp. 151–63.

'Keynesian Economics: The Search for First Principles', *Journal of Economic Literature* (1976), vol. 14, no. 4, pp. 1258–73; repr. in B. Snowdon and H.R. Vane (eds), *A Macroeconomic Reader* (1997, pp. 36–54). (See also 1983, ch. 6.)

'The Theory of Unemployment Reconsidered' (a review of E. Malinvaud), *Journal of Economic Literature* (1978), vol. 16, no. 3, pp. 1012–18.

'Friedman's Contribution to Methodological Controversy', *British Review of Economic Issues* (1979a), vol. 2, no. 4.

'Hicks' Contribution to Keynesian Economics', *Journal of Economic Literature* (1979b), vol. 17, no. 3, pp. 970–88; repr. in J.C. Wood and R.N. Woods (eds), *Sir John Hicks: Critical Assessments* (1989, pp.187–208). (See also 1983, ch. 5.)

'Deficient Foresight: A Troublesome Theme in Keynesian Economics', *American Economic Review* (1982), vol. 72, June, pp. 480–7; repr. in G.K. Shaw (ed.), *The Keynesian Heritage* (Aldershot, 1988, pp. 67–74). (See also 1983, ch. 4.)

Keynesian Economics: The Search for First Principles (1983).

Further Reading

Carling, A.H., 'The Unified Solution of the Cross/Coddington Model of the Bargaining Process', *Public Choice* (1977), vol. 32, pp. 11–38.

Clower, R.W., 'The Keynesian Counterrevolution: A Theoretical Appraisal', in F.H. Hahn and F.P.R. Brechling (eds), *The Theory of Interest Rates* (1965, pp. 103–25).

Cross, J.G., 'A Theory of the Bargaining Process, PhD Thesis, Princeton University (1964).

———, 'A Theory of the Bargaining Process', *American Economic Review* (1965), vol. 55, March, pp. 67–94.

Leijonhufvud, A., *On Keynesian Economics and the Economics of Keynes* (Oxford, 1968).

Victoria Chick

COHEN, Ruth Louisa (1906–91)

Cohen was born in London on 10 November 1906, and died in Cambridge on 27 July 1991. She was educated at Newnham College, Cambridge, where she read economics and studied with Richard KAHN, graduating with a first in 1929. After winning the Adam Smith Prize in 1930, she spent two years in the USA, at Stanford University and Cornell University, as a Commonwealth Fund Fellow. Upon her return to England in 1932, she became a research officer at the Oxford Agricultural Economics Research Institute, which published her *History of Milk Prices* (1936). Cohen 'was a militant agnostic but practised all the civic virtues of the large middle-class family from which she came' (Harcourt 1991). In the mid-1930s, these civic virtues led the Cohen family to turn their house near Berkhamsted into a halfway house for Jewish refugees and to finance the escape of several entire families, with Ruth spending all her spare time on this cause for several years (Kennedy 1991).

While at the Oxford Agricultural Economics Research Institute, Cohen engaged in a debate with the future Nobel laureate Ronald Coase about economic dynamics. In 1932, the Report of the Reorganisation Commission for Pigs and Pig Product had recommended intervention by marketing boards to dampen the observed four-year cycle in pig and bacon production, which it explained according to the 'cobweb' model (previously developed by Mordecai Ezekiel) that producers have static expectations of the production costs and output prices that will prevail from the production decision to marketing (see Cohen 1934). The amplitude of cycles around the price equilibrium would diminish, stay constant or increase, according to whether demand was more, equal or less elastic than supply. Coase and Fowler (1935) questioned the assumption of static expectations, insisting that producers try to forecast prices, and argued that even granting the assumptions of the cobweb model, it would predict a two-year cycle, rather than the observed four-year cycle. Cohen and Barker (1935), while joining Coase and Fowler, in rejecting some policy recommendations of the report, defended the report's use of the ration of corn prices to hog prices as a measure of production incentive, and constructed a numerical example of production incentives that would yield a four-year cycle. Coase and Fowler were unpersuaded (see Cloutier and Ruth 1997).

In 1939, Cohen's *The Economics of Agriculture* was published in the Cambridge Economic Handbooks series, and she was elected to a fellowship and lectureship at Newnham. The Second World War took her to the Ministry of Food (1939–42), and then the Board of Trade (1942–5). At the Ministry of Food, she took the lead in establishing the free provision of milk in all schools, a programme that was ended in the 1970s by Margaret Thatcher, then Minister of Education.

Cohen returned to Newnham at the end of the war, and was appointed as a university lecturer in the Faculty of Economics and Politics. 'Lecturing was definitely not her forte' (Harcourt 1991), and, although she continued teaching and writing, she found her metier as principal of Newnham from 1954 until her retirement in 1972. She was a determined, energetic and successful administrator, although 'often impatient, occasionally abrasive' (Edmonds 1991). Strikingly open, direct, and unstuffy in her dealings with everyone, including students, 'she chain-smoked through meetings and beat all-comers for speed at eating at High Table' (Harcourt 1991), and inspired widespread affection among colleagues and pupils.

After the Second World War, Cohen's publications dealt primarily with the regulation of mergers and monopolies (Cohen 1949, 1953). However, her greatest influence came not through her own writings, but from her participation in a Cambridge seminar discussing the paper later published by Joan ROBINSON as 'The Production Function and the Theory of Capital' (1954). Cohen pointed out the multiple solution possibility that later became famous, as reswitching of techniques, in the capital theory controversies between followers of Robinson in Cambridge, UK, and neoclassical economists at MIT in Cambridge, Massachusetts. The significance of 'the Ruth Cohen curiosum' was only gradually recognized (Harcourt 1972: 124–5; Johnson 1978). Consider two techniques A and B, each with a particular time-profile of inputs, for producing one unit of output. If a switch point such one would choose technique A at an interest rate higher than the critical value, and technique B at an interest rate lower than the critical value, technique B would be considered more capital-intensive. But suppose that there is another critical value, at a still lower interest rate, from which one would switch back to technique A (reswitching). It cannot then be concluded whether A or B represents a larger quantity of capital. If it cannot be decided whether the amount of capital is more or less, then the marginal product of capital can hardly be derived by differentiating output with respect to the amount of capital. Ironically, Cohen, an applied economist specializing in the down-to-earth subject of milk prices, achieved renown for an abstract point in formal theory.

After retiring, Cohen sat for Newnham Ward as a Labour member on the Cambridge City Council from 1973–87, warding off extravagant spending projects as chair of the finance committee from 1980–6. As a member of the development sub-committee, she insisted on visiting the sites of all planning applications even after she was confined to a wheelchair: 'her electrically-powered chariot became a familiar – and dangerous – sight in Cambridge' (Harcourt 1991).

BIBLIOGRAPHY

'Agricultural Reorganisation and Price Control', *Economic Journal* (1934), vol. 44, September, pp. 434–52.

(with J.D. Barker) (1935) 'The Pig-Cycle: A Reply', *Economica* (1935), new series, vol. 2, November, pp. 408–21.

The History of Milk Prices: An Analysis of the Factors Affecting the Prices of Milk and Milk Products (Oxford, 1936).

The Economics of Agriculture (1939).

'Milk Policy and Milk Prices', *Economic Journal* (1939), vol. 49, March, pp. 79–90.

'The New British Law on Monopoly', *American Economic Review* (1949), vol. 39, March, pp. 485–90.

'The Reports of the Commission on Monopolies and Restrictive Practices', *Economic Journal* (1953), vol. 63, March, pp. 196–209.

Further Reading

Cloutier, L.M. and Matthias, R. 'The "Pig-Cycle" Out of the "Cobweb": A Revisit of R.H. Coase's Contribution to Economic Dynamics', presented to History of Economics Society, Charleston, South Carolina (1997).

Coase, R.H. and Fowler, R.F. 'Bacon Production and the Pig-Cycle in Great Britain', *Economica* (1935), new series, vol. 2, May, pp. 142–67.

Edmonds, S.M., 'Economist with Milky Vision: Obituary of Ruth Cohen', *The Guardian* (1991), 3 August.

Harcourt, G.C., *Some Cambridge Controversies in the Theory of Capital* (Cambridge, 1991).

——, 'Obituary: Ruth Cohen', *The Independent* (1991), 31 July.

Johnson, H.G., 'Ruth Cohen: A Neglected Contributor to Contemporary Capital Theory', in E.S. Johnson and H.G. Johnson, *The Shadow of Keynes* (Chicago, 1978, pp. 167–72).

Kennedy, C., 'Letter: Ruth Cohen', *The Times* (1991), 19 August.

Robinson, J., 'The Production Function and the Theory of Capital', *Review of Economic Studies* (1954), vol. 21, no. 2, pp. 81–106.

Robert W. Dimand
Marie-Thérèse Maxwell Awadalla

COKE, Roger (*c.*1626–*c.*1703)

Coke was born around 1626, probably at Thorington in Suffolk, and died around 1703. He was the third son of Henry Coke of Thorington and grandson of the famous jurist Sir Edward Coke. He was educated at Cambridge but seems to have taken no exams, and wrote a treatise against HOBBES's *Leviathan* titled *Justice Vindicated from the False Focus put upon it by Thomas White, Gent., Mr Thomas Hobbs, and Hugo Grotius* (1660). He wrote a number of political and historical works including *A Detection of the Court and State of England during the four last Reigns and the Interregnum* (1694). He went into trade but seemed to have been less successful. Bad business speculations brought him into financial distress, and during his last years he appears to have been living on a small annuity paid by his family.

Coke seems to have been a capable mathematician, and he took a great interest in contemporary statistical works. To this extent he belongs to a generation of economists in England including Sir William PETTY, Gregory KING, Charles DAVENANT and others who are sometimes referred to as the 'political arithmeticians'. As a writer on economic issues, Coke is mainly known for two works of a more practical nature, *A Discourse of Trade* (1670) and *England's Improvement* (1675). He also published *Reflections upon the East-India and Royal African Companies* (1695), in which he discussed a popular theme of the period, the extent to which great chartered or joint-stock companies were beneficial, or not, for the country. He seems to have been quite doubtful whether they did provide benefits.

In the two first works mentioned above, Coke took as his point of departure a prejudice which was widespread during the 1670s, namely that England was losing out in competition with other trading nations, especially France. The main remedy for decaying trade was to liberalize it, he argued. Hence he denounced the closed trading corporations and maintained that they should be free to entry for all English citizens. He argued also for the repeal of the laws of naturalization, which in practice hindered the free importation of foreign workers. Moreover, in contrast to many during this period – including Josiah CHILD – he was critical of the Navigation Acts, arguing that they only served the interest of a minority of tradesmen who kept the foreign trade as a monopoly to themselves. Well ahead of most at this time, Coke also argued for the free importation of raw material and of foreign manufactures. Such importation would lead to increased competition, but also to more 'plenty and cheapness', from which the poor especially would gain.

Coke belongs to a large group of English writers in the end of the seventeenth century who are difficult to place amongst the kind of conservative mercantilism which conventional scholarship have believed dominated the economic thinking of this period. As with most of his generation of writers, he was eager to point out the advantages of an increased foreign trade:

that Trade is now become the Lady, which in the present Age is more Courted and Celebrated than in any former by all Princes and Potentates of the World, and that deservedly too; For she acquires not her Domination by the Horrid and Rueful face of Warr, shoes footsteps leave ever behind them deep impression of misery, devastation, and poverty, but with the pleasant aspect of wealth and plenty of all things conducted to the benefit of Humane life and Society, accompanied with strength to defend her, in case any shall attempt to Ravish or Invade her.

(1670: 334)

Moreover, Coke thinks of 'trade' in a wider sense than we would perhaps do. Hence he defines trade as 'an Art of Getting, Preparing and Exchanging things Commodious for Humane Necessities and Convenience' (1670: 338). Hence Coke was prepared also to include some aspects of what we would call 'production' in his definition of trade. This too was typical of the position taken by most economic writers during this period. Hence, it is rather unfruitful to argue – as many have done – that seventeenth-century economic writers believed that only trade, not production, was fruitful and created a surplus. Coke and others would not have drawn such a clear distinction as did those later writers, including Adam SMITH, who formulated a distinct 'mercantile system' as a typical feature of seventeenth and early eighteenth-century economic thinking.

BIBLIOGRAPHY

Justice Vindicated from the False Focus put upon it by Thomas White, Gent., Mr Thomas Hobbs, and Hugo Grotius (1660).

A Discourse of Trade, In Two Parts (1670; repr. in L. Magnusson (ed.), *Mercantilism: Critical Concepts in the History of Economics*, vol. I, 1995).

England's Improvement. In two parts: in the former is discoursed how the Kingdom of England may be improves in strength, employment, wealth. In the latter is discoursed how the navigation of England may be increased (1675).

A Detection of the Court and State of England during the four last Reigns and the Interregnum (1694).

Reflections upon the East-India and Royal African Companies (1695).

Further Reading

Heckscher, E.F., *Mercantilism I–II* (1994).
Magnusson, L., *Mercantilism: The Shaping of Economic Language* (1994).

Lars Magnusson

COLE, George Douglas Howard
(1889–1959)

Cole was born in Cambridge on 25 September 1889, and died in London on 14 January 1959. He was educated at St Paul's School, London and Balliol College, Oxford, where he graduated with a first-class degree in greats (*literae humaniores*). He was a prize fellow of Magdalen College, Oxford in 1913. He was a reader in economics at Oxford from 1925–44, and a fellow of Nuffield College from 1939–44. From 1944–57 he was Chichele Professor of Social and Political Theory. He also served as chairman of the Fabian Society, which he had joined while still a student, from 1939–46 and again from 1948–50, and was the Society's president from 1952–9. In 1918 he married Margaret Postgate; together, he and Margaret COLE wrote three political works and twenty-nine detective stories.

Although a professional economist, Cole was less interested in economic theory than in political theory, especially guild socialism. He also wrote on industrial relations, labour history and comparative economic systems.

Guild socialism, which attempted to synthesize socialism and anarcho-syndicalism, was a specific form of representative democracy: functional pluralism. As Cole wrote in his *Guild Socialism Re-stated*, 'It follows that there must be, in the Society, as many separately elected groups of representatives as there are distinct essential groups of functions to be performed' (1920: 33). Each factory, workshop, mine and so on defines one such group, and so must have its own representative council and internal autonomy. The administration of an industry is to be a federation of such groups, and in some cases, a rather loose federation, though this would vary from industry to industry (and by time and place) according to convenience. Some industries will need considerable centralization, but there is a presumption for decentralization. These federations of factories or workshops are the guilds; they, in turn, federate themselves for the administration of industry as a whole (1920: 124). This federation is not simple, however: the guilds federate themselves to form an economic administrative body for each city or rural district; the regional administration is at once a federation of industries and of towns and districts; the national administration is at once a federation of industries and regions.

Moreover, this interlocking multiple federalism in industrial administration is a model for society and for the state or 'commune' as a whole. In a more ordinary federation, an individual is a citizen of only one or another of the constituent states or provinces. But this cannot be so in a functionally constituted society; the functional groups in society cut across one another, and an individual is a member at the same time of several of them. He or she is a worker in an industry, a resident of a town or district, a consumer of this and that. Each individual must be a citizen in each group, represented in each, and thus the society must be at once a federation of overlapping groups of many different kinds, with their own respective competencies and powers.

Thus, in addition to the guilds, there are other functional bodies concerned with economic administration. At the least, there are consumers' councils or boards for the public utilities and for other private consumption (1920: 87). There may be many such councils, perhaps one for each industry (1920: 93). At the level of town or district, region, and nation, the various functional bodies federate themselves to form a 'co-ordinating body'. This 'co-ordinating body', the 'commune', is the minimal state of the guild socialist society. The decision-taking body of the commune is a joint board of representatives from the guilds, the consumers' boards, and other functional or territorial bodies. The guilds (workers) and the consumers are roughly equally represented (1920: 125). The decision-making process of the communal council is majoritarian. In addition to the communal council, however, there is also a guilds congress at each level, local, regional, and national. The guilds congress is the joint council of the guilds. Like the communal council, it is a representative body with co-ordinating functions as among the guilds. It does not have powers which ordinary usage would attribute to the state, but it may appoint the guilds' representatives to the communal council; alternatively they may be appointed directly by the guilds.

The production of civic services (public goods) is also to be carried on by guild organizations, the civic guilds. Corresponding to each civic guild or major grouping of civic guilds is a specialized citizens' council, which is to be consulted in the administration of the civic services. The civic guilds and the specialized citizens' councils are represented (about equally) on the communal councils; the civic guilds are also represented on the guilds congress.

Consumers' councils have the power to consult with the guilds about the prices, quantities of output, and qualities of the consumers' goods which the guilds produce. These things are decided, in the first instance, by negotiation with the communal council arbitrating in case of impasse. The prices of intermediate goods are determined by direct bargaining between the guilds concerned, with arbitration to the guilds congress in the case of impasse and further arbitration by the communal council if the guilds congress cannot arrive at a decision. The determination of prices may lead to operating cross-subsidies, for, as Cole remarks, 'It might be considered desirable...to sell a particular commodity at...less than the natural price based on its cost of production' (1920: 143). This involves a system of direct lump-sum transfers among the guilds, to cover the costs of production of some goods for sale below their 'natural' prices. These transfers are decided like other economic magnitudes under guild socialism: by direct negotiations among the guilds with arbitration by the next, more inclusive body in the case of impasse. The allocation of investment is to be decided and financed in the same way (1920: 143–5) as are wage schedules.

The civic services are funded by direct transfers between the industrial and civic guilds (1920: 146). Appropriation for the civic guilds is simply another case of negotiated cross-subsidy. Material incentives would not be used: incomes were to be independent of the state of the market and workers were to be 'put 'on their honour' to do their best (1920: 88–9). Thus, we seem to see the Guilds Congress generating something in the nature of a central economic plan, by negotiation. The plan comprises prescriptions for outputs and prices by industries, for wages and cross-subsidies, investments and gross taxes, among other things. Negotiation impasses are arbitrated by the communal council, which must in any case ratify the result.

This blueprint for a new society can be, and has been, criticized for its complexity, as though it multiplied committees and councils for their own sake. Cole himself raised that point in later years. But it is useful in conveying what a society that is thoroughly decentralized by function might look like, and thus to convey the meaning of functional pluralism.

As a complex and seemingly complete picture of a future society, guild socialism can fairly be described as utopian. However, it was a response to real forces at work in society, in the labour movement, expressed in syndicalism and industrial unionism (Cole 1971: 52–3). Guild socialism was not to be established by legislation or revolutionary dictatorship but by 'encroaching control' (Carpenter 1973: 77–80), as industrial unions wrested more and more control from employers through strikes and other measures, so that the unions gradually transform themselves into national guilds.

In the 1920s, Cole wrote on unemployment and the remedy for it in ways that foreshadow KEYNES's *General Theory*, but without the systematic basis and the multiplier concept. As he turned to writing on economic planning, Cole continued to call for the representation of consumers, as well as workers, in the planning process. His idea of planning focused first on the provision of basic needs, to be supplied via a social dividend, with the allocation of other goods and services through the wage-price mechanism. Cole also continued to advocate a maximum of workers' control in a planned economy, and looked forward to a gradual transformation of a planned economy into something along guild socialist lines.

Although Cole had broken with the Fabian Society over guild socialism, he later rejoined it and led in its reconstitution. From the late 1930s Cole was chairman and later president of the Society. He continued other attempts to organize socialist organizations on a broader scale, and remained a 'loyal grouser' within the Labour Party. His movement from one position to another after he gave up guild socialism might seem to be a product of uncertainty or opportunism, but it was not. Cole's position was always Fabian socialist in a broad generic sense.

The distinctly Fabian combination of meliorism and radicalism explains what might otherwise be seen as inconsistency or indecision in Cole's commitments and work. During the First World War and until 1923 he supported guild socialism, with encroaching control as its key strategy. In the 1920s as something of a premature Keynesian, he supported central government expenditures to reduce unemployment. Later, he would follow the Labour Party to support nationalization and a form of economic planning. In between there were many zigs and zags. It is not simply that these proposals followed what seemed to be opportunities to push a certain socialist ideal or to make the condition of the working class less onerous. Rather, for a Fabian, the ability of the proposal to improve the life of the working class here and now was, in itself, a test of its soundness both as socialism and as economic theory. If guild socialism could not make working people better off and at the same time advance some sort of socialist vision in society, then there was something wrong with the socialist vision no less than with the specific policies.

Cole's socialism was a moral viewpoint based on a clear and rather old-fashioned humanistic philosophy. For Cole, values are objective, so that moral statements are at the same time statements of fact (Carpenter 1970: 229). The moral critique of capitalist society arises from a personalist conception of the human individual. As a person, possessed of a free creative will, each individual has an irreducible value. This leads Cole to individualism, since 'only individuals could be ethical ends' (Carpenter 1970: 223). These same values lead Cole to socialism, since the existence of classes is the greatest threat to the autonomy of the individual. The classless society becomes the necessary condition for real individualism. Immensely creative, possessed of the moral autonomy to choose socialism despite his bourgeois class origins, and of the moral backbone to live according to the values he espoused and make himself a servant of the working class, Cole was an extraordinary man who thought himself quite ordinary, and built his worldview around that belief in his own ordinariness.

BIBLIOGRAPHY
The World of Labour (1913).
Self-Government in Industry (1917).
Guild Socialism Re-Stated (1920).
The Next Ten Years in British Social and Economic Policy (1929).
British Working Class Politics, 1832–1914 (1941).
A Century of Co-operation (1946).
Post-War Condition of Britain (1956).
Socialist Thought, 4 vols (1953–8).

Further Reading
Carpenter, L.P., *G.D.H. Cole: An Intellectual Biography* (Cambridge, 1970).
Cole, M., *The Life of G.D.H. Cole* (1971).
McCain, R.A., 'Anarchy as a Norm of Social Choice', in R. Leitner and G. Sirkin (eds), *Economics of Public Choice* (New York, 1980).
Wolff, R.P., *In Defense of Anarchism* (New York, 1970).

Roger Ashton McCain

COLE, Margaret Isabel (1893–1980)

Cole was born Margaret Postgate in Cambridge on 6 May 1893, the eldest child of John Percival and Edith Postgate and granddaughter of the reformer John Postgate. She died in London on 7 May 1980. She was educated at Roedean School, and like her mother before her, attended Girton College, Cambridge where she received a first-class degree in classics (1914). Initially a classics mistress at St Paul's Girl's School in London, she was won over to socialism in reaction to the imprisonment of her brother, Raymond W. Postgate, as a conscientious objector during the First World War. In 1917, she joined the Fabian (later 'Labour') Research Department, centre of the emerging guild socialism movement around the economist G.D.H. COLE, whom she married in 1918. The couple played a crucial role in revitalizing the Fabian Society following the eclipse of guild socialism in the 1930s, and, through the foundation of the New Fabian Research Bureau, helped establish the empirical base for many of the reforms of the post-war Labour government under Atlee.

While remaining active in the Labour Research Department and raising three children, in 1925 Margaret Cole began teaching for the Workers' Educational Association as an extra-mural tutor in social and industrial history. After the Second World War, she became a successful journalist and book critic, member (1943–65) and alderman (1952–65) of London County Council with a special interest in educational issues, and from 1965–7 was a member of the Inner London Education Authority. She served first as honorary secretary (1939–62) and then, up to her death, as president of the Fabian Society. She was awarded the OBE in 1965, and made DBE in 1970.

Although Margaret Cole's main contributions have been to political biography and the history of the labour movement – *Beatrice Webb* (1945); *Story of Fabian Socialism* (1961); *Life of G.D.H. Cole* (1971) – she was involved in several joint book projects with her husband *Condition of Britain* (1937), wrote various pamphlets, partly in labour economics (such as *Rate for the Job*, 1946), and developed an interest in the political economy of fascism in the *New Economic Revolution* (1937). While entertaining passing communist sympathies, her conceptual outlook overall was that of a non-partisan socialist who, having witnessed the failure of the trades union movement in the wake of the 1926 general strike, saw the future for democratic change in educational reform and an information revolution brought forth by low-cost printing technology *(Books and the People*, 1938).

As a feminist with a life-long commitment to a marriage with a husband of misogynist tendencies who later in life became increasingly dependent on her care, her position was that of balance and compromise, perceptively foreseeing the cultural changes new methods of contraception would entail (*Marriage, Past and Present*, 1938), and campaigning for more part-time employment opportunities for women (*The Road to Success*, 1936). Her prolific career as an activist and author found between 1923 and 1948 a belletristic, though largely undistinguished, complement in a range of detective and other stories authored jointly with her husband as 'GDH and M' (for example, *Death of a Millionaire*, 1925), following a collection of early poems.

BIBLIOGRAPHY
Margaret Postgate's Poems (1918).
(with G.D.H. Cole) *The Death of a Millionaire* (1925).
The Road to Success: Twenty Essays on the Choice of a Career for Women (1936).
The New Economic Revolution (1937).
(with G.D.H. Cole) *The Condition of Britain* (1937).
Marriage, Past and Present (1938).
Books and the People (1938).
Beatrice Webb (1945).
The Rate for the Job (1946).
Growing Up Into Revolution: Reminiscences (1949).
The Story of Fabian Socialism (1961).
The Life of G.D.H. Cole (1971).
Further Reading
Becchio, G., 'Margaret Cole (1893–1980)', in R.W. Dimand, M.A. Dimand and E.L. Forget (eds), *A Biographical Dictionary of Women Economists* (Cheltenham, 2000).

Cole, G.D.H., *Guild Socialism Re-stated* (1920).
Vernon, B.D., *Margaret Cole, 1893–1980: A Political Biography* (1986).

Matthias Klaes

COLERIDGE, Samuel Taylor (1772–1834)

Coleridge was born 21 October 1772 in Ottery St Mary, Devon, the son of a parson. He died in London on 25 July 1834. He was educated at Christ's Hospital and then Jesus College, Cambridge. Although he was originally destined for a career in the church, while at Oxford he developed interests in radical politics and Unitarianism and resolved to reject the priesthood. At the end of 1793 he left Cambridge and came to London, where he enlisted as a trooper in the 15th Dragoons under a false name; he was said to be a poor horsemen, but his officers liked him. Recognized and identified by a friend early in 1794, he was discharged from the army and returned to Cambridge. On a chance visit to Oxford that year he first met Robert SOUTHEY, and the two men formed a close friendship. He left Cambridge without a degree at the end of 1794. In 1795 he married Sara Fricker, of Bristol; Southey married Sara's sister Edith a week later.

Coleridge now settled in Bristol, where he began to write full time and published a number of works of poetry, having already begun to publish while still at Cambridge. He also edited a short-lived journal, and preached occasionally at Unitarian chapels. Short of money, he moved to house at Nether Stowey, Somerset. He continued to write, although not all of his works met with success. However, an intellectual circle began to grow around Coleridge, including Robert Southey, Charles Lamb, William HAZLITT and William

Wordsworth, who lived nearby. It was during this period that several of his most famous poems including, 'Christabel', 'Kubla Khan' and 'The Ancient Mariner', were written, although the two former were not published until many years later. He also developed an interest in philosophy and began a study of the Platonists, beginning with Plotinus; as Hedley (2002) points out, there was a natural connection between Platonism, especially of the Cambridge variety, and Unitarianism.

In 1798 Southey came to the attention of the brothers Thomas and Josiah Wedgwood, who offered him an annuity of £150 in order that he could devote himself entirely to poetry and philosophical studies. In company with Wordsworth, Coleridge went to Germany, settling ultimately at Göttingen and taking up the study of Kant and the later German philosophers. Learning German quickly, he translated Schiller's *Wallenstein*; the translation was published in 1800 and was a flop, though it is now regarded as a masterpiece. He returned to England in 1799 and lived in London for a time, contributing a few articles to the *Morning Post* and *Morning Chronicle*, but these were not well-received and Coleridge's career as a journalist was soon over. In 1800 he moved to Keswick, Cumberland, where he suffered from ill-health and began treating himself with laudanum, soon becoming addicted. During the following years he produced little work, and a journey to Malta and Italy did not improve his health.

In 1816 Coleridge returned to London. His health improved, he now became very productive once more, publishing not only poetry but a number of thoughtful prose works that set out his political and social views, including *The Statesman's Manual* (1816) and *A Lay Sermon* (1817). His earlier work which had met with such a poor initial response had now become fashionable, and he was regarded as something of an icon by the younger generation of poets and intellectuals. By 1822, however, his poor health had returned, and his strength gradually failed. *On the Constitution of the Church and State* (1829) is perhaps his last notable work.

Coleridge considered economics in the light of more general critiques of social and political forces. In *On the Constitution of the Church and State*, he argued for a balance between forces to create a moderate society. His most developed thinking on economics comes in *A Lay Sermon*, which begins as a consideration of the economic crisis following the end of the Napoleonic Wars and goes on to consider the role of commerce in society more generally. As Morrow (1990) points out, he believed that the commercial spirit had become too prominent in society, and while commerce played a necessary role in society, it should not be a substitute for the 'moral personality' that must be central to any idea of statehood. Coleridge himself wrote that 'I feel assured that the Spirit of Commerce is itself capable of being at once counteracted by the Spirit of the State, to the advantage of both (1817: 147).

This led him to a view that the state had a role to play in the regulation of commerce, the end of which should be the improvement of the lot of the people as well as the stimulation of commerce itself. In *A Lay Sermon*, he argues for land reform in order to reduce the power of the landholders over the labourers, and criticizes the abuses of the poor laws that lead to able-bodied labourers being paid out of the poor rates to subsidize agricultural work, money that should go to the genuine poor. Like Southey, he urged the education of the poor. Like Samuel Egerton BRYDGES, he believes the one of the chief drains on the economy is the large number of unproductive workers: 'And if I were question, as to my opinion, respecting the ultimate cause of our liability to distresses like the present...I should not hesitate to answer – the vast and disproportionate number of men who are to be fed from the produce of the fields, on which they do not labour' (1817: 150). But although he advocates reform, he is not a radical in this sense. Ashton (1996) depicts him as caught to some extent between opposing forces, seeing the need for reform but rejecting the more radical solutions advanced by BENTHAM. Economic improvement was very necessary, but not at the expense of social and moral welfare.

Coleridge also advocated reform of the revenue and abolition of the lottery. On taxation, he believed that complaints about the level of taxation were misguided; it is not the amount that is taken in taxes that matters, it is the amount each of us has left in our pockets after taxation that counts. If the money we have left 'is sufficient to satisfy our wants and needs, then we have no cause to complain' (1817: 110). The injury caused by taxation, he said, came not from the amount of taxation but from 'the time or circumstances from which they are raised, or from the injudicious mode in which they are levied, or from the improper objects to which they are applied' (1817: 109).

He pointed out also that the money taken in taxes is spent on ships, clothing and weapons for soldiers and so on, and so goes back into the economy. However, it is incumbent upon government to spend tax revenues quickly and so put these back into circulation. If tax money is not spent quickly, then the national wealth is affected. Another problem, he believed, was the large numbers of people employed unproductively in the civil service, whose existences was in effect paid for by the productive trades and agriculture.

Coleridge urged that financial management and expenditure should be managed more prudently, by both the state and the individual. He pointed out that people have a tendency to overspend when wages are high and money is in supply, and this means that the resulting crashes are all the more painful. He presented a rough outline of cycle theory, and attributes economic cycles to greed and overspending, again referring to the 'over-balance of the commercial spirit' (1817: 177). He argued that paper currency and the national debt were exacerbating the problem, and seems to have been a moderate bullionist.

A Lay Sermon, like most of Coleridge's prose writings, is flowery and punctuated by many asides. His influence on later economists was probably slight, although Turk (1988) argues that J.S. MILL drew heavily on Coleridge's eclecticism in his own critiques of BENTHAM's utilitarianism and Comte's positivism, and the influence of Coleridge led Mill to ultimately adopt a broader outlook. Coleridge is of interest today for his position between schools of thought; both a bullionist and a reformer, he brought a certain freshness and independence of thought and spirit to economics, and his views on cycle theory do not look out of place today.

BIBLIOGRAPHY
The Statesman's Manual (1816).
A Lay Sermon (1817; repr. in J. Morrow (ed.), *Coleridge's Writings*, vol. 1, *On Politics and Society*, Basingstoke, 1990, pp. 97–151).
On the Constitution of the Church and State, According to the Idea of Each (1829; 2nd edn 1830; repr. in J. Morrow (ed.), *Coleridge's Writings*, vol. 1, *On Politics and Society*, Basingstoke, 1990, pp. 152–220).

Further Reading
Ashton, R., *The Life of Samuel Taylor Coleridge, A Critical Biography* (Oxford, 1996).
Calleo, D.P., *Coleridge and the Idea of the Modern State* (Yale, 1966).
De Paolo, C., *Coleridge's Philosophy of Social Reform* (New York, 1988).
Hedley, D., 'Coleridge, Samuel Taylor', in W.J. Mander and A.P.F. Sell (eds), *Dictionary of Nineteenth Century British Philosophers* (Bristol, 2002, vol. 1, pp. 268–9).
Holmes, R., *Coleridge* (Oxford, 1982).
Morrow, J., *Coleridge's Political Thought: Property, Morality and the Limits of Traditional Discourse* (1990).
Turk, C., *Coleridge and Mill: A Study of Influence* (Aldershot, 1988).

Morgen Witzel

COLLET, Clara Elizabeth (1860–1948)

Collet was born 10 September 1860 in London, and died at Sidmouth, Devon on 3 August 1848. She was the second daughter of the radical editor and publisher Collet Dobson Collet and Jane Collet, née Sloan. She became a friend and correspondent of the MARX family and ENGELS in the late 1870s. She as educated at North London Collegiate School and University College, London (BA 1880, MA 1885); she was later the first woman elected a fellow of University College, in 1896. Collet later provided John Maynard KEYNES with recollections of her student days for his biographical essays on William Stanley JEVONS, who examined Collet in philosophy, and her long-time friend Herbert FOXWELL, whose economics lectures she attended. An active supporter of women's suffrage and women's legal rights, she supported herself as a student by teaching as an assistant mistress at Wyggeston's Girls' School, Leicester from 1878 to 1885, an occupation which led in 1891 to the presidency of the Association of Assistant Mistresses in Public Secondary Schools.

Collet studied political economy because it was a required subject for the London MA, but this study resulted in a long and distinguished career as an empirical social investigator. From 1888 to 1892, she worked as an investigator for Charles Booth's *Labour and Life of the People of London*, publishing chapters on women's work in volumes of that great survey in 1889 and 1891. Four decades later, she also published a chapter on domestic service in Sir Hubert Llewellyn SMITH's *New Survey of London Life and Labour* in 1931 (see Collet 1945). After working on Booth's Greater London Survey, Collet joined the public service as one of four assistant commissioners for the Labour Commission in 1892, then as labour correspondent for the Board of Trade from 1893 to 1903, as senior investigator for the Labour Department of the Board of Trade from 1903 to 1917, and then for the newly-created Ministry of Labour from 1917 to 1920. She served as a part-time member of trade boards from 1921 to 1932. Apart from her official reports on women's employment and wages, she published extensively in scholarly journals, as well as a book (Collet 1902). Her standing in the scholarly community is shown by her service on the Council of the Royal Economic Society from 1918 to 1941 and on the Council of the Royal Statistical Society from 1919 to 1935, and by her selection to write the articles on female earnings and female labour for the first edition of R.H.I. PALGRAVE's *Dictionary of Political Economy* in 1896. Peter Groenewegen (2000: 113) emphasizes Collet's skilful and critical use of statistics: 'she never drew conclusions which the data did not warrant and she never refrained from drawing conclusions from the evidence even if they were incompatible with her beliefs'. Among British economists and statisticians, Clara Collet was respected as an investigator and renowned as a raconteur who had known everyone from Marx and Booth to Francis EDGEWORTH (taking part in his 'tramping parties), Phillip WICKSTEED and the Indian planner and statistician P.C. Mahalanobis. She was the only person to publish in both the first and the fiftieth volumes of the *Economic Journal*.

BIBLIOGRAPHY
'Wages and the Standard of Living', *Quarterly Journal of Economics* (1891), vol. 5, no. 2, pp. 365–8.
'Women's Work in Leeds', *Economic Journal* (1891), vol. 1, no. 3, pp. 460–73.
Educated Working Women (1902).
'Charles Booth, The Denison Club, and H. Llewellyn Smith', *Journal of the Royal Statistical Society* (1945), series A, vol. 108, nos 1–2, pp. 482–5.

Further Reading
Groenewegen, P., 'A Neglected Daughter of Adam Smith: Clara Elizabeth Collet (1860–1948', in P. Groenewegen (ed.),

Feminism and Political Economy in Victorian England (Aldershot, 1994, pp. 147–73).
——, 'Clara Elizabeth Collet (1860–1948)', in R.W. Dimand, M.A. Dimand and E.L. Forget (eds), *A Biographical Dictionary of Women Economists* (Cheltenham, 2000, pp. 109–15).
Mahalanobis, P.C., 'Clara E. Collet', *Journal of the Royal Statistical Society* (1948), series A, vol. 111, no. 3, p. 254.

Robert W. Dimand

COLLINS, John (1625–83)

Collins was born at Wood Eaton, Oxfordshire on 5 March 1625, and died in London on 10 November 1683. At age thirteen he was apprenticed to the Oxford bookseller Thomas Allam, but the latter's business soon failed and Collins then found employment as a junior clerk in the household of the Prince of Wales. He left England upon the outbreak of the Civil War, and spent much of the period 1642–9 sailing with English merchant vessels in the Mediterranean. During the Ottoman invasion of Crete, Collins fought in the service of Venice, and he was present at the siege of Candia. During this time he also studied mathematics and accounting, probably learning the latter from one of the many Italian *scuole d'abaco* (literally, 'abacus schools') that existed to teach double-entry book-keeping and other accounting methods to apprentice merchants.

Returning to London following the end of the Civil War, Collins established himself as teacher of mathematics, including accounting methods. His first major work, *An Introduction to Merchants Accounts*, appeared in 1653. In the preface to this work, Collins notes that he intended it to follow on from an earlier work, *The Merchants Mirrour*, published in 1635 by Richard Dafforne (with some additional material added by the latter's son, John Dafforne). This was a large textbook on book-keeping, very much in the traditional style of earlier English works such as Hugh Oldcastle's *A Profitable Treatyce* (1543) and of still earlier Italian texts such as Luca Pacioli's *Summa de arithmetica* (1494).

Collins clarifies some of the longer and more obscure sections of Dafforne, and also offers some alternative methods of book-keeping. He poses a set of five questions or exercises concerning accounts, such as how to calculate the return on an investment in a mercantile or trading venture and how to keep accounts for goods being sold on consignment. Collins's own career would have allowed him knowledge of new accounting methods being developed in Italy which were not yet current in England. The text is clear and the material well-explained, and *An Introduction to Merchants Accounts* represents a considerable improvement over Dafforne's earlier work. It also shows the extent to which men from many walks of life were beginning to take an interest in the problems of trade and commerce.

Following the restoration of the monarchy in 1660, Collins held a number of government posts and wrote widely on mathematics. He was elected a Fellow of the Royal Society in 1664. He became one of the most widely respected mathematicians of the late seventeenth century: Isaac BARROW, a friend and colleague, called him the 'English Mersenne', and his correspondents included NEWTON, HALLEY, Flamsteed, Leibniz and Huygens. In a manner reminiscent of Charles BABBAGE in the nineteenth century, Collins argued that the application of science and especially of mathematics to industry and trade would increase national prosperity. His later works include a text on navigation for the use of the East India Company and several short works on the fishing industry. His library and papers were preserved after his death, and many of his scientific letters were reprinted in the nineteenth century.

BIBLIOGRAPHY
An Introduction to Merchants Accounts (1653).
The Mariner's Plain Scale New Plain'd (1658).
Salt and Fishery (1682).

Further Reading
Littleton, A.C., *Accounting Evolution to 1900* (Tuscaloosa, 1981).
Rigaud, S.P., *Correspondence of the Scientific Men of the Seventeenth Century* (Oxford, 1841).
Whiteside, D.T., 'Collins, John', in *Dictionary of Scientific Biography* (1995).

Morgen Witzel

COLQUHOUN, Patrick (1745–1820)

Patrick Colquhoun was born 14 March 1745 in Dumbarton, Scotland and died at Westminster, 25 April 1820. His father, Adam Colquhoun, was a magistrate and registrar of county records. Colquhoun's formal education at Dumbarton grammar school ended at sixteen when his father died. Engaged as an apprentice with tobacco firm Alexander Spiers and Company, he worked for the company in Virginia. In 1766 he returned to Glasgow and continued his career as a tobacco merchant. In 1775 he married his cousin, Janet Colquhoun; the marriage produced seven children, of whom four survived him.

Colquhoun formed a tobacco company in 1776. As a supporter of the war with the American colonies (he contributed to the raising of a regiment in Glasgow), he came to the attention of the government; in the early 1780s he used this connection to lobby for legislation favourable to Glasgow. He became deeply involved in public affairs in Glasgow: he was a member of town council, in 1782 he was elected Lord Provost of Glasgow (re-elected in 1783), in 1783 he was a founder and the first chairman of the Glasgow Chamber of Commerce, he was chairman of the management committee of the Forth and Clyde Canal, and he served on other public bodies as well. In 1797, Colquhoun was awarded an honorary doctor of laws degree by the University of Glasgow.

Colquhoun became a prolific writer of pamphlets during the 1780s, including two on the negative economic effects on British merchants of the war with the American colonies and eight on various aspects and problems of the cotton industry. After 1785, investigating the problems of the cotton industry and lobbying for legislative changes caused him to spend a good deal of time in England. In 1789 Colquhoun moved his family to London; his worsening financial situation led to bankruptcy in Glasgow in 1790. His activities brought him into contact with members of the Pitt government, especially the home secretary, Henry Dundas (later Viscount Melville).

In 1779 a short-lived police force was established in Glasgow. It failed shortly after for financial reasons, but the project remained a live issue and was investigated by a committee of town council, which issued a report in 1788. Although not a member of this committee, Colquhoun was undoubtedly aware of its recommendations, many of which he adopted in his own proposals in 1796 (Dinsmor 2003). In 1792, the Pitt government attempted to deal with the problems of crime and order in metropolitan London by establishing seven courts, each with three stipendiary magistrates. With Dundas's influence, Colquhoun was appointed one of these, an appointment he filled until 1818. With customary energy, he wrote a series of pamphlets dealing with the well-being of the lower classes. He was involved in founding a charity school and setting up soup kitchens, activities which led to additional pamphlets. He brought all this activity together in 1796 with the publication of *A Treatise on the Police of the Metropolis*. Successive revised and enlarged editions were published, the last in 1806. These were supplemented with additional publications on indigence, education and the police as he refined his theory.

Colquhoun has been known primarily as an early advocate of modern policing with an emphasis on prevention and as a harbinger of Sir Robert Peel's Metropolitan Police established in 1829. However, Colquhoun used the term 'police' in an earlier, much broader sense of 'policy' and 'anything contributing to the good order of society'. Certainly, his proposals for a 'criminal' police and for the 'marine' police are in line with a modern meaning of the term. However, the proposals for a 'municipal' police go far beyond into the realm of social policy, and this was where most of his emphasis on prevention rested. Although clearly in the tradition of the enlightenment and on some issues allied with reformers, Colquhoun was philosophically conservative, albeit with large doses of paternalism. He shared with many enlightenment thinkers a paradoxical approach to the 'lower orders' (McMullan 1998: 102–4). He could be scathing in his condemnation of their vicious and immoral habits, but he also believed that they were basically or potentially moral. His proposals for dealing with the lower orders were intrusive and authoritarian, but he had a deep concern for their welfare.

For Colquhoun, the basis of society was morality, which he seems to have understood principally in social terms. While he frequently coupled 'religion' with morality, he showed little interest in religion for itself and no traces of an Old Testament code in regard to sin and punishment. When properly inculcated and supported by the appropriate laws, religion and morality produced 'a conduct intentionally directed towards the Public Good'. Crime, public disorders of all kinds and even rebellion were traceable to departures from morality. Many things (evil influences and examples, temptations, destitution, lack of education and badly devised laws and legal system) subverted and seduced humans from their moral state.

His system of police was a very comprehensive approach of regulation, control and assistance to develop, maintain and restore (for those who had fallen into indigence and crime) this moral state. His objective was to maintain the lower orders in their place in the social order; he did not favour political reform: 'It is far better to improve and confirm a nation in the true principles of natural justice, than to perplex them by political refinements'. As a magistrate, Colquhoun supported the crackdown on radicalism and paid informers to gather information on those he thought were seditious (MacKay 1996).

This concern for the lower orders also had an essential economic dimension. In *The State of Indigence* (1799), Colquhoun argued, 'Labour is absolutely requisite to the existence of all governments; and it is from the Poor only that labour can be expected' (Neocleous 2000: 714). Poverty (defined by Colquhoun as the condition of having no means to acquire the necessities of life except through labour) was the spur to compel the lower orders to provide this labour; thus, poverty was essential for society and civilization, because without labour there could be no creation of wealth. Indigence, on the other hand, was the inability or unwillingness to satisfy one's necessities by labour. This was the real source of evil as the indigent sought to satisfy the necessities through begging, crime and prostitution. The main concern for Colquhoun was to prevent the lower orders from falling from the state of poverty into indigence and all too easily from there into crime. Society should address the causes of crime instead of harshly punishing the effects. Colquhoun did not believe that prevention could be perfect or that crime could be eliminated; hence, one aspect of his system of police was to create an effective criminal police.

Colquhoun joined with evangelical and Utilitarian reformers in advocating legal and prison reform. He condemned the existing approach that relied on severity of punishment (160 crimes for which the death penalty was prescribed) to deter crime. It was unjust ('punishing the petty pilferer with the same severity as the atrocious murderer'), it was cruel (allowing the lower orders to be ill educated and then punishing them for crimes which have originated in bad habits), and most seriously, it was also very ineffective. Because of the severity, many victims were unwilling to prosecute, juries were unwilling to convict, and many judges bent the law. With the low rates of apprehension, the probability of being caught and punished was too low to deter. Colquhoun argued that it was the certainty of punishment, not the severity, that deterred. The death penalty should be retained only for the most serious offences and for incorrigible offenders. A major objective of punishment should be the rehabilitation of the delinquent. Both execution and transportation deprived society of the offenders' labour; instead, he supported Jeremy BENTHAM's Panopticon scheme, where the labour of the convicted would pay for their incarceration and the offenders would be returned to society better prepared and disciplined to contribute their labour.

Approached by the West India merchants in London, Colquhoun investigated the problems of wastage and theft on the London docks. He published two pamphlets before his major book on this subject, *A Treatise on the Commerce and Police of the River Thames* (1800). His recommendations went beyond the setting up of a police force. He advocated eliminating the rights claimed by many workers to 'gleanings', cargo that had spilled, spoiled or been scraped from the holds of ships. Workers had an interest in ensuring that such gleanings were plentiful and this activity easily slipped over into outright theft. Colquhoun insisted that henceforth workers should be remunerated entirely in money wages. This fitted into *laissez-faire* theories of a flexible, modern class of wage labourers (Neocleous 2000: 718–20; McMullan 1998: 105–6). However, it also fitted into Colquhoun's insistence that workers should receive adequate wages to meet their subsistence needs and at the same time the temptation and opportunities for theft should be reduced as much as possible.

However, the criminal and marine police were not the most important aspects of prevention in Colquhoun's system of police. The major task of prevention was to be accomplished by a 'Municipal police' and by social policies, especially education and a more effective administration of the poor laws. Colquhoun argued emphatically that society should educate the children of the poor in order to develop the right habits. Education should be limited to the basics; this would make the poor more effective labourers, but would not give them ideas above their station. It should inculcate temperance, industry, and loyalty (MacKay 1996). Moreover, he insisted that instruction in religion (specifying the Church of England) be included to develop the essential moral sense at an early age.

Colquhoun advocated substantial changes to the administration of the poor laws. The settlement laws should be abolished; because assistance could only be received in one's parish of birth, workers were inhibited from moving to find employment. Also, in urban areas, the fiscal capability of parishes could vary enormously; some parishes had heavy concentrations of indigents and few wealthy ratepayers while others had the exact opposite. Poor relief should be funded by society as a whole through a national poor rate assessment. Initially, Colquhoun was attracted to workhouses, but later he grew disillusioned; he proposed that authorities should set up public works projects to provide employment if necessary. Nowhere did he express faith in free market forces to achieve his objectives or to maximize the creation of wealth, nor was he willing to accept the consequences of extreme disparities in income distribution. According to Colquhoun, society had an obligation to relieve destitution and to intervene actively to manage the moral and physical well-being of its lower orders.

Colquhoun was also known for his statistical estimation of the distribution of family incomes in *Treatise on Indigence* (1806) and especially *A Treatise on the Wealth, Power and Resources of the British Empire* (1814). This latter was one of the first full statistical surveys of the British Empire, and in the century that followed it had many imitators as Britain slowly developed awareness of its own imperial status. The work was also notable for its detailed picture of the incomes of the working classes, which were of considerable influence on subsequent generations of reformers. His figures were long accepted, but modern researchers have complained that Colquhoun failed to indicate what his sources were. Further, many conclude that his estimations were not very accurate (Schwarz 1979).

BIBLIOGRAPHY

Observations on the Present State of the Linen and Cotton Manufactures (1783).
Case of the British Merchants who Traded to America Previous to the Late War (London,1787).
Observations on the Relative Resources of the East India Company for Productive Remittance (1788).
A Representation of Facts Relative to the Sufferings and Losses of the Merchants Residing in Great Britain Who Carried on Trade to the United States of America (1789).
Explanation of the Plan Proposed for the Relief of Industrious Artisans, Mechanics and Labourers and Other Meritorious Poor (1795).
A Plan for the Purpose of Affording Extensive Relief to the Poor (1795).
A Treatise on the Police of the Metropolis (1796; revised edns, 1796, 1797, 1800, 1807.
A General View of the Depredations Committed on West-India and Other Property in the Port of London (1799).
A Treatise on the Functions and Duties of a Constable (1803).
A Treatise on Indigence (1806).
A Treatise on the Wealth, Power and Resources of the British Empire (1814; revised edn, 1815).

Further Reading
Dinsmor, A., 'Glasgow Police Pioneers', *The Scotia News* (2003, vol. 2, no. 1, (29 May 2003).
MacKay, L.P., 'Patrick Colquhoun', *Dictionary of Literary Biography* (1996) 158: 87–93.
McMullan, J.L., 'Social Surveillance and the Rise of the "Police Machine"', *Theoretical Criminology* (1998), vol. 2, no. 1, pp. 93–117.
Neocleous, M., 'Social Police and the Mechanisms of Prevention', *British Journal of Criminology* (2000), vol. 40, no. 4, pp. 710–26.
Schwarz, L.D., 'Income Distribution and Social Structure in London in the Late Eighteenth Century', *Economic History Review* (1979), vol. 32, no. 2, pp. 250–9.

Wally Mills

COOK, John (1608–60)

John Cook (sometimes Cooke) was born in Leicestershire some time in 1608. He was hanged, drawn and quartered at Tyburn in October 1660. He is said to have been educated at Oxford and as a young man, according to Ludlow (1894), spent a number of years abroad, living for several months in Rome and Geneva. By 1640 he was a barrister at Gray's Inn, where his acquaintances included the radical republican barrister John Bradshaw. Together, Cook and Bradshaw represented John LILBURNE in 1646 in the case that overturned Lilburne's conviction before the Star Chamber in 1637. This brought Cook to prominence in republican circles, and in January 1649 he was appointed solicitor for the Commonwealth and ordered to prepare the case against Charles I. Cook prosecuted the case against the king with considerable zeal, and he published several pamphlets during and after the trial, making the case against the king to the public.

As a reward for his services, Cook was made master of the hospital of St Cross in 1649 and, in 1650, chief justice of Munster. He became known as a zealous legal reformer in both England and Ireland, and Cromwell publicly praised him for his energy. However, by the mid-1650s he was increasingly disillusioned with the Protectorate. He had backed the army in 1647 during its occupation of London, and had regarded the New Model Army as the true instrument of the republic. Following the army's suppression Cook, like Bradshaw, came increasingly into conflict with Cromwell and his government, and in 1657 it appears that he was recalled from Ireland and possibly dismissed from his posts, though details are sketchy. Following the restoration, Cook fled to Ireland but was arrested almost immediately. As a leading regicide, Cook was specifically named in the Act of Indemnity as one of those to be tried for treason. He was one of ten men to be executed, the others including Francis Hacker and Daniel Axtel, who had commanded the king's guard during the trial, and Hugh Peters, who had preached Charles's funeral sermon.

Like many of those involved in the trial of the king, including Hacker, Axtel and Peters, Cook was a member of the Fifth Monarchy movement, a radical millenarian sect that preached republicanism as a means of preparing the way for the second coming of Christ, who would establish a new kingdom on earth. He was close to the movement's most eloquent spokesman, Major-General Thomas Harrison (also executed in October 1660). Among the Fifth Monarchy movement's tenets was a commitment to improving the lot of the poor, and Cook's pamphlet *Unum Necessarium* (1648), possibly written not long after he first became associated with the movement, is very much influenced by Fifth Monarchy ideas.

Care of the poor, says Cook, is a duty enjoined upon society by God, who 'suffers some to be poore, that rich men may have occasion to do good' (1648: 1). He argues, not for more giving to the poor – although he does suggest that magistrates should provide bread for 'every honest poore man' – but for a reform of the economic system that favours the rich over the poor. Charity, he says, 'consists as much in lending and selling to the poore at a moderate price, as in giving' (1648: 1). Unusually for such a tract, however, Cook does not believe in fixing the prices of staple commodities such as corn. During his continental travels he had seen how economies with fixed corn prices, such as that of Rome, did not necessarily deliver lower prices, or indeed sufficient quantities of corn to feed the poor. An honest free market, Cook thinks, is better than a regulated or fixed one. The role of regulation should be confined to preventing individuals from trying to manipulate the market to their own advantage. He is particularly harsh on those who hoard corn in order to drive prices up and create dearth, and argue that this practice should be deemed a treasonable offence. Like other Fifth Monarchists Cook also abhorred drunkenness, and called for alehouses to be closed down and inns to be 'reformed'. A state of sobriety, he believed, was necessary to industry and the economy.

BIBLIOGRAPHY

Unum Necessarium: or, The Poore Mans Case: being An Expedient to make Provision for all the poore People in the Kingdome (1648).

Further Reading

Capp, B.S., *The Fifth Monarchy Men: A Study in Seventeenth-Century English Millenarianism* (1972).

Ludlow, E., *Memoirs*, 2 vols, ed. C.H. Firth (Oxford, 1894).
Rogers, P.G. *The Fifth Monarchy Men* (1966).

Morgen Witzel

COPLESTON, Edward (1776–1849)

Edward Copleston was born at Offwell, Devon on 2 February 1776. He died Bishop of Llandaff 14 October 1849, and was buried in the ruins of his yet unrestored cathedral. He came from an ancient West Country family; his father and grandfather had both been educated at Oxford and become clergymen.

Copleston was educated at home until the age of fifteen, when he won a scholarship to Corpus Christi College, Oxford. He was elected fellow of Oriel College upon graduating BA (1795), and became successively tutor (1797), bursar, dean (*c.*1805) and provost (1814) of that college, then the centre of an effervescent revival of intellectual excellence at Oxford. He became vicar of St Mary's, Oxford, the university church, in 1800, and was elected professor of poetry in 1802. For more than twenty years Copleston remained one of the most powerful and influential of Oxford men, both in the university and in the greater world of high political society. In 1827 he was consecrated Bishop of Llandaff, quitted Oxford, and laboured devotedly in his diocese for the rest of his life, repairing the neglect and reforming the abuses of centuries. He required that each incumbent he instituted be fluent in Welsh. Every penny of his income from the bishopric (£500 per annum) he spent on charities within the diocese.

Though like most great scholars of that age, Copleston's academic interests ranged freely over a wide field, his interest in political economy went back at least to 1796. His prize essay on agriculture written in that year addresses many of the topics treated more fully in his famous *Letters to Peel* (1819). When Dugald STEWART's pupil and friend John William Ward (1781–1833), first Earl of Dudley, moved from Edinburgh to Oxford in 1799, he became a tutorial pupil of Copleston's. Thereafter there was continual communication, mutual respect and mutual criticism between the two men who dominated the intellectual lives of Edinburgh and Oxford respectively. There was a keen interest in political economy at Oriel during the first two decades of the nineteenth century, and several other fellows made contributions to the new science. Adam SMITH's *Wealth of Nations* and *Theory of Moral Sentiments* were acquired for the library, the *Edinburgh Review* was taken from the outset, and two volumes of *Pamphlets on the Bullion Question* (1810–11), marked 'Oriel College Common Room' in ink, are full of pencilled marginal comments, some by Copleston and some in other hands.

Copleston's *Reply to the Calumnies of the Edinburgh Review* (1810) had alluded to the study of political economy at Oxford and described the 'leading principles' of that science as a study (as we should now say) of equilibrium outcomes of market processes, hindered in most real-world cases by 'the friction of the machine'. Copleston acknowledged the centrality for economic theory of 'that principle of self correction which the analogy of nature teaches us is the universal law of her constitution'. But he was one of the first to see clearly that in the analytical 'short period' between one competitively determined social optimum and another – which in reality may last for years – substantial costs of adjustment must be borne by society, most of which would be shifted to the poorest and therefore weakest of its members. Social institutions such as the poor law, and rigidities introduced by more recent legislation suspending sterling convertibility and restricting the grain trade added to the 'friction in the machine'. By 1815 Copleston was a public figure whose advice on economic policy was sought by reformist

Tories such as Canning, Peel, BARING and HUSKISSON. Faced with widespread misery and social dislocation caused by severe post-war depression (1815–20), and encouraged perhaps by 'the refined and intellectual society' he encountered in Lord Grenville's circle, he composed his only systematic exposition of economic themes in two *Letters to the Rt. Hon. Robert Peel* (1819).

The first *Letter* (1819) analysed the 'Pernicious Effects of a Variable Standard of Value, especially as it regards the Condition of the Lower Orders and the Poor Laws'. The second *Letter* (1815), which is a continuation of the argument, considered the 'Causes of the Increase of Pauperism and...the Poor Laws'. Contrary to Malthusian opinion, the poor laws themselves have not been the cause of poverty. The chief cause of poverty has been inflation caused by the wartime expansion of Britain's inconvertible paper currency. The evil of inflation arises because the value of money is expected to be constant. Hence when prices begin to rise, expectations are falsified and redistributions of income and wealth occur that bear no relation to economic performance. Granted HUME's point that inflation stimulates the economy in the short run, this occurs because of what is now called 'money illusion' in the labour market. And though inflation 'deceives men to their own advantage' this has a cost, borne by 'the labouring class' whose income is fixed in nominal terms and who lack the bargaining power to re-contract. Though Copleston was aware of adaptive expectations, he did not regard steady-state inflation as a possible resting place. Like Friedman (1967), and for some of the same reasons, he held that the nature of inflation is to accelerate.

Copleston, who understood MALTHUS's argument better than did Malthus himself, showed that poverty of the kind the poor laws were intended to remedy could not be, and was not in fact, caused by those laws. For if the entire working class were fully employed at Malthusian equilibrium, each family would receive an income sufficient for its freely chosen size and standard of living. Save for the sick and disabled, poverty would be caused either by involuntary unemployment or by unanticipated inflation. Large-scale public relief would be required only if the able-bodied poor were unable, from macroeconomic causes, to earn the current socially determined subsistence wage. By careful use of such statistical evidence as then existed, Copleston showed that public attention had been drawn to the problem of poverty and the poor laws over the past two centuries only during and after periods of severe inflation.

Copleston's most famous pupil, Richard WHATELY, was later Drummond Professor of Political Economy at Oxford. He deemed that Copleston's 'work on the Currency...attracted much attention and probably exercised no small influence on the public mind'. RICARDO thought so highly of the second *Letter* that he made a detailed paragraph by paragraph summary. But save for his 'Dissertation on the State of the Currency' (1822) and *An Examination of the Currency Question* (1830), Copleston wrote no more on political economy, turning instead to more difficult and subtle philosophical inquiries into necessity and predestination.

Unlike many academic economists, Copleston was expert in domestic economy. He could add long columns of pounds, shillings and pence at sight with perfect accuracy. During his six years as bursar of Oriel he trebled the annual revenues of his college and liquidated all its debts. His personal fortune grew from £21 on 1 January 1800 to more than £20,000 by 1821.

Copleston was not an original thinker. His economic theory was, as he said, learned from 'the ordinary reading of the day'. But he was gifted with one of the most powerful analytical minds of his generation and what he grasped, which was a great deal, he held with a lucidity and penetration exceeding anything achieved by the more truly original Malthus or THORNTON, not to mention their other contemporaries. His importance for the history of economic thought lies in the fact that he formed Richard Whately, who in turned formed Nassau SENIOR; and in the less well-known fact that his synthesis of economic and theological ideas in the two *Letters to Peel* represents the intellectual high-water mark of 'Christian Political Economy' (Waterman 1991: 186–95).

BIBLIOGRAPHY
Reply to the Calumnies of the Edinburgh Review (1810).
A Letter to the Right Hon. Robert Peel, MP for the University of Oxford, on the Pernicious Effects of a Variable Standard of Value, especially as regards the Condition of the Lower Orders and the Poor Laws... (Oxford, 1819).
A Second Letter to the Right Hon. Robert Peel, MP for the University of Oxford, on the Causes of the Increase in Pauperism and on the Poor Laws (Oxford, 1819).
'A Dissertation on the State of the Currency', *Quarterly Review* (1822).
An Examination of the Currency Question and of the Project for Altering the Standard of Value (London 1830).

Further Reading
Waterman, A.M.C. (1991) *Revolution, Economics and Religion: Christian Political Economy, 1798–1833* (Cambridge, 1991).

A.M.C. Waterman

COTTERILL, Charles Forster
(c.1790–after 1856)

Cotterill was born some time around 1790, although the exact date is a matter of conjecture. His family came from south Staffordshire, and he himself first appears as a successful businessman and mayor of Walsall in the 1820s. In 1834 he retired from business and bought the manor of Ogley Hay, Staffordshire, becoming a justice of the peace. Rather than living the life of a country gentleman, however, he began developing the land, breaking up the manor and selling off parcels to developers who built houses and industries, including a steam-powered flour mill. Another parcel was sold to the builders of the Wyrley and Essington canal. By around 1840 Cotterill had developed or sold the entire manor of Ogley Hay and retired to London to live comfortably on the proceeds. He did not marry and had no issue, so his title to Ogley Hay died with him. The new town which Cotterill had begun is now the centre of the modern town of Brownhills.

In London, Cotterill wrote several works on economics and business, reflecting on his own experience and discussing some of the problems of the day. Unsurprisingly, he believed in free trade and land reform. *Agricultural Distress* (1850), later revised and re-issued as *The Civil Freedom of Trade* (1856), shows him to have mixed feelings on the subject of regulation. He is tentatively in favour of government interference in the economy, but says the key is to find a balance. Too much regulation leads to high prices and inefficiency, while too little, as in the case of the railways, leads to market chaos and financial crashes. The objective of regulation should be economic stability, and government should legislate with this as its sole view.

Somewhat unusually for the time, Cotterill says the crisis in agriculture is being caused not by the Corn Laws, but by overabundant harvests that have created an excess of supply and driven prices down. The Corn Laws were necessary to restore prices and ease the plight of the countryside. The laws, however, can only be a temporary expedient. In the long term, the vicissitudes of the seasons mean there will be continue to be shortages in some years and gluts in others. His answer is for the government buy up surplus corn in glut years, store it in depots, and then sell it onto the market in lean years. Market stabilization can thus be achieved by manipulating the actual supply, rather than regulating prices.

In his discussion of the railway companies (1849), Cotterill argues that the government made a mistake by allowing private enterprise to develop the railways freely without direction. Government should have planned and surveyed the routes, then allowed private companies to tender for their construction. The present system is highly wasteful, and has had serious consequences for the economy, with many localized bubbles when railway projects were promoted and then failed. Many companies have failed due to lack of capital or wastage of capital; others have built lines that turn out to be economically unviable, while still other areas that need railways are not getting them. He draws a distinction between the railway lines and the trains that run on them: he sees no problem with competing companies running coaches along the same lines, and believes that here the market can be allowed to work relatively freely. For the lines themselves, however, a degree of central planning and management is essential. His discussion of the railways has some similarities to that of John Stuart MILL, and Cotterill reaches some of the came conclusions; he believes that however unpopular a measure it may be, there are occasions when the state must intervene in the market.

BIBLIOGRAPHY

The Past, Present and Future Position of the London and North Western, and Great Western Railway Companies (1849).
Agricultural Distress, its Cause and Remedy, with a Preliminary Inquiry concerning the Civil Law of the Freedom of Private Enterprise (1850).
The Civil Freedom of Trade; or the Rights & Duties of Governments in their relation to the Natural Freedom of Private Enterprise (1856).
Letter to the Right Honorable Lord John Russell, M.P.: Public Granaries and the Cycle of the Seasons, in Connection with Trade and Agriculture (1856).

Katharine Norley

COURT, William Henry Bassano (1904–71)

Harry Court was born 12 October 1904 in Cirencester, the son of the manager of a W.H. Smith bookshop, and died in Birmingham on 30 September 1971. He won a scholarship to Cambridge, and in 1927 took up Choate and Rockefeller fellowships at Harvard. Returning to Britain in 1929, Court was appointed to a lectureship at Birmingham University in the Commerce faculty made famous by W.J. ASHLEY. After war service in the War Cabinet Historical Section, he returned to Birmingham to become professor of economic history in 1947, a post he held until retirement in 1970. He was an historian of great subtlety whose work was informed by wide reading in economic theory and in the history of ideas. He wrote with grace as well as clarity.

Court's original interest was political and military history but, under the influence of Edwin Gay, he began to move towards economic history whilst at Harvard. At Birmingham, where G.C. ALLEN and Eric Roll had already made important contributions to the region's history, Court made his own mark with *The Rise of the Midland Industries, 1600–1838 (1938)* wherein he demonstrated for the first time how complex and gradual was the development of the local economy. In doing so, he made a major contribution to the understanding of the origins of the Industrial Revolution in Britain. To convey the dynamism of the local economy, he made use of SMITH's 'division of labour' concept and Allyn

Young's extension of that concept in his famous article on increasing return. In presenting a picture of an economy in motion, Court made an advance on the Marshallian 'comparative statics' approach used by one of his heroes, Sir John CLAPHAM. By the time the book was published, Court was writing a pioneering essay on the origins of the theory of economic imperialism which showed that he had a talent for painting on a broad canvas as well as for detailed scholarship.

In 1951, as a direct result of his wartime work, Court published a book on the coal industry during the conflict. Three years later he produced his *Concise Economic History of Britain from 1750 to Recent Times*, a textbook full of subtlety, which held a high place in the teaching of the subject for many years. In his later years, partly under TAWNEY's influence, Court grew convinced that it was impossible to understand economic decision making in the past without regard to the social and cultural context in which it was made, a view expressed in *British Economic History, 1870–1914: Commentary and Documents* (1965). During convalescence from a serious illness in the mid-1960s, Court also wrote a short autobiography, 'Growing Up in an Age of Anxiety', which stressed this conviction and offered his own reading of the growth of history as a discipline of thought in Britain in the twentieth century. At the time of his death, he was working on a multifaceted study of the First World War only fragments of which found their way into print. Court was elected a fellow of the British Academy in 1969.

BIBLIOGRAPHY

The Rise of the Midland Industries, 1600–1838 (Oxford, 1938).
'The Communist Doctrines of Empire', in W.K. Hancock (ed.), *Survey of British Commonwealth Affairs*, vol. II, part 1 (Oxford, 1940).
Coal (1951).
A Concise Economic History of Britain from 1750 to Recent Times (Cambridge, 1954).

British Economic History, 1870–1914: Commentary and Documents (Cambridge, 1965).
Scarcity and Choice in History (1970). (Includes 'What is Economic History?', 'Growing Up in an Age of Anxiety' and 'The Years 1914–18 in *British Economic and Social History*.)

Further Reading

Young, A.A. 'Increasing Return and Economic Progress', *Economic Journal* (1928), vol. 38, pp. 527–42.
Cain, P.J., 'William Henry Bassano Court, 1904–71', *Proceedings of the British Academy* (1982), vol. 68, pp. 521–35.

Peter Cain

COURTNEY, Leonard Henry (1832–1918)

Courtney was born on 6 July 1832 at Penzance in Cornwall, and died in London on 11 May 1918. He was the eldest son of John Sampson Courtney, a banker, and his wife, Sarah Mortimer. Courtney began his working life in Bolitho's bank in Penzance. His outstanding mathematical abilities led to his being awarded financial assistance, and he went on to attend St John's College, Cambridge. In 1855 he was second wrangler and first Smith's Prizeman. He was also elected a fellow of the college. He went on to study law and was called to the Bar in 1858; in 1889 he became a senior member of Lincoln's Inn. Instead of pursuing a legal career, Courtney turned to journalism and the study of politics and economics. In 1865 he became the leader writer to *The Times* and produced over three thousand articles between 1865 and 1881. He also contributed to the *Fortnightly Review*.

From 1872 to 1875 Courtney was professor of political economy at University College,

London. He became interested in bimetallism – a system allowing the use of both gold and silver currency as legal tender at a fixed ratio to each other – and admired William Jennings Bryan's 'silver' speeches in the 1896 American presidential campaign. Courtney then left academic life to become the Liberal MP for Liskeard, a seat he held between 1875 and 1885. The constituency was merged into that of Bodmin in the 1885 reform of parliament, and Courtney then represented the newly created Bodmin constituency from 1885 to 1900 as a Unionist. In 1883 he married Catherine (Kate) Potter, the sister of Beatrice WEBB. They had no children.

Courtney served as Under-Secretary of State for the Home Office (1880–1), then moved to the Colonial Office (1881–2). He left the latter post to become Financial Secretary to the Treasury, resigning in 1884 because the proposed Reform Act did not contain proportional representation clauses. He was a supporter of Gladstone's economic and foreign policies until 1885, but joined the Liberal Unionists in opposition to Home Rule, saying that Ireland was unfit for self-government. Courtney went on to become chairman of committees and Deputy Speaker of the House (1886–92). Thereafter he did not hold office. However, he followed an independent path on many political issues and was not a 'party' man. After 1895 he found himself at odds with the Conservatives over foreign policy. He disagreed with the increasingly imperialist stance of the government, and opposed consistently the 'forward' policies in Egypt, the Sudan and South Africa: he had also opposed the annexation of the Transvaal in 1887. He denounced the Jameson Raid (1896), and during the Boer War was one of the leading 'pro-Boer' MPs.

His attitude towards events in South Africa forced Courtney's retirement from political life between 1900 and 1906. He stood unsuccessfully as a Liberal candidate in the 1906 election, and was then elevated to the House of Lords as Baron Courtney of Penwith. He spoke regularly in the House of Lords, urging a reduction in armaments and advocating alliances with both France and Germany. When the First World War broke out, he blamed it on the government's diplomatic failures. Courtney wanted to see a greater degree of freedom of both speech and conscience in Britain and was still trying to find some means of ending the war diplomatically when he died.

In the 1860s and 1870s Courtney was well known among his fellow economists. His friends and correspondents included J.S. MILL and J.E. CAIRNES, and the latter in particular supported him in his bid for the chair in political economy at University College. He was in favour of free trade and generally liberal in his views on economics. His writings on the subject are mostly to be found in his contributions to *The Times* and the *Fortnightly Review*, though he did produce a few pamphlets, such as *Direct Taxation: An Inquiry* (1860). Only in his later years did he begin to produce more writings, and most of these were on political and personal rather than economic subjects.

BIBLIOGRAPHY
Direct Taxation: An Inquiry (1860).
The Cobden Club and the Fiftieth Anniversary of the Repeal of the Corn Laws (1896).
The Working Constitution of the United Kingdom and its Outgrowths (1901).
The Diary of a Churchgoer (1904).
Peace or War (1910).

Marjorie Bloy

COWELL, John Welsford (*fl.* 1834–42)

From internal evidence in his writings, Cowell was either a lawyer or a minor landowner of East Anglia. No other details of his life are known. He served on a commission investigating the poor, chaired by the jurist Charles Hay Cameron, and produced a major part of the commission's report in 1834; it can be deduced that he himself had served at some time as an overseer of the poor. In 1843 he wrote a pamphlet on paper currency.

The report on the condition of the poor is a useful piece of work, drawing directly on detailed evidence collected in a number of parishes of Cambridgeshire and Norfolk, from questionnaires and personal interviews with overseers of the poor, clergy, local officials and the poor themselves. Cowell's section of the report is divided into three parts: the first concerns the general condition of the poor, the second examines the workhouses, and the third criticizes the laws respecting illegitimate children.

Cowell is highly critical of the poor laws throughout his report, claiming that they everywhere 'bring about a state of things in which the labouring class is thrown entirely on its own resources' (1834: 94). The laws punish the very behaviour they are meant to support. Those frugal poor who manage somehow to save even a modest amount of money are then debarred from poor relief, while those who remain idle and indigent may continue to claim relief. Cowell writes with approval of various schemes meant to weed out the undeserving claimants, in particular by forcing them to take work in exchange for their poor relief. Where such schemes are implemented, says Cowell, the deserving poor are usually only too happy to take work, while the more indolent members of the community quickly drop off the register.

Unlike other writers who supported the laws but condemned the manner in which they were administered, Cowell found both the poor and overseers of the poor trapped in a bureaucratic jungle, the latter forced to administer laws with which they did not agree, in a manner they knew to be harmful. He lauded those with the initiative to set up local schemes, and says these should be encouraged; meanwhile, the law itself required root and branch overhaul.

In his pamphlet on the currency, Cowell is critical of paper money which he believes, if issued in too great a quantity, produces distortions and disturbances in prices. He believes that metallic currency has intrinsic value, and comments that 'the appetite of mankind for precious metals is universal, ever constant and insatiable' (1843: 9). Gold and silver, he says, are 'universal commodities' (1843: 9). He proposes directly linking the issue of paper currency to the value of gold; thus the supply and value of paper money should follow the supply and value of gold. This, he believes, would prevent paper from creating further distortions beyond those already created by fluctuations in the value of gold. His proposals in this respect were very similar to those adopted in the Bank Charter Act of 1844. Elsewhere he suggests that the total value of paper currency in circulation ought never to exceed the total interest accruing on the national debt. Cowell is prepared to admit a role for paper money in the economy, but believes that because of its lack of intrinsic value, its excessive use can only be harmful.

BIBLIOGRAPHY

(with C.H. Cameron and J. Wrottesley) *Two Reports Addressed to His Majesty's Commissioners Appointed to Inquire into the Administration and Operation of the Poor Laws* (1834).

Letters to the Right Honourable Francis Thornhill Baring, on the Institution of a Safe and Profitable Paper Currency (1843).

David Ashbury

COX, Richard (1650–1733)

Cox was born at Bandon, near Cork on 25 March 1650, and died following a stroke on 3

May 1733 at Clonakilty, County Cork (his manor house at Dunmanway is also sometimes given as the place of death). The son of an army officer and a local gentlewoman, Cox was orphaned at the age of three and raised by his mother's family. In 1671, after apprenticing to a solicitor in Clonakilty, he came to London and was admitted to Gray's Inn, and was called to the bar in 1673. Rejecting several offers of work in London, Cox returned to Ireland in 1674, married, and appears to have rusticated for several years at Clonakilty before finally moving to Cork in 1681. Here he practised law and secured the recordership of Kinsale.

In Cork, Cox had a reputation for being a Protestant zealot. Upon the accession of the Catholic James II in 1685, he was stripped of his recordership and, fearing for his own safety, moved with his family to Bristol. Here he practised law and also wrote his most famous work, *Hibernia Anglicana*, a history of the English conquest of Ireland. Upon the arrival of William of Orange, Cox hastened to London to attach himself to the Protestant cause. He was offered a post as secretary to Sir Robert Southwell, one of William's most trusted officials, who became commissioner of customs and later secretary of state for Ireland. In this service, Cox returned to Ireland with William's army in 1690. He was present at the Boyne, where his information is said to have been of great value to the Protestant forces (though what this information was is not clear). He was made recorder and justice of the common pleas for Waterford in 1690, and military governor of Cork in May 1691. In this latter capacity he was a great success, raising irregular troops that harassed the Jacobite forces and reportedly killed several thousand rebels; he was also able to send supplies and troops to the army besieging Limerick, which was captured in September 1691. During this period he also became associated with the Duke of Ormond, whose patronage he acquired.

Cox was rewarded for his services with a number of honours. He was made a member of the privy council of Ireland in 1692, and was knighted later in the year; he was made a baronet in 1706. He was appointed one of the commissioners of forfeitures in 1693, but was removed from the commission in 1695 for defending the legal rights of Catholics. He retired to England in 1696, ostensibly on grounds of ill-health, but returned to Ireland before 1698. He was appointed chief justice of the common pleas in for Ireland in 1701, and readmitted to the privy council in the same year. Queen Anne called on him for advice on Irish affairs upon her accession in 1702, and thereafter relied on him, appointing him Lord Chancellor of Ireland in 1703. Cox held this post until 1707 and then again retired from public life for several years. He re-emerged in 1711 to become chief justice of the queen's bench in Ireland. Following Anne's death in 1714 his patron, Ormond, defected to the Jacobites, and Cox was dismissed from his post, ostensibly for refusing to comply with instructions from London, but almost certainly for political reasons. He remained in retirement until his death in 1733, devoting himself to building up his manor and plantation of Dunmanway, especially its linen industry.

Cox strongly supported the building up of domestic industries in Ireland, particularly linen but also woollen cloth. In a pamphlet stating the case for allowing Ireland exemption from the law prohibiting the import of woollen cloth into England, a protectionist measure designed to stimulate the English industry, he argued that economic prosperity was the quickest way to pacify Ireland. There are, he says, two ways of keeping conquered countries in subjection: by arms, or by colonies. The former option is dangerous and expensive; but colonies can create economic prosperity which will promote general happiness and make subject populations less likely to rebel. Allowing Irish woollens to be imported into England, Cox argues, will encourage Irish prosperity.

Rebutting the argument that allowing Irish cloth in England would mean a drain of

English wealth to Ireland, Cox points out that any money going to Ireland will remain largely in the hands of the English colonists, and so in time will be remitted back to England. England supplies Ireland with most of its commodities; English proprietors own about a third of the land of Ireland, the money they receive there being largely spent in England, especially on luxury goods. Most Irish exports are carried by English companies in English ships. He goes so far as to state that 'England gets more by Ireland than by the trade of the whole world besides' (1698: 3), and believes the balance of trade with Ireland to be worth £600,000 to England. He concludes by suggesting that a strong economy in Ireland would be the prelude not only to peace, but to union with England.

BIBLIOGRAPHY

Hibernia Anglicana: or, the History of Ireland from the conquest thereof by the English to this present time, 2 vols (1690–2).

Some Thoughts on the Bill Depending before the Right Honourable the House of Lords for Prohibiting the Exportation of the Woollen Manufactures of Ireland to Foreign Parts (1698).

Further Reading

Bennett, G., *The History of Bandon* (Cork, 1889).

Caulfield, R., *The Autobiography of Sir Richard Cox, Lord Chancellor of Ireland* (1860).

Gill, C., *The Rise of the Irish Linen Industry* (Oxford, 1935).

Morgen Witzel

CRAIG, John (1766–1859)

Craig was born at Glasgow in 1766, and died 29 December 1859 at Pegsborough, Co. Tipperary. He came from a family of merchants and pursued that business at Glasgow and Leith, and later was a manufacturer at Lasswade, near Edinburgh. He matriculated at Glasgow University 1778, as did his five sons. He was elected a fellow of the Royal Society of Edinburgh in 1818. Robert Craig, his second son, married a daughter of Thomas DE QUINCEY.

Craig is principally known for three works: a biography of his distinguished uncle John MILLAR, a work on political science and a shorter work on political economy. In his biography of Millar, professor of Civil Law at Glasgow, Craig discussed Millar's teaching, emphasizing that he followed the principle of propriety rather than utility.

His *Elements of Political Science* (1814) is one of the most comprehensive works on public finance of the period. In pursuit of the greatest happiness for all, political society has 'to protect the citizens from injury, to increase by combination the effects of individual exertions, and to improve the moral and intellectual faculties of man (1814, vol. 1: 271). These aims are translated into the duties of criminal law and national defence to achieve the first; redistribution of wealth, especially to maintain the poor, to fulfil the second; and educational and religious facilities to realize the third. His actual policy proposals were meagre. State education was to be limited to reading, writing and arithmetic: to encourage literacy, no illiterate would be allowed factory employment under the age of twelve, unless an orphan. Also he argued against state involvement in religion. He appreciated that a government has a role in regulating the economy by interfering with trade to stabilize corn prices, and through subsidization to stabilize other prices and encourage improvement.

He detailed the effects of schemes promoting equality. Property rights would be destroyed contrary to the feeling of society, the poor would work less, unemployment would increase as there would not be the funds to employ labour and there would be no incentive to save. He also discussed poor relief at length. Although he thought that helping the poor was the task of the individual, not the government, he had suggestions for the reform of the current system. He wanted the poor to receive less than the pay of a common labourer, and equal in amount across the country so that there would be no incentive to move from parish to parish. A statutory scheme would set up a fund with contributions from the rich through the poor rate and employee contributions. All contributions would be the same, as it would be difficult to estimate wealth and income

Craig's discussion of taxation is very detailed, beginning with his definition: 'The tax an inhabitant pays to the State consists of the quantity of enjoyment of which he is deprived' (1814, vol. II: 264). He argued for progressive taxation As the ordinary peacetime government was financed out of taxation leaving national capital intact, wars had to be financed by the sacrifice of private capital. The national debt should be gradually dissolved by setting aside 1 per cent of it annually for repayment.

Craig's fame chiefly rests on his *Remarks on Fundamental Questions in Political Economy* (1821), especially its value theory. He admits he is a follower of Say and an opponent of RICARDO's labour quantity approach to value, especially for ignoring differences in the quality of labour and for attempting to reduce capital to indirect labour. In search of an invariant standard of value, he follows MALTHUS's approach of employing an average of the price of corn and money wages. Craig clearly expounds the idea of subjective valuation: 'That a high price is paid for diamonds is of itself sufficient proof, that in some way or other they are capable of affording gratification to those who purchase them: for there is no standard for enjoyment but the opinions of men...'. Seligman praised Craig for asserting that utility is the basis of all value. Bruce (1938) thought Craig was on the verge of enunciating the marginal utility principle and that his ideas were in the twilight zone between classical and Austrian economics.

Craig also questioned Malthus's population theory. He rejected the view that population presses on the means of subsistence, and argued that a reluctance to give up comforts and social status would restrict family size. Craig also noted that postponed marriages could be as prolific as early ones.

In *Remarks*, he also reviewed the commercial state of Britain in the post-1815 period. Increased unemployment he regarded as the most serious effect of ending the war. He hoped that gradually jobs would be found in agriculture and manufacturing, and opposed large-scale public works. Whether financed by taxation on income or capital, these works would reduce demand elsewhere in the economy: an early example of the 'crowding-out' argument.

BIBLIOGRAPHY
An Account of Life and Writings of the Author, appended to the fourth edition of John Millar's *The Origin of the Distinction of Ranks* (Edinburgh, 1806).
Elements of Political Science, 3 vols (Edinburgh, 1814).
Remarks on Fundamental Questions in Political Economy; illustrated by a brief inquiry into the commercial state of Britain since the year 1815 (Edinburgh, 1821).

Further Reading
Bruce, T.B., 'The Economic Theories of John Craig, A Forgotten English Economist', *Quarterly Journal of Economics* (1938), vol. 52, pp. 697–707.
Seligman, E.R.A., 'On Some Neglected Economists', *Economic Journal* (1903), vol. 51, pp. 335–63.

Donald Rutherford

CREE, Thomas Scott (*fl. c.*1891–1903)

Cree was a Glasgow businessman and sometime member of the Philosophical Society of Glasgow. Attempts to trace other details of his career and activities have so far failed, and he remains known to us only through his writings, three works on economics and labour published in Glasgow between 1891 and 1903.

Cree's writings are of interest for two reasons: they are strongly critical of modern economic theory in general, and they contain a considered attack on contemporary theories of the labour market. It is the second of these which is of the most interest, first spelled out in *A Criticism of the Theory of Trades' Unions* (1891) and repeated with little variation in the two later works. This work was originally a paper given before the Philosophical Society of Glasgow, and was stimulated by a paper on the same subject a year earlier by Hubert Llewellyn SMITH, which had drawn heavily on the ideas of J.S. MILL. It is Mill who is the primary target of Cree's attack.

Cree begins by stating that he is not an opponent of trades unions *per se*, and believes they do much good in terms of providing welfare and education to their members (he later comments, however, that they also breed class hatred, leaving little doubt as to where his true feelings lie). He asks, however, whether they are an efficient and economically proper method for raising wages. As Cree interprets Mill and Smith, the laws of supply and demand do not fix prices absolutely, but rather determine a possible range of prices within an upper and lower limit, a kind of 'no man's land'. The exact price paid within this limit depends not on supply and demand, but on the astuteness and bargaining power of buyer and supplier. According to Mill and Smith, this means it is perfectly right and proper for workers to combine into unions in order to increase their bargaining power, and raising wages within the limits described is not economically harmful.

Cree denies the 'no man's land argument', at least in the case of labour. His view is that the operation of supply and demand must be seen not as the consequence of one bargain, but of a whole concatenation of previous exchanges which each have their influence on the final price. This means that, over a number of different bargains, the mean of the oscillations of price is an exact point, not a range of prices as Mill and Smith seem to suggest: 'There is not an inch of ground which can be called a no-man's-land within which the law of supply and demand does not operate. Every farthing of variation on the price has its effect on future supply and demand, just as every drop of water swells the sea.' (1891: 11).

This does not mean there are no variations in price, but the sensitivity of price depends almost entirely on the number of transactions. The market for fine art, in which the number of transactions is very low, might admit wide variations, but in the market for cotton or for consols the variations in price are no more than ¼ or ⅛ of 1 per cent. Thanks to its very large number of transactions, the labour market is a very sensitive one, and the laws of supply and demand operate very precisely. But combination destroys this market, 'and in doing so it destroys a gauge of the true price, delicate, sensitive, and self-acting, and, as Mr Mill and Professor Marshall admit, almost perfect; and it puts nothing in its place' (1891: 11). 'The true economical wage is the wage necessary to attract a sufficient number of men to do the work properly' (1891: 17), and the price fixed by unions is a false one and therefore dangerous.

Cree argues that bargaining through combination in any market is a 'rough and barbarous process, combining a maximum of uncertainty with a maximum of loss by friction' (1891: 36). The most sensitive market is that which has a high number of transactions which guide buyers and sellers more exactly to the true economic price. Cree is here groping, however crudely, towards a theory of perfect markets, though he has not yet introduced the role of information in any overt sense, and he does not prove that such a market in terms of labour is either actually extant or philosophical desirable. He remains, however, an interesting precursor of later theories in this field.

Cree criticized modern economists, especially Alfred MARSHALL but also Mill, Henry FAWCETT and Fleeming JENKIN, on the grounds that their work was overly abstruse and insufficiently practical. In *Business Men and Modern Economics* (1903) he complains about the 'new economists' who he says are moving away from considerations of practical commerce. He feels this is a mistake; a wholly theoretical science of economics, such as he believes is emerging, runs the risk of losing touch with the realities of commerce and the marketplace. Economic science and commercial practice must always have some relationship to each other if the former is to remain relevant.

BIBLIOGRAPHY
A Criticism of the Theory of Trades' Unions (Glasgow, 1891).
Evils of Collective Bargaining in Trades' Unions (Glasgow, 1898).
Business Men and Modern Economics (Glasgow, 1903).

Katharine Norley

CREED, James (*fl. c.*1752)

Nothing is known of Creed apart from a few references to himself in his own writing. His only surviving work, *An Impartial Examination of a Pamphlet, intitled Considerations on Several Proposals lately made for the Better Maintenance of the Poor* (1752), is an attack on the ideas of Charles GRAY. In it, Creed tells us that he was for many years a justice of the peace in Middlesex, Surrey and Kent, and he adds that at time of writing he had been confined for some years with a serious illness; the two points together suggest that he was then elderly or in late middle age.

His purpose in writing is to refute Gray, who he believes is in favour of dismantling the current system of poor relief and throw the whole burden onto private charity. He vigorously attacks this view, and argues that more state provision is necessary. In his time as magistrate, he says, he was 'frequently witness to the insufficiency of the laws, with regard both to the maintenance and employ of the poor' (1752: 19). He particularly supports legislation then being considered by parliament to improve the care and education of poor children. He refers frequently to the ideas on poor relief advanced by Sir Joshua CHILD and John CARY, and is particularly influenced by the latter, although he is not always specific in stating which proposals of Cary's he agrees with. In opposition to Gray, he calls for more publicly funded hospitals and infirmaries.

Creed expresses his views passionately, and these views were clearly shaped by his experiences as a magistrate. However, his attack on Gray is at least partially misjudged, for Gray, though conservative in his approach, was by no means in favour of tearing down the system of public welfare provision. Other targets could have been found more deserving of Creed's ire. It is possible that his illness somewhat affected his judgement in this matter.

BIBLIOGRAPHY
An Impartial Examination of a Pamphlet, intitled Considerations on Several Proposals lately made for the Better Maintenance of the Poor (1752).

Further Reading
Gray, C., *Considerations of Several Proposals late made for the Better Maintenance of the Poor* (1751).

Ann Kimber

CROKER, John Wilson (1780–1857)

Croker was born in Galway on 20 December 1780, and died in Dublin on 10 August 1857. He was educated in Cork and Portarlington before attending Trinity College, Dublin. In 1800 he entered Lincoln's Inn, and was called to the Irish bar in 1802. He began his literary career by publishing on theatrical matters; concurrently he began to establish a successful legal business in Dublin. In 1807 he joined the Munster Circuit, where he met Daniel O'Connell. Croker married Rosamund Pennell in 1806; the couple had one child, Spencer (1817–20).

Croker was MP for Downpatrick (1806–12) Athlone (1812–18), Yarmouth (1819), Bodmin (1820–6), Aldeburgh (1826–7 and 1830–2) and Dublin University (1827–30). He began his political life supporting Portland's ministry and favouring Catholic Emancipation: his maiden speech was on the state of Ireland. In 1808 he published *The State of Ireland, Past and Present*, which made Croker's political name and resulted in his appointment as chief secretary for Ireland in place of Wellington (1808). Croker became a close friend of Wellington, Peel and Canning, and he a founder member of the Athenaeum Club (1824).

In 1809 Croker became one of the founding contributors to the *Quarterly Review*, a Tory periodical, and wrote for virtually every issue between 1811 and 1845. Some of his work was so acerbic that writers claimed to have been 'hanged, drawn and *Quarterlied*'. His style earned him many enemies, but without his contributions, the *Review* would not have been as successful as it was.

From 1809–30, Croker was secretary of the Admiralty, soon proving his worth by proving that a high official had embezzled about £250,000. He grasped factual material readily, and built a reputation as a formidable parliamentarian. He was an incisive if sarcastic speaker. Although he supported Canning's ministry, Croker worked towards ensuring that Peel accepted leadership of the new 'conservative' party, a term that Croker coined in 1830. He resigned his post in 1830 when Wellington left office, and retired from politics in 1832. In opposition, he spoke powerfully against the Reform Act, even silencing Macaulay, who then indulged in personal invective against Croker. Croker retaliated later, calling Macaulay's *History of England* (1849) 'an historical romance'.

Croker defended Peel's *Tamworth Manifesto* (1834) and supported Peel's second administration. In December 1842, Peel approved an article of Croker's that was hostile to the repeal of the Corn Laws: Croker's anti-repeal essays were inspired by Peel and Sir James GRAHAM. By 1845, it had become clear that Peel was intending to repeal the Corn Laws, and as a confirmed protectionist, Croker felt betrayed. Wellington tried to persuade him that a refusal to repeal the legislation would put the ministry 'into the hands of the League and the radicals'. Croker was adamant that this was what repeal would do. Peel's repeal terminated their close friendship. Ironically, Disraeli – who made his political name by attacking the repeal – caricatured Croker as 'Rigby', a contemptible and hateful character *(Coningsby* 1844).

After 1850 Croker suffered from heart disease. In 1854 he stopped writing for the *Quarterly Review,* having contributed at least 260 articles on a range of topics: legal and historical matter, Ireland, the French Revolution, ecclesiastical affairs, travel and poetry.

BIBLIOGRAPHY
An Intercepted Letter from Canton (1804).
A Sketch of Ireland, Past and Present (1808; repr. 1884).
Key to the Orders in Council (1812).
Horace Walpole's Letters to Lord Hertford (1824).
Boswell's Life of Johnson (1831).
John, Lord Hervey's Memoirs of the Court of George II (1848).

Marjorie Bloy

CROMBIE, Alexander (1762–1840)

Crombie was born in Aberdeen some time in 1762, and died at his estate of Phesdo near Fordoun, Kincardineshire some time before 16 June 1840, the date of his obituary in *The Times*. He studied at Marischal College, Aberdeen, graduating MA in 1777 and later LL.D, probably in 1798. He was also ordained a minister in the Church of Scotland, but chose the career of schoolteacher over that of clergyman. He taught for several years in Aberdeen before moving to London. Here he established his own school, first in Highgate and later in Greenwich. He earned a substantial income from teaching and writing and became well-known as a scholar; his *The Etymology and Syntax of the English Language* (1802) and *Gymnasium Sive Symbola Critica* (1815) were widely used as textbooks for the study of Latin and English. His friends and correspondents included Joseph Priestley, Richard PRICE and Robert TORRENS; according to his own account, it was Torrens who first introduced Crombie to David RICARDO. He inherited the Phesdo estate from a cousin, and retired there from London a few years before his death.

In his own day Crombie was best known as a philosopher and theologian. His *Essay on Philosophical Necessity* (1793) is a reaction to James Gregory's *Philosophical and Literary Essays* of the previous year, which espoused the cause of 'philosophical liberty'. Crombie, influenced by Priestley and David HUME, argued instead for a doctrine of 'philosophical necessity', believing that the will is restricted and influenced by previous actions and circumstances. He later wrote an influential discussion on natural theology and the soul (1829).

Crombie's interests extended beyond philosophy and language, however, and he produced several works on economic issues, particularly those relating to labour. He was highly conservative on many issues, and in *The Strike* (1834) warns of the dangers to society should labour be able to organize and take action against employers. His most important work is a critique of Ricardo, specifically of the latter's equilibrium theory, in *A Letter to D. Ricardo* (1817). He refers to equilibrium theory, the idea that the currency of one country can never remain much more valuable than that of any other country for any length of time, and that in the long run currencies maintain an equilibrium of value with each other, as a 'fanciful hypothesis' (1817: 22).

Crombie begins his attack on Ricardo by stating a labour theory of value. Money, he says, is a commodity, and the worth of any commodity can only be measured by the quantity of labour that it can command:

> And, as labour is undertaken chiefly for the purpose of procuring the necessaries and comforts of life, the most correct measure of value, next to labour, is the quantity of those necessaries and comforts, for which any commodity may be exchanged. Money may be conveniently employed to express the value of labour, though that labour be itself the only real measure of value: but it is still to be remembered, that the labourer, in estimating his services, looks not at the money, which they may command, but at the portion of necessaries, conveniences and comforts, which that money may be able to purchase.
>
> (1817: 8)

As a result, says Crombie, the value of money fluctuates from country to country, and has done since time immemorial. At time of writing, an ounce of silver would command nearly double the quantity of labour in France that it would in Britain, and this was a direct result of differences in the supply of labour in each country.

Crombie goes on to attack several others of Ricardo's hypotheses. He does not agree with the latter's view that coin is only exported when there is a surplus in circulation. During the Napoleonic wars large sums of coin had been exported from Britain at a time of great scarcity in domestic circulation, largely as subsidies to foreign allies or to pay the expenses of the army in Spain. More generally, says Crombie, the widespread export of currency is often a symptom of a negative balance of trade, when currency must be exported to pay for goods coming in over and above the value of exports, and thus has little to do with the supply of coin in circulation. He also accuses Ricardo of muddled thinking with respect to gold: is the value of gold bullion determined by the value of gold coin, or vice versa? Ricardo, he says, seems to be saying both. Crombie then reiterates his own view that bullion and coin, though mutually convertible, cannot be regarded as identical. Both are commodities, and the value of both fluctuates like that of any other commodity. *A Letter to D. Ricardo* is an interesting and strong critique, but it suffers from muddled thinking and is often repetitive.

BIBLIOGRAPHY
An Essay on Philosophical Necessity (1793).
Letters on the Present State of the Agricultural Interest, Addressed to Charles Forbes, Esq., M.P. (1816).
A Letter to D. Ricardo, Esq, Containing an Analysis of his Pamphlet on the Depreciation of Bank Notes (1817).
Natural Theology (1829).
The Strike, or a Dialogue between John Treadle and Andrew Ploughman (1834).

Ann Kimber

CROSLAND, Charles Anthony Raven (1918–77)

Crosland was born at St. Leonard's-on-Sea, Sussex, on 29 August 1918, and died in Oxford on 19 February 1977. His father Joseph was a senior civil servant at the War Office, and his mother Jessie lectured at Westfield College, London. In many respects the family were typical of the professional middle classes between the wars. They lived in the leafy suburbs of north London, and were able to send Crosland to public school at Highgate. From there he went, with the support of a scholarship, to Trinity College, Oxford in 1937. Yet one distinguishing feature of this background was that the Croslands belonged to the Plymouth Brethren, a fervent nonconformist sect associated with a spartan lifestyle. In time Tony, as he was often called, rebelled against his upbringing by developing a strongly hedonistic streak: most people, he said, would be happy in life with a combination of 'sex, gin and Bogart' (Jefferys 1999: 28). But Crosland also carried much forward from his early life, for example his father's interest in public affairs and his mother's concern for rigorous scholarship. Above all, he accepted the Brethren conviction that all men and women were equal in God's eyes. This strong commitment to equality, combined with the anti-fascist mood at Oxford in the late 1930s, helped to shape Crosland's left-wing views and his interest in politics.

After the Second World War, in which Crosland saw active service in southern Europe, he returned to Oxford to complete his undergraduate studies, gaining a first in philosophy, politics and economics in 1946. When his tutor Robert Hall left to become an adviser to Attlee's Labour government, Crosland replaced him as Trinity's fellow in economics. Hall had helped his pupil to absorb many of the key economic texts of the day, notably Keynes's *General Theory*, and Crosland began to make his own scholarly contributions to the discipline. He wrote a series of short articles on topics ranging from the pricing policy of the National Coal Board to the distribution of labour. Days were spent in hard academic endeavour, but – in an effort to make up for lost years in the army – nights were given over to riotous living, gambling, smoking, drinking and womanizing. However, Crosland's career as an unusually glamorous academic economist was short-lived. He was most comfortable producing polemical pieces for socialist journals, and his mind was turning increasingly to politics. With the support of Hugh DALTON, Chancellor of the Exchequer from 1945–7, Crosland was adopted as a parliamentary candidate, and in 1950 he was elected as Labour MP for South Gloucestershire.

After his Oxford days, Crosland became increasingly convinced that the 'long-run problems of concern to Socialists are no longer mainly economic...It is sociologists the party needs' (Leonard 1999: 126). He nevertheless established his credentials as an intellectual in politics during the early 1950s with studies that reflected his background in economics. In 1952 he wrote for *The New Fabian Essays*, a collection which also contained contributions from other young MPs on the Labour centre-right such as Roy Jenkins, a close friend from undergraduate days at Oxford. Crosland's piece, 'The Transition from Capitalism', which was among the best received in the book, used a wealth of data to argue that the welfare and economic changes introduced since 1945 had produced a new type of post-capitalist society. In spite of such changes, he cautioned, Britain in the 1950s had not begun to approach the ideal of a 'classless or egalitarian society', a situation which could only be remedied by switching attention from economic to social reform, especially in the sphere of education.

Crosland's first full-length book, *Britain's Economic Problem*, published in 1953, brought his economic expertise to bear on Britain's balance-of-payments problem. Although published at a time when world trade was finally recovering from the effects of war, Crosland started from the assumption – borne out in later years – that the question of long-term solvency had not been addressed and that radical solutions were required. In place of traditional policies such as short-term cuts in public expenditure or 'fiddling with the Bank Rate', the real needs were for high levels of investment and industrial modernisation (1953: 207–22). In more partisan mode, Crosland accused the incumbent Conservative government of being obsessed with monetary techniques. Labour, he felt, struggling in opposition, desperately needed to develop a bold strategy, one that combined changes to the machinery of economic planning with the right distribution of investment between social and industrial expenditure. Reviewers were generally impressed. Among financial commentators not known for sympathy to the Labour cause, there was a guarded welcome. *The Financial Times* noted that Crosland did not appear to give 'two hoots' for the shibboleths of orthodox economists, even if towards the end of the book he became too much the party man.

Defeated at the general election in 1955, Crosland was free to put the finishing touches to a book that many came to regard as the finest of its type in the post-war period. *The Future of Socialism* was the culmination of the youthful, flamboyant phase of Crosland's life, as well as the most significant product of Labour 'revisionism' in the 1950s. In analysing changes since the war, Crosland again argued that pre-war capitalism had been changed beyond recognition. In thinking about how socialism needed to be redefined in consequence, he introduced a key aspect of the new revisionism: a distinction between ends and means. Too often, he felt, particular groups – notably Marxists – had appropriated the term 'socialism' to describe the means by which they would bring about reform. But as the proposed means had never commanded universal assent, it was best that any definition should stick to the ends in view. On this definition, socialism for Crosland was primarily about equality and welfare. It remained a relevant creed because in spite of post-war improvements, social distress was still widespread in 1950s Britain, class antagonisms remained strong, and the distribution of rewards and privileges was still highly inequitable. This constituted the 'ethical basis for being a socialist' (1956: 116).

What then was to be done? The core of *The Future of Socialism* contained Crosland's ideas for future policy. As well as continuing to improve welfare provisions such as the National Health Service, he hoped to see a 'social revolution' achieved through egalitarian reforms, notably to the education system and to the distribution of property. While wishing to go beyond equality of opportunity, he was not in favour of equality of outcomes. He did not wish to see 'the Queen riding a bicycle' (1956: 216). Society would look very different if his proposed changes were carried through, and it would be for a younger generation to look at the arguments afresh. As far as economic policy was concerned, Crosland noted the importance of growth for the realization of socialist objectives, though more attention was given at the time to his trenchant view that – while further measures of public ownership were needed – old-style state monopolies were 'wholly irrelevant to socialism as defined in this book' (1956: 495–7). The conclusion to the book contained some of its most striking passages, underlining Crosland's libertarianism and his conviction that social rather than economic issues should be accorded top priority in future. He urged not only cultural changes that might make Britain 'a more colourful and civilised country to live in', but also – in what amounted to a blueprint for the type of legislation introduced a decade later – the updating of restrictive laws on divorce, homosexuality, censorship and rights for women (1956: 520–4).

Labour fundamentalists were outraged by Crosland's assertion that nationalization should henceforth play only a minor role in socialist advance. Yet on the whole, *The Future of Socialism* was lauded as an exciting attempt to make socialism look relevant to the 'affluent society' of the 1950s. It provided a springboard for the development of Crosland's career in politics. He was close to Attlee's successor as Labour leader, Hugh GAITSKELL, who promoted revisionist policies and helped Crosland secure the nomination as Labour candidate for Grimsby, the parliamentary seat he represented from 1959 until the time of his death. In 1962 he brought together much of his thinking since 1956 in *The Conservative Enemy*, aimed at providing a 'programme of radical, social-democratic reform for the middle 1960s'. In what he later described as 'much the angriest of his books', Crosland attacked not just Macmillan's unpopular Conservative government, but also the extra-parliamentary New Left for clinging to 'an out-dated semi-Marxist analysis of society' (Jefferys 1999: 81). Despite lacking the freshness of his previous work, *The Conservative Enemy* won high praise. This was partly because Crosland's reputation as the high priest of revisionism was now firmly established, though it also stemmed from the concern even of his critics inside the party not to rock the boat ahead of what looked like a Gaitskell election victory. The sudden death of Hugh Gaitskell in early 1963 was a huge personal and political blow to Crosland. The triumph in the leadership contest that followed of Gaitskell's arch-enemy, Harold Wilson, meant that almost overnight Crosland went from the inner sanctum of party counsels to 'outer darkness' (Jefferys 1999: 89).

The best Crosland could hope for when Wilson became prime minister in 1964 was a middle-ranking government post. He was first appointed as deputy to George Brown at the Department of Economic Affairs, and then in 1965 he entered the Cabinet as Secretary of State for Education. In the more settled domestic circumstances of his second marriage to the American journalist Susan Catling (his first marriage in the 1950s ended in divorce), Crosland proved an effective and determined education minister, pushing ahead with the introduction of comprehensive secondary schooling. Yet he struggled to overcome the suspicions of the prime minister, especially as he insisted on promoting the idea of devaluation, a policy Wilson strenuously opposed. When devaluation became unavoidable in 1967, it proved a hollow victory for Crosland.

The government's reputation for economic competence collapsed, and Crosland – having moved a few months earlier to the Board of Trade – was passed over for the post of Chancellor of the Exchequer, made vacant by the resignation of James Callaghan. Wilson chose instead Roy Jenkins, a popular reforming Home Secretary. This was a defining moment in Crosland's political career, and marked the beginnings of a serious breach on Labour's centre-right. Crosland was convinced he was better qualified to tackle the demands of the Treasury than his younger friend and rival, and was left to languish first as President of the Board of Trade and then – in the dying days of the Wilson administration – at the Department of Local Government and Regional Planning.

Labour's loss of power in 1970 was followed by a fresh bout of in-fighting. As left-wing views gained ground among the rank and file, the social democratic wing of the party, far from reasserting itself as it did in the 1950s, began to disintegrate. Underpinning this process was the economic malaise of the 1970s, with inflation rampant, growth minimal and trade unions apparently 'out of control'. Other policy issues, notably Europe, also proved critical. The first two years in opposition were overshadowed by protracted disputes over Labour's attitude towards membership of the European Community. A minority of pro-Market MPs, grouped around Roy Jenkins, decided to back Heath's Tory government in pushing for British entry, despite suspicions about the value of membership in the eyes of most MPs and activists. The staunchly pro-European views of Jenkins were not shared by Crosland, who abstained in the crucial Commons vote. The followers of Jenkins were incensed by this 'betrayal' of the high priest of revisionism. Personality and policy differences thus combined to underline the increasing fragmentation among the inheritors of the Gaitskellite tradition.

By the time Labour won a narrow election victory in the spring of 1974, Crosland – who became Environment Secretary – had become almost a one-man champion of egalitarian socialism. Wilson's return to Downing Street coincided with the publication of Crosland's last book, *Socialism Now*. This addressed the issue of whether traditional revisionism required a complete overhaul in the wake of the oil crisis that sent shock waves through the world economy. Crosland acknowledged that it was legitimate to question if greater equality was still attainable. On this issue he insisted that revisionism remained more persuasive than the revived 'semi-Marxist thought' of the Labour left. The failures of the past decade, he argued, had little to do with nationalization. What was needed was not a move to Clause Four socialism but a 'sharper delineation of fundamental objectives', with careful costing and planning of reforms to make them part of a coherent package, not isolated achievements as when Labour was last in power. He then listed his own priorities, which included the reduction of poverty, the elimination of selection in secondary schools and the extension of industrial democracy (1974: 44–8).

Crosland was lucky in the timing of his book, which gave it much prominence, though he encountered sterner criticism than he had had in the past. He was attacked for being hazy not only about how to achieve higher growth, but also about how to secure the reduction of poverty that he said was the top priority. One Labour back-bencher, a supporter of Jenkins, wrote that *Socialism Now* was disappointing and had not provided a *Future of Socialism* Mark II. This clearly touched a nerve, for Crosland bluntly said at one point that he was 'too bloody busy' to rethink his whole philosophy. On another occasion he remarked: 'Keynes didn't write another *General Theory*' (Jefferys 1999: 176).

In the leadership contest that followed Wilson's resignation in 1976, Crosland came last of six contenders. His personal prospects nevertheless revived with the emergence as prime minister of an old ally, Jim Callaghan. When Roy Jenkins decided to leave British politics to take up the presidency of the European Commission, the future leadership of the Labour centre-right appeared to rest between Crosland, promoted by Callaghan to become Foreign Secretary, and Chancellor of the Exchequer Denis Healey. Crosland and Healey found themselves at loggerheads during the IMF crisis in the autumn of 1976, when the Foreign Secretary attempted to resist the draconian cutbacks required as the price of international support for the ailing British economy. The crisis did not, as some have claimed, mark a watershed in which Labour turned towards monetarism. Healey never had to draw on more than half the available loan and economic recovery in 1977 enabled him to celebrate 'Sod Off Day' – when Britain became free of IMF control – much earlier than anticipated. But as well as damaging the government's standing, the IMF crisis had shattering effects for Labour's social democrats. When Crosland died suddenly after a massive stroke early in 1977, the revisionist notion of achieving equality via economic growth and redistributive taxation looked dead in the water. The final nail in the coffin was the failure of Labour's strategy for working with the trade unions, culminating in the misery of the winter of discontent and the election of Margaret Thatcher's Conservative government in 1979.

After Crosland's death, his friends argued that his brand of socialism never became the overarching ideology that would have been likely if Hugh Gaitskell had lived, especially as Crosland was denied the Chancellorship in 1967 – the one post which would have put him in a position to propose alternatives to periodic bouts of deflation. His detractors claimed that his main error was to focus too much on the distribution of wealth and not enough on its creation. Yet he was not alone in being unable to produce any workable theory of growth in the testing circumstances of the 1970s. Whatever his failings, Crosland's career had been unique, wrote his American friend Daniel Bell, combining 'a reflective mind of great intellectual power' with 'the active life of a socialist politician' (Jefferys 1999: 231). As well as being a minister who had reached the highest rank below that of the premiership, *The Future of Socialism* in particular marked out Tony Crosland as one of the leading left-wing writers of the twentieth century. The brilliance of his prose and analysis made the book a vital reference point for a whole generation, capturing the post-war spirit of optimism that sought to reconcile liberty with equality, prosperity with fairness. In the eyes of Crosland, according to David Reisman, economics was 'the instrument that maximised the gains from capitalism's triumph in order to make possible the transition to reform' (Leonard 1999: 46).

BIBLIOGRAPHY
Britain's Economic Problem (1953).
The Future of Socialism (1956).
The Conservative Enemy. A Programme of Radical Reform for the 1960s (1962).
Socialism Now and Other Essays (1974).

Further Reading
Crosland, S., *Tony Crosland* (1982).
Jefferys, K., *Anthony Crosland* (1999).
Leonard, D. (ed.), *Crosland and New Labour* (1999).
Lipsey, D. and Leonard, D. (eds), *The Socialist Agenda. Crosland's Legacy* (1981).
Reisman, D., *Anthony Crosland. The Mixed Economy* (1997).

Kevin Jefferys

CROWTHER, Geoffrey (1907–72)

Crowther was born 13 May 1907 at Headingley, Yorkshire, and died suddenly at Heathrow Airport on 5 February 1972 while returning from Australia. He was the son of

Charles Crowther, professor of agricultural chemistry at the University of Leeds, and his wife Hilda. Crowther was educated first at Leeds Grammar School, where he proved to be academically gifted but easily bored, and then at Oundle. He entered Clare College, Cambridge where he read modern languages in his first year and then switched to economics. He was president of the Cambridge Union in his final year (1928). Contemporaries at Cambridge described him as being very confident and self-possessed (Edwards 1993: 696).

After winning an upper first in economics tripos, Crowther went to the USA in 1929 on a Commonwealth Fund Scholarship, and spent a year ostensibly attached to Yale University but in fact working on Wall Street, where he saw at first hand the after-effects of the financial crash. Returning to Britain, he worked briefly for a London bank, studied Irish banking affairs and became an advisor to the Irish government. In 1932 he married Margaret Worth from Wilmington, Delaware, and later that year was invited by Walter LAYTON to join the editorial staff of *The Economist*.

At *The Economist*, Crowther was part of an intake of influential young journalists including Graham Hutton and Douglas JAY. He worked particularly closely with Layton, and the two often collaborated on leader articles; Crowther was also the journal's specialist on America. Edwards, drawing on the recollections of Crowther's colleagues, comments that he and Layton developed a particularly strong mutual understanding, and Crowther became in effect Layton's intellectual heir (Edwards 1993: 730). When Layton stepped down from the editorship, remaining as chairman of *The Economist*, Crowther was the natural choice to succeed him.

Crowther inherited the post of editor on the night of the Munich agreement in 1938, and spent the entire night revising the journal as news came in; he finished the final draft of his leader article at 6 a.m. the following morning (Edwards 1993: 741). During the Second World War he spent periods as advisor variously to the Ministry of Supply, Ministry of Information and Ministry of Production, while still continuing to edit *The Economist*. During those years he developed a powerful intellectual partnership with Barbara WARD, and together they produced some of *The Economist*'s finest writing of the modern era. As editor, he continued Layton's strong commitment to internationalism; although hesitant about Bretton Woods, believing that on the whole it favoured American interests over those of Britain, he finally supported ratification. He also continued Layton's policy of hiring and encouraging female journalists, and argued for equal pay for women.

Crowther retired as editor in March 1956, shortly before Suez, but like Layton, stayed on as chairman. He was knighted in 1957, and created a life peer as Baron Crowther in 1968. However, the 1960s saw Crowther involved in a series of not always successful business ventures. His creation of the British Printing Corporation through the merger of two companies was fraught with difficulties, largely because Crowther himself had overlooked financial and structural problems in one of the merged companies. He became chairman of Trust Houses in 1960 and oversaw its merger with Forte in 1970 to become the nation's largest hotel group, but personal and policy differences with other members of the board became increasingly acrimonious, to the point where in 1971 Crowther himself supported a hostile takeover bid from Allied Breweries. This failed, and the boardroom climate grew still more bitter and may well have been a factor in Crowther's death at the age of sixty-four.

As well as a considerable journalistic output, Crowther also wrote the respected *An Outline of Money* (1940). He had earlier collaborated with Layton on the third edition of the latter's *An Introduction to the Study of Prices* (1938). The latter work was an extension of Layton's earlier study, collecting price data up to the mid-1930s but reaching much the same conclusions as had Layton in the original.

An Outline of Money is fairly introductory in nature, including chapters on the nature of money, the banking system, the value of money, the quantity of money, saving and capital, monetary policy, foreign exchange, exchange management and control, the gold standard and international equilibrium. Crowther repeats the familiar view that money has three functions: as a measure of wealth, a medium of exchange and a store of wealth (1940: 35). The second function is the most essential; other things may be used as measures of value or stores of wealth. For example, shares are a way to store wealth, but cannot be used to purchase goods.

In terms of the value of money, Crowther points out that money on its own has no intrinsic worth; its value is determined entirely by its exchange function. Thus the value of money is a problematic concept. There are three standard ways of expressing the value of money: first, in terms of the quantity of goods whose prices are quoted and recorded in public markets; second, in terms of the quantity of goods that the ordinary family consumes; and third, in terms of the amount of labour that a given quantity of money will buy. Using these three measures often results in three different values of money at the same time. This is clearly unsatisfactory and Crowther, following Layton, recommends establishing price indices to measure fluctuations and derive a more accurate and unified value of money.

An Outline of Money ends with a short analysis and criticism of C.H. DOUGLAS's writings on social credit. Crowther's other works include *Economics for Democrats* (1939), which includes strong support for the League of Nations – a view which Layton and Crowther had also expressed in the pages of *The Economist* – and two works on war finance.

BIBLIOGRAPHY
(with W. Layton) *An Introduction to the Study of Prices*, 3rd edn (1938).
Economics for Democrats (1939).
The Sinews of War (1939).
An Outline of Money (1940).
Paying for the War (1940).

Further Reading
Edwards, R.D., *The Pursuit of Reason: The Economist 1843–1993* (1993).

Morgen Witzel

CULPEPPER, Thomas (1626–97)

Thomas Culpepper the younger was born in 1626 at Leeds Castle, Kent, and died at Greenway Court, near Hollingbourne, Kent in 1697. He was the third son of Sir Thomas Culpepper (1578–1662), usually known as Thomas Culpepper the elder to distinguish him from his son, a gentleman of Kent who had been knighted by James I and served briefly as MP for Tewkesbury. Thomas Culpepper the younger entered University College, Oxford in 1640, later migrating to All Soul's; he apparently left Oxford without taking a degree. He was knighted shortly after the Restoration of Charles II, and upon inheriting Greenway Court from his father in 1662 (Leeds Castle passed to an elder brother and subsequently a cousin), established himself there and divided the rest of his life between Kent and London.

Culpepper the elder had in 1621 published *A Tract Against the High Rate of Usurie*, in which he suggested that the legal rate of interest should be lowered from 10 to 8 per cent. This tract was reprinted in 1641 with some additions. In 1640 Culpepper the elder had produced another pamphlet in which he argued for a further reduction of the interest rate from 8 to 6 per cent. Both these tracts which were referred to by Josiah CHILD in his discussion on lowering the legal interest in his *Brief Observations Concerning Trade and Interest of Money* (1668); Child also reprinted the 1641 re-issue of *A Tract Against the High Rate of Usurie*.

In the same year, 1668, Culpepper the younger republished his father's two tracts together with a preface. He also produced his own pamphlet, *Discourse Shewing the Many Advantages that will accrue to the Kingdome by the Abatement of Usury*, arguing that interest rates in England should be lowered to at least the level at which they stood in England's trading rivals. This was a period when the issue of possible state intervention in order to reduce the rate of interest by statute had been brought up by, amongst others, John LOCKE. Culpepper himself became involved in a protracted pamphlet dispute with Thomas Manley on the most desirable rate of interest. The discussion also provoked Child to reprint – and extend – his 1668 pamphlet under the new title, *A Discourse of Trade* in 1690.

The Culpeppers offer mainly moral arguments for the reduction of interest rates, although they certainly also were aware that such a reduction could be advantageous for trade and industry. However, their mainly moralistic discourse shares many similarities with early seventeenth century writers such as Gerard de MALYNES and Thomas MILLES, rather than with the later generation of writers on trade and economic issues after the middle of the century.

BIBLIOGRAPHY
Discourse Shewing the Many Advantages that will accrue to the Kingdome by the Abatement of Usury (1668).
The Necessity of Abating Usury Reasserted (1670).
Brief Survey of the Growth of Usury in England with the Mischiefs Attending it (1671).

Further Reading
Child, J., *Brief Observations Concerning Trade and Interest of Money* (1668).
Culpepper, T., *A Tract Against the High Rate of Usurie* (1621; repr. 1641, 1668)
Manley, T. *Usury at Six Per Cent. Examined* (1669).

Lars Magnusson

CUNNINGHAM, William (1849–1919)

Cunningham was born in Edinburgh on 29 December 1849, and died in Cambridge on 10 June 1919. His father, James, was a writer to the signet; His mother, Elizabeth Boyle Dunlop, was the second wife of James, and William was the youngest of three sons (there were a son and a daughter from the first marriage). He was educated at home until 1864 when he attended Edinburgh Academy. He entered Edinburgh University the following year. He had been brought up in a devoutly Presbyterian household, but in the summer of 1868 he spent three months at the University of Tübingen learning German. There he came under the influence of two Anglican scholars from America, and he resolved to become a priest in the Church of England. He graduated from Edinburgh in 1869 and in the same year entered Gonville and Caius College, Cambridge to read moral sciences, subsequently winning a scholarship to Trinity College. He was joint senior in the moral sciences tripos in 1872, took his MA in 1873 and was ordained deacon, becoming a priest a year later. He went on to serve as vicar of Great St Mary's, Cambridge (1887–1908) and Archdeacon of Ely (1907–19).

Cunningham had been an outstanding student at Cambridge, but in 1874 he failed to gain a fellowship at Trinity. Instead he began to lecture for the Cambridge Extension

Syndicate in Leeds, Bradford and Liverpool. His audiences were mostly working artisans and he learned a great deal about the economic and social problems of an industrializing society. In 1876 he married his cousin, Adele Dunlop of Dublin (there was one son and one daughter of the marriage). Soon after, he returned to Cambridge as assistant secretary, then secretary, to the Extension Syndicate and continued to teach and examine. In 1884 he became a university lecturer in history, teaching on the new paper on political economy and economic history, and in 1888 he was appointed a lecturer at Trinity College. He became a fellow of Trinity in 1891 and an honorary fellow of Caius in 1895. In 1891 he was appointed Tooke Professor of Economics at King's College, London, a post he held until 1897 whilst continuing to live in Cambridge. He lectured at Harvard in 1898–9 and again in 1914. He was a foundation member of the British Academy and president of the Royal Historical society from 1910 to 1913. His only son was killed in France in March 1918. Cunningham was survived by his wife and by his daughter, who published a memoir of her father in 1950.

The classes Cunningham gave in Cambridge and elsewhere were the basis of the work by which he is best remembered, the *Growth of English Industry and Commerce, during the Early and Middle Ages*. This was written quickly and published as a single volume in 1882, causing him later to express surprise 'that he should have managed to write such a good book in so short a time when he knew so little about the subject' (Cunningham 1950: 55). Over the years it grew into three monumental volumes, including two on 'Modern Times'. The fifth and final edition was published in 1910. As the enterprise expanded he was helped by former students and colleagues including Miss E.A. McArthur, Miss Elizabeth Lamond and especially Miss Lillian Tomn (later Professor Lillian Knowles). At times the work was almost too overloaded with detail, but its tone was authoritative. Subsequent generations of economic historians challenged Cunningham's interpretations, but he had given them a base from which to work.

Cunningham's studies of the past – and also a tour of India he made in 1881–2 – made him doubt the universal applicability of economic laws currently being elaborated by the neo-classical economists. The doubts developed gradually. In the preface to the *Growth of English Industry and Commerce* he wrote, 'economic history is not so much the study of a special class of facts, as the study of all the facts of a nation's history from a special point of view' (4th edn, 1905: 8). But what was the point of view that he had in mind? In the first edition he stated that 'the history of the eighteenth century in England could be conveniently studied as a series of illustrations of modern economic theory'. Further reflections had led him to change his mind. In his article, 'The Perversion of Economic History', published in the *Economic Journal* in 1892, Cunningham argued that economic laws were relative to time and place and did not enjoy universal application. Economic evolution was a complex process that was capable of understanding only through a thorough grasp of the facts. 'But there are some who do not feel the difficulties, who, with no practice in the weighing of historical evidence, and with the equipment of some two or three badly chosen books, will decide the most difficult problems off hand, or sketch the history of the world with easy confidence' (1892: 491–2). This was a broadside at Alfred MARSHALL, who in his *Principles of Economics* had included a relatively brief excursus into economic history that Cunningham dismissed as thin on knowledge and flawed in interpretation.

The dispute between Cunningham and Marshall was not without a personal edge. The latter had been elected to the Cambridge economics chair in 1884. Cunningham had also been a candidate, although he had held no great hope of success over the older man. But Cunningham was a university lecturer who did not enjoy the independence possessed by a college lecturer, and Marshall required him to teach formal political economy as well as economic history. More fundamentally, though, the argument between the two men was an English variant of the German methodological debate about whether economics should proceed by inductive or deductive reasoning. The German historical school had an influence on Cunningham's thinking, but his historicism was mainly home-grown, drawn from writers such as Thomas MUN, William PETTY and Adam SMITH.

Most important of all, the dispute was the outcome of a struggle for the professional independence of economics. Marshall and his colleagues were working to establish the scientific principles of economics that could be used to interpret the complex processes of economic behaviour. Cunningham had a different approach. Like most of his near contemporaries – ASHLEY, Cliffe Leslie, HEWINS, Ingram, Thorold ROGERS – he believed that a thorough knowledge of the political, economic and social institutions of the past was essential for the true understanding of economic behaviour. In a late work, *The Progress of Capitalism in England* (1916), he sketched in three stages of capitalistic growth that mirrored the work of German scholars, and in some respects foreshadowed Rostow's stages of economic growth. These were, firstly, a pre-capitalist form of organization (the natural economy), and secondly, capitalism in medieval cities where money was used and markets operated, but money and the ownership of capital did not shape personal relationships. In the third stage capitalism became a form of social organization in which the possession of capital defined the relationships between employers and the employed and determined the political and social structures in which they worked. The hope of the historical economists was that an intensive careful study of the successive stages of economic development would induce general explanations of economic behaviour. The hope was never fulfilled because the events of past rarely if ever explained themselves; theory was needed to explain the facts, just as facts were necessary to inform the theory.

At the distance of over a century, the arguments about inductive versus deductive methods in economics appear as little more than arid squabbles. Cunningham, whose nature was combative, certainly pushed his case too far and he was less than fair to Marshall. Indeed, Cunningham was himself sometimes willing to argue from general principles, especially in his earlier writings; his point was that the laws of economic behaviour have to be tested against the attitudes and institutions of the times. But the dispute was more than a petty quarrel; it had important consequences for the development both of economics and economic history. Following Marshall, economics came to be dominated by marginalism and high theory. Its methods and language created a technical barrier to entry into the profession except for those formally trained in the subject. Deductive economics became the mainstream of the discipline, and many academic economists were indifferent, or even mildly hostile, to economic history. For many decades there was relatively little cross-fertilization between the two approaches. As for economic history, its future in Britain lay in university history developments or in independent departments rather than within departments of economics. Whether this was good for the long-term health of the discipline is a debatable point. After the Second World War the interest of economists turned to the analysis of long-term economic growth, and there were major developments also in econometrics. These were of considerable benefit to the study of economic history in America, where the subject was normally located in the economics departments. For example, the briefly exciting emergence of econometric history occurred first in America. In Britain economic historians had always been interested in long-term growth but there was relatively little help from the economists. The intellectual cutting edge of economic history was now in the USA.

Cunningham's legacy to the discipline was nevertheless fundamental. He claimed, with justification, that his *Growth of English Commerce and Industry* laid the foundations of the subject in Britain. He believed, optimistically as it turned out, that economic history would forever be taught in the universities. His work established a strong empirical tradition demonstrated, for example, in the works of his pupil, Sir John CLAPHAM, who became the first professor of economic history in Cambridge in 1928. Clapham described Cunningham as one of the two outstanding economic historians of his time (other was Sir William ASHLEY). The Cambridge chair was not the first in Britain; the first, at Manchester in 1910, went to George UNWIN. Lillian Knowles, another of Cunningham's former pupils, had been appointed to a chair at the London School of Economics in 1921; she dedicated her book on the industrial revolution to his memory. Other chairs followed, and after the Second World War they multiplied in the new universities. By the end of the century many of these chairs had been abolished and departments closed down or merged into departments of history, economics or business.

The focus of Cunningham's economic history was on forms of economic organization: manors, gilds, trading companies, workshops and factories, financial and commercial institutions. This agenda fell rather out of fashion in economic history syllabuses during the 1950s and 1960s, in favour of demography and long-term trends in national income. But the approach later attracted the attention of institutional economists, such as Douglass North. They were led to this by their focus on private property and transaction costs. Economic progress, as economic historians had always known, involved one kind of economic institution replacing another, a factory, for example, in place of a cottage workshop. There was a cost – a 'transaction cost' – attached to the transition. The expected gains from the shift had to outweigh the cost otherwise it would not take place. In almost every form of economic organization somebody owned the resources. In other words, there was private property and the property owners would not incur the transaction cost unless they reaped the benefits. Cunningham might have appreciated the irony that economic structures had become part of the economists' agenda.

For Cunningham, along with many scholars influenced by the historical school, the state had an important role in promoting economic development. In the *Growth of English Industry and Commerce* he argued that Edward III pursued a coherent commercial policy designed to foster English foreign trade (he later, though, conceded to George Unwin that Edward III did nothing of the sort). Cunningham was an admirer of what he described as 'the great industrial code' of Elizabeth and her chief minister, Burleigh, and the commercial policies of the seventeenth and eighteenth centuries summed up in the word 'mercantilism'. Although he recognized the material benefits flowing from *laissez-faire* during the nineteenth century, he deplored many of its social consequences. Indeed, *laissez-faire* and free trade for him represented an aberration, a retreat from state policies of promoting the national interest.

As with his views on the generality of economic laws, Cunningham's antipathy towards free trade evolved gradually as his investigations of the economic past proceeded. Semmel dates his 'conversion' to protectionism to 'about 1902' (Semmel 1960: 191). Cunningham became a tariff reformer and a founder member of the Cambridge University Tariff Reform Association. Increasingly his economic, historical and polemical articles made the case for protection. His advocacy of tariff reform put him increasingly at odds with economic orthodoxy. Cunningham had become – perhaps he always had been – 'a great National Economist' (Semmel 1960: 189), arguing for the preservation and strengthening of the national state.

This stance led Cunningham, in one direction, to be a staunch opponent of socialism. Cunningham had sometimes thought of himself as a Christian socialist, but working-class socialism was a challenge to private property, which was a God-given institution. It was the Christian duty of property owners, as the guardians of wealth, to attend to the welfare of their workers and the unfortunates of society. In another direction it led him into a strongly held imperialism. It was the destiny of Britain (England, even) to be a leader of nations. He wrote in the conclusion to *Alien Immigrants to England* (1897) that England 'has come to be the mother of free states throughout the world, and the guardian of peoples who, though yet in tutelage, are learning under her guidance to live their own lives in a better way' (1897: 270–1). The belief in the importance of the nation state made him a strong supporter of the Boer War. His belief that it was England's destiny to make the world a better place enabled him to take comfort from the thought that when his son was killed in action in 1918, he fell in the service of his country.

William Cunningham was a Cambridge man, energetic in the defence of its interests as he saw them, although regretting that the university had not awarded him a chair. He had devoted students, especially at Girton, and he made over substantial royalties from his books to the college. Above all he was a priest in the Church of England. To Cunningham, the Church of England, the nation state and the university were all part of God's plan. He was assiduous in his duties as vicar of Great St Mary's for two decades. He knew his parishioners from the town and the university alike and attended faithfully to their spiritual and material needs. He was conscientious in his attention to business of the archdeaconry of Ely for twelve years. Dressed in his top hat and archdeacon's cloak, and with a bristling beard, he bestrode the streets of Cambridge like an Old Testament patriarch.

With the passage of time Cunningham's imperial vision has evaporated, and the once seemingly insoluble connections between church and state and places of higher learning, have dissolved. The confidence Cunningham had in the durability of the teaching of his subject has been dented by time. Subsequent economic historians in Britain fairly quickly rejected his belief in the power of governments to promote economic prosperity. But in the words of one occupant of the Cambridge chair, 'if economic historians of the next generation were able to devote themselves to specialized study, it was because the field was occupied for them and the foundation laid by Cunningham' (Postan 1971: 22).

BIBLIOGRAPHY
(For a full bibliography see A. Cunningham, 1950.)
Growth of English Industry and Commerce (1882; 5th edn, 3 vols, 1910).
'The Relativity of Economic Doctrine', *Economic Journal* (1892), vol. II, pp. 1–16.
'The Perversion of Economic history, *Economic Journal* (1892), vol. II, pp. 491–506.
(with E.A. McArthur) *Outlines of English Industrial History* (1895; subsequent edns 1898, 1904, 1910, 1913).
Alien Immigrants to England (1897).
The Progress of Capitalism in England (1916).

Further Reading
Coleman, D.C., *History and the Economic Past* (Oxford, 1987).
Cunningham, A., *William Cunningham: Teacher and Priest* (1950).
Foxwell, H.S., 'Obituary. Archdeacon Cunningham', *Economic Journal* (1919), vol. XXIX, pp. 382–90.
Knowles, L., 'Obituary. Archdeacon Cunningham', *Economic Journal* (1919), vol. XXIX, pp. 390–3.
Maloney, J., 'Marshall, Cunningham, and the Emerging Economics Profession', *Economic History Review* (1976), 2nd series, vol. XXIX, no. 3, pp. 440–51.

Postan, M.M., *Fact and Relevance: Essays on Historical Method* (Cambridge, 1971).
Semmel, B., *Imperialism and Social Reform: English Social-Imperialist Thought 1895–1914* (1960).

Leslie Clarkson

CUNYNGHAME, Henry Hardinge Samuel (1848–1935)

Cunynghame was born on 8 July 1848 at Penshurst, Kent. He died at Eastbourne at the age of 86 on 3 May 1935. He was descended from the ancient family of Milncraig, Ayrshire. His father was General Sir Arthur Thurlow Cunynghame and his mother, Frances, was the daughter of Field Marshal Viscount Hardinge. He was descended on one side from Lord Chancellor Thurlow, and on the other from Lord Chancellor Camden. He attended Wellington School and entered the Royal Military Academy, Woolwich, where in 1866 he won the Pollock Medal and Sword of Merit. Two years later he joined the Royal Engineers, but after a further two years, in 1870 at the age of twenty-two, Cunynghame resigned from a promising military career and entered St John's College Cambridge with a view to entering the legal profession. He read for the moral sciences tripos and there met Alfred MARSHALL (who had recently been appointed a College fellow). He graduated as second moralist in 1873. Cunynghame became one of Marshall's favourites, and was an early proponent of geometrical political economy, which became the subject of his famous text of 1904 entitled *A Geometrical Political Economy*.

On leaving Cambridge Cunynghame was called to the bar at the Inner Temple in 1875, and specialized in patent law. While practising law he also accepted a number of invitations which led him to a very varied career combining law and government. In 1894, Asquith made him an attractive offer to move full-time to the post of Legal Assistant Under-Secretary at the Home Office. He held that position for almost twenty years.

The experiences which led to this appointment began in 1880 when he became a special commissioner enquiring into the affairs of British Guyana. Thereafter he took up a number of other significant positions which included, in 1884, the role of assistant commissioner distributing the funds of the City parochial charities, in which position he was responsible for the founding of the London polytechnics (an innovation of great importance to the technical education of the young of London). He was secretary to the Parnell Commission (1888), the Behring Sea Arbitration (1892) and the Featherstone Riots Committee (1894). After Asquith appointed him to the Home Office he was, for example, a member of the Royal Commissions on Accidents to Railway Servants (1899) and on Food Supply in Times of War (1903). He also chaired the Royal Commission on Coal Mines (1906); in order to learn about coal mines and coal miners, he determined to travel extensively within the UK and literally saw work at the coal face. The Commission's work was informed and energized by Cunynhame's important and knowledgeable chairmanship, and was a precursor of the Coal Mines Act of 1911. He married Emily Harriette, daughter of Colonel Arthur Prescott (of the Bombay Cavalry) in 1893. He retired in 1913, and thereafter he and his wife spent much of their time at their villa in Nice. He was awarded the CB in 1900, and was knighted in 1908.

Cunynghame was a polymath and man of innumerable hobbies: he was a competent draughtsman, an enameller, a student and scholar of Hegelian philosophy, an authority on clocks, and an electrical engineer. He had, at one time, been vice-president of the Institute of Electrical Engineers and was an honorary member of the Royal British-

Colonial Society of Artists. He was also what could be described as an amateur economist (in the sense that he never took employment as an economist).

Of his contributions to economics, one has become shrouded in mystery and is akin to the economists' equivalent of Fermat's lost proof of his famous theorem. In the 1870s Cunynghame invented a machine for Marshall which facilitated the drawing of exact rectangular hyperbolae; the existence of this machine is known from various sources, including the article 'A Machine for Constructing a Series of Rectangular Hyperbolas with the Same Asymptotes' (*Proceedings of the Cambridge Philosophical Society*, 1873), but the text of the article was never printed and details of the machine are lost. In the later 1880s he was a regular member an economic discussion group which met at the Hampstead home of Henry Ramée Beeton, a group which included P.H. WICKSTEED, G.B. SHAW, H.S. FOXWELL and F.Y. EDGEWORTH. It is known that he presented a paper to the group in 1888 which was designed as a defence of Marshall's supply curve, which had been criticized by Wicksteed. In this privately published paper, Cunynghame introduced the concept of external effects in consumption and production. His arguments were developed in his *Economic Journal* paper, 'Some Improvements in Simple Geometrical Methods of Treating Exchange Value, Monopoly and Rent', of 1892. His other economic contributions comprised a paper of 1880, privately printed, entitled *Notes on Exchange Value*, a series of lectures on *The Political, Social and Industrial Condition in England* presented at Toynbee Hall for the London Society for the Extension of University Teaching (a copy of which is to be found in the Marshall Library reprinted from *The Charity Organisation* report of 1883), and a second *Economic Journal* paper, 'The Effect of Export and Import Duties on Price and Production Examined by the Graphic Method' (1903). In 1912 he delivered his presidential address to the Economic Science and Statistical Section of the British Association.

Cunynghame's *Economic Journal* paper of 1892 may be described as the first mathematical economics paper in that journal. The paper is notable for the argument that, in economics, the graphical method is superior to the analytical method in examining relationships between variables. This view does, of course, fail to acknowledge that a graph may exhibit some particular feature which the use of some general function $y = f(x)$ does not embody. Notwithstanding this objection to the graphical method, the paper introduced the idea of individuals having inter-dependent utility functions, and in examining production Cunynghame attempted to analyse some of the paradoxes of increasing returns. While Cunynghame is invariably referred to as one of Marshall's favourites, in correspondence with Edgeworth Marshall is critical of Cunynghame's concept of 'successive utility curves' and highly critical, even dismissive, of Cunynghame's concept of 'successive cost curves' (Marshall to Edgeworth, March 26 and 28, 1892). In developing the graphical method, Cunynghame's second *Economic Journal* article is notable for its innovatory use of back-to-back demand–supply diagrams to analyse markets which are inter-dependent. *Geometrical Political Economy* is largely synthetic, deriving its material from the two *Economic Journal* articles. Nonetheless, the very appearance of this introductory and interpretative text is symptomatic of the increasing acceptance at the beginning of the twentieth century of a mathematical approach to the subject matter of economics.

Cunynghame's final publication in economics was his lengthy presidential address to the Economic Science and Statistical Section of The British Association for the Advancement of Science. This was more a piece on method than methodology and maintained his earliest economic theme, namely that the graphical method has an important, in his view paramount, position in economic science. In this piece he also sought to argue that economics should be seen as one of the exact sciences, his test being that economic ideas can be demonstrated by means of geometry and mathematics.

BIBLIOGRAPHY
Notes on Exchange Values (1880).
Some Remarks on Demand and Supply Curves and Their Interpretation (1888).
'Some Improvements in Simple Geometrical Methods of Treating Exchange Value, Monopoly and Rent', *Economic Journal* (1892), vol. 2, pp. 35–52.
'The Effect of Export and Import Duties on Price and Production Examined by the Graphic Method', *Economic Journal* (1903), vol. 13, pp. 313–23.
Geometrical Political Economy (Oxford, 1904).
'Presidential Address to the Economic Science and Statistical Section of The British Association for the Advancement of Science', *Journal of The Royal Statistical Society* (1912), vol. 76, pp. 88–98.

Further Reading
Edgeworth, F.Y., 'Review of Cunynghame (1904)', *Economic Journal* (1905), vol. 15, pp. 62–71.
Keynes, J.M., 'Obituary: Sir Henry Cunynghame', *Economic Journal* (1935), vol. 45, pp. 398–406.
Ward, C.H.D. and Spencer, C.B. (1938) *The Unconventional Civil Servant: Sir Henry Cunynghame* (1938).

Adrian Darnell

CURRIE, James (1756–1805)

Currie was born at Kirkpatrick Fleming, Dumfriesshire, on 31 May 1756, and died of heart disease at Sidmouth, Devon on 31 August 1805. He was educated at parish schools in Dumfriesshire, where his father was a Church of Scotland minister, and then Dumfries grammar school. In 1771, aged fifteen, he emigrated to Virginia, where he worked for a mercantile concern at the town of Cabin Point; however, he suffered from ill health and the outbreak of the revolution in 1775 damaged his business. He decided to leave commerce and study medicine, and took passage to Britain in the spring of 1776. It took him a year to make the journey: several attempts to leave the colony were thwarted by rebels, and he was twice drafted to serve in the rebel army, but was able to buy himself out. Eventually he reached the Bahamas and finally Antigua where he found a passage to England, having endured fever and hurricanes and nearly been shipwrecked on several occasions.

Currie studied medicine at Glasgow, taking his MD in 1780, and intended to return to the West Indies to practice, but a combination of continued ill-health, bad weather and war forced repeated postponements of his departure, and he finally took up a post as physician in Liverpool and settled there. His practice prospered and he was elected a fellow of the Royal Society in 1792. By 1804 his health was in terminal decline, and he moved to Bath and then to Sidmouth, seeking a cure. His early death cut short a promising literary career. As well as medical papers, he wrote essays on a number of subjects and, around 1800, produced a popular and well-regarded biography of Robert Burns. He was familiar with the works of MALTHUS and Thomas REID and admired both men, and corresponded frequently with Dugald STEWART at Edinburgh, where his son attended some of Stewart's classes. Politically he was a left-leaning Whig; he admired Thomas Paine and thought the Declaration of the Rights of Man an essential step forward in human civilization. He became a close friend of Wilberforce, and was a vehement opponent of slavery.

In 1793 Currie published the pamphlet *A Letter, Commercial and Political, Addressed* to the Rt. Hon. William Pitt, under the pseudonym 'Jasper Wilson'. The pamphlet, which urged the end of war with France, was rebutted at once by Nicholas VANSITTART in *Reflections on the Propriety of an Immediate Conclusion of Peace* (1793). In early 1794 Currie's authorship of the pamphlet became widely known, and he was subjected to a number of personal attacks, especially from the anti-abolitionist Tory George CHALMERS. According to his son and biographer, Currie's medical practice also suffered for a time, and this may have been one reason why Currie henceforth confined himself to more neutral subjects in his writing.

Currie explicitly links the rise of pan-European wars with the new financial system based on credit and permanent national debt, a system which he regards as being designed specifically to facilitate war: 'the prevalence and extension of the war-system throughout Europe, [is] supported, as it has been, by the universal adoption of the funding-system' (1831, vol. 2: 423). Wars, he says, are becoming 'far more general, bloody, and expensive' (1831, vol. 2: 424). Quoting Sir Francis Bacon's dictum that 'knowledge is power', Currie says this is literally true: 'Wars thus originating in causes peculiar to a semi-barbarous state of society, have been extended in other respects by the progress of knowledge and its effects on the arts. To this we attributed many of the improvements in the science of destruction, and in the science of finance...' (1831, vol. 2: 424).

The whole system of national debts was invented in the first place to pay for wars, says Currie, and has grown for the same purpose ever since. He compares the national debt to a perpetual mortgage against the taxes and revenues of the state and notes that the people are by and large content to go along with this: 'The practice of mortgaging the public revenue during wars prevents people from feeling the immediate pressure of the expense, by transferring it in a great measure to posterity' (1831, vol. 2: 424). In other words, people prefer to see a rise in the national debt than a rise in the level of taxation. But, says Currie, this practice is fraught with danger; any nation that goes on borrowing will eventually become bankrupt. Britain is particularly at risk because its prosperity depends on commerce, and with war, commerce will fail or be harmed, meaning less revenue and more pressure from debt. Rather than fighting France, Currie urges that Britain seek to restore peace in Europe as soon as possible. The choice that faces Europe, he concludes, is between a system of general peace, or one of universal desolation.

BIBLIOGRAPHY
A Letter, Commercial and Political, Addressed to the Rt. Hon. William Pitt...by Jasper Wilson, Esq. (1793), repr. in W.W. Currie (ed.), *Memoir of the Life, Writings, and Correspondence of James Currie*, 2 vols (1831).

Further Reading
Currie, W.W., *Memoir of the Life, Writings, and Correspondence of James Currie*, 2 vols (1831).
Vansittart, N., *Reflections on the Propriety of an Immediate Conclusion of Peace* (1793).

Ann Kimber

D

DALRYMPLE, John (1720–89)

Dalrymple was born, probably at Edinburgh, some time in 1720, and died in London on 13 October 1789. His father was George Dalrymple, a younger son of the 1st Earl of Stair. He was educated privately and then studied law at Edinburgh, becoming an advocate of the Scottish bar in 1741. He then purchased a captaincy in the army, serving until 1745 when he attempted to inherit the title of Earl of Stair from his uncle, the 2nd Earl.

As a young man, Dalrymple had become a favourite of the 2nd Earl, and was nominated as the latter's heir. He accordingly assumed the title upon his uncle's death, but the succession was contested and in 1748 the House of Lords found favour with his cousin James, who became 3rd Earl of Stair. In 1768, however, following the death of the 3rd and 4th earls without issue, the title once again reverted to Dalrymple, who became officially the 5th Earl of Stair. In the interim he seems to have lived off the income of his estates in Scotland, which were considerable, and also became a shareholder in the East India Company.

Upon finally succeeding to the title, Stair entered public life. He first came to prominence through his opposition in the House of Lords to the introduction of new taxes in the American colonies, and received the thanks of the people of Massachusetts for presenting a petition against taxation on their behalf. The outbreak of war in America was a source of great gloom to him, and he frequently predicted that the war would lead to both military and financial disaster. This made him something of a laughing-stock in some quarters, and Horace Walpole referred to him as the 'English Cassandra'; but, rather like Cassandra, events proved many of his predictions correct.

Stair was particularly concerned with the national debt, which he described in his pamphlet *An Attempt to Balance the Income and Expenditure of the State* as a 'universal influenza' (1783: 3). He believed that the debt must be brought under control and the budget balanced before it was too late. Writing in 1783, he states facts starkly: government expenditure in peacetime amounts to a minimum of just over £16 million, with interest on funded debts and payment on unfunded debts accounting for over £9 million of this total. Against this, the government revenue amounts to a little over £12 million, leaving a shortfall of around £4 million. The deficit is being paid for with loans and more loans, a devil's bargain, says Stair, which can only end in disaster. The urgent need now is to find ways of balancing the budget to avoid increasing the debt still further. He repeated his call for a balanced budget and warned of disaster in a series of pamphlets, none of which had any measurable impact on government policy.

In *The Proper Limits of the Government's Interference with the Affairs of the East-India*

Company (1784), Stair defended the East India Company against an attempt to take the affairs of the Company into government management and to consolidate its debts with the national debt. Stair denounced this as illegal and unjust; the Company, though embarrassed, was not bankrupt and therefore government interference was unwarranted. To critics of the Company' rule in India and its methods of taxing the Indian populace, Stair retorted that the government itself must share responsibility on the issue: 'Having forced the Company to bear a share in all the foolish wars Britain involved herself in, money must be found' (1784: 11–12). He went on to state that reports of the Company's rapacity are greatly exaggerated and that if the crown were to assume direct rule, its methods would hardly be more liberal, so great was the government's own need for money. He urged support for Warren Hastings, then governor-general, on the grounds that he was a competent manager who would sort out the problems in India if left to his own devices. There is a strong suggestion of *laissez-faire* economics about this work; the East India Company would do best, Stair believed, if left unregulated.

BIBLIOGRAPHY

The State of the National Debt, the National Income and the National Expenditure (1776).
Facts and their Consequences, Submitted to the Consideration of the Public at Large... (1782).
An Attempt to Balance the Income and Expenditure of the State (1783).
State of the Public Debts (1783).
The Proper Limits of the Government's Interference with the Affairs of the East-India Company (1784).
Comparative State of the Public Revenue (1785).

Katharine Norley

DALTON, Edward Hugh John Neale (1887–1962)

Hugh Dalton was born at Neath, Glamorganshire on 26 August 1887, and died in London on 13 February 1962. His father, John Dalton, was a canon of St George's Chapel, Windsor and tutor and friend to Prince George, later King George V. Dalton was educated at Summerfields, Oxford and then at Eton and King's College, Cambridge. In his final year he read economics, studying under PIGOU and KEYNES. He also became a socialist and member of the Fabian Society, and it was through his association with the WEBBS that he chose to go on to become a research student at the London School of Economics. He also joined the Middle Temple, and was called to the bar in 1914. He served as an officer in the Royal Artillery during the First World War, seeing service in France and Italy; a number of his close friends, including the poet Rupert Brooke, were killed in the conflict, and this had an impact on Dalton's later thinking about politics and society.

After the war Dalton returned to the LSE, where he lectured on economics and was closely associated with Edwin CANNAN. He also taught economics classes for the Workers' Educational Association, and studied for his DSc, which was granted in 1921. He was Sir Ernest Cassel Reader in Economics at the University of London from 1925–36. His most famous work, *Principles of Public Finance*, was published in 1922, and although a work of fairly orthodox pre-Keynesian economics, it none the less won him a considerable reputation.

Dalton first stood as a candidate for parliament in 1922, but was not elected until 1924, for Peckham. In 1929 he was elected for Bishop Auckland and became a parliamentary under-secretary at the Foreign Office, but he lost his seat in 1931. From 1931–5 he travelled widely, visiting Russia, France, Germany and Italy, including a famous meeting with Mussolini where the two men evidently reminisced about their wartime experiences. Returning home, Dalton was re-elected for Bishop Auckland and held the seat until 1959. Already a member of the Labour Party's national executive, he served as party chairman in 1936–7. He had seen at first-hand the menace posed by the Nazis, and in the years before the Second World War was among those who warned of the dangers posed, an attitude which drew him into a closer relationship with Winston Churchill. In 1940 he joined Churchill's government as Minister of Economic Warfare; among his other tasks was the creation of the Special Operations Executive (SOE) to support sabotage and resistance movements in occupied Europe. In 1942 he moved to the Board of Trade, where he carried out a thorough reorganization.

Following Labour's victory in the 1945 general election, Dalton was appointed Chancellor of the Exchequer in the Attlee government. He oversaw the nationalization of the Bank of England and cut income tax. In 1947, however, Dalton suffered a series of setbacks; a new bond issue failed, there was a fuel crisis, the balance of payments was worsening and government debt was rising. Following KEYNES, Dalton adhered to a policy of cheap money, which in turn led to a financial crisis in November. His policies widely discredited, Dalton resigned as Chancellor in November 1947. He returned to Cabinet in 1948 as Chancellor of the Duchy of Lancaster, and played some role in the establishment of the Council of Europe; from 1950–1 he was briefly Minister of Town and Country Planning. He retired from politics altogether at the general election of 1959, and was made a life peer in 1960. He had also served as Master of the Drapers' Company in 1958–9. Although his political career had to some extent ended in failure, he had played an important role as mentor for a younger generation of Labour politicians, including Anthony CROSLAND, Evan DURBIN, James Callaghan, Dennis Healey and Hugh GAITSKELL.

Dalton's most productive period as an economist was in the early 1920s, when he cut a wide swathe at the LSE. Lionel ROBBINS, then a student, recalled: 'The name of Hugh Dalton stands out, both for the lucidity and force of his teaching…had he chosen to remain a professional economist I have no doubt he would have achieved a leading position in the academic world at large' (Robbins 1971). He produced three major works during this period: *Some Aspects of the Inequality of Incomes in Modern Communities* (1920); *Principles of Public Finance* (1922), for years one of the basic texts in the field; and *The Capital Levy Explained* (1923), all of which set out his socialist views on income redistribution and the role of the state in society. The later polemic *Practical Socialism for Britain* (1935) was intended as a manifesto for the Labour Party following the 1935 general election.

As an economist, Dalton remains most famous for his views on the use of taxation as a means of redistributing wealth, views set out in *Principles of Public Finance* and again more forcefully in *Inequality of Incomes* (1935). He argued that a redistribution of wealth from the rich to the poor would result in an overall increase of welfare, demonstrating this through a modified version of Bernoulli's theorem, and then concluded that direct taxation was the best means for achieving such redistribution. This became a core part of the Labour Party's economic and financial policies for the next decades.

BIBLIOGRAPHY
Some Aspects of the Inequality of Incomes in Modern Communities (1920).
Principles of Public Finance (1922).
The Capital Levy Explained (1923).
Practical Socialism for Britain (1935).
Inequality of Incomes (1935).
Call Back Yesterday: Memoirs 1887–1931 (1953).

Further Reading
Peacock, A., 'Dalton, Hugh', in J. Eatwell,

M. Milgate and P. Newman (eds), *The New Palgrave*, vol. 1 (1987, p. 747).
Pimlott, B. *Hugh Dalton* (1985).
Robbins, L., *Autobiography of an Economist* (1971).

Alan Ebenstein

DANIELS, George William (1878–1937)

Daniels was born in Swinton, Manchester some time in 1838, and died in Manchester in 1937. He was educated at Ruskin College and then Manchester University, taking an MA and MCom from the latter some time before 1910. He served the government as an advisor on trade during the First World War, and was appointed Stanley Jevons Professor of Political Economy at Manchester in 1920; he also became dean of the faculty of commerce and administration. He held both posts until his death.

At Manchester, Daniels was a colleague of George UNWIN, professor of economic history, and like Unwin he focused much of his attention on the history of the cotton industry in the north-west of England. Whereas Unwin had looked particularly at the career and impact of Samuel Oldknow, Daniels focussed instead on Samuel Crompton, whom he saw as the leader of a sort of 'second wave' of technological innovation following the initial breakthroughs of Kay and Arkwright. In the work that made his reputation, *The Early English Cotton Industry, with Some Unpublished Letters of Samuel Crompton* (1920), Daniels explored the development and organization of the cotton manufacturing industry and the impact of the new technologies of the late eighteenth century. He described in great detail the pre-industrial organization and especially the putting-out system, and then demonstrated the impact of Arkwright's water frame. An entire chapter was devoted to the opposition to Arkwright's patents, and then a further chapter to Crompton and the introduction of the mule. The final section of this chapter charts the social and economic changes that resulted from the introduction of these technologies, drawing on contemporary accounts such as those of William Radcliffe and Dr Gaskell.

Daniels concluded that the initial impact of technology on the ordinary workers was positive, and the cancellation of Arkwright's patent in fact led to a short period of prosperity. However, the lot of the weavers was soon worse than before. Previous historians and economists had assumed that it was the new technology and the factory system that led to this worsening of the plight of the worker, as the power of capital overcame the power of labour, but Daniels concluded that there was no reason to assume this was true. He conceded that there may have been an oversupply of labour that drove wages down, but this was not the deciding factor. Rather, said Daniels, the impact of the Seven Years War and the American Revolution were far more important and detrimental. Later, the Napoleonic Wars had the effect of concentrating and intensifying economic and social changes: 'the Napoleonic War thus becomes the dominant factor in the social and economic history of the later Industrial Revolution period' (1920: 147). The war distorted economic progress and 'the increased power of production, instead of improving the material welfare of the community, had to be devoted to the prosecution of the war; social development was thwarted and thrown back; and the relationship between employers and workpeople, with which the latter, in the middle of the eighteenth century, had shown their dissatisfaction and were striving through combination to modify, were continued and solidified, and left as a heritage to the nineteenth and twentieth centuries' (1920: 147).

Daniels went on to speculate that, had the Napoleonic Wars not occurred, the problem of industrial relationships would have been confronted at the time, rather than in the late nineteenth century. Quite possibly, different solutions to the problem would have been found. Whether this is true or not, he concluded, 'it may be said that the social retrogression and evils which mark the Industrial Revolution period are only in a very secondary sense to be attributed to the economic movement: the primary cause is to be found in the war in which the country was engaged' (1920: 147). It is an intriguing hypothesis, and Daniels was right to highlight the impact of the war, even if he was not altogether specific as to what that impact was. However, he probably overstated his case and underplayed the impact of technology and the factory system. Nevertheless, if only for its focus on the pre-Arkwright period, *The Early English Cotton Industry* provides a very useful picture of an industry and economy in transition. It is Daniels's only major work; his other publications were mostly short pamphlets, including one with John JEWKES on the impact of the post-First World War depression on the cotton industry.

BIBLIOGRAPHY

The Early English Cotton Industry, with Some Unpublished Letters of Samuel Crompton (1920).
(with H. Campion) *The Distribution of National Capital* (1926).
Capital, Labour and the Consumer (1927).
(with J. Jewkes) *The Postwar Depression in the Lancashire Cotton Industry* (1928).
(with H. Campion) *The Relative Importance of the British Export Trade* (1935).

David Ashbury

DARWIN, Leonard (1850–1943)

Darwin, fourth and last surviving son of Charles Darwin and Emma Wedgwood, was born at Down House near Downe, Kent on 15 January 1850 and died in London on 26 March 1943.

He entered the Royal Military Academy at Woolwich in 1868, and came second on the examination list, to his father's great joy. He served in the Royal Engineers, rising to the rank of major by 1890, and on scientific expeditions to photograph the transit of Venus. He taught at the School of Military Engineering at Chatham from 1877–82, and served in the intelligence division of the Ministry of War from 1895–90. He entered parliament in 1892 as Liberal-Unionist MP for Lichfield, holding the seat until 1895, during which time he began a serious study of economics. From 1908–11 he was president of the Royal Geographical Society.

Darwin's first work on economics, *Bimetallism* (1897) was reviewed by F.Y. EDGEWORTH, who commented: 'The name Darwin subscribed to the plan of examining arguments of both sides suggests scientific power and judicial impartiality' (Edgeworth 1898: 105). His *Municipal Trade* (1903) was widely discussed. KEYNES later summarized Darwin's argument: 'companies, looking mainly to profits, may, in the case of monopolies, ignore questions connected with public health, morals, order or convenience…but, if extensively undertaken, it tends to lower their efficiency. And a large number of voters being in the pay of the State adds greatly to the probability of corruption'. Keynes reported that 'Several generations of students were brought up on this most British approach' (Keynes 1943: 438–9). As Keynes's account suggests, there is a public choice element in Darwin's discussion. The Harvard lectures of 1907 extend considerations of corruption to encompass incentives to create non-transparent accounts.

The obituary notice in *Eugenics Review* provides insight into Darwin's role in the British eugenics movement: 'It was characteristic of Leonard Darwin that he had to be persuaded, against strong resistance, to succeed his cousin, Sir Francis Galton, as President of the Eugenics Society. He was too modest to acquiesce easily, but once convinced…he plunged himself into the work, and…formulated its policies and ideals (1943: 109). We do not know how he was persuaded to assume the office, but the dedication of his *Need for Eugenic Reform* to his father is suggestive: 'For if I had not believed that he would have wished me to give such help as I could towards making his life's work of service to mankind, I should never have been led to write this book' (1926: v). An open question is whether he regarded his 1929–34 campaign for voluntary eugenic sterilization (Box 1976: 196–7) as an implementation of his father's work. Recent attention has focused on how instrumental Darwin was in prompting R.A. Fisher to blend Darwinian evolutionary theory with Mendelian genetics (Box 1978; Bennett 1983), as well as his role in protecting Fisher from Karl Pearson's rejection (Bennett 1983: 14, 67–8).

Keynes's obituary notice for Darwin includes Arthur Keith's judgement (1943: 442) of Darwin's view of politics: 'He looked on politics as the art of applying science to the problems of government.' Darwin himself explained the need for eugenic policy: 'when we come to discuss eugenic reforms, we are apt to attach a somewhat different meaning to the word 'fittest'. The aim of eugenists is to alter human surroundings in such a way as to increase the chance of 'survival' of those types which are held to be more desirable...' (1926: 114).

BIBLIOGRAPHY

Bimetallism: A Summary and Examination of the Arguments for and against a Bimetallic System of Currency (1897).

Municipal Trade: The Advantages and Disadvantages Resulting from the Substitution of Representative Bodies for Private Proprietors in the Management of Industrial Undertakings (1903).

Municipal Ownership: Four Lectures Delivered at Harvard University (New York, 1907).

Organic Evolution: Outstanding Difficulties and Possible Explanations (Cambridge, 1921).

The Need for Eugenic Reform (1926).

Further Reading

Bennett, J.H. (ed.), *Natural Selection, Heredity, and Eugenics: Including Selected Correspondence with Leonard Darwin and Others* (Oxford, 1983).

Box, J.F., *R.A. Fisher: The Life of a Scientist* (New York, 1978).

Edgeworth, F.Y., 'Review of Leonard Darwin. *Bimetallism*', *Economic Journal* (1898), vol. 8, March, pp. 105–11.

Keith, A., 'Major Leonard Darwin', *Nature* (1943), vol. 151, April 17, p. 442.

Keynes, J.M., 'Obituary: Leonard Darwin', *Economic Journal* (1943), vol. 53, December, pp. 438–48.

'Leonard Darwin, 1850–1943', *The Eugenics Review* (1943), vol. 34, January, pp. 109–16.

David M. Levy
Sandra R. Peart

DAVENANT, Charles (1656–1714)

Davenant, or D'Avenant, was born in London some time in 1656, and died in London on 6 November 1714. His father was the poet and dramatist Sir William D'Avenant, who was rumoured (probably without foundation) to be the illegitimate son of William Shakespeare. Davenant was educated at Cheam grammar school and then entered Balliol College, Oxford in 1671, leaving without taking a degree. At age nineteen he wrote a tragedy, *Circe*, apparently thinking of following his father's career, but instead decided to study law. He claimed to have an LLD degree, though there is no record of any institution granting this degree. In 1683 he was elected MP for St Ives, and served as commissioner of excise from 1683–9. He lost this post upon the accession of William III, but it seems to have stimulated his interest in economics.

Davenant returned to parliament in 1698 as MP for Great Bedwyn. Though not a Tory, he was often in opposition to the government, particular over financial policy. William III disliked him, but Queen Anne – or her advisors – respected his abilities and he was appointed by her as secretary to the commission negotiating the union with Scotland. In 1705 he was appointed inspector-general of imports and exports, which again gave him opportunity to study the problems of trade at first hand. However, he produced little writing of note during this later period, and his most important work on economics remains *An Essay on the East India Trade* (1697).

Trade, to Davenant, meant wealth, and wealth meant power. Power and wealth were impossible without trade: 'The soil of no country is rich enough to attain a great mass of wealth, merely by the exchange and exportation of its own natural product' (1695: 2). In the case of England, Davenant believed that two particular forms of trade were responsible for the nation's wealth: the trade with the colonies in the West Indies, and the trade in spices, silks and other goods conducted by the East India Company. In order to pay for imports from these sources, however, it was necessary that the nation should also export, and here Davenant gave pride of place to the woollen cloth industry as the chief support of the national economy. He produced figures, of unknown provenance, to show that the annual contribution to the national income through a combination of imports and exports was £2 million, of which £600,000 came through the East India trade.

This combination of domestic manufactures and trade in foreign luxuries lay at the heart of Davnenant's policy recommendations. English woollens were the best in the world, and would find a ready market on the continent if they could be sold at a price low enough to beat local competition. At the same time, Europe was 'greedy' for the luxuries of the Indies, and by creating an entrepot for this trade – and by implication, excluding the Dutch from it – and re-exporting luxury goods such as silks and spices, England could profit from this trade as well. There lay the path to national wealth and, by extension, national power.

To Davenant it was obvious that trade was important, and it was equally obvious that one of the chief aims of government must be to facilitate trade: 'In a trading nation, the bent of all the laws should tend to the encouragement of commerce, and all measures should be there taken, with a due regard to its interest and advancement' (1695: 4). That perfect state of affairs does not exist in England, however: 'Instead of this, in many particulars, our former laws bring incumbrances and difficulties to it, and some seem calculated for its utter ruin; so little has it been of late years the common care' (1695: 4).

Another duty of government was to ensure peaceful conditions in which trade could flourish. War was the enemy of trade, Davenant argued, and pointed to the military threat posed to the vital trading posts in India; should these be lost, the nation would be greatly impoverished: 'And if we should come so to lose our hold in India, as not to trade thither at all, or but weakly and precariously, I will venture to affirm...that England will thereby lose half its foreign business' (1695: 12).

In *An Essay on the East India Trade*, Davenant comes across as a strong supporter of free trade: 'Trade is in its nature free, finds it own channel, and best directeth its own course: and all laws to give it rules and directions, and to limit and circumscribe it, may serve the particular ends of private men, but are seldom advantageous to the public' (1697: 14). In later years, however, he seems to have been more in favour of regulation; whereas in the 1690s he had thought that a favourable balance of trade could be achieved through market forces, a decade later he had begun to doubt this and supported tariffs to discourage cheap imports, especially of cloth.

Davenant described money as the servant of trade, and argued that national wealth consisted of commodities and the potential to produce and distribute them, such as fertile agricultural lands and good seaports. A supply of ready money was important in trade terms because those with money were in a better position to dictate terms to sellers of commodities; he seems to have had little interest in credit as a means of payment. In other areas his thought was typical mercantilist; he supported light taxation, primarily of luxury goods, and supported also the employment of the poor in industry in order to bring labour costs down and reduce the burdens of poor relief. In later years he revisited the work of William PETTY and Gregory KING and attempted to produce a statistical method of calculating the balance of trade. He also out a formula in support of King's theory of the effect of short supply of commodities on price, and estimated that a 50 per cent shortfall in the corn supply would produce a price increase of 500 per cent.

BIBLIOGRAPHY
An Essay on the Ways and Means of Supplying the War (1695).
Two Discourses on the Public Revenues and Trade of England (1695).
An Essay on the East India Trade (1697).
An Essay on the Probable Means of Making the People Gainers in the Balance of Trade (1699).
Essays on Peace at Home and War Abroad (1704).

Further Reading
Waddell, D., 'Charles Davenant (1656–1714): A Biographical Sketch', *Economic History Review* (1958), n.s. vol. 11, no. 2, pp. 279–288

Morgen Witzel

DAY, Alan Charles Lynn (1924–)

Day was born in Chesterfield in October 1924, son of Henry C. Day, MBE, a chartered accountant who was a public figure, and became mayor, of that town. Day was educated at Chesterfield Grammar School and Queens' College, Cambridge. There (with an interval of war service as a meteorological officer in the RAF) he studied economics and got a first. His exam papers so impressed one of his examiners, Richard SAYERS, that Day was asked to apply to join the London School of Economics as an assistant lecturer directly after his undergraduate work. Despite coming near the top of the Foreign Office and Civil Service exams, Day accepted a position at LSE after an informal interview with ROBBINS, MEADE and CARR-SAUNDERS.

Although Day came to LSE under the wing of Sayers in the money and banking sub-group of the economics department, there were joint lectures with the international trade group. When he was writing his book on the *Balance of Payments*, Meade had lectured on that subject; but once that book was completed (1951), he looked to pass those lectures on to Day. The latter enjoyed the challenge, and much of his more technical work in the 1950s was on the theory of international trade, including a methodological defence of Meade's procedures (1955; see also 1954b, 1954c).

Combining international trade with his work in the monetary field, plus an active interest in policy issues, led Day into the field of international monetary policy. This was a lively subject in the early 1950s, with a wide spread of views ranging from Fortress UK, protection (on the left, Thomas BALOGH) to complete convertibility (on the right, Roy HARROD). One of the key features in this debate was the prospective role for the sterling area and the sterling balances. Day jumped into the fray. Probably his best book is *The Future of Sterling* (1954a), and he also wrote numerous journal articles, both at a general political and more academic economic level, on this subject in the 1950s. He did not, however, know of the internal discussions in the Bank/Treasury (1952) on a dash for convertibility and floating (Fforde 1992), which were kept tightly secret. Day was pessimistic about being able to cope without continuing discrimination against the USA, about the likelihood of a future US depression, and about the efficacy of floating rates to stabilize the system without excessively adverse effects on UK living standards.

In this same period, the mid-1950s, he wrote a major textbook on money, *Outline of Monetary Economics* (1957), aimed at undergraduates at all levels. This was supplemented by a shortened and simplified version, *The Economics of Money* (1959), aimed at first-year undergraduates, and an American version, with S. Beza, in 1960. He did this not so much because he had any special line of argument to press, but because there was a gap in the market, with Geoffrey CROWTHER's *An Outline of Money* (1941) becoming dated, and Sayers's *Modern Banking* (1938) only covering part of the subject. The substance of the book was set out in a way that has stood the test of time, covering the nature of money, demand and supply of money, the determination of interest rates, the determination of real and nominal expenditures, and so on. What was so different then from now was the expository techniques; no algebra nor equations, no diagrams (except for the US version), the main technical tool being the multiplier with numerical (not algebraic) example, sparse references to the literature, and then mainly to books and not journal articles.

Day's only other major sally into monetary economics was a report, commissioned by Peter Jay as an addendum to *The Bankers Magazine*, to assess the debate between monetarists and keynesians, entitled 'Economic Strategies: Keynes, Friedman and their Disciples' (1986). This was a balanced and sensible report, though not widely noted, and made one regret that Day had moved away from monetary economics into other fields from the early 1960s onwards.

After a spell in the economic section of the Treasury (1954–6), Day became editor of the *National Institute Review* (1960–2), then published six times per annum. His interests moved towards transport economics, especially civil aviation, and he became adviser to Anthony CROSLAND, President of the Board of Trade, and then to the Civil Aviation Authority. He was also appointed to many official committees, notably the Layfield Committee on Local Government Finance, and, after becoming a full professor at LSE (1964), to several academic committees, a role made more time-consuming and difficult by the disturbances in 1968. His purely academic output fell away, but he substituted that for a regular weekly column in the *Observer*. He shared the Sunday economics slot from 1957 to 1964 first with Andrew Shonfield and then with Sam Brittan until 1964, when he was left largely on his own until Bill Keegan arrived in 1977. During these years he wrote his column some thirty, or even more, times a year. His columns focussed on transport (and aviation) issues; planning, rents and housing; international monetary matters with particular reference to Europe and the Common Market; and current short-term policy issues. They were a beacon of informed, liberal, good sense, and give an excellent feel for intelligent professional views at the time. It is to be hoped that he will make his collected columns available for students of the economic thought and policies of those decades.

Day dropped the column in 1979 when he became pro-director of LSE. The death of his first wife in 1981 and a major illness in 1982 were severe blows, which led to an early retirement in 1982 to a home in Kent to live with his second wife, Shirley.

BIBLIOGRAPHY
The Future of Sterling (Oxford, 1954a).
'A Geometrical Demonstration of Stability Conditions in International Trade', *Economia Internazionale* (1954b), vol. 7, no. 1, pp. 1–8.

'Relative Prices, Expenditure and the Trade Imbalance: A Note', *Economica* (1954c), vol. 21, no. 81, pp. 64–70.
'The Taxonomic Approach to the Study of Economic Policies', *American Economic Review* (1955), vol. 45, no. 1, pp. 64–78.
Outline of Monetary Economics (Oxford, 1957).
The Economics of Money (1959).
(with S. Beza) *Money and Income: An Outline of Monetary Economics* (New York, 1960).
'Economic Strategies: Keynes, Friedman and Their Disciples', The Alan Day Report, an addendum to *The Bankers Magazine*; pamphlet for *The Banking World* (1986).

Further Reading
Crowther, G., *An Outline of Money* (1941).
Fforde, J.S., *The Bank of England and Public Policy* (Cambridge, 1992).
MacDougall, D., *The World Dollar Problem: A Study in International Economics* (1957).
Meade, J.E., *The Theory of International Economic Policy*, vol. 1, *The Balance of Payments*, (1951).
Sayers, R.S., *Modern Banking* (Oxford, 1938).

C.A.E. Goodhart

DE QUINCEY, Thomas (1785–1859)

De Quincey was born near Manchester on 15 August 1785, and died on 8 December 1859 in Edinburgh. He was the son (fourth of eight children) of a successful linen merchant who was among the founder members of the Manchester Literary and Philosophical Society. His mother was a strong-willed, intelligent and pious woman whose friends included the evangelical bluestocking Hannah More. De Quincey was educated by private tutors and at Bath Grammar School, Winkfield School, Manchester Grammar School (from where he absconded) and Worcester College, Oxford (which he left before completing his final examinations). He showed acute intellectual and imaginative abilities from an early age, but his childhood was a markedly unhappy one: key events were the deaths of a favourite sister in 1791 and his father in 1792, his flight from school in 1802, and a period of homelessness and near-starvation in London (1803). In 1804, while a student, he began to take opium and eventually acquired a lifelong addiction to this drug whose effects upon the conscious and subconscious mind he would deeply explore and write much about, both discursively and creatively.

Already a passionate admirer of their poetry, De Quincey first met William Wordsworth and Samuel Taylor COLERIDGE in 1807, and soon became their close friend and neighbour; he lived in Dove Cottage at Grasmere from 1809–20. His first published essay was an appendix to Wordsworth's pamphlet on *The Convention of Cintra* which he saw through the press (1809). Even after their bitter estrangement, De Quincey continued to champion Wordsworth's and Coleridge's work, and his own writings show their deep influence. Living by his pen from 1819 onwards, De Quincey was a very prolific author. Still remembered chiefly for his autobiographical writings, most importantly *Confessions of an English Opium-Eater* (1821; revised and expanded, 1856) and *Suspiria de Profundis* (1845), he also wrote three novels – *The Stranger's Grave* (1823), *Walladmor* (1825) and *Klosterheim* (1832) – and some short stories and translations. Most of his work consists of essays originally written for periodicals including *Blackwood's Magazine* and *Tait's Edinburgh Magazine*. These cover a vast range of topics and encompass literary criticism, biography, history, politics, philosophy, theology, psychology, astronomy and philology, as well as economics.

De Quincey was heavily in debt almost constantly through his adult life. His earnings as a freelance writer were insufficient to maintain the standard of living he desired; he aimed at a high literary standard in his work, even if it meant missing a deadline to achieve it; he was by nature unreliable, trusting to his charm and power of persuasion to placate other people; and his drug addiction frequently incapacitated him for days or even weeks on end. Apparently, however, he was a devoted husband to his wife Margaret and a good father to their eight children, and by most accounts he was a brilliant and engaging personality whose company was widely welcomed.

De Quincey asserted that, 'my life has been, on the whole, the life of a philosopher' (1862–3: iv). Often describing himself as a 'philosopher', he probably meant this term to be understood primarily in the eighteenth-century sense of an articulate intellectual with wide interests, such as Edward Gibbon or Edmund Burke; but Grevel Lindop has suggested that De Quincey also has affinities with 'that heterogeneous body of European poet-philosophers – Kierkegaard, Nietzsche, Bergson, Heidegger – who helped to usher in the age of modernity and remain to inspire and interrogate it' (2000, vol. 1: xxi). De Quincey argued that a philosopher must combine 'a superb intellect in its *analytic* functions' with 'such a constitution of the *moral* faculties, as shall give him an inner eye and power of intuition for the vision and the mysteries of our human nature' ('Preliminary Confessions' in the 1821 text of *Confessions*); and both of these faculties are often demonstrated within De Quincey's work. In his discursive and critical writings, De Quincey's greatest insights mostly concern human psychology, and these give a special value to works such as 'On the Knocking at the Gate in *Macbeth*' (1825) and 'On Murder Considered as one of the Fine Arts' (1827). His eclectic knowledge and a tendency to explore any tangential point that occurs make almost all of his essays interesting and surprisingly informative (the titles sometimes bear little relation to their actual contents), but his scholarship, though competent and usually diligent, rarely achieves brilliance. De Quincey's writings on economics, usually displaying a sound grasp of the subject, rigorous logic and fluency of expression, rank among the best of what he termed his 'literature of knowledge'. However, his crowning merit is as a prose stylist, who influenced John RUSKIN, Walter Pater and Oscar Wilde, and it is mainly for this quality that De Quincey's essays continue to be read and admired.

De Quincey's main contribution in the field of economic theory was in popularizing the ideas of David RICARDO. He did so mainly through 'Dialogues of Three Templars', first published in the *London Magazine* in 1824, a series of three essays entitled 'Ricardo Made Easy', first published in *Blackwood's* in 1842, and a short book, *The Logic of Political Economy* (1844). Relating to this interest, he also wrote a number of essays refuting the ideas of Adam SMITH and Thomas MALTHUS and he occasionally applied a Ricardian interpretation of market forces in arguments to justify Tory policies and his own reactionary views on issues such as the Corn Laws and slavery, views which Ricardo would not have shared.

De Quincey's interest in economics began in 1818 when John Wilson, then editor of *Blackwood's*, sent him Ricardo's *Principles of Political Economy and Taxation* to review in that magazine. The review was never written, but reading this book made a profound impression on De Quincey, who hailed Ricardo as 'a transcendent legislator' in the field of political economy (1862–3, vol. 1: 255). According to De Quincey:

> Previous writers had been crushed and overlaid by the enormous weights of facts, details, and exceptions; Mr Ricardo had deduced, *a priori*, from the understanding itself, laws which first shot arrowy light into

the dark chaos of materials, and had thus constructed what hitherto was but a collection of tentative discussions into a science of regular proportions, now first standing upon an eternal basis.

(1862–3, vol. 1: 255)

However, he claimed that, seeing 'some important truths had escaped even "the inevitable eye" of Mr Ricardo', he composed a pamphlet entitled *Prolegomena to All Future Systems of Political Economy*, but, from his own inability to write a satisfactory preface and a worthy dedication to Ricardo, it was never printed (1862–3, vol. 1: 256). Whether or not that is true, De Quincey subsequently produced some notable writings explaining Ricardian economic theory and others which applied and developed it in new directions.

In his severe review of *The Measure of Value* by Malthus, which appeared in the *London Magazine* in December 1823, De Quincey vividly expressed his own preference for Ricardo, portrayed as a formidable intellectual adversary – 'whose arm...gives a blow like the kick of a horse' (1862–3, vol. 16: 480) – whom Malthus had been unwise to challenge in that treatise; De Quincey was then unaware that Ricardo had died in September that year. 'The Services of Mr Ricardo to the Science of Political Economy, Briefly and Plainly Stated', published the *London Magazine* in March 1824, was by turns a tribute to his economic mentor (news of whose death had now reached him), a detailed apology for his own tardiness in writing on economic theory, and a preface to the lengthy 'Dialogues of Three Templars on Political Economy, Chiefly in Relation to the Principles of Mr Ricardo' which appeared there in the following month. In that work, De Quincey granted Ricardo 'the entire merit of the discovery' that the ground of the value of all commodities lies in the *quantity* of the labour which produces them. This is the 'great principle which is the corner-stone of all tenable Political Economy; which granted or denied, all Political Economy stands or falls' (1862–3, vol. 4: 190). De Quincey carefully distinguished this principle from Adam Smith's seemingly similar formula which argues that it is the *value* of the productive labour involved which imparts value to any commodity (1862–3, vol. 4: 191–6). Consequently, contrary to Smith's view, 'it is Mr Ricardo's doctrine that no variation in either profits or wages can ever affect price; if wages rise or fall, the only consequence is that profits must fall or rise by the same sum; so again, if profits rise or fall, wages must fall or rise accordingly' (1862–3, vol. 4: 196).

De Quincey identified as Ricardo's 'two great doctrines', firstly, 'that no article can increase in price except from a previous increase in the quantity of labour necessary to its production: for here is no increase in the *quantity* of the labour, but simply in its value', and secondly, 'that no rise in the value of labour can ever settle upon price; but that all increase of wages will be paid out of profits, and all increase of profits out of wages' (1862–3, vol. 4: 199). Thus, he argued, 'the reason why all variations in the *value* of labour are incapable of transferring themselves to the value of its product is this, that these variations extend to all kinds of labour, and therefore to all commodities alike', because 'that which raises or depresses all things equally, leaves their relations to each other undisturbed' (1862–3, vol. 4: 200). Accordingly: 'Wages are at a high real value when it requires much labour to produce wages; and at a low real value, when it requires little labour to produce wages; and it is perfectly consistent with the high real value – that the labourer should be almost starving; and perfectly consistent with the low real value – that the labourer should be living in great ease and comfort' (1862–3, vol. 4: 233). De Quincey pointed out that Malthus's imprecise use of the word 'determine' caused him to conflate labour as a cause of value with labour as an effect of value, consequently confusing the wages paid for labour with the quantity of labour which is performed

(1862–3, vol. 4: 202–4). These 'Dialogues', generically similar to Walter Savage Landor's *Imaginary Conversations* (1824–9), provided a cogent and palatable explanation of the key principles and applications of Ricardian economics and were thus a genuine service to this magazine's readers, even including Samuel BAILEY, whose *Critical Dissertation on the Nature, Measure and Causes of Value* (1825) arose directly from this encounter with Ricardo's ideas, which he felt had to be systematically challenged.

At a time when the science of political economy was associated with Whiggism, and therefore eschewed by most Tories, it is remarkable that De Quincey, himself a staunch Tory and a frequent apologist for that creed, embraced it so fervently. De Quincey's work certainly helped to spread awareness and understanding of Ricardo's ideas in the 1820s, but at the same time as their credence was declining, except among proto-socialists such as William THOMPSON and Thomas HODGSKIN. Moreover, it is ironic that *Blackwood's Magazine*, dedicated to Tory values, published De Quincey's later Ricardian essays and thereby to some extent legitimized those ideas with its readership. Although Ricardo's name was revered by liberals and radicals for decades after his death and his writings studied by subsequent economic and political theorists, relatively few people actually subscribed to his theories of value, rent and profits. Thus De Quincey's enduring enthusiasm for Ricardo was somewhat eccentric.

'Ricardo Made Easy', a series of three essays for *Blackwood's* in 1843, formed the basis of De Quincey's only book on economics, *The Logic of Political Economy* (1844), a competent treatise, though lacking the clarity and freshness of the 'Dialogues' and occasionally also marred by unduly elaborate explanatory scenarios. It was reviewed in the *Westminster Review* by John Stuart MILL, who considered De Quincey 'very successful' as an exponent of Ricardo's ideas but 'would be more so if he had not a strange delight in drawing illustrations from subjects ten times more abstruse than what they are designed to illustrate' (quoted in Lindop 1981: 353).

In *The Logic of Political Economy*, De Quincey was no longer content to be mainly Ricardo's expositor, for now he confidently applied his theories far beyond the contexts of their formulation and to reach some conclusions which Ricardo himself would almost certainly have contested. De Quincey proposed that circulation in the economy results from the unfulfilled desires of consumers which induce a sense of scarcity. Examples of luxury goods, such as croton oil, salmon, Italian masterpieces, rhinoceroses and *Paradise Lost*, were presented to show affirmative and negative values, from either of which the price may be derived. Because the British public's curiosity to see rhinoceroses far exceeded the cost of obtaining them, the price of these animals was based on their affirmative value. Likewise, the negative value of an Italian masterpiece, the cost of producing it, was negligible compared with its affirmative value determined by its exceptional artistic merits and its known provenance. Both of these are cases of monopoly value. More usually, however, negative values prevail, as when the low cost of mass-producing copies of *Paradise Lost* means that it becomes affordable by nearly everyone and those who desire it probably already possess it; supply easily meets demand, so the retail price is pressed downwards. Very differently from Ricardo, who considered labour and land alongside capital as the central determinants of value, De Quincey was willing to treat them as commodities. He argued, for instance, that land will always be valued affirmatively, for what it can potentially yield more than what it requires to be productive.

Again unlike Ricardo's economic model, De Quincey entertained the factor of public faith which means that the supposed authenticity of products gives them much of their value, as in the cases of Italian masterpieces and – the most extreme illustration – holy relics. There are Christians who believe that a saint's relic is a conduit for supernatural power, perhaps to help achieve miracles; the value of this particular object is entirely dependent on those people believing in its authenticity. However adventurous De Quincey's exploration of economic activity, it was essentially Ricardian by proceeding from his recognition that a consumer can reasonably pay a higher price for a commodity than its intrinsic value seems to dictate; but more emphatically than Ricardo ever did, De Quincey suggested that the whole economy relies on public faith to function, because without faith there could be no exchange and without credit there could be no circulation. In his view, capital and debt are vital for economic life and for the healthy continuance of the body politic.

In *The Literature of Political Economy* (1845), J.R. MCCULLOCH (another stalwart disciple of Ricardo as an economist and – unlike De Quincey – sharing his wider political outlook as well) considered the 'Dialogues' to be 'unequalled, perhaps, for brevity, pungency and force', because they 'not only bring the Ricardian theory of value into strong relief, but triumphantly repel, or rather annihilate,' Malthus's objections to it (quoted in 1890, vol. 1: 154, editor's footnote); and he judged *The Logic of Political Economy* to be a 'very clever work', though also unduly 'scholastic' and 'tiresome and repulsive' (quoted in McDonagh 1994: 48). Overall, he wrote, De Quincey's contributions 'may, indeed, be said to have exhausted the subject' (quoted in 1890, vol. 1: 154, editor's footnote). Karl MARX acknowledged De Quincey's value as an interpreter of Ricardo's ideas in the rough draft of his own *Grundrisse* (cited by McDonagh 1994: 48, n. 16).

De Quincey's writings on economic theory not only performed a significant pioneering role in educating the public in this subject, especially by popularizing Ricardo's ideas (and thereby prolonging his influence), but they also withstand modern scrutiny fairly well and remain enjoyable to read, most particularly the 'Dialogues' in either respect. *The Logic of Political Economy* is De Quincey's most substantial work in this field and includes some original observations and speculations, but its contribution to economic thought is only a minor one, even in its historical context. Its main attractions are literary ones, as the author's fertile imagination and rhetorical skill are often employed to good effect on a subject which obviously delights him.

De Quincey's disorganised habits, the plethora of publishers who took his work, and the author's own revisions of many pieces, have caused considerable difficulties for scholars. Probably a substantial amount of De Quincey's work remains unidentified or lost. *Selections Grave and Gay* (1852–60), which was partly overseen by De Quincey, remains for the time being the most reliable edition of his writings, but complete sets of it are now rare. David Masson's edition of *Collected Writings* (1896–7) is not only far from complete but also heavily bowdlerized. Although it is the most easily accessible collection in libraries, and consequently has provided the texts used by most scholars, Masson's edition is so seriously flawed that it should be avoided if possible. A new collected edition of all De Quincey's assignable works is being prepared by a team of scholars led by Grevel Lindop, and will eventually total twenty-one volumes.

BIBLIOGRAPHY

Confessions of an English Opium-Eater (1821; revised and expanded, 1856).
The Logic of Political Economy (1844).
Suspiria de Profundis (1845).
Selections Grave and Gay, from Writings Published and Unpublished by Thomas De Quincey, 16 vols (Edinburgh, 1852–60; repr. as *De Quincey's Works*, 'Author's Edition', 1862–3).
The Uncollected Writings of Thomas De Quincey, ed. J. Hogg, 2 vols (1890).
The Collected Writings of Thomas De Quincey, ed. D. Masson, 14 vols (1896–7).

The Works of Thomas De Quincey, ed. G. Lindop et al. (vols 1–7, 2000; vols 8–9, 12–14, 17–18, 2001; further volumes in preparation).

Further Reading
Baxter, E., *De Quincey's Art of Autobiography* (Edinburgh, 1990).
Dendurents, H.O., *Thomas De Quincey: A Reference Guide* (Boston, 1978).
Eaton, H.A., *Thomas De Quincey: A Biography* (1936).
Goldman, A., *The Mine and the Mint: Sources for the Writings of Thomas De Quincey* (Carbondale, Illinois, 1965).
Gordon, J.B. (1985) 'De Quincey as Gothic Parasite: The Dynamic of Supplementarity', in R.L. Snyder (ed.), *Thomas De Quincey: Bicentenary Studies* (Norman, Oklahoma, 1985, pp. 239–62).
Groenewegen, P., 'Thomas De Quincey: "Faithful Disciple of Ricardo"?', *Contributions to Political Economy* (1982), vol. 1, pp. 51–8.
Heinzelman, K., *The Economics of the Imagination* (Amherst, Massachusetts, 1980).
Lindop, G., *The Opium-Eater: A Life of Thomas De Quincey* (1981).
McDonagh, J., *De Quincey's Disciplines* (Oxford, 1994).
Maniquis, R., 'Lonely Empires: Personal and Public Visions of Thomas De Quincey', in E. Rothstein and J.A. Wittreich (eds), *Literary Monographs*, vol. 8 (Madison, Wisconsin, 1976, pp. 111–27).
Roberts, D.S., *Revisionary Gleam: De Quincey, Coleridge, and the High Romantic Argument* (Liverpool, 2000).
Rzepka, C.J., *Sacramental Commodities: Gift, Text and the Sublime in De Quincey* (Amherst, Massachusetts, 1995).
Wellek, R., 'De Quincey's Status in the History of Ideas', in *Confrontations: Studies in the Intellectual and Literary Relations Between Germany, England, and the United States during the Nineteenth Century* (Princeton, New Jersey, 1965, pp. 114–52).

Martin Haggerty

DECKER, Matthew (1679–1749)

Decker was born in Amsterdam in 1679, and died in Richmond, Surrey on 18 March 1749. He was born into a Flemish commercial family, but was forced to flee Holland as a consequence of the Count of Alva's persecutions. Establishing himself as a merchant in London around 1702, he quickly became wealthy. From 1713–43 he was a director of the East India Company, serving twice as deputy governor (1720–1, 1729–30) and twice as governor (1725–6, 1730–33). His wealth gave him political influence, and he was elected Tory MP for Bishops Castle (1719-2) and appointed sheriff of Surrey in 1729. George I made him a baronet in 1716 after Decker entertained his monarch to dinner at his mansion on Richmond Green; according to tradition, the first pineapple grown in England was consumed at this meal.

Quite late in life, Decker published two extensive treatises on economic issues: *Serious Considerations on the Several High Duties which the Nation in General, as well as Trade in Particular, Labours Under, etc.* (1743), and *An Essay on the Causes of the Decline of the Foreign Trade, Consequently of the Value of the Lands in Britain, and on the Means to Restore All* (1744). The second work was widely read and reached seven editions by 1756. Its authorship was questioned by J.R. MCCULLOCH, but most authorities now acknowledge Decker to be the true author of the work, which undoubtedly contains more of interest than the first work. While *Serious Considerations* mainly includes practical descriptions of such things as the (positive) causal linkage between high duties and smuggling, and how duties instead could be replaced by an excise on houses, the *Essay* contains much more theory.

Historians of economic doctrine have mainly recognized Decker as a free trader well ahead of Adam SMITH, who might not have shared the latter's talents for abstract theory but who worked in the same spirit and was one of Smith's most important precursors. To some extent this is true. His starting point was undoubtedly the conventional one for his time, that in order for a country to prosper, more manufactures and trade were necessary. However, with regard to the means by which industry and trade should be augmented, Decker stood far from the *dirigisme* of, for example, Josiah CHILD. He believed in free trade as a general principle, and in the need to abandon duties and regulations in order to become more competitive. A proper 'knowledge of the true Nature of Trade', he said, can only lead to the conclusion that '...the cheaper things are, the more of them will be exported, and it is Exportation only that makes a Nation rich' (1744: 48). He even went so far as to say that 'Every Home Commodity in a free Trade will find its natural value' (1744: 49).

Decker presented a list of eight negative consequences stemming from high duties. First, high duties 'prevent our Country being an Universal Storehouse'. Second, they prevent an increase 'of our Navigation'. Third, high duties prevent the increase of sailors, 'the true Strength of this Nation'. Fourth, he says, they will lessen the capital of merchants. Fifth, they 'encourage and force the consumption of Foreign Superfluities' because – and this probably is a conclusion that not all would draw – 'The deerer outlandish Luxuries are, the more they are esteemed by our People of Taste.' Sixth, high duties on imports encourage smuggling. Seventh, they ruin manufacturing, especially the woollen cloth industry, and eighth and last, high duties 'sends away our Specie', or in other words, they turn the trade balance against England. This happens because England's trading partners retaliate and increase their own duties, so English goods become more expensive and no one will buy them. Decker believed in keeping wages low in order to maintain low costs of production and low prices. He believed in population growth, but at the same time stressed: 'That such as your Employment is for People, so many will your People be' (1744: 108).

However, at the same time we should beware of seeing Decker's ideas as drastically different from the general trend of thinking during this time. Hence, his free trade inclinations did not stop him from presenting a rather crude version of the balance of trade theory, pointing out that 'if the Exports of Britain exceed its Imports, Foreigners must pay the Balance in Treasure and the Nation grow Rich' (1744: 7). He said with regard to silver and gold that 'the more or less of these Metals a Nation retains, it is denominated Rich or Poor' (1744: 7). However, Decker seems to have been of two minds on this latter issue; later in the text he pointed out that raw materials imported and 'improved by the People's Labour at least twice' would thereby increase 'a Nation's Treasure in proportion' (1744: 8). He here seems quite close to the foreign paid incomes theory or the principle of a balance of labour (the importance of exporting more value-added wares than are imported).

BIBLIOGRAPHY
Serious Considerations on the Several High Duties which the Nation in General, as well as Trade in Particular, Labours Under, etc. (1743).
An Essay on the Causes of the Decline of the Foreign Trade, Consequently of the Value of the Lands in Britain, and on the Means to Restore All (1744).

Lars Magnusson

DEFOE, Daniel (1660–1731)

Defoe was born Daniel Foe in London in late 1660, and died in London 26 April 1731. He adopted the name 'de Foe' in 1695, possibly for business purposes. He was educated by an ejected minister, James Fisher, in Dorking, then at Charles Morton's dissenter academy, Newington Green (1674–9). Morton was later vice president of Harvard. Defoe was also a member of Samuel Annesley's congregation in Bishopsgate. Instead of entering the Presbyterian ministry, however, Defoe became a merchant and commodity speculator and then, at various times and often simultaneously, a shipping insurer, civet cat breeder, civil servant, part owner of a brick-and-tile works, hack writer, convict, journalist, political agitator, government spy, poet, newspaper editor, pamphleteer and novelist.

Defoe was active in the opposition to James II, fighting with Monmouth's cavalry at Sedgemoor. He opposed James's Declaration of Indulgence and joined William's army at Windsor in December 1688. He travelled widely and spoke several European languages. His fortunes were erratic. In mid-life, he claimed he had been rich and poor thirteen times. He was imprisoned seven times, pilloried three times and bankrupted at least twice. He confessed that both his business and political dealings were not always honest. He wrote for pay, and was often deeply troubled when attempting to reconcile his deeds with his conscience and his writings with his principles. He frequently lived in hiding from his creditors, political enemies and the law. In 1684, he married Mary Tuffley, daughter of a wealthy dissenting cooper. They had eight children; six survived. In the Spring of 1731, Defoe died as he had so often lived: weary, poor, frightened, in hiding from his creditors and enemies, but still writing. He had just finished *The Compleat English Gentleman* and he was well advanced with *Of Royall Education*.

Defoe was one of the most prolific writers in the English language. Until recently, he was credited with over 570 separate works, many of them running to several hundred pages and more. But P.N. Furbank and W.R. Owens (1994, 1998) and others have quite persuasively argued that the actual number that can genuinely be attributed to him is about half that. Defoe was also a masterful manipulator of the print market. He wrote on every subject of significant public controversy between the late 1680s and 1731. He experimented with a vast array of forms in both poetry and prose. He published anonymously, pseudonymously and, very occasionally, under his own name. He adopted many different *personae*, imitating his enemies and friends as well as those of his paymasters (Whig, Tory and commercial interests). He frequently argued on all sides of contemporary controversies, and it is often difficult to determine what his own position was on many issues. Today, Defoe is most famous for his fictional narratives, like the first part of the three-part *Robinson Crusoe* (1719), *Moll Flanders* (1722) and *Roxana* (1724). But during his lifetime and for most of the eighteenth century, Defoe was primarily known as a journalist, pamphleteer, social and political critic and satirical poet. His economic and political writings, frequently in the form of journalism, compose the foundation upon which his eighteenth century reputation rested.

In many respects, Defoe's political ideas were more effective than his economic ideas. In the paper wars of the early eighteenth century, Defoe created two distinct public *personae* to propagate his political and economic views. 'The Author of the True-born Englishman', named after a verse satire which was Defoe's most popular work during his lifetime, published mainly party political tracts and political theory. 'Mr. Review', named after Defoe's amazing periodical which appeared thrice weekly for most of its life from 19 February 1704 to 11 June 1713, published many of his most important economic tracts. Quite appropriately, however, there were significant overlapping concerns.

Among the writings of 'The Author of the True-born Englishman', three stand out as containing consistent and enduring expressions of Defoe's political ideas: *The True-Born Englishman* (1701), *The Original Power of the Collective Body* (1701) and *Jure Divino* (1706). All three extended arguments first deployed by Defoe in the controversies of the late 1690s about the possible threats to liberty posed by modern, professional standing armies. Defoe's defence of a professional army that was currently being advocated by William III's Whig government led him to reject the historical arguments of most earlier Whig justifications of the 1688 Revolution. The ancient contract constitution was a myth, the Normans had conquered England in 1066 and English liberty was modern, the outcome of a successful struggle between the people, the nobility and the monarch. In his three main works, Defoe generalized these arguments. Appeals to constitutional history and customary law were delegitimized. Reason and nature replaced them as the foundations of law and justice. James II's actions had dissolved the English constitution and the 1688 Revolution was justified as a legitimate expression of the people's right to resist, a right aided by a benevolent conqueror, William III. In short, Defoe replaced the highly questionable historical arguments of Old Whiggism by the rationalism of Modern Whiggism combined with Tory principles of a just conquest. In the broadest terms, Defoe had begun defending 'modern liberty' in commercial societies with parliamentary institutions against the 'ancient liberty' of slave-holding or agrarian societies. This distinction was only fully articulated more than a century later by Benjamin Constant in his *The Liberty of the Ancients Compared with that of the Moderns* (1819).

The impact of *The True-Born Englishman* was enormous. It far outsold even Richard Allestree's *The Whole Duty of Man* (1657). It established its own satirical sub-genre of true-born Welshmen, Scotsmen, Huguenots and English women. And the theoretical perspectives which it contained were very frequently attacked, defended, quoted and reworked in both poetry and prose throughout the eighteenth century, even by Thomas Paine in 1805. Defoe became an immediate celebrity, and was attacked by leading Tory propagandists, like Charles Leslie, as the chief Whig ideologist. He was accused of resurrecting the rationalist theories of papists and regicides and, in Tory propaganda, his name was linked with a long list of supposedly disreputable writers from Robert Parsons to John LOCKE. Indeed, Defoe has often been interpreted as versifying Locke's *Second Treatise of Government* (1690) in both *The True-Born Englishman* and *Jure Divino*. But this is an error: his sources were much more eclectic, ranging from the Old Testament, Samuel Pufendorf, Algernon Sidney and James Tyrrell to the commonplaces of contemporary Whigs and pro-Revolutionary Tories. His theories were rationalistic and dispensed with the historical myths of the Old Whigs, and hence they resembled Locke's in precisely those ways which led the Old Whigs to reject *Two Treatises* as an adequate defence of the constitutional revolution of 1688. But Defoe remained in his rationalism much more authoritarian and elitist than Locke. Yet still, Defoe's immensely popular, controversial and rationalistic theories, especially as presented in *The True-Born Englishman* and *The Original Power*, did much to clear the ideological ground for the acceptance of Locke as a Whig authority in the eighteenth century. His contemporary fame assured him a place, in John Dunton's words, as one of 'the chief Wits of the Age' well before he turned his pen to the novels upon which his enduring, literary reputation now rests.

Defoe's considerable volume of economic writings have fared less well in the eyes of historians of economic analysis than his political writings have in the eyes of historians of political thought. Schumpeter, for example, confines Defoe to a footnote and declares that 'even his most ambitious efforts in our field remained in the sphere of economic journalism' (1994: 372, n. 15). There is much to be said for this view. But in more recent years, a number of literary scholars and historians, including Maximilian Novak (2001), Laura Curtis (1979), Thomas Meier (1987) and J.G.A. Pocock (1975) have discovered much of interest in Defoe's economic writings. Nearly all of these writings were addressed to practical issues of the day. Hardly any of them rise to any theoretical heights. They are the works of an enthusiastic promoter of trade and commerce. 'Trade', Defoe wrote in the final issue of the *Review*, 'was the Whore I doated on.' And he continued to do so to the end of his life. His first work of any economic interest, *An Essay upon Projects* (1697), expresses the spirit of much of his writing. It contains about a dozen projects for public and private investment to remedy perceived socio-economic problems. The projects range from establishing banks, fixing highways and establishing a pension office to erecting academies for women. They express an almost utopian entrepreneurial enthusiasm which Defoe believed to be characteristic of his age. One of his last works, *Augusta Triumphans* (1728), continues in the same vein. It proposes the foundation of a university and a musical academy in London, as well as various measures to reduce crime and anti-social behaviour in order to make London 'the most Flourishing City in the Universe.' But such projecting had its down side. Defoe's own business failures led him to caution all aspiring tradesmen to beware of projectors' inflated claims (*The Complete English Tradesman*, I, ch. 4). The greatest danger, in these respects, came from the newly established traders in stocks. Defoe railed against the rumour-mongering and corruption of stock-jobbers in many pamphlets and newspaper articles from *The Free-Holders Plea* (1701) and *The Villainy of Stock-Jobbers Detected* (1701) to *The Anatomy of Exchange-Alley* (1719).

Although he was indisputably a proponent of commercial progress, there is much that is old-fashioned in Defoe's economic writing. He had no time for the emerging stock market. He was convinced that the woollen industry was the backbone of England's economic strength and supported every means possible to protect it. He was certainly no friend to innovations that streamlined production processes. The more hands a product passed through on its way from raw materials to retail shops, the better. For in this way, employment remained high. He could see no merit in John Law's banking proposals, insisting instead that all bills must be backed by specie. He was committed to common notions of a favourable balance of trade and he supported both colonization and the system of trade embodied in the Navigation Laws (1660–73). His moral, political and economic ideas were frequently at odds. Drunkenness and debauchery were the scourge of social life, until it came to defending the distilling industry in an almost Mandevillian fashion in a *Brief Case of the Distillers* (1726). Luxury and fashion were follies, but they were good for trade. Commerce with Catholic France should be limited, until Harley required him to argue the opposite in 1713. Slaves should be treated with discipline but not cruelty, but only because cruelty impaired them as an economic asset (*Review*, no. 8, p. 730). He defended the commercial monopolies of the East India Company and the Africa Company, but he opposed the provision of work for England's poor. There was, he claimed in *Giving Alms no Charity* (1704), sufficient work for the poor. They just had to go and find it.

But there were respects in which Defoe's economic ideas were unusual for his time. He was an (almost) consistent advocate of high wages, when most of his contemporaries advocated low wages to reduce production costs and increase sales. The one exception Defoe made was for servants. Their 'Exorbitent Wages', he argued in *Every-Body's Business, is No-Body's Business* (1725), had led to pride and insolence. But in manufacturing, Defoe was convinced that the high quality of English goods would always command a high price, hence care should be taken not to reduce the purchasing power of English workers. To Defoe, the inland trade was just as important as foreign trade in wealth creation. The circulation of goods was the barometer of economic well-being. Most of his economic writings display an intense patriotic pride in England's achievements and untapped potential as a 'trading nation', both domestic and foreign. They also display a steady didactic hand. Two of his major works, *A Tour thro' the Whole Island of Great Britain* (1724–6) and *The Complete English Tradesman* (1725–7), are clearly two such patriotic, didactic works. The first has been called 'a Paean of Business' (Meier 1987, ch. 3); the second was thought by Defoe's biographer William Chadwick to be not only Defoe's best book but 'the best book that ever was written in the English language' (Chadwick 1859: 454). But these same concerns to educate his readers about trade and business and to emphasize England's or Britain's advantages in these areas run through all of Defoe's lengthy works on trade from *A General History of Trade* in four parts (1713) to his contributions to the *Atlas Maritimus & Commercialis* (1728).

All of these works by Defoe provide a wealth of information for economic and social historians interested in the state of the British economy and economic relationships in the early eighteenth century. They are, as Schumpeter concluded, works of perceptive, well-informed and frequently witty economic journalism. But in one sphere, more has been claimed for Defoe. In several *Review* articles beginning in 1706 and in his *Essay Upon Publick Credit* (1710), Defoe both identified and defended the core institutions and values of the emerging commercial economy with its 'interdependence of land, trade and credit' (Pocock 1975: 449). The argument is persuasive. The context of Defoe's defence of public credit was party political. Against Tory attacks that all forms of property, save land, were 'transient or imaginary', Whigs like Defoe and Addison set out to analyse and defend credit, and hence mobile property, as equally valuable and real as fixed. They did so in part by drawing upon the same idiom as Machiavelli had done to describe *fortuna*. Credit was an unpredictable lady who might be placated but never tamed. Credit was inevitably unstable. But treated honourably, fairly and with constant attention, some stability and predictability might follow. Public credit depended not upon the persons of officeholders or which party was in power but upon public confidence in the reliability, stability and honourable practices associated with the offices of state. For Defoe, as for Addison, in Queen Anne's reign, this meant defending the 1688 Revolution Settlement and the Protestant succession. It meant opposing the more radical Tories and Jacobites. Defoe's economics ideas here were still inextricably connected to his politics.

Once again, then, Defoe's analysis of public credit and of the care needed to breed the necessary public confidence are of more historical than analytical interest. But Defoe does have an enduring legacy in the history of economic analysis. That legacy does not derive from his economic writings, nor from his political writings. It stems rather from the writings of a third of his public characters or *personae*: 'Robinson Crusoe'. Perhaps through the medium of Rousseau's praise for *Robinson Crusoe* in *Emile* (1762) or perhaps simply because of the enormous popularity that the first volume of *Robinson Crusoe* eventually achieved, MARX could report in 1867 that 'Robinson Crusoe's experiences are a favourite theme with political economists' (*Kapital*, I, I., 4, p. 90). This was undoubtedly the case then, and it is still the case today with frequent references in the economic literature to 'the Robinson Crusoe economy', the 'Robinson Crusoe fallacy' and so on. Defoe, it seems, unwittingly bequeathed to economists, as he did more wittingly to the authors of the many literary *Robinsonades*, a literary model, a thought experiment, to make of what they will. When Defoe himself came to reflect on the meaning of the work, as he did in his third volume, *Serious Reflections during the Life and Surprising Adventures of Robinson Crusoe. With his Vision of the Angelic World* (1720), the economic implications of his island economy were not in his mind. The work, he noted, was an allegorical presentation of the sufferings and successes of a real person, designed for the reader's moral and religious improvement. But as with all major works of fiction, subsequent readers of varying kinds with varied interests have found more in the book than the author knew was there.

BIBLIOGRAPHY
An Essay upon Projects (1697).
The True-Born Englishman (1701).
The Free-Holders Plea against Stock-Jobbing Elections of Parliament Men (1701).
The Villainy of Stock-Jobbers Detected (1701).
The Original Power of the Collective Body of the People of England (1702).
The Review (1704–1713), ed. A.W. Secord, 22 vols (New York, 1938).
Giving Alms no Charity (1704).
Remarks on the Bill to Prevent Frauds Committed by Bankrupts (1706).
An Essay at Removing National Prejudices against a Union with Scotland. Parts I and II (1706).
Jure Divino: A Satyr in Twelve Books (1706).
An Essay upon Publick Credit (1710).
An Essay upon Loans (1710).
An Essay upon the Trade to Africa (1711).
An Essay on the South-Sea Trade (1711).
A Brief Account of the Present State of the African Trade (1713).
An Essay on the Treaty of Commerce with France (1713).
Mercator: or, Commerce Retrieved (thrice weekly paper, 26 May 1713–20 July 1714).
A General History of Trade, and especially consider'd as it respects the British Commerce (1713).
Memoirs of Count Tariff, &c. (1713).
Some Thoughts upon the Subject of Commerce with France (1713).
Fair Payment No Spunge (1717).
The Anatomy of Exchange-Alley: or, a System of Stock-Jobbing (1719).
The Just Complaint of the Poor Weavers truly Represented (1719).
A Brief State of the Question, between the Printed and Painted Callicoes and the Woollen and Silk Manufacture (1719).
The Chimera: or, the French way of Paying National Debts, laid open (1719).
The Manufacturer (twice weekly paper, 30 October 1719–9 March 1721).
The Trade to India Critically and Calmly Consider'd (1720).
The Director (twice weekly paper, 5 October 1720–16 January 1721).
Brief Observations on Trade and Manufactures; and Particularly of our Mines and Metals, and the Hard-Ware Works (1721).
The Case of Mr. Law, Truly Stated (1721).
A Tour thro' the Whole Island of Great Britain (1724–6).
Every-Body's Business, is No-Body's Business (1725).
The Complete English Tradesman (1725–7).
A General History of Discoveries and Improvements (1725–6).
A Brief Case of the Distillers (1726).
A Brief Deduction of the Original, Progress, and Immense Greatness of the British Woollen Manufacture (1727).
Some Considerations on the Reasonableness and Necessity of Encreasing and Encouraging the Seamen (1728).
Augusta Triumphans: or, the Way to make London the most Flourishing City in the Universe (1728).
Atlas Maritimus & Commercialis (1728).
A Plan of the English Commerce (1728).
An Humble Proposal to the People of England, for the Encrease of their Trade (1729).
The Advantages of Peace and Commerce (1729).

A Brief State of the Inland or Home Trade, of England (1730).

Further Reading

Backscheider, P.R., *Daniel Defoe* (Baltimore, 1989).

Curtis, L.A. (ed.), *The Versatile Defoe* (1979).

Earle, P., *The World of Defoe* (1976).

Furbank, P.N. and Owens, W.R. *Defoe De-Attributions* (1994).

——, *A Critical Bibliography of Daniel Defoe* (1998).

Meier, T.K., *Defoe and the Defense of Commerce* (Victoria, BC, 1987).

Moore, J.R., *Daniel Defoe, Citizen of the Modern World* (Chicago, 1958).

Novak, M.E., *Daniel Defoe Master of Fictions: His Life and Ideas* (Oxford, 2001).

——, *Economics and the Fiction of Daniel Defoe* (Berkeley, 1962).

Pocock, J.G.A., *The Machiavellian Moment* (Princeton, 1975).

——, *Virtue, Commerce, and History* (Cambridge, 1985).

Rogers, P. (ed.), *Defoe: the Critical Heritage* (1972).

Schonhorn, M., *Defoe's Politics* (Cambridge, 1991).

Schumpeter, J.A., *History of Economic Analysis* (Oxford, 1994).

West, R., *Daniel Defoe* (New York, 1998).

Martyn Thompson

DENNISON, Stanley Raymond (1912–92)

Dennison was born on 15 June 1912 in North Shields, the son of an official in a local gas company. He died on 22 November 1992 in Newcastle upon Tyne. After completing a BA at Durham in 1933, Dennison became an affiliated undergraduate at Trinity College, Cambridge. He graduated with first-class honours in 1935. From 1935–9 he was an assistant lecturer at the University of Manchester, affiliated with the Economic Research Division. In 1939 he was elected to a chair in Economics at University College, Swansea. Between 1940 and 1944, he was chief economic assistant in the economic section of the War Cabinet Secretariat, working on air pollution, land utilization and medical remuneration, a job he pursued with the encouragement of John JEWKES. In 1946 he was awarded a CBE for his contribution to the war effort. Following the war, he became senior tutor and director of studies (economics) at Gonville and Caius College, Cambridge (1945–58), a period overlapping with Milton Friedman's visiting fellowship (1953–4). Dennison's later writings (for example, on education, on unions and other professional associations) reflect many parallels with the political views famously expressed by Milton and Rose Friedman (1979).

Following his time at Cambridge, Dennison was appointed to a chair in economics at The Queen's University of Belfast between 1958 and 1961, moving to the David Dale Professorship of Economics at the University of Newcastle upon Tyne between 1962 and 1972. From 1972 to 1979 he was vice chancellor of the University of Hull, and during this time served as a vice-chairman of the UK Committee of Vice Chancellors and Principals. Following his retirement, Dennison became an emeritus professor at the University of Hull. One of his last projects was a collaborative project with Oliver MacDonagh: *A History of Guinness 1886–1939: From Incorporation to the Second World War*. His other late work, the edited volume of Dennis ROBERTSON's works, *Robertson on Economic Policy*, was, according to Lord BAUER (1993) one of his greatest contributions.

In his non-academic roles, Dennison resisted the dominance of Keynesian economics in the post-war policy environment, expressing his pro-market views forcibly. He was chair of several Wages Councils and a member of the Review Body on Remuneration of Doctors and Dentists, as well as participating in a number of Departmental Committees of Inquiry. He was associated with the Mont Pelerin Society, established in 1947, and with the 1955 foundation of the free-market think-tank, the Institute of Economic Affairs.

In terms of his intellectual contributions, Dennison's *The Location of Industry and the Depressed Areas* (1939) was probably his most influential work. This book was a product of Dennison's research whilst in the Economics Research Department at University of Manchester. In it, Dennison analyses the existing literature on theories of industrial location, focussing on Alfred Weber's *Über den Standort der Industrien* (1909). Dennison rejects the technical aspects associated with the Weberian approach, and emphasizes that his own approach is not intended as a general theory of location. Nonetheless, key Weberian themes resurface in Dennison's work, most importantly in his analysis of the role of transport factors. After outlining the essence of his analytical arguments, Dennison goes on to dissect the problem of depressed areas in the UK. He presents statistical evidence to support the assertion that, during the 1920s and 1930s, the persistence of regional patterns of unemployment and decline reflected a problem of surplus labour, particularly in the North of England and Wales. Dennison explains this geographical divide in terms of theories of industrial location, and argues that the problem of depressed areas emerged from a series of changes in industrial structure. He asserts that, in resolving problems of regional decline, policy should be focussed on the need for increased labour mobility, both occupational and geographical. Dennison focuses on the limited efficacy of state intervention, foreshadowing his later preoccupation with the relative merits of *laissez-faire* solutions to economic problems. He argues that many of the policy initiatives undertaken to revive depressed areas (for example, those emerging from the Special Areas Act of 1934) had been fruitless. He emphasizes, however, that his analysis is diagnostic rather than prescriptive and concludes that problems of regional decline are complex and deeply seated, not necessarily amenable to general measures.

Much of Dennison's later work was collaborative. He worked with Dennis Robertson on the 1960 volume *The Control of Industry*, a re-working of Robertson's original 1923 volume of the same title. Robertson and Dennison argued that the 1923 volume had struck a chord because, with the advent of the infant socialist economy in Russia, there was a great interest in projects of radical industrial change. This preoccupation paralleled in the 1960s with the nationalization of many UK industries. Robertson and Dennison begin by outlining the three central economic questions: production; distribution; and control. They focus on the last, particularly on the problems associated with harnessing self-directing human activity in the context of government control. They go on to analyse the principles and development of modern industry and capitalism, focussing on large-scale industry. They assert that the evolution of organised industry and management, together with developments in workers' control, collectivism and communism had led to the problems of joint control in the 1960s. They argue that the transfer of governing powers to the worker should be completed but that workers' strength could be exploited by their representative institutions, leading to conflict and confusion. Policy lessons revolve around the insight that industry should develop representative institutions to match the unions as representative institutions for the workers. They conclude that the development of organised labour had created severe pressures for individual liberty; they emphasize that the immunities and privileges given to minority groups may no longer be appropriate in a world of powerful union corporations.

Stanley Dennison developed this *laissez-faire* theme in his 1984 critique of what he called the 'propaganda and distorted argument' circulated by Henry Neuburger in defence of the Low Pay Unit (1984: 63). The Low Pay Unit's aims were to protect workers against the monopsonistic tendencies of big employers, for example, by advocating minimum wage policies. Neuburger's theoretical defence of this strategy showed that wages set above the market-clearing equilibrium would not necessarily cause unemployment. Dennison produced a vehement critique of these theoretical arguments and the supporting statistical analysis. Instead, Dennison adopts a classical theory of the labour market, focussing on forces of perfect competition in the demand for and supply of labour. Dennison argues that his own analysis is not inconsistent with those expressed by KEYNES (1984: 77–8). This seeming inconsistency was justified by claiming that defences of the Low Pay Unit represented 'a confused mixture of fallacy and misapplication of distorted neo-Keynesian theory' (1984: 83). Dennison argues that Neuburger's approach was in essence 'objective analysis...subordinated to political aims' (1984: 86). Dennison concludes that the main causes of disadvantage and obstacles to advance were not market failures but rather government interventions, including minimum wages and restrictions on entry, such as into the professions (1984: 86).

Dennison also expressed his market-oriented approach in his policy prescriptions for education, reflecting a lifetime's interest in educational objectives. According to Lord Bauer (1993) he was a great teacher and influenced many students throughout his career. In *Choice in Education* (1984), he argues that the state is inferior to the market in meeting the objectives of individuals because of its focus on political objectives rather than social objectives. He argues that education is not a public good because the benefits and costs of education can be attributed to individuals. Reflecting his preference for applied analysis, he supports his arguments with a critique of the statistical analysis used to defend arguments for state education. He concludes that public education encourages political manoeuvring and excessive bureaucracy, all at the expense of taxpayers, voters and parents. Dennison practised as he preached and he actively supported the idea of an independent university, endowing research funds to the University of Buckingham, Britain's first independent university.

BIBLIOGRAPHY

The Location of Industry and Depressed Areas (1939).
(with D. Robertson), *The Control of Industry* (Cambridge, 1960).
'Economics without Prices: A Critique of the Low Pay Unit' in D. Forrest (ed.), *Low Pay or No Pay? A Review of the Theory and Practice of Minimum Wage Laws* (1984, pp. 63–87).
Choice in Education: An Analysis of the Political Economy of State and Private Education (1984).
(with J.R. Presley), *Robertson on Economic Policy* (1992).

Further Reading

Bauer, P., 'Professor S.R. Dennison, CBE' *The Caian: the Annual Record of Gonville & Caius College* (Cambridge, 1993).
Friedman, M. and Friedman, R., *Free to Choose: A Personal Statement* (1979).
Richardson, G.B., 'Review of *The Control of Industry* by D. Robertson and S.R. Dennison', *The Economic Journal* (1961), vol. 71, no. 283, pp. 615–7.
Robinson, A., 'Review of *The Location of Industry and the Depressed Areas* by S.R. Dennison', *The Economic Journal* (1940), vol. 50, no. 198/9, pp. 266–70.

Michelle Baddeley

DEVONS, Ely (1913–67)

Devons was born in Bangor, North Wales on 29 July 1913, the second of three boys and three girls. He died in London on 28 December 1967, being survived by his wife, the pianist Estelle Wine, two sons and a daughter. Devons's father was a Jewish rabbi and the family moved around the country, so that Devons was educated at Hanley High School, Portsmouth Grammar School and North Manchester Municipal High School. He attended Manchester University from 1931–4, graduating with first-class honours in economics, politics and modern history. He was awarded a Drummond Fraser Research Fellowship and used it to investigate British production statistics, which led to the award of an MA in economics in 1935 and his first publication (Devons 1935).

After university Devons began his career as an economic assistant to the Joint Committee of Cotton Trades Organisations in Manchester from 1935–9. At the outbreak of the Second World War he became a statistician for Cotton Control at the Ministry of Supply, but in March 1940 he joined the Central Economic Information Service in London, where he was responsible for collecting together the secret statistics generated in different departments of government, analysing them and making them available to policy makers in an intelligible form. He succeeded not only in collecting the statistics, but also in devising new formats and ways of presenting the data that continued to be used long after the war. In 1941 he moved to the post of chief statistician to the newly formed Ministry of Aircraft Production, and went on to succeed John JEWKES as the head of the planning department in 1944.

In 1945 Devons returned to Manchester University as Robert Ottley Reader in Applied Economics and was then Robert Ottley Professor in Applied Economics from 1948–59. From 1949–59 he was dean of the Faculty of Economic and Social Studies and his heavy administrative load gave him little time for writing, so that much of the work carried out during this period was published after he left Manchester. His conviction that theoretical economics was too narrow to provide a satisfactory analysis for policy makers led him to an active involvement in seminars in the departments of government, social anthropology and sociology, leading to the publication of *Closed Systems and Open Minds: The Limits of Naivety in Social Anthropology* (Devons and Gluckman 1964).

In 1959, despite having some reservations, Devons accepted the chair in commerce with special reference to international trade at the London School of Economics, when James MEADE moved to Cambridge. Meade was a hard act to follow, as Devons had no pretensions as a trade theorist and was not the first choice of the younger LSE economists, some of whom lobbied for the appointment of Harry JOHNSON. However, Devons made a major contribution to the development of the department of economics at the LSE after his appointment in 1962 as the first convenor (in other words, head) of the department. This was a time when the department was weakened by the exodus of many of the 'Young Turks' and the approaching retirement of most of the professors in the department. In a relatively short period, Devons took the initiative in attracting a number of leading economists to the LSE. Devons also played an important part in establishing the LSE's one-year taught masters degrees in economics and in mathematical economics and econometrics that were to be the models for those developed in many other institutions.

In 1965 Devons became seriously ill, remaining so throughout the last two years of his life. Despite the debilitating effects of his illness, he continued to teach and to pursue his administrative objectives within the economics department.

Devons's writings fall into three main groups. First, there are a number of publications on planning and economic organization, notably *Planning in Practice* (1950) and *Papers on*

Planning and Economic Management (1970), edited after Devons's death by Sir Alec CAIRNCROSS. Secondly, there are his writings on economic statistics, principally *Introduction to British Economic Statistics* (1956) and *Essays in Economics* (1961). Finally, there were several articles concerned with international trade. Of these, it is his contributions to the analysis of planning and economic management and the production of relevant statistics that were the most important and insightful, as they reflected the considerable practical experience he obtained during the Second World War.

BIBLIOGRAPHY
'Output Per Head in Great Britain, 1924–33', *Economic Journal* (1935), vol. 45, September, pp. 577–80.
'Productivity Trends in the United Kingdom', *Manchester School* (1939), vol. 10, January, pp. 55–61.
Planning in Practice (Cambridge, 1950).
'The Problem of Co-ordination in Aircraft Production', in D.N. Chester (ed.), *Lessons of the British War Economy* (Cambridge, 1951).
Introduction to British Economic Statistics (Cambridge, 1956).
Essays in Economics (1961).
'Understanding International Trade', *Economica* (1961), vol. 28, November, pp. 351–9.
(with M. Gluckman) *Closed Systems and Open Minds: The Limits of Naivety in Social Anthropology* (1964).
Papers on Planning and Economic Management, ed. A. Cairncross (Manchester, 1970).

Further Reading
Cairncross, A., 'Ely Devons: A Memoir' in E. Devons, *Papers on Planning and Economic Management* (Manchester, 1970, pp. 1–16).
Dahrendorf, R., *LSE: A History of the London School of Economics and Political Science, 1895–1995* (Oxford, 1995).

Johnson, H.G., 'Ely Devons', *LSE Magazine* (1968), June, p. 13.

Jim Thomas

DICKENS, Charles (1812–70)

Dickens was born 7 February 1812 at Landport, Portsea, Hampshire and died 9 June 1870 in London. He is buried at Westminster Abbey. He was educated at the Wellington House Academy and then at a school in Henrietta Street, Brunswick Square. The *Pickwick Papers*, published in 1836–7, launched his career as a writer; there followed *Oliver Twist* (1837–9) and *Nicholas Nickleby* (1838–9). His *American Notes* (1842) was based on his first American trip and reflects a horror of chattel slavery. Later novels include his *Tale of Two Cities* (1859) and *Great Expectations* (1860–1).

The year 1850 appears to mark a transition in Dickens's career. His subsequent novels *Bleak House* (1852–3) and *Hard Times* (1854), the latter dedicated to Thomas CARLYLE, have been judged by critics such as F.R. Leavis (1949) and Raymond Williams (1958) as witness to the materialistic content of nineteenth-century utilitarian political economy. Carlyle's 1849 'Negro Question' targeted 'Exeter Hall Philanthropy and the Dismal Science' for their 'sacred cause of Black Emancipation' (Carlyle 1849: 673). Similarly in *Bleak House*, Mrs Jellyby neglects her household for the benefit of African slaves (Dickens 1852–3: 35). The cover of the serial publication shows a middle-aged lady embracing two African children next to a sign reading 'Exeter Hall' (Levy and Peart 2001–2: 2).

Lord Denman, however, took issue with Dickens' anti-abolitionist position: 'he exerts his powers to obstruct the great cause of human improvement – that cause which in general he cordially advocates...We do not say that he actually defends slavery or the slave-trade; but he takes pains to discourage, by ridicule, the effort now making to put them down...The disgusting picture of a woman who pretends zeal for the happiness of Africa, and is constantly employed is constantly employed in securing a life of misery to her own children, is a laboured work of art in his present exhibition' (Denman 1853: 9). Denman linked Mrs Jellyby to articles in *Household Words* (Denman 1853: 11).

Dickens's attack on political economy occurs most memorably in *Hard Times* when Sissy Jupe encounters utilitarian political economy:

> after eight weeks of induction into the elements of Political Economy, she had only yesterday been set right by a prattler three feet high, for returning to the question 'What is the first principle of this science?' the absurd answer, 'To do unto others as I would that they should do unto me.'
> (Dickens 1854: 60)

But is the answer 'absurd'? J.S. MILL made the same argument: 'In the golden rule of Jesus of Nazareth, we read the complete spirit of the ethics of utility. To do as you would be done by, and to love your neighbour as yourself, constitute the ideal perfection of utilitarian morality' (Mill 1861: 218).

Dickens' characters re-emerged in the 1865 debates that followed the Eyre Controversy (Semmel 1962). Evangelicals, economists and evolutionists urged that Governor Eyre be held accountable for the massacre of former slaves. They were opposed by Carlyle, John RUSKIN and others. A *Punch* cartoon (23 December 1865) has the caption: 'The Jamaica Question. White Planter. "Am Not I a Man and a Brother, Too, Mr. Stiggins?"' (Levy and Peart 2001–02: 3). Stiggins is the red-nosed evangelical preacher in *Pickwick Papers*.

BIBLIOGRAPHY
Bleak House (1852–3; ed. G. Ford and S. Monod, New York, 1977).
Hard Times (1854; ed. K. Flint, 1995).

Further Reading
Carlyle, T., 'Occasional Discourse on the Negro Question', *Fraser's Magazine for Town and Country* (1849), vol. 40, pp. 670–9.
Denman, Lord, *Uncle Tom's Cabin, Bleak House, Slavery and Slave Trade* (1853).
Leavis, F.R., *The Great Tradition* (1949).
Levy, D.M. and Peart, S.J. (2001–2) 'Secret History of the Dismal Science', www.econlib.org. (16 January 2004).
Mill, J.S., 'Utilitarianism'. *Fraser's Magazine* (1861), vol. 64, pp. 391–406.
Semmel, B., *The Governor Eyre Controversy* (1962).
Stone, H., 'Charles Dickens and Harriet Beecher Stowe', *Nineteenth-Century Fiction* (1949), vol. 12, pp. 188–202.
Williams, R., *Culture and Society: 1780–1950* (New York, 1952).

David M. Levy
Sandra R. Peart

DICKINSON, Henry Douglas (1899–1969)

H.D. 'Dick' Dickinson was born in London on 25 March 1899, the son of a professional engineer who was also a biographer of early engineers. He died in Bristol on 11 July 1969. Educated at King's College, Wimbledon and at Emmanuel College, Cambridge, Dickinson graduated in economics in 1921 and in history in 1922. He was a research student at the London School of Economics between 1922 and 1924, his PhD thesis forming the basis of his first book, *Institutional Revenue* (1932). He taught at Leeds University from

1924 to 1947, being promoted from assistant lecturer to lecturer, and then to reader in the history of economic thought. A lifelong socialist, Dickinson was an active member of the Fabian Society and an enthusiastic tutor for the Workers' Educational Association. In 1947 he moved to Bristol University, where he was promoted to professor in 1951. After his retirement in 1964 he was briefly temporary professor at Queen's University, Belfast.

In *Institutional Revenue*, Dickinson revealed an affinity for both Austrian and Marxian economic theory; the book was an attempt to derive a theory of property income consistent with both strands of thought. His first important article, 'Price Formation in a Socialist Community' (1933), was also a response to Austrian analysis, this time to Ludwig von Mises's contention that rational economic decision-making was impossible under socialism. On the contrary, Dickinson maintained, 'only in a socialist community, where production can be carried out in the full light of statistical measurement and publicity, is it possible to realise the true principles of economic valuation... The beautiful systems of economic equilibrium described by Böhm-Bawerk, Wieser, Marshall and Cassel are not descriptions of society as it is but prophetic visions of a socialist economy of the future' (1933: 246–7). Dickinson's case was developed at length in *Economics of Socialism* (1939). He is sometimes interpreted as an advocate of market socialism in the Lange sense, but in fact his analysis was more nuanced than this: his socialist planners would raise and lower prices and observe the effects on the market, but they would also calculate demand and supply schedules as an aid to 'establishing the numerical values of the constants in the Walrasian equations of equilbrium' (1939: 105). In a more fundamental sense, however, Dickinson *was* a market socialist, since unlike his communist friend Maurice DOBB, he insisted that consumers and workers be given the maximum freedom in their purchasing and labour supply decisions.

Dickinson published relatively little after 1939, but two important mathematical articles from the mid-1950s deserve attention. 'A Note on Dynamic Economics' (1955) made early use of a CES production function and anticipated some aspects of the Swan–Solow neoclassical growth model, while 'The Falling Rate of Profit in Marxian Economics' applied a Cobb–Douglas production function to assess MARX's argument that in capitalism technical progress tends to reduce the profit rate. Dickinson concluded that Marx's intuition was sound. A neoclassical socialist of considerable distinction, it is unfortunate that Dicksinson did not publish more prolifically.

BIBLIOGRAPHY
Institutional Revenue (1932; repr. New York, 1966).
'Price Formation in a Socialist Community', *Economic Journal* (1933), vol. 43, pp. 237–50.
Economics of Socialism (1939).
'A Note on Dynamic Economics', *Review of Economic Studies* (1955), vol. 22, pp. 169–79.
'The Falling Rate of Profit in Marxian Economics', *Review of Economic Studies* (1956), vol. 24, pp. 120–30.

Further Reading
Dobb, M.H., 'Obituaries', *History of Economic Thought Newsletter* (1969), vol. 3, pp. 3–4.

J.E. King

DICKSON, Adam (1721–76)

Dickson was born at Aberlady, East Lothian in 1721, exact date unknown. He died at

Whittinghame, also in East Lothian, late in 1776 of injuries received in a fall from a horse. He took an MA from the University of Edinburgh some time after 1740 and then entered the church, taking up the ministry of Duns, Berwickshire in 1750. In 1770 he moved from Duns to Whittinghame, where he remained until his death.

Dickson was a notable and prolific writer on agriculture, and his *Treatise on Agriculture* (1762) was a summary of current knowledge about agricultural practices which combined the fruits of recent scientific research with personal observations of best practice on the farms of south-east Scotland. This work was followed by a number of essays on subjects such as tillage and manure. His later life was dedicated to compiling *The Husbandry of the Ancients*, which was published posthumously in 1784. This work drew on Roman texts on agriculture and compared ancient practices with those of the modern day. The book was highly popular and was also translated into French, but sadly Dickson's Latin was not up to the task of translating from Roman original texts, and later commentators found so many errors that the work was eventually judged to be valueless.

Dickson's ideas on economics grew out of both his interest in the problems of farming and his views on social welfare. In his *Essay on the Causes of the Present High Price of Provisions* (1773), he argues that 'the price of provisions is a matter of the greatest importance to society. When low, idleness is encouraged; and when high, the poor are distressed and manufactures suffer' (1773: 1). He goes on to state that the problem of high prices cannot be dealt with simply by price regulation, but that high prices are themselves symptoms of larger economic problems that must be identified and cured.

Dickson sees the price of provisions as depending on three things: the supply of provisions in the market, the extent of demand, and the overall state of the economy including especially the supply of money. Because all three of these fluctuate, there are difficulties in fixing the 'right' price for provisions; fluctuating supply, demand and money supply mean that the most beneficial price will differ from time to time. The important issue, Dickson implies, is not to fix the correct price, but to create a balance of supply, demand and economic conditions which allows prices to set themselves. He is clearly influenced here by the physiocrats, and he quotes from Montesquieu on several occasions.

In his own day, Dickson identified three factors that were pushing up prices. On the supply side, the increasing conversion of arable land to pasture in order to meet the public demand for beef was restricting grain supply, thus driving prices up. At the same time, a rising population was stimulating overall demand. It is to the issue of money supply, however, that he devotes the most attention. Following Montesquieu's views on the impact that the quantity of money in circulation has on prices, Dickson argues that while there is no doubt that money supply is increasing, thanks to the growth in banking activity, the circulation of money was not even but was instead open to severe fluctuations. He blames the increasing use of paper currency for this phenomenon: increased money supply leads in turn to more spending, and this also drives prices up.

Dickson also criticizes the increase of wealth based on bills of exchange (paper money) as 'imaginary riches', and he warns against the creation of excessive credit: he believes that if the supply of paper money and credit grows too quickly, the public will lose faith and an economic collapse will result. He then goes on to the need for reform of taxation, linking high taxation with price inflation. His proposals for reducing prices include (1) lower taxes, (2) tighter control of money supply and (3) new measures to increase the corn supply.

BIBLIOGRAPHY

An Essay on the Causes of the Present High Price of Provisions, as connected with luxury, currency, taxes and the national debt (1773).

Morgen Witzel

DIGGES, Dudley (1583–1639)

Digges was born in Barham, Kent, some time in 1583, and died at Chilham, Kent on 18 March 1639. His father was the celebrated mathematician Thomas Digges; his younger brother Leonard was a poet and friend of Shakespeare. Digges attended University College, Oxford, graduating BA in 1601. As a young man he spent some time at court and was at first friendly with the new king James I and VI, who knighted him 1607, but by 1614 Digges had fallen out with the court and was briefly imprisoned for offending the monarch. He then briefly entered the service of the Earl of Somerset. In 1618 Digges went to Russia as an emissary of the East India and Muscovy Companies to arrange a loan to the Tsar of Russia, but was unsuccessful in his mission. In 1620 he was one of the negotiators sent by the East India Company to the Netherlands to negotiate with the Dutch East India Company in order to settle the trade rivalry between the two companies, but this mission too was a failure.

From 1621–7 Digges served as member of parliament for Tewkesbury, and from 1628 represented Kent. He became an important political figure, and was often at the centre of parliamentary opposition to James I and Charles I. In 1627 he was again imprisoned for a speech giving offence to the king, but was released after making an apology. He was prominent among the opposition to Charles's minister, the Duke of Buckingham, and was a lifelong friend of George Abbot, Archbishop of Canterbury and a leading opponent of Buckingham. Digges was also one of the principal figures behind the Petition of Right in 1628. From 1636 until his death he served as Master of the Rolls. He was one of the founders of the Bermuda Company and was a shareholder in both the East India and Muscovy Companies, though it is doubtful if he ever made much money from these investments. However, his marriage to Mary Kempe some time before 1620 brought him the important manor of Chilham, and he was a moderately wealthy man at the time of his death.

A strong supporter of the East India Company, Digges campaigned for the governorship of the Company in 1614. He was unsuccessful, the post going instead to Sir Thomas Smith, but he continued to defend the Company against its detractors. In *The Defence of Trade* (1615), Digges argued that the Company was an important agent of national wealth. He compared its merchants to bees returning to the hive, bringing wealth to all the community: 'laborious bees, they clothe and feed the poore, and give the willing man imployment to gaine with them' (1615:2). Opponents of the Company believed that the national wealth was being exported to pay for silks and spices for the rich, but Digges argued that the reverse was true, claiming that the value of the goods imported by the Company exceeded the value of the specie it exported by £70,000 per annum. He pointed out that the Company imported not only luxuries but necessaries such as dyestuffs and drugs, and further that the Company was providing much employment in its own service and in the shipbuilding industry. Although primarily a work of propaganda on behalf of the Company, *The Defence of Trade* is also a strong defence of mercantilist principles.

BIBLIOGRAPHY
The Defence of Trade, in a Letter to Sir Thomas Smith, Knight, Gouvernour of the East-India Companie (1615).

Morgen Witzel

DOBB, Maurice Herbert (1900–76)

Dobb was born in London on 24 July 1900, and died in Cambridge on 17 August 1976. He was educated at Charterhouse and at Pembroke College, Cambridge, graduating in economics in 1922. Dobb spent the next two years as a research student at the London School of Economics, obtaining his PhD with a thesis on the history and theory of capitalist enterprise. In 1924 he returned to Cambridge as lecturer in the faculty of economics and politics, and taught there until his retirement in 1967. As both a communist and a divorced man Dobb was something of an outsider in Cambridge; it was not until 1948 that he was formally attached to a college (as fellow of Trinity). Eleven years later he was promoted to reader, together with Nicholas KALDOR and Joan ROBINSON, and in 1971 he became a fellow of the British Academy.

Already a socialist as an undergraduate, Dobb joined the Communist Party of Great Britain in 1922, playing an active role in many of its organizations, including the Plebs League, the Council of Labour Colleges and the Labour Research Department. He wrote for its journals, *Labour Research*, *Modern Quarterly* and *Marxism Today*, and was a tireless lecturer to working-class audiences. In 1925 Dobb made the first of many visits to the Soviet Union, and in 1952 he travelled extensively in India. He was in Poznan in early 1956 when the Polish workers' uprising was brutally suppressed by the authorities. Neither this nor the Hungarian revolution later in the year led him to resign from the Party. He remained a loyal member until the end, although he was sometimes critical of the dogmatic position taken by its leadership.

Dobb belonged to the last generation in which it was possible for an individual to make important contributions to economic history, to the history of economic thought and to economic theory. As a Marxist, he regarded this as the only sensible way to proceed. In his doctoral dissertation, which became his first book, *Capitalist Enterprise and Social Progress* (1925), he analysed the emergence and transformation of the capitalist enterprise since the eighteenth century as an essential foundation for understanding two centuries of profit theories and for his own criticism of modern analyses of capitalist incomes. When he wrote a brief introductory text on *Wages* (1928) for KEYNES's Cambridge Economic Handbooks series, Dobb devoted much of the book to describing the emergence of wage labour and the subsequent evolution of labour market institutions, along with a detailed account of the history of wage theories since Adam SMITH. By far his most important work on economic history, however, was *Studies in the Development of Capitalism* (1946). Here he explained the decline of the feudal system by its internal contradictions as a mode of production and the superior productive efficiency of the emerging capitalist system. Dobb criticized alternative explanations, including those of fellow Marxists like Paul Sweezy, which stressed external factors, above all the growth of trade. Production, he insisted, was more fundamental than exchange. A major historiographical controversy was provoked by Dobb's work, and is still continuing.

Dobb was equally committed to viewing 'the present as history', in Sweezy's evocative phrase. Thus he devoted almost one-quarter of *Studies in the Development of Capitalism* to a probing analysis of what he believed to be the decadence of post-1870 capitalism, which had been demonstrated once and for all by the events of the 1930s. Dobb had already written the first systematic economic history of the Soviet Union, initially published as *Russian Economic Development Since 1917* (1929) and then, transformed by Stalin's forced industrialization – and his own decision to learn Russian – as *Soviet Economic Development* (1948). There was a unifying principle in all Dobb's writing on economic history, which guided him also in his work as a historian of economic thought: everything hinges on the production of a social surplus, defined as total output minus the cost of producing it, and on the way in which this surplus is used. As MARX acknowledged, the classical economists had been the first to see this as the basis for a scientific political economy, and Dobb concurred. In his last book, *Theories of Value and Distribution Since Adam Smith* (1973), he distinguished two traditions. One, 'embracing most of the purely "exchange" or market theories...casts the economic problem in terms of "natural" or "universal" factors', while the other, 'by stressing social relations of production and/or income-distribution, [has] given prominence to the "institutional" factors and displayed economic problems in a mainly "institutional" shape' (1973: 26).

Implicitly, if not explicitly, this distinction ran through all his earlier work. By 1931, when he wrote a widely-read 'Introduction to Economics' for a popular audience, Dobb was already describing the emergence of supply and demand theory as being 'really no solution, but a retreat from the issue. It consisted in virtually abandoning the conception of objective real cost' (1931: 603–4). Six years later, in *Political Economy and Capitalism*, he developed this theme at much greater length. Marx's work, Dobb suggested, was the analytical culmination of classical political economy. Both the original neoclassical theorists and their successors in the inter-war period had renounced the surplus approach to economics, but they had failed to produce an acceptable alternative. 'Subjective economics', Dobb maintained, 'resting as it does on an attempt to interpret economic events in terms of the psychological behaviour of individuals, finds itself faced with a chaos of indeterminacy, where almost anything is possible' (1937: 218–19). In the 'random biographical notes' that he wrote in 1965 but which were published only in 1978, Dobb came very close to repudiating *Political Economy and Capitalism*, describing it as hastily written and superficial. A more reasonable judgement came from his former student, Ronald MEEK, who in his 1977 tribute to Dobb described the book as 'the first really *creative* contribution to Marxist economics ever to appear, at least in the English-speaking world' (1977: 336, italics in the original).

In the 1931 article, Dobb acknowledged the influence of his reclusive and deeply secretive Cambridge colleague Piero SRAFFA, who was working on the magnificent rehabilitation of classical political economy that would be published, thirty years later, as *Production of Commodities By Means of Commodities* (Sraffa 1960). In 1930, Sraffa had been entrusted by the Royal Economic Society with the task of editing RICARDO's writings for eventual publication. Work proceeded at a glacial pace until, in 1948, the Society asked Dobb to collaborate with Sraffa. Progress now accelerated sharply; the first volume of the *Collected Works*, Ricardo's *Principles of Political Economy and Taxation*, appeared in 1951 with a lucid introduction setting out the 'surplus interpretation' of Ricardo in great scholarly detail. The project was completed only in 1973. Dobb's intellectual contribution, though by no means negligible, was certainly less than Sraffa's; in practical terms, however, the *Collected Works* might never have appeared without him.

Sraffa had revealed very little to anyone about his own theoretical project, and after 1960 Dobb took some time to absorb the full significance of *Production of Commodities*. Slowly he came to realize that it contained both a profound critique of the orthodox theories of value, capital and distribution and a powerful case for the continued relevance of classical political economy. In 1970 he published an incisive article defending Sraffa's surplus approach as representing an important advance in Marxian economic theory. Originally published, somewhat obscurely, in the Dutch journal *De Economist*, Dobb's 'The Sraffa System and Critique of the Neoclassical Theory of Distribution', was reprinted in 1972 in the best-selling reader, *A Critique of Economic Theory*, edited by Kay Hunt and Jesse Schwartz, and proved extremely influential. It formed the basis for the concluding chapter of *Theories of Value and Distribution Since Adam Smith*, a book that brought Dobb's history of economic thought up to date. Sraffa's book had changed the course of economic theory, Dobb concluded; since the debates of the 1960s had so severely damaged orthodox analysis, 'nothing can ever be quite the same again' (1973: 266).

As already noted, Dobb's ideas on matters of economic theory developed *pari passu* with his work in economic history and the history of economic thought. His initial objection to the neoclassical theory of income distribution was that, even if the demand side had been settled by the principle of marginal productivity, the supply side remained undetermined. The conditions under which labour was supplied evidently depended on social institutions, including the distribution of wealth and of opportunities for education and training. Less obviously, but even more important, the apparently innocent notion of the 'supply price of capital' concealed a host of social and institutional determinants, among which the 'abstinence' of capitalists was probably the least significant. After 1960, Dobb came to accept Sraffa's critique of marginal productivity and to argue that the orthodox theory of capital was incoherent. In *Theories of Value and Distribution*, he returned to the question of income distribution, showing some sympathy for Nicholas Kaldor's model (anticipated by Michal Kalecki) in which the profit share was a function of the ratio of investment to income and of the propensity to save out of profits. Dobb himself had foreshadowed this approach in a 1929 article, 'A Sceptical View of the Theory of Wages' (reprinted in his essays, *On Economic Theory and Socialism*, 1955). Although he never totally repudiated the neoclassical theory of consumer demand, he persistently drew attention to the dependence of market demands upon the distribution of income and their susceptibility to manipulation by producers, which rendered the concept of 'consumer sovereignty' largely empty of meaning. For these reasons he took a highly critical – but not completely dismissive – view of mainstream welfare economics, which was the subject of the first half of his *Welfare Economics and the Economics of Socialism* (1969).

In his work on socialism Dobb was never a crude Stalinist, but his attitude adapted, continuously and apparently quite effortlessly, to the Party line. In 1928 he defended Lenin's New Economic Policy, insisting that War Communism had been nothing more than an inevitable temporary reaction to the civil war in Russia and was not (as some on the Left believed) a valuable experiment in the construction of a moneyless utopia. Five years later, criticising his friend H.D. DICKINSON, Dobb maintained that little if anything could be expected from the application of orthodox economic principles to the Soviet economy. Neoclassical welfare economics was largely useless, since dynamic considerations concerning the rate of growth were very much more important than questions of static resource allocation. He repeated these arguments, which were intended as a defence of Stalinist central planning, in the long chapter of *Political Economy and Capitalism* devoted to 'The Question of Economic Law in a Socialist Economy' and in the first (1948) edition of *Soviet Economic Development*. After 1953 Dobb took a close interest in the reform of the Soviet economy and wrote favourably on the development of optimal planning techniques and the greater use of markets. But he was not a market socialist.

When it came to Marxian economics, Dobb defended the labour theory of value as an indispensable tool for the analysis of capitalism and insisted on the need for value theory to be consistent with the theory of exploitation. Although he wrote (briefly) on the transformation problem, he never took much interest in the technical difficulties that arose from the distinction between values and prices of production. Indeed, he seems to have been the first Marxian economist writing in English to note that the labour theory of value had a qualitative as well as a quantitative dimension, and to give clear priority to the former. He took a rather eclectic approach to crisis theory, showing little enthusiasm for either the underconsumptionist or falling rate of profit elements in Marx's writings, but emphasizing the role of cyclical fluctuations in the reserve army of the unemployed, and therefore in real wages and the rate of exploitation. In this Dobb pointed towards the 'profit squeeze' or 'overaccumulation' perspective that would become important in Marxian crisis theory in the 1970s. He was sympathetic to Kalecki's treatment of capitalist macrodynamics, but was not greatly impressed by Keynes's *General Theory*. Dobb attributed the 'long boom' after 1945 to high levels of military expenditure; in this, and on questions of imperialism more generally, he was a rather orthodox Leninist.

His writings on development economics were a direct extension of his work on Soviet economic history. Against the neoclassical insistence that post-colonial countries should use techniques with very low capital-labour ratios appropriate to their status as low-wage economies with abundant labour reserves, Dobb argued that the crucial question was the size and rate of growth of the economic surplus. It might well be preferable for poor countries to use capital-intensive techniques with a large surplus product, even if this came at the cost of high unemployment in the early stages of development. In the long run, he maintained, growth would be faster, and unemployment lower, if the Soviet example were emulated.

Dobb was the first and perhaps the best of the Anglo-Marxist economists who explained, criticized and developed Marx's political economy in the four decades after 1930. Like Joan Robinson, Paul Sweezy and Ronald Meek, he wrote clearly and precisely, avoiding dogmatism, deliberate obscurity and pretentious Hegelian flourishes. He refined a version of Marxism that was perhaps less subtle, and certainly less philosophical, than that of his French, German and Italian contemporaries, but no less scholarly or politically committed. Paradoxically, he was also part of the Cambridge school of economics that began with MARSHALL and was buried, seven years after Dobb's death, with the demise of Joan Robinson and Piero Sraffa. In his 1987 entry in the *New Palgrave*, Amartya Sen described Dobb as 'a major bridge-builder between Marxist and non-Marxist economic traditions'. Above all, though, he was 'a great economist in the best of the broad tradition of classical political economy' (Sen 1987: 912).

BIBLIOGRAPHY
Capitalist Enterprise and Social Progress (1925).
Wages (Cambridge, 1928; subsequent edns 1938, 1946, 1956).
Russian Economic Development Since the Revolution (1928).
'An Introduction to Economics', in W. Rose (ed.), *An Outline of Modern Knowledge* (1931, pp. 593–623).
Political Economy and Capitalism: Some Essays in Economic Tradition (1937; repr. 1940).
Studies in the Development of Capitalism (1946; repr. 1963).
Soviet Economic Development Since 1917 (1948; repr. 1966).
On Economic Theory and Socialism: Collected Papers (1955).
An Essay on Economic Growth and Planning (1960).
Papers on Capitalism, Development and Planning (1967).
Welfare Economics and the Economics of Socialism (1969).
'The Sraffa System and Critique of the Neoclassical Theory of Distribution', *De Economist* (1970), vol. 118, pp. 347–62; repr. in E.K. Hunt and J.G. Schwartz (eds), *The Critique of Economic Theory* (1972, pp. 205–21).
Theories of Value and Distribution Since Adam Smith (1973).

'Random Biographical Notes', *Cambridge Journal of Economics* (1978), vol. 1, no. 2, pp. 115–20 (special memorial issue on Dobb).

Further Reading
Ashton, T.H. and Philpin, C.H.E. (eds), *The Brenner Debate: Agrarian Class Structure and Economic Development in Pre-Industrial Europe* (Cambridge, 1985).
Atley, T. and McFarlane, B., 'Maurice Dobb, Historical Materialism, and Economic Thought', in S.G. Medema and W.J. Samuels (eds), *Historians of Economics and Economic Thought: The Construction of Disciplinary Memory* (2001, pp. 63–92).
Feinstein, C.H. (ed.), *Socialism, Capitalism and Economic Growth: Essays Presented to Maurice Dobb* (Cambridge, 1967; includes a full bibliography of Dobb's writings to 1967).
Meek, R.L., 'Maurice Herbert Dobb (1900–1976)', *Proceedings of the British Academy* (1967), vol. 63, pp. 333–43.
Pollitt, B., 'The Collaboration of Maurice Dobb in Sraffa's Edition of Ricardo', *Cambridge Journal of Economics* (1988), vol. 12, no. 1, pp. 55–65.
Sen, A., 'Dobb, Maurice Herbert (1900–1976)', in J. Eatwell, M. Milgate and P. Newman (eds), *The New Palgrave*, vol. 1 (1987, pp. 910–12).
Sraffa, P., *Production of Commodities By Means Of Commodities* (Cambridge, 1960).

J.E. King
M.C. Howard

DODD, George (1808–81)

Dodd was born in 1808, possibly in London, and died in London on 21 January 1881. A professional writer, he built a reputation for high-quality work, dealing with a range of subjects. Initially he worked with the publisher Charles Knight, producing articles on industrial art in the *Penny Cyclopaedia* (1833–4) and the *English Cyclopaedia*, periodicals intended to educate the 'ordinary' public at affordable prices. Dodd also contributed to *London: The Land We Live In* and the *Penny Magazine* (1832–45), which had a sale of two hundred thousand by the end of its first year. On 29 June 1844, publication of the *Weekly Volumes* began. In it, Dodd contributed his accounts of *The Textile Manufactures of Great Britain*, dealing with chemicals, metals and manufactures. Dodd's great talent was his ability to present statistics in an appealing and understandable manner.

Dodd's *Days at the Factory* (1843) was a collection of forty-four articles written for the *Penny Magazine* between 1841 and 1844. It contained details of manufacturing processes including brewing and printing. Engravings that enhanced the text illustrated the articles. Dodd edited and, for the most part, wrote the *Cyclopaedia of the Industry of all Nations* (1851).

Using material supplied by A.C. Hobbs, Dodd produced the *Rudimentary Treatise on the Construction of Locks* in 1853. He raised the question of 'whether or not it is right to discuss so openly the security or insecurity of locks', arguing that since pick-locks already knew which locks were safe and which were not, it was only honest to give the information to the public: 'The unscrupulous have the command of much of this kind of knowledge without our aid; and there is moral and commercial justice in placing on their guard those who might possibly suffer therefrom.'

In 1856, Dodd published *The Food of London*, dealing with the variety, supply and distribution of food for the capital. In it, he describes public houses, saying that they 'have undergone great changes within the last few years. They have been transformed from dingy put-houses into splendid gin-palaces, from painted deal to polished mahogany, from small crooked panes of glass to magnificent crystal sheets, from plain useful fittings to costly luxurious adornments...'

At the end of the Crimean War in 1856, Dodd's *Pictorial History* was published. It contained maps, plans and wood engravings to illustrate the events that had received so much publicity. It also contained, for example, a list of the men who won the French *Légion d'Honneur*. In 1857, when Knight retired, Dodd began to write articles for Chambers's serial publications. Dodd's *Where Do We Get It, And How Is It Made?* (1862) described how 'everyday wants, comforts and luxuries' were supplied. He also complied the *Chambers' Handy Guide to London* (1862) and its companion *Kent and the Sussex Coasts* (1863).

Dodd contributed papers to the *Companion to the British Almanac* for over thirty years and his writing career lasted for almost fifty years. Most of his work was aimed at educating working people at a time when it was believed that 'knowledge was power' and when there was no state provision of education. His style was lucid and entertaining; the use of illustrative material proved to be popular.

BIBLIOGRAPHY
Days at the Factories (1843).
Curiosities of Industry (1852).
Rudimentary Treatise on the Construction of Locks (1853).
Pictorial History of the Russian War 1854–5–6 (1856).
A Chronicle of the Indian Revolt and of the Expeditions to Persia, China and Japan, 1856–7–8 (1859).
Where Do We Get It, And How Is It Made? (1862).
Railways, Steamers and Telegraphs (1867).
Dictionary of Manufactures, Mining, Machinery and the Industrial Arts (1871).

Marjorie Bloy

DONALDSON, John (*fl.* 1790–6)

Donaldson's identity is not known. We know from his own work only that he was born in Edinburgh, that his father had at some stage been briefly involved in linen manufacture, and that he himself had moved to London in his middle years where he supported himself by writing. In the 1790s he produced a number of pamphlets on a variety of subjects; he saw himself as a social reformer, but he was also interested in economics, chemistry, the theatre and manners. On economics, he wrote *Miscellaneous Proposals for Increasing Our National Wealth Twelve Millions a Year* (1790).

There were several persons by the name of John Donaldson active around the same time, including a prominent Perth merchant and corn dealer and an Edinburgh bookseller, both active in the 1770s; it is, however, difficult to link Donaldson to either of these. Another and somewhat more likely identification is with John Donaldson (1737–1801), the artist and author of the *Elements of Beauty* (1780). He too was born in Edinburgh, moving to London in the mid-1760s. He had a wide range of interests, including chemistry; he was described by contemporaries as being sarcastic and irascible, traits which could likewise be ascribed to the author of *Miscellaneous Proposals*. Some stylistic similarities are evident in their writing, although this is by no means conclusive. The author of *Elements of Beauty* describes his father as a glover, but this would not preclude the latter from also employing his capital in the linen industry at a time when there were many initiatives to encourage linen manufacture in Scotland. However, there is no firm evidence for this identification, and it must be regarded as tentative.

Miscellaneous Proposals is effectively an advertisement for Donaldson himself, who claims to have a 'patent' or system for economic improvement, including specifically finding employment for the poor, building up the fishing industry, stopping smuggling and putting an end to burglary and other crimes. He is vague about how exactly he will reach these goals, and deliberately does not give too much information on the grounds that he needs to protect his 'patent'. However, he says – repeatedly – if the government will employ him with suitable remuneration, he will put his plan into effect, to the benefit of the nation.

As far as can be glimpsed from the hints he drops, Donaldson seems to be arguing for a policy of public works to create full employment. Convicts and vagrants, for example, would be put to work improving roads and canals; others of the poor and unemployed would be employed in similar tasks. Because all the 'idle' people would be employed in these works they would have no time to commit crimes, and so crime would largely disappear. A more realistic proposal, for ensuring the navy was amply supplied with volunteer seamen without recourse to press-gangs, included a series of measures to increase pay and ensure better provision for the families of men serving at sea. Others of his proposals are much less workable, however, and a survey of his other writings reveals many similar ideas that appear to have little grounding in reality; though his letter to Pitt (1795) calling for hair powder to be banned for health reasons may not have been quite as mad as it must have seemed to contemporaries.

BIBLIOGRAPHY
Miscellaneous Proposals for Increasing Our National Wealth Twelve Millions a Year (1790).
Sketches for a Plan for an Effectual and General Reformation of Life and Manners (1794).
A Letter to the Rt. Hon. W. Pitt, on the Use of Hair-Powder (1795).
A Letter to the Rt. Hon. W. Pitt, Shewing how Crimes may be Prevented and the People made Happy (1796).

Katharine Norley

DOUBLEDAY, Thomas (1790–1870)

Doubleday was born in February 1790 in Newcastle upon Tyne. He died at Bulman's Village, Newcastle upon Tyne, on 18 December 1870. He was the son of George Doubleday, the head of Doubleday and Easterby, soap and vitriol manufacturers. Doubleday's uncle Robert was a distinguished classical scholar, theologian and philanthropist, who inspired Doubleday to a taste for literature. Doubleday became a partner in the company on his father's death, but took no active part in it. When the firm failed, Doubleday worked as registrar of births, marriages and deaths in the parish of St Andrew's in Newcastle, a post he held until he became secretary to the coal trade. In 1798 Doubleday published a small book of poems; in 1803 he published a tragedy. Both of them attracted attention for their quality. He also wrote three dramas: *The Statue Wife*, *Diocletian* and *Caius Marius*.

An early follower of COBBETT, Doubleday was active in the Reform Act agitation of the early 1830s. He was secretary of the Northern Political Union, which was led by Charles Attwood, and supported the reforming policies of Earl Grey and the Whigs through his speeches and writings. At the reform meeting held in Newcastle in 1832, Doubleday moved one of the resolutions. Subsequently, warrants were issued for the arrest of Doubleday and others on the charge of sedition. These were not served, as the government left office soon afterwards. In 1832 Doubleday published an *Essay on Mundane Moral Government* in which he advocated the theory of the existence of moral law.

Doubleday's integrity won him great respect. Having been disappointed by the terms of the Reform Act, which did not give the vote to working men, he and Charles Attwood presented an address to Earl Grey on behalf of the northern political union declaring the legislation to be unsatisfactory to the people. They went on to advocate some of the points later adopted by the chartists. Doubleday also opposed the 1834 Poor Law Amendment Act.

In 1842 Doubleday wrote *The True Law of Population Shown to be Connected with the Food of the People*. The outline of the piece first appeared in *Blackwood's Magazine* and attacked some Malthusian principles. Doubleday said that when a species was endangered through lack of food, the fertility increased and more offspring were produced. Conversely, when food was abundant, fertility fell. He thought that reduced fertility was attributable to overfeeding. The pamphlet caused considerable controversy. As an editor of *Blackwood's Magazine*, Doubleday wrote articles under a number of pseudonyms including 'Squire Shufflebotham of Gowk's Hall'. He also made numerous contributions to local newspapers and periodicals in the north-east.

Doubleday also wrote tracts on money; he criticized TOOKE's *Considerations* and published *A Political Life of Sir Robert Peel* (1856). He combined his literary taste with strong, outspoken political principles. He lived all his life in the north-east, which may have prevented his talent from being more widely recognized.

BIBLIOGRAPHY
True Law of Population (1842).
A Financial, Statistical and Monetary History of England from 1688 (1847).
A Political Life of Sir Robert Peel, an Analytical Biography (1856).
Matter for Materialists (1870).

Marjorie Bloy

DOUGLAS, Clifford Hugh (1879–1952)

Douglas was born in Stockport, Cheshire on 20 January 1879, and died at Dundee on 20 September 1952; he is buried in Aberfeldy on the shore of Loch Tay. Of humble origins, Douglas acquired qualifications in engineering, becoming a member of the Institute of Electrical Engineers in 1904. Subsequently, he worked as consulting engineer to a number of companies, including the Canadian General Electric Company, Lachine Rapids Hydraulic Construction, Buenos Aires and Pacific Railway, British Westinghouse Company in India and the Post Office Tube, London. During the course of his work as an engineer, he noted that the greatest impediment to implementation of schemes was not lack of skills, labour, materials or other resources, but shortage of money. He was frequently ordered to slow down work and lay off workers through lack of finance. During the First World War he joined the Royal Flying Corps, serving as assistant superintendent at Farnborough Aircraft Factory from 1916–18 and rising to the rank of major. While sorting out the accounts at Farnborough, he made the observations which formed the basis of his social credit economics.

At Farnborough, Douglas was responsible for improving the administration. By his own account, he concluded that the only way to ascertain how work was being allocated was to 'go very carefully into the costing which took place'. The existing costing system produced 'excellent information about what happened three years and two months before, but that was not of any use to me'. He needed 'news, not history'. Therefore he approached Sir Guy Calthorpe of the London and North Western Railway, who recommended the use of 'a tabulating machine' of the new type employed in his traffic statistics department. Douglas accordingly made use of those very early computers to explore financial flows at Farnborough, enabling him to analyse the dynamic characteristics of capitalist finance. It occurred to Douglas that by the end of the week, total wages and salaries were not equal to the cost value of the goods produced during that week. The two sums did not tally. For Douglas, the fact that it might be happening in every commercial business in the land, at the same point in time, was highly significant. He collected and collated information from over 100 large businesses in Britain, finding in each case that the total sums paid out as incomes (wages, salaries and dividends) were always less than total costs in the same period.

It followed that only a part of the final output coming onto the market at any point in time could be distributed through the incomes generated by current production. That fact formed the central thesis of Douglas's economics as later set out in the 'A+B theorem'. As industrial processes lengthened and became more complex, with increasing centralization of planning, the ratio of overheads to current incomes was constantly increasing, so that the distribution of the remainder depends increasingly on work in progress on future products. Whether valuable or not, the flow of industrial products must be continually increased (economic growth), financed by loan credit, export credits, sales below costs leading to bankruptcy and increasing centralisation of financial power, or by consumer borrowing. As early as 1918–19, in his first articles published in *The English Review*, Douglas predicted the modern dilemma of mass poverty through unemployment, growing inflation, debt and monopoly, with waste of human effort and of the earth's resources to maintain economic growth. Inevitably, economic warfare between nations would lead to military warfare as had already happened with the 1914–18 world war.

From his account, it emerges that Douglas's theories arose from his own original observations, rather than from familiarity with the work of established economists. However, his first book *Economic Democracy*, serialized in the guild socialist weekly *The New Age* in 1919, demonstrates a familiarity with the writings of J.A. HOBSON, Thorstein Veblen, Karl MARX and the full range of guild socialist thinkers of the time. His education in the political philosophy of guild socialism and socialist economics arose through his close collaboration, between 1918 and 1922, with Alfred Richard Orage, the multi-talented editor of the independent weekly *The New Age*. When he met Orage in the closing stages of the First World War, Douglas was a man of independent means, able to pursue his researches alongside running a yacht-building yard on Southampton Water.

The Douglas/*New Age* texts, the articles, books and pamphlets written between 1918 and 1922, were constructed in close collaboration with Orage, each book first appearing in serial form in *The New Age*. The substance of the publications of this period were set out as a compact *précis* in *Economic Democracy*, while subsequent publications provided amplification and elaboration of the main theme. The book lays out Douglas's basic tenets. Potentially, the wealth of the world is so great that competition over the existing supply is beside the point. In seeking to appropriate a greater share of the product for the worker, through securing control over administration, the Labour Party was tilting at windmills. Douglas's objective is to determine policy through gaining control over finance through the means of banks. Credit, the property of the community, should be administered by the community. Douglas was opposed to a state banking system, which would merely continue the process of centralization of unaccountable, unelected power. Therefore the community should use banks to pay a national dividend to all citizens. Observing the increasing centralization of power following the First World War and the formation of the League of Nations, Douglas predicted that financial amalgamations on the one hand and alliances of trade unions on the other heralded the crushing of individual authority and initiative in the work place and in the civic life of the community.

Douglas saw industry as representing a common cultural inheritance of human ingenuity, expressed through the application of technology. He attacked the market mechanism whereby finance controls technology in order to regulate the volume of output according to the dictates of profitability. Central to his view of an alternative economics was the importance of recognizing the right of all, regardless of employment status, gender or race, to share in the inheritance of human culture.

Douglas believed that the pace of technical progress, coupled to the creation of financial markets where ownership claims can be traded with anonymity, ease and liquidity, had replaced the personal nature of industrial competition by impersonal financial processes in which pecuniary gain through strategic purchase and sale is the key motivation. Under such a system, it becomes a competitive necessity to resort to 'credit finance' for leveraging business operations to speed up the financial turnover of capital.

Consequently 'capital' is redefined; it is no longer simply the aggregate market value of an enterprise's productive assets, for in modern industry the predominant part of 'capital' is the financial market's assessment of its future earnings potential. Such calculations based upon unverifiable expectations are inevitably inconsistent and uncertain. Douglas explored the relationship between production, income distribution and prices, concluding that financial institutions initiate production, direct it on grounds of financial profitability and effectively regulate the distribution of incomes.

Social credit analysis explored the relationship between real and financial credit. Real credit resides in the potential to create goods and services. It consists of natural resources, labour, machines and the common cultural inheritance of skills and technology developed over generations. For Douglas, real credit belongs to the community as a whole; he sees up to 95 per cent of the value created by the labour of any one individual being due to the 'increment of association'. While real credit focuses upon the supply of goods and services, financial credit involves the creation of money and other financial instruments.

Douglas then analysed the relationship between them. Money possesses value in so far as it relates to marketable goods and services. However, the function of money in a capitalist economy is 'to set in motion and direct real credit'. Before real credit in its various forms can be combined to generate the goods and services required by the community, producers require finance to purchase raw materials, labour and machines. Such finance is forthcoming only through the incentive of positive profit expectations.

Douglas argued that 'financial institutions determine credit-issue and price-making. Although they possess the capacity to determine production and distribution, the mechanisms whereby they allocate resources lie beyond democratic control'. As an alternative, Douglas envisaged a network of local industry-based banks co-ordinated under a national legislative framework. In principle, all workers, from management to shop-floor working within an institution, would share an interest in their producers' bank, along with consumers and the local community. His *Practical Scheme for the Establishment of Economic and Industrial Democracy: Draft Scheme with Commentary by A.R. Orage* was published as an Appendix to *Credit-Power and Democracy*, and reprinted in pamphlet form. In its focus upon locality, this approach differed radically from proposals for nationalisation of the banking system or from the continued growth of corporate finance.

From the publication of *Economic Democracy*, Douglas became an international figure. His theories were developed, debated and popularized through the social credit movement during the 1920s and 1930s, all his books going to multiple reprints and updated editions. Douglas's influence was such that he was invited to give evidence at the Canadian Banking Enquiry in 1923 and the Macmillan Committee in 1930. His work attracted the critical attention of ROBBINS, HAWTREY, Foster and Catchings as well as many other influential economists. The Douglas texts were an element in the development of KEYNES's theory of demand management, and were influential in the construction of MEADE's theories of international trade and income distribution. His work belonged to the broad body of contemporary opposition to emerging global corporatism represented in the writings of such figures as T.S. Eliot, G.K. Chesterton, Ezra Pound, Aldous Huxley, Wyndham Lewis and early opponents of factory farming methods, including H.J. Massingham.

The Monopoly of Credit (1931) extended further the theme of 'dividends for all', inspiring a vast literature on the alternatives to unemployment, over-production, degradation of the land, military warfare and poverty amidst plenty. In addition to his books Douglas produced hundreds of articles, pamphlets and speeches, all of which were extensively reprinted, circulating throughout Britain, Canada, the United States, Australia, New Zealand, South Africa, Scandinavia and elsewhere. In January 1934 Douglas drew an audience of 12,000 to Sydney Stadium, with a further 5,000 being turned away. In Alberta, a Social Credit Party swept to power on the strength of its widespread support amongst farming communities throughout Canada.

Although it was extremely difficult to detect flaws in his reasoning, Douglas was systematically attacked as an economic heretic and a crank. The main method of attack was misrepresentation. By summarizing Douglas's arguments inaccurately, and then refuting them *as* inaccurate, economic orthodoxy sought to stem the tide of his popularity. The final attack of this type focused upon Douglas's supposed but non-existent anti-semitism. By drawing his fire on the latter issue, his opponents succeeded in resigning his work to virtual obscurity.

BIBLIOGRAPHY
'The Delusion of Super-production', *English Review* (1918), pp. 428–32.
'The Pyramid of Power', *English Review* (1919), pp. 49–58, 100–7.
Economic Democracy (1920).
Credit-Power and Democracy (1920).
The Control and Distribution of Production (1922).
Social Credit (1924).
The Monopoly of Credit (1931).
The Alberta Experiment (1937).

Further Reading
Hutchinson, F., *What Everybody Really Wants to Know About Money* (Charlbury, 1998).
Hutchinson, F. and Burkitt, B., *The Political Economy of Guild Socialism and Social Credit* (1997).
———, 'The Contemporary Relevance of Clifford Hugh Douglas', *The Political Quarterly* (1999), vol. 70, no. 4, pp. 443–51.
Hutchinson, F., Mellor, M. and Olsen, W., *The Politics of Money: Towards Sustainability and Economic Democracy* (2002).
King, J.E., *Economic Exiles* (1988).

Frances Hutchinson
Brian Burkitt

DOUGLAS, Thomas (1771–1820)

Douglas was born at St Mary's Isle, Kirkcudbright, Scotland, the youngest son of Duncan Hamilton Douglas, 4th Earl of Selkirk, and Helen Hamilton Douglas. He died 8 April 1820 in Pau, France. He received his early education at Palgrave School in Sussex under the supervision of Anna Laetitia Barbauld, and attended the University of Edinburgh from 1785 to 1791, his mentor being Dugald STEWART and his closest friend Walter SCOTT. Although he did not graduate, he was an active member of the Speculative Society of Edinburgh. In the company of the vulcanologist Sir James Hall (his brother-in-law) and other members of his family, he spent the spring and summer of 1791 in Paris, observing the political scene and consorting with a number of the French intellectuals active in the French Revolution, including Lavoisier, Condorcet and Brissot de Warville. This experience reinforced both his bent towards political economy and his ambition to combine philosophical speculation with concrete experimental work, the hallmark of his career. After a few years touring the European continent, Douglas he returned to Scotland, becoming 5th Earl of Selkirk in 1799 (he also held the title Baron Daer and Shortcleuch). He was married on 24 November 1807 to Jean Wedderburn, in Inveresk, Scotland.

Soon after his inheritance of the title, Selkirk became involved in various schemes to recruit potential settlers for a colonization venture in North America. Early in 1803 he bought land in Prince Edward Island on the open market. He sent 800 Highlanders to Prince Edward Island aboard three ships in the spring of 1803, accompanying the party himself. He sent another party of 102 settlers to Upper Canada in 1804.

Upon his return to Britain from his North American tour, Selkirk began writing the manuscript that would become *Observations on the Present State of the Highlands of Scotland*, his major contribution to the debates over emigration and public policy for the Highlands, and his major work of political economy. In the book, Selkirk saw the real Highland question as one of alternate strategies of economic development. He recognized that small occupiers in the Highlands would inevitably be dispossessed by agricultural improvement, but insisted on their right to remove to North America, where they could continue their agrarian way of life. He exposed the regulatory legislation of 1803 to improve conditions on the trans-Atlantic passage as nothing but a cynical self-interested effort on the part of the Highland lairds to put a brake on the departure of their workforce. Selkirk offered two related propositions about Highland immigration in British America. The first was that Highlanders (and other ethnic groups) should be concentrated in 'national settlements' to preserve their traditional language, culture and manners. The second was that the Gaelic-speaking Highlanders in concentrated settlements would help prevent British America from falling to the Americans.

As a result of the positive reception of his book, Selkirk from 1807 to 1818 served as an elected Scottish member of the House of Lords and also served as Lord Lieutenant of Kirkcudbright (1807–15). Selkirk followed his early settlements with a later, more ambitious, experiment, placing Highlanders at the confluence of the Red and Assiniboine Rivers in what is now Manitoba. He died before he could report that this venture had been successful. In his time, Selkirk was one of the few British voices favourable to emigration to America. His vision was of employing waste land in the New World to allow emigrants to preserve their traditional languages and cultures, impossible in the changing industrial conditions of nineteenth-century Britain.

BIBLIOGRAPHY

Untitled pamphlet on poor relief in Scotland (c.1799).
Observations on The Present State of the Highlands of Scotland, with a View of The Causes and Probable Consequences of Emigration (1805; 2nd edn, 1806).
A Letter to the Peers of Scotland by The Earl of Selkirk (1807).
Substance of the Speech of the Earl of Selkirk, in the House of Lords, Monday, August 10, 1807, on the defence of the country (1807).
On the Necessity of a More Effectual System of National Defence, and the means of establishing the permanent security of the kingdom (1808).
A letter Addressed to John Cartwright, Esq. of the Committee at the Crown and

Anchor on the subject of parliamentary reform (1809).

Further Reading
Gray, J.M., *Lord Selkirk of Red River* (1963).
Martin, C.B., *Lord Selkirk's Work in Canada* (Oxford, 1916).

J.M. Bumsted

DOVE, Patrick Edward (1815–73)

Dove was born at Lasswade, near Edinburgh, on 31 July 1815, and died at Edinburgh on 28 April 1873 of complications following a stroke eleven years earlier. He was often known simply as Edward Dove, though he used both given names when publishing. The son of a naval officer, Dove had a somewhat turbulent education in England and France, and was expelled from one school for rebellion. In 1841, having come into money, he purchased an estate in Ayrshire near Ballantrae and devoted himself to the study of agriculture, philosophy, and marksmanship and gunmaking, interests which he seemed to share in equal measure. Though he suffered a financial loss in 1848 when some of his investments failed, his marriage the following year to Anne Forrester, daughter of an Edinburgh solicitor, seems to have restored his fortunes.

In 1850 Dove went to Darmstadt to study philosophy, and there wrote his first book, *The Theory of Human Progression* (1850). This book sets out the main elements of Dove's philosophical ideas, particularly his strong defence of individual liberty and freedom and the equation of progress with knowledge. Without knowledge and education, Dove maintained, society was doomed to stagnation, and lack of progress was the enemy of freedom. Freedom and knowledge, then, were closely linked. The book was admired on both sides of the Atlantic; Thomas CARLYLE and Charles Sumner both praised it, and Henry George later cited it as an influence.

Returning to England, Dove became a noted lecturer and writer. He edited the journals *Commonwealth* and *Imperial Journal of the Arts and Sciences*, was first general editor of the *Imperial Dictionary of Biography*, and contributed to the *Encyclopaedia Britannica*. His subject matter ranged from political economy through philosophy and theology to politics, history and field sports. A 'muscular Christian' of the same type as Charles KINGSLEY, Dove believed that people are most likely to remain free if given the means to defend their freedom. *The Logic of the Christian Faith* (1856) and *The Revolver* (1858) both make these points clearly. He invented a new design for a cannon with a rifled barrel, which compared unfavourably with the contemporary design of Joseph Whitworth and so was not adopted. He was also a founder member of the National Rifle Association and competed at the Association's first meeting at Wimbledon in 1860, winning prizes for marksmanship. In 1861, an active and vigorous man, he suffered a stroke which induced partial paralysis and also affected his mind. He remained an invalid until his death.

Dove's ideas on economics are to be found principally in three works, *The Theory of Human Progression* and the later *Elements of Political Science* (1854), which expands on the political and economic ideas of the former; and finally *An Account of Andrew Yarranton*, also published in 1854 and in later editions bound together with *Elements of Political Science*. Dove's principal idea on economics was that rents should belong to the nation, and this has often led to him being described as a Christian socialist. While other socialists such as Henry George admired his work, it is debatable whether Dove himself would have accepted this label; his politics and economics were strongly focused on individualism and freedom.

Given this, his argument on rents is a peculiar one, at odds with many of his other ideas. He begins by arguing, from a religious perspective, that the question as to whom the Earth belongs is a specious one; the Earth and all its lands belong to God. The real question should be, what is the proper distribution of the Earth among its inhabitants? The distribution of property, not property itself, is the key issue. The value of land, Dove goes on to say, lies in the productive power of those who work the land, not in the land itself. It follows that profits made by non-labouring landlords are in effect deductions from that value; all value is created by the labourers who actually do the labour, and any money taken from them reduces the value that they receive. In medieval times, grant of land to a noble by the king was in effect a grant of the future profits of the labourers on the land, not of the land itself.

Dove then goes on to show why this is wrong. Labourers, he says, create value from raw material, and he portrays labourers as value-creating agents, acting upon the object (land) in order to create a product (food). It is axiomatic, he says, that what is created remains the value of its creator; therefore the labourer has a theoretical right to retain the value he has created. Rent is the productive value of the soil, and all rent should therefore remain in the hands of the labourer. This is equally true of manufacturing as well as agriculture. The land employed for factories is made productive by the labourers in those factories; machinery is only 'brute matter made to exert skill and labour by human agency (1854: 289).

The problem as Dove sees it is how to ensure that all labourers reap a just reward for their labour. His solution is for all rents to go to the state, which would then in turn redistribute wealth. The benefits of such a system would be several: government could abolish customs and excise and have completely free trade; a single tax system would be employed; the manufacturing and agricultural classes would be united in a common interest; production would be increased to maximum efficiency; and every labourer would receive due reward for his work.

Dove's short work on YARRANTON is of only slight interest. He clearly admired Yarranton and approved of his ways of thinking even when he does not agree with him (Yarranton was a protectionist, Dove was a free trader, for example). He calls Yarranton the father of political economy, and says that he anticipated many modern economic problems. His fulsome praise of Yarranton somewhat obscures the fact that many other similar thinkers could be found in the same milieu.

BIBLIOGRAPHY
The Theory of Human Progression, and Natural Probability of a Reign of Justice (Edinburgh, 1850).
The Elements of Political Science (Edinburgh, 1854).
An Account of Andrew Yarranton, the Founder of English Political Economy (Edinburgh, 1854).
Romanism, Rationalism and Protestantism (Edinburgh, 1855).
The Logic of the Christian Faith (Edinburgh, 1856).
The Revolver, its Description, Manufacture and Use (Edinburgh, 1858).

Katharine Norley

DRAKE, James (1667–1707)

Drake was born in Cambridge in 1667, exact date unknown, and died in London on 2 March 1707. He was educated at Wivelingham and then Eton before attending Caius College, Cambridge, from which he received an MA in 1687. Drake then embarked on the study of medicine, moving to London and taking his MD degree in 1694. He was particularly interested in the study of anatomy, and his work resulted in his being elected a fellow of the Royal Society in 1701, and of the College of Physicians five years later. His *Anthropologia Nova, or a New System of Anatomy*, published in 1707, became a standard work in its field and went through several editions. Drake also had pretensions to being a dramatist, but seems to have produced only one play, *The Sham Lawyer*, in 1697. He was, however, among those who defended English theatre against Jeremy Collier, rebutting the latter's *Short View on the Immorality and Profaneness of the English Stage* in his *The Antient and Modern Stages Reviewed* (1700).

Much of Drake's energies during the last decade of his life were devoted to Tory politics. A vigorous pamphleteer, he repeatedly fell foul of the authorities. In 1702 an attack on the Whig government for allegedly plotting against Queen Anne resulted in his prosecution, trial and acquittal by the House of Lords. Two later pamphlets, perceived as giving offence to the religious authorities, were publicly burned in both London and Edinburgh. In 1706 Drake was again prosecuted for libelling members of the government and was acquitted, this time on a technicality. He would almost certainly have been prosecuted yet again, had he not contracted a fever in late February 1707 and died a few days later.

In 1702 Drake wrote and published a pamphlet entitled *An Essay concerning the Necessity of Equal Taxes*, one of his few publications during this period that did not result in open controversy. Drake argued that high taxation was having a depressing effect on trade and industry, and was also leading to higher levels of personal debt and a consequent rise in poverty and in usury. The source of the problem, he believed, was the excessive levels of interest being paid on government loans, anywhere from 8 to 14 per cent. It was because of this need to pay the interest on the national debt that taxes remained high, and Drake argued that this meant that the government was merely passing the burden of debt on to the people.

Drake proposed two remedies: first, to reduce the rate of interest payable on government loans to 6 per cent, broadly in harmony with the rate of interest charged to individuals and business concerns, and second, to tax the profits of usury and money-lending. The first would make government stocks less attractive and therefore people would be less likely to lend to government and more likely to invest in trade and industry, which would in turn create employment; it would also directly affect the amount of money the government had to pay its creditors, and Drake estimated that a saving of £100,000 per annum would result. The second would likewise reduce the attractiveness of government stocks, but would also raise revenue. Drake believed that the interest savings and tax revenue generated by his proposal would mean that government debt could be reduced, and so then could taxes. He failed to recognize that making government stocks less attractive would drive the price of the stock down and this in turn would force interests rate up. However, given Drake's political leanings, so directly in opposition to the government of the day, there was in any case little chance of this proposal being taken seriously.

BIBLIOGRAPHY

An Essay concerning the Necessity of Equal Taxes; and the Dangerous Consequences or the Encouragement given to Usury among us of recent years (1702).

Morgen Witzel

DRUMMOND, Henry (1786–1860)

Drummond was born in London on 5 December 1786, and died at Albury, Surrey on 20 February 1860. He was the son of the banker Henry Drummond and his wife Anne

Dundas, daughter of Henry Dundas, Viscount Melville. Following the early death of his father and his mother's remarriage, Drummond spent some years in the household of Lord Melville, where he met and became friendly with Pitt; it may have been this experience that encouraged him to go into politics. He was educated at Harrow, where Robert Peel and Lord Byron were among his contemporaries, and then Christ Church College, Oxford, where he spent two years but did not take a degree. In 1807, aged twenty-one, he toured Russia; returning home in 1808 he married his cousin, Lady Henrietta Hay.

Drummond entered parliament in 1810 as MP for Plympton. He was close to Perceval, and also to other young MPs such as Peel and John Wilson CROKER. He was made a partner in Drummond's bank in 1812, and in the same year introduced, with government support, a bill providing safeguards against the embezzlement of securities by bankers. However, in 1812 he gave up his seat on the grounds of ill health. He spent most of the next five years in idleness, travelling to Paris and to Naples but otherwise devoting himself to hunting and entertainment at his home in Surrey. In 1817, however, he had something of a religious conversion and, selling his house, resolved to go on pilgrimage to the Holy Land. Chance took him to Geneva, where he encountered Robert Haldane and took up the latter's campaign against Socinianism (a religious doctrine then current in Geneva, which denied the Trinity and the divinity of Christ). In 1819 for reasons that are unclear, Drummond abandoned Geneva and returned to England, buying the estate of Albury and Surrey. In 1825 he fell under the influence of the radical preacher Edward Irving, and in 1826 they co-founded the Holy Catholic Apostolic Church, in which Drummond held the position of 'apostle, evangelist and prophet'. Irving died in 1834, but Drummond continued to promote the organization, spending £16,000 to build a church on his estate. He was still nominally senior partner of the bank, but in 1843 the other partners succeeded in buying him out. In 1847 Drummond returned to parliament as MP for West Surrey and held the seat until his death. Notably, he defended the government during the Crimean War and spoke against the Divorce Bill of 1857.

Drummond's thinking was as erratic as his career, but in economics as in politics he remained a staunch Tory. His *Elementary Propositions Illustrative of the Principles of Currency* (1819) promoted the virtues of metallic currency and cautioned against the over-use of paper money. Although he made a point of supporting the budget no matter what government was in power, he was critical of high public spending and thought that it contributed to higher taxation and price inflation. In *On the Corn Laws* (1841), he defended the status quo and attacked the Anti-Corn Law League, urging his old friend Sir Robert Peel, then prime minister, to resist the League's demands. After the Corn Law debate he remained staunchly opposed to the radicals, whom he saw as anti-establishment and anti-monarchy (see for example *A Letter to Mr. Bright*, 1858).

Drummond's notable contribution to economics was his foundation of the chair of political economy at Oxford in 1825, later endowed by funds acquired when his partners bought him out of the bank. This was a major step forward in the teaching of economics at Oxford.

BIBLIOGRAPHY
Elementary Propositions Illustrative of the Principles of Currency (1819; subsequent edns to 1849).
Dialogues on Prophecy (1827).
Social Duties on Christian Principles (1830).
Causes Which Lead to a Bank Restriction Bill (1839).
On the Corn Laws (1841).
On Government by the Queen, and attempted Government from the People (1842).
Abstract Principles of Revealed Religion (1844).

History of British Noble Families (1846).
The Fate of Christendom (1854).
A Letter to Mr. Bright on his Plan for Turning the English Monarchy into a Democracy (1858).
A Letter to the Working Classes on Trades and Manufactures (1859).

Thomas Worth

DUNCAN, Jonathan (1799–1865)

Jonathan Duncan was born in 1799 in Bombay, where his father – also Jonathan Duncan – was governor. He died in Notting Hill, London on 20 October 1865. Initially Duncan was educated by a private tutor and then on 24 January 1817 he entered Trinity College, Cambridge. He was awarded a BA in 1821. Financially, Duncan was very secure and therefore he did not need to find employment. Instead, he became involved in literature and politics and published a number of pamphlets and books on a variety of topics. He was particularly interested in currency reform and economics.

In 1837–8 Duncan edited the first four volumes of the *Guernsey and Jersey Magazine*, in which he stated, that there was no history of commerce in the Channel Islands in any period earlier than the end of the sixteenth century. He also noted that every foreign breed of cattle was excluded from Guernsey. Another pronouncement was that the monks and canons of Mont St.-Michel in Normandy had been banished from the island and later established themselves in Guernsey at Mount St Michael of the Vale. Subsequently, the accuracy of these statements has been questioned.

From 1841, Duncan lived mainly in London, where he wrote and spoke on questions of land tenure and financial matters. He disapproved of the bullionist views of Sir Robert Peel, saying that the arguments were intended to deceive Peel's audience. Duncan also opposed the ideas of the banking reformers such as Samuel Jones Loyd OVERSTONE, which included limiting the amount of paper currency in circulation through a fiduciary issue and of allowing only the Bank of England to issue notes. Duncan said that the system was intended to 'sacrifice labour to usury'. However, Peel's government implemented the policies in the Bank Charter Act of 1844, which formed the basis of modern banking and fiscal policy.

Nevertheless, under the pseudonym 'Aladdin' in *Jerrold's Weekly News*, Duncan continued to attack the policies in a series of *Letters on Monetary Science*. In his pamphlet *The Bank Charter Act* (1858), Duncan considered the effects of the Act asking, 'ought the Bank of England or the People of England to receive the Profits of the National Circulation?'

Duncan's *Journal of Industry* appeared in 1850 but ran to only sixteen issues before collapsing. In 1854, immediately prior to the start of the Crimean War, he published a *History of Russia* for the National Illustrated Library. The book contained sixteen tinted plates and a number of maps of Russia; part of the content is a translation of the work of Rabbe.

BIBLIOGRAPHY

Remarks on the Legality and Expediency of Prosecutions for Religious Opinion (1825).
The History of Guernsey; with occasional notices of Jersey, Alderney, and Sark, and biographical sketches (1841).
The National Anti-Gold Law League. The Principles of the League explained, versus Sir R. Peel's Currency Measures, and the partial Remedy advocated by the Scottish Banks (1847).
The Principles of Money demonstrated, and Bullionist Fallacies refuted (1849).

The Bank Charter Act: ought the Bank of England or the People of England to receive the Profits of the National Circulation (1858).

Marjorie Bloy

DUNNING, John (1731–83)

Dunning was born at Ashburton, Devon on 18 October 1731, and died at Exmouth, Devon on 18 August 1783. The son of a local attorney, he was educated at Ashburton grammar school and then articled to his father's law practice. In 1752 he came to London and studied for the bar at the Middle Temple, becoming friendly with John Horne (later Horne TOOKE). He was called to the bar in 1756, and built up a successful practice. He was employed by the directors of the East India Company in 1762 to write a legal defence of the Company against the rival Dutch East India Company, which had complained that the British company was interfering with its trade in Bengal. This document helped to make Dunning's reputation as a lawyer. He also entered political life at about this time, and in 1768 he became a member of parliament for Calne, holding this seat until his death. From 1768–70 Dunning served as solicitor-general in several governments.

In 1774 Dunning was prominent in opposing attempts to tax the American colonies, foreseeing correctly that the attempt to do so would lead to a revolt. From 1776 onward he remained strongly opposed to the war in America, and was influential in persuading parliament to agree to negotiate peace terms in 1782. Despite his opposition to the war, he was friendly with George III, who settled a pension of £4,000 on him early in 1782. Dunning was made a privy councillor in the same year, and was also ennobled as Baron Ashburton and appointed chancellor of the Duchy of Lancaster. However, his health had begun to give way under the strain of so active a public life, and by the end of the year he had retired to Devon, dying early in the following year. He is buried in the parish church of Ashburton; his portrait, by Reynolds, is in the National Portrait Gallery in London.

Dunning was a lawyer rather than an economist, and his *A Defence of the United Company of Merchants of England Trading to the East-Indies and their Servants* (1762) is intended primarily as an answer to a legal complaint made by the Dutch East India Company. The work cites an array of correspondence with officials in India, and these give useful insights into the workings of the Company at a time when it was still establishing its government over recently conquered Bengal. Dunning defended not only the East India Company itself but also the trade that it created and its administration in Bengal, arguing that the economic benefits of the Company's rule were to the advantage of Britain and India alike. The work was sometimes cited by later generations of Company officers and civil servants as justification for expanding British rule in India.

Dunning was also the author of *A Letter to the Proprietors of the East-India Stock, on the subject of Lord Clive's Jaghire...* (1764), a strong criticism of Clive, the Company's military commander who accepted a large gift of money from local Indian princes following the Bengal war. Dunning argued that Clive's conduct was unacceptable, and opened up the Company as a whole to criticism from those who believed the conquest of Bengal was wrong and unjust.

BIBLIOGRAPHY

A Defence of the United Company of Merchants of England Trading to the East-Indies and their Servants... (1762).

A Letter to the Proprietors of the East-India Stock, on the subject of Lord Clive's Jaghire... (1764).

Further Reading
Roscoe, H., *Lives of Eminent British Lawyers* (1830).

Thomas Worth

DUNS SCOTUS, John (*c*.1265–1308)

John Duns Scotus (or 'the Scot') was born about 1265 at Maxton, Roxburghshire, and died in Cologne, Germany, supposedly on 8 November 1308. He probably received an early education at Haddington, then attended both Oxford and Paris universities where he studied theology. Little is known of Duns Scotus's life when young. His family may not have been noble, but they controlled large estates in the region of Maxton-on-the-Tweed. He probably entered the Franciscan order about 1280. The first date that can safely be assigned to Duns Scotus is 17 March 1291, when he was ordained priest at the church of St Andrews, Northampton.

The geographical course of Duns Scotus's studies in Oxford and Paris is a matter of considerable debate. It has been asserted that he must have spent most of his time at Oxford between 1283 and 1300 studying and teaching, while perhaps also lecturing in Cambridge. Yet other scholars claim that Duns Scotus's initial education at Paris took place during the 1290s. Documentary evidence places him at the Oxford convent in 1300, but the length of this stay in that abode remains uncertain. It seems clear that he was in Paris in 1302 and that he lectured there (possibly with some interruption) for several years, during which time he was granted bachelor's and then master's statuses, probably in 1304 and 1305 respectively.

In 1307, Duns Scotus was assigned to teach at Cologne for reasons that remain uncertain. Most probably, his presence there followed the standard Franciscan procedure of rotating its lecturing staff between its major houses of study. In any case, he died in Cologne the year following his arrival.

Duns Scotus's death, somewhat premature even by medieval standards, cut short a career that had just begun to blossom. Unlike other important scholastic figures, he had not yet commenced to produce a large body of commentary literature on the writings of Aristotle; only his exposition of the *Metaphysics* is deemed certainly genuine, although other commentaries (such as one on *De anima*) may derive from his hand. Thus, Duns Scotus's contributions to economic thought are slender. Without commentaries on Aristotle's *Nicomachean Ethics* or *Politics* to his name, his reputation in this field depends solely upon two distinct versions of his commentary on the *Sentences* of Peter Lombard, which seem to have been based on lecture notes of courses given at Oxford and Paris, respectively. It is the Oxford commentary, the so-called *Opus Oxoniense*, which was composed first but continually revised by Duns Scotus throughout his later travels, that forms the main basis for his standing among historians of economic ideas.

Peter Lombard's *Sentences* was the central and indispensable textbook of Christian theology during the later Middle Ages, and any aspiring schoolman was required to lecture on it. Virtually all of what is conceived to be Scotist economic thought is contained in the replies of the *Opus Oxoniense* to questions arising in Book IV, distinction 15, concerning the restitution of gains earned through improper or illicit means. As with most medieval theologians, economic issues for Scotus did not arise primarily in connection with the supremely positive goal of attaining eternal salvation. Rather, what we think of as 'economics' – questions of value, exchange, price, and so on – received attention in connection with sin and its punishment or avoidance. This viewpoint had only been reinforced by the transmission of Aristotle's moral and political theory, which treats acquisition of material goods as at best a necessary but base feature of human life.

In many ways, Duns Scotus's economic views were entirely in keeping with the ideas of his fellow schoolmen, such as the Dominican Thomas Aquinas. The salient principle at work is that just value in exchange requires a strict equivalence between those objects exchanged. The individual who engages in exchange relations that do not conform to this standard is not merely guilty of legally culpable activity (fraud), but of endangering the state of his eternal soul as well. Thus, the marketplace is fraught with moral and spiritual danger and must be regulated – by theological precepts as well as legal measures – for the sake of all the participants. Such scepticism about forms of unfettered, unregulated commerce among Christians predominated in scholastic literature (and beyond) throughout the Middle Ages.

Duns Scotus's object of opprobrium is not, as we may suspect, self-interest *per se*. He readily admits in the *Opus Oxoniense* that the parties to an exchange expect to achieve some advantage (*commodum*) that will fulfil their needs. What he condemns are transactions that benefit one of the parties out of proportion to the other, given the reasonable expectations of both sides. This insight stands at the core of the medieval theory of the so-called 'just price'. The just price represents a point of equilibrium in which those engaged in the exchange all have their expectations (understood explicitly in terms of the use values of the goods traded) realized. Such 'expectations' are not, however, subjective or perspectival. Instead, they are grounded in the use to which the items exchanged may be put to meet the needs of the persons involved in the trade. It follows for Duns Scotus and other scholastic thinkers that when such commerce excessively benefits one or another party, restitution is demanded (for reasons of spiritual safety if not temporal justice), quite regardless of the subjective satisfaction of the participants.

The dangers of economic transactions are multiplied for Duns Scotus when merchants and money are introduced into the social order. Duns Scotus acknowledges that the activity of the professional trader is not inherently vicious or demeaning. Commerce can be of great service to the public welfare, as when goods that are scarce in one location are brought by a merchant to that place from a region where they are more widely available. Thus, a profit from trade – beyond what is necessary to support the merchant and his family – may be justified, but strictly on the grounds of his industriousness and the risks he incurs. Yet market-oriented enterprises remain fraught, since the field for dishonest and unscrupulous practices is wider here than in other forms of labour. The standard Duns Scotus invokes for distinguishing between good and evil merchants is their usefulness in meeting the needs of other people, rather than their ability to enrich themselves.

Scholars have pointed out that Duns Scotus's model of commerce appears to be non-monetary, that is, he concentrates on the direct exchange of use-value for use-value, which assumes essentially a barter economy. Hence, money introduces further complications and an additional obstacle to moral and spiritual security. Like the preponderance of his fellow scholastic authors, Duns Scotus embraces the Aristotelian metallist theory, which holds that because money is made from a precious metal (gold, silver, and so on) it has an intrinsic value derived from its natural properties. Hence, the payment of coins in exchange for a commodity remains within the paradigm of the barter relation: it is the usefulness of the metal contained in the coins that defines its value in comparison with other goods.

The principle that the value of money is inherent in its metal content is central to the condemnation by Duns Scotus and other scholastics of the lending of money in return for the payment of interest, that is, usury (*mutuum*). Since metallic money is a 'sterile' thing and cannot reproduce or improve itself, there can never be justification for returning more money to a person from whom one has borrowed it than the original amount obtained. To enter into a contract that requires usurious terms of repayment is sinful. Any Christian hoping for salvation who demands or receives more than the principal endangers his soul unless he makes restitution. Classic scholastic economic thought permits no categories of exception to the rule that money cannot be fruitful and therefore its exchange must be strictly equal.

Duns Scotus reinforces his rejection of usury by examining various attempts to circumnavigate the letter of the theological injunction. For example, some asserted that money-lending contracts could licitly include a clause that required the payment of a penalty if the lent funds were not returned within a specified period of time. While not stipulating an interest rate necessary to the loan, Duns Scotus emphatically rejected these arrangements on the grounds that the money was no more valuable after the deadline than before it: its metallic worth was inherent to it. Thus, such penalties constitute a form of 'hidden' usury, since the lender is merely 'selling time,' a good that belongs to God alone. While Duns Scotus admits that the failure to return a loan on time might lead to a loss on the part of a lender who requires the money for a different purpose, he does not regard this as something that ought to be fixed in the contract. Rather, the wronged creditor must seek relief *ex post facto* for his damages in a court of law.

In the themes thus far surveyed, Duns Scotus's *Sentence* commentaries appear to be largely consonant with the core doctrines of scholastic economic theory. His most noteworthy deviation from convention arises from his treatment of the origins and basis of private property. Thomas Aquinas and succeeding schoolmen had argued that, while private property did not exist in nature before the Fall, it was nevertheless consistent with natural and divine law inasmuch as it emerged in post-lapsarian times as a discovery of human reason in order to eliminate conflicts between human beings and to realize earthly justice. This view was roundly rejected by Duns Scotus.

On the contrary, Duns Scotus maintained that private property is wholly artificial and without any warrant in the laws of God and nature. Rather, property rights exist only because of the legal authority and enforcement of the civil power, whose job it is to impose restitution of improperly acquired gains by means of its courts. As the guarantor of all property, the government of a territory, understood as the living embodiment of the law of the land, is seen by Duns Scotus as the final lord and arbiter of all uses of property by those subject to it. While the use of goods and resources may transfer temporarily to the hands of private persons, such possession must always remain congruous with the common good of society. Those who employ private property in a fashion hostile to the public welfare – either overtly, by harming their fellows, or implicitly, by neglecting their goods – may open themselves up to legitimate confiscation and reallocation. Against such government action, one has no recourse on earth.

Duns Scotus's advocacy of a legalistic and purely artificial conception of private ownership may be explained in several ways. As a leading Franciscan theologian, he doubtless embraced the teaching of his order at the time that material objects could be handled and consumed by friars without entering into their private or personal ownership. Rather, the goods used by Franciscans belonged to some other person or collectivity – the donor, the pope, or the order as a corporate unit, for instance. To insist that all licit private property was authorized by natural law, as Aquinas had done, would have constituted a direct challenge to this deeply held Franciscan principle.

At the same time, Duns Scotus could not have failed to be aware of the system of landholding that had evolved in England following the Norman Conquest. Unlike on the continent, all lords – from the mightiest baron to the lowliest knight – swore allegiance to the king directly as a condition for possession of their estates. Thus, the king was deemed to be the original owner of the whole realm, by whose grant alone any other possessors claimed valid title. Such 'original jurisdiction', as it has been termed, required that the king's courts and justices enjoy a monopoly of legitimate judgement concerning disputes between royal tenants. The king's superior law, far more than customary possession or *de facto* occupation, determined the arrangement of property rights.

The doctrine of the king's lawful supremacy in the determination of property ownership and control was a familiar one in thirteenth-century English political and legal writings. Likewise, later authors, such as William of Ockham (in his tract on the royal power to tax churches in England), Archbishop Richard Fitzralph (in *De Pauperie Salvatoris*), and John Wyclif, all proposed a very similar rejection of the naturalness of private goods in favour of the central role of royal law and government. Indeed, it may be possible to trace this theme within British political thought all the way to Sir Robert Filmer in the mid-seventeenth century, whose doctrines were the primary object of attack by John LOCKE in the *Two Treatises of Government*. Duns Scotus's views on the artificiality of property, then, place him in a venerable tradition of legal and social thought within the British Isles.

BIBLIOGRAPHY

Duns Scotus' Political and Economic Philosophy: Ordinatio Book 4, distinctio 15, quaestio 2, ed. A.B. Wolter (Santa Barbara, California, 1989).
Opera omnia (Paris, 1891–5).

Further Reading
Langholm, O., *Economics in the Medieval Schools* (Leiden, 1992).
Wood, D., *Medieval Economic Thought* (Oxford, 2002).

Cary Nederman

DURBIN

DURBIN, Evan Frank Mottram (1906–48)

Durbin was born in Bideford, Devon on 1 March 1906, and was drowned in a bathing accident in Cornwall on 3 September 1948. The son of a Baptist minister, he was educated at Taunton School before obtaining a scholarship to New College, Oxford, in 1924. There, he attended the influential 'Cole group' and became friends with Hugh GAITSKELL. He took his first degree in zoology, but then took a second degree, obtaining a first-class honours degree in PPE (politics, philosophy and economics), and won a Ricardo Fellowship at University College, London, before his appointment as an economics lecturer at the London School of Economics in 1930.

An unsuccessful Labour candidate for East Grinstead, Surrey in 1931 and for Gillingham, Kent, in 1935, Durbin entered the civil service as a wartime adviser, becoming a personal assistant to Clement Attlee, the Labour leader, in 1942. After his election as Labour MP for Edmonton in 1945, Hugh DALTON, Chancellor of the Exchequer, appointed him his Parliamentary Private Secretary. He became a junior Minister of Works in 1947, a year before his tragic accident. He had married Alice Marjorie Green in 1932, having a son and two daughters (one of whom, Elizabeth, is the main chronicler of his economic writings).

The attempt to understand, and to remedy, the economic crisis of the 1930s through the Labour Party led Durbin to associate with a number of young academic economists in the New Fabian Research Bureau, such as Colin CLARK and James MEADE. He was later accepted into the XYZ group, founded by Vaughan Berry in 1932 to overcome the Labour Party's ignorance of the City. This group included Nicholas Davenport, Hugh Gaitskell and Douglas JAY, and served as a nursery for budding Labour politicians as a result of the mentorship of Hugh Dalton. Meeting at private homes (such as

Davenport's stately mansion at Hinton Manor, near Oxford), they elaborated a credible economic policy with regard to price, money supply, investment policy and economic planning which provided the theoretical foundations for Labour's Interim Programme of 1937.

Durbin admitted that his work was eclectic rather than original, but his purpose was to develop a political project through his technical writings on the trade cycle and credit. This project was to demonstrate the total inadequacy of socialist dogmas popular with the quasi-Marxist Left in the Labour movement during the 1930s, a period of severe unemployment and poverty in the Labour heartlands of Scotland, South Wales and the North of England. He worked closely with Gaitskell to argue in technical terms that capitalism was capable of sustaining full employment and maximum output if guided by a directive planning mechanism. The alternative theories of underconsumptionism and monetary solutions to crisis then popular with sections of the Labour Party were painstakingly analysed in an attempt to show that capitalism was a dynamic system of economic growth despite its attendant miseries.

Durbin's *Purchasing Power and Trade Depressions* (1933), with which Gaitskell collaborated, was a criticism of the underconsumptionist views held by the Labour left (including G.D.H. COLE, who always argued that J.A. HOBSON rather than KEYNES was the more penetrating theorist of modern capitalism). Durbin argued that the excess of saving caused by low consumption (which the Hobson school believed lay behind the economic crisis), had always been characteristic of an expanding economy, and that the restriction of consumption was actually a precondition for the accumulation of capital for investment in new industry. While the savings that resulted from underconsumption could certainly hold back industrial expansion if held in the form of a hoard, they could also promote such expansion if they could be turned into investment. Consumption would be expanded, not held down, in the wake of increased investment because of the reduction in costs across the economy, and because of the increased physical productivity which would result from new economic activity. It was not the maldistribution of wealth, but the barriers to investment, which had led to the problems of the trade cycle. The answer to such problems lay not in any radical attack on the rich or the ruling class, but in reducing unemployment and poverty through the resumption of economic expansion.

His attacks on the radicalism of the Left did not lead Durbin to accept the unplanned market, however. Influenced by HAYEK's cyclical theory of sectoral imbalance, he argued that an excessive supply of money in the consumer sector had led to the crisis in the economy. While Hayek pointed to the scarcity of capital in the producers sector, he insisted that the relation between capital investment and the demand for consumption goods was determined by excess capacity and unemployment in the producers sector. This hoarding of capital was a direct consequence of a market left to the unplanned market, whose failure to convert savings into investment had caused sectoral imbalance and thereby an irrational contraction of the economy.

Durbin remained wary of Keynes's ideas, always holding that the trade cycle was the real problem in a capitalist economy, which only socialist planning could eliminate. He argued in *The Problem of Credit Policy* (1935) that an understanding of the trade cycle could explain the problems of the expansion and contraction of investment. He developed an analysis of the role of the money markets that foreshadowed Keynes's use of uncertainty in the *General Theory*, assessing the impact of rigidities on undermining confidence and the resulting preference for liquid resources to investment. He was particularly sceptical of the inflationary consequences of a policy of credit expansion (as advocated by Labour Keynesians such as

Oswald Mosley in 1930), believing that price stabilization by the state was not possible in a market economy, even in its transition to a planned economy. There was no certainty in such a situation that savings would not be hoarded rather than invested. In a socialist economy, however, both the direction and the size of a flow of credit could be controlled by the state.

Durbin's view of planning rested on the need for a central authority, directly responsible to the cabinet, to steer the course of economic development as a supplement to the individual decision-making of the market. He accepted that capitalism was theoretically an efficient system in regulating the relationship between supply and needs, and in ensuring economic growth through investment in new technical inventions. However, in practice, competition, inherited property and a private banking system ensured social inequality and class privileges that were unethical. Nevertheless, he was concerned that a central planning authority should not become insensitive to changes to fluctuations in the price of goods in the free market, responsive as such changes were to shifts in individual demand.

Unlike the Marxists and radicals of the Socialist League, Durbin welcomed a mixed economy as preserving the freedom of the market to choose jobs and goods, along with the incentive to innovate so essential to economic growth; at the same time, he looked to the state to sustain such growth through a general management of the economy and to ensure the social justice which would have been threatened by an unrestrained market. To overcome the Depression of the 1930s, therefore, he called for a mildly expansionary monetary policy through the use of low interest rates, a discriminatory tax policyboth to encourage private capital investment and keep inflation in check, and an agreement with the trade union movement to maintain stable incomes. By 1935, he had accepted the use of budgetary deficits as an important instrument in the control of inflation.

While Durbin is now mainly known for *The Politics of Democratic Socialism* (1940), a call for political moderation and opposition to the radicalism of the Labour left which became a crucial contribution to the later revisionist movement in the Labour Party, he promised a supplementary book on 'The Economics of Democratic Socialism', concerned with 'the economic organisation of a democratic and socialist economy'. It never saw the light of day except as unpublished notes, later discovered in Gaitskell's papers. Here Durbin sought to confront the problem of incentive in a planned economy, and extended his analysis of economic efficiency to his favoured realms of political theory and psychology by arguing that the question of motivation was essentially a psychological problem rather than one bound up in economic efficiency. It could be resolved, he believed, by the existing nature of political institutions, though he acknowledged the absence of any general theories of individual or group behaviour in the economy hampered his work in this field.

Durbin's commitment to economic planning was closely tied to his commitment to a particular blend of socialism. It was ethical (he had initially planned to follow his father in the ministry) and committed to a sense of fraternalism and community which was expressed through a deeply-felt nationalism. This was common to the group (witness the later hostility to the Common Market of Gaitskell and Jay), and Durbin's embrace of a sturdy sense of a robust Anglo-Saxon character led him to express a certain contempt for the Gallic character during the war. Only Sweden, with its mixed economy and welfare state, exerted a foreign influence on his political economy.

BIBLIOGRAPHY
Purchasing Power and Trade Depressions (1933).
The Problem of Credit Policy (1935).

'The Social Significance of the Theory of Value', *Economic Journal* (1935), vol. 45, December, pp. 700–10.
Personal Aggressiveness and War (1938).
How to Pay for the War (1939).
The Politics of Democratic Socialism (1940).
What Have We to Defend (1942).
'The Economic Problems Facing the Labour Government', in D. Munro (ed.), *Socialism: The British Way* (1948).
Problems of Economic Planning (1949).

Further Reading
Brivati, B., *Hugh Gaitskell* (1997).
Durbin, E., *New Jerusalems: The Labour Party and the Economics of Democratic Socialism* (1985).
Foote, G. *The Labour Party's Political Thought: A History*, 3rd edn (1997).
Morgan, K.O., *Labour People Leaders and Lieutenants: Hardie to Kinnock* (Oxford, 1987).

Geoffrey Foote

E

EDEN, Frederick Morton (1766–1809)

Eden was born 18 June 1766 Ashted, Surrey, and died at the offices of the Globe Insurance Company in London on 14 November 1809. His father, Sir Robert Eden, was governor of Maryland; his mother Caroline was the sister of Lord Baltimore. Eden matriculated at Christ Church College, Oxford in 1783, and graduated BA in 1787 and MA in 1789. Thereafter he went into business, founding the Globe Insurance Company and serving as its chairman until his death; he was also involved in a number of other commercial concerns. He inherited his father's baronetcy in 1784. In 1789 he married the daughter of a business colleague, and the marriage produced seven children; his eldest son, Sir Frederick Eden, was killed while serving in America during the War of 1812.

Eden's best known work is *The State of the Poor* (1797). While he is justly remembered for his contribution to the study of poverty – his data have even been used to estimate the probability of food being a Giffen good – his interests were more extensive and are now hard to locate. In his *Eight Letters on the Peace* (1802), Eden indicates significant liberal leanings, moderated by a recognition of the exigencies of war. He is fully aware that a commercial nation needs rich customers, while noting that commerce without arms is generally innocuous. Thus he wishes for a full economic recovery of France and the giving of commercial concessions to the French in India, observing that their trading posts there, so long as they were surrounded by the English, were of little consequence. Overall, Eden, with his qualified support for free trade and emphasis on providing employment at home, may be called a 'liberal mercantilist'.

Eden was moved to his inquiry by the state of the poor in 1794 and 1795. He began by sending questionnaires to clergymen in over 180 parishes. These he then supplemented with reports provided by 'a remarkably faithful and intelligent person', who spent more than a year gathering data for Eden. The questionnaire itself was closely modelled on that used by Sir John SINCLAIR in his *Statistical Account of Scotland*. Questions on religion were inserted by Eden because of HOWLETT's query as to whether the recent increase in numbers of the poor might be due to the rise of Methodism. Eden himself was fully aware that the primary causes of poverty were macroeconomic in nature, but he felt that this in no way diminished the responsibility of the state to alleviate the sufferings of the poor. While being a thorough individualist in all practical matters, there is a clear interventionist trait which runs through his writings: 'In every well-governed country, the doing no good is regarded the same as doing harm', a maxim which he applies to the owners of waste lands. Later in the work, Eden makes a longer plea for the regulation of educational syllabi on similar grounds.

Eden points out how the rich always have a cushion against hard times and are protected against the harshness of capitalist uncertainty, while the poor are always vulnerable and liable to fall into a pit from which they cannot emerge. The data he collected showed that about 75 per cent of the family budget was spent on food, and most of this was on bread. Hence Eden's data are a good testing ground for the existence of a Giffen good. The data are carefully marshalled, and Eden's occasional notes add much to the dry figures. Volume 1 is a review of all the policies for the relief of the poor. It is remarkable not only for the care with which Eden read his sources, and his care in citing them, but also for the breadth of his reading. Not only are all the familiar names, such as HOWLETT, Woodard, ACLAND and Burns, to be found, but also some obscure ones, such as Thomas Haweis.

In view of the delicacy with which Eden viewed the working of society, it is difficult to single out individual proposals for relief: 'No moral system can be formed at once on a regular plan, but must be modified according to circumstances: imperceptible additions, adopted with reference to what is retained, gradually swell into a complicated machine; and the whole composition produces effects, to which the subordinate parts have all contributed; but in what proportion, each has assisted, it often becomes impracticable to determine.' The poor laws were a good example of this complication. Eden wished to preserve the structure of the family, the independence of the worker and the continuation of friendly societies. He was very supportive of the friendly societies, and noted carefully how the members of these were from the ordinary poor, and yet the members of such societies had never been known to become a charge upon their parish.

One way of observing the care with which Eden read, as well as the independence of his mind, is by looking at three places where his views differed from those of Adam SMITH, an author whom he frequently quoted with approbation. To Smith's conjecture that vanity led the great feudal lords to give up their feudal powers in return for trinkets, Eden soberly responds that 'the inducements of a great proprietor to lessen the number of his retainers, and to let his estates, may, I think, be accounted for, upon more rational and more obvious motives than those of sordid vanity'. When Smith contends that manufacturing workers do not make good soldiers, Eden calls this a highly coloured characterization, and reports of the success of General Eliot with the tailors. As for Smith's claim that the corporation laws led to all good work being done in the suburbs, Eden flatly proclaimed his doubt whether there was 'a single corporation in England' to which Smith's claim applied.

Eden was much involved in practical issues such as the friendly societies and revitalizing the port of London. He did much valuable work in economics, but his careful reading, his attention to fact and his broad sympathies promised a great deal more. His early death must be counted a great loss for the development of classical economics.

BIBLIOGRAPHY

The State of the Poor; or an History of the Labouring Classes in England from the Conquest to the Present Period, 3 vols (1797).

Porto-bello, or, A Plan for the Improvement of the Port and City of London (1798).

An Estimate of the Number of Inhabitants in Great Britain and Ireland (1800).

Observations on Friendly Societies (1801).

Eight Letters on the Peace (1802).

Address on the Maritime Rights of Great Britain (1807).

Further Reading

Pyatt, F.G. and Ward. M., *Identifying the Poor: Papers on Measuring Poverty to Celebrate the Bicentenary of the Publication in 1797 of the State of the Poor, by Sir Frederick Morton Eden* (1998).

Salim Rashid

EDEN, William (1744–1814)

Eden was born at Windlestone Hall, Durham on 3 April 1744, and died at Beckenham, Kent on 28 May 1814. He was the third son of Sir Robert Eden and Mary Davison of Beamish, Durham. He was educated at Eton and Christ Church Oxford, receiving his BA in 1765 and MA in 1768. He read law in London, entering the Middle Temple in 1769. Eden was MP for Woodstock from 1774–84; on losing that seat, he was elected for Heytesbury. In 1776 he married Eleanor Elliot, sister of Sir Gilbert Elliot; they had eight daughters and two sons. The family lived at Eden Farm, Beckenham. Eden was elevated to the Irish peerage as Baron Auckland on 18 September 1789, becoming a British peer in 1793.

Hard-working and able, Eden built up a reputation as a formidable lawyer. In 1772 he published *Principles of Penal Law* in which he advocated using convict labour to carry out unpleasant or laborious public works instead of using transportation. Partly because of this book, Eden was appointed as an Under-Secretary of State in Lord North's ministry. He gave up his legal career for political life, specializing in economic and commercial matters. In 1776 he accepted a post at the Board of Trade and Plantations.

Eden was in charge of espionage in the American colonies after 1776. He established a huge spy network in Europe to report on Americans who sought aid for the fight against Britain. After France's intervention in the war in 1778, Eden went to America in an attempt to negotiate a peace settlement, returning without success in 1779. He became chief secretary of Ireland in 1780, and was elected as MP for Dungannon. He consulted Adam SMITH about free trade with Ireland; his major successes were the introduction of freer trade and the establishment of the National Bank of Ireland. In 1783 Eden and Smith discussed proposals for the regulation of trade with America following the end of the War of Independence.

Eden moved in and out of office with the various ministries between 1782 and 1785. He joined the Committee on Trade and Plantations under Pitt, and was sent to Paris to negotiate a reciprocity treaty that would bring about freer trade between Britain and France. With Pitt's approval, William Wilberforce attempted to include provisions against the slave trade, but nothing came of the plan. The Vergennes/Eden Treaty was signed in 1786. The terms were so favourable to Britain that even the parliamentary opposition under Charles James Fox was silenced.

After his success in 1785–6, Eden became a diplomat rather than a politician. He went as ambassador to Madrid in August 1787; from there he travelled to America on a commercial assignment, and in 1790 he visited Holland to negotiate for access to a Dutch naval squadron during the Nootka Sound incident. Later that year he conducted negotiations with Leopold II of Austria-Hungary and Frederick William II of Prussia over the settlement with Holland. He remained in Holland during the early years of the French wars, returning to England in 1793.

In 1796 Eden became chancellor of Marischal College in Aberdeen, rejoining Pitt's ministry in 1798 as Postmaster General and continuing in that post throughout Addington's ministry. He resigned in 1804, and died ten years later.

BIBLIOGRAPHY
Principles of Penal Law (1772).

Marjorie Bloy

EDGEWORTH, Francis Ysidro (1845–1926)

Edgeworth (who was actually christened Ysidro Francis) was born at Edgeworthstown, Co. Longford in Ireland on 8 February 1845 into an old established family of the Protestant Ascendancy. He died at Oxford on 13 February 1926. His grandfather, Richard Lovell Edgeworth (1744–1817) had been an inventor and eccentric in the grand tradition, a member of the Lichfield Circle around Erasmus Darwin, and an associate of David RICARDO, Dugald STEWART and Jeremy BENTHAM, while his aunt, Maria Edgeworth, was the celebrated novelist and educationalist. Edgeworth was educated at Trinity College Dublin, which he left without a degree, and then at Balliol College, Oxford, where he achieved a first class degree in *literae humaniores* in 1869. Although called to the bar in 1877, he never practised law, but instead pursued interests in mathematics, logic and political economy. The fact that he was largely self-taught in these subjects makes his later contributions to mathematical economics and to statistics all the more remarkable.

After almost a decade of subsisting on a variety of teaching jobs of low status and poorer pay, Edgeworth finally achieved academic recognition with his appointment as Tooke Professor of Economic Science and Statistics at King's College, London, in 1891. The following year he succeeded to the Drummond Chair of Political Economy at Oxford. He was elected a fellow of All Souls, and achieved many academic honours including becoming one of the original fellows of the British Academy. He was also the first editor of the *Economic Journal*, a role in which he continued, latterly as joint editor with John Maynard KEYNES, until his death. He never married, although at one time he tried, improbably, to court Beatrice Potter (subsequently WEBB).

Edgeworth made several important contributions to technical economic analysis, including his treatments of international trade theory, taxation and duopoly. The importance and originality of these contributions were only fully recognized after his death. However, Edgeworth's greatest significance in the history of economic thought was in developing a theory of bargaining, distribution and exchange which provided a bridge between utilitarian moral philosophy and the concepts of modern welfare economics. Indeed, his interest in questions of optimal distribution and the indeterminacy of bargaining situations was motivated by two overriding issues: how to bring mathematical precision into utilitarian reasoning and a related attempt to solve the problem that he claimed had defeated Helvetius, Bentham and other utilitarian thinkers, namely an explanation of the mechanism by which 'the force of self-love can be applied to support the structure of utilitarian politics'.

Edgeworth's first book was a slim volume of ninety-two pages entitled *New and Old Methods of Ethics: or Physical Ethics and Methods of Ethics* (1877). The book was directly stimulated by Henry SIDGWICK's *Methods of Ethics* and by the review of that book by Alfred Barratt. Edgeworth's originality was the application of mathematical techniques to determine the optimal utilitarian distribution. He argued that despite the inevitable 'roughness' (to use Sidgwick's word) of practical utilitarian reasoning there was no justification for not seeking to make our reasoning as precise as possible and this required that 'we keep before our minds the strict type of calculation that we should have to make, if all the relevant considerations could be estimated with mathematical precision'. In *New and Old Methods of Ethics* Edgeworth discussed, in mathematical terms, the possible meanings of the 'greatest happiness of the greatest number' and then moved to the core problem of his 'exact utilitarianism': 'Given a certain quantity of stimulus to be distributed among a given set of sentients...to find the law of distribution productive of the greatest quantity of pleasure.'

Edgeworth first analysed the problem by assuming that 'all the elements are equal as touching sensibility and capacity for pleasure' and that the total 'quantity of stimulus' is fixed. After formalizing the problem and applying Lagrangian mutliplier techniques,

Edgeworth came to conclusion that on these assumptions 'the law of distribution is equality'. However, once these assumptions are relaxed and both sensibility and the capacity for pleasure vary among individuals, unequal distributions would be justified: 'Unto him that hath greater capacity for pleasure shall be added more of the means of pleasure.' Further complexities were then examined using the same basic approach. Edgeworth wished to emphasize that utilitarianism implied equality of the means of pleasure only under the special set of assumptions described above, and in the general case the prescribed solution would be some form of inequality.

His analysis of the utilitarian optimal distribution was extended in *Mathematical Psychics* (1881). In this book, Edgeworth returned to many of the themes of the second part of *New and Old Methods of Ethics*. As JEVONS remarked in his review of the book, 'as the invisible energy of electricity is grasped by the marvellous methods of Lagrange, so may the invisible energy of pleasure admit of similar handling. The soul is likened to a steam car moving upon a plane in a direction tending towards the position of minimum potential electro-magnetic energy, but with inconceivably diversified degrees of freedom.' Edgeworth conceived of man, Jevons wrote, as a '*pleasure-machine*' and on this basis he 'undertakes to determine the distribution of means and of labour which shall be conducive to the highest aggregate of well-being'.

As well as extending Edgeworth's attempt to bring mathematical precision to utilitarian reasoning, *Mathematical Psychics* also gave analytical depth to his second over-riding concern, to show that self-interest and utilitarianism were ultimately compatible. In his first published work, a short note on Matthew Arnold's interpretation of Bishop Butler (1876), he had argued that egoism and utilitarianism could be subsumed under the same principle. Duty and interest were 'perfectly coincident' provided that individuals take a sufficiently long view of the effects of their actions, extending beyond their lifetime on earth. In *Mathematical Psychics* he returned to the question of how individuals motivated by narrow egoistic self-interest could come to embrace 'pure' utilitarianism in which they are concerned with the welfare of society as a whole.

Edgeworth's answer was set forth in the third section of *Mathematical Psychics*, which incorporated his 1879 essay 'The Hedonical Calculus' largely without changes. To understand the argument of this section, however, it is necessary to read it in conjunction with the preceding section, 'the Economical Calculus', in which Edgeworth analysed economic exchange in terms of indifference curves and the contract curve, both of which are now a standard part of welfare economics. The contract curve traces out the possible points of settlement between two traders, i.e. it is the loci of tangency between their sets of 'indifference curves' which denote a combination of two goods such that they yield equal utility. The final contract between the two traders must take place on the contract curve because any other point is such that one party may improve his situation without worsening the position of the other. However, whereas modern welfare economics makes extensive use of these conceptual tools as a component of demand analysis, Edgeworth's main emphasis was on distribution.

Edgeworth argued that with few competitors there would be indeterminacy in the rate of exchange. He criticized Jevons's theory of barter exchange, showing that under a system of 'recontracting' there will be, in fact, many solutions, an 'indeterminacy of contract'. Edgeworth's concept of a 'range of final settlements' was later resurrected by Martin Shubik (1959) as the game-theoretic concept of 'the core'.Edgeworth also articulated what eventually became known as 'Edgeworth's conjecture', namely that as the number of agents in an economy increase, the degree of indeterminacy is reduced. He argued that in the case of an infinite number of agents ('perfect competition'), contract becomes fully determinate and identical to the 'equilibrium' of economists.

However, as situations of 'perfect competition' are unlikely to be met in most markets, Edgeworth argued that the only way of resolving the indeterminacy of contract would be to appeal to the utilitarian principle of maximizing the sum of the utilities of traders over the range of final settlements. Since any point along the contract curve is a possible equilibrium, the precise position along the contract curve that the traders will settle on which depends on bargaining and negotiation. This gives rise to 'higgling dodges and designing obstinacy, and other incalculable and often disreputable accidents' and to avoid these causes of strife there was a need for a principle of arbitration which Edgeworth identified with utilitarianism.

Edgeworth first showed that the utilitarian distribution would represent a position on the contract curve, and hence would be in accordance with the self-interest of the contractors. This was a necessary condition for adopting utilitarianism as the principle of arbitration, since it entailed that the incentives confronting the contractors were such that they would not undo the utilitarian distribution through a process of further bargaining. Edgeworth further demonstrated that utilitarianism also satisfied a sufficient condition for use as a principle of arbitration. He argued that the contractors, when faced with uncertainty as to their prospects, would choose to accept a distribution in accordance with utilitarian principles. Confronted by equal a priori probabilities of the possible distributive arrangements, 'both parties may agree to commute their chance of any of the arrangements for...the utilitarian arrangement'. Thus the adoption of utilitarianism as a principle of distribution arose from a social contract in which the parties were faced with choice under uncertainty. Edgeworth's justification for utilitarianism thus anticipates twentieth century attempts to analyse distributive justice as essentially a problem of choice under uncertainty, as for example by Harsanyi and by Rawls.

Edgeworth's later work was a contribution to technical areas of economic analysis, including optimal taxation and international trade theory. In 1894, he published a survey of international trade theory in a series of articles in the *Economic Journal*. In it, he pioneered the use of offer curves and community indifference curves to illustrate its main propositions, including the 'optimum tariff'. In that same year, he engaged Eugen von Bohm-Bawerk in a brief controversy over the opportunity cost doctrine.

In 1897 Edgeworth published two major contributions to economic analysis. The first was a lengthy survey of taxation, in which he articulated his famous 'taxation paradox', in other words that taxation of a good may actually result in a *decrease* in price. His paradox was disbelieved by contemporaries, and was described as 'a slip of Mr Edgeworth' by E.R.A. Seligman, then the leading authority on public finance. However, many years later, Harold Hotelling rigorously proved that Edgeworth had been correct. Edgeworth also set the utilitarian foundations for highly progressive taxation, arguing that the optimal distribution of taxes should be such that 'the marginal disutility incurred by each taxpayer should be the same' (Edgeworth 1897). In the same year Edgeworth produced an article in the Italian journal *Giornale degli Economisti* on monopoly pricing, in which he criticized Cournot's exact solution to the duopoly problem with quantity adjustments as well as Bertrand's 'instantly competitive' result in a duopoly model with price adjustment. Instead, Edgeworth showed how price competition between two firms with capacity constraints and/or rising marginal cost curves resulted in indeterminacy.

Edgeworth also made important contributions to statistics. In his third book, *Metretike* (1887), he presented the application and interpretation of significance tests for the comparisons of means. In a series of papers in 1892, Edgeworth examined methods of estimating correlation coefficients. Among his many results was 'Edgeworth's Theorem' giving the correlation coefficients of the multi-dimensional normal distribution. For his efforts, he was elected president of Section F of the British Association for the Advancement of Science in 1889 and later served as president of the Royal Statistical Society (1912–14).

Edgeworth made a number of deeply original contributions to economics, but the power of his analysis was slow to be recognized. This was in part due to his elliptical style, in which long and intricate sentences were liberally laced with Greek quotations and invented words that could only be understood by those trained in the classics (for example, *brachistopone*, meaning the 'curve of minimal work'). More importantly, the technical mathematical apparatus he employed was beyond the grasp of most economists, let alone moral philosophers, of his time. Without warning, Edgeworth would glide seamlessly back and forth from his impenetrable prose to no less impenetrable mathematical notation and analysis.

A second reason why the originality of Edgeworth's contribution was not immediately recognized was that to many of his contemporaries, especially at Oxford and the Royal Economic Society, he was generally regarded as 'MARSHALL's man' and, indeed, he often showed excessive deference to Marshall's opinions. His professional activities also contributed directly to the ascendancy of the Marshallian neoclassical hegemony and the decline of alternative approaches in Britain around the turn of the century. He blocked the Oxford appointment of the self-confessed 'economic heretic' John A. HOBSON, and, in his editorial role on the *Economic Journal*, he seemed to adopt the editorial policy of rejecting papers which strayed from Marshallian line in their analytical approach or which threatened to strike up debates on methodology that might be uncomfortable to the Marshallian orthodoxy. The work of Lausanne School economists, like Barone, were routinely rejected, as were those of the English Historical school.

Nonetheless, as Marshall's reputation declined during the twentieth century, Edgeworth gradually emerged from his shadow. In the 1930s, some of his contributions were picked up by Paretians such as Harold Hotelling, John HICKS and Abba Lerner. The 1960s and 1970s were characterized by the flowering of an 'Edgeworthian' school, led by Martin Shubik, Gérard Debreu, Robert Aumann, Werner Hildenbrand and other mathematical economists. The development of game theory, in particular, gave renewed impetus to an exploration of some of Edgeworth's pioneering work on the indeterminacy of contract.

BIBLIOGRAPHY

'Mr. Matthew Arnold on Bishop Butler's Doctrine of Self-Love', *Mind* (1876)
New and Old Methods of Ethics (Oxford, 1877).
'The Hedonical Calculus', *Mind* (1879).
Mathematical Psychics: An Essay on the Application of Mathematics to the Moral Sciences (1881).
Metretike, or the Method of Measuring Probability and Utility (1887).
'On the Application of Mathematics to Political Economy: Address of the President of Section F of the British Association for the Advancement of Science', *Journal of the Royal Statistics Society* (1889).
'Theory of International Values, Parts 1, 2, and 2', *Economic Journal* (1894).
'La teoria pura del monopolio', *Giornale degli Economisti* (1897).
'The Pure Theory of Taxation', *Economic Journal* (1897).
Papers Relating to Political Economy, 3 vols (1925).

Further Reading
Bowley, A.L., *F.Y. Edgeworth's Contributions to Mathematical Statistics* (Oxford, 1928).
Bonner, J., *Economic Efficiency and Social Justice: The Development of Utilitarian Ideas in Economics from Bentham to Edgeworth* (1995).

Cready, J., *Edgeworth and the Development of Neoclassical Economics* (Oxford, 1986).

Hotelling, H. 'Edgeworth's Taxation Paradox and the Nature of Demand and Supply Functions', *Journal of Political Economy* (1932).

Hutchison, T.W., *A Review of Economic Doctrines 1870–1929* (Oxford, 1953).

Jevons, W.S., 'A Review of Edgeworth's *Mathematical Psychics*', *Mind* (1881).

Keynes, J.M., 'Francis Ysidro Edgeworth' in *Essays in Biography*, vol. X of *Collected Writings* (1972).

Shubik, M., 'Edgeworth Market Games', in R.D. Luce and A.W. Tucke (eds), *Contributions to the Theory of Games*, vol. 4 (Princeton, 1959).

Michael Taylor

ELIOT, Francis Perceval (1756?–1818)

Eliot was born at Kew, near London, probably in 1756 (some sources suggest 1755). He died in London on 23 August 1818. His father, General Granville Eliot (sometimes Elliot) was a soldier of fortune who had served in the armies of both Austria and France, and while in France had married the Comtesse de Matigny and had several children by her. After her death General Eliot returned to England and remarried; Francis Eliot was the second son of that marriage. The two families seem to have remained in contact following General Eliot's death, and there are records of correspondence between Francis Eliot and his half-brother Antoine Xavier Eliot, an officer in the French army.

Eliot himself had a much more quiet career. His education is not known, but by about 1780 he was employed by the civil service. In 1806 he was appointed a commissioner of audit, with an office at Somerset House, and he held this post until his death. He retained an interest in military affairs, and wrote several pamphlets on the yeomanry services; he also served as colonel of the Staffordshire Yeomanry, a volunteer cavalry regiment.

Eliot also wrote several pamphlets on economics and finance, the most important of which is *Observations on the Fallacy of the Supposed Depreciation of the Paper Currency of the Kingdom* (1811). This was written in response to the report of the Bullion Committee in 1810, which recommended the resumption of payments in gold and silver within two years, whether or not the country was still at war. Eliot attacked the Committee, and particularly the MP William HUSKISSON, one of its most prominent members. He argued that, contrary to the views of the Committee, there had been no depreciation in the value of the paper currency. Gold bullion, he says, is a commodity and as such its value can and does fluctuate. Paper money as a commodity has only the value of paper; its value lies in what it represents. What Huskisson and others take to be fluctuations in the value of paper money are in fact fluctuations in the value of commodities. Bank notes with a face value of twenty guineas still buy twenty guineas worth of goods or services. This stability, Eliot says, is a good argument for making bank notes legal tender in their own right, with no requirement for them to be redeemed.

Where Huskisson and others are in error, says Eliot, is in confusing the money of exchange with the money of account. Huskisson, he says, considers 'the guinea as the measure and standard of value, and the Bank-note as the proportional representative of that guinea' (1811: 31). On the contrary, 'the only original national measure of value is the pound sterling, in money of account, and was so long before a guinea was coined; for all monied value must be in account only, or it could never be ascertainably fixed to any valuation whatever' (1811: 31). In other words, while the value of gold bullion has indeed risen, a gold guinea still represents twenty-one shillings in money of account, and a pound note still represents twenty shillings, just as they had done in 1797 before the Restriction Act. While he concedes that an excess supply of money produces price inflation, he points out that this is not solely the fault of bank notes; an excess of gold or silver would have produced inflation in exactly the same way. What is wanted is a more careful management of money supply generally.

BIBLIOGRAPHY
Demonstration, or Financial Remarks: With Occasional Observations on Political Occurrences (1807).
Observations on the Fallacy of the Supposed Depreciation of the Paper Currency of the Kingdom (1811).
Letters on the Political and Financial Situation of the British Empire in the years 1814, 1815 and 1816 (1816).

Ann Kimber

ELLIS, William (1800–81)

Ellis was born in London on 27 January 1800 and died there on 18 February 1881. He was the fourth child of Andrew Ellis de Vezian, whose father emigrated from France, and Sophia Fazio. Ellis's father, an underwriter of marine insurance, dropped the name De Vezian after William's birth, becoming known as Mr Andrew Ellis. Little is known about William Ellis's early life except that he attended boarding school in Bromley from age six until thirteen, when he entered his father's business.

Around 1820 Ellis met James MILL and Jeremy BENTHAM and soon formed a life-long friendship with Mill's son, John Stuart MILL. Ellis joined the Utilitarian Society and became a central figure in the discussions of the younger Mill's study groups. During the 1820s, when the *Westminster Review* was founded by Jeremy Bentham, Ellis contributed four of the first thirteen economics articles and co-authored another with J.S. Mill. In these early articles, Ellis promoted Benthamite philosophy and Ricardian economics as propagated by the books of James Mill and J.R. MCCULLOCH. Two of Ellis's early articles were glowing reviews of the textbooks of Mill and McCulloch. His two articles on machinery (1825, 1826), however, broke new ground and exhibited a sophisticated understanding of comparative advantage and free trade. Ellis refuted RICARDO's notion that machinery might be detrimental to the working classes, and argued that exporting machinery was not harmful to the home country. Ellis also recognized the power of expected profits and separated savings from investment, thereby questioning the wages fund doctrine.

Having married in 1825, practical necessity forced Ellis to postpone his writing on economics. In 1827 he became manager of the Indemnity Mutual Marine Assurance Company, a company tottering on the brink of bankruptcy. Ellis rescued the company, becoming a prominent business leader. His financial condition thus improved, he influenced political economy by devoting large sums of time and money to spreading classical economic ideas. In 1835 he published a series of economics lectures that circulated in Mechanics Institutes and later published numerous books, pamphlets and articles on economics. Ellis was perhaps the only economist who attempted to educate all classes and make economic principles a major component of education. His unique contribution was founding and financing seven Birkbeck Schools beginning in 1848 that sought to teach children rules of good conduct, based on principles of political economy.

Ellis's methods were widely copied and his schools visited by members of parliament and other luminaries. In 1855, at Prince Albert's request he taught 'social economy' to the royal children. His teaching methods were carried to Italy and his books were translated into French, Dutch and Japanese. However, the working classes remained sceptical of the Ellis style of school, commonly perceiving them as propagandizing or worse. Few doubt that DICKENS's fictional Gradgrind school portrayed in *Hard Times* (1854) was a satirical treatment of the Birkbeck genre of schools, and such writings reinforced lower-class scepticism of schools promoted by upper classes. Nevertheless, Ellis is remembered as one of the most influential educators of the nineteenth century.

Ellis's later writings on economics were mainly textbooks or aids to teach economic principles and good conduct. In his schools and later writings Ellis used the phrase 'social economy' to reposition economics as a moral science included in social science, which he suggested considered not only 'the means of supplying physical wants', but also 'teaching and training, and self discipline, without which the desirable qualifications are not to be had in perfection' (1863: 10). His efforts to improve educational methods, promote economic literacy and his early *Westminster Review* articles are his most important legacies.

BIBLIOGRAPHY

'On Charitable Institutions', *Westminster Review* (1824, vol. 2, no. 3, pp. 97–121.
'James Mill's *Elements of Political Economy*', *Westminster Review* (1824), vol. 2, no. 4, pp. 289–310.
(with J.S. Mill) 'McCulloch's *Political Economy*', *Westminster Review* (1835), vol. 4, no. 7, pp. 88–92.
'On Exportation of Machinery', *Westminster Review* (1825), vol. 3, no. 6, pp. 386–94.
'On the Employment of Machinery', *Westminster Review* (1826), vol. 5, no. 9, pp. 101–30.
Conversations upon Knowledge, Happiness, and Education between a Mechanic and a Patron of the London Mechanics Institution (1829).
Lectures on Political Economy (Glasgow, 1836).
Outlines of Social Economy (1846).
A Few Questions on Secular Education (1848).
Questions and Answers Suggested by a Consideration of some of the Arrangements and Relations of Social Life (1848).
'The Distressed Needlewomen and Cheap Prison Labour', *Westminster Review* (1849), vol. 50, no. 99, pp. 371–94.
Introduction to the Study of the Social Sciences (1849).
'Relief Measures', *Westminster Review* (1850), vol. 53, no. 104, pp. 145–64.
'Classical Education', *Westminster Review* (1850), vol. 53, no. 105, pp. 393–409.
Progressive Lessons in Social Science (1850).
Education as a Means of Preventing Destitution (1851).
Lessons on the Phenomena of Industrial Life and the Conditions of Industrial Success (1854).
A Layman's Contribution to the Knowledge and Practice of Religion in Common Life (1857).
Philo-Socrates, 4 vols (1861–4).
Studies of Man, by a Japanese (1874).

Further Reading

Berg, M. (1980) *The Machinery Question and the Making of Political Economy: 1815–1846* (Cambridge, 1980).
Blyth, E.K., *Life of William Ellis* (1892).
Ellis, E.E., *Memoir of William Ellis* (1888).
Fetter, F.W., 'Economic Articles in the *Westminster Review* and Their Authors, 1824–1851', *Journal of Political Economy* (1962), vol. 70, no. 6, pp. 570–96.
Gilmour, R., 'The Gradgrind School: Political Economy in the Classroom', *Victorian Studies* (1967), December, pp. 207–24.
Miller, F.F., 'William Ellis and his Work as an Educationist', *Fraser's Magazine* (1882), February, pp. 233–52.

Sockwell, W.D., *Popularizing Classical Economics: Henry Brougham and William Ellis* (1994).
——, 'William Ellis: Contributions as a Classical Economist, Economic Educator, Economic Popularizer, and Social Economist', *Research in the History of Economic Thought and Methodology* (1994), vol.12, pp. 1–29.

William D. Sockwell

ENGELS, Friedrich (1820–95)

Friedrich (later Frederick) Engels was born on 28 November 1820 in Barmen (modern Wuppertal) in the industrial Ruhr near Düsseldorf in Germany. He died on 5 August 1895 in London; he had been continuously resident in Britain since late 1849, living in Manchester until 1869 and then in London during his retirement. Educated at the Gymnasium in Elberfeld, he never formally entered university, but rather attended lectures at the University of Berlin while posted there during 1841–2 on national service. Otherwise he was variously throughout his life a businessman and factory manager, journalist, literary critic, political pamphleteer, revolutionary and autodidact in philosophy, history, military science and economics.

Engels's career as an economist effectively took place before he began his formal association with Karl MARX in August 1844, when they met in Paris. Marx's lifework was a 'critique of the economic categories', eventually published as Volume 1 of *Das Kapital* (Capital) in 1867. The succeeding Volumes 2 and 3 (1885, 1894) were edited by Engels from manuscript materials, with occasional interpolations, not scrupulously marked. His reputation as Marx's editor is currently undergoing revision, as both the manuscript materials and his published versions themselves have begun to appear in the current *Marx-Engels Gesamtausgabe*. In so far as he is shown to have departed from Marx's work, his reputation as an editor will suffer, while his reputation as an economist is very unlikely to rise through this exposure of his independent thought. Reviewing Marx's earlier *Zur Kritik der politischen Ökonomie* (A Contribution to the Critique of Political Economy) (1859) in its year of publication, Engels introduced Marx's project to the world and summarized its methodology in two instalments; a promised third instalment covering Marx's economics never appeared.

Throughout his later life Engels's summaries of Marx's detailed economic arguments are perfunctory, whereas his formulation of a 'dialectics' applicable to nature, history and thought occupied him extensively. This resulted in the well-known volumes on which his reputation as 'first Marxist' now rests. In those works, specifically *Herrn Eugen Dührings Umwälzung der Wissenschaft* (Anti-Dühring) (1878) and extracted chapters published separately as *Socialisme utopique et socialisme scientifique* (Socialism: Utopian and Scientific) (1880), Engels reviewed the economic history of western civilization and outlined the history political economy, but produced nothing of his own as an economist.

However, in his early career up to mid-1844 Engels wrote as an economist, and was in fact a considerable influence on Marx, rather than the other way round. Engels's family background and early surroundings contributed very substantially to the formation of an economic outlook, and his personal inclinations gave this a very critical and even revolutionary turn at an early age. Barmen and Elberfeld were textile manufacturing towns, and Engels's great-grandfather had founded a business in lace and ribbon-making, from which Engels's father's generation had constructed a multi-national manufacturing and trading business with offices, factories and partnerships in Germany and England. At sixteen Engels joined the family firm, and at seventeen he did office work away from home in Bremen. At eighteen under an assumed name he published a scandalous exposé of working class conditions, factory pollution and smug middle-class hypocrisy in his hometown newspaper.

While not strictly economics in subject matter or reasoning, those works show that he took his observations of local production and consumption patterns with great personal intensity, linking them to the patterns of power and privilege that he found in the business community. Over the next few years Engels wrote numerous newspaper and magazine articles in both German and English on similar themes, culminating in his masterpiece *Die Lage der Arbeitenden Klasse in England* (The Condition of the Working Class in England) (1845). Of course, modern economics did not exist as yet; the philosophically more general and mathematically less rigorous discourse of political economy was the established mode of thought. While not a work of political economy either, Engels's sociological study of working class conditions referenced a number of notable works by political economists such as J.R. McCulloch, T.R. Malthus, Nassau Senior, Adam Smith and also Andrew Ure, professor of chemistry and natural philosophy at Glasgow and author of *The Philosophy of Manufactures* (1832). Engels was thus engaged with the subject and could read the major authorities in English.

After a brief and rather chilly first meeting with Marx (then editor of the liberal newspaper *Rheinische Zeitung* in Cologne in the Rhineland), Engels proceeded from Germany to take up a family post in Manchester. Engels had been writing for Marx's paper, which ceased publication in March 1843, and had evidently been commissioned to write for its political successor, the *Deutsch-französische Jahrbücher*, a periodical that only ever appeared on one occasion. He seems to have supplemented his discursive accounts of industrial conditions with a serious analytical investigation into political economy, seeing it from a communist perspective as not merely the science of commercial society but as its literal constitution. Commercial society is thus not merely described by economic concepts but rather those concepts are constitutive of it; hence they appear to describe it accurately and perforce scientifically. Engels had absorbed the philosophy as well as the politics of the most radical of the Berlin Young Hegelians during his time there, but unlike his colleagues, he had a 'feel' for economic life and for theorizations of its concepts. In that way he was unique. He wrote his critical essay on political economy in late 1843 and sent it to the editors in Germany at the turn of the new year.

Engels's *Umrisse zu einer Kritik der Nationalökonomie* (Outlines of a Critique of Political Economy) (1844) is a remarkable work on its own account. While it is read today, if at all, as a prefiguration of Marx's mature work, it is neither credited in relation to this work as generously as Marx himself famously did in print, nor is it taken seriously as an independent contribution to analytical thinking about the theories and concepts of commercial society. This is the sole major work by which Engels as political economist should be remembered and evaluated, yet it was not re-published in Engels's own lifetime. It was only re-circulated in the 1960s after the publication of the *Werke* edition of Marx and Engels's works and a subsequent translation into English.

Engels's approach was analytically engaged. He argued that in economic science, as in the industrial economy, the concept of private property was central, albeit historically, politically and morally problematic. It necessarily presupposed competition, which obscured the fundamental moral relationship between consumption goods, the stuff of human life, and the productive capacity of human labour to provide for all. For Engels, there was no way of reconciling private interest and public good in competitive practice, as individual interests would always be opposed in morally unpalatable ways.

A glorification of human relationships as competitive, in Engels's view, represented a hideous blasphemy on nature and humanity. Following the common schema in political economy, that the three great factors of production are land, labour and capital, he argued that land and capital were better situated in the competitive struggle than labour, and that this advantage would increase as competition itself provoked the concentration of these resources in fewer and fewer hands.

Arguing that workers were supplied through population growth to meet the demand for industrial labour, Engels deduced that capitalists and landowners would employ new technologies to economize on labour rather than to increase employment and output, thus putting labourers into destitution. Crises of underconsumption would ensue, and would of necessity get worse. Engels thus rejected a self-regulating view of market competition, and argued that the labour force would grow with each lurch from boom to bust, thus building the ranks of those subject to enforced unemployment and starvation. This analytical reductionism enabled him to discount the various ameliorative tactics that political economists had recommended, and that governments had in their limited ways sometimes deployed. In a striking theoretical move, he not only linked competitive trade with mutually destructive and enslaving wars but also with a logic of robbery as the law of the stronger, particularly when treaties and other political advantages were extracted from defeated competitors. Political economy was thus an apology for a system of licensed fraud and ruthless violence. And in a further burst of lateral thinking, he linked competitive market relations to black markets and crime, arguing that commercial society creates a demand for crime to be met by a corresponding supply.

Engels's politics was a radical inversion of the fatalism, conservatism or piecemeal reformism of the political economists with whose theories he was engaged. He argued that communists such as himself would resolve the theory of free trade into an inveterate monopolism, and that the abolition of private property was the only logical conclusion to those theoretical contradictions. In practice he identified a revolutionary impetus in the labour force, because they were the obvious and most needy beneficiaries of such a reform. His political message was buoyed up by the promise of rising numbers, in absolute terms and also relative to the other great classes in society. Far from rejecting modern industry, as many utopian socialists had done, Engels's communism presupposed its historical necessity and further development, albeit under community control of production through which a calculation of the common good would prevail. Thus his analytical attack on political economy as constitutive of, and an apology for, commercial society extended to a theorization of a replacement system that would abolish its central institution, private property, and with that the immorality and barbarity of competitive relationships among human beings.

While many of Engels's views can be found elsewhere amongst his friends and associates, as well as in other major writers on political economy, the analytical character of his thought is impressive, as is his extension of economic reasoning into areas now associated with sociology, politics, philosophy, demography, geography and criminology. Though his analysis does not push forward towards the marginalist revolution of the late 1870s, the basic views that it espouses have not gone away as criticisms either of modern economic science or of modern economic systems. If Engels had not subsequently become associated with Marx, it is quite possible that this short essay would have earned a place in the history of political economy and of the development, at least in theory, of collectivist rather than individualist economic systems. Marx, of course, did read Engels's article in manuscript, and arguably benefited from its unity of purpose, systematic approach and clarity of discrimination, all in rather short supply amongst his other Young Hegelian associates. He was only just getting to grips with the actual literature of political economy during this period (and only in French or German), and was obviously attracted to someone who could handle it so well in English. Most remarkably, Marx immediately drafted a conspectus that prefigured for the first time the critical investigation of the concepts of private property, trade and value, which became his life's work. As Engels settled into his role of supporting, supplementing and advertising Marx, he evidently lost interest in his own critical engagement with the economics of his day, and his excellent work in the *Outlines* passed into eclipse.

BIBLIOGRAPHY
Umrisse zu einer Kritik der Nationalökonomie (Outlines of a Critique of Political Economy) (1844).
Die Lage der Arbeitenden Klasse in England (The Condition of the Working Class in England) (1845).
(with K. Marx) *Manifesto of the Communist Party* (1848).
Herrn Eugen Dührings Umwälzung der Wissenschaft (Anti-Dühring) (1878).
Socialisme utopique et socialisme scientifique (Socialism: Utopian and Scientific) (1880).

Further Reading
Carver, T., *Friedrich Engels: His Life and Thought* (Basingstoke, 1989).
Claeys, G., 'Engels' *Outlines of a Critique of Political Economy* (1843) and the Origins of the Marxist Critique of Capitalism', *History of Political Economy* (1984), vol. 16, pp. 207–32.
Henderson, W.O., *The Life of Friedrich Engels*, 2 vols (1976).
Rigby, S.H., *Engels and the Formation of Marxism: History, Dialectics, and Revolution* (Manchester, 1992).
Steger, M.B. and Carver, T. (eds), *Engels After Marx* (University Park, Pennsylvania, 1999).

Terrell Carver

ESTCOURT, Thomas (1748–1818)

Estcourt was born 27 September 1748 at Tetbury, Gloucestershire, and died there on 2 December 1818. His father, Matthew Estcourt, was a gentleman and landowner in Gloucestershire and Wiltshire. He attended St John's College, Oxford in 1766, but appears not to have taken a degree. He inherited an estate from his uncle, Walter Estcourt, around 1750. He was sheriff of Gloucestershire in 1774–5, and held a commission in the Wiltshire yeomanry from 1794 onward. In 1782 he entered parliament, standing unopposed in a by-election in Cricklade and going on to hold the seat until 1806.

In parliament, Estcourt was a strong supporter of Addington, backing the latter loyally no matter what his position. He made few speeches in parliament, though notably in 1800 he opposed the removal and imprisonment of vagrants and he also urged the importance of the potato as a food crop to ward off famine both in Ireland and in England. His highest position was service on the Board of Agriculture from 1801–6. He resigned his seat in 1806, ostensibly on the grounds of ill health, but probably because his patron Addington (then Viscount Sidmouth) had fallen out of favour.

Estcourt's speeches show him to have had an interest in the problems of poverty, and his one publication, *An Account of the Result of an Effort to Better the Condition of the Poor in a Country Village* (1804), published at the direction of the Board of Agriculture, is an account of an experiment to remedy the problems of rural poverty in particular. This particular experiment took place in the parish of Long Newnton, Wiltshire, where landholders had agreed to make small parcels of land available to the poor. The thirty-two poor families of the parish were each offered a plot of land up to a maximum of an acre and a half, at a 'fair rent' of £1 12*s* an acre. Two conditions were set: first, the tenants agreed not to accept any money from the poor relief fund – should they do so, the land would be forfeited to the landlord – and second, one-quarter of each plot must be planted annually with potatoes, the rest being managed as the tenants saw fit.

Estcourt recorded that the great majority of the poor families took up the offer, and infirmity and age were the main reasons given by the few who declined. The first parcels of land were handed over in 1801, and Estcourt reported that since that time, none of those who had taken up the offer had received any money from the poor relief, and significantly, crime had dropped as well: 'It may not be improper to mention, that no warrant or summons has been issued against any poor person of this parish since A.D. 1800' (1804: 5). Thanks to the ability to grow most of their own food, the families remained free of debt and were starting to look forward to their future. As well as growing potatoes and other crops, some had invested in pigs and poultry and one family had even purchased a cow.

The benefits of encouraging self-sufficiency in this manner, says Estcourt, are felt by all classes, not just the poor. He strongly urges that similar schemes be adopted elsewhere and that landlords set aside land for this purpose. He adds, however, that charity is still necessary since the Long Newnton scheme showed that not everyone could work the land in this fashion, even if they wished to; in such cases, poor relief should continue to be offered with prejudice to those who needed it.

BIBLIOGRAPHY
An Account of the Result of an Effort to Better the Condition of the Poor in a Country Village (1804).

Further Reading
Thorne, R.G., *The History of Parliament: The House of Commons 1790–1820* (2000, vol. 3, pp. 714–15).

Ann Kimber

EVANS, Thomas (1763–c.1826)

Nothing is known of the early life of Thomas Evans. He first rose to prominence as a very active member of the radical London Corresponding Society in the mid-1790s, and for nearly thirty years he was a leading advocate of reform, particularly as the disciple of Thomas SPENCE. He was at different times a baker, a colourer of bawdy prints, a bookseller, a manufacturer of patent braces and spiral steel springs, the owner of a coffee house and then of a dissenting chapel where he charged fees for political lectures and debates. Always struggling financially, but determined to maintain his wife and son in reasonable circumstances, he moved in both constitutional reform and ultra-radical circles in London. Francis PLACE – with whom he had serious disputes – described him as ignorant, conceited and remarkably obstinate, but others described him as clever and energetic. He was certainly a man of some courage and resilience.

By 1795 Evans was a particularly active member of the London Corresponding Society, sitting on both the General Committee and the Executive Committee. He became secretary of the LCS in July 1797, but government repression encouraged him to move in more revolutionary circles. He began communicating with leading emissaries of the United Irishmen, who were seeking French military support for an armed rebellion, and he himself began forming a small revolutionary group in London, variously known as the United Britons, the True Britons and the United Englishmen. On 18 April 1798 he was arrested at a meeting of the United Englishmen with incriminating papers in his pocket. Although the government suspected him of high treason, he was never charged. None the less, the suspension of *habeas corpus* enabled the government to keep him in a succession of prisons until March 1801.

On his release Evans became involved in both moderate reform campaigns and in ultra-radical politics. He provided Francis Burdett with evidence of the harsh prison regime at Coldbath Fields gaol, and campaigned for Burdett in the Middlesex election of 1802 and the Westminster election of 1812. He also attended many meetings of ultra-radicals in 'free-and-easy' taverns in London and became an admirer and dedicated disciple of Thomas SPENCE, the propagator of a very radical Land Plan. When Spence died in 1814, Evans organized his funeral and set up a Society of Spencean Philanthropists. By 1815 there were four or five lodges meeting in different taverns on different nights of the week. Evans acted as librarian of the society, while his son was, for a time, its secretary. While the membership numbered only a few dozen stalwarts, it included at times such notorious ultra-radicals as Arthur Thistlewood, James Watson, Thomas Preston and Robert Wedderburn.

In 1816 Evans wrote and published the society's most important publication, *Christian Policy the Salvation of Empire*. This endorsed some of the essential features of Spence's Land Plan. It advocated the abolition of all private property and sought to put all private property (including water, mines and houses) under the control of the parishes. This property – now referred to as 'the people's farm' – was to be leased out on annual leases to the highest bidders. The money raised was to pay for the essential costs of central and local government, and the remainder was to be divided equally between every man, woman and child. The national debt would be liquidated and all taxes would be abolished. In this new world no one would be poor and yet industrious workers, artisans and small producers could do well. All this can be found in Spence's various expositions of his Land Plan, but Evans added new elements of his own. He largely ignored the question of political reforms, stressing that economic reforms must precede the reform of parliament, and he offered no description of a democratic republic of federated parishes in the manner of Spence. Indeed, he was ready to use parish rents to pay for the upkeep of a monarchy and a House of Lords, and to pay a salary to MPs and parish clergy. He also put much less stress than Spence on natural rights arguments. He believed that God had granted all property to all people in common, and he believed that Jesus Christ (a holy man, but not divine) had desired to re-establish this truly Christian society. But he also looked to historical evidence to justify his claims. He looked back to two periods when an agrarian commonwealth had actually been established: under Moses in biblical times, and in Saxon England under King Alfred. Unfortunately, the Saxon constitution and agrarian commonwealth had been destroyed in 1066, when invaders had imposed the 'Norman yoke' on the English people, had seized all their property and had instigated centuries of oppression.

In the years of distress after 1815, Evans associated with the ultra-radicals in London, though he carefully avoided any involvement in the Spa Fields Riots of December 1816 or the later Cato Street conspiracy. These precautions did not prevent the government from arresting him and his son in February 1817. Once more he was neither charged nor convicted of any crime, but the suspension of *habeas corpus* enabled the government to keep both men in prison until 20 January 1818. After his release, Evans tried to become more respectable, without abandoning his reforming ideas. He established a licensed chapel of Christian Philanthropists in Archer Street, Soho, where 'services' and political readings and debates were conducted several times a week. The fiery and blasphemous preacher and ultra-radical, the mulatto Robert Wedderburn, increasingly dominated these meetings. This eventually caused a complete breach, and Evans was left with a splinter group meeting in smaller premises. Early in 1820 Evans moved to Manchester, where his son was briefly in charge of the

Manchester Observer. While there, Evans publicly campaigned in support of the cause of Queen Caroline and privately published an admiring brief life of Thomas Spence. His son, however, was soon imprisoned for a year for seditious libel.

Shortly after his son's release, in April 1822, the family returned to London. There, Evans rallied to the defence of Richard Carlile, in trouble for his radical publications and encouraged the development of the London Mechanics Institution. Unwell and unemployed, Evans was last recorded on a public platform in early February 1824 at a meeting marking the birthday of Thomas Paine. Nothing more is heard of him and he appears to have died in the later 1820s.

BIBLIOGRAPHY
Address and Regulations of the Society of Spencean Philanthropists (1815).
Christian Policy the Salvation of Empire. Being a clear...examination into the causes that have produced the impending, unavoidable national bankruptcy (1816).
The Petition of Thomas Evans...to the House of Commons, 28 Feb. 1817 (1817).
Address of the Society of Spencean Philanthropists to all mankind, on the means of promoting liberty and happiness (1817).
Christian Policy in Full Practice among the People of Harmony (1818).
Address of the Society of Spencean Philanthropists, To all Mankind, On the Means of promoting Liberty and Happiness (1819).
A Brief Sketch of the Life of Thomas Spence (1821).

Further Reading
Chase, M., *The People's Farm: English Radical Agrarianism 1775–1840* (Oxford, 1988).
———, 'Evans, Thomas' in J.M. Bellamy and J. Saville, *Dictionary of Labour Biography* (Basingstoke, 1987, vol. 8, pp. 59–69).

Claeys, G., 'Thomas Evans and the Development of Spenceanism, 1815–16: Some Neglected Correspondence', *Bulletin of the Society of Labour History* (1984), vol. 48, pp. 24–30.
Evans, E.J., 'Evans, Thomas' in J.O. Baylen and N.J. Gossman (eds), *Biographical Dictionary of Modern British Radicals* (Brighton, 1979, vol. 1, pp. 165–6).
Hone, J.A., *For the Cause of Truth: Radicalism in London 1796–1821* (Oxford, 1982).
McCalman, I., *Radical Underworld: Prophets, Revolutionaries, and Pornographers in London, 1795–1840* (Cambridge, 1988).
Parsinnen, T.M., 'The Revolutionary Party in London, 1816–20' *Bulletin of the Institute of Historical Research* (1972), vol. 45, no. 112, pp. 266–82.
Thale, M. (ed.), *Selections from the Papers of the London Corresponding Society 1792–1799* (Cambridge, 1983).
Worrall, D., *Radical Culture: Discourse, Resistance and Surveillance, 1790–1820* (Detroit, 1992).

H.T. Dickinson

EVELYN, John (1620–1706)

Evelyn was born in Wotton, Surrey, on 31 October 1620, and died there on 27 February 1706. The son of a prosperous landowner, he was educated at Middle Temple, London, and then at Balliol College, Oxford, where he apparently neglected his formal studies in favour of the study of music and dancing. Most famous today for his *Diary*, the most detailed contemporary account of seventeenth-century English life and culture, Evelyn was a virtuoso who pursued an astonishing range of intellectual and cultural topics both as author and translator: architecture, antiquities, gardening, food, religion and natural philosophy. A founding member of the Royal Society, he is the author of the first book published under the auspices of the Royal Society, *Sylva: or A Discourse of Forest-Trees, and the Propagation of Timber in His Majesty's Dominions* (1664). Like many members of the early Royal Society – Robert Boyle, Robert Hooke, John Wilkins, William PETTY and Sir Robert Moray – Evelyn sought to understand how principles of natural philosophy could be used to improve the productivity and effectiveness of such fields as agriculture, manufacturing and medicine.

As early as the 1650s, Evelyn met Samuel HARTLIB and was thus introduced to a circle of reformers and experimentalists, all of whom were interested in practical applications of new discoveries. Many of these reformers (such as William Petty) laid the groundwork for what would become modern notions of economics. Hartlib noted in 1653 that Evelyn had started a history of trades (Evelyn would never complete this history), but he was already at work on his famous work on the reform of forestry, *Sylva*.

Sylva is a curious work, combining literary discourse, close observation of natural phenomena, clearly stated hypotheses, summaries of simple experiments and lengthy quotations from Greek and Roman literature. Evelyn makes it clear that his audience is gentlemen, not 'rustic woodmen'. Like Boyle's early works on chemistry, Evelyn tries to persuade gentlemen to become seriously interested in the cultivation of trees. Under Cromwell, Evelyn argued, England was deforested, and only through systematic, skilful practices could the forests be restored. Thus, the economics of forestry had a distinctly political undertone. Drawing on his own experience and observations, Evelyn demonstrates that economic productivity could be greatly enhanced through wise stewardship and more systematic evaluation of results. His economic projections for poplars, for example, illustrates the power of compound interest by projecting increased yields over many years.

Later works touch on economic issues. *Publick Employment and an Active Life prefer'd to Solitude* (1667) responds to George MACKENZIE's *A Moral Essay, preferring Solitude to Publick Employment* (1665). Evelyn stressed the public good being done by Robert Boyle (and, by implication, others who were publicly involved with the Royal Society) by showing that their works led to economic improvements. His *Navigation and Commerce* (1674) would appear to deal with economic issues, but it is instead a preface to a history of the Dutch Wars. For England, navigation had always been critical to economic prosperity, and to make the case, Evelyn draws on several centuries of history.

BIBLIOGRAPHY

Sylva; or a discourse of Forest-Trees...To which is annexed Pomona; Also Kalendarium Hortense; or, Gard'ners Almanac; Directing what he is to do Monethly throughout the Year (1664; revised edns 1670, 1679, 1706).

Publick Employment and an Active Life prefer'd to Solitude (1667).

Navigation and Commerce (1674).

A Philosophical Discourse of Earth, Relating to the Culture and Improvement of it for Vegetation, and the Propagation of Plants (1676).

Diary, ed. E.S. de Beer, 6 vols (Oxford, 1955; first published 1818).

Further Reading

Bédoyère, G. de la, *The Writings of John Evelyn* (Woodbridge, Connecticut, 1995).

Bowle, J., *John Evelyn and His World* (1981).

Hunter, M., *Science and Society in Restoration England* (Cambridge, 1981).

Keynes, G., *John Evelyn: A Study in Bibliophily and a Bibliography of His Writings* (1937; 2nd edn, 1968).

O'Malley, T. and Wolschke-Bulmahn, J., *John Evelyn's 'Elysium Brittanicum' and European Gardening* (Washington, DC, 1998).

Sharp, L., 'Timber, Science and Economic Reform in the Seventeenth Century', *Forestry* (1975), vol. 48, pp. 51–86.

Webster, C., *The Great Instauration: Science, Medicine and Reform, 1626–60* (1975).

John Harwood

F

FARRELL, Michael James (1926–75)

Farrell was born 9 May 1926, and died at Cambridge on 27 October 1975. He was educated at King Edward V School, Sheffield and read politics, philosophy and economics at New College, Oxford (BA 1949, MA 1953). He married Margaret Bacon in 1952; they had five sons. In 1957 Farrell contacted polio which paralyzed and crippled him.

In 1949, Farrell joined the Department of Applied Economics at Cambridge University, where Richard STONE was director. He was appointed a lecturer in the economics faculty in 1953, and was made a reader in 1970. He also visited and worked with Tobin at the Cowles Foundation, and was a visiting professor at both Berkeley (1966–7) and Carnegie-Mellon (1969). He was a fellow of Caius College, Cambridge from 1958.

In his relatively brief career Farrell made some lasting contributions to economic theory. He does not rank with such contemporaries as Arrow and Solow, but he did make path-breaking contributions. His comparative advantage was to be able to combine economic theory and the statistical testing of theories. His strengths were both as a theoretician and as a statistician/econometrician. Another feature of his published work is that it includes contributions to macroeconomics, microeconomics, applied econometrics and financial economics.

One important contribution was Farrell's work on the convexity assumption in the theory of competitive markets in 'The Convexity Assumption in the Theory of Competitive Markets' (1959). The objective of this paper was to 'examine how far the allocation of resources brought about by a perfectly competitive market remains optimal when indifference maps and production functions cease to be convex' (1959: 377). Farrell shows that any competitive equilibrium is a Pareto optimum, whether or not the assumption of convexity is made. Arrow refers to and uses Farrell's convexity contribution in his 'General Equilibrium': 'The assumption of convexity cannot be dispensed with in general theorums concerning the existence of equilibrium ... However, a line of thought developed by Farrell...suggests that the gap between supply and demand does not tend to increase with the size of the economy' (Arrow 1983: 124).

Another field in which Farrell made a lasting contribution was the measurement of production functions. His paper 'The Measurement of Production Efficiency' (1957), which aimed to 'provide a satisfactory measure of production efficiency – one which takes account of all the inputs (1957: 253) is his most quoted paper, stimulated by inter-country comparisons of productivity. Farrell distinguishes technical and allocative efficiency (the latter is the degree to which a firm uses the inputs in the least cost combination given their prices). He developed a method of measuring the technical efficiency of a firm by comparing its performance to the frontier production function for its industry. He also developed methods of estimating frontier production functions for industries, including using a linear programming model. He illustrated his methods using agricultural data for the USA.

BIBLIOGRAPHY

'An Application of Activity Analysis to the Theory of the Firm', *Econometrica* (1954), vol. 22, pp. 291–302.
'The Demand for Motor-Cars in the United States', *Journal of the Royal Statistical Society* (1954), Series A, vol. 117, pp. 171–93.
'The Measurement of Production Efficiency,' *Journal of the Royal Statistical Society* (1957), Series A, vol. 120, pp. 253–81.
'The Convexity Assumption in the Theory of Competitive Markets', *Journal of Political Economy* (1959), vol. 67, pp. 377–91.
'The New Theories of the Consumption Function,' *Economic Journal* (1959), vol. 69, pp. 678–96.
'On the Structure of the Capital Market', *Economic Journal* (1962), vol. 72, pp. 830–44.
'Profitable Speculation', *Economica* (1966), vol. 33, pp. 183–93.
'Some Elementary Selection Processes in Economics', *Review of Economic Studies* (1970), vol. 37, pp. 305–19.
'Philip Andrews and Manufacturing Business', *Journal of Industrial Economics* (1971), vol. 20, pp. 10–13.

Further Reading
Arrow, K.J., *Collected Papers*, Vol. 2, *General Equilibrium* (Oxford, 1983).
Fisher, M.R., 'Michael James Farrell 1926–1975', *Cambridge Review* (1975), November, pp. 47–8.
——, 'The Economic Contribution of Michael James Farrell', *Review of Economic Studies* (1976), vol. 43, pp. 371–82.

Cliff Pratten

FAWCETT, Henry (1833–84)

Fawcett was born on 26 August 1833, the son of a draper and Liberal mayor of Salisbury. He died in Cambridge on 6 November 1884. He was educated at Queenwood, a progressive school, King's College, London and Peterhouse and Trinity Hall, Cambridge. He was elected a fellow of Trinity Hall in 1856. In September 1858 he was blinded when his father accidentally shot him during a partridge shoot, but in spite of this disability he pursued an academic and a political career with distinction.

From an early age Fawcett was set upon a political career. Initially, he planned to be a lawyer in order to finance a career in politics, but blindness put an end to his legal ambitions and he switched to economics. In 1863 he was elected to the new chair of political economy at Cambridge University. Fawcett's contributions to economics were to popularize the views of the classical economists and apply classical economic theory. He seems not to have sought to question or develop existing theory. When he published the *Manual of Political Economy* in 1863, he viewed it as an easier and much shorter work than the *Principles of Political Economy* of his mentor and friend, J.S. MILL. Fawcett published six editions of the *Manual*, incorporating his research and views on contemporary economic issues and policies into successive editions.

Fawcett's primary interest was politics rather than economics. In 1865, he was elected MP for Brighton. In the 1874 election he was defeated at Brighton but quickly won an election to represent Hackney, a seat he held until his death. For many years he devoted the greatest part of his time and energy to Indian questions and was known as the 'Member for India'. He was a successful speaker and well-known as a politician, partly perhaps because of his blindness but also for his character and personality. He had a keen sense of justice and fair play.

Fawcett sought to apply the principles of economics to practical problems. The topics that he studied included the causes and consequences of combinations of employers and workers, strikes and co-operatives. He advocated co-operation, profit-sharing and co-ownership as ways of avoiding conflicts between employers and their employees.

Although Fawcett accepted classical economic theory and its *laissez-faire* implications, he showed flexibility on some issues, including regulation of the use of child labour and the introduction of compulsory education in agricultural districts. Nevertheless, he advocated emigration as a solution for unemployed textile workers, he was against restrictions being placed upon the hours of work for women, and he claimed that labour ought to be considered as a commodity, to be regulated like every other commodity.

In 1880 Fawcett published *Indian Finance*, in which he drew attention to the unsatisfactory administration and state of the public finances of India. He made a case for 'retrenchment', cuts in expenditure. He served as postmaster general in Gladstone's government from 1880 until 1884, during which time he introduced the parcel post and postal orders, lowered the price of telegrams and made changes to encourage people to bank small amounts of savings.

In 1867 Fawcett married Millicent Garrett; they had one daughter. Millicent Garrett FAWCETT took a prominent role in furthering the cause of the emancipation of women and, with Fawcett's assistance and support, expanding opportunities for women in higher education. Earlier he had taken an active part in the promotion of university reform. After his death, Millicent edited two further editions of the *Manual*.

BIBLIOGRAPHY
Manual of Political Economy (1863).
The Economic Position of the British Labourer (1865).
Pauperism: Its Causes and Remedies (1871).
(with M.G. Fawcett), *Essays and Lectures* (1872).
Free Trade and Protection: An Enquiry into the Causes which have Retarded the General Adoption of Free Trade (1878).
Indian Finance (1880).

Further Reading
Stephen, L., *Life of Henry Fawcett* (1885).
Goldman, L., *The Blind Victorian, Henry Fawcett, and British Liberalism* (Cambridge, 1989).

Cliff Pratten

FAWCETT, Millicent Garrett (1847–1929)

Millicent Garrett was born in Aldeburgh, Suffolk on 11 June 1847, and died in London on 5 August 1929. The Garretts were a wealthy business family: their political sympathies were strongly liberal and the milieu was a feminist one. There was strong family support for Elizabeth, one of her older sisters (afterwards Mrs Garrett Anderson) when she faced considerable obstacles in her ultimately successful attempt to obtain professional qualification as a medical practitioner.

Millicent was actively involved in a variety of reforming and political movements, and is best remembered as the leader of the constitutional section of the women's suffrage movement. She became a member of the first women's suffrage committee in 1867 – the year of her marriage to Henry FAWCETT – and made her first public speech on the subject the following year. For Fawcett, women's suffrage was an important pre-condition for other reforms and improvements in the status of women in an almost exclusively masculine state. But she also believed that, mainly through their domesticity 'women bring something to the service of the state different from that which can be brought by men' (1889: 9090). These were the broad tenets of the suffragists: those who sought to achieve votes for women on the same terms as men by means of rational argument conducted through speeches and pamphlets and pressure on politicians by petitions. Such constitutional methods set the National Union of Women's Suffrage Societies apart from the Women's Social and Political Union, founded in 1903 by Mrs Pankhurst and her daughter, whose members, known as suffragettes, engaged in more sensational and violent action, especially against property.

Both organizations suspended their campaigning on the outbreak of the First World War, but Millicent Fawcett was a prominent lobbyist when, in 1916, a conference was called by the Speaker of the House of Commons to examine a variety of issues concerning the parliamentary franchise. The subsequent legislation – the Representation of the People Act (1918) – extended the vote to women over the age of thirty with a basic property qualification. Ten years later and only one year before her death, Millicent Fawcett was in the gallery of the House of Lords to witness the final reading of the Equal Franchise Bill, which finally made male and female voters equal before the law at a uniform age of twenty-one.

In 1867 Millicent Garrett married Henry Fawcett, the blind professor of economics at Cambridge from 1863 until his death in 1884, and also Liberal MP for Brighton, and one of the leading parliamentary spokesmen for women's suffrage. Initially acting as his amanuensis, she subsequently produced her own best-selling textbooks *Political Economy for Beginners* (1870) and *Tales in Political Economy* (1874). In addition, she co-authored with her husband *Essays and Lectures on Social and Political Subjects* (1872), contributing eight of the fourteen chapters. These indicate the range of her interests including women's education (she was actually involved in the establishment of Newnham, a college for women students in Cambridge), women's suffrage, representative government and proportional representation (as a follower of John Stuart MILL), free education and the national debt. She opposed both of the latter: free education on the grounds that it would teach the poor that there was no need for thrift and self-restraint; the national debt principally because of its causes, expenditure on foreign wars and poor relief. She also published extensively in the pamphlet and periodical literature of the late Victorian period when her main contributions concerned women's suffrage, as well as their education and employment. Both before and after her husband's death, she lectured in political economy at Queen's College, London, and at King's College Department for Ladies, and was an active supporter of the University extension and adult education movement including the Working Men's College.

Within the context of both her writing and public activity, the education and employment of women were central concerns. In one of her earliest articles, published in 1868, she urged that girls' education should be greatly improved and that the range of occupations open to educated women should be extended. That remained a consistent objective, as is attested by her article on the use of higher education to women published in the late 1880s. She was equally averse to restrictions – especially by means of legislation – that were placed on the employment of women; hence her opposition to the Nine Hours Bill, presented to Parliament in 1873, and other measures that she believed threatened available employment for women. The primacy of her commitment to unrestricted women's employment helps to explain her support for women's trade unions, but this waned once the movement abandoned its opposition to protective legislation in the 1890s. Her support for a free market in labour had one exception, however. In the second half of the 1880s Millicent Fawcett allied herself – both publicly and by means of a series of articles – with those who sought to restrict the employment of children 'for gain', a campaign largely directed against the custom of employing children in the London theatres. The campaign, allied with broader concerns about child protection, led to the imposition of certain limited controls, which were subsequently extended in the early twentieth century.

Women's employment raised the issue of their remuneration, and specifically the question of equal pay. Fawcett set out her position in two articles during the 1890s. The essentials of her position were as follows. Because of the limited employment opportunities available to them, women tended to crowd into certain occupations, thereby causing their wages to be lower than men's. This idea, taken from J.S. MILL, was part of her rationale for women's trades unions. Their purpose was to ensure that women's interests and conditions were not overlooked. But her longer term strategy rested upon an increase in educational opportunities and in the number of professions and occupations open to women. 'What women most want is more training to enable them to pursue more skilled handicrafts and a larger number of professional occupations' (1892: 176). Those inter-related developments would enhance women's financial independence and economic status by improving their competitive position. The imposition of equal pay for equal work, on the other hand, she believed, would merely further restrict women's employment opportunities. This essentially *laissez-faire* approach was reinforced by her belief that wage levels should be determined only by the law of supply and demand. Equal pay requirements overlooked the disparities in the supply and demand for labour between different parts of the country. Wage rates, she believed, necessarily had to reflect such variations and market conditions.

In these debates of the 1880s and 1890s there was an interesting synergy between her thinking as a political economist, her personal involvement in educational concerns and her increasingly prominent commitment to the cause of women's suffrage. Yet in many respects her economic views remained static. Like her husband, she held to the principles of Ricardian economics (already in decline in England at the time she published her treatises on political economy in the 1870s) and the tenets of classical liberal individualism: competition, free trade, the primacy of the market and *laissez-faire* government. Paradoxically, Mrs Fawcett was also a woman of her time who played a major role – in both ideas and action – in creating a different world for the women of future generations.

BIBLIOGRAPHY

'The Medical and General Education of Women', *Fortnightly Review* (1868), vol. 10, pp. 554–71.
Political Economy for Beginners (1870).
(with H. Fawcett) *Essays and Lectures in Social and Political Subjects* (1872).
'National Debts and National Prosperity,' *Macmillan's Magazine* (1872), vol. 25, pp. 180–9.
Tales in Political Economy (1874).
'The Use of Higher Education to Women', *Contemporary Review* (1886), vol. 50, pp. 719–27.
'The Appeal Against Female Suffrage: A Reply', *Nineteenth Century* (1889), vol. 26, July, pp. 86–96.
'The Employment of Children in Theatres', *Contemporary Review* (1889), vol. 56, pp. 822–9.
'Mr Sidney Webb's Article on Women's Wages', *Economic Journal* (1892), vol. 1, pp. 173–6.
'Equal Pay for Equal work', *Economic Journal* (1918), vol. 28, pp. 1–6.

Further Reading
Rubinstein, D., *A Different World for Women: The Life of Millicent Garrett Fawcett* (Hemel Hempstead, 1991).
Strachey, R., *Millicent Garrett Fawcett* (1931).

David Gladstone

FELL, William (1758–1848)

Fell was born in 1758, probably at Brampton, Cumberland, and died at Shap, Westmoreland in March 1848. He was the younger brother of John Fell, a yeoman of Swindale Head Westmoreland. Fell found employment as a schoolmaster, first in at Manchester, then in Wilmslow, and finally in Lancaster. His one surviving son, Henry, went to live in Denmark.

Apart from teaching, Fell produced articles for the press and also published a number of other works. His *Hints on the Instruction of Youth* appeared in 1798, and in 1811 he wrote a criticism of Joseph Lancaster's system of education in which 'monitors' taught lessons by rote to other children. Following his retirement, Fell went to live at Clifton, near Lowther, Westmoreland where he owned a landed property of sufficient size to provide him with a reasonable standard of living. Fell disinherited his son and left the property to his brother's children.

Fell wrote two short works on economics, *Hints on the Causes of the High Prices of Provisions* (Penrith, 1800) and *A System of Political Economy* (Salford, 1808). The former suggests that the high cost of food and other commodities is due to artificially inflated prices caused by import restrictions, and suggests that Fell supports free trade. *A System of Political Economy* is largely an interpretation of Adam SMITH at a popular level and again supports free trade.

BIBLIOGRAPHY
Hints on the Instruction of Youth (Manchester, 1798).
Hints on the Causes of the High Prices of Provisions (Penrith, 1800).
A System of Political Economy (Salford, 1808).
Remarks on Mr. Lancaster's System of Education, in which his erroneous statements and the defects in his mode of tuition are detected and explained (Warrington, 1811).
A Sketch of the Principal Events in English History (Warrington, 1811; 2nd edition 1813).

Marjorie Bloy

FENTON, Roger (1565–1616)

Fenton was born in Lancashire some time in 1565, and died probably in London on 16 January 1615. He was educated at Pembroke Hall, Cambridge, where he received a doctorate in divinity some time before 1601. In that year he was made rector of St Stephen's Walbrook, resigning in 1606 to become vicar of Chigwell and, in 1609, rector of the parish as well. He served as chaplain to Sir Thomas Egerton, the lord chancellor, from around 1604 until an unknown date; possibly as late as 1611, as his *A Treatise of Usurie* is dedicated to Egerton. He also preached at Gray's Inn and to the Grocers' Company, and several of his sermons were published posthumously by Emmanuel Utie, who succeeded Fenton in the living of Chigwell. He was among the scholars who worked on the revised version of the Bible.

A Treatise of Usurie is Fenton's most substantial work. The bulk of the book is devoted to the condemnations of usury to be found in scripture, together with the opinions of canon and civil lawyers, the Church Fathers and pagan philosophers. However, Fenton is careful to define his subject rather more closely than many contemporary writers on the same subject. Usury, he says, is lending in hope and expectation of gain. He makes a distinction between usury *per se* and cases where goods are lent for use but with the lender retaining title to the property; thus someone who lends a house or a horse another to use for a period of time without transferring title is not engaging in usury, even if the lender charges a fee or rent for the service. Usury requires both goods and title to be transferred, and also requires a bond stating that the borrower will repay the money or goods with interest. This, says Fenton, implies consent by both parties, although he concedes that in some cases borrowers may not be aware that interest must be paid, and are thus innocent of the sin of usury (the lender, however, is not). Usury is also to be distinguished from rents, sales, exchange and other forms of economic activity. It is clear that Fenton intends to single out usury alone, and sees nothing harmful in these other forms of transaction.

It is on this transfer of both use and property that Fenton bases one of his major arguments against usury, claiming that the lender had no right to expect a return on something that was no longer his, even if only temporarily:

> I demand, then, during the time of the loane whose is the principall? Thine or the borrowers? It was thine before thou lent it, and it shall be thine at the day of payment; but during the time of the loane, it is the borrowers: for thou hast by covenant passed over both use and propertie to the borrower: so that during that time thou wilt not owne it; if it perish, it perisheth to the borrower, as to the right owner for that time. If it bee none of thine, then, but the borrowers for that time; I aske, by what right canst thou covenant to receive hire for the use of that which is none of the time, during the time it is not thine?
> (1611: 99)

He criticizes usurers for making money without taking risk. Their activities, he says, do not increase the stock of capital, but merely serve to concentrate capital in the hands of a few, and this is detrimental to the interests of the whole community: 'it is not good for a hive to nourish drones' (1611: 104). He also believes that usury encourages profligacy among the well-to-do, by providing them with money they would not otherwise have, and oppresses the poor, who are forced to borrow to make ends meet, and then borrow again to pay off the first debt. To those who argue that usury benefits the poor, who otherwise would lack the money for necessities, Fenton argues that if the poor need money, people should simply give it to them, or at least lend to them without gain.

Although Fenton notes the effects of usury, his criticism of it is, in the end, less than wholehearted. His definition of usury is a narrow one, and it seems clear that he is anxious not to criticize other forms of commercial activity, which he sees as being beneficial to the community and kingdom.

BIBLIOGRAPHY
A Treatise of Usurie (1611; 2nd edn, 1612).

Morgen Witzel

FERGUSON, Adam (1723–1816)

Ferguson was born at Logierait, Perthshire on 20 June 1723, and died at St Andrews on 22 February 1816. The son of a Presbyterian clergyman, Ferguson studied at St Andrews (MA, 1742) and Edinburgh, and was ordained a minister of the Church of Scotland in 1745. He served as chaplain to the Forty-Third Highland Regiment (the Black Watch) from 1745 until 1754; his first publication was a translation he had preached to the regiment in Gaelic during the Jacobite rebellion in 1745.

In 1756 Ferguson settled in Edinburgh, where he served as secretary to Lord Milton. He was elected to the Select Society of Edinburgh on 3 August that year, with David HUME presiding. In 1758 Ferguson became librarian of the Faculty of Advocates in succession to Hume, but resigned within a year in order to become tutor to Lord Bute's sons. In 1759 he was appointed to the chair of natural science at

Edinburgh College, and in 1764 transferred to the chair of moral philosophy. He published textbooks for his students in both natural and moral philosophy, and by all accounts was an excellent teacher. But it was not until his *Essay on the History of Civil Society* appeared in 1767 that he began to acquire a national reputation as a professor and author.

A witty political satire known as *Sister Peg* was published anonymously in London in December 1760 by Hume's friend and printer, William Strahan. This 188-page satirical allegory savages the opposers of a citizen militia for Scotland, and reconstructs the speeches in the House of Commons of both the opposers and supporters of the bill to extend the militia to Scotland, which had been defeated in the Commons in April 1760. The work has traditionally been attributed to Ferguson, and Hume's letter of 3 February 1761 acknowledging authorship has been entirely disregarded until recently. Opinion remains divided as to whether this continuation of Dr Arbuthnots *History of John Bull* was the work of Ferguson or Hume or both. But while the jury remains out, it is safe to say that *if* it was written by Ferguson then it is not only the most elaborate but also the most successful and most interesting of all his political pamphlets.

The *Essay on the History of Civil Society* traced the development of civil society from its 'rude' beginnings to its 'polished' forms, showing how this development was spontaneous, or how human institutions are 'the result of human action, but not the execution of any human design'. Along the way, Ferguson commented on many current issues, such as national defence, conquest, empire, political constitutions, the influence of climate upon the manners of a people, the history of arts and literature, the relation between the population and wealth of a country, and even the relations between the sexes. One of the distinctive features of the *Essay* is the attention paid to the bad effects of the division of labour in commercial societies, something that greatly impressed Karl MARX and, through him, many others since. The final parts of the book examine how nations decline and, in particular, how excessive luxury and the 'relaxation' of national spirit can corrupt political institutions and eventually lead to political slavery unless civic virtue is practised as well as preached.

When Hume read the *Essay* in manuscript, he strongly disapproved of it and advised against its publication, judging that it was not 'fit to be given to the public, neither on account of the Style nor the Reasoning'. Scholars have wondered exactly what Hume disliked about the *Essay*, but this is an unprofitable question to ask, given his remark that 'It is needless to enter into a Detail, where almost every thing appears to me exceptionable.' The *Essay* owed much to Montesquieu, and one of Ferguson's best friends suggested for this reason that it 'ought only to be considered as a college exercise'. Ferguson himself, in 1792, refused to revise the book because 'it is properly introductory & Stimulating of its Subject'. Introductory or not, Ferguson's *Essay* and other philosophical works reached an enviably large readership.

In 1778 Ferguson was appointed secretary to the Commissioners selected to settle Britain's dispute with her American colonies. In 1785 he retired from the chair of moral philosophy, publishing in 1792 a two-volume 'retrospect' of his lectures. This work, though seldom discussed, has the best claim to be considered his most mature reflections on moral philosophy. During his long old age he amused himself by composing essays which have only recently been published. His essay on 'The Principles of Moral Estimation' reconstructs contemporary criticisms of Adam SMITH's *Theory of Moral Sentiments*, and deserves to be better known.

BIBLIOGRAPHY

An Essay on the History of Civil Society (1767; 2nd, 3rd edns, 1768; 4th edn, 1773; 5th edn, 1782; 6th edn 1793).
The History of the Proceedings in the Case of Margaret, commonly called Peg, only

lawful Sister to John Bull, Esq (1760; 2nd edn, 1761; 3rd edn, Edinburgh 1761; 4th edn, 1776).
The History of the Progress and Termination of the Roman Republic (1783).
Principles of Moral and Political Science: Being Chiefly a Retrospect of Lectures Delivered in the College of Edinburgh, 2 vols (1792).
The Unpublished Essays of Adam Ferguson, 3 vols, ed. W.M. Philip (1986).
'"Of the Principle of Moral Estimation: A Discourse between David Hume, Robert Clerk, and Adam Smith": An Unpublished MS by Adam Ferguson', ed. E.C. Mossner, *Journal of the History of Ideas* (1960), vol. 21, pp. 223–32.
The Correspondence of Adam Ferguson, ed. V. Merolle, 2 vols (1995).

Further Reading

Brewer, A., 'Adam Ferguson, Adam Smith, and the Concept of Economic Growth', *History of Political Economy* (1999), vol. 31, pp. 237–54.
Hamowy, R., 'Adam Smith, Adam Ferguson and the Division of Labour', *Economica* (1968), vol. 35, pp. 249–59.
——, 'Progress and Commerce in Anglo-American Thought: The Social Philosophy of Adam Ferguson', *Interpretation* (1986), vol. 14, pp. 61–87.
Kettler, D., *The Social and Political Thought of Adam Ferguson*, Columbus, Ohio, 1965).

David R. Raynor

FIELDING, Henry (1707–54)

Fielding was born on 22 April 1707 at Sharpham Park in Somerset, and died on 8 October 1754 near Lisbon, Portugal. His maternal grandfather, Sir Henry Gould, was a King's Bench Judge, and his paternal grandfather, John Fielding, was a canon of Salisbury cathedral. His father was a general who had served under the Duke of Marlborough. Fielding was educated at Eton, where he developed his profound love of the classics, and also at the University of Leiden. He married Charlotte Cradock in 1734; she died in 1744, and Fielding remarried in 1747. During his early career, Fielding earned his living by writing and producing plays and enjoyed great success in the theatres of London. However, the passing of the Stage Licensing Act in 1737 effectively ended his theatrical career and he turned to the law, being called to the bar in 1740 and made a justice of the peace in 1748. Between 1728 and 1737, Fielding wrote a number of plays, including *The Grub Street Opera* (1731). He edited *The Champion* from 1739–41, *The Patriot* from 1745–6, *The Jacobite's Journal* in 1747–8 and *The Covent-Garden Journal* in 1752. His novels include *Shamela* (1741), *Joseph Andrews* (1842), *Tom Jones* (1749) and *Amelia* (1751).

Fielding is more readily associated with novels rather than with economics, but both these activities were shaped by his experiences in the courts. The people who came before him both stimulated his imagination and allowed him to understand the economic basis of crime. Fielding saw time and again how people could be pushed into crime by impoverished circumstances rather than by anti-social impulses. Unemployment, poor housing, access and addiction to cheap alcohol all created situations for unfortunate people to fall into crime. In the 1750s, Fielding wrote two pamphlets, *An Enquiry into the Cause of the Late Increase in Robbers* (1751) and *A Proposal for Making Effective Provision for the Poor – A Scheme for Hostels, Workshops and Infirmaries* (1753). In *An Enquiry*, Fielding argued that social changes over the last few hundred years had created a situation in which the 'commonalty' had been emancipated from feudalism and had acquired financial resources and freedom. He argued that this led many to try to emulate the upper classes' leisure pursuits, notably drinking and gambling. However, as the 'commonalty' did not have sufficient means to fund this, they were liable to fall into debt and ruin, and potentially into crime. Interestingly, Fielding also looked at the economic and medical impact of alcoholism: he was concerned that women who drank while pregnant gave birth not to healthy future workers, but to babies who in time would 'fill Alms-houses and Hospitals' (1751: 90). He also saw the fixing of wages at low levels as a method by which to lower the unit cost of British goods and to stimulate trade, and in doing so, to create further jobs to ease the problem of unemployment.

Fielding's views on social economy were taken further in *A Proposal*. He was concerned that a large number of the 'able' poor were unwilling to work, therefore weakening the economy. He argued that the best solution was to concentrate the poor in immense workhouses, which would also have a religious, reforming character. As a respected justice of the peace and member of London society, Fielding's views on the social and economic impact of crime were well received by his contemporaries. Although his economic pamphlets were overshadowed by his reputation as a novelist, they are still worth reading as a way of understanding the social and economic impulses behind the development of policing and the law in Britain.

BIBLIOGRAPHY
An Enquiry into the Causes of the Late Increase of Robbers (1751).
A Proposal for Making an Effectual Provision for the Poor (1753).

Further Reading
Battestin, M.C. and Battestin R.R., *Henry Fielding: A Life* (1989).
Thomas, D., *Henry Fielding* (1990).
Uglow, J., *Henry Fielding* (Plymouth, 1995).
Zirker, M.R., 'General Introduction', *An Enquiry into the Causes of the Late Increase in Robbers and Related Writings, The Wesleyan Edition of the Works of Henry Fielding* (Oxford, 1988).

Katharine Bradley

FIRMIN, Thomas (1632–97)

Firmin was born at Ipswich some time in June 1632, and died of typhoid fever in London on 20 December 1697. After apprenticing with a London mercer, Firmin established his own mercery in Lombard Street, probably in 1655. He made the shop into a prosperous business, and in 1676 handed over the management of it to his nephew so that he could devote more time to charitable work. In 1673 he was appointed a governor of Christ's Hospital; he lost this post briefly thanks to his opposition to James II, but was restored on the accession of William and Mary. In 1693 he became a governor of St Thomas's Hospital. He became interested in the welfare of prisoners, and worked to alleviate conditions in some of the harshest prisons.

Firmin's philanthropy took many forms. He helped to raise money for the victims of religious persecution in Poland and in Ireland, but he was best known for his attempts to provide work for the poor of London. Following the plague of 1665, Firmin set up a scheme whereby tradesmen thrown out of work could buy wool cheaply and make cloth, which Firmin would then guarantee to buy from them. The initial success of this encouraged Firmin in 1676 to begin providing flax to poor families which they could spin and weave into linen; again, Firmin would buy the finished cloth from them. The difference between his scheme and ordinary workhouses was that people carried out work in their own homes, rather than in an institution. Firmin continued the scheme until his death, but it never proved profitable and he was often forced to subsidize the workers out of his own money.

Firmin held deep religious convictions throughout his life, and included many clergymen and divines among his friends. John Tillotson, who later became Archbishop of Canterbury, was a close friend and also godfather to Firmin's son Giles. One of the strongest influences was the Unitarian clergyman John Biddle, who played a particular role in developing Firmin's views on charity and philanthropy. Like Biddle, Firmin believed that simply handing out alms to the poor was not enough; the real aim ought to be the prevention of poverty, not simply its alleviation.

Like his contemporary and friend Richard HAINES, Firmin believed that the causes of poverty were economic, and that the best way to assist the poor was to provide them with work. He disagreed with Haines as to how this should be done: the former believed that the best method was to provide workhouses where the poor could congregate and provide labour in exchange for food and money. Firmin argued that this could never succeed:

> I perceived that the only way to provide for our Poor, and to bring them to labour, is to provide such Work for them as they may do at their own Homes, which though never so mean and homely, is more desired than any other place, and the way which several Persons have proposed, of bringing them to a publick Work-house, will never effect the end intended.
>
> (1678: 4)

Firmin believed that the only measures to alleviate poverty that could succeed were those that allowed the poor to retain their dignity. He was concerned about the lack of skills by which people could earn a living, and suggested that parishes set up schools to teach every child a trade or a craft. As regards to trade he was a protectionist, calling for the prohibition of imported cloth and taking the view that a strong export trade in cloth would help alleviate poverty by providing greater employment for the poor.

BIBLIOGRAPHY

Some Proposals for the Imploying of the Poor, especially in and about London, and for the Prevention of Begging (1678; 2nd expanded edn, 1681).

Further Reading

Anon., *The Life of Mr Thomas Firmin, Late Citizen of London* (1698).

Cornish, J., *The Life of Mr Thomas Firmin, Citizen of London* (1780).

Dean, M. *The Constitution of Poverty* (1991).

Morgen Witzel

FISHER, Frederick Jack (1908–88)

Jack Fisher was born 22 July 1908 in Southend, Essex and died in London on 7 January 1988. He attended Southend High School, and studied history at the London School of Economics (LSE) where he took his BA (Hons) in 1928 and his MA (with distinction) in 1931, with a thesis on provincial industrial guilds under James I and Charles I. In 1930 he joined the London School of Economics as assistant in history, becoming assistant lecturer in 1935 and lecturer in 1939. His career was interrupted by the Second World War when he served in the Royal Air Force in East Africa and the Middle East with the rank of squadron leader. From 1943–6 he was seconded as deputy economic and financial advisor to the Minister of State in Egypt.

After the war Fisher returned to the LSE, and was promoted to reader in 1947 and professor of economic history in 1954, a post he held until retirement in 1975. At LSE he was widely known as an unenthusiastic administrator, informal head of department and a remarkable, stimulating, even 'scintillating', teacher. His dedication to his undergraduate and postgraduate students underpinned the careers of a generation of economic historians during the subject's heyday. From 1974 he chaired a seminar at the Institute of Historical Research on the economic and social history of early modern England, universally known as the 'Fisher Seminar', until a few years before his death, where he demonstrated his incomparable expertise as chairman, critic and debater. He did not suffer fools gladly, was a great iconoclast and had no time for pomposity or pretension. He served as president of the Economic History Society from 1974–7.

Fisher's published writings span the years 1933–71. Not a prolific author, he nevertheless published a number of highly influential articles on the economic history of early modern England. While he edited two important original sources, Thomas Wilson's *State of England, Anno Dom. 1600* (1936) and the *Letters relating to Lionel Cranfield's business overseas, 1597–1612* (1966), his legacy to economic history lies essentially in the stimulus and challenge of these articles, which show an abiding interest in the position of London within English economy and society, and a concern with the prospects for, and constraints upon, economic growth. His elucidation of the profound influence of London upon the wider economy, through its role in consumption, production, distribution and as a cultural catalyst, was laid out in two key articles on 'The Development of London as a Centre of Conspicuous Consumption' (1948) and 'London as an "Engine of Economic Growth"' (1971). Recent work has elaborated rather than refuted this thesis, which has been generalized to some of the larger provincial towns. His work on the London port books, published as 'Commercial Trends and Policy' (1940) and 'London's Export Trade' (1950), still underpins our understanding of English trade 1500–1640. More influential still have been his broad characterizations of the English economy, developed in 'The Sixteenth and Seventeenth Centuries: The Dark Ages in English Economic History?' (1957) and 'Tawney's Century' (1960). Acutely aware of the impossibility of confident generalization, rejecting the simplicity of received systems though willing to borrow the conceptual apparatus of economics and sociology, he elaborated a model of English economic development in which constraint dominated over appetite before 1640, yet intimated with remarkable foresight that further research would demonstrate the greater progress of the English economy in the later seventeenth century. While this latter view has been largely validated, it is only in recent years that his perhaps overly pessimistic analysis of the sixteenth and early seventeenth centuries has begun to be seriously questioned.

BIBLIOGRAPHY

'The Influence and Development of the Industrial Guilds in the larger Provincial Towns under James I and Charles I, with Special Reference to the Formation of New Corporations for the Control of Industry', unpublished MA dissertation, London School of Economics (1931).

'The Development of the London Food Market, 1540–1640, *Economic History Review* (1935), vol. 5, pp. 46–64.

The State of England, Anno Dom. 1600 By Sir Thomas Wilson (1936).

'Commercial Trends and Policy in Sixteenth-Century England', *Economic History Review* (1940), vol. 10, pp. 95–117.

'The Development of London as a Centre of Conspicuous Consumption in the Sixteenth and Seventeenth Centuries', *Transactions of the Royal Historical Society*, 4th series (1948), vol. 30, pp. 37–50.

'London's Export Trade in the Early Seventeenth Century', *Economic History*

Review, 2nd series (1950), vol. 3, pp. 151–61.
'The Sixteenth and Seventeenth Centuries: The Dark Ages in English Economic History?', *Economica*, new series (1957), vol. 24, pp. 2–18.
'Tawney's Century', in F.J. Fisher (ed.), *Essays in the Economic and Social History of Tudor and Stuart England* (Cambridge, 1961, pp. 1–14).
Calendar of the Manuscripts of the Rt. Hon. Lord Sackville of Knole, Sevenoaks, Kent: II, Letters relating to Lionel Cranfield's business overseas, 1597–1612 (1966).
'London as an "Engine of Economic Growth"', in J.S. Bromley and E.H. Kossman (eds), *Britain and the Netherlands, IV: Metropolis, Dominion and Province* (The Hague, 1971, pp. 3–16).

Further Reading
Corfield, P.J. and Harte, N.B. (eds), *London and the English economy, 1500–1700: F.J. Fisher* (1990).

Nigel Goose

FITZNIGEL, Richard (*c.*1130–98)

Richard FitzNigel (sometimes FitzNeal) was born about 1130, certainly before 1133, and died on 10 September 1198. He was educated at the monastery at Ely, where he lived for most of his youth. He was the illegitimate son of the Bishop of Ely, Nigel, who had served as treasurer to King Henry I. His unidentified mother is believed to have derived from English stock. Nigel and other members of his family fell from official grace during the reign of Stephen, and the first records of Richard's existence indicate that he was twice a hostage in Stephen's captivity as surety for his father's good conduct, probably in 1141–3 and again in late 1144.

When Henry II succeeded Stephen as king in 1154, Nigel was called upon to assist in the restoration of the Exchequer. Nigel seems to have arranged a series of administrative jobs for his son, culminating in his appointment as treasurer in 1158. Despite stories that Richard's rapid rise may be attributed to venal practices, his progress was not particularly remarkable in the context of the times.

While serving the king, Richard also entered into the administrative service of the church. He became archdeacon of Ely around 1160, and when his father, who left the king's service about 1165, became ill (eventually dying in 1169), he administered the affairs of the cathedral. At some point, probably during the 1160s, Richard received a papal dispensation for illegitimacy, since in later years he received preferment in succession as canon of St Paul's, archdeacon of Colchester and dean of Lincoln. He was elected Bishop of London in 1189.

Richard's ecclesiastical career was paralleled by his continued activity as a royal justice in the counties. He also served Henry II as an emissary to the Exchequer of Normandy in 1176. Service to the king proved financially remunerative; he was granted the income of several royal manors during the course of his career.

Richard's reputation turns less, however, on his administrative work than on his composition of the *Dialogus de Scaccario* (Dialogue of the Exchequer), a practical manual replete with detailed descriptive accounts of royal fiscal operations. Probably written between December 1176 and Easter 1179, the *Dialogus* contains a discussion between a Master (presumably Richard) and a Disciple concerning the organization and practices of the central financial mechanisms of Henry II's Exchequer. Richard's purpose in recording how and why this system functions is to pass on knowledge to future generations of royal servants. Thus, he declines to make grandiose claims for the content and the expression found in the *Dialogus*. Richard signals that the book is a work of practical advice, of the sort that was becoming more common by the end of the twelfth century, rather than a philosophical investigation. He proposes to draw on his own experience, instead of upon the wisdom of the ancients and arguments of subtle logic, to fill the pages of his volume. There is, in any case, serious doubt as to whether Richard's intellectual and verbal skills would have been up to such a task.

At the heart of the *Dialogus* is a theory of public management. Richard insists upon the king's need to gather wealth in order to rule effectively. Consequently, the work of the Exchequer in receiving, calculating and dispensing the royal treasury lies at the heart of government. The loyalty and honesty of royal fiscal administrators are made by Richard the *sine qua non* of a well-ordered society and a properly functioning government. Richard wishes to teach future generations of magistrates how to conduct themselves because he believes that upon them rests the burden of ensuring the continuation and glory of the king and of the realm. Richard may not be writing philosophy in the technical sense, but his book has a moral and political force.

BIBLIOGRAPHY
Dialogus de Scaccario, ed. C. Johnson (Oxford, 1950).

Further Reading
Hudson, J., 'Administration, Family and Perceptions of the Past in Late Twelfth-Century England: Richard FitzNigel and the *Dialogue of the Exchequer*', in P. Magdalino (ed.), *The Perception of the Past in Twelfth-Century Europe* (1992).

Cary Nederman

FLEETWOOD, William (1656–1723)

William Fleetwood was born in the Tower of London on 1 January 1656, the son of a clerk in the Ordnance Office. He died 4 August 1723 at Tottenham, Middlesex. He was educated at Eton and King's College, Cambridge (BA 1679, MA 1683, DD 1705).

A talent for preaching, first manifest in a sermon in 1689 at King's College to commemorate the founder, marked Fleetwood out for a great career in the Church of England. He was one of the most popular preachers of his day, often addressing the royal court and parliament. Eton awarded him a fellowship in 1689 and a living in the City of London at Farringdon, but he moved to the parish of Wexham, Buckinghamshire in 1706 to pursue his growing historical and antiquarian interests. Further preferment came quickly to him: he was canon of Windsor, then Bishop of St Asaph 1708, and finally Bishop of Ely 1714. His success came partly from his ability and partly through his loyalty as a Whig to the Hanoverian Succession and the Protestant Settlement. In a preface to his collected sermons in 1712 he mentioned the discord created by the Tories, who formed the majority in the House of Commons, and caused an uproar. The book was burned by the public hangman, but was reprinted by *The Spectator* and sold in thousands.

Fleetwood was a general scholar. His first work, on Christian and pagan inscriptions, was published in 1691. From the outset of his career, some of his sermons had an economic theme. Before the Lord Mayor of London in 1694, he argued against clipping coinage. Money he described as 'the common Measure of the Worth and Price of everything besides', which should be portable, durable and beautiful, hence the popularity of precious metals for coinage. He noted the losses to labouring people and to foreign commerce arising from debasement of the currency. In another London sermon in 1718, he strenuously made the case for debts to be paid. He attributed the ruin of many debt-ridden families to the desire to make a great fortune in a little time; previously, slower wealth accumulation had enabled families to retain their estates longer.

In his anonymous *Chronicon Preciosum* (1707), Fleetwood endeavoured to discover the relative value of estates in 1440 and 1700, to help a correspondent who would lose the fellowship of an Oxford college if he had outside income in excess of £5. Fleetwood set out to show how much bread, drink, meat, cloth and books could be purchased at the earlier and later dates. He tabulated the changing prices of many commodities, recorded stipends at different dates and stated the varying values of a host of gold and silver coins. Most of the prices grew at the same rate. He concluded that £5 in the fifteenth century would be worth £28 or £30 at the beginning of the eighteenth, some 260 years later. His approach was to chronicle price changes rather than to create a price index weighting the components according to each commodity's importance in a consumer's budget. This precursor to price indices was more in the spirit of TOOKE than of JEVONS and EDGEWORTH.

BIBLIOGRAPHY
A Sermon against Clipping (1694).
Chronicon Preciosum (1707, 1745).
The Justice of Paying Debts (1718).

Further Reading
Buss, R.W., *The Ancestry of William Fleetwood Bishop of St Asaph and Ely with a pedigree* (1926).
Chance, W.A., 'A Note on the Origins of Index Numbers', *Review of Economics and Statistics* (1966) vol. 48, no. 1, pp. 108–10.

Donald Rutherford

FLEMMING, John Stanton (1941–2003)

John Flemming was born in Reading on 6 February 1941, and died of cancer in Oxford on 5 August 2003. He was educated at Rugby school and Trinity College, Oxford, where he obtained a first in philosophy, politics and economics in 1962. He was awarded a studentship at Nuffield College, Oxford, and in 1963 was appointed fellow and lecturer at Oriel College. In 1965 he moved to an official fellowship of Nuffield College, a post he held until 1980. During 1968–9 he held a Harkness Fellowship in the United States, spending most of the year at Harvard. In 1980 became chief economist at the Bank of England; from 1984–8 he was economic adviser to the Governor of the Bank, and from 1988–91 he was an executive director of the Bank. In 1991 he became chief economist at the European Bank for Reconstruction and Development; two years later, in 1993, he returned to Oxford as Warden of Wadham College, a post he held till his death. He was elected an emeritus fellow of Nuffield College in 1980, fellow of the British Academy in 1991, a vice president of the Royal Economic Society, and he was awarded a CBE for his services to economics and his work on the environment in 2001. He received an honorary doctorate from Brunel University in 2003.

Flemming was managing editor of the *Economic Journal* from 1975–80, and before that had been involved in editing two other journals. He was a member of the Meade Committee on taxation, and of the Clare Group, an independent group of economists who produced widely read analyses of economic policy issues facing the UK. At Nuffield, he was bursar from 1970–9, managing its investments. He played a similar role as treasurer of the Royal Economic Society from 1992–98 at a time when the Society was beginning to take a more active role in promoting the profession of economics in Britain. He was involved with numerous organizations: the Royal Economic Society, the Institute for Fiscal Studies, the Economic and Social Research Council, the British Academy, the National Institute of Economic and Social Research, the Oxford Institute of Ageing, and Brunel University. He was a Member of the Royal Commission on Environmental Pollution.

Flemming's work spanned several fields of economics, though with a bias towards policy-related problems and macroeconomics. Though he used technical theory, much of his work was in a style that was more widely accessible. His early work was on saving and investment, where he was one of few people to explore the implications of capital market imperfections. This work, which paid great attention to wealth and the distribution of wealth, fitted in closely with the work on taxation that led to his first book, written with his Oxford colleague Ian Little, *Why We Need a Wealth Tax* (1974). During the mid-1970s he tackled the problem of inflation, writing what is probably his most widely-read book, *Inflation* (1976). A feature of this book was the emphasis Flemming placed on expectations, the importance of which economists were rapidly becoming aware during this period of high inflation. In analysing British economic problems, as well as discussing the macroeconomic side (wages, inflation and unemployment), he paid attention to the implications of policy for public finance, and to the microeconomic effects of economic policy, including effects on the distribution of income. As well as writing on macroeconomic issues, Flemming continued to work on taxation, tackling the subject both theoretically (looking at optimal taxation in dynamic, stochastic models) and in work more directly related to public policy such as the Meade Report. This followed on from his earlier book, advocating the replacement of income tax with an expenditure tax topped up with wealth and transfer taxes. Problems of inflation and unemployment, structural change, saving, investment and the distribution of wealth remained important during his time at the European Bank for Reconstruction and Development in 1991, when Eastern Europe was starting its transition towards a market economy.

In his economics, Flemming regularly used mathematical models. However, he did not confine his attention to what could be said using such methods. James Mirrlees (2003) said of him that he had the knack of thinking of good questions that were too difficult for others to handle and conjecturing answers that they could not verify. John Helliwell (2003) commented on his ability to know when to apply economic tools to problems and when not to do so. Flemming was widely respected by theorists and policy makers and by economists with a wide range of political and economic views.

BIBLIOGRAPHY
(with I.M.D. Little) *Why We Need a Wealth Tax* (1974).
Inflation (Oxford: Oxford University Press, 1976).

Further Reading
Blaug, M., 'Flemming, John Stanton', *Who's Who in Economics* (Cheltenham, 1999).
Helliwell, J.F. 'John Flemming', *The Independent* (2003), 12 August.
Mirrlees, J. and Hutton, W., 'John Flemming', *The Guardian* (2003), 25 August.

Roger Backhouse

FLETCHER, Andrew (1653–1716)

Fletcher was born in Saltoun, East Lothian in 1653, the son of the laird, and died on 15 September 1716 in London. He succeeded his father, Sir Robert Fletcher of Saltoun in 1665. His father brought Gilbert Burnet, the historian who was later Bishop of Salisbury, to be the parish minister and tutor to his sons. For five years Fletcher was taught Latin, history, geography, Greek, French and Italian then briefly attended Edinburgh and St Andrews universities. With a collection of six hundred books, largely theological, he had one of the leading libraries in Scotland.

Fletcher's political career, which was to earn him the nickname 'The Patriot' for his determination to preserve a separate Scottish parliament, began with his being a commissioner for the shire of Haddington in the Scottish parliament of 1678. His political opinions necessitated his flight to Holland in 1682. He supported Monmouth's rebellion in 1685, and was forced to flee to Spain for shooting the mayor of Taunton in a dispute over a horse. In 1686 he was found guilty of treason and lost his estates, not receiving them back until 1690. He accompanied the future King William to London in 1688, but soon was discouraged by the king's failure to recognize Scotland's rights. In 1693 he took a leading role in the setting up the Darien Company by introducing its projector, William PATERSON, to the minister for Scotland, the Marquis for Tweeddale. In the Darien venture, which financially ruined so many Scots, Fletcher subscribed personally £1,000.

The peak of Fletcher's parliamentary career was in the parliaments of 1703 and 1704. He argued strongly for limitations on the Scottish monarchy, and wanted the succession to the Scottish throne to be decided separately. He argued also that Scotland had been subordinated to England since the union of the crowns in 1603, and virtually accused the government of using bribes to effect the union of the Scottish and English parliaments. In 1708 he was arrested and briefly detained when a French fleet thought to be supporting the Jacobites was seen off the coast. In his latter years he travelled frequently to France, Holland and London, where he died unmarried.

Most of Fletcher's writing was done between 1697 and 1704 and focussed on Scotland's government, defence and economy, largely with a view to opposing the incorporation of Scotland into a new Great Britain. In his *Discourse Concerning the Affairs of Spain* (1698) he found a parallel case of a country which had declined and has the possibility of renewal. Fletcher argued that the establishment of a city near the straits of Gibraltar, the meeting place of the great seas, would revive the country. This was obviously similar to the Darien scheme to open up the isthmus of Panama, then underway in 1698 (Robertson 1997: 88n). Fletcher observed that the Spanish, through living off the precious metals from their American mines, had allowed manufacturing to decline and relied on the English, French and Dutch for imported necessities. He argued for re-population and religious toleration. As the population grew, agriculture would increase, then manufacturing, commerce and navigation would expand. The imitation of industrious foreigners would be important. The expansion of shipping would provide the basis for a powerful navy.

In an *Account of a Conversation* (1704), Fletcher reviewed the causes of decay in the Scottish economy. Because of the union of the crowns of England and Scotland in 1603, Scottish trade with several European countries had been severed, leading to a depression in Scotland which had pushed down rents. Also, many rich Scots had migrated to London thereby diverting demand from Scotland and exhausting its wealth. The government of Scotland had effectively moved to London. After a union incorporating Scotland, economic decline would be more rapid. With distinct sovereignty, Scotland would retain its wealth. Having several seats of government would tend to improve all arts and sciences and provide more entertainment. Union with England would also destroy Scottish agriculture and manufacturing, which could not compete with cheaper English substitutes. Fletcher noted that the Scottish population was declining because of famine, levies of soldiers and the failure of government policy to promote industry was encouraging emigration to Ireland. He did not narrow his policy recommendations to trade because governments ought to encourage trade, as mankind has the right to the product of its labour. God had created well-stocked agriculture so that the human population might grow. Fletcher argued for the dispersal of centres of economic power. He suggested that Europe should be divided into city-states, each consisting of an urban centre and the surrounding countryside.

Fletcher is most famous in economics for his policy response to the widespread poverty in Scotland after eight years of poor harvests. In the second of *Two Discourses* (1698), he noted that there were 200,000 vagrants wandering through Scotland: he attributed this nuisance originally to the freeing of slaves by Christians since the time of Constantine. Controversially, Fletcher set out arguments for a modified system of slavery to absorb the poor vagabonds. A 'slave', he pointed out, can either be absolutely controlled by another, or someone under certain limitations for the good of the commonwealth. Under Fletcher's scheme the 'slave' would be subject to laws rather than to a master, and would be given subsistence in return for executing services. To ensure there was a full coverage of this form of poor relief, 'every man of a certain estate' would take a proportion of the adult vagabonds to engage them in work such as hedging and ditching. They would train destitute children in mechanics creating in every substantial house a manufactory. The sick and infirm would be sent to almshouses.

Fletcher argued that widespread poverty had partly arisen due to high rents which were fixed in corn and not money, with the consequence that tenants could not afford suitable capital investment. He also proposed the drastic remedies of gradually abolishing the payment of interest, and redistributing land so that the limit to ownership would be the acreage cultivated by the farmer's own servants.

BIBLIOGRAPHY
A Discourse concerning the affairs of Spain (1698).
A Discourse of Government with relation to Militias (1698).
Two Discourses concerning the Affairs of Scotland written in the year 1698 (1698).
Speeches by a Member of Parliament which began at Edinburgh the 6th May 1703 (Edinburgh, 1704).
An Account of a Conversation concerning the right regulation of governments for the common good of Mankind (Edinburgh, 1704).
Political Works, ed. J. Robertson (Cambridge, 1997).

Further Reading
Scott, P.H., *Andrew Fletcher and the Treaty of Union* (Edinburgh, 1992).

Donald Rutherford

FLINN, Michael Walter (1917–83)

Flinn was born 22 October 1917 at Fallowfield, Manchester, and died 29 September 1983 in Gloucestershire. After attending William Hulme's Grammar School, Manchester, he worked for a cotton exporting business. During the war he was an officer in the Royal Artillery, and married a professional pianist, Grace, in 1943. Manchester University awarded him a BA in History 1950, diploma in education 1951 and MA 1952; he also received a D Litt from Edinburgh University in 1965. He taught at Grangefield Grammar School, Stockton-on-Tees and Isleworth Grammar School, Middlesex, and was a research assistant at Aberdeen University (1954–5). In 1959 Flinn was appointed to a lectureship at Edinburgh University. He was promoted swiftly, to a senior lectureship in

1964, a readership in 1965, and then a personal chair in social history in 1967. His early career as a schoolteacher helped him to write a textbook on economic and social history, which remained in print throughout his life. Always a keen administrator, he undertook the onerous tasks of being Principal Warden of Halls and Houses (1971–2) and dean of the Faculty of Social Sciences (1975–8), taking early retirement in 1978. He was president of the British Economic History Society (1980–83).

Flinn's thesis work for his MA on British overseas investment in iron ore mining, 1870–1914, gave direction to his research for the next fifteen years. His 1958 article, 'The Growth of the English Iron Industry, 1660–1760', emphasized data on new investment as a guide to the expansion of the iron industry; he also explained the industry's high costs. For ten years, Flinn investigated the late seventeenth and early eighteenth-century origins of the Crowley Ironworks. As the firm's records had been destroyed, Flinn used extant letters and reports of visitors to the works. He traced the development of nail-making into a large-scale firm practising paternalistic capitalism with an imaginative arbitration system. In his *Origins of the Industrial Revolution* (1966), he included an outstanding explanation of the social origins of the revolution (Saul 1984: vi).

Gradually Flinn turned to demography and related aspects of social history. He showed his mastery of the literature on sanitary reform in his edition of Edwin CHADWICK's report (1965), headed a team to study Scottish population changes, and later examined European demographic change. In his 1974 contribution to the standard of living debate, he concluded that most of the real wage gains, some 2–3 per cent annually, occurred in the period 1813–25.

In retirement, Flinn wrote the history of the British coal industry in the eighteenth century. From manuscript records of collieries, basic statistics on the industry were created to establish that the remarkable expansion in coal output had not incurred an increase in its real cost of production: the steam pump in particular coped with the drainage and ventilation problems of deeper mining. Flinn finished the reading of the proofs and the preparation of the index, and then died suddenly.

BIBLIOGRAPHY

'The Growth of the English Iron Industry, 1660–1760', *Economic History Review* (1958), second series, vol. XI, pp. 144–53.

An Economic and Social History of Britain, 1066–1930 (1961).

Men of Iron: The Crowleys in the Early Iron Industry (Edinburgh, 1962).

An Economic and Social History of Britain since 1700 (1963).

'Introduction' to *Report on the Sanitary Condition of Labouring Population of Gt. Britain by Edwin Chadwick, 1842* (Edinburgh, 1965, pp. 1–73).

The Origins of the Industrial Revolution (1966).

'Trends in Real Wages, 1750–1850', *Economic History Review* (1974), second series, vol. XXVII, pp. 395–413.

Scottish Population History (Cambridge, 1977).

The European Demographic System 1500–1820 (Brighton, 1981).

(with David Stoker) *The History of the British Coal Industry*, vol. 2, *1700–1820 The Industrial Revolution* (Oxford, 1982).

Further Reading

Saul, S.B., 'Obituary: Professor Michael W Flinn 1917–1983', *Economic History Review* (1984), new series, vol. 37, no. 1, pp. v–vii.

Donald Rutherford

FLORENCE, Philip Sargant (1890–1982)

Florence was born in Passiac, New Jersey on 25 June 1890, the son of the musician Henry Smythe Florence and the artist and writer Mary Sargant Florence. He died on 29 January 1982 in Birmingham. After education at Rugby School and Caius College, Cambridge, where he took an MA, he went to New York to study for his PhD at Columbia University. From 1917 to 1921 he was lecturer at the Bureau of Industrial Research and Bureau of Personnel Administration in New York. Much of his early interest in industrial economics, particularly in the sociology of labour, stems from this period. He married Lella Faye Secor in 1917, and the couple had two sons and two daughters; both the latter died young. Florence retained a lifelong affection for America, and at least one of his sons subsequently lived there.

Returning to Britain in 1921, Florence held a variety of posts at Cambridge until 1929, mainly at Magdalene College and in the Department of Economics. He was not entirely happy at Cambridge, however, and preferred to be closer to the industries and businesses that were the objects of his study. This led him to move to the University of Birmingham's Faculty of Commerce in 1929, where he remained for the rest of his career. He became professor of commerce, a post previously held by William ASHLEY; one of his inheritances from Ashley was a map of Britain, showing routes owned by different railway companies coded in different colours, that Ashley had used in his own lectures. His own lecturing style was engaging and articulate, and a former pupil, Michael BEESLEY, remembers him speaking from what appeared to be a 'compost pile' of notes. He attached great importance to observing and measuring phenomena, and had little time for speculative economics. Florence remained Professor of Commerce until 1955.

Florence served as dean of the Faculty of Commerce from 1947 to 1950, and was seen as the faculty's leading light for many years. He embodied the inter-disciplinary approach and breadth of interest, especially in actual industrial experience, that characterized the faculty in its early days, and his tenure as dean laid the groundwork for the later building up of the faculty by Gilbert WALKER. His family and the Walkers lived very close together at Highfields, near the university, with the Florences occupying the house and the Walkers the converted stables, and this became a social and intellectual centre for not only the faculty but many other members of the university; several famous artists also lived there. Lella Florence and her husband shared many artistic interests; both were also long-term supporters and advocates of the family planning movement.

For many years Florence held an evening industrial seminar at Birmingham, where local or national industrialists, civil servants, cabinet ministers and others were invited to reflect on some aspect of their own business practices and discuss these with the faculty, continuing over dinner. In 1969 the seminars were transferred to the new Graduate Centre for Management Studies and Florence, now nearly eighty, continued to chair the seminar, sometimes walking from his home across nearby parks to the Centre, a distance of about two miles. He was still active and writing at the time of his death at the age of ninety-two. He served on the council of the Royal Economic Society from 1930–61, and was a vice-president of the society from 1972 until his death. Florence was awarded the CBE in 1952.

Florence was particularly interested in industrial economics and on the sociological aspects of industry. His work often focused on theories of the firm and the impacts of human behaviour on economics and organizations. His early work on fatigue and industrial unrest (Florence 1918, 1924) convinced him that many of the problems faced by industry were not economic at all, but rather human in origin. That conviction comes through strongly in his work *The Logic of Organization* (1933) and its two follow-up studies, *Investment, Location, and Size of Plant* (1948) and *The Logic of British and American Industry* (1953). Political science and psychology, he says, are at least as important in the study of organization as is economics, and he is highly critical of the growing trend towards abstract analysis which leaves the human factor out of the equation (Florence 1953: 1–2).

In *The Logic of Organization*, Florence begins with an apparent paradox. The logic of organizations, he says, seems to suggest that big is best. 'Big' here means both large-scale production and large-scale organization (he makes the valuable point that many large organizations actually undertake production on a fairly small scale) (Florence 1933: 1–2). Combining both would make for optimum efficiency, which he defines as 'maximum return physical, pecuniary or psychological at minimum physical, pecuniary or psychological cost' (1933: 260). Throughout his work, Florence is careful to stress that efficiency is not solely about profit and cost; other human factors are at play as well, and the most efficient factory is not necessarily the one with the lowest cost ratios.

Yet, despite this supposed logic, and despite numerous individual examples to the contrary, industry as a whole has not moved towards large-scale production and organization. In both Britain and the USA, small firms continue to outnumber large ones, and continue to account for the majority of production and employment. Whence, then, is the source of this 'illogic'? Florence identifies three principal factors: (1) the individual and 'illogical' nature of human demand; (2) the burdens which large-scale organization places on management in terms of control; and (3) the tendency of people to feel less involved in and committed to larger organizations than smaller ones. All three of these are social and psychological factors which are often omitted by analysts who see the firm, and particularly its management, as primarily rational in nature: 'men engaged in business as administrators and investors are, no less than the labourers they employ, human beings, not, as is often assumed, hundred per cent efficiency experts' (1933: 263). Large-scale operation, then, does not necessarily result in efficiency.

The question of human relations in large organizations is also highly important: 'there is a specific loss of stimulus to the human factor psychologically connected with large-scale organization, and since scale of operation is partly dependent on scale of organization, this offsets the physical advantages of large-scale operation' (1933: 264). Paradoxically, large-scale organization creates individual inefficiency; workers identify less with the firm and more with their own interests. Again, this is a human problem, not an economic one.

What is the optimum scale for organizations in order to achieve maximum efficiency? Florence is undecided on this, and even doubts whether it is possible to reach such a measure; the conditions for optimum efficiency vary greatly from industry to industry, and the constantly evolving nature of competition and consumer demand mean that even the very measures of optimality tend to change. This, he points out, is the key problem with planned economies. It is not possible to plan production for optimum efficiency unless one can also plan *consumption*; and this, given the illogicality and irrationality of consumer demand, cannot be done (1933: 8). Far better to let the free market have its way, and ensure that companies are flexible and able to change and adapt their own organizations to meet the challenges of the market.

Florence does not develop a 'system' as such, and flexibility is not a word he uses frequently, but the thrust of his arguments is that businesses need to develop flexible systems, especially human systems. He calls for business organizations to be viewed as political entities, and speaks of the need to examine the firm's social systems; the powerful metaphor of the firm as church is used repeatedly. In *Investment, Location, and Size of Plant* (1948), he seems to move away from any idea of optimality at all, and instead argues that investment decisions need to be made on the basis of specific conditions at the time and place of operation.

Florence's work on labour inefficiency was very important in its day, as he showed for the first time how it was possible to measure the impacts of factors such as fatigue, illness, accidents and labour turnover on efficiency and profitability; he may have been the first writer to work out the actual financial costs of labour turnover (his methods of measurement remain broadly accurate) (Florence 1924). His later work looks at labour as a process, with various inputs – the workplace (including type and hours of work, physical conditions and social relationships), the wage (including amount and method of payment) and the worker (his or her personality, skills and training) – combining to produce what he calls the 'human factor'. The human factor is defined as a combination of the worker's *capacity* to work (how much he or she can do) and the worker's *willingness* to work (how much he or she will do). Inefficiencies in labour nearly always stem from a deficiency in one or the other aspects of the human factor. Such inefficiencies can be measured, Florence says, in the form of not only the quantity and quality of output, but also in areas such as accidents, absenteeism, strikes and industrial disputes, and labour turnover (Florence 1949). The human factor is an inevitable part of economic life; given that 'an economic system is part of the attempt to meet the needs of human beings from the natural and human resources at their disposal' (1949: 21), it is logical that human beings must be at the centre of any theory of economic activity. It is partly for this reason that Florence was opposed to unrestricted *laissez-faire* and prepared to tolerate a degree of state interference and participation in industry (Florence 1957).

One of the most important figures in British industrial economics, Florence was read and had influence on both sides of the Atlantic. His role in building up the Faculty of Commerce at Birmingham is one of his legacies, but so too is an eminently readable body of work which contributes greatly to our knowledge and understanding of industrial organization and the human face of economics.

BIBLIOGRAPHY
Use of Factory Statistics in the Investigation of Industrial Fatigue (New York, 1918).
Economics of Fatigue and Unrest (1924).
The Logic of Industrial Organization (1933).
Investment, Location, and Size of Plant (1948).
Labour (1949).
The Logic of British and American Industry (1953).
Industry and the State (1957).
Economics and Sociology of Industry (1964).
(with J.R.L. Anderson) *C.K. Ogden: A Collective Memoir* (1977).

Further Reading
Beesley, M.E., *Privatization, Regulation and Deregulation*, London: Routledge and Institute of Economic Affairs (1997, 2nd edn).

Stephen Littlechild
Morgen Witzel

FLUX, Alfred William (1867–1942)

Alfred Flux was born in Portsmouth on 8 April 1867 and died of pneumonia in Ladeplatts, Zealand, Denmark, on 16 July 1942. The son of a journeyman cement maker, he was educated at Portsmouth grammar school and entered St John's College, Cambridge, in 1884 as a minor scholar. He was bracketed first, or senior wrangler, in Cambridge University's mathematical tripos of 1887 and was elected a fellow of his college in 1889. Doubtless encouraged by Alfred MARSHALL, the leading light in Cambridge economics and also a fellow of St John's, Flux's interests seem to have turned rapidly from mathematics to economics. However, little is known of his activities or intellectual avocations prior to his leaving Cambridge in 1893 for Manchester, where he taught economics as Cobden lecturer (and later Jevons professor) at Owens College.

Finding the scope for economic teaching and research in Manchester too limited, Flux migrated to Canada in 1901 to take up a chair in economics at McGill University, Montreal. But in 1908 he abandoned his academic career and returned to Britain, entering government service as a statistician at the Board of Trade where he remained for the rest of his career. He became a leader in the process of expanding and refining the economic statistics published by the British government, maintaining meanwhile a close association with the activities of the Royal Statistical Society. He retired at age sixty-five in 1932 and moved to Denmark, the native land of his wife Emilie, whom he had married in 1897. He was made a CB in 1920 and received a knighthood in 1934 for services to statistics.

The publications emanating from the academic phase of Flux's career were able and varied, but did not quite live up to his early promise. Most important were three empirical studies of trends in international trade published in the *Economic Journal*, and a competent economics textbook (Flux 1904). Ironically, the contribution for which he is now best remembered was an aside in his first publication, a book review (Flux 1894) in which he observed that Euler's theorem on homogeneous functions could be invoked to prove WICKSTEED's result that paying factors their marginal products would just exhaust output given constant returns to scale in production. In the governmental phase of his career Flux published one book, his Newmarch Lectures (Flux 1924), but his most important publications appeared as articles in the *Journal of the Royal Statistical Society*, where he laid out the fundamental conceptual and procedural innovations that were transforming official statistics under his guidance. It is evident that, despite his impressive analytical skills, issues of pure economic and statistical theory failed to attract him. It was in furthering the often unsung and ephemeral task of measuring and describing economic outcomes that he found his true métier and had his main impact.

BIBLIOGRAPHY

'Review of Books by K. Wicksell and P. Wicksteed', *Economic Journal* (1894), vol. 4, June, pp. 305–13.

Economic Principles (1904; revised edn 1923).

The Foreign Exchanges, Newmarch Lectures for 1922 (1924).

John K. Whittaker

FORD, Edward (1605–70)

Ford was born in 1605 at Uppark, Sussex, and died in Ireland, probably in Dublin, on 3 September 1670. His family were Sussex gentry. Ford studied for a year at Trinity College, Oxford (1621–2), but did not take a degree. He next comes to public notice upon the outbreak of the English Civil War in 1641, when he joined the royalist cause and was commissioned a colonel, promising to raise a regiment of 1,000 men. He was also appointed High Sheriff of Sussex. In November 1642 Ford attempted to defend Sussex against Parliamentary forces under General William Waller. Outnumbered, he retreated before Waller's army and was besieged at Chichester, where he surrendered in December.

Ford's wife, the sister of the Parliamentary officer Major Henry Ireton, was able to arrange his release from captivity, and Ford rejoined the royalist army in mid-1643. Knighted by Charles I, he took command of a regiment of cavalry and served under Lord Hopton in the abortive campaign in West Sussex later that year. In December 1643 Ford was besieged by Waller in Arundel castle, and was forced to surrender for a second time early in 1644. He was imprisoned in the Tower of London, but escaped and made his way to France where he joined the court-in-exile of Queen Henrietta Maria. In 1647 he was sent back to England to negotiate with the leaders of the army and parliament in an attempt to secure the safety of the king, but seems instead to have connived at an attempt by the king to escape from custody, and was arrested and imprisoned for a third time. Thanks again to the good offices of Ireton, now a general and Cromwell's son-in-law, he received only a heavy fine, most of which was later remitted.

After this Ford seems to have become reconciled with Cromwell's regime, later accepting an appointment as First Lord of the Works. Barred from military service, he devoted himself instead to the study of engineering, especially hydraulics, and other scientific pursuits. He designed a scheme for bringing fresh water (or at least, water from the Thames) to all parts of London, and with support from Cromwell and Henry Ireton's brother John, then Lord Mayor of London, was able to put most of the scheme into effect. He also designed drainage schemes for farms and mines in Sussex, Kent and East Anglia. Following the Restoration, Ford developed a method of minting coins which was claimed to be effective against counterfeiters (Pepys notes this in his diaries, describing Ford in somewhat disparaging terms), but died before he was able to test this.

After the London fire of 1666, Ford produced a pamphlet offering ideas on how money could be raised to rebuild the city and also ensure that the country maintained a strong navy, a subject about which he had passionate views. Rather than increase taxation, Ford proposed the issue of a public stock, with an interest rate of 6 per cent to make it highly attractive and ensure rapid take-up. The funds thus raised would be more than sufficient to rebuild London and put the navy into a strong state of defence against external foes (Ford was thinking chiefly here of the Netherlands). Ford was strongly opposed to high taxation, which he believed was detrimental to the long-term health of the nation, and believed that a national debt could help to achieve national prosperity by allowing the state to support worthy projects.

BIBLIOGRAPHY

Experimented Proposals; how the King may have money to pay and maintain his Fleets with ease to his people. London may be rebuilt and all proprietors satisfied... (1666).

Further Reading

Stanford, C.T., *Sussex in the Great Civil War and the Interregnum, 1642–1660* (1910).

Morgen Witzel

FORSTER, Nathaniel (1726–1790)

Forster was born some time in 1726 in Crewkerne, Somerset, the son of a vicar, and died on 12 April 1790 at Colchester. His cousin, also Nathaniel Forster, was a noted scholar and editor of the works of Plato. Forster matriculated at Balliol College, Oxford in 1742, but then moved to Magdalen College from which he graduated BA in 1745 and MA in 1748. He was then elected a fellow of Balliol, from which he received a DD in 1778. His date of ordination is not known, but by 1764 he was rector of Tolleshunt Knights, Essex, and by 1777 was rector of Colchester.

Forster's interest in economic issues dates back to his time at Oxford, when he published *Reflections on the Natural Foundations of the*

High Antiquity of Government, Arts and Sciences in Egypt (1742). Later works include *An Enquiry into the Cause of the Present High Prices of Provisions* (1767), a short pamphlet on trade and several political tracts. *Reflections on the Natural Foundations* is of interest as an early example of the use of a method later called 'conjectural history' by Dugald STEWART. Here, Forster relates the interest and achievements of the Egyptians in agriculture, geometry and architecture to the peculiarities of Egypt's dependence upon the Nile. It is curious how the method of argument – such and such was clearly in the interest of the Egyptians and beneficial to them, hence this is how it must have happened – is taken as commonplace in the pamphlet. In defending the antiquity of Egyptian achievements, Forster is careful to point out that no impiety is involved since Bishop Warburton had already cleared the ground on this score.

This clerical background is no longer visible in the much more famous *An Enquiry into the Cause of the Present High Prices of Provisions*, which provides us with one of the earliest examples of the concept of *laissez-faire* entering English economic thought through the physiocrats. The introduction tells us that there are many causes for the present high price of provisions, some are deep-seated while others arise from temporary causes. Accordingly, the pamphlet is divided into two parts, the first treating of general causes and the second of temporary ones.

The first general cause, says Forster, is the increase of wealth in Britain, which he describes variously using the terms 'wealth', 'riches' and 'money', thereby reflecting a usage which was prevalent yet liable to confusion. He accepts the quantity theory of money as expounded by David HUME, and considers this a good general reason for the high prices that prevail. Unlike Hume, however, Forster lays the greatest emphasis upon employment. It is the subsistence of their people and their employment that should be the first priority of the state. Since the people could presumably feed themselves if employed, Forster soon comes to lay the first emphasis upon employment as the touchstone of economic policy. As agriculture provides the greatest employment, it should also be the most favoured sector. However, Forster doubts the value of specific interventions in order to achieve these goals. He notes that the statesman has to rely upon the passion of avarice when engaging in commercial legislation, and states that the role of law is to direct the passions appropriately, sometimes checking them, at others playing them off against each other: 'Thus are individuals happily made to contribute to the good of the public, without any such intention of their own, and sometimes even in spite of a contrary intention. The legislator here copies nature. And legislation would be perfect, could it exactly copy its great original' (1767: 17–18). This is perhaps the clearest statement in print, in the 1760s, of the directing role of the 'invisible hand'.

The reliance upon the French physiocrats is notable both in the way the thesis is phrased and in the rest of the pamphlet. Mirabeau and Rousseau are frequently referred to, and even Helvetius makes an appearance with the utilitarian maxim. One has to read the general philosophical maxims with care because the pamphlet not only aims at maximizing employment, it is also notably against encouraging luxury. Forster notes that luxury is relative, that human beings need to be aroused to action, yet the repeated thrust of his arguments is that luxury can bring ruin: 'from maturity to corruption is but a single step' (1767: 39). Later, after observing how the economic classes blend imperceptibly into each other in Britain, he observes that: 'In such a state as this fashion must have uncontrolled sway' (1767: 41).

Forster is classical republican and physiocrat in equal parts. The second part of the Enquiry goes into several specific topics, like exports, where Forster is a supporter of the bounty on corn; on engrossing, where he appears to support the free use of middlemen, and to particular discussions about horses, cattle, poultry and so on. The general method and the economic philosophy, with its unwavering devotion to the welfare of the ordinary labourer, are very clear; it is the treatment of particulars that sometimes shows confusion.

BIBLIOGRAPHY

Reflections on the Natural Foundations of the High Antiquity of Government, Arts and Sciences in Egypt (1742).
An Enquiry into the Cause of the Present High Prices of Provisions (1767).
An Answer to Sir John Dalrymple's Pamphlet on the Exportation of Wool (1782).

Salim Rashid

FORTESCUE, John (*c*.1395–*c*.1476/7)

John Fortescue was born about 1395 at Norris in Devon, the son of a minor nobleman, and died around 1477. He may have received some education at Exeter College, Oxford, and entered into the study of common law at Lincoln's Inn prior to 1420. He was governor of Lincoln's Inn on several occasions during the 1420s, and was elected to parliament several times between 1421 and 1436. Fortescue built a very successful (and apparently lucrative) career as a lawyer and justice in the royal service. He was named serjeant-at-law in 1430, rising to king's serjeant in 1441 and Chief Justice of the King's Bench in 1442. In this capacity as one of the king's leading legal lights, he performed both in the local administration as justice of the peace and commissioner and in the central government as a member of the king's council and parliamentary advisor. At the same time, through marriage, inheritance and royal patronage, Fortescue seems to have acquired a large network of estates. He was knighted for his service to the crown in 1443.

During the early stage of the Wars of the Roses, Fortescue was loyal to the Lancastrian cause. He witnessed the Battle of Towton in 1461, thereafter entering exile with Henry VI and his family, first in Scotland and then in France. He was attainted as a result, with his properties forfeited. It was during this period of exile that Fortescue produced the preponderance of his literary output. In addition to churning out pro-Lancastrian polemics, he wrote his central treatise on legal theory, *De Natura Legis Naturae*, and one of his main political tracts, *De Laudibus Legum Anglie*. When a Lancastrian invasion was organized in 1471, he returned to England with the royal family, only to be captured at the Battle of Tewkesbury. However, he quickly managed to re-enter royal favour following a published repudiation of his earlier writings on behalf of the Lancastrian cause. He became a member of Edward IV's council and composed an English language work of political theory, entitled *The Governance of England*, which he presented to the king. In 1475, he received a reversal of attainder that resulted in the restoration of his lands. His death occurred sometime after February 1476, and he was buried in the church of Ebrington, Gloucestershire.

Although primarily known for his legal and political thought, Fortescue has also been described as an important forerunner of modern political economy. He has sometimes – incorrectly – been reputed the author of a mid-fifteenth-century mercantile tract in poetry form, *The Libelle of English Policie*, which constitutes an important step forward in the promotion of a national economic programme. Fortescue's interest in economic matters must not be separated from his political and legal thought, the central tenet of which is that England has successfully realized the best type of constitutional system, which he terms *dominium regale et politicum* (royal and political lordship).

The terminology adopted by Fortescue derives from the work of St Thomas Aquinas and his student, Ptolemy of Lucca, who introduced a widely utilized distinction between both *dominium regale* (the rule of a king in his own right) and *dominium politicum* (constitutional or political rule, in which the people have a hand in governance). In *De Natura Legis Naturae*, Fortescue describes these two systems, then proposes a novelty: the existence of a third category that transcends the distinction between political and royal governments. Pointing to England, where laws and taxes are only imposed by the king with the consent of the whole community, Fortescue claims that we have before us a functioning instance of this conjoined system. In addition, Fortescue invokes the examples of Rome during the early Principate and scripturally depicted Israel under the Judges as other illustrations of such a regime.

Why should *dominium regale et politicum* be judged superior to either *dominium regale* or *dominium politicum*? This is a question that Fortescue takes up in two of his later works, *De Laudibus Legum Anglie* and *The Governance of England*. His view is twofold: first, he insists that there are distinct advantages to the king arising from the political character of his regime; second, and perhaps most significantly, he identifies clear and tangible benefits for those who are governed by a political and royal system. The fact that the monarch ruling politically as well as royally is limited by the laws that his subjects approve means only that he lacks license to decree and enforce unjust statutes. Such license is in no way appropriate to a king's true liberty; it does not fall within the legitimate power of the king to commit evil acts.

This practical standard for judging the superiority of 'mixed' government reflects, in turn, the fundamentally economic aim that Fortescue ascribes to government: the protection of the persons and goods of the realm from foreign invasion and internal injury. Like John LOCKE two centuries later, Fortescue upholds as the central responsibility of government the protection of the life, liberty, and estate of the inhabitants. This foregrounding of the material functions and duties of rulers resonates in Fortescue's explanation of why people should prefer the kind of regime typical of England, a constitution that he terms royal and political dominion (*dominium regale et politicum*). Because the people authorize the royal and political king by their consent, they would only chose to do so if they could be assured that they would continue in secure possession of their bodies and goods. If the king were able to deprive subjects of their lives and livelihoods, Fortescue contends, no one would willingly accede to such a system of government. If not quite a complete theory of a social compact, then Fortescue's explanation of the origin of *dominium regale et politicum* clearly articulates the connection between the people as the founding force and the king as essentially the guardian of the physical safety and well-being of the population.

The theme of reciprocity between regime type and the physical welfare of the people runs throughout both *De Laudibus Legum Anglie* and *The Governance of England*. Fortescue explicitly assesses the relative 'fruits' of a strictly royal constitution, as contrasted with royal and political government, by comparing the circumstances of France with those of England. The French monarchy is a strictly royal regime, lacking the element of popular consent. The king of France thus taxes its subjects arbitrarily and heavily, leading directly to the immiseration of the populace. Fortescue provides a very detailed depiction of this poverty – describing the diet, clothing and working conditions of the French nation – and lays the blame squarely on the royal system of rule through which France is governed. And just as the purely royal king causes such poverty, so he must constantly be on his guard, lest his subjects muster the courage to rise up and oppose him, contributing to the general instability of the realm.

The contrast with England, and its 'mixed' royal and political system, is striking.

According to Fortescue, the territory subject to the England, being ruled strictly according to the laws to which the people have given their approval, is wealthy and well-satisfied, even though it lacks the bountiful natural resources of France. Among other benefits, England is better prepared to arm itself and to defeat adversaries of the realm. On account of the legal structure, Fortescue says that the English king is restrained in his ability to lay claim to the goods of subjects, should he ever desire to do so. Fortescue recounts in great detail the structure of fiscal administration that bridles the king. On the one hand, the English king is assured a sufficient income to perform the tasks appropriate to his office, so that he will not be tempted to pursue illegal sources of income. On the other hand, the prerequisite of parliamentary approval conjoined with the independent authority of royal counsellors and magistrates form a check upon and barrier to the whims to which a king who reigns royally might easily succumb.

Consequently, the royal and political ruler takes it as integral to his office not to drain income away from his subjects into his own coffers, but to enact policies that enhance the wealth of the entire nation. In turn, the wealth of subjects that arises from royal and political rule acts as an assurance of public order. Inhabitants who enjoy material well-being are, in Fortescue's estimation, more willing and able to fight for their realm; they are less likely to engage in rebellious and seditious activities; and they possess the resources, not to mention the good-will, to subsidize the government in times of particular need. If subjects are contented with their physical lot, they will gladly subject themselves to the king and will perform their roles; but if their ruler adopts policies that impoverish them, they will express their displeasure directly and violently. Because it is by their own consent that subjects of a royal and political king are ruled, they cannot be involuntarily denied their goods and abused in their persons. On Fortescue's account, the immediate result of such government renders England a veritable earthly paradise.

BIBLIOGRAPHY

The Governance of England, ed. C. Plummer (Oxford, 1885).
On the Laws and Governance of England, ed. S. Lockwood (Cambridge, 1997).
The Works of John Fortescue, ed. Lord Clermont (1869).

Further Reading

Burns, J.H., *Lordship, Kingship and Empire: The Idea of Monarchy, 1400–1525* (Oxford, 1992).
Callahan, E.T., 'Blood, Sweat, and Wealth: Fortescue's Theory of the Origin of Property', *History of Political Thought* (1996), vol. 17, pp. 21–35.
Wood, N., *Foundations of Political Economy* (Berkeley, 1994).

Cary Nederman

FORTREY, Samuel (1622–81)

Fortrey was born 11 June 1622 in London, and died there in February 1681. His parents were Flemish refugees who had settled as merchants in London at the beginning of the seventeenth century. He was a clerk of the deliveries of the ordnance in the Tower of London, and seems also have been a member of the Privy Council. His combination of experience in trade and bureaucratic ability were typical of the group of 'consultant administrators', whom Joseph Schumpeter (1954) regarded as the social carriers of the more-or-less *dirigiste* doctrines that characterized much seventeenth-century economic writing and thinking.

Fortrey's only known work, *England's Interest and Improvements Consisting in the Increase of the Stores and Trade of this*

Kingdom (1663), became very influential and was referred to by many contemporary writers and politicians who searched for arguments for a more aggressive trade policy towards France. The opening passage of the work is quite conventional: the author emphasizes that 'Englands Interest and Improvements consists chiefly in the increase of our store and trade'. 'Store' he defines as all such commodities 'as either the soil, or people of this nation are capable to produce, which are either useful at home, or valuable abroad' (1673: 276). Hence, as he believes that the improvement of the mining industry, fishery and manufactories are crucial, he does not share the view – so often stated by seventeenth-century economic writers – that wealth only consists in money or can be increased by foreign trade. However, in this tract Fortrey's main interest is to present a calculation which shows that the value of exports to France amounts to only £1 million, while imports were £2,600,000. Although most certainly mistaken, this calculation without doubt served its purpose, namely to support heavy restriction on imports of luxury goods from France. In line with this argument, Fortrey suggests that, 'his Majesty would be pleased to commend to his people, by his own example, the esteem and value he hath of his own commodities, in which the greatest Courtier may be honourably clad, as in the best dress Paris or a French Taylour can put him in'. Hence to forbid the importation of Paris fashion and instead produce more of domestically would at least save us 'ten hundred thousand pounds a year to the advantage if the people' (1673: 290).

Fortrey also believes that the improvement of trade should in the long run lead to an export surplus. He presents an almost ideal type of the favourable balance of trade theory. Thus to the extent that 'our expectations of commodities would exceed our importations, a very great & signal advantage would accrue...is the profit we should then make of our returning money, by bills of exchange'. The consequence of the 'underballance of trade' was that money was drawn out of the country, 'whereby we are forced to give far more than the intrinsick value of the thing, to receive our monies beyond the sea, to supply our occasions' (1673: 293). Hence, according to Fortrey the problem with an unfavourable balance of trade is that it will lead to worsened terms of trade. Foreign goods will be more expensive to buy when the exchange rate is worsened. How to interpret passages like this – not uncommon in seventeenth-century British economic texts – has been a controversial issue since the days of Adam SMITH. However, it seems clear that Fortrey does not argue that wealth consists in gold and silver *per se*. Rather, he points to other problems which an 'underweight' might lead to, especially for the terms of trade.

BIBLIOGRAPHY
England's Interest and Improvements consisting in the increase of the Stores and Trade of this Kingdom (1663; repr. in L. Magnusson (ed.), *Mercantilism: Critical Concepts in the History of Economics*, vol. I, 1995).

Further Reading
Schumpeter, J., *History of Economic Analysis* (Oxford, 1954).

Lars Magnusson

FORTUNE, E.F. Thomas (*fl. c.*1796–1808)

Fortune was a London businessman who may also have been an investment broker. Nothing is known of his origins, or indeed of his life and career save what can be gleaned from his two major works, *An Epitome of the Stocks and Public Funds* (1796) and *A Concise and Authentic History of the Bank of England* (1797). He may have been alive in 1745, as he speaks of events surrounding the Jacobite rebellion with some knowledge; if so, he would have been quite a young man at the time. A short work on life annuities published in 1808 shows he was still active by that date, but after that nothing certain is known of him.

An Epitome of the Stocks and Public Funds is Fortune's best-known work. It was one of a number of handbooks for investors that appeared around this time, but is distinguished by its completeness and accuracy. The work contains summaries of the various public funds, annuities and stocks including navy bills, consols, exchequer bills, fractions, India stocks, imperial bonds, ordinance debentures, omnium, scrip and so on, with definitions of each, times of maturity, interest paid and other details. Also, from the second edition (also 1796) onward, the book included details of American funds and bank stocks, reflecting a growing interest by British investors in the American market. The book was highly popular and was frequently reprinted and updated by other hands, the last edition appearing in 1851.

A Concise and Authentic History of the Bank of England is, as the title suggests, a history of what had become by that time Britain's most important financial institution. Fortune also describes the organization and governance of the Bank, and includes a copy of its charter. Writing in the aftermath of the first Restricting Act, Fortune wonders at the motives behind the Act. The crisis of 1745 was, he says, far more severe, but there was no question then of restricting payments in gold and silver. He concludes that party political interests rather than economic needs are the driving force behind the new act, but does not specify how the parties might benefit. He does, however, argue that the Bank of England is quite capable of managing its own affairs and should be left to do so. He also agrees with Adam SMITH that the stability of the Bank of England is equivalent to the stability of the British government. The book also provides a history of the coinage and bills of exchange.

BIBLIOGRAPHY
An Epitome of the Stocks and Public Funds (1796; repr. 1797, 1820, 1826, 1833, 1838, 1851).
A Concise and Authentic History of the Bank of England, with Dissertations on Metals and Coin, Bank Notes and Bills of Exchange (1797).
National Life Annuities (1808).

Katharine Norley

FOWLE, Thomas Welbank (1835–1903)

Thomas Fowle was born on 29 August 1835 at Northallerton in Yorkshire's North Riding. He died at Oxford on 14 January 1903, and was buried in Islip. He was the son of the solicitor Thomas Fowle and his wife Mary Welbank, both from Northallerton. Between 1848 and 1853, Fowle was educated at Durham school and then Charterhouse. In 1854 he entered Exeter College, Oxford, but after a term, transferred to Oriel College on a scholarship. He was president of the Oxford Union and was also awarded his BA in 1858. His MA was given in 1861. In that year, he married Sarah Susannah Atkinson, from Richmond in the North Riding; the couple had seven daughters. Sarah died in 1874 and two years later Fowle married Mabel Jane Isaacs, the daughter of a West India merchant. There was one surviving daughter from this marriage, their son having died in 1895.

Fowle was ordained as an Anglican priest in 1859, and became the curate of Staines in Middlesex and then was appointed as the vicar of Holy Trinity church, Hoxton. In 1875 he became the rector of Islip church where he remained until he retired, due to illness, in 1901. He lived in Oxford until his death.

At Hoxton, Fowle promoted the building of new schools that were governed under a conscience clause. Hoxton had a large but poor population and this encouraged Fowle to develop his economic ideas on poor relief. He was opposed to the giving of outdoor relief, and after 1875, as rector of Islip and a poor law guardian, attempted to reduce it. Since this was the time of the agricultural depression, many agricultural labourers experienced great distress and poor relief often was their only means of survival. Fowle set up and managed an allotment system so that the agricultural labourers could grow their own food, rendering them less likely to claim poor relief.

Fowle wrote extensively on the application of poor relief. An article in the *Fortnightly Review* (1880) advocated the abolition of outdoor relief. This was followed by *The Poor Law* in 1881, in which he surveyed the history of the poor laws from the Elizabethan poor law (1601) to the passing of the 1834 Poor Law Amendment Act. In his studies, Fowle found that problems existed in all areas of poor relief: administration, the officials, settlement policies and the maladministration of workhouses.

Politically, Fowle was a Liberal. He supported the extension of the franchise to agricultural labourers (1884), but opposed home rule for Ireland, which took him into the ranks of the Liberal Unionists. He advocated the payment of old age pensions in his pamphlet *The Poor Law, the Friendly Societies and Old Age Destitution: A Proposed Solution* (1892). He was active in the campaign for the establishment of parish and district councils (1894).

As a latitudinarian Anglican minister, Fowle attempted to resolve the differences between the new ideas of evolution and the biblical accounts of the creation. He wrote three articles on the subject, which were published in *Nineteenth Century* (1878, 1879 and 1881). He also published theological articles such as *Types of Christ in Nature* (1864) and *The Reconciliation of Religion and Science* (1873).

Fowle's first-hand experience of rural social conditions enabled him to influence political opinion. He also gave practical help to agricultural labourers at a time of economic distress. His ideas on old age pensions were implemented in the 1908 budget.

BIBLIOGRAPHY
Types of Christ in Nature (1864).
'The Church and the Working Classes', in *Essays on Church Politics* (1868).
The Reconciliation of Religion and Science (1873).
The Poor Law (1880).
'Cellarius', *New Analogy* (1881).
The Poor Law, the Friendly Societies and Old Age Destitution: A Proposed Solution (1892).

Marjorie Bloy

FOWLER, William (1828–1905)

Fowler was born near Melksham, Wiltshire on 28 July 1828, and died at Tunbridge Wells some time in September 1905. He was educated at University College, London, where he took a BA in classics and mathematics (1848). He went on to study law (LLB 1850), and was called to the bar in 1852. From 1856–77 he was a partner in the firm of solicitors Alexander & Co. of Lombard Street, London. Thereafter he went into business and served as a director of several companies. He was a member of the Cobden Club, and served as Liberal MP for Cambridge from 1868–74 and again from 1880–85.

Fowler wrote several short works on land reform and on finance. His essays on land reform, especially *The Present Aspect of the Land Question* (1872), argued for the abolition of the limited ownership of land and for an extension of the principles of the free market to land ownership. Only when landowners were truly masters of their own land without encumbrance of law would they invest in the land to make it as productive as it should be. In *Limited Ownership of Land* (1874), Fowler rejected the report of the House of Lords committee of 1873, in particular its conclusion that landholders are stewards of the land for the coming generations, and that preserving this continuity is of prime importance. Fowler argued that most landowners did not in fact behave as stewards, and only if they could see benefit in their own lifetime would they invest in making land productive.

The Crisis of 1866 is Fowler's consideration on the financial panic of May 1866, which he regarded as unprecedented in scale, but still not much different from other panics that had come before. He sees panics in psychological terms, and believes they stem largely from a result of loss of confidence among financiers themselves: 'A vague fear seizes men's minds, leading to a general distrust, when, as a matter of course, unsound houses disappear under circumstances more or less alarming to others; and finally the alarm spreads and there ensues what is called a panic' (1866: 2). Fowler's discussion of the role of contagion in spreading financial panics is quite original and still remains of interest today.

In the particular case of May 1866, Fowler attributed the crisis to the rapid spread of limited liability companies, many of which were unsound. Concerns about risk had been building up for some time, but came to a head all at once. Such events were natural and inevitable in financial markets, said Fowler, and there was little point in trying to legislate against them. The primary issue was determining how, once started, panics could be quickly brought under control. In the case in question, he believed that the Bank of England had acted promptly and wisely and the markets had recovered swiftly. Like BAGEHOT, though in much less detail, Fowler argued that a key determinant of swift recovery would be whether the Bank had sufficient reserves to deal with crises.

Appreciation of Gold (1886) is a vigorous argument against bimetallism, especially in its American form; Fowler regarded silver as a standard of currency as being virtually obsolete. Though not a thinker of any great originality, Fowler is a typical example of the kind of thoughtful 'amateur' economist that gathered in late nineteenth-century institutions like the Cobden Club.

BIBLIOGRAPHY
The Crisis of 1866: A Financial Essay (1866).
Thoughts on 'Free Trade in Land' (1869).
The Present Aspect of the Land Question (1872).
Limited Ownership of Land: Remarks on the Report of the Committee of the House of Lords on Improvement of Land (1874).
Appreciation of Gold: An Essay (1886).
Indian Currency: An Essay (1899).

David Ashbury

FOXWELL, Herbert Somerton (1849–1936)

Foxwell was born 17 June 1849 at Shepton Mallet, Somerset, the son of a prosperous ironmonger and timber merchant, and died at Cambridge on 3 August 1936. He was educated at the Wesleyan Collegiate Institute in Taunton, and then London University (BA 1967); from there he went to St John's College Cambridge, where he took first-class honours in the moral sciences tripos in 1870. He remained at Cambridge for the rest of his life. He was elected a fellow of St John's in 1874, and appointed lecturer in economics in 1875. During Alfred MARSHALL's absence from Cambridge from 1877–85, he was the main honours teacher in economics at the university. Concurrently, he taught at University College, London, where he was professor of political economy from 1881, though this was less than a full-time position and the focus of his teaching activity continued to be Cambridge.

Foxwell had hoped to succeed Marshall upon the latter's retirement in 1908, but Marshall supported the appointment of A.C. PIGOU instead. Betrayed, Foxwell resigned from teaching at Cambridge and concentrated his teaching efforts instead at University College and the London School of Economics and Political Science, where he had been a regular lecturer in banking and currency since its inauguration in 1895. He succeeded W.S. JEVONS as professor of political economy at the University College, London in 1881. He had previously been elected fellow of the Royal Statistical Society in 1878, and a member of the Political Economy Club in 1882. He was a founder member of the British Economic Association (later Royal Economic Society), and served as its president from 1929–31. Foxwell retired from full-time teaching in 1927, but continued to be active in the field.

Foxwell published little during his career, concentrating for the most part on teaching. His most notable works were a long introduction to Anton Menger's *The Right to the Whole Produce of Labour* (1899), *Irregularity of Employment and Fluctuations of Employment* (1886), and 'The Economic Movement in England' (1887). In these works, Foxwell displayed strong historical erudition and clarity of thought. His introduction to Menger takes a fairly conservative position, and continues a theme common in Foxwell's early work, his rejection of David RICARDO. He held that Ricardo's influence was out of all proportion to his actual importance, and tried to point to the existence of other economic traditions.

A combination of ethical and historical views of economics informed much of Foxwell's thinking. In 'The Economic Movement in England', Foxwell again attacked the Ricardian tradition and argued for a more human-centred approach to economics. *Irregularity of Employment and Fluctuations of Employment* allied itself instead to the thought of J.S. Mill. He argued that free competition had produced both great wealth, but also great poverty, the latter stemming largely from economic fluctuations and the corresponding irregularity of employment. Writing at a time when socialist and anarchist movements were openly advocating violent revolution throughout Europe, Foxwell felt the key to labour peace was to be found in government intervention and restriction of unrestrained competition. He favoured counter-cyclical state spending in social welfare areas and public works, and supported monopoly regulation, profit-sharing and workers' co-operatives. He anticipated far better than most of his colleagues and peers much of the actual form of government intervention and policy during the twentieth century.

Papers on Current Finance (1919) considers the subject on which Foxwell's own later academic interests were concentrated, finance and banking. The book demonstrates a very wide knowledge of banking practices, both domestic and foreign, and looks at the relationship between finance and industry. Unfortunately, few others of Foxwell's lectures and papers on this subject have survived.

Foxwell's other great achievement was as a collector of books. By 1901 he had amassed a collection of some 30,000 items, which was purchased that year by the Goldsmith's Company and later presented to the University of London. Following this sale Foxwell immediately started a new collection, and by 1929 had amassed at least 4,000 items, this time much more historical in nature; this library was sold to Harvard Business School, where it forms the core of the Kress Library of Business and Economics. Today, the Goldsmiths and Kress collections form some of the most important resources for the study of the history of economic thought in the world.

BIBLIOGRAPHY
Irregularity of Employment and Fluctuations of Employment (1886).

'The Economic Movement in England', *Quarterly Journal of Economics* (1887), October.
'Introduction', in A. Menger, *The Right to the Whole Produce of Labour* (1899).
Papers on Current Finance (1919).

Further Reading
Coase, R., 'The Appointment of Pigou as Marshall's Successor', *Journal of Law and Economics* (1972), October.
Koot, G.M., 'Herbert Somerton Foxwell', *The New Palgrave: A Dictionary of Economics*, vol. 2 (1987).

Alan Ebenstein

FRYDE, Edmund Boleslaw (1923–99)

E.B. Fryde was born in Poland on 16 July 1923, and died on November 17 1999 at Aberystwyth. He came to the UK with his father, Mieczyslaw, who was a mathematician and socialist and who left Nazi Germany in 1938. Fryde went first to Bradfield College and then to Balliol College, Oxford, where he completed his DPhil thesis on the wartime finances of Edward III in 1946. From Balliol he went to Aberystwyth, where he spent the whole of his working life, first as a lecturer and then as a professor. His teaching covered not only political and social history, but also art history and historiography. In addition to his teaching, Fryde published widely on his areas of interest, and was one of the editors of the third edition *The Handbook of British Chronology*.

Much of Fryde's writing was concerned with the structure and mechanics of fourteenth century trade and royal finance, both in England and northern Europe. His doctoral thesis analysed in minute detail the complicated financial arrangements made by Edward III in order to fund the early phase of the Hundred Years War, and he used this study as a springboard for further work on the management of credit by medieval kings and merchants. His numerous articles in this area were gathered together in *Studies in Medieval Trade and Finance* (1983), a vital source of information for anyone working on the economic history of the period.

Fryde had a particular interest in the complexities of the wool trade between England and the Low Countries in the fourteenth century, and several of his articles are concerned with this issue. He used customs accounts in conjunction with accounts of key merchants in the trade to shed light on this vital component of the economy of England and the Netherlands. His interest in this trade also resulted in a biography of William de la Pole (1988), Edward III's most important private financier. His articles on public credit in England and the continent are highly valuable sources for students of medieval credit arrangements.

As well his substantial body of work about finance and credit, Fryde also wrote about Peasant's Revolt of 1381, and expanded on peasant and landlord relationships in *Peasants and Landlords in Later Medieval England, c. 1380–c. 1525*. In this work, he challenges the idea that the lot of peasants improved in the wake of the population decline of the fourteenth century; he also rejects the idea of the fifteenth century as a period of easy social mobility, preferring instead to emphasize the survival of feudal structures and economic stratification. In latter years Fryde turned his attention from northern to southern Europe. His last two books (one published posthumously) were concerned with the libraries of the Medici and with the Byzantine renaissance of the late thirteenth and fourteenth centuries.

BIBLIOGRAPHY
'The Great Revolt of 1381', *Historical Association* (1981), vol. 100.
Humanism and Renaissance Historiography (1983).

Studies in Medieval Trade and Finance (1983).
William de la Pole, Merchant and King's Banker (d. 1366) (1988).
Peasants and Landlords in Later Medieval England, c.1380–c. 1525 (1996).
Greek Manuscripts in the Private Library of the Medici 1469–1510 (1996).
The Early Palaeologan Renaissance (1261–c.1360) (2000).

Marilyn Livingstone

FULLARTON, John (1780?–1849)

John Fullarton was probably born in 1780, and died in London 24 October 1849. His mother was the daughter of Alexander Dunlop, professor of Greek in the University of Glasgow, and he himself married a Miss Finney of Calcutta, who died at Memphis (Egypt) in 1837. Provided with a wide and refined education, Fullarton took great interest throughout his life in art and literature, and travelled extensively through India, China, Egypt and Europe. From 1802 to 1813 he was an assistant surgeon in India; during this period he also became the editor of a Calcutta newspaper. Subsequently he made a fortune in banking, having entered the house of Alexander & Co., bankers of Calcutta, as a partner. In his early forties Fullarton went back to live in England. Here, he contributed several articles on political topics to the *Quarterly Review*, while travelling around the country and the continent in a coach specially fitted with a library and other luxuries. In 1833, as a fellow of the Royal Asian Society, he went again to India and in 1834 was entrusted with a mission to China. In 1838 his fortune was severely curtailed by the failure of his bankers: he moved from Lord Essex's house, in Mayfair, which he had purchased in 1823, to 12 Hyde Park Street, at which address he resided for the rest of his life.

As an economist, Fullarton is important as the author of *On the Regulation of the Currencies* (1844; 2nd edn, 1845), subtitled 'An examination of the principles on which it is proposed to restrict, within certain limits, the future issues on credit of the Bank of England and the other banking establishments throughout the country'. The book appeared shortly after TOOKE's *An Inquiry into the Currency Principle* (1844), and just after the passing of the Bank Charter Act of 1844 by whose provisions it had been inspired. *On the Regulation of the Currencies* made Fullarton an outstanding exponent of the Banking School. MARX included him among 'the best writers on money' (1883: 104n), and, according to GREGORY (1928: 81), Fullarton's book is 'perhaps the most subtle and most able production emanating from the Banking School'. Fullarton is chiefly interested in the critique of the principles which had inspired the regulation by law of the bank note circulation of the country: 'in fact', he writes towards the end of the book, 'the entire case [of the government bill] is one of principle, and on that ground must stand or fall; and it is on that account I have thought it necessary to treat the several questions of principle so fully' (1845: 174). He stresses at the beginning of the book 'the coincidence of his conclusions, in most of their leading features, with those of the eminent author of the "History of Prices", one of the most valuable contributions to economical science which the present century has produced' (1845: 5). However, as we shall see below, there are a few important questions on which Tooke and Fullarton's views are by no means coincident.

Sir Robert Peel's Act of 1844 rested its justification for restricting within certain limits the future issues on credit of the Bank on the assumed soundness of the currency doctrines. According to these doctrines, the value of a currency depended on its quantity, which the bankers were enabled at their pleasure to increase, and consequently raise the prices of all the commodities, thereby causing an adverse balance of payments, a fall of the exchange and a call on the Bank for gold to discharge the foreign debt. On this ground the Currency School deemed it indispensable, in order to avoid the oscillations of prices and the exchange, that the bank note circulation should at all times be made to fluctuate exactly as a purely metallic circulation would have fluctuated, and that this result could be obtained only by depriving the bankers of their power of over-issue.

Fullarton starts his critique by pointing out the absurdity of the emphasis placed by the Act on bank note circulation; as if, he argues, the action of any given facility of credit on prices depended on the particular piece of paper on which the amount of the credit may happen to be inscribed: 'nothing so preposterous can ever be maintained, as that the same payment, which contributes to a rise of the market when made through the instrumentality of bank notes, will have no such consequence if effected by the transfer of a bill of exchange, or by an adjustment of set-off in a banker's book' (1845: 40–1). Because of the great importance attached to bank note circulation, the fact was actually overlooked that by far the largest proportion of all the transactions of purchase and sale taking place in the country were carried through by other expedients of credit than bank notes, expedients of credit whose supply was inexhaustible and beyond the reach of credit restraint. This fact, according to Fullarton, should have made evident to everybody 'the utter hopelessness' of any attempt to control those transactions and the fluctuations of prices which they engender 'by any officious tampering with the free supply of so comparatively insignificant a portion of the whole mass of circulating credit as the bank notes, and that portion the least of any in affinity with those great operations of trade by which the course of prices and exchanges is really directed' (1845: 51). Moreover, out of the superabundance of existing forms of credit of one description or another, 'the bank-note circulation', he argued following Tooke, 'even if fully withdrawn, would in a very short time be replaced, not perhaps in all respects with exactly the same convenience, but amply and completely, and with very little assistance from gold. The innovation on established habits would be the chief difficulty' (1845: 48).

Fullarton then concentrates his attention on the allegation that bank notes are liable to be issued in excessive quantity at the discretion of the issuer, and that every such over-issue brings about a rise in the prices of commodities. He argues that the quantity of all 'currencies of credit', among which bank notes are included, can never be excessive because it is entirely regulated by the demand of the public. At difference from a government compulsory paper, which is 'introduced into the market by being made the medium of *payments*', credit-currencies are not 'paid away' (1845: 64, 66): they are not forced into circulation by authority but are limited by the demand for use; so they can never operate on prices by any excess of quantity, and therefore can never become depreciated or suffer a diminution of their purchasing power, as compared with the currencies of neighbouring countries. Concerning in particular the circulation of bank notes, Fullarton reminds the reader how 'Mr. Tooke has furnished the most elaborate and satisfactory proofs' that the expansions and contractions of the bank note currency which are often observed to accompany the fluctuations of prices 'are not the causes, but the consequences, of such fluctuations; they do not precede, but follow them' (1845: 101). The reason why, according to Fullarton, a rise of prices cannot be the effect of an expansion of bank circulation is simply that a circulation of notes cannot 'exist for any continuance in such a state of redundance as to raise prices' (1845: 121). He argues that the public 'can have no imaginable motive for desiring to possess themselves of a larger proportion of those notes than they absolutely require for use' (1845: 130). No merchant can ever desire to keep by him a larger sum in bank notes than is indispensably necessary for his payments, and 'the currency, if not wanted, finds its way back to the issuer' (1845: 97). Moreover, 'the tradesman, instead of keeping by him an unproductive hoard of such notes for his daily disbursements, will prefer paying them into a bank which allows him interest for the amount, without any prejudice to his perfect command over the principal. He will make his payments henceforth by cheque; and those cheques will, in the vast majority of cases, be adjusted by transfer or exchange, without any resort to money' (1845: 93). In sum, excess issues of notes would not be held if they did not match the preferences of holders for notes rather than deposits. But Fullarton rests his conviction that bank notes never can clog the market by their redundance chiefly on the argument that they are never issued but on loan, so that an equal amount of notes must be returned into the bank whenever the loan becomes due. This is the 'reflux' which he regards as 'the great regulating principle of the internal currency' (1845: 68), and it is its 'regularity' which, 'so long as a bank issues its notes only in the discount of *good* bills, at no more than sixty days' note' (1845: 206), would render impossible any redundance of the bank note issues.

Fullarton's 'great regulating principle of the reflux', however, is hardly sufficient to ensure that a circulation of credit-money can never be in such a state of redundance as to raise prices. Suppose the Bank issues its notes in exchange of securities; that is, by open market purchases. 'Overissue' then results first of all in a higher price of securities and a lower rate of interest, and the power of the Bank to add to the circulation and act as an originating cause on trade and prices ultimately depends on whether a fall of interest supplies the inducement to purchase commodities. Tooke was fully aware of this; he stressed that actual experience does not support the notion that the facility of borrowing at a low rate of interest supplies 'the *disposition* or *will*' to purchase commodities (Tooke 1844: 79). Fullarton does not seem to be aware of the crucial importance, for the validity of his views on the connection between money and prices, of the question of the effects of changes in the rate of interest on the inducement to purchase commodities. He feels confident that in order to understand that a credit-currency can never operate on prices by any excess of quantity, it is sufficient not to lose sight of the fact that its circulation is demand determined. But this fact, by itself, is insufficient to rule out the possibility of 'overissue', albeit through the channel of an over-demand for use, brought about by a fall of interest. In fact, if a lower rate of interest *had* the effect to raise private expenditure, the difference, insisted upon by Fullarton, between a credit-currency, whose quantity is regulated by the demand of the public, and a government compulsory paper, which is 'paid away', would become substantially irrelevant.

Fullarton does eventually discuss the question of the influence of the rate of interest on commodity prices, but with reference to the phenomenon of speculation, and also in this respect his and Tooke's positions differ. The consideration of speculation in commodities does not lead Tooke (see Tooke 1844: 82) to qualify his notion of a low rate of interest as a 'cause of cheapness', which leads to low rather than high prices. Fullarton somewhat distances himself from this way of reasoning (see the long and extremely cautious note on p. 170 of his book). He refers to the phenomenon of speculation which tends to take place in situations characterized by a diffused lack of profitable investment opportunities, and maintains that in such situations a low rate of interest *will* tend to raise prices, by the impulse which it gives to speculation in commodities: with a fall in the rate of interest, he argues, the capitalist finds his income reduced, and 'after waiting for several years in expectation that matters may take a favourable turn, he loses his patience, and, in his eagerness to regain his former position, he becomes disposed to listen with avidity to any project which holds out the expectation of a better return for his money' (1845: 169).

An important 'question of principle', among those which occupy centre stage in Fullarton's tract, is that of gold and convertibility. He shares with the other exponents of the Banking School the view that the integrity of the metallic standard must be kept intact, together with the obligation of full and constant convertibility of bank notes into gold on demand. This was in fact the only significant principle that the Banking School had in common with the Currency School. Fullarton's allegation is that bank notes, provided they are payable in gold on demand, are never liable to be issued in excess at the discretion of the issuer. The impossibility of a redundance of circulating bank notes is always referred to by him in association with 'a really convertible' state of the currency: 'a currency cannot be overissued so long as it is convertible'; 'a circulation of convertible notes cannot exist for any continuance in such a state of redundance as to raise prices'; 'the very constitution of a convertible currency makes it impossible that it can be issued in larger quantities than are required for use'. Propositions such as these are disseminated throughout the book.

But the arguments actually developed by Fullarton to rule out the possibility that a credit-currency (as distinct from a currency forced into circulation by authority) can persist in such a state of redundance as to raise prices, have hardly anything to do with the convertible state of the currency. As we have seen, those arguments are that the circulation of a credit-currency is demand determined, reflecting the needs of trade, and 'the great regulating principle of the reflux'. Fullarton himself, at a certain point of his exposition, admits that 'it is not so much by convertibility into gold, as by the regularity of the reflux, that in the ordinary course of things any redundance of the bank-notes issues is rendered impossible' (1845: 67). It can then be said that behind his insistence on the use of a metallic standard and on convertibility, as well as behind his opposition to a conventional currency, which is 'the creature of the law', there were both a preoccupation and a conviction. The preoccupation was that the positions of the Banking School on the connection between money and prices might be dismissed more easily by their confusion or association with those of the Birmingham economists (Thomas ATTWOOD and his followers), who advocated the abolition of the metallic standard, its replacement with a flexible and managed inconvertible paper currency, and were even in favour of high prices (maintained by inflation of the currency) to reduce the burden of debts.

As to the conviction behind Fullarton's insistence on the use of a metallic standard, he very soundly thought that the importance of a metallic standard and of keeping up a large stock of specie in the Bank of England derived essentially from the services that specie is capable of rendering to the nation:

> Could it be so ordered that the causes, which at present subject you to demands of this description, could be made to cease; could an interdict be laid for the future on short harvest and costly wars, could men who are deriving an income of only 2 per cent from their capital in this country be denied the liberty of transferring it to France, where it may be invested at an interest of 5 per cent...of what *use* would it be, I should be glad to know, to hoard up this money any longer?
>
> (1845: 207–8)

His point thus was that to part with gold would have amounted to 'a measure of isolation', to a surrender of power, both political and commercial; and that it was thanks to the metallic basis of the circulation that the Bank of England could be regarded as 'a vast granary, to which, in seasons of famine, the community is entitled to resort for succour' (1845: 157).

BIBLIOGRAPHY

On the Regulation of Currencies, being an examination of the principles on which it is proposed to restrict, within certain limits, the future issues on credit of the Bank of England and of the other banking establishments throughout the country (1844; 2nd edn, 1845).

Further Reading
Fetter, F.W., *Development of British Monetary Orthodoxy, 1797–1857* (Cambridge, Massachusetts, 1965).
Gregory, T.E., *An Introduction to Tooke and Newmarch's A History of Prices and of the State of the Circulation from 1792 to 1856* (1928; repr. 1962).
Marx, K., *Capital: A Critical Analysis of Capitalist Production*, vol. 1 (1883; 3rd edn 1896).
Tooke, T., *An Inquiry into the Currency Principle; the connection of the currency with prices and the expediency of a separation of issue from banking* (1844; repr. 1959).
Tooke, T. and Newmarch, W., *A History of Prices and of the State of the Circulation from 1792 to 1856*, 6 vols (1838–57; repr. 1928).
Viner, J., *Studies in the Theory of International Trade* (New York, 1937).

Massimo Pivetti

G

GAITSKELL, Hugh Todd Naylor (1906–63)

Gaitskell was born in Kensington, London on 9 April 1906, and died suddenly in London on 18 January 1963. He was the son of Arthur Gaitskell, an Indian civil servant, and his wife Adele. He was educated at Winchester and then New College, Oxford, where he read philosophy, politics and economics under Maurice Bowra and G.D.H. COLE, and gained a first-class degree in 1927. Gaitskell had already joined the Labour Party, and during the General Strike of 1926 he worked for a local strike committee as a driver. In 1927 he took a post as an extra-mural lecturer in Nottingham; in 1928 he was appointed lecturer in political economy at University College, London, and in 1938 he was promoted to reader and made head of department.

Gaitskell first stood for parliament, unsuccessfully, in 1935. During the Second World War he served as a temporary civil servant, working with Hugh DALTON at the Ministry of Economic Warfare and then again at the Board of Trade. In 1945 he stood for parliament again and was elected MP for South Leeds, holding the seat until his death. Thereafter his rise was rapid. He was a parliamentary secretary in 1946, Minister of Fuel and Power in 1947, Minister of State for Economic Affairs in 1950, and Chancellor of the Exchequer in October of that year, following the resignation of Sir Stafford Cripps. Gaitskell had married Dora Creditor in 1937, and they had two daughters. He was awarded the CBE in 1945.

At age forty-four, Gaitskell was now widely tipped as a future leader of the Labour Party. He espoused modernization of the Party, and became detested by its left wing, the more so when he vehemently opposed Russian communism and supported NATO and the American alliance. When Clement Attlee resigned in 1955, Gaitskell was elected leader of the Labour Party, defeating both Ernest Bevan and Herbert Morrison by a large margin. Although he lost the 1959 general election and was forced to fight off a challenge to his leadership in 1962, his popularity in the Party and the country was growing, and was enhanced still further when he opposed entry into the Common Market. Labour was well ahead in the opinion polls and Gaitskell would in all likelihood have become prime minister at the next general election. With his death, a light went out of British politics which has never since returned.

Gaitskell had never been a deep believer in Marxism, although early in his career he sometimes spoke in the language of class conflict; for example in his early essay *Chartism* (1929) and in a chapter for G.D.H. Cole's *What Everybody Wants to Know About Money* (1933). But by the middle of the decade he had become convinced the Marxism was wrong, both in theory and in practice; he once told Michael POSTAN that he 'found the whole system of dialectical notions hollow and boring' (Jenkins 1974: 165). He spoke of Marxism as one of the afflictions of German and Austrian socialism. He also had decided that social democracy in Britain would need a class base far wider than that provided by traditional Marxist analysis. At the same time, there was nothing of the Christian socialist in him. He turned away from religion early in his life, and it never again meant anything to him; nor did he ever seek to pretend otherwise.

The essence of Gaitskell's socialism was the search for more equality and a fairer society. He hated poverty and injustice. He wanted to make people happier: there was always a strong strand of unselfish hedonism in his philosophy. Towards these purposes he was, and remained, uncompromisingly radical; but it was ends and not means which made him uncompromising. He was in favour of the extension of public ownership, and probably overestimated, then for many years thereafter, the improvement of efficiency which state ownership or government intervention could bring. But even in the 1930s, he rejected the identification of socialism with nationalization, a view he repeated in the pamphlet *Socialism and Nationalisation* (1956). For Gaitskell, socialism always had to have the practical end of improving people's lives.

BIBLIOGRAPHY
Chartism: An Introductory Essay (1929).
'Four Monetary Heretics', in G.D.H. Cole (ed.), *What Everybody Wants to Know About Money* (1933).
(with E. Durbin) *How to Pay for the War: An Essay on the Financing of War* (1939).
Money and Everyday Life (1939).
In Defence of Politics (1954).
Socialism and Nationalisation (1956).
The Challenge of Co-existence (1957).
(with R.H. Tawney and R. Hinden) *The Radical Tradition: Twelve Essays on Politics, Education and Literature* (1964).

Further Reading
Jenkins, R., *Nine Men of Power* (1974).
Rodgers, W.T., *Hugh Gaitskell* (1964).

Roy Jenkins

GALE, Samuel (1747–1826)

Gale was born 14 October 1747 in Kimpton, Hampshire, and died 27 June 1826 in Farnham, Lower Canada. Trained as a surveyor, he moved to America about 1770, apparently as a paymaster in the British army. Two years later he was appointed to the lucrative office of deputy surveyor-general of New York. In 1773 he married the eldest daughter of Samuel Wells, land agent and judge of the Inferior Court of Common Pleas for Cumberland County (now Windham County, Vermont). Gale was appointed clerk of this court in 1774. He was well positioned to profit from land speculation on the New York–New Hampshire border, where he had been surveying disputed land grants for New York speculators, but this came to an abrupt end with the pre-revolutionary turmoil of 1775. After being jailed twice as a pro-British sympathizer, Gale became cashier for the deputy paymaster-general of the British army. In 1780 he switched to the position of itinerant paymaster in Virginia, the Carolinas and Florida, but his post-war case for a pension to compensate for loss of his professional income was weakened by his not having served in a military capacity. Furthermore, his property, although confiscated, had not been sold, and he was thus prevented from proving its irrevocable loss.

Gale attempted to strengthen his claim to an annuity by publishing *An Essay on the Nature and Principles of Public Credit* (1784), a complicated treatise on means of gradually extinguishing Britain's public debt. It was followed by two additional volumes under the same title in 1785 and another in 1787. In 1785 he received a small temporary annuity of £40, apparently later raised to £100.

In 1791 Gale accepted an invitation to Quebec by William Smith, the prominent New York attorney and politician who had become chief justice of Lower Canada. Gale became principal assistant to the surveyor-general, and later threw himself into the task of defending the claims of the Americans who had received warrants of survey after the townships north of international border were officially opened to settlement in 1792. Colonial officials in Quebec interfered with the land granting process initiated while Chief Justice Smith was chairman of the Executive Council's land committee, ensuring that they and their merchant allies were favoured instead. Gale was in London from 1799 to 1802 lobbying for the original American claimants, but the Privy Council finally rejected his petition.

Gale, seven of his brothers-in-law and two of his nephews had nevertheless received a total of 9,600 acres in Farnham Township in 1798. Gale settled there when he returned from London, accumulating a fine library and conducting a small practice as notary. Aside from championing local settlers who resisted the enforcement of militia laws that would oblige them to fight relatives and former friends during the War of 1812, he does not appear to have been active in public life. His only son, Samuel, became a prominent Montreal judge and a wealthy landowner.

The opening volume of *An Essay on the Nature and Principles of Public Credit* sets out Gale's basic ideas; the later volumes enlarge on the same themes, and the fourth also contains some reviews and discussions of the first. Gale begins ostensibly by investigating the real nature of the national debt, but it soon becomes clear that the work is a justification and defence of the concept. He divides the debt into three categories: perpetual annuities, determinate annuities which are repaid on a fixed term, and redeemable annuities or annuity stocks, and explains the basic mechanism by which the debt works. His justification begins from the premise that war is inevitable; and, with equal inevitability, war must be paid for. It might be possible to simply borrow money during the war and pay it back immediately at the end of the conflict, with interest; but this, says Gale, would offer no gain. The establishment of a sinking fund, however – if properly managed – can result in savings, as the peacetime interest rates on the sinking fund will always be lower than wartime interest rates on straightforward war loans. He does not go quite so far as Edward KING, who believes the national debt actually benefits the nation, but he strongly approves of borrowing during war and then repaying gradually during peacetime to take advantage of improvements in interest rates and financial conditions more generally.

From here Gale moves on to the subject of debt and money more generally. Interest rates, says Gale, are determined by the quantity of money to be lent and the quantity of money in circulation. The greater the amount of money in circulation, the more lenders have to lend, and so the laws of supply and demand dictate that interest rates will fall. However, more important than the quantity is the rate at which money circulates. If the circulation is brisk, then this means prices are lower and therefore a greater proportion of the money in circulation is available to be lent, pushing interest rates down; and vice versa. Money is a commodity, and interest is effectively the price of borrowing money.

Money itself is purely a circulating medium without intrinsic worth. Gale goes so far, in a footnote on p. 143, to suggest that money has nothing to do with the capital or wealth of the state; it is merely a means of exchange. The value of money fluctuates according to the speed of circulation, the quantity of money in circulation, and whether any other commodity is being used for exchange along with money. The comparative value of money in the end depends on the demand for it and the ease with which that demand can be met, just as with any other commodity. He concludes Volume 1 with postcripts on the principles of taxation and actual state of public credit.

BIBLIOGRAPHY
An Essay on the Nature and Principles of Public Credit, 4 vols (1784–7).

Further Reading
Hall, B.H., *History of Eastern Vermont from its Earliest Settlement to the Close of the Eighteenth Century* (New York, 1858).
Upton, L.F.S., *The Loyal Whig: William Smith of New York & Quebec* (Toronto, 1969).

J.I. Little
Morgen Witzel

GALTON, Francis (1822–1911)

Galton was born in Birmingham on 16 February 1822, and died on 17 January 1911 in Haslemere, Buckinghamshire. His mother was a daughter of Erasmus Darwin, and Charles Darwin was his cousin. He was educated at King Edward's School at Birmingham (1836–8), followed by a medical apprenticeship in Birmingham, a year (1839–40) at the medical school of King's College, London and then Trinity College, Cambridge (1840) where he read mathematics, graduating without honours.

Inheriting a substantial fortune on the death of his father in 1844, Galton embarked on an African exploration. Reflections on his travels were published in 1853. The explorations led him to an appointment the council of the Royal Geographical Society. In 1856 he was elected fellow of the Royal Society. He served as Secretary of the British Association from 1863 to 1867. His works include *Meteorographica, or Methods of Mapping the Weather* (1863) and *Finger Prints* (1892) which established the permanence of fingerprints across the life cycle.

Galton's contributions to mathematical statistics and, with W.R. GREG, to the creation of the 'science' of eugenics had a major impact on economics. In terms of the former, Stigler (1986: 265–6) documents how Galton, F.Y. EDGEWORTH and Karl Pearson developed statistical devices that served as substitutes for experiments. Galton's ideas on eugenics began as an argument against classical economics, arguing against MALTHUS's idea of checking population by delaying marriage. He believed that 'the practice of such a doctrine would assuredly be limited, and if limited it would be most prejudicial to the race…Those whose race we especially want to have, would leave few descendants, while those whose race we especially want to be quit of, would crowd the vacant space with their progeny… (Galton 1907c: 207).

Two devices which Galton developed for the study of eugenics illustrate his creativity and integrity. His method of composite photography attempted to identify inherited characteristics. He described the results: 'The individual faces are villainous enough, but they are villainous in different ways, and when they are combined, the individual peculiarities disappear, and the common humanity of a low type is all that is left' (1907c: 11). The case of Jewish composite photography (Galton 1885) is considered in Levy and Peart (2003). Secondly, at the age of eighty-five Galton asked how democratic policy might consider criterion of eugenic selection. He pointed out that a majority-rule democracy shares structure with the sample median (a word he coined), and he verified this conclusion with an ingenious experiment. He published the results in *Nature* (Galton 1907a, 1907b, reprinted in Levy and Peart 2002).

BIBLIOGRAPHY
Narrative of an Explorer in Tropical South Africa (1853).
Meteorographica, or Methods of Mapping the Weather (1863).
'Photographic Composites', *The Photographic News* (1885), vol. 29, pp. 243–45.
Finger Prints (1892).
'One Vote, One Value', *Nature* (1907a), vol. 75, pp. 414.

'Vox Populi', *Nature* (1907b), vol. 75, pp. 450–51.
Inquiries into Human Faculty and Its Development, 2nd edn (1907c).

Further Reading
Levy, D.M. and Peart, S.J., 'Galton's Two Papers on Voting as Robust Estimation', *Public Choice* (2002), vol. 113, pp. 357–65.
——, 'Statistical Prejudice: From Eugenics to Immigration', *European Journal of Political Economy* (2003).
Stigler, S.M., *The History of Statistics: The Measurement of Uncertainty Before 1900* (Cambridge, Massachusetts, 1986).
——, *Statistics on the Table: The History of Statistical Concepts and Methods* (Cambridge, Massachusetts, 1999).

David M. Levy
Sandra R. Peart

GEDDES, Patrick (1854–1932)

Geddes was born at Ballater on the Dee in Scotland on 2 October 1854, and died in Montpellier, France on 17 April 1932. The youngest of four children, he was educated in Perth, where the father was an officer in the Perthshire Rifles. On graduating from Perth Academy, he worked for two years at the Bank of Scotland before enrolling to study biology at the Royal School of Mines in London under the evolutionary biologist R.H. Huxley. Work as a biologist at London University College was followed by a period in Brittany and then at the Sorbonne. His numerous works written in 1878 and 1879 made Geddes a highly promising biologist at the age of just twenty-four. The British Association for the Advancement of Science employed him on a zoological station in Stonehaven in 1879 and then sent him on a research mission to Mexico, where he contracted an eye disease that prevented him from using the microscope and thus diverted him from biological research. Though possessing a letter of reference written by Charles Darwin in 1881, Geddes applied unsuccessfully for various university posts between 1880 and 1889 before obtaining the chair in botany at Dundee University, which he held until 1919.

On returning from Mexico in 1880, Geddes broadened his range of intellectual interests to include, among other things, economics. His major ideas are expressed in the economic works of 1884. He took part from 1885 in the redevelopment of Edinburgh's Old Town, thus beginning his career as a town planner. He went on to produce a vast number of books, articles, projects and studies on the planning or redevelopment of various cities. A complete list of his works is to be found in P.L. Boardman's *Esquisse de l'Oeuvre éducatrice de Patrick Geddes* (1936). Copies of his publications are held in the Strathclyde University Archives, Glasgow, together with projects and unpublished material.

Geddes saw education and the spreading of culture as essential elements in a process of developing the population to be carried out parallel to any redevelopment of the city, an idea that led him to embark on intense cultural activity. He founded the Edinburgh Social Union to promote the improvement of housing in the Old Town in 1885 and then the Outlook Tower (Camera Obscura), a workshop of analysis, observatory and museum of the city's social and physical phenomena, through which he launched various initiatives designed to promote Scottish culture. He organized a series of summer schools that ranged widely over the arts and sciences, inviting key figures in international culture to lecture in Edinburgh. The journal *Evergreen* was a result of this experience. His interest in student living conditions took concrete shape in the founding of University Hall, an independent hall of residence, and the Town and Gown Association.

He also founded the publishing house Patrick Geddes and Colleagues, and the Old Edinburgh School of Art.

Geddes was involved in the social planning of Cyprus in 1896, and took part in the 1900 Paris Exposition before leaving for the USA, where he lectured on the book *The Evolution of Sex* and met leading American intellectuals. He published *City Development: a Study of Parks, Gardens and Culture Institutes* in 1904. Together with his lectures at the London School of Economics and *City in Evolution* (1915), this constitutes the nucleus of his ideas on town planning.

Geddes moved to India in 1914 and stayed there until 1924, engaged in the planning of various cities and also teaching sociology at Bombay University from 1919, the year in which he designed the new Jewish university in Jerusalem. He returned to the United States in 1923 and held lectures in various universities on the evolution of cities organized by Lewis Mumford, his student and friend as well as champion of his ideas on town planning. Returning to Europe in 1924 he settled in Montpellier, where he worked on the rebuilding of Scots College. He was knighted in 1932, shortly before his death.

Geddes considered contemporary political economy backward with respect to what he described as the 'preliminary sciences', namely mathematics, physics, chemistry and biology. Though intrinsically connected with these disciplines by its very nature, economics failed to assimilate the extraordinary advances they achieved. These criticisms were also the subject of a brief correspondence with Léon Walras in November 1883. His primary target was the notion of utility, which he considered essentially metaphysical and unscientific. In order to understand what originates and determines the exchange value of goods, we must study their objective properties. Bread supplies a given amount of alimentary fuel. A diamond or a bunch of flowers supplies a quantifiable sensory stimulus that varies in accordance with Fechner's law. It is thus necessary to use physics, biology and the 'preliminary sciences' in general in order to measure these phenomena and give their analysis a scientific basis. The insistence on the need for quantitative measurement echoes the analysis of Le Play, whose works Geddes studied during his years at the Sorbonne.

This critical position led Geddes to a number of original ideas, the first of which has been taken up by environmental economists (Alier, 1987). Geddes was one of the first intellectuals to consider the fact that economies use exhaustible and non-renewable resources to produce energy. The exhaustibility of these resources is considered neither in the calculation of profits nor as an objective limit to economic development. Geddes credits JEVONS with having realized, contrary to his theory of marginal utility, that coal has an objective as well as a subjective value in that it represents a quantity of stored energy. Economics should study the relationship between existing stocks of coal and present and future demand. Geddes also thought it necessary to limit the wasting of energy (which could account, in his view, for as much as 99 per cent of the energy used) and to combat soot.

Geddes divided economic history into different ages according to the sources of energy used. Three initial ages – of stone, bronze and iron – making use of renewable sources of energy are thus followed by one in which non-renewable sources constitute the basis of an extraordinary increase in production with respect to the previous eras. He saw the economy as 'a machine, in which all phenomena are interpreted as integration or disintegration of matter, with transformation or disintegration of energy' (1884:15), which he represented in a diagram. The first column represents the amounts of raw materials and sources of energy available at the beginning of the production process. Among these he also includes the energy of human labour as measurable in terms of some sort of 'man power'. The next four columns represent the phases of extraction, processing, transport and exchange. For each phase, he indicates the quantity of raw materials and energy received from the previous phase, which he divides into a 'disintegrated and dissipated' part and a part that goes into the following stage/column. All the final products contain energy in a different form. More than a value added, the 'final product' is thus seen as the residual of the original amount of matter and energy.

If economics used physics in order to quantify energy correctly, it would become evident that 'the net amount of ultimate product may seem unwarrantably small in proportion to the gross amount of potential product; this smallness is intended to suggest the vast losses of energy and matter, often many times exceeding the product, due to the imperfection of our processes' (1884: 17). As these losses do not enter into the cost of production, the production process yields a profit as long as the cost of production is lower than that of the ultimate products. 'This surplus is the interest paid by Nature upon the matter and energy expended upon her during the process of production' (1884: 17). These considerations form the basis of the parallel frequently drawn between Geddes and the physiocrats.

Workers are seen as consumer-automata used in production and a part of final production as comprising a set of 'necessaries of life'. The definition of these is, however, no simple matter. The enormous differences between what are considered necessaries in different places but in similar objective conditions show that consumption must be regarded as consisting of at least two different parts. One is 'necessaries' and the other 'super-necessaries', which serve to stimulate the consumer's gustatory, visual and tactile sense organs and constitute so much *aesthesis*. The distinction between aesthetic and necessary elements must be drawn even for food and clothes. Nearly all the elements of the necessaries have 'super-added aesthetic sub-functions'. The economist should distinguish these different components and estimate the costs of production for each of them separately, which can only be done by using biology, physics and psychology.

A second original feature is the connection that Geddes establishes between economics and the theory of the evolution. Man's economic activity is to be seen as the result of an evolutionary process. As soon as they are differentiated from the state of protoplasm, the animal species perform economic activities that initially consist of hunting alone. More evolved animal species also produce shelters: birds' nests can be seen as an economic product. Some species attach some aesthetic sub-functions to their products. Means of production start to be produced at higher levels of intelligence, such as the roads and granaries of ants and the sticks and stones of the higher apes. With biological evolution, man became a 'tool-using animal' and the evolution of the production process began.

Technological innovation must also be seen as a result of the same evolutionary laws. As population increases, the advantages of simple co-operation clearly manifest themselves and 'then slight variations of individual and circumstance lead to the repeated performance of some one function by particular individuals, the efficiency and rapidity of its performance then alike improve, and the advantages of specialisation of function, or "division of labour" become obvious and tend to be continued and perpetuated' (1884: 26). The process of differentiation continues as circumstances render it advantageous or possible 'and the complicated co-operation of the ant-hill or the city arises' (1884: 26).

The differentiation of biological functions due to the difference of sex is seen by Geddes as the first economic differentiation provided by nature. This was the subject of *The Evolution of Sex*, written together with J.A. Thomson in 1889, and it formed the basis of the radical opposition to female suffrage for which Geddes is still often criticized. Progressive specialization in human societies is strengthened by heredity in the professions, which tends to form groups similar to castes. This specialization generates changes in the organisms of men performing particular functions. As for all living beings, the state of health of individuals is determined by their environmental conditions. Already acknowledged for food and housing, this influence was extended by Geddes to the quality of the atmosphere and conditions of social integration.

Geddes's approach to the theory of the city shared certain features with the economic ideas outlined above, namely an interdisciplinary approach, the influence of evolutionary biology, and attention to problems concerning energy and the environment. He saw the development of human communities as a primarily biological phenomenon in which great importance attaches to interaction between people, the environment in which they live, and the activities they perform. He used this triad of 'Folk, Work and Place' to conceptualize his central idea that social processes and spatial form are intimately related, and saw it as the basis for all analysis of actual urban conditions and all redevelopment projects.

Geddes was obviously influenced in this by Le Play, who used the conceptual triad 'Lieu, Travail, Famille' in maintaining the importance of the environment in determining the organization of societies. Geddes saw the triad 'Folk, Work and Place' as the counterpart of biology's rudimentary triad of Environment, Function and Organism. As evolutionary organisms, what he called 'human reefs', cities absorb energy from the surrounding environment, initially in the form of cereals and foodstuffs from the country. By transforming the way in which cities absorb energy, the Industrial Revolution introduced waste and the indiscriminate use of non-renewable sources of energy, aspects ignored by economics that should, according to Geddes, be examined by economists and town planners alike. He saw a confusion of the development of productive resources and the dissipation of energy also in the analysis of the process of urban development. Dissipation produces extraordinary wealth in financial terms but also has negative effects and makes the development of economies and cities intrinsically limited. Finally, Geddes introduced the distinction between 'palaeo-technological' and 'neo-technological' industrialization and urbanization, the former being based on coal and the latter on the use of renewable energy, which he identified optimistically with electricity. In actual fact, this was to prove renewable only when hydraulically generated and to raise environmental problems as complex as those Geddes pinpointed.

Geddes owed his reputation among contemporaries primarily to his work as an urban theorist and practical town planner. His contribution as an economist was of marginal importance as regards both his individual career and the development of political economy. His work as a town planner had an indirect influence on modern urban economics through his pupil and friend Lewis Mumford, whose work is often considered one of the first stages in that discipline. It is above all his original position with respect to the relationship between production and the use of energy that has recently led to his reappraisal by economists as a forerunner of environmental economics.

BIBLIOGRAPHY
The Classification of Statistics and its Results (1881).
John Ruskin Economist (1884).
'An Analysis of the Principles of Economics', *Proceedings of the Royal Society of Edinburgh* (1884).
(with J.A. Thomson) *The Evolution of Sex* (1889).
City Development: a Study of Parks, Gardens and Culture Institutes; a Report to the Carnegie Dunfermline Trust (1904).
Cities in Evolution: An Introduction to the Town Planning Movement and to the Study of Civics (1915).

Further Reading
Boardman, P.L., *Esquisse de l'Oeuvre éducatrice de Patrick Geddes* (A Sketch of

Patrick Geddes's Educational Work) (Montpellier, 1936).
Martinez-Alier, J., *Ecological Economics. Energy, Environment and Society* (Oxford, 1987).

Attilio Trezzini

GEE, Joshua (1667–1730)

Gee was born in 1667, probably in London, and died there in 1730. Little is known of his background, but by 1700 he had built up a thriving mercantile business and was trading with the American colonies. A Quaker, he was friendly with William Penn and was one of the seven mortgagees who helped rescue the colony of Pennsylvania when Penn ran into financial difficulties. He was also in partnership with Augustine Washington, father of the future American president; in 1718, Gee and Washington were partners in a company called Principio, which aimed to exploit iron ore resources in Maryland and, later, Virginia. It may be assumed that Gee had wide commercial interests in America and the West Indies.

Gee was the author of the widely read *The Trade and Navigation of Great Britain Considered* (1729). At least seven editions were published up to 1767. In this work, Gee argues that England must increase its manufactures in order to work up raw materials (especially wool) both domestically and from its growing colonial empire. 'Great Britain with its Dependencies is doubtless as well able to subsist within itself, as any Nation in Europe', Gee writes. 'We have an industrious enterprising People, as fits for all the Arts of War or Peace. (1729: 135). A continued import of textiles from abroad, especially France, would only lead to poverty and the decay of agriculture in Great Britain. Like Samuel FORTREY he argued that Louis XIV's decision to allow only French textiles for sale in France had been a master stroke, and should be copied by England.

Gee was a member of a group of writers who held similar views on the pivotal role of manufactures for economic growth. He was one of the collaborators in the famous paper *The British Merchant*, published twice weekly in 1713, which included Charles King, Henry MARTIN, Charles Cooke, Theodore Janssen, James MILNER and others. Gee is here described as a 'Merchant, was a very great Assistant and labour'd with much Industry in these papers'. The immediate cause for the publication of *The British Merchant* was the Treaty of Utrecht between France and Britain (1709) and the defence of the commercial clauses of the treaty published in another periodical at the time, *The Mercator*, written and published by Daniel DEFOE. In contrast to Defoe, the writers in *The British Merchant* found the treaty too liberal and argued for higher duties on especially manufactured textiles. In an article in *The British Merchant* entitled 'General Maxims in Trade' Janssen presented the general theoretical arguments behind the group's position. By exporting more manufactured goods than we import, Janssen said, we will be able to employ our own poor instead of providing employment to the poor of other countries. Some modern interpreters have referred to this argument for greater employment as 'the labour balance' or the theory of 'foreign-paid incomes' (Johnson 1939).

BIBLIOGRAPHY

The Trade and navigation of Great Britain Considered (1929; repr. in L. Magnusson (ed.), *Mercantilism: Critical Concepts in the History of Economics*, vol. IV, 1995).

Further Reading

Johnson, E.A., *Predecessors of Adam Smith* (New York, 1939).
Magnusson, L., *Mercantilism: The Shaping of Economic Language* (1994).

Lars Magnusson

GERVAISE, Isaac (1680–1739)

Gervaise was born in France in 1680, and died in London in 1739. His family were Huguenots, who emigrated to England following the Glorious Revolution of 1688. His father, Louis Gervaise, established a business as a hosiery merchant in London, and helped to finance the Royal Lustring Company. Isaac Gervaise followed his father into business, specializing in alamodes or lustrings, a kind of black silk fabric. He was granted a monopoly by parliament, but his business nevertheless seems to have stagnated. In 1699 he was made an elder and secretary of the Consistoire Church in Leicester Fields.

In 1720 Gervaise published a remarkable tract, *The System or Theory of the Trade of the World*, which set out to show how international trade worked in terms of a system with strong equilibrating forces. To this effect, he introduced a specie flow mechanism, formulated in a different manner from that of HUME thirty years later, but showing great similarities. Like Hume, Gervaise did not believe in the possibility of a country having a constant 'overplus' in its trade with other nations:

> When a Nation has attracted a greater Proportion of the grand Denominator [money] of the world, than its proper share; and the Cause of that Attraction ceases, that Nation cannot retain the Overplus of its proper Proportion of the grand Denominator, because in that case, the Proportion of poor and Rich of that Nation is broken; that is to say, the number of Rich is too great, in proportion to the poor so as that nation cannot furnish unto the World that share of labour which is proportion'd to that part of the grand denominator it possesses: in which case all the Labour of the Poor will not ballance the Expence of the Rich.
>
> (1720: 3)

What will then happen is simple: 'So that there enters in that Nation, more Labour than goes out of it, to ballance its want of Poor: And as the End of trade is the attracting Gold and Silver, all that difference of labour is paid in Gold and Silver, until the Denominator is lessen'd, in proportion to other Nations...' (1720: 3).

Gervaise's tract is very short and we do not know his views in any great detail. It is certainly speculative, and anachronistic, to argue – as is sometimes done – that Gervaise was a forerunner of a general equilibrium model. However, he obviously saw the international economy as a self-regulating order, steered by supply and demand, and presented his theory in an almost axiomatic way. He also analysed the international economy when discussing whether the state should support or intervene for the benefit of any specific manufacture. His argument was that such intervention is of no use, as 'No Nation can encourage, or enlarge its Proportion of any private and natural Manufacture, without discouraging the rest; because whether an Allowance be given, either to the Manufacturer, or Transporter, that Allowance serves, and is employed to attract the Workers from those other Manufactures, which have some Likeness to the encouraged Manufacture: So that what is transported of the encouraged manufacture, beyond nature, only balances the Diminution of others' (1720: 11). This approach foreshadows that of later eighteenth-century writers. In this sense Gervaise was an important thinker and deserves the high praise that, for example, Jacob Viner (1930) gives him as a forerunner of modern trade theory.

BIBLIOGRAPHY

The System or Theory of the Trade of the World (1720; repr. in L. Magnusson (ed.), *Mercantilism: Critical Concepts in the History of Economics*, vol. IV, 1995).

Further Reading

Magnusson, L., *Mercantilism: the Shaping of Economic Language* (1995).

Viner, J., 'Early English Theories of Trade I–II', *Journal of Political Economy* (1930), vol. 38.

Lars Magnusson

GIBBINS, Henry de Beltgens (1865–1907)

Gibbins was born on 23 May 1865 at Port Elizabeth, Cape Colony (now South Africa). He was killed on 13 August 1907, falling from a train in Thackley tunnel between Leeds and Bradford. He was the son of Joseph Henry Gibbins and his wife, Eleanor de Beltgens, from Stamford, Dominica in the West Indies. Gibbins was educated at Bradford Grammar School in Yorkshire and won a scholarship to Wadham College, Oxford in 1883. In 1888 he was awarded a BA; two years later, he won the Cobden prize for an economic essay at Oxford. In 1896 he received a DLitt from Dublin University. Gibbins married Emily Bell from Bradford; the couple had one daughter.

Having graduated, Gibbins began his working life as a teacher. From 1889 to 1895 he was employed as an assistant master at Nottingham high school. During this time he wrote a number of books on economic history. However, he discovered a religious vocation and was ordained a deacon in the Anglican Church in 1891, becoming a priest in 1892. His first appointment was as both deacon and curate at St Matthew's parish in Nottingham, where he served between 1891 and 1893. Gibbins was appointed as vice-principal of Liverpool College in 1895, and then headmaster of King Charles I school in Kidderminster in 1699. In 1906 he was appointed as the sixth principal of Lennoxville University (now Bishop's University), Quebec, an Anglican foundation. However, he was obliged to leave after a short time because of ill health, and returned to Britain.

Although his degree was in classics, Gibbins was interested in economic history during his time at Oxford and continued to study the subject for the remainder of his life. He contributed to Palgrave's *Dictionary of Political Economy*, and edited the Methuen series of publications on 'Social Questions of the Day' (1891) and also their 'Commercial' series (1893). Writing from a background of British imperialism, he had an Anglocentric view of history. For example, when writing about the Opium Wars of 1842 and 1857, he notes that 'regrettable as they were [they] established our commercial relations with the east generally upon a firm footing; and since then our trade with Eastern nations has largely developed' (1893: 114).

Gibbins believed that the social changes that had the most impact were those that were the most rapid. Belonging to the 'qualitative' school, his ideas dealt with the changes in social relations during the period of the Industrial Revolution. His best work is probably *Industry in England* (1896), a textbook which developed out of the shorter *Industrial History of England* (1890). It begins with prehistoric and Bronze Age industries and gives detailed accounts of Roman and medieval industry before turning to the modern period. In the introduction he notes that 'the history of industry is the history of civilization, and a nation's economic development must, to a large extent, underlie and influence the course of its social and political progress' (1896: 3).

BIBLIOGRAPHY
Industrial History of England (1890).
The History of Commerce in Europe (1891).
English Social Reformers (1892).
British Commerce and colonies (1893).
Economics of Commerce (1894).
Industry in England (1896).

Marjorie Bloy

GIFFEN, Robert (1837–1910)

Giffen was born at Strathaven, Lanarkshire on 21 July 1837, and died of heart failure at Fort Augustus in Scotland on 12 April 1910. Upon leaving school he went on to work as a clerk in a solicitor's office (1850–55) and then in a legal office in Glasgow – attending professional classes at Glasgow University – until 1860 when he began a career in journalism. He moved to London in 1862 and became sub-editor of *The Globe* (1862–6), moved to the *Fortnightly Review* (1866–8), and then served as assistant editor of *The Economist*, then edited by Walter BAGEHOT, from 1868–76. He then left journalism to pursue a third career as a civil servant, becoming chief of the statistical department of the Board of Trade (1876–82), assistant secretary to the Board of Trade and then controller-general of Commercial, Labour and Statistics Departments (1882–97). Giffen was instrumental in founding the Labour Department. He retired at the earliest permissible age, partly because of indifferent health. *The Times*, noting his loss to the field of economic statistics, hailed the benefits of the freedom this would give him to re-engage fully in public debate.

Giffen's contributions to the applied economics and economic policy debates of his time were extensive and significant. As a pioneering applied economist, his major concern was to marry economic theory and statistical measurement, arguing, in presidential addresses to the Royal Statistical Society and to Section F of the British Association for the Advancement of Science, the dangers of the one without the other. His own major contributions were as an economic statistician: MARSHALL described him as 'the prince of statisticians'. Here his strengths were not founded on the modern mathematical theory of his day so much as on 'common sense', 'an intuitive feel for the relative importance of numbers', and a 'power of penetration and discernment' which enabled him to extract truths from statistics 'whilst never losing his grip on the realities for which the figures stood' (*Economic Journal* 1910). He was the most significant early popularizer of inaccessible art of statistics. In the 1880s Giffen was in the forefront of attempts to provide accurate measurements of wage rates, national product and economic growth, and in a 1992 *Economic Journal* article he made the first attempt to tackle the problems of international statistical comparisons.

An undogmatic free-trader and *laissez-faire* liberal, Giffen was extensively and intensively engaged in the debating and development of economic and financial policy from the 1860s right up to his death in 1910. His contributions came through publications: books, lectures, academic articles, journalism, letters in the press, evidence to Royal Commissions and participation in clubs and professional associations.

A 'voluminous writer' whose many books included *American Railways as Investments* (1873), *Stock Exchange Securities* (1877), *Essays in Finance* (1880), *The Progress of the Working Classes in the last Half Century* (1884), *The Growth of Capital* (1890) and *The Case Against Bimetallism* (1892), Giffen was also a frequent contributor to the journals of the Royal Statistical Society and the Royal Economic Society. He did important work for Royal Commissions, presenting evidence to twelve commissions and select committees between 1876 and 1898 on the depression in agriculture, the depreciation of gold, gold and silver, the Port of London, the London Stock Exchange and financial relations between Great Britain and Ireland. Mason (1989) lists sixty-seven journal and periodical articles and lectures between 1867 and 1907; there were also fifty-four articles and letters in *The Times*, the main channel of his contributions to public debate after he joined the civil service.

As a founder member and, later, vice-president of the Royal Economic Society, Giffen played a leading role in the society's development. From 1882 to 1884 he served as President of the Royal Statistical Society. Invitations to serve as President of Section F of the British Association on two occasions provide further evidence of his standing in economic circles. For thirty-three years a devoted member of the Political Economy Club, he rarely missed a monthly dinner. His obiturists tell us that as a speaker he was 'weighty and lucid', as a companion humorous and kindly.

The Giffen Paradox was introduced, and vaguely attributed to Giffen, by Marshall in the demand chapter of the *Principles* from the third edition onwards:

> As Mr Giffen has pointed out, a rise in the price of bread makes so large a drain on the resources of the poorer labouring families and raises so much the marginal utility of money to them, that they are forced to curtail their consumption of meat and the more expensive farinaceous foods and, bread being still the cheapest food which they can get and will take, they consume more, and not less of it.
> (Marshall 1895: 208)

Stigler (1947) questions the attribution to Giffen, and there do seem to be no published references to the point in Giffen's writings prior to 1895. Nevertheless, modern introductory economics texts still refer to 'Giffen goods' as a particular type of 'inferior good'.

BIBLIOGRAPHY
(with B. Cracroft) *American Railways as Investments* (1873).
Stock Exchange Securities (1877).
Essays in Finance, first series, vol. 1 (1880).
The Progress of the Working Classes in the last Half Century (1884).
Essays in Finance, second series, vol. 1 (1886).
The Growth of Capital London (1890).
The Case against Bimetallism (1892).
'On International Statistical Comparisons', *Economic Journal* (1892), vol. 2, June, pp. 209–38.
Economic Inquiries and Studies, 2 vols (1904).

Further Reading
'Sir Robert Giffen (Obituary)', *Journal of the Royal Statistical Society* (1910), vol. 73, no. 5, pp. 529–23.
'Sir Robert Giffen (Obituary)', *Economic Journal* (1910), vol. 20, no. 78, June, pp. 318–21.
Marshall, A., *Principles of Economics*, 3rd edn (1895).
Mason, R.S., *Robert Giffen and the Giffen Paradox* (Oxford, 1989).
Stigler, G.J., 'Notes on the History of the Giffen Paradox', *Journal of Political Economy* (1947), vol. 55, no. 2, April, pp. 152–6.

Alan Hutton

GILBART, James William (1794–1863)

James William Gilbart was born in London on 21 March 1794, and died there on 8 August 1863. He worked in London as a bank clerk from 1812 until the financial crisis of 1825 when his bank, Everett, Walker and Co., stopped payment. After brief stints as a cashier in Birmingham and London, he moved to Ireland in 1827 to become branch manager of the Provincial Bank of Ireland, first in Kilkenny and then two years later in Waterford. When parliament passed a law permitting joint-stock banking in London in 1833, two different companies asked him to be their general manager. He accepted the post at the London and Westminster Bank, which became England's most successful bank under his administration. Besides administering the bank's day-to-day business, he also acted as agent for many of the growing number of joint-stock banks forming outside of London, and periodically battled the Bank of England's efforts to preserve what remained of its monopoly. Gilbart remained at the

London and Westminster until his retirement in 1860.

Gilbart's main contributions to economic thought were his many writings on the history, principles and administration of joint-stock banks, and his advocacy of *laissez-faire* in the issue of paper currency. He repeatedly revised his *Practical Treatise on Banking* (1827) throughout his life, offering updated advice on corporate governance, accounting methods, and the relationships among Britain's various financial institutions. Both this book and his *History and Principles of Banking* (1834) continued to serve as standard texts on banking long after his death. His work on currency mainly appeared in polemical tracts directed against Lord OVERSTONE's 'Currency School' and in a series of statistical articles tracing note-issuing patterns in England, Scotland and Ireland.

Gilbart's early years in London brought him into contact with such leading middle-class intellectuals as Thomas Macaulay, Edwin CHADWICK, John Stuart MILL and Edward BAINES, whom he met in the Athenian and Union debating societies. These influences were apparent in his *Practical Treatise*, which began its publishing life as an eighty-page manifesto on the merits of joint-stock banks. Such banks (legally defined as having more than six partners) had long existed in Scotland, but had been prevented from forming in England under the Bank of England's charter until 1826, and in London until 1833.

The description of joint-stock banking that emerged in successive editions of Gilbart's *Practical Treatise* was that of a progressive social force, very much part and parcel of the early Victorian 'age of improvement.' He claimed that joint-stock banks acted as 'public conservators of the commercial virtues' (1849: 387) which taught depositors how to be careful with their money, inspired clerks to advance through society by means of diligence and honesty, and fuelled economic growth with timely and well-judged loans. He generally praised the application of the corporate form to banking, including the entrustment of executive authority to professional managers like himself, and the clash of mercantile opinion among bank directors that allegedly guaranteed the perfect combination of caution and liberality. At times, however, he faulted directors for subordinating their managers' advice to the short-sighted demands of bank shareholders. Gilbart also discussed the geography of British banking, favouring the evolving English system (which prevailed from the 1840s until the 1890s) whereby London banking companies acted as agents for large provincial banks, the latter of which retained their regional autonomy and influence. He contrasted this system with the Scottish model of large centralized branch networks extending outward from Glasgow and Edinburgh.

Besides telling directors and managers of the new banking companies how to do their jobs, Gilbart also provided them with a history of their own, culminating in the joint-stock banks' dominance first of the Scottish, and then of the English financial market. His *History and Principles of Banking* went back to Roman times, but its main historical focus was on the Bank of England's evolving role as a regulator of the nation's currency and its continuing obstruction of the formation of sound commercial banks in England. The 'principles' section of the book was mainly descriptive, but it also sketched out arguments Gilbart would later develop on behalf of 'free banking'. Following shorter sections on savings banks and Scottish banks, he concluded his *History* by reprinting the London and Westminster's prospectus and first three annual reports. He updated his views on banking politics in *The Letters of Nehemiah* (1845), in which he praised Robert Peel's recent Joint-Stock Bank Act for strengthening that sector and criticized London's private bankers for continuing to exclude joint-stock banks from their clearing house.

Gilbart was a vocal and constant critic of the 'currency school' led by Samuel Jones Loyd (Lord Overstone) and George Warde

NORMAN, which claimed that the supply of paper money should be kept in fixed proportion to the amount of gold in the Bank of England. Currency school doctrine was behind the passage of the Bank Charter Act of 1844, which divided the Bank into issuing and banking departments and required the former to issue no more than £14 million beyond its bullion reserves. In evidence before Parliamentary Committees on banking (1837 and 1840) and in pamphlets like *Currency and Banking* (1841), Gilbart denied the currency school's premise that banks (especially the new joint-stock variety) were guilty of irresponsibly issuing more currency than their borrowers could productively invest. Instead, he attributed persistent instability in the money market to lingering aspects of the Bank of England's monopoly, such as the ban on note-issuing powers by London joint-stock banks and the survival of undercapitalized private banks. The fact that Thomas TOOKE's 'banking school' shared many of Gilbart's critiques of the currency school has caused many subsequent writers to lump them together. Unlike Tooke, however, who advocated a discretionary lending policy on the part of the Bank of England, Gilbart argued (along with the currency school) for *less* discretion by the Bank, which he claimed would be more safely brought about by competition from other issuing joint-stock banks than by artificially linking its note-issuing powers to its gold reserves.

Gilbart tried to bolster the empirical basis of his 'free banking' argument in a series of papers delivered to the London Statistical Society and the British Association for the Advancement of Science between 1852 and 1856 on 'the laws of currency' in England, Scotland and Ireland. In these papers, which relied on data generated by returns required under the 1844 Act, he detected seasonal patterns in privately issued bank notes, and inferred from these local regularities that any bank foolish enough to issue more notes than the regional market could bear would soon be driven out of business by its competitors. Summing up his findings in *The Logic of Banking* (1859), he argued that regional note circulation was 'not capricious or accidental, but...determined by the recurrence of the seasons and the state of trade in their respective districts' (1859: 460). In the Irish case, for instance, he rearranged the data to conform to the 'agricultural year' ending in August, then linked a succession of below-average issue levels to the poor harvests in the post-famine years of 1848–52.

Such arguments were successful enough at parrying the currency school's panacea of restricting the supply of paper currency, but neither Gilbart nor the currency school sufficiently accounted for the diminishing significance of bank notes in what was fast becoming a credit-based economy. Nor did Gilbart's assumption of continued regionalism in English banking remain justified for long; instead, large branch networks headquartered in London would be the norm by 1900. On the other hand, his vision of a world where the Bank of England regulated the money market in tandem with a collection of competing joint-stock banks did more or less accurately describe the future of the British money market.

BIBLIOGRAPHY

A Practical Treatise on Banking, containing an Account of the London and County Banks (1827; enlarged 5th edn, 1849).
The History and Principles of Banking (1834).
An Inquiry into the Causes of the Pressure on the Money Market during the year 1839 (1840).
Currency and Banking: A Review of some of the Principles and Plans that have recently engaged Public Attention (1841).
The Letters of Nehemiah, relating to the Laws affecting Joint-stock Banks (1845).
'On the Laws of Currency in Ireland,' *Journal of the Statistical Society of London* (1852), vol. 15, pp. 307–26.

'The Laws of the Currency,' *Journal of the Statistical Society of London* (1854), vol. 17, pp. 289–321.
'The Laws of the Currency in Scotland,' *Journal of the Statistical Society of London* (1856), vol. 19, pp. 144–69.
The Logic of Banking: A Familiar Exposition of the Principles of Reasoning, and their Application to the Art and Science of Banking (1859).

Further Reading
Alborn, T.L., *Conceiving Companies: Joint-Stock Politics in Victorian England* (1998).
Fetter, F.W., *Development of British Monetary Orthodoxy 1797–1875* (Cambridge, Massachusetts, 1965).
Gregory, T.E., *The Westminster Bank through a Century*, 2 vols (1936).
White, L., *Free Banking in Britain: Theory, Experience and Debate 1800–1845* (Cambridge, 1984).

Timothy Alborn

GILBERT, Thomas (*c*.1720–98)

Gilbert was born around 1720 at Cotton, Staffordshire, and died there on 18 December 1798. The son of a Staffordshire land-owning family, he read law at the Inner Temple and was called to the bar in 1744. In 1745 he served in a regiment raised to combat the Jacobite rising by Staffordshire magnate Earl Gower. He subsequently became Gower's agent, managing his Staffordshire and Shropshire estates and, under his patronage, represented two Staffordshire boroughs in parliament: Newcastle-under-Lyme (1761–8) and Lichfield (1768–94), Patronage also brought him several profitable offices, including a court post as Master of the Great Wardrobe (1763–82).

Gilbert's time as Gower's agent was during a period of generally rising agricultural prices and rents; he has been described as bringing to the management of the tenantry 'a new commercial attitude which spared little time for sentimentality' (Wordie 1982: 48), though also as displaying no special interest in the details of farming regimes. Industrial development commanded more of his interest, and contributed more to the development of his fortunes. In 1764, together with his brother, Gilbert became a partner in a new company set up by Gower to manage quarries and mines on his Shropshire estates. In 1788, he became a shareholder in the Shropshire canal company, designed to link the Ironbridge region to the Severn. He also held shares in the Trent and Mersey canal.

Gilbert's party political stance was largely dictated by his relationship with Gower: with him he first supported, then deserted the North administration. He was active among the St Alban's Tavern group of backbench MPs who tried to broker ways out of the political chaos which followed North's resignation in 1782, and subsequently gave his support to the younger Pitt. An able and industrious MP, he is best known for his attempts at poor law reform, but he also promoted important measures including consolidating and refining the laws on roads and turnpikes, and successfully promulgating an act to promote clerical residence by facilitating the release of funds to build clergy houses. He also sat on innumerable committees, and in 1784 was appointed chairman of the Committee of Ways and Means, the committee which vetted the government's fiscal programme.

Though he was on the commission of the peace for Staffordshire, Gilbert was not an active justice of the peace. It is unclear how and why he first became interested in poor law reform. His brother was involved in the management of poor relief at parish level, and possibly Gilbert had some such experience too, though his pamphlets never evoke personally won knowledge or understanding. It is possible that his interest in such matters developed entirely within parliament. His first reform proposal, outlined in a pamphlet of 1765, echoed many previous proposals: Gilbert suggested that counties should henceforth serve as administrative units, and that committees of gentlemen in each county should take over the general direction of relief and should establish central workhouses in which a broad swathe of relief recipients might be confined. Probably in response to criticism, he modified his proposal before bringing in a bill in 1766: counties were no longer to be required to adopt the scheme, but might do so if a majority of large landowners opted for it. Thus modified, the bill passed the Commons; its rejection in the Lords was apparently a jab at the faction with whom Gilbert acted, rather than a judgement on the bill itself.

Gilbert persisted in his reform endeavours on and off for more than twenty years, making further serious attempts to secure sweeping reform legislation in 1775–6 and 1786–7. In the 1770s he chaired a parliamentary committee that sought returns, first from those urban and rural parishes that had experimented with incorporations and central workhouses, and secondly from parishes throughout the country, detailing their expenditure on the poor. Returns of the latter kind had been sought in 1696 and 1751; novel to the 1770s, in the context of a general trend towards giving greater publicity to parliamentary proceedings, was the decision to publish both sets of returns. Gilbert also circulated his proposals and invited comment. Relief costs had increased in the 1760s (in part a result of rising population and prices) and poor relief reform schemes therefore attracted much interest; many towns, counties and rural regions were ready to experiment. It is not surprising that Gilbert's proposals were discussed at some county meetings. Much of the feedback was hostile. Men with more hands-on experience than Gilbert censured what they took to be the impracticality of his proposals, and questioned their applicability across widely varying local economies and societies.

Perhaps because of this hostile feedback, but also probably because the outbreak of the American war militated against schemes entailing local taxation or borrowing, Gilbert allowed discussion to lapse until the early 1780s. When he took up the cudgels again, in the closing years of the war, he acknowledged continuing fiscal constraints and therefore proposed only modest reforms. Ironically, only at this time did any of his relief schemes to result in legislation. 'Gilbert's Act' of 1782 empowered ratepayers in each parish to decide whether to amalgamate with other parishes to form a larger unit. If they chose to do so, further provisions came into effect. Overall administrative responsibility passed into the hands of a common administrative body, which was to establish a workhouse for the maintenance of children and the elderly, but not the able-bodied poor. In the face of criticism, Gilbert had modified his earlier schemes in two major ways. First, he had vested power to launch the scheme not, as initially, in major landowners, but instead in small ratepayers. The effect of placing this power in the hands of presumptively hypercautious spenders was expected to be to reduce take-up of the act. His second major modification was to narrow the task assigned to the workhouse, which was now to house not the able-bodied, but only the helpless young and old.

Gilbert did not regard the 1782 act as a satisfactory terminus, and in 1786–7, against a background of peace and economic recovery, he once again pressed upon parliament a sweeping scheme of reform. Though material circumstances were more favourable, the tide of opinion had however by then turned further against the tradition of reforming thought on which he drew. The utility of large, expensive institutions was increasingly questioned; there was concern about the effect of heavy relief costs on the middling and poorer sort; the hypothesis that welfare schemes operate primarily to create dependency was in vogue. Interest therefore focussed on low-cost relief schemes designed to nurture independence –

on, for example, contributory schemes. Against this background of criticism, Gilbert modified his proposal. In its final form, his scheme focussed above all on the creation of larger administrative units and committees to govern them. Taking on board the argument that conditions differed across the nation, he gave such committees discretion as to the kinds of relief they might endorse; he simply wished to see significant policy-shaping powers vested in bodies of higher social status and greater spatial reach than parish vestries. With an eye to reducing tax burdens, he launched a parliamentary investigation into the extent, nature and status of charitable endowments; the thought being that these might be re-deployed to reduce relief costs. At the same time, he commended alternative approaches to the problem of poverty: through, for example, the formation of friendly societies and imposition of moral discipline.

Despite the efforts that he made to adapt to changing opinion, Gilbert's efforts once again came to naught. It was argued that prolonged parliamentary discussion was causing planning blight in the localities; if parliament could not agree how to proceed, it had better leave the matter to local initiative. It seems probable that, even in its revised form, Gilbert's scheme still seemed too institutional for rapidly changing tastes. Gilbert passed some of his working papers on to the younger Pitt, who as prime minister in 1796, introduced his own reform bill, but Pitt's bill departed further than any of Gilbert's schemes from the institutional reform tradition, accepting the parish as the unit of initiative, and concentrating rather on diversifying relief strategies to include encouragement to cow-keeping and education.

Historically, Gilbert's name is primarily associated with a 'humanitarian' phase in poor relief thinking. However, this judgement appears to be a retrospective construct, having little to do with Gilbert's own concerns. He is better understood as an entrepreneur and manager, both in his professional and in his parliamentary life. His initial poor-law reform proposals were unoriginal, deriving straightforwardly from a well established tradition of thought about how to make relief management more efficient; Gilbert simply judged that the time was ripe for a kind of general reform often previously broached. Because he took on board the need to manage public opinion about such proposals, his ideas evolved in practice in interesting ways between the 1760s and 1780s, in response to currents of thought that sometimes stressed humanitarian, sometimes quite other values. Throughout Gilbert appears rather as a follower than as a leader of opinion.

In addition to the pamphlets which he certainly wrote – pamphlets setting out his poor law reform proposals – Gilbert is traditionally credited with the editorship of *A Collection of Pamphlets Concerning the Poor* (1787). The pamphlet incorporates some of the returns to Gilbert's enquiries, but internal evidence suggests that it emanates from another, almost certainly Scottish source: it was co-published in Edinburgh and London by members of the Elliott family, and attends to Scottish circumstances in a way uncharacteristic of English pamphlets at this time. Specimen books of accounts for the parish poor provided by the editor list poor with Scottish surnames; finally, the copy in Cambridge University Library includes a note, in an eighteenth-century hand, that one phrase is 'a Scotchism'. It may well have come from John M'FARLAN's pen. The collection implicitly constructs an alternative tradition of thought about poor law reform to that on which Gilbert drew. The editor constructed this alternative view largely from English material, but his choice was probably affected by his Scottish viewpoint: Scotland notionally had a relief system similar to the English, but many Scottish parishes levied no poor rates, and relief, when paid, was paid at a lower level.

The author of this work built on much previous work in his assemblage of quantitative data about poverty and relief costs. He echoed widely held views when he criticised overseers for spending too lavishly; suggested that the poor were spoiled by high wages and prone to dependence; and lamented the multiplicity of alehouses and the paucity of schools and prisons for the correction of the idle. He was in line with mainstream opinion in the 1780s when he favoured more schools and contributory relief schemes. But instead of advocating the creation of unions of parishes as the infrastructure for an improved regime, he urged the improvement of parish government, notably through the establishment of select vestries; a course that would be adopted (with a nod in the direction of Scottish example) in 1818–19.

BIBLIOGRAPHY

A Scheme for the Better Relief and Employment of the Poor: Humbly Submitted to the Consideration of the Members of both Houses of Parliament (1765).
Plan for the Better Relief and Employment of the Poor, for Enforcing and Amending the laws respecting Houses of Correction and Vagrants; and for improving the Police... With Bills intended to be offered to Parliament, etc (1781).
Considerations on the Bills for the better Relief and Employment of the poor...intended to be offered to Parliament this Session (1787).
A Collection of Pamphlets concerning the Poor: with Abstracts of the Poor's Rates; Expenses of Different Houses of industry, &c. and Observations by the Editor (1787). (As noted, the attribution of this work to Gilbert is not correct.)

Further Reading

Brooke, J., 'Thomas Gilbert', in J. Brooke and L. Namier (eds), *History of Parliament: The House of Commons 1754–1790* (1964).
Slack, P., *The English Poor Law, 1531–1782* (Cambridge, 1995).

Thorne, R.G., 'Thomas Gilbert', in R.G. Thorne (ed.), *History of Parliament: The House of Commons 1790–1820* (1986).
Trinder, B., *The Industrial Revolution in Shropshire* (1981).
Wordie, J.R., *Estate Management in Eighteenth-Century England: the Building of the Leveson-Gower Fortune* (1982).

Joanna Innes

GLASS, David Victor (1911–78)

Glass was born in the East End of London on 2 January 1911, the son of a journeyman tailor and grandson of Polish immigrants, and died in London on 23 September 1978. He was educated at the local voluntary school, the Raine's Foundation School, and the London School of Economics where he graduated in 1931 with a second-class honours BSc (Econ), taking geography as his special subject. From 1932–40 he had his first acquaintance with demographic studies, first as research assistant to W.H. BEVERIDGE in 1931, then as a research worker with Lancelot Hogben in the department of social biology at the LSE (1935–7). He worked with Alexander CARR-SAUNDERS on improving population statistics as its research secretary at the Population Investigation Committee (1936–40), and went on to be the committee's chairman (1959–78). His PhD thesis was published as *Population Policies and Movements in Europe* (1940).

In 1940 Glass went to the USA as a Rockefeller Fellow, and soon took up war work as deputy director of the British Petroleum Mission in Washington, DC. He then returned to London as assistant director for overseas statistics at the Ministry of Supply. From 1944–9 he worked for the Royal Commission on Population and from 1946–50 served as UK representative on the UN

Population Commission. Through running a master's course in demography and travels to Asia, he had much influence on the study of population in developing countries. In succession to R.R. Kuczynski he was appointed reader in demography at the LSE in 1945 and was promoted to professor of sociology in 1949; he succeeded Morris Ginsberg to the Martin White Chair of Sociology in 1961. In 1947 he founded the journal *Population Studies*, with E. Grebenik as joint editor. He was the first president of the British Society of Population Studies 1974. His many honours included fellowships of both the British Academy (1964) and the Royal Society (1971), reflecting his mathematical grasp of demography. He declined a knighthood because of his long-standing beliefs on equality and social justice. Glass was a talented pianist and a bibliophile who accumulated a notable collection of books on population, enabling him to write on Gregory KING and other founders of the subject. His wife Ruth, whom he married in 1942, was also a sociologist.

Much of Glass's early writing in the 1930s was for the *Eugenics Review*. He surveyed population policies that were responding to the contemporary fear of a declining population. He used net reproduction rates to estimate the ability of a country to maintain its population size. Further, he was engaged in predicting population sizes; for example, in 1943 he forecast the population of Britain and other major countries for 1980. The geographical breadth of his early studies showed how determined he was to be cosmopolitan in his demographical research. In his contribution on fertility to a symposium published as *Political Arithmetic*, he indicated his ability to handle long sweeps of data by analysing data for England and Wales covering the period 1851–1934. He established that the link between real wages and the marriage rate of unmarried males aged 20–44 was weakening, and noted that greater employment of women, unemployment and health insurance were eroding the relationship.

In his *Population Policies and Movements in Europe* (1940), Glass established his central position in British demography at the early age of twenty-nine. In this monograph, after glancing at pro-natalist population policies as old as the Babylonian *Code of Hammurabi*, he looked at instances of such policies in France, Belgium, Italy, Germany and Scandinavia, noting the intensity of policies in the 1930s. A mixture of marriage loans, family allowances and cash grants attempted to arrest the contemporary decline in the birth rate. Glass criticized governments for their paltry incentives, trying 'to buy babies at bargain prices' (1940: 371). He also noted that Germany was attempting to increase its population through propaganda and repressive measures to control conception and child-bearing. In a concluding section on population trends, he mused over the significance for a country of a declining population. He was optimistic enough to believe that encouraging immigration and pursuing economic and social planning would prevent disaster. Instead of recommending population decline as a way of reducing unemployment, Glass, using his understanding of the new macroeconomics, suggested a fall in the interest rate and, as an effective policy, increasing the propensity to consume by redistributing income (1940: 367).

The difficulties Glass faced as a demographer were well outlined in his 1966 lecture to the Royal Society. He discussed the boldest of demographical tasks, forecasting total populations. Partly he saw it as the perennial task of making sense of mortality and fertility data, and partly as the prediction of components of the population. He argued that general laws on population were devised in the nineteenth century by opponents of MALTHUS, whereas in the seventeenth and eighteenth centuries demographers had wanted to know how rapidly the population doubled. By 1901 CANNAN had moved to the more sophisticated question of discovering the ratio of births per marriage which would maintain a stationary population, given unchanged probabilities of marriage and survival. Glass was less keen on searching for the general laws determining the life table. He thought the later use of the concept of the net reproduction rate encouraged demographic forecasting. While admitting that demographers cannot predict the total population decades ahead. Glass believed it was possible to make smaller forecasts of populations already in existence, for example, to provide a fifteen-year manpower plan. Short-term forecasts of births would continue, helped by taking into account the effects of contraception.

Early in his career Glass showed an interest in the wider sociology of population studies. In *The Town* (1935), he sought to trace the influence of the town on its inhabitants. He argued that urbanization could only occur if conditions favoured large-scale trade, there was a monetized system of exchange and high agricultural productivity to feed rural and urban populations. He expected continued population decline through the falling birth rate and a shrinkage in size of urban settlements. As the town is the foundation of our current civilization, he warned that the consequences of urban decline would be widespread.

Glass's major contribution to sociology was his work on social mobility. His research demonstrating the difficulties encountered by ex-elementary school pupils entering Oxford and Cambridge universities was published in *Political Arithmetic* in 1938, but his more famous foray into the subject consisted of papers in an anthology published in 1954 following on from Morris Ginsberg's early studies. A research project at the London School of Economics seeking to understand social selection and differentiation coincided with his elevation to a chair. Sample survey data on the occupations of the persons chosen and their fathers and fathers-in-law were gained from interviews conducted in 1949. Occupational classifications were used to devise a social hierarchy, and those classifications were checked to confirm that it was generally acceptable as a measure of social status. Social mobility was defined as movement between seven broad social categories, the highest being professional and high administrative, and the lowest unskilled manual. The methods used, a refinement of contemporary techniques of Italian statisticians, produced indices of association and dissociation between occupations of parents and children. 'Perfect' mobility, the equal probabilities of movement for persons of all social origins to other social status categories, was considered. Glass approved of a high degree of social mobility, as he believed it increased economic and social efficiency and utilized a person's capacities more fully. Proudly, he asserted that this was the first investigation of its kind.

BIBLIOGRAPHY

The Town (1935).
'Changes in Fertility in England and Wales: 1851–1931', in L. Hogben (ed.), *Political Arithmetic* (1938, pp. 161–212).
(with J.L. Gray) 'Opportunity and the Older Universities. A Study of the Oxford and Cambridge Scholarship System', in L. Hogben (ed.), *Political Arithmetic* (1938, pp. 418–70).
Population Policies and Movements in Europe (Oxford, 1940).
Introduction to Malthus (1953).
Social Mobility in Britain (1954).
'The Third Royal Society Nuffield Lecture: Demographic Prediction', *Proceedings of the Royal Society of London. Series B, Biological Sciences* (1967) vol. 108, no. 1011, pp. 119–39.

Further Reading
Borrie, W.D., 'David Victor Glass 1911–1978', *Proceedings of the British Academy* (1982), vol. LXVIII, pp. 537–60.
Grebenik, E., 'David Victor Glass (1911–1978)', *Population Studies* (1979), vol. 33, pp. 5–17.
Halsey, A.H., 'Sociology as Political Arithmetic (The Glass Memorial Lecture)', *The British Journal of Sociology* (1994), vol. 45, pp. 427–44.

Hobcraft, J.N., 'David Victor Glass (1911–1978)', *Population Index* (1978), vol. 44, pp. 621–9.

Marshall, T.H. and Laslett, P., 'David Glass: An Appreciation', *The British Journal of Sociology* (1979), vol. 30, pp. 1–4.

Donald Rutherford

GODWIN, William (1756–1836)

William Godwin was born on 3 March 1756 at Wisbech, Cambridgeshire, to a family of strict Calvinist dissenters. He died in London in New Palace Yard adjoining the Houses of Parliament on 7 April 1836. After a thoroughly classical and Christian education, at the age of seventeen he attended Hoxton College, a dissenting academy in London. Five years of intensive study prepared him for a brief career as a dissenting minister and a much longer career as a philosopher, novelist, historian and journalist. His studies of theology were undermined by a passionate reading of Holbach and Helvétius, and he left his church appointment in Buckinghamshire to become a professional writer in London in the 1780s.

By the late 1780s Godwin attained some distinction as a political commentator in the *New Annual Register* and in a number of books. He exploded upon the revolutionary 1790s with his *Enquiry Concerning Political Justice* (1793), that weighed a social order based on monarchy, aristocracy, property, and an established church against an egalitarian society of responsible individuals. *Political Justice* was followed immediately by a fictional account of domestic injustice, *Things as they Are; or the Adventures of Caleb Williams* (1794). The two works brought Godwin initial fame, but a Britain driven by war against the French Revolution turned rapidly against the ideals that his works consistently espoused. He continued to write, and to write effectively, but the reception of his works was usually tainted by the prejudices of a violently opposed ideology.

Godwin's economic theories stem from overarching concerns with justice and equity. Justice argues that 'the good things of the world' are 'a common stock, upon which one man has as valid a title as another'. To negotiate possession is the function of justice which places the general good over private nature. The unequal distribution of property is an evil that upsets the natural equality into which all are born as subject of a common nature seeking common benefits.

His main forays into the ethics of property are found in four publications: in Book Eight of *Political Justice*, in his book of essays, *The Enquirer* (1797), and in two responses to MALTHUS: *Thoughts Occasioned by the Perusal of Dr. Parr's Spital Sermon* (1801) and *Of Population* (1820). Book Eight of *Political Justice* is the foundation of his economic position. He defines property as things that may add to 'benefit or pleasure' such as food, clothing, and housing, 'the good things of the world', and distinguishes among four classes: subsistence, the means of intellectual and moral self-development, inexpensive gratifications, and luxuries. The last he rejects as evil.

Godwin also distinguishes among degrees of property rights. The first degree are things of most intense personal benefit; the second degree is the right to the produce of one's own industry, the third degree, devoid of right, is to the power of disposing the produce of another's industry. Godwin's 'rights' are moral rights and not sanctions for either confiscation or hoarding. His arguments are anti-Mandevillian in locating the greatest evil in appropriating another's industry to purchase luxuries.

Godwin's essays 'Of Riches and Poverty' and 'Of Avarice and Profusion' in *The Enquirer* develop the attack on luxury and inequality in *Political Justice*. He argues that money is not a commodity but a means of exchange and that there is no wealth in the world other than human labour. Money confers on a few the power of compelling others to labour for their benefit. Those with such power traditionally keep the wages of labourers and artisans at subsistence level. Thus a new luxury means a new burden. If productivity demands it, subsistence will require more hours of labour per day. Living conditions for the worker never improve. Regarding the lives of those fated to a bare and uncertain subsistence, he asserts that to be born to poverty is to be born a slave: a life of poverty is brief, without enjoyments, without leisure to improve the mind; the only happiness lies in fitful moments when pain is absent. The ideal, he argues, is 'a state of cultivated equality' based on all sharing the labour required for the production of the necessaries of life. When one's labour is not appropriated by another, the production of life's necessities demands less time and leaves individuals longer lives, fewer cares, and many more hours for self-development.

Godwin's purpose was to change people's ideas about property. The only genuine revolution for Godwin is a revolution of opinion. For him, economic inequality is the main source of social disaster because it creates selfishness, servility, the suppression of ideas, and hindrance of the free development of individuals. Both rich and poor are less complete as a result of a social structure that values property too highly.

The economics of Thomas Robert Malthus are inimical to Godwin's. With contrasting views of property, it was inevitable that they would clash. Indeed their careers contrast, for Malthus's popularity rose as Godwin's declined. The first edition of *An Essay on the Principle of Population* (1798) devotes a third of its length to Godwin's arguments in *Political Justice* and *The Enquirer*. Malthus dismisses Godwin's egalitarianism as fiction contrary to 'fixed laws of human nature', and responds with his notorious ratios that show population increasing geometrically while food production increases only arithmetically. Godwin's cultivated equality will result inevitably in a population increase that will outstrip food supply. The result will be a world of vice and misery until death restores the balance.

Godwin's *Thoughts Occasioned by the Perusal of Dr. Parr's Spital Sermon ... being a reply to the attacks of Dr. Parr, Mr. Mackintosh, the author of An Essay on Population, and others* (1801) offers only a brief response to Malthus. Godwin reiterates his rebuttal of similar arguments in Book Eight of *Political Justice*: that overpopulation is a remote concern, the earth's capacities for food production are far from fully employed, that under conditions of equality people would practice restraint and limit their offspring to what the land can support. However, Malthus's subsequent editions found confirmation of a disturbing population increase in the census data of the United States. His fifth edition of 1817 condemned any improvements in political and social conditions and found sympathetic support among the heavily taxed classes of war-indebted Britain.

Of Population (1820) is Godwin's second and final response to Malthus and his social attitudes. This 626-page examination of evidence and arguments challenges Malthus's reliance on the census figures of the United State on the grounds that they ignore massive and unrecorded immigration. He offers the more accurate census figures of Sweden as evidence of no implacable increase in population. He describes the improvements in productivity resulting from modern methods of cultivation, and notes how little of the arable land in Britain is devoted to human nourishment. He rejects Malthus's conviction that human beings cannot control their own passions; and finally he directs scorn at the pusillanimity of the Malthusian vision, finding even in Adam SMITH humane arguments that better wages and living conditions for working people benefit the whole society.

Godwin is the first and most profound British advocate of philosophical anarchism. By focussing on human need, he offers new perspectives on capital and production. He is a man of the enlightenment and shares some of the optimism of the French philosophes in his vision of human possibility. His dislike of government is founded on the conviction of the evil it does and will do since it is organized on authority rather than benevolence.

His life was a model of industry. To support his growing family he wrote essays, novels, histories and children's books. He also managed a publishing house devoted to works for children. Despite all this industry, he was never far from poverty. A concluding irony of Godwin's long life is that government benevolence saved him from destitution. In 1833 Lord Grey conferred upon him the post of Yeoman Usher of the Exchequer, a sinecure that gave him a small residence and a pension of £200.

BIBLIOGRAPHY

An Enquiry concerning Political Justice, and its Influence on General Virtue and Happiness (1793; repr. 1796, 1798).
Things as they Are; or the Adventures of Caleb Williams (1794).
The Enquirer (1797).
Thoughts occasioned by the Perusal of Dr. Parr's Spital Sermon ... Being a reply to the attacks of Dr. Parr, Mr. Mackintosh, the Author of An Essay on Population, and Others (1801).
Of Population (1820).

Further Reading
Fleisher, D., *William Godwin: A Study in Liberalism* (1951).
Marshall, P.H. (ed.), *The Anarchist Writings of William Godwin* (1986).
Monro, D.H., *Godwin's Moral Philosophy* (Oxford, 1953).
Priestley, F.E.L, 'Introduction', *Enquiry Concerning Political Justice by William Godwin* (Toronto, 1946).

St Clair, W., *The Godwins and the Shelleys* (New York, 1989).

Kenneth Graham

GONNER, Edward Carter Kersey (1862–1922)

Edward Carter Gonner (he seems to have acquired his third forename only after graduation) was born on 5 March 1862 in London, and died in Liverpool on 24 February 1922. He was the second son of Peter Kersey and Elizabeth Gonner. At his matriculation in October 1880 his father's occupation was recorded as 'gentleman', which probably implies only that he had retired from his business in the silk trade and possessed sufficient means to pay the fees. Gonner was educated at Merchant Taylors' School, London, and at Lincoln College, Oxford, from which he graduated with first-class honours in modern history in 1884. His introduction to economics came through the lectures of Alfred MARSHALL, for whom he was a star pupil, during Marshall's brief appointment at Oxford, 1883–4. During the following year he was a lecturer for the London Extension Society, and in 1885 obtained his first academic post as lecturer in political economy at University College, Bristol. In 1888 he successfully applied for the post of Lecturer in Political Economy and Commercial Education at the recently founded (1881) University College, Liverpool. In 1891 he was appointed to the newly-created Brunner Chair of Economic Science, a post he held until his death.

Gonner pursued scholarly interests in economic theory, economic history and social development at the highest level, but was not an ivory-tower don. He pioneered efforts to reach a wider, non-traditional audience and established courses of economics lectures for bank clerks, classes for night workers, which were always crowded, and a formal curriculum of commercial education. He was an engaging lecturer and exerted a remarkable hold on students and colleagues. He was active in the administration and development of the college and later the university (from 1903), and in 1905 helped to found (and directed) the School of Social Science. This latter was concerned with the training of social workers associated with the university settlement, and here Gonner worked with Eleanor Rathbone among other early campaigners for social improvement.

Gonner was president of Section F, Economics and Statistics, of the British Association in 1897 and again in 1914. In 1913 he was vice-president of the economic history sub-section of the International Historical Congress in London. He was a member of the Royal Commission on Shipping Conferences (1906–9) and from 1917 he was economic adviser to the Ministry of Food in London; he was later appointed director of Statistics. His work continued after the Armistice in 1918 and the transfer of the Ministry's functions to the Board of Trade. He also led a team charged with the compilation of a history of food statistics and food control during the war. He was appointed CBE in 1918 and KBE in 1921. In 1890 Gonner had married Nannie Ledlie, the sister of the High Sheriff of Cork, and they had a son and three daughters. Between 1918 and 1920 the son and two of the daughters died. Under the weight of these bereavements and the strains of his many activities, Gonner's health, never robust, was further weakened and he died after a short illness.

Gonner's published works fall into a number of apparently little-related fields, and this lack of specialization has been adduced as the reason for his failure to find greater, lasting prominence. His three most substantial works are, first, his critical edition of RICARDO's *Principles of Political Economy and Taxation* (1891), together with the related edition of Ricardo's principal economic essays (1923) and his evaluation of the case made by Ricardo's critics (1890); second, his interpretation and synthetic re-presentation of the social and economic teachings of Johann Karl Rodbertus (1899); and third, his very considerable work of economic history on the causes and consequences of the agricultural enclosure movement, *Common Land and Inclosure* (1912).

In the second rank of Gonner's publications stand *Interest and Saving* (1906), his critical examination of the case for public ownership and control; *The Socialist State: Its Nature, Aims and Conditions* (1895); and an essay on German economic development in the nineteenth century (1912). There were also important articles in the *Economic Journal* and the *English Historical Review*, an introduction to a collection of the economic and statistical studies of John Towne Danson (1906) and two textbooks, *Political Economy* (1888) and *Commercial Geography* (1894). He also contributed to major dictionaries.

Despite the apparently disparate nature of his output, there is a strong underlying theme. That theme is social betterment, and Gonner's whole career is witness to his commitment to this end. With respect to the method of its achievement, he took a keen interest in the idea of the stages of development of society, through need and greed to the higher forms (*The Social Philosophy of Rodbertus*, 1899). He rejected socialism, in the sense of state ownership and control, in favour of competition and natural economic processes (*The Socialist State*, 1895). Gonner greatly admired the ideas, if not the exposition and method, of Ricardo, who believed that social well-being depended on the distribution of wealth between rent, wages and profits. Though Ricardo's work demonstrated the consequences of the employment of capital, he had no developed theory of capital accumulation and this Gonner supplied (*Interest and Saving*, 1906). He believed that, wherever possible, hypothesis should be supported by empirical evidence, and Gonner's study of the enclosure movement, *Common Land and Inclosure* (1912), can be seen as a monumental case-study, in which he rejected the dramatic simplicity of the socialist, conflictual interpretation in favour of a view of the movement as 'continuous and as due in the main to the operation of large economic, and, so to say, normal causes' (1912: v). Finally, in the process of betterment, education can widen appreciation of the higher forms and, therefore, the destination, while social work can help to alleviate the stresses of the journey.

BIBLIOGRAPHY

Political Economy: An Elementary Text Book of the Economics of Commerce (1888).
'Ricardo and His Critics', *Quarterly Journal of Economics* (1890), vol. 4, pp. 276–90.
Principles of Political Economy and Taxation, by David Ricardo (1891).
'The Survival of Domestic Industries', *Economic Journal* (1893), vol. 3, pp. 23–32.
The Socialist State: Its Nature, Aims and Conditions: Being an Introduction to the Study of Socialism (1895).
The Social Philosophy of Rodbertus (1899).
Interest and Saving (1906).
'Introduction', in J.T. Danson, *Economic and Statistical Studies* (1906).
Common Land and Inclosure (1912; repr. 1966).
'The Economic History', in J.H. Rose *et al.*, *Germany in the Nineteenth Century* (Manchester, 1912, pp. 79–99).
Economic Essays by David Ricardo (1923).

Further Reading
Beveridge, W.H., 'Professor Sir Edward Gonner' *Economic Journal* (1922), vol. 32, June, pp. 264–7.

Gordon Fletcher

GOODWIN, Richard Murphey (1913–1996)

Goodwin was born 24 February 1913 in Newcastle, Indiana and died in Siena, Italy on 6 August 1996. He was educated first at Harvard where he studied political science, writing an essay on a critique of Marxism for his graduation thesis. He then went to Oxford as a Rhodes scholar and read philosophy, politics and economics for his bachelor's degree, working with Roy HARROD and Henry PHELPS-BROWN. He then returned to Harvard where he finished his PhD on British monetary history, a project which he had begun under the guidance of Phelps-Brown. He joined the economics department at Harvard as an instructor and stayed there until 1949, when he left for Cambridge after some disagreement with his elders. He remained at Cambridge until 1980, when he retired to Siena.

Goodwin's major contributions are to a study of investment and its role in generating undamped but irregular fluctuations in economic activity. Ragnar Frisch had shown that cycles could be generated by a combination of a deterministic structure and periodic shocks. This model requires the random shocks to have a periodicity to make the fluctuations undamped and sustained. Goodwin succeeded instead in devising non-linear models of investment behaviour which guaranteed deterministic cyclical outcomes which were undamped. The key was a non-linear accelerator which reacted to changes in income, as well as a gap between actual and desired capital stock. Since investment also generated income via the multiplier, the falling off of investment when the gap in capital stock was closed gave an endogenous turning point for the end of the boom. This clutch of essays, reproduced later in Goodwin (1982), occupied him in his Harvard phase.

Another pioneering insight was that a Leontieff-type input output matrix for the economy could be used to demonstrate the working of the multiplier through changes sectoral production activity. 'The Multiplier as a Matrix' (published later in Goodwin (1983)) is totally original in bridging together the thinking of KEYNES and Leontieff. Goodwin was also able to show the connection between growth and linearity by using the Perron–Froebenius theorem (brought to his attention by one of his students, Robert Solow). This was the first use of the theorem in Western economics, Morishima having used it in his Japanese work (see Di Matteo 2000). A further generalization of the relation of eigenvalues of a linear system with their economic logic allowed Goodwin to extend SRAFFA's standard commodity to as many such constructs as the number of distinct eigenvalues of the linear system.

Perhaps his best and most influential paper was 'A Growth Cycle', written for the Maurice DOBB Festschrift (Feinstein 1967). This is an elegant use of the Volterra–Lotka predator–prey schema to generate growth and cycles in a deterministic fashion. The pair of equations relate to a real wage bargain on lines of a linearized Phillips curve and a Cambridge type classical saving-investment behaviour in which workers consume wages and capitalists save and invest all the profits. The system has an equilibrium which ensures a natural growth rate which absorbs all labour force, but the equilibrium is never approached even asymptomatically. If the system does not start in equilibrium, it cycles perpetually. Yet the system does not break down in an apocalyptic Marx–Rosa Luxemburg fashion either. Capitalism lives on as a dynamic disequilibrium system. Extensions and modifications of this system are several and some are included in Goodwin et al. (1984).

It was this insight of a perpetual dynamic disequilibrium which occupied much of Goodwin's energy during his period in Siena. The original 1967 model was found to be structurally unstable, but Goodwin was able to develop this property by linking his work to the newly emerging chaos theory in the 1980s (Goodwin 1990). He also collaborated with a younger colleague Linello Punzo to develop the idea of dual instability in price and quantity adjustment in linear systems, in a major work on capitalist dynamics (Goodwin and Punzo 1987).

Capitalism and its disequilibrium, cyclical yet growth-imbued behaviour, fascinated Goodwin all his life. But while many have been fascinated by the same problem, few if any have succeeded in bringing to bear rigorous methods of non-linear mathematics and combining it with a talent for simplicity and elegance as did Richard Goodwin. He blended together in a unique fashion classical and Keynesian economics with modern mathematical techniques. He was also a talented painter and a wine connoisseur of some note, attributes which gave pleasure to his friends and fellows of Peterhouse, Cambridge college.

BIBLIOGRAPHY
'A Growth Cycle', in C. Feinstein (ed.), *Socialism, Capitalism and Economic Development* (Cambridge, 1967).
Essays in Economic Dynamics (1982).
Essays in Linear Economic Systems (1983).
(with M. Krueger and A. Vercelli), *Non-Linear Models of Fluctuating Growth* (Berlin, 1984).
(with L. Punzo) *The Dynamics of a Capitalist Economy* (Cambridge, 1987).
Chaotic Economic Dynamics (Oxford, 1990).

Further Reading
Di Matteo, M. 'Richard Murphey Goodwin', in P. Arestis and M. Sawyer (eds), *A Biographical Dictionary of Dissenting Economists* (Cheltenham, 2000, pp. 240–9).
Feinstein, C. *Socialism, Capitalism and Economic Development* (Cambridge, 1967).

Meghnad Desai

GOSCHEN, George Joachim (1831–1907)

Goschen was born on 10 August 1831 in Stoke Newington, and died suddenly at his home at Seacox Heath, Kent, on 7 February 1907. He was the eldest son and second of seven children born to William Henry Goschen and his wife, Henrietta Ohmann. He was educated at schools in Blackheath (1840–2) and Saxe-Meiningen (1842–5) before attending Rugby and then Oriel College, Oxford (1850). He gained a double first in classics and was an active member of the Oxford Union, becoming famous for his speeches on political and literary topics; he was president of the Union in his final year. He graduated in 1853.

Goschen then went into the family business of Frühling and Goschen. In 1854 he went to 'New Granada' (Colombia) in South America to look after the family's business affairs. He spent two years there learning about commercial matters; on his return he continued to work with his father and made a name for himself in the commercial world: his nickname was 'the fortunate youth'. In 1856, at age twenty-seven, he became a director of the Bank of England. On 22 September 1857 he married Lucy Dalley; the couple had two sons and four daughters.

Entering politics in 1863, Goschen was the Liberal MP for the city of London from then until 1878. He supported policies such as the secret ballot, the abolition of tithes and the removal of the religious test for Oxbridge candidates. This latter brought Goschen into direct conflict with Lord Robert Cecil (Lord Salisbury). Goschen also supported the disestablishment of the Irish Church. However, he differed in his approach to foreign affairs from fellow Liberals such as John BRIGHT and Richard COBDEN. Goschen had first-hand experience of politics in countries other than Britain; he had dealings with other nations in his business life as well as in political life and he built up an extensive network of contacts in Europe.

Lord John Russell succeeded Palmerston as prime minister in 1865 and appointed Goschen vice-president of the Board of Trade in November, because of Goschen's knowledge of economics and commerce and his ability to debate effectively. In January 1866 Goschen became chancellor of the Duchy of Lancaster and joined Russell's cabinet, leaving the family business in order to pursue a career in politics. He played an active role in the debates for the reform of parliament along with other Liberals and became president of the poor law board in Gladstone's first ministry (1868). In that post, he attempted to bring some order to the administration of poor relief in rural areas. His proposals led to an outcry from the landowners who did not wish to see their powers diminished and the plans were abandoned. In March 1871 he was appointed as First Lord of the Admiralty, where his administrative abilities were invaluable in bringing credibility to a department that had been criticised for inefficiency.

In 1876, while he was a backbencher during Disraeli's ministry, Goschen was chosen as the representative of British holders of Egyptian bonds, and went to Cairo to investigate and report on the country's financial situation. He and the French representative worked together on behalf of their respective bondholders and succeeded in negotiating the establishment of Anglo-French control over Egypt's finances. On his return in 1877, Goschen found himself at odds with the Liberal party over a proposed reform of the franchise. He told his constituents in London that he would not stand as a candidate in the next general election; however, he was returned for Ripon in 1880. Gladstone offered him the post of Viceroy of India, which he declined. He did accept the post of special ambassador to the Porte, however, and left for Constantinople in May 1880. The aim of the government was to force the Sultan to implement the agreement reached by the Treaty of Berlin (1878). Goschen was in Turkey until June 1881, successfully settling the Greek and Montenegro frontier questions.

Goschen found political life difficult during Gladstone's second ministry, not least because he disliked the radical leanings of such men as Sir Charles Dilke and Joseph Chamberlain, both of whom appeared to be rising stars in the Liberal Party. Often, Goschen opposed the government's policies, particularly on issues such as the extension of the franchise and Gladstone's policies concerning Ireland, South Africa and Egypt. He declined the post of Leader of the House in 1884 and voted against the government on a motion of censure over the events in the Sudan and the fall of Khartoum. Gladstone's policies were blamed for the perceived disaster. Following the 'Hawarden kite' of 1885, when Gladstone announced his conversion to the idea of Home Rule for Ireland, Goschen and Lord Hartington became the founders and most active members of the Liberal Unionists. He resigned from the Reform and Devonshire Clubs in protest at Liberal policies. He strenuously opposed the first Home Rule Bill for Ireland (1886), his speeches bringing him again to political prominence but resulting in him losing his Edinburgh seat in the general election of that year. He stood unsuccessfully as a candidate in Liverpool then was elected for St George's, Hanover Square.

From December 1886 until the end of the ministry, Goschen served as Chancellor of the Exchequer in Salisbury's Conservative government following the resignation of Lord Randolph Churchill. During that time Goschen was responsible for meeting the increasing monetary demands of the government while reducing the national debt. In March 1888 he converted the debt in what a very large operation for the time. He dealt with three blocks of 3 per cent stock: the first block of £166 millions could be redeemed at face value without notice. The second block comprised £69 millions of 'reduced' stock and the third block was of £323 millions of 'consols'. These two blocks could be redeemed only with notice and in large sums. He created new consols that carried an interest of two and a three quarters per cent as a substitution. The immediate saving on interest was only about £1,400,000 and the final total was a saving of only double that amount.

In the same year, Goschen reduced income tax to sixpence in the pound and cut the tobacco tax, and in 1890 he reduced the tea tax by twopence. At the same time, he was able to raise sufficient money to allocate £2.9 million to local governments in 1888 and even larger funds in the subsequent two years. He funded increases in the army and navy estimates by levying a one per cent estate duty on real or personal estates exceeding ten thousand pounds. As a firm believer in 'Britain's wooden walls' – a strong navy to protect Britain and her empire and to guarantee world peace – he raised enough money to pay for a special naval building programme in 1889. He also provided two million pounds for free education in 1901.

During the late nineteenth century, British trade expanded greatly, culminating in a boom in 1900. However, there had been much overspeculation in South American nations and in November 1890 Barings' Bank looked set to crash; its liabilities were over £21 million. Although the governor of the Bank of England, William Lidderdale, asked Goschen to intervene to save the City's financial institutions, the Chancellor refused to pledge state money to save a private company. He did offer to suspend the Bank Charter, but that was as far as he would go. Lidderdale was able to raise sufficient money from private concerns to save Barings, which became a joint stock company as a result.

Gladstone formed his fourth ministry in 1892, and Goschen again strenuously opposed Liberal plans for home rule in Ireland. He formally joined the Conservative party and became a member of the Carlton Club. The ministry lasted for less than two years, and Salisbury's succeeding ministry was strengthened by the addition of other Liberal Unionists including Hartington and Joseph Chamberlain. Goschen was appointed once more as First Lord of the Admiralty. He then decided to retire from political life, resigning in October 1900. He intended to spend the remainder of his life at the family home at Seacox Heath in Kent, but instead, he was elevated to the House of Lords as Lord Goschen of Hawkhurst. In 1903 he opposed Joseph Chamberlain's proposals for the reintroduction of protectionist tariffs; joining the Duke of Devonshire and other Conservative free traders, he worked to prevent the implementation of a policy that he thought would be disastrous for Britain. The free traders were successful: in December 1905 the Liberals were returned to power on a free trade platform.

As a mark of the respect for Goschen's work, he was elected as lord rector of Aberdeen university in 1874 and again in 1888. In 1890 he was elected to a similar position at Edinburgh university. He was chosen as chancellor of Oxford university in 1903 and was awarded an honorary DCL at Oxford in 1881. He was also given honorary LLDs at Aberdeen and Cambridge universities in 1888. After his retirement from the House of Commons, Goschen spent time completing the *Life and Times of Georg Joachim Goschen*, his grandfather, a publisher and 'man of letters' in Leipzig; it was published in 1903. He also published *Essays and Addresses on Economic* Questions (1905), comprising his contributions to the *Edinburgh Review* and the texts of some of his speeches.

Goschen's major contribution to economic ideas was his *Theory of the Foreign Exchanges*, published in 1861. In this work, he pointed out that the diversity in specie accounted only for a small part of the banking costs that occurred during foreign trade and currency exchange. He said that, for example, there were only minimal expenses incurred in sending gold between Britain and France but even so, in order to maintain parity, the Bank of England ought to raise its rate by steps of one per cent at a time instead of the customary half of one per cent. The Bank of England implemented Goschen's suggestion; this enabled the country to survive the economic crisis of 1862–5 because the bank had an adequate gold reserve to maintain public confidence. The book was acclaimed by leading financiers and businessmen all over the world and it was translated into most of the main European languages.

George Goschen had a long and successful career in politics and as Chancellor of the Exchequer, he was second to none. His opinions on most matters were moderate and he proved himself to be remarkably consistent in his views. Invariably, he opposed home rule for Ireland but he supported the extension of education for all. Outside of his political commitments, he was a church commissioner and was in favour of the extension of university teaching in London. He opposed the religious test imposed by Oxford and Cambridge universities. He held deep religious convictions and was a scholar of the first order. His knowledge of foreign affairs was extensive and he worked hard to master the details of his departments. He built up Britain's finances, generated public confidence in the Exchequer and fought for what he believed was right.

BIBLIOGRAPHY
Theory of the Foreign Exchanges (1861; repr. 1932).
Life and Times of Georg Joachim Goschen (1903).
Essays and Addresses on Economic Questions (1905).

Further Reading
Elliott, A.D. *Life of Lord Goschen* (1911).

Marjorie Bloy

GRAHAM, James Robert George (1792–1861)

Graham was born 1 June 1792 at the family home at Netherby in Cumberland, and died there on 25 October 1861. He was the son of

Sir James Graham and his wife Lady Catharine Stewart, the daughter of the seventh Earl of Galloway. His family had lived at Netherby since the early seventeenth century and had held a baronetcy since 1629. Graham was educated in Dalston, Cumberland, then Westminster School and then at a school in Bampton, Berkshire. He entered Christ Church College, Oxford in 1810 but left two years later without a degree. He lived in London for a short time and then went to Spain and later to Sicily where, in 1813, he was asked to act as the private secretary of a diplomat, Archibald, Lord Montgomerie. Montgomerie fell ill and the major work involved in the mission devolved to Graham. The two went from Palermo to Rome and Genoa, returning to England in 1814.

From 1818 to 1820 Graham was Whig MP for Hull. He re-entered parliament in 1826 and served as an MP until his death, representing Carlisle (1826-7), Cumberland (1827-37; 1852-7), Pembroke (1838-41), Dorchester (1841-7) and Ripon (1847-52). He supported Catholic emancipation, parliamentary reform and free trade. He served as First Lord of the Admiralty (1830-4; 1852-5) and Home Secretary (1841-6). In July 1819 he married Fanny Callander of Craigforth, Stirlingshire. Lady Graham died in October 1857.

Graham's first foray into politics proved to be expensive. He had Whig sympathies and his father, a Tory, refused to help him into parliament. Graham chose to stand as a 'stranger' in Hull, his election costing him £6,000: he had to borrow the money to finance the campaign. He was not a good speaker and he did not have sufficient money to offer himself for election in 1821. He then returned to Cumberland where he lived near Netherby and devoted himself to managing the family estates. Graham was an 'improving landlord', who also found time to consider the leading political questions of the day. He was interested in political economy and in 1826 he published *Corn and Currency*. The pamphlet demonstrated that governmental attempts to control the exchange rate and price of goods were of little use. It also showed that the Corn laws, passed in 1815, and currency rates were interlinked. Even as early as 1826, Graham favoured the removal of government restrictions from both trade and banking, and he urged people to oppose the Corn Laws which he felt were driving up wages and depressing profits. He wrote that 'the capital of a nation is but the accumulation of the profits of its inhabitants' (1826: vii).

In 1824, Graham's father died and he inherited the baronetcy. This launched Graham into local politics. He was instrumental in the reform of county finances, and consequently was elected as the Whig MP for Carlisle (1826), transferring to become the county MP in 1828. He became an ally of Lord Althorpe and William HUSKISSON, and made his political name as a reformer in a speech (1830) calling for the reduction of official salaries, particularly those of privy councillors. In Grey's ministry, Graham was First Lord of the Admiralty, and reformed the department's finances. However, he insisted that the government ought to be able to press men into the Royal Navy and opposed legislation that would have exempted men who had served for five years from further impressments.

Graham was one of the four men to whom the framing of the Reform Bill was entrusted, although his speeches were not successful. As a speaker, Graham had a very pompous style that was not appreciated by MPs. Even so, the legislation finally became law in 1832. In 1834, Joseph HUME presented a motion for repealing the Corn Laws, which Graham opposed, having evidently changed his position since the 1820s (he was later a moving force behind their repeal). In the same session, Graham introduced an unsuccessful bill to reform the exchequer office. When the administration proposed a reform of the Irish church, Graham resigned because he believed that there had been sufficient constitutional reform already; in any case, he was a staunch Anglican and firmly believed in the necessity for an established Church. In 1834 Melbourne's ministry collapsed and Graham was offered, but rejected, a ministerial position by the incoming prime minister, Sir Robert Peel.

Peel's first ministry was short-lived, lasting only from December 1834 to April 1835, but increasing in strength all the time. Meanwhile, Graham had made himself unpopular with the Whigs and with his constituents. In June 1835 he crossed the floor of the House to join the Conservatives. This cost him his seat for Cumberland in 1837. In 1838 he was elected as lord rector of Glasgow university but in his inaugural speech, his references to the relations between church and state alienated his audience.

Although Graham continued in public life, the loss of his home constituency embittered him for many years. In the House of Commons he attacked the Whigs, with whom he had begun his parliamentary career. In 1841, in a speech supporting Peel's motion of 'no confidence' in the government, Graham's attack on Lord Melbourne was particularly vicious and was partly responsible for the collapse of the Whig ministry. In September 1841, Graham became Peel's Home Secretary, having a well-deserved reputation for administrative competence. He was hard-working, tenacious and had a sound grasp of financial principles, but was perhaps not well suited to the post of Home Secretary as he also had an unfortunate manner: he was confrontational and lacking in tact. 'It was significant that he performed well in the bluff, direct, outspoken and authoritarian world of the navy. He...knew his own mind and expressed it, he was intolerant of idleness, inefficiency, or even ambiguity...Above all, he had a strong streak of authoritarianism. His application of these qualities at the Home Office was at once noticeable' (Donajgrodzki 1977: 103).

Graham undertook a massive overhaul of government-run prisons, having visited many of them to gather information at first hand. He took a personal interest in the administration of the poor law and was happy to reprimand Edwin CHADWICK for overstepping his allocated powers. However, many of his proposed pieces of legislation either failed or had to be withdrawn, so unpopular was Graham as a minister and MP. He lost half of the legislation that he advocated, including bills on prison discipline, a county courts bill and a bill intended to regulate the medical profession (Donajgrodzki 1977: 105). Because of Graham's personal shortcomings and his unwillingness to compromise, the education clauses in the 1844 Factory Act had to be withdrawn and a bill for the reform of church courts had to be abandoned. His comment in 1843 that 'concession to Ireland had reached its limits' alienated many and did nothing to enhance Graham's reputation. In 1844 he admitted that he had authorized the opening of private letters: he did not say that it was done at the request of Lord Aberdeen, the foreign secretary. This issue damaged Peel's government and Graham was the scapegoat for the affair.

However, as a close colleague of Peel, Graham provided support for Peel's economic measures. During the course of the ministry Graham was won over to the idea of an income tax, a policy that initially he resisted. He wanted to see the reduction in tariffs and was delighted with the budget of 1842. In 1845, he was one of only three members of the cabinet to fully support Peel's proposals to suspend the duties on grain immediately, to call parliament and modify the existing Corn Laws. Graham thought that the Anti-Corn Law League was 'the most formidable movements in modern times' and did not want to see it control affairs in parliament. Throughout the Corn Law debates of 1845–6, Graham gave Peel his wholehearted support in the face of strong opposition from the Tories and Conservatives.

In 1845 a potato blight appeared throughout the British Isles, bringing hunger in many places but carrying the threat of famine in Ireland. Graham believed, as did Peel, that the

Corn Laws had to be abandoned. According to Graham, the sliding scale that had been in place since 1842 'would neither slide nor move, and that was its condemnation'. He was overt in acknowledging his conversion to free trade, causing a breach between himself and Lord Stanley, who was a confirmed protectionist. When Peel resigned in June 1846, Graham found himself part of the rump of 'conservatives' in parliament. This group – the Peelites – refused to be absorbed by either of the main political parties, remaining independent of both and eventually becoming the basis of the Liberal Party in 1859. In 1847, Lord John Russell offered the post of Governor-General of India to Graham, who refused it once more: he had already turned down similar offers from Lord Melbourne and Peel. He also refused a post at the Admiralty. As a backbencher, he served on a variety of committees, and when Peel died in July 1850, Graham found himself to be one of the leading Peelites in parliament. As such, he headed the campaign that opposed Disraeli's attempts to reintroduce protectionism. Graham was offered posts in both Whig and Tory ministries, all of which he refused to accept. When the Earl of Aberdeen formed his ministry in 1852, Graham returned to the Admiralty, where he continued to make administrative reforms in the name of efficiency. The Crimean War (1854–6) increased Graham's workload and brought down Aberdeen's ministry, but Graham continued to serve as First Lord of the Admiralty in Palmerston's ministry until the government agreed to an enquiry into the conduct of the war. Graham then resigned and returned to the backbenches until 1861, when he died during the parliamentary recess.

BIBLIOGRAPHY
Corn and Currency (1826).

Further Reading
Donajgrodzki, A.P., 'Sir James Graham at the Home Office', *Historical Journal* (1977), vol. 20, no. 1, pp. 97–120.

Erickson, A.B., *The Public Career of Sir James Graham* (Oxford, 1952).
Parker, C.S., *Life and Letters of Sir James Graham* (1907).
Torrens, W.M., *Life and Times of Sir James Graham* (1863).
Ward, J.T., *Sir James Graham* (1967).

Marjorie Bloy

GRAUNT, John (1620–74)

Graunt was born on 24 April 1620 in Cornhill, London, and died of jaundice in London on 18 April 1674. His father was a draper, and aged sixteen, Graunt himself began a four-year apprenticeship in the drapery business. He then joined his father's business and became very prosperous. He married Mary Scott, who bore him a son and three daughters. He was Renter Warden of the Draper's Company in 1670, having already become a captain in the Trained Band (the London militia). Among other business interests he was a governor of the New River Company and was involved briefly in the Duke of Ormond's attempts to expand the Irish woollen cloth industry by encouraging Flemish weavers to migrate to Ireland. Brought up a Puritan, he later dabbled with Socinianism before finally converting to Roman Catholicism. A cultured man with an interest in art, he collected prints of many great houses and antiquities. The Great Fire of 1666 destroyed his property and thereafter his fortunes declined.

Graunt published his *Natural and Political Observations Made Upon the Bills of Mortality* in 1662. It made him immediately famous; when he presented the work to the Royal Society, Charles II personally recommended Graunt be accepted as a fellow into the society. However, it has proved to be a difficult work to categorize; it was formerly regarded as a work of 'political arithmetic' (a term derived from the work of Sir William PETTY), but is now generally regarded as one of the founding works of modern demography.

Natural and Political Observations is based on an extensive study of mortality statistics published by the City of London, as well as parish records of baptisms and funerals. On the basis of this information, he drew conclusions concerning infant and child mortality, relative fertility and mortality in urban and rural areas, average total fertility of women, relative numbers of women and men in the population, comparisons between different causes for mortality, urban migration, population doubling times and overall population levels. The work has long been of interest for its insights into the degree of medical understanding, and also for some of its more picturesque phrasing; for example, the table of vital statistics for the city of London lists 'bit by a mad dog' and 'made away themselves' among its causes of death.

Much more importantly, however, Graunt was attempting to do many of the things that modern demographers do, developing better knowledge of both productive lifespans and causes of death, and also estimating total population. He attempted to collect exact statistics, which are presented in tables as appendices to the main report. In a series of short chapters, Graunt sets out the conclusions he draws from the analysis of these statistics. Many of these are both common sense and yet radical; for example, observing that there are higher death rates among the larger parishes on the edge of the city, he hypothesizes that these parishes have higher populations which puts more strain on the overseers of the poor and their services. A re-organization of London parish boundaries so that all parishes are more equivalent in terms of area and population could reduce death rates.

Graunt was well aware of the novelty of what he was doing and the uses to which his statistics could be put. In his concluding chapter, he argued that the first duty of the state was to provide peace and plenty for its inhabitants. It had been recognized for some time that in order to do so, the Crown and its advisors needed to have exact information about the land and its resources, and writers such as William HARRISON had attempted to provide geographic surveys. But, argued Graunt, this knowledge was of limited value without corresponding knowledge of the population of the country, what resources are required for its maintenance – particularly for the poor and the ill – and what their productive capacity might be. He believes he has gone some way towards answering these questions for London, and hints without saying so directly that the same kind of study should be done elsewhere. The hint was taken, and in the following century many such studies were undertaken, often with divergent and surprising results.

Graunt's scholarly contributions were more greatly appreciated in the late twentieth century as historians turned increasingly to social history, based on the lives of ordinary people. During the same period, world population has more than doubled, and the science of demography has become renowned. As both a social surveyor and a demographer, John Graunt may be regarded as a pioneer.

BIBLIOGRAPHY
Natural and Political Observations made upon the Bills of Mortality (1662; ed. W.F. Willcox, Baltimore, 1939).

Further Reading
Stephan, E., 'John Graunt', www.ac.wwu/ed/~stephan (29 January 2004).

Norman West

GRAY, Alexander (1882–1968)

Gray was born on 6 January 1882 at Dundee, the son of an art teacher, and died on 17 February 1968 in Edinburgh. He married Alice Gunn, daughter of an Edinburgh solicitor, in 1909; they had one son and three daughters. Gray was knighted in 1947. He was educated at Dundee High School and then at Edinburgh University where he was awarded a first in mathematics in 1903 and, after study at Paris and Göttingen, another first, in economic science, in 1905. He came second in the civil service examinations to John Anderson, later Chancellor of Exchequer in 1943, his fellow student and lifelong friend. Gray spent sixteen years in the civil service chiefly working on social insurance before he turned to an academic career as professor of economics at Aberdeen (1921–35) and then Edinburgh (1935–55). He was a short ruddy-faced man noted for his frugal Calvinism and Rabelaisian humour. No student forgot his robust teaching nor the sight of him playing the organ in the Pollock Hall as his Edinburgh University ordinary class of four hundred students assembled to hear his pungent lectures.

During the First World War Gray's propaganda work for the government included the task of reading German and Dutch newspapers. This led to translation work such as R. Grelling's *J'accuse*, a book of Swiss authorship arraigning German ministers for provoking universal war. His beer-swilling student days left a fondness for German and Danish ballads which he translated in his leisure hours into Scots. He also published scores of his own poems in Scottish newspapers.

When Gray changed to an academic profession, his ability as a civil servant was not forgotten. He was a member of the Royal Commission on national health insurance (1924–6) and of the White Fish Commission (1935). Later he was chairman of many courts of inquiry under the Industrial Courts Act and of appeals tribunals of the Ministry of Labour (1939–45). In his occasional addresses he was determined to apply the lessons of his civil service work. In *Family Endowment* (1927), he attacked schemes of income redistribution. He thought welfare payments based on 'needs' would undermine private property, as someone with a greater need could claim one's assets and would violate the principle of equal pay for equal work. He dissected thoroughly different types of child allowance.

His enduring fame rests on his *The Development of Economic Doctrine* (1931). Gray modestly claimed that this was intended as a student introduction to the subject. The progression of topics, some on schools of economics and some on leading economic writers, started in a standard way with an analysis of the economic writings of Greece and Rome and then surveyed economics in the Middle Ages, mercantilism, the physiocrats, Adam SMITH, MALTHUS and RICARDO. Once he had paid homage to the more familiar economic thinkers he considered writers such as Lauderdale, Rae, Sismondi, Muller, List, Carey and Bastiat. He expounded the later classical writers such as Say, SENIOR, J.S. MILL and CAIRNES, finishing off with MARX and the Austrian School. Throughout it is clear that he handled several languages with ease and could think theologically. Why students find the book appealing is undoubtedly its jaunty style and fearless judgements. The author had enough self-confidence to describe *The Wealth of Nations* as a disorderly book and its author, Adam Smith, as 'sometimes singularly confused' (1931: 123). Gray acknowledged in his epilogue that economics has become more of a method than a doctrine, but asserted that in a time of conflicting schools of economics there is much to be learned from past economic thinkers: 'No point of view, once expressed, ever seems wholly to die; and in periods of transition like the present, our ears are full of the whisperings of dead men' (1931: 370). Frank Knight praised the treatment of Marx, noting significant omissions such as Malthus's rent theory and Senior's utility theory, but thought overall that: 'The exposition combines clearness and accuracy with stylistic freshness and charm in an extraordinary degree' (Knight 1932: 713).

Gray researched radical writers for twenty-two years to write *Socialist Tradition* (1946). The range of 'socialists' discussed is large and surprising. There is a thorough discussion of the Greek, Jewish and Christian origins of socialist ideas, and much on utopias, anarchism and French writers. In this survey of 517 pages, Marx and ENGELS together merit only thirty-seven pages but the ephemeral guild socialists receive twenty-six pages. The idiosyncratic nature of this mixture is partly due to his working definition of socialists: 'all who, urged by a passion for justice or equality, or by a sensitiveness to the evils of the present world, seek a better world, not by way of reform, but by...a fundamental change in the nature and structure of society' (1946: 2).

Gray is honest about his heroes and villains. He likes Fourier and St.-Simon but despises Marx, Lassalle and Rousseau. The book is memorable for its vivid judgements. Aquinas's doctrine of 'callings' is division of labour by divine decree (1946: 59). Life is always 'weary, flat, stale and unprofitable' in utopias as life has reached a static stage (1946: 63). Babeuf's pathetic faith in education is 'found only in those who have been denied it' (1946: 104). He refers to his orthodox economist contemporaries as brought up on 'Tales from the Viennese Woods' (1946: 280). 'It did not take a Karl Marx to come from Trier to the British Museum to tell us that the poor, more often than not, had a rough deal in history' (1946: 329). 'The peculiar position which Lenin occupies among his companions in this volume is that somehow he got things done' (1946: 484). Gray concludes from his vast readings that we need a prophet of liberalism to protect the individual at a time when state intervention is in danger of leading to totalitarianism (1946: 513–14).

Gray's labours attracted many reviewers. Sweezy admired the quality of the writing but quibbled about the inclusion of anarchists such as GODWIN in a work on socialism. He regarded the treatment of St.-Simon and Fourier as the best part of the survey; the chapter on Marx was 'uninformative and unreliable' (Sweezy 1947: 466). SHOVE noted that as a consequence of Gray presenting his work as a collection of studies he 'fails to emphasise the extent to which socialism is, in essence, the antithesis of capitalism'; the book appears to be too much of a fools' gallery, 'almost, indeed...he regards the whole socialist and anarchist tradition as a huge joke' (Shove 1946: 444). HAYEK acknowledged that *Socialist Tradition* would become the standard work and thought it not unjust to expose early socialists as 'maladjusted cranks and phantastic idealists' (Hayek 1947: 154). He regarded Gray's treatment of Marx as reliable and just.

Gray was renowned as a public speaker. His 1948 lecture *Adam Smith* claimed that 'the essence of Smith's doctrine is semi-theological in character...a 'Natural Order' divinely ordained... The Almighty...has endowed man with inclinations which have a purpose and a design' (1948: 7), and thus restrictions of any kind impede the will of God. He noted the inconsistencies in Adam Smith and asserted it is 'a tribute to the greatness of Smith that all schools thought may trace to him their origin and inspiration'. In his 1952 lecture *The Rise of the Welfare State* he again used Smithian economics to assert that the earthly planner frustrates the divine plan. He distinguished the welfare state from social insurance, and complained that schemes of the latter lacked co-ordination produced inadequate benefits, treated the sick unevenly and emphasised unemployment too much. But the welfare state alternative worried him: 'the Welfare State, in its unbounded benevolence, may find itself driven to a degree of regimentation and control which would make it in essence a government at least mildly totalitarian in character' (1952: 160). The sentiments in that lecture echoed his inaugural lecture at Edinburgh of 1935, *Some Observations on Planning*, in which he warned that governmental attempts to plan undermined our democracy and were likely to fail in the endeavour to eliminate uncertainty because of what are now called exogenous shocks. In his address *Economics: Yesterday and Tomorrow* of 1949, he warned that the most fundamental contemporary problem was 'determining the limits of the economic activity of the State' (1949: 513). He complained that the welfare state had become the 'Santa Claus State' and that liberty and equality are natural enemies. To be free we must be unequal: incentives would be the acid test of the stability of our future economy.

Alexander Gray was a robust nineteenth-century liberal with enough native humour to mock the creeping socialism of his day. His talents – mathematical, linguistic, poetical, literary and administrative – were enormous. He still amuses, but his promising early career did not blossom as much as one would have expected, perhaps because he sat too long at a civil servant's desk before returning to academe.

BIBLIOGRAPHY

Scottish Staple at Veere: A Study in the Economic History of Scotland (1909).
The True Pastime: Some Observations on the German Attitude Towards War (1915).
The Upright Sheaf: Germany's Intentions After the War (1915).
Some Aspects of National Health Insurance (1923).
Family Endowment: A Critical Analysis (1927).
Gossip: A Book of New Poems (1928).
The Development of Economic Doctrine: An Introductory Survey (1931).
Arrows: A Book of German Ballads and Folk-Songs Attempted in Scots (1932).
The Socialist Tradition: Moses to Lenin (1946).
Adam Smith (1948).
Historical Ballads of Denmark (1958).
J'accuse! By a German (1958).
A Timorous Civility: A Scots Miscellany (1966).

Further Reading
Hayek, F.A., 'Review of The Socialist Tradition. Moses to Lenin', *Economica* (1947) new series, vol. 14, pp. 154–6.
Knight, F.H., 'Review of The Development of Economic Doctrine: An Introductory Survey', *Journal of Political Economy* (1932), vol. 40, pp. 711–13.
Knight, M.M., 'Review of The Socialist Tradition: Moses to Lenin', *American Economic Review* (1947), vol. 37, pp. 198–201.
Shove, G.F., 'Review of The Socialist Tradition: Moses to Lenin', *Economic Journal* (1946), vol. 56, pp. 443–6.
Sweezy, P.M., 'Review of The Socialist Tradition: Moses to Lenin', *Journal of Political Economy* (1947), vol. 55, pp. 465–66.

Donald Rutherford

GRAY, Benjamin Kirkman (1862–1907)

Gray was born in Blandford, Dorset on 11 August 1862, the son of a Congregational minister, and died at Letchworth, Hertfordshire on 23 June 1907. At the age of fourteen he went to work in a warehouse in the City of London, but a Christian conversion when sixteen caused him to resume his studies and return to Blandford to be a schoolteacher. He went in 1886 to New College, London to train for the Congregational ministry. His reading of economics, psychology and philosophy there enabled him to gain the Ricardo Economic Scholarship at University College, London. It was difficult for him to gain a ministerial appointment because of his unorthodox theology, but in 1892 he undertook social work at Belgrave Chapel, Leeds and gave lectures to co-operative societies and labour clubs. Increasingly a mystic and free thinker, he moved to Unitarianism and became a Unitarian minister at Warwick (1894–7). In 1898, the year of his marriage to Eleanor Stone, he took up social work at Bell Street Domestic Mission, Edgware Road, London, as well as forming the Christian Social Brotherhood. Failing physical strength brought his resignation in 1902. In 1905 he gave a lecture course on 'The Philanthropy of the Eighteenth Century' at the London School of Economics, and visited Germany to study the practice of municipal philanthropy.

Gray is principally remembered for his history of English philanthropy. Philanthropic action he described as 'the process of modifying the existing distribution of wealth in the interests of the more unfortunate classes, and of doing this with a view to improvement in the quality of life' (1905: ix). The sources for the book were largely the reports of the endowed charities; Sidney WEBB read the manuscript. Gray was keen to assert that philanthropy comes from an exercise of the free will and is not forced by the legal right of beneficiaries. He saw 1833 as the crucial year for voluntarism for the first building grant for schools was given by the government. Gray had to admit that philanthropy ultimately fails as it does not terminate evils.

Gray's other extant writings were assembled for posthumous publication. His most subtle writing was 'The Ethical Problem in an Industrial Community'. Drawing on a romanticism fostered by William Blake and the Lakeland poets, he attempted to tackle the difficulty of relationships between individuals in a heavily populated society. What is needed is the social imagination to see that 'each individual has symbolic, much more than individual, significance' (1910: 178). With 'a progressive interdependence in external form with the growth of industrial society there is a need practically to find a representative or symbolic quality in unknown persons' (1910: 183). However, he admitted there was also a need for social control. In *Philanthropy and the State of Social Politics* (1908) he usefully produced a sevenfold classification of the forms of state intervention. Annexation is the first type when the state takes over a private concern, as it did with lunatic asylums and elementary schools. Partition occurs when the state takes over part of the voluntary activity. There can also be co-operation, supervision, co-ordination (state and voluntary action in parallel) and delegation when the state asks the voluntary sector to execute its programmes.

Gray was at his most practical in discussing two German schemes, for co-operative housing and for worker democracy. In 'Co-operative Housing in Berlin', he was impressed that the jointly owned communal residence housed all types of worker, thus reducing class warfare (1910: 250). He describes a profit-sharing arrangement at the Carl Zeiss factory in 'Abbé's Theory of Industry'. Workers at the Zeiss company in Jena received wages under a system which prevented the highest paid earning more than ten times the rate for a competent adult labourer, as well as a fluctuating amount of profits and a retirement pension. Gray was especially impressed that the scheme was created by a legal statute so that workers were independent of their employer (1910: 263).

BIBLIOGRAPHY

A History of English Philanthropy from the dissolution of the monasteries to the taking of the first census (1905).

A Modern Humanist: Miscellaneous Papers of B Kirkman Gray, ed. H.B. Binne (1910).

Philanthropy and the State of Social Politics, ed. E.K. Gray and B.L. Hutchins (1908).

Donald Rutherford

GRAY, Charles (1696–1782)

Gray was born in Colchester in 1696, the son of a prosperous Colchester glazier who was an alderman of the town, and died there in 1782. He married well, acquiring a substantial estate in Colchester, practised successfully as a barrister, and in 1741 stood for Colchester as an opponent of the Walpole government and the local corporation. Having won his seat, he took legal action against the corporation which led to its dissolution. His father opposed him in both local and national politics, and cut him out of his will. Gray served as MP for the town from 1741–54, and again from 1761 until old age forced his retirement in 1780. According to one contemporary judgement, he was 'rather too full of strange reformations'. Contemporaries often termed him a Tory, probably because he was not only a fiercely independent politician and a critic of political oligarchy and corruption, but also a devout Christian. He had antiquarian interests; he worked to preserve the fabric of Colchester castle, in which he lived, and he helped to found the British Museum. He was also a humanitarian, observing with concern the condition of the poor at home and the impact of British trade and settlement on other parts of the world, not least on African slaves.

Gray's 1751 pamphlet, *Considerations on Several Proposals lately made for the Better Maintenance of the Poor*, represented a contribution to a policy debate that had taken shape in the aftermath of the War of the Austrian Succession (1739–48). At this time, some critics began to advocate the complete dismantling of the poor laws, arguing that the poor should be funded only by voluntary charity. Others argued that poor relief should be shifted away from a parish base and administered in larger administrative units, capable of maintaining large workhouses. Two legislative schemes along these latter lines were introduced into parliament in the early 1750s. Gray was essentially a conservative in this context, defending the principle of public relief and arguing for the merits of the parish as an administrative unit; at the same time he opposed the taking of infirmaries – which were then proliferating on the basis of voluntary charity – under any form of local government control.

Gray was undoubtedly influenced in part by the experience of the Colchester 'Corporation of the Poor' which had established in the 1690s, a decade which saw several such local experiments in the creation of larger relief units. The corporation of the poor was dissolved as a consequence of the dissolution of the town corporation. In Gray's view this was good riddance: large establishments were relatively costly (after the corporation's abolition, expenditure fell); they also lent themselves to political 'jobbery' and served as battlegrounds for faction. Gray advocated instead more active magisterial supervision of local administration, through a system of district petty sessions where overseers of the poor and keepers of penal 'houses of correction' could be called to account.

Gray's criticism of privileged and exclusive institutions linked into a broader attack on partial fiscal and commercial policies, which, as he saw it, served to embitter what should have been a harmonious relationship between land and trade. Gray's resistance to change provoked two published critiques, one by James CREED, and in 1760 he returned to the fray himself, reiterating his doubts in the face of revived talk of change, as most recently embodied in Commons resolutions of 1759.

BIBLIOGRAPHY

Considerations on Several Proposals lately made for the Better Maintenance of the Poor (1751; 2nd edn, 1752).
Further Considerations on the Laws relating to the Poor, by the author of Considerations... (1760).

Further Reading
A Letter to the Author of Considerations... (1752).

Creed, J., *An Impartial Examination of a Pamphlet intitled, Considerations...* (1752).

Cruickshanks, E., 'Charles Gray', in R. Sedgwick (ed.), *History of Parliament: The House of Commons 1715–54* (1970).

Namier, L., 'Charles Gray', in J. Brooke and L.B. Namier (eds), *History of Parliament: The House of Commons 1754–90* (1964).

Rogers, N., 'Confronting the Crime Wave: the Debate over Social Reform and Regulation, 1749–1753', in L. Davison, T. Hitchcock, T. Keirn, and R.B. Shoemaker (eds), *Stilling the Grumbling Hive: The Response to Social and Economic Problems in England, 1689–1750* (New York, 1992).

Joanna Innes

GRAY, John (1724–1811)

Little is known of Gray save that he was assistant private secretary to the Duke of Northumberland when the latter was Lord Lieutenant of Ireland (1762–3). His writings included both recommendations for improving the Irish economy and wider discussions of public finance. In a pamphlet of 1779, he argued for the establishment by statute of a National Bank of Ireland to provide greater security for the currency. The proposed bank would issue bank notes in competition with private issues, and cut interest rates by one-half of 1 per cent to stimulate agriculture and manufacturing.

A recurrent theme in Gray's writings is taxation. In his *Plan* of 1785, he examined public expenditure and taxation in Great Britain and Ireland. Gray pointed out that the public did not suffer greatly from taxation because tax revenues returned to the economy through government spending. He argued in favour of land taxation, even for Ireland, as it would provide funds for the stimulation of Irish manufacturing and trade and the building of new ports. The land tax would stimulate smaller landholders to greater productivity in order to be able to pay the tax. Gray also had a broader notion of 'tax' as inessential expenditure. Spending could be reduced by dismissing physicians if all adopted a rural lifestyle, by setting up a land register to eliminate the need for lawyers, and by cutting the number of menial servants. In 1786 he proposed a tax on retailers who are idle and unproductive, as manufacturers could sell directly to consumers.

In his *The Income Tax Scrutinised*, Gray argued that as most of the national income was derived from agriculture taxes on rents should provide the bulk of government revenue: a tax of four shillings in the pound would be sufficient for the provision of national defence. Every county town would have a land register with information on rents. He deplored taxes on profits, the home trade and specific commodities. He also argued for a land bank, partly as it would bring down interest rates.

Gray also had a scheme for stabilizing bread prices in London, described in a pamphlet of 1798. Taxation and public subscriptions would raise finance for granaries in London and other large cities to store grain for eight years. Judicious purchases and release of stocks would effect price stability. He also attempted to correct the 'errors' of Adam SMITH and the French physiocrats. Gray had some sympathy for the French economists, and agreed that people should live close to the land, with even manufacturing dispersed to the countryside. His criticisms of Smith included the failure to indicate the incidence of taxes on the rent of land relative to that of tax on other sources of income.

BIBLIOGRAPHY

An Essay Concerning the Establishment of a National Bank in Ireland (1779).

A Plan for finally settling the Government of Ireland upon Constitutional Principles, and the chief cause of the unprosperous state of that country explained (1785).

The Policy of the Tax upon Retailers Considered, or a Plea in Favour of our Manufacturers (1792).

The Essential Principles of the Wealth of Nations Illustrated in Opposition to Some False Doctrines of Adam Smith and others (1797).

A Proposal for Supplying London with Bread at a Uniform Price from One Year to Another, according to Annual Assize (1798).

The Income Tax Scrutinised and Some Amendments Proposed to Render it more Agreeable to the British Constitution (1802).

Donald Rutherford

GRAY, John (*c.*1799–1883)

Gray was born about 1799, and died on 26 April 1883 at Upper Norwood, London. His origins are rather shadowy, though he was said to be of Scottish extraction and it was in Scotland that he spent much of his life. According to his own account, he attended Repton School, Derbyshire, began work in London at fourteen, developed an interest in social questions and by his early twenties had formulated ideas similar to those of Owenite reformers. In 1825 he published *A Lecture on Human Happiness*, a socialistic analysis designed to show how those whose labour created wealth were exploited by the useless classes. Drawing on the statistical material in Patrick COLQUHOUN's *Treatise on the Wealth, Power and Resources of the British Empire* (1814), Gray maintained that the productive classes enjoyed only a fifth of the wealth they produced. His remedy was to change the institutions of society to promote the happiness of man rather than perpetuate his misery. He saw co-operative communities as a means of replacing capitalism and was drawn to the Orbiston estate near Motherwell in 1825. On witnessing the community that Abram Combe was establishing there, Gray was struck by its inadequacies, and he stated these in pamphlet form as *A Word of Advice to the Orbistonians*. Remaining in Scotland, he began various publishing ventures and appears to have struggled financially for a while, although later in life he prospered in business.

In 1831 Gray published *The Social System: A Treatise on the Principle of Exchange*. As in his earlier work, he held that the producers of wealth were deprived of most of the fruits of their labour, but he scaled down the moralistic and communitarian arguments associated with Owenism. Instead, his remedy was based on a central authority, termed by him the National Chamber of Commerce. The chamber would open national warehouses, value goods, decide wages and generally organize the economy. A central bank would also be created, a proposal elaborated in his next book, *An Efficient Remedy for the Distress of Nations* (1842). He also sought in this book to rebut critics of the *Social System*, including those of T. Perronet THOMPSON, who had associated him with St.-Simonism in the *Westminster Review*. Nevertheless, as he moved away from Owenism, there was an element of St.-Simon's ideas in Gray's later schemes, which, although he placed more emphasis on economic remedies, retained visionary elements.

By the late 1840s Gray writings were preoccupied with currency reform. Apart from this issue, he saw little wrong with the economic system and there was no longer a need for the communitarianism or the centrally directed economy favoured in his early works. In 1847, after *The Times* had declined to print a letter on the currency question, Gray challenged the paper to discuss the issues for a sum of five hundred guineas, a tactic he adopted in *Lectures on the Nature and Use of Money* (1848). In this book, which was sent to every MP and other public figures, he offered the sum of a hundred guineas to anyone who refuted his arguments. Rejecting the co-operative ideas of his youth, Gray contended that the competitive system would flourish if the monetary system were reformed in a way that removed the need for an expanding supply of gold and silver.

J.S. MILL added a lengthy footnote to the second edition (1849) of his *Principles of Political Economy* noting the ingenuity of Gray's scheme, while denying that producers were hampered by the supply of precious metals. MARX too commented on Gray's ideas, though after acknowledging that *The Social System* had been the first book to develop systematically a theory of labour time as the measure of value, he mocked the timid reformism of the *Lectures on the Nature and Use of Money*.

In his later years Gray ceased to write. He retained an interest, with his brother James, in two newspapers they had established, the *North British Advertiser* and the *Ladies' Own Journal* (the two were amalgamated in 1874). In the 1860s he moved to London, living at Faldonside House, Upper Norwood, where he died in 1883. So fully did he disappear from public life that, as in the history of socialism began to be written, it was assumed he had died in the 1850s. Gray was also rediscovered by historians of economic thought, although scholars such as Esther Lowenthal (1911) characterized him, somewhat misleadingly, as a Ricardian socialist. He was thus misunderstood for some time, and, while the details of his life became better known through the work of Janet Kimball (1948), there was a tendency, as with Alexander GRAY (1947), to see him as a cranky and increasingly less revolutionary anticipator of Marx. Later writers, however, have offered a more nuanced analysis of his writings. Claeys (1987) argues that, although Gray placed greater trust in *laissez-faire* mechanisms, he retained some of his early concepts and contributed to popularizing both Owenite and later socialist ideas. Thompson (1998), who links Gray's economic views with those of John Francis Bray, relates his thought to the strengthening of industrial capitalism in the 1830s and 1840s, one effect of which was to elicit new solutions to society's ills.

BIBLIOGRAPHY

A Lecture on Human Happiness... (1825).
A Word of Advice to the Orbistonians on the Principles which ought to Regulate their Present Proceedings, 29th June 1826 (1826).
The Social System: A Treatise on the Principle of Exchange (1831).
An Efficient Remedy for the Distress of Nations (1842).
The Currency Question. A Rejected Letter to The Times. Challenge to The Times to Discuss the Subject for the Sum of 500 Guineas (1847).
Lectures on the Nature and Use of Money (1848).
Edinburgh Monetary Reform Pamphlet, No. 1. Committee of Enquiry into the Validity of the Monetary Principle Advocated in Gray's Lectures (1849).

Further Reading

Claeys, G., *Machinery, Money and the Millennium: From Moral Economy to Socialism, 1815–1860* (Oxford, 1987).
Gray, A., *The Socialist Tradition: Moses to Lenin* (1947).
Kimball, J., *The Economic Doctrines of John Gray, 1799–1883* (Washington, DC, 1948).
King, J.E., 'Utopian or Scientific? A Reconsideration of the Ricardian Socialists', *History of Political Economy* (1983), vol. 15, pp. 345–73.
Lowenthal, E., *The Ricardian Socialists* (New York, 1911).
Martin, D.E., 'Gray, John', in J.M. Bellamy and J. Saville (eds), *Dictionary of Labour Biography*, vol. 6 (1983).
Saad-Filho, A., 'Labor, Money and "Labour-Money": A Review of Marx's Critique of

John Gray's Monetary Analysis', *History of Political Economy* (1993), vol. 25, pp. 65-84.

Thompson, N.W., *The People's Science: The Political Economy of Exploitation and Crisis 1816-34* (Cambridge, 1984).

———, *The Real Rights of Man: Political Economies for the Working Class 1775-1850* (1998).

David E. Martin

GREEN, Harold Alfred John (1923-76)

John Green was born in Birmingham on 23 February 1923, and died on 4 January 1976 in Kent. He was educated at Oxford, obtaining a BA in philosophy, politics and economics in 1947 and an MA in 1948, and Massachusetts Institute of Technology, where he obtained his PhD in 1954. His academic career spanned the Atlantic, with positions at Clark University (1948-50), Brown (1952-4), Manchester (1954-5), Keele (1955-8), California at Santa Barbara (1958-9), Toronto (1959-73) and Kent at Canterbury (1973-6).

Green was an economic theorist who, typically for someone of his generation, applied techniques to problems in a variety of fields: the term structure of interest rates; public sector resource allocation under risk; the structure of consumer preferences; the measurement of capital; and investment and growth. He could reasonably be described as the economic theorist's theorist, for a common pattern in his articles was to provide an elegant exposition of and solution to technical problems arising in the economic theory of his day. For example, a paper on revealed preference theory investigated certain difficulties that arose in work by Hedrik Houtthaker and Paul Samuelson. A paper on 'Growth Models, Capital and Stability' opened by saying that its purpose was part expository, part critical. Throughout, he applied up-to-date techniques to solve technical problems arising in the contemporary theoretical literature. He published in many of the leading academic journals.

Given his acknowledged abilities as an expositor of economic theory, it is perhaps not surprising that Green is well known for his two books. The first, *Aggregation in Economic Analysis* (1964), provided a survey of a field that nowadays receives less attention than its significance deserves. This is the conditions under which (for example) a group of commodities can be aggregated and treated as though they were a single commodity. The absence of any rigorous solution to the problem means that economists generally ignore it, usually by making assumptions that rule it out (such as that an economy produces a single homogeneous commodity). Green's conclusion was that, given that economists are typically concerned with prediction, and that this involves statistical methods, decisions about appropriate aggregation procedures should be considered as part of statistical decision theory. However, while he conjectured that this was the way forward, he did not solve the problem.

His second book, *Consumer Theory* (1971), was a textbook that offered one of the clearest and, given the level of rigour, one of the most accessible surveys of this aspect of economic theory available during the 1970s. The theory involved was probably as rigorous as it was possible to be given the nature of the mathematical training received by economics students at this time. For many students, Green's book was their introduction to proper consumer theory.

BIBLIOGRAPHY
Aggregation in Economic Analysis (Princeton, 1964).
Consumer Theory (1971).

Further Reading
Neufeld, E.P. and Dobell, A.R., 'Harold, Alfred John Green, 1923–76', *Canadian Journal of Economics* (1977), vol. 10, no. 1, pp. 130–1.

Roger Backhouse

GREG, William Rathbone (1809–81)

Greg was born in 1809 in Manchester, the son of a mill owner, Samuel Greg. He died at Wimbledon, Surrey on 15 November 1881. He was educated at Carpenter's school in Bristol and then at the University of Edinburgh. In 1828 Greg became manager of one of his father's mills in Bury, and in 1832 he went into business for himself. His career as an author began in 1842 when an essay was published by the Anti-Corn Law League. Business failure induced a career change to full-time essayist, at which he excelled. He published more than 150 articles and essays, twelve in 1852 alone. His second marriage, to the daughter of the publisher of *The Economist*, James WILSON, is worthy of notice because it was through Greg that Walter BAGEHOT met Wilson and went on to become editor of the journal.

Greg combined the free-trade conclusions of economic liberals with the racial attitudes of Thomas CARLYLE. He consistently opposed the views of political economists such as J.S. MILL regarding racial equality. He recognized that Mill's proposals for Ireland relied on the presumption that the Irish were capable of making sound economic decisions. In Greg's judgement, by contrast, the problem with Ireland was the Irish: 'till you change the character of the Irish cottier, peasant-proprietorship would work no miracles', and Mill erred by 'never deign[ing] to consider that an Irishman is an Irishman, and not an average human being...an idiomatic and idiosyncratic, not an abstract, man' (Greg 1869: 78). Greg took no public stand on Governor Eyre's actions in the Jamaican revolt of 1865, but his judgement on the events leading up to controversy is in line with that in Carlyle's 1849 'Negro Question'. The Negro race required guidance, Greg asserted, to survive. His 1866 essay, retitled 'The Doom of the Negro Race', was suppressed from the 1873 collection of his *Literary and Social Judgements* by his American publisher.

Greg was not, however, persuaded by the entire Carlylean enterprise. He favoured free exchange amongst equals. He also argued against making an economic case in the form of a novel; his review of Charles KINGSLEY's *Alton Locke* pointed out that in fiction, one can make up any relationship one wants. The review praises only Kingsley's portrayal of a lightly fictionalized Thomas Carlyle. The culmination of Greg's influence might well have been the notice which Charles Darwin gave Greg in *The Descent of Man*. In 1864, Alfred Wallace had argued that the principle of natural selection does not apply to humans because humans sympathize with the infirm. Coining the phrase, 'non-survival of the fittest', Greg responded that humans should suppress sympathetic tendencies and create the new model person (Greg 1875: 119). Darwin (1871: 138–9) quoted Greg's claim (Greg 1868: 360) that racial degeneration occurs when the improvident Irish outbreed the provident Scots. The racial strain in eugenic thinking owes much to Greg.

BIBLIOGRAPHY

English Socialism: Mistaken Aims and Attainable Ideas of the Artizan Class (1850).

'The Jamaica Problem', *Fraser's Magazine for Town and Country* (1866), vol. 73, March, pp. 277–305.

'On the Failure of "Natural Selection" in the Case of Man', *Fraser's Magazine for Town and Country* (1868), vol. 78, September, pp. 353–62.

'Realities of Irish Life', *Quarterly Review* (1869), vol. 126, pp. 61–80.
Literary and Social Judgements (Boston, 1873).
Enigmas of Life (Boston, 1875).

Further Reading
Darwin, C., *The Descent of Man, and Selection in Relation to Sex* (1871; repr. in P.H. Barret and R.B. Freeman (eds), *The Works of Charles Darwin*, vol. 21, New York, 1989).

David M. Levy
Sandra R. Peart

GREGORY, Theodore Emanuel Gugenheim (1890–1970)

Theodore Gregory was born in London on 10 September, 1890, and died in Athens on 24 December 1970. He was educated at St Owens School in Islington, at Stuttgart, and at the London School of Economics. He was appointed assistant lecturer at the LSE in 1913, serving in that capacity until he became Cassel Reader in International Trade in 1920. He served as Sir Ernest Cassel Professor of Economics from 1927–37, and as dean of the Faculty of Economics in the University of London from 1927–30. Gregory also served as professor of social economics at Manchester University from 1930–2. Beginning in 1929, Gregory served the British and Indian governments in a variety of capacities: as a member of the Macmillan Committee on Industry and Finance (1929–31); as economic advisor to the Niemeyer Mission to Australia and New Zealand (1930); as economic advisor to the government of India (1938–46); as a member of the Irish Free State Banking Commission (1934–7); and as chairman of the (Indian) Food Grains Policy Committee (1943). He was knighted in 1942, and was later named Honourable Fellow of the London School of Economics and Commander, Austrian Order of Merit, and was awarded the Order of George I (Greece).

Gregory taught money, banking, and international trade at the LSE during a period in which the institution intentionally styled itself as a counterweight to Cambridge University. By 1930 the LSE had attracted a distinguished faculty which approached economics from a decidedly different direction than did the typical Cambridge economist. 'There appears to have been considerable agreement among the senior LSE economists: Robbins, Hayek, Gregory, Plant, Benham, on both doctrinal and policy matters…Hayek, Robbins, Plant, and Gregory were all defenders of the market and critics of socialist economic planning' (Coats 1993: 384, 386). Known for 'his wide contacts and his roving intellectual interests' (Robbins 1971b: 85), Gregory introduced a generation of LSE students to contemporary continental and American thought. He also introduced them to the ideas of earlier generations, continuing the tradition of 'serious attention…to the history of economic thought' begun by LSE predecessors such as Edwin CANNAN (Coats 1993: 385).

Gregory began his teaching career as Europe plunged into war, and the disintegration of the international economic order loomed large in Gregory's thinking throughout his career. According to perhaps his most illustrious student, 'he inclined to a sombre view of the future, expressed sometimes with almost despairing emphasis' (Robbins 1971a). Perhaps this was because Gregory did not see a worthy successor to the classical gold standard that disappeared with the Great War. He had no faith in the 'new economics' of paper money, arguing in the Joseph Fisher Lecture at the University of Adelaide (25 August 1930) that attempts to inflate the economy would be 'fatal…a very risky and dangerous expedient'.

Gregory wrote extensively on monetary and international issues. His first books, *The Gold*

Standard and Its Future (1921) and *Tariffs: A Study in Method* (1921), displayed a technician's understanding of the mechanics of a commodity–money system, as well as of the technical details of international trade. Gregory supported a return to gold after 1930, a position consistent with his general sympathy with Austrian economics, which had made strong inroads into the London School of Economics in the 1920s. Ludwig von Mises (1935: 229–30), in a review of the third edition of Gregory's *The Gold Standard and Its Future*, hailed its final chapter as 'a brilliant examination of the pros and cons of the return to gold'.

Although he is best known for his work on monetary and international topics, one of Gregory's first notable publications was in the history of economic thought. In 'The Economics of Employment in England, 1660–1713' (1921) Gregory assessed the attitudes of English writers during the mercantilist era towards workers, employment, and wages. His work drew a favourable response from Schumpeter (1954: 272). Gregory's 'Introduction' to TOOKE and NEWMARCH's *History of Prices* (1928) represents a searching evaluation of Thomas Tooke's (and, to a much lesser extent, John FULLARTON's) banking school theories of money and monetary policy from the position of one whose basic sympathies lay with the currency school. However, even modern readers, familiar with the theory of competitively supplied currencies and the monetary approach to the balance of payments, and hence more inclined to find merit in banking school arguments, must be impressed with the depth of Gregory's understanding of international monetary theory and his detailed knowledge of what Tooke had written and said over a period of four decades.

The following year Gregory published a volume of *Select Statutes, Documents and Reports Related to British Banking, 1832–1928*, for which he wrote another detailed introduction. Despite the many claims upon his time by the governments of Great Britain and Ireland in the 1930s, he found time to write the definitive history of the Westminster Bank (1936), a book which made a valuable contribution to nineteenth-century British monetary history.

Gregory was not a path-breaking theoretician, but his considerable theoretical skills, combined with his ability to sensibly apply theory to important problems, led the British government to call upon him repeatedly for advice. In addition, he was a first-rate teacher who inspired a generation of students. This combination made him an important figure in British economics during the inter-war period.

BIBLIOGRAPHY

'The Economics of Employment in England, 1660–1713', *Economica* (1921), vol. 1, pp. 37–51.
The Gold Standard and Its Future (1921).
Tariffs: A Study in Method (1921).
Foreign Exchange Before, During, and After the War (1925).
The Present Position of Banking in America (1925).
The First Year of the Gold Standard (1926).
'Introduction' to T. Tooke and W. Newmarch, *The History of Prices* (New York, 1928).
'Introduction' to *Select Statutes, Documents and Reports Relating to British Banking, 1832–1928* (1929).
The Westminster Bank through a Century (1936).

Further Reading

Coats, A.W., *The Sociology and Professionalization of Economics* (1993).
Mises, L. von, 'Review of *The Gold Standard and Its Future*, 3rd ed.', *Economica* (1935), new series, vol. 2, no. 6, pp. 229–32.
Robbins, L. 'Obituary: Sir T. Gregory,' *The Times* (1971a), 3 February, p. 14.
———, *Autobiography of an Economist* (1971b).
Schumpeter, J.A., *History of Economic Analysis* (New York, 1954).

Neil Skaggs

GRENVILLE, William Wyndham
(1759–1834)

Grenville was born on 24 October 1759, the third son and sixth of nine children born to George Grenville and Elizabeth Wyndham. He died on 12 January 1834 at Dropmore Lodge, Buckinghamshire, having suffered several strokes. Grenville was educated at Eton and Christ Church College, Oxford. He graduated in 1780, and was admitted to Lincoln's Inn soon afterwards, but was never called to the bar. Academically, he was very gifted and had a keen interest in and extensive knowledge of classical literature. He spent much time editing the correspondence of his uncle, William Pitt, first Earl of Chatham. Grenville entered parliament in 1782 as MP for the family's borough of Buckingham, continuing to represent the constituency until he was elevated to the peerage in 1790. In 1792, he married Anne Pitt, the daughter of Thomas Pitt, first Baron Camelford. The couple had no children.

Grenville held ministerial office continually during his parliamentary career. He was Chief Secretary for Ireland between August 1782 and May 1783 while his brother, Earl Temple, was Lord Lieutenant. He was offered ministerial positions by Pitt the younger (his cousin) throughout his premiership, and was paymaster general between December 1783 and March 1784. For a short time in 1789 he was Speaker of the House of Commons, and he then became Home Secretary; in 1791 he became Foreign Secretary.

When the French Revolution broke out, Grenville advocated British neutrality as the best means of avoiding conflict, but when France declared war of Britain, he supported the first coalition of European powers. He also supported repressive domestic legislation to maintain law and order in Britain. In 1790, as Baron Grenville, he took over the post of leader of the House of Lords. He resigned along with Pitt over the king's attitude towards Catholic Emancipation in March 1801, following the passing of the Act of Union with Ireland. However, he did not have confidence in Addington's abilities to conduct the war, and spoke forcefully in opposition to the new government. He also abandoned Pitt, who did not respond to Grenville's proposal for a pact between the political 'outs'; Grenville and Charles James Fox then worked together in a combined opposition. In 1804 when Pitt returned to power, Grenville refused to accept office without Fox. This completed the separation of the cousins.

Grenville formed a ministry in 1806 to continue the government and the fight against France, and Fox became his Foreign Secretary. However, Fox died in September 1806, which meant that the ministry had to be reconstructed. Grenville continued to support Catholic Emancipation, and when the king refused to consider it, he resigned. He spent the rest of his political career in opposition. However, it was his ministry that steered the legislation abolishing the slave trade through parliament.

In 1800, Grenville protested against Pitt's proposal to strengthen the protectionist laws, saying that he 'was convinced ... of the soundness of Adam Smith's principles of political economy'. Not surprisingly, at the end of the French Wars, Grenville supported the principle of free trade and opposed the passing of the Corn Laws. He argued that 'public prosperity is best promoted by leaving uncontrolled the free current of national industry'. He continued to support Catholic Emancipation, but by 1822 he virtually had retired from politics. In retirement he produced a couple of short works on economics based largely on his own experiences. Although he had helped oversee the sinking fund while serving in Pitt's government, in later life he doubted its expediency and believed that the national debt had grown too high. He also wrote on John LOCKE, expressing some support for the latter's views on money.

BIBLIOGRAPHY
Letters Written by the Late Earl of Chatham to his Nephew, Thomas Pitt, Esq. (1804).
Essay on the Supposed Advantages of a Sinking Fund (1828).
Oxford and Locke (1829).

Marjorie Bloy

GRESHAM, Thomas (c.1518–1579)

Gresham was born in his father's house in Milk Lane, London in about 1518, and died suddenly of a stroke in London on 21 November 1579. He was the second and younger son of Richard Gresham by his first wife Audrey, daughter of William Lynne of Southwick in Northampton. Nothing is known of his childhood, save that he was deprived of a mother's care at the age of three or four; and that he was subsequently sent to Cambridge and admitted as a pensioner at Gonville College. On leaving Cambridge, Gresham was apprenticed by his father around 1535, at the age of seventeen, to his uncle John Gresham. In 1543 he was admitted a member of the Mercer's Company.

Having found by the mid-1530s that his eldest son, John, preferred life as a member of the lesser gentry, Richard Gresham began seriously moulding the career of his younger son. During the years 1535–47 he himself withdrew from the management of that branch of the 'House of Gresham's' activities which was concerned with the pursuit of the traditional mercer's trade at the Netherlands marts, and in the process set about grooming Thomas to take his place. To this end, during the years of Thomas's apprenticeship (1535–43) he began to reveal to his younger son the mysteries of exchange dealings, employing him in operations on behalf of the Crown and preparing him for a partnership his father's business empire. To this full gamut of training in mercantile and financial skills Richard Gresham, now also added other elements. He augmented his now favoured younger son's existing knowledge of classical languages with a pragmatic education in contemporary tongues, French and Flemish. By securing Thomas's admission to Gray's Inn he provided him with at least a cursory knowledge of law.

Nor did Thomas Gresham waste these opportunities. In three short years following his admission to the freedom of the Mercers' Company in 1543 Thomas Gresham fulfilled every aspiration that his father had of him. In 1544, at the age of twenty-six, he took to himself a wife, Anne Ferneley, widow of the mercer William Read, who brought with her two young sons by her first marriage and Read's business. In March 1547 she bore him a son Richard (d. 1564). In 1546 he assumed the headship of the Netherlands branch of the 'House of Gresham's' commercial operations, successfully running in difficult conditions the enlarged business until his assumption of the post of royal agent in the Netherlands in the winter of 1551–2. Then, by his own account, he closed the account book in which he had recorded all his business since 1546 and finally turned his back on his mercantile activities.

Thereafter, until 1567, he undertook the management of English royal finances at Antwerp under three monarchs, Edward VI, Mary and Elizabeth, receiving a knighthood in 1559 for his services to the crown. It was at this time that he composed the memoranda on the exchange which have established his reputation as an economic theorist. In these memoranda, composed in a spirit of self-advertisement in 1553, 1558 and perhaps in 1559, he explained the mysteries of the exchange to his political masters, the Privy Council.

In the 1558 memorandum, which has a clear attribution to Gresham, the theoretical framework underpinning his rudimentary understanding of the mechanisms of the exchange was revealed. A discussion of contemporary monetary usage, conceived as operating within a monometallic, silver standard, and showing only an intuitive appreciation of the contemporary bimetallic situation, was seen as establishing the importance of mint price parities in determining the 'natural' rate of exchange. The interest rate element encompassed within the terms of 'merchant' exchange transactions was also clearly elucidated, as was its relationship to the balance of trade. He also in this context made proposals aimed at creating a level playing field in English commodity markets, advocating the suspension of the privileges of Italian traders and German merchants of the Hanseatic League who enjoyed tax concessions which gave them a competitive advantage over their English counterparts. The manuscript is throughout pervaded by a pragmatic rather than a theoretical approach to his subject matter and is very different in form to the memorandum of 1559 whose attribution to Gresham by de Roover (1949) has been seriously challenged (Challis 1983; Lloyd 2000).

It was this latter document of doubtful provenance, however, which became one of the main pillars of that 'Gresham myth', established in the late sixteenth and early seventeenth centuries. Known only by two transcripts, the so-called John Dee manuscript and another manuscript in the Public Record Office, both of which are dated 1576 and are copies derived either directly or indirectly from a common and earlier original, this document is very different in form to the 'Information' of 1558. The 'Memorandum' is divided into five sections or parts. The first part deals chiefly with the coinage and gives certain rules for determining the mint par. Other topics are discussed in more or less detail. These included the difference between the pound tale (of 240 pence counted by number) and the Tower pound weight of silver (of 324 grams weight), the ratio between gold and silver, recent changes in English and foreign currencies and the difficulty of determining mint par. In order to eliminate the evils arising from a divergence of the two measures, the author recommends a de-monetization of all the base moneys in circulation and their recoinage into fine moneys of a uniform character.

The second part is concerned with the more technical aspects of foreign exchange. The author explains the difference between natural and merchant's exchange, gives a list of the principal European exchange centres and explains the terms sight, single, double and half usance. Next comes a long list of twenty-four devices, by which the financiers allegedly tried to manipulate the exchange. They are accused of culling out the heavier coins and exporting them, of operating with borrowed funds and attempting to corner money and commodity markets. The fourth part suggests various ways of thwarting them and of raising the exchange: strict enforcement of sumptuary legislation, repression of usury, the establishment of low internal prices and costs and an improvement of the terms of trade. The author also advocated the creation of a reserve of foreign balances, which might be used on occasion to prop up the exchange. The fifth and final part of the manuscript is an anomalous account of the balance of trade in 1354.

From its incorporation in John Dee's library in 1576, the manuscript was copied and recopied for circulation within a small circle of men interested in public affairs or in the promotion of trade and industry. Then with 'the foreign exchange controversy' of the 1620s, when German and Baltic debasements precipitated an acute English trade crisis (Supple 1959), it was utilized by all the major participants in the debate. At that time it acquired a new status and a new provenance. The authorship was attributed to Gresham, who long before had established the 'myth' of his unrivalled expertise in matters concerning the 'exchange'. Gresham perpetuated this self-glorifying 'myth', moreover, by embodying it in stone in the Royal Exchange, built to his orders between 1565–71, and Gresham College, established by the terms of his will after his death. According to MISSELDEN, in around 1622, there were several copies of the so-called 'Gresham Memorandum' in circulation, and he himself possessed one. This is certainly the tract over which Misselden and MALYNES came to blows. The twenty-four devices particularly appealed to Malynes, who published this entire section in his major work, *Consuetudo vel Lex Mercatoria* (1622) and also in his tract, *The Maintenance of Free Trade*. Since this tract was a direct attack upon Misselden, the latter retorted with charges of plagiarism, only to spoil his own case by incorporating part five of the 'Memorandum' in his own work, the *Circle of Commerce* (1623). For more half a century, until 1686, as the debate rumbled on and each of these works passed through edition after edition, both the 'Memorandum' and the now almost mythical Gresham were greeted with popular acclaim, until in the aftermath of the Glorious Revolution they passed once more into obscurity.

Then in the early years of Victoria's reign, Gresham was 'rediscovered'. When the Royal Exchange was destroyed by fire in 1838, its founder was reinstated as a public figure. Enough interest was caused for Gresham College to be rebuilt and newly funded. A street in the City of London and an insurance company were named after him, and a most comprehensive biography of his life and career as a public servant for the Tudors was published (Burgon 1839). He even had the honour to have a law of economics – 'that bad monies cannot circulate alongside good and drive them out' – wrongly attributed to him (Macleod 1858). The Victorians had recreated him in accord with their own popular notion of an upwardly mobile public figure in the manner of Samuel Smiles. It is perhaps this image which is the greatest testimony to the true talents of Thomas Gresham: not as an original economic theorist, but as the maker of myths.

BIBLIOGRAPHY

'Memorial given by Thomas Gresham unto the Queen's Majesty,' 13 November 1553 (Public Record Office, Kew, SP 69/2/74).
'Information of Sir Thomas Gresham, Mercer, touching the fall of the exchange, 1558' (1558; repr. in J.W. Burgon, *The Life and Times of Sir Thomas Gresham*, 1839, vol. I, pp. 483–86; and in R.H. Tawney and E. Power, *Tudor Economic Documents*, London, vol. II, pp. 146–9).
'Memorandum for the Understanding of the Exchange', ed. R. de Roover in *Gresham on the Foreign Exchanges* (Cambridge, Massachusetts, 1949, pp. 289–309).

Further Reading

Bindoff, S.T., *The Fame of Sir Thomas Gresham* (1973).
Blanchard, I., 'English Royal Borrowing at Antwerp, 1544–1574', in M. Boone and W. Prevenier (eds), *Finances publiques et finances privées au bas moyen âge. Actes du colloque tenu à Gand le 5–6 mai 1995* (Leuven-Apeldoorn, 1996).
———, 'Thomas Gresham, ca. 1518–1579', in A. Saunders (ed.), *The Royal Exchange: Essays on the History and Topography of a London Institution* (1997, pp. 11–19).
———, 'Sir Thomas and the House of Gresham: Activities of a Mercer-Merchant Adventurer', in F. Ames-Lewis (ed.), *Sir Thomas Gresham and Gresham College: Studies in the Intellectual History of London in the Sixteenth and Seventeenth Centuries* (Aldershot, 1999, pp. 13–23).
Buckley, H. 'Sir Thomas Gresham and the Foreign Exchanges', *Economic Journal* (1924), vol. 34, pp. 589–601.
Burgon, J.W., *The Life and Times of Sir Thomas Gresham Compiled Chiefly from his Correspondence Preserved in Her Majesty's State-Paper Office: including notices of many of his contemporaries*, 2 vols (1839).
Challis, C.E., 'On the Authorship and Dating of the Memorandum, "For the Understanding of the Exchange"', *Bulletin of the Institute of Historical Research* (1983), vol. 56, pp. 34–45.
Fetter, F.W., 'Some Neglected Aspects of Gresham's Law', *Quarterly Journal of Economics* (1931–2), vol. 46, pp. 480–95.

Lloyd, T.H., 'Early Elizabethan Investigations into Exchange and the Value of Sterling, 1558–1568', *Economic History Review* (2000), second series, vol. 53, no. 1, pp. 60–83.

Macleod, H.D., *The Elements of Political Economy* (1858).

Newman, J., 'Thomas Gresham: Private Person rather than Public Figure', *History Teaching Review, Year Book* (1993), vol. 7, pp. 13–22.

Salter, F.R. *Sir Thomas Gresham* (1925).

Supple, B., *Commercial Crisis and Change in England, 1600–1642: A Study in the Instability of a Mercantile Economy* (Cambridge, 1959).

Ian Blanchard

GROSSETESTE, Robert (c.1168–1253)

Grosseteste, or Bighead, was born in about (perhaps slightly before) 1168 in Suffolk to a minor Anglo-Norman family. He died during the night of 8 October 1253 at his manor of Buckden, Huntingdonshire. He was primarily educated in the arts (quite possibly in the schools at Oxford that predated the founding of the university), although some exposure to theology at the University of Paris has been ascribed to him.

The evidence for Grosseteste's early life is slim. Prior to 1198, he was a member of the household of William de Vere, Bishop of Hereford, a fact mentioned in a letter of Gerald of Wales. Grosseteste is styled a master (of arts, it is assumed) by Gerald. Hereford was renowned for its cathedral school, the curriculum of which included the Greek and Arabic learning that was beginning to circulate through Europe.

Grosseteste spent much of his later career at Oxford, to which he moved (probably not for the first time) soon after 1214. He not only taught theology there for two decades, but also served as the school's chancellor during its formative years. In 1229, Grosseteste accepted an invitation to lecture on theology at the newly founded Franciscan school at Oxford. He produced a large and varied literary output, including philosophical treatises and commentaries, theological tracts and biblical exegesis, and translations from Greek texts, as well as sermons and letters. Much of his work remains unedited.

While still teaching at Oxford, Grosseteste commenced a career in ecclesiastical administration. From 1229 until 1232 he was archdeacon of Leicester, and in March 1235 he was elected Bishop of Lincoln. Thereafter he became enmeshed in ecclesiastical politics, attending the Council of Lyons in 1245 and lobbying Rome (unsuccessfully) against its program of centralized appointments to important clerical offices. Yet he continued to engage in philosophical studies even as he produced large volumes of pastoral and administrative literature. Grosseteste was widely acclaimed as a churchman as well as a scholar throughout Europe – known simply as *Lincolniensis* – by the time of his death in 1253.

During the 1140s, while fully engaged in the business of a bishop, Grosseteste produced the first widely disseminated complete Latin translation of Aristotle's *Nicomachean Ethics*, a work that constituted a central source of later economic thought. Although Grosseteste probably based his work on an earlier partial translation of the *Ethics*, his rendering was sufficiently cogent and fluid to become the standard version of the text for the rest of the Middle Ages. The *Ethics* incorporates Aristotle's views about economic justice, the origins and nature of money, need, economic value, and many other topics that were increasingly relevant to the commercializing society of the thirteenth century. Grosseteste also added to his translation a number of study aids and guides, such as a summary of the major themes of the *Ethics*, a compendium of earlier commentaries on the work, and his own personal commentary and glosses (most of the latter surviving only in fragmentary form).

Moreover, as an ecclesiastical administrator, Grosseteste composed various works that attempted to apply economic ideas to practical issues. For example, he wrote a letter to the Countess of Winchester concerning the expulsion of the Jews from Leicester in 1231 that discussed at length the nature of usury, couched in the terms of canon law but in a manner consonant with the soon-to-be-revived Aristotelian teaching on the topic. In particular, Grosseteste went beyond the strictly biblical condemnation of usury to argue that it was contrary to nature, regardless of who engaged in it.

BIBLIOGRAPHY
Ethica Nicomachea Translatio Roberti Grosseteste Lincolniensis, ed. R.A. Gauthier (Leiden, 1973); *The Greek Commentaries on the Nicomachean Ethics of Aristotle in the Latin Translation of Robert Grosseteste*, ed. H.P.F. Mercken (vol. 1, Leiden, 1973; vol. 2, Leuven, 1991).
Opera Roberti Grosseteste Lincolniensis (Turnhout, 1995–).

Further Reading
McEvoy, J., *The Philosophy of Robert Grosseteste* (Oxford, 1982).
———, *Robert Grosseteste* (Oxford, 2000).
Southern, R.W., *Robert Grosseteste: The Growth of an English Mind in Medieval Europe* (Oxford, 1986).

Cary Nederman

GUILLEBAUD, Claud William (1890–1971)

Guillebaud was born in Cambridge on 2 July 1890, and died there on 23 August 1971. He was educated at Repton, Manchester University and St John's College, Cambridge. He was appointed a fellow of St John's in 1915 and a lecturer in the economics faculty at Cambridge University in 1926. He was senior tutor at St John's from 1952 to 1956 and a reader in the faculty from 1955 until his retirement in 1957. He was married with two daughters. His mother was sister to Alfred MARSHALL, and Guillebaud later acted as executor to Marshall's widow, Mary Paley MARSHALL, after her own death in 1944.

There were three strands to Guillebaud's career: teaching, research and administration. His lecture courses included trade and finance, elementary principles and wage regulation. He is remembered for two contributions to economics, an edition of Marshall's *Principles of Economics* and his arbitration of labour disputes. The task of editing the *Principles of Economics* and tracing the development of Marshall's economics was spread, 'off and on' and with a break during the Second World War, over a quarter of a century from 1934. Denis ROBERTSON described the task as 'an almost inconceivably laborious operation'. In an article in the *Economic Journal* in 1961, Guillebaud described the preparation of the two-volume edition. The first volume reproduces the eighth and final edition of the *Principles* corrected for misprints. The second volume indicates from which edition each sentence, paragraph or section of the eighth edition originates, and whether there was any change of sense or emphasis. His own conclusion was that the work threw an 'instructive light' on 'the way in which (Marshall) expressed his thought'.

In 1928 Guillebaud published a study of German Works Councils, which he had observed from 1919 until 1926. The study reports the generally successful development of the works councils, the difficult political and economic background, including rapid inflation, and the frictions within trade unions. At the end of the 1930s, Guillebaud reported his studies of the German economy in *The Economic Recovery of Germany* (1939). Such studies based on international comparisons became a popular and rich area of applied economics after the Second World War.

Following the war, Guillebaud was invited by the Tanganyika Sisal Growers Association to conduct a survey of the sisal industry, the leading industry in Tanganyika. While he was undertaking the survey, he was invited to make recommendations on the form of joint consultations between employers and labour appropriate to the circumstances of the industry. In 1966 he published the third edition of *The Sisal Industry of Tanganyika*, a careful and thorough description of the development of the industry.

In a review of HAYEK's *Road to Serfdom* written in 1944, recognizing the importance of the book, Guillebaud commented: 'The British people do not, in fact, believe in hard and fast logical solutions; they much prefer to compromise' (1944: 215). His approach to labour relations was based on this perception. During the 1950s and 1960s Guillebaud was involved in the arbitration of labour disputes in a wide range of industries, including baking, road haulage, bespoke tailoring and agriculture. From 1952 until 1959 he was an independent member of the Industrial Disputes Tribunal. In 1958 he was appointed Chairman of the Railway Pay Committee of Inquiry. The report of the Committee, published in March 1960, describes the complexity of wage structures, lack of earnings statistics and the difficulties of making comparisons across industries. The report, which was based on comparisons with pay in other industries, recommended an increase of approximately 8 per cent for manual grades, and a radical simplification of the wage structure and higher differentials for certain categories. The report provided the basis for a speedy resolution of a difficult dispute, and resulted in substantial increases in pay for employees in the railway industry. The Guillebaud formula for resolving the dispute was later viewed as incompatible with the operation of incomes policies, but arbitration based on comparability returned when incomes policies were abandoned. In a short monograph of fifty-four pages, Guillebaud (1970) described the arts of conciliation and arbitration of industrial disputes and drew on his experience of settling disputes.

BIBLIOGRAPHY
The Works Council (Cambridge, 1928).
The Economic Recovery of Germany (1939).
'Hitler's New Economic Order for Europe', *Economics Journal* (1940), pp. 449–60.
The Social Policy of Nazi Germany (New York, 1941).
Review of *The Road to Serfdom* by F.A. Hayek, *Economica* (1944), vol. XI, p. 215.
'The Teaching of Economics in the United Kingdom', in International Economic Association, *The University Teaching of Social Sciences: Economics* (Paris, 1954).
Report of the Railway Pay Committee of Inquiry (1960).
'The Variorum Edition of Alfred Marshall's Principles of Economics', *Economics Journal* (1961), vol. LXXI, pp. 677–90.
The Sisal Industry of Tanganyika, 3rd edn (Welwyn, 1966).
The Role of the Arbitrator in Industrial Wage Disputes (Welwyn, 1970).

Cliff Pratten

H

HAINES, Richard (1633–85)

Haines was born some time in early May 1633 at Sullington, Sussex, and died in London on 29 May 1685. He farmed at Sullington throughout most of his life, but despite an interest in agriculture and science, he seems not to have been a very successful farmer and had to sell land on several occasions. He was well known in London as well as among the gentry of Sussex, and seems to have had friends at court. A polymath, he wrote on economy and trade as well as agriculture and science.

Haines believed that the English economy was in decline for two reasons: first, the volume of manufactured goods produced within the country was declining, and second, the volume of imported goods was rising. He particularly condemned rising imports of goods which could be made in England, singling out linen cloth in particular, but also mentioning salt, saltpetre and iron. He argued that imports of these goods should be banned, and that efforts should be made to stimulate their domestic manufacture. Other products, 'especially such as are superfluous and injurious to the well-being of the Kingdom' (1674: 4) should also be prohibited from import; for example, people should be forced to give up importing French brandy, and drink beer brewed in England instead. He also suggested that the coinage should be devalued to make the English market less attractive to foreign merchants.

Creating a favourable balance of trade, Haines believed, would also provide employment and reduce poverty. From 1672 onward he became increasingly interested in the problem of poverty. His solution was the workhouse, which would provide both work and shelter for the poor and indigent. In the early 1670s he travelled to Holland and studied the Dutch workhouse system, which impressed him greatly. He believed that a system of workhouses in every county, with people employed at spinning and weaving either wool or linen cloth would result in a gain to the nation of some £5,000 per day. In *A Method of Government for such Publick Working Almshouses* (1679), Haines suggested that vagrants and criminals could also be put to work in the workhouses. Even criminals sentenced to hang could have their sentences commuted to being confined to a workhouse for life or a term of years. Thus the labour of every person in the nation could be made useful.

BIBLIOGRAPHY
A Model of Government for the Good of the Poor and the Wealth of the Nation (1672).
The Prevention of Poverty; or a Discourse on the Causes of the Decay of Trade, Fall of Lands, and Want of Money throughout the Nation (1674).
A Breviat of Some Proposals Prepared to be Offered to the Great Wisdom of the Nation...for the Speedy Restoring of the Woollen Manufacture, by a Method practised in other Nations (1679).

The Proposals for Promoting the Woollen-Manufactory, Promoted (1679).
A Method of Government for such Publick Working Alms-houses as may be Erected in every County for bringing all idle hands to Industry (1679).
England's Weal and Prosperity Proposed: or, Reasons for erecting Publick Work Houses in every County (1681).

Further Reading
Haines, C.R., *A Complete Memoir of Richard Haines, 1633–1685* (1899).

Morgen Witzel

HALE, Matthew (1609–76)

Hale was born at Alderley, Gloucestershire 1 November 1609, and died there on 25 December 1676. The son of a barrister, Hale was orphaned at the age of five and was brought up by his guardian, the puritan Antony Kingscot. He was educated at Magdalen Hall, Oxford, where he enrolled in 1626. Originally intending to take holy orders, he soon changed his mind. As a skilled fencer, he briefly considered an army career but ultimately decided upon law. He entered Lincoln's Inn in 1629, where he befriended William PRYNNE and John Vaughan and studied under William Noy and John Selden. He was called to the bar in 1636 and developed special expertise in the law of treason, eventually defending a number of Charles I's allies, including Sir John Bramston (1641), Archbishop William Laud (1643–4), the Duke of Hamilton (1649) and the presbyterian royalist Christopher Love (1651).

Hale's legal connections were advanced by his marriage to Anne Moore in 1640. Her uncle, Geoffrey Palmer, became attorney-general upon the Restoration. The marriage, however, was not very successful. Anne gave birth to ten children (only two of whom survived) but, according to Aubrey, Hale 'was a great cuckold'. His second marriage, to his servant in 1656, was socially less acceptable but apparently more fulfilling. Through all his domestic troubles, however, Hale's career was a great success. His law practice was sufficiently flourishing by 1648 for him to buy substantial lands. Although a royalist in the 1640s, he swore allegiance to the Commonwealth in 1649 and became a leading figure in the Hale commission (1652) for law reform. In 1654 he was elected to parliament, and in the same year Oliver Cromwell appointed him a justice of the common pleas, a position which he relinquished on Cromwell's death in 1659. He sat in Richard Cromwell's parliament (1659) but played no major part. He became active once more in the Convention Parliament of 1660. He proposed that an original contract be drawn up and signed by parliament and Charles II, but his motion to this effect was defeated by Monck's supporters. As one of the managers of the joint conference of Lords and Commons, he was influential in moulding the Restoration settlement. He took part in the commission for the trial of the regicides. Later in the same year, he was appointed Lord Chief Baron of the Exchequer, and was also knighted. One of his last actions in the 1660 parliament was to introduce a bill for the comprehension of presbyterians into the Church of England. The bill was defeated by the Anglican majority, but Hale continued to press for less severe treatment of dissenters until his death. Between 1666 and 1672, he worked on a statutory tribunal resolving disputes between owners and tenants of property destroyed in the Great Fire of London. In 1671 he was created Chief Justice of the King's Bench. Ill-health obliged him to resign in early 1676, and he died on Christmas Day the same year.

As a practitioner of law through all the changes of regime between the 1640s and the 1670s, Hale gained a reputation for being 'wonderfully charitable and open handed' and for being a great lawyer who 'would never suffer the strictness of the law to prevail against conscience' and who 'would make use of all the niceties and subtleties of law when it tended to support right and equity'. His one famous misjudgement that proved this rule led to the conviction and execution of two women for witchcraft, in a case tried at the Bury St Edmunds assizes in 1662. Too late to make any practical difference, Hale regretted that he had omitted to give any directions to the jury about the highly questionable evidence that had been brought against the two accused.

Hale was reputedly a 'godly man', and his puritan commitments coloured everything he wrote, including his economic writings. He wrote extensively on natural philosophy, religion and, especially, jurisprudence, though he published relatively little in his lifetime. In natural philosophy, or science, his purpose was to prove the Creator's existence and to interpret the physical laws of nature as divine commands. He adopted a neo-Aristotelian philosophy of nature, but replaced Aristotle's final causes by divine intention. Drawing upon the sometimes rather eccentric writings of Jan Comenius and John Baptist van Helmont, Hale sought a middle way between the mechanistic views of the universe which he encountered in Descartes and Robert Boyle and the vitalism of Henry More and the Cambridge Platonists. His own, far from rigorous conclusions appeared in his last published work, *Contemplations, Moral and Divine* (1677), which argued that all that happened in the world was motion in obedience to God's will.

Hale's specifically religious writings focused mainly on practical devotion and the issue of 'comprehension' rather than the toleration of dissent. He moved from an early commitment to Calvinism to a later, more liberal latitudinarianism. In later life, he became very close to Richard Baxter, and used his own prominent legal position to help several dissenters who ran foul of the Act of Uniformity. During the Restoration, Hale joined forces with John Wilkins, John Tillotson and Edward Stillingfleet, the leading members of the comprehension movement. Their point was not to tolerate dissent, but to rationalize the Anglican Church so that moderate dissenters could be comprehended within it. Although Hale opposed the strictness of Restoration laws against dissent, he never doubted that secular authorities were obligated to defend a national church and to enforce conformity to it. Part of his reasoning was summed up in a judgement in 1676, where he established that blasphemy was a crime at common law since rejecting religion meant dissolving all obligations upon which civil society was founded. In any case, he argued, the Christian religion was, in fact, part of the laws of England. There was no question of tolerating atheists or papists, since the first bred anarchy and the second bred tyranny. The experience of the civil wars led him to refuse toleration for those varieties of religious dissent, such as the Quakers, that claimed special access to divine inspiration. He also consistently opposed beliefs in religious ministers' powers of excommunication. Such powers, he argued, must always belong to the secular authority.

In his jurisprudential writings, Hale attempts to reconcile the contractualism of his mentor, John Selden, with the common law mentality of Edward Coke. The surprising result, as a modern commentator has remarked, is that Hale anticipates many of the essential features of BURKE's philosophy. His most enduring book, *The Analysis of the Law* (1713), transformed Coke's ideas of ancient, immemorial, unchanging custom and the 'reason' of the common law. By eschewing abstract reasoning, Hale developed a theory of law as customary and continuously changing in response to circumstances. The work gained high praise from the great twentieth-century legal historian, William Holdsworth.

In a number of manuscripts, circulated among friends and colleagues in the 1660s and 1670s, Hale took issue with Thomas HOBBES. Against Hobbes, he asserted that natural laws were the commands of God and that contracts were binding ultimately because of God's rewards and punishments to man's immortal soul. Hobbes had also attacked Coke's view that the reason of law was what professional common lawyers identified it to be. The reason of law was certainly 'artificial reason' for Hobbes, but it was the artificial reason of the sovereign. In response, Hale refashioned the organizing ideas contained in his work. Coke was right to identify an intricate, rational coherence underpinning the system of laws and he was also right to insist that this coherence was only evident to the professional eyes of trained common lawyers. Hobbes was right to locate the legislative power exclusively in the sovereign's hands. But both Coke and Hobbes were wrong in failing to see that the general consent of the subjects was necessary to fit new law into an existing, intricate system. As a matter of historical experience, legal obligation stemmed from popular consent, not from the will of a sovereign and not from the wisdom of a judge. One product of Hale's preoccupation with the writings of Hobbes, Grotius, Seldon and Coke is of importance for his economic ideas. He developed a labour theory of private property which has some affinities to that of John LOCKE. Private property was logically prior to government, and hence could not be modified without the individual's consent.

Assessments of Hale's contribution to the history of economic thought have usually focused on two, posthumously published works: *A Discourse touching Provision for the Poor* (1683), and Chapter 10 of *The Primitive Origination of Mankind* (1677). Part of the latter was separately published by George CHALMERS in 1782 as *An Essay on Population*. The first work offers a project to reform the Jacobean and Elizabethan poor laws. It anticipates some of the main provisions of the 1834 poor law. Problems of poverty were, Hale argued, worse in England than anywhere else in Europe. Crime was rampant, social and political instability were increasing. The well-intentioned Elizabethan poor laws placed too heavy a burden on individual parishes. Local overseers were not enforcing the poor laws for fear of retaliation by their neighbours. Charity was insufficient to bridge the gap. A culture of indolence, begging and theft was spreading, and an enormously important economic resource was being wasted. Hale's solution was to make groups of parishes responsible for a shared workhouse. In the final section of the pamphlet, Hale undertook to show that such workhouses could be economically viable, employing all of the able-bodied poor while paying them a reasonable, living wage. If adopted, his project would create a culture of industry to replace that of indolence and England would then flourish, socially, politically and economically. Hale's project has been interpreted as an early example of the economic projects of DEFOE's 'Projecting Age'. The poor were merely an unemployed 'productive resource' (Appleby, chap. 6). But as Charles Whibley noted long ago and rather aggressively in his 1927 edition of Hale's pamphlet, there is much more to Hale's argument than this. In Whibley's words, Hale's was 'the work not of an economic pedant but of a Christian gentleman'.

The same must be said of Hale's essay on population. To be sure, Nicholas BARBON frequently cited its argument about the continuous, overall increase in the world's population in his economic pamphlets of the 1680s and 1690s. Much more recently, Schumpeter (1994: 253) placed Hale's work in the context of William PETTY, the rise of 'political arithmetic' and the gradual acquisition of statistically reliable facts about socio-economic life. There is some justification for this. For Hale, in part, set out to show through statistical calculation and historical comparison that the population of England had increased greatly since the Norman Conquest. His chosen method was to compare the houses and households of selected localities as recorded in Domesday Book with their equivalents in 1670. His conclusion was that even though England had suffered major disasters of 'disease, pestilence, wars, civil wars, emigrations, famines', still its population had increased more than twentyfold since the Conquest.

But to see these essays by Hale on the poor law and on population as anticipations of what would later be said and done by others far better, far more effectively and far more rigorously is to miss Hale's point entirely. Both projects were anchored in his religious beliefs. These beliefs are explicit in *The Great Audit: With the Account of the Good Steward*, first published in 1805 but written shortly before his death. The whole duty of man, Hale shows, can be derived from two 'truths.' The first was that the 'Great Lord of the World hath placed the children of men in as his Stewards' (1805: 253). The second was the parable of the talents. Stewardship was key. The world was God's estate. Man's duty was to cultivate the bodily and intellectual talents loaned to him by God and to apply them in successful estate-management. In accounting for his own life, Hale attributed his work for the poor as a direct application of the parable of the talents. And he considered all his intellectual enquiries, including containing the chapter on population, as an exercise in explaining God's ways to men. So the most appropriate intellectual context for understanding Hale's economic writings is not solely mercantilist concerns with the poor as an unproductive resource and population growth as the engine of economic growth, nor is it the gradual emergence of classical political economy: it is rather the much older tradition of Christian neo-Aristotelianism. In this context, Hale's economic writings are of a piece. They are the works of a man who understands himself to be the manager of God's estate. His project for efficient workhouses was the direct application of the injunction to do for the 'least' of men as one would do to God. His calculation of the progressive increase in world population was an account of God's bounty with respect to mankind. It was, after all, a chapter in a book designed to combat atheism.

BIBLIOGRAPHY
Contemplations, Moral and Divine (1677).
The Primitive Origination of Mankind, Considered and Examined According to the Light of Nature (1677).
A Discourse touching Provision for the Poor (1683; repr. ed. C. Whibley, 1827).
A Discourse of the Knowledge of God and of our selves (1688).
The Analysis of the Law: being a scheme, or abstract, of the several titles and partitions of the Law of England, digested into method (1713).
The Great Audit: With the Account of the Good Steward, ed. T. Thirwall (1736).

Further Reading
Appleby, J.O., *Economic Thought and Ideology in Seventeenth-Century England* (Princeton, 1978).
Cromartie, A., *Sir Matthew Hale, 1609–1676: Law, Religion and Natural Philosophy* (Cambridge, 1995).
Heward, E., *Matthew Hale* (1972).
Pocock, J.G.A., *The Ancient Constitution and Feudal Law: A Study of English Historical Thought in the Seventeenth Century* (Cambridge, 1987).
Schumpeter, J., *History of Economic Analysis* (1994).

Martyn Thompson

HALES, John (*c*.1516–1572)

Hales (also Hayles) was born in 1516 or shortly before, probably at or near Canterbury, and died in London on 26 December 1572. As a young man he suffered an accident that left him lame for life. He appears to have received no formal education, and claims to have taught himself four languages including Greek. From around 1525 he was in service in the household of a distant relative, Sir Christopher Hales, master of the rolls, but there seems to have been a falling out between them, possibly because Hales saw no chance of preferment upon his reaching adulthood. In 1534 he sought employment with Thomas Cromwell, and by the following year was a clerk in Cromwell's household. By 1537 he was was assisting Ralph Sadler as a senior clerk in the Wardrobe. He became prosperous and in the early 1540s bought several properties in London and Coventry, notably the former Hospital of St John in Coventry, where he later founded a school, the Henry VIII's Free School.

The fall of Cromwell saw Hales dismissed from his posts, but the accession of Edward VI brought him back into prominence thanks to his friend Sadler, now a privy councillor and adherent of the Duke of Somerset. Hales was returned to parliament as MP for Preston in 1547, and in 1548 made a member of the Commission of Enclosures in the Midlands. He became an opponent of enclosure and also attacked abuses such as purveyancing and regrating, the buying up of commodities by rich merchants at low prices who then sold them at high prices. He introduced several bills on these subjects into the House of Commons, all of which failed. Hales's parliamentary career was cut short with the fall of Somerset, and he was briefly imprisoned in the Tower of London. Released, he made plans to leave the country, and was already in exile in Germany when Mary came to the throne. Hales's activities with other exiles and German reformers led to the confiscation of his property in 1557, but all was restored to him by Elizabeth following her accession. He was again appointed a clerk of the Wardrobe and became MP for Lancaster in 1563, but fell out of favour for writing a pamphlet on the succession.

A Discourse of the Common Weal of the Realm of England is the most notable work associated with Hales. It was probably written in the autumn of 1549, during Hales's most active period in parliament, but did not appear in print until 1581. The only author attribution in the first published version was the initials WS, leading one eighteenth-century printer to re-issue it as the work of William Shakespeare. Lamond and CUNNINGHAM, editors of the 1893 edition, note that the work was sometimes attributed to Sir Thomas SMITH, and surmise that WS might be William Smith, Sir Thomas's nephew and leader of the failed Ards plantation in Ireland, known to have been a friend of Hales. They conclude, however, that Hales was the author. This has since been rejected by Dewar (1965) and Bindoff (1982), both attributing the work to Smith. He and Hales were near contemporaries in age and were both members of the circle of intellectuals around the Duke of Somerset, and shared similar views on many subjects, meaning that cross-influence is likely no matter who the actual author was. As with Sir Thomas Smith's own *De Republica Anglorum*, the problem of attribution of Tudor political tracts remains a difficult one.

The *Discourse* takes the from of three dialogues between various speakers. Lamond and Cunningham note that the setting for the dialogues is likely to be Coventry, where the 1548 Commission of Enclosures often sat. The two principal speakers are the Knight, whom they surmise to be Hales himself, and the Doctor, who is believed to be Hugh Latimer, Bishop of Worcester and a noted opponent of enclosure. Other characters including merchants, local officials, tradesmen and husbandmen, were probably based on worthies of Coventry.

The first dialogue begins with an attack on enclosure, blaming it for the decay of agriculture and, in part, for the consequent shortage of food and high prices. The work then goes on to discuss the state of trade and the decay of the coinage, arguing that good coin has nearly all been exported to pay for imported goods and what remains in circulation is short in supply and of poor quality. This compounds the problem, as even when goods are available, there is a lack of money with which to pay for them. The dialogue warns that the shortage of money has consequences for the nation as a whole, as without money the crown is unable to pay and equip armies.

The second dialogue goes on to suggest the regulation of prices and also of imported goods to protect local industry, and argues for prohibiting the export of wool. It does not call for trade to be prohibited altogether, but rather to be regulated in such a way as to provide benefit for the kingdom. A further discussion of money highlights the problem that coin, no matter what it be made of, must have the confidence of the people, otherwise its worth will decline; for this reason the dialogue is strongly against debasement of the coinage, or indeed any alteration. People require coins to be familiar, not only in substance and quantity but also in name, and tend to distrust novelty. The third dialogue enlarges further on the themes of the first two.

Causes of Dearth (1548), fully attributed to Hales, also speaks of the rise of poverty and the decay of agriculture, and attacks regrating and purveyancing. It also calls for more money to be set aside for the poor and better provision to be made for them. *Causes of Dearth* sets out the programme of reform which Hales attempted to pursue in parliament until the fall of Somerset. Unlike Smith and others of the Somerset circle, Hales was never to regain his old prominence and never got another chance to press for his reforms.

BIBLIOGRAPHY
Causes of Dearth (1548; repr in Lamond and Cunningham, xlii–xlv)
Bill on Decay of Tillage (1548; repr in Lamond and Cunningham, xlv–lii)
A Discourse of the Common Weal of the Realm of England (1581; ed. E. Lamond and W. Cunningham, Cambridge, 1893).

Further Reading
Bindoff, S.T., *The House of Commons 1509–1558*, vol. 2 (1982).
Dewar, M., 'The Authorship of the *Discourse of the Commonweal*', English *Economic History Review* (1962), ser. 2, vol. 19, pp. 388–400.

Morgen Witzel

HALL, Charles (1738?–1825?)

Hall was born probably in 1738 or 1739, and died some time after June 1825. The date of birth has been suggested on the basis of his matriculation date at the University of Leyden. However, in a letter to Thomas SPENCE, probably written in 1807, he refers to himself as being 'over seventy'. He was said to be eighty-six years of age upon his release from the Fleet prison in 1825.

Hall matriculated at the University of Leyden in 1765 and later graduated with the degree of MD for a thesis on pulmonary consumption, before moving to practice in England. His *Family Medical Instructor* was published in Shrewsbury in 1785 and that may suggest that he practised in this area, but we know for certain that he was living and working in Tavistock at the time of the publication of his major work, *The Effects of Civilization on the People in European States* (1805). It was this book, republished in 1813, 1820 and 1850, together with a pamphlet entitled *Observations on the Principal Conclusion in Mr Malthus's Essay on Population*, that brought him to public notice and, in particular, to that of some of the followers of Robert OWEN, such as John Minter Morgan; the latter reprinted Hall's work in his Phoenix Library series in 1850. It was Morgan too who furnished most of what we know about the later years of Hall's life. A German edition of the work – *Die Wirkuungen er Zivilisation auf die Massen* – was also published in Leipzig in 1905 in a series of major socialist works edited by Georg Adler.

Hall was arrested in Somerset in December 1816 for failure to discharge a debt of £157, and remained incarcerated in the rules of the Fleet prison for eight and a half years. Morgan tells us that 'he had friends who would have released him from prison but he was confined through a lawsuit – as he considered unjustly; and rather than permit the money to be paid he had resolved to remain incarcerated for life' (Morgan 1834: 21). In fact he was discharged from the Fleet on 21 June 1825, though it is reasonable to assume that he died shortly thereafter.

It was Hall's medical experience of the consequences of contemporary poverty and industrial activity that led him to consider the effects of an emergent industrial and commercial civilization. As he saw it, the primary consequence had been to confirm and exacerbate the division of rich and poor that had originated when the appropriation by 'some daring spirits' of what had previously been 'common to all', had eventuated in an unequal distribution of landed property.

With the seizure of common land went the acquisition of 'all things as compose wealth', and these in turn gave 'command and direction of the labour of those who are not possessed of any of them' (1805: 49–50). Thus, for the labourer denied access to the land by enclosures or other means, there was 'an absolute necessity under the penalty, the heaviest of all penalties, namely the deprivation of such things as are necessary to his and his family's existence, for submitting to the things thus imposed upon him to do' (1805: 44). It was this power to submit labour to the dictates and desires of the rich that Hall believed had produced a reallocation of productive resources from agriculture to 'various refined manufactures' with the consequent growth of industrial and commercial activity. And with 'hands [being] drawn off powerfully from agriculture and coarse manufactures such as produce the things they [the labourers] themselves make use of', production was skewed in favour of luxuries and semi-luxuries with a dearth of necessities and working-class impoverishment resulting (1805: 44–5).

Moreover, manufacturing and commerce also provided further opportunities for the appropriation of what labour produced. As Hall saw it, manufacturers and traders possessed 'such things as the possessors of the necessaries of life [the landowners] stand in need of'. They could therefore be considered as:

possessed of a certain share of the land, and the produce of it. They have a claim on it resembling that of a mortgagee, who has a property in land equal to the interest of the sum he advances on it…Now, therefore, this *capitalist*, this manufacturer is in reality a possessor of land, and like him, has in his power and disposal a certain quantity of the necessaries of life…[and] forces his workmen to work for him, and to give him a share of what his work produces in the same manner as…the proprietors of land or possessors of the necessaries of life do.

(1805: 71–2)

Possessed of this power, the manufacturer and the tradesman would buy labour or the product of labour for less than their value, selling them dear, in particular to the landowner. Here Hall went further than agrarian socialists such as Thomas SPENCE. His argument was that the capacity to direct labour and to appropriate the greater part of what labour produced derived from the land and from circulating capital. The capitalist and the landowner both played a part in labour's impoverishment. Yet his anti-capitalism had physiocratic foundations. Landed property remained the 'basis, the source and the substance of all wealth' (1805: 73). The power of capital derived from its indirect control over the produce of land and thence the land itself, even if Hall's critique of existing economic arrangements was directed against the owners of capital as well as the owners of land.

Hall was also clear that such exploitative economic relations laid the basis for social antagonism. As he saw it, because 'every rich man [was] to be considered as the buyer and every poor man as the seller of labour. It [was] for the interest of the rich man to get as much of the work of the poor man and to give as little for it as he can; in other words to get as much of the labour and to give the labourer as little of the produce of the labour as possible.' It was therefore 'obvious that the interest of the buyer and seller [of labour and goods] is, in every case opposite' (1805: 111).

The rapid expansion of commercial and manufacturing activity oriented to the satisfaction of the desires of the rich not only effected a material impoverishment of labour, through a diminution in the resources allocated to the provision of necessities, it also had damaging repercussions of a social, physiological and psychological nature. Here Hall took up and developed the ideas of Adam SMITH on the deleterious consequences of the progressive subdivision of labour. Manufactures involving an extensive division of labour tended 'to the utter exclusion of all rational improvement of the mind'; 'they lessen the stature of man: they misshape his body: they enervate and diminish his strength and activity and his ability to bear hardships – they depress the spirit and vigour of his mind' (1805: 157).

In contrast, Hall's ideal society was essentially rural. It was to be a society dominated by small, independent and largely self-sufficient proprietors who, literally and metaphorically, reaped where they had sown; who would not wield the kind of economic power that could produce a misallocation of resources and who could improve their material condition only by their own honest endeavour. In a letter to Thomas Spence, Hall wrote that, 'I think that what we should aim at is to go back a good way towards our ancestral state: to that point from which we strayed, retaining but little of that: only (to wit, of the coarser arts) which civilization has produced together with certain sciences' (Claeys 1981: 317). Manufactures would exist only as an adjunct to an economy overwhelmingly agrarian in nature. Moreover the micro and macroeconomic self-sufficiency that characterized such an economy would obviate or reduce the need for market exchange, and with that would go the inequities that inhered to buying cheap and selling dear. In such a simple, equitable, frugal, agrarian economy, 'what a man had would be little liable to be taken from him by another, [and] all strife about *meum* and *tuum* would be nearly at an end' (1805: 268).

In discussing how such a vision might be realized, Hall distinguished between the practical and the ideal. As practical remedies for existing evils, he suggested the abolition of the law of primogeniture and the prohibition, or heavy taxation, of refined manufactures. Ideally, though, the land should be collectively owned and then distributed in such a manner as to lay the basis for a commonwealth of small independent producers.

Writing during the throes of an industrial transformation of the British economy, Hall was one of those who had difficulty accommodating the material possibilities that was creating. He has been described by many commentators as a socialist, or socialist critic, of nascent industrial capitalism but such a categorization is not entirely satisfactory (see, for example, Beer 1953; Cole 1959). He certainly formulated a critique directed both at landowners *and* capitalists, rent *and* profit. Moreover, he looked to a collective ownership of the key productive resource of the economy. Yet he saw economic power as rooted, directly or indirectly, in the land, and he embraced not the liberating material abundance that industrialization was making possible, but a Godwinian frugality devoid of the corruption, intellectual atrophy, coercion and debilitating working conditions that inhered to luxury consumption. That said, as the popular support for the Chartist Land Plan makes clear, if it cannot be denominated socialist, his imaginative vision of a smallholders' commonwealth would continue to strike a chord with a significant section of the British working classes well into the nineteenth century.

BIBLIOGRAPHY
The Family Medical Instructor (Shrewsbury, 1785).
The Effects of Civilization on the People of European States (1805; repr. 1813, 1820, 1850).
Observations on the Principal Conclusion in Mr. Malthus's Essay on Population (1805).

Further Reading
Beer, M., *A History of British Socialism*, 3rd edn, 2 vols (1953).
Claeys, G., 'Four Letters Between Thomas Spence and Charles Hall', *Notes and Queries* (1981), vol. 226, pp. 317–21.
Cole, G.D.H., *Socialist Thought: The Forerunners, 1789–1850* (1959).
Dinwiddy, J., 'Charles Hall, Early English Socialist', *International Review of Social History* (1976), vol. 21, pp. 256–76.
Morgan, J.M., *Hampden in the Nineteenth Century*, 2 vols (1834).
Stafford, W. *Socialism, Radicalism and Nostalgia, Social Criticism in Britain, 1775–1830* (Cambridge, 1986).
Thompson, N., *The Market and its Critics, Socialist Political Economy in Nineteenth Century Britain* (1988).

Noel Thompson

HALLEY, Edmond (1656–1742)

Halley, was born in London on 8 November 1656, the son of a prosperous soap-boiler. He died on 14 January 1742 in London. Educated in the classics and mathematics at St. Paul's School, he entered The Queen's College, Oxford, in 1673, leaving without a degree in 1676. That year, with financial support from his father, Halley undertook a voyage to St Helena with the purpose of charting the stars visible in the southern hemisphere. Two years later he presented his mapping of the southern constellations to Charles II. Shortly thereafter he was awarded, on the king's intercession, an MA degree from Oxford.

In 1678, at the age of twenty-two, Halley was elected a fellow of the Royal Society, an organization he later served for some years as secretary. In 1682 he married Mary Tooke; of their several children, two daughters and one son survived to adulthood. On a visit to Cambridge University in 1684, Halley met Sir Isaac NEWTON. Subsequently he played a key role in guiding Newton's *Principia* all the way from manuscript to publication. In 1703 Halley was appointed Savilian professor of geometry at Oxford. In his 1705 work, *Synopsis of the Astronomy of Comets*, he argued that notable comets seen in 1531, 1607 and 1682 were in fact the same body and that it would return in 1758, a correct prediction that led to the posthumous naming of 'Halley's comet'. In 1720 Halley succeeded John Flamsteed as astronomer royal at Greenwich.

Halley's significance to economics derives from his pioneering construction of a life table based on mortality statistics for the city of Breslau in Silesia (now Poland). John GRAUNT had published a rudimentary life table for London in 1662, as had William PETTY for Dublin in 1683. Halley, working from Breslau data for the years 1687 through 1691, formed a grid in which the risk of death was given for every age from birth to one hundred. This provided the actuarial basis for a proper determination of life insurance premiums as well as for calculating the fair value of annuities for life. Halley demonstrated how to use vital statistics, probability theory, and discounting techniques to value an annuity not only upon a single life but also upon two or three lives jointly. He disavowed any universal applicability for his results: other cities might be more or less 'salubrious' than Breslau, with mortality rates correspondingly lower or higher. Also, a table based on only five years' data could not be considered as accurate as one based on a longer period of observations. Halley expressed the hope that others would conduct studies similar to his in other cities. His paper on the life table and its financial applications appeared in the 1693 *Transactions* of the Royal Society, a journal in which he published about eighty scientific papers over many years.

BIBLIOGRAPHY

'An Estimate of the Degrees of the Mortality of Mankind drawn from curious Tables of the Births and Funerals at the City of Breslau, with an attempt to ascertain the Price of Annuities upon Lives', *Philosophical Transactions of the Royal Society* 17 (1693), pp. 596–610.

Further Reading
Bonar, J., *Theories of Population from Raleigh to Arthur Young* (1931).

Geoffrey Gilbert

HAMILTON, Henry (1896–1964)

Hamilton was born on Islay on 2 March 1896, and died at Aberdeen on 4 May 1964. He was educated at Dunoon Grammar School, and graduated MA from the University of Glasgow in 1919 and was awarded a D.Litt in 1925. His early academic posts were in Birmingham, as lecturer in social studies at the Selly Oak Colleges from 1920–1 and as an extension lecturer in economics at the University of Birmingham from 1921–5. In 1925 he became a lecturer in economic history at the University of Aberdeen, where he remained for the rest of his life, becoming Jaifrey Professor of Political Economy in 1945.

Though Hamilton was latterly a professor of economics, he was first and foremost an economic historian. His first major study, inspired by his early years in Birmingham, was *The English Brass and Copper Industries* (1926), a pioneering study of industrial organization which was neglected in later years by many, including Hamilton himself after his move to Aberdeen. In the forty years he spent there, and so for most of his productive life, he concentrated almost exclusively on the economic history of Scotland. In the 1920s the serious study of this subject was almost non-existent. Hamilton gave a solid foundation for much subsequent work in *The Industrial Revolution in Scotland* (1932). As the study of the field has expanded enormously, with the increasing availability of relevant records and the application of new techniques, his achievement is in danger of being underestimated, even forgotten. Inadvertently, Hamilton contributed to the neglect. Though he showed his skill in the handling of original sources in two editions of papers, *Monymusk Papers* (1945) and *Life and Labour on an Aberdeenshire Estate* (1946), circumstances forced him to wider and often less scholarly activities.

In the Second World War Hamilton and one other member of staff carried the burden of all teaching in economics and economic history at Aberdeen. Thereafter his early interest in industrial organization and in the supply of manpower led to various public appointments locally and nationally, including the chairing of four wages councils. After his appointment as a professor of economics he made a valiant effort to re-establish his early commitment to the discipline, but with only qualified success. In 1948 he published more studies of industrial organization, of the white fish industry of Aberdeen and of the granite industry. At much the same time his early interest in extension work led to his popular but time-consuming *History of the Homeland* (1947). A later diversion was his general editorship of three volumes in the Third Statistical Account of Scotland: the counties of Aberdeen (1960), Banff (1961) and posthumously, Moray and Nairn (1965).

Hamilton was never apologetic about his diversion of effort and he rejected any suggestion that he should be an isolated specialist. Such diffusion of effort had unfortunate effects on the consolidation of his pioneering work on Scottish economic history. For over ten years before his death he worked on a major study of the eighteenth century, but he never had the time and perhaps increasingly the inclination to keep abreast of the range of sources becoming available or of the new techniques being applied to their analysis. When it did appear, *An Economic History of Scotland in the Eighteenth Century* (1963) still relied heavily on his earlier work and never made the mark on the development of the field which his comprehensive study of thirty years earlier had done. The result is that his achievement has been underestimated by many, but that may be the fate of the pioneer. Without his work the study of the economic history of Scotland would not have evolved as it has done.

BIBLIOGRAPHY
The English Brass and Copper Industries to 1800 (1926).
The Glorious Revolution in Scotland (1932).
Selections from the Monymusk Papers (1713–1755) (Edinburgh, 1945).
Life and Labour on an Aberdeenshire Estate 1735–1750 (Aberdeen, 1946).
History of the Homeland (1947).
'The White Fish Industry' [section on Aberdeen], in M.P. Fogarty, *Further Studies in Industrial Organization* (1948, pp. 108–29).
'The Granite Industry', in M.P. Fogarty, *Further Studies in Industrial Organization* (1948, pp. 181–208).
An Economic History of Scotland in the Eighteenth Century (Oxford, 1963).

R.H. Campbell

HAMILTON, Robert (1743–1829)

Hamilton, the eighth son of Gavin Hamilton, was born at Pilrig in Edinburgh on 11 June 1743. He died in 1829 and is buried at St Nicholas churchyard in Union Street, Aberdeen. He matriculated at the University of Edinburgh, where he studied Greek, logic, metaphysics, law and mathematics. After graduating from the University of Edinburgh, at his father's request he reluctantly took a job with the banking office of William Hogg and Son. In 1769 he became rector of Perth Academy, a position that was vacant after the death of John MAIR. In 1779 he was appointed to the chair of natural philosophy at Marischal College, Aberdeen. A student described him as very learned and excellent, but most eccentric.

Hamilton's major work is *An Introduction to Merchandise*. Volume 1 was published in 1777 and consists of three parts, on (1) arithmetic, (2) algebra and (3) bills of exchange, promissory notes and receipts, British monies, weights and measures. Volume 2 was published in 1779 and consists also of three parts, on (4) Italian book-keeping, (5) practical book-keeping and (6) the state of British trade, custom house laws, mercantile laws and public funds. An abridged version of *An Introduction to Merchandise* was published in 1788 under the same title; the fifth edition of the shortened version was published in 1802, and in 1820 a new version, partly rewritten by Elias Johnston, was published.

Many accounting textbooks were published in England and Scotland in the seventeenth and eighteenth centuries. Most of them were written for the textbook market, especially for academies and grammar schools for merchants' sons and heirs, such as Mair's *Book-keeping Methodiz'd* (1736). However, a new tendency was on the increase. This was the development of practical accounting books, which were strongly applicable to the practice of foreign trades in North America. Hamilton's *An Introduction to Merchandise* played the role not only of a forerunner of such practical book-keeping manuals for foreign trade, but also as a precursor of management accounting and cost accounting manuals. However, he has had no proper recognition for his achievement. In the words of Mepham (1988: 97), 'Hamilton was just too far ahead of his time'.

Hamilton's other works include *Reflection on Peace and War* (1790), *An Inquiry Concerning the Rise and Progress, The Redemption and Present State, and Management of the National Debt of Great Britain* (1813), and posthumously, *The Progress of Society* (1830) and *Essays* (1831).

BIBLIOGRAPHY
An Introduction to Merchandise, 2 vols (Edinburgh, 1777–9).
Reflection on Peace and War (1790).
An Inquiry Concerning the Rise and Progress, The Redemption and Present State, and Management of the National Debt of Great Britain (1813).
The Progress of Society (1830).
Essays (1831).

Further Reading
Bywater, M.F. and Yamey, B.S., *Historic Accounting Literature: A Companion Guide* (1982).
Chatfield, M. and Vangermeersch, R., *The History of Accounting, An International Encyclopedia* (1996).
Mepham, M.J. *Accounting in Eighteenth Century Scotland* (1988).

Izumi Watanbe

HAMILTON, Rowland (fl. 1863–92)

Little is known about Hamilton apart from his own statement that in 1875 he was an honorary secretary to the Standing Committee on Education. He wrote several works on the social sciences, especially on economics and education, between 1863 and 1892, and wrote on various subjects concerning education in the *Transactions of the National Association for the Promotion of Social Science* from 1873–84. His main economic works were *The Resources of a Nation* (1863) and *Money and Value* (1878), both written in the realm of mainstream classical ideas and theories. The classical character of his inquiries is inferred from his treatment of some special issues. For example, he was an advocate of the free trade doctrine and adopted the market equilibrating mechanism of prices and quantities (1863: 131–2; 1878: 170–1, 289). He stressed that supply price is determined by the cost of production, while the demand price mainly by utility (1863: 116–7; 1878: 100–1, 124). He treated the market wage rate on the basis of the wage fund doctrine (1878: 217), while he paid special attention on the division of labour and organization as the main sources of economic progress (1863: 18–20, 23; 1873; 1878: 186–9).

Monetary analysis is the main theme of his 1878 work, *Money and Value*. Hamilton's analysis has a positive and normative character, while his writing style is more explanatory than exploratory and strictly scientific. By accepting the role of the quantity theory of money, he explained the function of the various substitutes of metallic money and analytically portrayed the banking system and credit (1878: 35–6, 70–2, 224–74). He also distinguished among the various effects of domestic and international currencies (1878: 317–45), and described the specific effects of the changes in the value of money on continental economies and especially on the Indian economy (1878: 346–92).

Hamilton's pioneering idea in *Money and Value* has to do with the existence of economic uncertainty and its role and effects on the function of entrepreneurship, topics which he also mentioned in other works, notably *The Resources of a Nation* and an article, 'General Relations of Employers and Employed' (1874).

He considered the entrepreneur to be an active factor in economic development absolutely separable from capitalist (1878: 210–11). He recognized that the entrepreneur is inspired by two motives: the profit motive, and the freedom he enjoys in running his own business (1878: 210, 218–19). He attributed the active role of the entrepreneur to be the direction, responsibility and control of his enterprise and the introduction of various innovations, while the passive role is the bearing of the ultimate risk and uncertainty (1878: 29–30, 214–16, 257). The uninsured ultimate risks that are assumed by the entrepreneur in running and expanding his enterprise, justify the net profit which is his fair reward (1878: 216–17). He considered that wage, rent and interest – which, following SENIOR, he justified as the reward of abstinence – are contractual incomes, while net profit is the only residual of distribution.

The special historical literature on the phenomenon of entrepreneurship has paid no notice to Hamilton's contribution to the theory of entrepreneurship. However, he made a significant and independent contribution to this subject, and was a pioneer in connecting the existence of uninsured risks and uncertainty to the function and reward of the entrepreneur. Furthermore, his theory of entrepreneurship and profit bears a strong resemblance (Karayiannis 1992) to those developed independently by Richard Cantillon's *Essai sur la Nature du Commerce en General* (1755) and Frank Knight's *Risk, Uncertainty and Profit* (1921).

BIBLIOGRAPHY
The Resources of a Nation: a Series of Essay (1863).
'General Relations of Employers and Employed', *Transactions of the National Association for the Promotion of Social Sciences* (1874).
'Introductory Observations on Primary Education', *Sessional Proceedings* (1875), pp. 267–74.

Money and Value: An Inquiry into the Means and Ends of Economic Production (1878).
'Thrift in Great Britain', *Economic Journal* (1892), vol. 2, pp. 290–301.

Further Reading
Comment on Hamilton's *Money and Value: An Inquiry into the Means and Ends of Economic Production*, *The British Quarterly Review* (1878), vol. 68, pp. 248–9.
Karayiannis, A.D., 'Rowland Hamilton's Neglected Contribution on Risk, Uncertainty and Profit', in S. Todd Lowry (ed.), *Perspectives in the History of Economic Thought: Contributions to the History of Economics*, vol. 8 (Aldershot, 1992, pp. 80–9).

Anastassios D. Karayiannis

HAMMOND, John Lawrence Le Breton (1872–1949)

Lawrence Hammond was born 18 July 1872 at Drighlington in the West Riding of Yorkshire. He died at Hemel Hempstead, Hertfordshire on 7 April 1949. He was one of eight children of the Rev. Vavasour Fitz Hammond, a Church of England vicar, and Caroline Annie Webb. He married Lucy Barbara Bradby on 5 July 1901; they had no children. Hammond learned his liberalism from his father, who was active in Liberal circles in the West Riding. He was educated at Bradford Grammar School and then in 1891 went up to St John's College, Oxford, where he read classical moderations and *literae humanaires*. His tutor at Oxford was Sidney Ball, a friend of Arnold TOYNBEE and a disciple of T.H. Green. Toynbee's call for historical research in economic history, combined with a commitment to social reform, provided the essential framework for the Hammonds' interpretation of the Industrial Revolution. Hammond was also influenced by the Oxford medieval historian and Christian Socialist A.J. Carlyle, and by his friendship with the historian H.A.L. Fisher. Both taught him the new and painstaking methods of historical research then being advanced at Oxford.

Upon his graduation from Oxford in 1894 with a second, Hammond embarked on a career as a journalist and writer. He wrote for a number of Liberal newspapers, edited a revived *Speaker*, was for many years associated with *The Nation*, and served as correspondent at the Paris Peace Conference for the *Manchester Guardian*. He joined the *Guardian* in London in 1925. During the late 1890s, he was among a group of young Liberals who sought to create a 'new liberalism' while rejecting a socialist path. His essay on education, for example, both demonstrated his increasingly historical bent and his willingness to use the state to provide the education essential to a free democratic society (Hammond 1897). During the Boer War he articulated a fervent anti-imperialism (Hammond 1900). In the years before the Liberal election victory of 1906, Hammond embraced a liberal programme of land taxes, a progressive income tax to pay for old age pensions, factory acts, education, land reform, public employment for the unemployed and various schemes of rural reform and urban beautification. Despite his distaste for military values, he served as an artillery training officer during the First World War. As a result of his work on reconstruction, he published anonymously his plans for extensive state support for reconstruction after the war (Hammond 1918) and supported the Joint Industrial Councils, advocated by G.D.H. COLE.

Although Beatrice and Sidney WEBB urged him to stand as a Labour candidate for parliament in 1918, Hammond remained a liberal. He reluctantly supported Labour in elections from 1922, but he always worried about the party's close ties to the Trades Union Congress and its increasing class consciousness. During the inter-war period he was a strong supporter of democratic national self-determination for small states and international institutions to guarantee their freedom. The rise of Fascism led him to support Churchill's calls for rearmament during the 1930s. By the 1940s, Hammond's liberal advocacy had moved from Gladstone's parsimonious approach to public spending to an embrace of a mixed economy that owed more to the spirit of J.S. MILL than to socialism. It was these liberal ideas that he enshrined in his historical writing for, as Hammond's biographer concluded, 'history, Hammond believed, was a schooling in citizenship' (Weaver 1997: 51).

In addition to his journalism and books and essays on politics, Hammond published four major historical works: *Charles James Fox: A Political Study* (1903), *C. P. Scott and the Manchester Guardian* (1934), *Gladstone and the Irish Nation* (1938) and posthumously, *Gladstone and Liberalism* (1952). With Barbara HAMMOND, he published *Lord Shaftesbury* (1923) and *James Stansfield: A Victorian Champion of Sex Equality* (1932). The Hammond Papers at the Bodleian Library, Oxford, show that both did a great deal of research for these works but it was Barbara Hammond who did most of the careful transcribing from documents, while Lawrence Hammond turned their research into eminently readable books that sold in large numbers. Their social and economic histories were widely used as texts in universities, and were especially popular in adult education classes and among the educated public.

When the Hammonds began their research in social and economic history, historical economists were the dominant school of economic history in Britain. Although the Hammonds were severely critical of the neo-mercantilism and social-imperialism of the historical economists, they shared the latter's inductive critique of classical political economy. In *The Village Labourer*, first published in 1911, they traced England's agrarian transformation from the enclosure movement of the eighteenth century to the rural rising of 1830. The Hammonds were the first to use the Home Office papers and to interpret the agrarian unrest not as mere riots, but as popular reform movements against the advancement of large-scale capitalist agriculture supported by the doctrines of classical political economy. R.H. TAWNEY argued that the careful and original research of the Hammonds provided documentation for Toynbee's charge that political causes had been at the root of Britain's system of large-scale agriculture (Tawney 1960: 278). The Hammonds, who were heavily indebted to classical scholarship, did not fully accept the desirability of making England primarily an industrial nation. Indeed, they called for the reintroduction of a species of peasant proprietors designed to revitalize the countryside, promote personal and family development, and bring stability and permanence to the countryside. They were not, however – as has often been argued – simply romantic critics defending an old England. Their study of rural England was an indictment of the actions and ideology of the ruling classes of the time toward the common people.

The Hammonds next turned their attention to the effects of modern industry on the traditional artisans of the towns. *The Town Labourer* (1917) described the rise of a 'new Civilization' that had added 'the discipline of a power driven by a competition, which seemed as inhuman as the machines that thundered in the factory and shed', to the poverty of the old domestic system (1917: 16). They concluded that this revolution had 'raised the standard of comfort of the rich', but had 'depressed the standard of life for the poor' (1917: 31). Moreover, they declared that the dislocation brought by the rise of modern industry had been made harsher by the ruling class's fear of social and political revolution. This fear, stimulated by evangelical religion, had added intensity to the war of the ruling classes on the workers' demands for political and social redress. They argued that classical political economy had richly deserved its reputation as the 'dismal science', and, with the historical economists, were especially critical of RICARDO:

Ricardo's brilliant and rather labyrinthine deductive reasoning has led later students to the most diverse conclusions...But of the character of his immediate influence there can be no doubt...[it was] to create the impression that every human motive other than the unfailing principle of self-interest might be eliminated from the world of commerce and industry; that the forces of supply and demand settled everything; that the laws governing profits and wages were mechanical and fixed.

(1917: 176)

In his plans for reconstruction after the Great War, Hammond argued that classical economics, and its neoclassical offspring, were too individualistic, fatalistic and determinist. He urged that economics adopt a more complex human psychology, rooted in history and the new social sciences, which recognized the need for co-operation and public welfare in social and economic policy (1918: 10–26). The third volume of the labour trilogy, *The Skilled Labourer* (1919), concentrated on telling the detailed stories of the efforts of workers, such as miners, weavers, spinners and framework knitters, to protect their trades against degradation by both their masters and the new machines. The volume concludes with a superb narrative of Luddism, seeing it as essentially an effort at reform.

The Rise of Modern Industry (1925) placed the Industrial Revolution in a broad context. The Hammonds saw the Commercial Revolution of the early modern period, and especially the Atlantic trade dependent upon slavery, as one of the chief sources of European economic growth. They chronicled the rise of steam power, enclosures and the destruction of custom in industry. They characterized the

Industrial Revolution as a cataclysmic revolution in economic and social life akin to the French Revolution in politics, and concluded that the economic man of classical economics had not been 'a mere nightmare of the new textbooks', but had become an 'omnipotent force in a world existing for a single purpose' (1925: 158).

The pessimistic interpretation of the Industrial Revolution embodied in the work of the Hammonds was questioned by, among others, J.H. CLAPHAM, who maintained that the standard of living for workers between 1780 and 1850 had improved rather than declined, and insisted that a rising standard of living was the consequence of the rise of modern industry, competition, technology and increasing economic freedom. Although the Hammonds were reluctant to engage in the minutiae of academic scholarly debate, in 1930 they responded to Clapham in the newly created *Economic History Review*. It was here that Lawrence Hammond framed the classical debate over the social consequences of the Industrial Revolution, as one between the 'optimists', from T.B. Macaulay and most of the classical economists to Clapham, and the 'pessimists', from Robert SOUTHEY and the critics of classical economics to Toynbee and the historical economists. While Hammond criticized some of Clapham's statistics, he quickly conceded the possibility that the standard of living of many workers during the classic period of industrialization may have improved. Nonetheless, he continued, the Industrial Revolution was accompanied by a significant rise of 'discontent' as demonstrated by the social unrest of the period. The optimists, he argued, influenced by a scientific outlook, looked at life as the conquest of nature and material gain. In contrast, the pessimists, influenced by a classical and humanist education, were more interest in the 'quality of life'. He contrasted the beauty of Greek and Roman civilization, and its philosophical and spiritual fellowship, with that of England:

If you look at the life of the age of the Industrial Revolution in this spirit you are struck at once by its extraordinary poverty. What did Manchester and Leeds offer to the workman? It had destroyed his contact with nature and turned him from a craftsman into a man serving the routine of a great industry...it did not offer him the dignity of political rights or the excitement of a share in the government of a great society: it did not offer him the fellowship of common pleasure or common culture symbolized in the magnificence of his city. It offered him one incentive and only one, the hope of becoming rich.

(1930: 223)

The Hammonds abandoned the standard of living debate on the grounds of statistics. As it turned out, they did so much too early since the statistical debate remains unresolved to this day. Instead, they argued in *The Age of the Chartists, 1832–1854: A Study of Discontent* (1930, reissued in 1934 as the *Bleak Age*) that, despite Britain's vast increase in wealth during the Industrial Revolution, the period saw a dramatic increase in social unrest, a decline of leisure and the dignity of work in many trades, an increase in urban squalor and rural poverty, political repression and the growth of class consciousness.

Despite the challenge of Clapham and others to the Hammonds' interpretation of the Industrial Revolution, their books were the most widely read on the subject until they were replaced by the new empiricist and much more optimistic orthodoxy exemplified by T.S. ASHTON's *The Industrial Revolution* in 1948. Their emphasis on the attack upon custom and the imposition of a 'new discipline' upon society, as well as the resistance of the workers through collective action, anticipated much of E.P. Thompson's *The Making of the English Working Class* (1963), as well as more recent work in cultural history. In economics their historical work gave substance to the nineteenth-century critics of political economy as the 'dismal science'. They were inspired historians of the alienation so widely felt and expressed during the period of industrialization. Historiography has moved well beyond many of the conclusions of the Hammonds, but their remains much to be learned from their liberal humanist interpretation. Not the least of this is that good history, including good economic history, must do more than deal with statistics and the 'economic man'. For history to be influential beyond the academy, as the Hammonds demonstrated, it must deal with the ideas and experience of the period by telling the stories of real people and must speak to the spirit of the age in which it is written.

BIBLIOGRAPHY
'A Liberal View of Education', in *Essays in Liberalism by Six Oxford Men* (1897).
(with F.W. Hirst and G. Murray) *Liberalism and the Empire* (1900).
Past and Future (1918).
'The Industrial Revolution and Discontent', *Economic History Review* (1929–30), vol. 2, pp. 215–28.
The Growth of Common Enjoyment (Oxford, 1933).
(with Barbara Hammond) *The Village Labourer, 1760–1832: A Study of the Government of England Before the Reform Bill* (1911).
(with Barbara Hammond) *The Rise of Modern Industry* (1925).
(with Barbara Hammond) *The Town Labourer, 1760–1832* (1917; repr. New York, 1968).
(with Barbara Hammond) *The Skilled Labourer* (1919).

Further Reading
Clapham, J.H. 'Economic History: Survey of Development to the Twentieth Century', *Encyclopedia of the Social Sciences*, vol. 5 (New York, 1931).
———, *An Economic History of Modern Britain*, vol. I, *The Railway Age* (Cambridge, 1926).

Koot, G.M., 'Historians and Economists: The Study of Economic History in Britain, ca. 1920–1950', *History of Political Economy* (1993), vol. 25, no. 3, pp. 641–75.
Weaver, S.A., *The Hammonds: A Marriage in History* (Stanford, California, 1997).
Tawney, R.H., 'J.L. Hammond', *Proceedings of the British Academy* (1960), vol. 44, pp. 267–93.

Gerard M. Koot

HAMMOND, Lucy Barbara (1873–1961)

Lucy Barbara Bradby was born 25 July 1873 near Hoddesdon, Hertfordshire, and died on 15 November 1961 at Hemel Hempstead, Hertfordshire. She was the youngest of seven children of Ellen Johnson and the Rev. Edward Henry Bradby, then headmaster of Haileybury College. Her father, a Christian socialist, resigned his position in 1885 to take up a post at Toynbee Hall. She was educated at St Leonard's School in St Andrews, and then entered Lady Margaret Hall, Oxford in 1892. She was by all accounts a clever as well as a handsome woman with flaming red hair who attracted admirers; she was also captain of the hockey team at Lady Margaret Hall. In 1896 she became the first woman at Oxford to win a double first in classical moderations and greats.

Although she won a fellowship at Lady Margaret Hall which might have launched her into an academic career, Bradby returned to London to work for the Women's Industrial Council on the improvement of working-class women's social and political conditions. In 1901 she gave an address to the International Congress of Women in Berlin entitled 'Equal Pay for Equal Work'. She was part of a remarkable group of London women who played a major role in investigating social issues through their work on Charles Booth's study, *The Life and Labour of the People of London*, and also in establishing the discipline of economic history in England. Politically she was an advanced Liberal, a supporter of women's suffrage and an ardent anti-Boer War activist. She had known Lawrence HAMMOND both at Oxford and London, and conducted some research for him while he was editor of *The Speaker*. They were married by Rev. Samuel Barnett on 5 July 1901. Barbara Hammond contracted tuberculosis in 1905, one consequence of which was that she was unable to have children.

Despite her feminism, her superior education and the spirited independence she maintained for the rest of her life, when Barbara Bradby married Lawrence Hammond, she became known primarily as a participant in the remarkably productive partnership. Together, the Hammonds published eight major books and fought for many liberal causes. While not everyone agreed with their wholesale critique of classical political economy, their books were widely regarded as the standard interpretation of the social consequences of the Industrial Revolution in Britain during the 1920s and remained influential through the 1960s. Their friend R.H. TAWNEY once told them that their achievement lay 'in destroying the historical assumptions on which our modern slavery is based, unknown both to the slaves and the masters' (Clarke 1978: 189). After Lawrence Hammond's death in 1949, the obituary notice in the *Economic History Review* noted that even though the Hammonds had not held academic appointments, 'in the end even the Universities could not escape the spell and even CLAPHAM [the foremost British economic historian of the time], strongly as he disagreed with the Hammonds' verdicts directed much of his teaching and his writings to the issues raised by the Hammonds' ('Obituary; 1949: 143).

What each brought to their joint work is difficult to disentangle. However, Tawney's judgement of their individual contributions appears to be corroborated by the Hammond correspondence at the Bodleian Library, Oxford. Tawney noted that 'the research – in the sense of the collection and analysis of the materials, particularly the statistical materials, for their works, without which the books could not have been composed – owed most to Barbara, and that the nobility of style, the dignity of outlook and breadth of view reveals most clearly the hand of Lawrence Hammond' (Tawney 1961). It was Barbara Hammond who wrote the moving chapters on child labour in their books (Weaver 1997: 138), and she also contributed the sympathetic attitude toward the countryside and the natural environment that marked their books.

As well as their joint work, Barbara Hammond published two works on her own. The first was a paper on urban death-rates in the early nineteenth century in the first volume of the new journal of the Economic History Society, whose publication signalled the creation of economic history as a professional discipline (1926–9). The other was an essay, 'The Battle for Open Spaces', in 1936. From the early 1930s, she was deeply involved in the political movement to preserve open space. In her essay she chronicled how 'a small body of men once saved a great deal of English scenery from vandal Governments' (1936: 119). She told the story of how new agricultural methods and fertilizers, as well as an attitude on the part of the government 'that every tract of land might be beneficially enclosed' (1936: 122), created immense pressure to develop remaining wasteland commons and royal forests and how a preservation movement emerged, beginning with the Commons Preservation Society of 1865, to provide open space for allotments, recreation and wild-life habitats near population centres. She noted with satisfaction that 'the delight taken by the intelligentsia during the 'sixties' and 'seventies' of the last century in striding over the country was of great service to the community' (1936: 130). She believed that the educated elite had an individual moral responsibility to convince the government to take collective action for the preservation of open space, and that a civilized society needed public amenities provided by the state.

BIBLIOGRAPHY
(with J.L. Hammond) *The Village Labourer, 1760–1832: A Study of the Government of England Before the Reform Bill* (1911).
(with J.L. Hammond) *The Town Labourer, 1760–1832* (1917; repr. New York, 1968).
(with J.L. Hammond) *The Skilled Labourer* (1919).
'Urban Death Rates in the Early Nineteenth Century', *Economic History Review* (1926–29), vol. I, pp. 419–28.
'The Battle for Open Spaces', in J.A.K. Thompson and A.J. Toynbee (eds), *Essays in Honour of Gilbert Murray* (1936, pp. 119–40).

Further Reading
'Obituary of J. L. Hammond', *Economic History Review* (1949), second series, vol. I, nos 2–3, pp. 143.
Berg, M. 'The First Women Historians', *Economic History Review* (1992), vol. 45, no. 2, pp. 308–29.
Clarke, P., *Liberals and Social Democrats*, (Cambridge, 1978).
Koot, G.M., *English Historical Economics, 1870–1926: The Rise of Economic History and Neomercantilism* (1987).
'Obituary of Barbara Hammond', *Manchester Guardian* (1961), 17 November.
Tawney, R.H., 'Obituary of Lucy Barbara Hammond', *Manchester Guardian* (1961), 20 November.
Weaver, S.A., *The Hammonds: A Marriage in History* (Stanford, California, 1997).

Gerard M. Koot

HARRIS, Joseph (1702–64)

Harris was born at Talgarth in Breconshire in 1702, and died at the Tower of London on 26 September 1764. As a young man he worked as a blacksmith, but by 1728 he was living in London. Clearly well educated, he contributed a number of papers on astronomy and magnetism to *Philosphical Transactions*, and wrote later works on optics and mathematics. He probably joined the Royal Mint some time in the 1730s, and in 1748 he was appointed assay master at the Mint, a post he held until his death.

Harris's treatise *Essay upon Money and Coins* has been described by Schumpeter (1954: 291, n 9) as one of the best eighteenth-century works in the field of monetary analysis. In the first part, published in 1757, Harris analysed the true nature and theory of money, while in the second part, published in 1758, he used historical data in justifying some of his conclusions relating to the influence of money on economic growth. In the context of this discussion, he also made contributions to various non-monetary issues of economics. More specifically, by abandoning the mercantilist doctrine concerning the content of wealth, he argued instead that land and labour are its main sources (1757: 9, 25). He adopted a Platonic explanation of the division of labour as a product of the various talents and inclinations of men, and a cause for the formation of society (1757: 18). By the division of labour, the productivity of labour is increased as every person becomes expert and skilful in his own particular art (1757: 19). Thus, in regard to the determination of wage rate, he emphasized training time, risk, dexterity and skill as elements which regulate the prices of labour and services of different sorts (1757: 17). He emphsized the role of exchange in promoting wealth, and justified internal trade as saving time and adjusting market operation, and a factor for increasing employment (1757: 21–3). For Harris, the desire for wealth and motives of self-interest were of paramount importance for economic growth (1757: 20, 22, 27–8).

Harris, probably building on PETTY and Cantillon, developed a real cost theory of relative values (1757: 12–13) and in turn influenced Sir James STEUART (Karayiannis 1991) and probably also Adam SMITH. He believed that things in general are valued, not according to their real uses in supplying the necessities of men, but rather in proportion to the land, labour and skill that are requisite to produce them (1757: 12). In other words, the value of goods is mainly determined by these factors; in the majority of the products, labour is the main ingredient of value. Therefore, the wages of the lower class, 'as well the common artificers as the husbandmen, seems to be the main and ultimate standard that regulates the values of all commodities' (1757: 17). But how is the real subsistence wage of labour, the most important determinant of value, itself determined? Harris's answer to this question has a modern content. He recognized that if we regard the minimum subsistence level as that needed to maintain the labourer and his family in ordinary food and clothing (1757: 15), its value is determined ultimately by the productivity of labour and land (1757: 10, 15, 19n).

By distinguishing between market and real variations of value, Harris stressed that the first is determined through a demand and supply process, while the second is determined mainly by its intrinsic value, which must include the prime cost and the profits taken by the several dealers (1757: 56). However, he emphasized that the market price is mainly determined by demand (1757: 52, 76). Thus he turned against consumption of imported luxury goods, while stressing that increasing the demand for domestically produced goods also increased the demand for labour, and increased the wealth of the nation (1757: 27–8).

Harris adopted the idea that foreign trade is established because of the mutual interest of trading nations, and thus usually increases their economic dependence. He then built upon the vent of surplus doctrine previously developed by Adam Smith as a necessary precondition for international trade. By analysing the balance of trade, he maintained that the gains from international trade are to be estimated in terms of the net amount of foreign primary goods that have been imported against the export of labour (in other words, ready manufactured goods) (1757: 24).

Harris also built upon the specie-flow mechanism in international trade, introduced by Cantillon and Isaac GERVAISE. He considered that the main role in international exchange is played by real economic factors such as labour productivity and the rate of demand for goods. He described well the mechanism of the par of exchange (1757: 82–6), which is based upon precious metals for the promotion of international trade. After describing the inconveniences of barter economy, he analysed the functions of money as a medium of exchange and a measure of value. He held that a good having internal value is more suitable for use as money than other things like paper, which do not incorporate labour value. He argued against the debasement of money as it destroys the confidence of people in the general standard of exchange (1757: 43), and was supportive of monometalism and mainly of the silver standard (1757: 46–7). Although Harris recognized and accepted the quantity theory of money (1757: 52–4; 1758: 28–9), he also stressed (1757: 59–62) that an increase of the quantity of money increases consumption, production and employment. Thus, he considered that the influence of the amount of money in circulation does not proportionately alter the level of prices, as the labour productivity may be also changed and because of the possibility of hoarding (1757: 73). He also analysed the various sources for increasing the volume of money in circulation (1758: 20–1), and argued against the alternation of the money standard and the money level of prices (i.e., inflation) which he claimed to be a harmful cause for reducing the real rate of the contractual incomes (1758: 24–5, 32–3)

BIBLIOGRAPHY
Essay upon Money and Coins, Part I (1757), Part II (1758).

Further Reading
Hutchison, T., *Before Adam Smith: The Emergence of Political Economy, 1662–1776* (Oxford, 1988).
Johnson, E.A., *Predecessors of Adam Smith: The Growth of British Economic Thought* (1937; repr. New York, 1965).
Karayiannis, A.D., 'Sir James Steuart on Value and Prices', *Spoudai* (1991), vol. 24, no. 2, pp. 167–90.
Schumpeter, J.A., *History of Economic Analysis* (New York, 1954).

Anastassios D. Karayiannis

HARRISON, William (1534–93)

Harrison was born in London on 18 April 1534, and died at Windsor some time before 22 November 1593, the date on which his will was proved. He was educated at Westminster School and then St Paul's School, and was briefly at Cambridge before going on to Christ Church, Oxford; he received his BA in 1556 and MA in 1560. He had already by the latter date taken up a post as chaplain to Lord Cobham, and became rector of Radwinter, Essex, early in 1559. He was also vicar of Wimbush in Essex from 1570–81, and was finally appointed canon Windsor in 1586; he held this post and the rectory of Radwinter until his death, but resided thereafter at Windsor. He married Marion Isebrande, and the couple had a son and two daughters.

At some point in the early 1560s Harrison became acquainted with the queen's printer, Reginald Wolfe, then planning his 'universal cosmography', and agreed to become involved in the project. When Wolfe died in 1576, the scope of the project was greatly reduced, and it was instead planned to produce a history and geographical survey of the British Isles. Harrison's role was to produce the survey of England, and the result was his famous *Description of England*, which was finally published in conjunction with Holinshed's *Chronicle* in 1577. Two other works by Harrison, a chronology of English history and a compendium of weights and measures, were never published and remain only in manuscript form. *The Description of England* became very popular in its own day for its gossipy style and vivid descriptions, and later writers would rely on him heavily; parts of the work found their way almost word for word into Sir Thomas SMITH's *De Republica Anglorum*. As the latter work was compiled around 1565, we can deduce that Harrison wrote the first draft of *Description of England* before this date, although it was almost certainly revised heavily before publication.

The *Description of England* is a highly personal and quirky description of England, appearing to rely as much on anecdote as on analysis and observation, and despite the high opinions of later generations of historians, it is a book which must be read with caution. Volume 1 is a geographical survey of England, especially its rivers; Volume 2 looks at food, diet and custom, including one chapter on the poor and another on fairs and markets, and Volume 3 is a survey of industries and agriculture. When discussing the poor, Harrison classifies them into three groups: those who are poor by impotence (orphans, lepers, the blind and the lame); those who are poor by casualty (the sick, wounded soldiers, those who lose their estates); and the thriftless poor, whom he subdivides into idlers, rioters and vagabonds. He then describes the provision made for the first two groups through hospitals and asylums. Finally he lists, with evident relish, the punishments meted out to the latter group, along with sundry colourful slang names for different kinds of criminal, such as 'rufflers' and 'uprightmen'.

The chapter on fairs and markets is of more interest. Harrison sees markets as being one of the great strengths of the kingdom, providing much economic benefit, but he argues that the market system is also very much abused by dishonest traders. He calls in particular for more stringent enforcement of the assize of bread, and also for an end to the practices of dishonest purveyors and middlemen who drive down the price of agricultural produce in the country, particularly at harvest time, and then sell at excessive profits in urban markets such as London. He alleges that fraud and other illegal activities are commonplace in English markets, and gives a number of anecdotal examples.

The account of the industries and economic activity of England in Volume 3 is interesting, but again Harrison fails to give much in the way of hard evidence. Overall, he provides useful background 'colour' to the English economy in the second half of the sixteenth century, but little by way of fact.

BIBLIOGRAPHY
Description of England (1577; vols 2 and 3 repr. 1877; abridged version ed. L. Withington, 1889).

Morgen Witzel

HARROD, Roy Forbes (1900–78)

Harrod was born on 13 February 1900 in Norwich and died on 8 March 1978 in Holt, Norfolk. He was the only son of Henry Dawes Harrod, 'the son of a very distinguished antiquary', and Frances Harrod, 'a writer and painter', sister of the Shakespearean actor Johnston Forbes-Robertson. Harrod was first educated at home, 'one of high literary and artistic culture', then attended St Paul's School for one year and Westminster School in London, where two of his masters, 'Sargeaunt and Smedley, had a permanent influence on [his] life, a greater one than did any don at Oxford' (Harrod 1980). At New College, Oxford, Harrod gained first-class honours in ancient history and philosophy in 1921 and modern history a year later, and was then invited to take up economics in view of a studentship (fellowship) at Christ Church College, where he spent the rest of his academic life. He was granted two terms' leave to become acquainted with the subject, one of which was spent in Cambridge under KEYNES's guidance; on his return to Oxford, he attended EDGEWORTH's last set of lectures (which he vividly described in Harrod, 1937 and in correspondence with Keynes, Harrod 2003). Nevertheless, he considered himself largely self-taught (letter to Lindemann, 24 February 1926, in Harrod, 2003).

Harrod's innate interests, philosophy and politics (his original aim was to win a seat in parliament for the Liberal Party, although in the early 1930s he sympathized with Labour and later in his life he sought a nomination for the Conservative Party), frequently interacted with his economic thinking. He wrote his first book, *International Economics* (1933), following his despair over the debate on tariffs (he was a keen believer in free trade). He derived the idea that the most appropriate starting point for the study of the cycle was not a state of rest but one of moving equilibrium, from a shared presupposition in debates on economic policy taking place within the New Fabian Research Bureau, Harrod and MEADE being the 'Keynesians' in Oxford, and DURBIN and GAITSKELL the 'Hayekians' in London (Harrod 1934a; Besomi 1999: 38–42). His reflections on the inductive basis of knowledge – which he eventually expounded in *Foundations of Inductive Logic* (1956), in Harrod's own opinion the best of his writings (Harrod 1980: 617) – supplied the methodological basis for his research in economic dynamics and guided his participation in the empirical inquiry of the Oxford Economists' Research Group on prices and interest in the late 1930s (Besomi 1999: 117–26 and 1998a, respectively).

Harrod's seminal contributions to economics date mainly from the 1930s: in the later part of his life he recast, further elaborated and specified his views, often exploring their relevance for economic policy (in which he always maintained a keen interest), without however equalling the peaks of high theory reached in the inter-war years (Brown 1980: 26). His name is thus associated with the pioneering stages of imperfect competition theory, with the development of the foreign trade multiplier, and with the analysis of economic dynamics in terms of the interaction of the multiplier and the acceleration principle.

In his first important publication, Harrod (1930) expounded the concept of 'marginal revenue': although he was anticipated in print by T.O. Yntema in the USA, Harrod had submitted an earlier version of his paper to *The Economic Journal* in July 1928, and can therefore in full right be considered a co-discoverer of the concept (see Harrod's own account of this 'rather boring question of priorities' in an 'egoistic footnote' to 1951: 159–60, 1967: 65 and 1972: 394). This was followed by the construction of the long-period cost curve as the envelope of short-term cost curves, by the formulation of the marginal revenue in terms of the elasticity of demand (Harrod 1931), and by a debate with Joan ROBINSON and Gerald SHOVE on free entry into trade in relation to the 'normal' rate of profit and of long-trade equilibrium in different market conditions, which took place both in correspondence (the exchanges, dated March 1933, are reproduced in Harrod 2003) and in print (Harrod 1932, 1933).

Meanwhile, Harrod wrote a textbook on *International Economics* (1933) which overstepped the scope of the Cambridge Economic Handbooks series in which it was included. In particular, he formulated the concept of the 'foreign trade multiplier' to argue that a surplus or deficit in the balance of payments sets in motion the forces bringing it back to equilibrium via successive adjustments in the rates of wages and/or in the level of income (and therefore of imports). His policy conclusion (as summarized in a letter to ROBERTSON of 29 April 1933, in Harrod 2003) was, 'that improvement in the foreign current credit account has the same potentiality of giving employment as public works. But if that potentiality becomes an actuality (that is, is not countered by hoarding or some such process) the increased employment will wipe out the balance. The extra credit will be offset by an extra debit.'

A survey of the recent progress in the theory of imperfect competition, which Harrod wrote in 1934, linked his reflections on this topic with his new interest in trade cycle theory. The conclusion that imperfect competition is compatible with equilibrium at increasing returns suggested to him the possibility that equilibrium is not stable. This would establish the conditions for the possibility of endogenous and permanent displacements from equilibrium, while if equilibrium were stable movement could only be explained as the result of causes external to the system (Harrod 1934: 465–70). Harrod did not pursue this specific line of research further, but the epistemic principle that a 'rational explanation' of the trade cycle requires equilibrium to be unstable remained at the heart of his approach. A mechanism capable of generating the required instability was expounded in *The Trade Cycle* (1936): it consisted in the interaction of the Keynesian multiplier, which explains how an increase in investment gives rise to an expansion of income, and the acceleration principle ('the Relation', in Harrod's terminology), which explains investment as a result of the need of equipment for facing the increase in demand made possible by an augmented income.

One of the possible results of such an interaction is a state of moving equilibrium, characterized by growth at a constant rate (depending on the propensity to save and the acceleration coefficient). Such a state, however, is unstable, as any deviation from it tends to be amplified rather than damped. The cycle, in Harrod's view, results from growth inducing changes in the co-efficients (the propensity to save increases as income increases, and the multiplier therefore falls), which reduce the rate of advance. A reduced increase of income implies less investment, which in turn gives rise to a still smaller advance in income, and eventually to its reduction. The downward phase is cumulative, but at a certain point it brings about shifts in the values of the coefficients which eventually determine the reversal of the direction of movement: a reduced income decreases the propensity to save, and renewal of obsolete machinery are made more convenient by a decreased rate of interest. Progress is also cumulative, up to the point when the increase of income brings about its own demise.

One of Harrod's most frequently cited contributions is an 'Essay in Dynamic Theory' (1939), where he couched the multiplier-accelerator mechanism into a formula for the equilibrium rate of growth which was further elaborated in *Towards a Dynamic Economics* (1948). In both these writings, Harrod focussed mainly on his formulas for the rates of growth at one point of time (the 'warranted' rate, describing the moving equilibrium; the 'actual' rate, namely, the one registered ex-post; and the 'natural' rate, describing the maximum rate attainable by the system given the available resources) and barely outlined their consequences on the theory of the cycle. Although the fundamental ingredients were clearly expressed (the instability of equilibrium is discussed at length, and there are precise references to changes in the values of the parameters), the debate which followed – also due to the shift in the economists' interests in the 1950s and 1960s – concentrated on the growth formulas, interpreted as expressing long-period trends rather than referring to a single point in time (Harrod had to limit the validity of his equation to one instant only as his mathematical tools did not allow for inclusion of changeable co-efficients, and everything had to be re-calculated instant after instant). Harrod's complaints notwithstanding, 'growth theory' was born and was associated with his name and that of Evsey Domar, who had independently formulated equations similar to Harrod's (Domar 1946; Harrod 1959a).

The debate which followed bore valuable fruit, but was characterized by some major misunderstandings of Harrod's ideas. The Harrod–Domar equation was the starting point of both neoclassical and neo-Keynesian growth theories, and some of Harrod's specific points gave rise to interesting debates (in particular his proposal for the classification of technological progress on lines alternative to that of HICKS: see Besomi 1999a). Some of the misapprehensions originated from Harrod's own ambiguity and lack of precision in the formulation of his assumptions. In particular, his notion of the 'warranted rate of growth' was qualified in no less than six different ways (McCord Wright 1949: 326), opening the way to at least as many interpretations of the equilibrium behaviour of the system or of individual entrepreneurs. Moreover, the assumptions as to the entrepreneurs' reaction to disequilibrium positions were not explicitly stated, leaving room for different hypotheses to be grafted onto the basic equation, giving rise to different conclusions regarding the system's stability.

Some misinterpretations were instead characterized by careless reading of Harrod's writings. This was partially due to the very success of Harrod's theory: once it became a 'classical' it was widely quoted, and second-hand citations of statements taken out of context became frequent. The cycle part was ignored altogether, as was Harrod's provisos regarding the fluctuations in the values of the co-efficients. The point that instability was a *premise* to trade cycle theory was therefore lost, and instability was understood as resulting from the rigidity in Harrod's formulation. Neoclassical growth theorists (in particular Yeager 1954 and Solow 1956) argued that Harrod ignored that the capital/output ratio (the acceleration co-efficient) can vary in consequence of the abundance or scarcity of capital and thereby adjust growth to its (full employment) equilibrium rate by causing substitution of production factors. Neo-Keynesian growth theorists, on the other hand, attributed Harrod's instability principle to the rigidity in the propensity to save and to his ignoring changes in the distribution of income (in particular Kaldor 1954: 843–4 and Robinson 1970: 732). Only when Harrod's original formulation (1936) was reconsidered by researchers in non-linear dynamics (the forerunner being Goodwin 1951; for an extensive discussion and a survey see Pugno 1992 and 1998, respectively) and re-read in their full context (beginning from Kregel 1980) his points could be fully understood. In particular, the instability principle is vindicated by the feature of non-linear models whose phase diagram represents convergence to limit cycles or strange attractors surrounding an unstable steady point (for a survey of the interpretations of Harrod's dynamics, see Besomi 1998).

For more than two decades Harrod seems to have been struggling between the enjoyment of having his name attached to one of the most widely discussed fields in economics, and the disappointment of seeing his pet ideas eponymously linked to interpretations he could not share. He started fighting back from the mid-1960s. At first he contested that he was proposing an actual *model* of growth, as opposed to 'a way of thinking' dynamic problems (Harrod 1968). Then he rejected Joan Robinson's interpretation of growth theory, and, in yet unpublished correspondence, he accused her of not having read his writings with sufficient care and having misrepresented him (undated letter of May 1970 in Harrod's Papers at Chiba University of Commerce, Ichikawa, file IV-1089-1107), stressing that what matters is not much the warranted rate of growth but its interaction with the actual and natural rate. In other words, he claimed pride of place for the analysis of disequilibrium behaviour (Harrod 1970). Eventually he drastically revised his 1948 book and re-published it as *Economic Dynamics* (1973), taking up all the parts on the cycle he had discarded from his 1939 'Essay in Dynamic Theory' (now published as Harrod 1996) under the pressure of shortage of space and of the editor's criticisms.

Harrod's bibliography includes not only numerous writings in the topics already mentioned, but is rather varied in kind and exterminate in size (two partial bibliographies are published in Eltis *et al.* 1970 and as Scott 1971). Among his books there are five pamphlets published during and shortly after the war, seven books on monetary theory and policy, five more books on policy issues, and two biographies: a memoir of Lord Cherwell (1959), and the official *Life of John Maynard Keynes* (1951), which he wrote in two years of intense and very productive work, mastering a huge mass of documents but skipping over some details he did not deem opportune to make public. Harrod also wrote numerous articles for the press on policy matters and other issues (in the inter-war years, for instance, he frequently wrote on the population problem), and exchanged and preserved thousands of letters with friends, colleagues, politicians, philosophers and many others.

Harrod was knighted in 1959, received a number of honorary degrees, was president of the Royal Economic Society (1962–64), took over the editorship of the *Economic Journal* from Keynes in 1945 and held it to 1961, was Nuffield reader in international economics from 1952 to 1967, was invited to a number of visiting professorships in the USA after his retirement from Christ Church and Nuffield. But he failed to secure for himself a professorship at Oxford, and narrowly missed being awarded the Nobel prize in economics (for further details on his life and career see Blake 1970; Hinshaw 1978; Phelps Brown 1980).

BIBLIOGRAPHY

'Notes on Supply', *Economic Journal* (1930), vol. XL, June, pp. 233–41.

'The Law of Decreasing Costs', *Economic Journal* (1931), vol. XLI, December, pp. 566–76.

'Decreasing Costs: An Addendum', *Economic Journal* (1932), vol. XLII, September, pp. 490–92.

'A Further Note on Decreasing Costs', *Economic Journal* (1933), vol. XLIII, June, pp. 337–41.

International Economics (1933).

'Doctrines of Imperfect Competition', *Quarterly Journal of Economics* (1934), vol. 48, May, pp. 442–70.

'The Expansion of Credit in an Advancing Community', *Economica* (1934), new series, vol. 1, August, pp. 287–99.

The Trade Cycle: An Essay (1936).

'Scope and Method of Economics', *Economic Journal* (1938), vol. XLVIII, September, pp. 383–412.

'An Essay in Dynamic Theory', *Economic Journal* (1939), vol. IL, March, pp. 14–33.

Towards a Dynamic Economics (1948).

The Life of John Maynard Keynes (1951).

Foundations of Inductive Logic (1956).

The Prof: A Personal Memoir of Lord Cherwell (1959).

'Domar and Dynamic Economics', *Economic Journal* (1959), vol. LXIX, September, pp. 451–64.

'Increasing Returns', in R.E. Kuenne, *Monopolistic Competition Theory: Studies in Impact. Essays in Honor of Edward H. Chamberlin* (New York, 1967).

'What is a Model?', in J.N. Wolfe (ed.), *Value, Capital and Growth: Papers in Honour of Sir John Hicks* (Edinburgh, 1968, pp. 173–91).

'Harrod after Twenty-One Years: A Comment', *Economic Journal* (1970), vol. LXXX, September, pp. 737–41.

'Imperfect Competition, Aggregate Demand and Inflation', *Economic Journal* (1972), vol. LXXXII, March.

Economic Dynamics (1973).

'An Essay in Dynamic Theory (1938 Draft)', ed. D. Besomi, *History of Political Economy* (1996), vol. 28, no. 2, pp. 253–80.

The Collected Interwar Papers and Correspondence of Roy F. Harrod, ed. D. Besomi (Cheltenham, 2003).

Further Reading

Besomi, D., 'Failing to Win Consent. Harrod's Dynamics in the Eyes of his Readers', in G. Rampa, L. Stella and A. Thirlwall (eds), *Economic Dynamics, Trade and Growth: Essays on Harrodian Themes* (1998, pp. 38–88).

———, 'Harrod and the Oxford Economists' Research Group's Inquiry on Prices and Interest, 1936–1939', *Oxford Economic Papers* (1998), new series, vol. 50, October, pp. 534–62.

———, *The Making of Harrod's Dynamics* (1999).

———, 'Harrod on the Classification of Technological Progress: The Origin of a Wild-Goose Chase', *Banca Nazionale del Lavoro Quarterly Review* (1999), vol. 208, March, pp. 96–118.

Blake, R., 'A Personal Memoir', in W.A. Eltis, M.F. Scott and J.N. Wolfe (eds), *Induction, Growth and Trade: Essays in Honour of Sir Roy Harrod* (Oxford, 1970, pp. 1–19).

Brown, E.H.P., 'Sir Roy Harrod: A Biographical Memoir', *Economic Journal* (1980), vol. XC, March, pp. 1–33.

Domar, E.D., 'Capital Expansion and Growth', *Econometrica* (1946), vol. 14, pp. 137–47.

Eltis, W.A., Scott, M.F. and Wolfe, J.N. (eds), *Induction, Growth and Trade: Essays in Honour of Sir Roy Harrod* (Oxford, 1970).

Goodwin, R.M., 'The Nonlinear Accelerator and the Persistence of the Business Cycle', *Econometrica* (1951), vol. 19, no. 1, pp. 1–17.

Hinshaw, R., 'Sir Roy Harrod', *Journal of International Economics* (1978), vol. 8, pp. 363–72.

Kaldor, N., 'The Relation of Economic Growth and Cyclical Fluctuations', *Economic Journal* (1954), vol. LXIV, March, pp. 53–71.

Kregel, J.A., 'Economic Dynamics and the Theory of Steady Growth: An Historical Essay on Harrod's "Knife-Edge"', *History of Political Economy* (1980), vol. 12, no. 1, pp. 97–123.

McCord Wright, D., 'Mr. Harrod and Growth Economics', *Review of Economics and Statistics* (1949), vol. XXXI, no. 4, November, pp. 322–28.

Pugno, M., *Roy F. Harrod. Dall'equilibrio dinamico all'instabilità ciclica* (1992).

———, 'On the Research on Harrod's Contribution to Economic Dynamics: A Note', in G. Rampa, L. Stella and A. Thirlwall (eds), *Economic Dynamics, Trade and Growth: Essays on Harrodian Themes* (1998, pp. 89–106).

Rampa, G., Stella, L., and Thirlwall, A. (eds), *Economic Dynamics, Trade and Growth: Essays on Harrodian Themes* (1998).

Robinson, J.V., 'Harrod after Twenty-one Years', *Economic Journal* (1970), vol. LXXX, September, pp. 731–7.

Scott, M.F., 'List of Articles and Letters by Sir Roy Harrod', mimeograph deposited in the libraries of Nuffield College, Oxford, Yale and the University of Pennsylvania (1971).

Solow, R.M., 'A Contribution to the Theory of Economic Growth', *Quarterly Journal of Economics* (1956), vol. LXX, no. 1, February, pp. 65–94.

Yeager, L.B., 'Some Questions about Growth Economics', *American Economic Review* (1954), vol. XLIV, no. 1, March, pp. 53–63.

Young, W., *Harrod and his Trade Cycle Group: The Origins and Development of the Growth Research Programme* (1989).

Daniele Besomi

HARTLEY, David (1705–57)

Hartley was born at Luddenden, near Halifax, Yorkshire in June 1705, and died at Bath on 28 August 1757. He received his education at Jesus College, Cambridge, of which he became a fellow in 1727. As it was obligatory in those days, he gave up the fellowship on marriage in 1730. His first wife died in childbirth in 1731. Although he did not take a medical degree, he practised medicine in various cities. In 1742 he moved to Bath, where he stayed until his death. Like many of his contemporaries, Hartley suffered severely from stones of the bladder. His critical research into a popular remedy against this painful physical illness made him famous even on the Continent. His second marriage, in 1735, provided him with the financial means to live an active intellectual life.

As with many of his contemporaries, Hartley moved in his philosophical interests between medicine, moral philosophy and natural theology, as witnessed by the title of his best-known book *Observations on Man, His Frame, His Duty, and his Expectations* (1749). But while most eighteenth-century philosophers showed some explicit interest in what came to be known as political economy, there is little to be found on this subject in Hartley's work. His influence on the work of Jeremy BENTHAM, James MILL and associationist psychologists like Alexander Bain in Victorian England was considerable, however, and so for a proper understanding of this later period, some knowledge of Hartley's work is indispensable.

Hartley is commonly seen as one of the fathers of the association psychology that was to dominate the nineteenth century, until this theory came under pressure from more physiological and experimental-based approaches and theories. There are some fine ironies at work here, as we will see. Hartley's ideas stemmed from two different sources. One, his theory of vibrations, was suggested to him by the last part of NEWTON's *Principia* and the queries attached to the *Opticks*; the other, the association of ideas, stemmed from John LOCKE and John Gay, a faithful follower of Francis HUTCHESON. The *Observations* promised the study of man on a firm Newtonian basis. The book aimed to ground mental processes in man's physiology, and to deduce the consequences for moral philosophy and religion. Even though Hartley felt uneasy about the beliefs of the Church of England – he abandoned the idea of becoming an Anglican minister because of this – the conformity of his theory with natural religion was for him never into doubt.

In the first book, Hartley proposed the 'hypothesis' that mental states were the result of small vibrations of the nerves, which he called vibratiuncles. These vibratiuncles should not be seen as vibrations of a chord, but as vibrations of small particles of which the white medulary substance of the nerves, spinal marrow and the brain is assumed to consist. These particles vibrate in an elastic ether without noticeable resistance, just as Newton had suggested that all celestial bodies move in an imponderable and all-pervading ether. These small vibrations are transmitted from the nerves to the brain, thus forming the basis of sensations and actions of the body. These sensations are then combined to complex ideas and perceptions by means of association. It is important to emphasize that associations in the mind have no status independent from their material correlates. All formation of mental sensations, perceptions and ideas are the result of vibratiuncles of the medulary substance.

The remainder of the first book elaborates the consequences of this fundamental idea for the operation of the senses, the formation of the ideas and the passions, and its implications for voluntary and involuntary action. The second volume is devoted to moral philosophy and religion. Hartley's theory is thoroughly materialistic, mechanistic and necessitarian. Man did not have the 'Power of beginning Motion'. By contrast, 'all human Actions proceed from Vibrations of the Nerves of the Muscles, and these from others, which are evidently of a Mechanical Nature, as the automatic Motions' (1749: 501–3).

Hartley's philosophical views only rose to prominence after the Unitarian dissenter and natural philosopher Joseph Priestley published a demolishing criticism of one of Scotland's leading philosophers of mind, Thomas REID, teacher of Dugald STEWART and founder of the so-called common sense school of philosophy. The subsequent debate between Reid and Priestley on the merits of Hartley's views centred on his alleged violation of Newton's famous *regulae philosophandi* and on his materialism and necessitarianism, two themes that would carry over well into the nineteenth century. Reid pointed out that Hartley's hypothesis of vibratiuncles could not be brought into line with (what was then commonly taken as) Newton's views on induction. Priestley's abridged edition of Hartley's *Observations*, published in 1775, and the further controversy this edition raised, subsequently did much to spread Hartley's ideas. Priestley left out all of Hartley's discussions on religion, and left an even stronger materialistic and necessitarian impression than was already present in Hartley's original work. In his foreword Priestley wrote with his characteristic acerbity that, 'my mind is no more *in my body*, than it is in the moon' (1775: xx).

The Mills took the opposite stance to Hartley's work. Hartley had emphasized that his theory of associations and his theory of vibrations could be considered independently, even though associations and vibrations were closely linked, and this was James Mill's starting point in his *Analysis of the Phenomena of the Mind* (1829). Disregarding any intrusion of physiology into psychology, Mill treated the association of ideas as a theory of the mind in its own, that could bow on separate, introspectively acquired evidence. This point was of prime importance in John Stuart MILL's defence of a separate science of political economy that was yet as scientific as physics. In his defence of a separate science of psychology, in the *Logic* (1843), John Stuart Mill emphasized much the same issue, pointing out that the 'vexed question' of a physiological underpinning of the laws of mind had been solved too hastily by Hartley with his conjecture of vibratiuncles and was as yet as undecided as it was then. John Stuart Mill's extreme reliance on introspection as a certain route to truth did much to retard the introduction of empirical methods of inquiry into political economy. Only with the re-emergence of psychophysiology in Victorian Britain, in the work of Laycock and Carpenter amongst others, that had only indirect links to Hartley's and Priestley's materialism, did political economists like JENNINGS and JEVONS consider anew how to combine empirical research with theory.

BIBLIOGRAPHY

De lithontriptico a Joanna Stephens nuper invento dissertatio epistolaris (1741).
Observations on Man, His Frame, His Duty, And his Expectations (1749; repr. Hildesheim, 1967).
Various Conjectures on the Perception, Notion, and Generation of Ideas (1746; repr. New York, 1967).

Further Reading
Allen, R.C., *David Hartley on Human Nature* (Albany, New York, 1999).
Priestley, J., *Hartley's Theory of the Human Mind, on the Principle of the Association of Ideas; with Essays Relating to the Subject of It* (1775).
Warren, H.C., *A History of the Association Psychology* (New York, 1921).
Yolton, J.W., *Thinking Matter: Materialism in Eighteenth-Century Britain* (Oxford, 1984).

Harro Maas

HARTLIB, Samuel (*c.*1600–1662)

Hartlib was born in about 1600 in Elbing, Prussia (now Elblag, Poland) to a wealthy German merchant and his English wife, and died in London on 10 March 1662. Educated in Brieg, Hartlib studied at Cambridge (1625–6) without taking a degree, and settled permanently in England in 1628. He married Mary Burningham on 20 January 1629, and the following year set up a boys' academy in Chichester, which failed almost immediately, taking most of his financial resources with it. The rest of his life was spent in London, where he lived on the sponsorship of kindred spirits and somewhat irregular state funding for his services to the 'public good'.

Hartlib's interests were encyclopaedic, and he was a tireless promoter of the advancement of learning in general, which, following the hint in Daniel 12:4, he saw as a prerequisite for Christ's second coming. He was not an economic thinker in his own right, but he was a friend and patron of many who were, most notably William PETTY, Benjamin Worsley, Henry ROBINSON and William POTTER.

Probably in collaboration with John Dury, Hartlib drew up detailed and imaginative proposals for a publicly funded 'office of address' that would help transmute his ideals into reality. This institution was to double as a labour exchange and a means of establishing and fostering contacts between scholars in any field, wherever they were based. Though the idea was looked on favourably by many of the more radical members of parliament during the Civil War and Commonwealth periods, it never came to fruition, but Hartlib went a good way to fulfilling at least its latter projected function single-handedly. He made himself the centre of an informal, international network of 'intelligencers' keen to exchange new ideas on everything from metaphysics to bee-keeping. He edited and/or published a great number of works collated (often without the authors' knowledge or consent) from the voluminous correspondence that passed through his hands, though it was probably the correspondence itself that represented his greatest contribution to the intellectual life of his age.

Amid the gloriously chaotic profusion of his publications and his manuscript legacy, there is little that can be unequivocally attributed to Hartlib himself. He was more interested in stimulating discussion than in promoting particular agendas, and had no qualms about juxtaposing mutually contradictory views, without acknowledging the source of either, in a single publication. He is often misrepresented as the originator of opinions and proposals that in fact he only cited or publicized.

It is certain, though, that social justice and the use of technology to improve the human lot were high among his priorities. Husbandry and agriculture particularly interested him for this reason, and in compilations such as *Samuel Hartlib His Legacie* (1651) and *The Reformed Common-wealth of Bees* (1655) he helped disseminate a range of new practical techniques – some of them real advances, some wild flights of fancy – to a wide public. He also published Arnold and Gerard Boate's *Irelands Naturall History* (1652), a pioneering if politically loaded exercise in land surveying and economic analysis, and in *A Discoverie* (1653), William Potter's proposal for a national bank depending on land holdings rather than bullion for its reserves. He circulated assorted more or less innovative and realistic insurance schemes, and he agitated for legislation to promote full employment and poor relief.

As Hartlib saw things, his intellectual 'Legacie' lay not in his own opinions or writings, but in his labours to preserve and make widely accessible the views of others. On those terms, he was and remains spectacularly successful.

BIBLIOGRAPHY

Considerations tending to the happy accomplishment of Englands Reformation in Church and State. Humbly presented to the Piety and Wisdome of the High and Honourable Court of Parliament by Samuel Hartlib (1647).

A Further Discoverie of the Office of Publick Addresse for Accommodations (1648).

Londons Charity inlarged, stilling the Orphans Cry...By S.H. a well-wisher to the Nations prosperity, and the Poors Comfort (1650).

A discourse of Husbandrie used in Brabant and Flanders: shewing the wonderfull improvement of Land there; and serving as a pattern for our practice in this Commonwealth (1650).

Samuel Hartlib his Legacie: or An Enlargement of the Discourse of Husbandry used in Brabant and Flaunders; wherin are bequeathed to the Common-Wealth of England more Outlandish and Domestick Experiments and Secrets in reference to Universall Husbandry (1651; repr. 1652, 1655).

Irelands Naturall History...Now Published by Samuel Hartlib (principally compiled by Arnold and Gerard Boate, variously attributed to both or either) (1652).

A Discoverie for Division or Setting out of Land as to the best Forme. Published by Samuel Hartlib Esqr. (1653).

The Reformed Common-wealth of Bees. Presented in several Letters and Observations to Samuel Hartlib Esqr. With The Reformed Virginian Silk-worm (1655).

The Hartlib Papers, 2nd edn, CD-ROM comprising transcriptions and facsimiles of the bulk of Hartlib's surviving papers (Sheffield, 2002).

Further Reading

Greengrass, M., Leslie, M. and Raylor, T. (eds), *Samuel Hartlib and Universal Reformation: Studies in Intellectual Communication* (Cambridge, 1994).

Leslie, M. and Raylor, T. (eds), *Culture and Cultivation in Early Modern England: Writing and the Land* (Leicester, 1992).

Turnbull, G.H., *Hartlib, Dury and Comenius: Gleanings from Hartlib's Papers* (Liverpool, 1947).

Webster, C., *The Great Instauration: Science, Medicine and Reform 1626–1660* (1975).

John Young

HAWTREY, Ralph George (1879–1975)

Hawtrey was born on 22 November 1879 in Langley, Middlesex, to George Proctor Hawtrey (a teacher at St. Michael's preparatory school, established by Ralph's grandfather) and Eda Strahan. He died at Cambridge on 21 March 1975. He studied at Eton and in 1898 went to Trinity College Cambridge, obtaining a first in mathematics in 1901. His only formal economic studies were in preparation for the civil service examinations. He entered the Civil Service in 1903 and, after a year in the Admiralty, he went to the Treasury. In 1919 he was appointed director of financial enquiries, a position he held until his retirement in 1947. Though his ability was recognized, he was kept at a certain distance from the process of policy formation. During this period he was a visiting professor at Harvard in 1928–9, and after his retirement he was Price Professor of International Economics at the Royal Institute of International Affairs in London. At Cambridge he was one of the Apostles, influenced by G.E. Moore, and was associated with the Bloomsbury group, through whom he met his wife, the concert pianist Hortense Emilia Sophie d'Aranyi. On his death, he left behind two complete book manuscripts on ethics. He was awarded the CB in 1941, was knighted in 1956, and was elected a fellow of the British Academy.

From his first book, *Good and Bad Trade* (1913), Hawtrey argued that the business cycle was caused by monetary factors. His theory was based on a distinctive view of the relationship between credit and spending. When a bank grants a new loan, the credit that is created in the form of new bank deposits will be spent, generating income for those who receive the money. This will raise spending, which in turn will generate further income. This process will continue until the money in circulation is returned to the bank, paying off the original loan. Credit is thus a revolving fund, continually being created and destroyed. The money supply, which he called the 'unspent margin' of purchasing power, increases or decreases according to whether creation of credit exceeds or falls short of credit that is paid off. Because loans are taken out in order to be spent, there is a direct link between the granting of new credit, the resulting change in the money supply and spending. Thus although Hawtrey emphasized the importance of money, he may also be viewed as a proponent of the income–expenditure approach to macroeconomics.

Hawtrey emphasized the short-term interest rate as the transmission mechanism of monetary policy. The bank rate, the rate set by the Bank of England, was therefore the key policy instrument. His confidence in the bank rate stemmed from the experience of the years immediately after he came to economics, in 1903, when variations in the bank rate appeared to be able to increase and reduce spending. His theoretical reason for the bank rate having such a strong effect was that he believed commodity markets were dominated by dealers; they held stocks of goods financed by a volume of credit that was very large in relation to their turnover, making them very sensitive to interest rate changes. (Perhaps this reflected the role of dealers and merchants in late Victorian and Edwardian England.) Interest rate changes worked through causing dealers to adjust their inventories, changing their orders from producers who, in turn change their production with consequent effects on employment. Hawtrey held this belief in the power of short-term interest rates throughout his career, even when other economists began, in the 1920s, to emphasize the long-rate; he disagreed strongly with KEYNES when, in his *Treatise on Money* (1930) he focused the long rate. Hawtrey saw no reason to believe that long-term investment responded significantly to interest rate changes. Only a year after Keynes's *General Theory* was published, Hawtrey published *A Century of Bank Rate* in which he backed up his view of how monetary policy worked with extensive historical evidence.

Hawtrey's view of the investment market led him to develop a version of the Treasury View, the doctrine that increased government spending financed by borrowing could not create additional employment. Saving was determined by income and determined investment, the two being equated by the rate of interest. He focused not on the stock of outstanding debt but on new issues. Thus borrowing money to finance public works reduced the flow of saving going to the private sector, reducing investment. If fiscal policy was to increase employment, it had to be associated with an increase in the money supply. He supported money-financed government deficits as a way of raising employment, but only under extreme circumstances when monetary policy would not work. Under normal circumstances, his priority was keeping interest rates low.

However, although Hawtrey differed from Keynes over interest rates, their theories had much in common. It was Hawtrey, not Keynes, who introduced the phrase 'effective demand' into macroeconomics (as early as 1913), though in his review of the *General Theory* he was too polite to point this out. He was a pioneer of the savings-investment approach on which Keynes, from his work with Dennis ROBERTSON in the 1920s, based his work. He assumed that saving was related to income, and in 1930 he worked out examples of a multiplier process. He raised doubts about Keynes's treatment of saving and investment, not so much because he was stuck in a 'classical' world as because he saw issues about which Keynes was somewhat vague, such as the difference between planned and actual investment. He also applied his saving-investment analysis to problems of international finance. He agreed with Keynes that the economic system was inherently unstable. However, where Keynes located instability in long-term expectations relevant for decisions to invest, Hawtrey emphasised instability of credit in the short-term. When prices rise, dealers wish to increase their stocks (on which they will receive a capital gain), which raises demand. As desired stocks will typically be related to the level of demand, a rise in stocks raises investment more than proportionately. Falling prices have the reverse effect. Fluctuations in income would be magnified. Lags in the process accounted for observed cycles in output.

Hawtrey supported the gold standard after the First World War because he believed that it was very important that there was confidence in the monetary standard. If sterling was devalued once, there was no reason why it would not be devalued again, undermining that confidence. However, he was not prepared to accept the gold standard at any price. He was very concerned that there might be a shortage of gold after 1919 which, if all countries returned to gold, would cause falling prices. To remedy this he proposed, to the International Financial Conference at Genoa in 1922, a gold exchange standard. Gold reserves would be held in London, New York and Paris, and central banks in other countries would hold reserves of sterling, dollars or French francs. Gold would then be required only for settlements between these three currencies. All currencies would be convertible into gold, either directly or indirectly. Much less gold would be required than if all countries held gold and all payments imbalances were settled using gold, rather than in foreign currency. To reduce demand still further, gold coins would not circulate and convertibility would be into bullion. However, though such a scheme would economize on the use of gold, it would cause other problems. There was a danger that credit would expand on the basis of a small and unchanging gold reserve. The gold exchange standard might replace deflation with inflation. He was also concerned that demand for gold might fluctuate, causing fluctuations in its price. To remedy this, Hawtrey proposed a scheme that would stabilize the price of gold in terms of a world price index. This was a significant proposal for it implied using the gold exchange standard as a way to co-ordinate activist monetary policies in different countries in the interests of the system as a whole. His resolutions were passed by the Genoa conference, but due to doubts held by many central bankers, the follow-up meetings necessary to implement such a policy were never held.

When the Bretton Woods system was set up in 1944, Hawtrey raised similar doubts. The gold exchange standard could work only if there was international co-operation. The value of gold would depend on the monetary policies of all countries taken together, even though individually they would behave as though the value of gold was given. It was necessary, therefore, that a mechanism be found to bias domestic policies in one direction or another, according to the needs of the world situation. Concerted action would be required to stabilize the value of gold, preventing both inflationary and deflationary movements from getting out of control.

In Britain, Hawtrey accepted the arguments for returning to gold at the old parity in 1925, but his belief in the importance of short-term interest rates made him unhappy about the level to which interest rates were raised to support the pound. He advanced a number of alternative policies, including the radical one of exporting a large quantity of gold to the USA to cause inflation there, reducing the imbalance in international price levels caused by returning to the old parity. He also believed that raising Bank Rate to 6.5 per cent in 1929, when the USA had begun to enter a recession, was a big mistake. Underlying both decisions was a view that in times of recession (and he thought Britain had been in a recession since 1921) high interest rates had particularly strong negative effects.

Hawtrey was much more influential than he is often given credit for. Despite his disagreements with Keynes, they remained close and Keynes considered him a constructive critic. His income approach was much closer to the approach to which Keynes moved in the 1920s than to more traditional theory. It seems likely that his influence on Keynes, who acknowledged his help in the *General Theory*, was very significant. Hawtrey also had a very important effect on American monetary economics. *Currency and Credit* (1919), arguably his most important book, was widely used as a textbook in Harvard as well as in Cambridge. He has been credited with introducing the idea of stabilization policy. Several American economists praised his work, the most important being Allyn Young who went so far as to recommend Hawtrey as his replacement when he left Harvard for the LSE in 1926. The monetary economics of Young and Laughlin Currie (Hawtrey's teaching assistant during his year at Harvard) owed much to Hawtrey. They took from him a belief in the power of monetary policy and the importance of designing policies to stabilize credit. Currie, like Hawtrey, offered a monetary interpretation of the Great Depression. This package of ideas, associated with Harvard in the 1920s and early 1930s, later influenced the Chicago School through Henry Simons and Jacob Viner, and thence Milton Friedman. Though they differed on the inherent instability of credit, Hawtrey's views on fiscal policy and employment were close to those of Friedman.

Hawtrey was unusual in being one of the world's leading monetary economists while holding a government position, and the great influence he had on his students during his single year at Harvard suggests that his situation outside academia might considerably have reduced his influence. As the leading economist at the Treasury, he is notorious for being the supporter of the so-called Treasury View, a view that went against the consensus of opinion among academic economists. He came to be seen as an illustration of what the 'classical economics', lambasted by Keynes, was really like. In the wake of the Keynesian revolution, Hawtrey was rapidly neglected: he spurned the mathematical and statistical approaches to economics that were becoming fashionable; he drew on detailed historical knowledge to support his theoretical claims; his theory was based on assumptions about the way markets worked that appeared more relevant to Edwardian Britain than to more modern economies; and his work was seen as having been superseded by Keynesian economics. However, though he did provide the theoretical case for the Treasury View, Hawtrey remained close to Keynes and played a significant role in the development of Keynesian economics, having been a pioneer of the income-expenditure approach to macroeconomics. It could even be argued that in this respect, Keynes came round to Hawtrey's position during the late 1920s and early 1930s.

Hawtrey's views on monetary policy were remarkably consistent throughout his long career. His theoretical framework, emphasising the link between money and spending, short term interest rates and the instability of credit, lay beneath all his policy views, from the Treasury View to his views on the Bretton Woods system. Though he disagreed with Keynes on government spending to alleviate unemployment and on the merits of the return to gold in 1925, they shared a commitment to the need for stabilization policy. It could be argued that it was quite an achievement for the same person to be involved in the Keynesian revolution and, via Harvard, to be the origins of Chicago monetary economics. To do both while remaining a Treasury official, with no long-term academic position, was even more remarkable.

BIBLIOGRAPHY
Good and Bad Trade: an Inquiry into the Causes of Trade Fluctuations (1913).
Currency and Credit (1919).
Monetary Reconstruction (1923).
Bretton Woods: For Better or Worse (1946).
The Economic Problem (1926).
The Gold Standard in Theory and Practice (1926).
Trade and Credit (1928).
Economic Aspects of Sovereignty (1930).
Trade Depression and the Way Out (1931).
The Art of Central Banking (1932).
Capital and Employment (1937).
A Century of Bank Rate (1938).
Economic Destiny (1944).
Bretton Woods for Better or Worse (1946).
Economic Rebirth (1946).

Further Reading
Black, R.D.C., ' Ralph George Hawtrey, 1879–1975', *Proceedings of the British Academy* (1977), vol. 63, pp. 363–97.
Davis, E.G., 'R.G. Hawtrey, 1879–1975', in D.P. O'Brien and J.R. Presley (eds), *Pioneers of Modern Economics in Britain* (1981, pp. 203–33).
Deutscher, P., *R.G. Hawtrey and the Development of Macroeconomics* (1990).
Hicks, J.R. 'Hawtrey', in *Economic Perspectives: Further Essays on Money and Growth* (Oxford, 1977).
Howson, S. 'Monetary Theory and Policy in the 20th Century: The Career of R.G. Hawtrey', in M. Flynn (ed.), *Proceedings of the Seventh International Economic History Conference* (Edinburgh, 1978, pp. 505–12).
———, 'Hawtrey and the Real World', in G.C. Harcourt (ed.), *Keynes and his Contemporaries* (1985, pp. 105–24).
Laidler, D., 'Hawtrey, Harvard and the Origins of the Chicago Tradition', *Journal of Political Economy* (1993), vol. 101, pp. 1068–1103.
———, *Fabricating the Keynesian Revolution: Studies in the Inter-War*

Literature on Money, the Cycle, and Unemployment (Cambridge, 1999).

Roger Backhouse

HAYEK, Friedrich August von (1899–1992)

Hayek was born in Vienna on 8 May 1899, and died in Freiburg-in-Breisgau, Germany on 23 March 1992. He came from an academic background, and was related to the philosopher Wittgenstein. He was educated at the University of Vienna, served in the First World War, and then entered the Austrian civil service in which he spent the years 1921–6. Hayek was director of the Austrian Institute for Trade Cycle Research (1927–31), an organization and a position both created for his benefit by Ludwig von Mises; then visiting professor at the London School of Economics (1931–2), Tooke Professor at LSE (1932–49), and professor of social and moral science (on the Committee on Social Thought) at the University of Chicago (1950–62). He then moved to Germany, becoming professor of economics at the University of Freiburg (1962–9).

It was when Hayek came under the influence of Mises, whom Hayek acknowledged was probably the decisive influence upon him, that he left the civil service and entered into academic work. But unlike Mises, who was a forceful and aggressive personality – perhaps understandably given the slights which he experienced in Vienna – Hayek was a more retiring and scholarly individual, yet one who showed enormous moral courage in maintaining positions of the correctness of which he felt intellectually convinced, in the face not merely of hostility but of attacks amounting at times to defamation.

Despite his enormous scholarly knowledge, gained from reading incessantly in a wide variety of languages, Hayek seems to have had initially a fairly narrow training in economics in the Austrian tradition, grounded in the work of Menger, Wieser and Böhm-Bawerk. Nonetheless he came to read extraordinarily widely in the literature of economics, and to feel something approaching contempt for the narrowness of reading of many English economists, especially those in Cambridge.

It was undoubtedly Mises who broadened Hayek's outlook and encouraged him to read widely. Not only did Mises bring home to Hayek the importance of key strands in the Austrian tradition – general, as against the Anglo-Saxon partial, equilibrium analysis, and subjectivism – but he directed his attention to the way in which these elements pointed to the functioning of a market system and to the inherent contradictions in pretensions to be able to plan the economy. As Hayek's views on this issue developed, so the weight which he attached to the different parts of the Austrian economics he had inherited changed. When introducing Menger's works in 1934, he stressed the importance of subjectivism and the key role of this in the analysis of markets, because of the fundamental role of *individual* decisions. He also attached considerable importance to the work of Wieser, particularly his treatment of marginal utility and of the earnings of factors of production. Initially, he stressed the importance of Menger's *Grundsätze* (1871) and of Wieser's *Der Natürliche Werth* (1889). But subsequently, partly as a response to his reading of Adam SMITH, Adam FERGUSON and Edmund BURKE, he came to stress the importance of the *evolutionary* context of economic activity. The market system, and key elements such as money, were evolved through human experience and functioned in a way which had been adapted through time to operate as efficiently as possible, given the limited knowledge of any one individual. Thus, in his later references to Menger, he laid more emphasis on Menger's 1883 *Untersuchungen* in which Menger developed these evolutionary themes.

The emphasis upon subjectivism and individual decisions provided the basis for Hayek's sustained and fundamental criticism of important, and highly fashionable, elements in twentieth-century thought. Subjectivism was linked by Hayek to the idea of introspection. This in turn led to an emphasis upon decision taking by each individual, on the basis of limited information. The individual did not have objective data, but preferences. The interaction of the preferences of a large number of individuals produced market values. On this basis, Hayek criticized the attempt to apply the methods of science to the much more complicated world of economics. He was scathing about 'scientism', both of what might loosely be called the Baconian variety and also – once Popper had convinced him that Baconianism was not how real scientists behaved – of the falsificationist variety. The methods of natural science simply did not apply to economics. He was also extremely critical of the attempts by writers like Comte, Hegel and MARX to develop historical 'laws' of economic, political, legal and social development. This in turn led to detailed criticism of what he called 'constructivism', the idea that a society could be built according to some kind of blueprint.

This critique was put forward by Hayek in a number of publications, but amongst the most important are two series of articles in *Economica* which appeared as 'The Counter Revolution of Science' in 1941, and as 'Scientism and the Study of Society' in the years 1942–3. The critique of the work of writers like Comte and Saint-Simon in particular, and the detailed and pitiless spotlight which Hayek shone on their pretensions, was one of the great exercises in intellectual history. Moreover, Hayek was able to show how much was due to these sources in the work of later writers, notably Hegel and Marx; it was from Saint-Simon that Marx took the idea of the class struggle.

Attempts to treat the world, in which observable phenomena resulted from the unobservable interaction of the subjective evaluations of countless individuals, in such a way were bound to fail. Indeed, there was a nice irony that people who proclaimed themselves positivists thought that pseudo-scientific 'laws' relating to such metaphysical entities as 'society', 'the economy', 'capitalism' and 'the class struggle' could be discerned – and discerned by observation – and made the basis of social and economic policy. This paradox was at its most acute in the contention by Comte, and by subsequent enthusiasts for planning, that while the weakness of the human mind produced a chaotic society, a human mind was also capable of planning for society as a whole.

Thus a planned society would necessarily fail. As Hayek, who lived long enough to see the events of 1989 unfold, contended, a society and economy could not function without markets. It was possible for the state to decide upon the production of goods; and consumers could be forced to take what was available, although – as happened in practice – the end result was shortages, unsold goods and a thriving black market. But there was no way of approximating, even in the crudest manner, the operation of factor markets. Factor markets had to operate through the valuation of factor services, reflecting consumer preferences in the form of derived demand. Cost of production literally had no meaning outside a market system, which gave market values to factor services. Thus there was absolutely no way that the economy could be run as a single factory, as even some natural scientists seemed naively to believe.

Such was Hayek's academic isolation, however, perhaps especially in Britain, a country to which he was devoted, that the myth that Hayek (and Mises) had been shown to be wrong about planning by such theorists of the planned economy as Lange and Taylor continued to be retailed for generations, especially to undergraduates. Yet as Hayek pointed out patiently – indeed with great restraint – all that these writers had shown was that the Lausanne (Walras–Pareto) conditions had to be observed in any static optimization; what they had singularly failed to show was how these conditions could be achieved under planning. (There was even a naive belief at one stage that the development of computational power would somehow overcome any problems in the implementation of this.) As Hayek stressed, Lausanne conditions could not be achieved without markets. Moreover, such conditions related only to static equilibrium, and not to a society in which tastes, technology and resources were all evolving dynamically over time, as envisaged by writers from Smith onwards.

Thus the concept of evolution is again of key importance to Hayek. Linked to that of evolution is the idea of unintended consequences. Individuals pursuing self-interest achieve, through their interaction, results beneficial to society as a whole – as argued by Smith with his example of the butcher and the baker – and (and this was Hayek's own particular emphasis) the institutions in which these individuals operate (the legal and other framework for the market) evolved over time so as to compensate for the limited information and restricted motivation of self-interested individuals, and thus to produce social benefit.

Hayek, ever the scholar, attached particular importance to the work of Bernard MANDEVILLE, whose *Fable of the Bees* was well known in the eighteenth century, in bringing forward the doctrine of unintended consequences. But, in the evolution of the legal and other framework of the market, Hayek attached enormous importance to the Anglo-Saxon common law tradition, an importance which reflected also his affection for Britain. This tradition protected individual liberty and, in so doing, enabled institutions to evolve in a beneficial way; it was contrasted by Hayek with the continental tradition of liberalism, which transmuted effortlessly into authoritarianism, socialism and economic planning. Not only did this affect the liberty of individuals; it had unintended consequences of its own which, because the actions of the state were the result of actions of individuals acting outside the constraints, and the information mechanisms of the market were not beneficial but the reverse.

Hayek's writings on macroeconomics have to be seen against the background of the idea of unintended consequences, and of the harm which could be done to macroeconomic stability by arbitrary interference with an equilibrium resulting from the market registration of individual preferences. Hayek was at his scholarly best in dealing with the history of monetary thought, and he was responsible for the production of a very fine edition of Henry THORNTON's *Paper Credit*. But his macroeconomic analysis is firmly grounded in the work of Mises (whose own work in turn stemmed from Wicksell), and in discussing the work of earlier writers he was wont to look for anticipations of this line of thought.

The key point in the Mises–Hayek analysis is that monetary expansion upsets general equilibrium and produces macroeconomic disequilibrium. Monetary expansion involves lowering the lending rate below the marginal rate of profit with which, in the previous equilibrium, it had been equated. Rather than looking at this in terms of its effect on the *general* price level, as in a straightforward quantity theory approach, Hayek insisted that what mattered was an alteration in the *relative* prices of consumption and investment goods. This alteration distorted factor markets, by bidding resources away from the production of consumption goods into the production of investment goods. This shifted the supply schedules for consumption goods to the left, raised their prices, and imposed 'forced saving' upon consumers. This forced saving was thus contrasted with voluntary saving, an increase in which would automatically free resources for an expansion of investment goods output.

However, the bidding away of resources from the consumption goods industries raised factor rewards, shifted the demand curve for consumption goods to the right, restored output of those goods as factors were re-attracted into the production of consumption goods, and restored the original relative price level of consumption goods and investment goods, but at a higher *absolute* price level. Those embarked upon investment schemes were thus faced with another round of bidding away resources from the consumption goods industries. This they sought to do by securing yet further expansion of credit. There could be several rounds of this sort before the banks, their own liquidity imperilled, called a halt to further expansion of credit. Once they called a halt, there would be a depression. There would be uncompleted investment projects, and unemployed labour. The only way in which the initial equilibrium could be restored would be through a general fall in prices *and* wages, so that labour could return to the consumption goods industries, and the relative output of consumption and investment goods would be restored to one reflecting the preferences of consumers for consumption and saving.

As a part of this analysis, Hayek introduced something which he called 'The Ricardo Effect'. The label was misleading; the effect is not to be found in the passages from RICARDO which Hayek cites. It simply involves the proposition that a fall in real wages will encourage the use of less capital intensive methods of production. It was in fact a point which Wicksell had made *in criticism of* Ricardo's claim that the introduction of machinery would create unemployment. It does however fit into Hayek's analysis of depression, where a fall in real wages helps to reduce unemployment. More fundamentally, the rises in the prices of consumption goods, as a result of monetary disequilibrium, would reduce real wages; this would make less capital intensive methods of production profitable, thus reducing the stimulus to investment provided by monetary expansion.

It required considerable moral courage for Hayek, ROBBINS and others to put forward such an analysis, with the associated policy recommendations of sweating out the depression and inducing wage reductions, in the conditions of the 1930s. It was particularly unfortunate that their analysis was based upon an error of fact.

They believed that US money supply had continued to expand, when in fact it had fallen sharply from 1929 onwards. As late as 1932, Hayek appeared to be under this misapprehension. Thus, even had the analysis itself been unassailable, it was based upon a crucial error of fact in its assumptions.

However, the conflict with KEYNES which, given the grip of Keynes, Keynesians and Cambridge on British intellectual life, did Hayek great personal harm, dated from well before this policy stance became the focus of criticism. Keynes and Hayek had apparently first come into conflict in the late 1920s; and in 1931 Hayek published a hostile review article dealing with Keynes's 1930 *Treatise on Money*. In the Cambridge style, Keynes's acolytes then rushed to defend him in print. Hayek seems to have been upset as much as anything by the subjective originality of Keynes's *Treatise*, which clearly owed a great deal more to Wicksell than Keynes was prepared to acknowledge, perhaps even to himself.

At a personal level, there was a rapprochement between Keynes and Hayek during the Second World War. Indeed, Keynes found rooms for Hayek in Cambridge, when LSE was evacuated from London to escape bombing during the war. But Hayek remained critical of Keynes on an intellectual level, while the hostility to Hayek of Cambridge economists of the generation of the so-called 'Circus', notably Richard KAHN and above all Joan ROBINSON, remained intense. Keynesianism undoubtedly triumphed. Hayek withdrew from the field of macroeconomics. He later claimed that he did not review Keynes's *General Theory* of 1936 because he thought that Keynes would change his mind yet again, as he had done between his *Treatise* and his *General Theory*.

However, there was a much more fundamental issue. It is to be found in Hayek's struggles with capital theory. The Böhm-Bawerk concept of a period of production was not essential to Hayek's macroeconomic theory. It was perfectly possible to put forward such a theory without reference to a period of production, as Mises and Robbins both did. But Hayek simply appeared unable to let the matter go. He drove himself during the war to the point of intellectual exhaustion, in trying to develop the Austrian capital theory. The first fruit of this was his *Pure Theory of Capital*, published in 1941. But this was supposed to be only the first stage; to be a development of the Austrian theory of capital which would provide, in the second stage, the springboard with which to attack the fundamental Keynesian idea that a rise in aggregate demand would in turn increase investment, which would then increase income and thence employment. Thus the second part of the work on capital theory was supposed to provide the basis for a critique of the Keynesian multiplier.

Hayek was clearly too exhausted intellectually to do this; and he may well have feared, at least subconsciously, that such a plan was doomed to failure, as subsequent critics like Mark Blaug have argued it was. But there was another reason for his failure to persevere with his critique of Keynes. Hayek had come to be alarmed by the rise to dominance amongst British intellectuals, especially of the younger generation, of socialist ideals. He now regarded socialism which, as Skidelsky has shown, Keynes opposed valiantly in the Treasury during and immediately after the war, as the major threat to a free society. Compared with this, the inflationism of Keynesian macroeconomic policies was less important. Indeed, Keynes and Hayek were much closer on this issue than is generally realized. Keynes wrote approvingly to Hayek of the latter's *Road to Serfdom* which its author believed – rightly – had finished his career as an academic economist. In this 1944 book, much reviled but hardly ever read, Hayek argued that the growth of economic planning would lead progressively to the loss of individual liberties. There seems no doubt that he was seriously alarmed by those who, like his colleague at LSE, Harold Laski, believed that the war-time economy, a single-objective command economy *par excellence*, represented some kind of ideal which – and this is the thing which really alarmed Hayek – should be continued after the war with Germany ended. Hayek's alarm was intensified by the fact that, as *The Road to Serfdom* shows, he knew very well where the roots of Nazism lay, not just in Hegel and his followers, but in the strong German anti-capitalist tradition.

Looked at – and, more importantly, read – more than half a century after its original publication, it is difficult to understand the vituperation – indeed in some cases, like that of Herman Finer, defamation – which Hayek's *Road to Serfdom* attracted. But it marked the end, for practical purposes, of Hayek's career as an economist. He moved, very fruitfully, into much broader questions of political and legal philosophy, producing such very substantial works as *The Constitution of Liberty* (1960) and *Law, Legislation and Liberty* (1973–9), in which he was able to deploy his extraordinary erudition in explaining, in much greater detail than before, his philosophy of the evolving framework of a free economy and society. The more strictly economic work which he wrote was almost all a restatement of his earlier macroeconomic theory, and it is to Hayek's work between the 1920s and the late 1940s that we have to look for Hayek as an economist.

Indeed, it was largely for this work that Hayek was – with a nice irony, jointly with Gunnar Myrdal – awarded the Noble Memorial Prize in Economics in 1974. While paying tribute to the blending of political and economic considerations in Hayek's work as a whole, which enabled his name to be put forward together with that of Myrdal, it was his work in macroeconomics (which, as the 1970s inflations progressed, became of renewed interest), and his critique of central planning, which the Nobel committee mentioned in particular. It was, however, at least some recognition for an economist who, at the height of his powers, was regarded as a significant rival to Keynes, but who was later pushed into isolation and at one time appeared to be in danger even of oblivion.

BIBLIOGRAPHY
Monetary Theory and the Trade Cycle, trans. N. Kaldor and H. Croome (1933).
'Carl Menger', *Economica* (1934), new series, vol. 1, pp. 393–420; repr. as 'Introduction' to reprint of Menger's *Grundsätze der Volkswirtshaftslehre* (1934).
The Pure Theory of Capital (1941).
'The Counter Revolution of Science', *Economica* (1941), new series, vol. 8, February, pp. 9–36; May, pp. 119–50; August, pp. 281–320.
'Scientism and the Study of Society', *Economica* (1942–4), new series, vol. 9, August 1942, pp. 267–91; vol. 10, February 1943, pp. 34–63; vol. 11, February 1994, pp. 27–39.
The Road to Serfdom (1944).
The Constitution of Liberty (1960).
'Dr Bernard Mandeville', *Proceedings of the British Academy* (1966), vol. 52, pp. 125–41.
'Three Elucidations of the Ricardo Effect', *Journal of Political Economy* (1969), vol. 77, no. 2, pp. 274–85; repr. in *New Studies in Philosophy, Politics, Economics, and the History of Ideas* (1978).
Law, Legislation and Liberty, 3 vols (1973–9).
Collected Works of F. A. Hayek, ed. W.W. Bartley III, S. Kresge and B. Caldwell, 20 vols (1988–). (This project set is due for completion in 2008.)

Further Reading
Blaug, M., *Economic Theory in Retrospect*, 4th edn (Cambridge, 1985).
Caldwell B. (ed.), *Contra Keynes and Cambridge: The Collected Works of F.A. Hayek*, vol. 9 (1995).
Hicks, J., 'The Hayek Story', in *Critical Essays in Monetary Theory* (Oxford, 1967).

Kresge, S. and Wenar, L. (eds), *Hayek on Hayek*, (1994).
Menger, C. *Grundsätze der Volkswirtschaftslehre* (Vienna, 1871; repr. 1934).
——, *Untersuchungen über die Methode der Socialwissenschaften und der Politischen Oekonomie insbesondere* (Leipzig, 1883; repr. 1933).
Skidelsky, R., *John Maynard Keynes*, Vol. 3, *Fighting for Britain 1937–1946* (2000).
Thornton, H., *An Enquiry into the Nature and Effects of the Paper Credit of Great Britain* (1802; repr. ed. F.A. Hayek, 1939).
Wieser, F. von, *Der Natürlich Werth* (Vienna, 1889).

D.P. O'Brien

HAYNES, John (*fl.* 1698–1715)

Nothing is known of Haynes save that he was a member of the commission appointed for the prevention of wool exports, established in 1698 under the direction of Sir Henry Goodrick. He wrote several pamphlets on the illegal export of wool and the effect of this on the domestic textile and garment industries, and offered suggestions for more effective enforcement of the law. His largest and most detailed work is *Great Britain's Glory*, published in 1715 and re-issued as *Provision for the Poor* in the same year. No further references to him have been found.

Haynes opens *Great Britain's Glory* with a strong statement of the importance of trade:

It will undoubtedly be granted on all hands, that the only way to make a nation both rich and happy, is to enlarge its commerce and employ the poor; the first of these will be a means to make it the possessor of the productions of other countries, and its traffick very extensive; the other to procure business for the indigent, so that the advantage obtained by trade may be difused to the lowest of its members, and prevent their falling into divisions, tumults, rebellions, debauchery and thiving, the dire effects of poverty and laziness.

(1715: 2)

The manufacture of woollen cloth is the most important industry in Britain, says Haynes; a prosperous industry exporting cloth will create a favourable balance of trade, while a diminished industry will create an unfavourable balance and will also result in large-scale unemployment. The success of the cloth manufacturing industry is therefore vital to the national interest. Like many of his contemporaries, Haynes bemoans the continued smuggling of wool to France, and calls for the laws against it to be toughened and more strictly enforced. He goes on to calculate in detail the loss to the country in terms of income and employment, showing how many people could be employed and at what wages, if the wool that was clandestinely exported could be kept in the country and used in domestic manufacture. He backs up his assertions by showing how many people are employed in the silk industry, using raw silk imported from Turkey and Italy; though small by comparison, the silk industry exports its products and is adding to the national wealth. Woollen cloth could likewise be exported, and Haynes goes on to discuss new markets that could be exploited in Russia, Persia and India. The book then describes the measures then being used to prevent wool smuggling and the problems faced by the commissioners, and concludes with a renewed plea for more stringent measures to be taken.

BIBLIOGRAPHY

A View of the Present State of the Clothing Trade in England (1706).
Proposals Humbly Offered to the Honourable House of Commons, for the More Effectual Prevention of the Exportation of Wool, &c. from England and Ireland into Foreign Parts (1714).
Great Britain's Glory, or an Account of the Great Numbers of Poor employ'd in the Woollen and Silk Manufacturies (1715; second edn published as *Provision for the Poor: or, a View of the Decay'd State of the Woollen Manufactory, with Remarks on the Causes and Evil Consequences thereof*, probably also 1715).

Morgen Witzel

HAZLITT, William (1778–1830)

Hazlitt was born in Maidstone, Kent on 10 April 1778, and died in London on 18 September 1830. After four years in America during his childhood, Hazlitt was educated at a local school in Wem, Shropshire, where his father settled as Unitarian minister, and then at the prestigious but short-lived dissenting academy at Hackney in London, the New College. There Hazlitt studied under Joseph Priestley, among others. Upon deciding not to enter the Unitarian ministry, which had been his father's express wish, Hazlitt took up the study of painting in order to make a living while he pursued his philosophical and literary interests. In this he was followed by his brother John, who was a moderately successful portrait painter. In a way wholly characteristic of his passionate and enthusiastic nature, Hazlitt became intensely interested in painting, and during the Peace of Amiens (1803) went to Paris to study in the Louvre. As his extant art works show, he was more than competent; but since he could not bear to do less well than his idols Rembrandt, Titian and Claude, he soon reverted to his philosophical and literary ambitions.

Hazlitt had begun writing a treatise on politics, and the work which after a long struggle became his *Essay on the Principles of Human Action*, while he was still at the New College in Hackney. After ten years of labour, the *Essay* was published in 1806. Not long after he married Sarah Stoddart, who had a small property in Wiltshire. They were able to live on her means while he wrote and prepared lectures to give in London. In 1812, as a result of a war-induced national economic crisis which reduced their income, Hazlitt had to find regular salaried employment. On the strength of his published works (then three books), he entered journalism as a writer of reviews, editorials, features and 'think pieces' as they are now known, working for the *Morning Chronicle*, then the main rival of *The Times*. He was an immediate success, and within a few years was famous – or notorious – for his radical views, his support for Napoleon, his alleged lax morals, his feisty and rebarbative powers as a polemicist and debater in print, and the power and freshness of his ideas. From then until his death in 1830 he was never without a home in one or another newspaper or magazine, and many of his articles were collected and published in book form during his lifetime.

In the judgement of critics from his own time until now, Hazlitt was one of the greatest writers of prose in the English language, and arguably the greatest exponent of the essay – the personal, miscellaneous, free-flowing prose composition which, in hands like Hazlitt's was both an art form and a protean vehicle for debate and discussion. His wider cultural views were firmly based in his philosophical principles, and he was arguably the best and most important critic of the early nineteenth century's Romantic epoch, making original contributions to the appreciation of art, theatre and literature. His essays fill twenty volumes in the standard edition of his works, making him a major figure in English literature and thought. His essays are littered with philosophical discussion and debate, and like David HUME, he believed that philosophy should be read and debated by the general educated public, not just a coterie of scholastics.

Hazlitt was far from being only a theoretician. He was also a robust political polemicist and journalist who, at the expense of his own chances for advancement in worldly terms – unlike his early friends Coleridge and Wordsworth, he never received establishment honours or a government pension – defended a radical stance that was not just unpopular but actively persecuted in its day. He attacked privilege and monarchy, and was a life-long partisan of the founding principles of the French Revolution, which were democratic, socialist, and based on a new and bold conception of human rights and secular freedoms. For this reason he opposed the unjust and unnecessary war waged by the crowns of Europe against France's republican revolution, and was devastated when the Bourbon regime was at last restored in Paris, because it meant that absolutist monarchies had conquered the efforts of a people to cast of feudalism and to construct a new society based on liberty, equality and fraternity.

Although there is much in Hazlitt's political writing that has economic overtones, he also addressed economic issues directly, notably in 1807 in his three published letters in reply to T.R. MALTHUS's *Essay on the Principle of Population*. The *Essay*, first published a decade before (in 1798), asserted the doctrine that unless its procreative activity is restrained in some way, a population will increase in geometrical ratio while food supplies will increase only in arithmetical ratio. Malthus regarded this as an ineluctable law of nature, and argued that this law, rather than social or political arrangements, is what causes poverty: for as soon as the poor get a little richer, they simply have more children, thereby returning themselves to subsistence level. Hazlitt's 'letters' opposing Malthus appeared above the signature 'AO'. Between the appearance of the third, on 23 May 1807, and August of that year, he had written two more and a series of critical comments on passages excerpted from Malthus's book. He gathered all this material into a single volume under the title *A Reply to the Essay on Population*, which was published by Longman, Hurst, Rees and Orme. In the preface Hazlitt, acknowledged that his scheme of arrangement made for both repetition and divagation, and that some of his reviewers might complain – as they had done of other works – that his style was 'too flowery'; so, in ironic reference to his 'metaphysical choke-pear', he said that he would, if they preferred it, 'undertake to produce a work as dry and formal as they please, if they will undertake to find it readers.'

What prompted Hazlitt to reply to Malthus at this juncture, nearly a decade after the latter's book appeared, was the introduction of a bill in parliament on 19 February 1807 which, if passed, would have had the effect of substituting education for the dole. The Bill was brought forward by Samuel Whitbread – a good-hearted man whom Hazlitt said nevertheless had too little real understanding of the poor – with the intention of establishing a free national education system. Hazlitt had his doubts about the value of such a thing in the then prevailing state of society (he had his doubts too about the extension of Christian missions to the new industrial proletarians of the northern cities, on the grounds that attempting to moralize at them would have the reverse effect). But he was chiefly concerned to rebut the Malthusian ideas that underlay suggestions for reform of poor laws in general. These ideas had been iterated by their author in the form of a *Letter to Samuel Whitbread* after the failure of the Bill, during whose attempted passage Malthus was to be seen in the precincts of the House of Commons, lobbying MPs with a copy of his *Essay* in his hand. Hazlitt felt he had to attack.

His letters were as full of *ad hominem* argument against Malthus as analysis and refutation of his views – a fact which, Hazlitt said in his preface, he could not help and would not apologize for. He despised Malthus's principles, which urged acceptance of the view that war, famine and starvation are 'benevolent remedies by which nature has enabled human beings to correct the disorders that would arise from a redundance of population'. He despised also Malthus's espousal of the principle of self-interest – which Hazlitt has so vigorously repudiated in his own *Essay* – and rejected his call on the 'lower classes of society' to limit their numbers by 'moral restraint'. Malthus's imputation of enlarged sexual appetite among the poor prompted Hazlitt's graphic attack on the upper classes' far greater inducements to licentiousness: the undress fashions of the women, the bawdy plays they attended, the provocations and opportunities of balls and great parties. It was not that Hazlitt was against sex (on the contrary); rather, he was against the hypocrisy and condescension of Malthus's view, and tore at the mask of pieties that covered it, as when Malthus recommended that parsons should discourage the poor from marrying, and if the poor insisted nevertheless, parsons should lecture them not to have children they cannot support. If a poor man still pays no heed then, said Malthus, let him marry and breed, but: 'When nature will govern and punish for us, it is a very miserable ambition to wish to snatch the rod from her hand and draw upon ourselves the odium of executioner. To the punishment of nature therefore he should be left, the punishment of want. He has erred in the face of the most precise warning, and can have no reason to complain of any person but himself when he feels the consequences of his error.' The consequences are of course death by starvation first of his children, then of himself. Malthus does not question a system that tolerates the accumulation of so much economic resource in the hands of a few that the many have to strive or starve for want of a share. He simply argues that the latter must starve if they do not strive, and do not deprive themselves of the comforts of love. Hazlitt was disgusted and enraged by this, which explains the vehemence of his attack.

Hazlitt had two chief arguments against Malthus. First, when society finds itself inconvenienced by increase of population, it will adjust the size of families by a natural self-regulating feedback mechanism, the process of new families not having so many children as was standard in the previous generation. This idea seems not to have occurred to Malthus. Secondly, neither the poor nor anyone else are as sexually and procreatively incontinent as Malthus himself must, said Hazlitt, be, for he seems to be generalising from his own unrepresentatively hot-blooded case to all men. Of the two criticisms, the former tells.

The polemical character of Hazlitt's *Reply* and its frank discussion of sexual matters might have been one reason why all but one of the periodicals ignored it; only the *Monthly Review* ran an article on it, in May 1808, and then only to hold its nose over Hazlitt's 'disgusting and preposterous' defiance of all 'modesty, breeding, and a sense of decency', to which they give this 'slight notice...as a warning to others'.

BIBLIOGRAPHY
Essay on the Principles of Human Action (1806).
A Reply to the Essay on Population (1808).
Complete Works of William Hazlitt, ed. P.P. Rau (1928–32).

Further Reading
Baker, H., *William Hazlitt* (Cambridge, Massachusetts, 1962).
Grayling, A.C., *The Quarrel of the Age: The Life and Times of William Hazlitt* (2000).
Houck, J.A., *William Hazlitt: A Reference Guide* (Boston, 1977).
Kinnaird, J., *William Hazlitt, Critic of Power* (New York, 1978).
Park, R., *Hazlitt and the Spirit of the Age* (Oxford, 1971).
Wardle, R.M., *Hazlitt* (1971).

A.C. Grayling

HEATHFIELD, Richard (*c*.1775–1859)

Heathfield died in London in 1859. Nothing is known of his origins or background. The flyleaf of *Elements of a Plan for the Liquidation of the Public Debt of the United Kingdom* (1819) refers to him as 'gent.', but this probably indicates only that he had become wealthy through business and had purchased a landed estate. A connection with engineering and surveying is indicated in some of his technical works. His writings, which are considerable, date from the period 1819–51 and cover subjects relating to engineering and transport and several works on the national debt. His last book was *Fallacies of Taxation* (1851).

In his 1819 work, Heathfield begins by contemplating Britain after the end of the Napoleonic Wars. Trade and manufacturing were strong and the country was undoubtedly powerful, but there were also many weaknesses. Among these Heathfield lists the system of public debt, unemployment, the poor laws and low standards of education. The last three, he says, lead to a large extent from the first: 'relief from the burthen of the public debt, appears to be indispensable to the successful institution of corrective or remedial measures, with reference to all departments of social life' (1819: 3). He goes on to explain that the debt acts as a drag on industry and commerce:

Industry is the vital principle of property; abstracted from labour, the land, the spindle, and the loom, are likewise inert and unproductive; a free course to honest exertion, and protection and compensation to the industrious, are, therefore, first principles in the social compact. A public debt, whatever the circumstances in which it may originate, unavoidably bears adversely upon those principles: the duties and taxes, inseparable from a public debt, enhance the price of all productions, particularly the price of domestic agricultural produce...

(1819: 3)

Debt leads to taxation, which in turn depresses consumption and slows the economy. Any public debt, once assumed, should be cleared as quickly as possible. Heathfield is against debt in principle, believing that unrestricted credit leads to speculaton, and is among those who believe that the Bank of England has allowed too much paper currency into circulation.

Having established the 'evils' of the national debt, Heathfield then turns to the problem of clearing it. He argues that if all private property in the United Kingdom, whether owned domestically or by foreigners, were subject to an immediate levy of 15 per cent of its value, the national debt could then be cleared and, subsequently, taxes reduced or abolished. The principal sum of the levy could be paid by property holders over a period of years, but with interest accruing so as to encouraging early payment. He stresses that this charge would be levied not only on land but also on ships, commercial property and so on.

In *Fallacies of Taxation*, Heathfield objects not to taxation in principle, but to what he terms 'unncessary' taxation. He is particularly opposed to taxes on goods: 'The impulses to industry are commensurate with consumption, the extent of which is, as the ability to purchase, not as the power to consume; – the ability to purchase is as the circulation of money from hand to hand, the vigour of this circulation depends on the condition of each individual throughout the social body' (1851: 3–4). High taxes on particular goods – and he names tobacco, tea, spirits and malt as the most heavily taxed – lead to non-consumption. This in turn interrupts the circulation of money: 'the non-consumption of one branch of supply, keeps in check the current of demand for other supplies. The less, for instance, the consumption of the products of home agriculture, the less the demand, in exchangfe, for the production of the town' (1851: 4). 'The whole is a vast system of barter, and the non-consumption of one class of productions narrows the demand for other classes. In the present state of the world, the limit to barter, and the consequent great check to industry, is occasioned by the introduction of artificial increments of cost, incident to a high revenue system' (1851: 5).

Excessive taxation also leads to crime, especially smuggling and fraud, which he believes on tobacco alone are costing the country £4 million annually. Smuggling in turn he equates with 'moral degradation', and argues that high taxation literally forces people into crime. His conclusion is that indirect taxation should be repealed or greatly reduced, and a new and fairer system which taxes income and property instituted.

BIBLIOGRAPHY
Elements of a Plan for the Liquidation of the Public Debt of the United Kingdom (1819; repr. 1820).
Further Observations on the Practicability and Expedience of Liquidating the National Debt of the United Kingdom (1820).
Addenda to Mr Heathfield's Second Publication on the Liquidation of the Public Debt (1820).
Thoughts on the Liquidation of the Public Debt, and on the Relief of the Country from and Distress Incident to a Population Exceeding the Demand for Labour (1829).
Commentaries on the Mining Ordinances of Spain (1830).
Commercial Docks on the Southern Coast of England (1838).
Fallacies of Taxation (1851).

David Ashbury

HENDERSON, Hubert Douglas
(1890–1952)

Henderson was born in Beckenham, Kent, on 20 October 1890, the son of John Henderson, a Glasgow banker. He died in Oxford on 22 February 1952. Henderson was educated at Aberdeen Grammar School, Rugby School and Emmanuel College, Cambridge, where he studied mathematics and then economics just prior to World War I taking first-class honours in the economics tripos in 1912. During this period of his life Henderson became increasingly interested in Liberal Party politics, an interest that would eventually lead to his becoming secretary and then (1912) president of the Cambridge Union. After being declared unfit for military service in the First World War, Henderson joined the Cotton Control Board in 1917 as secretary. In 1919 he became a teaching fellow at Clare College, Cambridge, where he found intellectual company with John Maynard KEYNES, then a fellow of King's College, Cambridge.

The pairing of Henderson and Keynes should come as no surprise. Both were trained within the Marshallian tradition of economic thought, and both were sympathetic to liberal politics. Keynes, the elder of the two, had already made a name for himself in political circles, and Henderson had become increasingly active in helping arrange the first Liberal summer schools. Their similarities led the two men to discover a mutual interest in analysing the role of government policy, an interest which drew them even closer professionally. For example, when Henderson published *Supply and Demand* in 1922, Keynes supplied the introduction. After Keynes became chairman of *The Nation* and the *Athenaeum* in 1923, he offered Henderson the editorship. This platform allowed the two men to collaborate in a way that greatly increased the visibility of their ideas.

In the early 1920s, prevailing macroeconomic thought on unemployment was largely classical. If unemployment was observed, then that unemployment was thought to be voluntary. As a decade, the 1920s became a period of increased unemployment, an observation that led to Keynes suggesting the existence of involuntary unemployment, where downward rigidity in the nominal wage contributed to an excess supply of labour. As liberal economists like Henderson and Keynes noted the unemployment problems surrounding them, their collective prescription was that of government intervention. In 1924, Henderson published Keynes's article 'Does Unemployment Need a Drastic Remedy?' in the *Nation*, where their shared beliefs were discussed in a general fashion. This article was a first step in the direction of moving toward the more applied stage of formulating policy. Over the next year, Henderson was asked to join other liberal economic thinkers to provide an academically acceptable economic foundation for David Lloyd George's Liberal Party. In 1927, Henderson's role was expanded when Walter LAYTON, chairman of the Liberal Industrial Inquiry group, made Henderson and Keynes responsible for guiding Liberal Party economic policy.

While in this position, Henderson helped produce the Inquiry Group's 1928 report, *Britain's Industrial Future*, which was also referred to as the Liberal Yellow Book. The Yellow Book was both a political and economic tool. As an economist, Henderson used this opportunity to further a new understanding as to how government should address problems of high unemployment. As part of the Liberal Party's policy-making arm, Henderson's work was obviously also used to gather in votes for the party.

In 1929, Henderson was an important contributor to the Liberal Party article, 'We Can Conquer Unemployment'. Keynes and Henderson also reworked some earlier articles from the *Nation* into a pamphlet entitled *Can Lloyd George Do It?*. The intent of this work was to further promote Keynes and Henderson's ideas regarding the use of public works to resolve problems of unemployment, but was also produced to address conservative criticisms about the financing of these public expenditure proposals. The conservative fear was that debt financed public expenditure would diminish private investment. In retrospect, an important contribution of this work involved Keynes and Henderson's discussion of the 'cumulative force of trade activity'. These views are considered an early reference to the role of the expenditure multiplier. Their discussion did not provide any formal multiplier analysis or theory, however, because they were unable to determine the actual value of the multiplier effect.

Henderson left his post at the *Nation* in 1930, after being persuaded to accept an appointment as secretary of the newly formed Economic Advisory Council (EAC). The EAC was a formal advisory group established by J. Ramsay MacDonald, and included both industrialists and intellectuals. Their charge was to regularly advise the prime minister on economic policy decisions.

After serving on the EAC for five years, Henderson accepted a research fellowship at All Souls College, Oxford, in 1934. In this new capacity, he became acquainted with economists like Roy HARROD and James MEADE. Harrod and Henderson became members of the Group of the Royal Institute of International Affairs, and were responsible for producing the *Report on The Future of Monetary Policy* in 1935. It was with Harrod and Meade that Henderson founded the Oxford Economists' Research Group (OERG), a group Henderson chaired from 1936 until 1938. During this time, Henderson developed the research path for the OERG, a procedure that involved interviews with entrepreneurs and led by a team of Oxford fellows. In 1938, Henderson took a leading role in creating the academic journal *Oxford Economic Papers*, serving eventually as a member of the editorial board. Henderson also helped organize the Oxford Institute of Statistics during this period as well.

The 1930s also saw the beginning of a change in Henderson's attitude to Keynesian thought. For example, in a letter to Keynes, Henderson wrote that Keynes's support of expansionary fiscal policy ignored the dangers of budget deficits. He also began to take issue with various other points raised by Keynes as well, from the use of monetary policy to expand the economy to the possible existence of a multiplier effect from government spending. Henderson also began writing more critically on the use of abstract approaches to economic theory. For example, in correspondence with Henderson, Harrod describes Henderson's comments on such work as saying that discussion of 'elasticities and varying costs is a great waste of time and really injurious to the advance of economics'. Henderson's specific response to such charges by stating that he believes abstract theorizing to have value if the theory can suggest 'the right questions to ask'.

During the Second World War, Henderson was an advisor to the Treasury and in 1942 was knighted for his contributions to both country and discipline. He went on in 1944 to become a member and later chair of the Royal Commission on Population, a position he occupied until 1949. He was chairman of the Statutory Committee on Unemployment Insurance from 1945 to 1948, and was appointed Drummond Professor of Political Economy at Oxford in 1945. In 1951, Henderson was elected warden of All Souls, but resigned on medical grounds six months later. He died within a month of his resignation.

BIBLIOGRAPHY
Supply and Demand (1922).
(with J.M. Keynes) *Can Lloyd George Do It?* (1929).

Further Reading
Clarke, P. *The Keynesian Revolution in the Making: 1924–1936* (Oxford, 1988).
Liberal Party, *We Can Conquer Unemployment* (1929).

'Sir Hubert Henderson 1890–1952', *Oxford Economic Papers* (1953), new series, vol. 5, supplement, pp. 5–6.

Dimand, R.W., *The Origins of the Keynesian Revolution*, Stanford, California, 1988).

Barry Haworth

HEWINS, William Albert Samuel (1865–1931)

Hewins was born in Wolverhampton, West Midlands on 11 May 1865, the second son of Samuel Hewins, a middle-class Midlands metal merchant. He died at his home in London on 17 November 1931. He attended Wolverhampton Grammar School, from whence he obtained the Hatherton Scholarship to Pembroke College, Oxford. He graduated in 1887 with a second class in the final mathematical school, having obtained a first class in the mathematical moderations in 1885. In addition to his studies in mathematics, he had been drawn to economics by the adverse effects of the economic downturn in the 1870s on his family's business. At Pembroke, he was taught by Sir C.H. Firth and undertook economic and social studies of England in the seventeenth century. From early on, however, he rejected the methodology of classical political economy in favour of a more historical approach. In 1892, Hewins married Margaret, the daughter of James Slater of Bescot Hall, Staffordshire. They had a son and two daughters.

After he graduated, Hewins became involved in the University Extension Movement and from 1887 to 1895 he lectured, mainly in the North of England, to working-class audiences on economic and social issues, including trade unionism and factory legislation. He had plans for improving the operation of the University Extension Movement, but these were left unfulfilled when Sidney WEBB invited him to become the first director of the newly founded London School of Economics and Political Science (LSE).

Hewins served as director of the LSE from 1895 until 1903. He was also Tooke Professor of Economic Science and Statistics at King's College from 1897–1903 and lecturer in modern economic history in the University of London in 1902–3. Hewins was chosen as director by Webb, who wanted economics at the LSE to be different from that taught by Alfred MARSHALL at Cambridge. However, while Marshall was unhappy at with some of the criticisms of Cambridge economics made by Hewins (Coats 1967), and CANNAN in his LSE lectures was highly critical of Marshall, the LSE finally produced Lionel ROBBINS rather than an English historical school of economics.

Hewins had studied the major mercantilist writers early in his academic career, and he contributed many biographical entries to the *Dictionary of National Biography*. His sympathies with their positions led him to argue that mercantilism provided ideas that were relevant to the issues arising over policy of free trade. From the 1890s, Hewins had been arguing the case for 'constructive imperialism', which involved 'the deliberate adoption of the Empire as distinguished from the United Kingdom as the basis of public policy, and in particular, the substitution in our economic policy of imperial interests for the interest of the consumer'. In 1903 he wrote a series of articles for *The Times* under the signature of 'An Economist' in favour of imposing tariffs to revive British industry, choosing anonymity to avoid involving LSE in the controversy. Later that year, when Joseph Chamberlain established the Tariff Commission, Hewins resigned as Director of the LSE to become the secretary of the Commission, a position he held until 1917, and was then its chairman from 1920 to 1922. He was a close personal advisor in regular contact with Chamberlain until the latter's death in 1914, and he also provided economic advice on tariff reform to the prime minister, Arthur Balfour, particularly between 1903 and 1906.

Hewins fought three unsuccessful elections before being elected as Conservative MP for Hereford City, a seat that he held between 1912 and 1918. During his time in Parliament, he spoke frequently and passionately in favour of tariff reform. In 1917, David Lloyd George appointed Hewins Under-Secretary of State for the Colonies, a post he held until 1918. In 1918 Hereford City was merged in the South Herefordshire seat and Hewins was not invited to stand in the new constituency. Despite three attempts to win the seat in Swansea West (in 1922, 1923 and 1924) he failed to return to Parliament.

In 1923, Hewins was appointed Chairman of the Economic Development Union, an organization that argued that the unification of the Empire was the only solution to the problem of growing unemployment. He continued his vigorous campaigning for tariff reform, using statistical information collected by the Tariff Commission to support the case. Two of his publications from this period (1924, 1929) cover the history of tariff, presenting his personal, though inevitably partisan, account of the tariff campaign. By the time of his death he had made a significant contribution to the campaign for tariff reform by providing an historical critique of free trade and arguing the case for the relevance of mercantilism.

BIBLIOGRAPHY
English Trade and Finance in the 17th Century (1892).
Lecture on Tariff Reform (1907).
Trade in the Balance (1924).
The Apologia of an Imperialist (1929).

Further Reading
Coats, A.W., 'Alfred Marshall and the early development of the London School of Economics: some unpublished letters', *Economica* (1967), vol. 34, November, pp. 408–17.

Dahrendorf, R., *LSE: A History of the London School of Economics and Political Science, 1895–1995* (Oxford, 1995).
Wood, J.C., *British Economists and the Empire* (1983).

Jim Thomas

HEYSHAM, John (1753–1834)

Heysham was born 22 November 1753 at Lancaster, and died at Carlisle on 23 March 1834. His father was a shipowner, and his mother came from a prominent Westmoreland family. Heysham attended a Quaker school in Westmoreland before serving a five-year apprenticeship with a surgeon. In 1774 he entered the medical college at the University of Edinburgh, where he wrote (in Latin) a thesis on canine rabies. He received his MD degree in 1777. The following year, he started his medical practice in Carlisle. He married in 1789 and was eventually the father of seven children; he survived his wife by some three decades. A public-spirited man, Heysham served as a justice of the peace in Carlisle. He introduced smallpox vaccination to Carlisle, leading the way by vaccinating his own month-old daughter. He worked with the local clergy to establish, in 1782, a clinic for the poor, and he served as its first physician. In the same year, Heysham published a pamphlet describing a recent episode of 'jail fever', or typhus, in Carlisle, including recommendations for future treatment of the disease. His biographer, Lonsdale (1870), credits him with 'an eye for business and money-making'. He was the founder of a cotton-spinning mill and, for a time, the manager of an iron foundry.

Heysham's significance for economics derives from the careful statistical observations he made in Carlisle over an extended period of time and the use to which they were put. Soon after his arrival in Carlisle, Heysham began keeping systematic records of births and deaths in the town's two parishes. The accuracy and age-specific detail of his records for 1779–87 enabled Joshua MILNE, after an extensive correspondence with Heysham, to compute a life table showing survival probabilities for every age cohort of the population. Milne published the 'Carlisle table' in 1815, and it soon earned recognition as a major advance over the previous standard, Richard PRICE's 'Northampton table' of 1783. The flaws in the Northampton table had caused English life insurance companies to charge excessive premiums on policies, and the government to miscalculate the long-term cost of life annuities issued in connection with funding operations. Milne's new table, based on Heysham's data, put all such calculations on a sounder footing. It remained a touchstone of insurance calculations for half a century.

BIBLIOGRAPHY
An Account of the Jail Fever, or Typhus Carcerum: as it Appeared at Carlisle in the Year 1781 (1782).
Observations on the Bills of Mortality in Carlyle for the Year MDCCLXXXVII (Carlisle, 1788).

Further Reading
Armstrong, W.A., 'The Trend of Mortality in Carlisle between the 1780s and the 1840s: A Demographic Contribution to the Standard of Living Debate', *Economic History Review* (1981), vol. 34, no. 1, pp. 94–114.
Armytage, W.H.G., 'John Heysham: a Carlisle Bicentenary', *British Medical Journal* (1953), vol. II, pp. 1156.
Lonsdale, H., *The Life of John Heysham, M.D., and his Correspondence with Mr. Joshua Milne relative to the Carlisle Bills of Mortality* (1870).
Milne, J., *A Treatise on the Valuation of Annuities and Assurances on Lives and Survivorships; on the Construction of Tables of Mortality; and on the Probabilities and Expectations of Life*, 2 vols (1815).

Geoffrey Gilbert

HICKS, John Richard (1904–89)

Hicks was born at Warwick on 8 April 1904, and died at Oxford on 20 May 1989. His father was a journalist working for a local newspaper in the Midlands. He was educated at Clifton School and then studied mathematics at Balliol College, Oxford, to which he had won a scholarship, in 1922. In 1923 he moved to the study of philosophy, politics and economics, taking a second-class degree in 1926. His first post was as a temporary lecture at the London School of Economics, which then turned into a permanent position; Hicks remained at the LSE until 1935, teaching alongside contemporaries such as Lionel ROBBINS, Friedrich von HAYEK, Nicholas KALDOR and Roy ALLEN.

From 1935–8 Hicks was a fellow of Gonville and Caius College, Cambridge. It was during this period that he wrote his first major work, *Value and Capital*. From 1938–46 he was professor of economics at the University of Manchester. He then moved to Oxford, first as fellow of Nuffield College (1946–52), then Drummond Professor of Political Economy (1952–65), and finally fellow of All Souls College (1965–71). In 1935 he married Ursula Webb, a distinguished public finance specialist, and collaborated with her in the preparation of numerous works on public finance theory and application. Ursula HICKS died in 1985. John Hicks was a member of the Royal Commission on the Taxation of Profits and Income in 1951. He became a fellow of the British Academy in 1942, was knighted in 1964, and was awarded the Nobel Prize in

Economics (jointly with Kenneth J. Arrow) in 1972.

John Hicks is a major figure in the history of British economics, one of a great line of economists that runs from SMITH through RICARDO and MILL to EDGEWORTH, MARSHALL and KEYNES. Yet he also represents a break from that tradition. In *Value and Capital* he recorded his explicit desire to understand better the interrelations of markets, and felt that the work of the Lausanne school and of Wicksell offered the best chance of so doing. However, he felt there was something missing from the work of these economists. There was 'a certain sterility' in Walras; Pareto's work is limited by a lack of attention to capital and interest; Wicksell's work, which does tackle capital and interest but lacks knowledge of Pareto (which his own work pre-dated). Wicksell could not take his analysis beyond what Hicks calls 'the artificial abstraction of a stationary state'. In communicating with a readership which he presumes to be English, familiar with Marshall, and unfamiliar with the works of the Lausanne school (not at that time available in the English language), Hicks explains his proposed course in words which perfectly capture his position:

> I shall summarize such parts of their [the Lausanne school] work as I need in the course of my own argument. I shall take for granted not Pareto's value theory but the more familiar value theory of Marshall; and this will have some advantages, since I do not regard Pareto's theory as being superior to Marshall's in all respects. One of the things we have to do is to fill out Pareto's theory in those respects where it is defective compared with Marshall's.
>
> (1939a: 5)

Hicks begins by applying the theory of consumer demand to the most basic general equilibrium of markets model, pure exchange between consumers involving only goods and personal services. He shows that stability is problematic. In particular, price changes cause income effects. To resolve these issues Hicks required a method for treating stability in a general multiple commodity market system.

There were three natural approaches to dynamism. If he had turned to NEWTON, Hicks might have drawn on the huge body of highly developed contemporary scientific knowledge concerning dynamics which existed in his time in a highly developed form. Samuelson followed this route and was able to elucidate the basics of economic dynamics as well as anyone has ever done. However, some economic dynamics had been developed by older writers. Cournot's approach was closest to physics, and the best; Walras also had a dynamics, which Hicks rightly found to be unsatisfactory. There was also some work on economic dynamics in the work of English-language economists. In particular, Alfred Marshall had developed a pseudo-dynamics in the form of his period analysis for the partial equilibrium of a market served by many firms. As it stood, this model was not at all what Hicks required: it was partial equilibrium with no obvious means of extending it to general equilibrium. Hicks borrowed the method and adapted it to include dynamics and comparative statics in a simultaneous equilibrium model.

There was another deeper difficulty, however. Marshall's dynamics was not genuine dynamics. His model applies to a market initially in long-period equilibrium which receives a permanent shock, such as a sudden and permanent rise in demand. Three defining model variables are assumed to adjust at such sharply differential rates that three different types of equilibrium are reached successively according to whether one, two or all three of these variables have adjusted to the post-shock state. The variables at issue, in decreasing order of adjustment speed, are: market price; output or fast adjusting factor input; and capital stock or slow adjusting factor input. Then the successive equilibria are respectively: the market-period equilibrium;

short-period equilibrium and long-period equilibrium (1939a: 119–22).

Hicks took this model and adapted it to general equilibrium analysis by replacing lagged adjustment of factor inputs by lagged adjustment of prices (1939a: 68). Such a description of price adjustment, as Samuelson pointed out, is artificial and does not correspond to true dynamic stability. This point, while valid, turned out not to matter as much as one might expect. The point is that general stability does not have usable implications, so we are always forced to consider special cases. Hicks's Marshallian method captured these. In particular, Hicks found that substitution effects needed to dominate if the system was to be well-behaved; own price effects should be larger than cross-price effects. These findings paved the way for later mathematical economic modelling using gross substitutability and diagonal dominance. McFadden (1968) shows that Hicks's stability method is valid in precisely those cases in which partial equilibrium analysis constitutes a valid approximation. Those cases in turn are the only ones in which general equilibrium stability and comparative statics results can be rigorously shown. In that exact sense, partial equilibrium analysis is all that we have. As Hicks said:

> Either we have to face up to the difficulty, and allow deliberately for the fact that supplies (and ultimately demands too) are governed by expected prices quite as much as by current prices; or we have to evade the issue by concentrating on the case where these difficulties are at a minimum. The first is the method of Marshall; the second (broadly speaking) is the method of the Austrians.
>
> (1939a: 117)

Hicks's non-Austrian intertemporal economics is quickly constructed and explained. For the prices of future goods which markets do not provide, agents are given expectations. To be exact, this means that agents have inside their heads prices which they treat as if they were definite data, although they are in fact subjective and can be incorrect and biased in any manner. Hicks notes that treating uncertain values as if they are definite cannot be absolutely right, and he mentions the possibility of adjusting point expectation prices upwards or downwards to correct for their dispersion, without developing this idea formally. Did he sense that he would run into serious problems if he were to attempt the complete simultaneous definition of the certainty equivalent levels of a number of different prices?

A similar problem is encountered in Keynes's General Theory, where expectations are treated in an exactly parallel manner and suitable adjustments to their values are supposed to reflect both the presence of subjective risk and possibly variable willingness to undertake it. No doubt Keynes is the source of Hicks's conception. Even supposing that to be the case, Hicks applies the idea of subjective price expectations in a distinctly different manner from Keynes. He looks at the implications of subjective price expectations for the general equilibrium of current markets and thus derives one of his great contributions to economic theory: temporary equilibrium.

In his discussion of interest in Chapter 11 of *Value and Capital*, Hicks concentrates on money loans and money rates of interest. The strict temporary equilibrium case in which only current goods are traded for current goods, although those trades reflect expectations concerning the relative prices at trades will take place in the future, is reinforced by the presence of a subset of futures markets in which trades involving future deliveries take place today, in the present period. Examining the determination of the rate of interest, Hicks considers whether the rate of interest is determined entirely by the real economy, and whether it is a flow equilibrium or a stock equilibrium that occurs in money markets. He regards the first issue as genuine, and firmly takes the view that monetary influences do matter for the determination of the rate of interest. But, unlike Keynes, he rightly holds that flow equilibrium and stock equilibrium are simply two ways of looking at the same general equilibrium of markets.

In the final chapter of Part III of *Value and Capital*, Hicks made some of his most important and distinctive contributions. He cut a path through this jungle of measurement of income problems by making use of a bold and powerful concept, 'Hicksian income'; that level of real income which an individual, or a firm or a society, could spend in perpetuity. This is a much more permanent concept of income than is a current net cash flow measure.

In Part IV, Hicks rejects previous ground rules for constructing a theory of capital as they had been understood previously. He is not willing to contemplate any kind of long-run or perfect equilibrium model. His method is to analyse a sequence of temporary equilibria, one following another. The chief problem to be overcome in order to do so is to model how price expectations are adjusted from one period to the next in the light of experience. He found intriguing the Böhm-Bawerk idea that capital is equivalent to waiting, and later explored it systematically in *Capital and Time* (1973). Böhm-Bawerk was clearly exposed as a special case: a fascinating special case perhaps; but a very special case without doubt.

Hicks's conception of equilibrium is profoundly asymmetric with regard to goods and time. Present goods are united in all having definite prices, whereas most future goods have prices which are manifest in the first period only as subjective expectations. It is allowed that one good, call it 'money', can be traded at definite prices between present and future periods. Even in that case, speculation plays a role. That is because, even if rates are quoted today for loans of all durations, the levels which short rates will take in future periods are not known for certain. For this reason, an agent needing to borrow long may choose to speculate that short rates will fall, and borrow short, planning to re-finance the loan by means of subsequent short borrowing. This strategy is risky, as many nations confirmed in the 1980s, because short rates may not fall as expected, and may indeed rise, as is obvious from theoretical consideration.

As time moves on, agents experience current prices, and revise their expectations in the light of their experiences. This gave Hicks the opportunity to elaborate one of his finest intellectual constructs: the elasticity of expectations. He shows that for a sequence of temporary equilibria to be well behaved, the responsiveness of price expectations to current experience must not be too large.

Allowing money to be the good which directly bridges time periods, because there are active forward markets for lending and borrowing money, permits Hicks to construct a theory of the demand for money. Uncertainty concerning future relative prices encourages the holding of money, for which the own rate of return is given for certain by the money market, against the productive holding of other goods, which are subject to return uncertainty.

Capital and Growth (1965) was the product of afterthoughts concerning, and continuing discontents with, *Value and Capital*. It was forged in intellectual interchanges with Michio Morishima during the latter's visit to All Souls College (Morishima 1994). In the new work, Hicks put aside the assumption that even current markets always clear. Instead, he now considered the fix-price economy, in which all or many current prices are fixed at arbitrary levels. Despite being strongly influenced by Keynes in the 1930s, Hicks had rejected the assumption of sticky prices, which was why his temporary equilibrium, for all its evident non-optimality, was not Keynesian in character. On the other hand, fix-price general equilibrium is notoriously difficult to analyse. If *Capital and Growth* was not a huge success, this is partly because it offers that great reasonableness plus a certain vacuity which is all-too-easily the product of fix-price reasoning.

The other problem was the new dynamics. Hicks created the concept of the traverse, being the path followed by an economy as it moved from one steady state to another. It is a clever construct, the transfer taking the form of the successive adjustment of different and broader classes of variables. Yet the old question reasserted itself: is this genuine dynamics? To judge by the profession's response, the answer was no. Growth modelling at that period was making use of Newtonian dynamics, and that corresponded better to the taste of the time.

In *Capital and Time* (1973), Hicks provides a Neo-Austrian theory, so called because he greatly generalizes the special cases considered by Böhm-Bawerk and Hayek. By examining inter-temporal processes, in which dated inputs and outputs are jointly produced, Hicks created an elegant technique. For example, terminable processes, which can be cut off at any time, behave differently from non-terminable processes. The approach employed in *Capital and Time* places its emphasis on the inter-temporal substitution effects of relative price changes. That those are not the only consequences of price changes is clear, of course, because the capital model of *Value and Capital* demonstrates exactly that point.

Hicks's flagrant disregard of the boundary between general equilibrium and macro/money theory comes as a surprise. It seems that while he was working on the formal text on microeconomics and general equilibrium that is the first half of *Value and Capital*, Hicks re-read Keynes's General Theory. Enthused by the new macroeconomic theory, Hicks could easily have abandoned his researches into general equilibrium. Instead, he chose to take the Lausanne School general equilibrium of markets and to make it respond to Keynes's questions. It is no contradiction to say that this enterprise was less than entirely successful, but what Hicks did achieve was of monumental importance. He did more than apply the general equilibrium model; he first refined it and gave to it its modern specification. Then he extended it to encompass capital theory. However, Hicks was not contented with the static long-run view of capital which he found in Wicksell, and he used an implicit axiom: capital equals dynamics.

What made Hicks's contribution important is not the answers which he provided to classic questions, although there are some of those. Rather, it is the development of entirely new questions and new ways of viewing the fundamental issues of economic theory. Thus, even when his answers are far from perfect, Hicks effectively redefined the field. With hindsight, it is remarkable so formidable a theorist should write, 'at first I regarded myself as a labour economist, not a theoretical economist at all'. Lionel Robbins is given the credit for interesting Hicks in theory: 'he moved me from Cassel to Walras and Pareto, to Edgeworth and Taussig to Wicksell and the Austrians – with all of whom I was more at home at that stage than I was with Marshall and Pigou' (1963: 306).

Hicks's huge output is that of a man who worked largely on his own. Even when, unusually, he reacted to the work of others, as in *A Revision of Demand Theory* (1956), or with the famous IS/LM model, his approach is so distinctive that it is recognizably his own. This may be a distinctively English style. If some found Hicks so aloof as to be arrogant, many more were impressed by his openness to ideas and discussions of all kinds. In making the 1972 Nobel Prize award to Hicks, the Committee mentioned 'general equilibrium and welfare economics'.

Hicks's writings on welfare economics comprise work on four connected fields of interest: the foundations of welfare economics, including the famous compensation test; the valuation of social income; the definition and measurement of consumer's surplus; and, lastly, the measurement of capital. *The New Welfare Economics* owed its inception to Kaldor (1939). The problem at issue is fundamental to the justification of recommendations offered by economists. The notion of a 'Pareto improvement' – a change that would make no individual worse off and at least one better off – was familiar, but was seen to be limited as a basis for recommendations, as all actual changes harm someone. In Robbins's telling example, economists could not state scientifically that the abolition of the Corn Laws was a good thing because this reform harmed landlords.

Attempts to resolve this problem depended on compensation tests. The chief contributors to this debate, including Hicks, do not all emerge with great honour, as ambiguity concerning the question of whether compensation must be paid in order for the improvement to count muddied the waters. A well-argued solution to this problem was proposed by Little (1950), but this required explicit value judgements concerning income distribution, hence negating the original intention of the exercise, which had been to remove value judgements from welfare economics. For Hicks's mature views on these questions see 'The Scope and Status of Welfare Economics' (1975).

The problem of income measurement is closely allied to the issue of welfare improvements, and Hicks discusses social accounting in *The Social Framework* (1942), and the valuation of social income in a paper of that title (1940). He concludes that the measurement of income could mean measurement in terms of utility or measurement in terms of cost, and that the two measures are in general different. The problem of how to treat indirect taxation and government expenditure on goods and services led Hicks into controversy with Kuznets. The usual practice is to measure prices at factor cost and to value public services at cost. Hicks's position may be briefly summarized as follows: (1) as there is no market test where public goods are concerned, the taxation which pays for them is not a reliable measure of their value to the consumer; and (2) even if consumers were to be regarded as choosing public expenditure, the appropriate price weights would not be average costs but marginal costs.

In the 1932 edition of *The Theory of Wages*, Hicks remarks that, 'there has been no date this century to which the theory that I was putting out could have been more inappropriate.' G.F. Shove's review identified a number of the shortcomings, notably the relatively weak treatment of the supply side of labour markets and the consequently limited ability to treat unemployment. These legitimate criticisms apart, there were very considerable merits. By concentrating on the long-run determinants of wage rates, Hicks was able to examine some of the most interesting influences at work. He saw changes in the demand for labour as consisting of two components quite analogous to the income and substitution effects in demand that he was to investigate later. A lower wage rate leads to an expansion of output, because the cost curve has fallen, which induces a higher demand for labour. In addition, a lower wage rate induces the adoption of more labour intensive methods of production, which increases the demand for labour for a given output. Also, there is the idea that because capital tends to accumulate faster than labour, technical progress tends to be labour saving; and there is the first-ever attempt to model a labour dispute which may culminate in a strike, and more besides. He also models wage bargaining under the threat of a strike.

Hicks's first response to the *General Theory* is described in detail in 'Recollections and Documents' included in *Economic Perspectives* (1977). However the response for which he is best known was an expository piece, 'Mr Keynes and the "Classics"' (1937), a piece that perfectly fulfilled the innate demand for a more accessible account of the essentials of Keynes's argument. It is important to make clear that what was provided was more than a simplification of Keynes. Hicks replicated faithfully Keynes's various specifications, but by working with a two-sector model produced a framework which resulted in a simple diagram – the IS/LM diagram – which became an ideal tool for basic macroeconomic analysis. Hicks's way of presenting the argument is in some ways superior to that adopted in the General Theory, because the original IS/LM model brings out very clearly how the relative price of capital and consumption goods enters into the determination of the solution, a point which is somewhat obscure in Keynes. It is ironic that one of the arguments later advanced against the IS/LM model, admittedly with simpler versions than Hicks's in mind, was that it omitted an essential feature of Keynes, the relative price of capital and consumption.

In the hands of others, the IS/LM model often became merely a model of an economy with all prices fixed, and was sometimes misused. However, it made the General Theory intelligible to a whole generation, not because it left out the subtleties, but because it captured the part of Keynes's message which is amenable to formalization.

A Contribution to the Theory of the Trade Cycle (1950) explains cycles as the outcome of the interaction between the multiplier and the accelerator. These systems are linear in their simplest formulations when they lead to cycles which are almost certainly either damped or anti-damped. A floor on or a ceiling to the level of economic activity may be added to keep the solution within bounds. The underlying solution, Hick's main model, may be damped, in which case the cycle will have to be kept alive by the frequent intervention of random shocks.

Late in his career Hicks published several series of lectures. In *Causality in Economics* (1979), he reacts to the 1974 IEA conference on 'The Micro-foundations of Macroeconomics'. Hicks's definition of causality is reminiscent of Hume, but without induction being importantly involved. There is a touch of philosophical amateurism about this work. The last chapter provides a statement of Hicks's views on the meaning of probability and on econometric methodology.

A Theory of Economic History (1969) is an ambitious sortie into foreign territory, but is the product of deep thought and reading. The main idea, that economic history is tied up with the development of the market, is one that few would question. However most historians would be tempted by a safe position according to which developments of ideas, knowledge, social institutions and so on, would all be seen as progressing in parallel with the development of the market, which consequently would enjoy no special status as a motive force. Put simply, Hicks's account gives a leading role to the market, although he does not go so far as to argue that the market drives history.

BIBLIOGRAPHY
The Theory of Wages (1932; 2nd edn, 1963).
(with R.G.D. Allen) 'A Reconsideration of the Theory of Value', *Economica* (1934), vol. I, part I, February, pp. 52–76; part II, May, 196–219.
'A Suggestion for Simplifying the Theory of Money', *Economica* (1935), vol. 2, February, pp.1–19.
'Mr Keynes and the "Classics"', *Econometrica* (1937), vol. 5, April, pp. 147–59.
Value and Capital (Oxford, 1939).
'The Foundations of Welfare Economics', *Economic Journal* (1939), vol. 49, December, pp. 696–712.
'The Valuation of the Social Income', *Economica* (1940), vol. 7, May, pp. 105–24.
The Social Framework (Oxford, 1942).
'The Valuation of the Social Income: A Comment on Professor Kuznets' Reflections', *Economica* (1948), vol. 15, August, pp. 163–72.
A Contribution to the Theory of the Trade Cycle (Oxford, 1950).
A Revision of Demand Theory (Oxford, 1956).
'The Measurement of Real Income', *Oxford Economic Papers* (1958), vol. 10, June, pp. 125–62.
Essays in World Economics (Oxford, 1959).
Capital and Growth (Oxford, 1965).
Critical Essays in Monetary Theory (Oxford, 1967).

A Theory of Economic History (Oxford, 1969).
Capital and Time: A Neo-Austrian Theory (Oxford, 1973).
'Recollections and Documents', *Economica* (1973), vol. 40, February, pp. 2–11.
The Crisis in Keynesian Economics (Oxford, 1974).
'The Scope and Status of Welfare Economics', *Oxford Economic Papers* (1975), vol. 27, no. 3, pp. 307–26.
Economic Perspectives (Oxford, 1977).
Causality in Economics (Oxford, 1979).
Collected Essays on Economic Theory (Oxford, 1981–3).

Further Reading
Bliss, C., 'Hicks, John Richard', in J. Eatwell, M. Milgate and P. Newman (eds), *The New Palgrave: A Dictionary of Economics* (1987, vol. 2, pp. 641–6).
——, 'Hicks on General Equilibrium and Stability', in H. Hagemann and O.F. Hamouda (eds), *The Legacy of Hicks: His Contributions to Economic Analysis* (1994).
Kaldor N., 'Welfare Propositions in Economics and Interpersonal Comparisons of Utility', *Economic Journal* (1939), vol. 49, pp. 549–52.
Kennedy, C., 'Capital Theory', in H. Hagemann and O.F. Hamouda (eds), *The Legacy of Hicks: His Contributions to Economic Analysis* (1994).
Little, I.M.D., *A Critique of Welfare Economics* (Oxford, 1950).
McFadden, D., 'On Hicksian Stability', in J.N. Wolfe (ed.), *Value Capital and Growth: Papers in Honour of Sir John Hicks* (Edinburgh, 1968).
Morishima, M., 'Capital and Growth', in H. Hagemann and O.F. Hamouda (eds), *The Legacy of Hicks: His Contributions to Economic Analysis* (1994).
Samuelson, P.A., *Foundations of Economic Analysis* (Cambridge, Massachusetts, 1947).
Sraffa, P., 'The Laws of Return Under Competitive Conditions', *Economic Journal* (1926), vol. 25, pp. 535–50

Christopher Bliss

HICKS, Ursula Kathleen (1896–1985)

Ursula Hicks was born Ursula Kathleen Webb on 17 September 1896 in Dublin, and died at Porch House, Blockley, Gloucestershire on 16 July 1985. Her parents, of whom she was the only daughter, were from Ulster and were members of the Society of Friends. Educated at Alexandra School in Dublin, Ursula Webb was pupil during part of the long tenure of headmistress Isabella Mulvany (1881–1927), who instilled the ethos that no career was off-limits for women. She then attended Roedean School in Brighton and read modern history at Somerville College, Oxford (BA 1918). After almost a decade of working, first briefly at the Ministry of Agriculture, then at the Workers' Educational Association (WEA), Webb was again to pursue studies, at the London School of Economics (BSc. Econ, 1934, MA 1936). She married John Hicks in 1935. She became a foundation fellow of Linacre College, Oxford (1964), and also a fellow of the Institute of Social Studies, The Hague. In addition to many visiting professorships, she was awarded a honorary doctorate in Economics from The Queen's University of Belfast.

It was her work experience with the WEA that first turned her interests to economics. The goal with which the Workers Educational Association was founded in 1903 was to provide opportunities for humanistic learning for adults from all walks of life, but especially for those who were socially and economically disadvantaged. In this work environment, she encountered many of the principles and theories of the contemporary world of economic dissenters. The newly radical connection between access to education and socio-economic change also resonated with the earlier influence of the Society of Friends in the Adult School Movement. Education was a strong focus in the Webb family as well as for the new socio-economic idealists, and this was a strong earlier influence.

In some biographies, Ursula Webb is explicitly identified as the daughter of renowned Fabians, Sidney and Beatrice WEBB. Although no genealogical link whatsoever has been established between these key socialists and this offspring of Irish Quakers, there is an important institutional one. In the early 1900s, as chairman of the trustees named in the will of fellow Fabian Henry Hunt Hutchinson, Sidney Webb, with instructions to dispose of the estate for 'socially progressive purposes', pushed to have the money used to encourage the research and study of economics. Consistent supporters of labour and human rights and strong internationalists, the Webbs had by 1929 left their mark on the institution Ursula Webb would attend. Undoubtedly, it was her experience in London, studying and teaching amongst an impassioned group of young economists from 1929 to 1936 at the LSE, which cemented her interest in economics, however stimulated it might have been before that time.

At the LSE, Webb's graduate supervisor was Lionel ROBBINS, newly appointed to the chair in political economy in 1929. The publications on which he was at work during her student days, *Essay on the Nature and Significance of Economic Science* (1932), and *Economic Planning and International Order* (1937), informed his teaching and advising, as it did his correspondence. Her thesis, published as *The Finance of the British Government 1920–1936* (1938), reflected Robbins's conviction of the potential dangers of government fiscal mismanagement: 'men, no matter how well intentioned they may think themselves, cannot be trusted not to abuse and distort the natural working of the market order'. Writing on a subject which was already being highlighted by KEYNES, she observed that, 'it is now generally agreed that the great extension of government influence on the economic system necessitates a much more thorough treatment of the economic aspect of public finance than was called for in the nineteenth century' (1938: xxxv). From her initial publication, she went on in 'Standards of Local Expenditure' (with J.R. Hicks) (1943), 'The Terminology of Tax Analysis' (1946), and *Public Finance* (1947) to refine her analysis of the cherished routes of government intervention, expenditure, taxation and monetary policy, into finely tuned functional macroeconomic classifications. The most important subject of her economic science was public finance, whether applied to standards for national accounting, circumstances of an economy under fluctuation or to the governments of newly developing states.

Ursula Webb and John Hicks had both attended an econometrics conference in Leiden in 1933, but she presumably became better known to him as managing editor and cofounder of *The Review of Economics* (as she had named *The Review of Economic Studies*, whose first issue appeared in October 1933). He then recommended her to Erik Lindahl to help him translate some essays into English. Webb and Hicks married in December 1935 in London. In the summer of 1935 John Hicks accepted a lectureship at Cambridge University, and in September the couple bought a brand-new house on Trumpington Road for £1,800. Although prevented by this move from being appointed to the lectureship Hicks was vacating at the LSE, as Robbins had hoped she would, Ursula Hicks subsequently found a number of teaching opportunities in Cambridge. She was also very busy preparing her thesis for publication, and by 1939 she and her husband had begun joint projects.

In 1938 John Hicks became Stanley Jevons Professor of Political Economy at Manchester University, and the couple moved to Prestbury, near Manchester. From 1941-5 Ursula Hicks commuted to Liverpool University where she was head of the economics department. In 1946 they moved to Oxford, where John Hicks became official fellow of Nuffield College (1946), and Drummond Professor of Political Economy (1952), and Ursula Hicks became university lecturer in public finance (1946), based on the increasing renown of her first book. In 1964 she became senior fellow of Linacre House, and then fellow emeritus in 1966. The couple moved themselves and their immense library to the Porch House at Blockley, earlier home of John Hicks's aunt, Winifred Stephens Whale. Having no children of their own, both were close to their extended families, which included Ursula's cousins in Dublin, but it was academe which absorbed them to the core. As unchanging over the decades as she had once described the British system of public finance, Ursula Hicks served as managing editor of the *Review of Economic Studies* for twenty-eight years, until October 1961. After his wife's death in 1985 at age eighty-nine, Sir John Hicks wrote of missing his 'fellow-worker for fifty years', having to write 'in monastic seclusion, without the benefit of continual discussion'. Upon his death, their library and home passed, as willed, to Oxford University.

The reality of economic inequality repeatedly commanded Hicks's attention. She felt challenged by the sentiment that 'it would be a good thing to mitigate inequality', as Robbins once put it in a letter to HARROD, and thought too that it must be due to 'a deficiency of a system of free market', with which taxes and other means of redistribution could deal. Her initial academic orientation, history, led her to pursue the issue first through the evidence of historical data to produce 'general principles of thought' which economists could apply to public finance problems including policies of growth and development.

Thus, linked to her initial historical interest in the institutions of public finance within Great Britain came an examination of their possible comparison with those of other countries and, even more dominant, their application in the developing world. Perhaps inspired by a year as visiting professor at Chicago and Harvard in 1946, Hicks admitted that the best she could do before 1948 to demonstrate her strong belief in the benefit of international comparisons was to include figures from the USA, a country which remained for her 'the most interesting and relevant comparison with the United Kingdom'. Attuned from the start to the connection between institutional structure and public finance, she advanced the view in 1938 that the US Constitution would 'probably have assumed a considerably different form from the one it has now developed' if it had incorporated certain British institutions, such as the Treasury, in its organization of national finances, and even its cabinet, designed after the accession of Charles II. Although her focus on England continued well through *British Public Finances: Their Structure and Development 1880-1952* (1954), in which she observed basic structural changes in public finance over a longer, 'striking' period in UK history, Hicks was drawn from the early 1950s to address both growth and development economics. It was almost as if the two additional priorities of the economic radicals of her youth, support for scientific research concerning poverty and enhancement of leadership in local communities, were emerging influences from her past.

Hicks had argued (1938) that public borrowing and monetary policy cannot successfully be divorced from expenditure and fiscal policy, and she went on to broaden the issue of raising productivity in the advanced countries to include Third World development. *Development from Below: A Study of Local Government and Finance in Developing Countries of the British Commonwealth* (1961) is the first main statement of her perspective on local-state relations in initiatives for development. A series of stints overseas – as visiting professor at the Delhi School of Economics, as economic adviser for the UN in India (1950), with the Revenue Allocation Commission in Nigeria (1950), in Jamaica as co-commissioner with her husband (1954), for the Central Bank in Ceylon (1957), as Fiscal Commissioner in Uganda (1962) and also in the Eastern Caribbean (1962) and in Eastern Nigeria (1964), became the main immediate source of Hicks's new orientation. These experiences in applied economics ran simultaneous to her lecture course at Oxford University; attended by a generations of international students, the course took book form as *Development Finance: Planning and Control* (1965).

'Development countries', as she called them, were appropriate fields to her for the application of the well-established techniques of the advanced countries, but, to avoid 'much waste of funds and material, disappointment and frustration', she insisted, these have to be adapted to the new setting's very different and 'imperfectly known' conditions, in terms of climate, resources, population changes, and so on. At a Working Party Conference in Exeter in 1959, Hicks, who edited its proceedings (1961), highlighted the urgency for guidance in these matters, since many of the countries in question were 'emergent' in two ways: at the same time as attempting accelerated development, they 'are experimenting with federal constitutions.' She argued that the success of a federal constitution depends on a division of political and fiscal powers both to correspond with 'the initial desired political and economic degree of integration' and to allow 'easy adjustment to keep the respective powers appropriate' over time.

As her later writings, such as *Federation of the East Caribbean Territories* (1963) or *Financing Metropolitan Government* (1967), reflect, Hicks was called upon to propose immediate, concrete measures of politico-economic organization to entities as diverse as proximate island nations and urban metropolitan unions, particularly those to allow for direct revenue sources for that level of government. Slightly later in *The Large City: A World Problem* (1974), she described the difficulties in implementing her vision for a metropolitan environment: 'decongested at the centre and growing in an organized fashion at the periphery'. By her last work on larger political unions, *Federalism – Failure and Success: A Comparative Study* (1978), she had moved well beyond one of the major fiscal concerns of her first book, roads and transport, having already noted that 'becoming too attached to the material aspects alone of an economic union as, for example, to the organization of transport and routes, might actually aggravate the socio-economic situation'. Nonetheless, perhaps in tribute to her first and major intellectual contribution, in a late publication, 'City Transport and Circulation Problems in the Less Developed Countries with Special Reference to India' (1972), she focused once again on this most-discussed aspect of regional economic development. Her ever-optimistic economic conclusion was that through cost equalization at the margin, a wise community will obviously not limit itself in the matter of transport, but will develop each particular type that is cost effective.

Ursula Hicks was important both as an academic advocate and a pragmatic advisor for public finance. John Hicks, in his own first major writing, acknowledged that his work had 'profited from the constant reminder' which he had 'from her work, that the place of economic theory is to be the servant of applied economics'.

BIBLIOGRAPHY

The Finance of the British Government 1920–1936 (1938; 2nd edn, 1970).
'Standards of Local Expenditure: A Problem of the Inequality of Incomes', *National Institute of Economic and Social Research Occasional Paper* (1943), vol. 6, no. 3.
'The Terminology of Tax Analysis', *Economic Journal* (1946), vol. LVI, pp. 39–50; repr. in *Readings in the Theory of Taxation* (1959).
Public Finance (1947; revised edn, 1951; 2nd edn, 1955; 3rd edn, 1968).
British Public Finances: Their Structure and Development 1880–1952 (1954).

Federalism and Economic Growth in Underdeveloped Countries: A Symposium (1961).
Development from Below. A Study of Local Government and Finance in Developing Countries of the British Commonwealth (1961).
Federation of the East Caribbean Territories (1963).
Development Finance: Planning and Control (1965).
Financing Metropolitan Government (1967).
'City Transport and Circulation Problems in the Less Developed Countries with Special Reference to India', Report of a Seminar on Transport (All India) held at Dharwar, Mysore, India (1972).
The Large City: A World Problem (1974).
Federalism – Failure and Success: A Comparative Study (1978).

Further Reading
David, W.L., *Public Finance, Planning and Economic Development: Essays in Honour of Ursula Hicks* (1973).
Hamouda, O.F., *John R. Hicks: The Economist's Economist* (Oxford, 1993).
Shoup, C.S. and Musgrave, R.A. (eds), *Readings in the Theory of Taxation* (Evanston, Illinois, 1959).

Omar F. Hamouda

HIGGS, Henry (1864–1940)

Higgs was born 4 March 1864 in Cornwall, the eleventh of thirteen children of Samuel Nicholas Higgs, master butcher, and his wife Anne. He died in Brighton on 21 May 1940. Of obscure and humble origins, which influenced his career choice and made essential the early attainment of financial security for his family, Higgs took full advantage of the meritocratic opportunities offered by a newly reformed civil service. Entering as a lower division clerk in 1881, he passed the competition for Class I in 1884, and for the next fifteen years served in the secretary's office of the General Post Office. Transferring to the Treasury in 1899, he attracted the attention of its Permanent Secretary, Edward Hamilton, from whom he learnt of the intricacies of Britain's public finances and which he in turn communicated in a series of books (1914, 1917, 1919, 1924), many of them originating in his frequent periods as Newmarch lecturer. He became private secretary to a succession of ministers, culminating with Henry Cambell-Bannerman when prime minister from 1905–8. He served as a special commissioner to Natal in 1902–3 and as inspector-general of finance in Egypt from 1912–15. He retired in 1921 as principal clerk. Higgs married Winifred Sarah South in 1908, and they had at least one child.

Upon securing his position within the established civil service in 1884, Higgs then enrolled in University College, London intending to pursue legal studies. He took his LLB in 1890 and was called to the bar, but it was economics rather than the law which quickly captivated him. He fell early under the influence of H.S. Foxwell, whose political economy lectures he attended in 1885–7, and thereafter his energies were increasingly devoted to economics and to the burgeoning economics profession. Quickly adept at the subject, he won a scholarship in 1886 to continue his studies at University College and the following year began lecturing in economics at Toynbee Hall. It was under Foxwell's influence that he then began his lifetime interest in the physiocrats, and in particular in Richard Cantillon, who was the subject of early papers (1891, 1892) and of his most significant contribution to the history of economic thought, his translation for the Royal Economic Society (RES) of Cantillon's *Essai* (1931). These were the fruits of long years spent vacationing in the Bibliothéque Nationale, as also was the published version of his series of lectures on the physiocrats (1897). (They were also made possible by the relaxed work schedule required of a late nineteenth-century civil servant.) However, and contrary to most accounts of Higgs's career, his first major economics paper was not on Cantillon but on a later French economist, Le Play (1890), whose writings on family budgets and labour statistics were an inspiration for the other work in which he was then engaged, as a member of one of the background studies for Charles Booth's investigations into London life and labour. He thus also published on working-class family budgets (1893; Booth et al. 1896), and was part of the advocacy coalition pressing the Board of Trade to improve the quantity and quality of official economic and social statistics (Collet 1940: 549–50).

Higgs is primarily regarded not for these writings but for his contribution to the British economics profession at an important early stage of its development. He was one of the founding members of the British Economic Association (later Royal Economic Society, RES), serving as the Association's first secretary and, with F.Y. EDGEWORTH, was joint editor of its *Economic Journal* between 1892 and 1905. While he continued too long on the RES Council, being still an active but unhelpful contributor to its meetings until his death (see J.M. KEYNES's bittersweet obituary, 1940), as Austin ROBINSON noted in the RES centenary volume: 'in his time and in [our] early history...Higgs played a major part and deserves a place in our memories...carrying on his shoulders in the early critical years much of the burden of keeping the Society and its *Journal* alive at a time when others failed to do so' (Robinson 1990: 164, 168). He displayed similar administrative and interpersonal skills in his re-editing of the *Palgrave Dictionary of Political Economy* (1923–6) and in his completion of various projects initiated but abandoned by Foxwell, most notably the publication of W.S. JEVONS, *The Principles of Economics* (1905) and *A Bibliography of Economics* (1935).

BIBLIOGRAPHY

'Frédéric Le Play', *Quarterly Journal of Economics* (1890), vol. 4, no. 4, pp. 408–33.

'Richard Cantillon', *Economic Journal* (1891), vol. 1, no. 2, pp. 262–91.

'Cantillon's Place in Economics', *Quarterly Journal of Economics* (1892), vol. 6, no. 4, pp. 436–56.

(with C. Booth and E. Aves) *Family Budgets, being the Income and Expenses of twenty-eight British Households, 1891–1894* (1896).

The Physiocrats: Six Lectures on the French Économistes of the 18th Century (1897).

(with H. Jevons) *W.S. Jevons, The Principles of Economics: A Fragment of a Treatise on the Industrial Mechanism of Society and Other Papers* (1905; repr. New York, 1965).

The Financial System of the United Kingdom (1914).

National Economy: An Outline of Public Administration (1917).

A Primer of National Finance (1919).

Palgrave's Dictionary of Political Economy, 3 vols (1923–6).

Financial Reform (1924).

Bibliography of Economics, 1751–1775 (Cambridge, 1935).

Further Reading

Cantillon, R., *Essai sur la Nature du Commerce en Général*, ed. H. Higgs (Cambridge, 1931).

Collet, C.E., 'Henry Higgs', *Economic Journal* (1940), vol. 50, no. 4, pp. 546–55, 558–61.

Keynes, J.M., 'Henry Higgs', *Economic Journal* (1940), vol. 50, no. 4, pp. 555–8.

Robinson, E.A.G., 'Fifty-Five Years on the Royal Economic Society Council', in J.D. Hey and D. Winch (eds), *A Century of Economics: 100 Years of the Royal Economic Society and the Economic Journal* (Oxford, 1990, pp. 161–92).

Roger Middleton

HILL, Alsager Hay (1839–1906)

Hill was born on 1 October 1839 at Gressonhall Hall in Norfolk. He died in Boston, Lincolnshire on 2 August 1906. He was the second son of John David Hay Hill and his wife Margaret Collett of Hemel Hempstead. Hill was educated at Brighton College (1850–4), Cheltenham College (1854–7), Caius College and then Trinity Hall, Cambridge. While at Cambridge, he formed the 'Chit Chat' debating club and became treasurer of the Union. He was awarded his LLB in 1862. He entered the Inner Temple on 3 October 1860 and was called to the bar on 26 January 1864. He joined the south-eastern circuit, but soon turned his attention to social issues and left the legal profession.

Hill began writing poetry when he was still at school, an activity that continued for the rest of his life. He published *Footprints of Life* in 1857 when he was still at school and *A Household Queen* in 1881. In 1877, Hill was elected a member of the Athenaeum, and was also president of the Cheltonian Society (1877–8). During his later years, he retired to Boston in Lincolnshire. He was buried at the family estate at Gressonhall.

Hill was an almoner for the Society for the Relief of Distress in the east of London, an organization set up in 1860. From its foundation in 1869, he was prominent in the work of the Charity Organisation Society; he was its honorary secretary until 1870 and an active member of its council until 1880. The aim of the COS was to provide better administration for charity relief, emphasizing the need for self-help. At this time there was great concern that charity and self help were conflicting issues. Hill was vice-president of the National Sunday League from 1876 until 1890: this movement advocated 'rational' recreation on Sundays. Hill also was a supporter of the Working Men's Club and Institute Union.

Hill wrote a number of pamphlets on poverty and unemployment. The most important of these was *Our Unemployed* (1867), in which he noted the effects of unemployment on the poor and suggested a national system of labour registration. He was one of the first people to draw public attention to the problems of unemployment, and wrote a number of letters to newspapers in 1868 about the ineffectiveness of the poor law, asking for a more 'scientific' classification of paupers. On a more practical level, in 1871 Hill established the 'Employment Inquiry Office and Labour Registry' in Soho: this was the origin of labour exchanges. When the office moved to Covent Garden it was renamed as the Central Labour Exchange. As director, Hill tried to help applicants to find work or to arrange emigration; he also advised clients on how to obtain assistance. In his *Statutes for the People* (1871), Hill tried to give the working classes access to cheap legal advice. Concurrently, Hill founded and edited the *Labour News*, a nationally available publication in which both employers and workmen could advertise. This publication was not profitable and drained Hill's financial resources so that when he retired, he had little upon which to live.

BIBLIOGRAPHY
Footprints of Life (1857).
Rhymes with Good Reason (1870–1).
Lancashire Labour and London Poor (1871).
Impediments to the Circulation of Labour (1873).
The Unemployed in Great Cities (1877).
A Household Queen (1881).
Vagrancy (1881).

Marjorie Bloy

HILL, Edwin (1793–1876)

Hill was born on 25 November 1793 in Birmingham. He died on 6 November 1876 at 1 St. Mark's Square, Regent's Park, London, and was buried in Highgate cemetery. He was the second son and one of eight children born to Thomas Wright Hill and his wife Sarah Lea: the family originated in Kidderminster and was Unitarian by faith. Hill was an elder brother of Sir Rowland Hill, the inventor of the penny post. He was educated at his father's school at Hill Top, on the outskirts of Birmingham. He married Anne Bucknall from Kidderminster. The couple had ten children, seven of whom survived their father.

Hill started work at the Fazeley Street rolling mills in Birmingham, eventually becoming manager of the works. However, he gave up this employment in 1827 in order to join his brother Rowland in establishing a new school at Bruce Castle, Tottenham. This replaced Hazelwood, the Hills's school in Birmingham. The Hill family held everything in common, and appointed Edwin as arbitrator of the property, which by 1827 amounted to several thousand pounds.

Rowland Hill established the penny post in 1840, and Edwin Hill was appointed as supervisor of stamps at Somerset House. He controlled the manufacture of the stamps until his retirement in 1872. Hill had always been interested in inventions and had great skills in mechanics. He improved the stamp-producing machinery, and with Warren de la Rue, was responsible for the invention of an envelope-folding machine. This machine was produced in direct response to the increase in the number of letters sent following the introduction of the penny post, and could produce sixty envelopes a minute, provided the children operating it fed in the paper fast enough. It was displayed at the Great Exhibition.

In 1856 Hill published the *Principles of Currency: Means of Ensuring Uniformity of Value and Adequacy of Supply*. Here he proposed that 'government should prepare and issue under the authority of parliament an adequate amount of interest-bearing securities, almost identical with exchequer bills; and that these be made a legal tender for their principal sum, together with their accumulated interest up to the day of tender, according to a table to be printed upon the face of each bill.'

Hill also published *Criminal Capitalists* (1870–2), a series of pamphlets that made suggestions for crime reduction. His ideas concerned the owners of lodging houses who knowingly provided accommodation for criminals and shops where stolen goods could be disposed. Hill proposed to combat crime by first catching and prosecuting the landlords, thus depriving criminals of 'safe houses' and points of sale for the stolen goods.

BIBLIOGRAPHY
Principles of Currency: Means of Ensuring Uniformity of Value and Adequacy of Supply (1856).
Criminal Capitalists (1870–2).

Marjorie Bloy

HILL BURTON, John *see* Burton, John Hill

HILTON, Rodney (1916–2002)

Hilton was born in Middleton, Manchester on 17 November 1916, and died in Birmingham on 7 June 2002. He was educated at Manchester Grammar School and Balliol College, Oxford, where his fellow students included the historian Christopher Hill and the future politician Denis Healey. He was also active in left-wing politics, and a member of the Labour Club. He completed his DPhil in 1939, writing a thesis on the rural economy of Leicestershire from the thirteenth to the fifteenth centuries, applying the Marxist analysis to the emergence of agrarian capitalism. He joined the army in 1940, and served with the Eighth Army in Palestine and Syria, North Africa and then Italy. Discharged at the end of the Second World War, he took up a teaching post at the University of Birmingham in 1946, remaining there until his retirement in 1982. He was appointed professor of medieval social history in 1983.

After the war, Hilton was an active member of the Communist Party, along with other high-profile academic figures such as E.P. Thompson, Eric Hobsbawm, Christopher Hill and Maurice DOBB. He was a member of the Communist Party Historians Group that in 1952 founded the journal *Past and Present*, devoted to study of the history of the working classes. Like many Marxists, Hilton became disillusioned with the party, and resigned following the Soviet invasion of Hungary in 1956.

Hilton applied Marxist theories to English rural history in his thesis, published as *The Economic Development of Some Leicestershire Estates in the Fourteenth and Fifteenth Centuries* (1947) and in what many see as his best work, *The English Peasantry in the Later Middle Ages* (1975). He saw feudalism as a mode of production, and defined the rural peasantry as a distinct class, 'as determined by its place in the production of society's material needs; not as a status group determined by attributed esteem, dignity or honour' (1975: 12). This approach enabled Hilton to analyse the medieval rural economy not only in terms of class conflict but also inter-class co-operation and co-dependence. But he was never a strong ideologue, and in the words of Christopher Dyer, 'took medieval peasants seriously, as people with ideas, who were able to organise themselves in purposeful actions' (Dyer 2002). He placed much value on evidence and sources, and was one of the first historians to advocate the use of archaeological evidence; critical in his own field, where documentary evidence was sometimes lacking; for a number of years at Birmingham, he participated annually in local archaeological digs. Close engagement with the sources and the evidence was a strong trait of Hilton's work.

Later projects included studies of class rebellion in the Middle Ages, especially of the Peasants' Revolt of 1381, and also of the Robin Hood legend. Late in his career Hilton transferred his attention to medieval towns; his last work, *English and French Towns in Feudal Society: A Comparative Study* (1995), looked at similarities and differences in urban development on both sides of the English Channel. Through much of his career, Hilton worked closely with contemporary French historians and spoke frequently at conferences (he was a fluent speaker of French). He likewise had a considerable following among Spanish historians, and a number of his works were translated into Spanish.

Despite the waning of Marxism, Hilton's work has stood up well to the test of time, thanks largely to his close attention to evidence and sources. His emphasis on the peasantry of the Middle Ages as a distinct economic and social class with a strong identity has carried over into many other fields of investigation. He had indeed much in common with Michael POSTAN, who at the time was considered Hilton's ideological rival, but who in fact investigated many of the same problems and came to at least some of the same conclusions. A quiet and modest man, Hilton was a fine teacher who inspired a generation of later historians. He suffered from Alzheimer's disease in later life, which sadly put an end to his work before its time.

BIBLIOGRAPHY
The Economic Development of Some Leicestershire Estates in the Fourteenth and Fifteenth Centuries (1947).

The English Peasantry in the Later Middle Ages (1975).
The Transition from Feudalism to Capitalism (1976).
Bond Man Made Free: Medieval Peasant Movements and The English Rising of 1381 (1977).
Class Conflict and the Crisis of Capitalism (1985).
English and French Towns in Feudal Society: A Comparative Study (1995).

Further Reading
Dyer, C., Obituary, *The Guardian* (2002), 10 June.
Kaye, H.J., *The British Marxist Historians: An Introductory Analysis* (Cambridge, 1984).

Morgen Witzel

HIRST, Francis Wrigley (1873–1953)

Hirst was born 10 June 1873 at Huddersfield, Yorkshire and died 22 February 1853 at Singleton, Suffolk. He was one of five children of a wool merchant, Alfred Hirst, and his wife, Mary Wrigley; his mother was a distant cousin of the Liberal politician H.H. Asquith. He was educated at Clifton school and then won a scholarship to Wadham College, Oxford in 1891, where he took a first in *literae humaniores* in 1896 and was also president of the Oxford Union. In 1896 he went to London to study at the London School of Economics, then the Inner Temple, and was called to the bar in 1899. He practised law but did not flourish, apparently preferring a more contemplative way of life and becoming increasingly interested in writing.

At Oxford he had met Lawrence HAMMOND, and both were contributors to the volume *Essays on Liberalism* in 1897, Hirst's contribution being on 'Liberalism and Wealth'. This book brought Hirst to the attention of senior figures in the Liberal Party, and he was asked to contribute to a life of Gladstone, a project that brought him into contact with Lord Morley, who became a friend and patron. He began writing essays for *The Speaker*, then edited by Hammond, and then for *The Nation*; he published a biography of Adam SMITH in 1904. His reputation as a liberal writer and thinker was now confirmed, and in 1907 he was appointed editor of *The Economist*. Here he gathered an exceptional team of journalists, including Walter LAYTON, himself a future editor of the journal, and future Italian president Luigi Einaudi. Peace, liberty and economy were the key themes of Hirst's tenure at *The Economist*, but the former in particular became harder to support after 1914. Hirst, who had opposed the Boer War, was unhappy about British commitment to the First World War, and pressure from government helped to bring about his dismissal in 1916.

Hirst then turned to writing on a full-time basis, and through the 1920s and 1930s produced a stream of important works including further work on Gladstone and then *Wall Street and Lombard Street* (1931), *Liberty and Tyranny* (1935) and *Economic Freedom and Private Property* (1935). In all three of these latter works and in others such as *The Need for Public Economy* (1931), Hirst argued for the maintenance of liberal economic values: private property, free trade, low taxation, low government expenditure, and the absence of the state from economic affairs. He has been called libertarian rather than liberal, and certainly the libertarians would have found much to support their own case; but the heart of Hirst's argument is not so much about personal freedom as to say that the economy functions best when left to regulate itself. This of course put him very much at odds with J.M. KEYNES and his followers, who were arguing much the opposite; Roy HARROD once commented, damning with faint praise, that Hirst's views were shallow but delightfully presented. There is a more than a hint here of the contempt of the academic for the outsider, and heterodox though Hirst's views were at this time, they were far from shallow. Like F.A. HAYEK, he has been consistently presented as being far more right-wing than he really was; in fact, he was nothing more or less than one of the last nineteenth-century free trade liberals.

His shunning by the Cambridge school did not appear to bother Hirst, and he continued to write and work very actively. As well as his books, he produced newspaper articles and a stream of caustic letters to *The Times*, and served as a governor of the London School of Economics. He was a regular visitor to the USA, where his sister was professor of classics at Columbia University; unsurprisingly, his views found much more popular acceptance than in Britain. There he caused a mild furore by referring to the welfare state as 'the Beveridge hoax' (in *Principles of Prosperity*, 1944) and predicting that it would lead to high taxes and industrial decline. He had stood unsuccessfully for parliament on a liberal ticket in 1919, but from 1930 on withdrew into a kind of intellectual isolation, apparently quite happy to challenge any and all economic and political orthodoxies. Despite this he remained a warm and sociable man with many friends, even among his intellectual enemies.

BIBLIOGRAPHY
'Liberalism and Wealth', in *Essays in Liberalism by Six Oxford Men* (1897).
(with J.L. Hammond and G. Murray) *Liberalism and the Empire* (1900).
Free Trade and Other Fundamental Doctrines of the Manchester School (1903).
Adam Smith (1904).
The Stock Exchange: A Short Study in Investment and Speculation (1911).
The Political Economy of War (1915).
Gladstone as Financier and Economist (1931).
Wall Street and Lombard Street (1931).
The Need for Public Economy (1931).
Money: Gold, Silver and Paper (1933).
Liberty and Tyranny (1935).
Economic Freedom and Private Property (1935).
Free Markets or Monopoly (1941).
Principles of Prosperity (1944).

Further Reading
F.W. Hirst, *By His Friends* (1958).
Edwards, R.D., *The Pursuit of Reason: The Economist 1843–1993* (1993).

Morgen Witzel

HOBBES, Thomas (1588–1679)

Hobbes was born at Westport (now a part of Malmesbury), Wiltshire on 5 April 1588. He died 4 December 1679 at Hardwick, Derbyshire. He was brought up by his uncle Francis, a prosperous glover, and educated at Magdalen Hall, Oxford (BA 1607). He then took a position as a tutor in the service of the Earl of Cavendish. He later said that the next years, spent with the young earl, were the happiest part of his life. He travelled in to France in 1610–13, and met Francis BACON in 1621, handling the translation into Latin of the latter's *Essays*. In 1628 he became tutor to the son of Sir G. Clifton, and returned to Paris in 1629, where he studied physics, mathematics and Euclid's *Elements*. His third tour to the continent (1634–37), in company with his pupil, gave him the chance to meet Mersenne, who in turn introduced him to Gassendi and Descartes. Hobbes was admitted to this circle, to which he remained attached the rest of his life. He also got to know Huygens, and visited Galileo at Florence.

Back in England in 1640, Hobbes published the first draft of his *Elements of Law, Natural and Politic.* The same year the Long Parliament met, and Hobbes saw himself in danger and left for France. In Paris, he taught mathematics to the Prince of Wales, later Charles II. There also, he published *De Cive* (1642) and his great book *Leviathan* (1651), a theory of the society and the State. The criticism he received from the future Charles II, the French clergy and the Anglican ministers, hurt badly. Later (1651), the book was printed in London. Taking advantage of Cromwell's amnesty, Hobbes returned to England in 1653, and published, between 1655 and 1658, *De corpore* and *De homine*. The Restoration (1660) coincided with the end of his public life; Hobbes spent the rest of his life reading and writing his autobiography.

Hobbes starts from the positivist logic dominant in the intellectual atmosphere of the seventeenth century, which considers man as a being who always moves in the environment of means and excluded from consideration the existence of a final cause in actions. The method he uses is rationalist, deduced from certain initial premises. The human being is the inventor of the word, his most precious gift and the touchstone of his rationality. Rationalism situates us before one of Hobbes's central problems: the limits of reason in its approach to reality.

The primary human impulse is to preserve one's own life and to avoid death. Passions are movement. Reason understands means only as the instruments by which each person may obtain a comfortable life. This leads him to remain always in a naturalistic plane. It is a formulation of optimistic rationalism: 'reason itself cannot err'. This is the nucleus of his rationalist platform: 'reason it selfe is always Right Reason', what is reasonable must be true. His thesis is that all problems can be resolved by means of 'right Reason constituted by Nature'.

In Hobbes's thought we encounter the essential elements of the so-called bourgeois mentality, linked by birth and later evolution to capitalist ideology. Such a manner of understanding society is termed 'chrematistic'. Hobbes's *Leviathan* contains an idea of human beings which contains elements of the model of 'economic man' (particularly individualist) and Hobbes was the first author to elaborate this conception.

Hobbes is the father of mainstream English thought, displaying a series of features which all later authors of the school would share: a philosophical nominalism based on linguistic logic; opposition to abstract metaphysics; an evolutionary materialism; a pragmatic and utilitarian mentality in questions of ethics and politics; agnosticism and religious indifference; moral philosophy based on sentiment; an individualism of freedom as basic vital attitude; an inclination towards liberalism; and a fascination for the scientific method. Hobbes based his entire speculative edifice on four empirical principles: fear, security, selfishness and domination or property. It is difficult to resist seeing in these presuppositions the principal pieces of the capitalist puzzle: fear and the desire to assure the peaceful possession of acquired property lead to a selfish (individualistic) attitude. It suffices to add that by acting in this manner, the welfare of society is achieved, and we arrive at the Smithian invisible hand.

Hobbes finds inadequate the motives of traditional society (reason that guides man to virtue) for a realist platform which includes economic criteria. He proposes an alternative theory based in what is most radical and strongest in man, his passions and interest. Gain is the main motive in men's actions. The value of a man is his price, what is offered for the use of his power. From that point are deduced the characteristics of this new man who will be the object of study by economic science: the person is levelled to the set of things which enter the transactions of the market; his value is that which is paid to use what he has; the demand for his services conditions his price; the buyer is the one with the power in the transaction. Hobbes finds no other moral base for establishing the value of things. Man's work is merchandise; the market sets its value. The equality of things' value is proven by the very fact of exchange. Notably, Hobbes was in favour of taxing consumption rather than income, arguing that any tax should be put on the value of goods consumed rather than labour supplied. Fair taxation should take note of our propensity to consume, while the frugal labourer who spent little should be rewarded for his efforts.

Hobbes had a bourgeois mentality, and used a model which corresponds to a mercantile capitalist society. Work is considered as merchandise. The traditional concept of justice is abandoned. For economic man, it is not so much political rights as security in the market that matters; capitalist liberalism inherits from Hobbes its individualistic base and its bourgeois financial platform.

BIBLIOGRAPHY
Essays (Paris, 1621).
Translation of Thucydides (1629; repr. 1634, 1676).
The Elements of Law, Natural and Politique (1640).
De Cive (Paris, 1642; London, 1651).
Leviathan (Paris and London, 1651; Amsterdam, 1668).
De Corpore (1655).
De Homine (1658).
Problemata Physica (1662).
Considerations upon the Refutation, Loyalty, Manners, and Religion of Thomas Hobbes (1662).
T. H. Opera philosophica quae latine scripsit (Amsterdam, 1668; repr.1839–45).
Autobiography (1672).
The Behemoth: History of the Causes of the Civil Wars of England (1679; repr. 1681).
Vita, carmine expressa (1679).
Dialogue between a Philosopher and a Student of the Common Law of England (1681).
Historia Ecclesiastica, Carmine Elegiaco concinnata (1688).

Further Reading
Benson, B., 'Emerging From the Hobbesian Jungle', *Constitutional Political Economy* (1994), vol. V, pp. 129–58.
Bobbio, N., *Thomas Hobbes and the Natural Law Tradition* (Chicago, 1993).
Chapell, V.C. (ed.), *Thomas Hobbes* (New York, 1992).
Gauthier, D., *Morals by Agreements*, (Oxford, 1986).
Green, A.W., *Hobbes and Human Nature* (New Brunswick, New Jersey, 1993).
Hoffman, P., *The Quest for Power: Hobbes, Descartes, & Emergence of Modernity* (Atlantic Highlands, New Jersey, 1996).
MacPherson, C.B., *The Political Theory of Possessive Individualism: Hobbes to Locke* (1962).
Myers, M.L., *The Soul of Modern Economic Man: Ideas of Self-Interest, Thomas Hobbes to Adam Smith* (Chicago, 1983).
Robertson, G.C., *Opera Omnia* (1886).
Rider, R., 'War, Pillage, and Markets', *Public Choice* (1993), vol. 75, pp. 149–56.
Schmitt, C., *The Leviathan in the State Theory of Thomas Hobbes: Meaning and Failure of a Political Symbol* (Westport, Connecticut, 1996).
Thomas, K., 'The Social Origin of Hobbes' Political Thought', in K.C. Brown (ed.), *Hobbes Studies* (Cambridge, 1965).
Tönnies, F., *Life and Works of Thomas Hobbes* (1932).

Jesùs M. Zaratiegui

HOBSON, John Atkinson (1858–1940)

Hobson was born in Derby on 6 July 1858, and died in London on 1 April 1940. His ashes were dispersed in the Garden of Remembrance, Golders Green Crematorium. He was second of four children to Josephine (née Atkinson) and

William Hobson, founder and proprietor of the *Derbyshire Advertiser and Journal*. His older brother, Ernest Hobson, coached J.M. KEYNES for the tripos in mathematics and was Sadleirian Professor of Mathematics at Cambridge University.

Hobson began his education in economics while still in his teens with courses offered by the Cambridge University Extension Movement, using texts by J.S. MILL and Millicent Garrett FAWCETT. He went on to Lincoln College, Oxford on an open scholarship achieving a second in classics, a third in *literae humaniores* and a blue in the high jump. Although his examination performance was not distinguished, he credited his classical education with liberating him from the materialistic and utilitarian ethos of the Victorian age.

Upon completing his degree at Oxford, Hobson taught school in Faversham and later, Exeter. While in Exeter, he met A.F. MUMMERY, the businessman and famous mountaineer. Mummery persuaded Hobson of the truth of the oversaving doctrine, that business depressions can be caused by insufficient consumer spending. The oversaving doctrine had long been considered a fallacy in economics, and initially Hobson resisted Mummery's arguments. But he was eventually convinced, and together they wrote *The Physiology of Industry* (1889). The book was poorly received, with F.Y. EDGEWORTH writing a sharply negative review. At the time, Hobson had given up school teaching to work as a university extension lecturer in economics and literature. The publication of his book, however, led H.S. FOXWELL to recommend that he not be allowed to teach economics. Establishment economists considered the doctrine of oversaving not only scientifically wrong, but pernicious in its effect of discouraging the saving deemed necessary for economic progress. The book was vindicated, to a large extent, when Keynes gave it a lengthy tribute in his *General Theory on Employment, Interest and Prices*.

Hobson and Mummery put greater emphasis than did Keynes on the problem of balancing the growth in productive capacity with the growth in consumption. Their implicit model bears more resemblance to the Harrod–Domar growth model than to Keynes's more static construction. It contains an early account of the acceleration principle that states that investment spending will pick up when output levels are stimulated with increased consumption. Hobson and Mummery saw the chief problem as an insufficiency of consumer demand relative to productive capacity, and recommended measures to put more purchasing power into the hands of the poor, whereas Keynes put more emphasis on stimulating investment spending.

By 1887, Hobson had given up his teaching post and had moved to London to pursue his writing career. His output of books, pamphlets and official reports was prodigious. Throughout the rest of his life he was to produce, on average, almost one major work a year. He was also an active journalist. Besides contributing a weekly column to his father's newspaper in Derby, he wrote numerous reviews and articles in various progressive periodicals (see Pheby 1994: 252–77 for a complete bibliography of his writings).

Hobson was active in the Ethical Movement, giving frequent public lectures during which he tested ideas that found their way into his books. Well connected within the progressive intelligentsia in London, Hobson was one of the original members of the Rainbow Circle, a diverse group that met monthly to discuss economic and political issues. He also enjoyed the weekly lunches of the writers and editors at the *Nation*, where he was dubbed 'jester-in-chief' for his ready wit. Hobson attended meetings of different socialist groups, although he never felt fully comfortable with any particular sect. Friends who were influential while he was in his thirties included future Labour Prime Minister Ramsay MacDonald and the more conservative J.M. Robertson, the author of *The Fallacy of Saving*.

Hobson's friendship with one of the Fabian essayists, William Clarke, led to a contract to write a survey of capitalism, published in 1894 as *The Evolution of Modern Capitalism*. This was used as a text in many colleges and did much to rebuild Hobson's battered reputation. Hobson contrasted his straightforward, common-sense approach with that of MARX, whose Hegelian dialectic and labour theory of value, he thought, only led to confusion.

In 1899, an article by Hobson on the Boer War prompted L.T. Hobhouse to suggest to his editor at the *Manchester Guardian* that Hobson be sent to South Africa to serve as a correspondent. Hobson met with leading political and business figures in South Africa, and was startled by the degree of influence that business interests had in determining foreign policy. His experiences are recorded in *The War in South Africa* (1900) and formed the basis two other books, *The Psychology of Jingoism* (1901) and *Imperialism: A Study* (1902). Fellow Derby native Herbert SPENCER wrote to Hobson praising the *Psychology of Jingoism*. Hobson had read Spencer's *Study of Sociology* at a young age and noted that it had 'a profound influence' (1938: 23).

Imperialism: A Study is the most famous of Hobson's writings, in large part because it was prominently and approvingly cited by V.I. Lenin in his own *Imperialism, the Highest Stage of Capitalism*. Hobson argues that the economic 'taproot' of imperialism is the profit seeking of business elites, who as a result of oversaving at home, seek out foreign markets. He provides statistical evidence that the overall costs of imperialist expansion exceed the benefits, buttressing his position that business interests are the primary beneficiaries and the motivating force behind the expansion. He later conceded, however, that he was led by his experience in South Africa to 'an excessive and too simple advocacy of the economic determination of history' (1938: 63).

In 1900, Hobson once again irritated the economics establishment with the publication of *The Economics of Distribution*. In this work, he attempted a unified theory of distribution in which all factors of production potentially earn a monopoly rent. He criticized neoclassical distribution theory for its neglect of differences in bargaining power as a determinant of prices, maintaining that a surplus obtains in any transaction and that it will be secured by the transactor with the greater bargaining power. His theory led him to the conclusion that the market economy leads to an unfair distribution of income. He wrote of this conclusion that it was: 'my most destructive heresy, and therefore the one for which I have least succeeded in gaining attention, even in the form of hostile criticism, from the orthodox economists' (1938: 168).

Hobson's criticisms of neoclassical economics were indeed dismissed, rather than refuted, by economists such as Alfred MARSHALL and Joseph Schumpeter. They tended to believe that his views were based on a misunderstanding, due to his lack of formal training. Undeterred, Hobson continued to work to develop his alternative economics of welfare, writing numerous books including *The Social Problem: Life and Work* (1900) and *Work and Wealth: A Human Valuation* (1914).

In the mid-1890s Hobson had been asked by Sir Charles Mallet to write a book on John RUSKIN. Hobson was ignited by Ruskin's phrase 'there is no wealth but life', making it the central tenet of his emerging humanist economics. He rejected the idea of economics as a distinct discipline that could safely ignore political, psychological, ethical and sociological factors, and believed that the reduction of economics to a mathematical science led to significant distortion.

Hobson married the daughter of a prominent New Jersey lawyer, and was to spend many months travelling in the United States and Canada giving lectures and learning about American capitalism. He noted a more ruthless competition than was found in Great Britain, and expressed concern about rising monopoly power. He was friendly with Henry D. Lloyd,

Lincoln Steffens and others who were labelled 'muck-rakers' in what Hobson termed 'the Press of the profiteers' (1938: 68). Other American associates with whom he expressed sympathy included sociologists E.A. Ross and Thorstein Veblen. His book *Veblen* (1936) provides a succinct and readable introduction to Veblen's ideas.

Hobson was active in the anti-war movement in Great Britain, and in 1916 resigned from the Liberal Party in protest over the entry into the war and its protectionist policies. He was on the executive committee of the Union of Democratic Control, which was started by a group of politicians who were against secret diplomacy. His *Richard Cobden: The International Man* (1918) emphasizes Cobden's distrust of foreign statecraft and his advocacy of free trade as a means to peaceful relations between nations. In 1918 Hobson was defeated narrowly when he ran as an Independent for a seat in the House of Commons. Although he did not join the newly formed Independent Labour Party, he served on its policy committee and drafted a proposal for a living wage in 1925.

The economic aftermath of the war strengthened Hobson's conviction that politics and economics should be brought together in an organic union. Hobson is considered to be one of the architects of Britain's welfare state, and indeed, many of his policy recommendations were eventually enacted. Besides measures to even the distribution of income, he advocated a shorter working day and workplace health and safely regulations. Sceptical about the workability of full-fledged socialism, he envisioned a mixed economy in which private entrepreneurs would operate along side state-run industries providing for basic consumption needs.

In 1929, Hobson participated, along with Keynes and others, in a series of luncheons organized by Prime Minister Ramsay MacDonald, prior to his setting up an Economic Advisory Council. Although Hobson was not among those selected for the Council, he was offered a peerage in 1931. Hobson refused it in protest over the Labour government's economic policies.

Towards the end of his life Hobson reflected on the question of whether it is possible to conduct a disinterested study of society. His *Free Thought in the Social Sciences* (1926) presents a pessimistic view on the possibility of progress in the social sciences, no doubt reflecting some of his disappointment in being unable to convince mainstream economists of the truth of his positions. In his short autobiography, *Confessions of an Economic Heretic* (1938), Hobson pursued the theme further. He acknowledged that his life's work in economics was out of step with the orthodoxy and had gained him little recognition, but nonetheless affirmed his personal confidence in its value.

BIBLIOGRAPHY

(with A.F. Mummery) *The Physiology of Industry: Being an Exposure of Certain Fallacies in Existing Theories of Economics* (1889).
The Evolution of Modern Capitalism: A Study of Machine Production (1894).
John Ruskin: Social Reformer (1898).
The Economics of Distribution (1900).
The War in South Africa: Its Causes and Effects (1900).
The Social Problem: Life and Work (1900).
The Psychology of Jingoism (1901).
Imperialism: A Study (1902).
Work and Wealth: A Human Valuation (1914).
Richard Cobden: The International Man (1918).
Free-thought in the Social Sciences (1926).
Veblen (1936).
Confessions of an Economic Heretic (1938).

Further Reading
Allet, J., *New Liberalism: The Political Economy of J. A. Hobson* (Toronto, 1981).

Freeden, M. (ed.), *Reappraising J.A. Hobson: Humanism and Welfare* (1990).
Pheby, J. (ed.), *J.A. Hobson After Fifty Years: Freethinker of the Social Sciences* (New York, 1994).
Schneider, M., *J. A. Hobson* (1996).
Townshend, J., *J. A. Hobson* (Manchester, 1990).

Fiona Maclachlan

HOBSON, Samuel George (1870–1940)

Hobson was born in Belfast to an Ulster Quaker family in 1864. After working as a technical journalist and merchant, he joined the Fabian Society and the Independent Labour Party in the early 1890s, standing unsuccessfully for Parliament as a Labour candidate for East Bristol in 1895 and for Rochdale in 1906. By 1910 he had left the ILP and the Fabians, feeling that they had lost the revolutionary vision of socialism, and contributed a series of articles to the influential periodical, *New Age*. These were collected and published in book form as *National Guilds: An Inquiry into the Wage System and the Way Out* in 1914. Hobson protested when the first edition appeared under the name of A.P. Orage, the *New Age*'s editor, and the second edition appeared under Hobson's name; in fact Hobson drafted and Orage revised the text, and both were responsible for its final form. Hobson's book ran through three editions between 1914 and 1920, and was translated into several languages; it proved to be extremely influential on the intellectual formation of the Guild Socialist movement in Britain through the writings and activities of G.D.H. COLE. His 'personal life was not invariably impeccable' (Cole 1971) and some of his business enterprises in Latin America seem to have been shady. He died in 1940, probably in London.

Hobson was inspired by the medievalism of Arthur PENTY, but was less concerned with the horror at industrialism and more with the problems of capitalism and the modern state as the enemy of fulfilling human potential. He rejected state socialism along with capitalism because both treated human labour as a mere commodity in the marketplace, excluding it from all control over the management of the economy. It was the system of wages which led to the subjection of labour to the employer, and Hobson looked to the trades unions to move beyond their present role of negotiating the sale of labour power to taking up the cause of the emancipation of labour from the whole system by which it was bought and sold. At a time of union militancy in which syndicalist ideas of union control were popular among sections of the left, Hobson argued that the union should monopolize the sale of labour, forcing the employer to pay the wage bill directly to the union, which would then take responsibility for distributing that wage among the work force. In this way, the unions would be placed in a position where taking control of ownership, and control of industry would become a formality The unions would then become national guilds, co-operating with other guilds to satisfy human economic needs. The state, as the representative of the community, held the final authority over industrial affairs and would be the owner of the tools of production while the guilds were trustee of productions. While the state could arbitrate the more difficult conflicts between the guilds, Hobson sought to exclude it from economic affairs as much as possible.

BIBLIOGRAPHY
National Guilds: An Inquiry into the Wage System and the Way Out (1914).
Pilgrim to the Left (1938).
Further Reading
Cole, M., *The Life of G.D.H. Cole* (1971).

Cole, G.D.H., *A History of Socialist Thought* (1956).
Foote, G., *The Labour Party's Political Thought: A History*, 3rd edn (1997).
Glass, S.T., *The Responsible Society: The Ideas of Guild Socialism* (1966).

Geoffrey Foote

HODGES, James (fl. 1695–1705)

Almost nothing is known of James Hodges apart from the fact that he was a Scot and wrote a series of pamphlets in both London and Edinburgh in the late seventeenth and early eighteenth centuries. The flyleaf of one of his works describes him as a gentleman. He opposed the Darien Colony on the grounds that that the Scottish occupation of the colony was illegal, the territory being the property of Spain; among the supporters of the project, he singled out Andrew FLETCHER for particular criticism. He also opposed the Act of Union, and wrote a pamphlet rebutting DEFOE. Curiously, contemporaries in Scotland regarded him as being an agent provocateur in the service of London much as Defoe himself was (Prebble 2000).

Hodges's major work on economics is *The Present State of England, as to Coin and Publick Charges* (1697), and he later refined some of his views in *Considerations and Proposals, for Supplying the present Scarcity of Money, and Advancing Trade* (1705), the latter work being primarily concerned with Scotland. Hodges's starting point is the linkage of money supply with economic strength; a strong economy is one with considerable quantities of money in circulation, while a weak one has little money and suffers from the hoarding of coin. Lack of money leads to lack of credit, diminished trade, and an inability to pay for national defence. He emphasises the need for a reliable and secure system of credit, which he describes as 'undoubtedly one of the best and readiest ways of supplying the want of money' (1705: 1).

In 1697 Hodges believed that England was suffering from a crippling shortage of money, and required an additional £6 million in circulating money for economic health to be restored. Part of the deficit could be made up by calling in all privately held gold and silver plate, which Hodges valued at £3.2 million. The remainder of the shortfall could be made up by increasing the value of money. This, as Hodges acknowledged, was a controversial topic at the time, and there would be many difficulties involved in doing so, and he went on to state that ideally it would be preferable to mint new money than to raise the value of that already in circulation. In the present crisis, however, the latter measure would have to suffice as the country had no access to supplies of bullion from which new money could be minted. Hodges added that raising the value of money would have an additional benefit in that it would call out privately hoarded coin, which would then enter circulation and increase the money supply.

Much of the second half of *The Present State of England* is a sustained rebuttal of LOCKE, who had argued that the value of money could not be arbitrarily changed. According to Hodges, Locke had stated that 'the intrinsick value of silver, considered as money, is that estimate which common consent hath placed on it' (1697: 132). But this statement, Hodges says, is contradictory: an intrinsic value is something inherent in a thing itself, internal to it, not something which is put upon it by others. Placing an intrinsic value on something from the outside is, he says, like putting on your clothes by swallowing them (1697: 132). So, the value of silver is either intrinsic to silver, or it is placed upon silver by society, but not both. Here, says Hodges, is a fundamental error which negates Locke's entire theory. One part of the statement is true and one part is false, and all Locke's further propositions are drawn from the false part. Thus he rejects Locke's two further propositions, 'silver is the measure of commerce by its quantity, which is the measure also of its intrinsick value', and 'an equal quantity of silver is always equal in value to an equal quantity of silver'.

Lest the reader be in any doubt, Hodges makes it clear that he believes that the value of money is the value placed on it by society, and is not intrinsic to it. He points out that at different times and in different places, different values have been put on silver. This happens as the values of other commodities, purchasable with silver, rise and fall:

> Tho one ounce of silver will sometimes buy one bushel of wheat, and two ounces two bushels, and so in double quantity hath double value; yet at another time when there is dearth or scarcity...then the two ounces of silver, which formerly could buy two bushels of wheat, will only buy one...because the raising of the value of wheat to double doth lower the value of silver to the one half, tho in the same quantity.
>
> (1697: 143)

Hodges goes on to call for a system of credit that will ensure a strong money supply: 'Credit duly imploy'd in trade, and duly encouraged, must effectually produce increase of money, enabling it to make it self good, at long run, to all who trust it' (1705: 2). He believes that the system at present, where individual banks advance credit on their own reputations is inherently risky. It would take only a few failures to shake faith in the credit system and drive people back to reliance on coin alone. Repeating several times the proposition that 'it is easier to advance credit than to restore it', Hodges says it is essential to have a system that is seen to be sound and has widespread backing. Such a system ought to be national in scope, backed by assets that 'the whole nation is most generally concerned in, and the distribution of the profits whereof is to be most universal' (1705: 6). When establishing a credit system, he says, governments must never lose sight of the fact that the primary goal of such a system is the advancement of trade and the increase of national prosperity. He says also that measures need to be taken to stimulate the use of credit, and to discourage those who fail to use it. In Scotland, Hodges advocated the setting up of a fund of £100,000 based on the public revenue, on which bills could then be issued. To encourage acceptance of bills drawn on this credit, Hodges proposed that all ordinary taxes and excise be raised by ten per cent, but all those paying taxes by means of exchequer bills should have a ten per cent discount off the total to be paid. A similar fund could be established backed by the assets of the African Company.

BIBLIOGRAPHY
The Present State of England, as to Coin and Publick Charges (1697).
Considerations and Proposals, for Supplying the present Scarcity of Money, and Advancing Trade (Edinburgh, 1705).

Further Reading
Prebble, J., *Darien* (Edinburgh, 2000).

Morgen Witzel

HODGES, William (1645?–1714)

Hodges was born in London, probably in 1645, and died there on 31 July 1714. His early career is obscure, but he is known to have been the son of a London merchant and probably entered and later took over his father's business. Hodges built up a large overseas trading business, with particularly strong connections in Spain, establishing a partnership with two other London merchants in Cadiz around 1690. In exchange for arranging loans for the government, he was created a baronet in 1697. He seems to have been popular as well as wealthy, and a large crowd attended his funeral.

Hodges wrote a number of pamphlets on economic and social matters. Being connected as he was with the maritime trade, he was particularly concerned with matters of national defence and trade security. He deplored the condition of the Royal Navy and in several pamphlets, notably *Humble Proposals...* (1695), *Great Britain's Groans* (1695) and *Ruin to Ruin* (1699), he argued for reform of the Navy, in particular for providing proper pay to seamen to allow them to support themselves and their families. He believed a strong navy was essential to security both at home and overseas.

Hodges's other principal work, *The Groans of the Poor, the Misery of Traders, and the Calamity of the Publick* (1696) is a work on money and money supply. He believed that there was a severe shortage of money in England, thanks to an unfavourable balance of trade which had led to large-scale exports of currency. He suggested that the overall drain amounts to four or five million pounds sterling, though he did not say over what period this drain occurred. He claimed that some taxes in London could be paid due to lack of silver with which to pay them, and that much of the money still in circulation was cracked or milled and therefore of less value.

It is important that sufficient quantities of money be kept in circulation, says Hodges, for without money trade becomes impossible and the country starves. He calls for poor quality coins to be called in and reminted, but his primary proposal is for the raising of new money through bills. His proposal is for £4 million in bills to be issued over the course of a year, the bills to be backed by a new land tax; but he believes the bills will increase trade, and hence prosperity, to such an extent that any new tax would not be burdensome. He believes there would be a multiplier effect, with the £4 million bills generating some £40 million in trade over the course of the year. The issuing of the bills, says Hodges, should be carried out by a national bank controlled by the government. He suggests the bills themselves could be similar to those currently issued by the Bank of England, which itself could serve as a useful model for how to organize a national bank.

BIBLIOGRAPHY

Humble Proposals for the Relief, Encouragement, Security and Happiness of the Loyal, Couragious Seamen of England... (1695).

Great Britain's Groans: or, an Account of the Oppression of the Seamen of England (1695).

The Groans of the Poor, the Misery of Traders, and the Calamity of the Publick (1696).

Ruin to Ruin, after Misery to Misery: Being the Distressed State of the Seamen of England (1699).

Morgen Witzel

HODGSKIN, Thomas (1787–1869)

Hodgskin was born in Chatham, Kent, on 12 December 1787, and died in Feltham, Middlesex, on 21 August 1869. His father was assistant storekeeper at Chatham Naval Dockyard. In 1800, at the age of twelve, Hodgskin joined the navy as a first-class volunteer. He swiftly climbed through the ranks, winning commendations for bravery on more than one occasion, and taking part in the operations that preceded Nelson's victory at Trafalgar. By 1809 Hodgskin had reached the rank of first lieutenant; thereafter, however, his career fell victim to the general rundown in the service that followed the naval defeat of the French. As his hopes of promotion faded, his behaviour became increasingly erratic, and in

1812 he was court martialled for sending an insubordinate letter to a senior officer and for wilfully allowing a prisoner in his charge to escape.

Dismissed from the service and left, in his own words, 'a disappointed and discontented man', Hodgskin immediately penned his first book, a valedictory piece entitled *An Essay on Naval Discipline* (1813), and set off for Edinburgh to take classes at the university. In the spring of 1815 he came to London with a letter of introduction to Francis PLACE, the radical tailor of Charing Cross, and entered into the utilitarian circle of Jeremy BENTHAM and James MILL. Place helped to organize a Continental trip to further Hodgskin's education and, with letters of introduction provided by Bentham and Mill, Hodgskin travelled to Paris in 1815, taking courses at the university, then moving on to Rome in 1816 and travelling back to Holland via Switzerland, Austria, Bohemia, Moravia and a lengthy spell in Germany. Hodgskin spent most of 1817 in Hanover, following a plan drawn up by Bentham and Mill to study the government and society; this eventually led Hodgskin's second book, *Travels in North Germany* (1820).

By the time of its publication, however, Hodgskin had started to break with the Benthamites and to develop his own ideas about economics. Instrumental in sparking his interest may have been his acquaintance with Jean-Baptiste Say. Much to Place's amusement, these two rather shy men had initially been tentative in each other's company, but during Hodgskin's stay in Paris had attained a level of intimacy that allowed them to freely argue political economy over dinner. If Say was the catalyst for Hodgskin's interest, it was David RICARDO who provided the clarifying point around which Hodgskin could organize his ideas. Place had sent Hodgskin a copy of Ricardo's *Principles of Political Economy* soon after it was published in 1817, in the hope that he would become a disciple. Instead it encouraged Hodgskin to develop a critique of the whole of political economy, as Mill and Ricardo propagated it. This critique was developed, in letters to Place and in debates with John Ramsay MCCULLOCH, during Hodgskin's three-year spell working in Edinburgh as a hack journalist and a language tutor. By the time he returned to London in 1823, to take the position of parliamentary reporter at the *Morning Chronicle*, Hodgskin's analysis was complete. All that was lacking was an audience. And this Hodgskin found among the mechanics of London after working on the early editions of J.C. Robertson's *Mechanics Magazine* and helping to establish the London Mechanics Institution (now Birkbeck College, University of London) in 1824.

Between 1825 and 1832 Hodgskin published his three most important works of political economy: *Labour Defended against the Claims of Capital* (1825), *Popular Political Economy* (1827) and *Natural and Artificial Right of Property Contrasted* (1832). They represent a three-stage critique of the political economy of Mill and Ricardo. *Labour Defended* arose as a direct response to the struggles in 1824 and 1825 to first repeal, and then to re-impose, the Combinations Acts outlawing trade union activity. Writing under the pseudonym 'A Labourer', Hodgskin's explicit intention was to complement intellectually the physical battle being waged by the trade unions. His title, *Labour Defended*, was a self-conscious parody of Mill's *Commerce Defended* (1808), and his aim was to dispute the claims of capital as justified by Mill and Ricardo. His method was an etymological examination of the ideas associated with 'capital'. Drawing on the principles of LOCKE and Horne TOOKE, Hodgskin asked 'what is capital?' 'what form does it take?' and 'is it productive?', concluding that the ideas associated with the term were false, delusive and illusory. To his own satisfaction, Hodgskin exposed capital as nothing more than so many different aspects of the process of labouring, the relations among labourers and the products of labour. Capital was not a 'thing' but a cabalistic word that veiled a relation between men –

labourers and capitalists – by suggesting the interposition of a mythical substance. Capital, as later in MARX, was not an independent factor of production but a social relationship through which one class expropriated the produce of another. With Ricardo's view of capital exposed, Hodgskin was quick to point out that Ricardo's relative overpopulation thesis and Mill's wages fund 'fell baseless to the ground'.

The second instalment of Hodgskin's critique of political economy focused on the Malthusian population principle. This had been a bugbear of radicals since it was first proclaimed in 1798, and Hodgskin provided the most convincing answer yet in his *Popular Political Economy* (1827). The book was adapted from four lectures Hodgskin had delivered at the London Mechanics Institution the previous year, and took British political economy to task for neglecting the importance of knowledge and observation in economic growth. In doing so Hodgskin explicitly aligned himself with the French political economists, especially Say, who had placed 'the effects of observation and knowledge in a proper point of view'.

Far from heralding misery and vice, Hodgskin found the increased knowledge and ingenuity which sprang from an increasing population more than offset the increased demand for food. There were, he argued, two reasons for this. The first, as even MALTHUS had understood, was that 'necessity was the mother of invention'. The second was equally simple: if two heads were better than one, then 'each one of four thousand heads, and of four million heads, will necessarily have still more wisdom and still more knowledge than when there is only one head in existence'. This position distinguished Hodgskin from Adam SMITH, who he felt had confused the causal order, and reduced the effects of the progress of knowledge to the division of labour. For Hodgskin, the division of labour was itself the result of progress in knowledge of the material world. The two mutually promoted each other, but 'observation must have preceded division of labour'. In this way Hodgskin removed those limitations on the division of labour that Smith had thought would ultimately produce a stationary state. As long as population increased so too would the division of labour, and increasing returns could continue indefinitely.

Having denied Ricardian relative overpopulation and Malthusian absolute overpopulation, Hodgskin was left with the question 'whither evil?' If, as he had argued, the political economists had misidentified the population principle as the root of the suffering of the labourers, and there was no limitation on the division of labour, he was left to explain the cause of suffering. It lay, he concluded, in social regulations. All the mistakes of Ricardo and Malthus and their popularizers, such as Mill, lay in a failure to follow Smith in delineating the natural from the artificial. When the multiplication of the labourers was merely compared to the wants of the capitalists for their services, then their poverty could be 'justly attributed' to that multiplication. What Hodgskin pointed out was that the productive power of society as a whole augmented with an increasing population. Malthus and the political economists had not contradicted this; they had only said that the proportion of that produce received by the labourer diminished with an increase of population. Both propositions were true. Total production had increased, and the labourers' share diminished because a class who stood apart from the labourers was siphoning off the benefits of increased production. The next stage in his argument was to examine the social regulations that allowed this to occur.

Again writing under the pseudonym 'A Labourer', Hodgskin's *Natural and Artificial Right of Property Contrasted* (1832) was structured as eight letters addressed to Lord BROUGHAM. But just as *Labour Defended* had been principally directed against Mill's exposition of Ricardo's theory of capital, so the

Natural and Artificial was principally directed against Mill's exposition of Bentham's theory of rights, in particular the claim that all rights were derived exclusively from government. Mill had made this case in two articles for the *Encyclopaedia Britannica*, 'Government' and 'Jurisprudence'. Hodgskin was unable to accept Mill's argument on two grounds. Firstly, it denied that society was natural, and, in consequence, gave government unlimited power. Secondly, when applied to the right of property, the argument justified the exactions of capital and the Malthusian population principle. To counter these points, Hodgskin drew a distinction between a *natural* and an *artificial* right of property that took its inspiration from the 'workmanship model' of John Locke. This allowed Hodgskin to make clear that property rights arose naturally and were being violated in contemporary society.

As in Locke, Hodgskin's theory of property was rooted in a psychological conception of individuality. It rested, that is, on prior property rights. Since one's body was one's property, and its produce (labour) was also one's property, it followed that labour's product was one's property. But whereas Locke had consigned the 'natural law of appropriation' to a past state, Hodgskin found it existent 'in full force at all times and places'. Even more strongly than Locke, therefore, Hodgskin wished to mark the fact that 'antecedently to all legislation, and to any possible interference by the legislator, nature establishes a law of appropriation by bestowing as she creates individuality, the produce of labour on the labourer'. Unfortunately, in society an artificial right of property had arisen, which broke the intimate relation between labour and property and allowed a class of idle men to appropriate property to themselves by controlling access to land and capital. The payments received by the landowners, the tax gatherers, the priests and the capitalists were all violations of the natural right of property because they were not received as a reward for labour. Rather, they were received because government and law (force and fraud) had established them. This thwarting of the decrees of the Almighty necessarily entailed evil. The limitations on production which Ricardo, Malthus, Mill and, to a lesser extent, Smith had identified, were the by-products of the artificial right of property. It was this, rather than any disproportion between capital and labour or the 'niggardliness of nature', that was the root of misery and want.

Underlying all Hodgskin's economic writings was an essentially theological assumption about the beneficence of nature. Hodgskin was first and foremost a deist, a believer in God's naturally harmonious order. In the 1840s this led him to become an advocate of an absolute free trade, which was consistent with his radicalism and reinforced his Providential assumption of a set of harmonious natural laws governing all societal relations. For Hodgskin, free trade was more than an economic doctrine; it was a *Weltanschauung* providing a moral imperative to govern all areas of life. By consistently applying the distinction between a natural 'society' and an artificial 'government', Hodgskin tipped his endorsement of free trade into a providential anarchism consistent with his earlier writings. Moreover, he made his case for free trade within the context of the critique of political economy he had developed in the 1820s, and saw free trade culminating in the overthrow of existing, artificial, property rights.

Hodgskin's works were briefly popular among political radicals and some Owenite socialists and co-operators, but he never achieved the impact his undoubted intellect deserved. After 1832 he buried himself in Whig journalism, only emerging in the winter of 1842–3 to lecture both the Chartists and the Anti-Corn Law League on the need to recognize the harmonious, providential, natural order that was violated by the violence and poverty of the artificial social order. These two lectures, *Peace, Law and Order* (1842) and *A*

Lecture on Free Trade in Connexion with the Corn Laws (1843), coincided with a new turn in Hodgskin's career. He became a free trade journalist, spending fifteen years working for James WILSON at *The Economist*, where he responsible for instilling the virtues of clear exposition and a dogged commitment to free trade that characterize *The Economist* even today. He was left reluctantly in 1857, aged sixty-nine but still full of life, and immediately arranged two public lectures which revived the argument of the *Natural and Artificial Right of Property Contrasted* that the law of property was a 'parent crime' from which all other crimes flowed. The second lecture concluded by arguing that the only way to overcome the criminality of society was to let all laws perish by an extension of the free trade principles of 1842. Hodgskin promised to justify these 'striking opinions' in a work he was preparing for the press entitled 'The Absurdity of Legislation Demonstrated'. This work, which might have been Hodgskin's *magnum opus*, never saw the light of day. The last twelve years of his life were spent producing a weekly column for the *Brighton Guardian*.

BIBLIOGRAPHY

An Essay on Naval Discipline shewing Part of Its Evil Effects on The Minds of The Officers, On The Minds of The Men, And on The Community, With An Amended System By Which Pressing May Be Immediately Abolished (1813).

Travels in North Germany Describing The Present State of the Social And Political Institutions, Agriculture, Manufactures, Commerce, Education, Arts And Manners In That Country, Particularly In The Kingdom of Hannover, 2 vols (Edinburgh, 1820).

Labour Defended against the Claims of Capital or the Unproductiveness of Capital proved with Reference to the Present Combinations amongst Journeymen (1825).

Popular Political Economy: Four Lectures Delivered At The London Mechanics' Institution (1827).

The Word Belief Defined and Explained (1827).

The Natural and Artificial Right of Property Contrasted: A Series of Letters Addressed Without Permission, To H. Brougham, Esq. M.P. F.R.S & C... (1832).

Peace, Law and Order. A Lecture Delivered in the Hall of the National Association, on 29 September 1842 (n.d.).

A Lecture on Free Trade In Connexion with The Corn Laws; Delivered At The White Conduit House, on January 31, 1843 (1843).

What Shall We Do With Our Criminals: Don't Create Them. A Lecture Delivered At St. Martin's Hall, May 20th 1857 (1857).

Our Chief Crime: Cause And Cure. Second Lecture, On What Shall We Do With Our Criminals? Delivered At St. Martin's Hall, June 3, 1857 (1857).

Further Reading

Halévy, E., *Thomas Hodgskin* (1956).

Hunt, E.K., 'Value Theory in the Writings of the Classical Economists, Thomas Hodgskin and Karl Marx', *History of Political Economy* (1977), vol. 11, pp. 322–45.

Jaffe, J., 'The Origins of Thomas Hodgskin's Critique of Political Economy', *History of Political Economy* (1995), vol. 27, pp. 493–515.

Lowenthal, E., *The Ricardian Socialists* (New York, 1911).

Stack, D., *Nature and Artifice: The Life and Thought of Thomas Hodgskin, 1787–1869* (1998).

Stark, W., *The Ideal Foundations of Economic Thought: Three Essays on the Philosophy of Economics* (1943).

Thompson, N., *The People's Science: Popular Political Economy of*

Exploitation and Crisis, 1816–1834 (Cambridge, 1984).

David Stack

HODGSON, William Ballantyne (1815–1880)

Hodgson was born on 6 October 1815 in Edinburgh, and died in Brussels 24 August 1880 when attending an international teachers conference. He was educated at the High School of Edinburgh, and entered Edinburgh University at the age of fourteen. Opposed to his father's plans for him to become a lawyer, he became a freelance lecturer on literature, education and phrenology, as well as a newspaper editor for a few months. He was appointed secretary (1839), then principal (1844) to the Mechanics' Institute of Liverpool. Here he expanded the teaching staff from 48 to over 60 and the numbers of those in attendance at day and evening classes, as well as establishing a girls' school in 1844. He was awarded an LLD by Glasgow University in 1846, and was principal of Chorlton High School, Manchester from 1847–51. In 1857 he gave evening lectures on physiology in Edinburgh, and in 1858 he was appointed an assistant commissioner of the Royal Commission to inquire into the state of primary education in England.

After residence in London from 1863–70 and an examinership in political economy at the University of London, Hodgson was appointed the first professor of commercial and political economy and mercantile law at Edinburgh University in 1871. W.S. JEVONS, a referee, praised his wide and intimate knowledge of economic literature. The chair was a novelty in Scotland, although economics had long been taught as part of moral philosophy: Hodgson reversed this by bringing morality into economics. From childhood he was involved in the Liberal Party, supporting free trade and the abolition of slavery and regretting the British conquest of India. He made several speeches in support of Gladstone in the Midlothian campaign of 1880. He was liberal too in theology, opposing church schools and approving of only the blandest multi-faith religious education. He was married twice and fathered two sons and two daughters, one of whom married his professorial successor, Joseph Shield NICHOLSON.

In a career dedicated to education, Hodgson often lectured on educational reform. He argued passionately for an extension of women's education because of the mental equality of men and women. Boys and girls should have the opportunity to study all school subjects and sit the same examinations. He questioned the teaching of the classics to the exclusion of science. Also, proper training of teachers was his repeated plea.

In his Edinburgh lectures as professor Hodgson reviewed J.S. MILL and attacked RUSKIN, starting with supply and demand analysis then turning to capital, labour, rent, value, money and banking. He insisted that political economy taught 'how men might enrich themselves only so far as might be advantageous to the community' (Woodhead 1888: 22). There was in his lectures a breadth of thought coming from his deep knowledge of the history of economics and familiarity with contemporary French and Italian economic literature. His class averaged fifty students, despite it being an optional course. He lectured on 110 days of the year, speaking out of the side of his mouth.

In *The True Scope of Economic Science* (1870), Hodgson argued that it was wrong to see economics as the route to self-enrichment, otherwise it would in the short term be advocating theft and fraud. Instead, there is a direct relationship between social morality and social prosperity. Social prosperity is the consequence of human acts resulting from human character. On many occasions he discussed the connection between health, or wholeness, and wealth, and denounced drunkenness. In support of temperance in 1871, he argued that if people abstained from liquor for six years the national debt could be paid off and the number of policemen halved. In his Edinburgh inaugural lecture he said that economics is 'the science of exchange' and that 'exchange is but the economic phase of human brotherhood, of mutual dependence, each providing for others' wants directly, and only indirectly for his own' (1871: 21).

In the great Victorian debate on competition versus co-operation, Hodgson supported both sides. In 1870 he declared that competition is to be regarded as general freedom and excessive only if dishonest. Restrictions on competition, for example, controlling the number of apprentices, can be harmful by causing persons to be in a less desired occupation. Competition keeps prices near actual costs and, according to Montesquieu, produces a just price. Monopoly is deplored as 'the parent of scarcity, dearness and badness, removes the incentives to honest effort, and encourages fraud as well as indolence', whereas 'freedom, effort, struggle, competition, are salutary' (1871: 22). But he also praised co-operation, as his 1876 address showed. He argued that division of labour means co-operation to a common end, and capital and labour are mutually indispensable. Co-operation can reduce the waste of having many distributive outlets, but there can still be competition between different co-operatives in the quality of goods.

Hodgson as economist is perhaps best known for his lectures on Turgot. He saw in the latter's writings justification for his major economic attitudes. Turgot believed in a universal morality founded on human nature and in the justice of pursuing one's self-interest without infringing the rights of others. Inequality of conditions is praised for encouraging the industrious and making possible capital accumulation. Libertarianism in the free setting of prices and free trade, and the freedom of the press is exalted.

BIBLIOGRAPHY
Competition (1870).
The True Scope of Economic Science: A Lecture Delivered March 1st, 1870 (1870).
Turgot: His Life, Times and Opinions (1870).
Inaugural Address. 3 November 1871 (1871).
The Inaugural Address delivered at the opening of the Eighth Annual Co-operative Congress Glasgow. April 17th, 18th, 19th, 1876 (1877).

Further Reading
Meikleljohn, J.M.D., *Life and Letters of William Ballantyne Hodgson, LLD* (Edinburgh, 1883).
Woodhead, E., *Student Recollections of Professor Hodgson* (Edinburgh, 1888).

Donald Rutherford

HODSON, Septimus (1768–1833)

Hodson was born in Yorkshire in 1786, and died in London on 12 December 1833. He is perhaps better known as the husband of the writer Margaret Hodson (1778–1852). The couple were married on 16 October 1826 at South Kirby in Yorkshire; it was Hodson's second marriage, and they had no children. In 1832, the couple were living near Ripon: it is from there that Margaret Hodson's last work, *The Lives of Vasco Nunez de Balboa and Francisco Pizarro* was published. Hodson himself studied medicine and received a Bachelor of Medicine Degree at Cambridge, and then took holy orders. He went on to become the rector of Thrapston, Northamptonshire. He was appointed as chaplain in ordinary to the Prince of Wales: that is, he was in actual and constant service and was responsible for conducting the day to day services for Prince George. Hodson was also a preacher at the asylum for female orphans at Lambeth and published a number of sermons.

In 1795, Hodson published his *Address on the High Price of Provisions in this Country*. A series of bad harvests had put wheat in short supply and consequently the price of bread had risen sharply. The situation was made worse by the growing population and the French Wars. This meant that grain could not be imported from Europe. Things were so bad that famine was a distinct possibility, and there was a fear among the ruling classes that the lower orders might be tempted to emulate the French and revolt. There had been a spate of food riots in the spring of 1795. It was in response to this situation that Hodson produced his pamphlet. The bulk of the pamphlet is a call for the authorities to regulate the price of corn and defuse the situation, but Hodson was aware also of the problems that such regulation might bring, especially in terms of driving up wages. He saw regulation as a short-term necessity to solve an urgent and pressing problem.

BIBLIOGRAPHY
Address on the High Price of Provisions in this Country (1795).

Marjorie Bloy

HOLLAND, John (d. 1722)

Details of Holland's early life are not known. He describes himself as English, and may have been born in London. He spent much of his professional life in London, where he was a merchant of the Staple and later a member of the Mercer's Company. Despite his association with the Bank of Scotland, he does not seem to have lived permanently in Edinburgh. He died at his home, Brewood Hall in Staffordshire, some time in 1722.

Most of what we know about Holland comes from his own account of his later life, when he had partially retired. In the early 1690s he was persuaded by friends to lend his support to a projected Bank of Scotland. His efforts on behalf of the project saw it carried successfully through: the Bank of Scotland was established by an act of the Scottish Parliament in 1695, and the first branches opened in 1696. Holland was elected the first governor of the Bank and succeeded in establishing it on a firm footing, seeing off challenges from the Bank of England and from the Indian and African Company, which was also trying to set up a bank. Holland succeeded largely because he was a prudent financial manager who distrusted speculation and refused to offer excessive returns on investment.

Holland's career is perhaps most notable for his virulent feud with William PATERSON, who had promoted the Bank of England and was also a leading force in the Indian and African Company's attempt to set up a bank, using the company's capital. Holland stopped short of accusing Paterson of outright fraud, but he maintained that Paterson was mis-using his stockholders' money and was guilty of deception and dishonesty. Paterson's friends in turn accused Holland of being an East India Company spy (he had had dealings with the East India Company during his earlier career) and of trying to wreck the Indian and African Company's trade. The clash is recounted in *A Short Discourse on the Present Temper of the Nation with Respect to the Indian and African Company* (1696).

Holland's prudent approach to banking led him to view events in London in the early eighteenth century with dismay. In *The Ruine of the Bank of England, and all Publick-Credit Inevitable* (1715), he argued that the national debt was far too high, and that there was real danger of a run on the Bank of England. The fact that an earlier run on the Bank in King

William's reign had been successfully prevented, he said, was no guarantee that a similar run could be prevented now. The Bank's stock was now much larger and the debt much higher, and there were few ways of avoiding a collapse:

> The Bank indeed stands upon the same Legs that it ever did, to wit, the Government Security; but the Superstructure, the Body, is no so vastly Great and Bulky, so many Millions, that if it Falls, it may be easily conceiv'd by any considering Man, that all the Adventurers, and all their Friends into the Bargain, will not be able to help it up again.
> (Holland 1715: 3)

High debt was leading to high taxation, but at the same time declining national prosperity meant there would soon be nothing left to tax. Holland argued for fiscal prudence, for a reduction on the interest on government stocks and for stopping payments to government funds, and also to the South Sea Company. He clearly foresaw the South Sea Bubble, and was putting forward a programme of measures to prevent it. In the second half of this work he chronicles his efforts to lobby key members of the government, notably Viscount Townshend and Sir Robert Walpole, but to little effect.

BIBLIOGRAPHY
A Short Discourse on the Present Temper of the Nation with Respect to the Indian and African Company; and of the Bank of Scotland (1696).
The Ruine of the Bank of England, and all Publick-Credit Inevitable (1715).

Further Reading
Forrester, A., *The Man Who Saw the Future* (2003).

Morgen Witzel

HOLROYD, John Baker (1735–1821)

Holroyd was born in 1735 in Ireland, and died at Sheffield Place, East Sussex on 30 May 1821; he was buried in Fletching church. He was the second son of Isaac Holroyd and his wife, Dorothy Penn. Holroyd entered the army in 1760 and became a captain in the Royal Foresters; the regiment was disbanded in 1763. Between 1763 and 1766 Holroyd travelled in Europe, and in 1768 he succeeded to the estates of his mother's family and assumed the name of Baker; the following year he purchased the estate of Sheffield Place. Holroyd was married three times. In 1767 he married Abigail Way of Richmond, Surrey, who died in 1793. They had a son who died young, and two daughters. On 26 December 1794 he married Lucy, daughter of the first Earl of Chichester, who died in 1795; finally, on 9 January 1798, he married Anne, daughter of the second Earl of Guilford. They had one son and a daughter.

In February 1780 Holroyd was elected as MP for Coventry, standing again for the constituency in September. The election was violent, so a new election took place in November. Holroyd was declared to be duly elected following a petition to parliament. When Lord George Gordon presented the Protestant Association's petition to the House of Commons on 2 June 1780, Holroyd told him: 'Hitherto I have imputed your conduct to madness, but now I perceive that it has more of malice than madness in it'. Holroyd was active in suppressing the subsequent Gordon Riots.

On 9 January 1781 Holroyd was raised to the Irish peerage as Baron Sheffield of Dunamore, Meath; on 17 December 1783 he became Baron Sheffield of Roscommon. After 1781 he sat as MP for Bristol, taking an active part in debates. He opposed Wilberforce's motion for the abolition of slavery in 1791. On 29 July 1802 he was raised to the peerage of the United Kingdom as Baron Sheffield of Sheffield, Yorkshire. He was created Earl of

Sheffield and Viscount Pevensey in the Irish peerage on 22 January 1816. He was made president of the Board of Agriculture in 1803, and Privy Councillor and a lord of the Board of Trade in 1809.

Holroyd was considered an authority on matters concerning commerce and agriculture, and his estate at Sheffield Place was regarded as a model of farming. He wrote a number of pamphlets on the woollen industry, the corn laws and the poor laws, none of any great originality, and generally was a conservative in terms of his economic thinking. In 1783, Holroyd wrote *Observations on the Commerce of the American States* in opposition to a bill introduced by Pitt in 1783 that proposed to relax the Navigation Laws in favour of America. Holroyd opposed this on the grounds that free trade with America would open up British businesses to dangerous competition. This led to a long controversy, and finally to the abandonment of the proposal. However, Holroyd was not a dogmatic protectionist. His *Observations on the Manufactures, Trade, and Present State of Ireland* (1785) attempted to prove that Irish prosperity could only be maintained by a friendly connection with Great Britain. Holroyd supported the union with Ireland in parliament, and believed that free trade between Britain and Ireland would be economically good for both parties.

Beyond these, his economics writings attracted little attention. Holroyd was a close friend of Gibbon, whom he met in 1764, and he is perhaps best known for editing Gibbon's posthumous works.

BIBLIOGRAPHY

Observations on the Commerce of the American States (1783).
Observations on the Manufactures, Trade, and Present State of Ireland (1785).
Observations on the Project for Abolishing the Slave Trade (1790).
Observations on the Corn Bill now depending in Parliament (1791).

Strictures on the Necessity of inviolably maintaining the Navigation and Colonial System of Great Britain (1804).

Marjorie Bloy

HOLYOAKE, George Jacob (1817–1906)

Holyoake was born on 13 April 1817 at Inge Street, Birmingham, and died at Brighton on 22 January 1906, and after cremation at Golder's Green his ashes were buried in Highgate cemetery. He was the eldest son and second of thirteen children born to George Holyoake and his wife, Catherine Groves. Holyoake was apprenticed to a tinsmith, then worked as a whitesmith. He became a student at the Old Mechanics' Institute (1834), later teaching mathematics in Sunday schools (1836–7) and at the Mechanics' Institute. His first marriage took place on 10 March 1839 to Eleanor Williams. who died at Brighton in January 1884. The couple had four sons and three daughters. In 1886 he married Jane Pearson.

Holyoake wrote a number of biographies, including books on Richard Carlile (1848), Tom Paine (1851), Robert OWEN (1859, 1866), John Stuart MILL (1873) and Joseph Rayner Stephens (1881). He tried to enter parliament successively for Tower Hamlets (1857), Birmingham (1868) and Leicester (1884) but could not afford to go to the poll. He joined the Birmingham reform league in 1831 and became a moral force Chartist, and eventually was a member of the Chartist executive. He was present at the Bull Ring riots at Birmingham on 15 July 1839.

In 1837 Holyoake attended Robert Owen's meetings, and became a confirmed supporter of co-operation. The following year he gave his first lecture on socialism and co-operation, and joined the Association of all Classes of all Nations. In 1840 he applied to teach at the

Birmingham Mechanics' Institute but was rejected. He became an Owenite Social Missionary in Worcester and then in Sheffield. Concurrently he was an editor of *The Oracle of Reason*. On 24 May 1842, Holyoake lectured at Cheltenham Mechanics' Institution, where he replied to a question and was then arrested for blasphemy. On 15 August 1842 he was tried, convicted and sentenced to six months' imprisonment at Gloucester Assizes. He was the last man in England to be imprisoned on a charge of atheism. On his release, Holyoake opened a shop in London selling radical texts. He was secretary of the anti-persecution union, demanding freedom of theological thought and speech.

Holyoake became the national figure of secularism, founding and editing *The Reasoner* (1846–61). He was a key promoter of legislation to legalize secular affirmations (1888), a supporter of Italian nationalism and a devoted Gladstonian Liberal. He advocated extension of the franchise, and defended the secret ballot. In 1851 he helped form the Association for the Repeal of the Taxes on Knowledge. In 1853 he started a bookselling and publishing business; he ignored the newspaper tax and published unstamped journals denouncing the Crimean War (1854). The fines he incurred totalled £600,000. In 1874 he received an annuity by public subscription. He still wrote copiously, starting a new periodical, *The Secular Review* (1876). Holyoake twice travelled in the United States and Canada. Later in life he moved to Brighton, where he was president of the Liberal Association.

Holyoake's enthusiasm for co-operation never waned. He edited *The Movement* (1843) and presided at the opening of the Toad Lane store, Rochdale in 1845. In 1858 he wrote *Self-Help by the People*, a history of the Rochdale Pioneers. In 1870 he was one of the founders of the Co-operative Union, and in 1877 he completed *The History of Co-operation in England*. The spread of co-operative ideas owed much to Holyoake's enthusiasm.

The History of Co-operation in England is a comprehensive study of its subject, looking at Owen and his precursors and discussing the various strands of the co-operative movement, utopian, socialist and so on. As Holyoake himself emphasizes, it is primarily a study of people, and contains pen sketches of many leading figures, and many minor ones, in the movement; he believes that it is through the study of people's actions, not abstract theory, that we touch on economic realities. The focus throughout is practical and pragmatic. He defines co-operation as 'self-help, self-dependence and such share of the common competence as labour shall earn or thought can win' (1875–77: 6). The emphasis is on participation; the co-operative movement excludes 'no one who works', but the emphasis remains squarely on the individual.

BIBLIOGRAPHY
Self-Help by the People (1855).
Principles of Secularism (1859).
A History of Co-operation in England, 2 vols (1875–7; repr. 1906).
The Co-operative Movement To-day (1891).
Sixty Years of an Agitator's Life, 2 vols (1892).
Public Speaking and Debate (1895).
Bygones Worth Remembering (1905).

Marjorie Bloy

HOPE, John (1739–85)

Hope was born in London on 7 April 1839, and died at Newcastle upon Tyne on 21 May 1785. He was an obscure member of a notable family; his grandfather was first Earl of Hopetoun, and his father was for a number of years MP for Linlithgow. Hope was educated at a private academy in Enfield, near London, and then joined a merchant house in London, but was not temperamentally suited to a career in commerce. In 1768 the patronage of his uncle, the second Earl of Hopetoun, gained him the parliamentary seat of Linlithgow in succession to his father, but he lost the seat two years later; thereafter he seems to have had no fixed occupation. His wife Mary, the daughter of a Middlesex gentry family, committed suicide in 1767, leaving three sons. All three of these went on to become notable in their respective careers: the eldest, Charles, became Lord Granton and president of the Court of Session in Edinburgh; the second, John, became a general, served under Wellington in Spain with some distinction and was knighted; the third, William, joined the navy, served with Nelson, and became an admiral and was likewise knighted.

Most of Hope's writings took the form of meandering poems, such as *Occasional Attempts at Sentimental Poetry by a Man of Business* (1769), which show him to have had little talent for either business or poetry. His *Letters on Credit* (1784), originally a series of articles for the *Public Advertiser*, show, however, a more thoughtful and analytical side to his character. The articles were originally written in reply to a broadside by one 'E.M.', who had produced a pamphlet arguing that credit was a 'destructive cancer'. Hope defends the principle of credit, arguing that credit becomes necessary particularly when much of the economy depends on overseas trade and goods take a long time in transit. He admits there are abuses of credit, and is concerned about these; he notes that he is writing in the immediate aftermath of the failure of the Air Bank, and believed that this incident had exposed inherent instability in the banking system.

Hope goes on to argue that the state should back the credit system in order to restore stability and instil greater confidence in the system. In the end, he says, all credit is founded not on money, but on the trust or confidence that two parties have in each other. That trust is the foundation of all credit systems. To refuse to accept another's credit is to refuse to trust them; to refuse to accept credit offered by the state is to distrust the state, and is therefore close to treason.

On the issue of coinage versus paper money, Hope argues that paper currency represents real value in right, not in terms of its convertibility to gold and silver but in the 'lands, products, manufactures, and all kinds of saleable commodities' of the kingdom (1784: 36). Paper money is backed up by the whole wealth of the kingdom, not just that proportion that exists in the form of previous metals. He recognizes the critical role played by the Bank of England in guaranteeing the stability of the paper currency and the credit system, and comes at times close to Francis BARING's later description of the Bank as the lender of last resort, though he does not use this term.

MCCULLOCH dismissed Hope's views as being of little worth. This may be too harsh; while there is little that is truly original, Hope is representative of a particular school of thought, and his views on the necessity of trust if a credit system is to function remain important.

BIBLIOGRAPHY
Occasional Attempts at Sentimental Poetry by a Man of Business (1769).
Letters on Credit, second edition, with a Postscript, and a Short Account of the Bank of Amsterdam (1784).

Further Reading
McCulloch, J.R., *The Literature of Political Economy* (London, 1845).

Ann Kimber

HORNE TOOKE, John (1736–1812)

John Horne was born on 25 June 1736 near Leicester Square, London, and died at his home in Wimbledon, Surrey on 18 March

1812. He was the youngest son of a prosperous poulterer. He was educated at Westminster School and Eton College before going to St John's College, Cambridge, in 1755; he graduated in 1758. Before that he had already enrolled at the Inner Temple to study law. His parents wanted him to enter the church instead, and he reluctantly bowed to their wishes. He was ordained a priest on 23 November 1760 and he took up a living at New Brentford, in Middlesex. Although staunchly anti-Catholic and always a supporter of the established church, he had no very firm religious beliefs and no real sense of vocation. He made extended visits to France and Italy between 1763 and 1767. In France he met David HUME, Adam SMITH and Laurence Sterne, and became friendly with John Wilkes who was then living in political exile.

Back in Britain in 1765 Horne wrote a short pamphlet, *The Petition of an Englishman*, which expressed sympathy for the anti-ministerial stance taken up by Wilkes. When Wilkes returned to England in 1768, hoping to be returned to parliament, Horne agreed to support him as a candidate for Middlesex. He remained active through the repeated by-elections in Middlesex in 1768–9, and he sought in vain to prosecute those he held responsible for killing some Wilkite supporters in the St George's Fields massacre on 10 May 1768. He was a founder member and driving force behind the Society of the Supporters of the Bill of Rights (the SSBR). The treasurer was William Tooke, who became Horne's patron for many years thereafter. In early 1771, however, Horne became engaged in a bitter dispute with Wilkes over the purposes of the SSBR. Wilkes persuaded a majority of members to agree that the first objective of the society was to pay off his debts, while Horne wanted the society to dedicate itself to wider political objectives. The dispute between the two men widened when the celebrated 'Junius' attacked Wilkes for dividing the anti-government camp of reformers.

In 1773 Horne resigned his church living and resumed his study of the law. He sought to be called to the bar in 1780 and in 1782, but he was rejected on both occasions on the grounds that he was still in holy orders. This failure to enter the profession, which he believed was his true vocation, made him more cynical. During this period he fathered three children by two different mistresses. He never married and nothing is known of these mistresses.

In February 1774 Horne used his political and legal talents to assist his patron, William Tooke, who was in dispute with the De Grey family over the latter's efforts to enclose land. He published a long letter in the *Public Advertiser* accusing Fletcher Norton, the Speaker of the House of Commons, of ignoring petitions against the bill. He was summoned to appear before the House of Commons for breach of privilege, but he was discharged because there was insufficient evidence against him. His intervention, however, embarrassed many MPs and helped to persuade the House of Commons to drop the offending bill. In gratitude, Tooke promised to make Horne one of his heirs and urged him to add his surname to his own. In 1782 Horne changed his name to Horne Tooke to please his patron, although when William Tooke died in 1802, he left Horne Tooke only a modest inheritance.

As early as 1770 Horne had recognized that the grievances of the American colonists were similar to those voiced by metropolitan radicals like himself. In 1775 he was shocked by the outbreak of war with the colonies. He placed an advertisement in four newspapers seeking to raise subscriptions for the dependants of those Americans killed at Lexington and Concord, and accused the king's troops of murdering these colonists. On 4 July 1777, Horne was charged with seditious libel for putting his name to this advertisement. Horne freely admitted the act, but denied that this action was seditious libel. He argued semantic terms with his judge, Lord Mansfield, but lost the argument, was convicted and was sentenced to serve a year in the King's Bench prison. Although he was allowed to reside in a small house beyond the prison walls, his health was permanently impaired by his sentence.

In 1780, still opposed to the American war, Horne co-operated with Richard PRICE in publishing *Facts addressed to the Landholders, Stockholders, Merchants...of Great Britain and Ireland*. Price contributed Chapters 2 and 8, which dealt with the heavy financial burdens that the American War imposed on the country. Horne wrote the other chapters, which stressed the political costs of the war. He accused the ministry of misusing crown influence in order to corrupt parliament, and he castigated parliament for not resisting crown influence and for prolonging the war. His most positive arguments were advanced in support of economic reforms designed to curb crown influence. This led him to ally with Christopher Wyvill, whose Yorkshire Association was just starting to wage a major campaign in support of economic reform.

Horne joined the Middlesex Association in 1780 to support economic reform, and the Society for Constitutional Information (SCI) in 1781 to campaign for parliamentary reform. He advanced his own views in *A Letter to Lord Ashburton* in 1782. In this pamphlet, he fully supported the case for economic reform, believing that both the crown and the aristocracy had too much influence on the composition of the House of Commons. He did not wish to abolish the monarchy or the House of Lords, however. He confined his reform proposals to making the House of Commons more representative of the independent men in the country. He advocated more frequent general elections and equal-sized and single-member constituencies. He wished also to widen the electorate, but he thought that universal manhood suffrage was at present impractical. He thought the franchise should be denied to the poor and the ignorant, but it should be extended to rate-paying householders. Disillusioned with the Fox–North coalition of 1783, he pinned his hopes of reform on the young William Pitt. He campaigned against Charles James Fox in the celebrated Westminster election of 1784, and later produced a brilliant satirical study of Fox and Pitt on the one hand and their respective fathers on the other, in *Two Pair of Portraits* (1788).

In addition to his various political activities, Horne devoted himself to the serious study of the origins and usage of the English language. Convinced that he had been sent to prison in 1777 because of a dispute over the meaning of a simple phrase, he wrote a pamphlet, *A Letter to J[ohn] Dunning* (1778), on the meaning of the single word 'that'. This study was substantially expanded in *Epea Pteroenta: Or, the Diversions of Purley* (1786), which was written at Purley Lodge, one of the homes of William Tooke. This work attracted very considerable attention. It was expanded and republished in 1798 and a second substantial part, with the same title, appeared in 1805. These sold well enough to earn Horne Tooke a considerable income. In his last years he worked on a third part, but, dissatisfied with this, he burned his papers (along with his voluminous correspondence) shortly before his death.

Horne Tooke's interest in politics revived with the outbreak of the French Revolution in 1789. He stood for election at Westminster in 1790, lost, and was successfully sued by Fox for refusing to pay his share of the election expenses normally paid to the returning officers. He was very soon active in the Revolution Society, the SCI and the Friends of the Liberty of the Press. In the chair of the SCI, he advocated parliamentary reform at home, praised the French for their efforts to promote liberty, and condemned the efforts of Austria, Prussia and then Britain to overthrow the French Revolution by force of arms. He advised Thomas Hardy on how to draw up rules and regulations for the London Corresponding Society, and he encouraged this society to make contact with the many radical societies being established across the country. He criticized BURKE's *Reflections* and recommended Paine's *Rights of Man* to many plebeian radicals (while claiming to oppose Paine's republican views). While outspoken in his condemnation of political corruption and the government's repressive policies, it is not clear what political reforms he himself desired. From William HAZLITT to the present day he has left commentators uncertain as to exactly how radical his aims were. Hazlitt, in an essay on Horne Tooke in *The Spirit of the Age*, accused him of enticing others into dangerous political activities, while steering clear of these himself.

Horne Tooke's caution, however, did not prevent him being arrested on 16 May 1794, and kept in prison for six months before being put on trial for high treason on 17 November. Though ably defended by Thomas Erskine and Vicary Gibbs, he himself took an active role in his trial. He examined many witnesses himself and made many witty observations on the conduct of his trial. His trial lasted six days, but it took the jury only eight minutes to acquit him. He emerged from prison a popular hero.

Although, thereafter, Horne Tooke acted in a more circumspect manner, he never abandoned his interest in politics or in political reform. He continued to oppose the war with France and to criticize Pitt's economic policies and his repressive measures. In 1795 he stood once more for election at Westminster. He came a distant third, although he received 2,819 votes. On the hustings he gave a witty and sarcastic speech which raised the issues of the war, heavy taxation and widespread economic distress. He is also credited with having drafted a substantial pamphlet, *The Causes and Effects of the National Debt and Paper Money on Real and Natural Property, in the Present State of Civil Society*, published posthumously during the financial crisis of 1818. This work maintains that all property originates in labour and yet the lazy landowners live in luxury while labourers live in poverty. It attacks the whole system of public credit and the heavy taxes raised by the Exchequer. This whole financial system increases the power of the government, enriches the moneyed interest, and ultimately impoverishes the poor. While taxes may be paid initially by wealthy landowners and merchants, these men ensure that the burden is ultimately shifted onto the poor by raising prices or lowering wages. The only solution is for the government to refuse to pay the interest due on the national debt, apart from that portion owned by those with no more than one hundred pounds invested in government stock.

After this election, Horne Tooke increasingly acted as the political mentor of Francis Burdett. He encouraged Burdett in his inquiries in 1798, 1800 and 1802 into the harsh conditions in the Cold Bath Fields prison, where many radicals were incarcerated, and he later campaigned to have Burdett elected as a member for Middlesex in 1802 and for Westminster in 1807. To his surprise, Horne Tooke himself was invited in 1801 by the 'half-mad' Lord Camelford to stand at the by-election at Old Sarum, a notorious pocket borough. Although he had previously attacked such corrupt boroughs, Horne Tooke could not resist this offer. He entered parliament on 16 February 1801, took the oath and participated in various debates, particularly on the war and on economic hardship. Almost at once, however, Lord Temple challenged his right to sit in the House of Commons because he was in holy orders. Horne Tooke insisted that he was no longer a clergyman and that, in any case, the law was far from clear on the issue. Henry Addington, the prime minister, then secured a bill to debar deacons and priests from sitting in the House of Commons. Horne Tooke retained his seat until parliament was dissolved in June 1802, but the new law prevented him being re-elected.

Horne Tooke spent the last decade of his life shaping the political views and supporting the political career of Francis Burdett and continuing his serious study of the English language. Increasingly in bad health, suffering from dropsy in particular, he became famous for presiding over Sunday lunches at his home in Wimbledon. There a host of able men in a wide variety of fields made the journey out from London to take part in jovial, witty and combative discussions on a very wide range of subjects. He died in this house in 1812, and planned to be buried in his own garden. His daughters and numerous friends ensured instead that he was buried at St Mary's parish church in Ealing. His impressive library was sold off, with many of his best books being bought by Burdett.

BIBLIOGRAPHY
The Petition of an Englishman (1765).
A Letter to J. Dunning (1778).
(with Richard Price) *Facts: Addressed to the Landholders, Stockholders, Merchants, Farmers, Manufacturers, Tradesmen, Proprietors of Every Description, and Generally to all the Subjects of Great Britain and Ireland* (1780).
A Letter to Lord Ashburton (1782).
Two Pair of Portraits (1788).
Proceedings in an Action for Debt Between the Right Honourable Charles James Fox, plaintiff, and John Horne Tooke, Esq., defendant (1792).
The Speeches of John Horne Tooke during the Westminster Election, 1796; with his two addresses to the electors of Westminster (1796).
The Causes and Effects of the National Debt and Paper Money on Real and Natural Property, in the Present State of Civil Society (1818).
Diversions of Purley, 2 vols (1829; repr. ed. R. Taylor, 1993).
The Prison Diary (16 May–22 November, 1794) of John Horne Tooke, ed. A.V. Beedell and A.D. Harvey (Leeds, 1995).

Further Reading
Aarsleff, H., *The Study of Language in England, 1780–1860* (Princeton, 1967).

Barrell, J. *Imagining the King's Death: Figurative Treason, Fantasies of Regicide 1793–1796* (Oxford, 2000).
Bewley, C. and Bewley, D., *Gentleman Radical: A Life of John Horne Tooke 1736–1812* (1998).
Graham, J., *The Nation, The Law and The King: Reform Politics in England, 1789–1799*, 2 vols (Lanham, Maryland, 2000).
Howell, T.J., *A Complete Collection of State Trials* (1818, vol. 25, pp. 1–748).
Smith, O., *The Politics of Language 1791–1819* (Oxford, 1984).
Stephens, A., *Memoirs of John Horne Tooke*, 2 vols (1813).
Thomas, P.D.G., *John Wilkes: A Friend to Liberty* (Oxford, 1996).
Wharam, A., *The Treason Trials, 1794* (Leicester, 1992).
Wilkes, J., *The Controversial Letters of John Wilkes Esq., the Rev. John Horne, and their principle* [sic] *adherents* (1771).
Yarborough, M.C., *John Horne Tooke* (New York, 1926; repr. New York, 1966).

H.T. Dickinson

HORNER, Francis (1778–1817)

Francis Horner was born in Edinburgh on 12 August 1778, and died 8 February 1817 in Pisa. His father was John Horner, an Edinburgh merchant; his mother, Joanna, was the daughter of John Baillie, a writer to the signet. Horner went to Edinburgh High School in 1786, and entered Edinburgh University in 1792. He left the university at the end of the summer term in 1795, turning to the study of law. In 1800 he was called to the Scottish bar. In 1803 he moved to London and became a student of Lincoln's Inn in preparation for being called to the English bar. Also in 1802, along with Sydney Smith, then living in Edinburgh, and a group of young Scots, he founded the *Edinburgh Review*. This was to become one of the most important journals in the history of economics; although other contemporary journals carried numerous articles on economics, none equalled the *Edinburgh Review* in the importance of what they published. Horner, along with John Ramsay MCCULLOCH and Nassau SENIOR, essentially determined the economic content of the *Review*.

Between 1802 and 1806 Horner published eight economics articles, and six on other subjects, in the *Review*. Even before this date he was thinking about monetary issues. For example, on 17 March 1797, less three weeks after the Bank Restriction Act, he wrote to his father: 'All political reasonings point out the increase of paper currency as a pernicious evil; but it is hoped, that matters may yet go on well, provided it be used only as a temporary expedient' (1843: 156). By 1802 his knowledge of economics extended well beyond the monetary field. He wrote to the Duke of Somerset (at the suggestion of the Duke's brother) with a list of important economic works and an outline of their contents. In his letter, he showed a wide knowledge of both English and French writings. Nor did he confine himself to reading what had been published. When his friend John Allen went to the continent a few months later, Horner gave him a list of twenty-eight queries on economic and political matters on which to seek information.

In 1806 Horner entered the House of Commons as member for St Ives. He lost that seat in the election of 1807, but through a by-election became member for Windsor later that year. He then stayed in parliament until 1812, when he had to make room at Windsor for a nephew of Lord Carrington, the patron of the seat. He was, however, offered a seat for St Mawes by the Marquis of Buckingham in 1813; that seat he retained until his death. From 1806 to 1809, he was a member of the commission adjudicating on the claims of the creditors of the Nabob of Arcot.

Horner's most famous parliamentary effort is his co-authorship of the *Report of the Bullion Committee*, the Committee appointed in 1810, on his motion, to 'inquire into the cause of the high price of gold bullion, and to take into consideration the state of the circulating medium and of the exchange between Great Britain and foreign parts'. The other authors of the report were Henry THORNTON and William HUSKISSON, and the report recommended a resumption of gold convertibility after a period of two years. The report, important both to nineteenth-century monetary affairs and to future monetary historians and historians of economic thought, was compiled after only thirty-one days of sittings by the Committee. There was widespread debate over the report until the following year, when it was rejected by parliament.

Horner was interested in many other economic issues as well. It is worth remarking, however, that he often in his recommendations modified the conclusions to which his economic analysis had led him. He was much more ready than, for example, David RICARDO to temper the conclusions of his analysis with his views on morality. For example, in 1808 a bill that 'proposed with the consent of the masters as well as that of the journeymen, to limit the excessive depreciation of the wages of those employed in the weaving of Cotton' was brought before the House of Commons. Horner was opposed to the measure. But, according to Hansard, 'however strong his conviction was of the impropriety of the principle on which this measure was founded, he thought the application of such a numerous and deserving class of individuals merited every attention; and perhaps in discussing the remedy which had been proposed by the right honourable gentlemen one might be discovered' (Hansard, vol. XI: 426). Seven years later, Horner wished to strengthen the measure proposed by Sir Robert Peel to regulate the employment of apprentices in cotton mills. He did, however, always pay heed to economic theory, and urged others to do the same.

Commenting on some remarks made in the February 1815 debate on the Corn Laws, he said: 'But as to political economy generally, upon which ground could gentlemen pretend to depreciate its character, unless they meant to depreciate the exercise of reasoning upon the subject under the consideration of the committee?' (Hansard, vol. XXIX: 1032).

Particularly between 1814 and 1816, Horner was also involved in debates over British foreign policy. Until Napoleon's abdication in 1814 he had supported the war, but thereafter he was very critical of the government's foreign policy. When Napoleon returned from Elba, Horner urged that Britain should take no hostile action unless Napoleon had first committed an act of aggression. He remained critical of British policy after Waterloo, attacking the peace treaties. He urged the dangers of forcing on France a government to which its people objected. This view on foreign policy was opposed to that of many of the main figures in the Whig Party, including the Marquis of Buckingham, through whose patronage Horner had obtained a seat in Parliament. Horner therefore offered his resignation to the Marquis, but this was refused and Horner kept the seat until he died in 1817.

Horner's main contributions to economics are his co-authorship of the Bullion Report, and his early review of Thornton's *Paper Credit*. His influence was very considerable. His approach was important: economic policies should be analysed by the tools of economics, used in conjunction with the relevant facts, and these facts should include the experience of other countries. His influence was also spread through the *Edinburgh Review*, and not just through his own writings: he encouraged others to write on economic matters as well. The circulation of the *Review* was wide: the original printing of the first issue was 750 copies but by 1807, only five years later, 5,000 copies were printed.

Horner's review of Henry Thornton's *An Enquiry into the Nature and Effects of the Paper Credit of Great Britain* was first published in 1802, and consisted of an article of some thirty pages in the *Edinburgh Review*. This article played a major role in diffusing Thornton's ideas. Hayek noted that the review glossed over some of the finer points of Thornton's analysis, but that Horner 'gave an exposition of the argument of the book in a form which was considerably more systematic and coherent than the original version', (Hayek 1939: 51).

Horner was a man of wide intellectual interests and great intellectual vigour. In February 1808, Sydney Smith wrote of him to Francis Jeffrey: 'Of our friend Horner I do not see much. He has four distinct occupations, each of which may fairly occupy the life of a man not deficient in activity: the Carnatic Commission, the Chancery Bar, Parliament, and a very numerous and select acquaintance' (Smith 1953, vol. 1: 133). In 1802 he joined the King of Clubs, a club subsequently joined by MALTHUS and Ricardo. In 1807 he joined Brooks, a predominantly Whig club which Ricardo joined in 1818. Again like Ricardo, he belonged to the Geological Society of London. He was a member of the African Institution, an organization strongly interested in the suppression of the slave trade, where he encountered members of the Clapham sect. Though not a member of that sect, Horner shared their views on slavery and on education, and sought to advance these both in and out of Parliament. In 1797, Horner translated Euler's *Elements of Algebra* from the French and wrote a short biography of Euler. He also planned, but did not carry out, a translation of the philosophical and political writings of Turgot.

Horner's health was not robust. It broke down in the summer of 1816, and in October of that year he left England. At the end of November he reached Pisa, where he died a few months later. He was buried in the Protestant cemetery at Leghorn. When on 3 March 1817, moving the writ for a by-election for the seat of St Mawes (which Horner had held at his death), Lord Mawes paid a glowing tribute to Horner, and was supported by many others including Canning. Even before his death, tributes were paid to him describing his intelligence, industry and good judgement. James MILL wrote to Ricardo when Horner was in Italy: 'He will be a very great loss – even his absence this winter is grievously to be deplored – when so many foolish, and I fear, some villainous, scheme of finance will be proposed and listened to' (Ricardo 1951–5, vol. VII: 85). Ricardo wrote in reply: 'The absence of Horner is indeed a great loss. I meet with no-one who does not lament his illness. Whatever he has undertaken he has done well, and has always avoided the error into which I think Brougham is apt to fall, he never goes beyond the mark, he never endeavours to prove too much' (Ricardo 1951–5, vol. VII: 89–90).

BIBLIOGRAPHY

A Memoir of the Life and Character of Euler (1822).
Memoirs and Correspondence of Francis Horner MP, ed. L. Horner (1843).
The Economic Writings of Francis Horner in the Edinburgh Review, 1802–6, ed. F.W. Fetter (1957).
The Horner Papers: Selections from the Letters and Miscellaneous Writings of Francis Horner, MP, 1895–1817, ed. K. Bourne and W.B. Taylor (Edinburgh, 1994).

Further Reading
Ricardo, D., *The Works and Correspondence of David Ricardo*, ed. P. Sraffa (Cambridge, 1951–5).
Smith, N.C., *The Letters of Sydney Smith* (Oxford, 1953).

Geoffrey Wood

HOUGHTON, John (c.1640–1705)

Houghton was born, probably in London, the son of an apothecary. A tentative birth date of 1640 has been assigned to him, but that may not be reliable. He died in London in September or October 1705. He studied for a year at Corpus Christi College, Cambridge, but then discontinued his studies and returned to London. He became an apothecary, opening a shop in Gracechurch Street and doing a thriving business in luxury goods such as coffee and chocolate. He appears to have become quite prosperous, and devoted his leisure time to science, particularly the improvement of agriculture and husbandry. He was elected a fellow of the Royal Society in 1680, and was for several years a member of the Royal Society's committee on improving agriculture.

Houghton's major achievement was the editing of a periodical, *A Collection of Letters for the Improvement of Husbandry and Trade*, from 1681–3, and its successor, *A Collection for Improvement of Husbandry and Trade*, from 1692–1703. The first series, though short-lived, included contributions from figures such as John EVELYN. The second, with the backing of the Royal Society, was considerably larger and ran for twelve years, with issues appearing irregularly at intervals of two to three months. A four-volume collection of articles from both series, edited by Richard Bradley, appeared in 1727.

Lord Ernle, in his history of English agriculture, referred to Houghton's work as the first attempt to develop a scientific periodical on agriculture. Most of the works are technical, many contributed anonymously, on a wide variety of topics relating to farming and livestock. Articles of specific economic interest are few, but occasional contributions try to summarise the debate on issues related to farming such as enclosure and poverty. Often the articles are judicious, trying to show both sides of the debate. There are also occasional reviews of other publications; the very first issue contained a review of Thomas FIRMIN's

Some Proposals for the Imploying of the Poor (1678), setting out its contents but neither praising nor condemning the work itself. There are occasional articles on trade, mostly listing overseas markets for various commodities. The journals are a mine of information for anyone wishing to understand best practice in English agriculture at the beginning of the eighteenth century. Houghton's short pamphlet on credit (1683) is explanatory but contains no original ideas.

BIBLIOGRAPHY
England's Great Happiness: or, a Dialogue between Content and Complaint (1677).
A Collection of Letters for the Improvement of Husbandry and Trade (1681–3).
An Account of the Bank of Credit in the City of London (1683).
A Collection for Improvement of Husbandry and Trade (1692–1703).

Further Reading
Bradley, R. (ed.), *Husbandry and Trade Improved*, 4 vols (1728).
Ernle, Lord, *English Farming: Past and Present* (1912).
Glaisyer, N., 'Readers, Correspondents and Communities: John Houghton's *A Collection for the Improvement of Husbandry and Trade* (1692–1703)', in A. Shepard and P. Withington (eds), *Communities in Early Modern England* (Manchester, 2000, pp. 235–51).

Morgen Witzel

HOWLETT, John (1731–1804)

Howlett was born in Warwickshire in 1731, and died at Bath in 1804. He studied at Oxford from 1749 to 1755. After an interval in which his movements are unknown, from 1762 he served as curate of two country parishes, first Boughton, then Hunton, both near Maidstone. These low-level posts suggest a man without powerful connections. In 1782 – possibly on the strength of his new reputation as an author – he was appointed to the parish of Great Dunmow, Essex, where a healthy stipend (augmented in 1786 by a further appointment as vicar of Badow) helped him to support a more affluent life-style, and to travel across southern England and to France.

Even before he was first published, Howlett somehow managed to build some connections: notably with agricultural writer Arthur YOUNG; the socially and statistically curious bishop of Chester, Beilby Porteus, and Alexander Wedderburn, Lord Loughborough, shortly to become Pitt's Lord Chancellor (whose interest in such matters dated back to his Scottish university days). Howlett's first foray into print, at the age of fifty, was *An Examination of Dr Price's Essay on the Population of England and Wales* (Maidstone, 1781). Thereafter he published nine other pamphlets, and also two sermons. Especially notable are *An Enquiry into the Influence which Enclosures have had upon the Population of England* (1786) and *The Insufficiency of the Causes to which the Increase of the Poor's Rates and our Poor have generally been ascribed* (1788). He also sent more than a dozen contributions to Young's periodical, *Annals of Agriculture*. The topics which interested him – population, agriculture, the state of the poor, patterns of health and disease, and the interrelations between these – were urgent and contested ones in an era of rising agricultural prices and poor rates. Howlett combined zeal in amassing relevant data with a reflective interest in the wider significance of his findings; also, a willingness to stake out controversial positions. This made his work of interest to a network of like-minded enquirers, with some of whom he corresponded.

Howlett was an 'optimist' on the population question. Unlike Richard PRICE, he thought that the population of England was rising, and that the rise in food prices was in part the result of this: not evidence of agricultural collapse or dereliction. He was similarly optimistic in his assessment of the impact of enclosures: a comparison of population trends between sample enclosed and unenclosed parishes persuaded him that enclosures were not driving people from the land. His views on the state of the poor, though consonant with his other views, were by contrast pessimistic, insofar as he thought that rising poor rates reflected a real increase in poverty, and not either administrative failure or the increasing idleness of the common people. In his view, wages were lagging behind prices. Nor indeed was poor relief filling the gap: the difference was being taken out of 'the blood and bones of the poor'. Howlett did not follow the many among his contemporaries who hoped to encourage the poor to contribute more to their own support through benefit societies: in his view, the rigours of their situation made this impracticable.

These views influenced Howlett's response to the French Revolution. During the years of terror, when many feared that like scenes might yet be enacted in England, Howlett, though endorsing the efforts of the 'Association for the Protection of Liberty and Property against Republicans and Levellers' to rally support for the constitution, nonetheless deprecated propaganda suggesting that all was well in England, arguing the poor had real grounds for grievance, which anyone concerned to preserve social peace would do well to address. Troubles in France itself were, as he saw it, in part the product of yet more dire social conditions (conditions he had observed and about which he had also written).

A hallmark of Howlett's writings is his insistence on the need carefully to assess a full range of evidence. He criticizes Price for lining up only evidence which supports his 'pessimistic' conclusions, and also for failing to engage effectively with criticism. Howlett demonstrated pertinacity and ingenuity in amassing data to test hypotheses. In order to test the impact of enclosures on population, for example, he identified a range of recent enclosure acts from the statute books, then wrote to the clergy of those parishes and of a sample of non-enclosed parishes asking them to copy down baptism and burial data from parish registers and send him the results. He was nonetheless also prepared to push inadequate data further than it would easily go: his 1786 *Essay on the Population of Ireland* (a country he never visited) has a notably slender empirical base.

BIBLIOGRAPHY

An Examination of Dr Price's Essay on the Population of England and Wales (Maidstone, 1781).

Observations on the Increased Population, Healthiness, &c. of the Town of Maidstone (Maidstone, 1782).

An Enquiry into the Influence which Enclosures have had upon the Population of England (1786).

An Essay on the Population of Ireland (1786).

The Insufficiency of the Causes to which the Increase of the Poor's Rates and our Poor have generally been ascribed...and a Slight General View of Mr Acland's Plan for Rendering the Poor Independent (1788).

Further Reading

John, A.H., 'Introduction' to J. Howlett, *Enclosure and Population* (Farnborough, 1973).

Glass, D.V., *Numbering the People: The Eighteenth-Century Population Controversy and the Development of Census and Vital Statistics in Britain* (Farnborough, 1973).

Joanna Innes

HOYLE, William (1831–86)

William Hoyle was born in 1831 in Rossendale valley, Lancashire, into a poor family. He died on 26 February 1886, either at Tottington, Lancashire, or in Manchester. Hoyle's education seems to have included some elements of the 'Protestant work ethic' of hard work and thrift. Consequently, in 1851 he was able to start up a business as a cotton-spinner in partnership with his father at Brooksbottom near Bury, Lancashire. In 1859 he built a large mill at Tottington. By 1872 the Tottington mill had nine hundred looms and also had some spinning machines. William Hoyle & Co. owned both the Bottoms Hall spinning mill and another mill, known as Potter Factory. Hoyle married in 1859 upon his move to Tottington. The Hoyles brought in labour from impoverished agricultural areas, thus satisfying the laws of supply and demand. However, there were accusations that the company ruined the town because 'outsiders' who worked for less money were brought in and the Hoyles were able to lower wages to their employees.

In nineteenth-century England, almost anyone could open an alehouse and there were no licensing hours. The drunkenness of the working classes became a social concern, and the temperance movement began around 1826. In 1863, Hoyle became one of the founders of the Lancashire and Cheshire Band of Hope and temperance union. He was its honorary secretary until his death and remained an active member of the temperance movement.

In 1869 Hoyle published a *An Inquiry into the long-continued Depression in the Cotton Trade* which was revised, extended and published in 1871 as *Our National Resources, and How They Are Wasted*. Through this book, Hoyle became a recognized authority on the statistics of the drink question. He estimated that one-sixth of the population of England and Wales fell below the poverty line because of alcohol consumption. He followed up the book with a number of short publications and letters to the *Times* on the subject. Partly through his work, the 1874 Licensing Act was passed, limiting the opening hours of public houses.

Hoyle was a supporter of the United Kingdom Alliance, a temperance movement that included the 'Blue Cross' organization for young people. He was also interested in the introduction into England of Good Templarism, an organization that taught the ideals of temperance, peace and brotherhood. In connection with these organizations he wrote many pamphlets and letters. His *Hymns and Songs for Temperance Societies and Bands of Hope* were very popular.

BIBLIOGRAPHY
Our National Resources, and How They Are Wasted (1871).
Crime in England and Wales in the Nineteenth Century (1876).

Marjorie Bloy

HUME, David (1711–76)

Hume was born David Home on 7 May 1711 in Edinburgh, and died there on 25 August 1776. He was the youngest son of the lawyer Joseph Home of Ninewells, who died in 1713. David, together with an elder brother and a sister, was brought up by his mother Katherine in a strongly Calvinist environment. Like John Stuart MILL, he had the experience of a deep crisis as a young man. He was educated as a lawyer at the University of Edinburgh 1726–9, which he left without having earned a degree. By this time he already had developed a strong interest in philosophy. He was influenced by the Stoics and also by the pioneers of empirical methods in science such as BACON and NEWTON and thinkers on the modern political philosophy and natural law including Grotius, HOBBES, Pufendorf and LOCKE. Later in his life, he met eminent contemporary thinkers such as Benjamin Franklin, Edmund BURKE and Edward Gibbon. During his stays in France, Hume became conversant with some of the French thinkers. His correspondence with Rousseau (the friendship with whom ended in discord after Hume had brought him to England) was published in 1766. Over and above all, Hume prized his friendship to thinkers of the Scottish enlightenment, amongst them Adam SMITH. Like Smith, Hume spent a fatherless childhood, avoided marriage and (to the best of our knowledge) fatherhood.

Hume did not have an academic career. Attempts by friends to endow him with an academic chair were turned down twice: in 1744 (ethics and pneumatical philosophy at the University of Edinburgh) and in 1752 (logic at the University of Glasgow). His reputation as a critic of established religion no doubt was amongst the reasons for these failures. The portfolio of his occupational activities is richly diversified, including posts in trade and as a tutor, as a secretary on diplomatic missions, as librarian to the Faculty of Advocates in Edinburgh (giving him access to a major library, which was of some importance for the historical research resulting in his multi-volume *History of England*, 1754–61), as ambassador in Paris and as Under-Secretary of State. Enjoying modest financial independence based on a small patrimony, he devoted considerable periods of his life (including his stay in France from 1735–7) exclusively to his philosophy. His theoretical *magnum opus* (*A Treatise of Human Nature*, 1739–40) was received by the public with disappointingly little enthusiasm. As Hume himself famously put it in his short published autobiography, it fell dead-born from the press. In the light of his influence on eminent thinkers like Adam Smith and Immanuel Kant, this is a serious misjudgement.

The self-perceived failure to gain adequate distinction as a philosopher induced Hume to change the expository mode of his writing. He never again wrote a book which is comparable to the *Treatise* with its rigorous conceptual analyses and thought experiments. On the one hand, he developed a more essayistic style. On the other hand, he increasingly relied on historical examples as a device for expounding his arguments and for the kind of limited generalizations which he deemed possible in the application of what he called 'experimental philosophy' to moral subjects (psychology, political and social theory, including economics). The historical turn in his writing has an highly important substantial aspect: for Hume (who reflected on the impracticality of controlled experiments in the moral sciences in the Introduction to the *Treatise*), and the natural experiments afforded by history were the main source of empirical material for social, political and economic theory.

In his *Essays: Moral and Political* of 1741–2, Hume styled himself 'as a kind of resident or ambassador from the dominions of learning to those of conversation' (1993: 2). This anonymously published collection of twenty-seven essays was the first of more than a dozen such collections which were to appear during his lifetime. These collections included revised versions of some of the older essays as well as new ones. A final revised and authorized collection of thirty-nine essays appeared shortly after Hume's death (*Essays Moral, Political, and Literary*, 1777). This collection also included the bulk of his essays dealing with more technical issues in political economy, which first had appeared in the *Political Discourses* in 1752. In his essays, a broad variety of political, philosophical, cultural, historical, demographical and economic themes is covered.

Hume's *Enquiries* (1748–51) are attempts to make available a more accessible version of his philosophy. The more interesting of the *Enquiries* is the *Enquiry Concerning the Principles of Morals* (1751), which Hume believed to be by far the best one of his writings. Hume offers us here new insights on the status and function of institutions such as private property, which reflect the advances he made as a social theorist and economist. Whereas in the third book of the *Treatise* (*Of Morals*), his main concern was the explanation of the individual motifs of moral behaviour in general and for accepting the rules of justice in particular (normative psychology), in the *Enquiry* the emphasis was somewhat shifted to the socio-psychological aspects of morality and its evolution. With respect to moral theory, the *Treatise* and the *Enquiry* are complementary. Regarding the more foundational parts, the *Treatise* clearly is the more profound piece.

In terms of the subjects covered, Hume's thought is enormous in scope. Moreover, his thinking underwent considerable changes in exposition and emphasis. Both aspects contributed to a lack of awareness of its systematic character and the nature of the interrelationships between what were seen as isolated parts. This clearly applies to his economic writings. Representing only a small portion of his *oeuvre*, some of his economic essays were well-known amongst economists. Read as self-contained pieces in isolation from the remainder of his work, the ideas articulated in these mostly rather short essays typically were attributed the status of interesting forerunners to later systematic developments. Yet they often relate to Hume's broader project in terms of method as well as in terms of content. Not only economists failed to acknowledge that Hume is one of the most interesting pre-classical authors with regard to foundational problems of social and economic theory and the political economy of the emerging market society. Many philosophers (whose reading of Hume was focused on issues such as epistemology) failed to see that the *Treatise* is also a major achievement in political philosophy. Important parts of it deal with changes in the nature of moral ties between individuals in the emerging market society and the concomitant development of institutions (for instance the pivotal role of justice as stability of possession).

The programme and the most important corner-stones of this approach are to be found in their fully-fledged form in the *Treatise*. Human social life must be seen as a part of nature in a wider sense. Hence we are in need of a de-mystifying account of human agency and social life which must be explained in terms of the methods of modern science. This applies particularly to phenomena such as morality which typically used to be derived from super-natural powers. For Hume, this explanation has to be non-reductive in the sense that he puts great emphasis on the need to understand the distinct status of various types of moral obligation, of natural virtues like beneficence, property rights, promissory rights, rights to command obedience and so forth. This rules out simple utilitarian or contract-based explanations of the normative infrastructure of modern civil society. Hume sees that the concept of contract presupposes a kind of normative infrastructure belonging to the sphere of human social artifice, which itself is in need of explanation (and which, of course, must not be based on contract in order to avoid circularity). The first step in his endeavour to establish 'experimental moral philosophy' is therefore to study human nature, that is the way in which our biologically given nature, human cognition, human reason and the passions work and how they do (or do not) motivate human action.

According to Hume, study of human nature is basic for all sciences as it clarifies their epistemological foundation. It is of particular importance for what he calls experimental moral sciences in which the analysis of the principles of human nature has immediately to be complemented by an analysis of the conditions and forces of the external environment. Confronting the principles of human agency with an adequate account of these external conditions allows for limited generalizations regarding human behaviour and its pattern in particular environmental, social and institutional contexts. Under some suitable institutional premises, we may even expect 'general and certain' predictions 'as any which the mathematical sciences afford us', as Hume (1993: 14) declares in the essay *That Politics May be Reduced to a Science*.

Hume's analysis of human nature as well as the descriptions of environmental conditions as expounded in the *Treatise* offer conceptualizations pivotal in economics (rationality, scarcity, utility, public goods). For instance, in the chapter on the origin of government of the *Treatise* (1739–40: III.ii.7), Hume provides an analysis of the co-ordination failure linked to what modern economists call public good problems. Hume aims at a realistic account of mental mechanisms, of the cognitive and emotional processes mediating the force of the passions which ultimately drive choices. Reason conceptually plays a serving role. It imposes formal requirements on us which are embedded in a complex texture of motivating forces and mediating mechanisms. What reason 'requires' (correcting distortions of imagination, myopic perspectives, or partiality) in an abstract sense is one thing. The extent to which these requirements actually contribute to the human faculty of reflective correction of errors is a quite different thing, depending on emotional and cognitive mechanisms and their biases and on empirical circumstances triggering some of these biases. Moreover, Hume is interested in socio-psychological mechanisms such as sympathy, along with other mental mechanisms and reason helps to explain the evolution of artificial virtues (justice) and artificial human institutions such as stable private property, contracts and the government.

Hume rejects all attempts to make reason the explanatory basis of morality or other phenomena in the social world. We owe to Hume the canonical account of reason as the 'slave of passions' characterizing reason as guiding the agent with respect to the means which are necessary/sufficient to attain some given end. Intrinsic ends, wanting things valued for their own sake and not for their instrumental value, cannot be irrational. This focus on instrumental rationality may be taken as an informal version of individual rationality as a kind of formal coherence among preferences and choices (as captured by the axiomatic systems proposed by Frank RAMSEY or Leonard Savage) which is now common among economists. Modern economics extended this means-oriented concept of rationality to the social level as the quest for efficiency in the allocation of scarce means. This leads us to the role of *scarcity*, which is crucial for Hume's account of external conditions of human agency. He emphasizes the role of scarcity in imposing its logic upon socio-economic institutions in general, making it very clear that his explanation of justice as an artificial virtue as well as the role of private property and of the government hinge on scarcity and would fail under conditions of abundance as well as under conditions of ubiquitous absolute poverty. Understanding the role of scarcity, he also did not fail to grasp the function of the price system as mechanism of resource allocation, as is shown not only in his economic essays but also in various passages in the *History of England*.

It needs to be emphasized that, for Hume, human agency is by no means completely determined by the immutable elements of human nature. The psychological pattern of economic motivation is endogenous with respect to social mechanisms and historical processes, such as the process of economic growth, the rise of commerce and civil society in which he was much interested. Hume's interest in history was motivated by the observation that macro-processes provide fertile ground for application of experimental moral science because they are likely to be driven by increasingly robust and stable patterns of motifs, which tend to be fostered and stabilized by the institutional patterns emerging during this process. In addition, he remarked that the effects of pure chance and whimsical idiosyncrasy tend to be eliminated in the context of such macro-processes due to the law of large numbers. In *Of the Rise and Progress of the Arts and Sciences*, Hume summarizes the reason for this in a 'general rule': '*What depends on a few persons is, in a great measure, to be ascribed to chance, or secret and unknown causes: what arises from a great number, may often be accounted for by determinate and known causes*' (1993: 57; italics in original). According to Hume, the world is still too young to allow for many general truths in human affairs, but in the *History of England* he managed to show the systematic interrelations between social and economic changes in the formative period of modern society, or more precisely, how changes in the historical environment affected the way in which human passions operated and thereby stimulated economic growth.

This fits well within Hume's more general project of a natural history of the evolution of the network of social ties which is the main task of empirical moral science. Hume endorses an optimistic view concerning the potential of the commercial society and economic growth for promoting human values. In addition to the more narrowly utilitarian aspects of increasing opportunities for consumption experiences and leisure, he emphasizes the enlargement of the scope for entrepreneurial activity. Moreover, growing economic interdependence brings more people into contact with each other and thereby provides enlarged opportunities for social moral learning. Economic growth and the growth of knowledge go hand in hand. Ethical learning, the growth of scientific knowledge and the growing awareness of economic interdependence all foster the understanding of the advantages of political institutions built on individual liberty and stability of possession. In this context, his arguments in defence of the manifold advantageous effects of luxury deserve to be mentioned as a particularly crisp attempt to model some of the benign interrelationships between economics, politics and ethics (in *Of Refinement in the Arts* and *Of Commerce*).

Hume's ethical-political optimism notwithstanding, his view of socio-economic processes does not take the form of the Panglossian view according to which whatever is, is best. His distance to this view is profoundly related to his fundamental concern that valuation and motivation are two entirely different things. This tenet informs the translation of his general theory of agency into psychological microfoundations for social and economic theory. Hume gives self-interest its due but also provides us with a stock of non ad hoc arguments which allow us to go beyond self-interest. In particular, his accounts of the motivational patterns referring to social or professional classes (landowners, priests) make immediately clear why motivational patterns are not necessarily benign or welfare enhancing. These generalizations are derived from confronting human nature with the specific circumstances under which certain classes of individuals live. Consider the following paradigmatic passage from the essay *Of Interest*:

There is no craving or demand of the human mind more constant and insatiable than that for exercise and employment; and this desire seems the foundation of most of our passions and pursuits. Deprive a man of all business and serious occupation, he runs restless from one amusement to another... Give him a more harmless way of employing his mind or body, he is satisfied and feels no longer that insatiable thirst after pleasure. But if the employment you give him be lucrative, especially if the profit be attached to every particular exertion of industry, he has gain so often in his eye, that he acquires, by degree, a passion for it, and knows no such pleasure as that of seeing the daily increase of his fortune. And this is the reason why trade increases frugality, and why, among merchants, there is the same overplus of misers above prodigals, as among the possessors of land there is the contrary.

(Hume 1993: 182–3)

There are three aspects of this passage which are of interest. First, it leads us into Hume's economic psychology, presenting in a nutshell his pluralistic theory of economic motivation, within which three independent types of motifs play a role: (1) the craving for exercise and employment, (2) the desire for pleasure, amusement and leisure (which is more specific than and kept distinct from consumption necessary for bare biological subsistence) and (3) the desire for wealth accumulation. Second, it shows how the idea of endogeneity of preferences is given substance when it is combined with a pluralistic psychology of motivation and a suitable account of class-related patterns, and how it may become a key to the explanation of socio-economic changes in history. Third, the way in which the idle and prodigal landowner is modelled suggests that understanding some historically found patterns of motivations in no sense does entail their justification. For Hume, the structure of the good is accounted for by some concept of utility, but this structure does not immediately translate into the 'corresponding' psychological mechanisms, and much less into social structures, mechanisms or institutions which have the tendency to promote the good.

Amongst Hume's contributions to economics in a narrower sense, his quantity theory specie flow model is perhaps the most widely quoted (*Of the Balance of Trade*). As in the case of his attempt to explain the level of interest in terms of supply and demand for real capital discussed below, this model can be seen as part of his analysis of the historical progress of commercial civilization and his attempts to de-mystify peculiar economic phenomena pertinent to it. His arguments are linked to two main ideas: the power of self-regulating forces and the emphasis on the level of *real* economic activity and industrial progress determining the centre of gravitation of the system (he makes explicit use of the physical analogy). Hume argued that the amount of specie in a country regulates itself by gravitating to an equilibrium characterized by a balanced relation between imports and exports. Attempts to enhance the amount of specie by trade restrictions (which may be favoured by mercantilist policies) are futile, as the concomitant rise in domestic prise level will hurt exports and boost imports, thereby leading to an offsetting outflow of specie.

On similar quantity theory grounds, Hume argues that (contrary to doctrines endorsed in the mercantilist period) the rate of interest is not determined by money supply. As an increase in the amount of money *ceteris paribus* must lead to a proportionate increase in the general price level, the demand for borrowing in turn must increase at the same rate, thereby leading to the same equilibrium rate of interest as before. Rather, the rate of interest is ultimately determined by a host of socio-economic factors which determine demand and supply of real capital. These factors are crucial for the growth process of the commercial society in general because they influence (1) the size of the economic surplus, (2) the proportion of this surplus which is transformed into supply of real capital – and not borrowed by idle classes for consumption purposes as it was the case in feudalism – and (3) the demand for real capital. But in economic as well as in philosophical matters, Hume was no dogmatist: In a further essay expounding the basic logic of quantity theory (*Of Money*), it is argued that the economic processes triggered by the *increase* in money supply (but not its higher level) may spur economic activity.

One of the most brilliant and in a certain respect most interesting of the economic essays is the four-page piece *Of the Jealousy of Trade*. Hume tries to show that for an advanced trading nation like Great Britain it is impossible that the flourishing trade of foreign countries depresses domestic prosperity and hurts domestic industry (as he argued elsewhere, the case may be different for backward and poor countries). The bulk of the essay deals with providing arguments in support of the contrary thesis according to which foreign prosperity even is a necessary condition for domestic prosperity. The theoretical basis for these arguments deserve special attention because they show that he did not only understand the allocation function of market price systems, but to some extent also the role of markets in mediating a dynamic process of differentiation, learning, technological improvement, diffusion of technologies and innovation, coming close to a concept of competition as a discovery process. It is made clear that for Hume the history of the modern growth process is not captured by the idea of quantitative expansion.

Another essay presenting a rich array of arguments on a few pages concerns the political economy of taxation. One general message of this essay may be summarized as follows: excessively high taxes may discourage industry, but a certain amount of suitably administered taxation may spur economic activity. Moreover, Hume addresses the question of tax incidence, coming up with the sketch of a model linking incidence to the economic reactions to taxation. Even more interestingly, he introduces an insight which resembles some arguments of neo-Hobbesian Leviathan theory of taxation. It refers to a disadvantage of poll taxes as compared to what in the optimal taxation literature are called distortionary taxes (he also discusses taxes on consumption). According to Hume, poll taxes have no endogenous limit so that the sovereign may impose them in an arbitrary fashion and may raise them to an extent which depresses or even ruins economic activity. Tax avoidance by choices implying a reduction of the tax base is seen as a desirable self-regulating mechanism. Excessive raises in tax rates will lead to a sufficiently great diminution of the tax base as to reduce tax revenues. Hume concludes with a more general politico-economic reflection: the power of a sovereign to impose a system of taxation is correlated to a decent state of affairs as it makes obsolete more despotic and arbitrary ways of securing power.

Regarding public debt (*Of Public Credit*) it is impossible to summarize all the arguments, most of which emphasize the dangers of public credit. But Hume (1993: 206) also argues that public debt may be 'of some advantage to commerce, by diminishing its profits, promoting circulation, and encouraging industry'. His ultimate blow against those who endorse public debt as an innocuous method of public finance refers to the famous argument 'that the public is no weaker on account of its debts, since they are mostly due among ourselves'. Hume's (1993: 208) counter-argument relies on the auxiliary hypothesis that it *is* definitely possible to overburden a nation with taxes. If so, it may be overburdened by public debt as well. In this context, Hume invokes a strand of thought structurally similar to the idea that public debt is just postponed taxes. Hume concludes: 'But if all of our present taxes be mortgaged, must we not invent new ones? And may not this matter be carried to a length that is ruinous and destructive?'

If we compare Hume's economic thought to that of his friend Adam Smith, both provide fine examples of how to take a richer economic psychology on board, while at the same time being aware of economic mechanisms and processes which make part of that psychology redundant for economic explanations. One of the most salient differences in their economic thought is the description of the socio-economic environment. While for Smith various forms of specialization processes including mechanisms of cumulative causation play the key role in the institutional evolution characterizing modern society, Hume's explicit accounts of the phenomenon of the division of labour are more static. In the passages expressing his grasp of some of the dynamic effects of trade and exchange (such as the links between trade and diffusion of technology), he does not elaborate the idea of dynamic specialisation in a way comparable to Smith. But in many other respects, David Hume is much more than a predecessor.

BIBLIOGRAPHY

A Treatise of Human Nature (1739–40; ed. L.A. Selby-Bigge, revised P.H. Nidditch, Oxford, 1978).

An Enquiry Concerning Human Understanding (1748; revised edition ed. E. Steinberg, Indianapolis, 1993).
An Enquiry Concerning the Principles of Morals (1751; ed. J.B. Schneewind, Indianapolis, 1983).
Essays, Moral, Political, and Literary (1777; revised edition ed. E.F. Miller, Indianapolis, 1987).
The History of England, from the Invasion of Julius Caesar to The Revolution of 1688 (1754–61; ed. W.B. Todd, 6 vols, Indianapolis, 1983).
The Philosophical Works of David Hume, ed. T.H. Green and T.H. Grose, 4 vols (1882).
Writings on Economics, ed. E. Rotwein (Edinburgh, 1955).
Selected Essays, ed. S. Copley and A. Edgar (Oxford, 1993).

Further Reading
Baier, A.C., *A Progress of Sentiments* (Cambridge, Massachusetts, 1991).
Mossner, E.C., *The Life of David Hume* (Oxford, 1954).
Price, J.V., *David Hume* (1968; 2nd edn, 1991).
Smith, N.K., *The Philosophy of David Hume* (1941).
Stroud, B., *Hume* (1977).

Richard Sturn

HUME, Joseph (1777–1855)

Hume was born on 22 January 1777 at Ferryden, near Montrose, Scotland, the son of a shipmaster, and died 20 February 1855 at Burnley Hall, Norfolk. He went to school at Montrose Academy, where his closest friend was James MILL, and then studied medicine at Aberdeen and Edinburgh, acquiring the Certificate of the London Corporation of Surgeons and an MD from Marischal College, Aberdeen. He went to India in 1797 as an assistant surgeon in the marine service of the East India Company, and later became a supplier of food and clothing to the army. In 1808 he returned to Britain with a fortune of £40,000. He embarked on a tour of the British manufacturing districts to study labour conditions, concluding that employers were too powerful and the poor in need of education. In 1812 he paid the Duke of Cumberland £10,000 to gain the parliamentary seat of Weymouth and Melcombe Regis. When he was abandoned later that year by the Tories for consorting with the Whigs, Hume sued for breach of promise, as he expected to be MP for life, and gained £1,000 compensation.

Hume engaged in the affairs of the East India Company from 1812–18 as a stockholder, and argued that the Company should allow free trade. In 1815 he married Mary, the daughter of another stockholder, Joseph Burnley. Failing to become a director, he turned into a fierce critic of the Company's financial management. He was appointed manager of the Panton Street Provident Institution for Savings, an institution for working men's savings, in 1815. He also continued his career in politics, and was MP for Aberdeen Burghs (1818–30), Middlesex (1830–7), Kilkenny (1837–41) and Montrose Burghs (1842–55).

In the House of Commons Hume was a frequent and boring speaker. He campaigned long for parliamentary reform, presenting a Little Charter advocating triennial parliaments and an extension of the franchise to all ratepayers. His other causes included Roman Catholic Emancipation, equality for Jews, abolition of stamp duty on newspapers, and the repeal of the Six Acts and the Combination Acts. He chaired the House of Commons Select Committee on Income and Property Tax (1851). During long debates he maintained his stamina by eating fruit he had stuffed into his pockets.

From the beginning of his parliamentary career Hume had a distinctively libertarian attitude towards economic issues, unlike his more radical approach to education, which created a long association with Francis PLACE. When speaking on the framework knitters in 1812, Hume fervently opposed exclusive privileges for particular occupational groups and the regulation of industry. Uncontrolled competition, with no wage regulations and no prescribed standards for the quality of goods, he argued, would be beneficial to both capitalists and artisans. Free mobility of labour within and between countries was recommended. Benefit societies should not support strikers as this interferes with free and open competition. He believed that unions would be unnecessary in a free market for labour. Initially in 1844 he opposed factory safety regulations because they restricted the employment of labour, but later approved of giving children time to attend school.

The monetary debates of the early nineteenth century interested him. His views on coinage in 1816 were that there should be notes issued for less than £10 and that silver should be used for shillings and copper for pennies. He wanted an end to the competition between notes and gold coin. He approved of a move towards metrification by making a pound equal to 10 shillings, 100 pennies and 1,000 farthings. In 1827 he opposed the grant of more powers to the Bank of England because it was a monopoly. In 1839 he again mentioned the increase in the currency as the cause of rising prices, but wanted a mixed currency with paper convertible into gold. He accused the Bank of England of making money cheap by increasing its securities and engaging in the absurd practice of lending at four different rates of interest.

For years Hume preached the need for cuts in government expenditure. In his drive for economies, he caused more than half of the votes on economic matters in the House of Commons from 1823–30. Repeatedly he asserted that indirect taxes and protective duties could be cut if the government spent less. His opposition to many wars and to coercion in Ireland, as well as his attack on sinecures, were partly to save expenditure. The cost of maintaining the poor through the poor laws worried him. His support for the Poor Law Amendment Act also sprang from his belief that the change would encourage industry and morality among the poor. As he told his friend George Sinclair in August 1819, 'Economy with me is the order of the day, and I look on that as the best reform that can be attempted... Taxation and extraordinary expenditure...are the diseases of the State, and reduction of expenses...will cure it.'

BENTHAM said that Hume was the 'only true representative the people [of England] ever had'. Palmerston, in a tribute in the House of Commons said of him that 'he took the lead in almost every branch of improvement which has of late years been carried into practical operation'. Halevy (1955: 309) summed him up more savagely as having 'a heavy mind, but later won a reputation for himself by his pigheadedness in discussing budgets and in obtaining the necessary economies...'

BIBLIOGRAPHY

A letter addressed to the Right Honourable the Chancellor of the Exchequer and the substance of a speech of Mr Joseph Hume, on the third reading of the Bill for preventing frauds and abuses in the frame-work-knitting manufacture, and in the payment of persons employed therein (1812).

Thoughts on the New Coinage, with Reflections on Money and Coins, and a new system of coins and weights on a simple and uniform principle (1816).

An Account of the Provident Institution for Savings (1816).

Speech of Joseph Hume, Esq. MP on the Bank of England, and state of the currency made on 8 July 1839 (1839).

Further Reading

Chancellor, V., *The Political Life of Joseph Hume 1777–1855* (1986).

Halevy, E., *The Growth of Philosophic Radicalism* (Boston, 1955).
Huch, R.K. and Ziegler, P.R., *Joseph Hume: The People's MP* (Philadelphia, 1985).

Donald Rutherford

HUSKISSON, William (1770–1830)

Huskisson was born on 11 March 1770 at Birch Moreton Court, Warwickshire, and died on 15 September 1830 at Heaton, Manchester after being struck by a train. His father was William Huskisson of Oxley near Wolverhampton; his mother was Elizabeth Rotton, who died in 1774. Huskisson was sent to school in 1775, initially to Brewood, then to Albrighton, Staffordshire and Appleby, Leicestershire). In 1783 he went to Paris where he lived with and was educated by his maternal uncle, Dr Gem, the physician to the British embassy. It was through his uncle's connections that Huskisson met Benjamin Franklin and Thomas Jefferson, as well as many leading British politicians. On 6 April 1799 Huskisson married Elizabeth Mary Milbanke, the daughter of Admiral Mark Milbanke; they had no children.

In 1790, William Huskisson (senior) died. Huskisson inherited the small, heavily encumbered family estates at Oxley, which he was obliged to sell. He needed employment because he had no other source of income. Ten years later, he inherited Dr Gem's estate at Eastham, Sussex, and another in Worcestershire: these lands gave him a private income.

In 1830, Charles Greville (Wilson 1927: 1, 316) said, 'Huskisson was about sixty years old, tall, slouching, and ignoble-looking. In society he was extremely agreeable, without much animation, generally cheerful, with a great deal of humour, information, and anecdote, gentlemanlike, unassuming, slow in speech, and with a down-cast look, as if he avoided meeting anybody's gaze.'

After entering the political arena, Huskisson held a number of posts. He was Under Secretary for War and the Colonies in 1795 and Secretary of the Treasury in 1804, a post to which he returned in 1807. He was the colonial agent for Ceylon between 1811 and 1823, resigning from this position when he became President of the Board of Trade because he felt that the two offices were incompatible. He was Commissioner for Woods and Forests from 1814 to 1823. In 1827 he became Colonial Secretary and Leader of the House. His major contribution to the economic life of Britain included the opening of colonial trade to foreign competition, relaxing the Navigation Acts, promoting free trade and reducing import duties.

Huskisson began his political life as a Tory and saw the events of the French Revolution at first hand. In 1790 he joined the French 'Club of 1789' which supported the idea of a constitutional monarchy in that country. It was to this group that he read his discourse on the currency, a subject that interested him for the rest of his life. Also in 1790 he became the private secretary of Lord Gower, the British ambassador in France. When diplomatic relations with France were severed in 1792, Huskisson returned to England. Pitt introduced Huskisson to George Canning, who invited Huskisson to become secretary to the Admiralty. Canning and Huskisson became political allies and close friends until Canning's death in 1827.

In 1793 the Aliens Act was passed, preventing French Republicans from coming to England but allowing émigrés to travel freely. Huskisson was appointed to a newly created post in which he made arrangements for émigrés to travel to Britain. He proved himself to be a competent administrator, and in 1795 he was given employment as Under Secretary at War. Here, he met Lord Carlisle, who offered Huskisson the parliamentary seat of Morpeth in 1796. Aware that he was a poor speaker, he did not make his maiden speech until 1798. As a member of Pitt's government, he resigned in January 1801 but continued in post until March so that the new incumbent could learn the necessary duties. The following year, Huskisson stood as a parliamentary candidate at Dover; he was defeated and did not return to political life until February 1804, when he was elected as MP for Liskeard. In May 1804, following his return to office, Pitt appointed Huskisson as Secretary to the Treasury. Other parliamentary constituencies that Huskisson represented were Harwich (1807–12), Chichester (1812–23) and Liverpool (1823–30).

After Pitt's death, Huskisson chose to oppose Lord Grenville's new Whig government as a backbencher. In July 1806 he proposed a number of financial measures that the government implemented. Huskisson began to acquire a reputation as an economist. In 1808 he became involved in the reorganization of the relationship between the Treasury and the Bank of England at a time when paper money was depreciating. In 1810, Huskisson published *The Question Concerning the Depreciation of our Currency Stated and Examined*, which helped to establish his reputation as one of the country's leading economists. He was a member of the Bullion Committee of 1810, which recommended the resumption of cash payments by the Bank of England within two years whether or not Britain was still at war with France. Other members of the committee included David RICARDO, Francis HORNER, Spencer Perceval and Henry THORNTON. The debates on the report continued until 1811, when it was rejected by parliament.

Huskisson made many speeches on fiscal matters, but rarely spoke on other issues. He supported Catholic emancipation but rarely contributed to matters concerning foreign affairs. By March 1813 he was demanding changes to import duties. The following year, he joined Lord Liverpool's ministry where he worked with men such as Robert Peel and Frederick Robinson. Huskisson became a Privy Councillor in July 1814, and was one of the key supporters of the 1815 Corn Laws. In 1816 he was prominent in the debates on bank restrictions, favouring the idea of leaving the Bank of England to decide on the length of time it would continue the limitation on gold payments. In 1819 he became a member of the parliamentary committee of inquiry into the return to cash payments by the Bank of England. The report recommended this should be done in four stages between February 1820 and May 1823. Britain returned to the gold standard on 1 May 1820. Unfortunately, the rapid reduction on note issues brought a fall in the price of goods and caused widespread unemployment.

Huskisson was a member of the Committee of Inquiry into Agricultural Distress, established in 1821, and was the main author of the final report, even though his views on taxation made the agriculturalists distrust him. He opposed Lord Londonderry's proposal to lend £4 million for the relief of agricultural distress, and was instrumental in defeating the government's resolution on the report of the committee. Consequently, he tendered his resignation. It was rejected by Lord Liverpool, who went on to appoint Huskisson as Treasurer of the Navy in January 1822 and then as President of the Board of Trade in April that year, with cabinet rank. The latter appointment allowed Huskisson to apply his specialist skills and knowledge to economic matters. His sophisticated free trade ideas made him stand out among his cabinet colleagues.

In February 1823 Huskisson was chosen to stand as MP for Liverpool upon Canning's retirement from the constituency. It was thought that he was the only Tory who was capable of pacifying Liverpool's merchants, who had been hard hit by the Corn Laws. Huskisson was soon considered to be the representative of merchants' interests in parliament. In the space of about two years, he was responsible for the introduction and passing of legislation for regulating the manufacture of silk, for the Merchant Vessels' Apprenticeship Act, for legislation to remove restrictions on the manufacture of Scottish linen and also for a Registration of Ships Act. In 1825 he and James Deacon Hume consolidated the entire revenue legislation into eleven Acts. At the same time, Huskisson amended the revenue laws to introduce freer trade. Duties on imported cotton goods were reduced to a flat rate of 10 per cent; duties on woollen imports were fixed at 15 per cent; similar reductions were introduced on glass, paper, bottles, pottery, sugar, copper, zinc and lead. In 1824–5 he reduced the duties and taxes on such varied items as coal, wool, iron, coffee, wine, rum, hemp and silk. Huskisson argued that lighter taxes would increase sales and improve the economic basis of the country. Under his auspices, indirect taxes were reduced by £12 million without any marked adverse effect on government revenues.

Frederick Robinson had begun the overhaul of the Navigation Laws and commercial legislation. This work was continued by Huskisson, who was responsible for the Reciprocities Duties Act of June 1823. The legislation began the removal of the protectionist system by imposing duties and drawbacks on all goods, regardless of the origin of the carrying vessel. The Act allowed the new regulations to be extended to any country that was willing to reciprocate; it also provided for the continuation of restrictions to countries that were not.

Although Huskisson had supported the implementation of the Corn Laws in 1815, he came to have doubts about their effectiveness and began to work towards lifting the restrictions that had been imposed. The Corn Laws generated no revenue for the government, but they did restrict foreign trade at a time when British manufacturing was increasing rapidly. The Corn Laws prohibited the import of foreign grain until domestic grain reached eighty shillings a quarter. This artificially forced up the price of bread, limiting the amount of disposable income available for the purchase of manufactured goods. This affected manufacturing industry that relied heavily on domestic sales for its profits. In 1822, David Ricardo demanded that the corn duties should be removed gradually, starting with a flat rate of twenty shillings and being lowered by one shilling a year until the duty was reduced to a more acceptable, but fixed, ten shillings a quarter. Huskisson preferred a sliding scale because it was more flexible than a fixed duty. During the autumn of 1826, Huskisson began to prepare a new corn bill, but the proposed legislation was abandoned because of the Duke of Wellington's opposition.

During the early 1820s, many Britons were speculating in America. Huskisson saw the dangers of this, but his warnings were ignored; when the panic came in 1825, his policies of free trade were accused of causing it. The government intervened swiftly and prevented a major crash, and Huskisson spent much of 1825 dealing with America. He was involved in negotiations over the north western border between Canada and America and the navigation rights in the St Lawrence river. Another issue which concerned him was the slave trade in America. For all this work, his constituents, predominantly Liverpool merchants, presented him with a plate dinner service.

On 12 April 1827, Huskisson's friend George Canning succeeded Lord Liverpool as prime minister, but died on 8 August 1827. The new prime minister, Lord Goderich (Frederick Robinson), offered Huskisson the colonial office and leadership of the House of Commons. He accepted once he had been persuaded that this was the only way of continuing Canning's policies. Internal disputes in the cabinet led to Goderich's resignation and he was succeeded as prime minister by Wellington who wanted to continue the protection of agriculture. In 1828, Huskisson and Wellington managed to agree to introduce a sliding scale for corn duties. Huskisson recommended that the scale should become operational when grain reached sixty or sixty-two shillings a quarter. The Act provided for a sixty-six shilling threshold. Imports with a nominal duty of one shilling were allowed when domestic grain fetched seventy three shillings a quarter; at the other end of the scale, imports were prohibited when domestic grain cost fifty two shillings or less. Huskisson accepted Wellington's scale on the grounds that it was better than nothing. They came into conflict again over a proposed minor reform of parliament; Huskisson voted against the government, and then offered to resign if Wellington thought it would be in the interests of the ministry. Much to Huskisson's surprise, his resignation was accepted.

Huskisson's health was failing by this time, and he attended parliament less frequently. He supported Catholic emancipation in 1828, and made a number of speeches in favour of parliamentary reform in 1829. He attended the funeral of George IV in July 1830, and then attended the official opening of the Manchester to Liverpool railway on 15 September that year. The accident-prone Huskisson was run down by one of the trains and died nine hours later, becoming the first ever railway fatality. Charles Greville described the events:

> While the Duke's car was stopping to take in water, the people alighted and walked about the railroad; when suddenly another car, which was running on the adjoining level, came up. Everybody scrambled out of the way, and those who could got again into the first car. This Huskisson attempted to do, but he was slow and awkward; as he was getting in some part of the machinery of the other car struck the door of his, by which he was knocked down. He was taken up, and conveyed by Wilton and Mrs. Huskisson (who must have seen the accident happen) to the house of Mr. Blackburne, eight miles from Heaton. Wilton saved his life for a few hours by knowing how to tie up the artery; amputation was not possible, and he expired at ten o'clock that night. Wilton, Lord Granville, and Littleton were with him to the last. Mrs. Huskisson behaved with great courage.
> (Wilson 1927: 319)

Huskisson was given a public funeral in Liverpool on 24 September. Robert Peel, who was Home Secretary in Liverpool's ministry and had worked closely with Huskisson, continued many of his free trade policies. Peel repealed the Corn Laws in 1846, bringing Huskisson's work to its logical conclusion; the Navigation Laws were repealed in 1849. Britain's conversion to almost total free trade came during Gladstone's first ministry, again building on the foundations laid by Huskisson.

BIBLIOGRAPHY
The Question Concerning the Depreciation of our Currency Stated and Examined (1810).

Further Reading
Fetter, W.F., 'The Politics of the Bullion Report' *Economica* (1959), new series, vol. 26, pp. 99–120.
Lingelback, A.L., 'William Huskisson as President of the Board of Trade', *The American Historical Review* (1938), vol. 43, no. 4, pp. 759–74.
Wilson, P.W. (ed.), *The Greville Diary* (1927).

Marjorie Bloy

HUTCHESON, Archibald (c.1660–1740)

Hutcheson was born around 1660 in Stranocum, County Antrim, and died, probably in London, on 12 August 1740. Details of his early education are not known, but he studied law at the Middle Temple from 1680 and was called to the bar in 1683. In 1688 he took up the post of attorney-general for the Leeward Islands and spent the next fifteen years in the West Indies. Although a Presbyterian, he was broad-minded in matters of religion and numbered several leading Catholic noblemen among his patrons, and he was frequently suspected of Jacobite tendencies. In the Indies, he allowed freedom of worship to Catholics, and in 1691 he was charged with subversion and failing to swear allegiance to William III.

In 1704 Hutcheson returned to London to practise law, and here numbered the Duke of Ormond among his clients, although he seems to have been careful to keep Ormond at arm's length and did not get involved in the latter's politics. Ormond nonetheless relied upon him for legal and financial advice, and as a favour arranged for Hutcheson to be elected MP for Hastings in 1713. Hutcheson returned the favour by strongly defending Ormond at the time of the latter's impeachment in 1716, which again brought accusations that he was a closet Jacobite.

At the time of his election, however, Hutcheson was travelling on the continent, where he made contact with senior ministers at the court of Hanover, and he became identified as a leading member of the 'Hanoverian Tories', members who had broken with the Jacobites and were interested in rapprochement with the Whigs. His later speeches in parliament often showed real sympathy for the Whigs, and both contemporaries and later historians have found it difficult to tell exactly where he stood; historians of parliament have complained that Hutcheson was 'a political gadfly, variously described as a Whig or a Tory, but who seemed comfortable with neither party' (Cruickshanks et al. 2002: vol. 4, p. 449). Indeed, Hutcheson's broad-mindedness and ability to see both sides of a question must have been a disadvantage in the highly polarized politics of the time.

Hutcheson served on the Board of Trade from 1714–16, but held no other public offices until he resigned his seat in parliament in 1727; he was thereafter appointed one of the Lords Commissioners of the Carolina colonies. He had earlier been made a Fellow of the Royal Society (1808). He married four times, but there was no issue apart from a single daughter from the third marriage.

From 1716 into the early 1720s Hutcheson was a vigorous and strident critic of the South Sea Company, and published a stream of pamphlets attacking its management and its purpose. He continually pointed out errors and frauds in the accounts of the South Sea Company, and warned of disaster. He believed that there would be a crash and that investors would lose their money, and the only way to prevent this was for the Company to be brought under government control. In 1720 he called for the directors of the South Sea Company to be prosecuted and their estates seized to pay the Company's debts. In 1721 he argued that investors were partly to blame, and that if the stock of the South Sea Company had been realistically valued, it might have had a chance of survival.

Hutcheson was slightly less scathing about the Bank of England and East India Company, which he regarded as at least competently run, but he argued that the whole issue of the national debt had been mishandled from the beginning. In *Some Calculations and Remarks Relating to the Present State of the Publick Debts and Funds* (1718), he maintains that the various funds set up to manage the debt, including the South Sea Company, the Bank of England and so on, were bad bargains for the public. He condemns equally all governments since the Revolution of 1688, saying that they have merely trod in each others' footsteps without looking for alternative ways out of the dilemma. Rather than relying on private companies to raise the funds, Hutcheson calls for government to take over sole responsibility for the national debt, and in particular for the establishment of a sinking fund backed by a land tax and malt tax. This, he argues, could pay off the debt completely within thirty years. He also urges the restoration of a favourable balance of trade and preventing the export of gold and silver.

BIBLIOGRAPHY
Some Calculations and Remarks Relating to the Present State of the Publick Debts and Funds (1718; repr. 1720).
An Estimate of the Present National Debt (1718).
A Collection of Calculations and Remarks Relating to the South Sea Scheme and Stock (1720).
A Collection of Treatises Relating to the National Debts and Funds (1721).
Some Paragraphs of Mr Hutcheson's Treatises on the South-Sea Company (1723).
An Abstract of all the Public Debts Remaining Due at Michaelmas, 1722 (1723).
An Abstract of an Account Stated by some of the Clerks at the South-Sea House (1723).

Further Reading
Crookshank, J., *Some Seasonable Remarks on a Book by Archebald Hutcheson, Esq., Relating to Public Debts and Funds* (1718).
Cruickshanks, S., Handley, S. and Hayton, D.W., *The House of Commons 1690–1715*, vol. 4 (2002).

Morgen Witzel

HUTCHESON, Francis (1694–1746)

Hutcheson was born on 8 August 1694, and died in Dublin on 8 August 1746; he was buried in St Mary's Churchyard, Dublin. His father, John, was a Presbyterian minister in Armagh, and Hutcheson spent his early years at nearby Ballyrea. In 1702 he went to live with his grandfather at Drumalig in order to attend school near Saintfield. At the age of fourteen he moved to a small denominational academy in County Down. In 1711 he entered Glasgow University, where he was influenced by Robert Simson (mathematics), Gerschom Carmichael (philosophy) and Alexander Dunlop (Greek).

Hutcheson was elected to the chair of moral philosophy in Glasgow in 1730. It was as a lecturer that he made his mark on the university: brilliant and stylish, using English rather than Latin, Hutcheson's career amply confirms the accuracy of Adam SMITH's reference to the 'abilities and virtues of the never-to-be-forgotten' professor. Hutcheson lectured five days a week on natural religion, morals, government, and jurisprudence. On three days he commented on classical theories of morality, thus contributing (with Dunlop) to a revival of classical learning in Glasgow and forming an important channel for the dissemination of Stoic philosophy; a discipline which was to have a profound influence on Adam Smith.

Hutcheson remains of continuing interest to the student of political economy, not least because, like Smith and HUME, he did not see himself as an economist so much as a philosopher who placed the study of economic phenomena in a broad social context. All three started from a position that was neatly stated by Hutcheson's correspondent, Adam FERGUSON, when he noted that 'both the earliest and the latest accounts collected from every quarter of the globe, represent mankind as assembled in troops and companies'. The basic task was to explain how it was that a creature endowed with both self and other regarding propensities was fitted for the social state. The responses, which varied in character, were to be found in the way in which Hutcheson, Hume and Smith addressed the central question which was so neatly posed by the latter, namely: 'how and by what means does it come to pass, that the mind prefers one tenor of conduct to another, denominates the one right and the other wrong; considers the one as the object of approbation, honour and reward, and the other of blame, censure and punishment?' (*Theory of Moral Sentiments*, VII, i. 2). In dealing with this question, both Hume and Smith agreed with Hutcheson's emphasis on immediate sense and feeling as distinct from reason.

When we turn to Hutcheson, and especially to his major work, *A System of Moral Philosophy* (1755), it is to discover marked similarities with the work of his successor, especially in the context of his belief that, 'We may see in our species, from the very cradle, a constant propensity to action and motion' (1755: 21). But in some respects the position is subtler than that stated by Smith. While Smith was correct in identifying Hutcheson with the school of thought that found virtue to consist in benevolence, there is equally no doubt that Hutcheson gave a prominent place to self-love:

> Our reason can indeed discover certain bounds, within which we may not only act from self-love consistently with the good of the whole; but every mortal's acting thus within these bounds for his own good, is absolutely necessary for the good of the whole; and the want of self-love would be universally pernicious. But when self-love breaks over the bounds above mentioned, and leads us into actions detrimental to others, and to the whole; or makes us insensible of the generous kind affections; then it appears vicious, and is disapproved.
> (1755: III. v)

As in the case of Smith, what is critically important is man's desire to be approved of: 'an high pleasure is felt upon our gaining the approbation and esteem of others for our good actions, and upon their expressing their sentiments of gratitude; and on the other hand, we are cut to the very heart by censure, condemnation, and reproach' (1755: 25). On Hutcheson's argument, an important source of control is represented by a capacity for judgement, including moral judgement, which is linked to man's deployment of internal senses such as the 'sympathetic' which differ from external senses such as sight, sound, or taste, and 'by which, when we apprehend the state of others, our hearts naturally have a fellow-feeling with them' (1755: 19).

In practice, Hutcheson places most emphasis on the moral sense whose exercise (reinforced by the senses of honour and of shame) encourages the individual to virtuous action, and to the practice of restraint. It was Hutcheson's contention that men were inclined to, and fitted for, society: 'their curiosity, communicativeness, desire of action, their sense of honour, their compassion, benevolence, gaiety and the moral faculty, could have little or no exercise in solitude' (1755: 34).

This discussion was to lead to Hutcheson's treatment of natural rights and of the state of nature in a manner that is reminiscent of LOCKE. He also advances the Lockian claim that the state of nature is a state not of war but of inconvenience which can be resolved only by the establishment of government in terms of a complex contract. This has been described as the 'Real Whig position' (Winch 1978: 46; Robbins 1954) and may explain the considerable influence of Hutcheson's political ideas in the American colonies (Norton 1976). Hutcheson's 'warm love of liberty' was attested by Principal Leechman in his introduction to *A System of Moral Philosophy* (1755: xxxv–xxxvi) a sentiment that was echoed by Hugh Blair (Winch 1978: 47–8) in a contemporary review of the book.

While agreeing that an essential precondition of social stability is some system of 'magistracy', Adam Smith (like Hume) was to emerge as a critic of the contract theory. It is also well known that he rejected the idea of a moral sense as a 'peculiar sentiment, distinct from every other' (*Theory of Moral Sentiments* VII, iii. 3. 15). In addition, he criticised Hutcheson for seeming to imply that self-love was 'a principle which could never be virtuous in any degree or in any direction' (VII, ii. 3. 12). But for the economist, it is important to note that Hutcheson distinguished often more clearly than did Smith between approval and moral approbation. As Hutcheson put it: 'A penetrating genius, capacity for business, patience of application and labour are naturally admirable and relished by all observers, but with quite a different feeling from moral approbation' (1755: 28).

Five major topics are covered in Hutcheson's *System*, which is generally assumed to follow closely the content of his lecture course as a whole. The economic analysis is not given in the form of a single coherent discourse, but rather is woven into the broader treatment of jurisprudence. Perhaps for this reason, Hutcheson's work did not attract a great deal of attention from early historians of economic thought. But the situation was transformed as a result of Edwin CANNAN's discovery of Smith's *Lectures on Jurisprudence*. Cannan recalled that:

> On April 21, 1895, Mr Charles C. Maconochie, Advocate, whom I then met for the first time, happened to be present when, in course of conversation with the literary editor of the *Oxford Magazine*, I had occasion to make some comment about Adam Smith. Mr Maconochie immediately said that he possessed a manuscript report of Adam Smith's lectures on jurisprudence, which he regarded as of considerable interest.
> (Cannan 1896: xv)

While Cannan's reaction may be imagined, the lectures had the effect of confirming Hutcheson's influence upon his pupil on a broad front, but especially in the area of economic analysis (as distinct from policy). For what Cannan discovered was that the *order* of a large part of Smith's course, and its content corresponded closely with what Hutcheson was believed to have taught. It is this correspondence that served to renew interest in Hutcheson's economics with remarkable speed. Quite apart from Cannan's introduction to the *Lectures*, the same theme is elaborated in his introduction to the 1904 edition of the *Wealth of Nations*. The link had also been noted, following the publication of the *Lectures*, in PALGRAVE's *Dictionary of Political Economy* (1899) and received its most elaborate statement in W.R. SCOTT's *Francis Hutcheson* (1900). The most modern treatment of this kind is to be found in W.L. Taylor's influential work, *Frances Hutcheson and David Hume as Predecessors of Adam Smith* (1965).

But Cannan noted something else, namely that it may be that the 'germ of the *Wealth of Nations* is to be found in Hutcheson's treatment of value' (Cannan 1896: xxvi). It is this topic that forms the central feature of the remainder of the present argument although it will be convenient to begin with Hutcheson's views on the division of labour where his influence on Smith may be particularly obvious. Before we pass on to these subjects, however, it should be noted that Hutcheson's work on economic topics has its own history. It is evident that he admired the work of his immediate predecessor in the chair of moral philosophy, Gerschom Carmichael, and especially his translation of, and commentary on, Samuel Pufendorf. Carmichael's influence as a student of ethics and of jurisprudence has been frequently celebrated, notably by Sir William Hamilton who stated that he may be regarded 'on good grounds, as the true founder of the Scottish school of philosophy' (Taylor 1965: 253). Later, W.L. Taylor concluded that:

> The interesting point for the development of economic thought in all this is the very close parallelism between Pufendorf's *De Officio* and Hutcheson's *Introduction to Moral Philosophy*. Each man covered almost exactly the same field. The inescapable conclusion is that Francis Hutcheson took over almost in whole, from Carmichael, the economic ideas of Pufendorf.
> (Taylor 1965: 289)

A key issue for both Hutcheson and Pufendorf arose from the comparison of the social as distinct from the solitary state; or, as Pufendorf put it, it would seem to have been more wretched than that of any wild beast, if we take into account with what weakness man goes forth into this world, to perish at once, but for the help of others; and how rude a life each would lead, if he had nothing more than what he owed to his own strength and ingenuity. On the contrary, it is altogether due to the aid of other men, that out of such feebleness, we have been able to grow up, that we now enjoy untold comforts, and that we improve mind and body for our own advantage and that of others. And in this sense the natural state is opposed to a life improved by the industry of men.

(Pufendorf 1927: ii. 89)

This broad line of argument was developed in the *System* (Hutcheson 1755, book 2, ch. 4) where he offered two specific economic applications. First, he noted that the '*joint* labours of twenty men will cultivate forests, or drain marshes, for farms to each one, and provide houses for habitation, and inclosures for their stocks, much sooner than the *separate* labours of the same number' (1755: 289). Secondly, Hutcheson drew attention to the importance of the *division* of labour:

Nay 'tis well known that the produce of the labours of any given number, twenty, for instance, in providing the necessaries or conveniences of life, shall be much greater by assigning to one, a certain sort of work of one kind, in which he will soon acquire skill and dexterity, and to another assigning work of a different kind, than if each one of the twenty were obliged to employ himself, by turns in all the different sorts of labour requisite for his subsistence, without sufficient dexterity in any. In the former method each procures a great quantity of goods of one kind, and can exchange a part of it for such goods obtained by the labours of others as he shall stand in need of. One grows expert in tillage, another in pasture and breeding cattle, a third in masonry, a fourth in the chase, a fifth in iron-works, a sixth in the arts of the loom, and so on throughout the rest. Thus all are supplied by means of barter with the works of complete artists. In the other method scarce any one could be dextrous and skilful in any one sort of labour.

(Hutcheson 1755: 288–9)

The discussion of the division of labour implied that members of society are interdependent in respect of the satisfaction of their wants. It also led to two further analytical developments: security of property and the problem of value in exchange (see especially Brown 1987). Much of the discussion in Book 2, chapter 6 of the *System* is concerned with 'the right of property'. But Hutcheson also noted that:

If we extend our views further and consider what the common interest of society may require, we shall find the right of property further confirmed. Universal industry is plainly necessary for the support of mankind. Tho' men are naturally active, yet their activity would rather turn toward the lighter and pleasanter exercises, than the slow, constant, and intense labours requisite to procure the necessaries and conveniences of life, unless strong motives are presented to engage them to these severer labours. Whatever institution therefore shall be found necessary to promote universal diligence and patience, and make labour agreeable or eligible to mankind, must also tend to the public good; and institutions or practices which discourage industry must be pernicious to mankind. Now nothing can so effectually excite men to constant patience and diligence in all sorts of useful industry, as the hopes of future wealth, ease, and pleasure to themselves, their offspring, and all who are dear to them, and of some honour too to themselves on account of their ingenuity, and activity, and liberality. All these hopes are presented to men by securing to every one the fruits of his own labours, that he may enjoy them, and dispose of them as he pleases.

Nay the most extensive affections could scarce engage a wise man to industry, if no property ensued upon it.
(Hutcheson 1755: 320–1)

Hutcheson attached a great deal of importance to freedom of choice and in fact concluded this phase of the argument by rejecting any suggestion that 'magistrates' may be involved, passages that may well have attracted the attention of the youthful Smith (Hutcheson 1755: 322–3).

It is Hutcheson's treatment of value that shows most clearly the influence of Pufendorf and of Carmichael. Pufendorf's analysis received its most elaborate statement in the *De Jure*, in the long chapter 'On Price' (book 5, ch. 1). The most succinct statement, on which Carmichael commented, is to be found in the *De Officio* (book 1, ch. 14). Hutcheson opened his analysis of the problem by pointing out that the 'natural ground of all value or price is some sort of use which goods afford in life', adding that 'by the use causing a demand we mean not only a natural subserviency to our support, or to some natural pleasure, but any tendency to give any satisfaction by prevailing custom or fancy, as a matter of ornament or distinction' (Hutcheson 1755: 53–4). He continued:

> But when some aptitude to human use is presupposed, we shall find that the prices of goods depend on these two jointly, the *demand* on account of some use or other which many desire, and the *difficulty* of acquiring, or cultivating for human use. When goods are equal in these respects men are willing to interchange them with each other; nor can any artifice or policy make the values of goods depend on any thing else. When there is no *demand*, there is no price, where the *difficulty* of acquiring never so great: and where there is no *difficulty* or labour requisite to acquire, the most universal *demand* will not cause a price; as we see in fresh water in these climates. Where the demand for two sorts of goods is equal, the prices are as the difficulty. Where the difficulty is equal, the prices are as the demand.
> (Hutcheson 1755: ii. 54)

Hutcheson then added two points which are reminiscent of Pufendorf in commenting on issues that affect supply price and the rate of exchange. First, he argued:

> In like manner by difficulty of acquiring, we do not only mean great labour or toil, but all other circumstances which prevent a great plenty of the goods or performances demanded. Thus the price is encreased by the rarity or scarcity of the materials in nature, or such accidents as prevent plentiful crops or certain fruits of the earth; and the great ingenuity and nice taste requisite in the artists to finish well some works of art, as men of such genius are rare. The value is also raised, by the dignity of station in which, according to the custom of the country, the men must live who provide us with certain goods, or works of art. Fewer can be supported in such stations than in the meaner; and the dignity and expense of their stations must be supported by the higher prices of their goods or services. Some other singular considerations may exceedingly heighten the values of goods to some men, which will not affect their estimation with others. These above mentioned are the chief which obtain in commerce.
> (Hutcheson 1755: ii. 54–5)

As regards the rate of exchange, Hutcheson commented:

> In commerce it must often happen that one may need such goods of mine as yield a great and lasting use in life, and have cost a long course of labour to acquire and cultivate, while yet he has none of those goods I want in exchange, or not sufficient quantities; or what goods of his I want, may be such as yield but a small use, and are procurable by little labour. In such cases it cannot be expected that I should exchange with him. I

must search for others who have the goods I want, and such quantities of them as are equivalent in use to my goods, and require as much labour to produce them; and the goods on both sides must be brought to some estimation or value.

(Hutcheson 1755: ii. 53)

But although these positions do not differ significantly from those of Pufendorf, Hutcheson does seem to have taken notice of two additional points. First, he seems to suggest, as the above quotation indicates, that goods will exchange at a rate that will be in part determined by the quantity of labour embodied in them (a point later taken up by Smith). Secondly, he noted in a passage that may have been 'foreshadowed' by Pufendorf, that some commodities: 'of great use have no price, either because they are naturally destined for community, or cannot come into commerce but as appendages of something else, the price of which may be increased by them, though they cannot be separately estimated' (Hutcheson 1747: 200; quoted in Taylor 1965: 66).

The discussion of value in exchange led Hutcheson on quite logically to consider the medium of exchange, namely money, and here too he followed an old tradition which had already been commented upon by Pufendorf. In the *De Officio* (book 1, ch. 14) the latter noted the inconvenience of exchange by barter: 'But after men departed from their primitive simplicity and various kinds of gain were introduced, it was readily understood that common value alone was not sufficient for the transactions of men's affairs and their increased dealings.' Once more, Hutcheson followed suit in explaining the problems of barter and the need to establish a standard or 'common measure' when settling the 'values or goods for commerce'.

The qualities requisite to the most perfect standard are these: it must be something generally desired so that men are generally willing to take it in exchange. The very making any goods the standard will of itself given them this quality. It must be *portable*; which will often be the case if it is rare, so that small quantities are of great value. It must be *divisible* without loss into small parts, so as to be suited to the values of all sorts of goods; and it must be *durable*, not easily wearing by use, or perishing in its nature. One or other of these prerequisites in the standard, shews the inconvenience of many of our commonest goods for that purpose. The man who wants a small quantity of my corn will not give me a work-beast for it, and his beast does not admit division. I want perhaps a pair of shoes, but my ox is of far greater value, and the other may not need him. I must travel to distant lands, my grain cannot be carried along for my support, without unsufferable expense, and my wine would perish in the carriage. 'Tis plain therefore that when men found any use for the rarer metals, silver and gold, in ornaments and utensils, and thus a demand was raised for them, they would soon also see that they were the fittest standards of commerce, on all the accounts above-mentioned.

(Hutcheson 1755: ii. 55–6)

The familiar arguments concerning the need for coinage and the dangers of debasement follow (Hutcheson 1755, book 2, ch. 12), while there is also a hint of the need to find an invariable measure of value at least over long periods of time.

In conclusion, as we have seen, Edwin Cannan considered that Hutcheson's emphasis on the utility of the goods to be acquired and on the disutility of effort needed to create the goods to be exchanged, with the attendant emphasis on demand and supply-side considerations, provided the 'kernel' of the *Wealth of Nations*. Taylor, on the other hand, suggested that Smith's concern with material welfare (Taylor 1965: 193) served to obscure the line of argument set out by Hutcheson. Robertson and Taylor in fact concluded that: 'it does not appear inexplicable that Adam Smith no longer paid so much attention to the lines of argument taken over from Hutcheson, which had served well enough in the *Lectures*' (Robertson and Taylor 1957: 194–5). What Robertson and Taylor did not note was that Smith's preoccupation with a real measure of value may also have owed much to Hutcheson.

Readers of the *Wealth of Nations* and *The Theory of Moral Sentiments* will need no reminding that Smith did not conceive of welfare as measurable in real terms along. In Smith's view, happiness is a state of mind and he was well aware of the social and psychological costs of economic growth. Indeed, it is this perspective that returns us to the form of argument stated above, where it was noted that both Hutcheson and Smith emphasized that men desire to be approved of and that this approval was itself a source of satisfaction. Smith used this argument in disposing of MANDEVILLE's 'licentious doctrine'. He argued in effect that the pursuit of gratification is not inconsistent with propriety and indeed should be consistent with it. Hutcheson concurred: 'there is no necessary vice in the consuming of the finest products, or the wearing of the dearest manufactures by persons whose fortunes can allow it consistently with all the duties of life. But what if men grew generally more frugal and abstemious in such things? More of these finer goods could be sent abroad' (Hutcheson 1755: 320; Taylor 1965, ch. 4).

BIBLIOGRAPHY
Inquiry into the Original of our Ideas of Beauty and Virtue (1725; 2nd edn, 1726).
A Short Introduction to Moral Philosophy (Glasgow, 1742; 2nd edn 1747).
A System of Moral Philosophy (1755).

Further Reading
Brown, V., 'Value and Property in the History of Economic Thought', *Oeconomia* (1987), vol. 7.

Cannan, E., *Adam Smith's Lectures on Justice, Police Revenue and Arms* (Oxford, 1896).
Hutchison, T., *Before Adam Smith: The Emergence of Political Economy* (Oxford, 1988).
Meek, R.L., 'New Light on Adam Smith's Lectures on Jurisprudence', *History of Political Economy* (1976), vol. 8.
Naldi, N., 'Gerschom Carmichael on Demand and Difficulty of Acquiring', *Scottish Journal of Political Economy* (1993), vol. 40.
Norton, D.F., 'Francis Hutcheson on America', *Studies on Voltaire*, ed. T. Besterman (Oxford, 1976).
Pesciarelli, E., 'On Adam Smith's Lectures on Jurisprudence', *Scottish Journal of Political Economy* (1986), vol. 33.
Robbins, C., 'When is it that Colonies May Turn Independent: An Analysis of the Environment and Politics of Francis Hutcheson', *William and Mary Quarterly* (1954), vol. 11.
——, *The Eighteenth Century Commonwealth Man* (New York, 1968).
Robertson, H.M. and Taylor, W.L., 'Adam Smith's Approach to the Theory of Value', *Economic Journal* (1957), vol. 67.
Scott, W.R., *Francis Hutcheson, His Life, Teaching and Position in the History of Philosophy* (Cambridge, 1900).
Skinner, A.S., *A System of Social Science: Papers Relating to Adam Smith* (Oxford, 1966).
Taylor, W.L., *Francis Hutcheson and David Hume as Predecessors of Adam Smith* (Durham, North Carolina, 1965).
Winch, D., *Adam Smith's Politics: An Essay in Historiographic Revision* (Cambridge, 1978).

Andrew Skinner

HYNDMAN, Henry Mayers (1842–1921)

Hyndman was born in London on 7 March 1842, into a wealthy merchant family, and died in London on 22 November 1921. He was educated privately and then at Trinity College, Cambridge. Although he was a prominent socialist he never pretended to be anything other than upper class in demeanor and lifestyle, which was supported by his stockbroking activities. His entry in *Who's Who* gave 'cricket and racquets' as his favourite recreations.

Hyndman was an influential popularizer of Marxian economics, especially in the 1880s and 1890s. He began as a radical Tory but was slowly converted to Marxism, despite an early and irredeemable quarrel with MARX and ENGELS. In 1881 he established the Social Democratic Federation, which he always dominated, and he maintained a close but uneasy relationship with socialism in Britain throughout the last forty years of his life. Inconsistent on the question of imperialism, as on many other issues, Hyndman became increasingly anti-German, and had the unfortunate distinction of setting up a National Socialist Party in 1916, two years before Adolf Hitler. He opposed the Bolshevik revolution, but continued until the end to advocate socialism with a patriotic tinge.

Hyndman was an uncritical defender of Marx's theory of value and exploitation. He is perhaps best known for his forthright and entertaining attack on neoclassical value theory in a lecture with the title 'The Final Futility of Final Utility', which he reprinted in his *Economics of Socialism* (1896). This supposedly new and revolutionary theory, he claimed, was nothing but an obscure restatement of the old supply and demand theory of Bastiat and LAUDERDALE. As for the much-vaunted analytical rigour of the new theory, Hyndman simply sneered: 'the *débris* of shattered arguments are not rendered more formidable by being enveloped in useless mathematical formulae' (1910: 259–60).

More seriously, Hyndman complained that JEVONS had proved completely incapable of explaining economic crises. This was indeed a fundamental weakness not only in contemporary neoclassical economics but also in Fabian socialism. As J.A. HOBSON noted in his introduction to the 1932 reissue of *Commercial Crises of the Nineteenth Century* (1892), Hyndman's own writings on crises were largely descriptive, repeating the Marxian mantras about the antagonistic and anarchic nature of the capitalist mode of production but failing to develop any sort of theoretical argument. But Hyndman's insistence that crises were inevitable under capitalism, were increasing in severity and could only be eliminated under socialism, did contribute to the influence of his writings in the growing socialist movement at the end of the nineteenth century.

BIBLIOGRAPHY
Commercial Crises of the Nineteenth Century (1892; repr. 1932, 1967).
The Economics of Socialism: Marx Made Easy (1896; repr. 1922).

Further Reading
Hobson, J.A. (1932) 'Preface to the Second Edition' in H.M. Hyndman, *Commercial Crises of the Nineteenth Century* (1932, pp. vii–viii).
Johnson, G., 'Hyndman, Henry Mayers (1842–1921)', in J. M. Bellamy and J. Saville (eds), *Dictionary of Labour Biography*, vol. 10 (Basingstoke, 2000, pp. 101–11).
Tsuzuki, C., *H.M. Hyndman and British Socialism* (Oxford, 1961).

J.E. King

I

INWOOD, William (1771?–1843)

Inwood was born in Highgate, near London, around 1771, and died in London on 16 March 1843. He trained initially as a surveyor and estate manager, but was best known in his own day as an architect. He was particularly noted for several churches and chapels in London, including St Pancras New Church, Somers Town Chapel and Regent Square Chapel, and he also designed Westminster Hospital. He was frequently assisted by his two sons, Henry and Charles, who became notable architects in their own right. He also taught architecture and produced a number of notable architectural drawings.

Inwood originally compiled his *Tables for the Purchasing of Estates, Freehold, Copyhold, or Leasehold, Annuities, &c. and for the Renewing of Leases...* for his private use in a professional capacity, but was persuaded to publish them for the first time in 1811. Although similar tables had been compiled and published in the past, what makes Inwood's tables valuable, as he himself says, is that each table is accompanied by an explanation and examples, making the tables easier to understand for the non-specialist. The final publication included five groups of tables concerning the following subjects: (1) purchasing and renewal of leases over varying terms; (2) values of annuities; (3) life expectancy and rates of mortality; (4) tables for converting pennies in a pound, and weeks of the year, to decimal rates; and (5) rates of compound interest. The whole formed a handy guide for surveyors, estate managers and others engaged in similar lines of work. That the work was seen as valuable is evidenced by the fact that it was still in use in the early twentieth century, being re-issued for the thirty-third time in 1930.

Today, the tables of greatest interest are probably those of the third group. Inwood presents a series of tables comparing life expectancy and mortality in London and in Northampton, and concludes that the residents of the latter were likely to live longer and suffer from lower mortality rates at all ages. For example, out of every 1,000 persons born in London, 242, or about 1 in 4, lived to the age of 35, but in Northampton the figure was 344, or about 1 in 3. Only 147 Londoners would live to the age of 50, but 245 residents of Northampton could expect to do so. One out of 15 Londoners reached the age of 67, but one in eight people in Northampton did so.

BIBLIOGRAPHY

Tables for the Purchasing of Estates, Freehold, Copyhold, or Leasehold, Annuities, &c. and for the Resnewing of Leases... (1811; 2nd edn 1820; 3rd edn 1824, reprinted thirty-three times to 1930).

Ann Kimber

J

JACK, Daniel Thomson (1901–84)

Jack was born in Glasgow on 18 August 1901, and died on 15 December 1984. He was educated at Bellahouston Academy, Glasgow and the University of Glasgow, where he won prizes in philosophy and political economy. After holding academic posts at the University of Glasgow and the University of St Andrews, he was appointed to the David Dale Professor of Economics at King's College, Newcastle-upon-Tyne in 1935, a post he held until 1961. This was initially part of Durham University, but became the University of Newcastle in 1963. During the Second World War, Jack served in the Ministry of Labour under Ernest Bevin, became an expert on collective bargaining, and became a member of the Industrial Disputes Tribunal. He acquired a reputation as an effective arbitrator in industrial disputes in Britain, and was author of the 'Jack Report' on the Ford Motor Company. He helped set up institutions for collective bargaining in East Africa and was an active member of the Royal Commission on East Africa. He worked on many public bodies, including being Chairman of the Air Traffic Licensing Board (1960–70).

From 1925 to 1940 Jack wrote a series of short books on topical economic issues. Some, however, failed to go into their subjects with as much depth as would be desired and were criticized by reviewers, including Ralph HAWTREY. *The Economics of the Gold Standard* (1925) discussed the mechanism of the gold standard, but not the economic issues that KEYNES was raising at the time. The issues of deflation and exchange rate adjustment that were posed by the return to gold were mentioned in his preface, but not discussed as his main concern was with the long run. These concerns also characterized his book on European currencies (1927), where the main theoretical frameworks employed were the the quantity theory of money and purchasing power parity. He used these to analyse the links between money, exchange rates and government finance.

His *International Trade* (1931), like his *Currency and Banking* (1932), was written for students and businessmen. It offered a descriptive account of its subject, with simple discussions of relevant theory. Policy issues such as the role of international investment, tariffs, dumping and Britain's post-war problems were also discussed. More novel was his *Studies in Economic Warfare* (1940). This traced economic warfare to the wars between Britain and France from 1793 to 1815, and after a chapter on international law, offered a detailed analysis of the 1914–18 war. Jack applied the lessons from that war to 'the War of 1939', drawing the conclusion that economic warfare would not precipitate a quick German collapse, but that weaknesses in the German economy would become evident as time passed. After the war, his interests turned to employment, labour relations and economic development, as a participant in events rather than an observer.

BIBLIOGRAPHY
The Economics of the Gold Standard (1925).
The Restoration of European Currencies (1927).
The Crises of 1931 (1931).
International Trade (1931).
Currency and Banking (1932).
Studies in Economic Warfare (1940).
'Full Employment in Retrospect', *Economic Journal* (1952), vol. 62, no. 248, pp. 731–49.
'Is a Wages Policy Desirable and Practicable?' *Economic Journal* (1957), vol. 67. no. 268, pp. 585–90.

Roger Backhouse

JACOB, William (1762–1851)

Jacob was born in 1762; his parentage and education are unrecorded, as is his early career. He died in London, at eighty-nine, on 17 December 1851. Beginning in 1794 he appears in London directories as merchant, warehouseman and linen merchant, at 36 Newgate Street. In 1800–4 he also traded from the Droitwich salt warehouse, Upper Thames Street. He was one of the few English merchants to develop direct trade connections with South America. In 1807, described as 'a Gentleman well versed in various branches of Natural Knowledge', and recommended by people like Humphry Davy, he was elected a fellow of the Royal Society.

In November 1804 Jacob sent his pamphlet on war with Spain to William Pitt. By 1806 he was providing the government with economic and military information about Spanish America. In the 1806 general election he took the seat for Westbury (possibly by purchase) and was active in debates on mercantile questions. After unsuccessfully contesting Great Yarmouth at the 1807 general election, in 1808 he re-entered parliament for Rye, a Treasury borough, and again spoke on trade and colonial questions. He was also involved in local government, and was elected alderman for the ward of Lime Street in 1810 but gave up that position in 1811 when his business went bankrupt. In 1812 he moved to Chelsham Lodge, Surrey, and did not again stand for parliament. For the next ten years he farmed between 300 and 400 acres in Kent and Surrey.

In 1814 and 1815 Jacob published books 'on the protection required by British agriculture'. After travelling in Germany, France and the Low Countries, in 1820 he published another on their agriculture and industry, with particular reference to British Corn Laws and trade. He wrote or collaborated on eleven articles in the *Quarterly Review* between 1812 and 1832, and contributed to Constable's supplement to the 5th edition of the *Encyclopaedia Britannica* (1822–4). His writing gained him favourable notice at a time when farming was becoming less profitable. In 1820 he sought but failed to succeed Arthur YOUNG as secretary of the Board of Agriculture. In April 1822, dating from the Revenue Enquiry Office, he reported that he was one of the commissioners (along with Thomas Wallace, vice-president of the Board of Trade) about to be sent for an extended period to Edinburgh and Dublin (to Macvey Napier, BL Add.Ms. 34, 613/48-9). Instead, he accepted an appointment as comptroller of corn returns at the Board of Trade. He acquired a house on Cadogan Place, London, where he lived for the rest of his life. He continued to travel on the continent, both on holiday and as a government agent studying the corn trade of northern Europe. His highly praised reports, published in 1826 and 1828, were a novelty at the Board of Trade, relying on his observations rather than on official statistics and continental publications. However, some contemporaries as well as later writers questioned his conclusion that abolition of protective Corn Laws would not increase imports of grain even when British yields were low and prices high.

William HUSKISSON had suggested the research that led to Jacob's two-volume *Historical Inquiry into the Production and Consumption of the Precious Metals* (1831). From 1832 to 1838 he was treasurer of the Royal Society of Literature. In January 1842 he retired from the Board of Trade on a pension and a substantial inheritance from his barrister son Edward, who had died in 1841.

BIBLIOGRAPHY
Historical Inquiry into the Production and Consumption of the Precious Metals (1831).
For identification of Jacob's contributions to the *Quarterly Review,* see J.B. Cutmore, 'Further *Quarterly Review* Attributions, Wellesley Index, Volume I,' *Victorian Periodicals Review* (1994), vol. 27, no. 4, p. 319; J.B. Cutmore, 'The Early *Quarterly Review*: New Attributions of Authorship,' *Victorian Periodicals Review* (1995), vol. 28, no. 4, pp. 305–7, 319; W. Houghton et al, *The Wellesley Index to Victorian Periodicals 1824–1900* (1972), vol. 1, pp. 703–13, vol. 2, p. 1206; and H. Shine and H.C. Shine, *The Quarterly Review Under Gifford* (Chapel Hill, North Carolina, 1949).

Further Reading
Brown, L., *The Board of Trade and the Free-Trade Movement 1830–1842* (Oxford, 1958).
Collinge, J.M., 'Jacob, William,' in R.G. Thorne (ed.), *The House of Commons 1790–1820* (1986, vol. 4, pp. 290–1).
Matthews, R.C.O., *A Study in Trade-cycle History: Economic Fluctuations in Great Britain 1833–1842* (Cambridge, 1954, pp. 35–40).

Eileen Curran

JARROLD, Thomas (1770–1853)

Jarrold was born at Manningtree, Essex on 1 December 1770, and died in Manchester on 24 June 1853. He was educated at the University of Edinburgh, from which he reportedly took a degree in medicine, though this cannot be confirmed from the university's own records. He established a medical practice in Stockport some time before 1806, but by 1810 had relocated to Manchester, where he lived and worked for the remainder of his life. He published several medical works, and also on the poor laws. He is best known for his *Dissertations on Man* (1806), written while at Stockport and intended as a direct assault on the theories of MALTHUS.

Jarrold's attack on Malthus follows the general lines of the second edition of the *Essay on Population,* so it useful to review the structure of Malthus's argument. The general principles asserting the power of population to grow immeasurably faster than food is stated and proved by the claim that population has the capacity to grow geometrically while food supply can only grow arithmetically at best. This leads to an inevitable conflict where the growth of population must be restrained by some checks. Malthus refers to these as misery and vice one on occasion, and also as the preventive and positive checks. After proving his thesis in a few early chapters, almost all the rest of the *Essay* is taken up with a review of the state of population in many different countries. This review is meant to show that population in all countries is subject to positive and preventive checks, and that whenever any of these checks has been relaxed, population has grown at great speed.

Jarrold begins by taking issue with the idea that population has a definite rate of growth if left unchecked. If this is not assumed, then the American data, which formed Malthus's principal support, ceases to be relevant. Jarrold then follows Malthus through his tour of the world and critically examines the evidence presented. In Siberia, in America, in Germany and in Norway, he finds defects in Malthus's facts and reasoning. Jarrold was perhaps the first to show how Malthus had tampered with Sussmilch's data to 'prove' his own case; an argument made much more explicitly by SADLER some thirty years later.

In this compact critique of the *Essay on Population*, Jarrold's medical knowledge shows in his observation that organic food has been found in the belly of all fish except the herring. The most original points made by Jarrold relate to his adumbration of the predator–prey model. He clearly notes that organic life is dependent upon food that itself grows at a geometric rate. This too is a point elaborated upon with greater clarity by Sadler.

Some of the sharpest points Jarrold raises are about the implied pessimism of the Malthusian view. Population presses so hard upon food that the young marry only when their elders have died and thereby make room for the next generation. Malthus had written the callous words: 'If a child is born into a world already possessed...cannot get subsistence from his parents...he has no claim of right to the smallest portion of food, and in fact has no business to be where he is. At nature's mighty feast there is no vacant cover for him; she tells him to be gone...' To this Jarrold indignantly replied, 'But at nature's mighty feast, none are bishops, but all are men' (1806: 21), and went on to argue that unless men reformed their ways they had no right to complain of God's provision. Jarrold (and William HAZLITT) were among the first to be publicly outraged by these sentiments, and Malthus withdrew the offending passage in later editions.

Jarrold looked upon marriage as one of the great sweeteners of life: 'The principal cause [of marital infelicity] is, a struggle for power: the mutual study to please, which is the charm of courtship, by not being made the business of life, is the principal source of the evil of it' (1806: 56). It is an appropriate comment upon the age that neither Malthus nor any of his contemporaries ever doubted that marriage and children were most desirable: indeed, so desirable that people would raise families at the earliest opportunity. However, the Malthusian worldview attacked such a picture, and it is a common theme of all the critics of Malthus that the *Essay* chose to paint ordinary life with such dark hues. Few of them, however, wrote with the force and elegance of Thomas Jarrold.

BIBLIOGRAPHY

Dissertations on Man, Philosophical, Physiological, and Political; in Answer to Mr Malthus's Essay on the Principle of Population (Stockport, 1806).
A Letter to S. Whitbread, Esq., on the Subject of the Poor Laws (1807).
Dissertations on the Form and Colour of Man (Stockport, 1808).
Instinct and Reason Philosophically Investigated (Manchester, 1836).

Salim Rashid

JAY, Douglas Patrick Thomas (1907–96)

Douglas Jay was born in Woolwich, Kent on 23 March 1907, into a middle-class family, the son of a Conservative London County Councillor. He died in London on 6 March 1996. He was educated at Winchester (with other future Labour luminaries such as Hugh GAITSKELL and Richard Crossman), and then at New College, Oxford, before becoming a financial journalist in the 1930s, working for *The Times*, *The Economist* and the Labour newspaper, the *Daily Herald*. Influenced by his tutor, Lionel ROBBINS, and by the economic writings of Gaitskell, he joined the New Fabian Research Bureau and Nicholas Davenport's XYZ club of Labour-sympathising economists in the City. His book *The Socialist Case* (1937) was an important step in helping the Labour party to accept a Keynesian analysis into its socialist programme, though Jay himself pointed out that his ideas were developed independently of KEYNES's *General Theory*. After a wartime career as a civil servant, Jay was elected Labour MP for Battersea North in 1946; he continued to represent the seat until 1983.

As Economic Secretary to the Treasury between 1947 and 1950, Jay worked with Gaitskell against two more powerful ministers, Stafford Cripps and Harold Wilson, to persuade the Cabinet to accept devaluation in 1949. He served as Financial Secretary to the Treasury in 1950–1 and was a leading Gaitskellite in the party struggles between left and right in the 1950s. Appointed President of the Board of Trade in 1964, he was successful in promoting exports and reviving regional development, but his virulently nationalist opposition to the Common Market led finally to his exclusion from the Wilson government in 1967. He then took up a fellowship at All Souls College, Oxford, and in 1987 was created Baron Jay of Battersea.

In *The Socialist Case*, Jay sought to demonstrate the relevance of Keynesian policies of demand management for achieving socialist economic goals. He rejected the radical fervour of the quasi-Marxist Labour left in the 1930s, and pointedly refused to relate economic problems of unemployment and trade depression to the social and political issues of class power in capitalist society. Instead, he pointed to the mal-distribution of wealth and resources as the cause of the poverty which blighted working-class existence. His socialism manifested itself as an elaboration of a radical Keynesianism, which had the aim of ending social inequality.

This concern with inequality rather than power led Jay to interpret the market economy in traditional neoclassical terms; he saw it as a fundamentally sound system in which supply and demand were regulated by price in a theoretically elegant mechanism of resource allocation. However, Jay also argued that this system was elegant only in the realm of theory, and failed to correspond to a real world in which inequality, poverty and waste appeared endemic. The reason for the discrepancy between theory and reality lay in the failure of neoclassical economics to recognize the difference between demand and need. The needs of the hungry were not satisfied because, lacking disposable income, they were excluded from the definition of demand as effective purchasing power. While the functions of land, capital and enterprise were necessary, their actual rewards were partially unearned because of the distortion of wealth between the classes. The abstinence of the wealthy merely meant that they were waiting rather than working for prosperity; their refusal to invest was a result of a timidity and caution that resulted in a hoarding of money outside the working economy.

To resolve these problems, Jay called for the regulation of the market economy by an interventionist state. This would take the form of the public ownership of the Bank of England, a taxation policy that would redistribute hoarded wealth by measures such as the abolition of inheritance, and managed monetary policy to regulate the trade cycle. As such policies would lead to the gradual disappearance of the inequality of incomes, the fundamental equilibrium of the market economy would reassert itself, free of the distortions caused by differential purchasing power.

Jay was unhappy, however, with the idea that state intervention was a panacea for all problems. He argued that while natural monopolies such as gas and rail transport were just candidates for public ownership, both small companies and large, well-established industries which were efficient under private ownership should be protected from the bureaucratic powers of a central planning mechanism, which would create economic inefficiencies by its disruption of the market relationship between supply and demand. He believed that nationalization was usually wrong, in that it would create a state monopoly that would be insensitive to consumers by its extraction of a monopoly profit from the public. Jay believed that, in order to overcome this problem, competition between public and private companies should be encouraged: for example, a nationalized rail company could compete with privately owned road transport companies for the benefit of economic efficiency and consumer service. The benefits of planning were therefore limited; it could reduce insecurity and social inequality, but if carried too far it would result in the loss of consumer freedom and the creation of unnecessary and dangerous state monopolies in industry.

BIBLIOGRAPHY
The Socialist Case (1937).
Who is to Pay for the War and the Peace (1941).
Socialism in the New Society (1962).
After the Common Market (1968).
Change and Fortune (1980).
Sterling: A Plea for Moderation (1985).

Further Reading
Foote, G., *The Labour Party's Political Thought: A History*, 3rd edn (1997).
Morgan, K.O., *Labour People Leaders and Lieutenants: Hardie to Kinnock* (Oxford, 1987 pp.109–14).
——, *Labour in Power 1945–51* (Oxford, 1984, pp.379–88).

Geoffrey Foote

JENKIN, Henry Charles Fleeming
(1833–85)

Fleeming Jenkin was born on 25 March 1833 near Dungeness in Kent, where his father was serving in the coastguard. He died in Edinburgh on 12 June 1885 of complications following an operation on his foot. He was educated at Edinburgh Academy, where he won a number of prizes. James Clerk Maxwell was his senior, and Peter Guthrie Tait his classmate. In 1846, Jenkin and his mother moved to Frankfurt-am-Main; his father joined them soon after. In 1847 the family moved to Paris, and after the 1848 revolution to Genoa. In Paris Jenkin studied French and mathematics, and in Genoa, where he was the first protestant student at the university, he studied natural philosophy and got his MA with first-class honours. After completing his studies, Jenkin worked as an engineer with the Fairbairn works in Manchester, in Switzerland, and then at the Penn engineering works at Greenwich. Through Elisabeth Gaskell, he became acquainted with Alfred Austin. Despite his poor financial situation, he married Austin's only daughter, Anne Austin, in 1859.

Jenkin importantly contributed to the design and laying of submarine cables from 1855 onwards, and remained involved in this field through much of his professional life. He became acquainted with William Thomson, Lord Kelvin, in 1859, and they collaborated frequently in later years, through their partnerships for the telegraph and in their work for the British Association's Committee on Electrical Standards. In this collaboration, Jenkin proved to be the more practical man, although, for example, his speculations on the nature of matter are important to understand Thomson's own conception of matter. Jenkin was appointed as professor of engineering at University College, London in 1866, and moved to a similar chair in Edinburgh in 1868. Jenkin's professorship considerably eased his financial position, and the new position enabled him to continue his engineering activities as well, which finally started to pay off.

Though Jenkin's major contributions to the sciences clearly are in engineering, his interests were far from limited to that field. The two-volume compilation of his papers give an indication of his interests in literary and philosophical subjects as well, and also his ardent and lifelong interest in theatre and drama. Jenkin showed great interest in the sanitary conditions of the working poor, and founded the Sanitary Protection Association for the supervision of houses with regard to health. He wrote a penetrating criticism of the *Origin of Species* that Darwin considered most valuable he had read, and that forced the latter to re-examine arguments about the age of the earth. Jenkin's many essays, books and articles show an acute mind. His lengthy article of 1877 on the use of graphical methods for determining the efficiency of mechanism was honoured with the Keith Gold Medal from the Royal Society of Edinburgh. This article supplied, in William Thomson's words, 'the elements required to constitute from Reulaux's kinematic system a full machine receiving energy and doing work' (1887, vol. 1: clix).

Between 1868 and 1872, Jenkin published three articles in political economy that form a small but important contribution to the subject. In the first article of 1868, on the possibility of trade unions permanently benefiting their members, Jenkin criticized the classical wage fund theory as begging the question. Only on the assumption of a fixed wage fund could it be argued that the wage was fixed as well, but this was to 'misapply the doctrine of demand and supply'. Jenkin argued that demand and supply were a function of prices, and of consequence the, wage was not a fixed magnitude but dependent on the state of the market. In this first article, Jenkin also showed great sympathy for the demands of the trade unions to improve legislation, which would thus improve the functioning of the labour market. Far from sharing the 'fear' of the Victorian middle-class for trade unions, Jenkin considered them to something needed and of potential benefit to the nation as a whole.

Jenkin's sympathy for the workers also emerges in his unpublished essay 'The Time-Labour System', in which he essentially argues for a fixed annual wage contract. Jenkin perceptively examines the differences between the labour market and the markets for commodities, and argues that those who fear that fixed wage contracts are a hindrance to the well-functioning of the labour market conflate two different concepts of competition, that is, 'competition in excellence' and 'competition in price'. Fixed annual wage contracts not only spur the self-esteem of the workman, but in fact also smooth wage changes in the market, which is to the benefit of all.

Jenkin's best-known article is his 'Graphic Representation of the Laws of Supply and Demand, and Their Application to Labour', published in 1870. The article shows Jenkin's great ingenuity in the use of graphs not only as means of illustration but also as tools of discovery. He also suggested ways of empirically estimating these curves. By means of his curves, he investigated William THORNTON's 1869 attack on John Stuart MILL's wage fund theory, especially Thornton's examples of non-clearing markets. This article prompted Stanley JEVONS to write and publish his own *Theory of Political Economy* (1871). Jenkin also extended this graphic analysis to the effects of taxation on the gains and losses of buyers and sellers through exchange. A last unpublished essay, 'Is One Man's Gain Another Man's Loss?', investigates the consequences of trade on wealth in a barter economy by means of a beautiful closed circuit diagram (1887, vol. 2: 150).

Fleeming Jenkin has been seen as a precursor of marginalism, but he never embraced Jevons's theory of marginal utility. His correspondence with Jevons that followed on his first published essay on trade unions shows his objections. Though needs and motives were important variables in Jenkin's explanatory scheme, he was reluctant to trace his descriptive relationship between prices and demand or supply back to Jevons's 'more complex algebraic representation' (1887, vol. 2: 108). For Jenkin, 'the causes which help to form the opinion' of traders in the market were simply 'too numerous…so that their opinion of the utility of the article does not ultimately affect the price' (1887, vol. 2: 98–9).

BIBLIOGRAPHY
Papers Literary, Scientific, &c., ed. S. Colvin and J.A. Ewing, with a memoir by Robert Louis Stevenson, 2 vols (1887).
The Graphic Representation of the Laws of Supply and Demand and Other Essays on Political Economy (1931; repr. 1996).

Further Reading
Brownlie, A.D. and Lloyd Prichard, M.F., 'Professor Fleeming Jenkin, 1833–1885, Pioneer in Engineering and Political Economy', *Oxford Economic Papers* (1963), vol. 15, no. 3, pp. 204–16.
Morris, S.W., 'Fleeming Jenkin and The Origin of Species: A Reassessment' *The British Journal for the History of Science* (1994), vol. 27, pp. 313–43.
Smith, C., 'Engineering the Universe: William Thomson and Fleeming Jenkin on the Nature of Matter', *Annals of Science* (1980), vol. 37, pp. 387–415.
Smith, C. and Wise, M.N., *Energy and Empire: A Biographical Study of Lord Kelvin* (Cambridge, 1989).
Uemiya, S., 'Jevons and Fleeming Jenkin', *Kobe University Economic Review* (1981), vol. 27, pp. 45–57.
White, M.V., '"That God-Forgotten Thornton": Exorcising Higgling after On Labour', *History of Political Economy* (1994), vol. 26, annual supplement, pp. 149–83.

Harro Maas

JENNINGS, Richard (1814–91)

Jennings was born in 1814, probably in London, and died in 1891. Very little is known about him, but it may be assumed that he came from a well-to-do family as he was educated at Eton and Trinity College, Cambridge. He was called to the bar afterwards, and then became Deputy Lieutenant and High Sheriff of Carmarthenshire.

Jennings wrote two books in political economy, of which his *Natural Elements of Political Economy* (1855) would prove especially influential. This is not so much due to the book itself: its sparkling insights are overshadowed by confused expressions of thought, and it is predominantly because of Stanley JEVONS's remarkably positive references to the book that Jennings is still remembered today. Perhaps because of his education at Cambridge, Jennings showed himself hostile to the economics of J.S. MILL and RICARDO, and promised to establish the subject on a new, scientific footing. His bents were clearly physicalist. Rather than searching for the ultimate causes of human action in man's (mental) motives, as John Stuart Mill had delimited the subject of political economy, Jennings aimed to reduce these motives to their physiological basis. In these attempts Jennings relied on the new psycho-physiological theory of reflex action developed by Henry Maudsley and especially William Carpenter, that had become prominent in Britain after Marshall Hall's pioneering work in the 1830s. Jennings's *Social Delusions Concerning Wealth and Want* (1856) was largely devoted to economic policy issues and the 'art' of economics. He was a critic of *laissez-faire*, and a proponent of strong government intervention in the economy. His proposals for tax reform display a sense of social engineering that is line with the physicalist principles laid out in the *Natural Elements*.

Though Jennings's physicalism was, even by the standards of his day, speculative rather than foundational, the idea of reducing man's motives to man's 'physical groundwork' (the words are Jevons's) would become ever more prominent in the last quarter of the nineteenth century, as witnessed from Jevons's own work, Thomas Huxley's highly controversial 1874 essay 'On the Hypothesis that Animals are Automata', and especially Francis Ysidro EDGEWORTH's incisive remarks on the subject in *New and Old Methods of Ethics* (1877). There runs a straight line from Jennings's *Natural Elements* to Edgeworth's 'hedonic barometer'.

Among Jennings's ideas are his clear perception of the idea of diminishing marginal utility, a hunch as to the possibility of using calculus to formulate this idea more rigorously, a strong emphasis on the importance of consumption for economic theory, and a further emphasis on the need to test the hypotheses of theory by using statistics. All these ideas were grist to the mills of Jevons, who seized upon them as 'a clear statement of the views which I have also adopted' (Jevons 1871: 18).

At the time Jennings's *Natural Elements* was barely discussed by any authoritative political economist, with the important exception of John Eliot CAIRNES, who devoted a note and an appendix in his 1857 *Lectures* to criticizing Jennings's views. This criticism is best summarized in Cairnes's visionary statement that 'if political economy is treated in this way, it is evident that it will soon become a wholly different study from that which the world has hitherto known it' (Cairnes 1857: 231). Precisely for this reason, Jennings's work is still justly remember as an early contribution to the marginalist revolution in economics.

BIBLIOGRAPHY
Natural Elements of Political Economy (1855, repr. New York, 1969).
Social Delusions Concerning Wealth and Want (1856).

Further Reading
Black, R.D.C., 'Richard Jennings', in J. Eatwell, M. Milgate and P. Newman (eds), *The New Palgrave: A Dictionary of Economics* (1998, vol. 2, p. 1008).
Cairnes, J.E., *The Character and Logical Method of Political Economy* (1857).
White, M.V., 'The Moment of Richard Jennings: The Production of Jevons's Marginalist Economic Agent', in P. Mirowski (ed.), *Natural Images in Economic Thought: 'Markets Red in Tooth and Claw'* (Cambridge, 1994, pp. 197–230).

Harro Maas

JENYNS, Soame (1704–87)

Jenyns was born in London on 1 January 1704, and died of a fever on 18 December 1787, also in London. His father, Sir Roger Jenyns, was a gentleman of Cambridgeshire. Jenyns was privately tutored and then in 1722 was admitted as a fellow-commoner of St John's College Cambridge, but he left in 1725 without taking a degree. He embarked on a career as a writer, producing several small volumes of poems, and later entered politics. From 1742–80 he represented either Cambridgeshire or Cambridge borough in the House of Commons, with the exception of the period 1754–8 when he represented Dunwich in Suffolk. In 1755 he was appointed a commissioner of the Board of Trade and Plantations.

While in politics Jenyns continued to write, producing prose essays as well as poetry. He was known as a writer on theological matters, and his *Free Inquiry into the Nature and Origin of Evil* (1757) and *View of the Internal Evidence of the Christian Religion* (1776) were both popular, the latter going through several editions. Dr Johnson publicly derided the first work in a review for the *Literary Magazine*, and this led to a feud between the two men that lasted until Johnson's death.

Acquaintances regarded Jenyns as having a great interest in trade and economics, and he was a frequent speaker on these subjects in the House of Commons. In *The Objections to the Taxation of our American Colonies* (1765) he argued in favour of taxing the American colonies. He saw no reason not to levy taxes in America, and scoffed at the idea that people should not be taxed without their consent; he argued that many English people were also taxed without their consent, as they could not vote and had no representation in Parliament, which levied taxes. Why, he asked, should the American colonists should be favoured over Englishmen in this regard?

Jenyn's most notable work on economics, *Thoughts on the Causes and Consequences of the present high Price of Provisions*, appeared in 1767. He ascribes the high cost of foodstuffs, especially corn, to two causes: 'the increase of our national debts, and the increase of our riches; that is, from the poverty of the pubic, and the wealth of private individuals' (1790, II: 165). The high taxes being levied to pay off the national debt are, says Jenyns, increasing the prices of many goods, and he shows how taxation creates not only higher prices for the goods being taxed, but general inflation:

> every new tax does not only affect the price of the commodity on which it is laid, but that of all others, whether taxed or not, and with which, at first sight, it seems to have no manner of connection. Thus, for instance, a tax on candles must raise the price of a coat, or a pair of breeches: because, out of these, all the taxes on the candles of the wool-comber, weaver, and the taylor, must be paid; a duty upon ale must raise the price of shoes, because from them all the taxes upon ale drank by the tanner, leather-dresser, and shoemaker, which is not a little, must be refunded.
> (1790, II: 166)

Even though there is no tax on corn, says Jenyns, the many other taxes that the farmer must pay inevitably raises the price of corn so that the farmer can earn enough to pay for other goods.

On the increase in wealth, Jenyns notes that 'the first, and most obvious effect of the increase of money, is the decrease of its value, like that of all other commodities; for money being but a commodity, its value must be relative, that is, dependant on the quantity of itself, and the quantity of the things to be purchased with it' (1790, II: 171) He argues that high money supply automatically leads to inflation, an effect which can be observed in every country down through the centuries. He notes too that there are winners and losers in inflationary times; merchants and traders, he says, nearly always gain, but those on fixed incomes lose.

BIBLIOGRAPHY
Free Inquiry into the Nature and Origin of Evil (1757).
The Objections to the Taxation of our American Colonies, by the Legislature of Great Britain, briefly considered (1765).
Thoughts on the Causes and Consequences of the present high Price of Provisions (1767).
View of the Internal Evidence of the Christian Religion (1776).
The Works of Soame Jenyns, ed. C.N. Cole (1790).

Further Reading
Cole, C.N., *Sketches of the Life of Soame Jenyns, Esq. with a short account of his family*, preface to *The Works of Soame Jenyns* (1790).

Thomas Worth

JEVONS, Herbert Stanley (1875–1955)

Jevons was born in Manchester in 1875, the son of the eminent political economist William Stanley JEVONS. He died in 1955. He was educated at Giggleswick Grammar School, then attended University College, London and Trinity College, Cambridge, and also studied at the Geological Institute, Heidelberg. From 1902–4 he was lecturer in mineralogy and geology at the University of Sydney. Returning to Britain, in 1905 he was appointed lecturer in economics at the College of South Wales and Monmouthshire, Cardiff; he was later Fulton Professor of Economic and Political Sciences there. From 1911–14 he was engaged in housing reform and garden city projects.

In 1914 Jevons went to India as first professor of economics at the University of Allahabad. It was here that perhaps his most important organizational work was done. Allahabad was at the time establishing its reputation as one of the leading universities in North India, and Jevons built up the teaching of economics there virtually from nothing. He also reached out to other economics departments in India and was a driving force behind the foundation of the Bengal Economic Association in 1916, along with other figures such as Gilbert SLATER, J.C. Coyajee, C.J. Hamilton and J.S. Chakravarti. In 1918 Jevons was present at the meeting, chaired by Hamilton, which inaugurated the Indian Economic Association. He went on to become its president in 1922, and had a hand in the foundation of the *Indian Journal of Economics*. Jevons also served as professor of economics at the University of Rangoon.

As an economist, Jevons followed very consciously in the footsteps of his father, William Stanley Jevons. He produced two editions of the latter's *The Theory of Political Economy*, one published in 1911, the other posthumously in 1957. His preface to the latter edition shows his views plainly:

> It is still a matter of controversy whether economics should be regarded as a calculus of pleasure and pain or, more correctly, of positive and negative feeling, or whether it should be treated as the science of preferences in the satisfaction of human wants. For myself, I believe that those who refuse or neglect to study the psychological basis of economics as one branch of the science of human behavior are less likely than those who do so to arrive at sound conclusions.
> (1957: v)

Jevons's first notable work was *The Sun's Heat and Trade Activity* (1910), a theory of trade cycles based on W.S. Jevons's paper 'The Solar Period and the Price of Corn' of 1875. Central to H.S. Jevons's version were empirical findings that trade activity on average has a peak every three and one-half years, while the sun's energy, indirectly measured through sunspots, has major cycles every eleven years and minor cycles lasting three and one-half years. To explain the transmission mechanism from the sun's activity to trade, Jevons argued that industry has seven or ten-year cycles fitting into the lowest multiples of three and one-half years. Industrial cycles could not be as short as agricultural cycles, as it takes time to change methods and businessmen's mental activities. Jevons undertook extensive data collection and analysis to test his approach. Wheat yields of the United States in the period 1870–1902 were on average 11.2 years, compared with average sunspot cycles of 11.125 years. The US agricultural output index had cycles of 3.7 years. Finally, he correlated changes in the agricultural sector with the rest of the economy, pointing out the severe effects of a downturn in agricultural incomes. He thought cyclical unemployment could not be cured by accumulating buffer stocks in years of good harvests: he preferred wages to vary with industrial activity.

Jevons's work on the coal trade portrays the industry's great days when it employed five million men. Again building on the work of his father and making use of his own technical expertise as a geologist, he considers the coal question as the 'working out of the easily gettable coal' (1915: 719). His father had pessimistically stated that coal supplies could run out because he had looked at only the resources of the nation. Jevons suggested that coal production would switch to new locations, finally reaching Siberia, Central Asia,

Central Africa, South America and the Polar regions. Thus coal reserves would last hundreds of years, but by 2040 a commercial substitute for coal would be possible. He speculated that the new sources of energy would not be water power or oil, but tidal and solar energy.

Faced with the trade depression of the 1930s, Jevons set himself the task of devising a workable form of co-operative socialism in *Economic Equality in the Co-operative Commonwealth*. He proposed a path from competition to co-operation, beginning with the transfer of ownership of land and the means of production to co-operative societies, philanthropic institutions, state or public institutions. The state would control industry within the framework of a plan and private co-operatives would run it. Adults would be controlled by a 'registrar of occupations', who would ensure that everyone was employed in an authorised occupation. Jevons called his system 'communism'. Fearlessly, he advocated the equality of all remuneration to avoid sectional jealousies. The satisfaction of pleasant work and a sense of duty to the community would provide incentives to work.

While in India, Jevons also wrote on money and exchange. Much of his work in this field was stimulated by the rapid destabilization of the silver-standard rupee over the years 1917–22, which was came as a surprise to him as it did to most people. He speculated on whether a gold standard might be possible, and concluded by 1922 that it was not. His work on money is not so much important in its own right as it is indicative of an emerging nationalism in Indian economic thinking and a recognition that the Indian economy could exist independent of that of Britain.

BIBLIOGRAPHY
The Sun's Heat and Trade Activity (1910).
The British Coal Trade (1915).
The Economics of Tenancy Laws and Estate Management (Allahabad, 1921).
The Future of Exchange and the Indian Currency (Allahabad, 1922).
Money, Banking and Exchange in India (Simla, 1922).
The British Steel Industry (1932).
The Causes of Fluctuations of Industrial Activity and the Price-Level (1933).
Economic Equality in the Co-operative Commonwealth (1933).

Further Reading
Jevons, W.S., *The Theory of Political Economy* (1871; subsequent edns ed. H.S. Jevons, 1911, 1957).

Tom Tomlinson

JEVONS, William Stanley (1835–82)

Stanley Jevons was born on 1 September 1835 at 14 Alfred Street, Liverpool, and was accidentally drowned on 13 August 1882 at Bulverhythe, near Hastings. He was the ninth child of Thomas Jevons, a prosperous iron merchant, and his wife Mary Anne, daughter of William Roscoe (1753–1831), 'Liverpool's cultural pioneer *par excellence*' (Chandler 1953: xv.) Jevons's formal education began at the Mechanics' Institute High School in Liverpool in 1846, and in 1850 he was sent to University College School in London. From there he entered University College in 1851, studying chemistry as his main interest, and in 1853 was awarded the gold medal for chemistry in the College examinations. At this time Jevons seems to have had no intention of making an academic career, and did not even plan to complete the course for his BA degree, preferring to return to Liverpool and seek a career in some type of manufacturing involving chemical processes. In this he might have succeeded, but was not given the opportunity to try. At the end of the summer term of 1853, when he was not yet eighteen, his chemistry professor, Thomas Graham, told Jevons that he had been asked to find someone fitted to fill the post of assayer at a new branch of the Royal Mint to be established in Sydney, and that he was prepared to recommend him for the appointment.

At first Jevons was inclined to refuse because of his age and inexperience, but his father urged him to think carefully before turning down such a well-paid post. Thomas Jevons's own business had failed after the railway building boom of the 1840s ended in the crisis of 1847, leaving his family in straitened circumstances. Jevons then accepted the appointment and, after spending some time training in Thomas Graham's assaying laboratory in London and in the Paris Mint, sailed for Australia in July 1854, arriving in Sydney on 6 October. For the next eighteen months Jevons found the work of setting up the apparatus and initiating the processes of assaying and coining demanding and hard. Thereafter the work of the Mint became almost a sinecure, usually occupying him for no more than an hour or two each working day. He had time to spare for a variety of interests of his own, of which meteorology was initially the most important. This formed the foundation for more comprehensive studies of the climate, not only of New South Wales but of all Australia. Jevons's systematic studies of Australia later extended to much more than its climate – to its 'geography, geology, topography, flora and social and economic character and policy' (Konekamp 1972: 22).

While still a student in London, Jevons had begun a spare-time study of what he later called 'the industrial mechanism of society', focussing initially on the classification of trades and extending to the growth and structure of the city. Soon after coming to Australia he began to make a similar study of Sydney; but other economic problems in the infrastructure and external trade of New South Wales also attracted his attention. In 1856 and 1857 this led him to seek to improve his knowledge of political economy by extensive reading of its leading authors, from Adam SMITH to J.S. MILL.

Early in 1858, Jevons had decided that 'it is my mission to apply myself to such subjects and it is my intention to do so.' He soon carried that intention into effect, resigning from his lucrative post at the end of 1858 in order to return to London and complete his BA degree at University College.

Having left Australia in the spring of 1859 and taken six months to travel homewards via South and North America, Jevons resumed his studies almost immediately and graduated in the first division in October 1860. He remained at University College for a further two years to complete the MA degree in a course which covered political economy, logic and philosophy, and in the examinations for these he was awarded the gold medal as the best candidate in 1862. In those two years Jevons also published fourteen papers on climatology, chemistry and political economy, including one which was to become a classic, his 'Notice of a General Mathematical Theory of Political Economy', read for him before the Economic Science and Statistics section of the British Association at Cambridge in September 1862. Along with this he sent another paper, 'On the Study of Periodic Commercial Fluctuations'. This latter dealt with a theme which was to recur in his later work on trade cycles; the former was to prove a harbinger of a revolution in the theory of value.

Yet at the time, as Jevons himself wrote in his personal journal, it was 'received without a word of interest or belief' (1972–81, vol. I: 188) and the year which followed his success in the MA examinations was an anxious one for him, without any settled employment. Nevertheless he continued his creative work in both political economy and logic, publishing in the spring *A Serious Fall in the Value of Gold Ascertained*, a pamphlet of 73 pages. In this Jevons tackled the question of the effect of recent gold discoveries on the general price level in the United Kingdom, a question to which various economists had given varying answers. Jevons subjected it to rigorous statistical analysis and, as KEYNES wrote, he 'had to solve the problem of price index numbers practically from the beginning; and it is scarcely an exaggeration to say that he made as much progress in this brief pamphlet as has been made by all succeeding authors put together' (Keynes 1936: 120). It was a masterpiece, and came to be recognized as such; but by the end of 1863 it had sold only seventy-four copies.

Even before this, Jevons had realized that he could not hope to make a living by his pen in London. His cousin, Henry Enfield Roscoe, who had been appointed to the chair of chemistry at Owens College, Manchester in 1857, had suggested to Jevons at Christmas 1862 that he should apply for a post as general tutor to the students at Owens College, which was soon to be filled. It was a small post, involving much work for little pay, so Jevons was at first reluctant to commit himself. In April 1863, he changed his mind and agreed to take up the tutorship from the opening of the next session.

Jevons held this post for two years, but did not allow it to interfere with the progress of his own work in logic and political economy. He spent the summer of 1863 completing his first book on logic, *Pure Logic: or the Logic of Quality Apart From Quantity*. In the summer vacation of 1864 he returned to London to work at the British Museum Library on 'the question of exhaustion of coal, which I look upon as the coming question', as he wrote to his brother Herbert (1972–81, vol. III: 58). Britain's position as the leading industrial economy in the world at that time depended on possessing cheap and plentiful coal supplies. In the early 1860s, fears that these might someday, perhaps soon, run out had begun to be widely heard. So Jevons, who had still a reputation and a career to make, saw that 'a good publication on the subject would draw a good deal of attention' (1972–81, vol. III: 52). Just as he had done with the question of gold supplies, he set out to replace vague speculations with statistical facts. Jevons's conclusion was, not that British coal supplies would soon be exhausted, but that the development of heavy industry had produced a rate of increase of coal consumption, which could not be sustained without large increases in the cost of mining coal; and this in turn must tend to weaken Britain's ability to compete against newly industrializing countries.

Jevons's 'good publication' *The Coal Question* appeared in the spring of 1865, but did not become an immediate best-seller. Ultimately this was to work in his favour. In October 1865 Jevons was appointed a substitute lecturer in logic and political economy at Owens College, and was able to resign his ill-paid tutorship. Early in 1866 the trustees of Owens College decided to reorganize its professorships and to advertise a new chair of logic, mental and moral philosophy and political economy, for which he duly applied. At about the same time, J.S. Mill, then MP for Westminster, spoke in the House of Commons in support of an amendment favouring reduction of the national debt before changes in taxation, and drew attention to the arguments for such a policy put forward by Jevons in *The Coal Question*. Gladstone, then Chancellor of the Exchequer, accepted the point and soon Jevons was able to write to his sister Lucy: '*The Coal Question* gets on apace. The papers are hammering away about it... The more one's name is named now, the better for my professorship appointment' (1972–81, vol. III: 101).

Although he was clearly a strong candidate for that appointment, Jevons remained deeply anxious and doubtful about the outcome until it was officially confirmed to him by the trustees on 31 May 1866. On taking up this new post, Jevons found not only that the work involved was 'much more easy, familiar and congenial', but also that his personal finances were much improved. He was now able to contemplate marrying and setting up a home; in October 1867 he became engaged to Harriet Ann Taylor, a daughter of John Edward

Taylor, founder and proprietor of the *Manchester Guardian*. They were married on 19 December 1867 and had one son and two daughters.

About a year before his marriage, Jevons 'began thinking about logic again seriously' (1972–81, vol. I: 208) At first his thoughts took the form of grafting some extensions onto the *Logic of Quality as apart from Quantity*, which he had published in 1864. On 11 February 1867 he wrote in his journal, 'I have now fully decided on commencing at once a complete work on logic...the work will require several years of hard thinking, reading and writing. I should wish to produce a work which will not only embody a new and luminous system but will be readable and read by many'. This was to become *The Principles of Science*, published in two volumes in 1874. This comprehensive 'treatise on logic and scientific method' Jevons regarded as 'the most important book I can ever hope to produce'.

Although, for at least six years, writing *The Principles of Science* was Jevons's main occupation, it did not prevent him from writing and publishing many other papers and books, including *The Theory of Political Economy* (1871), the work on which his enduring international reputation as an economist was to rest. He decided to write it when Fleeming JENKIN, professor of engineering at Edinburgh, with whom Jevons had corresponded in 1868, published a paper in 1870 on 'The Graphical Representation of the Laws of Supply and Demand' without acknowledging Jevons's previous work in this area. Jevons felt that the time had come to publish his 1862 'General Mathematical Theory of Political Economy' in a fuller form, and to assert his priority in it. He was able to develop it into a book in a remarkably short time because its essentials had long been clear in his mind. He sent the manuscript to Macmillan in March 1871 and the first edition appeared in October of the same year.

In the preface, Jevons stated precisely what the book was intended to do: 'In this book I have attempted to treat Economy as a Calculus of Pleasure and Pain...' (1871: 44). It was, in other words, an application of Benthamite utilitarianism to the economic problem as Jevons saw it. In the introduction, he boldly advanced 'the somewhat novel opinion that *value depends entirely upon utility*', and followed it with another, equally novel statement: '*our science must be mathematical, simply because it deals with quantities*' (1871: 77, 78). Taking Bentham's theory of pleasure and pain as his starting point, Jevons argued that 'to satisfy our wants to the utmost with the least effort...in other words, to *maximise pleasure* is the problem of Economics.' Its solution required, first, the development of a theory of utility, to explain how pleasure is derived from the consumption of commodities. In this, Jevons first stated the 'law of variation of utility', and distinguished between total utility and what he called 'degree of utility', the concepts on which so much of the theory of consumer behaviour was later to be founded. But 'utility arises from commodities being brought in suitable quantities and at the proper times into the possession of persons needing them and it is by exchange...that this is effected' (1871: 126). The theory of exchange thus becomes the central core of the book, set between the theory of consumption and the theory of supply or production. This latter Jevons assumed first to be the result of labour alone, which involves the disutility of painful exertion. Then the utility provided by consumption and the disutility involved in production are related by the process of exchange, in which values are established.

Jevons rounded off his *Theory* with two further chapters, one on rent and one on capital. The purpose of the brief chapter on 'Theory of Rent' is to show how when labour is combined with land in production, a surplus over the 'necessary recompense' for the pain of labour can arise. But in the 'Theory of Capital', Jevons regards capital as 'a distinct branch of our subject' because 'we might have the advantages of capital without those of exchange...Economics, then is not solely the science of Exchange or Value; it is also the science of Capitalisation'. Both can increase the sum of utility: capitalization essentially by affording the means of carrying on what the Austrian economist Eugen Böhm-Bawerk was later to call 'roundabout methods of production'.

This sketch of the contents of *The Theory of Political Economy* shows it to be a major departure from, and advance on, the classical theory of value and distribution, yet almost as far from what later came to be regarded as orthodox neo-classical economics. For Jevons, whose earlier reputation was that of 'a recognised statistical writer', it was a challenging work in economic theory which proved the truth of what he had once said of himself, but never claimed publicly: 'I am better in theory than I am in fact' (1972–81, vol. III: 42). Among the small community of British economists at the time, the book had at first a mixed and lukewarm reception, but in continental Europe it received more understanding and attention; and from it ultimately Jevons gained an international reputation as an economic theorist.

In late 1871 and after, Jevons returned to the completion of *The Principles of Science*, but by May 1872 he had to admit that 'I seem to have exhausted my nervous system by overwork' (1972–81, vol. III: 249). His doctor insisted that he should take a complete break from work for the summer of 1872 and Jevons reduced his teaching load by half during 1872–3. Even then he felt obliged to seek leave of absence for the next academic year in order to finish the book. Torn between his sense of obligation to Owens College and his desire to escape or reduce his burden of teaching and return to London, Jevons went through a long period of uncertainty about his own future. In 1875 the secretary of University College, London, made it known to Jevons that he could have the refusal of the chair of political economy there, previously held by J.E. CAIRNES.

The lighter duties of this post attracted Jevons and he finally accepted, taking it up in October 1876. He hoped that it would also allow him more freedom to write and publish, but certainly did not look on it as a sinecure. In the first year of his tenure of the chair, Jevons doubled the number of lectures and attracted an increased number of students to his classes. Subsequently he reverted to lecturing only once a week; nevertheless, the old tension between the demands of teaching and those of writing soon reappeared. In the spring of 1878 overwork was again threatening his health, and lecturing and examining became an increasing burden to him. In October 1880, Jevons decided to resign the professorship, not without some regret (1972–81, vol. V: 110), but he did not cut down on his writing commitments. Though he found lecturing stressful, Jevons had a talent for presenting the elements of his subjects clearly. He published a *Primer of Logic* in 1876 and a *Primer of Political Economy* in 1878. These little books sold in thousands to students the world over for the next fifty years.

Nor was Jevons lacking in original ideas for research during these years in London. Of these the best known – and at the same time the least successful – was his attempt to explain the decennial trade cycle by the hypothesis of a causal relationship, direct or indirect, between it and sunspot activity. Always fascinated by the concept of periodicity, Jevons first put forward the idea that these particular periodically varying phenomena were related as cause and effect in a paper presented to the Economic Science section of the British Association in August 1876. Although in subsequent years and numerous papers he formulated it in a variety of ways, he was never able to show that the hypothesis was adequately supported by the available statistical data. Nevertheless, even in his last completed paper on an economic subject ('The Solar–Commercial Cycle' in 1882; 1972–81, vol. VII, pp.108–11) he still held to his belief that the objections advanced against this theory were 'far from being conclusive, and I may hope in time to give them a satisfactory answer.'

After he had freed himself of teaching commitments, Jevons set about revising the many articles and pamphlets he had written on economic subjects, with the intention of collecting them into two volumes, one to be entitled *Investigations in Currency and Finance*, incorporating his well-known papers in the monetary field, and the other entitled *Methods of Social Reform*. The papers in this volume, taken together with his last completed book, *The State in Relation to Labour* (1882), provide an account of Jevons's views on state intervention versus private enterprise in economic and social affairs. Those views were typically Benthamite: the greatest good of the greatest number was the only deciding principle he would allow in such questions.

Jevons left much work unfinished, including a planned major book, *Principles of Economics*, when, on holiday with his wife and family at Bulverhythe in August 1882, he made an unwise decision to go swimming. Apparently as a result of the shock of the unusually cold sea, he suffered a heart attack and drowned.

From the time of his graduation as a Master of Arts of the University of London until his death, Jevons's career lasted just over twenty years. In that time, the quantity of work, both theoretical and applied, which he had accomplished in economics alone was remarkable; but it was also work of the highest quality and originality. Jevons possessed a rare ability to generate ideas which have proved to be of continuing interest, and to raise questions which still stimulate others to further research.

BIBLIOGRAPHY
A Serious Fall in the Value of Gold Ascertained (1862).
Pure Logic: or the Logic of Quality Apart From Quantity (1863).
The Coal Question: An Inquiry concerning the Progress Of the Nation, and the Probable Exhaustion of our Coal-mines (1865).
The Theory of Political Economy (1871; repr. 1970).
The Principles of Science: A Treatise on Logic and Scientific Method (1874).
Money and the Mechanism of Exchange (1875).
The State in Relation to Labour (1882).
Methods of Social Reform (1883).
Investigations in Currency and Finance (1884).
Papers and Correspondence of William Stanley Jevons, 7 vols, vol. I ed. R.D. Collison Black and R. Könekamp, vols II–VII ed. R.D. Collison Black (1972–81).

Further Reading
Chandler, G., *William Roscoe of Liverpool* (1953).
Keynes, J. M., 'William Stanley Jevons, 1835–1882: A Centenary Allocution on his Life and Work', in *Essays in Biography*, vol. 10 in *Collected Writings of John Maynard Keynes* (1936).
Konekamp, R., 'Biographical Introduction', *Papers and Correspondence of William Stanley Jevons*, vol. 1 (1972).
Schabas, M., *A World Ruled by Number: William Stanley Jevons and the Rise of Mathematical Economics* (Princeton, 1990).

R.D. Collison Black

JEWKES, John (1902–88)

Jewkes was born in June 1902 in Barrow-in-Furness, Cumberland and died 18 August 1988 in Oxford. Much of the first part of his life was spent in the north-west of England. Educated at Barrow Grammar School, he graduated from Manchester University with and MComm degree in 1924 and, following a two-year stint as assistant secretary to the

Manchester Chamber of Commerce, became a lecturer in economics at Manchester in 1926. He visited the USA as a Rockefeller Foundation Fellow (1929–30), and on his return in 1930 published a study of the efficiency of American manufacturing industry, where he considered the possible causes of the greater productivity of American industry compared with that in the UK. He looked at the relative scale of enterprises, the use of labour and capital and the relative profitability of firms in the two countries. Already it is possible to perceive Jewkes's cautious interpretation of economic data. Instead of looking for evidence that business decisions in one country were right and in the other wrong, Jewkes tended rather to search for explanations or rationalizations for observed differences. He also undertook *An Industrial Survey of Cumberland and Furness* (1933), with Allan Winterbottom, and studied the historical evolution and the structure of the Cotton Industry.

Cotton played an important role in the industrial development of the north-west, and Jewkes studied the structure of the industry, the location of its constituent parts, its adjustment to post-war depression and the operation of its labour markets. His work discussed the size distribution of factories and firms, the gradual technical specialization of factories in spinning or weaving (unlike the USA), the trend towards geographical specialization of weaving in north Lancashire and spinning in the south, the effects of technological change and of overseas competition. His early work raised the issues which would eventually come to define his career. If conscious planning and control is a necessary part of economic life, what is the appropriate size and scope for these administrative and planning units? Why were looms in the United States located with spindles but not predominantly so in England? When will things be done separately and when together? If separate firms undertake different parts of a process of production, co-ordinating their activities by buying from upstream and selling to downstream firms, will these decentralized market transactions achieve better results than fully integrated administrative arrangements?

With unemployment in the early 1930s at historically unprecedented levels, Jewkes and his wife Sylvia Butterworth (whom he had married in 1929 and who was to become an important collaborator in much of his work) produced a report on *The Juvenile Labour Market* (1938). They used a survey of two thousand children leaving school in 1934 in five Lancashire towns: Ashton-under-Lyne, Atherton, Burnley, St Helens and Warrington. Jewkes's work on juvenile unemployment reveals the same meticulous observation of the actual operation of markets and businesses as they adjusted to new circumstances, and provided a 'down-to-earth', 'common sense' and intensely practical approach to microeconomics.

Neither did Jewkes at this stage espouse any particular 'ideological' hostility to government intervention. Although recognizing the difficulties and limitations, he supported vocational guidance for children, schemes to compel employers to notify vacancies to a Juvenile Employment Office, routine medical inspections before leaving school, and efforts to improve the information available to parents and children. He was aware of the frictions that accompanied the market process – as witnessed for example by the 'extreme immobility of juvenile workers' (1938: 60), leading to great differences in rates of juvenile unemployment that could persist in towns only a few miles apart. He was aware of the problems of local monopoly power and local dependence on a single main employer – in the case of his own town, Barrow-in-Furness, the firm of Vickers-Armstrong. The future scourge of the planners and champion of competitive markets could write about 'the grossest forms of exploitation' (1938: 89) in a book published by the Left Book Club.

During the Second World War Jewkes was director of the economic section of the War Cabinet Secretariat (1941), director general of statistics and programmes at the Ministry of Aircraft Production (1943) and principal assistant secretary at the Office of the Minister of Reconstruction (1944). His direct experience of the operations of state agencies in these years was greatly to influence Jewkes's postwar work in economics, and to do so in a way that distinguished him from others of his generation. Far from inducing a sense of confidence in the benign potential and rationality of state planning mechanisms, Jewkes was more impressed by their waste and inefficiency, even when the authorities were invested with wartime powers and were pursuing a single over-riding collective aim.

Jewkes continued his academic career at Manchester, having become professor of social economics in 1936 and holding the Stanley Jevons Chair in Political Economy between 1946 and 1948. The latter year saw the publication of his great critique of state planning *Ordeal by Planning*. It established the trademarks that were to be associated with Jewkes's work in the future: deceptive simplicity and clarity of writing; homely and practical examples; the remorseless application of elementary economic principles; the ability to break down complex and multifaceted social questions into sub-components capable of separate consideration; and finally the courage to draw conclusions startlingly at odds with the temper of the age, such as: 'There can be nothing but bitterness and ruin waiting for those who create, or suffer to be created, a centrally controlled economy' (1948: 9).

This conclusion, so unpalatable to contemporary opinion, was derived from some simple observations about the realities of economic and social life. Scarcity imposed the necessity of choice. Choice implied the perception of opportunity cost. In a world of continual change and dispersed knowledge (if consumption and production decisions were supposed to have something to do with people's preferences as well as technical possibilities) central planners could never know what opportunity costs were. The control of prices by a central authority undermined their role as co-ordinating devices and information transmitters. Prices could no longer be used as independent sources of information about the prevailing supply and demand conditions, but instead represented reflections of the central authority's own highly imperfect assessments of opportunity costs. Efforts to overcome this lacuna in knowledge, argued Jewkes, would result in gradually rising intervention in local decisions, the imposition of elaborate reporting devices, deception, self-delusion, outright lying, the debasement of language, increasing infringements of individual liberty, rising economic instability and, finally, economic collapse. The system of state planning desired by many in order to achieve greater 'rationality' in the use of resources completely frustrates the achievement of any such goal. Jewkes was not, of course, the sole originator of these ideas, associated as they are with more celebrated scholars such as Friedrich von HAYEK. But Jewkes had unrivalled grasp of the arguments and presented them in a way calculated to persuade the general reader and not merely the trained philosopher.

Jewkes moved to Oxford in 1948 as a fellow of Merton College and as professor of economic organization. After 1969 he held an emeritus fellowship at Merton. In the years after the war, Jewkes was a member of several advisory committees and Royal Commissions, notwithstanding his strongly expressed critique of state planning. He was a member of the Fuel Advisory Committee (1945); the Cotton Industry Working Party (1946); the Royal Commission on Gambling, Betting and Lotteries (1949); and the Royal Commission on Doctors' and Dentists' Remuneration (1957–60). Perhaps it is not surprising that during the 1950s, with his views reinforced by his time as a visiting professor in Chicago (1953–4), Jewkes became a major critic of the nationalized industries, the British Broadcasting Corporation (BBC) and the National Health Service (NHS). In each case, the state-imposed monopoly power and the claims made for improved co-ordination and more socially 'rational' or 'fair' resource use were subjected to the same tireless de-construction process that Jewkes employed in *Ordeal by Planning*.

In the case of the nationalized industries, Jewkes saw all the problems of state planning on a somewhat smaller scale. What had Britain received in return for granting monopolies to important sectors? The experiment had been 'barren of anything fruitful or novel' (1953: 164). His reflections on public versus private enterprise were further developed in the Lindsay Memorial Lectures (1964) which he gave after returning from a period as visiting professor at Princeton (1961). In the case of the BBC, his major criticisms (1953: 210–214) were levelled against the suppression of consumers' preferences, attempts to buttress its monopoly by stifling foreign broadcasts from Luxembourg, and actions designed to inhibit technical innovation especially in 'wire broadcasting'. Indeed, the tendency of monopoly to suppress innovation was a major theme running through Jewkes's work. He argued that the creation and maintenance of monopoly power was particularly difficult in broadcasting and the tide of technical changes ultimately decisive. If, even in these internationally dynamic conditions, local monopoly power in the UK had resulted in resistance to innovation, what losses might there be in those areas where new and useful ideas 'have not the same inherently overwhelming power to assert themselves' (1953: 213)?

Jewkes recognized that the pursuit of equality had been an important motivation leading to the foundation of the NHS in 1948, and he avoided explicit criticism of this objective. He did allow himself to observe, however, that he could not see how the objective of health equality could reasonably be given 'practical shape' and that where, as a result of administrative necessity, some practical shape emerged, attempts to achieve it were likely to be self-defeating and add to inequality. As with the nationalized industries, he concentrated on showing that there were inevitable and substantial opportunity costs associated with the construction of social organizations that depend upon the suppression of the price mechanism. He wrote a memorandum of dissent to the Royal Commission (1960) in which he criticized the recommended pay award for being too low to ensure the required flow of new doctors into the profession. More fundamentally, however, his real complaint was that a committee should be trying to calculate the ideal remuneration of doctors in the first place. Planned or hierarchically determined prices (whether of doctors' services or medical treatment) would simply result in rationing, ignorance of consumers' wants and distortions to the effort of NHS staff. The NHS, in Jewkes's opinion, seemed 'doomed to remain second or third-rate' (1978: 87).

From his early work on the structure of the cotton industry onwards, Jewkes was aware that innovation both in institutions and in technology was a central force in economic progress. He therefore saw the market process as a continuing generator of new methods as well as a means of adapting to them. Government policy towards invention, technical innovation and pure science was of great interest to him. In *The Sources of Invention* (1958), Jewkes and his co-authors produced short histories of the major inventions of the first half of the twentieth century. These case studies were then used to discuss the roles of the large research establishments and individual inventors. Jewkes emphasized that generalizations about the sources of invention are bound to be difficult, but the importance of individual determination in overcoming the inertia of bureaucrats or the hostility of threatened interests is well documented. His interpretation of the evidence contradicted the view associated with Schumpeter and (later) with Galbraith, that large-scale enterprises with monopoly power encouraged technical dynamism. Jewkes's reading of the historical record led him to distrust the role of long-established large organizations with empires and vested interests to protect.

Jewkes's views on government policy towards science and technology were, as usual, out of step with the times. Governments worried that markets failed to allocate adequate resources to pure science (because of its public good characteristics) or 'high technology' (because private businesses were too risk averse and overlooked socially beneficial spillovers). Comparisons with Russia and other countries led some to conclude that the UK was falling behind. Jewkes (1960: 7) observed that, even soon after the launch of Russia's Sputnik, 'it surely cannot be denied that Russia is capable of inflicting upon herself massive misdirections of her resources'. These misdirections of resources, argued Jewkes (1972), also characterized British efforts to support 'high-technology' projects in the 1960s. The primary motivation of government efforts to boost high technology, Jewkes surmised, was fear of economic competition from other countries: 'Such fears are understandable, highly contagious and largely without foundation' (1972: 8). He was sceptical of causal links between overall spending or government spending on science and technology and economic growth, and he warned against the politicization of decision making and emphasized the difficulty of calling a halt to costly mistakes when public sector projects were involved.

Between 1969 and 1974, Jewkes followed Arthur Shenfield as the director of the Industrial Policy Group (IPG). This group comprised the chairmen of between fifteen and twenty large companies who had become dissatisfied with government policy towards business. Papers were produced on the selective employment tax (a tax on employment in the service industries) the case for overseas direct investment, industrial structure, the nature of competition, monopoly and mergers policy, and the connection between economic growth profits and investment. As usual, the free market agenda pursued by Jewkes was not received well by the mainly corporatist establishment of the time. The president and the director general of the Confederation of British Industry were uncomfortable *ex officio* members of the group, and eventually found it necessary to record a note of dissent when an IPG Paper on 'Economic Growth, Profits and Investment' criticized fiscal investment incentives and argued instead for general cuts in the level of taxes on company profits. Jewkes himself judged the IPG as 'the failure of an experiment', and reflected upon the hostile general atmosphere of the time: 'It is easy to forget that up to 1974 there was hardly one important newspaper that robustly defended private enterprise...' (1978: 182).

Jewkes's writing reveals the interplay of many themes. Before the formal study of 'public choice' was developed by the Virginia School in the 1960s and 1970s, Jewkes was an intuitive 'public choice' economist. Before the publication of articles on the economics of bureaucracy, Jewkes fully comprehended the incentive problems implied by that form of organization. Before Ronald Coase's analysis of transactions costs had been refined, Jewkes's approach to the integration versus disintegration problem was consistent with this emerging tradition. He saw the size and scope of factories and firms as the result of economic forces, including incentives, decision making and control which, in competitive market conditions, imposed limits on the growth and size of firms. On the other hand he realized that in conditions where the co-ordination of continual changes in product was required, internal organization and vertical integration might (again within limits) be favoured. It was, he argued, the development of man-made fibres and the great variety of new fabrics based upon them that led after 1945 to a reversal of the trend, discernible since 1884, towards less integrated firms in the cotton industry in the UK.

The analysis of economic change was at the heart of Jewkes's approach to economics. His interest in the importance of individual enterprise and initiative meant that he dealt with the themes of 'Austrian Economics'. He wrote about entrepreneurship, technical change and the economics of information. Yet he did not become an icon of the Austrian School and adopt its more radical ideas. He was always a classical liberal and, for example, consistently defended the role of the state in the field of anti-monopoly policy. He was closer in spirit to the Ordo-Liberals of post-war Germany, and wrote an introduction to Walter Eucken's book *This Unsuccessful Age* (1952). He met Eucken at the first meeting of the Mont Pèlerin Society at Vevey in 1948. As his introductory essay betrays, he was occasionally prone to bouts of optimism about the capability of democratic societies to learn from collective mistakes and impose limits on the scope of government intervention. Perhaps, he mused, Keynesian employment policies might not lead to rampant inflation and growing state intervention 'when the appropriate institutional checks and safeguards have been erected against these dangers' (1952: 25). Similarly he always hoped, perhaps against his better judgement, that the anti-monopoly agencies of the state could 'stick to their last' and confine themselves to their main task. 'The primary purpose of any investigating Commission is to satisfy itself whether competition exists or not' (1977: 54); and by competition, he meant real competition, not textbook versions of 'perfect competition' which, indeed could never exist.

Another characteristic of Jewkes's writing was his often-repeated view of the economic system as an 'organic' entity. In this, he followed the tradition of Alfred MARSHALL. Firms of differing sizes and forms were in a complex and mutually dependent system that evolved through time, changing gradually in response to local entrepreneurial initiatives. Failed experiments were as important to the operation of this system as successful ones and industrial policy would be destructive if it blundered around encouraging larger units in the name of efficiency, but undermining the ecological balance. The main thing, for Jewkes, was that 'the vast processes of trial and error that go on constantly through the operation of free markets' should not be inhibited (1970: 20). Just as he wrote on the themes of 'Austrian Economics' without being recognized as a member of the school, however, so he drew from evolutionary thinking without contributing to modern evolutionary economics.

By the criteria of modern academic life, it is apparent that Jewkes was not a great economic theorist. He made no great theoretical breakthroughs or conceptual advances in the manner of his close contemporary, Ronald Coase. But he was a political economist of the highest order. The focussed attention of those capable of making theoretical advances can lead them to errors to which Jewkes could never succumb. He distrusted the heavy formalism of much modern economic theory, the mathematical model building and the econometric techniques. Given his ecological and evolutionary conception of the economy, this is not surprising. Econometric forecasting faced the same problems as weather forecasting or predictions of long-term climate change. It was not that these techniques could never be useful, but only that the 'scientific mystique' should not blind us to their dangers and shortcomings. But, as we have seen, in spite of his scepticism about econometric modelling, Jewkes was an empiricist. His support for market processes rested on the twin supports of basic Marshallian economic theory and close observation of business life.

Jewkes's work was under-rated in his lifetime. There were several causes of this. The clarity of his writing combined with his use of literary and sometimes polemical devices militated against attracting the regard of serious scholars, who were increasingly adopting a somewhat sterile and de-personalized style as proof of their scientific detachment. This growth of professionalism, however, did not lead to greater popular understanding of economic principles. In Jewkes's work, the arguments are always clear and straightforward. Any priesthood, in contrast, generally prefers its truths to be more obscure and difficult to interpret in order to protect its monopoly. The lack of theoretical pretension and the use of the most elementary economic ideas contrasted with the tools employed by the supporters of planning, who were developing general equilibrium models, input–output analysis, growth theory, multi-equation econometric forecasting models and so forth. Finally, his entire professional life from the mid-1920s to the late 1970s coincided almost exactly with the advance of socialist ideas. He stood out against the 'zeitgeist'.

Jewkes's influence is impossible to calibrate precisely. His effect, like that of George Eliot's provincial heroine Dorothea Casaubon, has been 'incalculably diffusive' and therefore probably much greater than meets the superficial eye. Certainly the channels of his influence flowed freely through his teaching, through his independent writing, through his support of the Institute of Economic Affairs and through his membership and presidency of the Mont Pèlerin Society. An obituary written by Lord Harris of High Cross in 1988 paid tribute to Jewkes with the following assessment: 'Jewkes deserves the lion's share of the credit for encouraging the intellectual rejuvenation of the market economy.' Jewkes lived long enough to see some of the results of this rejuvenation, including the market reforms of the 1980s and much of the privatization programme in the UK. He did not see the final collapse of the planned systems of Eastern Europe, whose post-war record fully vindicated his dismal prognosis in *Ordeal by Planning*. He was triumphantly correct about central planning, because he applied simple economic ideas consistently and courageously from the beginning of his career to the end. To read Jewkes is to realize that economics does still have some claim to be the 'queen of the social sciences'. It is a claim hopelessly compromised by those who tried to add to her dominions and her prestige by dressing her in ever more elaborate and extravagant garb and by making ever more exaggerated claims on her behalf. Jewkes was the ambassador of a discipline modestly attired, jealous of her territory but at peace with her neighbours, aware of her limits but whose laws were not prudently to be disdained.

BIBLIOGRAPHY

(with G. Daniels), 'The Post-war Depression in the Lancashire Cotton Industry', *Journal of the Royal Statistical Society* (1928), vol. 153.

'The Localisation of the Cotton Industry', supplement to the *Economic Journal* (1930), vol. 91.

'The Efficiency of American Manufacturing Industry', *Economic Journal* (1930), vol. 40, no. 4, pp.581–98.

(with A. Winterbottom) *An Industrial Survey of Cumberland and Furness: A study of the social implications of economic dislocation* (1933).

(with A. Winterbottom) *Juvenile Unemployment* (1933).

(with E.M. Gray) *Wages and Labour in the Lancashire Cotton Spinning Industry* (Manchester, 1935).

(with S. Jewkes) *The Juvenile Labour Market* (1938).

'The Population Scare', *The Manchester School* (1939), October.

Ordeal by Planning (New York, 1948).

'Monopoly and Economic Progress', *Economica* (1953), vol. 20, pp. 197–214; repr. in *A Return to Free Market Economics? Critical Essays on Government Intervention* (1978, pp.192–210).

'The Nationalisation of Industry', *The University of Chicago Law Review* (1953), repr. in *A Return to Free Market Economics? Critical Essays on Government Intervention* (1978, pp.139–69).

(with D. Sawers and R. Stillerman) *The Sources of Invention* (1958).

'British Monopoly Policy 1944–56', *The Journal of Law and Economics* (1958), vol. 1, pp.1–19.

'How Much Science?', *The Economic Journal* (1960), vol. 1, pp. 1–16.

(with S. Jewkes), *The Genesis of the British National Health Service* (Oxford, 1961).
(with S. Jewkes), *Value for Money in Medicine* (Oxford, 1963).
Public and Private Enterprise (Keele, 1964).
(with S. Jewkes), 'Britain out of Step', in *Monopoly or Choice in Health Services?* (1964).
(with S. Jewkes), 'A Hundred Years of Change in the Structure of the Cotton Industry', *The Journal of Law and Economics* (1966), vol. 9, pp. 115–34.
(with P. Chambers and Lord Robbins), *Economics, Business and Government* (1966).
'No Industry Without Enterprise', in *Growth through Industry: A Reconsideration of Principles and Practice before and after the National Plan*, (1967, pp. 3–14).
The Structure and Efficiency of British Industry (1970).
Government and High Technology (1972).
Delusions of Dominance (1977).
A Return to Free Market Economics? Critical Essays on Government Intervention (1978).

Martin Ricketts

JOHN, Arthur Henry (1915–78)

Arthur John was born in South Wales in 1915. He died in London on 30 October 1963. He was educated at Port Talbot County School and the London School of Economics, where he obtained first class honours in the BS (Econ) in 1936. He completed a PhD at Cambridge under Sir John CLAPHAM in 1939, later published as *The Industrial Development of South Wales*. During the Second World War he served in the Royal Air Force, after which he worked briefly as a university administrator at LSE and at Nottingham. By 1950 he had been appointed a lecturer in the economic history department at LSE. He was appointed to a chair in 1964. He became active in LSE's administration, serving as pro-director of LSE from 1970–3, and was on the council of the Economic History Society for over twenty years.

John's study of South Wales traced the region's industrial development in two stages: in the first, iron and copper smelting dominated, and in the second, coal mining. The transition came around 1850 with the development of the railways. He traced the many implications of railways for the region, from the decline of Bristol as a centre for Welsh trade to their encouraging the movement of farmers away from the land. South Wales industrial development differed significantly from that of other coalfield areas. There was no previous tradition of industrial development, and the region relied on access to raw materials that could be worked with unskilled labour. The social structure of the region severely limited the supply of capital, which implied a particularly large role for outsiders, causing the gap between masters and workers to be larger than elsewhere.

With his history of Alfred Booth and Co., John moved away from the history of his native region, but his work continued to have a regional dimension, for the history of Booth and Co., a trading and later a shipping company, was bound up with the history of Liverpool. It marked a shift in his interests away from industry to trade, evidenced by use of Miles Nightingale, a drysalter of the City of London, to illuminate economic conditions at the time of the Seven Years War and the reasons why economic activity accelerated in the middle of the century. His more general writings on the British economy focused on the early eighteenth century, the period before the industrial revolution. However, he retained an interest in Welsh history, contributing to the *Glamorgan County History* shortly before his death. He also wrote a short history of the LSE library.

BIBLIOGRAPHY

The Industrial Development of South Wales, 1750–1850 (Cardiff, 1950).

'War and the English Economy, 1700–1763', *Economic History Review* (1955), vol. 7, no. 3, pp. 329–44.

A Liverpool Merchant House: Being the History of Alfred Booth and Company, 1863–1958 (1959).

'Agricultural Productivity and Economic Growth in England, 1700–1760', *Journal of Economic History* (1965), vol. 25, no. 1, pp. 19–34.

'Miles Nightingale – Drysalter: A Study in Eighteenth-Century Trade', *Economic History Review* (1965), vol. 18, no. 1, pp. 152–63.

The British Library of Political and Economic Science: A Brief History (1971).

(with G. Williams) *Glamorgan County History*, vol, 5, *Industrial Glamorgan* (Cardiff, 1980).

Further Reading
The Times, Obituary, 13 Feburary 1939, p. 4.

Roger Backhouse

JOHN OF SALISBURY (1115/20–1180)

John of Salisbury was born between 1115 and 1120 in Salisbury (Old Sarum), Wiltshire, apparently to a minor noble family, and died on 25 October 1180 at Chartres, France. He was educated at Salisbury and Exeter cathedral schools, and studied in Paris between 1136 and 1147 with Peter Abelard, Gilbert of Poitiers, Robert Pullan and many other important teachers of his age.

In 1148, John entered the service of the archbishop of Canterbury, Theobald, in whose employ he became a leading advisor, secretary and diplomat to the ecclesiastical and courts of England and the continent. He produced a philosophical and satirical poem, the *Entheticus de dogmate philosophorum*, in 1154, which he dedicated to the newly appointed chancellor to King Henry II, Thomas Becket, a former member of Theobald's household.

John fell out of favor with Henry II in late 1156 and was forced into internal exile, commencing a period of intense writing that generated his two major prose contributions to philosophy, the *Policraticus* and the *Metalogicon*, both of which were substantially completed by 1159. The *Policraticus* constitutes a philosophical memoir of court life, encompassing moral theology, satire, speculative philosophy, legal procedure, self-consolation, and biblical commentary as well as political theory. The *Metalogicon*, which may be appropriately read as a methodological companion to the much longer *Policraticus*, addresses the curriculum current in the Paris schools of John's day and surveys many of the philosophical controversies that raged during the mid-twelfth century.

After Theobald's death in 1160 and Becket's elevation to the archepiscopacy, John withdrew from active public life. The Archbishop's emerging conflict with Henry II, however, compelled John to chose sides, and he eventually went into exile in France (although not with Becket's entourage). John was among those present at Canterbury on the day of Becket's martyrdom, although he fled prior to the archbishop's assassination by Henry's knights. The remainder of John's life was dedicated to promoting the memory of St Thomas of Canterbury, for which he was rewarded with preferment as Bishop of Chartres in 1176. He died at Chartres in 1180 and is buried at the abbey church of Notre-Dame-de-Josaphat.

John's main contribution to the discussion of economic questions may be found in the *Policraticus*. In the fifth and sixth books, he employs an extended analogy between the political community and the human organism, which includes a positive valuation of artisan and agricultural occupations, whom he describes as the 'feet' of the body. John argues that the natural needs of human beings dictate the design and organization of the parts of the community. Thus, the creation and exchange of the goods required to achieve the physical well-being of the members of society form the basis of public economic relations. The body politic ought to be arranged so as to facilitate the intercommunication of such tasks and functions for mutual advantage.

John's model of the economy is directed toward production for use rather than for the market. In his view, this is what nature dictates. Consequently, he criticizes commercial activity aimed solely at personal profit, and he associates such commerce with the circulation of money. According to John, money is antithetical to the 'natural' circulation of goods and services necessary for the maintenance of human life. Yet ultimately he does not reject the accumulation of liquid wealth, especially by rulers, at least so long as its purpose is clearly understood to be the pursuit of the interests of the communal good. His position therefore reflects a tempered realism. He accepts a limited commercial and monetary economy, while recognizing the serious moral and spiritual pitfalls posed by the introduction of market-driven forms of economic interaction.

BIBLIOGRAPHY
Metalogicon, ed. J.B. Hall and K.S.B. Keats-Rohan (Turnhout, 1991).
Policraticus I–IV, ed. K.S.B. Keats-Rohan (Turnhout, 1993).
Policraticus, ed. C.C.J. Webb (Oxford, 1909); Policraticus: Of the Frivolities of Courtiers and the Footprints of Philosophers, ed. and trans. C.J. Nederman (Cambridge, 1990).

Further Reading
Nederman, C.J., 'The Virtues of Necessity: Labor, Money, and Corruption in John of Salisbury's Thought', *Viator: Medieval and Renaissance Studies* (2002), vol. 33, pp. 54–68.
——, *John of Salisbury* (Tempe, Arizona, 2003).

Cary Nederman

JOHNSON, Harry Gordon (1923–77)

Johnson was born in Toronto on 26 May 1923, and died in Geneva on 9 May 1977, following a stroke. He was the son of Herbert Henry (also called Harry) Johnson, a newspaperman who became secretary of the Ontario Liberal Party (1929–43), and Frances Lily Muat, a graduate teacher who later took a postgraduate degree in psychology and joined the Institute of Child Study at the University of Toronto. He was educated almost entirely privately before embarking on his university education at Toronto (BA 1943, MA 1947), Cambridge (BA 1946, MA 1949) and Harvard (MA 1948, PhD 1958). His first academic appointment was as acting professor of economics at St Francis Xavier University in Nova Scotia (1943–4). His subsequent appointments were at Toronto (1946–7), Cambridge (1949–56) where he was a fellow of King's (1950–6), Manchester, as professor of economics (1956–9), Chicago (1959–77) with a simultaneous full-time appointment at the London School of Economics (1966–74), and a part-time appointment at the Graduate Institute of International Studies, Geneva (1976–7). He held substantial visiting appointments at Toronto (1952, 1967), Northwestern (1955), Stanford (1955), Yale (1972–3) and Queen's (1975), and spent shorter periods as a visitor at several other universities. His activities were somewhat restricted following a stroke in October 1973; he suffered a second stroke in Geneva, of which he died.

Johnson's contribution to the profession included important editorships: *The Review of Economic Studies* (1950–9), *The Manchester School* (1956–9), *The Journal of Political Economy* (1960–6, 1970–4) and *Economica* (1966–74). He was the best editor of his generation, particularly gifted at discovering and then developing contributions from young authors, and spending considerable time rewriting their work to bring out their essential contributions in succinct terms.

Throughout his career, Johnson was best known as an international economist. His seminal technical contributions to trade theory included a careful analysis of the optimum tariff and retaliation in game-theoretic terms, analyses of equilibrium and disequilibrium growth in a two-country world economy, the transfer problem, the cost of protection and scientific tariff-making, and the theory of effective protection and the nature of optimal policy in a world of domestic distortions. He also made important contributions to the policy literature on customs unions, including the earliest attempt to quantify the effects of Britain joining the European Common Market, and to the literature on trade policy and economic development. His contributions to international monetary economics included a seminal article, 'The General Theory of the Balance of Payments' (1958), and subsequently, in pulling together and aggressively publicizing the monetary approach to the balance of payments. Inevitably, throughout the 1960s and 1970s, he was an important participant in discussions on the developments in and the reform of the international monetary system.

From the beginning, Johnson also maintained an interest in monetary economics, although he tried, unsuccessfully, to avoid conflict with his senior colleagues in the field in both Cambridge and Chicago. After two contributions – a December 1960 review of the contributions of KEYNES's General Theory after twenty-five years, and a 1962 survey of developments in monetary theory and policy – his authoritative status in the field was established and he became known, particularly to a generation of graduate students, for his regular surveys of the developing literature and his LSE lecture notes, *Macroeconomics and Monetary Theory* (1971). His stature in the field meant that during his LSE period he played an important role in the development and encouragement of the study of monetary economics in Britain, largely through the Money Study Group, of which he was founder-chairman. Through the Group he made important theoretical contributions to the discussion of the conditions for efficiency in the monetary system, which played an important role in shaping British discussions in the 1960s and 1970s. His institution-building in Britain also extended beyond the monetary field to the Trade Policy Research Centre, which encouraged the academic study of policy issues and the dissemination of research results to the more general public. Finally, he was an important figure in the institutionalization of what he regarded as more professional economics in Britain (and also in Canada), both through the development of professional associations and in the design of graduate programmes.

One of the characteristics of Johnson's later work was his increasing interest in the history and characteristics of economics as a profession, including differences in national styles of professing economics, the role of the economist in policy discussions and debates, the influence of differing institutional structures on the development of the subject, and the development of revolutions and counter-revolutions in the subject. Also, as he grew older, he became a speculative, 'big thinker' in international economics, most notably in his Wicksell Lectures, *Comparative Cost and Commercial Policy Theory in a Developing World Economy* (1968).

Johnson's influence was heightened by his ubiquity. He was an indefatigable conference participant who was invariably asked to sum up at the end of the sessions and draw out the implications of what had been said for the development of the discipline. He was also the perpetual visiting lecturer, willing to go to obscure places to spread the gospel of scientific economics. Finally, he was ever-ready, perhaps too ready, to publish, sometimes in too-obscure places to help fledging journals, but he collected the best of his more than five hundred professional papers in a series of volumes beginning in 1958.

BIBLIOGRAPHY
International Trade and Economic Growth: Studies in Pure Theory (1958).
Money, Trade and Economic Growth: Survey Lectures in Economic Theory (1962).
Economic Policies Towards Less Developed Countries (1967).
Essays in Monetary Economics (1967).
Comparative Cost and Commercial Policy Theory for a Developing World Economy (1968).
Aspects of the Theory of Tariffs (1971).
Macroeconomics and Monetary Theory (1971).
Further Essays in Monetary Economics (1972).
Technology and Economic Interdependence (1975).*On Economics and Society* (Chicago, 1975).
The Shadow of Keynes: Understanding Keynes, Cambridge and the Keynesian Revolution (Oxford, 1978)

Further Reading
Bhagwati, J., 'Harry. G. Johnson', *Journal of International Economics* (1977), vol. 7, pp. 221–9.
Corden, W.M., 'Harry Johnson's Contributions to International Trade Theory', *Journal of Political Economy* (1984), vol. 92, pp. 567–91.
——, 'Harry Johnson's View of the Scientific Enterprise', *American Journal of Economics and Sociology* (2001), vol. 60, pp. 641–6.

Laidler, D., 'Harry Johnson as a Macroeconomist', *Journal of Political Economy* (1984), vol. 92, pp. 592–615.
Lipsey, R.G., 'Harry Johnson's Contributions to the Pure Theory of International Trade', *Canadian Journal of Economics* (1978), vol. 11 supplement, pp. 34–54.
——, 'Harry Johnson as a Mentor of Young Economists', *American Journal of Economics and Sociology* (2001), vol. 60, pp. 611–18.
Tobin, J., 'Harry Gordon Johnson, 1923–1977', *Proceedings of the British Academy*, (1978), vol. 64, pp. 443–58.

Donald Moggridge

JOHNSON, William Ernest (1858–1931)

Johnson was born at Llandaff House, Cambridge on 23 June 1858, and died in Northampton on 14 January 1931. He was the son of William Henry Farthing Johnson and Harriet, née Brimley. His father ran the once famous day school at Llandaff House, an educational establishment which had been run by the Johnson family from 1823; his mother taught languages at the school and was also matron. Johnson was one of five children: his elder brother, George William, became an eminent civil servant, and his sister Harriet took over the school after their father's retirement in 1893 and ran it until 1925. Another sister, Alice was the long-standing editor and research officer to the Society for Psychical Research.

Johnson was a sickly child and was seriously ill when eight years old; he suffered asthma attacks thereafter and had chronic bronchial ill-health. In consequence, much of his education was interrupted. He was educated first at the Perse School and later as a boarder at the Liverpool Royal Institution School, but while there his health was so poor that he was advised to spend the winter of 1877 in France. He won a mathematics scholarship to King's College, Cambridge, in 1879, and in 1882 was eleventh wrangler. In 1883 he graduated with a first in the moral sciences tripos (of which economics was an integral part). He then embarked upon a teaching career, first as lecturer on psychology and education at the Cambridge Women's Training College. Henry SIDGWICK had long recognized Johnson's abilities, and with his support Johnson became university lecturer in the theory of education in 1893–8, becoming also university lecturer in moral sciences in 1896. In 1902 he was appointed the Sidgwick Lecturer (and fellow of King's College) when the lectureship was endowed in Sidgwick's memory. For many years he lectured on psychology, logic and mathematical economics; in the most severe winters he delivered his lectures from his house, rather than his room in King's. He married Barbara Keymer Heaton in 1895, with whom he had two sons; she died suddenly in 1904 and henceforth his sister Fanny took over the running of the household, devoting her life to him and his children. He suffered a stroke in 1927 and, though he recovered much of his speech he remained in failing health and died four years later.

Johnson's academic career may be described as that of an inspirational, if unorthodox, lecturer. He is best remembered as a philosopher, and in particular as a logician, but as a pioneer of mathematical economics, he deserves rather more credit than he is generally accorded. He was not a prolific publisher: he wrote a textbook, *Trigonometry*, published in 1889, but a combination of poor health, some diffidence and his own very high standards prevented him from publishing much else before his sixties. His college fellowship, awarded in 1902, was for a fixed term, and whenever the issue of its continuance arose the college sought evidence of his endeavours and achievements; reports from his colleagues and pupils always proved sufficient, for there was nothing by way of publications, and his position was always renewed. Of those colleagues who would have supported him, one can undoubtedly include KEYNES, who would have been familiar with Johnson's work in economics through his active membership of the Cambridge Economic Club, and his lectures in logic and probability. Keynes's *Treatise on Probability* (1921) contains generous acknowledgement and indebtedness to Johnson, but Johnson's own work in the area, the treatise *Logic* (1921–4), was only published following the encouragement and insistence of one of his pupils, Miss Naomi Bentwich. A further volume, on probability, was planned and was in preparation at the time of death, but the volume was never published. Upon publication of *Logic*, Johnson gained immediate recognition outside Cambridge, the highlight of which was his election as a fellow of the British Academy in 1923.

Johnson's publications are relatively few in number for one of significant influence, and his total output in economics is known to number three papers: two presented to the Cambridge Economic Club (1891 and 1894) and one which was published in the *Economic Journal* (1913). His paper of 1891 sought to offer a solution to the price-taking, profit-maximizing firm, embedded within a general equilibrium system. He set out the first-order marginal conditions for a solution, but failed to note any second-order conditions and, as profit was treated as a residual, a full marginal productivity theory was not apparent in this paper. His paper of 1894 was written jointly with C.P. Sanger, a mathematician and economist who made numerous contributions to economics (including over fifty contributions to the *Economic Journal*, many of them book reviews). This paper contained some major innovations in utility and value theory, notably the explicit use of a general interdependent utility function, rather than the more common additively separable form. This treatment of the preference function then led to a general treatment of the concept of consumers' surplus in the context of interdependent goods.

The paper of 1913 in many ways developed the joint work with Sanger. It represents a most significant and important contribution to utility theory Here Johnson, apparently in ignorance of Pareto's work, analysed consumer choice in terms of the ratios of marginal utilities, thus freeing the theory of choice from the shackles of cardinal utility. Indifference curve analysis was not, until HICKS and ALLEN (1934), in common use; Johnson used the now familiar indifference curve and budget line, and provided a critical analysis of the convexity of an indifference curve and its consequences (and in particular its *non*-consequences: he showed that negatively-sloping expenditure curves and positively-sloping demand curves are consistent with convex indifference curves). In describing his graphical representation, he pointed out that 'there are no lines in the figure which measure utility itself', and argued that economics does not 'need to know the marginal (rate of) utility of a commodity. What is needed is a representation of the *ratio* of one marginal utility to another. In fact, this ratio is precisely represented by the *slope* at any point of the utility [indifference] curve' (1913: 490, italics in original). This is a major advance in the use of ordinal, rather than cardinal, utility. However, not acknowledging Pareto's work led, as Schumpeter (1954) suggested, to a 'not unnatural resentment on the part of Italian economists'; yet 'this important paper contains several results that should secure for its author a place in any history of our science' (1952: 1063n). That Johnson's work did not receive widespread acclaim from contemporaries may be due to its use of a sophisticated level of mathematics which was not in common use amongst economists at the time, and its very use of indifference curves. It was not until the comprehensive analysis of Hicks and Allen in the 1930s that the neglected and prescient contributions of Johnson (and Slutsky 1915) became more widely, and properly, recognized.

BIBLIOGRAPHY

'Exchange and Distribution', *Cambridge Economic Club* (1891), pp. 1–6.
(with C.P. Sanger) 'On Certain Questions Connected with Demand', *Cambridge Economic Club* (1894), pp. 1–8.
Treatise on Trigonometry (1889).
'The Pure Theory of Utility Curves', *Economic Journal* (1913), vol. 23, pp. 483–513.
Logic (Cambridge, 1921–4).

Further Reading

Braithwaite, R.B., 'Obituary: W.E. Johnson', *The Cambridge Review* (1931), 30 January, p. 220.
Broad, C.D., 'William Ernest Johnson, 1858–1931', *Proceedings of the British Academy* (1952), vol. 17, pp. 491–514.
Hicks, J.R. and Allen, R.D.G., 'A Reconsideration of the Theory of Value Parts I and II', *Economica* (1934), vol. 1, pp. 52–76 and 196–219.
Keynes, J.M., *A Treatise on Probability* (1921).
Schumpeter, J.A., *History of Economic Analysis* (1954).
Slutsky, E., 'On the Theory of the Budget of the Consumer', *Giornale degli economisti*, (1915), ser. 3, vol. 51, pp. 1–26.

John J. O'Connor
Edmund F. Robertson
Adrian Darnell

JONES, Richard (1790–1855)

Jones, of Welsh origin, was born in Tunbridge Wells in Kent in 1790, where his father was a solicitor, and died at Haileybury, Hertfordshire on 26 January 1855. He was of poor health as a child, and because of this it was decided that he should not follow his father into legal practice. At relatively advanced age he was sent to Cambridge, entering Gonville and Caius College in 1812 to read mathematics; he was senior wrangler. At Cambridge, he easily moved in the same circles as Charles BABBAGE, John Herschel, and his close friend William WHEWELL. Jones finished his studies in 1816 and entered into the offices of the church, where he served as a vicar at various places in Sussex. His affiliation with the Church of England cannot be separated from his political conservatism and his strong belief in the providential order of nature. Jones shared these political and religious convictions with Whewell, and they were important motive forces for both men's strong resistance to the political radicalism and religious agnosticism of the Benthamites and Ricardians.

Jones became professor of political economy in 1833 at the newly established King's College, London, an institution expressly founded as a countervailing influence to University College, London, in the founding of which Jeremy BENTHAM and James MILL had been instrumental. University College, where Bentham's body still surveys the scene, had been established in 1826 and was the first institute where so-called dissenters of the Church of England could receive higher education. In 1835 Jones succeeded MALTHUS at the East India College at Haileybury. His *Essay on the Distribution of Wealth and on the Sources of Taxation, Part 1: Rent*, published 1831, in which he articulated his objections to Ricardianism and formulated an alternative approach, certainly contributed to his election.

Jones was actively involved in the formulation of the Tithe Commutation Bill in the 1830s. He became a member of the tithe commission on behalf of the Archbishop of Canterbury in 1836, and remained on the commission until it closed its activities in 1851. Tithes were payments in kind to the church and may now be considered small beer, but at the time the commutation of the tithes, that is, the conversion of money payments, was a very important issue. In his last years Jones was a member of the Charity Commission. In 1859 Jones published his *Literary Remains*, largely consisting of lectures he had given at King's College and Haileybury College. The Haileybury lectures, largely devoted to labour, were highly praised by Karl MARX.

It is difficult to see Jones's life and work except through the eyes of William Whewell, who took much interest in his engagements with political economy. The extensive correspondence between the two men, now in the archives of Trinity College, Cambridge, gives witness to the tedious writing process from which Jones's only work on political economy to be published during lifetime, his *Essay on the Distribution of Wealth and on the Sources of Taxation* finally saw the light in 1831. Even when parts of the manuscript were already at the printers, at the costs of the trustees of Cambridge University Press, Whewell still had to bully Jones to produce more manuscript. Whewell heavily edited Jones's literary remains, omitting duplicate works and bringing more clarity into the exposition, and could not see them published without a 'prefatory notice' which, he hoped, would be 'rejoiced' by Jones's many and illustrious friends.

Despite Jones's manifest difficulties in writing, his 1831 book and the *Literary Remains* (1859) prove him an acute critic of Ricardian political economy, and an original thinker in his own right. He is commonly seen as the most important propagator of an inductive approach to political economy, in opposition to the deductive, a priori approach of the Ricardians and many other contemporary political economists, Nassau SENIOR in particular. Consistent with his inductivism, he strongly emphasized and encouraged the collection of statistical data and the detailed study of the historical and geographical differences in the social organization of the production of wealth. This made him a precursor of the

English Historical School, and an attractive source of insights for his most insightful reader, Karl Marx. Marx was so impressed by Jones's writings that he devoted a roughly seventy pages to a discussion Jones's theories of rent and labour in his *Theories of Surplus Value*. For Marx, Jones was the first to see the historical determinacy of economic laws, and he considered Jones's work in this and many other respects 'a fundamental advance over Ricardo'.

From 1822 onwards, Jones worked on his inductively based theory of political economy, of which only the first volume, on rent, would be published. His fundamental objection to the Ricardian theory of rent (the origin of which he attributed to Malthus, not mentioning James ANDERSON), was that rent was universally explained by differences in fertility between marginal and intra-marginal soils. Jones took further issue with the political consequences the Ricardians drew from their theory, the opposition of the landed interests to those of capital and labour in particular. Both these generalizations were in Jones's view only based on scant observations which subsequently were declared universally true. The Ricardians thus violated what Jones considered the true basis of all sound scientific inference, BACON's inductivism. By taking recourse to historical and geographical data, Jones claimed to remedy this sorry state of affairs. In response to MCCULLOCH's claim that RICARDO did not use the term rent 'in the ordinary and vulgar sense of the word', Whewell in his preface to Jones's works pointedly asked the reader 'to decide for himself which subject of inquiry is better worth his notice, – the rents that are actually paid in *every* country, or the Ricardian rents, which are *not* those actually paid in *any* country' (1859: xii–xiii).

Both historical and contemporary data taught Jones that rent payments were crucially dependent upon the social organization of production. This organization was in most parts of the world very different from that in England (and Holland), and Jones aimed to show that the rent schemes of these advanced countries was the exceptional rather than the general case. Jones distinguished between 'primary' and 'secondary' rents, or 'peasant' and 'farmer' rent, and further distinguished the first class of rent into several sub-classes. Primary (or peasant) rent was a conventional payment for the use of the soil, and was completely independent of its (grade of) fertility. In a phrase with which Marx was much taken, Jones wrote that rent 'has usually originated in the appropriation of the soil, at a time when the bulk of the people must cultivate it on such terms as they can obtain, or starve' (1831: 11). Jones further distinguished peasant rent payments in serf rents, metayor rents, ryot rents and cottier rents, depending on the specific tenure systems in which the rent payments were made. He showed especially an extensive knowledge of Asiatic rent tenure systems. Most of the book was devoted to a meticulous discussion of these different tenure systems, and only the last chapter was devoted to a discussion of farmer's rents, the tenure system the English were almost uniquely acquainted with.

For this comparative approach, Jones is acknowledged as the founder of the comparative analysis of economic systems. Jones emphasized that the English scheme of rent payments only came into existence one a 'race of capitalists' has made its appearance that took its place between the landowners and the peasants. This new class did not find its origin in agriculture but in manufactures, where craftsmen in the course of time 'arranged themselves' under its management. Once capitalists were there, they sought the most profitable use for capital in whatever business, including agriculture. It was only in such circumstances, where rent became basically identical to 'surplus profit', that the fertility of the soil became of importance. What the Ricardians presented as the natural state of affairs thus was fundamentally dependent upon social and historical circumstances. Jones also made it a matter of importance to show that there was no fundamental opposition between the landed interests and the interests of the other two classes in society (labour and capital). He proved himself in this regard an early critic of McCulloch's wage fund theory, that McCulloch (and others) took as a fixed magnitude. Jones persistently pointed out that there was nothing in the state of society to validate this assumption. His firm belief in the providential order of nature, and his conservative attachment to the old institutes of Britain, was of course of importance in his denial of any conflict of interests between the landlords and the other classes in society. In contrast, Jones emphasized the fundamentally disruptive consequences for the social order of the emergence of this new class in society, the capitalists:

> We see changes constantly affecting this economical conformation, and the institutions and forms of society it gives birth to...The great agent in all these changes, in the configuration of society, the moving power from which they proceed is *capital*...The ties which formerly bound the community together are worn out and fall to pieces; other bonds, other principles of cohesion, connect its different classes; new economical relations spring into being...Not only is the great body of non-agriculturists almost wholly in the pay of capitalists, but even the laboring cultivators of the soil...are their servants too.
> (1859: 555–58)

Jones's book would be an important factor in convincing the still very young British Association for the Advancement of Science (BAAS) that something scientific could be done in political economy, in contrast with the allegedly unscientific 'rabble-rousing' of the political radicals – that is, in contrast with Ricardo's a priorism and its disruptive political proposals. In 1833 the BAAS established Section F, devoted to statistics and political economy, and in 1834, Jones (with Charles Babbage and others) took the lead in the establishment of the Statistical Society of London, later the Royal Statistical Society. To exclude the 'deamon of opinion', its act of constitution explicitly stated that the works of the society should be devoted to the collection of numerical data only, preferably in tabular form. Soon after its establishment, Jones got so deeply involved in the tithe commission that he lost his interest in what, in the early 1830s, had been his deepest concern: the promotion of an inductively based investigation of the laws of political economy.

As said, apart from Marx and the English Historical School, Jones has received little appraisal. The classical political economists did everything possible to depreciate the value of his contributions, as might be expected. McCulloch dismissed it as 'superficial', and John Stuart MILL considered it a 'copious repertory of valuable facts' – as Whewell noted, a most effective strategy to dismiss the worth of someone's work. Yet, Mill basically adopted Jones's classification of rent tenure systems in his own *Principles*. After Eugen Böhm-Bawerk wrote that Jones 'adds nothing important to our knowledge', economists by and large forgot about him, and about his message of the historical determinacy of the laws of political economy.

BIBLIOGRAPHY
An Essay on the Distribution of Wealth and on the Sources of Taxation (1831; repr. New York, 1964).
Literary Remains Consisting of Lectures & Tracts on Political Economy, ed. W. Whewell (1859; repr. New York, 1964).

Further Reading
Cannon, S.F., *Science in Culture: The Early Victorian Period* (New York, 1978).
Goldman, L., 'The Origins of British "Social Science": Political Economy, Natural Science and Statistics, 1830–1835', *The Historical Journal* (1983), vol. 26, pp. 587–616.
Grossman, H., 'The Evolutionist Revolt against Classical Economics, II, In England – James Steuart, Richard Jones, Karl

Marx', *The Journal of Political Economy* (1943), vol. 51, pp. 506–22.

Henderson, J.P., *Early Mathematical Economics: William Whewell and the British Case* (Lanham, Maryland, 1996).

Marx, K., *Theories of Surplus Value* (1969).

Rashid, S., 'Richard Jones and Baconian Historicism at Cambridge', *Journal of Economic Issues* (1979), vol. 13, pp. 159–73.

Harro Maas

JOPLIN, Thomas (c.1790–1847)

Thomas Joplin was born probably in 1790, although no record of his birth has been traced. He died at Böhmischdorf near Freiwaldau in Silesia on 12 April 1847. The family were timber merchants from County Durham, around a village called Satley, but had settled in Newcastle upon Tyne by the time of Joplin's birth. The difficulties encountered by banks in Newcastle after 1815 naturally affected the business community, including Joplin; and it seems to have been one particular case of such difficulties, in which he was asked to act as guarantor for a bank, which led to the first edition of his *On the General Principles and Present Practice of Banking*, which appeared in 1822. It went through a number of editions subsequently, growing into a sort of manual for the establishment of joint stock banks.

Joplin quickly concluded that the only basis for a sound banking system was the introduction of joint stock banking, which operated successfully in Scotland, into England. Such a development encountered the apparently unyielding obstacle of a Bank of England monopoly of joint stock banking, and one of the two important aspects of Joplin's career involved an assault, which was to prove largely successful, upon this monopoly position. The other important aspect of Joplin's career was as a macroeconomic theorist of remarkable originality.

Joplin's campaign to establish joint stock banks really began to bear fruit from the mid 1820s, following the financial crisis of 1825. The monopoly of the Bank of England was confined to within 65 miles of London, from 1826, although the joint stock banks subsequently established had to operate without the protection of limited liability. Apart from paving the way for others to establish joint stock banks, Joplin himself managed to establish the Provincial Bank of Ireland in 1824, which was a joint stock bank operating with branches, of the kind that he advocated to replace local partnerships, and then, in 1833, he took the battle to the Bank of England and established the National Provincial Bank of England.

Joplin was handicapped in his business relationships both by a personality which was extremely inflexible and abrasive, and by his north-eastern origins which could even have rendered his speech barely intelligible to the financial establishment in London, clearly marking him as an outsider. At all events, he left the Provincial Bank of Ireland within two years of its foundation (though with financial compensation); and he was ousted from the National Provincial Bank of England within a further two years of its foundation. He subsequently engaged in various unsuccessful business ventures, while attempting to obtain compensation from not merely the English bank which he had founded but from the joint stock banks in general, whose activities he had defended. In his attempts to secure compensation he was apparently – this is his own account – obstructed by an unnamed individual who was very probably J.W. GILBART.

If Joplin had done nothing else, his extraordinary drive and energy in establishing the foundation of the modern banking system in Britain would have entitled him to considerable recognition albeit, sadly, posthumous. But Joplin also developed, in parallel with his banking activities, a structured macroeconomic model with, drawn from this, plans for wholesale reform of the banking and monetary system. These were far-reaching, and in many ways superior to what his establishment contemporaries in the currency and banking schools were arguing; but Joplin was not to live to see himself vindicated, dying, after years of financial difficulties, in April 1847, just months before the October financial crisis erupted and followed the course that he had predicted.

Joplin's macroeconomic model had a distinctly Keynesian flavour. For equilibrium, expenditure should equal income. The income stemmed from production; the expenditure was on consumption and investment. Savings would equal investment plus borrowing for consumption, if the market for loans was allowed to clear (1823, 1825, 1839, 1844a).

However, for Joplin, all this had to be seen in the context of an open economy. Then expenditure was equal to output plus net imports. Aggregate demand depended on the money supply, and changes in aggregate demand would have multiple effects on the level of income. An increase in the money supply would increase aggregate demand; this would increase demand for the contents of existing inventories, and this demand would in turn be transmitted to the producers of the goods held in inventories (1823, 1833, 1833–4, 1838). Joplin thus had concepts in common with HAWTREY, as well as with KEYNES.

The subsequent rise in output would involve both increased employment and, with a less than perfectly elastic aggregate supply schedule, an increased price level (1825, 1828). However, an increased price level could result in a balance of payments deficit, which would then reduce the money supply, aggregate demand, and prices, to levels at which there was external balance. If, conversely, there were a fall in the money supply, it would be possible for income and expenditure to come into balance at less than full employment. Thus depression was due to a lack of aggregate demand (1825, 1844a, 1844b).

It is clear from this that changes in the money supply were of vital importance in determining the level at which income and expenditure were equal for the economy. Joplin thus identified, like his currency school contemporaries, a problem with a paper currency since, unlike a metallic currency, there was no direct and necessary link between the balance of payments and the money supply. Moreover, a paper currency allowed banks to lend money without there being prior saving, thus introducing the possibility of an inequality between the supply of saving and the amount of loans (1826, 1832, 1844a). There was a further possibility which escaped his currency school contemporaries. They regarded the Bank of England as providing the high-powered money base of the whole system. But Joplin argued that there was in fact a dual circulation. The Bank of England notes, and bank deposits, supplied the financial circulation; the money supply which determined the price level of goods and services was, however, the country bank note issue which, although of roughly the same size of that of the Bank of England, had a velocity of circulation approximately four times that of notes issued by the Bank (1823, 1825, 1826, 1828, 1831, 1832).

This country bank note circulation was however issued under conditions which ensured monetary disequilibrium. Rather than allowing the market for loans to clear so that, as required by his model, investment plus borrowing for consumption were together equal to saving, the country banks held the rate of interest fixed at around what was, until 1833, a legal maximum of 5 per cent, and issued or withdrew bank notes equal in amount to the gap (whether positive or negative) between savings and the demand for loans (1822, 1825, 1826, 1827, 1828). While individual banks would be constrained by clearing from expanding their issues when their competitors were not doing so, the country banks as a whole could increase their issues together, without experiencing adverse clearing individually, and this might happen if they all experienced a similar buoyancy in the demand for loans (1823, 1825, 1826, 1828, 1839, 1841, 1844a).

All this ensured that the country bank note issues did not move in the same direction as would a metallic currency, directly affected as the latter would be by gold flows resulting from balance of payments deficits or surpluses. Thus there was no corrective effect on the price level, which depended on these country bank notes, when there was external disequilibrium.

In addition to this, there was a very specific problem associated with the London money market. This bore the burden of flows of gold across the exchanges (1839, 1844a). Gold imports all ended up in London; and they thus increased the reserves in the London money market. But the incoming gold was initially purchased by the country banks with their own notes. There was thus a double effect. The country banks' note issue increased, and their reserves held in London increased also, for they used the gold purchased to increase their London deposits and holdings of gilt edged securities. At the same time, the London banks acquired Bank of England notes for the gold, which they had purchased from the country banks by creating deposits on behalf of the latter. Since, unlike the country loan market, the London market cleared at a flexible interest rate, this increase in their own reserves allowed them to increase their own lending at a lower rate of interest. Thus, on the one hand, both they and the country banks were separately increasing the availability of funds; on the other, the London banks were, like the country banks, lending not as a result of increased saving but as a result of the effects of the balance of payments (1823, 1825, 1826, 1828, 1832, 1833, 1841, 1844a, 1844b, 1845a, 1845b).

This in turn meant that the prescription of the currency school – to reduce the circulation of Bank of England notes in the event of a balance of payments deficit and a gold outflow – was a recipe for disaster. For such a reduction would draw upon the precautionary reserves of the London banks, and bring about a financial panic, rather than reducing the circulation of the country banks and thus lowering the price level. Indeed, Joplin argued consistently from 1825 that the correct course of action when there was a danger of financial pressure, because of a gold outflow, was for the Bank of England to *increase* its lending freely to the financial sector.

Joplin did not consider that all variations in aggregate demand were due to variations in the money supply. There were also problems of fiscal policy: Joplin attributed the post-Napoleonic war depression to a reduction in government expenditure. If government reduced its borrowing, this would reduce aggregate demand. At the same time it would mean that savings were greater than the demand for loans, whether for investment or consumption, one major borrower having withdrawn from the market (1823, 1828).

Joplin recognized that the position of the Bank of England itself was very difficult. On the one hand, the prevailing conventional wisdom, at least from the 1820s onwards, was that the Bank should regulate its note issue with respect to the balance of payments, on the assumption that it controlled aggregate demand through provision of a monetary base. If it did regulate its issue of notes in this way, it was likely to produce a financial crisis, Joplin believed, as had indeed happened in 1825 (1841, 1844a, 1844b). But if it did not, there was no correction of the disequilibrating changes in the money supply which had originated with the country banks (1832, 1841).

As Joplin saw it, the correct way forward was not to impose upon the Bank an automatic rule that its issues must fluctuate with its gold holdings (above the so-called 'fiduciary' minimum note issue) but to get rid of the two competing and unsynchronized sources of variations in the money supply, and to introduce a national money supply which itself would vary as an identically circumstanced metallic currency would have done (1837, 1838, 1839, 1844b, 1845a). Thus a balance of payments deficit or surplus would be self-correcting, and the market for loans would be allowed to clear.

The mechanics of the plan involved the establishment of a Board of Commissioners, which would purchase bullion and issue bullion receipts. (Joplin's proposals predate RICARDO's *Plan for the Establishment of a National Bank*, 1824.) These receipts could then be exchanged at any bank for new notes. The bank purchasing the bullion receipt would have a credit with the Commissioners (1823, 1825, 1826, 1832, 1839, 1840, 1841). Conversely, when these banks were faced with a demand for bullion for export, they would buy back their own notes, in exchange for drafts on the Bullion Commissioners who would, in turn, exchange the drafts for bullion. All this would unify not merely the national money supply, linking it to the balance of payments in a way that ensured equilibration, but unify also the loan market so that the London money market would no longer have its special, and very vulnerable, position, and financial panics could be avoided.

Under normal circumstances, changes in aggregate demand would be small, and the expectation would be of macroeconomic equilibrium. However, in the event of a catastrophe, such as harvest failure, Joplin suggested – with considerable courage – that the exchange rate between the domestic currency and gold should be allowed to float freely, until normal times had returned (1826, 1828). If there were not already enough in Joplin's proposals to alienate both the currency and banking school writers, this on its own would have been sufficient: both sides accepted the idea that maintenance of the convertibility of the note issue into gold was of fundamental importance.

To any one familiar only with the writers of the currency and banking schools – OVERSTONE, NORMAN and TORRENS on the one hand, TOOKE, FULLARTON and WILSON on the other, to name the major figures – Joplin's extraordinarily sophisticated and far-reaching analysis and policy recommendations come as a revelation. The model is so well worked out that it is possible to state the entire system of relationships in mathematical form (O'Brien 1993, ch. 14). Joplin was also extremely advanced methodologically, compared with his contemporaries, in that he spoke explicitly of testing hypotheses against data. Moreover, when such tests are carried out – when Joplin's hypotheses are confronted with data on a scale which was not available to him – they stand up remarkably well (O'Brien 1993, ch. 13).

It is very unfortunate that Joplin's prophecies were ignored. It is certainly arguable that the 1840s and 1850s would have been spared much macroeconomic turbulence had Joplin been an influential insider rather than a perpetual outsider.

BIBLIOGRAPHY

Outlines of a System of Political Economy (1823).
An Essay on the General Principles and Practice of Banking, in England and Scotland (1823).
An Illustration of Mr. Joplin's Views on Currency, and Plan for Its Improvement; together with Observations applicable to the Present State of the Money Market; in a Series of Letters (1825).
Views on the Subject of Corn and Currency (1826).
An Essay on the General Principles and Present Practice of Banking (1827).
Views on the Corn Bill of 1827 and Other Measures of Government (1828).
The Plan of a National Establishment for Country Banking, and the Principles by which it is Recommended (1831).
An Analysis and History of the Currency Question (1832).
A Digest of the Evidence on the Bank Charter taken before the Committee of 1832 (1833).
Case for Parliamentary Inquiry into the Circumstances of the Panic: in a Letter to Thomas Gisborne, Esq., M.P. (1835).

An Examination of the Report of the Joint Stock Bank Committee (1837).
Articles on Banking and Currency from 'The Economist' Newspaper (1838).
On Our Monetary System &c. &c. with an Explanation of the Causes by which the Pressures on the Money Market are Produced, and a Plan for their Remedy, which can be carried into immediate effect, without any derangement, and with the approbation of the banks, both private and public, by which the currency is issued (1839).
Prospectus of an Association to Promote the Establishment of a Uniform Currency under One General Head (1840).
The Cause and Cure of Our Commercial Embarrassments (1841).
Currency Reform: Improvement not Depreciation (1844).
An Examination of Sir Robert Peel's Currency Bill of 1844 (1844).
An Examination of Sir Robert Peel's Currency Bill. Second Edition with Supplementary Observations (1845).
Mr. Joplin's Circular to the Directors and Managers of the Joint Stock Banks (1845).

Further Reading

Crick, W.F. and Wadsworth, J.E., *A Hundred Years of Joint Stock Banking* (1936).
——, 'Some New Light on Thomas Joplin', *Economica* (1936), new series, vol. 3, pp. 323–6.
Hawtrey, R., *Currency and Credit*, 3rd edn (1928).
O'Brien, D.P., *The Classical Economists* (Oxford, 1975).
——, *Thomas Joplin and Classical Macroeconomics* (Aldershot, 1993).
Ricardo, D., *Plan for the Establishment of a National Bank* (1824; repr. in P. Sraffa (ed.), *Works and Correspondence* (Cambridge, vol. 4, pp. 271–300).
Thomas, S.E., *The Rise and Growth of Joint Stock Banking* (1934).
Thornton, H., *An Enquiry into the Nature and Effects of the Paper Credit of Great Britain* (1802; repr. ed. F.A. Hayek, 1939).

D.P. O'Brien